SCOTT, FORESMAN

World Geography

A Physical and Cultural Study

*The journey
of a thousand
miles begins
with one step.*

Chinese proverb

SCOTT, FORESMAN

World Geography

A Physical and Cultural Study

Harm J. de Blij

Gerald A. Danzer

Roger A. Hart

Dorothy W. Drummond

Scott, Foresman and Company

Editorial Office: Glenview, Illinois
Regional Offices: Sunnyvale, California • Atlanta, Georgia
Glenview, Illinois • Oakland, New Jersey • Dallas, Texas

Authors

Dr. Harm J. de Blij is a Professor of Geography at the University of Miami. He also serves as editor of *National Geographic Research,* the scientific journal of the National Geographic Society. In addition, he is the author of some 30 books and more than 100 articles, all dealing with various aspects of geography. Dr. de Blij has organized and participated in several geography teacher-training seminars, and studied and traveled in many parts of the world.

Dr. Gerald A. Danzer is a Professor of History at the University of Illinois at Chicago. He directs the MA program in the teaching of history, and specializes in the history of cartography and the development of cities. He has published articles and reviews in many journals and has taught geography at both the high school and junior high school levels.

Dr. Roger A. Hart is a Professor of Geography on the faculty of the Environmental Psychology Program of The Graduate School and University Center of The City University of New York. He is also the Director of the Center for Human Environments. Professor Hart is the author of several publications on children's geographic behavior and geographic learning.

Dorothy W. Drummond is an Instructor of Geography at St. Mary-of-the-Woods College in Terre Haute, Indiana. She has conducted many workshops for geography teachers and is the president-elect of the National Council for Geographic Education. In addition, she has coauthored several geography textbooks and traveled extensively in Asia, Africa, Europe, and the Americas.

Academic Consultants

Dr. William Renwick
Department of Geography
Miami University
Oxford, Ohio

Dr. Lawrence Wolken
Department of Economics
Texas A&M University
College Station, Texas

Dr. Norman Bettis
Department of Curriculum and Instruction
Illinois State University
Normal, Illinois

Linda S. Wojtan
Social Studies Development Center
Indiana University
Bloomington, Indiana

Frank McCray
Cross-Cultural Education Consultant
Instructor, Anoka Ramsey and Normandale Community Colleges
Woodbury, Minnesota

Critical Thinking
Kevin O'Reilly
Social Studies Teacher
Hamilton-Wenham Regional High School
South Hamilton, Massachusetts

Reading Comprehension
Robert A. Pavlik
Chairperson, Reading-Language Arts Department
Cardinal Stritch College
Milwaukee, Wisconsin

Lorraine Gerhart
Cardinal Stritch College
Milwaukee, Wisconsin

Teacher Consultants

Constance Manter
Chairperson, Social Studies Department
Groton-Dunstable Regional Secondary School
Groton, Massachusetts

Marsha Miller
Teacher, World Geography
Edward White Senior High School
Jacksonville, Florida

Nicholas Sakellaris
Teacher, World Geography
Westover Senior High School
Fayetteville, North Carolina

Gail Stasky
Assistant Superintendent of Schools
Ludlow, Massachusetts

The authors and publisher would like to thank the above consultants for their reviews of *Scott, Foresman World Geography* during its developmental stage. They contributed valuable comments, chapter by chapter, on both the content and the level of difficulty. Their assistance has helped make *Scott, Foresman World Geography* a practical classroom text.

CONTENTS

UNIT 1

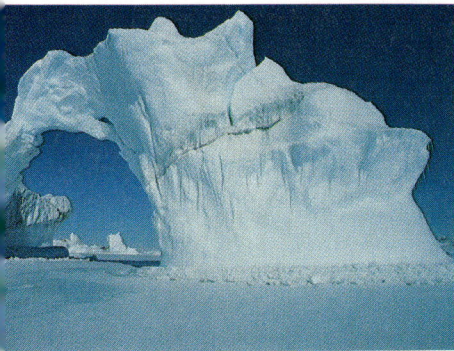

The Physical Earth   1

UNIT 2

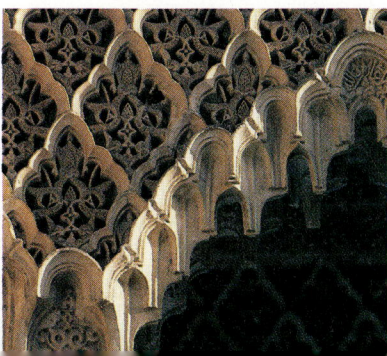

The Human World   78

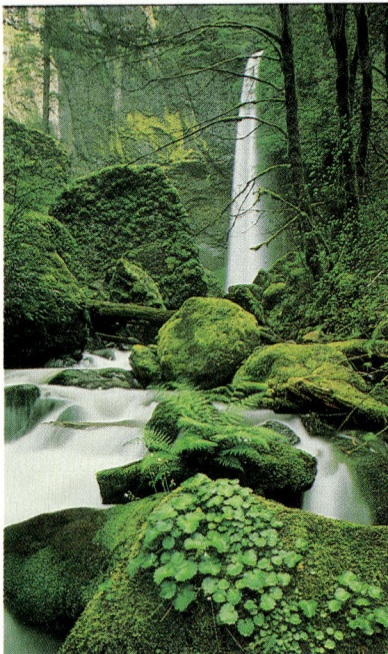

UNIT **3**

The United States and Canada 118

Maps, Diagrams, and Special Lessons

Maps

Charts, Tables, and Diagrams

Special Lessons

Case Studies

Map Lessons

Sources for chart, table, diagram and map data: U.S. State department, the World Bank, the United Nations

Scott, Foresman World Geography

Scott, Foresman World Geography has been organized so that you will find it easy to use. The book is divided into ten units and 30 chapters, with special lessons, a variety of maps, and an extensive reference section.

Unit Organization

Each unit begins with a two-page opener that includes the unit title, a photograph, an introductory statement, and a list of chapters in the unit.

Each unit concludes with a **Unit Review and Test**. This includes a chapter-by-chapter summary, an in-book practice test, and a **Writing for Understanding** activity that will help you develop and improve writing skills that relate to geography.

Chapter Organization

Each chapter begins with a full-page photograph, an introductory statement, and a list of sections in the chapter.

The end of each chapter features a two-page **Chapter Review** that includes Section Summaries, Using Geography Skills, Using Social Studies Skills, and an in-book practice test.

Section Organization

Each section begins with a **Preview** that lists the key places and terms that appear in the section. The **Preview** also includes a short number of pre-reading questions that focus on the section's main ideas. Finally, a locator globe helps you locate key places on a global perspective. A sample preview appears to the right.

The number of questions in the preview correspond to the number of subsections within the section. Each subsection begins with a heading in **dark type**. Each preview question asks you to read to find out certain information. As you read the section, periodically refer back to these preview questions to see if you can answer them.

The key terms listed in the **Preview** appear in **dark type** in the section. Each key term is defined when first used in the section. Definitions for every key term also appear in the glossary along with the page number on which the term is first used.

The study of world geography includes many places and people, some of which may be unfamiliar to you. Many of these new names will be followed by their pronunciations. A guide to pronunciation can be found on page 657.

Scott, Foresman World Geography features more than 150 maps. Each map in a section has a **Map Study** caption, which asks questions to help you grasp the map's meaning and practice your map-reading skills.

By skimming a section and reading the key places, key terms, preview questions, and headings, you will get a good idea of what the section is about and what to study. In addition, carefully look over the photographs, diagrams, and charts in the section as you read.

At the end of each section is a **Section Review**. Completing the **Section Review** will help you locate key places, identify key terms, and review the main ideas of the section. At the end of each **Section Review** is a question that will ask you to put your critical thinking skills to work. A sample **Section Review** is shown to the right.

Map Lessons

A **Map Lesson** appears at the end of each chapter right before the **Chapter Review**. These lessons provide details coverage of a range of map-reading skills. Some map lessons, such as "Reading a Newspaper Map" and "Interpreting a Road Map," will help you practice maps skills that are a part of everyday life. Other lessons relate to reading and using maps that provide such geographic information as land use, temperature, population density, and topography. Still other lessons will help you use maps to learn about history, politics, and economics. Each map lesson is identified in your textbook with the symbol above.

Case Studies

Each unit contains a **Case Study** that provides an in-depth look at a contemporary issue that relates to geography. Each case study is identified with the symbol above and includes a preview to help guide your reading.

Atlas and Reference Section

An extensive **Atlas and Reference Section** begins on page 619. It includes the following:

Atlas. Sixteen detailed political and physical maps are featured in the **Atlas**.

Facts About Countries. This eight-page section features a complete and updated list of the nations of the world with a flag and geographical data for each. Refer to this section to check a country's capital, area, population, languages, or important products.

Gazetteer. The **Gazetteer** is a geographical dictionary that provides brief descriptions and locations of the key places in *Scott, Foresman World Geography*. Pronunciations and page references for each place are also given.

Glossary. The **Glossary** provides definitions for each of the key terms listed in the text with the page on which they first appear.

Index. The **Index** provides general and specific references to help you locate text information quickly.

Preview

Key Places
Where are these places located?
1 Transylvania
2 Adriatic Sea

Key Terms
What does this term mean?
Balkanize

Main Ideas
As you read, look for answers to these questions.
- What makes Romania unusual among the countries of Eastern Europe?
- How is Bulgaria distinct in this geographic realm?
- Why are Yugoslavia and Albania unique among their neighbors?

Section 2 Review

Locating Key Places
Locate the following places on the map on page 379: Transylvania, Adriatic Sea

Identifying Key Terms
Define the following term: Balkanize

Reviewing Main Ideas
1. Explain how Romania is unusual among the countries of Eastern Europe.
2. Why is Bulgaria unlike its neighbors?
3. What makes Yugoslavia and Albania different from other Eastern European countries?

Thinking Critically: Assess Cause and Effect
Each of these Balkan countries has populations of diverse ethnic backgrounds because of fairly recent border changes. What have been the effects of this ethnic diversity on the countries of this realm?

UNIT 1

The Physical Earth

Welcome! You are about to explore our planet Earth.

What Is Geography?

In this chapter you will learn about maps and the study of geography.

Sections

1 The Vision of Geography

2 Maps and Globes

The Vision of Geography

Preview

Key Places
Where are these places located?
1 sun
2 earth
3 moon
   See the drawing below.

Key Terms
What do these terms mean?
physical geography   cultural feature
human geography   region
natural feature

Main Ideas
As you read, look for answers to these questions.
• How is the earth unique in our solar system?
• What is geography?
• What are the branches of geography?
• How does the study of geography help people?

My two space flights have changed my perception of the earth. Of course, Apollo 11 also changed my perception of the moon, but I don't regard that as being nearly so important. . . . The moon is so scarred, so desolate, so monotonous, that I cannot recall its tortured surface without thinking of the infinite variety the delightful planet earth offers: misty waterfalls, pine forests, rose gardens, blues and greens and reds and whites that are missing entirely on the gray-tan moon. . . . I can now lift my mind out into space and look back at a midget earth. I can see it hanging there, surrounded by blackness, turning slowly in the relentless sunlight. . . . If I could use only one word to describe the earth as seen from the moon, I would ignore both its size and color and search for a more elemental quality, that of fragility. The earth appears "fragile," above all else. I don't know why, but it does.

Michael Collins,
Carrying the Fire: An Astronaut's Journey

Earth is unique because its location allows for the necessities of life.
Michael Collins was a member of the historic Apollo 11 mission, the team that, in 1969, first landed on the moon. While his fellow astronauts explored its surface, Collins viewed the moon from his orbit in space. His lofty position also enabled him to see the earth in a new way.

Our planet, Earth, is part of a family of nine planets that orbit a star that we call the sun. Revolving around many of these planets are satellites like the earth's moon. Earth is the third planet from the fiery sun, lying between Venus and Mars. Its orbit thus maintains a fragile balance between the extremes of fire and ice. If

Facing page: **Mapmaker Jaime Quintero updates a large relief map of the United States.**
Page 1: **A view from space shows planet Earth.**

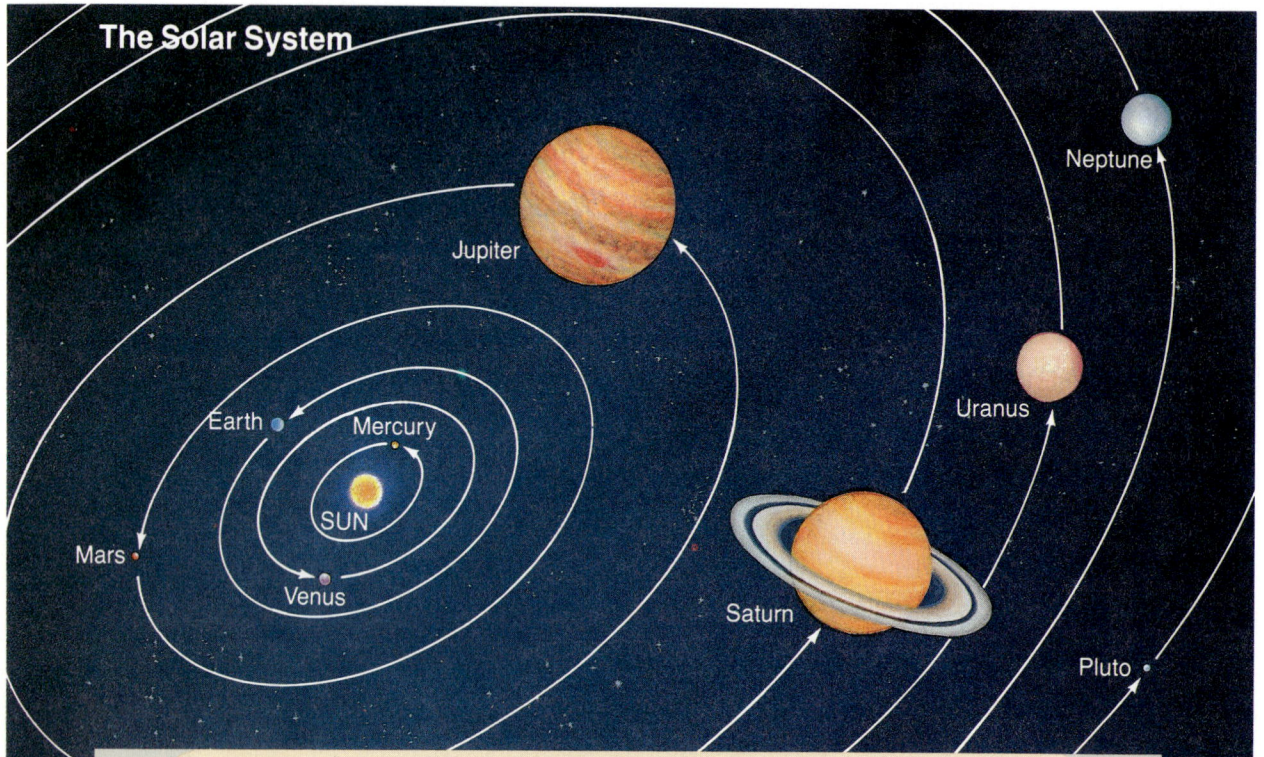

The Solar System

The sun is about 865,000 miles in diameter, much larger than Jupiter, the largest planet. The size of each planet and its average distance from the sun is given in the table below.

Planet	Average Distance from Sun (Millions of Miles)	Diameter (Miles)
Mercury	36	3,100
Venus	67	7,700
Earth	93	7,900
Mars	142	4,200
Jupiter	484	89,000
Saturn	887	75,000
Uranus	1,784	32,000
Neptune	2,795	28,000
Pluto	3,675	1,500

Earth had an orbit closer to the sun, like Venus, it would suffer tremendously scorching temperatures up to 850° F. If its orbit were as far away from the sun's warmth as that of Mars, Earth would be a frozen wasteland. Although the moon circles the earth and follows a similar path around the sun, it is lifeless. The moon is so small that its gravity is not strong enough to keep water and oxygen molecules from flying off into space.

In contrast to the moon, Earth possesses plentiful water and oxygen, both necessities for life as we know it. Our atmosphere of oxygen and nitrogen filters incoming sunlight, helping to keep the earth's seas from boiling away or freezing solid. When Collins described the earth's "misty waterfalls, pine forests, [and] rose gardens," he was describing features that are unique to our planet.

Geography is the study of where and why.

Geography can be a study of almost anything on the earth—people, animals, plants, mountains, earthquakes, rivers, oceans, continents, or hurricanes. The list could go on and on. Geography, though, looks at these subjects from a unique perspective. The study of geography is most interested in the locations and relationships of things on the earth. Take, for example, the scientists who study the earth's natural vegetation. The researchers' first question might be: Where do certain kinds of plants grow naturally?

To answer this question, they would begin by mapping the location of different kinds of plants all over the world. On such a map, the plants would form patterns. Palm trees, for example, would be concentrated in some areas and absent in others. In this same way, the location of almost anything can be mapped. Once drawn, the distribution, or pattern of location, becomes clear.

Mapping, however, is only the first step in the study of geography. The main goal is to find answers to some basic questions and concerns: (1) Why are things located where they are? (2) How are things related to each other and to their location? (3) Why is a thing's location significant or important to people?

To answer these questions, people often compare the distribution of one thing with the distribution of another. For example, you would see that a world map of the distribution of palm trees places most of them near the Equator. To find out the reason for this distribution, you could also check a map showing the distribution of other factors you suspect might be related, such as temperature and precipitation.

Besides maps, geographers have many other tools at their command. For example, geographers may draw information from such sources as population data or satellite images. In addition, other experts, such as geologists or political scientists, may provide new viewpoints from which to study the "where" and "why" questions of geography.

There are two main branches of geography.

Geography can be divided into two main branches or divisions: **physical geography** and **human geography**. Physical geography focuses on **natural features**, those landforms, water bodies, climates, geologic events, and vegetation patterns that occur in nature. Physical geographers study natural phenomena, such as earthquakes or rivers, glaciers or thunderstorms, tropical vegetation or rare arctic blooms.

Human geography, on the other hand, is concerned with **cultural features**. These physical or social structures show how humans have organized or changed the natural world. Human geographers, therefore, study such features as cities, religions, agriculture, or architecture.

They also examine the social, economic, historical, and political structures of human life. Political scientists, for example, often focus on geopolitics—a way of thinking about the importance of geographic positions, especially how they affect the control of resources and lines of communication.

There are two ways to study physical and human geography, topically and regionally. The topical approach involves studying one aspect of geography at a time. Within physical geography, an example of a topical approach is the study of soils. Within human geography, an example is the study of where and why different forms of architecture occur.

On the other hand, with a regional approach, the geographer studies all the aspects of a particular region. A **region** is a part of the earth that is marked by features that make it different from neighboring areas. In physical geography, a regional approach would involve not just examining soil but examining all the physical aspects of a mountain chain or an earthquake region. In human geography, a regional approach would mean examining not just architecture but all aspects of a particular culture region. A culture region is an area where there are clear similarities in human behavior and beliefs. For example, an area where most people speak Arabic and practice the Islamic religion could be considered a culture region.

Geography helps make people better caretakers of the earth.

As you study geography, you will see how human beings are linked to events occurring all around the globe, within the depths of the earth, and high in the atmosphere. By better understanding how the many elements of life on earth are tied together, you will be better equipped to deal with challenges that may arise in the future concerning food shortages or loss of natural environments.

Along with knowing how to protect our planet, a citizen of the earth should have a rich understanding and appreciation of all its regions and treasures. The study of geography, and the development of your geographic imagination, can lead you on your way. Your trained eyes will come to notice more detail in the environments through which you travel. Visual images will begin to accompany place names on the world map. The Amazon River will not be just another river to you. It will be a great python snaking through a hot, steamy rainforest. India won't be just another distant country. It will become the intriguing land that holds its breath for the quenching rains that come only once a year. Most of all, geography is an adventure. It is a journey in which your most important tool is your imagination.

Section 1 Review

Locating Key Places
Locate the following on the diagram on page 3: sun, earth, moon

Identifying Key Terms
Define the following terms: physical geography, human geography, natural feature, cultural feature, region

Reviewing Main Ideas
1. In what ways is Earth unique in our solar system?
2. What are some important questions of geography?
3. What are the two main branches of geography? How are they different from one another?
4. Why is geography a useful field of study?

Thinking Critically: Evaluate Sources of Information
This chapter states that if Earth were as close to the sun as Venus, its temperatures could reach as high as 850° F. With which of the following sources of information would you feel most confident in verifying this figure: a recent article on space research in your local newspaper, this year's NASA space report, an encyclopedia article on Venus, or a 1973 book on the planets? Explain your reasoning.

SECTION 2

Maps and Globes

Preview

Key Places
Where are these places located?
1 Equator
2 Prime Meridian
See the globe below.

Key Terms
What do these terms mean?
parallel   longitude
latitude   hemisphere
meridian

Main Ideas
As you read, look for answers to these questions.
• How are places located on maps and globes?
• What purposes do maps serve?
• What are essential features of all maps?

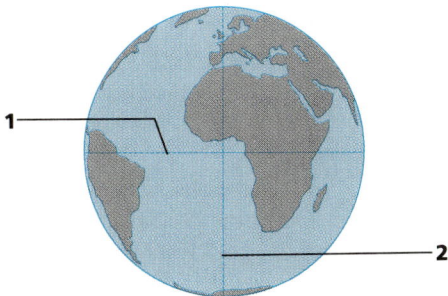

Now when I was a little chap I had a passion for maps. I would look for hours at South America, or Africa, or Australia, and lose myself in all the glories of exploration. At that time there were many blank spaces on the earth, and when I saw one that looked particularly inviting on a map (but they all look that) I would put my finger on it and say, "When I grow up I will go there."

Joseph Conrad, *Heart of Darkness*

Grid systems enable us to locate places on maps and globes.

The English novelist Joseph Conrad wrote these words around 1900. A former ship captain, Conrad understood the passion for travel and exploration that strikes many people as they look at maps. In this geography book, you'll find many kinds of maps. Perhaps they'll inspire you to travel to faraway places. For now, you can begin a journey of imagination, a trip that will take you to all parts of the globe. You'll encounter towering mountains and fiery volcanoes, lush green pastures and icy glaciers. You'll visit the seven continents and the four oceans as well as hundreds of smaller places—rivers, lakes, deserts, cities, towns, and villages.

But how do travelers, geographers, and mapmakers know where all these places are located? For Jaime Quintero, the mapmaker whose picture is shown in the chapter opener on page 2, to begin the enormous job of plotting out every major city, mountain, river, and lake in the United States, he had to have a system in mind. How else would he, or any other cartographer (mapmaker), know exactly where to place Mount St. Helens, Lake Michigan, or New Orleans?

To locate places on earth, cartographers invented a system made up of imaginary crisscrossing lines. These intersecting lines form what is called a grid system. One of the major points of reference in this grid system is an

The Global Grid System

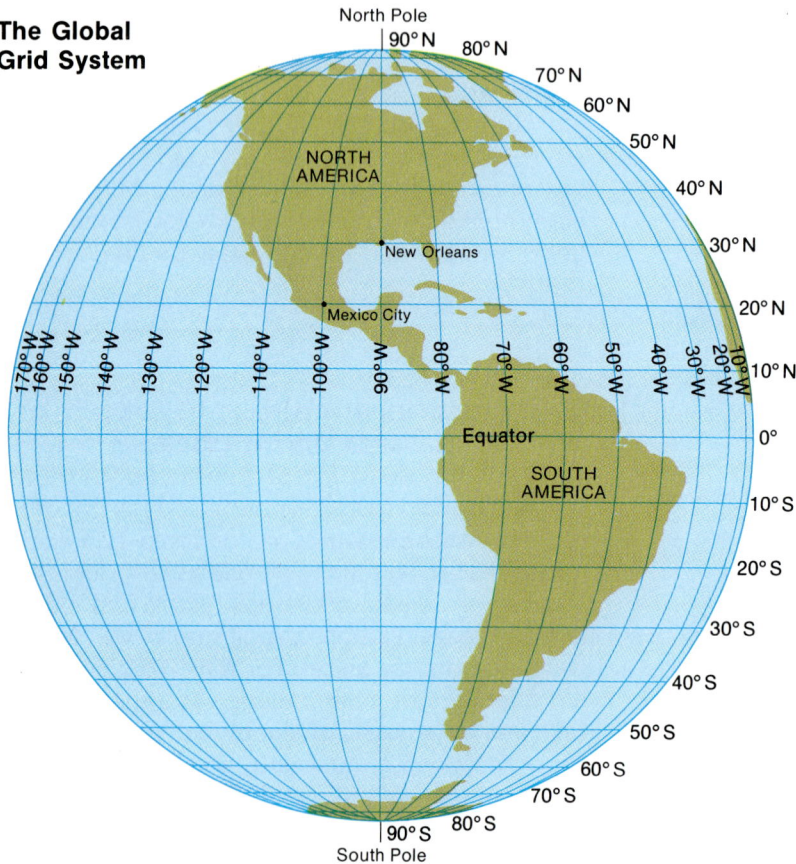

North Pole

90° N
80° N
70° N
60° N
50° N
40° N
30° N
20° N
10° N
0°
10° S
20° S
30° S
40° S
50° S
60° S
70° S
80° S
90° S

South Pole

NORTH AMERICA

New Orleans

Mexico City

Equator

SOUTH AMERICA

170° W
160° W
150° W
140° W
130° W
120° W
110° W
100° W
90° W
80° W
70° W
60° W
50° W
40° W
30° W
20° W
10° W

Map Study

The global grid system locates places on earth. New Orleans is located at 30°N and 90°W. Where is Mexico City located?

imaginary line known as the Equator. The Equator circles the earth, halfway between the North and South poles. It belongs to a set of lines running east and west around the globe called **parallels**. The distance between these lines is used to measure **latitude**. In this system, the Equator represents zero degrees latitude. Because the earth, like any sphere, has a circumference of 360 degrees, the distance between the Equator and either pole is 90 degrees, or one-fourth of the total circumference. Locations between these extremes are identified according to their distance from the Equator, measured as a number of degrees north or south of the Equator. The distance between lines of latitude is the same everywhere because these lines

are parallel to one another. New Orleans, Louisiana, for example, is located 30 degrees north of the Equator, or 30° N.

Running north and south on the globe, meeting at the two poles, are **meridians**, imaginary lines used to measure **longitude**. Just as the Equator serves as the starting point for measuring latitude, another imaginary line, called the Prime Meridian, acts as the starting point for longitude. Another name for this line is the Greenwich Meridian, derived from the name of the observatory in London, England, through which the line passes. Longitude is measured in degrees east or west of the Prime Meridian. The dividing line between east and west longitude is the 180° meridian, located in the Pacific Ocean.

This meridian is halfway around the globe from the Prime Meridian. The distance between lines of longitude is not the same everywhere because these lines are not always parallel. New Orleans, then, is located 90 degrees west of the Prime Meridian, or 90° W.

Using this system of latitude and longitude, the exact location of any place on earth can be clearly defined. In this system, the Equator and Prime Meridian serve another function. The two lines divide the earth into **hemispheres**, or half-spheres. The Equator divides our planet into the Northern Hemisphere and the Southern Hemisphere. The Prime Meridian divides the earth into the Western and Eastern hemispheres. The diagrams below and on page 10 show these hemispheres. You can see that New Orleans lies both in the Northern and Western hemispheres.

This system of latitude and longitude is used on both maps and globes. On road maps, how-ever, another grid system may be used. This other system, called a letter-number grid system, also relies on a similar formation. Its lines, how-ever, do not represent parallels and meridians. Instead, the lines serve as reference marks sim-ply for the map on which they exist. In such a system, lines run left to right and top to bot-tom, forming a pattern of rectangles on the map. These rectangles are then labeled by let-ters, set across the top and bottom, and num-bers, set down the sides of the map. Location is identified by the letter-number combination of the particular rectangle. The road map of part of Mexico on page 11 shows you how this grid system looks.

Different maps serve different purposes.
Maps are made to serve special functions. Many different types of maps are used for the study of geography. Each serves a different purpose

The Equator

North Pole

Northern
Hemisphere

0° Equator

Southern
Hemisphere

South Pole

0° Equator
20°N
40°N
ASIA
60°N
EUROPE
80°N
ARCTIC + North Pole
PACIFIC   OCEAN
OCEAN
AFRICA
ATLANTIC
OCEAN
NORTH
AMERICA

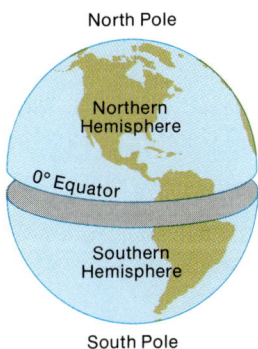

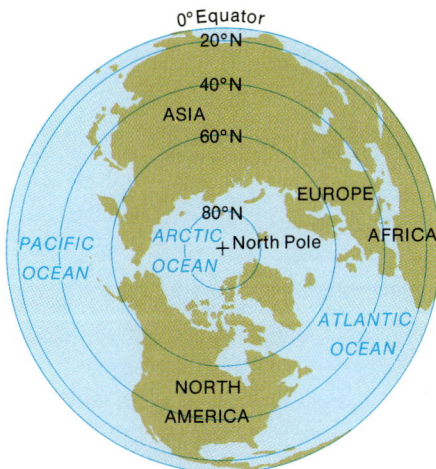

The Northern Hemisphere

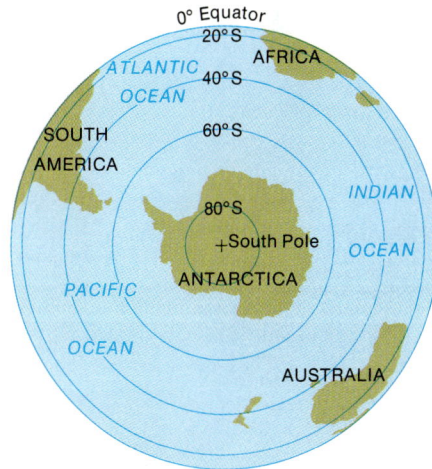

0° Equator
20°S
AFRICA
ATLANTIC
OCEAN
40°S
SOUTH
AMERICA
60°S
INDIAN
80°S
+ South Pole
OCEAN
PACIFIC
ANTARCTICA
OCEAN
AUSTRALIA

The Southern Hemisphere

Map Study

The Equator divides the earth into two hemispheres: the North-ern and the Southern hemispheres. Which one has the most land?

for the user. Some of the more common ones are political maps, physical maps, and special-purpose maps.

Political maps, as their name implies, identify political boundaries between or within countries, states, provinces, counties, or cities. Physical maps show the landforms, such as mountains, valleys, and plains, that shape a landscape. Special-purpose maps can represent any topic the cartographer wishes to illustrate. Examples are climate maps, road maps, and maps that show population distribution.

All good maps have five standard features.

Basically, every map needs to have a title, date, scale, key, and direction symbol or latitude-longitude grid.

Title. No good map is complete without a map title. The title allows the reader to identify the map's subject matter at first glance. The title should identify the part of the world it covers, and should indicate briefly the purpose of the map. For example, a possible map title is: "The World: Ocean Currents."

Date. Knowing the date that the map was made is essential because nothing on earth stays the same forever. Changes occur: a new hospital or highway is built, a forest is cut down, a country changes its name. By including the date on a map, the cartographer is telling the reader how a particular area looked at a specific point in time. You can determine when many of the maps in this book were made by looking at the copyright date of the book on page iv.

Scale. One of the most important parts of any map is the scale. A scale allows the reader to compare distances on the map to distances

The Prime Meridian

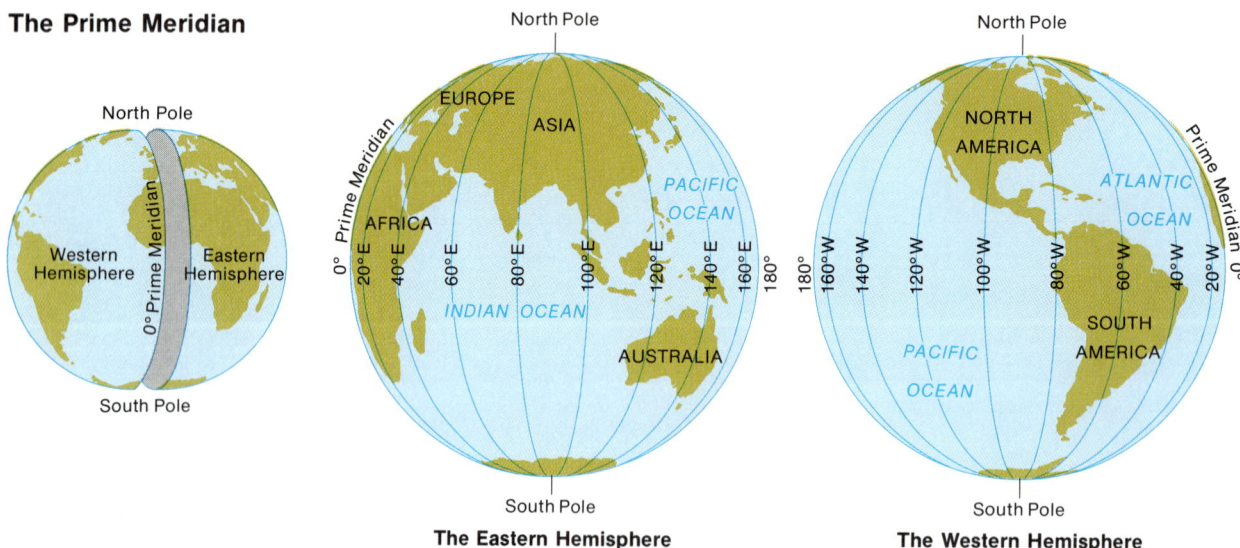

The Eastern Hemisphere

The Western Hemisphere

Map Study

The Prime Meridian divides the earth into two hemispheres: the Eastern and the Western hemispheres. Which one has the most land? In which is North America located?

Road Map: Northern and Central Mexico

Legend:
- Toll Expressways
- Free Expressways
- First Class Highways
- Second Class roads
- Points of Interest
- Mileage between dots

0   100   200 Miles
0   100   200 Kilometers

PACIFIC OCEAN

N

Map Study

Road maps often use a letter-number grid system. In which square is Mexico City located? Where is El Paso, Texas?

on the earth's surface. For example, a scale might tell you that one inch measured on a particular map is equivalent to 100 miles on the ground. The scale is determined by the type of information, or amount of detail, in the particular map. If you were just beginning to do some

exploration in an area and wanted some general information about locations of cities or national parks, you might decide to use a small-scale map. A small-scale map shows a large area of land with a small degree of local detail. Once you had chosen a particular city or park to visit, you would then need a large-scale map. This type of map represents only a small area on earth, but shows greater detail than a small-scale map. A large-scale map of a city might include the art museum, public zoo, or police stations.

In your experience with maps, you might have seen three different ways to show the scale. The simplest way is to describe the scale in words, perhaps writing "1 inch equals 50 miles." The scale can also be expressed as a ratio comparing units of distance, as in "1:2,000,000." This type of scale is known as a fractional scale. In the example given, 1 unit on the map (for example, one inch or one centimeter) represents 2 million of the same units on the earth's surface. The third, and most common, way to represent the scale is a bar scale. This scale is a straight line with distances marked out on it, with each mark representing a set number of miles or kilometers on the earth's surface. See the example on the road map on page 11.

Map key. Like the other essential elements of a map, the key serves a special function. The map key is the guide to the symbols used on a particular map. For example, the key on the Mexican road map tells you that a heavy purple line represents a toll expressway, and a yellow line indicates a smaller road. On another map, the key might show that the color blue covers areas where the average July temperature measures between 50 and 70 degrees. In either situation, the map key is the great decoder, unlocking the secrets of the map.

Direction symbol or latitude-longitude grid. A map must include some means of indicating direction. One common direction symbol is a compass rose, a diagram that indicates the basic cardinal directions of north, south, east, and west. A compass rose might also show the intermediate directions lying in between, such as northeast and southwest. A second common

direction symbol, used on the Mexican road map, is a simple arrow pointing to the north. This symbol leaves it up to the reader to determine the other directions. The third method of showing direction is to use the latitude-longitude grid system to mark out the directions. This method gives the most information to the map reader.

Now that we've reviewed the essentials of maps and mapmaking, you're ready to begin your journey around the earth. Your map skills should be top-notch, so you'll be able to find your way across any mapped area you encounter. Bon voyage!

Section 2 Review

Locating Key Places
Locate the following places on the map on page 620: Equator, Prime Meridian

Identifying Key Terms
Define the following terms: parallel, latitude, meridian, longitude, hemisphere

Reviewing Main Ideas
1. What are the two main systems used to locate places on maps and globes? How are these systems alike? How are they different?
2. What different purposes are served by physical, political, and special-purpose maps?
3. What five standard features do all maps need?

Thinking Critically: Make Hypotheses
The Equator cuts the earth in half. Since the earth is a giant ball, it could have been cut in half at any location. Why do you think geographers located the Equator where they did?

MAP LESSON

Comparing Maps of Different Scale

Congratulations! You've won the grand prize trip to Paris—all expenses paid. Before you depart, you'll need to plan out what to see and do. How much can you fit into ten days? Using the maps on this page may be helpful.

Using several different maps is often more useful than using just one. When each map has a different scale, you can picture an area from many different viewpoints. Remember that the scale of a map shows you how the distance on the map relates to the real distance on the earth. Because this relationship is constant across the map, the scale can be expressed as a ratio or fraction.

To make maps easier to read, mapmakers usually use a simple device called a bar scale. This type of scale is shown in the lower left corner of each of the maps on this page.

In each case, the bar scale uses a simple distance, such as two or twenty miles or kilometers. The length of the bar tells you how long this distance appears on any part of the map. This type of scale gives you a good estimate of the actual distances on the earth. If you wanted to be more accurate, however, you could copy the markings of the scale onto a piece of paper, and use the paper "ruler" to measure more exact distances on the map.

Review

Your hotel for the trip will be located on the Luxembourg Gardens near the University of Paris. If you wanted to walk about two miles away from your hotel, in any direction, which of the following Paris landmarks would be within walking distance? About how far away is each landmark?
a. the Cathedral of Notre Dame
b. The Museum of Natural History
c. Orly Airport
d. the Arch of Triumph
e. the Eiffel Tower

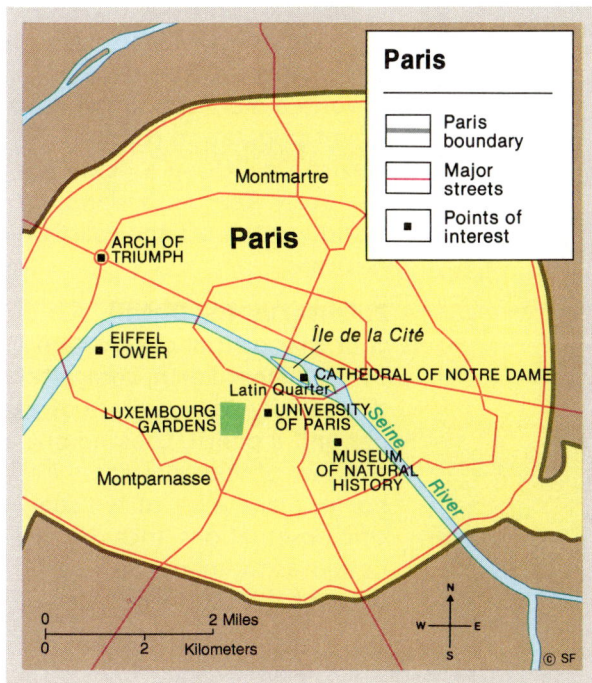

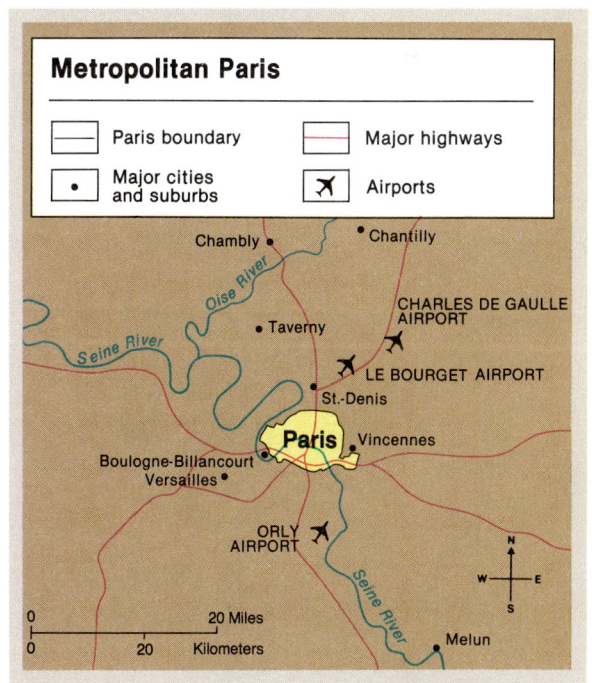

Paris

	Paris boundary
	Major streets
■	Points of interest

Montmartre

ARCH OF TRIUMPH

Paris

EIFFEL TOWER

Île de la Cité

Latin Quarter

CATHEDRAL OF NOTRE DAME

LUXEMBOURG GARDENS

UNIVERSITY OF PARIS

Seine River

Montparnasse

MUSEUM OF NATURAL HISTORY

0 ___ 2 Miles
0 ___ 2 Kilometers

© SF

Metropolitan Paris

	Paris boundary
●	Major cities and suburbs
	Major highways
✈	Airports

Chambly ●

● Chantilly

Oise River

CHARLES DE GAULLE AIRPORT

Seine River

● Taverny

LE BOURGET AIRPORT

St.-Denis

Paris

Vincennes

Boulogne-Billancourt
Versailles ●

ORLY AIRPORT ✈

Seine River

Melun ●

0 ___ 20 Miles
0 ___ 20 Kilometers

13

Review

Section Summaries

1. The Vision of Geography

The study of geography involves a special way of looking at the earth. Geography considers the distribution of such things as population, climate, and religion. The study of geography also questions why things are located where they are, and how things are related to one another. Physical and human geography are the two main branches of geography. Physical geography focuses on natural features, and human geography studies cultural features.

2. Maps and Globes

There are two systems for locating places on maps and globes: a latitude and longitude grid system and a letter-number grid system. Maps can serve many special purposes. Maps usually have such standard features as a title, date, scale, map key, and direction indicator.

Using Geography Skills

Reviewing the Map Lesson

The map of France below shows you a different viewpoint than the maps in the map lesson. To do this, the map uses a different scale.

Imagine that your vacation to Paris includes a side trip to any place within 200 miles. Which of the following places would you be able to visit?

a. Belgium
b. Switzerland
c. the Mediterranean Sea
d. Luxembourg
e. Spain

Using Social Studies Skills

1. Locate and Gather Information.

A first step in the study of geography is knowing your reference sources. Tour the geographic references in your school or community library. Some useful sources are the *Scott, Foresman World Atlas,* Rand McNally *Goode's World Atlas,* a world almanac, and *Webster's New Geographical Dictionary.* Using a world almanac, find the most recent population count of Mexico City. Using a world atlas, locate Kangaroo Island, an island located off the coast of Australia.

2. Observe for Detail.

As your first official observation of the planet Earth, complete this activity. Take a piece of paper and a pencil. Looking out a window of your classroom or home, make a list of ten specific observations. Include such details as the name and address of the hardware store across the street, the color of the bird flying by, the license plate of the car parked in the nearby lot, or the one-inch crack in your window. Be as specific and complete as possible.

Testing for Understanding

Locating Key Places
Match these descriptions with the key places listed below.
1. imaginary line that divides the earth into the Eastern and Western hemispheres
2. the earth's nearest star
3. parallel that divides the earth into the Northern and Southern hemispheres
4. third planet from the sun
5. lifeless satellite that orbits our planet
a. sun
b. earth
c. moon
d. Equator
e. Prime Meridian

Recalling Key Terms
Define these terms in your own words.

Section 1
physical geography
human geography
natural feature
cultural feature
region

Section 2
parallel
latitude
meridian
longitude
hemisphere

Reviewing Main Ideas
Section 1
1. Why can Earth maintain life better than Venus or Mars?
2. What questions define the special perspective of geography?
3. How do the two main branches of geography differ?
4. How can the study of geography help you be a better caretaker of the earth?

Section 2
1. Describe the two main systems for locating places on maps and globes.
2. Describe three different types of maps and explain the purpose of each.
3. List five essential features found on all complete maps.

Thinking Critically
1. Evaluate Sources of Information. For a camping trip in eastern Tennessee, which two of the following pieces of information would be most useful to you? Write a paragraph explaining your reasoning.
- a road map of the United States
- a physical map of Tennessee
- a political map of the United States
- a population distribution map of Tennessee
- a trail map of the Appalachian Mountains

2. Make Hypotheses. Imagine being a geographer 4,000 years ago. How would your work be different from the work of geographers today? Why would the job be easier today? Why would it be more difficult?

Shaping the Earth's Surface

In this chapter you will learn about the shaping of the earth's surface.

Sections

The Moving Plates of Our Planet

Preview

Key Places
Where are these places located?
1 Alps
2 Himalayas
3 Pacific Ocean
  See the globe below.

Key Terms
What do these terms mean?

core	plate tectonics
mantle	convection
crust	subduction
fossil	

Main Ideas
As you read, look for answers to these questions.
• How is the earth structured?
• How has the earth changed over time?
• How do plates affect the earth's landmasses?

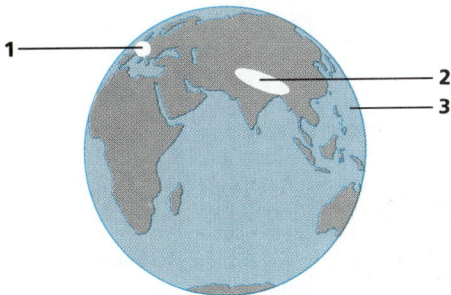

And holding the paper close to his eyes, moving from the last letter to the first, with trembling voice he read the message. It went like this:

> *In Sneffels Yoculis craterem kem delibat umbra Scartaris Julii intra calendas descende, audas viator, et terrestre centrum attinges. Kod feci. Arne Saknussemm.*

Which bad Latin may be translated as follows:

> *Descend into the crater of Snaeffels Jokull that lies under Scartari's shadow just before the calends of July, audacious traveler, and you will reach the center of the earth. I did it. Arne Saknussemm.*

Jules Verne,
Journey to the Center of the Earth, 1864

The earth is made up of distinct layers.

In Jules Verne's adventure story, three travelers find a secret passage to the center of the world. Is such a trip possible? So far, no one has been able to go very far below the earth's surface. In fact, the deepest anyone has been able to drill is only about 5 miles. The earth, however, has a diameter of almost 8,000 miles. Consequently, geologists—those scientists who study the composition of the earth—must use other means to journey to its center.

One of these means relies on vibrations. Whenever there is an earthquake or a major explosion such as a nuclear test, a series of vibrations is sent from the point of the disturbance. These vibrations are similar to the ripples formed when a stone is thrown into a pond. The vibrations travel first toward the center of the planet,

Facing page: **Ghostly wind-sculpted rocks seem to march silently across an Australian sand dune.**

then head back out to the surface. As the vibrations travel through the earth, they travel at different speeds and with different patterns depending upon the material through which they pass. By measuring the vibrations from the same explosion at various locations around the planet, geologists have confirmed that the earth is made up of distinct layers consisting of different materials.

These layers seem to have formed because of the way the earth developed over time. Scientists theorize that early in its history, the earth was so hot that much of it was molten, or melted. Gradually, some of the lighter material floated toward the surface, while iron and nickel, which are both heavy metals, moved to the center of the planet, forming its **core**. The core is believed to be divided into an outer liquid core and an inner solid core. The diagram below shows that the outer core is surrounded by a thick layer of very hot and heavy liquid rock called the **mantle**. The material of the mantle is molten and has the consistency of putty. The surface of the earth is a very thin layer of lighter solid rock known as the **crust**. This layer acts as the earth's skin and varies from about 6 miles in thickness beneath the oceans to about 25 miles beneath the continents.

The earth has changed dramatically over billions of years.

Consider this statement for a moment: Most scientists believe that the crust of the earth formed 4.5 billion years ago. Can you even imagine 4.5 billion years?

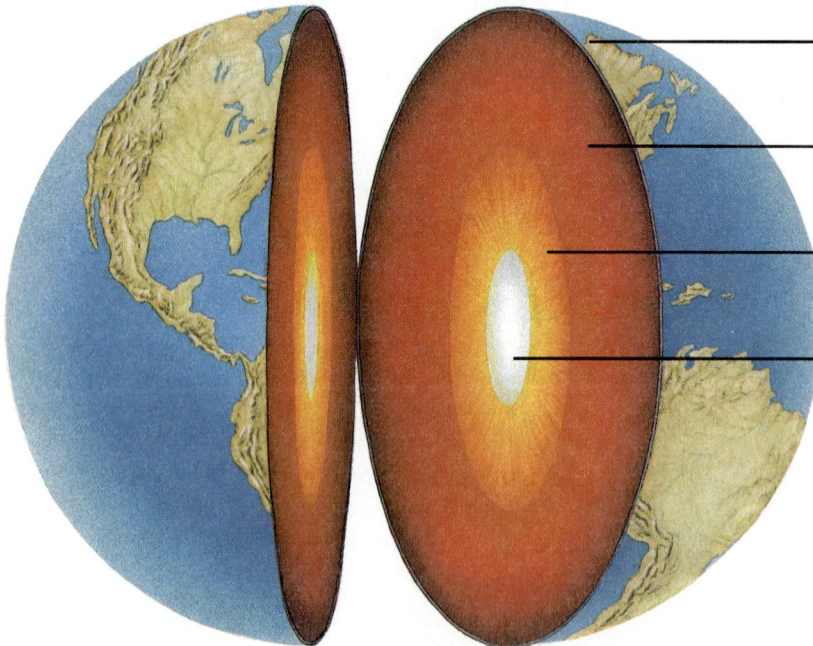

The Earth's Interior

Crust
Solid rock
6–25 miles

Mantle
Liquid rock
1,800 miles

Outer core
Liquid iron and nickel
1,400 miles

Inner core
Solid iron and nickel
1,600 miles

To understand the earth's history, you must use your imagination to consider time from a new perspective. Imagine a silk moth in a garden. After it develops its wings, the giant silk moth *Ailanthus* lives for only two or three days. During that brief time, the moth tours summer's gardens, lighting on flower after flower. To the silk moth, the flower garden has existed always and will exist forever. How can it know that flowers fade and die and that seasons change? Its eternity is but a two- or three-day sliver of time.

Human beings live 70 to 80 years in a world that has existed for billions of years. Like the moth in the garden, our existence is so brief that the earth to us does not appear to change very much. The seasons come and go, but the earth and its landforms seem to stand solid and last forever.

Although our brief view does not allow us to see much, the earth does change. It changed greatly before you were born, and it will change much after you have died. Since its beginnings, the surface of the earth has continually shifted and heaved. Its landforms have risen and fallen, and its surface features have been transformed over and over again.

Geologists have been able to piece together the history of these changes from various clues discovered in our planet's rock formations. Some of these clues have been buried in the rocks as **fossils**, those hardened remains or traces of ancient plants or animals. Other clues lie in the structures of the rocks themselves. From their investigations, geologists have divided the earth's long life into several major divisions of time, called eras. The earliest-known stage, encompassing all time before 600 million years ago, has been named the Precambrian era. About 80 percent of all geologic time falls within this era. During the Precambrian period, the oldest rocks of the continents formed.

Precambrian time was followed by three major eras. These time divisions are based largely on events that changed the shape or composition of the earth's crust, such as the building of mountain ranges. Eras are also marked by the kinds of plants and animals that flourished at the time. The three divisions are known as Paleozoic, or ancient life; Mesozoic, or middle life; and Cenozoic, or recent life.

The Paleozoic [pā'lē ə zō'ik] era, lasting from 600 million years ago to 225 million years ago, is a time that fascinates mining engineers today. This era produced the beginnings of the fossil fuels we know as coal, oil, and natural gas. These fuels formed from the remains of decaying plants and animals. This was also a time when some of the mountains we now recognize were being formed.

The Mesozoic [mes'ə zō'ik] era, lasting from 225 million years ago to 65 million years ago, is the era we now associate with lumbering dinosaurs. These large creatures existed at a time when the Rocky Mountains were just beginning to take shape.

The Cenozoic [sen'ə zō'ik] era, beginning about 65 million years ago, shaped the earth's surface to the point where we recognize it today. Several more familiar mountain ranges began to form: the European Alps, the Asian Himalayas, and the mountain chains that rim the Pacific Ocean. It also became noticeably colder during the Cenozoic era. During several periods called ice ages, much of the earth's surface was covered with large sheets of ice. The movement of the ice scoured much of North America, northern Europe, and Asia. When most of the ice finally melted, the height of the oceans rose, drowning many land areas and changing the shape of the world's coastlines. At the same time, many of the earth's lakes were carved out and filled in by the movement and melting of the glaciers.

Throughout its history, the earth has changed considerably. Scientists have only recently begun to understand the mighty forces that continue to change the shapes of the continents and oceans on this planet.

Plates move the earth's landmasses.

Scientists have long tried to explain the patterns of land and sea on the earth's surface. Nearly a century ago, a German scientist, Alfred Wegener, developed a theory that the continents were once united in an enormous single landmass he called Pangaea. He believed that over time, Pangaea broke into two pieces which he named Laurasia and Gondwanaland. According to Wegener's theory, these two super-continents eventually drifted apart to form the seven continents we know today. Wegener's proof lay in the shapes of the modern continents. Look at the world map on pages 620–621, and you can see that South America and Africa seem to fit together like large pieces of a jigsaw puzzle.

Other discoveries lent support to the theory. Fossils that were found on the Atlantic coast of South America matched those found on the Atlantic coast of Africa. In another case, fossils of ancient sea creatures were discovered high in the Himalayas in Asia, thousands of miles from any ocean. These discoveries brought more scientists into Wegener's camp, and prompted more research on the question of whether the landmasses were once joined together.

Not until the 1960s, however, did scientists begin to come up with any proof for this theory of "continental drift." The ocean floors were then being mapped for the first time. Through detailed mapping, scientists discovered that there were mid-ocean mountain ranges snaking around the globe. For millions of years, molten rock has oozed out of cracks along these ridges from deep within the earth's mantle. The rock cools as it reaches the water and eventually hardens. When drilling into the sea floor near these ridges, scientists detected a pattern. The oldest rocks are those that are farthest from the ridges. Apparently, molten rock rises to the surface in the ridges, pushing the sea floor outward. Slowly, the sea floor expands, pushing the continents bordering the ocean apart.

Most scientists now believe that the continents or sections of continents are carried on giant plates of crustal rock much like packages moving on a conveyor belt. The ocean floor discoveries led to the development of the theory of **plate tectonics**. This theory holds that the earth's crust is made up of around 20 moving plates. (See map at right.) These plates carry both the earth's continents and sea floor. In some places these plates are spreading apart, and in other places they are colliding or scraping against each other.

The plates are spreading apart at the mid-ocean ridges, where new sea floor is being created. The process thought to be responsible for this plate movement is known as convection. **Convection** is the transfer of heat from one place to another by the circulation of heated particles of a gas or liquid. In the earth's mantle, convection works in a simple cycle: hot molten rock, called magma, rises; as it rises, it cools; as it cools, it starts to sink again. When the hot rising magma reaches the cooler layer of crust, some of it escapes through the vents of mid-ocean ridges. This heated material then becomes part of the spreading sea floor. If enough of the magma accumulates, a volcanic island such as Iceland may result.

Where the plates are coming together, different formations are created. In some areas the edge of one plate is forced under the edge of another plate. This process of one plate sliding

Map Study

Earthquakes often occur at the boundaries of the earth's moving crustal plates. What are the plates that cause earthquakes in southern Europe?

The Earth's Plates

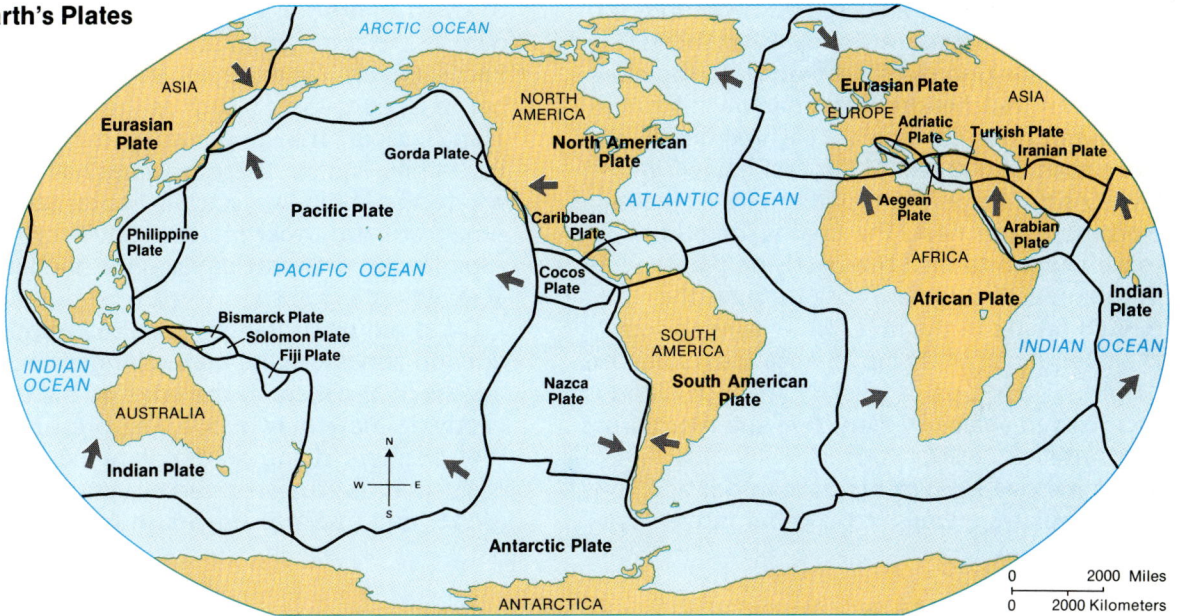

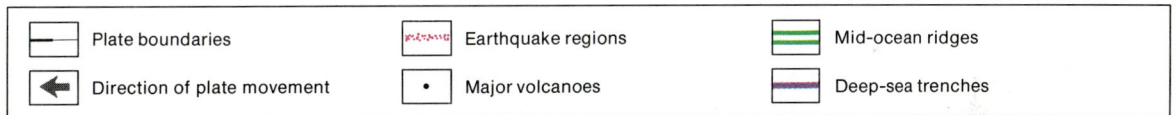

ARCTIC OCEAN

ASIA

Eurasian Plate

Philippine Plate

Gorda Plate

NORTH AMERICA

North American Plate

Pacific Plate

PACIFIC OCEAN

Caribbean Plate

Cocos Plate

Bismarck Plate
Solomon Plate
Fiji Plate

INDIAN OCEAN

AUSTRALIA

Indian Plate

Nazca Plate

SOUTH AMERICA

South American Plate

ATLANTIC OCEAN

Eurasian Plate

EUROPE

ASIA

Adriatic Plate

Turkish Plate
Iranian Plate

Aegean Plate

AFRICA

Arabian Plate

African Plate

Indian Plate

INDIAN OCEAN

N
W E
S

Antarctic Plate

ANTARCTICA

0   2000 Miles
0   2000 Kilometers

| | Plate boundaries | | Earthquake regions | | Mid-ocean ridges |
| | Direction of plate movement | • | Major volcanoes | | Deep-sea trenches |

Effects of the Moving Plates

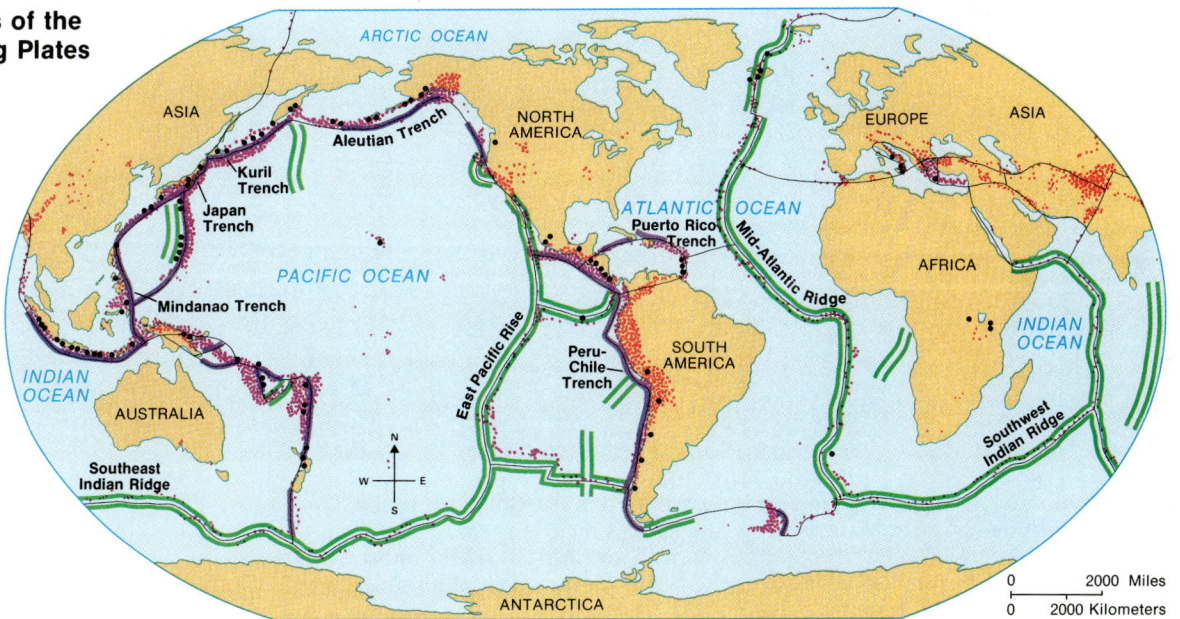

ARCTIC OCEAN

ASIA

NORTH AMERICA

Aleutian Trench

Kuril Trench

Japan Trench

Mindanao Trench

PACIFIC OCEAN

INDIAN OCEAN

AUSTRALIA

Southeast Indian Ridge

East Pacific Rise

Puerto Rico Trench

Peru-Chile Trench

SOUTH AMERICA

ATLANTIC OCEAN

Mid-Atlantic Ridge

EUROPE

ASIA

AFRICA

INDIAN OCEAN

Southwest Indian Ridge

N
W E
S

ANTARCTICA

0   2000 Miles
0   2000 Kilometers

© SF

beneath another is called **subduction**. In a subduction zone, an ocean trench often forms where the sinking plate descends into the mantle. Ocean trenches are deep, narrow ditches in the ocean floor, sometimes reaching depths of more than 24,000 feet (4.5 miles) below sea level. As the edge of the plate sinks, its movement generates heat. The heat is sometimes intense enough to melt the overlying plate, allowing tunnels of magma to rise through the melted breaks in the rock. These tunnels form the beginnings of chains of volcanoes; some examples of this type of volcano are such island arcs (curved chains of islands) as the Aleutians and Antilles.

The massive movements of sea floor and continental plates give rise to another intense type

of earth-shattering event, earthquakes. Earthquakes are common in subduction zones. The Pacific Ocean, for example, is ringed by a number of deep trenches, such as the Mindanao Trench, Japan Trench, Aleutian Trench, and Peru-Chile Trench. These trenches have formed where the Philippine, Pacific, Nazca, South American, and other plates meet. They have all experienced dramatic earthquake and volcanic activity.

Great mountain ranges are also typical of subduction zones. As one plate plunges into the depths of the mantle, the edge of the other overlying plate may buckle. The pressure upon the continent riding on the plate may be so great that its crustal material is pushed both together and upward. The South American Andes

How the Plates Move

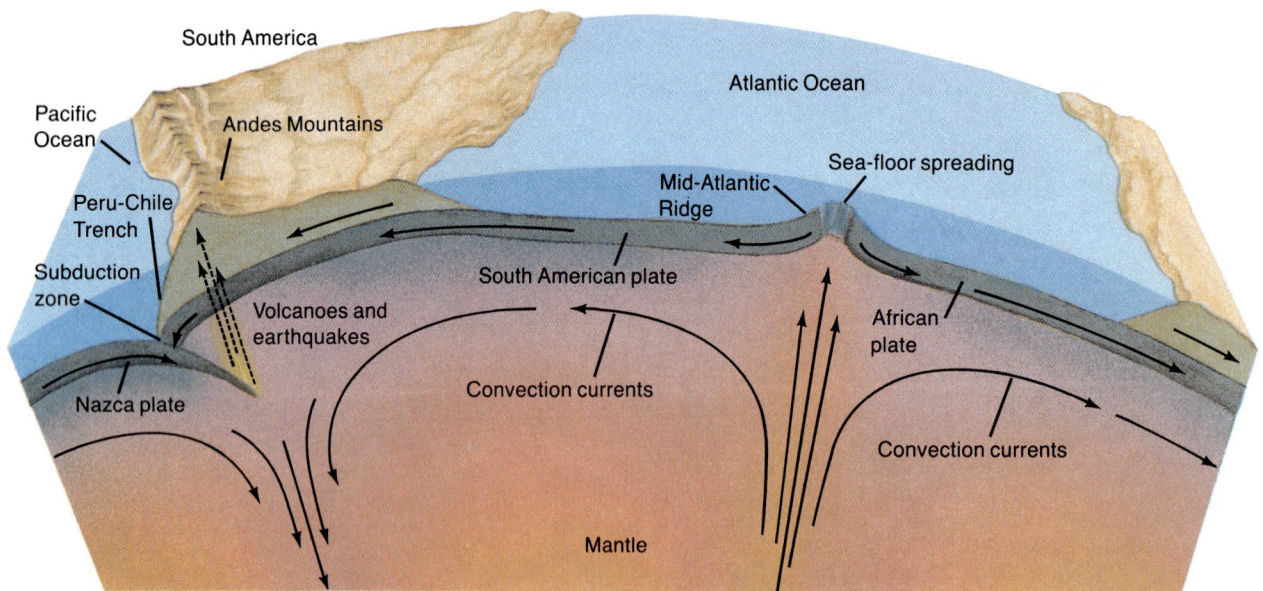

This diagram gives a general view of how the earth's crustal plates move, causing continental drift. Material from the earth's mantle rises up at the Mid-Atlantic Ridge, pushing the South American and African plates apart. As it moves, South America slides over the Nazca plate, which plunges down into the mantle, forming a deep ocean trench.

Molten lava oozes from a volcano, creating new landforms.

Drifting Continents

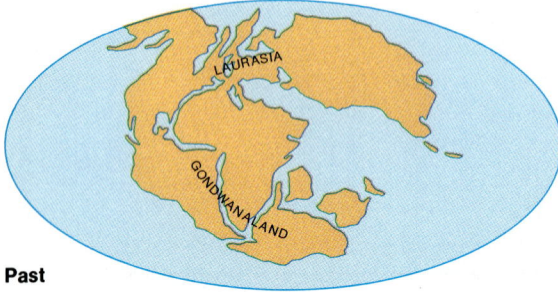

Past

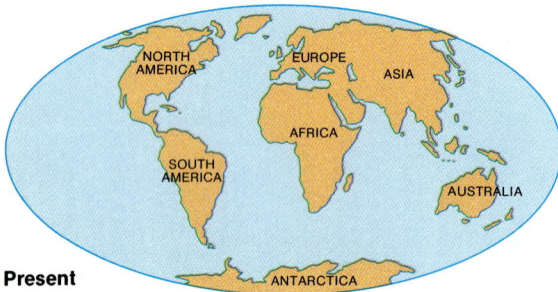

Present

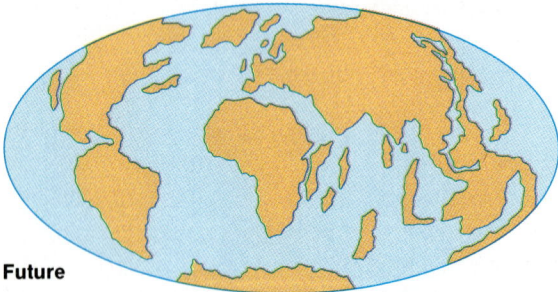

Future

Map Study

The top map shows the world as it may have looked about 200 million years ago. In the middle is the world today. The bottom map shows the world as it may look 10 million years from now. Will Asia and Africa be closer together or farther apart?

and the Asian Himalayas have been formed in this way.

Slow-motion collisions and separations of plates occur over millions of years. The movement, however slow, can be measured. For example, activity at the Mid-Atlantic Ridge is forcing the Atlantic Ocean to expand about one inch per year. This means that at the end of the school year, your desk will be measurably farther away from the continent of Europe than it was in September. Some people also believe that the west coast of California, which is located on a moving plate separate from the rest of the continental United States, will become an island in several million years.

Section 1 Review

Locating Key Places
Locate the following places on the map on page 622: Alps, Himalayas, Pacific Ocean

Identifying Key Terms
Define the following terms: core, mantle, crust, plate tectonics, convection, subduction

Reviewing Main Ideas
1. If you were to slice the earth in two, what distinct layers would you find?
2. How do scientists believe that the earth has changed in the past 600 million years?
3. How does the movement of plates explain the present-day pattern of earthquakes, volcanoes, and ocean trenches around the Pacific Ocean?

Thinking Critically: Analyze Comparisons
An analogy, which shows similarities between two different items, can sometimes be used to explain an abstract idea in terms of something more familiar. In this section, an analogy comparing the lifespan of a moth in a garden to that of human beings on earth is used to illustrate the immensity of the earth's history; that is, *a* (human being) is to *b* (earth) as *x* (moth) is to *y* (garden). Think of an analogy of your own that illustrates the size relationship between the earth's crust and the earth's diameter.

The Earth's Uplifting Forces

Preview

Key Places
Where are these places located?
1 Hawaii
2 Andes
See the globe below.

Key Terms
What do these terms mean?

elevation	plains
mountains	compression
hills	folds
plateaus	faults

Main Ideas
As you read, look for answers to these questions.
- How are the earth's landforms shaped?
- What is volcanism?
- What causes earthquakes?
- How does plate tectonics build mountains?

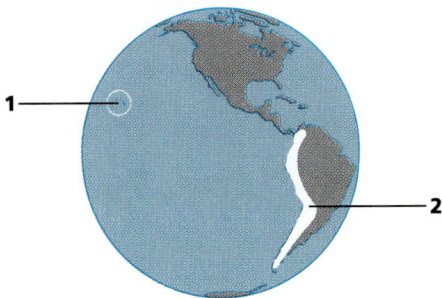

And then one day . . . an eruption of liquid rock occurred that was different from any others that had preceded. It threw forth the same kind of rock, with the same violence, and through the same vents in the earth's core. But this time what was thrown forth reached the surface of the sea. There was a tremendous explosion as the liquid rock struck water and air together. Clouds of steam rose miles into the air. Ash fell hissing upon the heaving waves. Detonations shattered the air for a moment and then echoed away in the immensity of the empty wastes.

[Rock] had at last been deposited above the surface of the sea. An island . . . had risen from the deep.

James Michener, *Hawaii*

Powerful forces shape the earth's landforms.

Novelist James Michener's words provide a dramatic description of the birth of Hawaii, one of our 50 states. The state of Hawaii is a chain of islands in the Pacific Ocean formed on the tops of huge undersea volcanoes.

If you were to drive across the continental United States from east to west, you would see a wide range of landforms. You would see volcanoes, cliffs, canyons, mountains, craters, swamps, sand dunes, and grassy rolling plains. Landforms are classified primarily by their **elevation**, or distance above or below sea level. **Mountains** are landforms that are highest in elevation, reaching heights of thousands of feet above sea level. **Hills** are lower and often more rounded on top. **Plateaus** are flat areas that rise higher in elevation than the surrounding area. **Plains** are flat or gently rolling areas that are generally low in elevation. Locate these four kinds of landforms on the world map on pages 26–27.

The Andes Mountains

Rolling hills of England

Fertile plains of Ohio

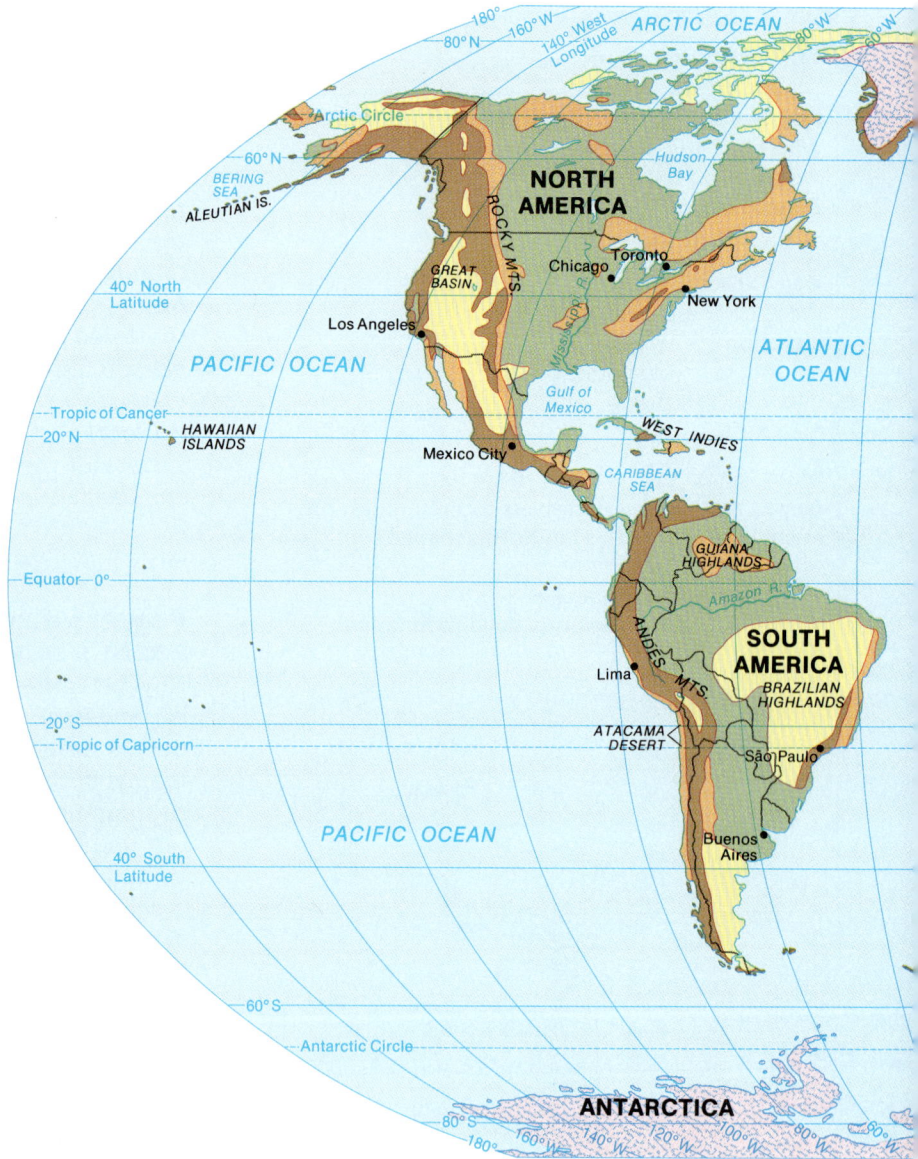

Map Study

Note that most of Africa is a huge plateau. What kind of scenery would you expect to find in western South America? In central North America?

ARCTIC OCEAN

160° E

180°

80° N

ICELAND

100°

80° E

60° E

40° E

20° E

0° Prime Meridian

AND

Arctic Circle

60° N

London

Moscow

URAL MTS.

Ob River

NORTH SEA

BALTIC SEA

EUROPE

ASIA

ALPS

Paris

Volga R.

CAUCASUS MTS.

CASPIAN SEA

GOBI

Beijing

40° N

BLACK SEA

Huang R.

Tokyo

ATLAS MTS.

MEDITERRANEAN SEA

PLATEAU OF TIBET

Chang (Yangtze) River

Shanghai

PACIFIC OCEAN

Cairo

HIMALAYAS

EAST CHINA SEA

SAHARA

RED SEA

THAR DESERT

Tropic of Cancer

SOUTH CHINA SEA

20° N

Calcutta

Bombay

PHILIPPINE ISLANDS

Niger R.

ARABIAN SEA

Nile R.

AFRICA

Zaire R.

Nairobi

Equator—0°

Congo R.

Lake Victoria

Jakarta

NEW GUINEA

Kinshasa

INDIAN OCEAN

ATLANTIC OCEAN

MADAGASCAR

20° S

KALAHARI DESERT

AUSTRALIA

Tropic of Capricorn

GREAT VICTORIA DESERT

Johannesburg

N

Sydney

40°

W   E

S

0   1000   2000 Miles

0   1000   2000   Kilometers

Scale accurate for the Equator

60° S

Antarctic Circle

20°

Prime Meridian

40° E

60° E

80° E

120° East Longitude

140° East Longitude

160°

80° S

180°

ANTARCTICA

© SF

World:
Landform Regions

Mountains

Hills

Plateaus

Plains

Ice-covered land

Except for the occasional scars made by plowing or mining, landforms may seem unchanging, frozen in time. In fact, the land is constantly being uplifted and worn down by two powerful types of forces. Internal forces—those energies from deep inside the earth's fiery mantle—produce volcanoes and mountains. External forces—wind, water, ice, and gravity—wear down the mountains and other landforms built up by the internal forces. If the earth's internal forces ceased pushing the land into irregular shapes, the surface would gradually be worn flat by the external forces. Eventually, the earth would become as astronaut Michael Collins saw it from space—"smooth as a billiard ball."

In this section you will read about the internal forces driving the earth's development. The next section will introduce you to the external forces. Think back now to what you've read in the last section about plate tectonics. Most scientists believe that all upheavals of land can be traced back to the convection currents that flow within the mantle. The convection currents cause the crustal plates to spread, collide, and scrape. When such massive movements occur, enormous pressure is released. Three kinds of geologic activity take place because of this pressure: volcanism, earthquakes, and mountain building. They result in the formation of landforms.

Volcanism is a means of building landforms.

Volcanism is the general term for volcanic activity. Molten rock rises from within the earth's mantle and is released in the form of lava during a volcanic eruption. The lava cools and eventually hardens into solid rock. As subsequent eruptions occur, the rock accumulates and volcanic mountains are born.

Volcanoes do not occur randomly. Unless you live in a volcanic region, a volcano probably will not spring up at your front door. Look back at the map on page 21. Note that most volcanic eruptions tend to occur at or near the boundaries of crustal plates. For example, look carefully at the rim of the Pacific Ocean. You'll find the "Ring of Fire," an immense circle of volcanic activity that runs all around the ocean. The eruptions of El Chinchon in Mexico in 1982 and Washington State's Mount St. Helens in 1980 are

A fiery volcano creates a small island off the coast of New Zealand. Located on a plate boundary, New Zealand has many active volcanoes.

recent examples of the volcanic activity taking place in this ring of fire.

As we discussed in the last section, volcanoes usually occur at plate boundaries because of plate tectonics. Where two plates are spreading apart, or where they come together, lava emerges from the cracks. The lava eventually forms a volcano. Volcanic activity is common all around the globe. The sliding of plates has created enormous volcanic mountain chains that sweep around the Pacific Ocean, including the islands of Indonesia, the Philippines, and Japan.

Moving plates also cause earthquakes.

Like volcanoes, three-fourths of the world's earthquakes occur in the Pacific Ring of Fire. They occur near the boundaries of plates, either near subduction zones or where two plates scrape against each other. Within this ring, earthquakes are common in Indonesia, Japan, Alaska, California, Mexico, Central America, and western South America. There are also many earthquakes in other areas of plate activity— along the mid-oceanic ridges, the Mediterranean Sea, Turkey, Iran, Pakistan, and the Himalayas. The rest of the world's earthquakes seem to form in response to weaknesses in the earth's crust. These weaknesses may result from ancient cracks in the earth's rock layers. One noteworthy example of an earthquake zone far from any known plate boundary lies near New Madrid, Missouri.

An earthquake shakes an area by releasing immense amounts of energy in the form of seismic, or shock, waves. The process begins when pressures from shifting plates force the earth's rock layers to fracture or break. The energy freed by this break is released through the surrounding rock and is felt above the ground as an earthquake.

Using special instruments, scientists can determine the location and strength of an earthquake. The Richter scale, developed in 1935 by Charles F. Richter, a seismologist, is the most common tool for identifying the force of an earthquake. The scale measures the strength of the quake, with each step up the scale indicating an increase in strength by a power of 10. For example, an earthquake measuring 7.0 is ten times as powerful as one measuring 6.0. The strongest earthquake ever measured registered 8.9 on the Richter scale.

Plate tectonics builds mountains through folding and faulting.

Many of the earth's great mountain ranges have formed at points where two plates have collided. One of the major means of mountain building is compression. **Compression** is a force that makes an object smaller through applied pressure or squeezing. When one plate is causing another plate to submerge, great pressure is applied to the overriding plate. This pressure forces the surface rock of the plate to compress into a series of giant wrinkles called **folds**. These folds are what we now recognize as the earth's great mountain ranges.

To picture the folding process of the rock, you can conduct a brief experiment. Start with a stiff piece of material such as a tablecloth or napkin on a flat, smooth surface. Lay the material down on the surface. Put your left hand on the left edge of the material, and your right hand on the right edge. Your two hands represent two different crustal plates about to collide. Slowly, move your left hand toward your right hand, keeping both hands on the material. You should find that the material will compress into a series of folds. The same basic process occurs with the rock.

Compare the world landforms map on pages 26–27 to the world plate map on page 21. Locate the major mountain ranges of North America, the Andes of South America, the Alps of Europe, and the Himalayas of Asia. Scientists believe that these huge mountain ranges are folded mountains that developed in places where plates collided.

Even though they are not all near present-day plate boundaries, remember that some mountain ranges were formed a long time ago when the continents were in a different position. For example, the Appalachian Mountains along the east coast of the United States were probably formed at a time when North America was joined to northern Europe. At the time, 200 to 300 million years ago, the Appalachians and the mountains of northern Europe were located along the borders of plates which eventually spread apart to form the Atlantic Ocean.

Besides folding, mountains are also built as a result of faulting. When rock strains under the pressure of colliding plates, it often splits into fractures. The resulting fractures, or breaks in the rock, are called **faults.** If the pressure from the plates continues, the slabs of rock between the faults begin to overlap like shingles on a roof. As the diagram below (left) shows, these rock "shingles" are eventually lifted up into mountains.

Mountain Building
Mountains are built through folding, faulting, and volcanic action. These processes often occur at the same time.

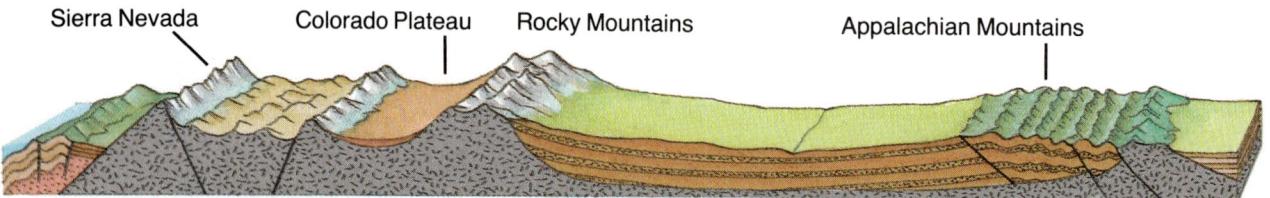

Sierra Nevada   Colorado Plateau   Rocky Mountains   Appalachian Mountains

Fault-Block Mountains

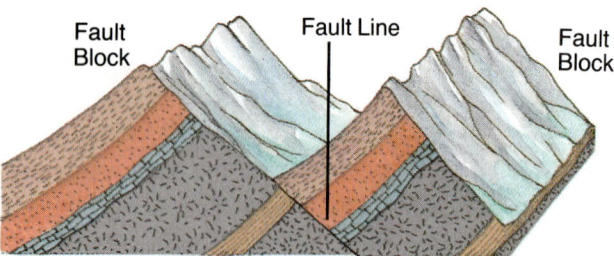

Fault Block   Fault Line   Fault Block

The Sierra Nevadas developed as the earth's crust cracked into huge blocks that were then tilted. Fault-block mountains usually have a steep face on one side and a gentler slope on the other.

Folded Mountains

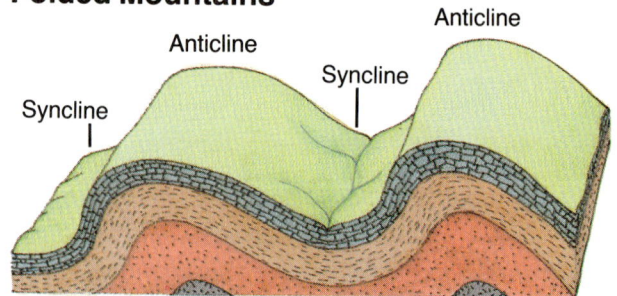

Anticline   Anticline   Syncline   Syncline

The Appalachians formed long ago when two plates collided, pushing the crust into long folds. The tops of these folds are called anticlines; the bottoms are called synclines. The earth's largest mountain ranges, such as the Himalayas, Andes, Rockies, and Alps, are all folded mountains.

Faults also occur at points where two moving plates scrape past one another as they travel in different directions. The best-known example of this type of fault in the United States is the San Andreas Fault in California. The fault lies along the line where the Pacific Plate is moving northwest past the North American Plate at an average speed of 2.5 inches per year. The scraping of the two plates has produced several severe earthquakes in the area surrounding the fault.

Volcanoes

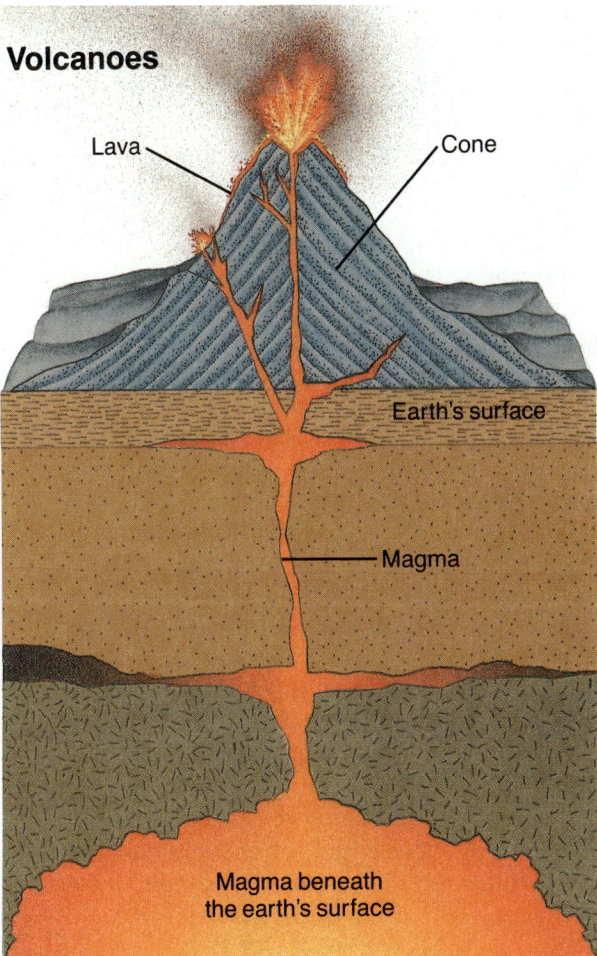

Lava

Cone

Earth's surface

Magma

Magma beneath the earth's surface

Section 2 Review

Locating Key Places
Locate the following places on the map on page 622: Hawaii, Andes

Identifying Key Terms
Define the following terms: elevation, mountains, hills, plateaus, plains, compression, folds, faults

Reviewing Main Ideas
1. How do internal forces shape the earth's landforms?
2. How does volcanism build landforms?
3. How does plate tectonics create earthquakes?
4. Describe two ways in which mountain ranges are formed.

Thinking Critically: Analyze Comparisons
On page 29 the folding process of rock on the earth is compared to the folding of a tablecloth or napkin. Reread that paragraph. How strong is that comparison? What similarities do the two processes being compared have? What differences?

Some western volcanoes, like Mount St. Helens and Mount Rainier, were formed by an old crustal plate that slid underneath the western United States. The entire state of Hawaii in the Pacific Ocean is located on the tops of huge undersea volcanoes.

SECTION 3

The Earth's Destructive Forces

Preview

Key Places
Where are these places located?
1 Great Lakes
2 Rocky Mountains
3 Appalachian Mountains
See the globe below.

Key Terms
What do these terms mean?

weathering	continental ice sheet
erosion	alpine glacier
deposition	

Main Ideas
As you read, look for answers to these questions.
- What three external forces shape landforms?
- How does the weathering of rock occur?
- How does erosion occur?
- What does deposition accomplish?

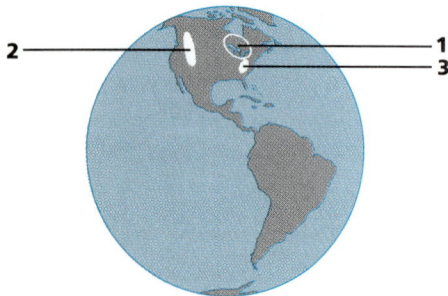

Then from the south, where storms breed in the senseless deep, a mighty wave would form and rush across the world. Its coming would be visible from afar, and in gigantic, tumbling, whistling, screaming power it would fall upon the little accumulation of rocks and pass madly on. . . .

[The] action of wind and rain and cooling nights began to pulverize the newly born lava, decomposing it into soil. When enough had accumulated, the island was ready.

James Michener, *Hawaii*

Weathering, erosion, and deposition shape landforms.

In Section 2 you learned that mountains are formed by the tremendous uplifting of forces deep within the earth. In this section you will learn how the earth's destructive forces shape these mountains and many other kinds of landforms, as James Michener described in *Hawaii*.

The Appalachian Mountains, as an example, are one of the world's oldest mountain ranges and reach about 6,000 feet above sea level. Compared to higher mountain ranges such as the Rocky Mountains or the Alps, the Appalachians seem more like high hills. For millions of years, ice, wind, water, and gravity have worn away the sharp peaks and precipices of the Appalachians. Their rounded slopes serve to demonstrate the effects.

The type of transformation exhibited by the Appalachians occurs in three stages. The first stage is the break-up, or **weathering**, of rock into fragments. The second stage is **erosion**, or the carrying away or transportation of the rock fragments. The third stage is **deposition**, which is the laying down of the rock fragments in a new location. The complete process can eventually result in the creation of entirely new landforms and a remodeling of the earth's surface.

If these wearing-down actions were to continue undisturbed for millions of years, the landscape would become a simple, flat surface. The leveling process, however, is usually countered by the internal forces of mountain building. Earth's internal and external forces are both at work at the same time. Therefore, landforms are either being built or torn down, depending upon which forces are stronger at that particular time.

Weathering occurs in two major forms.

During weathering, the first stage of transformation, the rock structures of the landform are broken down into smaller pieces. Two main types of weathering exist, mechanical weathering and chemical weathering. Both can occur at the same time.

Mechanical weathering. Have you ever seen buckling in a sidewalk? This buckling is the result of the same phenomenon that causes rocks to split and fracture. This phenomenon is mechanical weathering, the break-up of rock formations through physical stresses. In the case of concrete sidewalks, growing tree roots are often the cause of such buckling. Their expanding bulk puts pressure on any cracks or openings in the rock, forcing the sidewalk to heave or break. In cold regions mechanical weathering can also occur through frost action. Water enters the cracks between rocks and freezes into ice crystals when the weather turns cold. Since frozen water takes up more space than liquid water, pressure is applied to the rock, causing it to split.

In areas that remain dry for most of the year, mechanical weathering also occurs through salt-crystal growth. When an area has been dry for a long period of time, water is drawn up from below the surface. This water contains dissolved salt, which is left behind when the water evaporates. Like ice crystals, these salt crystals can ex-

pand enough to damage even rock. A common example occurs when salt is applied to streets to prevent the build-up of ice in cold-winter areas. The resulting potholes are evidence of salt damage.

Chemical weathering. Unlike mechanical weathering, chemical weathering actually involves a chemical change in the rock. A number of different chemical substances cause rock to break down. One form of chemical weathering occurs when water combines with decaying plant matter and root secretions. The water becomes a weak acid that can dissolve some of the minerals in the rock. Once part of the rock dissolves or changes, the whole rock begins to disintegrate.

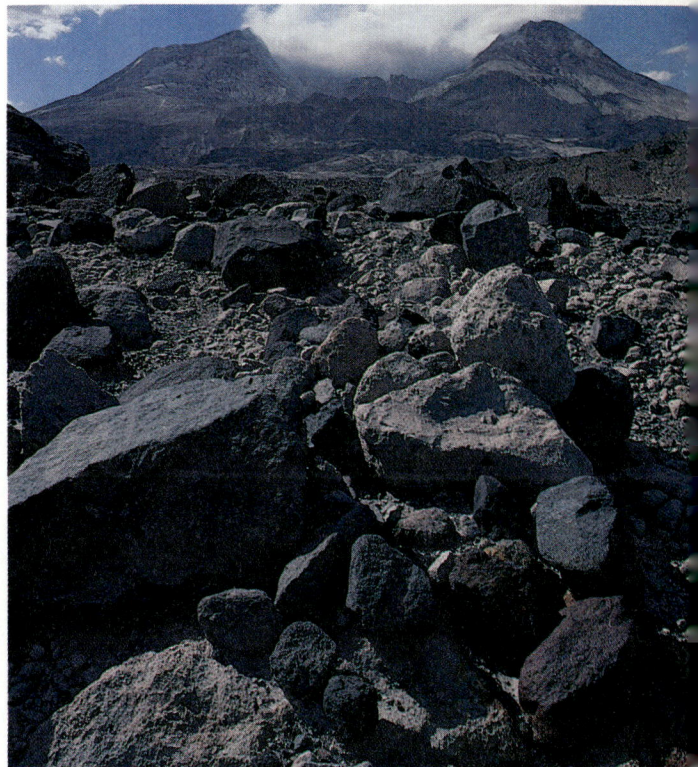

Weathering breaks up a mountain into smaller pieces.

Erosion occurs in four main ways.

After the rock of a mountain has begun to break into smaller pieces, the loosened rock pieces are eroded away. By this process, they are transported from one place to another. The erosion process can be fueled by gravity, water, ice, or wind.

Mass wasting. When gravity is involved, the erosion process is called mass wasting. If you've ever tried to build a sand castle, you should be familiar with the process of mass wasting. Mass wasting is the movement of soil or rock by the force of gravity. The loosened material moves down, but not far, from its original site. For your castle, if you added more sand or a large amount of water, the structure may have collapsed from the added weight. The slopes of landforms react in a similar way. Gravity forces pieces of rock or soil, usually from the top layer of earth, to move down the slope. Sometimes, this movement can cause a whole section of the slope to collapse and slide. This large-scale slide can take along soil, rocks, boulders, and anything else in its path. These major landslides are sometimes initiated by earthquakes. More often, though, a heavy rain, helped down the slope by gravity, pushes along the rock and soil already loosened by weathering.

Water erosion. When gravity is assisted by water, much more soil and rock debris is eroded from slopes. When rain falls, some of the water sinks into the ground. The water that cannot be absorbed runs along the surface of the soil. Where the surface is heavy with vegetation, erosion is less severe. Trees and ground cover serve to hold most of the soil in place. In areas with less vegetation, however, raindrops hit hard on the bare earth, causing massive soil displacement. Particles of soil loosen and are washed away. The water forms tiny streams on slopes. Eventually, these streams grow bigger and be-

gin to carve out gullies, or narrow ditches in the earth.

Streams and rivers are powerful vehicles of erosion. Sediment, made up of fine particles loosened from soil and rock, is carried from smaller streams into larger rivers. The steeper the bed of a stream, the faster the water flows and the more sedimentary material the stream can carry. As it moves, the water carves deeper into its own bed, changing the depth, width, and course of its path.

Waves are another major cause of water erosion. Waves can weaken and shatter cliff faces, wash away beaches, and cause the coastline to retreat.

Ice erosion. At first glance, ice does not look as though it is an agent of erosion. It seems solid and still, harmlessly melting away in the spring. In fact, ice moves, and when it does, it changes almost everything in its path. Without the great sculpturing ability of ice, we would not enjoy the Great Lakes of Canada and the United States, the fiords of Norway, or the dramatic silhouette of the Matterhorn in Switzerland.

Two main forms of ice erosion occur. The first form is continental ice sheets. Ten to fifteen thousand years ago, 30 percent of the earth's surface was covered by great sheets of ice. These **continental ice sheets** were huge blankets of ice, some measuring more than two miles thick in places. Such ice sheets had covered large parts of the earth before, and many scientists believe they will move out from the poles again.

When the last great continental ice sheets melted about 10,000 years ago, the evidence of their force remained. The ice had ripped off layers of soil and rock in Canada, going so far as to expose the ancient rock formations known as the Canadian Shield. Many great depressions were gouged out by the retreating ice. When the ice melted, five of these basins filled with

A glacier in southern Argentina meets the sea.

water and formed the Great Lakes. Today two continental ice sheets still remain. They cover Greenland and Antarctica.

Alpine glaciers are the second form of ice erosion. **Alpine glaciers** are blocks of ice that form at high elevations when more snow falls than melts in a year's time. They form in depressions in mountain slopes. Snow collects in these holes and compacts into glacial ice. As the size of the glacier increases, gravity begins to force the glacier downhill.

As a glacier moves, rocks freeze onto its underside and edges. These rocks become the glacier's teeth and grind the slope as the ice moves. All the way down the mountain, the glacier picks up more and more material from the surface. With its snout, the glacier pushes boulders and rocks ahead of it. In the process large amounts of soil and rock material are removed from their original location.

Wind erosion. Wind is an important force in eroding surfaces, working in two distinct ways. In one way the wind lifts particles off the ground and rolls them along the surface. This action removes any loose soil particles and is especially effective when the sand or soil lacks moisture. In the other way, wind pushes sand against rock surfaces, wearing the rock down like a sand-blasting machine. Wind is an especially powerful force of erosion in desert areas where there is little vegetation to break its path.

Deposition creates new landforms.

The third stage of the mountain transformation process is deposition, the laying down of the loosened rock fragments. Water, ice, and wind all eventually unload their collections of rock and soil fragments in a different location from where the material started its journey. These collections eventually accumulate enough to form new and different landforms.

35

Rivers and streams are often the creators of new landforms. Once a river accumulates more sediment than it can carry, it begins to deposit some of the material in its path. The river may then slowly widen its path, eventually forming a valley where it can drop its sediment. Often, a floodplain may result. A floodplain is a landform made up of low-lying land that floods periodically, when snow melts or during a rainy season. Floodplains form some of the most important agricultural regions in the world because of the rich sediment deposited there during floods.

The next step of the river's journey takes it to the sea. Once the river reaches the sea, it deposits all of the sediment it has carried on its long trip. One physical geographer estimates that it would take a train with 24,600 boxcars to carry as much sediment as the Mississippi River carries to the Gulf of Mexico every day. The sediment that is dropped there at the entrance to the sea eventually forms a fan-shaped area of land known as a delta. To reach the sea, the river now must flow across the delta in many small streams.

As in water erosion, waves also play a role in the deposition of eroded materials. Along the many stretches of seacoast, waves deposit the sand and pebbles they picked up on other beaches. In this way waves often serve as the redistributors of material around the world's beaches.

In a similar fashion, ice moves rock and soil around the globe. When the ice sheets moved across the continents of the world, they picked up much of the material over which they passed. When the ice sheets melted, they deposited their cargo of soil and rock in other locations. The midwestern United States was one of the recipients of such a deposit. The result is some of the most fertile soil in the world.

Once a glacier melts, it leaves its debris—all the stones, soil, and sand it collected on its journey—in heaps called moraines. Moraines, which look like ridges or piles of rock, are familiar landforms in New England communities such as Cape Cod and Martha's Vineyard, or in Wisconsin and Michigan.

One important form of landform transformation remains to be discussed. The activities of human beings have also been powerful tools in the alteration of soil and rock formations around the world. Such actions as the mining of rocks, the damming of rivers, and the clearing of forests have all had effects on the natural environment. Some actions have speeded up the processes of transformation and others have slowed them down. Either way, we human beings have left our mark.

Section 3 Review

Locating Key Places
Locate the following places on the map on page 622: Great Lakes, Rocky Mountains, Appalachian Mountains

Identifying Key Terms
Define the following terms: weathering, erosion, deposition, continental ice sheet, alpine glacier

Reviewing Main Ideas
1. What are the three main steps of landform transformation?
2. How are mechanical and chemical weathering alike? How are they different?
3. Describe the common forms of water and ice erosion.
4. How does deposition help create new landforms? Give two examples.

Thinking Critically: Predict Effects
Predict the possible effects of erosion on the following environments: a desert, a cornfield, and a forest filled with many small plants and trees. Explain your reasoning.

SECTION 4

Case Study: The Earth's Vanishing Coastlines

The following case study is adapted from the article, "Where's the Beach," from Time *magazine, August 10, 1987. This case study describes the problem of coastal erosion along the entire shoreline of the United States.*

Preview

Key Places
Where are these places located?
1 West Coast
2 East Coast
3 Gulf Coast
See the globe below.

Key Terms
What do these terms mean?
ecosystem
greenhouse effect

As you read, look for answers to these questions.
• How have humans changed the world's coastlines?
• How have storms and ocean levels changed the world's coastlines?
• How can coastal erosion be controlled?

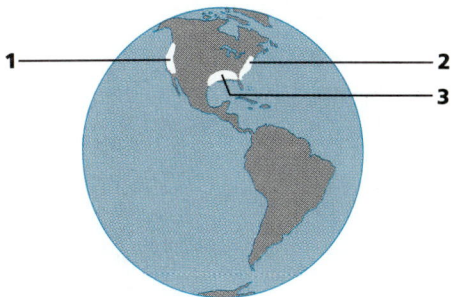

Humans have overdeveloped coastal areas.

The scourge of coastal erosion is felt worldwide, especially in such countries as Britain, West Germany, and the Netherlands, where ocean-front property has been heavily developed. In the United States, entire coastal areas are disappearing into the sea. Almost every mile of shoreline is affected in every state that borders an ocean, as well as those on the five Great Lakes.

Coastal erosion in the United States has been hastened by one main problem—Americans' passion for living and vacationing at the seashore. That has led to a boom in the development of U.S. coastal areas since World War II.

"If we had known 30 years ago what we know now, New Jersey and much of the rest of the country would be in better shape," admits New Jersey Governor Thomas Keane. "We wouldn't have built in those areas, and we wouldn't allow people to build in those areas." Even now, however, billions of dollars worth of coastal development—some would say runaway overdevelopment—cannot simply be abandoned. Says Chris Soller of the National Park Service, "It's a tough tightrope to walk. Our whole concept of property rights clashes with the natural process."

In the past few decades, as property owners began to demand that coastal areas stay put—by buying up seaside property and erecting multimillion-dollar beachfront houses, condominiums, hotels, and resorts on shifting sands—the natural process of erosion began to matter to growing numbers of Americans. However these development projects accelerated the damage to U.S. coastal areas.

How? On the West Coast, houses perched atop cliffs create new run-off patterns for rainfall and irrigation; combined with seepage from septic [sewage] systems, the drainage weakens the land itself. On the East and Gulf coasts, the major problem is destruction of beaches and sand dunes that normally check the ocean's force. Of particular concern are the 295 barrier islands that protect most of the U.S. coast from Maine to Texas. Not surprisingly, they are considered prime development spots: Atlantic City, NJ; Virginia Beach, VA; and Hilton Head, SC; among others, were all built on barrier islands.

It is mainly the dunes, explains the National Park Service's Soller, that keep coastal areas, including barrier islands, intact. 'The natural process is for dunes to roll over on themselves,' he says. When the ocean breaks through, 'what was once the secondary dune becomes the primary dune. The beach retreats as the ocean level rises. When you have houses on the beach, there's no place for the dunes to move.'

Along a broad expanse of southern Louisiana, between the Atchafalaya and Mississippi rivers, a million acres of wetlands have disappeared since 1900. "It's a catastrophe that's happening to the wetlands. You're looking at the genocide [murder] of an entire ecosystem," says Oliver Houck, a Louisiana environmental lawyer. [An **ecosystem** is a physical environment with the community of various organisms that inhabit it.] Indeed, the loss of the state's marshes affects more than just local residents: the area provides almost 30% of the nation's fish harvest and 40% of the fur catch, and is a winter habitat for some two-thirds of the migratory birds in the Mississippi flyway.

Storms can sometimes collapse shoreline houses. Homeowners in Los Angeles, California, survey what is left of their property.

High ocean levels and storms erode coastlines.

Shoreline erosion, however, is worsened by less well understood—and perhaps more ominous—factors. Over the past 100 years, the ocean has risen more than a foot, a rate faster than any time in the past millennium. Sea-level fluctuations are part of a natural cycle, but scientists suspect that this one may be different. They believe it is magnified by a fundamental change in world climate caused by a phenomenon called the greenhouse effect. The **greenhouse effect** takes place when carbon dioxide, produced when fossil fuels such as coal, oil, and gas are burned, enters the atmosphere in large amounts.

While carbon dioxide allows the warming rays of the sun to reach the earth, it blocks the excess heat that would normally reradiate out into space. As a result, the atmosphere is gradually growing warmer, thus melting the polar ice caps and raising sea levels. It may be years before scientists determine just how significant the greenhouse effect is—but they know the process is accelerating. Sea levels are expected to rise a foot in just another half-century.

Periodically, a warm-water current in the Pacific shifts eastward in a pattern called El Niño, a Spanish eponym for the Christ Child, so called because it appears off South America around Christmastime. The result: higher sea levels, unusually high tides, and severe winter storms along the western coast of the Americas. During the most recent occurrence of El Niño, sea levels along the California coast rose an average of 5 inches. With the added tides and storms, the effects were catastrophic.

Anti-erosion measures that might be expected to last for years can be wiped out by a single storm. The worst storm to hit the Northeast in this century was the hurricane of 1938, which killed at least 600 people on the East Coast.

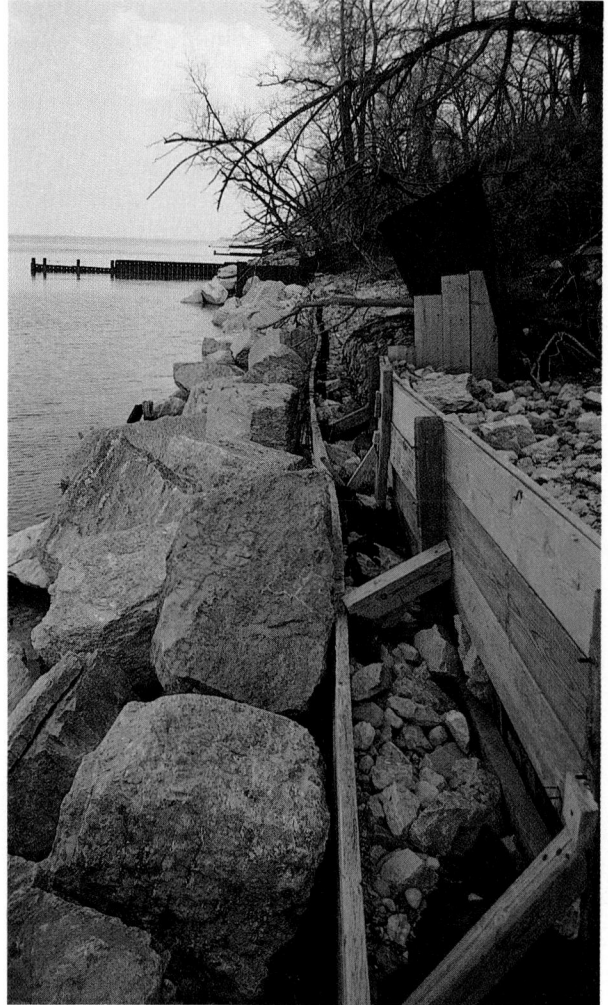

Property owners along Lake Michigan built this barrier against erosion.

Property damage was assessed at $3.2 billion (in 1987 dollars). Norbert Psuty, director of the Center for Coastal and Environmental Studies at Rutgers University notes that the eastern U.S. has enjoyed the relative peace of a "low-storm phase" for the past 25 years. "Because of continued development in high-hazard areas, the

39

longer this phase continues, the worse the damage will be when a big storm finally hits."

Some measures can control coastal erosion.

The growing damage to oceanfront property has generated a host of makeshift solutions to erosion. On Galveston Bay, desperate ranchers have positioned junked cars on the shore to prevent the water from washing away roads. On Long Island, beach residents shore up dunes with driftwood and old tires. And in Carlsbad, California, the community has come up with a number of ideas, from planting plastic kelp to laying a sausage-like tube along the beach in order to trap the sand normally washed away during high tide.

There are more substantive approaches to beach protection. When properly designed and built, they can slow beach erosion. Nevertheless, most are ineffective in the long run and can actually worsen damage. A seawall, for example, may protect threatened property behind it, but often hastens the retreat of the beach in front as waves dash against the wall and scour away sand.

A variant on the seawall that can also hasten erosion is riprap—rocks and boulders piled into makeshift barriers to absorb the force of incoming waves. While seawalls and riprap run parallel to the beach, barriers called groin fields extend directly out into the water. Made of short piers of stone extending from the beach and spaced 100 yards or so apart, they can slow erosion by trapping sand carried by crosscurrents. But down current, the lack of drifting sand can result in worse erosion.

The simplest and most effective response to coastal erosion would be to prevent people from living at the edge of the sea. That is not likely, "Abandonment is a joke," scoffs Folly Beach, Florida, Mayor Richard Beck. He notes

that his island is almost completely developed and tourism is just too valuable an income source.

Those who resist a balanced policy of coastal management whether they are motivated by greed or by a genuine concern for the well-being of coastal communities, will probably lose in the end—to the sea. Says Coastal Geologist Cary Griggs: "In the long run, everything we do to stop erosion is only temporary."

Section 4 Review

Locating Key Places
Locate the following places on the map on page 624: West Coast, East Coast, Gulf Coast

Identifying Key Terms
Define the following terms: ecosystem, greenhouse effect

Reviewing Main Ideas
1. How has overdevelopment caused severe erosion of coastal areas?
2. Why are high ocean levels and storms dangerous to coastal development?
3. How can measures to slow coastal erosion in one area cause greater erosion in another?

Thinking Critically: Make Decisions
You are on the city council of a major city on the West Coast. A developer comes before the council with a plan for homes and a shopping center to be placed very near the ocean. Your city desperately needs the income this venture would bring. However, erosion of the coastline will occur if the development is placed too near the ocean. Using arguments from this case study, convince the developer that his or her plan should be changed. Propose alternate solutions to the development.

Understanding Map Projections

Imagine that you are a mapmaker. How would you show the earth's surface on a flat piece of paper? Most maps are not entirely accurate because of a basic property of the earth's surface—it is curved. How can you show the surface of a sphere, which is a three-dimensional object, on a two-dimensional sheet of paper?

To look at the problem in another way, think of the earth as an orange with the continents outlined on the peel. To transfer the image from the orange to the sheet of paper, you would first cut the orange and take off the peel. Then, you would need to stretch and tear the peel to get it to lie flat on the paper. As a result, the map would have interruptions where the tears occurred and distortion where the peel was stretched.

Map projections are scientific attempts to solve or reduce the problem of distortion, which changes the shape and size of the continents. Map projections even out the distortions and place the tears at regular intervals.

Many different types of map projection have been developed. Each one has some distinct advantages and disadvantages. Look at the two examples shown below. On the left is a Mercator, the most commonly used projection for a world map. Its advantages include showing true directions and accurate shapes of land and water. It does not, however, show the true size of land near the poles.

The map projection on the right is an interrupted projection. One of its advantages is that it shows the true size and shape of the earth's landmasses. Distances on this projection, however, are distorted, especially across water.

Two other common projections are the polar and Robinson. The polar projection, used on page 168, shows the accurate shape and size for polar areas, but can only show one hemisphere at a time. The Robinson is discussed in the chapter review.

Review

1. Compare the size of Alaska on the two maps. Which map comes closer to showing Alaska's real size in relation to the rest of the world?
2. Locate Australia on each map. In reality it is due south of Japan. Which map shows this relationship better?
3. Only one of these maps really portrays the entire world. Which one is it? What does the other projection leave out?

Mercator Projection

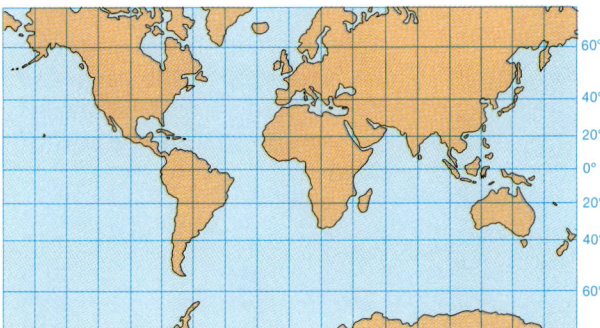

Interrupted Projection

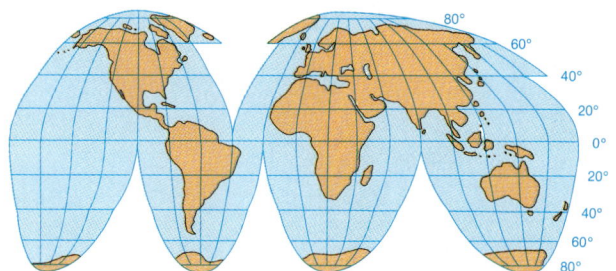

CHAPTER 2

Review

Section Summaries

1. The Moving Plates of Our Planet Over time, the materials in the interior of the earth formed layers: the core, mantle, and crust. Changes in the structure and position of the continents and oceans in the crust are believed to be caused by convection currents in the mantle. Huge moving plates constantly changed the face of the earth.

2. The Earth's Uplifting Forces The internal forces fueling plate tectonics have shaped the diverse landforms of the earth—mountains, hills, plateaus, and plains. The power of plate tectonics can be seen in the intense volcanic and earthquake activity at or near plate boundaries. The moving plates are also responsible for the earth's mountain ranges through the processes of folding or faulting.

3. The Earth's Destructive Forces External forces are constantly at work leveling the landforms built up by internal forces. The transformation of landforms has three steps: weathering, which breaks up the rock into smaller fragments; erosion, which carries away the rock fragments; and deposition, which lays down the rock in a new location.

4. Case Study: The Earth's Vanishing Coastlines Overdevelopment, high ocean levels, and storms are changing the face of the world's coasts. Although much is being tried to slow the natural erosion process, most measures are temporary. Some measures hasten erosion of nearby shores.

Using Geography Skills

Reviewing the Map Lesson
The Robinson projection combines some of the best features of the two projections shown in the map lesson. Study the map below and answer these questions.
1. Do the sizes of the continents appear to be accurate?
2. Do the shapes of all landmasses appear to be accurate?
3. Where does the most distortion of size or shape occur on the map projection?

Using Social Studies Skills

1. Sequence Historical Data and Information. Create a time line that shows the sequence of the earth's geological eras. As you list the eras, note below the names of the major events or developments that occurred at that time. You may wish to refer to an encyclopedia. You may also wish to illustrate the time line with drawings of what you think the earth looked like during the different eras.

2. Organize and Express Ideas in Written Form. A well-written paragraph begins with a strong, clear topic sentence. The rest of the paragraph serves to explain or detail that topic statement. Every sentence should be related and supportive. Any unnecessary ideas or facts should be omitted. Begin with the following topic statement: "Plate tectonics have shaped the earth's surface." Write a well-organized paragraph that develops this idea.

Robinson Projection

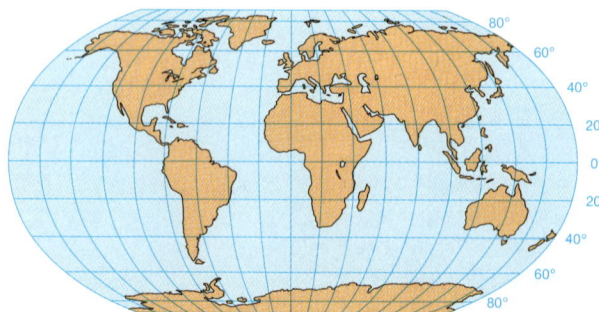

80°
60°
40°
20°
0°
20°
40°
60°
80°

Testing for Understanding

Locating Key Places
Match these descriptions with the key places listed below.
  1. an American chain of islands
  2. large lakes in North America
  3. land in United States bordering the Pacific Ocean
  4. mountain range in Asia
  5. mountain range in eastern North America
  6. land in United States bordering the Gulf of Mexico
  7. mountain range in Europe
  8. mountain range in western North America
  9. ocean rimmed by Ring of Fire
10. mountain range in South America
  a. Rocky Mountains
  b. Appalachian Mountains
  c. Andes
  d. Alps
  e. Himalayas
  f. Pacific Ocean
  g. Great Lakes
  h. Hawaii
  i. West Coast
  j. Gulf Coast

Recalling Key Terms
Define these terms in your own words.

Section 1
core
mantle
crust
fossil
plate tectonics
convection
subduction

Section 2
elevation
mountains
hills
plateaus
plains
compression
folds
faults

Section 3
weathering
erosion
deposition
continental ice sheet
alpine glacier

Section 4
ecosystem
greenhouse effect

Reviewing Main Ideas
Section 1
1. Describe the different layers of the earth.
2. How are the three eras following the Precambrian era of the earth's history distinguished from one another?
3. How are volcanoes and earthquakes related to the theory of plate tectonics?

Section 2
1. How have forces shaped the major landforms on the earth's surface?
2. How does volcanism cause the formation of landforms?
3. How are earthquakes related to plate tectonics?
4. Describe two ways that mountain ranges form.

Section 3
1. What three external forces shape landforms on earth?
2. Describe the two major forms of weathering.
3. Describe several ways that water and ice erosion occur.
4. How does deposition help create the fertile floodplains of the world?

Section 4
1. How is overdevelopment related to the erosion of coastlines in the United States?
2. In what ways do high ocean levels and storms pose a danger to coastal developments?
3. How do measures to combat erosion sometimes cause erosion of other areas?

Thinking Critically
1. Predict Effects. Picture a forest of evergreen trees on a steep mountain slope in the northern United States. What do you think the consequences would be if all of the evergreens were removed by fire or by a lumber company? Consider the effects on the soil and plant and animal life of the forest.

2. Identify Assumptions. Geographers have noted that North America is a little further from Europe each year. From this, the geographers concluded that a long time ago North America and Europe were closer together. What assumptions did they make?

Climate, Soils, and Vegetation

In this chapter you will learn about the causes and diversity of climate, soils, and vegetation on the earth.

Sections

1 The Sun's Effect on Climate

2 Wind, Water, and Climate

3 World Climate Patterns

4 The Earth's Soils and Vegetation

The Sun's Effect on Climate

Preview

Key Places
Where are these places located?
1 Tropic of Cancer
2 Tropic of Capricorn
3 Arctic Circle
4 Antarctic Circle
   See the globe below.

Key Terms
What do these terms mean?
tropics   equinox
middle latitudes   solstice
polar regions

Main Ideas
As you read, look for answers to these questions.
• What factors determine the climate of a region?
• How does the sun-earth relationship affect climate?
• What causes seasonal climate variation?

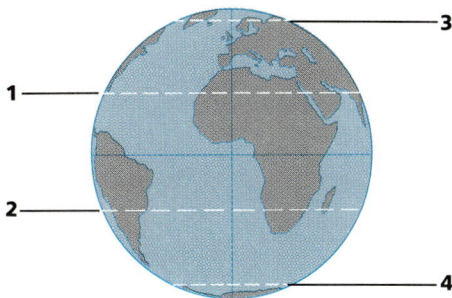

Wind high and cold, low the sun,
Short his course, sea running high.

Cold has caught the wings of birds;
Season of ice—these are my tidings.

Anglo-Saxon poem, 9th century

Four main factors determine climate.

Take a minute to look out the window. What is the weather like out there? Is it rainy, warm, cloudy, cold, sunny, snowy? Is the weather at this particular time typical for your area? If you had to describe your weather over a year's time to a stranger, what would you say?

What you would describe is the climate of your region. Weather is the day-to-day condition of the atmosphere. Climate is the pattern created by the kind of weather a place has over a long period of time. Many different factors influence climate, and climate, in turn, influences many elements of life.

The most important influence on the earth's climate is the position of the earth in relation to the sun. The earth's tilt on its axis affects the distribution of heat and light, causing different parts of the world to receive more or less solar energy. These differences are related to latitude. A particular place's position relative to the sun also affects daily and seasonal variation of temperature and precipitation.

A second influence on a region's climate is the circulation of the atmosphere. The pattern of winds and air masses plays a major role in determining climate.

A third influence on climate is the nearness of the area to large bodies of water. Lakes and

Facing page: **A whirling tornado approaches a farm in Kansas. These violent storms may occur when air masses from Canada and the Gulf of Mexico meet on the Great Plains.**

oceans supply moisture for precipitation and serve as moderating influences on temperature. The climate of a place will also usually be influenced by the presence of warm or cold currents flowing in a nearby ocean.

Finally, the nature of the landscape—whether mountainous, hilly, or flat—has an influence on climate. The type and position of landforms and their altitude cause local variations of regional climate patterns.

The sun-earth relationship causes global climate differences.

The sun is the earth's primary source of energy. It provides energy in the form of solar radiation, that is, heat and light. This energy does not strike all places on the earth equally, however. As you know, the earth rotates on its axis every 24 hours as it orbits around the sun. This rotation means that different parts of the earth are facing the sun at different times during our 24-hour day. The side of the earth turned toward the sun has daylight, while the other side, turned away from the sun, experiences night.

When the sun's energy strikes the earth, it warms those places on which it shines. It is therefore generally warmer during the day, where the sun is shining, than it is at night. The sun also warms some parts of the world more than it warms other parts. To understand this situation, try this experiment. Take a flashlight and shine it straight down at a table or desktop. You will see a small, but intense, circle of light. If you tilt the flashlight at an angle, you will find that the light covers a larger area, but it is less intense.

The same occurs with the sunlight striking the earth's surface. As you can see in the diagram on page 47, the sun's rays are most direct, and therefore most intense, at or near the Equator. The sun's rays hit the places away from the

Day and Night

The earth rotates on its axis, making one complete turn every 24 hours. The side facing the sun experiences day, while the side turned away from the sun has night.

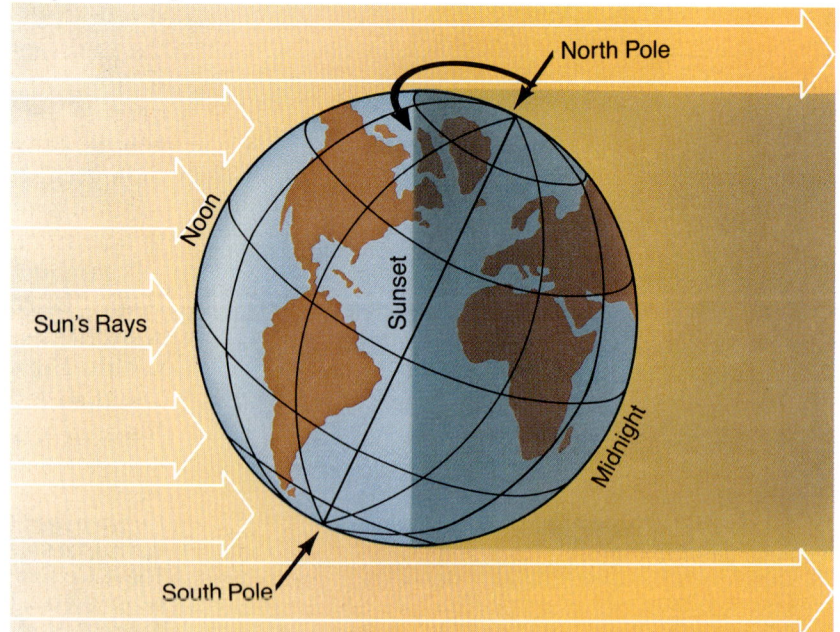

Equator at an angle, as in the flashlight demonstration. Therefore, solar radiation near the poles is spread over a larger area, is less intense, and provides less heat.

You can rely on this general rule for understanding the earth's differing climates: Temperatures decrease as one travels away from the Equator toward either pole. Using this rule, the world can be divided into three latitude zones: tropical, middle, and polar.

The zone closest to the Equator is called the low latitudes, or **tropics**. The tropics extend from 30° N to 30° S. Because of their nearness to the Equator, the tropics are usually hot all year round. High altitudes or cool ocean currents, however, can sometimes keep the tropics cooler than expected. Note that within the tropics lie special parallels, the Tropic of Cancer (23½° N) and the Tropic of Capricorn (23½° S). Depending on the time of the year, the sun is always somewhere overhead at noon in the region between these two special parallels.

Between 30° and 60° N and 30° and 60° S, the sun shines at more of an angle than near the Equator. Within this zone, known as the **middle latitudes**, temperatures tend to be less consistently hot than in the tropics. As the millions of Americans who live in this zone know, however, there is actually a wide range of temperatures in this region.

The zone located between 60° to 90° N and 60° to 90° S is called the high latitudes, or **polar regions**. Here, the sun's rays strike at a very low angle. The solar heat is therefore diffused over a large area, decreasing its intensity and warmth. These polar regions are the coldest on the earth. Within the polar regions are two special parallels: the Arctic Circle (66½° N) and the Antarctic Circle (66½° S). Depending on the time of year, the lands between these circles and the poles experience 24-hour days and 24-hour nights.

Why Latitude Affects Climate

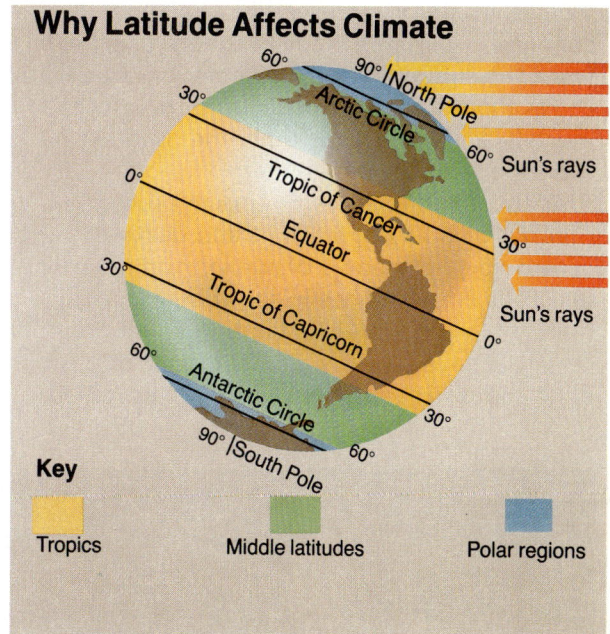

Key

Tropics　　　Middle latitudes　　　Polar regions

The tropics are warm because the sun's rays strike the earth directly. The polar regions are cold because the sun's rays strike the ground at a sharp angle and spread out over a large area. The rays also have to travel through a thicker layer of atmosphere, where energy is scattered and absorbed.

The sun-earth relationship causes seasonal climate variation.

As you have just seen, the relationship between the sun and the earth causes differences in world climate. In addition, the position of the earth as it revolves around the sun plays a major role in how intense the sun's energy is at any given time and location. As the earth revolves around the sun on its yearly orbit, the 23½° tilt of its axis remains the same. Therefore, on this orbit, parts of the earth will be tilted toward the sun, and other parts will be tilted away from it. These differences cause seasonal changes in climate. The hemisphere tilted toward the sun experiences summer because it receives more direct solar rays, and therefore, more heat. At the same time, the other hemisphere experiences winter.

As the earth revolves around the sun, the number of hours of daylight and darkness varies according to the angle of sunlight on a particular place. At two times in the year, approximately March 21 and September 22, all places on earth have a nearly equal amount of daylight and darkness. These two days are called **equinoxes**, and they mark the first day of either spring or fall. If you traveled to any place on earth on either of these days, you would experience about 12 hours of daylight and 12 hours of darkness. The equinoxes occur at the two times when the tilt of the earth causes the poles to be about the same distance from the sun. At this time the sun is directly over the Equator.

Two other days mark special events in the earth's revolution around the sun, the winter and summer solstices. A **solstice** is one of two days a year when either the North or South

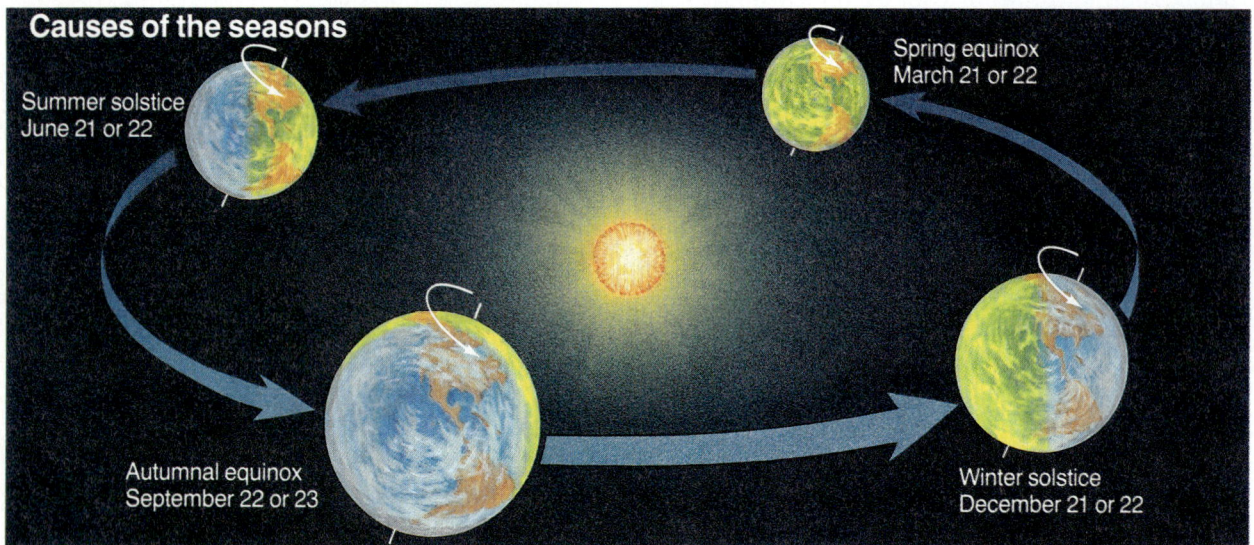

Causes of the seasons

Summer solstice
June 21 or 22

Spring equinox
March 21 or 22

Autumnal equinox
September 22 or 23

Winter solstice
December 21 or 22

The diagram above shows the seasons for the Northern Hemisphere. They are reversed for the Southern Hemisphere. The seasons change because the earth is always tilted in the same direction but the parts of the earth receiving the sun's direct rays change as the earth revolves.

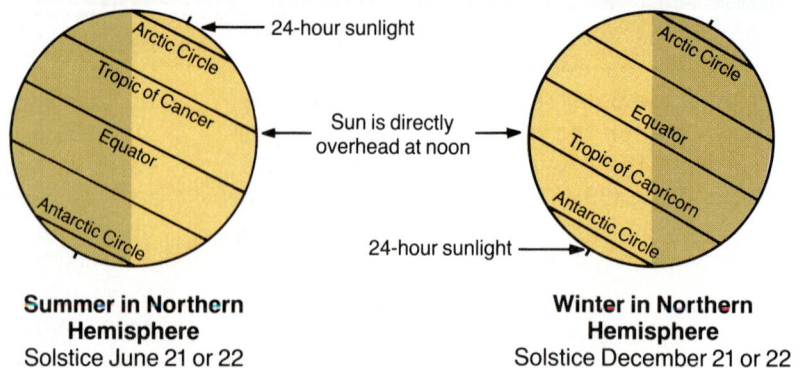

Arctic Circle
Tropic of Cancer
Equator
Antarctic Circle
24-hour sunlight
Sun is directly overhead at noon

Summer in Northern Hemisphere
Solstice June 21 or 22

Arctic Circle
Equator
Tropic of Capricorn
Antarctic Circle
24-hour sunlight

Winter in Northern Hemisphere
Solstice December 21 or 22

Swedes hold a summer festival honoring the midnight sun.

(However, in the Southern Hemisphere, it occurs around December 21.) North of the Arctic Circle, there is daylight for all 24 hours of this day. This situation occurs because the North Pole is tilted as far toward the sun's rays as it will get all year. For this reason northern Sweden, Norway, and Finland are called the "Lands of the Midnight Sun." At the same time, because of the tilt of the earth, no sunlight at all shines on places south of the Antarctic Circle. Winter is just beginning in the Southern Hemisphere.

As you have seen, the constantly changing relationship between the sun and the earth plays a major role in the climate experienced around the globe. It controls the temperatures of our world, the seasons of the year, and the lengths of our days. The sun, however, does not work alone. There are many other factors that also influence climate that we will discuss in the next section.

Section 1 Review

Locating Key Places
Locate the following places on the map on page 622: Tropic of Cancer, Tropic of Capricorn, Arctic Circle, Antarctic Circle

Identifying Key Terms
Define the following terms: tropics, middle latitudes, polar regions, equinox, solstice

Reviewing Main Ideas
1. Describe the four factors that determine climate.
2. How does the sun-earth relationship cause differences in climates across the latitude zones?
3. How does the earth's tilt cause seasonal variations in hours of daylight and climate?

Thinking Critically: Make Hypotheses
Suppose the earth were tilted 40° instead of 23½°. How would that change the climate at the Arctic Circle and the Tropic of Cancer?

pole is as close to the sun's rays as it will be all year. The winter solstice marks the first day of winter and the shortest day of the year. This day usually occurs around December 21 in the Northern Hemisphere and June 21 in the Southern Hemisphere. On December 21 the South Pole is closest to the sun and the North Pole is tilted as far away from the sun as it will get all year. As a result, there is no sunlight at all north of the Arctic Circle. (See the diagram at left.)

The summer solstice marks the longest day of the year in terms of hours of sunlight. In the Northern Hemisphere, it occurs around June 21.

49

SECTION 2

Wind, Water, and Climate

Preview

Key Places
Where are these places located?
1 Gulf Stream
2 Atlantic Ocean
   See the globe below.

Key Terms
What do these terms mean?
hydrologic cycle   prevailing winds
relative humidity   front
precipitation   rain shadow
Coriolis effect

Main Ideas
As you read, look for answers to these questions.
• What physical rule determines how air moves?
• How are the earth's waters recycled?
• How does the movement of air and water affect the earth's energy balance?
• How does a place's location on a continent influence its climate?
• How do landforms affect climate?

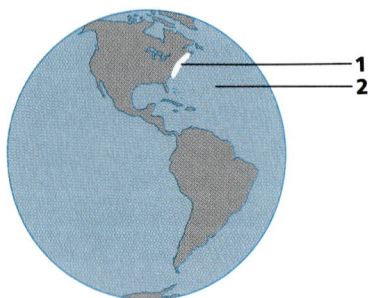

Snakelike, it whipped through space slithering along for miles. . . . As the seconds went by, it seemed to increase in volume until it was a huge roiling caldron of heated darkness. . . . [It] stabbed at the fields and sucked huge portions up, spinning them in the darkness. The winds were moaning, almost howling. . . .

Then there was an utter stillness on the plains, and the whole world seemed to glow.

Science Digest

The rules of convection determine how air moves.

Violent storms, like the tornado just described, are caused by the uneven heating of the earth's surface. So are many other weather and climate conditions. As explained in the last section, the sun warms the earth unevenly, causing the earth to be hot year-round in the tropics, seasonally hot-and-cold in the middle latitudes, and always cold in the polar regions. These basic climate patterns are further modified by other influences, such as the circulation of the atmosphere.

The atmosphere circulates according to a simple rule. As you just learned in the last chapter, in a liquid or a gas, convection transfers heat from one place to another in the form of currents. The basic rule for air, which is made up of gases, is that warm air rises and cool air sinks. The reason for this rule has to do with weights and pressures. The gases that make up air have weight. This weight is expressed as air pressure, which is the force caused by the weight of the air. When air molecules are densely packed, the air is heavy. Air pressure is therefore high. When molecules are more spread out, the air is lighter. Air pressure is low.

When air is cool, its molecules are slow-moving and packed tightly together. The air is dense and heavy, resulting in high air pressure. As heat is added to the air, the molecules move faster and faster, bumping into one another more and more often. Each of these collisions

The Circulation of the Atmosphere

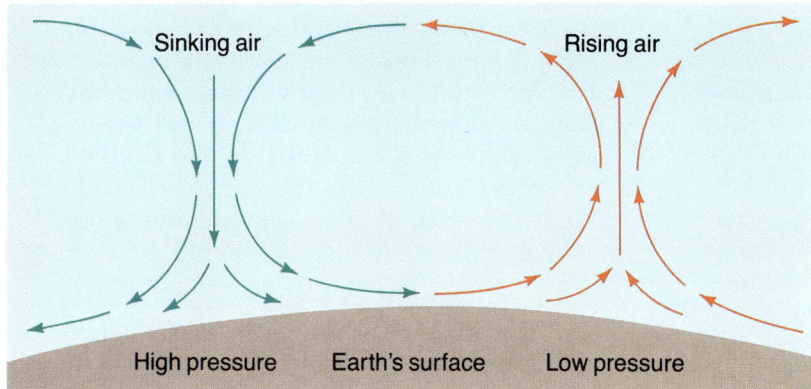

Sinking air

Rising air

High pressure   Earth's surface   Low pressure

Warm air rises, creating a low pressure area. Air from a high pressure area moves into the low pressure zone, creating winds.

gives off heat energy, warming the air. As the air warms further, the spaces between molecules increase, causing the air to become lighter and less dense. The air pressure drops accordingly. The warmed air, now lighter in weight, rises.

As the air moves into higher altitudes, however, it too grows cooler and heavier and begins its fall back to earth. Eventually, the cooler air will rush along the earth's surface to fill the space being left by the rising air. (See diagram above.) Thus, the cycle continues.

Just as the cool air rushed in to take the place of the warm rising air, air from high pressure areas will always move toward low pressure areas. The motion created by this movement of air is what you use to fly a kite—the wind. Wind always blows from high to low pressure areas. The greater the difference in pressure, the stronger the wind.

The hydrologic cycle circulates the earth's waters.

Earth is the only planet in our solar system where water can be found in all three forms: solid ice, liquid water, and water vapor. Water changes its form through the **hydrologic cycle**, in which water continuously circulates between the earth and its atmosphere.

In one step of the cycle, liquid water changes to water vapor by the process of evaporation. In a liquid, water molecules are always in motion. At times, some molecules break away from the surface and escape into the air as water vapor. When the water is warmed, its molecules, like air molecules, move faster. When they move faster, more of them escape into the air. In this way, when the sun heats the surfaces of bodies of water, evaporation occurs at a faster rate.

When water molecules fill the air, they add to the humidity of the air. When only a few water molecules are in the air, the relative humidity is low. As more molecules arrive, the relative humidity rises. **Relative humidity** is the amount of moisture actually in the air compared to the amount the air can hold at a given temperature. It is expressed as a percentage, and is often an important part of a daily weather report. When this percentage approaches 100, the speed of evaporation slows down because there is less and less room for more water molecules. Air reaches its saturation point—the point at which it cannot hold any more water vapor—at 100 percent humidity.

Warm air, however, can hold more water vapor than cool air. If, at some time, air cools beyond its saturation point, the excess water vapor will turn to water droplets or ice crystals.

This step of the hydrologic cycle is called condensation. You will see condensation in the form of clouds, fog, or dew.

As more water vapor condenses, the droplets in the clouds grow. They become heavier, and eventually fall to the ground as **precipitation**. Depending on the temperature, precipitation can take the form of rain, snow, sleet, or hail. It returns water from the air back to the earth, sometimes falling directly back into the oceans and sometimes taking a more indirect route over land, under the ground, and through small streams or rivers. (See diagram below.)

The Hydrologic Cycle

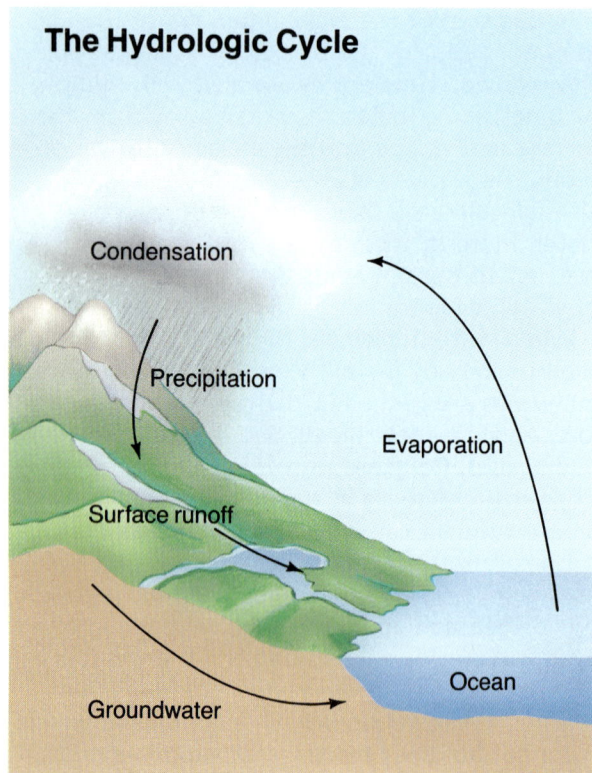

Condensation

Precipitation

Evaporation

Surface runoff

Ocean

Groundwater

This simple diagram illustrates how water moves continuously from sea to air to land to sea over and over again.

The movement of air and water helps balance the earth's energies.

The movement of air and water around the earth is an important factor in the maintenance of climate patterns. If air and water did not move around the planet, the heat of the sun would destroy all life on earth. The tropics would get hotter, with the sun scorching the earth and plant life. The polar regions would get colder, and their icecaps would grow larger.

The movement of air. The earth, however, does stay in balance. The atmosphere, along with the oceans, transports heat energy around the globe, creating a global energy balance. Air always moves from high pressure areas to low pressure areas. Thus, the cold air from the poles moves toward the Equator to replace the warm rising air there. The warm air near the Equator flows up and out toward the poles. This process goes on continuously, preventing the polar regions from getting colder and the tropics from getting hotter.

Let us now see what happens to these cycles of air circulation because of the earth's rotation. Rotation affects everything that moves, from ocean currents to spaceships, and—yes—even the wind itself. Without rotation, all winds would flow north and south. With rotation, the winds bend. In the Northern Hemisphere, the winds bend to the right of the direction in which they are blowing. In the Southern Hemisphere, they bend to the left. This tendency of winds to bend because of rotation is called the **Coriolis effect**, named after a French engineer who studied the winds.

The combination of high and low pressure areas and the Coriolis effect affects the directions in which all winds blow. The most dominant winds in any area are called the **prevailing winds**. They vary from zone to zone. Two sets of prevailing winds blow out of the high pressure area that exists at about 30° latitude. This area itself is practically windless. In the tropics, the trade winds blow from the northeast or southeast—depending upon the hemisphere. The trade winds blow toward the Equator. In the middle latitudes, the westerlies take over, blowing toward the subpolar low pressure area and bending to the northeast or southeast. Finally, in the high latitudes, the prevailing winds are cold winds called polar easterlies. They blow outward from the polar high toward the subpolar low, with the Coriolis effect bending them to the west in both hemispheres.

The movement of water. Like the winds, oceans are affected by convection currents and the earth's rotation. Just as air circulates heat and cold between the Equator and the poles, so ocean currents circulate hot and cold water around the planet. Not all of the tropical water reaches the poles, however. As the currents reach about 30° N and S, the warm currents begin to cool. Some of this cooled water turns and proceeds back to the Equator.

As the map on page 54 shows, a clear pattern has developed for the circulation of ocean currents. Warm currents, like the Japan Current and the Gulf Stream, move toward the poles on the east sides of the continents. Cold currents,

High and Low Pressure Belts

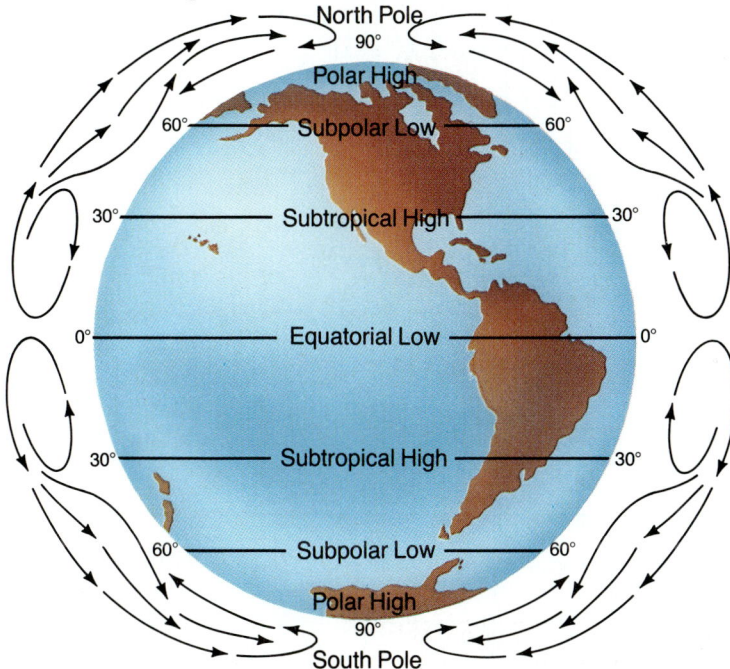

North Pole
90°
Polar High
60° — Subpolar Low — 60°
30° — Subtropical High — 30°
0° — Equatorial Low — 0°
30° — Subtropical High — 30°
60° — Subpolar Low — 60°
Polar High
90°
South Pole

Prevailing Winds

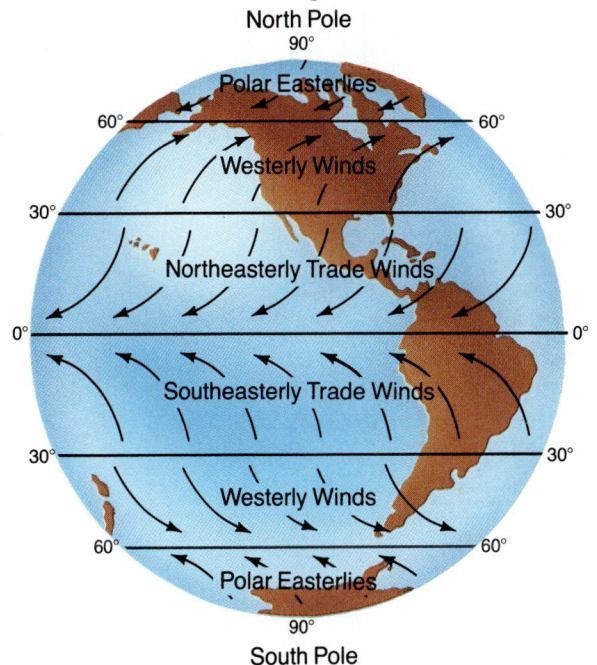

North Pole
90°
Polar Easterlies
60° — Westerly Winds — 60°
30° — Northeasterly Trade Winds — 30°
0° — 0°
Southeasterly Trade Winds
30° — Westerly Winds — 30°
60° — Polar Easterlies — 60°
90°
South Pole

High and low pressure belts and the Coriolis effect create the prevailing winds shown at right. The sun's intense heat causes the Equatorial Low. The poles' bitter cold causes the Polar Highs. Temperature differences between ocean and continent create the Subpolar Lows and the Subtropical Highs.

like the California and Canary currents, return along the west sides of the continents. This pattern often causes distinct differences in climate conditions between places on the two sides of the world's oceans.

Ocean currents have important cooling and warming effects on the continents they adjoin. As an example, find the Gulf Stream on the map below. As you can see, it originates in the Carib-bean Sea, in the tropics, and becomes the North Atlantic Drift. The current flows across the Atlantic Ocean, traveling northeastward because of the Coriolis effect. The North Atlantic Drift eventually laps against the northwestern shores of Europe. Because the North Atlantic Drift is so warm, the prevailing westerly winds over Europe are warmed by the waters. These winds, in turn, warm the land. As a result, the northwest

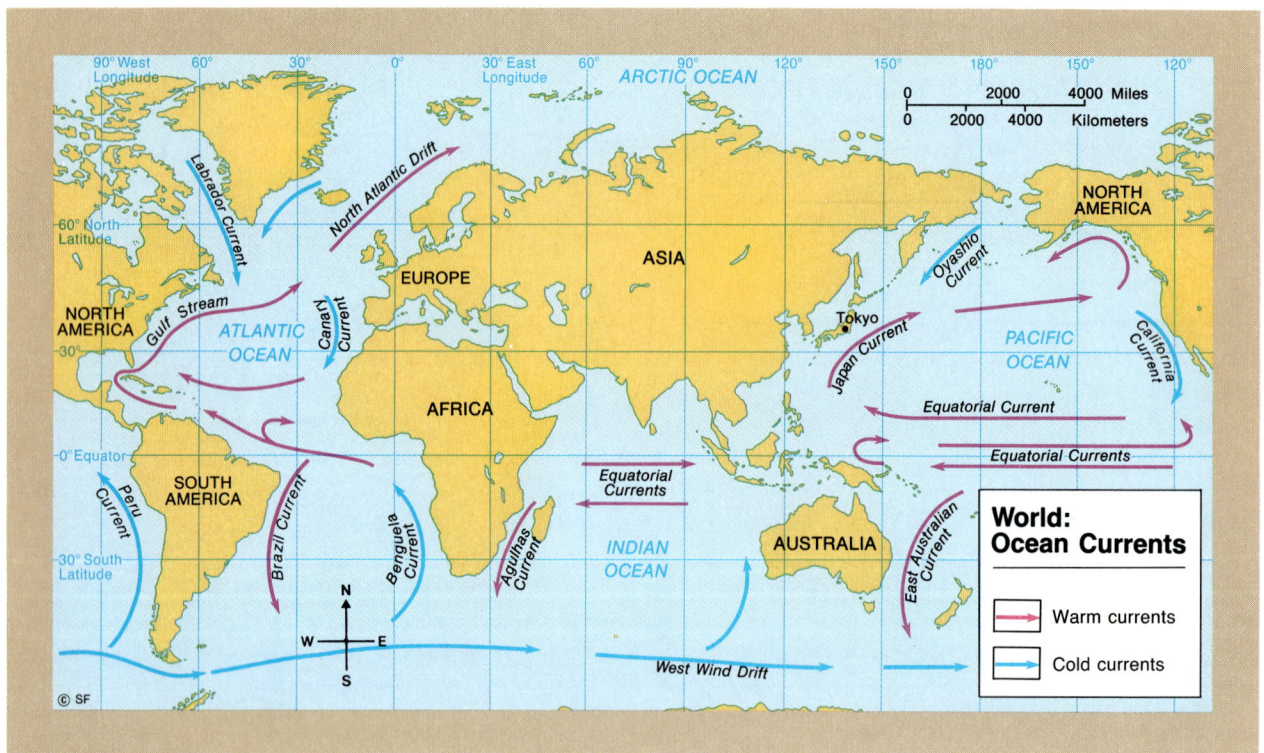

Map Study

Note that warm currents move north or south from the Equator along the east sides of continents, while cold currents move toward the Equator along the west sides of continents. Why does northwest Europe have a mild climate even though it is located very far north?

coast of Europe experiences very mild winter climates.

A place's location on a continent influences its climate.

Besides the effects of living near a warm or cold ocean current, living near a large body of water can greatly influence the climate of your home. Think about this situation: Have you ever been at a beach, lake, or swimming pool in the summer and noticed that the sand or pavement was too hot for you to walk barefoot on it? Once you reached the water, you probably experienced cool relief. Why? Basically, water and land vary in their heating capacities. Under the sun's radiation, land surfaces heat up quickly. They also lose that heat quickly.

Water, on the other hand, takes a long time to heat, and it retains that heat for a longer period of time. When solar radiation hits water, it penetrates several feet below the surface. Because the sun's heat can spread out so far, the water can absorb more solar energy without much change in its temperature. Once it is warm, water stays warm longer than land, acting as a reservoir of heat energy.

Places that are near large bodies of water generally have milder climates than places far away from water. Let's look at the Northern Hemisphere. As summer begins, the land heats up quickly, while the water retains some of winter's chill. If you live in a northern state, you may have had the experience of going to swim in a large lake or ocean on a 90° June day, only to find the water had yet to climb above 60°.

The air above the land and water has similar characteristics—warm summer air over the land and cool air over the ocean. If you follow the basic rule of convection, you can imagine that the warm air over the land rises, and the cool sea air rushes in to replace it. With some additional help from cooling sea breezes, coastal areas stay cool even as inland places swelter. In the winter the situation is reversed. The land

turns cold, while the water is still warmed by the heat of the summer sun. The principle of convection works to move some of this stored up warmth from the air above the water to land areas near by.

The different heating capacities of land and water cause differences in air pressure. For example, the North American continent heats up in summer, warm air rises, and a low pressure area forms over the interior of the continent. Cooler high pressure areas hover over the oceans where the surface stays comparatively cool. Since air always moves from a high to low pressure zone, air moves inland. This situation tends to bring moisture from the oceans to the interior of the continent, showing up as rain.

The differing high and low pressure areas, over either the land or oceans, in turn, serve as the birthplace of many of the world's weather patterns. Basically, when blocks of unlike air collide, a boundary between the two air masses becomes instable. This border area is called a **front**. Foul weather and storms follow these fronts. In middle and high latitudes, these storms often produce tornadoes and thunderstorms.

Landforms modify regional climate.

Major landforms will change a region's normal climate patterns. Mountains, for example, interrupt the flow of the atmosphere around them. This interference creates climate conditions that differ from the surrounding region.

If you are a hiker or skier, you might already have discovered that climates on mountain slopes are colder than those in lower elevations. Even near the Equator, you might find yourself stumbling into a snowstorm if you're high enough into the peaks of the Andes in Ecuador. Why do you think this is so? The answer goes back to what you've learned about air: hot air rises, and as it rises, it cools. As you move higher into the atmosphere, the air becomes lighter and less dense. Its pressure is lower than the air

Mountains and Rain Shadows

As winds pass over large bodies of water, they pick up moisture. They drop it as rain or snow on the windward slopes of mountains, creating a rain shadow desert on the leeward side.

Windward slope

Moist wind

Leeward slope

Dry wind

Ocean

Mountain

Rain shadow desert

below it. There are fewer air molecules bumping into one another generating heat. Without the energy from those collisions, the air temperature drops. Thus, the higher the altitude, the colder the temperature of the air, and the colder the climate. As a rule, for every 1,000 feet above sea level, the temperature drops about 3° F.

Mountains, besides being high in elevation, also affect local weather patterns. They act as fences to the movement of air. When air hits a mountainside, it is forced upward since it can't go through the mountain. As this air rises, it begins to cool. In cases where the air has traveled across oceans to reach a coastal mountain, interesting effects take place. This ocean air is carrying moisture in the form of water vapor. On its journey up the mountain slope, the air cools and its saturation point lowers. When saturated, the air spills most of its moisture on the windward side of the mountain. This side, closest to the ocean, receives plentiful rainfall.

As the air moves up and over the mountain, it loses its moisture. The mountain slope away from the wind, the leeward side, therefore receives almost no rainfall. The mountain has created a **rain shadow** desert. On the map on page 58–59, note the rain shadow desert east of the Andes Mountains.

Section 2 Review

Locating Key Places
Locate the following places on the map on page 54: Gulf Stream, Atlantic Ocean

Identifying Key Terms
Define the following terms: hydrologic cycle, relative humidity, precipitation, Coriolis effect, prevailing winds, front, rain shadow

Reviewing Main Ideas
1. What physical rule affects how air moves?
2. Describe the way the earth's waters are recycled.
3. How do air and ocean currents affect the earth's energy balance?
4. How is the climate of a coastal area different from that of an inland area?
5. How do mountains cause local variations in regional climate?

Thinking Critically: Make Hypotheses
An area lies on the western coast of a middle-latitude continent. Using what you have read in this chapter, what might you conclude about the area's climate?

SECTION 3

World Climate Patterns

Preview

Key Places
Where are these places located?
1 the Gobi
2 the Sahara
3 Mount Kilimanjaro
See the globe below.

Key Terms
What do these terms mean?
convection rainfall
permafrost

Main Ideas
As you read, look for answers to these questions.
- How are most climate regions classified?
- What are the major types of climate regions around the earth?

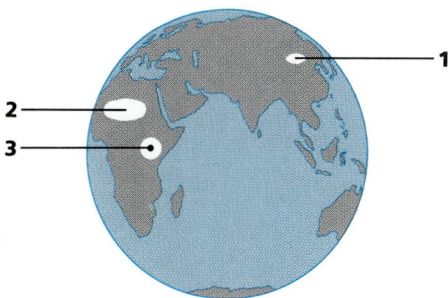

The Western Desert is the driest part of the Sahara. There, the sun could evaporate 200 times more rain than actually falls. In some places generations pass without a rain. . . . Thus, rains are memories of old men in this desert. To them a storm is that of sand or dust, and weather is the howling wind.

National Geographic

Most climate regions are classified based on Köppen's research.

The lack of rain in the Sahara characterizes one kind of climate region, a desert. Such regions are easy to classify because they have less than 10 inches of rainfall each year.

The natural world is so complex, however, that it is difficult to invent a simple set of categories into which all climates fit neatly. Long ago, scientists struggling with this problem noticed that a close relationship exists between the distribution of certain types of plants and certain types of climate. For example, some plants grow only in cold regions, and others grow only in hot or dry regions.

Early in this century, Wladimir Köppen, a German botanist and climatologist, saw this relationship. He began to correlate vegetation regions with average measures of temperature and precipitation collected from places around the world. He drew boundary lines on a world map to enclose areas that had similar temperatures and precipitation.

By 1918 Köppen had designed a system that serves as the basis for most commonly used climate classification systems today. The climate map on pages 58–59 is adapted from Köppen's system. Each classification represents a different climate region. Keep in mind that climate conditions change gradually from region to region. The boundary lines are not exact borders but are instead wide fuzzy transition zones between regions.

57

World: Climate Regions

Tropical climates

- Tropical rainforest
- Savanna

Dry climates

- Steppe
- Desert

Mild climates

- Marine west coast
- Humid subtropical
- Mediterranean

Continental climates

- Humid continental, warm summer
- Humid continental, cool summer
- Subarctic

Polar climates

- Tundra
- Ice caps

High altitudes

- Highlands
- Uplands

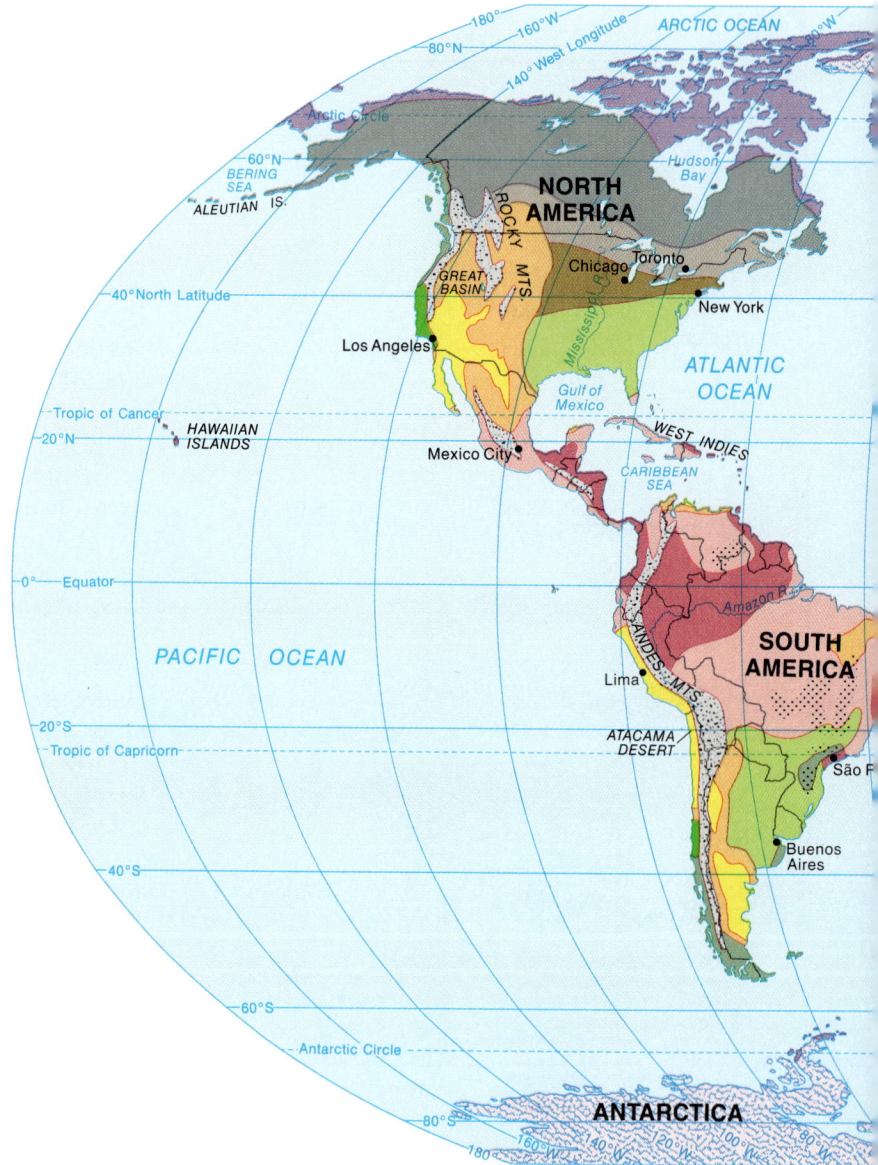

ARCTIC OCEAN

NORTH AMERICA

BERING SEA

ALEUTIAN IS.

ROCKY MTS.

GREAT BASIN

Chicago

Toronto

New York

Los Angeles

Gulf of Mexico

ATLANTIC OCEAN

Mexico City

WEST INDIES

CARIBBEAN SEA

HAWAIIAN ISLANDS

Hudson Bay

Arctic Circle

60°N

40°North Latitude

Tropic of Cancer

20°N

0°—Equator

PACIFIC OCEAN

20°S

Tropic of Capricorn

Lima

ANDES MTS.

ATACAMA DESERT

Amazon R.

SOUTH AMERICA

São P.

40°S

Buenos Aires

60°S

Antarctic Circle

80°S

ANTARCTICA

180° 160°W 140° West Longitude 80°N

180° 160°W 140° 20°W 100°W 80°W

Map Study

Which climate zone is most common along the Equator? Which zone is most common in northern North America and northern Asia?

58

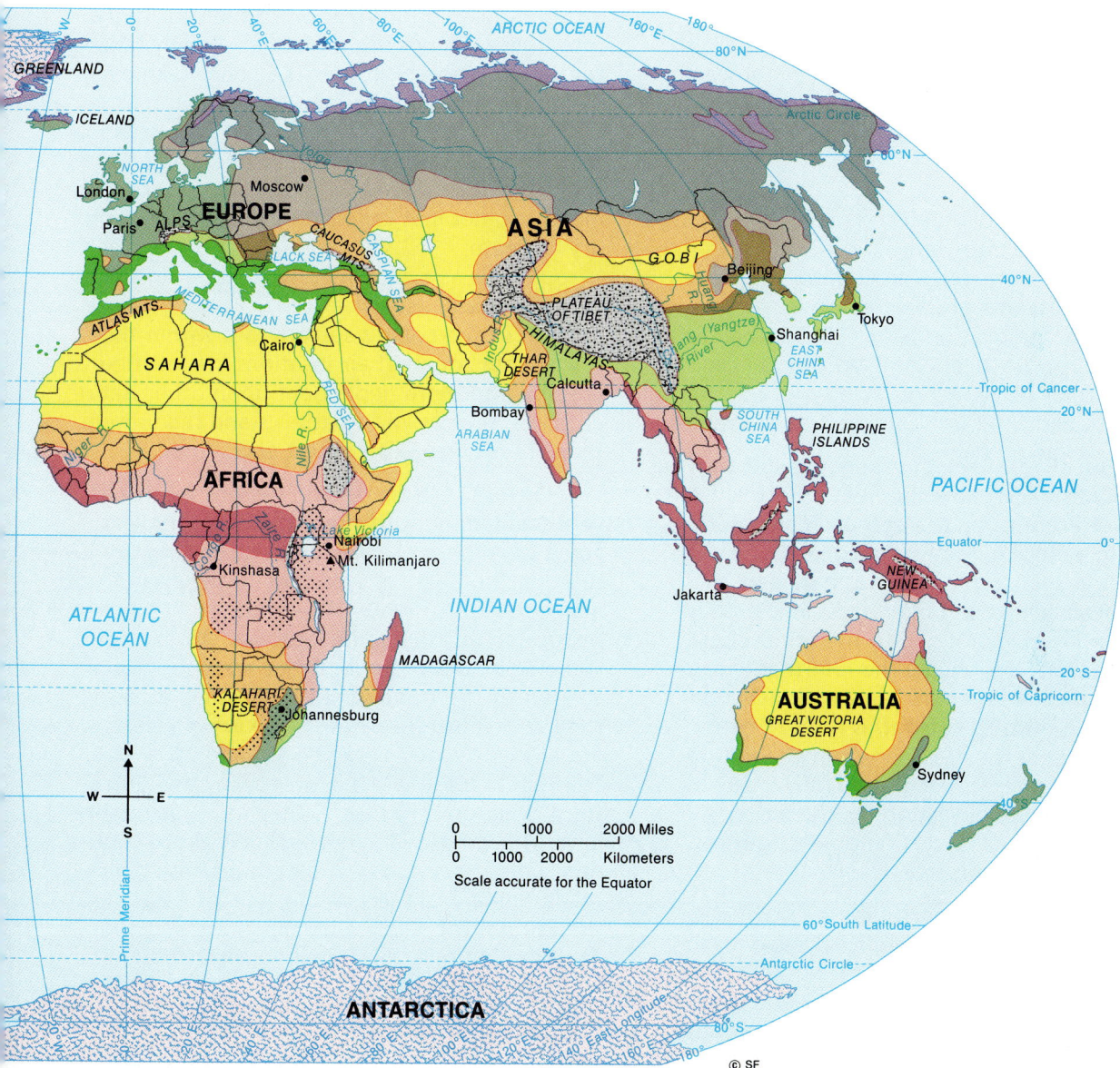

GREENLAND

ICELAND

ARCTIC OCEAN

Arctic Circle

London

Paris

NORTH
SEA

ALPS

EUROPE

Moscow

Volga R.

ASIA

CAUCASUS
MTS.

BLACK SEA

CASPIAN SEA

ATLAS MTS.

MEDITERRANEAN SEA

Cairo

SAHARA

Niger R.

RED SEA

Nile R.

THAR
DESERT

PLATEAU
OF TIBET

HIMALAYAS

GOBI

Indus R.

Huang R.

Beijing

Tokyo

Shanghai

EAST
CHINA
SEA

Chang (Yangtze)
River

Tropic of Cancer

Calcutta

Bombay

ARABIAN
SEA

AFRICA

Zaire R.

Congo R.

Lake Victoria

Nairobi

Mt. Kilimanjaro

Kinshasa

SOUTH
CHINA
SEA

PHILIPPINE
ISLANDS

PACIFIC OCEAN

Equator

ATLANTIC
OCEAN

INDIAN OCEAN

Jakarta

NEW
GUINEA

MADAGASCAR

KALAHARI
DESERT

Johannesburg

AUSTRALIA

GREAT VICTORIA
DESERT

Tropic of Capricorn

Sydney

N
W   E
S

0   1000   2000 Miles
0   1000 2000   Kilometers
Scale accurate for the Equator

Prime Meridian

East longitude

60° South Latitude

Antarctic Circle

ANTARCTICA

© SF

There are six major types of climate regions.

Within this system, based on that of Köppen, six general types of climate regions cover the earth. Each of these general groupings are subdivided into more specific climate regions.

Tropical climates.

When you think of tropical climates, one word should pop into your mind—hot. The tropical climates straddle the Equator and receive large amounts of solar radiation. As you can see from the map on pages 58–59, they lie almost entirely between the Tropic of Cancer and the Tropic of Capricorn. Two types of tropical climate exist, tropical rainforest and savanna.

1. Tropical rainforest. Whenever you turn on a hot bath and allow the heat and steam to fill a closed room, you are approaching the conditions of a tropical rainforest climate. The thermometer in such a climate reads between 75° and 90° F all year round. Rain falls almost daily and is quickly evaporated into the atmosphere because of the great heat. The rain that is common to this climate region is called convection rainfall. **Convection rainfall** is a result of convection forces in the air. As the sun's radiation intensifies, the heated air begins to rise according to the rule of convection. As the air rises, it cools and lowers its saturation point. Both condensation and precipitation result.

2. Savanna. To the north and south of the tropical rainforest climate regions lie the savanna regions. Like the tropical rainforest, the savanna is hot all year round. Unlike the tropical rainforest zones, however, these regions receive heavy rains for only half the year. The convection rainfall comes during the half of the year when the sun is directly overhead. At this time the solar radiation is most intense. For the other half of the year—the winter—the earth is in a different position in relation to the sun. Therefore, these regions are no longer directly below the sun, and the high pressure zones take over, weighing down on the land and bringing little or no rain. Thus, over a year's time, the savanna regions experience hot, wet summers and warm, very dry winters. For this reason the savanna climate is sometimes called the "tropical wet and dry" climate.

Dry climates.

Much of the earth's surface falls within the dry climate zones. Their locations are less tied to latitude and more dependent upon other natural forces, such as wind patterns and high mountains. Two types exist, desert and steppe.

1. Desert. Desert climate regions receive a very small amount of precipitation every year. Some of these areas are dry because they are located in the heart of a continent, far away from major sources of water. These deserts tend to be located in the middle latitudes. An example is the Gobi in Mongolia. Other areas are dry as a result of the trade winds that sweep across the lower latitudes. These trade wind deserts are always located between 10° and 25° N or S. The thirsty trade winds blow toward the Equator picking up moisture as they move across the land. The winds will cross over the entire continent unless stopped by high mountains or plateaus. Some examples of this type of desert are the Sahara, the Baja California in Mexico, the Atacama in Chile, the Namib in southern Africa, and most of Australia.

2. Steppe. Rain does fall in the steppe regions of the world. The amount of precipitation cannot support large forests, but there is enough moisture to sustain scattered trees, thorny bushes, and low grasses. Locate these regions on the map on pages 58–59. You can see that they tend to hug the world's desert regions. Steppe regions can be found near rain shadows as well.

Mild climates.

Mild climate regions experience few extremes of temperature or precipitation. Mild climates can be found in many different places around the world. They tend to exist under two circumstances. Some mild climate regions exist on the borders of the low latitude zones. Others lie on the coasts of continents in the middle latitudes, right in the path of the westerlies blowing inward from the ocean. Three types of mild climates are spread out across the earth's surface: marine west coast, humid subtropical, and Mediterranean.

1. Marine west coast. Imagine a typical English scene as you'd see in an old detective movie: a person in a trenchcoat, collar up, all huddled against a chilling rain. Like all stereotypes, exceptions are likely to exist in the English climate. But some truth remains. As you can see on the climate map, the British Isles have a marine west coast climate. Like other areas in this climate region, they lie between latitudes 30° and 60°, on the receiving end of the westerly winds. The westerlies bring a steady supply of rain throughout the year.

In North and South America, where high mountains block the movement inland of the westerlies, the marine west coast climate is limited to narrow strips along the coasts of such areas as southern Chile and Washington State. In western Europe, however, no such barriers block these moisture-laden winds. The marine west coast climate extends well into eastern Europe as a result.

2. Humid subtropical. Like the marine west coast climate, the humid subtropical climate gets a good amount of precipitation in a year's

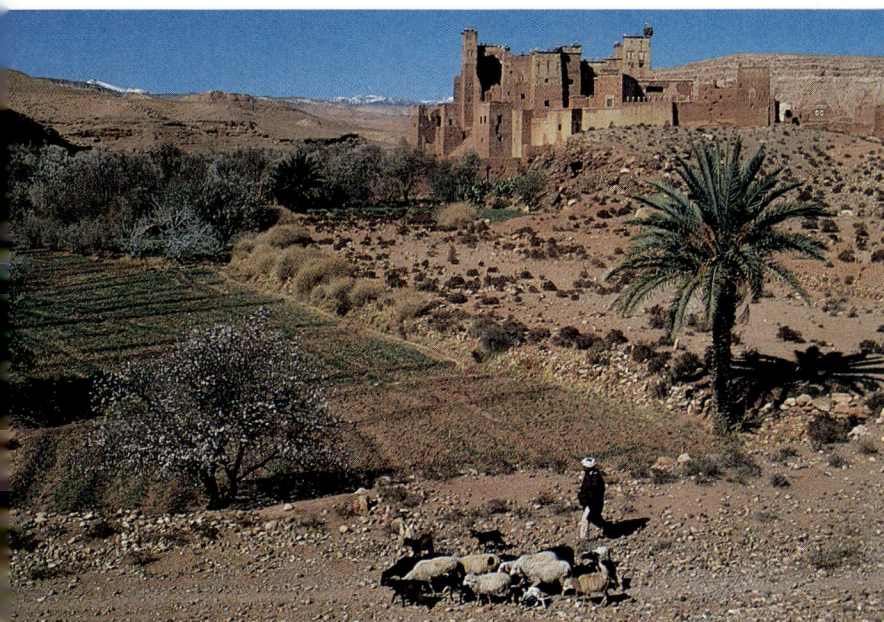

Small farms dot the Sahara where water is available. This small field is in Morocco.

time. Temperatures, however, tend to be warmer in these regions than in the marine west coast areas, because humid subtropical areas tend to be closer to the Equator. Locate places with humid subtropical climates on the map on pages 58–59.

Places with a humid subtropical climate have warm ocean currents offshore. In the summer, winds blow from high pressure areas in the ocean to low pressure areas inland. As they cross over warm currents, the winds absorb moisture that they bring to land. In the brief winter, humid subtropical areas are cool, but not cold, and usually drier than in the summer. Farmers in these regions, such as the southeastern United States and eastern Asia, enjoy a long growing season with plentiful moisture.

3. Mediterranean. Imagine an ideal vacation spot: clear, sunny skies, dry air, mild temperatures, a gentle breeze . . . all on a glorious sandy beach. Parts of Spain, France, Greece, Australia, Chile, and California all qualify. These locales boast a Mediterranean climate. Most also enjoy a site on the western coasts of continents between latitudes 30° and 45° N or S. Their mild climates are further distinguished by a distinctly wet and a distinctly dry season. The summers are sunny and dry under the influence of the trade winds. The winters tend to be wet with moisture brought by the westerlies.

Continental climates.

As their name implies, continental climate regions extend over large areas in the interior and eastern parts of continents. They are located primarily between 40° and 70° N. Because the Southern Hemisphere has almost no land in this latitude zone, the continental climate regions are all located in the Northern Hemisphere. They tend to be far from the moderating influence of oceans, and experience a wide annual range of temperatures. Hot summers and cold winters are common. Three main types of

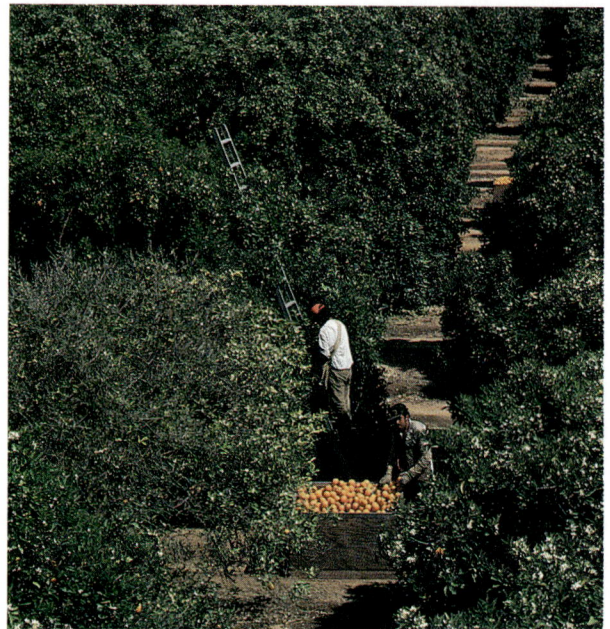

Oranges thrive in Florida, a humid subtropical zone.

continental climates have been classified: (1) humid continental, warm summer, (2) humid continental, cool summer, and (3) subarctic.

1. Humid continental, warm summer. This continental climate region enjoys the longest, warmest summer of the three. Summer temperatures sometimes soar above 100° F in such places as the north central United States. In the summer, people may seek relief on streetside porches where a cool breeze might blow past. In the winter, however, the same streets will be filled with people bundled up in heavy coats and hats to protect themselves from the cold wind and driving snow. Winter temperatures often plunge well below freezing.

2. Humid continental, cool summer. The far northern United States, Canada, eastern Europe, and the western section of the Soviet Union all experience the cool but short summers of this category of the humid continental climate. Winters are bitterly cold, causing frostbite to be a common concern in these areas. Summers tend to be shorter and cooler than in the warm summer continental areas.

3. Subarctic. Reaching still further north, this continental climate region extends over huge areas of land in the Soviet Union, Canada, and Alaska. Here, winter temperatures may last for eight months of the year, remaining below 0° F for months at a time. Summers, though brief, can bring temperatures up into the 70s.

Summer's balminess, though pleasant, is really only a "skin-deep" phenomenon in subarctic regions. Below the surface lies a layer of permanently frozen soil called **permafrost**. During the warm season, the top layer of soil thaws enough to sustain plant life.

Polar climates.

Polar climates extend from near the Arctic and Antarctic circles toward the North and South poles. Long cold winters and brief summers characterize this climate. Two types of polar climate exist, tundra and icecap.

1. Tundra. The frigid cold of the tundra climate region extends across the far northern reaches of Canada, Scandinavia, the Soviet Union, and Alaska, and encircles the coastlines of Greenland. Winters are long, cold, and whipped by gale-force winds, with summers lasting only one and a half to two months of the year. Summer temperatures may reach to 70° F, allowing the growth of tundra blossoms and mosses.

2. Icecap. The polar icecap regions are the coldest of any regions on earth. Temperatures rarely nose above freezing. The area is usually covered by ice or snow of enormous depths. Though they do not resemble the common image, icecap regions are, in effect, deserts. Cold air can hold little moisture because of its low saturation point, so precipitation comes in very

small amounts. Icecap regions often receive less than two inches of precipitation per year.

High altitude climates.

Unlike other climate regions, the climates of upland regions and mountainous areas vary according to both altitude and latitude. As you move up a mountain, the climate becomes harsher and harsher as you go higher and higher. Mountains near the Equator approximately mimic the changes in climate from Equator to pole. For example, if you stood at the base of Mount Kilimanjaro in eastern Africa, you would be standing in a tropical climate region. You would probably be very warm in just shorts and a T-shirt. As you trekked higher, you would advance gradually into colder temperatures. You would begin to shiver and need heavier clothing. As you approached the summit of the mountain, you would need real arctic gear, complete with warm mittens, socks, and a hat. At the top, which is covered with ice, the peak has a climate like that of a polar icecap.

Section 3 Review

Locating Key Places
Locate the following places on the map on page 58: the Gobi, the Sahara, Mount Kilimanjaro

Identifying Key Terms
Define the following terms: convection rainfall, permafrost

Reviewing Main Ideas
1. What is a common system for classifying climate?
2. Describe the characteristics of the major climate regions around the earth.

Thinking Critically: Identify Assumptions
A traveler is packing a suitcase for a trip to Manaus, Brazil. She is packing suntan lotion, T-shirts, shorts, a hat, sunglasses, a raincoat, and an umbrella. What is she assuming about the climate of this part of Brazil? Are her assumptions correct?

SECTION 4

The Earth's Soils and Vegetation

Preview

Key Places
Where are these places located?
1 Antarctica
2 Greenland
See the globe below.

Key Terms
What do these terms mean?
humus
biome
deciduous

Main Ideas
As you read, look for answers to these questions.
• How are soils important to plant life?
• How do plants relate to one another?
• How are biomes spread out around the planet?
• How have human beings affected the natural environment?

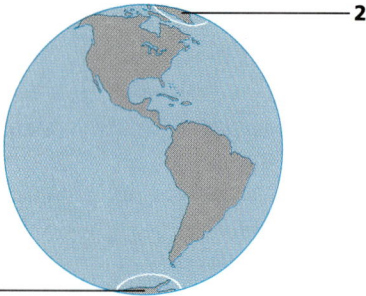

Ingredients
weathered rock, in fragments
dead plants
live bacteria
live, active earthworms, insects, and other animals
available moisture

Directions
Preheat environment to the local temperature. Make sure water is available. First, break the rock down into small fragments. The mineral composition of the rock will affect the chemical flavor of the soil, so choose your rock type accordingly. Then, add plants—trees, shrubs, grasses, mosses—any or all. They must, however, be dead. This organic material is the critical ingredient for the success of this soil recipe. Next, add the bacteria. The bacteria will break down the plants into **humus,** *the dark brown or black product of decayed plants and animals. Finally, to mix, add the insects, earthworms, and the available moisture. Set them loose to stir the mineral ingredients together with the humus. Cook at local temperature.*

Soils are critical to life.
The recipe you've just read shows that many ingredients contribute to the making of soil. To most nonfarmers soil is just ordinary "dirt." In fact, for farmers and scientists, thousands of names exist to describe different types and variations of soils. These people recognize that soil is a critical element in the growth of plant life and is especially valuable in the production of much of the world's food. Understanding soil is essential to understanding the problems and possibilities for farming and human survival in all parts of the world.

Climate controls the making of soil. It affects the speed at which all the decaying and mixing processes take place. For example, a climate with heavy rain and frost action may speed up the weathering process. Also, the warmer and wetter the climate, the denser the vegetation and the quicker the decayed material breaks down into humus. In dry, cold climates, soil may accumulate at the slow rate of one foot every thousand years.

Soil varies in infinite ways. It can be fine or coarse, filled with humus or deprived of nutrients, sandy or clay, rich or lacking in minerals. The variations depend on the climate and the quality and quantity of ingredients in any one place. These variations result in a world pattern of soil that is closely related to the world pattern of climate and vegetation regions. Soil is closely linked to the plants that grow in it. If the soil is rich and fertile, plants can more easily grow in it. If the soil lacks minerals or humus, plants will need special qualities to grow there. Likewise, soil depends upon plants to furnish the organic material from which it forms. The close relationship between climate, soil, and vegetation is reflected in the pattern of vegetation regions around the world, each with its own special qualities.

Plants live together in communities.

In any one area, a particular combination of plants lives together in a harmonious balance. This combination of plant life is called a plant community. The plants live together where they do because their needs for food, water, and light are complementary. As an example, some ground-level mosses and ferns may need to live in a shady area. Tall leafy trees may be able to provide that shade.

Large plant communities that share common plant and animal life and a distinctive climate are called **biomes**. The plants, animals, and other living organisms that live together in a biome rely on each other and on the soil that forms the basis of the environment.

Different biomes are spread in patterns around the earth's surface.

Over millions of years, all living things have adapted to survival in particular environments. Animals, plants, and soils together form an interdependent system that is uniquely suited to their environment and climate. Following is a description of several different biomes identified according to the types of vegetation that grow around the world. The five main categories of vegetation regions are forest, grassland, desert, tundra, and highland. As you read, locate the regions on the map on pages 66–67.

Thick growths of moss carpet trees in Washington State.

World: Natural Vegetation Regions

- Broadleaf forest— rainforest
- Broadleaf forest— deciduous
- Broadleaf forest— other
- Needleleaf forest
- Mixed forest (broadleaf and needleleaf)
- Grassland
- Desert—little or no vegetation
- Desert—scrub with grassy patches
- Tundra
- Ice-covered land
- High mountains (vegetation varies with elevation)

Map Study

Use this map to find the natural vegetation region near Toronto, Canada. In what direction would you travel from Toronto to find the nearest ice-covered land?

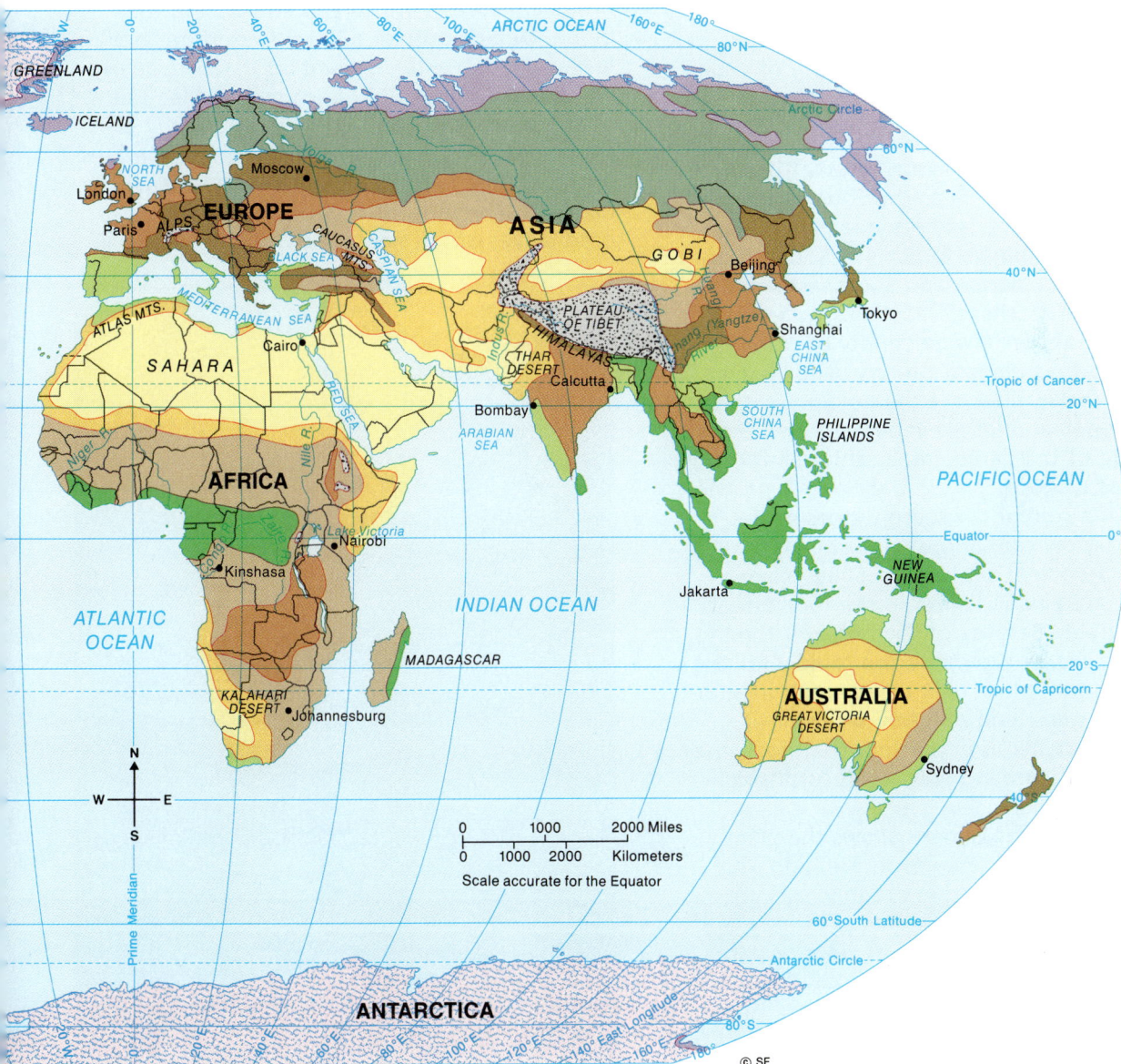

GREENLAND

ICELAND

ARCTIC OCEAN

Arctic Circle

80°N

60°N

NORTH SEA

Moscow

London

EUROPE

Paris

ALPS

CAUCASUS MTS.

BLACK SEA

CASPIAN SEA

Volga R.

ASIA

GOBI

Beijing

40°N

Tokyo

ATLAS MTS.

MEDITERRANEAN SEA

Cairo

RED SEA

SAHARA

PLATEAU OF TIBET

HIMALAYAS

Indus R.

Chang (Yangtze) River

Shanghai

EAST CHINA SEA

THAR DESERT

Calcutta

Tropic of Cancer

20°N

Bombay

ARABIAN SEA

SOUTH CHINA SEA

PHILIPPINE ISLANDS

PACIFIC OCEAN

Niger R.

Nile R.

AFRICA

Zaire R.

Lake Victoria

Nairobi

Kinshasa

Equator

0°

NEW GUINEA

ATLANTIC OCEAN

INDIAN OCEAN

Jakarta

MADAGASCAR

20°S

KALAHARI DESERT

Johannesburg

AUSTRALIA

GREAT VICTORIA DESERT

Tropic of Capricorn

Sydney

N

W   E

S

0   1000   2000 Miles
0   1000   2000   Kilometers

Scale accurate for the Equator

40°S

Prime Meridian

60°South Latitude

Antarctic Circle

ANTARCTICA

80°S

140° East Longitude

© SF

Forest biomes.

Forests are the most common type of vegetation in the world. They also require more rainfall than any other major category of vegetation. Many variations of the forest biome exist, but five principal ones are described here.

1. Broadleaf forest—rainforest. This type of forest thrives at or near the Equator in areas of high temperatures and abundant rainfall. The rainforest is native to parts of South and Central America, Africa, and Southeast Asia, where rainfall reaches at least 100 inches a year. Rainforests support a wide variety of plant species under an elegant canopy of tall leafy trees. The leaves filter out the hot sunlight, creating an open and lightly vegetated area below. The image of the dense, impassable rainforest is just not accurate.

Without a cold or dry season, trees of the rainforest grow continuously. Most of the tallest trees are broadleaf evergreens. Some leaves, however, are always falling so the forest floor remains green. Because of the hot, wet climate, the fallen leaves decompose too rapidly for the bacteria to turn much of it into humus. In addition, heavy rains tend to leach, or dissolve, many of the minerals in the soil. Therefore, the soil of the lush, green rainforest is surprisingly poor and infertile.

Adaptation to the climate allows the plant community to thrive. Tree roots are long, shallow, and many-branched in order to suck up available moisture and nutrients as quickly as possible. Other plants survive as vines or parasitic organisms, living and feeding off other plants instead of directly off the soil.

2. Broadleaf forest—deciduous. Deciduous broadleaf forests are spread out around the globe. **Deciduous** [di sij'ü əs] trees drop their leaves and become dormant, or inactive, yearly when the local weather becomes hostile. Many of the trees have adapted to the distinctly different seasons found in the continental climates. In the middle latitudes, trees lose their leaves in order to survive severe cold. The brightly colored leaves of fall signal the onset of winter in

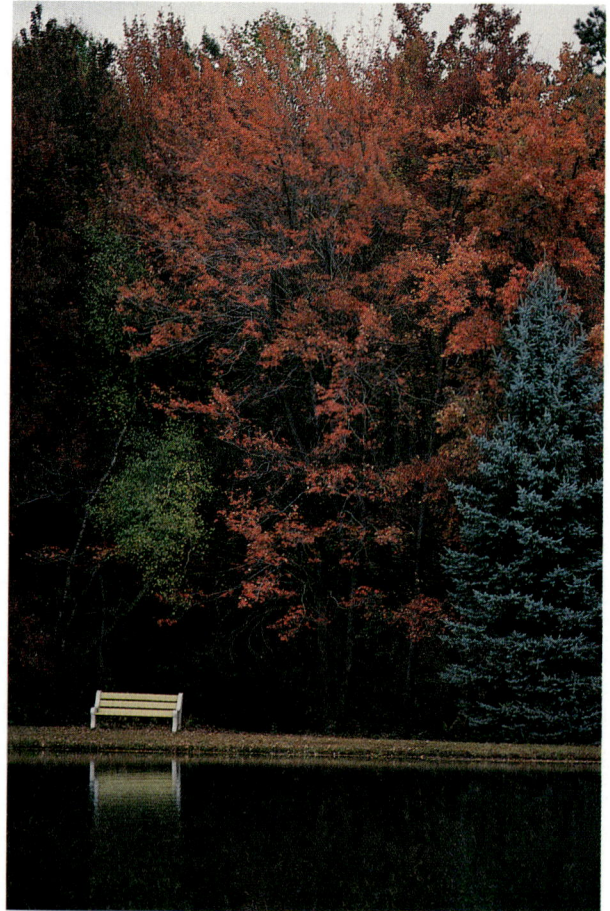

Red, purple, and bronze color the deciduous trees of Pennsylvania each fall.

parts of the Soviet Union, Canada, China, and the United States. In the low latitudes, the deciduous trees generally become dormant in response to drought conditions. The dry seasons of Africa, India, and Southeast Asia trigger deciduous leaf loss in native trees there.

The trees need to drop their leaves in order to protect themselves. In cold climates, if leaves continued to hold water in the winter, the water in them would freeze and destroy both the leaves and the trees. In both cold and dry seasons, trees cannot afford to give off their normal amounts of moisture into the air when they are not receiving moisture from the frozen or dry soil.

In deciduous forests a variety of trees grow to reach many different heights. Such species as oaks, elms, and maples grow differently from one another. The result is far different from the open feeling of the rainforest. Because more sunlight is able to pass through the top layers of the trees, a wider variety of smaller trees, shrubs, ferns, and plants can grow.

Soils in the middle latitude deciduous forests are rich in humus since they are fed by the annual leaf loss. The leaves, however, tend to make the soil somewhat acidic. Some leaching of minerals also occurs because of abundant rainfall. Trees are able to adapt to the situation by extending their roots deep into the earth. The long roots break up buried rock, increasing the mineral content of the soil.

3. Broadleaf forest—other. Several other types of broadleaf forest exist around the world, but the most common type is the Mediterranean scrub forest. This biome variation is uniquely adapted to Mediterranean climate regions, where winters are mild and wet, and summers are hot and dry. Mediterranean scrub forests tend to be located on the coastlines of the Mediterranean Sea, and smaller coastal areas of California, Chile, South Africa, and Australia. (See the map on pages 66–67.)

The Mediterranean scrub forest is made up of low bushes and small trees. Most of the plants have such drought-resistant qualities as small, leathery leaves. These leaves are designed to retain moisture during the dry summer months. Other adaptations protect the scrub forest from the common problem of fire. Because of the threat of fire in the dry seasons, tall trees have little chance or time to properly take root. Smaller trees, however, have developed deep root systems. With long roots, plants can survive and resprout after fires have burned off their foliage.

4. Needleleaf forest. This type of forest covers a massive area of land stretching across North America, Europe, and Asia. Needleleaf trees thrive mainly between latitudes between 50° and 65° N in regions where the subarctic climate reigns. The forest in this subarctic region is known as the *taiga.*

Needleleaf trees are more successful than deciduous trees in surviving the long winters of the subarctic climate. Needleleaf trees are also found in areas of the humid subtropical climate region that have poor leached soils.

The needleleaf trees have adapted in a number of ways to subarctic climate conditions. Their small needlelike leaves and thick bark hold in moisture. These features protect the moisture from the cold, dry air of the subarctic winter. In addition, needleleaf trees are evergreens that keep their green leaves all year. Because the trees do not have to use energy to form new leaves every spring, they can begin to use the sun's energy to grow as soon as warm conditions return. They can therefore take full advantage of the limited amount of sunlight.

Although evergreens have no regular season of falling leaves, they still produce a thick mat of needles on the forest floor. The tough acidic quality of the needles, however, prevents the build-up of much humus. Therefore, the soil is relatively poor and infertile.

5. Mixed forest (broadleaf and needle-leaf). As we have discussed earlier in this chapter, all regions are not entirely separate from each other. Overlaps occur and various combinations of plant life are always apt to develop. The mixed forest variation is one such example. This vegetation region contains a wide variety of trees, both broadleaf and needleleaf. It can be found in many parts of the world, and in several different climates. Generally, these forests are located in the middle latitudes or at high altitudes. Clusters occur in Europe, Canada, Mexico, Chile, China, Japan, the Soviet Union, and the eastern United States, and along the Himalayan Mountains in Asia.

Grassland biomes.

Many different types of grasslands are found around the globe. They vary in temperature, soil condition, and seasonal pattern of precipitation.

In the low latitudes, grasslands take the form of savannas. Savannas are grasslands with few or scattered trees. If you think of typical African wildlife films, you can picture a savanna. Lions stalk zebras and antelope through areas of tall grass, and giraffes reach high to nip the leaves off the isolated acacia trees. Savannas are located north and south of the rainforest. They cover a large portion of tropical latitude in Africa, South and Middle America, India, and Southeast Asia.

Savannas are greatly affected by the sun's relationship with the earth. Our planet's changing position relative to the sun creates a distinct wet and dry season for savannas. During the rainy season, the grasses commonly grow to 10 to 16 feet high. In contrast, during the dry season, the grasses turn yellow and strawlike, catching fire quite easily.

In the middle latitudes, grasslands were once found in abundance across broad stretches of North America, the Soviet Union, and northern China. Smaller areas were located in South America, especially Argentina. These broad zones of grassland cover areas where precipitation is not quite sufficient for growing trees. Depending upon how much moisture is available in a particular area, the grasses can vary from three to six feet in height. In the driest areas, the shorter grasses are called steppe grasses. The steppe grasses grow in short tufts separated by patches of bare ground. Where there is more moisture, taller grasses known as prairie grasses can grow.

One effect of the relatively sparse rainfall in the grassland regions is that little leaching of minerals and nutrients takes place. As a result, middle-latitude grasslands produce the world's most fertile soils. The soils are rich in humus and packed with minerals. For this reason, most of the world's prairie grasslands have been cleared and plowed under to make farmland for such crops as wheat and corn. Most steppe areas, however, receive too little rainfall for crops and are used for grazing.

Desert biomes.

A popular image of the desert is one of deep drifting sand dunes as far as the eye can see, the only sign of life being an isolated palm-fringed oasis. In fact, this image portrays an extreme form of desert, which accounts for only a small percentage of the world's desert lands. In most deserts a wide variety of plants and animals are sustained. To see a desert after a substantial rainfall would change your image of this biome. The desert would be covered with a blanket of brightly colored flowers.

As you've read, desert vegetation can be found in two major locations. In the middle latitudes, desert vegetation tends to be found in

Desert blooms add color in Baja California, a region in northwest Mexico.

tected by sharp spines and a thick skin. Another solution to the water shortage uses the plant's roots. Some desert plants send shallow roots out over a large area of land in order to catch any drops of rain that might fall.

Another way to survive in the desert is to disappear . . . or at least to appear to disappear. During droughts, some plants rely on their seeds. Their seeds, hidden underground, become inactive in very dry conditions. They remain dormant, waiting until enough rain has fallen to get through the plant's life cycle.

Because little plant debris falls to the desert floor, soils tend to be low in organic matter and, consequently, humus. The desert's lack of rain eliminates the problem of leaching, however, and the soils are usually rich in minerals. As a result, they often respond well to irrigation farming. Some deserts are able to be quite productive with the addition of water.

Tundra biomes. Compare the tundra regions on the vegetation map on pages 66–67 with the same areas on the climate map on pages 58–59. As you probably guessed, tundra vegetation generally grows in tundra climate regions. The tundra reaches into the extreme cold of the high latitudes, stopping where the land becomes covered with ice.

Permafrost is an important feature of tundra climate areas. The top layer of soil thaws for only a few months of the year, and the lower layers never thaw at all. Therefore, most plants must go through their entire cycle of growth and reproduction during the short time that the top layer of the permafrost is thawed. Only grasses, mosses, lichen, low shrubs, and a few flowering plants can survive in this harsh environment. They huddle low to the ground, staying buried under the snow. There, they are protected from the strong, cold winds of the Arctic.

People generally believe that the lands surrounding the poles, including Greenland, Antarctica, and the Canadian Archipelago, are

the middle of continents. In the low latitudes, desert vegetation is likely to be located poleward of the savanna, between latitudes 20° and 30°.

The vegetation in deserts may vary dramatically. Some deserts have little or no vegetation at all. Other deserts are covered with scrub with grassy patches. Look at the vegetation region map to locate the different types of desert vegetation around the world.

Desert plants have adapted in several different ways to their dry environment. Many desert plants are able to store moisture for long periods of time. Some retain moisture with the help of glossy leaves and thick bark. The cactus plant is able to hold large amounts of water in its tissue. To keep away thirsty animals, cacti are pro-

barren. This area is covered by snow and ice year round and maintains temperatures far too cold to support most plant life. Surprisingly enough, however, researchers in Antarctica have found a few hardy species of moss and lichen that have been able to adapt to this harshest of environments. Two species of flowering plant have also been discovered.

Highland regions. Highland environments are a mosaic of vegetation zones. As you have learned, the higher you climb up a mountain, the colder the climate becomes. Vegetation follows this change in climate. On a single mountainside, you may find a progression leading from a tropical rainforest through a treeless grassland or needleleaf forest up to tundra vegetation at the peak.

Human beings have greatly changed the natural environment.

You've just read about the earth's natural vegetation regions. In actuality, many people would argue that there are no longer any true natural environments on our planet. One species, the human being, has so successfully learned to use tools that almost all of the earth has been visited and to some degree changed.

As a test, imagine a world without greenhouses, indoor houseplants, zoos, or pets. In such a natural world, you might never see a parakeet or a gardenia outside of their natural habitats. They would only be found in the particular parts of the world in which they live naturally. No forms of watering, heating, or fertilizing would keep them alive outside of that habitat.

In populated areas the natural landscape has been dramatically altered. Instead of a deciduous forest, you have the concrete streets and steel skyscrapers of New York City. Instead of a steamy tropical rainforest, you have Rio de Janeiro. In these and other areas worldwide, such human activities as cutting, burning,

farming, mining, and building have altered natural growth.

Even the seemingly positive action of "saving" a forest area from a fire caused by lightning is human interference. A fire started by natural means is often a healthy and necessary way for a forest to release new nutrients from the soil and rock, restore a balance of plant and animal life, and replenish its energy.

In our efforts to cast the world into new shapes, we human beings must remind ourselves that we are just one part of a global life system. When we act on the environment, a chain of reactions is set off which can move through the entire system of our earth.

Section 4 Review

Locating Key Places
Locate the following places on the map on page 620: Antarctica, Greenland

Identifying Key Terms
Define the following terms: humus, biome, deciduous

Reviewing Main Ideas
1. How are soils related to vegetation?
2. Why are plants linked to each other in biological communities?
3. Describe the major biomes around the earth.
4. How have human beings changed the natural environment of the earth?

Thinking Critically: Make Decisions
Antarctica is one of the last places on earth to be reached by human beings and remains one of the least touched. Large stores of valuable oil and minerals have been found buried within the ice. The cost and difficulty of mining would be high, and there is a possibility of loss or reduction of rare plant and sea animal life. If the decision were yours, would you mine Antarctica? If so, who should own the riches? Write a persuasive paragraph explaining your decision. You may want to find more information in your library.

Using Temperature Maps

Suppose that you were going on a January ski trip and wanted to know where the climate wouldn't be too hot or too cold. What resources could you use?

A temperature map would be a good tool in this case. It is really two maps in one—a locator map and an isotherm map. This temperature map, for example, has a base map of Europe and the Soviet Union and an overlay of isotherms.

Isotherms, from the Greek words "iso" (equal) and "therm" (heat), are lines that connect places on a map having the same temperature. For the map below, the title tells

you that the isotherms, shown in red, connect places in Europe and the Soviet Union having the same average temperature during January.

Places located along the same isotherm share a common average temperature. If a place is located between isotherms, its temperature lies between the temperatures marked on the neighboring lines.

For example, find the words "Soviet Union" on the map. The area lies between the two isotherms marked "+10" and "−10." You can then conclude that the average temperature is between +10 and −10 degrees Fahrenheit.

In other cases, temperatures are not so clearly identified.

Note that the British Isles have an isotherm marked "+40" cutting through them. How can you tell what the temperatures are on either side of the line?

The patterns on the map suggest that climates get warmer as one moves closer to the Atlantic Ocean. You can infer that temperatures range from above 30 in the east to below 50 in the west.

Review

1. What is the coldest average temperature marked on the map?
2. Where is the warmest place on the map located?
3. What is the temperature range for the Soviet Union?

Europe and the Soviet Union: Average January Temperatures (°F)

CHAPTER 3

Review

Section Summaries

1. The Sun's Effect on Climate
The sun is the primary influence upon the earth's climate. Other influences are the circulation of air, the nearness of an area to large bodies of water, and the nature of the landscape. The earth can be divided up into three latitude zones: the tropics, which are hot; the middle latitudes, which are moderate; and the polar regions, which are cold.

2. Wind, Water, and Climate
The movement of air and water are two important influences on a region's climate. Convection currents direct the flow of air in clear patterns around the earth's atmosphere. This movement of air produces winds, which, along with ocean currents, maintain a global energy balance. A place's location on a continent and the local landforms also affect its climate patterns.

3. World Climate Patterns
Climates may be classified in many different ways. The following climate categories are found in one basic system: tropical (the hottest and wettest), dry (with very little precipitation), mild (with few extremes of climate), continental (located in the interior of northern continents), and polar (the coldest on earth). High-land areas are unique because their climates are determined by both altitude and latitude.

4. The Earth's Soils and Vegetation
Differences in soil quality, temperature, and precipitation have caused the development of several distinct plant and animal communities called biomes. The earth's four major biomes are forest, grassland, desert, and tundra. Human beings have altered or displaced many of the earth's natural biomes.

Using Geography Skills

Reviewing the Map Lesson
Use the map below to answer the following questions.
1. What is the land area featured on this temperature map?
2. Which areas have the warmest January temperatures?
3. What is the range of temperatures for Japan? Use the map on page 621 to help locate the islands.

Using Social Studies Skills

1. Detect Stereotypes. This chapter describes a popular image, or stereotype, of the desert as a nearly lifeless stretch of sand with a palm-fringed oasis. List common stereotypes for other climate or vegetation regions, and give facts that show how each is an oversimplification.

2. Synthesize Information. You've read about climate and vegetation regions. Choose one vegetation region and write a paragraph about how its climate affects its plant life. Use the maps on pages 58–59 and 66–67 as references.

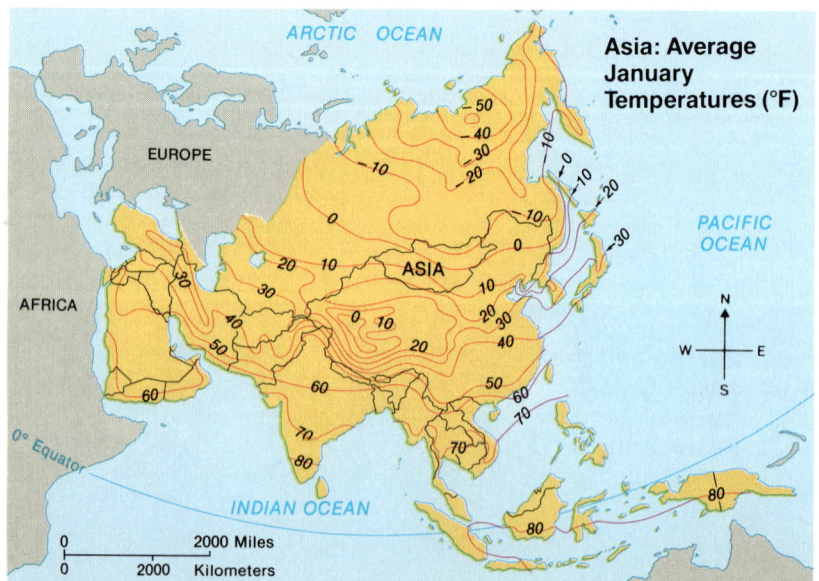

Asia: Average January Temperatures (°F)

Testing for Understanding

Locating Key Places
Match these descriptions with the key places listed below.
1. a middle-latitude desert in Mongolia
2. an ocean current that flows northeastward over the Atlantic Ocean
3. the 66½° N parallel
4. a landform in eastern Africa with a highland climate
5. the 23½° S parallel
6. a large body of water through which the Gulf Stream passes
7. the 23½° N parallel
8. the world's largest desert
9. the 66½° S parallel
10. island in Northern Hemisphere with huge icecap
a. Tropic of Cancer
b. Tropic of Capricorn
c. Arctic Circle
d. Antarctic Circle
e. Gulf Stream
f. Atlantic Ocean
g. the Gobi
h. the Sahara
i. Mount Kilimanjaro
j. Antarctica
k. Greenland

Recalling Key Terms
Define these terms in your own words.

Section 1
tropics
middle latitudes
polar regions
equinox
solstice

Section 2
hydrologic cycle
relative humidity
precipitation
Coriolis effect
prevailing winds
front
rain shadow

Section 3
convection rainfall
permafrost

Section 4
humus
biome
deciduous

Reviewing Main Ideas
Section 1
1. What are the four main influences on climate in a region?
2. How does the sun-earth relationship affect world climate?
3. What causes seasonal variation in the amount of sunlight a place receives?

Section 2
1. Describe the forces that influence how air moves.
2. How does the hydrologic cycle circulate the earth's waters?
3. What are the effects of the movement of air and water around the earth?
4. How does a place's location on the coast of a continent influence its climate?
5. What is the effect of a large mountain on an area's climate?

Section 3
1. How are the earth's climates commonly classified?
2. What are the main types of climate regions according to our system?

Section 4
1. Explain the relationship between soils and vegetation.
2. Why do plants live together in communities?
3. What are the major biomes distributed around the earth's surface?
4. Give three examples of how human beings have altered the natural environment.

Thinking Critically
1. **Identify Assumptions.** In a geographical study to determine why wild roses grow where they do, a scientist chooses to compare a map showing the distribution of wild roses with world maps of temperature and precipitation distribution. On what assumptions, or basic beliefs, might the scientist be relying?

2. **Predict Effects.** Many scientists predict that the temperature of the earth's oceans will rise one or two degrees in the next 100 years. One consequence is expected to be that the ice at the poles will begin to melt. What other consequences do you think a rise in temperature would have on the earth's atmosphere and overall climate?

Review

Summarizing the Unit

Chapter 1 What Is Geography? Geography is a specialized study of the earth. Its tools include maps and globes. Its concerns revolve around several major questions: where things are located, why they are located there, how they are related to the other things around them, and what is the significance of location. Geography can either be a physical or human study, concentrating on natural or cultural features of the earth.

Chapter 2 Shaping the Earth's Surface Earth has changed much throughout history. Plate tectonics, fueled by convection currents, is thought to be shaping most of the earth's landforms. The massive movement of plates causes sea-floor spreading, continental drift, and mountain building. Plate boundaries are often areas of intense volcanic and earthquake activity. The building up of the earth's landforms is always countered by forces of deterioration. For example, many American coastlines are now being eroded.

Chapter 3 Climate, Soils, and Vegetation Climate is the pattern of weather a place experiences over a long period of time. It is determined by many factors, but is influenced primarily by the sun and its changing relationship with the earth. This and other influences create distinct climate regions around the planet. These climate regions in turn affect the types of soil and vegetation that develop around the globe.

Using Writing Skills

The skill of effective writing is important in the study of geography. It helps to define, explain, describe, compare, analyze, evaluate, or persuade.

The process used in writing about geography topics is the same as that used for any writing. Four steps take you through from beginning to end: prewriting, writing, revising, and presenting. These steps need not be isolated. Writing may take place as you prewrite, prewriting and revising as you write, and writing as you revise.

The following guidelines will introduce you to the writing process. In later unit reviews, other features will help you develop effective writing skills.

(1) Prewriting involves choosing an appropriate topic and developing ideas about your purpose, audience, and facts.
(2) Writing is putting your first draft on paper as quickly as possible without worrying about spelling or grammar.
(3) Revising involves several activities intended to turn your first draft into a well-written final copy.
(4) Presenting, or publishing, means sharing your work with your chosen audience.

Activity Writers often need a nudge to begin their work. One effective warm-up is free-writing, in which a writer spends a set amount of time writing down anything that comes to mind.

To experience freewriting, select any general topic from this unit (for example, the earth, maps, climate). Take ten minutes to write down everything that comes to mind about that or a related topic. Don't worry about spelling or punctuation; just write without stopping.

Test

Key Terms (20 points)

Match each term with the correct definition.

1. a layer of permanently frozen soil
2. the carrying away of rock fragments that were removed by weathering
3. a part of the earth marked by features that make it different from neighboring areas
4. the tendency of winds to bend because of rotation
5. the distance above or below sea level

a. region
b. elevation
c. erosion
d. Coriolis effect
e. permafrost

Main Ideas (30 points)

1. Earth is unique in our solar system because _____.
a. it is the only red planet
b. it is a perfect sphere
c. it is the only planet with a moon
d. it has life-maintaining elements
2. Physical geography would be better than cultural geography if you wanted to study _____.

a. the major religions of the world
b. the earthquake zones of the Pacific Ocean
c. the history of government in Bali
d. the way buildings have protected people from harsh climate conditions

3. The _____ are the three main layers of the earth.
a. the core, surface, and crust
b. the outer core, inner core, and magma
c. the crust, mantle, and core
d. the crust, magma, and core
4. Volcanoes and earthquakes are most likely to occur _____.
a. in the Atlantic Ocean
b. in the middle of the sea
c. along fault lines
d. along plate boundaries
5. _____ is a major influence on the climate of an area.
a. The relationship between the sun and earth
b. The relationship between Earth and Mars
c. The nearness to a pond
d. The occurrence of cold or warm fronts
6. For air, the basic rule of convection is _____.
a. cold air rises, warm air sinks
b. warm air rises, cold air stays the same
c. cold air rises, warm air floats
d. warm air rises, cold air sinks

Thinking Critically (20 points)

1. Make Hypotheses. Explain how geography would help historians and economists answer questions in their fields.

2. Evaluate Sources of Information. Which three of the following maps shown together would most clearly illustrate the climate conditions in Alaska: maps showing annual rainfall, average summer temperatures, population distribution, annual precipitation, average winter temperatures, predominant winds, or air pressure? Explain why you chose these three maps.

Place Location (30 points)

Match the places listed below with the letters printed on the map.

1. Equator
2. Prime Meridian
3. Tropic of Cancer
4. Tropic of Capricorn
5. Arctic Circle
6. Antarctic Circle

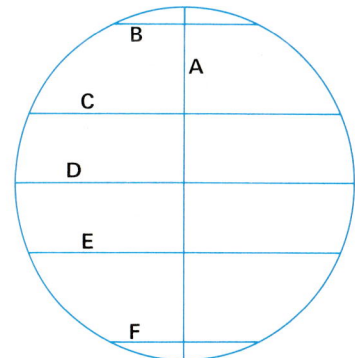

The Human World

In this unit you will read about human geography.

Chapter 4 Patterns of Population

Chapter 5 Patterns of Culture

CHAPTER 4

Patterns of Population

In this chapter you will read about where people live
and why they live where they do.

Sections

1 Where People Live

2 How Populations Change

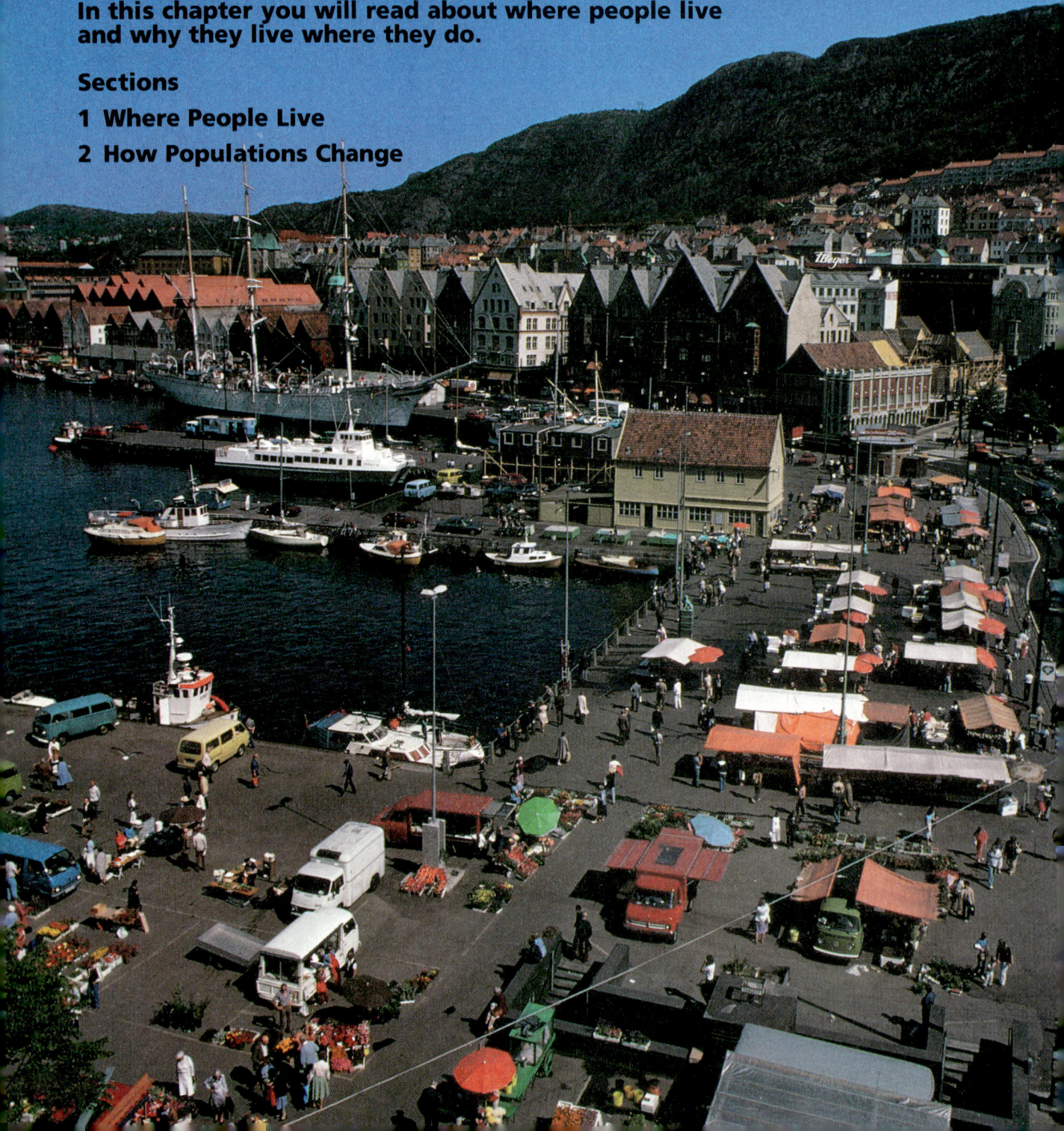

SECTION 1

Where People Live

Preview

Key Places
Where are these places located?
1 East Asia
2 South Asia
3 Europe
See the globe below.

Key Terms
What do these terms mean?
population distribution   situation
population density   metropolitan area
site   megalopolis

Main Ideas
As you read, look for answers to these questions.
• What influences where people live?
• Where do most of the world's people live?
• How are communities defined?

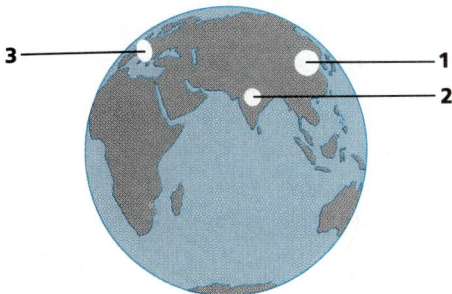

ZAGREB, Yugoslavia (AP)—The United Nations on Saturday [July 11] proclaimed an 8-pound newborn boy the world's 5 billionth inhabitant, and began worldwide celebrations to welcome baby Matej Gaspar.

Chicago Tribune, July 12, 1987

Geography and history influence where people live.

With the birth of the baby Matej [mä tā'], the human population of our small planet reached five billion—5,000 million people on a planet that is 75 percent water and ice! People live all over the globe: in warm coastal regions, on high mountain tops, on grassy plains, and in steamy rainforests. A map of population distribution, like the one on page 83, shows you where people generally live. **Population distribution** is the way people are spread out around the earth. The map shows you both where many people live and where only a few make their home. **Population density** is the average number of people living in each square mile or kilometer of a certain area.

Many factors influence where people live around the world. Some of these are growing conditions, climate, resources, and location. One of the most immediate concerns is human survival. To survive, people need food and fresh water. Throughout history people have tended to settle where these needs could be met most easily. Thus, fertile river valleys on flat or rolling land have become some of the most crowded areas on the earth. In such river valleys, farming is relatively easy and productive, and fresh water is readily available.

Facing page: **Bergen, Norway, lies on the edge of an icy fiord. Water has always been an important concern for populations.** *Page 78:* **Tokyo, Japan, is a very densely populated city.**

Other geographical factors also work to attract and maintain populations. Pleasant or mild climates, plentiful natural resources, and nearness to rivers or oceans all attract people. For example, a location on a river or coastline is desirable because it provides access to fishing and routes for trade, transportation, and communication with other people. In addition, some natural water bodies and landforms can serve as an important means of defense for a community. To defend themselves people have used natural barriers such as mountains, rivers, deserts, and islands. Where an effective form of defense existed naturally, the area was more desirable to its settlers.

History has also influenced where people live. Over time people have often settled where others have been successful before them. The early residents of an area set a historical precedent for others to follow. Tradition then plays a strong role in encouraging people to stay in the land of their ancestors.

Population clusters, however, do not always develop in the most ideal geographical conditions. Many groups of people have had to make dramatic changes to their environments in order to survive in their chosen home. Other groups have made the changes in their own lifestyles. For example, the desert has always been a difficult place to find enough fresh water and food to support permanent settlements. To survive, desert dwellers have traditionally led a nomadic, or wandering, life. They travel with their tent homes and animals in search of fresh water and food.

Most of the earth's population lies in four major clusters.

As you can see from the population distribution map on the next page, four large population clusters extend across part of the earth's surface. They are in East Asia, South Asia, Europe, and eastern North America.

Each of these large clusters lies near major rivers or ocean coasts. All are in areas well-suited for farming. Simple farming, with its demands for water, remains an important way of life for many of the earth's people. In this modern age of huge cities and mechanized farming, hundreds of millions of people still bend to the soil to plant with their hands the crops for another season's survival.

East Asia. Today the largest population cluster on the earth lies in East Asia. It includes China, Japan, North and South Korea, and Taiwan. Altogether about 1.3 billion people—more than a quarter of all humanity—live in this East Asian cluster. Many of the people are urban dwellers, living in such large cities as Tokyo, Shanghai, Beijing, and Seoul.

One woman, a busdriver, described what everyday life is like in the crowded capital city of China. "Beijing is inhabited by about seven million people, and sometimes it seems they're all trying to get on my bus at once. My biggest headache is . . . not the cars . . . it's the cyclists. About three million of them. At one of the busiest crossroads the police counted 25,000 cyclists an hour during the peak period."

Most people, however, live in small rural East Asian villages. Three out of every four people walk each day to work in the farm fields near their homes. Shoulder to shoulder they plant the rice and sow the wheat. In many areas of East Asia, rivers have deposited fertile soils. In addition, moisture from rainfall and river water helps to maintain productive farming.

South Asia. The second largest population cluster lies in South Asia, the section of the continent south of the Himalaya Mountains. South Asia includes India, Pakistan [pak'ə stan], Bangladesh [bäng'glə desh'], Nepal [nə pôl'], and Sri Lanka [srē'läng'kə]. India alone has more than 760 million inhabitants. Together the other countries have another 240 million.

The population distribution map shows that most people live either along the coastlines or along a major river. As elsewhere, farming usually occurs near rivers, including the Indus River in Pakistan and the Ganges River in India.

Europe. The third largest population cluster is in Europe. Instead of one dominant country, like India or China, Europe includes several well-populated countries, each with between 50 and 60 million people. The largest countries in Europe are West Germany, Italy, France, and Britain. Throughout Europe most people live in large cities and towns. Rivers and coastal locations have played an important role in the development of this area, not only for agriculture but for travel, transport, and communication as well. Europe has other geographical benefits as well, including plentiful mineral resources, mild climates, and wide areas of flat plains.

Eastern North America. Compared to the three great Eurasian population clusters, the fourth cluster in eastern North America is relatively small. This concentration of people extends roughly from southern Canada to North Carolina along the east coast of the continent. The origins of this cluster of people date back

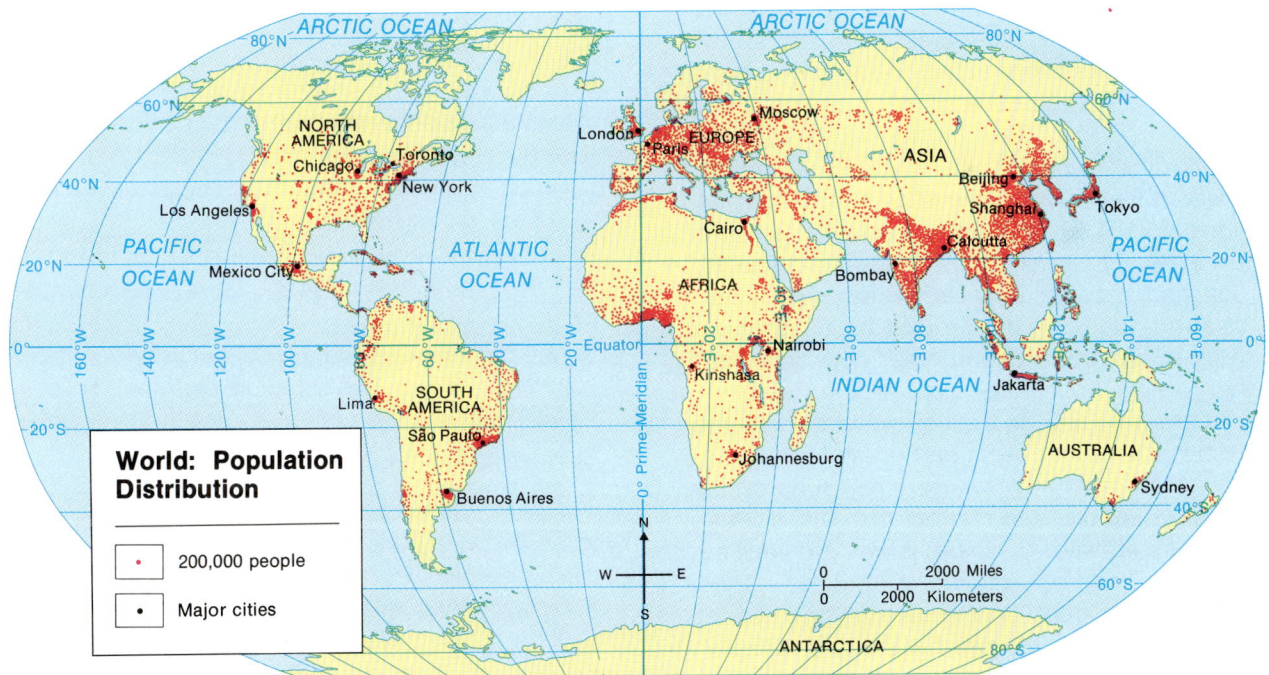

World: Population Distribution

· 200,000 people

· Major cities

Map Study

This map shows where the world's people live. Locate the four major population clusters discussed in this section. Use this map and the Atlas map on pages 620–621 to name some countries in each area.

to the first European settlements of America. Fueled by industrial progress in the 1800s, cities in this area, including Boston, New York, Newark, and Philadelphia, became major manufacturing centers. The cities began to attract millions of people in search of work. Today these cities have almost grown together to form a continuous urban complex.

Communities can be defined by location, function, and relationship.

Most of the people around the earth's surface live in communities. These communities vary from region to region and from culture to culture. They can, however, be classified into different types of categories.

First, a community can be defined by its location. The location has two aspects—site and situation. A place's **site** refers to the physical characteristics of the specific place. A city's site could be on a bay, in a valley, in the middle of an island, or at high altitude. A place's **situation** refers to its position in relation to the surrounding region. A city's situation could be that it is surrounded by enemies or accessible by water.

Second, a community can be defined by its function. Communities provide both goods and services, but some communities provide more than others. Therefore, a hierarchy of settlements can be set up. At the lowest step of the ladder is a hamlet. A hamlet usually has less than 100 inhabitants and very few services, limited perhaps to a gas station and general store. One step above is a village, which provides a wider range of services for its residents, as well as for the residents of the surrounding hamlets. A village is more likely to have a post office, church, restaurant, and grocery stores. The next step up is a town, which provides a greater variety of functions and services for the town and surrounding villages and hamlets. A town probably has even more specialized stores and occupations. Each step further up the ladder yields both a larger number and a wider variety of services and functions.

Third, a community can be defined according to its relationships with other communities. To begin, consider a large city. A city usually is surrounded by smaller towns and villages for which it provides jobs, services, entertainment, and transportation. These smaller towns, called suburbs, have a close relationship with the larger city. The city and suburbs together are called a **metropolitan area**. When many metropolitan areas grow together, as in eastern North America, they become a **megalopolis** like the area encompassing Boston, New York City, Philadelphia, Baltimore, and Washington, D.C. The cities within the large unit are well connected by air, rail, and car, and often share business and political relationships.

Section 1 Review

Locating Key Places
Locate the following places on the map on page 620: East Asia, South Asia, Europe

Identifying Key Terms
Define the following terms: population distribution, population density, site, situation, metropolitan area, megalopolis

Reviewing Main Ideas
1. What features influence where people choose to live on the earth?
2. Where are the four clusters in which most of the earth's people live?
3. Describe three ways that communities can be defined.

Thinking Critically: Assess Cause and Effect
Using the population distribution map on page 83, choose one location that has many people living there and one that has few people. Which factor do you think is most important in causing the population level to be high or low in each location? Use any maps in the book for help.

How Populations Change

Preview

Key Places
Where are these places located?
1 Japan
2 China
3 France
   See the globe below.

Key Terms
What do these terms mean?

census   migration
natural growth rate   demographic transition

Main Ideas
As you read, look for answers to these questions.
• How has world population changed throughout history?
• How is population measured?
• How do population rates vary around the earth?

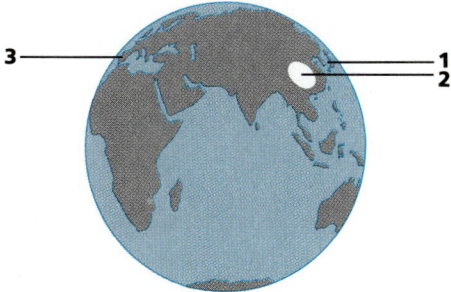

If the 2,000 years between A.D. 1 and 2000 could be turned into the 24 hours of a day, imagine how fast the world's population would be growing.

12:00 Midnight: 200 million people on the earth
7:48 p.m.: Population doubles to 400 million
10:12 p.m.: Population doubles to 800 million
11:00 p.m.: Population doubles to 1.6 billion
11:36 p.m.: Population doubles to 3.2 billion
By 11:59, the population will once again double.

World's population has increased dramatically over the past 300 years.

As the population clock shows, the world's population has taken less time to double each and every time. Consider these figures: the earth's population took from the beginning of history to about 1820 to reach 1 billion people, a span of several thousand years. Yet only 12 short years were required for the population to grow from 4 to 5 billion between 1975 and 1987.

As these numbers and the population growth graph on page 86 make clear, the world's population, after starting out slowly, has skyrocketed in the past few centuries. A population explosion has developed. Why? Many changes have contributed to the shift in growth patterns—improved health care and knowledge, advanced farming technology, and changes in societal needs and values.

Early in history, the earth's population was quite small and grew very slowly. Scientists estimate that there were around 200 million people on the earth about 2,000 years ago. Disease, war, and famine kept the number of deaths high, so population growth was held down. For example, a disease known as the bubonic plague once ravaged many parts of Europe and Asia. In fact, between 1348 and 1370, this disease, known as the Black Death, killed about one-third of the entire population of Europe.

85

By 1650 the earth's population had almost tripled and was now about 600 million. Around this time things began to change for the world's people. Farming methods improved. More food was produced, and more efficient ways of storing and distributing the food were put into use. Thus, less of the food was lost to disease, rotting, or animals.

In addition, increased contact with other parts of the world introduced new types of food to people. For example, one major import into Europe was the potato, brought from Peru. At first viewed with suspicion, the potato soon became an important staple food for many Europeans. The crop was easy to grow on a small area of land and required few tools. A family of six could obtain the bulk of their yearly food supply from a single acre of potatoes in a good year. Thus, the potato and other new imports improved the diets of Europeans and helped their populations to grow.

During the 1800s, populations around the world began to grow even larger. At about this time, Europe, Russia, and the United States were experiencing the dramatic changes and effects of the Industrial Revolution. Medical discoveries and scientific advances of the 19th century allowed more people to live longer, thereby increasing the population.

Population is measured by an official count or by comparing rates.

Most of the figures on population that we use throughout this book exist because the countries of the world periodically engage in an official count of their populations. This official count is known as a population **census**. In the United States, a population census is conducted

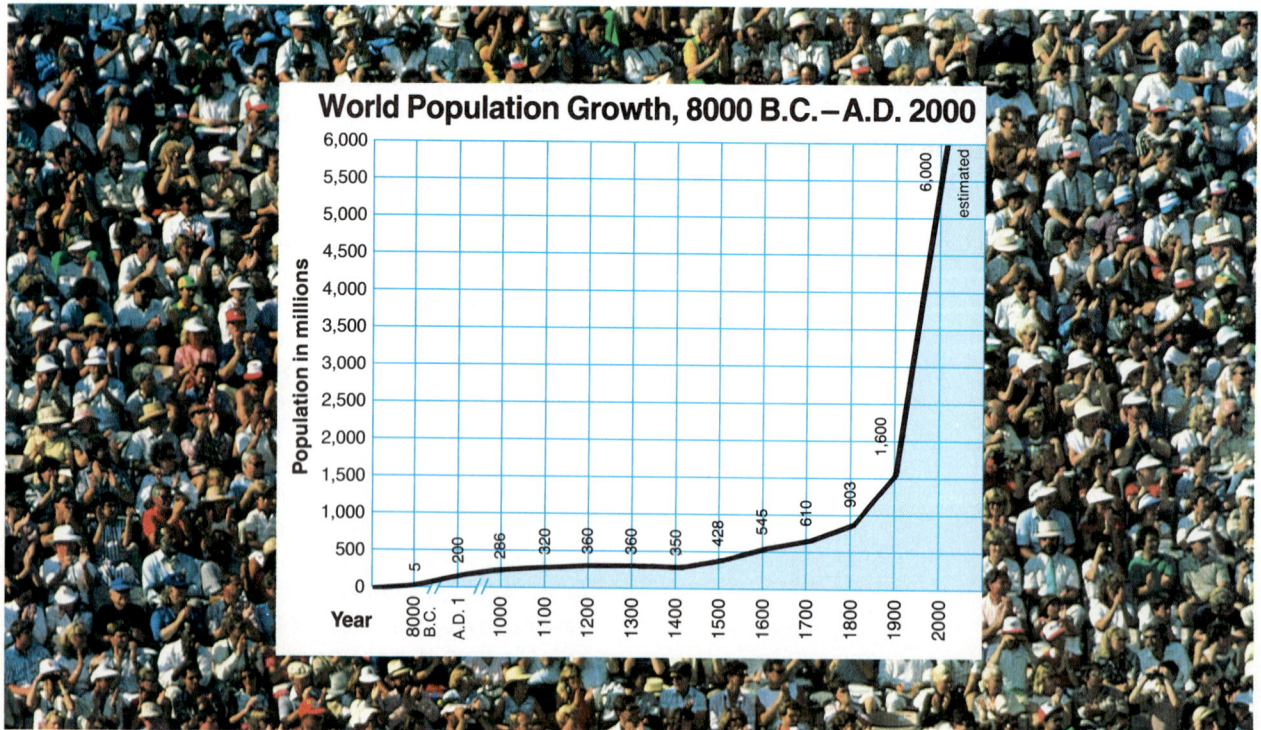

World Population Growth, 8000 B.C.–A.D. 2000

every ten years. To get an accurate count of the American population, census takers try to contact every person or family in the country either by mail or in person. In some other countries, population counts are not very accurate because of geographical, political, or economic reasons, such as the desire to downplay overcrowding, isolated regions, poor communication, or lack of money.

In countries where it is difficult to do an official census, another method is used. The population count is taken by calculating three measures called the crude birth rate, the crude death rate, and the migration rate. The crude birth rate is the number of live births during each year. It is reported either as the number of births that occur for every thousand people in the country or as a percentage. For example if there were 32 births for every thousand people, then the crude birth rate would be 32/1000 or 3.2%.

Similarly, the crude death rate is the number of deaths for the same period. It is also expressed for every thousand people or as a percentage. If there were eight deaths for every thousand people in one year, the crude death rate could be expressed as 8/1000 or 0.8%. To determine if the overall population were growing or declining, you would need to look at the **natural growth rate**. This measure is the difference between the crude birth rate and the crude death rate. For the example above, the natural growth rate would be 32 births minus 8 deaths for every thousand, or 2.4%. If there are more deaths than births, the percentage will be a negative number. The population is therefore declining and experiencing "negative growth."

Populations can also change by means other than births or deaths. **Migration**, the movement and settlement of people from one place to another, also affects many populations. When people leave a country to move to another, they are called emigrants from their old country and immigrants to their new country. Thus, to get a full sense of population change

for an area, you would use this simple formula: Births − Deaths + Immigrants − Emigrants = Population Change.

In many countries the effects of migration are small. In other countries, however, migration has dramatic effects. For example, each year the United States receives many more people through immigration from places such as Asia, Mexico, and other parts of Latin America than it loses through emigration.

Population migration does not only occur between countries. People often migrate within a country's borders, thereby affecting the relationships between regional areas. The most notable migrations are from the rural to the urban areas of the world, especially in developing countries. Birth rates tend to be higher in rural areas than in urban areas. Rural dwellers often move to cities in search of work. As a result, many cities around the globe are growing at a rapid pace.

Growth rates vary with industry, tradition, and government.

Population rates vary from country to country, within a country itself, and from year to year. Average rates of population growth for the world as a whole could, therefore, present a misleading impression. In reality, some populations are growing rapidly, some are growing slowly, and others are actually declining.

All around the world, however, population changes take place in fairly predictable patterns. Demographers—scientists who study human population—have found four basic stages of population change, the sequence of which has been called the **"demographic transition."** Generally, countries move from stage to stage as they move from low-technology agricultural economies to high-technology industrial and service societies.

In the first stage, called the high stationary stage, population grows very slowly. Countries at this stage have agricultural economies. Since families generally need many children to help out with farming, birth rates are high. Disease, war, and famine, however, keep death rates high as well, especially for infants. As a result, the population stays fairly constant over time. Few countries are still in this stage.

In the second stage, called the early expanding stage, improved medical practices and farming technology cause death rates to decline. Birth rates tend to stay high since the tradition of having large families remains strong. Thus, populations grow quickly. Many expanding countries in Africa, Middle and South America, and Asia are now in this second stage.

In the third stage, called the late expanding stage, birth rates begin to drop because of economic and societal changes. Death rates are low. As a result, the population grows but at a slower pace than in the second stage.

In the fourth stage, the low stationary stage, both birth and death rates are low, and there is little or no population growth. The United States, Canada, Japan, Australia, New Zealand, the Soviet Union, and most European countries are now at this stage. These countries are highly urbanized and industrialized, and most citizens enjoy high standards of living. Most people in these countries choose to have fewer children than their parents.

Government policy can sometimes change the normal course of demographic transition. For example, China is a basically agricultural country with more than a billion people. In recent years, the government has tried aggressively to stop further population growth. Government policies encourage citizens to postpone marriage and penalize those who have more than one child. Abundant posters and billboards promote the benefits of a one-child family. Although China's population should be rapidly growing, according to the normal stages of growth, its rate of growth has been slowed as a result of the government's influence.

In contrast, France has found itself losing population. Women are having fewer children and emigration rates are high. As a result, the country is experiencing "zero population growth." In response, the government has tried to encourage people to have more children by advertising and offering economic benefits to parents.

As you've read in this section, population rates vary both around the world and over time. Overall, however, the earth's population is growing, and growing fast. When you consider that much of the earth's surface is water or otherwise uninhabitable, you begin to realize that population growth is not simply filling up empty areas of the earth. In most situations the most heavily populated areas of the earth are the ones that are gaining more and more people every day. As demands for more food, water, and other goods grow, many experts are concerned that adequate supplies will not be available.

Section 2 Review

Locating Key Places
Locate the following places on the map on page 620: Japan, China, France

Identifying Key Terms
Define the following terms: census, natural growth rate, migration, demographic transition

Reviewing Main Ideas
1. How has the earth's population grown over time?
2. In what two ways is population measured?
3. What three factors cause population rates to vary?

Thinking Critically: Evaluate Sources of Information
As discussed in this section, population counts are not always accurate. What political, economic, or other conditions do you think may cause over- or under-reporting of a country's population?

Population Distribution Maps

Population distribution maps are special purpose maps that show how population is spread out around a chosen area. This particular map shows the United States with its state boundaries. Alaska and Hawaii are treated separately.

Two types of data are placed on the base map. First, a red dot is drawn on the map for every 10,000 people living in a particular place. In rural or wilderness areas, these dots are generally far apart. In urban areas, however, the dots are so close to one another that they blur together.

Review

1. Which major population cluster lies midway between Chicago and San Francisco?
2. Which major population center lies furthest north?
3. Which major population center lies in southeastern Texas?

United States: Population Distribution

- · 10,000 people
- • Major cities

CHAPTER 4

Review

Section Summaries

1. Where People Live In general, people live where they can make a living more easily. People look for food and fresh water, a pleasant or mild climate, natural resources, and nearness to waterways. As a result, most of the earth's population lives in East Asia, South Asia, Europe, and eastern North America. In these and other areas, people established communities that can be defined by their location, function, or relationship with other communities.

2. How Populations Change After maintaining a slow, steady growth pattern for thousands of years, the earth's population exploded about 300 years ago. Advances in farming, sanitation, and science helped more people live longer lives. Population is measured in an official count, called a census, or by using the crude birth, death, and migration rates. Population growth varies from place to place and from time to time. Industrial growth, tradition, and government policies all affect the rates at which populations grow or decline.

Using Geography Skills
Reviewing the Map Lesson
Use the map below to answer the following questions.
1. How may people does each dot represent on this map?
2. What part of Canada is the most heavily populated?
3. Name five major cities in Canada.
4. Which region of Canada is the least heavily populated?

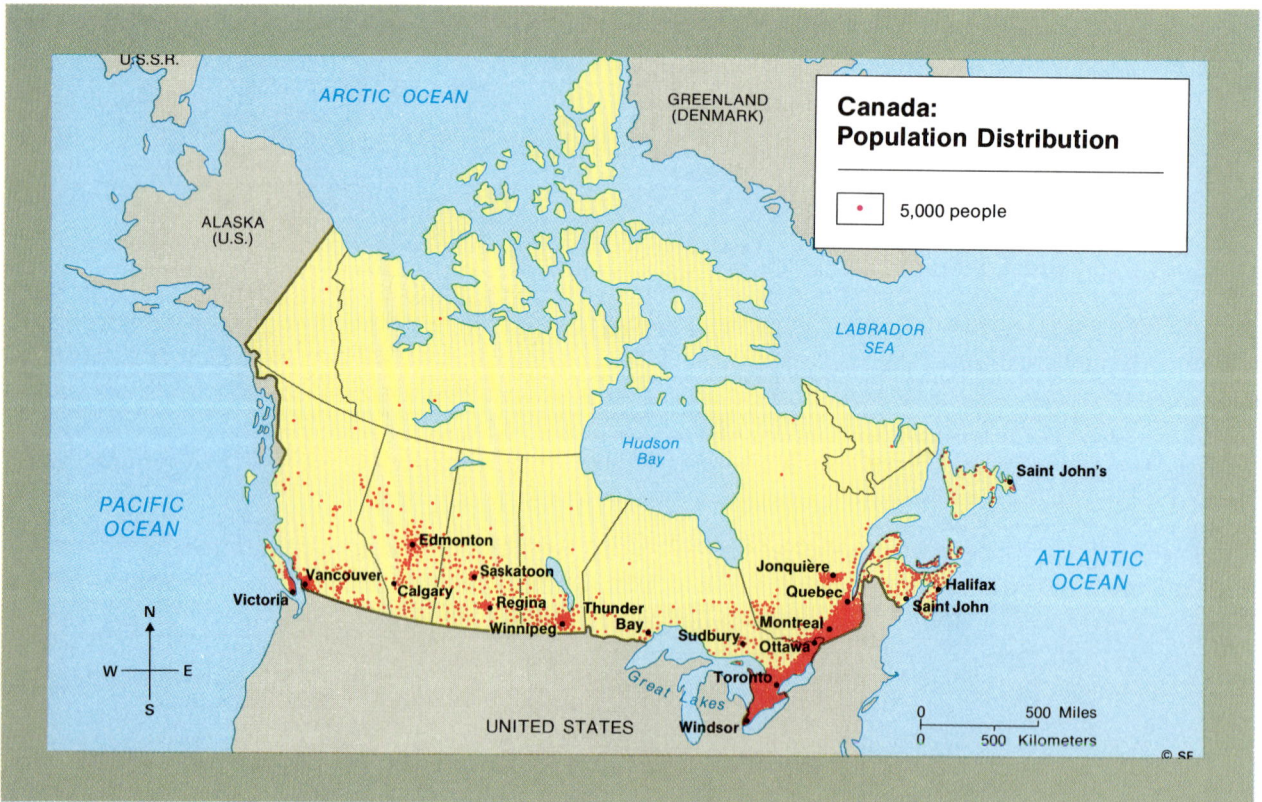

Canada: Population Distribution

• 5,000 people

Using Social Studies Skills

1. Sequence Historical Data and Information. Using the chart below of the European population from A.D. 1000 to 2000, make a line graph showing the changes in population.

Year	Population in millions
1000	36
1100	44
1200	58
1300	79
1400	60
1500	81
1600	100
1700	120
1800	180
1900	390
2000	800 (estimate)

What do you think caused the drop in population between 1300 and 1400?

2. Draw Inferences. You've learned in this chapter where the world's people live and why they live where they do. Look now at your own community. Why do you think people live there? Use the information in this chapter to infer why your community developed where it did. What geographical or historical conditions have brought people there? Write a paragraph explaining your reasoning.

Testing for Understanding

Locating Key Places
Match each description below with the name of the place.
1. a population cluster that includes France, Germany, and Italy
2. a country whose government set up laws to limit population growth
3. the largest population cluster on the earth
4. a country that is working to fight a declining population
5. a population cluster that includes India and Pakistan
6. an urbanized Asian country with little population growth
a. East Asia
b. South Asia
c. Europe
d. Japan
e. China
f. France

Recalling Key Terms
Define these terms in your own words.

Section 1
population distribution
population density
site
situation
metropolitan area
megalopolis

Section 2
census
natural growth rate
migration
demographic transition

Reviewing Main Ideas
Section 1
1. How do geography and history affect where people live?
2. Where are most of the world's people clustered?
3. How can communities be defined?

Section 2
1. How has the world's population changed over the past 300 years?
2. In what two ways can population be measured?
3. Why do population rates in a country vary over time?

Thinking Critically
1. Identify Assumptions. Imagine that a person decides to migrate to another country. What assumptions do you think that person is making about his or her new home, and about the process of moving itself? Consider reasons why someone would migrate.

2. Predict Effects. What would you expect to happen if the earth's population continued to increase dramatically over the next hundred years? What effects might you see on the world's food and water supply? What political consequences would you predict?

Patterns of Culture

In this chapter you will read about the cultural origins and practices of people around the world.

Sections

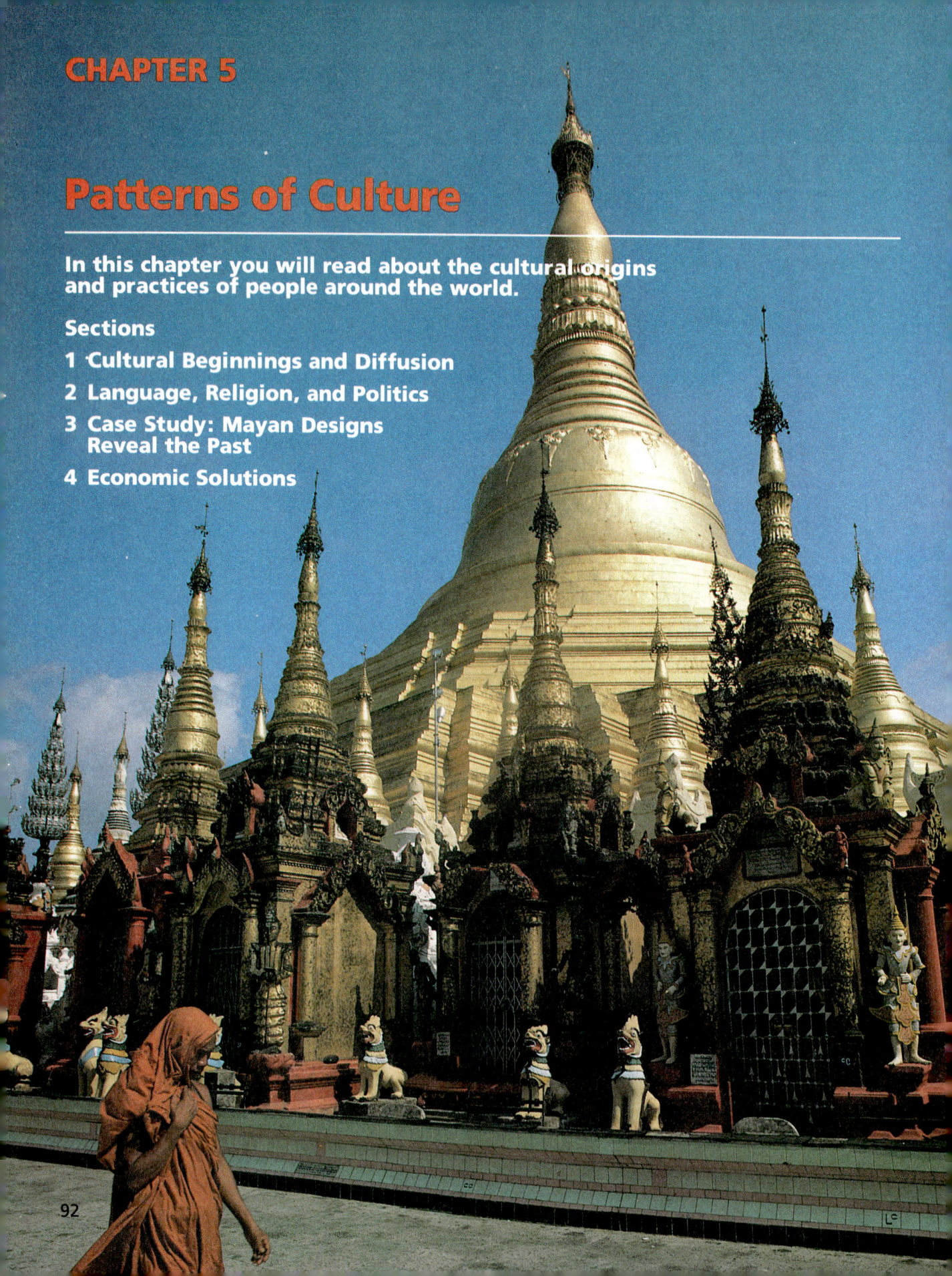

Cultural Beginnings and Diffusion

Preview

Key Places
Where are these places located?
1 Tigris River
2 Euphrates River
3 Huang River
   See the globe below.

Key Terms
What do these terms mean?
culture
culture hearth
cultural diffusion

Main Ideas
As you read, look for answers to these questions.
• What is culture?
• How does culture spread?
• How is the culture reflected in the landscape?

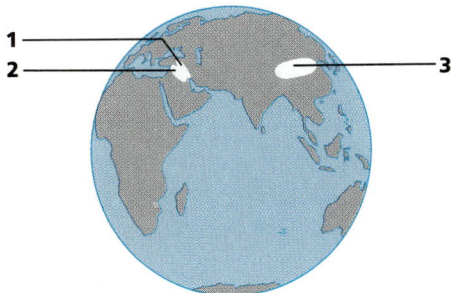

No matter how hard a man tries, it is impossible for him to divest himself of his own culture, for it has penetrated the roots of his nervous system and determines how he perceives the world.

E. T. Hall, cultural anthropologist

Culture is the human part of the environment.

As E. T. Hall noted, your culture is inescapable. **Culture** is everything, material and nonmaterial, that a society has learned and passed along to its members. Culture expresses the way of life of a given people at a particular time. Material culture is everything that we make or build—our utensils, farming methods, foods, clothes, buildings, tools, and communication systems. Nonmaterial culture is everything that we believe in or practice—our religion, language, laws, ideas, music, values, and political systems.

Culture is not something that you were born with, like your eye color. Rather, culture is learned, slowly and without much effort. Children learn from many sources of culture, such as their family and friends, television and movies. They gradually learn the customs and rules of their culture by watching, listening, and participating.

Everyone has a culture, but all cultures differ. People in various cultures speak different languages, practice different religions, and build their homes differently. Some people eat with chopsticks, some with forks, and still others with their fingers.

Culture spreads by diffusion.

Cultures, like people, change over time. Advancing technologies affect how people travel, eat, work, and play. The way you live today is

Facing page: **The magnificent Shwe Dagon Pagoda in Rangoon, Burma, reflects the country's strong Buddhist faith.**

probably very different from the way your grandparents lived at your age. Your children's lives will probably be different from your own. The history of a culture is the story of hundreds, sometimes thousands, of years of change and development.

Culture hearths. The origins of many modern-day cultures began thousands of years ago in the world's earliest culture hearths. A **culture hearth** is the center and major source of a particular culture, a place from which new ideas, values, and practices have spread.

Culture hearths, some ancient and some modern, have emerged throughout history. Two early culture hearths emerged between the Tigris and Euphrates rivers in Mesopotamia and along the Huang River in China. These ancient culture hearths were also among the world's first civilizations. They were able to be successful largely because they were located in fertile valleys and basins of major river systems. Effective farming techniques brought food surpluses. As a result, some people could afford to devote time to the arts, religion, and trading instead of farming. Ideas about government developed. Through trade, cultural traditions began to spread outward to the surrounding areas.

Cultural diffusion. From the early culture hearths to the surrounding areas, from large cities to rural areas, and from one country to another, new ideas and inventions spread. The process by which a culture trait or innovation moves from one culture to another is called **cultural diffusion.** Innovations do not usually spread unchanged however. Sometimes ideas are quickly adopted just as they are, and sometimes they are modified to fit another way of life. Other times, they are rejected completely.

The reasons an idea is or is not accepted vary. Some cultures are very open to new ideas and welcome change. Others hold very firmly to their customs and traditions and choose to re-

ject anything that doesn't fit with their social or religious values. Some cultures are destroyed by conquering peoples, and others may be geographically isolated from outside influences. Ideas may travel slowly to these isolated cultures, losing their impact with each passing day and mile. The farther from their source, in both time and distance, the less likely innovations are to be adopted.

An illustration of two groups who responded differently to the arrival of new ideas comes from Kenya in East Africa. Among Kenya's people are the Kikuyu [ki kü'yü], who were farmers, and the Masai [mä sī'], who were and are nomadic cattle herders. When the European colonists arrived in Africa, the Kikuyu adopted British ways. The Masai instead resisted change and for many years continued to practice their traditions. Now, however, even the Masai are changing their ways. The vast quantities of open land they require to maintain their nomadic life are being claimed and fenced in. The Masai are also meeting strong resistance to their lifestyle from other Kenyans.

The cultural landscape is most evident in clothing and architecture.

People of every culture adapt and transform their physical environment by constructing buildings upon it, farming its land, channeling its water, and creating means of travel and communication across it. People leave traces of their use of the natural world in railroad tracks, dams and canals, and the patterns of farm fields. The interaction between a culture and the natural environment produces the cultural landscape. Two important elements of the cultural landscape are clothing and architecture. Each reflects how human beings in a particular culture have responded to the physical conditions of their environment.

Clothing. Clothing serves many functions in a culture. It covers and protects from the cold, rain, snow, or sun. In this sense, it is part of the material culture of a people. In another sense, clothing is also part of the nonmaterial culture since clothing serves the function of projecting images of fashion, independence, youth, or business competence. A person's clothing, in most cultures, is used to demonstrate belonging or status. A soldier's uniform or a priest's religious robe each presents an image of importance and authority.

A group's location has traditionally affected the clothes its members wear. Local climate, natural resources, and accessibility to outsiders have long dictated styles and materials of clothing. In many cold northern regions of Asia, North America, and Europe, people relied on the heavy furs and skins of reindeer and caribou to keep them warm and dry. In hotter regions of the world, people have worn clothes made of lighter materials such as cotton.

Tradition also plays a role in clothing choices. In many Muslim cultures, for example, women are required to wear a head-to-toe cloak and veil. This form of dress reflects the Muslim belief that women should be concealed in public.

Today many changes have occurred in the way people cover their bodies. Advances in the ways we can control our environment, such as central heating and air conditioning, have given many of the world's people freedom in what to wear. In addition, increased global contact and communication have made people more aware of fashions and styles.

Architecture. Like clothing, a culture's architecture, or the way buildings are designed and built, is molded both by environmental and societal concerns. Thus, architecture reflects a culture's physical environment—climate, natural materials, and landforms—as well as its values, traditions, history, and outside contact. The

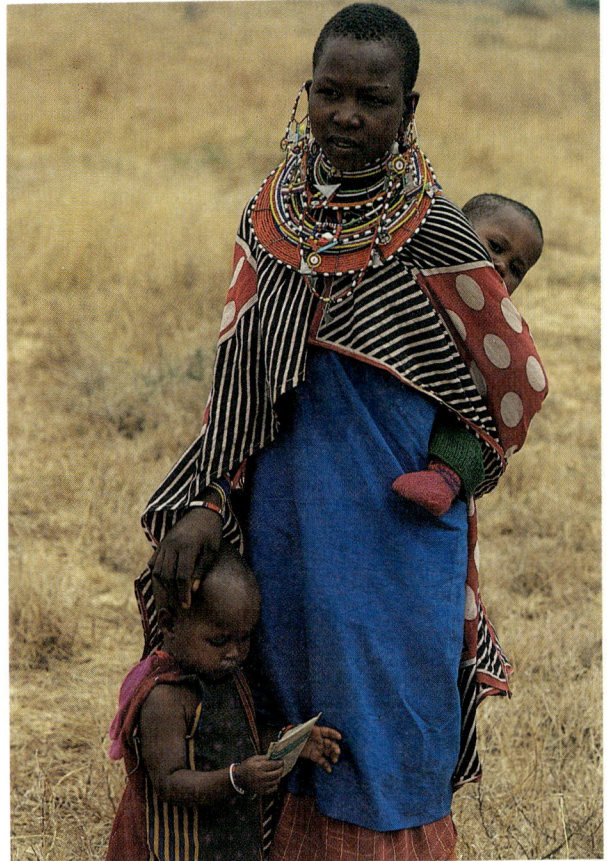

Masai women of East Africa wear bright jewelry and clothing.

combination of all these influences produces different effects in every culture.

Architecture, like clothing, serves many functions. It serves governmental, religious, commercial, public, and domestic purposes, and the style of the building varies with each use.

The architecture of government buildings today often reflects the traditional values of the culture's political history. For European and American government structures, for example, architects often return to the styles of ancient Greece, where many of our democratic ideals originated. These buildings present a powerful image, with imposing size and stone columns.

Religion plays an important role in the cultural landscape of many cultures around the world. In countries where the Islamic religion prevails, tall, slender towers called minarets pierce the skyline from atop Muslim mosques. Throughout Europe and the Americas, churches and cathedrals are common reminders of a Christian heritage.

Commercial architecture dominates many of the earth's urban communities. Tall skyscrapers are a common sight in many American and European cities, as well as in other modern cities around the globe. The urban cultural landscape, with its huge towers of steel and glass, reflects the predominance of commerce in modern life.

Public architecture includes schools and universities, libraries and hospitals, museums and sports arenas. The styles are often quite efficient and functional—appropriate for the public purpose of the buildings. In some cultures, however, such public buildings as universities and museums are carefully designed to show respect for education and the arts.

Domestic architecture reflects most closely how people in a culture live—how they choose to build their homes and decorate their immediate surroundings. In most parts of the world, the style of a home depends on the local climate and the availability of building materials.

In the United States, housing choices vary according to climatic conditions. For example, houses in rainy or snowy areas often have steep roofs to keep the rain or snow from building up. Because of gentler weather conditions, houses in dry areas tend to have flatter roofs.

Building materials vary all around the world. Where it is available and inexpensive, wood is a popular choice for homes. In areas without abundant trees, houses may be built from mud, stones, or grass. In some parts of Europe and North America, building bricks are often made of oven-baked clay. Likewise, in hot, dry areas like parts of Africa and South and Middle America, houses are often made out of dried mud. Traditionally, many houses in hot areas were built out of grasses, bark, and leaves covered with dried mud. Now, however, more modern building materials, such as corrugated aluminum, are often used.

Housing styles reflect not only weather and available materials, but also the lifestyle of the people who build the homes. For nomadic peoples, housing materials must be portable. Their lifestyle demands that they move frequently, so their homes must go along with them. As a result, nomads often live in tents made of lightweight cloth or animal skins. Whether it be a tent, an apartment, or a two-story colonial, a home is one of the most important parts of the cultural landscape.

Section 1 Review

Locating Key Places
Locate the following places on the map on page 622: Tigris River, Euphrates River, Huang River

Identifying Key Terms
Define the following terms: culture, culture hearth, cultural diffusion

Reviewing Main Ideas
1. How is culture defined?
2. How does culture move from place to place?
3. What are two elements of a cultural landscape? How do they reflect the culture?

Thinking Critically: Recognize Values
You read in this section that values are an important part of culture. Explain what values are shown in each of the following: fences around yards, huge mansions, beautiful libraries, camping trailers, and golden temples.

SECTION 2

Language, Religion, and Politics

Preview

Key Places
Where are these places located?
1 India
2 Israel
3 Saudi Arabia
See the globe below.

Key Terms
What do these terms mean?

language family	authoritarian system
lingua franca	communism
democracy	

Main Ideas
As you read, look for answers to these questions.
- How did our modern languages evolve and spread?
- What are the major world religions?
- How are political systems related to culture?

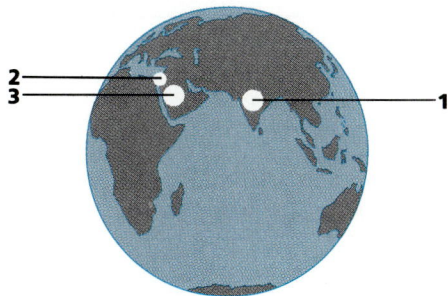

Language is the amber in which a thousand precious and subtle thoughts have been safely imbedded and preserved.

R. C. Trench, *The Study of Words*

Modern languages evolved and spread from a few common sources.

Just as the yellow amber stone forms with each new bit of fossilized plant remains, language has evolved with each new word, thought, or idea. Through language, people communicate with one another. They communicate their ideas, their needs, and their feelings. Without a shared language, people would find it difficult to develop and pass along a common culture. Language therefore becomes important in expressing and sharing culture.

In the world today, however, thousands of different languages are spoken. Within these languages, many dialects, or variations, exist as well. The English language, for example, has very different vocabularies and pronunciations when it is used in Britain, the United States, Canada, Australia, and around the world. In addition, different variations of language can be found in specialized technical, diplomatic, or business fields. Around the world, local needs, activities, resources, and attitudes are reflected in the language or dialect spoken.

Although there are many different languages in use around the world, scientists believe that many of them share common origins. Languages with similar vocabularies and structures belong to the same **language family**. Thirteen major language families exist in the world today. The map and diagram on page 98 show these broad groupings and some of the main languages they include.

One of the most widespread language families is called Indo-European. It has been traced back to a single tongue that has long been forgotten. Linguists—scientists who study

97

2.2 billion
Indo-European

Germanic
Dutch-Flemish
English
German
Danish
Icelandic
Norwegian
Swedish
Yiddish, etc.

Armenian

Albanian

Baltic
Lithuanian
Lettish

Slavic
Bulgarian
Czech
Macedonian
Polish
Russian
Serbo-Croatian
Slovak
Slovene
Ukrainian, etc.

Romance
Italian
French
Portuguese
Romanian
Spanish, etc.

Celtic
Breton
Irish Gaelic
Welsh, etc.

Indo-Iranian
Afghan
Bengali
Hindi
Farsi
Kurdish
Sanskrit
Singhalese
Urdu, etc.

Hellenic
Greek

Other Language Families

1 billion
Sino-Tibetan
Burmese, Chinese, Thai, Tibetan, etc.

110 million
Ural-Altaic
Finnish, Hungarian, Mongolian, Turkish, etc.

330 million
Sub-Saharan African
 Bantu, Fulani, Kikuyu, Xhosa, etc.

70 million
Southeast Asian
Vietnamese, Khmer, etc.

230 million
Malay-Polynesian
Hawaiian, Indonesian, Maori, etc.

10 million
Latin American Indian
Quechua, Guarani, Arawak, Carib, etc.

190 million
Dravidian
Malayalam, Tamil, Telugu, etc.

2 million
North American Indian
Aztec, Algonquian, Iroquoian, Siouan, etc.

180 million
Japanese-Korean

80,000
Inuit-Aleut

180 million
Semitic and Related Languages
Arabic, Hebrew, Amharic, Berber, etc.

50,000
Australian Aboriginal

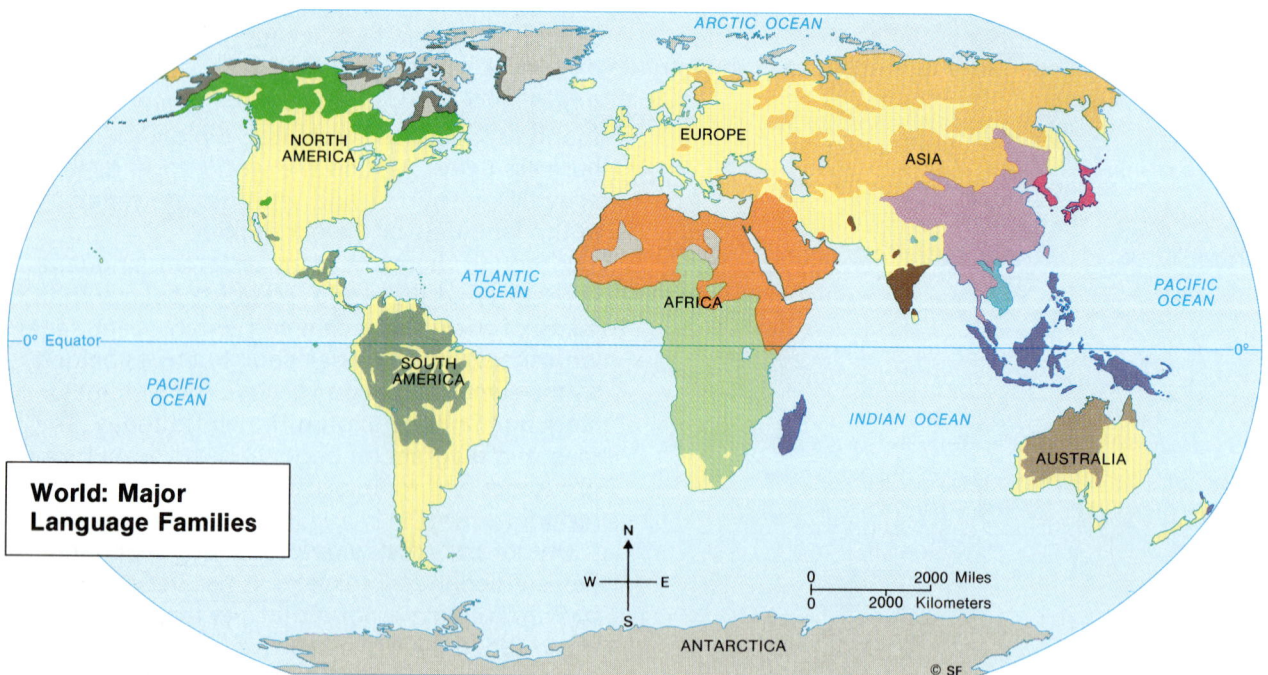

World: Major Language Families

language—call it Proto-Indo-European. The speakers of this language probably lived in what is now the southwestern part of the Soviet Union, near the Black Sea, more than 5,000 years ago. From this place of origin, the population migrated west into Europe, southeast into what is now India and Iran, and north farther into the Soviet Union. In moving, the original language splintered into many related languages, including English, Russian, French, German, Hindi, and Farsi. The words used for "mother" in many of these languages illustrate the similarity—"madre" (Spanish), "matka" (Polish), "mütter" (German), "ma" (Hindi), and "mère" (French).

Languages like the Indo-European ones spread out by cultural diffusion. They may move into new areas when the people who speak the languages migrate. They may also move into an area when its speakers conquer, colonize, or otherwise dominate the native language. In both of these ways, English has spread out from the islands of Britain into North America, Australia, New Zealand, and India.

Around the world, languages have developed in response to the needs of people involved in trade, commerce, and general communication with people who speak different languages. A language that is widely used as a means of communication among speakers of different languages is called a **lingua franca**.

Some established languages may become a lingua franca for reasons of practicality. English, for example, has become one of the most dominant languages of the world because it is the major language of international commerce. To do business in the United States or in many other places around the globe, people must

Facing page: **Which language family shown on the chart has the most speakers? Name some of its branches.**

understand the English language.

Another type of lingua franca contains words and expressions borrowed over time from different languages. An example is the language of Swahili, which developed mainly in the eastern African countries of Kenya, Tanzania, Uganda, and Mozambique. This lingua franca is a combination of the native Bantu language and Arabic, which was spoken by Arab traders in this region.

There are several major world religions.

Religions, like languages, share common origins and paths of diffusion. Religious diffusion takes two main courses, with the religion either moving with its followers or being spread by missionary efforts. In the first method, people carry their religion along with them when they leave their homeland because of war, natural disaster, or other reasons. In the second method, people travel to new places in order to spread their beliefs and attract new followers to their religion.

Around the world, religions maintain belief systems that, to many people, offer comfort, support, and hope. They provide a structure for the way people think about the world and live their lives. Following is a discussion of the belief systems and geography of five of the major world religions.

Hinduism. The Hindu religion is the oldest of the five major religions. It began to develop about 4,000 years ago in India, but it has no single founder or system of beliefs. Instead, it has many diverse gods and beliefs. One important belief is the theory of *karma,* which holds that all beings, human or animal, have souls, and that karma determines the birth attributes of each new soul. The ideal of the religion is for the soul to move upward to the most sacred level through reincarnation. If a person leads a life of good deeds and strong faith—achieving a good karma "score"—his or her soul will move upward, perhaps into the body of a scholar or holy person. If he or she leads a bad life, the soul will move downward, perhaps into the body of an animal.

From its origins, the Hindu religion spread eastward across India and into Southeast Asia. Today it is found primarily in India, where 85 percent of the country's 760 million people are Hindu. Hinduism is also found in spots around the globe where Indians moved in colonial times, particularly in East and South Africa, the Caribbean, and the Pacific Islands.

Buddhism. Buddhism appeared in India during the 6th century B.C. as a protest against miseries associated with Hindu beliefs about reincarnation. The religion was founded by Gautama Siddhartha, a prince from what is now Ne-

pal, who was called the Buddha, or the Enlightened One. The Buddha attracted large numbers of followers by preaching that salvation could be achieved by anyone. Salvation and enlightenment would come to those who practiced honesty, self-knowledge, selflessness, and kindness to all beings.

The Buddhist religion spread very slowly over the next 200 years. Then a powerful Indian emperor named Asoka became a convert to the faith. He promoted Buddhism not only in India, but also in Southeast Asia. Over time, Buddhism declined in the land of its origin but it remains strong today in Southeast and East Asia.

Judaism. Judaism, the religion of the world's Jews, is the oldest world religion to originate west of India. Judaism developed about

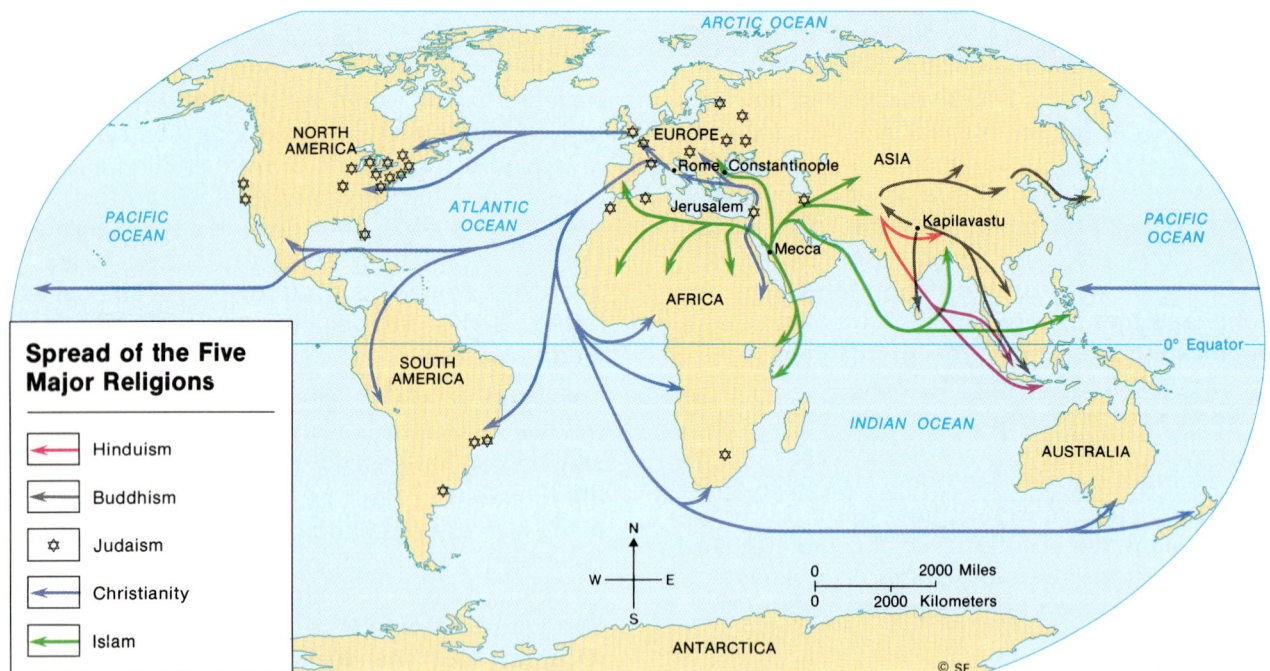

Spread of the Five Major Religions

←	Hinduism
←	Buddhism
✡	Judaism
←	Christianity
←	Islam

Map Study

This map shows how the five major religions have spread around the world. Where did most religions originate? To which continents did Christianity primarily spread?

1800 B.C. in present-day Israel. In the early years of the religion, Judaism was unique because its followers believed that there is only one God, the creator of the universe and of all people. This monotheistic faith—belief in one God—differed from the polytheism—belief in many gods—of the surrounding peoples. Basically, Jews believe it is their task to spread God's message to all people on earth to work for a just and peaceful world. They believe that God demands kindness and moral conduct from all people, Jews and non-Jews.

From its origins in Southwest Asia, Judaism has spread to many countries around the globe, especially the United States, the Soviet Union, and Europe. In addition, the creation of the Jewish state of Israel in 1948 reestablished the original center of Jewish culture and tradition.

Christianity. Christianity is a religion that grew out of Judaism. When Jesus was born in Bethlehem, near Jerusalem in what is now Israel, many people believed that he was the Messiah of whom the Jewish prophet Isaiah had spoken. He was believed to have come to end evil and establish justice and goodness around the earth.

Within Christianity there are many different branches and beliefs. All the religious branches follow the teachings of Jesus Christ and his disciples, but the interpretation of these teachings varies from church to church. Christian religious groups maintain many different practices, ceremonies, and customs. Some prominent branches are Roman Catholicism (prominent in South America, Italy, France, Spain, Ireland, and parts of the United States), Protestantism (prominent in much of Europe and the United States), and the Eastern Orthodox faith (prominent in Greece and Eastern Europe).

The diffusion of Christianity occurred both by the migration of followers and missionary work. Originally Christianity spread toward Europe during the period when Rome ruled in the Mediterranean regions. Much later, many Christians left Europe, during the era of colonialism. Through these movements, Christianity reached large parts of North, Middle, and South America. Colonial pressures, combined with missionaries, brought Christianity to much of Sub-Saharan Africa, parts of India, and the Philippines. Today Christianity is the most widespread and largest of the major religions.

Islam. Islam, the faith of the Muslims, is the youngest of the major religions. It is based on the teachings of Muhammad, a prophet born in A.D. 570 in what is now Saudi Arabia. According to Muslim belief, Muhammad received the truth directly from God (called Allah in Arabic) in a series of revelations. The Muslim holy book, the Koran, is the result of these communications. Like Jews and Christians, Muslims believe in one all-seeing and powerful God who demands justice and goodness.

Islam contains several different branches. Two major groups, Sunni Muslims and Shiite Muslims, have been involved in a disagreement for many centuries. They disagree primarily about who

Muslims pray together in a mosque in Dahran, Saudi Arabia

was meant to succeed Muhammad after his death.

Before the Islamic religion developed, the Arab world was very divided. Muhammad was able to unify the Arab peoples, increasing their power and leading to dominance in the region. Islam spread outward in all directions from Saudi Arabia. Large Muslim populations can now be found throughout North Africa, Southwest Asia, Pakistan, India, Bangladesh, Malaysia, and Indonesia, along with clusters in the Philippines, Europe, the Soviet Union, and the United States.

Political systems reflect a culture's values and organization.

Like languages and religions, political systems vary from culture to culture. Ever since the development of the first culture hearth, people have felt the need for some form of organization to make and enforce rules of behavior, to ensure security, and to provide guidance. Political units developed in response to these needs. Families and kinship groups served as the first political units, and as families joined forces, more complex group organization became necessary.

As communities grew larger, the state emerged as a vital political unit. In modern usage the word "state" is similar to the words "country" and "nation," but subtle differences exist. States have people, territory, and laws, and operate within clearly defined boundaries. The state has sovereignty, or absolute authority to rule and conduct foreign affairs. Each state has its own form of government.

Today Americans use the word "state" primarily to refer to one of the 50 United States. Our states do not have complete sovereignty, or absolute, power so they do not fit the common definition. Instead, the term "country" is more related to the common meaning of "state." A country, such as Mexico, is a sovereign political organization. Similarly, a nation is a political

Political parties play major roles in democracies. Here, the delegates at the 1984 Republican convention participate in a display of patriotism.

unit, but the word may also have ethnic meaning, such as in the Navajo nation. The boundaries of a nation are not as much physical as emotional or cultural. A nation-state combines these last two units. It is a country whose political boundaries are roughly the same as the boundaries of the ethnic group that occupies it. Two examples are France and Japan.

The political systems that govern the various units have four key ingredients. They are (1) an ideology, which states the values and goals of the system; (2) institutions such as schools, hospitals, and prisons; (3) leaders and decision-makers; and (4) membership, including citizens or subjects. Each political system used around the world, both in the past and present, has developed a unique way of fitting these ingredients together. That whole reflects the values, needs, resources, and general culture of the people it serves.

Various types of political systems can be found around the globe. In theory, distinct differences exist between the various systems. In practice, however, these distinctions often tend to be blurred. Individual leaders and local cultures adapt the principles of the theoretical forms of government to their own needs and situations.

In theory, two major forms of government exist today—democracy and the authoritarian system. **Democracy** is a system in which all citizens are involved in the forming and running of the government. The ideology of this system respects individual rights and freedoms, and ensures participation by all. In a direct democracy, all citizens have the opportunity to take an active part in making laws and decisions. In an indirect democracy, citizens elect representatives to make the laws and political decisions for them.

In an **authoritarian system**, by contrast, one or a few individuals have complete, or nearly complete, power. Monarchies were an early form of authoritarian government. In most monarchies, kings and queens gained their power by heredity, that is, through their families. Today most monarchs, like the Queen of England, play only ceremonial roles. Another form of authoritarian system is the dictatorship. Dictators often come to power by force, overthrowing the old government in a revolution. In this system, absolute power can be held by a single person. In most cases, human rights and freedoms are not observed. An oligarchy, another authoritarian system, is rule by a few select people. In some cases, a handful of important families governs and influences a country.

Communism is a system that combines both authoritarian political and socialist economic philosophies. It is based on the ownership of land, factories, and other means of production by the community as a whole, or the state. In a communist system such as exists in the Soviet Union and China, all power lies with the communist political party. The leaders of this party control the activities, resources, and movement of the entire country.

Section 2 Review

Locating Key Places
Locate the following places on the map on page 620: India, Israel, Saudi Arabia

Identifying Key Terms
Define the following terms: language family, lingua franca, democracy, authoritarian system, communism

Reviewing Main Ideas
1. How did languages diffuse from their early sources?
2. Briefly describe the beliefs of the five major world religions.
3. Name two elements of a culture that are reflected in its political system

Thinking Critically: Recognize Values
What values might leaders of a democracy hold? Of an authoritarian system?

Case Study: Mayan Designs Reveal the Past

Preview

Key Places
Where are these places located?
1 Guatemala
2 Chiapas
See the globe below.

Key Terms
What do these terms mean?
motif
huipil
vestment

Main Ideas
As you read, look for answers to these questions.
• What has given anthropologists new insights into the Maya culture?
• How is the ceremonial huipil used?
• What figures appear in Maya clothing?

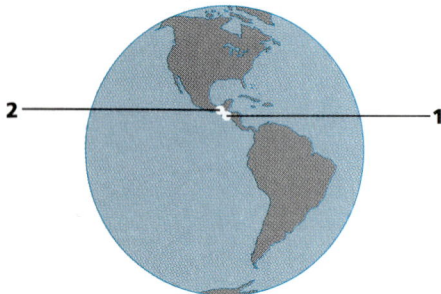

The following case study comes from the article, "Garments Offer Fresh Look at Ancient Maya," from the New York Times, *September 29, 1987. You have read in this chapter how culture is reflected in clothing. In this case study, you will learn how the culture of the ancient Maya, an Indian people who live in southern Mexico and Central America, is reflected in the ceremonial clothing of their modern descendants.*

Ceremonial weaving has brought new insights into the Maya culture.

In their ceaseless fascination with all things Mayan, anthropologists have left few sculpted stones unturned or jewel-filled tombs unopened in the jungles of Guatemala and Mexico. But for a long time they generally overlooked evidence of the enigmatic [puzzling] ancient culture that is as obvious as the clothes on the backs of today's Maya descendants.

A revival of one of the most beautiful art forms of the Maya people, the weaving of ceremonial garments rich in symbolism, has given anthropologists new insights into a mythology and vision of the cosmos that has persisted over 2,000 years.

In 14 years of research in Chiapas, the southernmost state of Mexico, Walter F. Morris, an American anthropologist, found that the geometrical **motifs** [distinctive figures in designs or paintings] woven into modern garments were very much like those used for hundreds of years before the Spanish conquest. Now, as then, he said, the ceremonial garment, known as a **huipil** [wē pēl'], is embellished with fields of diamond-shaped patterns representing the cosmos, figures of ancestors emerging from the underworld and symbols of a reptillian Earth-lord and toad, representing rain and fertility.

These motifs have been observed often in the sculpture, painting, and pottery found in ruins of the Maya civilization at its peak, between A.D. 300 and 900. Interviews with modern weavers, many of whom said they were inspired by "sacred dreams," led Mr. Morris to a detailed interpretation of the ancient symbolism.

By surrounding themselves with these . . . designs, Mr. Morris wrote, the weavers of the garments in ancient times were, "symbolically at the center of the world, close to the precious ancestors who interceded on the ruler's behalf with the gods who control order, rain, and the continuation of life on the surface of the Earth."

The great Maya civilization, which developed a hieroglyphic writing system [which uses pictures instead of words], a sophisticated knowledge of astronomy, and monumental pyramids, collapsed suddenly and mysteriously about 1,000 years ago. About four million Maya descendants live in southern Mexico and Central America, preserving the myths, songs, language and ceremonies of their celebrated heritage.

Christopher Jones, a specialist in Maya hieroglyphics at the University Museum of the University of Pennsylvania, said several studies had established the surprisingly close cultural link between today's Maya and the pre-Columbians, despite the overlay of Roman Catholic religion and Spanish influence. Modern ceramics in Guatemala, he said, bear a striking resemblance in style and symbolism to that of the ancient culture.

The huipil is used to clothe statues and is worn during festivals.

In 1983, Mr. Morris concentrated his work on

Modern Maya women and child display their elaborate woven artistry.

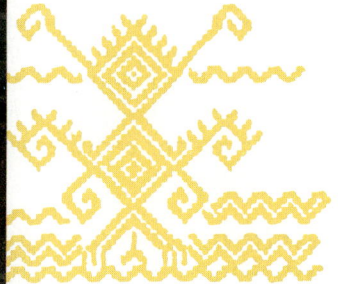

Harry N. Abrams, Inc. Photo Jeffrey Jay Foxx. Drawing Pedro Meza.

the weavers in the . . . community of Santa Maria Magdalenas Aldama in the highlands of Chiapas. Fewer than 20 women in the area, he said, know how to weave the ceremonial huipil in which intricate designs are created by placing colored threads in the fabric as it is being woven on a type of loom that has been used for more than 2,000 years.

The huipil, a rectangular **vestment** [a robe or gown], is placed on the statues of saints at the village church or worn by the women at festivals. The revival of the old craft is said to have begun in Magdalenas in the late 19th century when a woman had a dream in which the community's patron saint appeared and demanded that the woman make her a new huipil.

The ceremonial huipil consists of three pieces of cotton cloth, two sleeve sections sewn to the central section that drapes the body to the waist. The design is brocaded in homespun wool of red, yellow and black as well as some commercial yarns of green, orange and pink.

Although each design is a distinctive version of the weaver's vision of the universe, Mr. Morris said, a typical huipil is one where the central section is almost completely covered with rows of diamond-shaped patterns. Each unit consists of a main diamond symbolizing the square Maya world with a small diamond in the center as the sun and other diamonds in each corner of the world.

The inner diamond has a line that connects it to the upper and lower diamonds, depicting the path of the sun from east to west. Two curls on each side of the central diamond are the wings of a butterfly, woven as a metaphor for the sun's movement and the transformation from day to night.

Symbolic designs appear in Maya clothing.

There are 24 rows of this design and 24 repetitions of the butterfly pattern, with small dots and shadings of color that apparently correspond with numbers of symbolic importance to the Maya. For example, the Classic Mayas believed there were nine layers to the underworld and 13 layers in the heavens.

Other geometrical symbols prominent in traditional huipils are the woven figures of the toad, Earthlord and the rain god, all three being manifestations of the power of life and death. The Earthlord lives in a cave and controls the growth of plants and souls of the dead; the figure is shown holding flowers, and the toad next to him has a flowering headdress. The rain god creates the clouds and is shown in the heavens. And the toads, which symbolize femininity and fertility, appear on all three sections of the garment and seem to integrate the huipil's mythological significance, according to Mr. Morris.

Although the style and individual designs vary in each highland community, Mr. Morris concluded, "the symbolic concepts have changed little in the last millennium."

Section 3 Review

Locating Key Places
Locate the following places on the map on page 220: Guatemala, Chiapas

Identifying Key Terms
Define the following terms: motif, huipil, vestment

Reviewing Main Ideas
1. How have anthropologists developed new insights into the Maya culture?
2. When are ceremonial huipils worn by the Maya?
3. What do the designs showing gods symbolize on Maya clothing?

Thinking Critically: Identify Assumptions
What assumptions does the following speaker make: "I'm amazed that 1,500 years ago the Maya knew astronomy and had writing."?

Economic Solutions

Preview

Key Places
Where are these places located?
1 United States
2 Soviet Union
See the globe below.

Key Terms
What do these terms mean?
resource
market economy
command economy
gross national product (GNP)
per capita income (PCI)

Main Ideas
As you read, look for answers to these questions.
- How do different cultures meet the needs and wants of their people?
- How are different types of industry defined?
- How are resources distributed among nations?

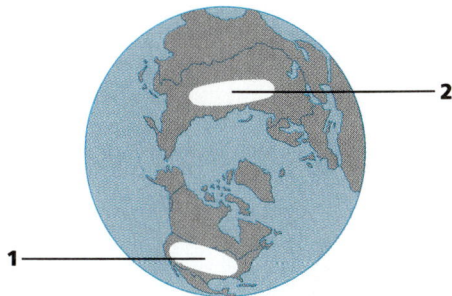

If a merchant has given to an agent corn, wool, oil, or any sort of goods, to traffic with, the agent shall write down the money value, and shall return that to the merchant. The agent shall then take a sealed receipt for the money that he has given to the merchant.

Code of Hammurabi, around 1700 B.C.

Cultures meet needs and wants through different economic systems.

Hammurabi, a king of ancient Babylon, had a set of 300 laws, including the one you just read, recorded on a stone column almost 4,000 years ago. Many of these laws reflected the government's attempt to promote justice and public welfare through fair economic practices. Hammurabi's Code became the basis for many other legal systems in Southwest Asia.

As you learned in Unit 1, different parts of the world contain different landforms, minerals, climates, soils, and vegetation. In other words, these places contain different and unequal amounts and values of resources. A **resource** is any supply, skill, or aid that will meet a need. Resources can be natural, such as trees, oil, or water; human, such as skilled workers or managers; or capital, such as finances or machinery used to produce goods.

The ways people use these resources to meet their needs and wants are called economic systems. A system must exist to deal with scarcity—how to use and distribute a limited supply of resources in a society with conflicting needs and wants.

Each society must answer these four basic economic questions: (1) What should be produced? (2) How much should be produced? (3) What methods of production should be used? (4) How should the goods and services be distributed?

Various groups of people have developed many different economic systems to answer these questions. In the past many societies had a traditional economy, in which custom and tradition were used to answer the four economic questions. No country today, however, uses a completely traditional economic system.

Since the 1800s, two types of system have emerged as ideological opposites: market and command economies. A **market economy** is an economic system in which the four factors of production—land, labor, capital, and entrepreneurship—are owned by individuals. In a market economy, the four questions are answered by the people who buy and sell goods and services. People are free to choose their own work and make other economic choices and decisions. They compete with others in order to earn profits, which become their private property.

A **command economy**, by contrast, is a system in which most of the factors of production are owned by the government. The government, by way of central planning, answers the questions of production and distribution. Citizens have very few choices to make.

In the real world, there are no pure market or command economies. Instead, as the diagram below shows, most modern economies have developed as mixtures of the two forms. In the United States, for example, most people believe in a market economy but live in daily contact with the government-run postal service and social security system.

Command economies also have their divergent elements. Communism, as practiced in the Soviet Union and China, relies on a command economy in which the communist party dictates economic decision-making. Even in these two countries, some people are beginning to get permission to own property and run their own businesses.

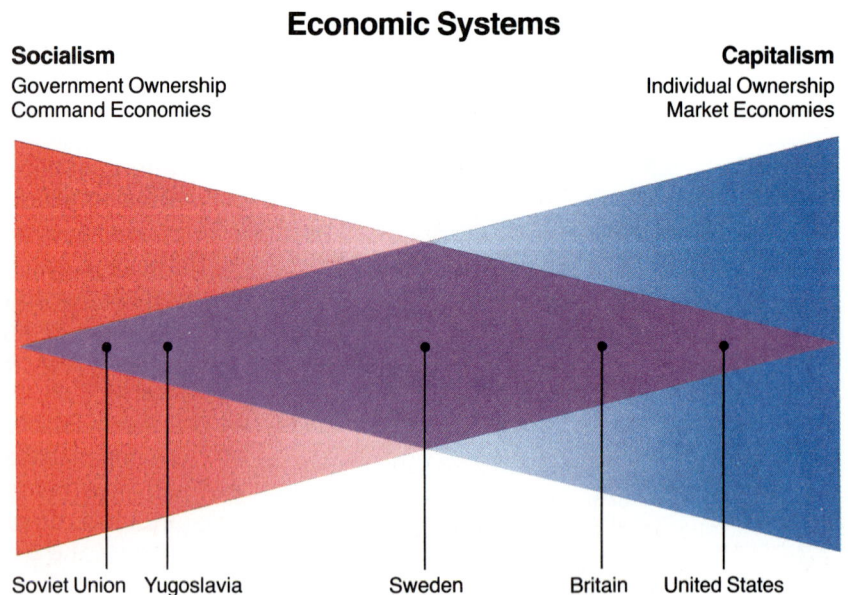

Economic Systems

Socialism
Government Ownership
Command Economies

Capitalism
Individual Ownership
Market Economies

Soviet Union   Yugoslavia   Sweden   Britain   United States

Industries can be defined as primary, secondary, and tertiary.

Each of the economic systems that you've just read about maintains three different types of industries—primary, secondary, and tertiary. Primary industries are the most basic. They usually involve taking things from the earth—farming, hunting, forestry, mining, fishing, and herding.

Secondary industries involve manufacturing, in which raw materials are made into products. The raw materials are first gathered through the primary industries, then used to make everything from breakfast cereals to pizzas, plastic toys to railroad cars.

Tertiary industries in turn encourage increased production of the other two types of industry. Tertiary industries include service fields such as education, tourism, banking, and sales.

To take a closer look at how industries work, consider agriculture. As described earlier, farming is one of the main primary industries. Within the industry itself, however, you'll find many different types of farming.

Subsistence agriculture. The most basic form is subsistence agriculture. People who practice this type of farming grow food only for their family's survival. Today few societies around the earth practice subsistence farming in the pure sense of the term. Even where traditional tools and techniques are still used, most farmers consider, to some degree, the demands of the marketplace.

Commercial agriculture. At the other end of the scale is commercial agriculture, in which farmers grow food to sell in the marketplace. The types and quantities of crop grown depend upon the needs and desires of consumers, those people who buy the product.

Commercial farming is the kind of farming most widely practiced throughout the United States. In this country most crops are grown using scientific techniques and advanced equipment. Another type of commercial agriculture is

Workers pick tea leaves on a Japanese hillside.

plantation farming. A plantation is a large farm, usually in a tropical or subtropical location, on which crops are grown for export.

Such plantations need large amounts of capital—often provided by foreign corporations—because they usually exist in isolated underdeveloped areas. Transport and communication systems must be built, along with housing for workers who live on the plantation. These workers tend such tropical cash crops as bananas, coffee, pineapple, sugar cane, cotton, and rubber—usually without the aid of modern machinery or techniques.

Plantation agriculture usually disrupts the traditional way of life of these tropical people. Under the plantation system, workers grow crops, not for the use of their people, but to send out of the country for export. In some cases, countries become dependent upon a single plantation crop. When world prices fall for that crop, the country intensely feels the drop in income.

Peasant agriculture. Between the extremes of subsistence and commercial farming lies peasant agriculture. This type of farming combines elements of the two extremes since farmers use what they need to feed their families and sell the rest. It is most common today in the world's traditional societies. In some cases, farmers establish permanent settlements where they use fertilizers and irrigation techniques.

This is also true of another type of peasant agriculture known as shifting cultivation or "slash and burn" agriculture. Here, however, farmers move from place to place. This type of farming is commonly practiced in remote, densely forested tropical areas of South America, Africa, and Southeast Asia.

Farmers begin to clear the forested land by "slashing" down small trees and underbrush.

Next, they kill the larger trees by stripping away sections of bark. Finally, when all the vegetation is dried out by the sun, the farmers set fire to the area. In the clearing, they plant such cash crops as beans, yams, and bananas.

As you learned in Chapter 3, however, the soil in a tropical rainforest is fairly poor in mineral content. As a result, after two or three years of heavy cultivation—with no fertilization—the soils lose their nutrient value. Once the soil is depleted, it can not produce good crops. The farmers move on to new plots of forested land, and weeds take over.

Resources are distributed unequally among nations.

Resources—natural, human, and capital—are distributed unevenly around the globe. Some

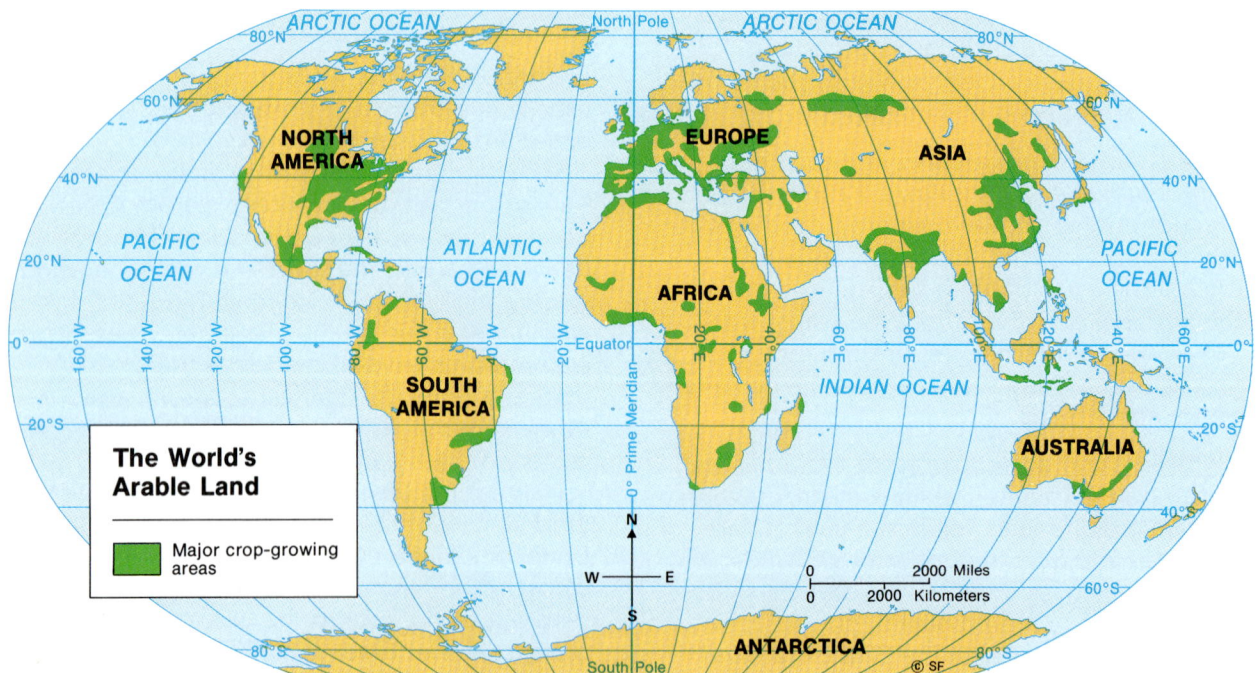

The World's Arable Land

Major crop-growing areas

Map Study

This map shows the limited amount of productive farmland on the earth. Compare this map to the population distribution map on page 83. What conclusions can you draw?

countries have abundant mineral resources and some have climates that are ideal for productive farming, but other countries are located where physical or economic conditions are less than perfect.

In the late 1700s and 1800s, European powers, with their superior weaponry, conquered peoples and established colonies all over North and South America, Africa, and Asia. From their colonies, Europeans received raw materials that helped fuel their developing industrial revolution. In turn, the colonies purchased manufactured products from Europe.

The relationships that developed during this time, along with internal political conditions, left some countries ahead and others behind, in terms of economic development. If you could compare the countries of the world as you would different individual's bank account statements, you would see great differences. According to certain measures, some countries would be labeled very rich and some very poor.

In making world comparisons, the wealthy countries are sometimes called developed, with the poorer countries called developing or underdeveloped. These countries are also called "industrialized" or "traditional." One way to measure a country's wealth is by looking at its **gross national product (GNP)**—the total worth of all goods and services produced in a country in a year.

Another way is to divide the GNP by the total population. The resulting figure is the **per capita income (PCI)**—the value of goods and services available for each person. The map below shows how per capita income—or

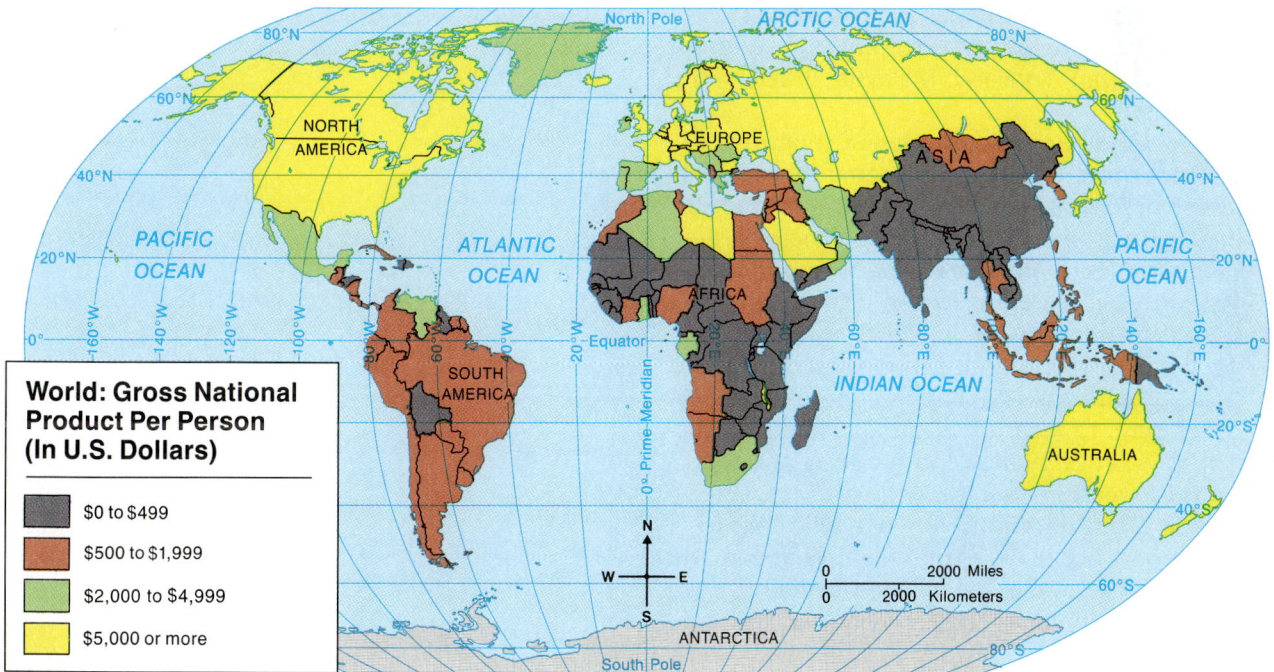

World: Gross National Product Per Person (In U.S. Dollars)

- $0 to $499
- $500 to $1,999
- $2,000 to $4,999
- $5,000 or more

Map Study

Use the Atlas map on pages 620–621 to locate three countries that export oil: Venezuela, Saudi Arabia, and Libya. How do these countries differ from the countries surrounding them?

gross national product per person—is distributed around the world.

Developed countries are usually the most modern and urbanized in the world. Their infrastructures—power and telephone lines, roads, and transport systems—are in place and working smoothly. The developed nations include the United States, Canada, most of Europe, Israel, Australia, New Zealand, Japan, Singapore, and the Soviet Union. These countries are usually the ones that have low birth rates, low death rates, and high rates of literacy—the number of people who can read and write. Developed countries have a wide variety of industries, but most workers are employed in services. The average per capita income usually exceeds $5,000 a year.

Developing countries have many of these same characteristics, but a large part of their society is still rural. Average incomes are climbing but are still low in comparison to developed countries. Examples of developing countries are Korea, Taiwan, Thailand, Malaysia, Brazil, and Argentina.

Traditional, or underdeveloped countries, by contrast, have a per capita income that may be less than $500 a year. Generally they have high birth rates and low literacy rates. Their infrastructures are inadequate for building up industry. Most people are involved in primary activities, primarily farming. In comparison, about 3 percent of Americans are farmers.

Along with the GNP and PCI, there are many other ways to measure wealth. In some traditional societies, money and property are not signs of wealth or success. The most respected person is not necessarily the one who lives in the largest house. In a traditional village in West Africa, for example, the village storyteller, the person who holds children spellbound with tales of the community's history, has the respect of everyone. The storyteller is the one who is regarded as truly wealthy, the one who is rich in culture and tradition.

Section 4 Review

Locating Key Places
Locate the following places on the map on page 620: United States, Soviet Union

Identifying Key Terms
Define the following terms: resource, market economy, command economy, GNP, PCI

Reviewing Main Ideas
1. What are the three main economic systems by which cultures meet their needs and wants?
2. What are the three major types of industry?
3. What are the three types of nation created by the unequal distribution of resources?

Thinking Critically: Identify Assumptions
The terms "developed", and "developing" or "underdeveloped," are sometimes used to describe countries with different levels of material or economic wealth. What assumptions do you think users of these terms hold about wealth?

Population Density Maps

There are two popular ways to show population data on a base map, by distribution and by density. In Chapter 4, a world population distribution map used dots to show how many people lived in a given area. Turn to page 83 to review this map.

The map on this page uses the second method and is called a population density map. Instead of showing how many people live in a given area, the density map shows how closely the people live together. The key tells you how many people live in each average square mile or kilometer. On this particular map, residential patterns are divided into four categories: "Under 2 (people per square mile)," "2 to 25," "25 to 125," and "Over 125." In general, the first three categories show rural or un-populated areas. The fourth shows both productive agricultural regions and urban areas. To more clearly indicate cities, the map would need to show areas with more than 250 or 500 people per square mile.

Review

Name the color which represents each of these areas on the map.
1. The areas of the world where it is too cold, hot, or dry to support much economic activity.
2. Areas of ranching, herding, gathering, lumbering, or mining that often border wilderness areas. These areas usually support less than 25 people per square mile.
3. Areas of between 25 and 125 people per square mile that are usually agricultural regions with only a few urban centers.

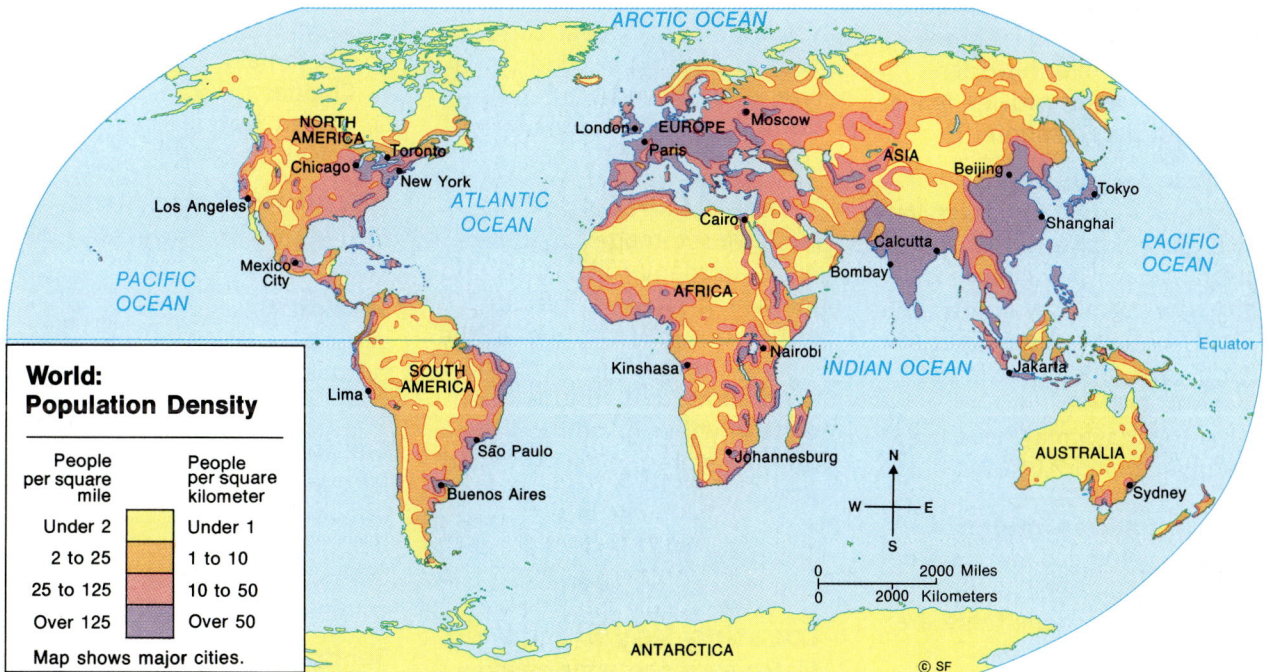

World: Population Density

People per square mile	People per square kilometer
Under 2	Under 1
2 to 25	1 to 10
25 to 125	10 to 50
Over 125	Over 50

Map shows major cities.

Review

Section Summaries

1. Cultural Beginnings and Diffusion Culture is the part of the environment made or adapted by people. Culture originates in culture hearths. Through cultural diffusion, ideas and innovations spread around the world. The cultural landscape, seen clearly in clothing and architecture, shows how a culture and environment interact.

2. Language, Religion, and Politics Language, religion, and political systems all had origins in our past. Modern languages often share common origins and have similar words. Many major world religions also share similar histories. Political systems provide leadership and organization.

3. Case Study: Mayan Designs Reveal the Past Woven garments worn by present-day Mayas have brought forth new insight into ancient Maya culture. Special garments, called huipils, use symbols and designs that reveal how the Maya may have lived and worshiped 2,000 years ago.

4. Economic Solutions. Cultures develop economic systems to meet their needs and wants. Within each system, there are three types of industry—primary, secondary, and tertiary. The resources used by these industries—natural, human, and capital—are distributed unevenly around the earth, creating inequalities.

Using Geography Skills
Reviewing the Map Lesson
Use the map on the next page to answer these questions.
1. Which color shows the highest population density?
2. What is the range of density for Northern Ireland?
3. Why is the population density low in northern Scotland?

Using Social Studies Skills
1. Analyze Information. Make a list of 20 things around you that identify your culture, such as clothing or music. Analyze whether each item represents material or nonmaterial culture.

2. Detect Stereotypes. People have set images or stereotypes for many cultures around the world. Think of five cultures. For each, write down the images that first come to your mind about that culture. Then write whether or not you think that the stereotype is valid and why.

Testing for Understanding
Locating Key Places
Match each description below with the name of the place.
1. the country where Islam began
2. a Mexican state
3. a modern communist country
4. the north and east boundary of Mesopotamia
5. a river in China
6. a nation with a market economy
7. a country of Maya culture
8. the country where Judaism and Christianity began
9. the south and west boundary of Mesopotamia
10. the country where Hinduism and Buddhism developed.
a. Tigris River
b. Euphrates River
c. Huang River
d. India
e. Israel
f. Saudi Arabia
g. Guatemala
h. Chiapas
i. United States
j. Soviet Union

Recalling Key Terms
Define these terms in your own words.

Section 1
culture
culture hearth
cultural diffusion

Section 2
language family
lingua franca
democracy
authoritarian system
communism

Section 3
motif
huipil
vestment

Section 4
resource
market economy
command economy
GNP
PCI

Reviewing Main Ideas
Section 1
1. How is culture related to the environment?
2. How is culture spread from one place to another?
3. How do clothing and architecture reflect cultural landscape?

Section 2
1. In what way did languages spread?
2. What are some of the beliefs of the five major world religions?
3. What do political systems reflect about a culture?

Section 3
1. How have anthropologists found clues to Maya culture?
2. How is the ceremonial huipil used by the Maya?
3. Which Maya gods usually appear on the Maya clothing?

Section 4
1. Name the three major economic systems.
2. Name three types of industry.
3. What are three defined types of country?

Thinking Critically
1. Make Hypotheses. Many foods, such as spaghetti, have come from other cultures. Make a list of popular foreign foods. How do you think these foods got here?

2. Identify Assumptions. Does any one kind of building in your community stand out as being more impressive than the others? What assumptions can you make about what your city feels is important or valuable?

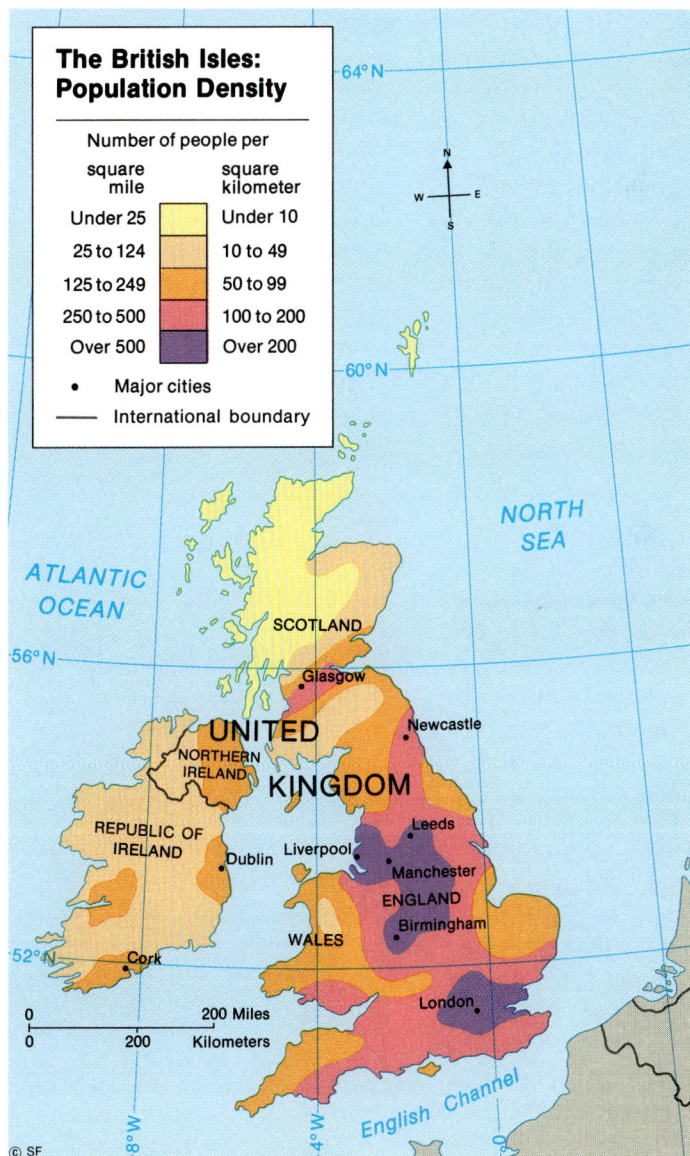

The British Isles: Population Density

Number of people per

square mile	square kilometer
Under 25	Under 10
25 to 124	10 to 49
125 to 249	50 to 99
250 to 500	100 to 200
Over 500	Over 200

• Major cities
— International boundary

Review

Summarizing the Unit

Chapter 4   Patterns of Population Geography and history are both important in determining where people live. Physical features—natural resources or mild climates—and cultural features—such as tradition—both play a role. In the past 300 years, the world's population has increased dramatically to more than 5 billion. The populations of individual countries or cities can be counted in a census, and growth rates can be calculated by considering births, deaths, and migrations. These rates change according to a society's industrial growth, tradition, and government policy.

Chapter 5   Patterns of Culture Culture is the part of the environment—material or nonmaterial—that is made or adapted by people. A society's culture is expressed through its clothing, architecture, language, religion, politics, and economics. The cultural landscape reveals how culture interacts with the physical environment. Cultural traits or innovations can spread from one place to another through cultural diffusion. Several languages and religions have spread all around the world by way of conquest, travelers and modern communications.

Using Writing Skills

In Unit 1 you learned that the writing process involves four steps: prewriting, writing, revising, and presenting. You began the writing experience with a freewriting activity. Other elements of prewriting are choosing a topic and developing ideas.

Just how though do you go about getting and fleshing out ideas? One tool that many writers use is the photograph. Pictures often offer a rich visual image from which to draw both ideas and information. In many cases photographs will lead you to further research a particular culture by stimulating your interest.

Look at the photograph below for example. What thoughts does the photograph stir? What can you learn about the culture of this society in India?

Activity. Use the photograph on this page—or select another one in this unit—to develop ideas for a writing experience. The freewriting techniques you learned about may help you. Make a list of several ideas or themes from which you could later write an essay or story.

Test

Key Terms (20 points)

Fill in each blank with the correct term listed below.

1. Clothing and architecture are expressions of _____.

2. Most Americans believe in the freedom and participation afforded by _____.

3. To find out where people live, you study a _____ map.

4. _____ is often important in determining a nation's growth rate.

5. Examples of a natural _____ are minerals, water, and soil.

a. population distribution
b. migration
c. culture
d. democracy
e. resource

Main Ideas (30 points)

Select the best answer.

1. Near what resource do most of the world's people live?
a. mountains
b. fresh water
c. minerals
d. coal

2. As societies become more industrialized, what usually happens to birth rates?
a. they stabilize
b. they increase rapidly
c. they increase slowly
d. they decline

3. Which of the following represents nonmaterial culture?
a. clothing
b. buildings
c. food
d. language

4. Which world religion is the most widespread?
a. Christianity
b. Hinduism
c. Judaism
d. Buddhism

5. How have anthropologists recently learned about ancient Maya symbolism?
a. from archaeological digs
b. from modern ceremonial garments
c. by studying written records
d. from modern Maya stories

6. Which of the following is an economic system based on individual ownership of the factors of production?
a. democracy
b. command economy
c. market economy
d. socialism

Thinking Critically (20 points)

1. Predict Effects. What effects do you think that our modern systems of communication —satellites, computers, movies —will have on the process of cultural diffusion? Do you foresee the various parts of the world becoming more similar or more different?

2. Analyze Comparisons. In this unit different types of political and economic systems were discussed and compared. How might these comparisons be affected by individual or societal bias? Discuss whether or not it is possible to accurately compare systems that are used in societies that differ in historical and physical attributes.

Place Location (30 points)

Match the places below with the letters printed on the map.
1. Japan
2. China
3. India
4. Israel
5. the United States
6. the Soviet Union

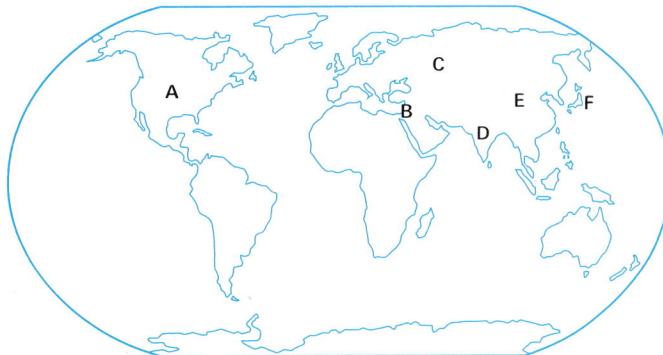

The United States and Canada

In this unit you will study two important democracies.

A Physical and Cultural Overview

In this chapter you will read about the two largest countries in North America.

Sections

Land Regions of the United States and Canada

Preview

Key Places
Where are these places located?
1 Piedmont
2 Great Basin
See the globe below.

Key Terms
What do these terms mean?
continental shelf
fall line

Main Ideas
As you read, look for answers to these questions.
- What forces shaped the landforms of the United States and Canada?
- What are the major plains regions of the United States and Canada?
- What landforms border the plains regions of the United States and Canada?

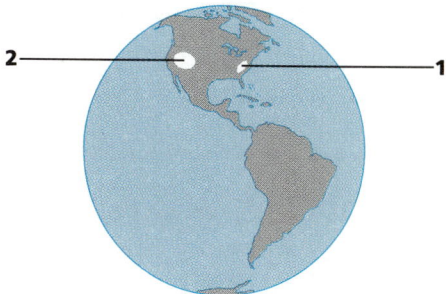

Rivers cut a path on flat lands.
The mountains stand up.
The salt oceans press in
And push on the coast lines.
The sun, the wind, bring rain
And I know what the rainbow writes across the east or west in a half-circle:
A love-letter pledge to come again.

Carl Sandburg, *Cornhuskers*

Internal and external forces shaped the United States and Canada.
Carl Sandburg was glorifying the Rocky Mountains and the Appalachians, the oceans that bracket the United States and Canada, and the plains that sweep along the Atlantic Ocean and between the mountain chains. You read in Chapter 2 of the powerful internal and external forces that shaped and erased the first features of the continents. These same forces created the United States and Canada that we know today.

Laying the foundation. Like every continent, North America is built on a basement of hard granite formed about 3.8 billion years ago during the Precambrian era. Today this ancient granite is exposed in several areas of the United States and Canada. The largest of these areas is the Canadian Shield, a region of Canada and the United States made up mainly of plains.

Folding, faulting, and uplifting. About 225 million years ago, the plates beneath North America, Africa, and Europe collided. This movement uplifted and folded the earth's crust to form the Appalachian Mountains and plateaus. In addition to the highlands formed by folding,

Facing page: **These machines dominate an Idaho field of wheat, which is a principal crop of the United States and Canada.**
Page 118: **The Rocky Mountains, shown here in Banff National Park, join these two countries.**

121

ASIA

ARCTIC OCEAN

BEAUFORT SEA

GREENLAND (DENMARK)

BERING SEA

Barrow
ALASKA (U.S.)
Fairbanks

Baffin Bay

Anchorage
Gulf of Alaska
Dawson

Arctic Circle

Juneau

CANADA

Hudson Bay

LABRADOR SEA

Churchill

Goose Bay

Edmonton
Saskatoon
Calgary

Victoria
Puget Sound
Vancouver
Seattle
Columbia River
Portland

Regina
Winnipeg

St. John's

SAINT PIERRE AND MIQUELON (FR.)

Thunder bay

GREAT LAKES

Quebec
Montreal
Ottawa ⊛
Laval

St. John

Halifax

Minneapolis
St. Paul

Milwaukee
Chicago

Mississauga
Hamilton
London
Detroit
Toledo

North York
Toronto
Buffalo
Cleveland
Pittsburgh
Columbus
Cincinnati

Boston

Newark
New York City
Philadelphia
Baltimore
Washington, D.C. ⊛

San Francisco
Oakland
San Jose

Salt Lake City

Denver

Omaha

UNITED STATES

Missouri R.

Kansas City
St. Louis
Indianapolis

Ohio R.

Los Angeles
Long Beach
San Diego

Colorado

Albuquerque

Phoenix
Tucson

Tulsa

Nashville
Memphis

Norfolk
Greensboro
Raleigh
Charlotte

Atlanta

PACIFIC OCEAN

30° North Latitude

El Paso

Fort Worth
Dallas

Mississippi R.

ATLANTIC OCEAN

Bermuda (U.K.)

120° West Longitude

Austin
San Antonio

Houston

Rio Grande

New Orleans

Jacksonville

Gulf of California

Gulf of Mexico

MEXICO

Miami

BAHAMAS

Tropic of Cancer

CUBA

DOMINICAN REPUBLIC

PUERTO RICO (U.S.)

ANTIGUA-BARBUDA

JAMAICA

HAITI

SAINT CHRISTOPHER AND NEVIS

BELIZE

GUATEMALA

HONDURAS

WEST INDIES

CARIBBEAN SEA

DOMINICA
SAINT LUCIA

SAINT VINCENT AND THE GRENADINES

BARBADOS

GRENADA

EL SALVADOR

NICARAGUA

CENTRAL AMERICA

COSTA RICA

PANAMA

TRINIDAD AND TOBAGO

SOUTH AMERICA

United States and Canada
Political

International boundaries
⊛ National capitals
• Other cities

PACIFIC OCEAN

Honolulu

HAWAII (U.S.)

20°N

N
W   E
S

0   250   500 Miles
0   250   500 Kilometers

0   100 Miles
0   100 Kilometers

some Appalachian ranges, such as the Blue Ridge, were formed by faulting. Blocks of the earth's crust pushed themselves over other parts of the crust. The resulting breaks in the earth's crust are called thrust faults.

Between 80 million and 10 million years ago, volcanic activity in western North America gave rise to the Rocky Mountain ranges. A volcanic core in the earth pushed up the material in a weak section of the crust, forming mountains. Folding and faulting are believed to have occurred in the process.

In many cases, pressure inside the earth's mantle produced mountains without faulting. The granite basement pushed up and arched the rock on the surface to create dome mountains. The Black Hills of South Dakota and Wyoming are examples of dome mountains.

Rushing water and moving ice. Water and ancient sheets of ice sculpted and scoured the United States and Canada. Water shaped the mountains and valleys of the Appalachians. Thrust faults sandwiched ancient granite between newer, softer layers of sandstone and limestone. Over time, mountain streams eroded the top layers, and the ancient granite once located below the surface of the mountains became the mountaintops. In addition, the streams cut out valleys and deposited sediment, which helped make up the valley soil.

In the course of the last 3 million years, a continental ice sheet advanced and receded over North America several times. In the mountains, the rough underside of the glaciers carved out jagged peaks. In the Central Lowlands, the glaciers smoothed surfaces instead. You read in Chapter 2 how glaciers scoured away at the ancient rocks of the Canadian Shield and stripped it of soil. Meltwater from the glaciers deposited this rich soil on plains to the south of the shield. Later, winds redistributed some of this fine soil—called loess [lō'is]. Meltwater also created thousands of lakes, most notably the Great Lakes.

By the time the last glacier receded, North America was divided into the seven main landform regions we see today. Most landforms in each region share the same geological origins.

There are three major plains regions.

Flat or gently rolling lands that are low in elevation make up three major regions: the Canadian Shield, the Atlantic Coastal Plain, and the Interior Plains. As you read about these regions, locate them on the map on page 125.

The Canadian Shield. The Canadian Shield covers one-half the total area of Canada and part of the United States. The southeastern edge of the shield tilts upward to form a region of hills. This mineral-rich region reaches into eastern Canada, Minnesota, Wisconsin, Michigan, and the northeastern states.

The Atlantic Coastal Plain. Find the Atlantic Coastal Plain on the map on page 125. This region extends in a curving arc along the eastern and southern coasts of North America. Along the Gulf of Mexico, this plain is often called the Gulf Coast. The plain is mainly flat with some rolling hills and is made up of clay, sand, and silt deposited by rivers. The Atlantic Coastal Plain extends beyond the land boundaries shown on the map and gently slopes into the sea for several miles. The underwater part of the plain is known as the **continental shelf**. The shallow places formed by the shelf, called banks, are teeming with fish.

Much of this coastal region is submerging below the surface of the ocean. As a result, flooding and erosion have occurred. Other parts of

Map Study

What is the capital of Canada? The United States? Name five cities in each.

This lush swamp, in Palmdale, Florida, supports rich wildlife.

the region, however, such as the islands off Cape Hatteras, North Carolina, are emerging slowly above the water. Between the islands and the mainland are bays and lagoons. From the mainland, rivers wash sediment that is gradually filling in the quiet waters. Slowly these areas will become swamps similar to the Great Dismal Swamp of Virginia and North Carolina and the Okefenokee Swamp of Georgia and Florida.

The Interior Plains. The plains that emerged from under an ancient inland sea form the base of the Interior Plains. The largest landform region in North America, the Interior Plains has two parts: the Central Plains and the Great Plains. Although generally flat, the Great Plains slant gradually upward as you move west. This slant was caused as rivers flowing down from the Rocky Mountains deposited sediment there for millions of years. The closer to the Rockies, the thicker the deposits and the higher the land.

Plateaus, hills, and mountain systems border the plains regions.

Two giant groups of mountain ranges—the Appalachian Mountains and the Rocky Mountains —set the eastern and western boundaries of the Interior Plains. Equally important are two other landform regions formed mainly of mountains, hills, and plateaus: the Intermontane Plateaus and the Pacific Mountain Region.

The Appalachian Mountains. Long, smooth-topped mountains stretching from eastern Canada into central Alabama form the spine of the Appalachian Mountains. Between the Appalachian Mountains and the Atlantic Coastal Plain lies an area of foothills called the Piedmont. The Piedmont rises sharply above the plain because its hard Precambrian rock has been able to withstand erosion. Rivers flowing seaward rush from the Piedmont onto the softer plain, carving deep valleys as they go. Many waterfalls and rapids form at the fall line, just east of the Appalachians. A **fall line** marks the end of layers of hard rock of a plateau and the beginning of a softer rock layer of a plain.

Beyond the Piedmont, long, narrow valleys are squeezed between the ridges of the Appalachian Mountains. West of the Blue Ridge lies the Great Valley, which stretches almost the entire length of the Appalachian system. Farther west are higher mountains and the plateaus.

The Appalachian Mountains are rich in resources. Pressure from the great weight of overlying layers of sedimentary rock hardened layers of decaying trees and ferns into coal. Today mining companies scoop the coal from the large seams exposed on the sides of mountains.

Map Study

What are three major mountain ranges and three major rivers in this realm?

United States and Canada
Physical

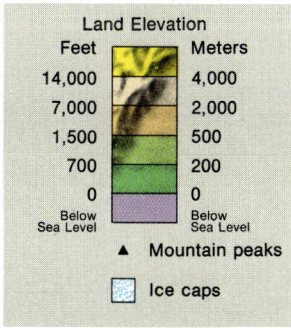

Land Elevation

Feet		Meters
14,000		4,000
7,000		2,000
1,500		500
700		200
0		0
Below Sea Level		Below Sea Level

▲ Mountain peaks

Ice caps

White lines represent international boundaries.

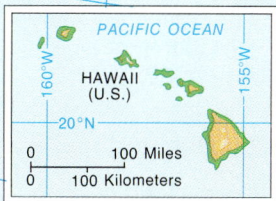

0   250   500 Miles
0   250   500 Kilometers

ASIA

ARCTIC OCEAN

Bering Strait
Pt. Barrow
BEAUFORT SEA
Queen Elizabeth Is.
Greenland
Iceland
Arctic Circle

BROOKS RANGE
Yukon
Victoria I.
Baffin Bay
Baffin I.
Davis Strait

BERING SEA
ALASKA PENINSULA
ALASKA RANGE
Mt. McKinley
Kodiak I.
Gulf of Alaska
Great Bear Lake

COAST MOUNTAINS
Alexander Arch.
Queen Charlotte Is.
Vancouver I.
Puget Sound

Great Slave Lake
Lake Athabasca
Peace
Reindeer Lake
Saskatchewan R.

Hudson Bay
CANADIAN SHIELD
UNGAVA PENINSULA
LABRADOR PENINSULA
LABRADOR
LABRADOR SEA

Newfoundland
Gulf of St. Lawrence

Mt. Rainier
COLUMBIA PLATEAU
Snake R.
Lake Winnipeg
Lake of the Woods

CASCADE
COAST RANGES
SIERRA NEVADA
Mt. Whitney
Pt. Conception
ROCKY MOUNTAINS
GREAT BASIN
Great Salt Lake
DEATH VALLEY
MOJAVE DESERT
GRAND CANYON
COLORADO PLATEAU
Colorado R.

GREAT PLAINS
BLACK HILLS
Platte
Missouri R.

INTERIOR PLAINS
CENTRAL PLAINS
Lake Superior
Lake Michigan
Lake Huron
Lake Erie
Lake Ontario

OZARK PLATEAU
Arkansas R.
Ohio
Red R.
Mississippi R.

APPALACHIAN MTS.
PIEDMONT
COASTAL PLAIN
Cape Cod
Long I.
Chesapeake Bay
Cape Hatteras

PACIFIC OCEAN

ATLANTIC OCEAN
Bermuda Is.

COASTAL PLAIN
Cape Canaveral
FLORIDA PENINSULA
Lake Okeechobee
Gulf of Mexico
Bahama Is.
Tropic of Cancer

Rio Grande
YUCATÁN PENINSULA
ISTHMUS OF TEHUANTEPEC

West Indies
Cuba
Greater Antilles
Jamaica
Hispaniola
Puerto Rico
Leeward Is.
Lesser Antilles
Windward Is.

CARIBBEAN SEA

CENTRAL AMERICA
Nicaragua
ISTHMUS OF PANAMA

SOUTH AMERICA

PACIFIC OCEAN
HAWAII (U.S.)
0   100 Miles
0   100 Kilometers

© SF **125**

The Rocky Mountains. A series of high, rugged ranges that stretch from Alaska into New Mexico make up the Rocky Mountains. Geologists think that small earth movements continue to push up some of these mountains as much as one foot every 500 years. Almost impenetrable in most places, the mountains open up in Wyoming at South Pass. This pass is the easiest place to cross the Rockies.

The crest of the Rockies forms the Continental Divide, an irregular line from north to south which separates the rivers that flow westward from those that flow east. Many great North American rivers begin in the Rockies. The Colorado, the Snake, the Columbia, the Platte, and the Missouri are just a few.

The Rocky Mountains contain the largest deposits of gold, silver, and other precious metal ores in the United States. These ores lie close to the surface in mineral-rich granite, allowing for easy mining. In fact, early miners sifted gold from the sediment washed by streams down the mountainsides.

The Intermontane Plateaus. *Intermontane* means "between the mountains." This region is located between the Rocky Mountains and the Sierra Nevada. It includes the Columbia Plateau and the Colorado Plateau. Find the Intermontane Plateaus on the map on page 125.

The sedimentary rocks of the Intermontane Plateaus were formed at the same time as those in the Interior Plains, but the Intermontane Plateaus were raised higher. Later, rivers divided the plateaus with spectacular canyons, including the world's most spectacular—the Grand Canyon.

In the center of the region lies the Great Basin, which is shaped like a bowl. Here rivers drain into marshes or salt lakes, like the Great Salt Lake, because no outlet is available to the ocean. Death Valley, the lowest point in North America, lies within the Great Basin.

The Pacific Mountain Region. To the west of the Intermontane Plateaus lie the high mountains, narrow valleys, and low coastal ranges that make up the Pacific Mountain Region, the region that includes the Coast Mountains of Canada and the Cascades and Sierra Nevada of the United States.

These ranges and valleys are the result of faulting and folding rock. The rock along the fault is easily affected by erosion. In addition, the cliffs along the Pacific Coast are steadily eroded by the ocean. Long ago, the ocean flooded such areas as San Francisco Bay and Puget Sound, which were once river valleys. At the same time, rivers in the region deposit soil in valleys and deltas. As in every other region, some forces build up while others wear down.

Section 1 Review

Locating Key Places
Locate the following places on the map on page 125: Piedmont, Great Basin

Identifying Key Terms
Define the following terms: continental shelf, fall line

Reviewing Main Ideas
1. How were the landscapes of the United States and Canada created?
2. Name the three main plains regions of the United States and Canada.
3. What main landform regions border the main plains regions of the United States and Canada?

Thinking Critically: Make Hypotheses
You read in this section about some of the physical characteristics of the United States and Canada. Based on these characteristics, where would you predict the best farming to be? Explain your answers. What other factors influence agriculture?

Climate, Soils, and Vegetation

Preview

Key Places
Where are these places located?
1 Colorado Plateau
2 Columbia Plateau
  See the globe below.

Key Terms
What do these terms mean?
tornado
hurricane
timberline

Main Ideas
As you read, look for the answers to these questions.
- What are the major types of climates in the United States and Canada?
- What are the two main groups of soils in this geographic realm?
- What are the main types of vegetation in the United States and Canada?

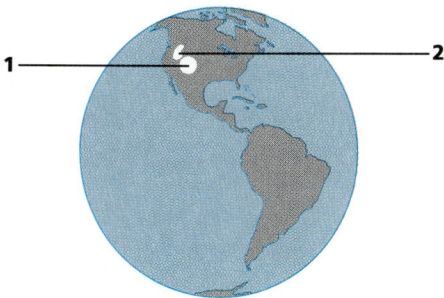

White, floating clouds,
clouds like the plains,
come and water the earth.
Sun, embrace the earth
to make her fruitful.
Moon,
lion of the north,
bear of the west,
badger of the south,
wolf of the east,
shrew of the earth,
speak to the cloud people for us,
so that they may water the earth.

Aline Amon Goodrich, "Rain Song"

The United States and Canada have three main types of climates.
This Zia song accompanied a complex ritual calling for rain. These Indians of New Mexico saw the moving clouds as part of an ongoing process linked with life itself. Cloud patterns mark the masses of air surrounding the earth. The air profoundly affects our climate, soil, and vegetation and supports all forms of life.

The three main types of climates in the United States and Canada are continental, mild, and dry. They are influenced by six major air masses shown on the map on page 128: (1) the Polar Canadian air mass from Canada's cold interior; (2) the Tropical Gulf air mass from the Gulf of Mexico; (3) the Tropical Atlantic air mass from the Caribbean Sea; (4) the Polar Pacific air mass from the ocean off the Aleutian Islands; (5) the Tropical Pacific air mass from the waters near the Hawaiian Islands; and (6) the Tropical Continental air mass from the southwestern deserts of North America.

The polar air masses move southward. The tropical air masses move northward. The air masses can further be divided into continental and maritime types, reflecting their origin over land or water.

Continental climates. Northern Canada and Alaska have subarctic and polar climates with cold, dry winters that may last as long as 10 months. The Central Plains have no large mountain ranges to block the Polar Canadian air mass, so this cool air sweeps across the lowlands toward the Gulf and Atlantic coasts. Sometimes the cool air reaches as far south as Florida, causing unusually low temperatures and frosts.

The Tropical Gulf air mass also meets no resistance as it spreads north. As a result, the cool and warm air masses often collide over the plains, whipping up storms and tornadoes. A **tornado** is a destructive whirlwind that forms over land.

More importantly, collision of the Gulf and Polar air masses brings snowy winters and rainy summers in southeastern Canada and in the northern United States. In these latitudes the climate is classified as humid continental, cool summer. Farther south, a humid continental, warm summer climate takes over. In both climate areas, the average difference in temperature between the warmest and coldest months is 50°F or more.

Mild climates. Maritime air masses help keep most coastal climates in the United States and Canada mild. Because water temperature changes more slowly than land temperature, winds blowing from over the ocean cool coastal areas in summer and warm them in winter. As a

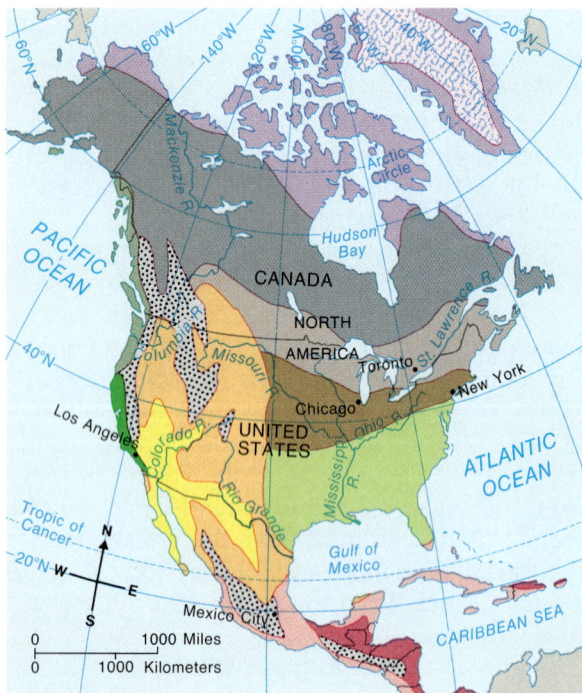

United States and Canada: Climate Regions

Tropical climates
- Tropical rainforest
- Savanna

Dry climates
- Steppe
- Desert

Mild climates
- Marine west coast
- Humid subtropical
- Mediterranean

Continental climates
- Humid continental, warm summer
- Humid continental, cool summer
- Subarctic

Polar climates
- Tundra
- Icecap

High altitudes
- Highlands

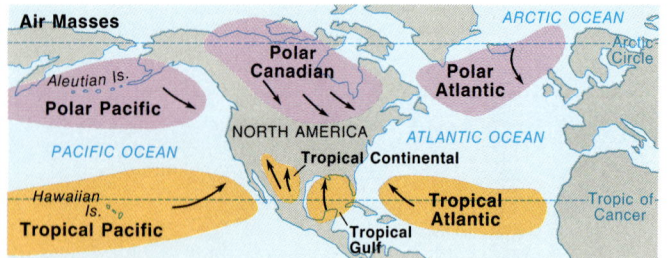

Map Study

These maps show the different climate regions and air masses found in the United States and Canada. What climate prevails in the Southeast? Which air masses might affect this area?

This California surfer enjoys the warm Mediterranean climate.

result, the average difference in temperature between the warmest and coldest months in areas with mild climates is 40°F or less.

The Tropical Gulf and the Tropical Atlantic air masses create a humid subtropical—or warm and wet—climate in the southeastern United States. Although moist south winds sometimes travel as far north as southern Canada, the northern limit of the warm humid subtropical climate area is about 35° N Latitude.

Weather from the Caribbean Sea and the Gulf of Mexico, however, is not always balmy. Occasionally during the summer, **hurricanes**—winds that spin at speeds of 70 miles or more an hour—move inland. These storms often uproot trees and damage roads and houses in their path.

A narrow, mountainous strip of the United States and Canada that extends from the southern tip of Alaska to northern California has a marine west coast climate. This climate is best described as mild and rainy. The Polar Pacific air

mass is loaded with moisture. Prevailing westerly winds carry the moisture inland, dropping it as rain or snow on the west-facing slopes of the coastal ranges.

Farther south, the California coast has a warm, dry Mediterranean climate. Winters are mild, and summers are hot. In winter the westerlies prevail, bringing moisture. The Tropical Pacific air mass that prevails in summer brings little rain, for the winds are cooled off-shore by a south-flowing cold current. Thus, they hold little moisture.

Dry climates. The interior basins of the western United States have a dry desert or semi-arid steppe climate. The Tropical Continental air mass that sweeps northward from Mexico brings dry summers and dry winters to the Great Basin and the Colorado Plateau. The Columbia Plateau is dry because it lies in the rain shadow of the coastal ranges. Winds evaporate moisture instead of carrying it. The southern part of this inland area is hot or warm the year round. The northern area has cold winters.

The Great Plains also have a steppe climate. During eight months out of the year, the winds from the west lose most of their moisture before they reach the Great Plains. In the summer, however, the area alternates between dryness from the Tropical Continental air mass and moisture from Gulf air masses.

The major soils are humid and arid or semiarid.

As you read in Chapter 3, climate and plants affect soil, just as soil and climate influence plants. Pedologists, or soil scientists, have analyzed many different soil types in the United States and Canada. Each soil type is affected by the kinds of rock it came from and the conditions under which it was formed. Soil is also affected by plants and animals. However, climate is the basis for dividing soils into two main groups: humid and arid or semiarid.

Humid soils. Areas with ample rainfall are said to have humid soils. Such soils tend to be fertile because they usually contain decaying plant matter that holds water and nutrients.

Not all humid soils are rich, however. Soils that developed under northern needleleaf forests tend to be less fertile because they contain acid leached from the blanket of pine needles that covers the forest floor. Such soils from Alaska to Newfoundland support coniferous forests but not much agriculture. Acidic soils are also found in conifer-covered areas of the southeastern United States. Throughout the humid subtropical climate area, the plentiful rain continually leaches minerals from the soil. Because of the long growing season, however, farmers who add fertilizers to such soils can still produce good crops—except in the acidic-soil, "piney-woods" areas.

Arid to semiarid soils. Grasslands, deserts, and tundras have arid to semiarid soils. The most fertile of all the important soil groups lies in areas with moderate to light rainfall in the western part of the Interior Plains and the Great Plains. Much of this rich soil did not originate in the Interior Plains but was carried there by glaciers and winds. Then grasses enriched this soil as they decayed. There is little leaching of minerals where rainfall is light or moderate. In Iowa and other farm states, this fertile soil is sometimes 80 feet deep.

Deserts tend to have young, mostly sandy soils. Although low in organic matter, these soils can be made fertile if irrigated and fertilized.

Forests, grasses, and desert plants are three types of vegetation.

Towering oaks, swaying prairie grass, and blooming desert paintbrush each require a certain combination of soil and climate. These and most other kinds of vegetation in the United States and Canada can be classified as forests, grasses, or desert plants. Compare the maps on pages 128 and 130 to help you understand the relationships between natural vegetation and climate. Find where you live on each map.

Forests. Evergreens such as fir, pine, and spruce need moisture but few nutrients. These

United States and Canada: Natural Vegetation Regions

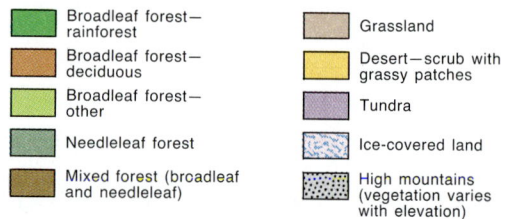

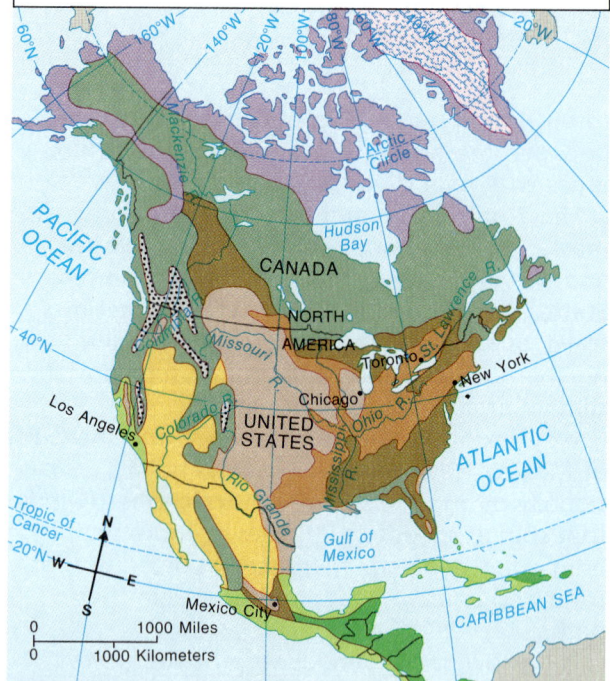

- Broadleaf forest—rainforest
- Broadleaf forest—deciduous
- Broadleaf forest—other
- Needleleaf forest
- Mixed forest (broadleaf and needleleaf)
- Grassland
- Desert—scrub with grassy patches
- Tundra
- Ice-covered land
- High mountains (vegetation varies with elevation)

Map Study

What types of natural vegetation dominate the middle of this realm?

trees thrive in thin soils like that on the Canadian Shield and in the leached-out soils in the southeastern part of the Atlantic Coastal Plain.

Evergreen forests also cover the slopes in many mountain regions. However, high in the mountains, the trees become fewer and fewer and finally disappear. The boundary above which trees cannot grow is the **timberline**. Temperatures above this point are too low for trees to grow.

Forests of deciduous trees such as oaks and maples once covered the northern Atlantic Coastal Plain and the eastern part of the Central Plains. These kinds of trees need plenty of rain and alkaline soil, which is rich in such minerals as calcium. Calcium-rich limestone is an ingredient in the soil of both of these regions. Furthermore, the well-developed humus of the Central Plains holds water like a sponge, slowing leaching even where rainfall is plentiful.

Grasses. The prairie grasses of the Central Plains naturally grow to more than eight feet in height. This height is supported by an extensive system of roots. A piece of prairie sod 18 inches square may contain as many as 13 miles of closely packed roots. These roots hold the soil firmly in place. They also return life-giving nitrogen to the soil.

Clumps of deciduous trees also grow along water courses on the prairie. In fact, forests are the type of vegetation one would expect in the area, based on its climate and soil. However, glaciers destroyed the original forests. After the glaciers melted, grasses grew up to prepare the way for the trees.

Fires set by lightning and by early hunters burned the prairies and destroyed the seedling trees. The grasses returned, but the trees often did not.

Now corn and soybeans have replaced most of the grasses. Prairie preserves, like the Konza of central Kansas, are all that remain of what once was described as a "sea of grass."

The Great Plains are drier than the Central Plains, so the natural vegetation there is mainly scattered clumps of short grasses. In the flat, fertile areas to the east, the predominant vegetation today is wheat. Like steppe grass, wheat requires less water than corn or prairie grasses.

Mosses, lichens, and short grasses cover the tundra. Their brief growing seasons and tenacious roots are ideal adaptations to the permafrost. These same plants also grow above the timberline in mountain regions.

Desert plants. The most adaptive plants in North America grow in the deserts and on the dry plateaus. Cactuses store water in their thick stems. Some desert trees send their roots deep down to tap underground rivers. Wildflower seeds in the desert lie underground for most of the year. After spring rains dissolve their hard protective coats, the seeds quickly sprout, and blossoms cover the ground.

Section 2 Review

Locating Key Places
Locate the following places on the map on page 125: Colorado Plateau, Columbia Plateau

Identifying Key Terms
Define the following terms: tornado, hurricane, timberline

Reviewing Main Ideas
1. What are the primary types of climates in the United States and Canada?
2. Describe the different groups of soils in the United States and Canada.
3. Describe the main types of vegetation in the United States and Canada.

Thinking Critically: Predict Effects
As you read, the Great Plains in the United States are basically flat, treeless, and semiarid. What effects did these geographic characteristics probably have on the first pioneers who settled here?

Settling the United States and Canada

Preview

Key Places

Where are these places located?

1 Bering Strait
2 Jamestown, Virginia
  See the globe below.

Key Terms

What do the following terms mean?
shifting cultivation
conquistadors

Main Ideas

As you read, look for answers to these questions.

- How did the first Americans survive?
- Why did the Spanish, the French, and the English come to what is now the United States and Canada?
- How did people from Africa affect the economy and culture of the United States and Canada?

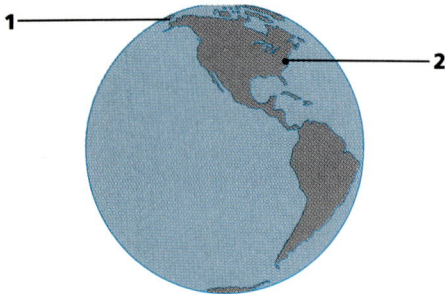

It is hard now to imagine, but it is a matter of record that a mid-eighteenth-century mariner approaching the American strand could detect the fragrance of the pine trees about 60 leagues, or 180 nautical miles, from land. . . . On landing . . . he could see the trees themselves, arrayed in such formidable ranks that they were attacked and felled in careless numbers by settlers eager to get at the untilled soil beneath; he could see beaver pelts and deerskins brought to market, tokens of a teeming animal life in the interior; he might hear about the fish, spawning in such numbers and growing to such size . . . that the ease of catching them had become a legend and a joke.

Richard Hofstadter, *America at 1750*

The first Americans used the resources around them.

In 1750 the natural resources of the land that is now the United States and Canada seemed so abundant as to almost hinder settlement. Travelers and writers expressed surprise, more than 200 years after Columbus's discovery, at the newness and wealth of the land around them.

Although new to the Europeans who came there after 1492, the North American continent had been home for centuries to hundreds of Indian groups. The Indians planted, fished, and hunted to keep their families alive.

People disagree as to who the first Americans were and exactly when they came here. However, some experts believe that the first people of North America crossed from northeastern Asia over a land bridge about 27,000 years ago.

During the last Ice Age, much of the earth's water was locked up in glaciers. As a result, waters had receded from the Bering Strait, the strip of water that now separates North America from Asia near the Arctic Ocean. The land below the Bering Strait and the nearby seas emerged above water, connecting Asia with North America.

When Europeans came to North America after 1492, they met Indians who were the descendants of these first Americans. The Indians by the 1500s had spread from the Alaskan Peninsula to the tip of South America and belonged to hundreds of distinct groups, with different physical characteristics, different languages, and different customs. The way of life a group followed depended heavily on the land and other resources nearby. For this reason, historians often identify the cultures of the American Indians by the regions where they lived, such as Eastern Woodland or Plains Indians. The following descriptions illustrate how the people of these two cultures used their environment. Within each culture region, many groups existed whose ways of living varied widely.

Eastern Woodland Indians. Groups of early Eastern Woodland Indians like the Delaware and Creek hunted and fished for food and gathered nuts, roots, and berries. These Indians also were farmers, practicing **shifting cultivation**. In this type of farming, the Indians cleared fields by cutting down the large trees and burning over the area. The women planted crops of corn, squash, and beans between the stumps. After a few years, the farmers would move to another area.

Plains Indians. Some groups of early Plains Indians such as the Assiniboines [ə sin′ə boinz] were nomad wanderers who followed herds of buffalo. The buffalo supplied the hunting people of the plains with meat and with hides for tepees, bedding, and clothing.

Other groups of early Plains Indians such as the Pawnee hunted buffalo but farmed as well. Their simple tools could not break through the dense prairie sod. As a result, they lived along rivers where the soil was easier to plow.

Europeans came for economic and religious reasons.

The Spanish fleet of Christopher Columbus was soon followed by explorers and settlers from England, France, and other European countries. The explorers came in search of adventure and gold. They also came to spread and freely practice Christianity.

The Spanish in the New World. The leaders of the first Spanish expeditions, known as **conquistadors** [kon kē′stə dôrz], were mainly ruthless conquerors. Juan Ponce de León accompanied Columbus on his second voyage. Later, Ponce de León helped defeat the Indians of Puerto Rico and was rewarded with the governorship of that island. Ponce de León set sail in 1513 for a fabled island in search of gold and slaves and a fountain whose waters made old people young. He landed on a peninsula that he called Florida, thus becoming the first Spaniard to explore the North American mainland. A conquistador named Hernando de Soto came to

U.S. and Canadian Place Names

United States

Colorado	Spanish, "red"
Detroit	French, "narrow place"
Mississippi	Chippewa, "great river"
Texas	Caddo, "friends" or "allies"
Virginia	English, honors "Virgin Queen" Elizabeth I

Canada

Montreal	French, "Mount Royal"
Ontario	Iroquois, "beautiful lake"
Quebec	Algonquin, "place where the river narrows"
Saskatchewan	Cree, "fast flowing river"
Toronto	Huron, "meeting place"

Florida in 1539 looking for gold. Hundreds of miles later, he found not gold but the Mississippi River. De Soto hoped to follow the river to the Pacific and then to the riches of Asia. Instead, he died of a fever, and his followers buried him in the Mississippi.

Friars—Catholic missionaries and teachers—came with Columbus and other explorers. Spanish friars came to Florida and to what are now Texas, Arizona, New Mexico, and California. The friars baptized Indians and had the converts build mission towns. The friars gave their towns names that reflected their Spanish origin and Catholic religion, like San Francisco (named for St. Francis) and Santa Fe (city of the "Holy Faith").

The Spanish introduced new crops, which included figs, peaches, oranges, and watermelons, to the region. They also brought the first horses, sheep, and cattle.

In addition, the Spanish and other Europeans carried new diseases to the continent. Measles, mumps, and smallpox were unknown in the area before that time. Lacking immunity to these germs, hundreds of thousands of Indians died from the new diseases. Europeans in turn carried new forms of disease back to Europe. The Indian cultures also gave Europe hundreds of new plants, including potatoes, corn, peppers, tomatoes, chocolate, peanuts, and tobacco.

French explorers and fur traders. Like De Soto, early French explorers searched for the Northwest Passage—a waterway that would take them across North America to the Pacific and eventually to Asia. Among the most important explorers were Jacques Cartier and Samuel de Champlain. Although Cartier and Champlain failed to find a waterway to Asia, they provided a wealth of information for mapmakers.

By the late 1600s, the French were more interested in American riches than Asian ones. Beaver fur hats were popular in Europe, so fur trading was extremely profitable. The French traded goods such as knives, metal pots, and cloth to the Indians in exchange for furs.

The English wanted a share of the fur trade, and this rivalry led to the French and Indian War. The English won the war in 1763. The French lost all their North American land to England except for their Caribbean colony of Haiti.

The English settlements. The English, along with other European groups, came to North America to settle. Many had left their homes in order to escape religious persecution. In North America they sought the freedom to worship as they wished. The English established their first permanent colony in North America in 1607. They settled a swampy but easily defensible site 40 miles up the broad, beautiful James River in what is now Virginia. Year after year, hundreds of English colonists came to Jamestown, Virginia, usually to die from Indian attack, starvation, or disease. Then colonist John Rolfe discovered that tobacco could be raised on a large scale. Tobacco became a major agricultural product of Virginia, helping it become a thriving colony.

Pilgrims landed on the forbidding coast of what is now New England in 1620. They soon discovered that the soil in most places was only a thin layer over rock. The people of New England were forced to make their living in other ways—fishing, building ships, and carrying fish, lumber, and other raw materials to England.

After the Revolutionary War, Americans in the new United States enlarged their shipping and started new industries apart from England. Canadians remained loyal to the British Empire. About one-fifth of the American colonists also had remained loyal to the British, and thousands of Loyalists migrated from the 13 colonies to Canada during the Revolutionary War.

Africans and their descendants helped build the U.S. economy.

Black sailors from Africa accompanied many of the first explorers—Ponce de León, De Soto, and probably even Columbus. A black explorer from Morocco named Estevanico, for example, was the first non-Indian in Arizona and New Mexico.

However, the best known of the early black immigrants were the Africans who first came to Virginia unwillingly in 1619. They were indentured servants, forced to serve masters for a specified time. Soon, Virginia lawmakers declared all black people in the colony permanent servants, or slaves.

Slavery was not confined to the southern colonies. Crispus Attucks, one of the victims in the Boston Massacre early in the Revolutionary War, was a runaway slave from Framingham, Massachusetts. Free black people also lived throughout the colonies, and many served in the Revolutionary War.

After the United States was established, black workers continued to contribute significantly to its economy and culture. In Africa black people had known for centuries how to make useful objects of iron. As black slaves in America, they used these skills as iron workers and blacksmiths. They also worked as farmers, carpenters, barrel makers, brick makers, and bricklayers, sometimes as slaves and after the Civil War as free persons.

Section 3 Review

Locating Key Places
Locate the following places on the map on page 624: Bering Strait, Virginia

Identifying Key Terms
Define the following terms: shifting cultivation, conquistadors

Reviewing Main Ideas
1. How did the first Americans survive? Give an example from your text.
2. Why did Europeans first come to the land that is now the United States and Canada?
3. How did black Americans help build the economy of the United States?

Thinking Critically: Recognize Values
When Europeans came to North America, their first settlements could not have survived without food, furs, and other resources supplied by the Indians. What values do you think the Indians had that were similar to or different from Europeans?

This black family was among the early homesteaders in the land that is now Nebraska.

The United States and Canada Today

See the globe below.

Preview

Key Places
Where are these places located?
1 Sunbelt
2 Toronto
3 Montreal
4 Vancouver
See the globe below.

Key Terms
What does this term mean?
cabinet system

Main Ideas
- What do Americans and Canadians have in common?
- Where do most Americans and Canadians live?
- What influences have shaped American and Canadian cultures?

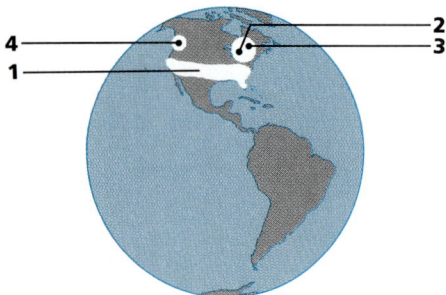

Give me your tired, your poor,
Your huddled masses yearning to breathe free,
The wretched refuse of your teeming shore,
Send these, the homeless, tempest-tost to me,
I lift my lamp beside the golden door!

Emma Lazarus, "The New Colossus"

Americans and Canadians share similar ways of life.

The words of Emma Lazarus, inscribed on the base of the Statue of Liberty in New York Harbor, have welcomed millions of immigrants to the United States since 1886. Today's immigrants see the same words on a wall of the Reception Hall at New York's international airport.

More than half a million new residents are admitted to the United States each year. About 10 percent are refugees fleeing violence, hunger, and oppression in their native lands. Most immigrants are highly skilled and well-educated people coming in search of the freedom and economic opportunity that is at the heart of our American heritage. Canada, too, is a nation of immigrants, annually welcoming thousands of refugees. This continual influx of new Americans and Canadians shapes both countries, giving them fresh momentum and new goals.

Both the United States and Canada cover huge territories. However, systems of communication and transportation have created a certain sameness in both countries as compared with other parts of the world. A family from Dallas could move to Philadelphia or to Toronto without experiencing much culture shock. Members of the family could live in a similar residence, find the same foods at supermarkets, enjoy the same entertainment, and work at similar jobs.

The Americans. Despite many similarities, differences do exist, especially among Americans themselves. *E pluribus unum,* "out of many,

On July 4th, Americans of all backgrounds join together to celebrate the birthday of the United States.

one" is the motto of the United States. The motto suggests the diverse backgrounds of its people. Out of a population of more than 240 million, about 83 percent have European origins. Of these, 6 percent are Hispanic. Hispanics—people living in the United States whose culture is of Latin American origin—make up a large and growing part of the population today in major cities such as Miami, Chicago, Los Angeles, and New York. Some Hispanics trace their ancestors to the earliest Spanish settlers. Most are immigrants or descendants of immigrants from Mexico, Cuba, Puerto Rico, and other Central and South American countries.

Some Americans are descendants of the original English and French colonists. The Appalachians are home to groups of people descended from the Scots-Irish (Northern Irish) immigrants who arrived in the 1700s. Many other Americans are descendants of Irish and Germans who came in later waves of immigration. Still other people in the United States have descended from Scandinavians, Italians, Russians, Jews, Greeks, Poles, and other Europeans.

Black Americans, who trace their ancestry to Africa, make up 12 percent of the population. Four percent of the population are Asians, most of whom have Chinese, Japanese, Korean, Indian, Filipino, or Vietnamese backgrounds. One percent are Native Americans.

The Canadians. Almost half—about 45 percent—of the more than 27 million Canadians are descendants of immigrants from Britain—England, Wales, Scotland, and Northern Ireland. Twenty-nine percent of Canadians are of French origin, and 23 percent have other European backgrounds. About 2 percent are Inuit or Indians. Less than 1 percent are of African or Asian descent.

Three-fourths of all Americans and Canadians live in or near cities.

At one time, most Americans and Canadians lived in rural areas. They worked mostly at primary industries such as farming, mining, and lumbering. After the Civil War in the United States and after World War II in Canada, secondary industries grew rapidly. More and more people moved to cities to work in factories that made such products as machinery, fabrics, and automobiles. More recently, the North American economy has relied more and more on tertiary industries, supplying services such as medical care, entertainment, and transportation. As a result, about 75 percent of all Americans and Canadians today live in or near cities.

Population shifts. Cities in the northeastern and central parts of the United States long have been the major population centers for many reasons. These cities were the sites of the earliest colonial and pioneer settlements. In addition, they are almost always located near the ocean or a large river, allowing for easy access and trade.

By the early 1900s, however, many people had moved west. The Gold Rush of 1849 had brought thousands of people to California, Colorado, and other mineral-rich areas. During the mid-1900s, cities in the Sunbelt—the southern and southwestern United States—began to attract millions of people looking for a warm climate and low living costs. Dallas, Texas; Denver, Colorado; and Phoenix, Arizona, were among the cities that grew rapidly at this time.

Cities and suburbs. Until the 1950s, the centers of population and business were in the cities themselves. Since then the surrounding suburbs have expanded greatly, and many central cities have decreased in population.

As you learned in Chapter 4, a large city and its suburbs make up a metropolitan area. The United States has about 330 metropolitan areas. The three largest are New York with 18 million people, Los Angeles–Long Beach with 12 million, and Chicago with 8 million. The urban sprawl from Boston, Massachusetts, to Washington, D.C., and including metropolitan New York is an enormous megalopolis. Find these large metropolitan areas on the map on page 122. In which areas might other cities merge to form a megalopolis?

Canada has 23 metropolitan areas with 100,000 or more people. The largest metropolitan area is Toronto, Ontario, with 3 million people. Montreal, Quebec, is a close second with about 3 million people. Vancouver, British Columbia, has a population of 1 million. Locate each of these Canadian cities on the map on page 122. Despite rapid growth, Canadian cities so far have avoided some of the traffic jams and other urban problems that plague cities in the United States.

American and Canadian cultures mingle old and new traditions.

American and Canadian cultures are rooted in European traditions. Other cultural traditions, however, have also had influence, particularly African, Asian, and Native American Indian.

Language and culture. The dominant elements of culture in the United States and Canada—language and laws, for example—have English roots. Immigrant groups, however, often try to preserve their ancestral heritage. Most groups have assimilated, adopting the English language and values. However, almost two-thirds of French Canadians speak only French, the official language of the province of Quebec. The deeply rooted Spanish traditions of the southwestern United States and closeness to Mexico have encouraged many Hispanic people to speak mainly Spanish. Similarly, the Cajuns of Louisiana speak a unique mixture of French and English.

Music, art, and architecture in the United States and Canada have all reflected the influence of Europe. Even Indian and Inuit crafts were changed when traders brought new materials like beads and wool to the continent.

Over the years, however, uniquely American themes in music, literature, painting, and architecture have developed. For example, African rhythms and spirituals with African origins led in the United States to a new style of music—jazz. Jazz rhythms and sounds have changed music throughout the world. In the field of architecture, skyscrapers were first built in Chicago and New York City in the 1800s. Today's skyscrapers have changed the appearance of modern cities everywhere.

These musicians share their artistry at the Chicago Jazz Festival.

Religions. Most Americans and Canadians have a Christian heritage. Many varieties of Christianity that are practiced in the United States and Canada today were first brought over from Europe by the colonists. Many of these early settlers—Puritans, Roman Catholics, and Quakers, for instance—came to North America in order to worship as they pleased. Two new Protestant sects originated in the United States—the Church of Jesus Christ of Latter-day Saints, also known as the Mormon Church, and Christian Science.

The largest single religious denomination in North America is Roman Catholic. This denomination includes about 52 million Catholics in the United States and 10 million in Canada. About 79 million other Americans belong to Protestant religious groups. Members of Protestant churches include Baptists, Methodists, Presbyterians, Lutherans, and Episcopalians as well as other smaller denominations. Six million Americans are Jews. Four million belong to Eastern Orthodox churches. Several million people are Muslims, Buddhists, or Hindus.

In Canada, after the Catholics, members of the United Church of Canada make up the second largest denomination. Members of the Anglican Church of Canada make up the third largest group. Canada also has many Presbyterians, Lutherans, and Baptists. Jews, Muslims, Buddhists, Hindus, and Sikhs are also represented.

Because North Americans are predominantly Christians and Jews, the Judeo-Christian influence is most evident in everyday life. Public schools and post offices are closed on Sunday, the Christian sabbath. Judeo-Christian mottoes, such as "In God we trust," are carried on money and state seals. Christian and Jewish religious groups operate thousands of schools, hospitals, and other institutions.

Political systems. The Declaration of Independence and the Constitution of the United States were inspirations to many democracies that formed after that of the United States. The framers of these documents, however, drew their ideas from European thinkers. The Declaration of Independence shows the influence of John Locke. This English philosopher developed the idea that people had natural rights to life, liberty, and property, and that governments must protect these rights. The French Baron de Montesquieu studied the laws and governments of ancient Greece and Rome. Montesquieu's concept of the separation and balance of powers in government is the basis for the U.S. government under the Constitution, which has lasted more than 200 years.

Canada became an independent nation only as recently as 1931. Not surprisingly, then, the Canadian government follows a cabinet system similar to that of Britain. Under a **cabinet system**, the officials who hold the executive powers of the government are directly responsible to the legislature, or lawmaking body. The House of Commons, the lower house of Canada's legislature, chooses the chief executive, the prime minister. In addition, the British monarch is the official but nonfunctional ruler of Canada.

Section 4 Review

Locating Key Places
Locate the following places on the map on page 122: Sunbelt, Toronto, Montreal, Vancouver

Identifying Key Terms
Define the following term: cabinet system

Reviewing Main Ideas
1. How are Americans and Canadians alike?
2. How did changes in industry bring changes in where most Americans and Canadians live?
3. Describe three areas in which American and Canadian cultures are based on European traditions.

Thinking Critically: Identify Assumptions
What assumptions lie behind the open-entry immigration policy? What assumptions are made by those who oppose open entry?

These two buildings—the U.S. Capitol on the left and the Canadian Parliament on the right—house the legislatures of these democracies.

Interpreting Road Maps

Suppose you wanted to drive around a part of the country, or world, with which you were unfamiliar. How would you get around? A road map would be your best guide to major streets and highways.

A road map will give you an overview of the area's transportation network. It will show you where you are, and how to get somewhere else. A road map may also tell you what you might see along the way—points of interest, capitals, or campgrounds.

The first road maps were actually made for bicyclists. The streets were labeled with local names instead of the numbers that are used today. These numbers first came into use in the 1920s as the state and U.S. highway systems were being developed.

This highway map shows all three types of numbered highway—interstate, federal, and state. Each is identified by a symbol that appears on the map key. Interstate highways cross state lines, and were designed for long-distance travel. Federal and state roads are built and maintained by the respective government.

This map also contains valuable information for the traveler. For example, you can figure out the distance between two cities by checking the number printed between any two arrows. From the map you can see that there are 27 miles between Tallahassee and Monticello.

Review

1. What highway would take you directly between Tallahassee and Jacksonville?
2. What type of highway is this?
3. Which state highway runs along the Atlantic coast of Florida?
4. How far is it between Monticello and Greenville?
5. What is the best route from Cedar Key to Jacksonville?

Florida: Road Map

- 🛡 Interstate highways
- ⬡ Federal highways
- ◯ State highways
- ⬖ 25 ⬗ Mileage between points
- ⭐ Capital
- ■ National Park System
- Ⓒ Major public camping area
- • Points of interest
- - - - Time zone boundaries

© 1988 R.R. Donnelley & Sons Company

141

CHAPTER 6

Review

Section Summaries

1. Land Regions of the United States and Canada

The landforms of this region were formed and shaped by internal and external forces such as plate tectonics and the movement of ice and water. Major landform regions include three plains regions: the Canadian Shield, the Atlantic Coastal Plain, and the Interior Plains. In addition, there are the Appalachian and Rocky mountains, the Intermontane Plateaus, and the Pacific Mountain Region.

2. Climate, Soils, and Vegetation

Three main climate regions cover the United States and Canada: continental, mild, and dry. The type and movement of six main air masses help to determine the climate patterns of the region. These climate patterns affect the soils of the region, which are divided into two main types: humid soils and arid or semiarid soils. Together, the climates and soils of the area encourage the main types of natural vegetation: forests, grasses, tundra, and desert plants.

3. Settling the United States and Canada

Indians, the first North Americans, used the abundant natural resources they found around them to survive. Europeans came next, to find treasure, new land, and religious freedom. Spanish, French, and English settlers claimed parts of the land that is now the United States and Canada. Other early residents of the region came unwillingly as slaves from Africa. These black slaves contributed significantly to the area's economy and culture.

4. The United States and Canada Today

Americans and Canadians share similar values and ways of life. In addition, communication and transportation have linked the two countries in a way that makes them culturally similar. One similarity is that most residents of both countries live in or near cities. Another similarity is that both cultures mingle old and new traditions—in language, culture, religion, and political systems.

Using Geography Skills

Reviewing the Map Lesson

Use the Indiana-Ohio road map below and the map key on page 141 to answer these questions.

1. What highway offers the most direct route between Indianapolis and Cincinnati?
2. How many miles lie between these two major cities?
3. What type of road connects Greenfield and Connersville?
4. What is the best way to travel between Bloomington and Greencastle?
5. What is the state capital of Indiana?

Using Social Studies Skills

1. **Organize and Express Ideas in Written Form.** A well-written paragraph should have a topic sentence that focuses all the ideas in the paragraph. Choose a topic sentence that describes how you feel to be an American. Then, write a paragraph that explains and supports your topic sentence. Use details that relate to the United States' physical or cultural features.

2. Observe for Detail. Find a book on Canada in your school or community library. In the photographs or text, look for details that show how the United States and Canada are similar. Look for clues in the pictures of houses, stores, restaurants, churches, cars, or people.

Testing for Understanding

Locating Key Places
Match each description below with the name of the place.
   1. the southern and southwestern United States
   2. a steppe plateau region in the United States
   3. the largest metropolitan area in Canada
   4. a desert region in the western United States
   5. the first permanent colony in North America
   6. a large city in British Columbia, Canada
   7. a bowl-shaped region in the Intermontane Plateaus
   8. a strip of water separating North America from Asia
   9. an area of foothills between the Appalachian Mountains and the Atlantic Coastal Plain
   10. a large Canadian city in French-speaking Quebec
   a. Piedmont
   b. Great Basin
   c. Colorado Plateau
   d. Columbia Plateau
   e. Bering Strait
   f. Jamestown, Virginia
   g. Sunbelt
   h. Toronto
   i. Montreal
   j. Vancouver

Recalling Key Terms
Define these terms in your own words.

Section 1
continental shelf
fall line

Section 2
tornado
hurricane
timberline

Section 3
shifting cultivation
conquistadors

Section 4
cabinet system

Reviewing Main Ideas
Section 1
1. What shaped the landscape of the United States and Canada?
2. Name the three major plains regions of the United States and Canada.
3. What four regions border the plains areas of the United States and Canada?

Section 2
1. What three climates cover most of the United States and Canada?
2. Name the two main types of soils of the region.
3. Name the three major types of natural vegetation in the United States and Canada.

Section 3
1. What did the first Americans use to survive?
2. For what reasons did the three groups of Europeans described come to the region?
3. How did black Americans affect the culture and economy of their new home?

Section 4
1. How are Americans and Canadians similar?
2. Where do most Americans and Canadians live? How has this changed in recent years?
3. What European traditions have influenced American and Canadian cultures?

Thinking Critically
1. Analyze Comparisons. How strong is the following comparison argument? "Farmers in the United States are smarter and work harder than other farmers because they produce more crops per year than do foreign farmers."

2. Predict Effects. When the first English colonists landed at Jamestown, they encountered a new environment. In what ways did geography shape the American character?

CHAPTER 7

The United States

In this chapter you will learn about life in the four census regions of the United States.

Sections

The Northeast

On the coastal rocks of northern New England the sea is an immediate presence, compelling, impossible to ignore. Its tides rise and fall on their appointed schedule, draining coves and re-filling them, lifting boats even with their wharfs or dropping away to leave them stranded and useless.

Rachel Carson, "Our Ever-Changing Shore"

Preview

Key Places
Where are the following places located?
1 Boston
2 New York City
3 Philadelphia
4 Pittsburgh
See the globe below.

Key Terms
What do these terms mean?
reforestation
electronics

Main Ideas
As you read, look for answers to these questions.
- How do land and climate shape life in the Northeast?
- How do people in the rural Northeast earn a living?
- How do people in the urban Northeast earn a living?
- Which cities form a megalopolis?

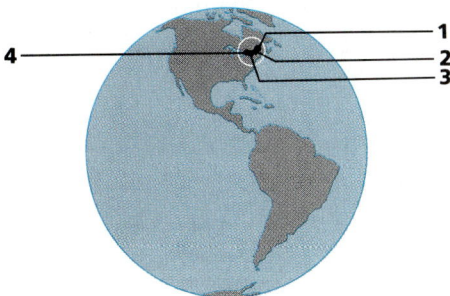

Land and climate challenge the people of the Northeast.

The sea borders all but two states of the Northeast, providing jobs, resources, and a place for recreation. The riches of the sea make up for the poverty of the land, which is mostly rocky and ill-suited for farming. Rachel Carson, marine biologist and author, explained that a sandy coastal plain once bordered all of the Northeast but now lies under the sea off New England.

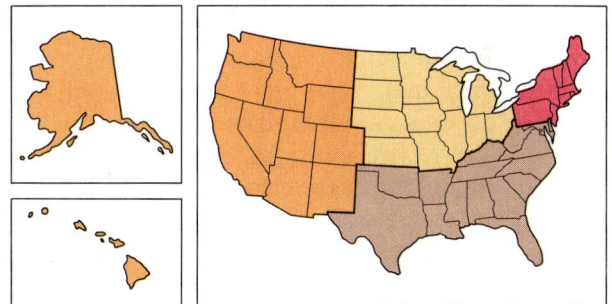

United States Census Regions

| Northeast | South | Midwest | West |

Map Study

This map shows the U.S. census regions. What are the four regions named?

Facing page: **Dodger Stadium lights up Los Angeles, the second largest American city.**

Six states—Maine, New Hampshire, Vermont, Massachusetts, Rhode Island, and Connecticut— generally are called New England. Captain John Smith, a founder of Jamestown, named New England when he first mapped the area in 1614. The three other northeastern states—New York, New Jersey, and Pennsylvania— are called Middle Atlantic states because they once lay in the middle of the English colonies. The Appalachian Highlands are the Northeast's main landform region. The Atlantic Coastal Plain covers parts of New York, New Jersey, and Pennsylvania.

In addition to rocky soil, New England also has a short growing season. The cold Labrador Current from the north cools the air that blows from the Atlantic to the coast. As a result, the summers are cool and the winters long, cold, and wet. The Gulf Stream, a warm current from the south, warms the climate in the Middle Atlantic states.

On the map on page 147, you can see several major rivers running through the Northeast to the coast. Many shorter rivers not shown on the map also cut through this region.

In colonial days, rivers were the main highways. Most rivers emptied into seaports such as Portsmouth, New Hampshire, and Providence, Rhode Island. These seaports grew into centers of trade. The rivers were also a source of water power, and factories grew up along the fall line.

Rural northeasterners make their living in primary industries.

Rural northeasterners, today as before, make a living in primary industries. The main activities are farming, fishing, forestry, and mining.

Farming. Only 13 percent of New England is farmland, and the short growing season limits the kind of crops farmers can grow. Dairy products—milk, cheese, and eggs—and beef cattle account for most agricultural income in New England.

The Middle Atlantic States are flatter than New England. Thanks to the Gulf Stream, these states also have a longer growing season. As a result, Middle Atlantic farmers raise a greater variety of foods such as oats, rye, and buckwheat as well as grapes, fruit, and tobacco.

Fishing, forestry, and mining. Many northeasterners fish for a living. The Georges Bank off the Massachusetts coast is teeming with cod, flounder, ocean perch, sea herring, and various shellfish.

Forest products are also important. White pines once covered the Northeast. Colonists used them for ship masts, pitch, and turpentine. Later, loggers felled hardwoods such as ash, beech, maple, and cherry for building railroads. Today **reforestation**, or replanting of forests, ensures abundant lumber for the pulp and paper industry.

Mining is another major industry in the Northeast. Miners in New England quarry—dig out—granite, a hard stone used for building and for tombstones, and marble, a hard white or colored limestone valued in sculpture and architecture. In Pennsylvania people mine coal, which is used to generate electricity and heat homes.

People of the urban Northeast engage in many industries.

Today almost 80 percent of the 49 million northeasterners live in or near cities. Most of these people are involved in trade, service industries, or manufacturing.

Trade. The total value of goods going through the port of New York is greater than that of any other city in the United States. As a result, the surrounding area has become a giant trading center.

Finance and other service industries. To meet the needs of trade and manufacturing, service industries such as banking and insurance have developed. New York City is a financial center. The New York Stock Exchange, where traders buy and sell stock in corporations, influences not only the United States but the world economy.

Manufacturing. Urban areas of the Northeast are centers for many kinds of manufacturing. The New York City area leads in printing and publishing and in the manufacture of cloth-ing. Massachusetts manufactures machinery and electronic products. **Electronics** is the branch of physics that deals with electrons in motion and which makes machines like transistors, lasers, computers, and television possible. Pittsburgh is a major steel-making center. The steel industry in Pittsburgh and in other U.S. cities has suffered a decline in recent years, however, because of a decreased demand and foreign competition.

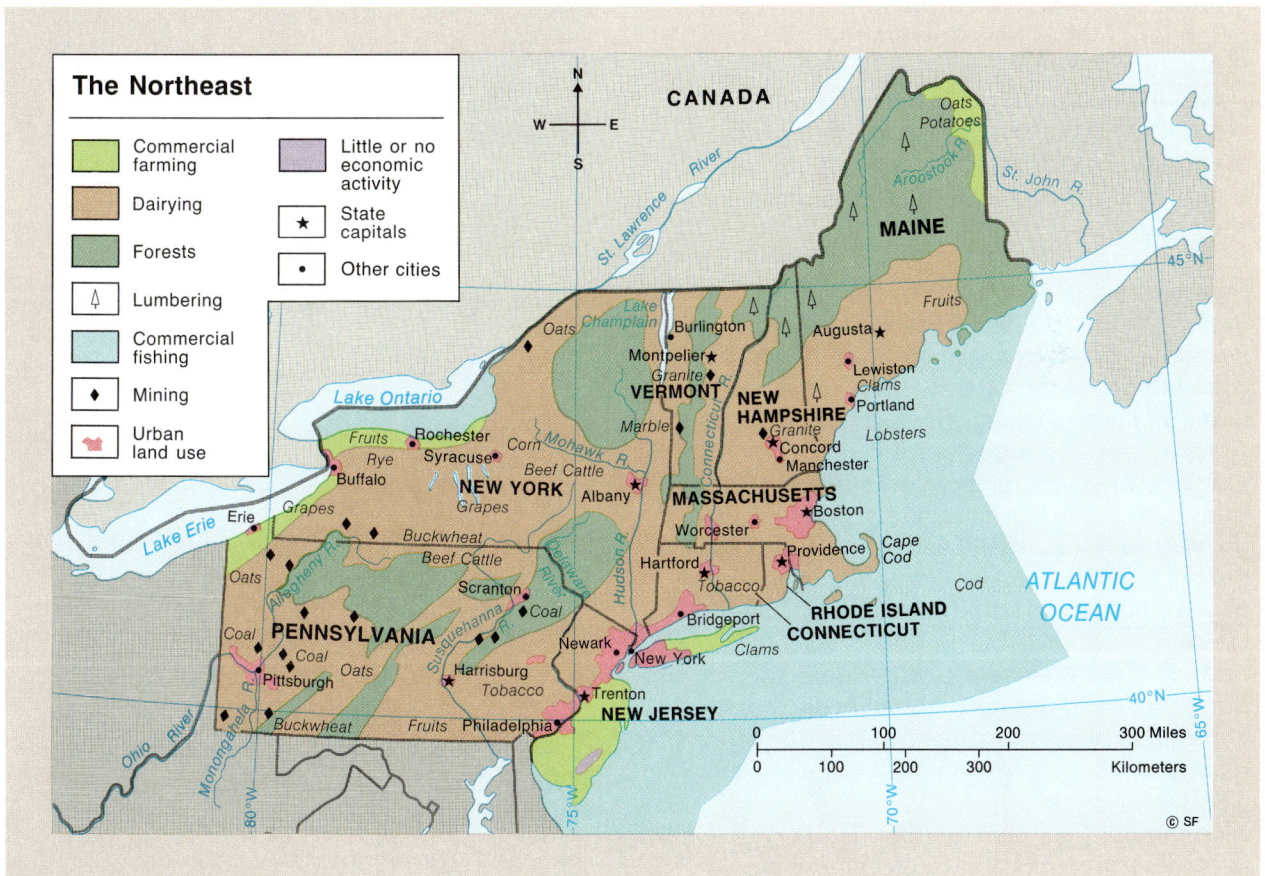

The Northeast

Symbol	Activity
	Commercial farming
	Dairying
	Forests
	Lumbering
	Commercial fishing
	Mining
	Urban land use
	Little or no economic activity
★	State capitals
•	Other cities

Map Study

This map shows the major cities and principal agricultural and industrial products of the Northeast. What are some of the economic activities of this geographic region?

Several northern cities have merged into a megalopolis.

The largest concentration of people in the Northeast extends from Boston through New York City and beyond the Northeast to Washington, D.C. This megalopolis also includes Philadelphia. Except for scattered open spaces, cities, towns, and suburbs occupy this heavily developed urban corridor.

Millions of immigrants have entered the United States through the port of New York, especially between 1845 and 1914. Many immigrants stayed in the area, creating such ethnic neighborhoods as New York's Little Italy and Boston's South End Irish town. More recently, Asian immigrants have moved in.

Migrants from other areas of the United States also have formed neighborhoods in the big cities. Black Americans first moved up from the South in the 1890s to settle in Harlem, part of Manhattan Island. More black southerners moved into the Bedford-Stuyvesant district of Brooklyn in the 1920s. Today Harlem and Bedford-Stuyvesant are among the largest black communities in the United States. Recently, many Spanish-speaking Americans have moved to New York City from Puerto Rico.

The central cities offer many cultural attractions such as museums, theaters, and symphony orchestras. For example, each day thousands of people visit New York's Metropolitan Museum of Art, the largest art museum in the United States.

Many businesses have crowded into the downtown areas of northeastern cities. One solution is to build skyscrapers, mainly for offices. Manhattan has more than 30 skyscrapers rising 500 feet or more.

Commuter lines enable urban workers to live in far-flung suburbs and to escape the crowding, high taxes, and high rents of the cities. For the same reasons, many businesses have fled to the suburbs.

Many immigrants, such as these Cambodians, have started businesses all over America.

Section 1 Review

Locating Key Places
Locate the following places on the map on page 147: Boston, New York City, Philadelphia, Pittsburgh

Identifying Key Terms
Define the following terms: reforestation, electronics

Reviewing Main Ideas
1. How have the rocky soil and cool climate challenged the people of the Northeast?
2. What kinds of jobs do people in the rural Northeast do?
3. In what ways do most people in the urban Northeast make a living?
4. Which large cities of the Northeast form an important megalopolis?

Thinking Critically: Make Hypotheses
Look at the map showing the six major North American air masses on page 128. Why do you think the Northeast would be a major target of acid rain?

SECTION 2

The South

Preview

Key Places
Where are these places located?
1 Washington, D.C.
2 Miami
3 New Orleans
4 Houston
   See the globe below.

Key Terms
What do these terms mean?
forest conversion   estuary
bayou   petrochemical

Main Ideas
As you read, look for answers to these questions.
• What are the landforms and climate like in the South?
• How do rural southerners earn a living?
• Why has the population of southern cities grown in recent decades?
• How do urban southerners make their living?

Spring had come early that year, with warm quick rains and sudden frothing of pink peach blossoms and dogwood dappling with white stars the dark river swamp and far-off hills. . . . The moist hungry earth, waiting upturned for the cotton seeds, showed pinkish on the sandy tops of furrows, vermilion and scarlet and maroon where shadows lay along the sides of the trenches. The whitewashed brick plantation house seemed an island set in a wild red sea.

Margaret Mitchell, *Gone with the Wind*

The South has wide plains areas and a warm climate.

For many years, "the South" conjured up images of prosperous plantations like Tara and southern belles like Scarlett O'Hara. In the background were many minor characters, mostly black slaves, picking cotton and doing household chores.

The South, if it was ever like the South of *Gone with the Wind,* is a far cry from that today. New people, new businesses, and new wealth have come to the South, along with new answers to what being part of the South means. In this section, you will read about this new South and the people who live and work there, the newcomers and those who have been there for years.

On the map on page 150, find the 16 states that make up the South. Notice that the South includes Washington, D.C., the seat of our federal government. This federal district, also known as the District of Columbia, is governed directly by Congress.

You can see from the map that almost every state in the South has large areas within the Atlantic Coastal Plain or the Gulf Coastal Plain. Part of the Appalachian Highlands, the Blue Ridge Mountains area extends from West Virginia, western Virginia, and North Carolina into western Georgia.

149

With its large plains and warm weather, the South is well-suited to farming. However, as you read in Chapter 6, heavy rainfall has leached nutrients from the soil, making some areas more suited for forests than farmland. Other farming areas lack adequate rainfall and must be irrigated. The southern states also have rich mineral resources.

Rural southerners make their living from primary industries.

For many years, the economy of the South was based almost entirely on primary activities, mainly farming. Manufacturing, however, has grown in importance since the 1950s.

Farming and soil erosion. For southern farmers, the most precious resource is soil. To-

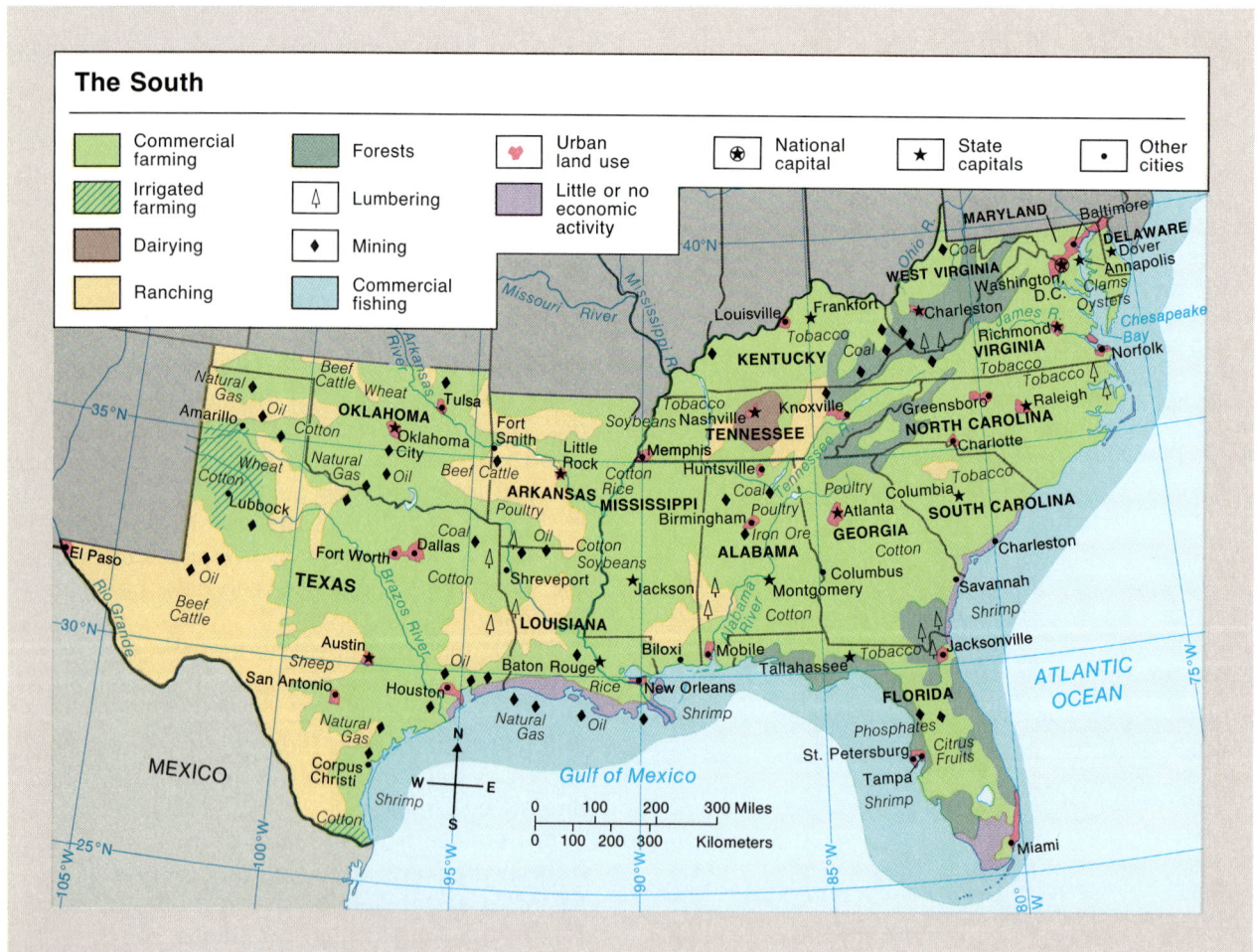

The South

Commercial farming	Forests	♥ Urban land use
Irrigated farming	⚑ Lumbering	Little or no economic activity
Dairying	♦ Mining	⊛ National capital
Ranching	Commercial fishing	★ State capitals
		· Other cities

Map Study

This map shows the major cities and principal agricultural and industrial products of the South. What are some of the economic activities of this geographic region?

These workers produce intricate textiles in North Carolina.

day most farmers try to stop erosion by raising crops on terraces that go around hills rather than in rows that run up and down them. Many farmers now also grow soybeans, which need little tilling and restore nitrogen to the soil. Badly eroded areas such as the southern Piedmont have been planted with trees for the production of pulp and lumber.

In southwestern states such as Texas and Oklahoma, low rainfall is the cause of soil erosion. Nearly half of all the cotton acreage in the United States is located in Texas. During the frequent dry spells, tilling allows the soil to dry out and turn to dust. This dust blows away with the first strong wind.

Forestry. The mild, rainy climate in the southeastern states is ideal for growing trees. The fastest-growing trees are southern pines used to build houses and for pulp to make paper. Pine sap also is used to produce rosin [roz'n] and turpentine for paints and varnishes.

In some parts of Arkansas and Alabama, logging companies burn down or poison stands of hardwood trees and plant forests of the more marketable pines in their place. This process of supplanting one kind of tree with another is called **forest conversion**.

Southern craft workers lament the destruction of the hardwoods. Cabinetmakers search out slabs of walnut, cherry, and maple from 400-year-old trees. North Carolina produces more hardwood furniture than any other state.

Fishing. The volume of fish caught and their value are greater in the South than in any other region of the United States. The states with the largest income from fishing are Louisiana, Texas, and Florida. Sluggish, marshy inlets along the Gulf Coast of Louisiana produce much of the shellfish consumed in the United States. The inlets, called **bayous** [bī'üz] are a major source of shrimp.

Another important fishing ground is Chesapeake Bay, where fishing boats from Virginia and Maryland take in oysters, softshell crabs, and striped bass. The bay is an **estuary,** a broad mouth of a river into which the tide flows. In fact, the Chesapeake receives many rivers: the Susquehanna, the Potomac, the Rappahannock, the York, and the James among others.

Mining in the South. Petroleum is another important resource in the South. Louisiana alone has 4,000 offshore oil wells. Texas, however, is the country's leading producer of petroleum and natural gas. Oklahoma is another important source. The South leads in the production of many other minerals. Florida produces three-fourths of the country's phosphate, used in fertilizers. Tennessee mines the most zinc. Arkansas mines most of the nation's bauxite, used in making aluminum. West Virginia, Kentucky, Alabama, and Tennessee mine huge quantities of coal.

Many people recently have moved to southern cities.

During the last few decades, change has been the hallmark of the South. For example, in 1940 two-thirds of the population of Virginia was rural. Almost 50 years later, more than two-thirds of all Virginians live in cities and suburbs.

151

Displaced farmers. A major reason for this shift in the southern population is the mechanization of farming. On southern farms in the 1920s, a mule pulled the plow. Farmers chopped the weeds and picked the crops. Producing one bale of cotton took 150 hours of labor. Today machines do the job in only 5 hours. As a result, fewer workers are needed on southern farms.

Many displaced farmers have moved to medium-sized southern cities. To provide jobs and boost the economy, state and local governments in the South offer tax breaks to businesses that build plants there. These tax breaks plus low wage costs have lured many businesses south.

Newcomers. The population of the South has grown as well as shifted. Florida and Texas are the two most rapidly growing southern states. In Florida the number of people rose from about 2 million in 1940 to nearly 12 million in 1988. In Texas the growth has been just as spectacular.

A major reason for southern growth is an influx of northerners. The short, mild winters in the South attract many workers and professionals from the Northeast and the Midwest. Thousands of northern retirees called "snowbirds" also regularly spend their winters in Florida.

Hundreds of thousands of immigrants from Cuba, the Caribbean islands, and other Latin American countries have come to Miami and South Florida since 1950. Many thousands of Mexican immigrants also enter the South each year, often through El Paso, Texas.

Urban southerners work in a variety of industries.

Changes in the South are most evident in its cities. Old commercial and transportation centers have developed new industries, and young industrial centers take advantage of the region's human and natural resources. Here are some examples.

This mural in Miami's Little Havana serves as an interesting backdrop for the Hispanic neighborhood's many activities.

Washington, D.C. Government has been the main business in Washington, D.C., since George Washington chose this site for the nation's new capital in 1791. The city grew slowly at first, but population soared during the Civil War and again in World War I. In the 1930s, when the size of the federal government mushroomed, Washington's population rose from 485,000 to 665,000, close to its present size. The population of its suburbs continues to rise, now spreading far into Virginia and Maryland.

Millions of tourists come to the Washington area each year to see the White House, the Capitol, the Supreme Court, museums, and monuments. Thousands of people work in jobs that provide tourist services.

Miami, Florida. Miami lies at the heart of an urban area that extends more than 100 miles along the Atlantic and is the only major city on the United States mainland with a tropical climate. The warm, sunny climate has made Miami a major tourist center. Thousands of service workers cater to the tourist trade at Miami's parks, golf courses, and luxury hotels.

In addition to being a tourist center, Miami is also a transportation center. Miami International Airport is one of the largest cargo airports in the world. More Latin American visitors enter the United States at Miami than at any other airport. Miami has also become a major international banking center.

New Orleans, Louisiana. Located near the mouth of the Mississippi River, New Orleans has been a major port for 200 years. Today New Orleans is the second busiest U.S. port and handles more foreign goods than any other port. New Orleans also capitalizes on its French heritage to attract a large tourist trade.

A major attraction in New Orleans is the French Quarter, or Vieux Carre [vyə ka rā']. This is a square where the first French and Spanish settlers lived. World-famous ironwork trims porches and balconies of the 200-year-old build-

ings that line its streets. Vendors sell tourists *café au lait* [ka fā' ō lā']—coffee and milk—and *beignets* [bān'yāz]—sugary pastries.

Houston, Texas. With a population of more than 3.5 million, Houston's metropolitan area is the largest in the South. Many people in Houston work in petrochemical industries. **Petrochemicals** are chemicals made from petroleum or natural gas, including plastics, paint, and fertilizer. Houston factories also make products such as steel, books, beer, paper, cement, and machinery.

The Gulf Intracoastal Waterway runs all along the Gulf Coast from Texas to Florida, linking Houston to the Mississippi River at New Orleans. As a result, Houston has become a world-class port. Cotton, rice, lumber, and livestock are some of the goods shipped from Houston.

Section 2 Review

Locating Key Places
Locate the following places on the map on page 150: Washington, D.C.; Miami, New Orleans, Houston

Identifying Key Terms
Define the following terms: forest conversion, bayou, estuary, petrochemical

Reviewing Main Ideas
1. How do the land and climate of the South differ from that of the Northeast?
2. In what ways do most rural southerners make a living?
3. What factors have contributed to the recent population growth of southern cities?
4. How do people make a living in these southern cities: Washington, D.C.; New Orleans; Houston; Miami?

Thinking Critically: Predict Effects
You've read that the population of the South has been growing very rapidly. What effects do you think this growth will have on southern cities and the South in general?

SECTION 3

The Midwest

Preview

Key Places
Where are these places located?
1 Chicago
2 Detroit
3 Indianapolis
4 Kansas City, Missouri
  See the globe below.

Key Terms
What do these terms mean?
agribusiness
foreign trade zone
duty

Main Ideas
As you read, look for answers to these questions.
- What are the land and climate of the Midwest like?
- How do people earn their living in the rural Midwest?
- What industries provide jobs in midwestern cities?

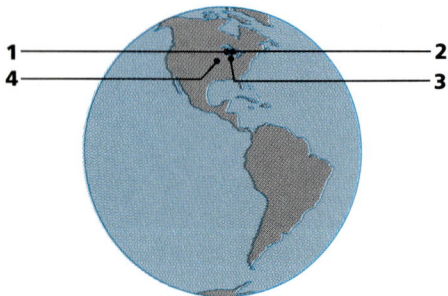

The prairie's sweep is flat infinity,
The city's rise is perpendicular to farthest star,
I stand where the two directions intersect,
At Michigan Avenue and Walton Place,
Parallel to my countrymen,
Right-angled to the universe.

Jean Toomer, "Brown River, Smile"

The Midwest is mostly plains, with a climate of distinct seasons.

The flatness of the Midwest is its most striking feature. This is so whether the observer stands in the middle of a country field or at a busy intersection in Chicago, the largest city in the Midwest and the third largest city in the United States. Midwesterners, like the poet Jean Toomer, can be sure they are standing "right-angled to the universe." In this section, you will read about the land and people in the Midwest today and how both are tied to the rest of the country and to the world.

Find the 12 states of the Midwest on the map on page 155. The Interior Lowlands is the main landform region. The Canadian Shield borders the Midwest to the north in Minnesota, Wisconsin, and Michigan. What plains region begins in the western Midwest states?

Glaciers left their mark on the Midwest, stripping the soil from areas close to the Great Lakes and depositing it farther south in parts of Ohio, Indiana, Illinois, and Iowa. Cold winds from Canada cause snowy winters. Warm, wet air from the Gulf of Mexico brings rain in summer.

Midwestern farmers supply food for the United States and the world.

Midwestern farmers grow most of the corn and much of the wheat in the United States today. Soybeans also have become a major crop in the Midwest during the last few decades. In addition, Midwestern farms produce other field crops, fruits, livestock, and dairy products.

Midwestern farm belts. Iowa, and parts of Ohio, Indiana, Illinois, Minnesota, Missouri, Kansas, Nebraska, and South Dakota have a hot, rainy growing season, which is ideal for corn. These states produce 40 percent of the world's corn and thus make up the Corn Belt. The climate farther west is cooler and drier. Wheat is grown there because wheat needs less rain than

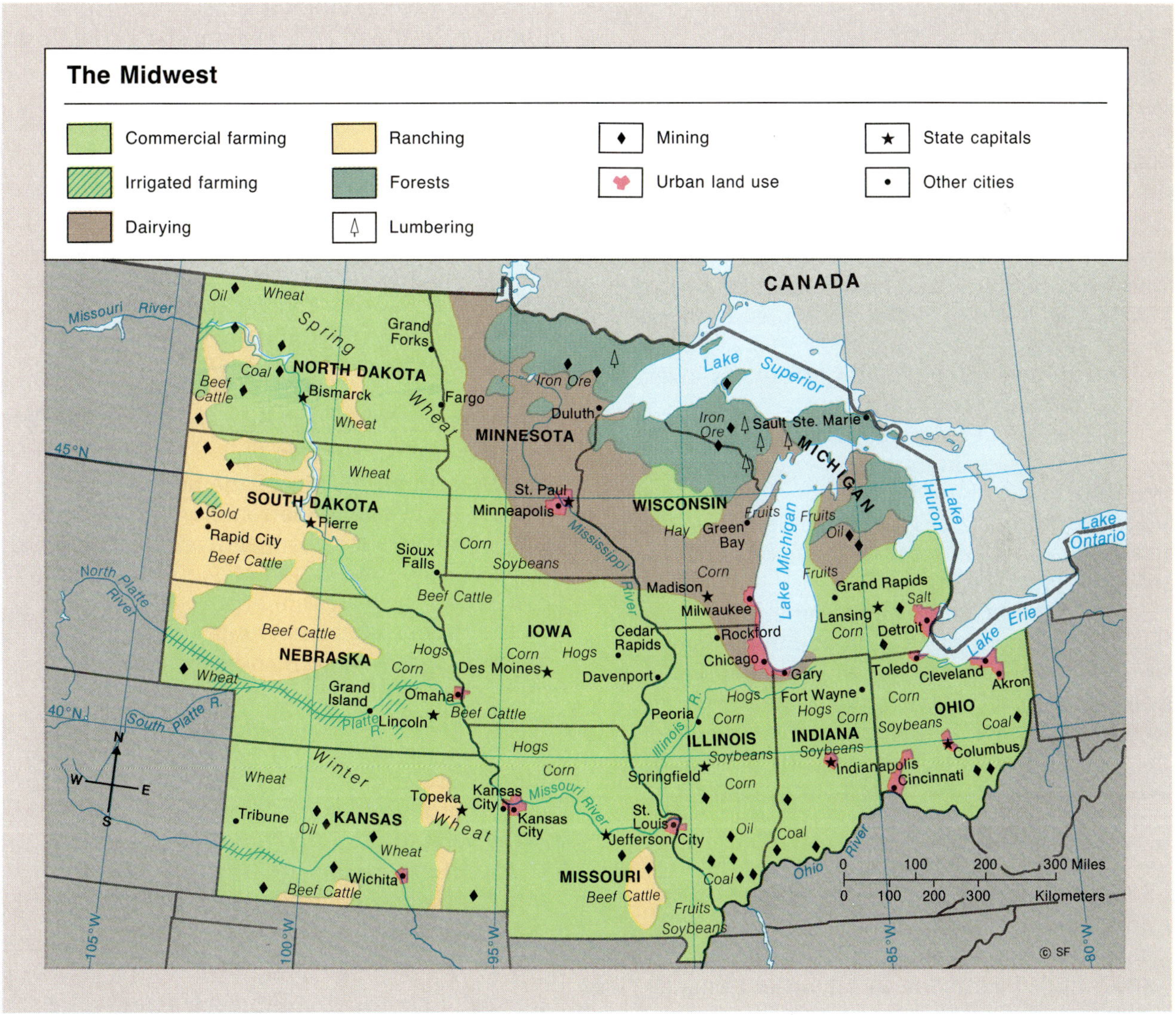

The Midwest
Commercial farming
Irrigated farming
Dairying
Ranching
Forests
Lumbering
Mining
Urban land use
State capitals
Other cities
CANADA
NORTH DAKOTA
SOUTH DAKOTA
NEBRASKA
KANSAS
MINNESOTA
IOWA
MISSOURI
WISCONSIN
ILLINOIS
INDIANA
OHIO
MICHIGAN
Lake Superior
Lake Michigan
Lake Huron
Lake Erie
Lake Ontario
Missouri River
Mississippi River
Ohio River
North Platte River
South Platte R.
Platte R.
Illinois R.
Spring Wheat
Winter Wheat
Bismarck
Grand Forks
Fargo
Pierre
Rapid City
Sioux Falls
Minneapolis
St. Paul
Duluth
Madison
Milwaukee
Green Bay
Sault Ste. Marie
Lansing
Grand Rapids
Detroit
Toledo
Cleveland
Akron
Columbus
Cincinnati
Indianapolis
Fort Wayne
Gary
Chicago
Rockford
Peoria
Springfield
St. Louis
Jefferson City
Kansas City
Topeka
Wichita
Tribune
Omaha
Lincoln
Grand Island
Des Moines
Cedar Rapids
Davenport
Iron Ore
Oil
Coal
Gold
Salt
Wheat
Corn
Hogs
Soybeans
Beef Cattle
Hay
Fruits
0 100 200 300 Miles
0 100 200 300 Kilometers
45°N
40°N
105°W
100°W
95°W
85°W
80°W
N
S
E
W
© SF

Map Study

This map shows the major cities and principal agricultural and industrial products of the Midwest. What are some of the economic activities of this geographic region?

corn.

Parts of Michigan, Wisconsin, and Minnesota are known as the Dairy Belt. Raising dairy cows and other livestock such as hogs, cattle, and chickens is actually the principal business of the Midwest. Much of the grain and soybeans grown in the area is fed to livestock.

Farming as big business. Farms in the Midwest are highly mechanized. Tractors pull the plows and huge combines harvest the crops. Even raising livestock in the Midwest is mechanized. At midwestern dairies, for instance, machines clean the stalls, milk the cows, and pipe the milk to cooling tanks. On some dairy farms, cows wear computerized neckbands that control exactly how much corn and protein each animal can consume.

Many farmers can no longer afford the investment in farmland and machines that make farming profitable. More and more acres are being farmed by **agribusinesses**, which produce, process, and distribute food products. Food-processing corporations run some agribusinesses. Families own most of them, hiring other people to work them.

Farms in the Midwest supply Americans with much of the food they eat. In addition, many farm products from the Midwest are shipped around the world. Countries like Japan with little farmland buy U.S. grain. Larger nations like China and the Soviet Union also buy millions of tons of grain from the United States. These countries have fertile fields but lack the ideal climate of the Midwest.

Farm problems. The demand for U.S. farm products has fluctuated widely from year to year. World food shortages in the 1970s triggered a huge investment in American farming. At the same time, U.S. experts helped poor, weak countries learn to grow more food. As a result, American food exports have dropped, and some farmers have gone out of business.

Many businesses in the towns and medium-sized cities of the Midwest are related to farming—food processing and the manufacture of farm machinery, for example. As small farms began to fail in the late 1970s and 1980s, many farmers left to find jobs in cities. As a result, businesses in towns and medium-sized cities lost money. Some companies, like those that made or sold farm machinery, closed plants.

Since then new companies have moved to the towns and medium-sized cities of the Midwest. Some of these companies are Japanese-owned. Japan, which has one of the most powerful economies in the world, is able to supply the heavy flow of needed capital. Japanese companies produce soy sauce in Walworth, Wisconsin, television sets in Franklin Park, Illinois, and cars and motorcycles in Maryville, Ohio.

A variety of industries provide jobs in midwestern cities.

More than three-fourths of the people in the Midwest today live in metropolitan areas. Some major employers are the meatpackers in Omaha, Nebraska, the breweries in Milwaukee, Wisconsin, the flour mills in Minneapolis, Minnesota, and the rubber factories in Akron, Ohio.

Many city jobs are in manufacturing. The Great Lakes area is rich in iron. Since steel is made from iron, the making of steel and steel products is important in the Midwest. Gary is an important steel making city in Indiana, the leading steel producing state. Factories in Chicago use the steel to produce railway cars, locomotives, and farm machinery. However, the steel industry's biggest customer is the automotive industry. Its center is Detroit, Michigan, where factories turn out cars, buses, and trucks.

Recent changes in manufacturing. Automotive sales fell off in the 1970s. Owners of small farms could not afford new machinery, and people were buying more cars from other countries, especially Japan. As a result, American steel and automobile plants cut back production. During the 1980s some 100,000 workers lost their jobs in Michigan, Indiana, and Illinois. Some workers took new jobs in light manufacturing, especially electronics.

The heavy manufacturing industries recovered slowly. By 1986 some steel and automotive plants again were making profits. Highly efficient, small mills in Indiana, Ohio, Pennsylvania, Michigan, Texas, and other states proved more profitable than the large integrated mills handling every step in the steelmaking process.

Trade, transportation, and service. Chicago, Indianapolis, and Kansas City, Missouri, are all important manufacturing centers. These three cities also offer jobs in trade, transportation, and service industries related to health, government, and tourism.

Chicago's position on the Great Lakes makes it the transportation center of the Midwest and a prime source of jobs in shipping. The opening of the St. Lawrence Seaway in 1959 made Chicago one of the busiest inland ports in the world, linking Chicago and the Great Lakes with the Atlantic Ocean. O'Hare, the city's major airport, is one of the world's busiest.

The Midwest, including this area near Ely, Minnesota, has many natural recreation areas.

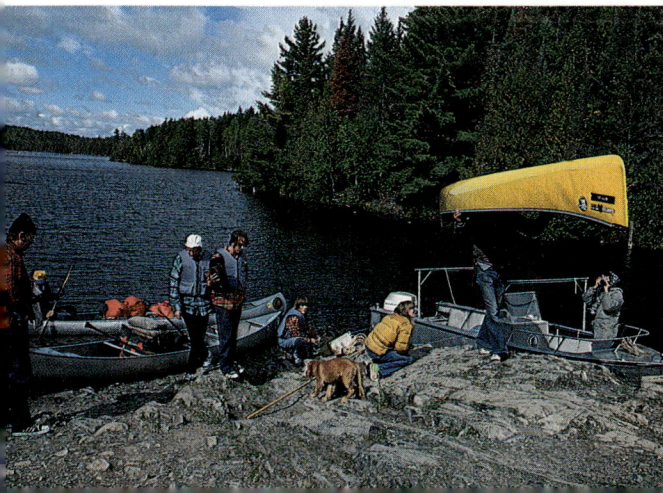

In addition to its role as a center for manufacturing, trade, and transportation, Indianapolis, Indiana, is rapidly becoming the sports capital of the United States. In 1987 Indianapolis hosted athletes from all over the Western Hemisphere at the Pan American Games. Every year fans watch basketball at Market Square Arena, football at the Hoosier Dome, and car racing at the Indianapolis 500.

Kansas City, Missouri, is the leading market for winter wheat, farm machinery, and frozen foods in the United States. In addition, one of the world's largest foreign trade zones is located in limestone caves beneath the city. A **foreign trade zone** is an area in the United States where importers pay no duties. A **duty** is a tax on imported goods. Companies in Kansas City's foreign trade zone import parts, and workers assemble them to make finished products.

Section 3 Review

Locating Key Places
Locate the following places on the map on page 155: Chicago, Detroit, Indianapolis; Kansas City, Missouri

Identifying Key Terms
Define the following terms: agribusiness, foreign trade zone, duty

Reviewing Main Ideas
1. Describe the land and climate of the Midwest.
2. How do people earn their living in the rural Midwest?
3. What kinds of jobs do people do in midwestern cities?

Thinking Critically: Recognize Values
The family farm is increasingly being replaced by agribusiness. What values are reflected in family farms and agribusinesses?

Case Study: Tribune, Kansas

Preview

Key Places
Where is this place located?
Tribune, Kansas
  See the globe below.

Key Terms
What do these terms mean?
county seat
speculator
fallow

Main Ideas
As you read, look for answers to these questions.
* Why did Tribune become the county seat of Greeley County, Kansas?
* How did Simon Fishman bring prosperity to Tribune?
* What is Tribune like today?
* What American institutions hold the people of Greeley County together?

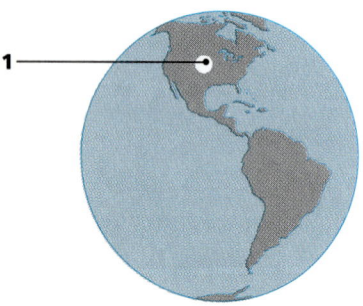

1 ——

The following case study comes from the article, "The Simplest of Counties," in Focus magazine, Summer, 1987. This case study describes the unique character of Tribune, a small town in sparsely populated Greeley County, Kansas. As you read, think about American values and attitudes.

Tribune became the county seat because of its central location.

The Kansas legislature of 1872, considering the shortgrass prairie covering the High Plains in the western part of the state, decided that the time had come to complete the subdivision of Kansas into counties. It was common knowledge in those days that residents should be no more than a day's ride—about 15 miles—from the county seat where they would have to go to take care of land claims, taxes, and legal matters.

Look today at the counties of western Kansas—say the seven lined up against the Colorado border—and you will see that they're tidy enough to stack up like crates in a shipping container.

The middle county of the seven was named after Horace Greeley, a famous newspaperman. But giving the county a well-known name

GREELEY COUNTY **KANSAS**
• Tribune

Map Study
This map shows the counties of Kansas. What shape is common?

wasn't enough to guarantee settlement, and for more than a decade it was little more than an empty shell, with fewer than a dozen people. One of them was a man named Girard. He was an Indiana veteran of the Civil War who, once in Greeley County, decided to lay out a county seat. [A **county seat** is the town or city where the county government is located.] And remembering Mr. Greeley, named it Tribune. Sensibly, Girard chose a site in the center of the county and laid it out as a grid, with east-west streets named for other towns in Kansas and north-south streets named for prominent Kansans.

The town might have vanished if not for Jay Gould, who in the summer of 1887 ran his Missouri Pacific Railroad straight through Greeley County and nicked the southern edge of Tribune.

A properly imposing stone courthouse was built in Tribune in 1890, but the county, which in the summer the railroad was built boasted 2,600 residents, was already losing people; by 1900 its population had dropped to 500. Most of those who left had been **speculators** [people who buy and sell land with the hope of making a profit from future price changes]. They departed as soon as it became clear that this part of Kansas, with 15 inches of precipitation annually, was too dry for corn.

Simon Fishman helped make Tribune prosperous.

Tribune's fortunes changed with the arrival in 1920 of a Russian immigrant named Simon Fishman, who opened a mercantile store and, more important, a land office. It was Fishman who brought the first tractor to Greeley County, Fishman who showed that winter wheat—if the fields were fallowed every other year—could be a profitable crop in the county. [A **fallow** field is plowed and left unseeded for a season or more.] He also bought land, plowed it, seeded it, and sold it as established farms. Though dwarfed by newer ones, there is still an elevator

at Tribune with Fishman's name faintly legible on it. But perhaps Fishman's real monuments are the 450,000 acres of cultivated land in the county and the 160,000 acres of wheat grown on it annually.

Tribune today is a small rural town.

Tribune has expanded since Girard's day. A western addition long ago more than doubled its extent, to about 12 blocks east-west and seven north-south. The main street, Broadway, is really no more than a named segment of Route 96, the north-south highway. . . . Broadway crosses a residential street called Greeley Avenue. Here is the county's one traffic signal, a blinking red light swinging on a cable, and here are the county's one supermarket and its one clothing store, which doubles as the county drugstore. The county's one bank is on the southwest corner of the same intersection, and from it you can see the county's one gas station.

The courthouse is a block away from the bank, to the northeast. The old stone building was retired in 1975 and is now a museum with photographs and firearms. . . . The new courthouse is next door, and it is an attractive one-story brick building. . . . Drop by the city hall—in an old store on Broadway—and you will

The county's only stoplight stands guard over Tribune.

learn that Tribune has about 400 residences. You can see for yourself that they have never been very prosperous. . . . Many of them share a special bit of Greeleyana—front porch columns cast in cement and decorated not in any classic style but in a bound-rods motif. Perhaps it's a corny reminder of the tribunes of antiquity [tribunes were representatives of the people in ancient Rome], but in a way it doesn't seem an inappropriate reminder of the fact that communities are made, not given.

Strong beliefs hold the people of Greeley County together.

This is a county that has pared American institutions down about as fine as they can get. There are still fewer than 2,000 people here, with a thousand in Tribune, a subordinate cluster at Horace, and the rest scattered about. Look at a county map and you see nothing but the simple square of the county itself, with two roads crossing in the center of the blank space at a spot marked Tribune. Most Americans who have never set foot in the county can predict what . . . Tribune is like: a courthouse, of course, a few stores but with people often making expeditions to bigger towns farther away, quiet streets, more pickup trucks than cars probably, a school, and a hospital. And though none of this seems remarkable to most people in this country, from a more detached point of view it's almost fantastic. Do the people of Greeley County know how lucky they are to have graded roads and a half-hour drive to town? . . . Tribune's supermarket on Easter weekend was advertising a special on fresh strawberries. In April on the High Plains!

That's the amusing part. The miraculous part is that when you've spread Americans and American institutions this thin, the fabric holds, does not unravel. The county clerk is happy to tell you how she spends her $3 million annual budget—more than half on the schools. The county sheriff keeps his car parked in front of the jail wing of the new courthouse, and over the weekend you never hear the car's siren or see it speeding about. Greeley is just about the poorest of Kansas counties; the average income is about two-thirds of the state's average. No doubt, too, the wheat business is tough. . . . But the people of the county live together peaceably, without the slightest thought that the rules that hold them together could lose all force, could dissipate, could leave them in a chaos of their own making. How hard it is to create such a fabric elsewhere on this planet! How simple it seems here, how everyday, the work of ordinary people doing only the obvious!

Section 4 Review

Locating Key Places
Locate the following place on the map on page 155: Tribune, Kansas

Identifying Key Terms
Define the following terms: county seat, speculator, fallow

Reviewing Main Ideas
1. Explain why Tribune became the county seat for Greeley County.
2. How did Simon Fishman's ideas about land cultivation help Tribune prosper?
3. How is Tribune different today than it was in the early 1900s?
4. How does the belief in American institutions hold the people of Greeley County together?

Thinking Critically: Evaluate Sources of Information
The writer of the article you have just read has a definite point of view about Tribune, Greeley County, and the people who live in these places. What is this author's point of view? Support your opinion with excerpts from the article. How does the author's point of view affect how you look at the information?

The West

Preview

Key Places
Where are these places located?
1 Central Valley
2 Colorado River
3 Santa Clara County
4 Los Angeles
See the globe below.

Key Terms
What do these terms mean?
ground water   chip
dry farming   freeway

Main Ideas
As you read, look for answers to these questions.
- What two groups of states make up the West?
- How do western farmers and ranchers use the land and climate?
- What kinds of natural resources does the West have?
- How are people in and near western cities dealing with problems of population growth?

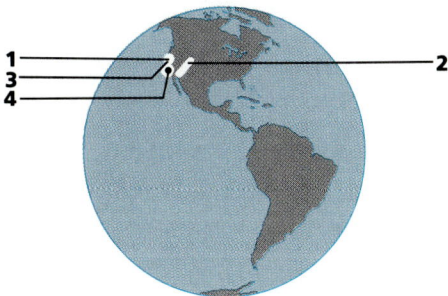

As I was a-walkin', one mornin' for pleasure,
I spied a young cowboy a-lopin' along:
His hat was throw'd back, and his spurs was a-jingle,
And as he rid by he was singin' this song.

Tip-pee ti-yi-yo, git along little dogies;
It's your misfortune and none o' my own,
Yip-pee ti-yi-yo, git along little dogies,
The plains o' Wyoming will be your new home.

A traditional cowboy ballad

The West includes the Mountain West and the Pacific West.

When people think of the West, they often picture a lonesome cowboy, driving longhorn cattle down a dusty trail. In the background are windswept plains, snowcapped mountains, or towering rock formations. The West has all of these landscapes and more. In this section, you will read about the natural and human resources of the West. You will find out how westerners today use and protect these resources.

The West is divided into two parts: the Mountain West and the Pacific West. Find the 13 western states on the map on page 162. You can see from the inset map that 2 of the 13 states—Alaska and Hawaii—do not touch the rest of the United States. Alaska, Hawaii, and the other states of the Pacific West all border the Pacific Ocean.

The West includes the wettest place in the United States—Mount Waialeale [wī äl'ā äl'ā] in Hawaii—and the driest and hottest place—Death Valley in California. Turn back to the map on page 128. What are the main climate regions in the West? You can see from the map that only land close to the Pacific Ocean has humid climates. Most of the West receives less rain and snow than other parts of the United States.

The West has the lowest population density of all the regions in the United States. Yet the West is the country's fastest-growing area. By the year 2000, its population will have increased more than 44 percent. How westerners control this growth and use their resources will determine the quality of life in the West of the future.

Western farmers and ranchers adapt to the land and climate.

Western farmers grow more than 200 different kinds of crops. Idaho produces more potatoes

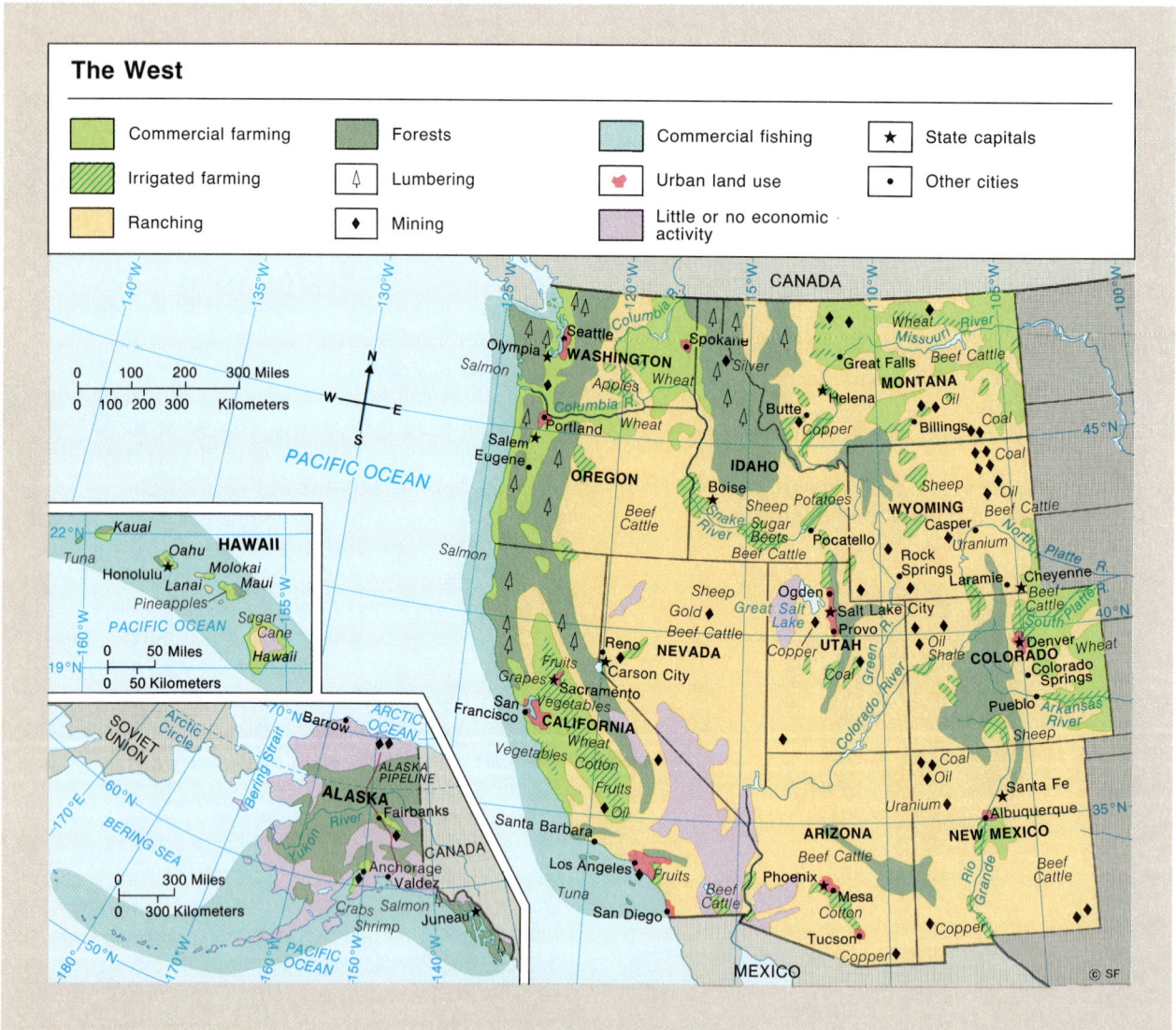

The West

Commercial farming	Forests	Commercial fishing	★ State capitals
Irrigated farming	⌂ Lumbering	Urban land use	• Other cities
Ranching	◆ Mining	Little or no economic activity	

Map Study

This map shows the major cities and principal agricultural and industrial products of the West. What are some of the economic activities of this geographic region?

than any other state. Washington is famous for its apples, and Hawaii is known for its pineapples and sugar cane. More than half the nuts, fruits, and vegetables grown in the United States come from California. The most productive farmland in California is the Central Valley. Farmers there grow grapes, peaches, oranges, almonds, potatoes, rice, and cotton.

Irrigation. The generally dry climate of California's Central Valley and of the Imperial Valley farther south is better suited to ranching than farming. Irrigation, however, has made growing fruits and vegetables more profitable than raising cattle.

Like California, many other areas of the West have rich soil but little rainfall. To make use of this nutrient-rich soil, every western state has at least some irrigated farmland. Generally, farmers irrigate their fields by supplying additional water from rivers or wells.

Mountain streams serve as the major source of water in the West. Large areas of the West depend for their water on the Colorado River. Los Angeles and 12 other cities of southern California use water carried by aqueduct from the Colorado. The Colorado is one of the few rivers with more water at its source than at its mouth. So much water is diverted that little is left by the time the river finally reaches the Gulf of California in northern Mexico.

Tapping underground water. Farmers who irrigate often use wells that draw on available ground water. **Ground water** is water that flows or seeps downward and saturates the soil. The upper level of this saturated soil is called the water table. Most of the world's fresh (unsalty) water is ground water. Westerners sometimes overdraft, or use more ground water than the rainfall replaces, risking a water shortage.

Farming without irrigation. Some farmers in the West raise wheat, rye, peas, hay, and bar-

Cattle graze in the desert west of Tucson, Arizona.

ley without irrigation. These farmers practice dry farming. **Dry farming** depends entirely on melting snow and rainfall to provide moisture for crops.

One dry farming method involves leaving parts of a field fallow. The fallow soil absorbs water that falls as rain or snow during the year, and this moisture nourishes the crop planted the following year.

Ranching in the West. Most of the Mountain West is made up of rugged plateaus. Its slopes and rocky soil are unsuited for farming but ideal for grazing. Thus beef is the leading farm product.

In extremely dry areas of California, Colorado, New Mexico, and Montana the ranchers raise sheep. Unlike cattle, sheep need little water. They thrive on tough grass and can crop the shortest blades even shorter.

The West has tremendous energy, mineral, and forest resources.

The West is an important source of energy, including such fuels as petroleum and natural gas.

Alaska and California are major producers of petroleum. Large deposits of coal are found in Montana and Wyoming.

Ten billion barrels of petroleum lie under Prudhoe Bay on Alaska's northern Arctic Coast. Prudhoe Bay has the largest accessible oil field yet found in North America. However, the bay's ice-choked waters prevent tankers from carrying the petroleum to market. Instead, a pipeline completed in 1977 delivers oil from Prudhoe Bay to tankers in Valdez on the southern coast of Alaska. The pipeline's 800-mile-long course crosses 3 mountain ranges, more than 300 rivers and streams, and nearly 400 miles of permafrost tundra. Geographer Ron Redfern described the pipeline's construction as "a feat comparable only to the building of the pyramids of Giza or the landing of a man on the Moon."

During the 1970s, petroleum companies began working on deposits of oil shale in Utah, Colorado, and Wyoming. Through a costly process, petroleum can be extracted from oil shale, which is a fine-grained sedimentary rock formed on ancient lake bottoms. When the price of oil dropped in the 1980s, however, production of petroleum from oil shale fell off.

Many people came to the West when gold and silver were discovered there in the 1800s. Gold and silver mines experienced a new boom in the 1980s. Old mines that once were considered exhausted are being reopened in Nevada, California, Utah, Montana, and Colorado.

The mining boom is the result of new technology and the high price of gold and silver. Miners now spray metal ore with liquid cyanide [sī'ə nīd] to separate the metal from the rock. This process can make a profit from a ton of ore containing a fraction of an ounce of gold. With older methods, only much richer ore was worth mining.

Other minerals also are mined in the West.

Arizona and Utah produce copper, and Oregon is the major producer of nickel.

Lumbering is another important industry in the West. Oregon, Washington, and California produce almost half the lumber used in the United States. The most expensive lumber comes from California redwoods, ranging from 500 to 2,000 years old. Recently, a lumber company started cutting down the redwoods at an unprecedented rate. Environmentalists sued the company and stopped the cutting—for now.

People in cities are controlling growth through planning.

The West is the fastest-growing region in the United States. Most of the growth is taking place in and around western cities. California's Santa Clara County and Los Angeles are good examples.

Santa Clara County. This area, which includes San Jose and Palo Alto, became the national center of the electronics industry in the 1960s. Nearby universities made the county an ideal site because the scientists there were a valuable source of ideas and knowledge. Great wealth flowed to the county, which soon was nicknamed "Silicon Valley." Silicon is the hard, dark gray substance used in making computer chips. A single tiny **chip** of silicon can serve as either the central processing unit or memory for a computer. Since 1958 the number of components that can be squeezed onto a chip has increased from five to several million. As a result, computers have become much smaller, faster, and cheaper.

As buildings fill up the land in Santa Clara County, pollution from car exhaust fills the air and chemical wastes poison the ground. City planners hope to tap the valley's great wealth and human resources to solve these problems.

Los Angeles. This sprawling metropolis is America's second largest city, and people flock there to find many different kinds of jobs. New-

The L.A. freeway provides transportation for millions.

comers soon discover that Los Angeles has fine beaches, warm weather, and many other attractions. Sports fans enjoy baseball at Dodger Stadium and football at Memorial Coliseum. The city's parks have baseball fields, golf courses, and tennis courts. The Los Angeles Music Center for the Performing Arts and dozens of other theaters offer plays, concerts, operas, and ballets.

Newcomers to Los Angeles sometimes have trouble finding a home there. The city has little land left to build on, and this land is very costly. Most of the newer buildings in the city are glass, steel, and concrete towers with hundreds of apartments or offices.

People generally drive to work because train and bus service is limited. Los Angeles has 650 miles of freeways. A **freeway** is a highway with no tolls, stop lights, or stop signs. The freeway system makes driving an automobile the quickest way to get around in the city.

Facing challenges. Growth has created problems for Los Angeles. One of these prob-

lems is smog. Car exhaust mixes with fog to cloud the air. California has lessened this problem by forcing automakers to manufacture cleaner cars. Los Angeles also plans to build a subway system.

Other western cities want to avoid the growing pains that plague Santa Clara and Los Angeles. Voters in San Diego, California, have declared parts of the city off-limits to new construction. Officials in Albuquerque, New Mexico, try to weigh the good and bad points before adding new areas to the city. In Portland, Oregon, one of the West's fastest-growing high-technology centers, tough zoning laws ensure that some land will be preserved for recreational uses. These people believe that planning will make their cities better—if not bigger—places to live.

Section 5 Review

Locating Key Places
Locate the following places on the map on page 162: Central Valley, Santa Clara County, Colorado River, Los Angeles

Identifying Key Terms
Define the following terms: ground water, dry farming, chip, freeway

Reviewing Main Ideas
1. Name the states that make up each group of the West.
2. What methods do western farmers and ranchers use to adapt to the land and climate of the region?
3. Describe the natural resources of the West.
4. How have people in urban areas of the West dealt with problems of population growth?

Thinking Critically: Make Decisions
Tunnels now draw water from the western to the eastern side of the Continental Divide. Do you think this is a good idea? In areas where the water supply is limited, what solutions can you see for dividing the water fairly?

SECTION 6

The United States and the World

Preview

Key Places
Where is this place located?
1 Persian Gulf
   See the globe below.

Key Terms
What do these terms mean?
guerrilla   trade deficit
embargo   superconductor
alliance

Main Ideas
As you read, look for answers to these questions.
• How does United States foreign policy influence other regions of the world?
• How does foreign competition affect American industries?
• Why is technology important to the American economy?

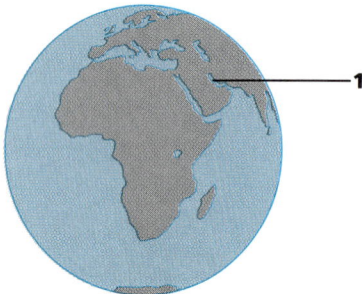

The ocean does not separate us from lands of our duty and desire—the oceans join us, rivers never to be dredged, canals never to be repaired. . . . Cuba not contiguous! Porto Rico not contiguous! Hawaii and the Philippines not contiguous! The oceans make them contiguous. And our Navy will make them contiguous. . . . We cannot retreat from any soil where Providence has unfurled our banner; it is ours to save that soil for liberty and civilization.

Senator Albert J. Beveridge, September, 1898

U.S. foreign policy reflects a superpower rivalry.

A major change took place in American policy toward other countries as a result of the Spanish-American War in 1898. Before that time the United States had been concerned about expansion within its continental boundaries. As the war ended, the United States found itself with foreign possessions—Cuba and Puerto Rico in the Caribbean and, halfway around the world, the Philippines and Guam. Americans like Senator Beveridge debated whether or not to keep these possessions.

Since the end of World War II, the United States has had worldwide power that the Congress in 1900 could not even have envisioned. Its military strength, however, is matched by that of the world's other superpower—the Soviet Union—which is committed to the spread of the communist system.

Central America. Since long before the Spanish-American War, Central America had been an area of great concern to the United States. Today our government's main goal there is to maintain governments that are friendly to the United States and free of foreign, particularly communist, influence.

For many years, dictators have run the governments of most countries in Central America. One such dictator was Anastazio Somoza Debayle of Nicaragua. In 1979 Somoza was overthrown in a popular revolution led by the Sandinista movement. The revolutionary government the Sandinistas established initially had broad-based support. In time, however, radical or left-wing elements began to dominate the movement.

Guerrillas known as contras—for counter-revolutionaries—began attacking Sandinista supporters in Nicaragua. A **guerrilla** is a member of a band of fighters—not part of a regular army—who use sabotage, ambush, and hit-and-run attacks to harass the enemy. Throughout the 1980s the United States sent funds and weapons to the contras, sometimes through secret and illegal means. In addition, American

Reagan and Gorbachev shake hands on a 1987 arms agreement.

President Ronald Reagan ordered an **embargo**, or trade restrictions, on trade between the United States and Nicaragua.

Western Europe. After World War II, the United States and the Soviet Union emerged as opposing superpowers. To maintain this status, they built up large arsenals of nuclear weapons.

Since the end of World War II, Americans and Soviets have continued to develop powerful new weapons systems. The expense of these systems and the risk of their accidental use has led to extensive talks aimed at reducing or eliminating nuclear weapons.

President Reagan proposed in 1983 the Strategic Defense Initiative (SDI), a system then untested and still largely theory. This system of space-based defense against nuclear missiles was nicknamed "Star Wars." Its purpose was to detect nuclear missiles launched anywhere on earth and destroy them.

The American and Soviet governments are not the only ones concerned with arms control and nuclear defense. European members of the North Atlantic Treaty Organization (NATO) also have a stake in these issues. NATO is an **alliance**—a joining of independent nations by a treaty. The map on page 168 shows the countries that belong to NATO.

At the end of World War II, the Soviet Union took over most Eastern European countries. After the war, Western Europeans feared that the Soviet Union would take over their countries too. So the North Atlantic Treaty Organization (NATO) was formed to counter this Soviet threat. By the 1980s the United States had placed hundreds of nuclear missiles and more than 300,000 soldiers at NATO bases in Western Europe. In 1987 Reagan and Soviet leader Mikhail Gorbachev agreed to reduce nuclear arms.

Southwest Asia. The United States is also involved in Southwest Asia, an area rich in oil. Japan and Europe depend on oil imports from

Southwest Asia. Locate two of the oil countries—Iran and Iraq—on the map on page 620. These countries have been at war throughout most of the 1980s. Tankers moving oil through the Persian Gulf have been attacked. In 1987 the United States government began sending American ships to protect the oil tankers. Some Americans argued that if the United States did not protect the tankers, the Soviet Union would. The United States did not want Soviet power in the Persian Gulf.

Two Southwest Asian countries—Egypt and Is-

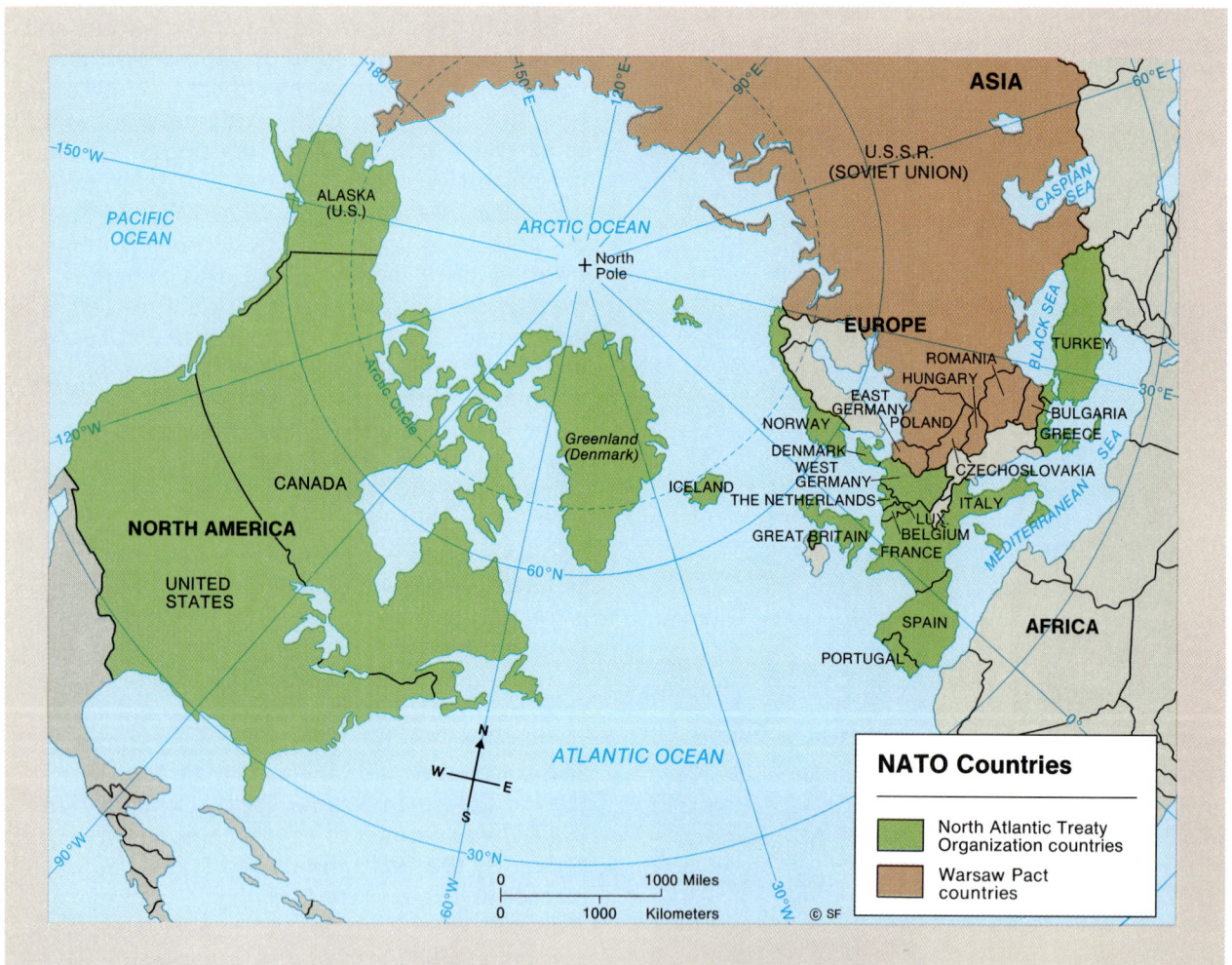

Map Study

This map is a polar map. It shows how the NATO countries would appear if you were looking down on them from above the North Pole. At what points are NATO countries closest to Warsaw Pact countries (those influenced by the Soviet Union)?

rael—receive heavy aid from the United States. The two countries were formerly enemies, but in 1979 U.S. President Jimmy Carter arranged a peace between them. Most other Arab states still oppose Israel.

Foreign competition creates hardships for American industries.

After World War II, the United States provided military support for Japan and West Germany, rather than allow its defeated enemies to re-arm. Japan and West Germany worked hard to rebuld their industries, installing modern factories with up-to-date technology. At first, their workers received much lower pay than workers in the United States.

In the 1950s and 1960s, U.S. industrial products led in worldwide sales, but Japanese, German, and other foreign products were beginning to offer competition. By the 1970s the world demand for American-made industrial goods was slipping. Meanwhile, foreign-made automobiles, radios, cameras, television sets, steel, clothing, and other products flooded the American market.

Trade imbalances. By the 1980s Americans were importing more goods than they exported. The fall in exports by U.S. industrial products for a time was offset by overseas sales of American grain. The production of grain, however, improved worldwide, and so by the mid-1980s, American grain sales, too, were way down. When the value of a country's imports exceeds the value of its exports, a **trade deficit** exists. The trade deficit brought hard times for American industries. As consumers bought imports rather than American goods, many older factories closed, and many workers lost their jobs.

The remaining factories, however, were producing more efficiently than ever before. Prices for American goods did not rise as fast as prices for foreign-made goods—American goods were now more efficiently made, foreign workers

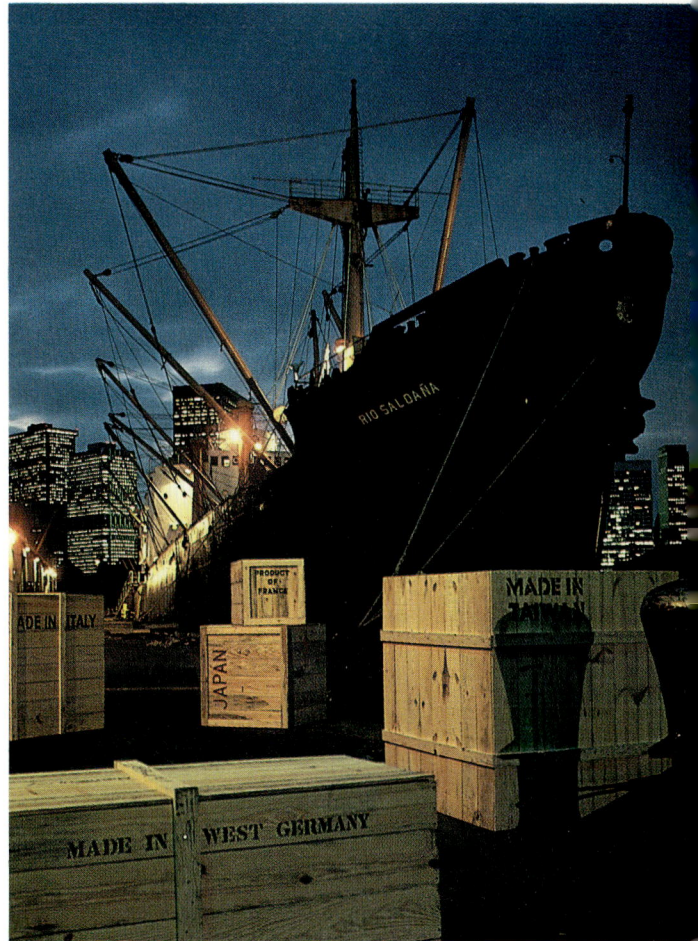

Goods from all over the world are shipped as import trade to the United States.

now received higher wages, and the value of the dollar had fallen. In effect, the United States was working to end its trade imbalance.

Interdependent economies. Ironically, the same countries that help slow our economy also help keep it going. Overseas investors buy stock in American companies and invest in the United States itself through the purchase of government bonds. A bond is a certificate of debt that

169

a government issues with the promise to pay back the buyer with interest. The United States has needed extra money to pay its bills, because of the trade deficit.

The Japanese and West Germans tend to save or invest much of their money instead of spending it. American officials are asking the Japanese and West German governments to encourage their citizens to spend more and thus create markets for American exports.

The leaders of both countries realize that their economies can thrive only as long as the American economy remains healthy so Americans can continue to buy imports. Also, successful American companies earn profits for foreign investors.

An effective way for the Japanese to protect their investments is by starting companies in the United States. Japanese, German, British, Dutch, Canadian, and other foreign companies all own industrial plants in our country. These plants employ American workers and pay U.S. Taxes, but their profits go to overseas investors. American companies have similar overseas ventures.

Technology promises to renew the American economy.

Electronics is an American industry that has boomed over the last couple of decades, especially in the computer field. In factories, computer-controlled robots now do many routine jobs. Millions of offices now use microcomputers to save time and money. Computers are also used to help teach, to communicate messages, to diagnose diseases, and for many other purposes.

Promising news for American industry lies in the development of new, tough plastics and ceramics. These innovations are being used to improve products once made of more costly materials—bridges, ice-skating rinks, helicopter rotors, lightweight motors, rustless knives, and scissors that never need sharpening.

Exciting developments today are in ceramic superconductors and genetic engineering. A **superconductor** is a material that conducts electricity without resistance. Ordinary materials such as copper wire resist the flow of electricity and so waste energy. Once superconductors are perfected, they may be used to produce smaller and faster computers, batteries that last indefinitely, and trains that move above the ground at high speed.

Genetic engineering is a way of altering the basic gene strength of living organisms to combat disease. It holds promise of producing improved crops and livestock, along with healthier and longer lives for humans.

Section 6 Review

Locating Key Places
Locate the following place on the map on page 621: Persian Gulf

Identifying Key Terms
Define the following terms: embargo, alliance, guerrilla, trade deficit, superconductor

Reviewing Main Ideas
1. In what ways does the United States influence other regions of the world?
2. How does foreign competition affect the United States?
3. Explain why technology is important to the American economy.

Thinking Critically: Predict Effects
Do you think the United States should import capital from Japan and other countries? What benefits might result? What disadvantages might you predict?

MAP LESSON

Reading Topographic Maps

If you were a hiker, civic planner, or oil explorer, you would find a map like this very useful. The U.S. Geological Survey has published thousands of detailed topographic maps like the one pictured here of Crater Lake in Oregon.

These maps show both the physical and cultural features of the subject area. The lines on the map, called contour lines, connect places of equal elevation above sea level. Any place located on a line is at the elevation written on that line. Places in between lines are at elevations between those marked on the two lines. Lines that are close together show rapid elevation change, indicating a steep slope.

Green areas on the map represent forest cover. Along with color, symbols are commonly used on topographic maps. Symbols may represent roads, buildings, or mines.

Review

Are these statements true or false? Correct those that are false.

1. Crater Lake is surrounded by a gently sloping landscape.
2. Wizard Island reaches 6,940 feet above sea level.
3. The park headquarters are near Pumice Point.
4. Phantom Ship is really a small island.
5. Eagle Point is lower than Applegate Peak.

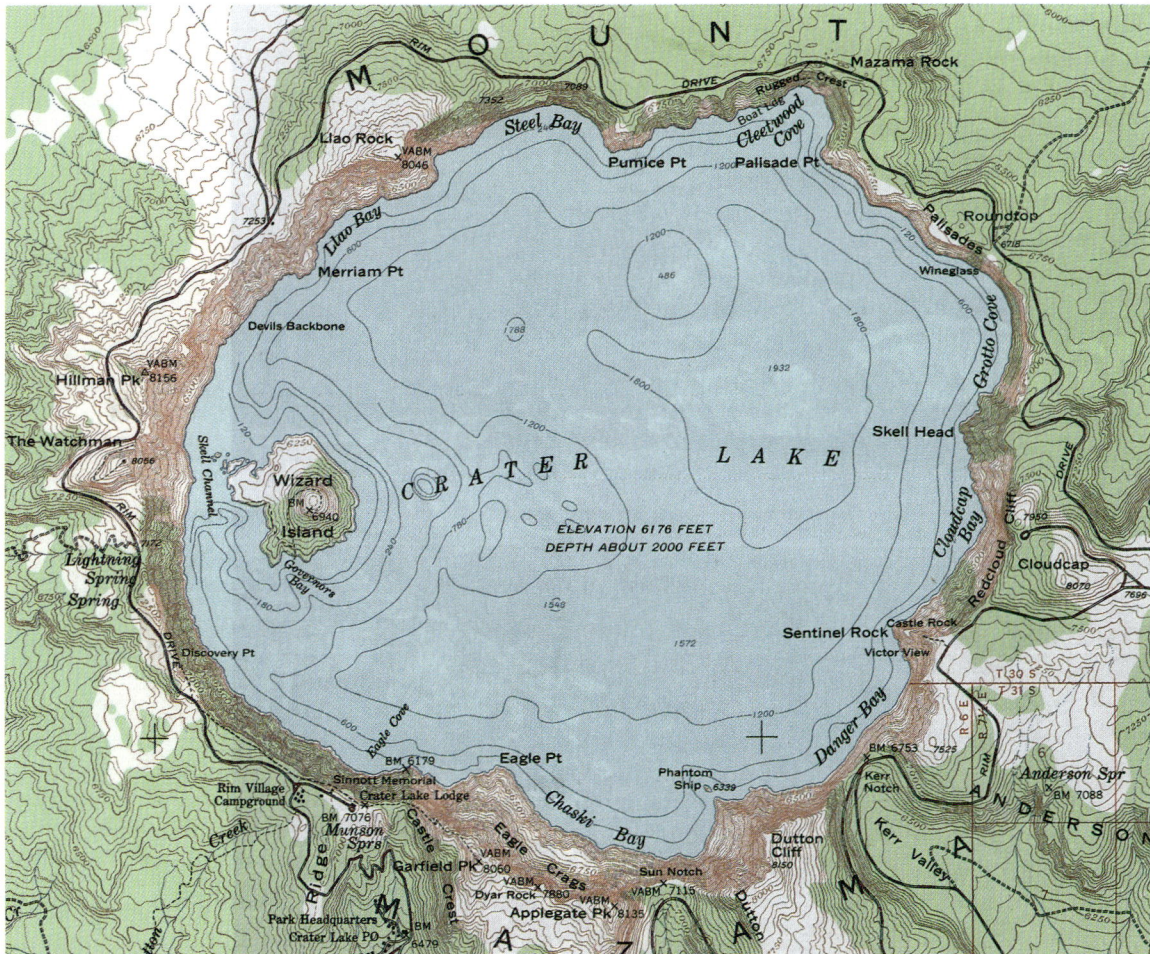

Review

Section Summaries

1. The Northeast Rocky soil and a cool, wet climate make farming difficult in much of the Northeast. Rural northeasterners do farm, and they also engage in fishing and forestry. People of the urban Northeast work in jobs related to trade, finance, and manufacturing.

2. The South Wide plains areas and a warm climate make the South ideal for farming. Rural southerners also make a living from logging, fishing, and mining. Population of southern cities has grown recently. Government, tourism, shipping, and oil-related industries attract workers to Southern cities.

3. The Midwest Level land and warm, wet summers make agriculture big business in the Midwest. In addition, the location of the Midwest has made its cities important centers for manufacturing, trade, transportation, and tourism.

4. Case Study: Tribune, Kansas The small town of Tribune became the county seat of Greeley County, Kansas, because of its central location. Although Tribune remains a small rural town, its citizens reflect the essence of American institutions and values.

5. The West The West is divided into two groups of states—the Mountain West and the Pacific West. The dry climate challenges its farmers and ranchers to use the available water efficiently. In addition to farm products, the West is an important source of energy, minerals, and lumber.

6. The United States and the World The rivalry between the United States and the Soviet Union affects other governments, especially in Central America, Western Europe, and Southwest Asia. Foreign competition has resulted in trade imbalances that have weakened the American economy.

Using Geography Skills

Reviewing the Map Lesson

Use the topographic map on page 171 to answer these questions.
1. What is the deepest point in Crater Lake?
2. What is the elevation of Applegate Peak?
3. What is the name of the bay near Wizard Island? What is the name of the nearest channel?

Using Social Studies Skills

1. Distinguishing fact from opinion. Copy and read an article from a recent newspaper or news magazine about trade relations with Japan. Highlight statements of opinion with a marker. Remember that facts can be verified, but opinions state feelings or beliefs.

2. Translating information from one medium to another. Use the information below to make a line graph that compares the 1970 and 1980 populations of the four U.S. census regions. Show the different regions with different colored lines. The following populations have been rounded to the nearest million. Northeast (1970:49, 1980:49); Midwest (1970:57, 1980:59); South (1970:63, 1980:75); West (1970:35, 1980:43).

Testing for Understanding

Locating Key Places

Match each description below with the name of the place.
1. largest city in the Midwest
2. a center for petrochemical industries in the South
3. Pennsylvania city, part of the Northeast's megalopolis
4. a financial center that is the largest city in the United States
5. a major government city
6. automotive center
7. New England city, part of the Northeast's megalopolis
8. major port city noted for its French heritage
9. center for Latin American-based tourism and finance
10. second largest U.S. city
a. Boston
b. New York City
c. Philadelphia
d. Washington, D.C.
e. Miami
f. New Orleans

g. Houston
h. Chicago
i. Detroit
j. Los Angeles

Recalling Key Terms
Define these terms in your own words.

Section 1
reforestation
electronics

Section 2
forest conversion
bayou
estuary
petrochemical

Section 3
agribusiness
foreign trade zone
duty

Section 4
county seat
speculator
fallow

Section 5
ground water
dry farming
chip
freeway

Section 6
guerrilla
embargo
alliance
trade deficit
superconductor

Reviewing Main Ideas
Section 1
1. How have the land and climate shaped life in the Northeast?

2. How do people in the rural Northeast earn a living?
3. How do people of the urban Northeast earn a living?
4. Which large cities of the Northeast form a megalopolis?

Section 2
1. How do land and climate in the South differ from the Northeast?
2. How do people in the rural South earn a living?
3. What factors have brought workers to southern cities?
4. How do people earn a living in Washington, D.C.? Miami? New Orleans? Houston?

Section 3
1. Describe the land and climate of the Midwest.
2. How do people in the rural Midwest earn a living?
3. How do people earn a living in the urban Midwest?

Section 4
1. How did Tribune become the county seat for Greeley County?
2. What ideas about farming helped Tribune prosper?
3. How is Tribune different today than in 1900?
4. How does the belief in American institutions support the people of Greeley County?

Section 5
1. What are the two groups of states that make up the West?
2. What methods help western farmers and ranchers adapt to the region's land and climate?
3. What are the West's most

important natural resources?
4. How have people of the urban West solved problems related to rapid population growth?

Section 6
1. How does the United States influence other regions of the world?
2. How does foreign competition affect American industries?
3. Why is technology important to the American economy?

Thinking Critically
1. Assess Cause and Effect. Think about what you've read about population trends in the United States. What factors do you think have caused people to move—from rural to urban areas, and from one census region to another?

2. Make Decisions. Acid rain is a serious issue between the United States and Canada. Make a proposal to resolve the problem. Think of the perspectives of the various groups involved.

Canada

In this chapter, you will explore Canada—the second largest country in the world.

Sections

Eastern Canada

Preview

Key Places
Where are these places located?
1 Bay of Fundy
2 Halifax
3 St. Lawrence River
4 Ottawa
   See the globe below.

Key Terms
What do these terms mean?
province   bilingual
territory   separatist

Main Ideas
As you read, look for answers to these questions:
● How do natural resources affect the people of Newfoundland?
● What economic activities support the Maritime Provinces?
● What kind of culture does Quebec have?
● What are the major occupations in Ontario?

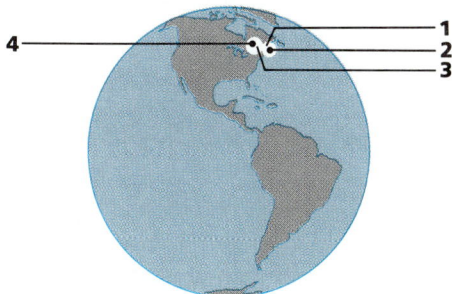

Were the soil as good as the harbors, it would be fine; but this [coast] should not be called Terre Neuve [new land], being composed of stones and frightful rocks and uneven places; for on this entire northern coast I saw not one cartload of earth, though I landed in many places. . . . To conclude, I am inclined to regard this land as the one God gave to Cain.

Jacques Cartier, *Première Relation*

The people of Newfoundland depend on natural resources.

Explorers often exaggerated the wealth and beauty of newly discovered lands. Not so Jacques Cartier, the founder of France's New World empire. When Cartier made his first voyage to Newfoundland in 1534, he remarked that the land was a fit place of punishment for Adam and Eve's son Cain after he had killed his brother Abel. For years, Newfoundland's harsh and barren coast was mainly a place to cut, salt, and dry the cod, salmon, and seals caught in abundance there.

Newfoundland is one of Canada's ten **provinces**—political divisions like the states in the United States. Canada also includes two huge regions that are still **territories**—areas that have only a limited governmental structure because so few people live there. Canada's provinces and territories are shown on the map on page 176. Eastern Canada includes five provinces besides Newfoundland—Nova Scotia, Prince Edward Island, New Brunswick, Quebec, and Ontario. Locate these provinces on the map.

You can see on the map that Newfoundland province is made up of two parts—a mainland area, known as Labrador, and the island of

Facing page: **Snow-blanketed mountains form a magnificent backdrop for a lone skier in western Canada.**

175

Canada

🟩 Commercial farming	🟨 Ranching	◆ Mining	🟪 Little or no economic activity	⊛ National capital

Commercial farming

Irrigated farming

Dairying

Ranching

Forests

Lumbering

Mining

Commercial fishing

Urban land use

Little or no economic activity

National capital

Provincial or territorial capital

Other cities

Map Study

The map shows political and economic information about Canada. What is the provincial capital of Manitoba? What minerals are found in Quebec?

176

Newfoundland. Labrador is part of the Canadian Shield, which curves around Hudson Bay and makes up about half of Canada. The island of Newfoundland is an extension of the Appalachian Highlands.

Resources from the sea always have been important in Newfoundland. For centuries, Beothuk Indians hunted seals, walruses, and seabirds off the coast. Europeans established their first permanent outposts, or fishing villages, during the 1600s. Most of the settlers were English.

About 579,000 people live in Newfoundland today. Twenty thousand of them earn a living from fishing. However, mining is the province's leading economic activity. Iron ore is mined and processed in western Labrador, and natural gas is obtained off the coast.

The Maritime Provinces depend on many industries.

The Maritime Provinces include Nova Scotia, Prince Edward Island, and New Brunswick. These provinces are part of the Appalachian Highlands and are mostly hilly.

The first Europeans in what is now the Maritime Provinces were French. Their land, known as Acadia, was developed to support fur trade with the Micmac Indians. The French Acadians built dikes to keep out the sea and began to farm the rich, swampy land along the Bay of Fundy. Britain finally took over Acadia in the 1700s, scattering the Acadians from Maine to Louisiana. Still, one-fourth to one-third of the people in the Maritime Provinces are descended from the Acadians. Most of them are bilingual. **Bilingual** means having the ability to speak two languages, in this case French and English.

Nova Scotia. Today Nova Scotia is the most populous Maritime Province, with 880,000 people. About one-third of the people live in rural areas and work at farming, fishing, forestry, and mining. Farmers near the Bay of Fundy produce fruit and dairy products. On Cape Breton, a hilly island in the northeast, miners extract coal, salt, and gypsum—a mineral used to make fertilizer. The leading center of manufacturing in Nova Scotia is Halifax, which is also an important seaport and the provincial capital.

Prince Edward Island. Since colonial days, people on Prince Edward Island have made a living by farming. The island's deep soil produces potatoes, fruits such as strawberries and blueberries, and field crops such as oats and corn.

Scenery is another important resource on Prince Edward Island. Its beautiful scenery has helped make tourism a major industry.

New Brunswick. Forestry is an important part of New Brunswick's economy because forests cover most of the province. Wood is fed into pulp and paper mills to produce newsprint, the paper on which newspapers are printed.

One of the newer industries in New Brunswick is the production of electricity. The province has a nuclear power station as well as oil-fueled and hydroelectric stations. Quebec, Nova Scotia, Prince Edward Island, and the state of Maine buy electricity from New Brunswick.

The culture of Quebec is predominantly French.

Quebec has the largest area of all the Canadian provinces and the second largest population. Its main landform region is the Canadian Shield. As you can see from the population distribution map on page 90, however, the most heavily populated area is the fertile valley of the St. Lawrence River.

Four out of five people there speak French. For 200 years in Quebec, the Anglophone, or English-speaking, minority dominated the Francophone, or French-speaking, majority. Children who spoke French at home were taught in English at school. Traffic signs were written in English, not French.

This square in Montreal is named for Jacques Cartier. He was the first European explorer to reach the site that became Montreal.

Quebec's independence movement. During the 1960s Francophones who called themselves the Québécois [kā'be kwä'] began asserting political power. Legislators elected by the Québécois declared French the official language of the province in 1974. Many Québécois were **separatists.** That is, they wanted to separate from Canada and form an independent country.

In the early 1980s, Quebec experienced an economic slump, partly because some major companies left the province. Using only French, they said, made business across provincial boundaries difficult. Soon the problem of unemployment overshadowed the separatist issue.

Life in Montreal. With a population of almost 3 million, the metropolitan area of Montreal is the second largest in Canada. You can see on the map on page 176 that Montreal is in a commanding position on the St. Lawrence River, not far from the Great Lakes. Montreal also lies near the eastern end of the St. Lawrence Seaway, making the city an international port and transportation center. In addition to transportation, the St. Lawrence River supplies hydroelectric power for factories. Montreal is a center for oil refining, food processing, and textile manufacturing.

Montreal's Old Town is a major tourist attraction. This district's gothic churches, horse-drawn carriages, and cobblestone streets let visitors imagine themselves in a French city back in the 17th or 18th century.

Many Ontario jobs are in farming, mining, and service industries.

Like Quebec, Ontario is dominated by the St. Lawrence River and the Canadian Shield. A lowland area borders Hudson Bay. Grain from the interior is shipped from the Hudson Bay port of Churchill during the summer.

Ontario's farmland is much richer and more extensive than in Quebec. Ontario also has more towns and cities. In fact, more people live in Ontario than in any other Canadian province.

Primary industries. Most farming in Ontario takes place on its southern peninsula. Breezes from nearby Lakes Ontario, Erie, and Huron warm the air over the peninsula during the winter and prolong its growing season. Two-thirds of Ontario's agricultural income is from livestock and products such as milk, eggs, and poultry.

Piles of iron ore stand ready for rail transport in Ontario.

Ontario is Canada's leading producer of salt, gold, silver, platinum, zinc, nickel, and copper. Salt is mined under Lake Huron near Goderich. The metals are drawn from the Canadian Shield.

Service industries. More than half of Ontario's population lives and works in metropolitan areas. The city with the largest population in Ontario and in Canada is Toronto. More than 3 million people live in Toronto and its suburbs, and most of them work in service industries, especially finance. The city's stock exchange is second in size in North America only to that of New York City.

Government is the largest employer in Ottawa, Canada's capital. England's Queen Victoria named Ottawa the capital in 1858 because she thought Montreal was too French and Toronto too English. Government workers come from all parts of Canada and around the world. As a result, Ottawa has a more cosmopolitan atmosphere than most cities.

Section 1 Review

Locating Key Places
Locate the following places on the map on page 176: Bay of Fundy, Halifax, St. Lawrence River, Ottawa

Identifying Key Terms
Define the following terms: province, territory, bilingual, separatist

Reviewing Main Ideas
1. How do natural resources affect life in Newfoundland?
2. What jobs do people in the Maritime Provinces do?
3. How do the people of Quebec differ from other Canadians?
4. Describe the jobs people have in Ontario.

Thinking Critically: Make Hypotheses
Use the map on page 176 to locate the capitals and major cities of eastern Canada. Why do you think they are located where they are?

179

Western and Northern Canada

Preview

Key Places
Where are these places located?
1 Winnipeg
2 Edmonton
3 Arctic Archipelago
See the globe below.

Key Terms
What do these terms mean?
métis
archipelago

Main Ideas
As you read, look for answers to these questions.
- What economic activities are important in the Prairie Provinces?
- How has the location of British Columbia affected its economy?
- What changes opened the development of the northern territories?
- How has life among Canada's Inuit and Indians changed?

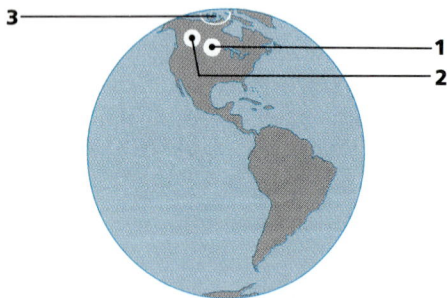

The wind is still sweet, but there is no wildness to it and it no longer seems to have wandered a great way over grass and flowers. It now smells of dry straw and bread.

Mary Hiemstra, *Gully Farm*

The Prairie Provinces are important for their farming and mining.

Canadian writer Mary Hiemstra described how farm fields had replaced wild prairies in Saskatchewan, her home. Saskatchewan is the middle of the three Prairie Provinces, which also include Manitoba to the east and Alberta to the west. Much of this wide, flat to rolling prairie belongs to the Interior Plains. Other large areas lie within the Canadian Shield, and part of western Alberta is in the Rocky Mountains.

The Prairie Provinces together with British Columbia make up western Canada. Northern Canada includes the Northwest Territories and Yukon Territory. Locate the provinces of western Canada and the territories of northern Canada on the population distribution map on page 90. Can you guess from the map why the Northwest and Yukon territories are not provinces?

Manitoba. Although 85 percent of Manitoba's 1 million people are native-born Canadians, the province is more ethnically diverse than any other. Many Manitobans have British origins. Others are descendants of settlers who came from Russia, Iceland, Poland, and other countries in the 1890s and early 1900s. One hundred thousand Manitobans are Cree, Sioux, or Ojibwa Indians or métis [mā tēs']. A **métis** is a Canadian with both European and American Indian ancestors.

Manitobans in rural areas work in trapping, fishing, mining, and farming. The province is a leading producer of nickel, gold, copper, and zinc. In the southwest is a rich deposit of petroleum. Manitoba's richest farmland is also in the southwest. Farmers there raise cattle and crops such as oats, wheat, and barley.

Riders compete in the Chuck Wagon Race, part of the Calgary Stampede rodeo held each year in Calgary, Alberta.

About 600,000 Manitobans live in the capital city of Winnipeg. Some people work in manufacturing, often processing the raw materials from rural Manitoba. Two examples are the city's meat-packing plants and clothing factories that use goose down, the soft underfeathers from geese, to make coats and vests.

Alberta and Saskatchewan. Like twins, Alberta and Saskatchewan share many characteristics. Both provinces are dry as a result of being in the rain shadow of the Canadian Rockies. Both provinces were settled by the same immigrant groups: Scots, Germans, Ukrainians, and Hungarians.

Alberta and Saskatchewan also have similar economies. Both provinces rely heavily on wheat and cattle. The provinces export wheat to the whole world, including the Soviet Union and China. Alberta is Canada's leading producer of petroleum. Saskatchewan is second.

Differences between the provinces do exist. Alberta's population of more than 2 million is double Saskatchewan's population. Edmonton, Calgary, and other Alberta cities have become major urban centers as a result of the oil industry. Saskatchewan has remained largely rural. Calgary was the site of the 1988 winter Olympics.

British Columbia's location has shaped its industries.

The Rocky Mountains and the Pacific Mountain Region are the main landform regions in British Columbia. The Rocky Mountains virtually cut off British Columbia from the rest of western Canada. As a result, British Columbia was the first province to consider separating from Canada. In the mid-1800s the British prevented the break by building the Canadian Pacific Railroad between the province and the east.

Shipping in British Columbia. Vancouver is British Columbia's largest city. With a population of more than 1 million, it is the third largest metropolitan area in Canada. It is also a leading port, where ships from any port on the Pacific come and go. When the Canadian Pacific Railroad made Vancouver its western terminal, cargo and passenger ships from Asia began using it as their North American port of entry. Eventually, the transportation systems that ran through Vancouver spanned the globe.

Someday Prince Rupert in the far north may rival Vancouver as a major Pacific port. The government of Alberta has funded development of facilities there for handling grain, coal, and forest products.

Primary industries. The economy of British Columbia depends heavily on natural resources. Forest products such as lumber, pulp, and newsprint account for half of the province's income. The mining of coal, lead, zinc, and copper also contributes heavily to the economy. Fishing and farming are important as well.

Improved transportation has opened the northern territories.

The Northwest Territories and the Yukon Territory are mostly tundra with poor soil and a cold climate. The main landform regions are the Canadian Shield, the Interior Plains, the Rocky Mountains, and the Pacific Mountain Region. The Northwest Territories includes one of the largest archipelagos in the world— the Arctic Archipelago. An **archipelago** [är′kə pel′ə gō] is a group of islands. The Arctic Archipelago includes hundreds of thousands of square miles of cold, barren land in the freezing Arctic Ocean.

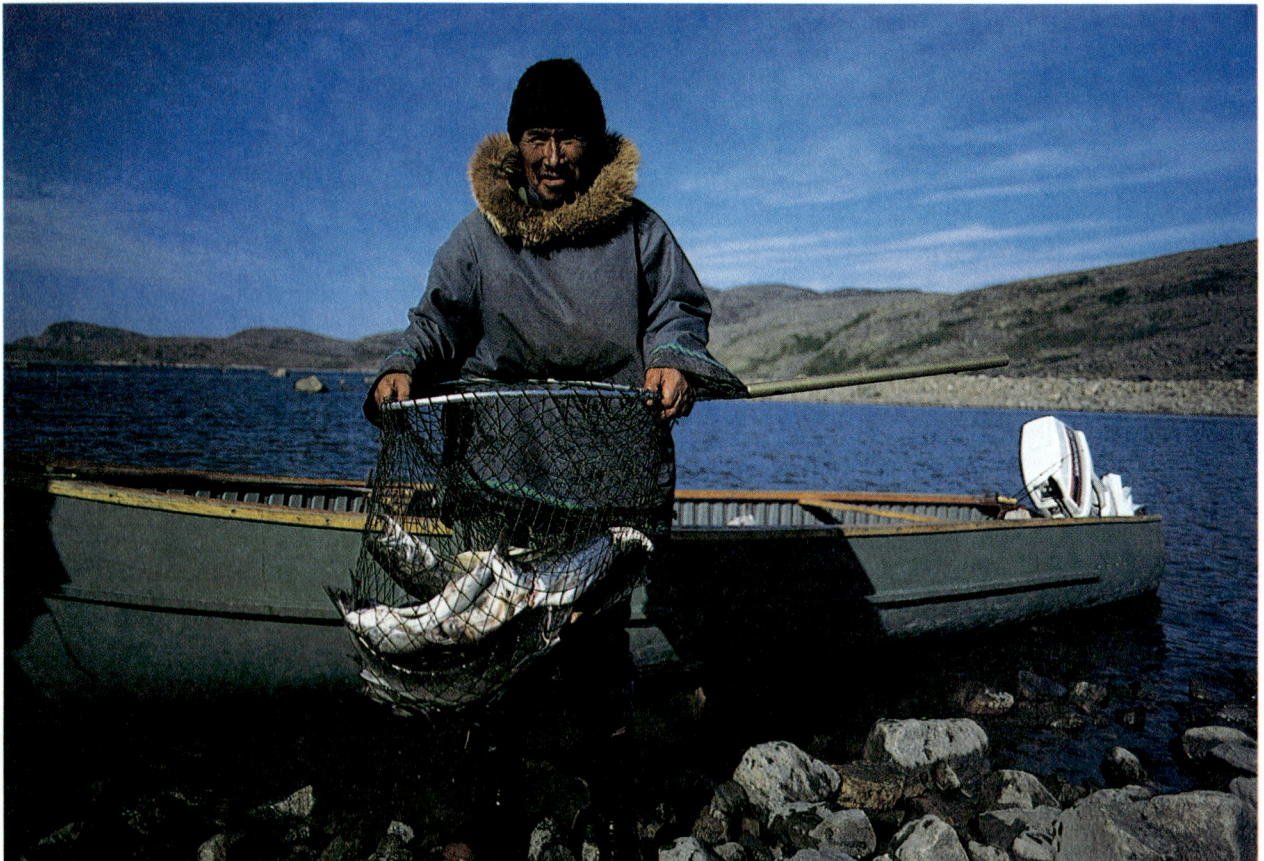

Canadian waters support both individual fishers and large commercial fleets. This Inuit fisherman pulls in his catch of fish.

Most newcomers arrived in the Yukon Territory after gold was discovered there in 1896. Prospectors from all over the world rushed to the gold fields at the junction of the Klondike and Yukon rivers. The city of Dawson sprang up nearby and at the height of the gold rush boasted a population of 25,000. When the mines were played out in 1904, Dawson's population dwindled. Today most of Dawson's 800 residents make their living helping tourists recapture the excitement of the Klondike gold rush.

A wealth of minerals still lies beneath the surface of the land in the territories: zinc, lead, gold, silver, copper, and asbestos. At one time these rich deposits were virtually untapped. Suitable transportation for carrying out the ore did not exist. The harbors and rivers in the territories are frozen most of the year, and building roads over the permafrost tundra proved difficult.

During the 1950s, however, new technology made possible the construction of the Alaska Highway through Yukon Territory. A railroad was also built from Alberta to the Hay River in the Northwest Territories in 1965. To aid in the development of petroleum reserves, another road was built through the Northwest Territories to a port on the Arctic Ocean in 1973. As a result, mining and population in the territories have increased.

Many Inuit and Indians have adopted modern ways of living.

Although the Northwest and Yukon territories make up two-fifths of Canada's land area, only about 75,000 people live there. About one-fourth are Canadian Inuit [in'ü it], also known as Eskimos. A smaller number are northern Indians, including Slaves and Hares.

At one time the Inuit wandered from place to place, hunting and fishing to meet their needs. In the winter the Inuit hunted seals. In the summer they caught salmon and hunted whales,

seals, and caribou, a type of reindeer. The Inuit used the animals for food and made tents and clothing from the skins and hides. They fashioned tools and other objects from stone, ivory, and whale bone.

Today most Inuit and Indians live in permanent settlements like Baker Lake and Chesterfield Inlet on Hudson Bay. There they work for oil and mining companies and buy their food and clothing in stores. The modern Inuit and Indians live in frame houses instead of skin tents and travel in snowmobiles or motorboats.

Although some Inuit and Indians still hunt, fish, and trap for a living, increasingly their lives have become more like that of other Canadians. Ironically, as their unique way of life disappears, the original Inuit and Indian place names in the far north are now being restored.

Section 2 Review

Locating Key Places
Locate the following places on the map on page 176: Winnipeg, Edmonton, Arctic Archipelago

Identifying Key Terms
Define the following terms: métis, archipelago

Reviewing Main Ideas
1. What kinds of jobs are important in the Prairie Provinces?
2. How has the location of British Columbia helped its economy?
3. Why have the natural resources of the northern territories been developed only recently?
4. How has life changed for Canada's Inuit and Indians?

Thinking Critically: Analyze Comparisons
Think about what you have read about western and northern Canada. Are these parts of Canada more like eastern Canada or more like the corresponding areas of the United States? Give examples from the text to support your opinions.

Canada's Relations with the United States

Preview

Key Places
Where is this place located?
1 Sudbury, Ontario
  See the globe below.

Key Terms
What do these terms mean?
tariff
free trade
protectionism
subsidy

Main Ideas
As you read, look for answers to these questions:
• How are the economies of the United States and Canada linked?
• How do U.S. films, television, and music affect Canadian culture?
• How does the United States affect Canada's environment?

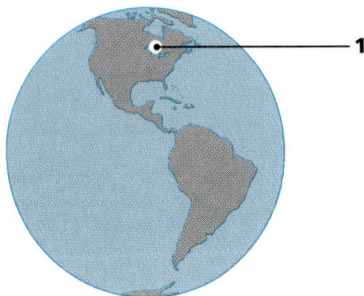

We all know that the Canadian nation . . . came into being because our ancestors repudiated the most important single event in the history of the western hemisphere, the American Revolution. Canada exists today because they said no to that. . . . The reason was basic. . . . They wanted to survive as a people, and it was as simple as that.

Hugh MacLennan, *The Colour of Canada*

The U.S. and Canadian economies form a major trading partnership.
The United States and Canada share many things besides their 4,000-mile-long common border. Life on either side of the border can be much the same, as you have read. However, because the United States has 10 times as many people as Canada and because 95 percent of the Canadian people lie within 200 miles of this border, U.S. influence in Canada is strong.

Trade is an important tie binding the Canadian economy to that of the United States. The United States and Canada are major trading partners. In 1986 the United States sold more goods to Canada than to any other country. As the table on 185 shows, Canada ranked second to Japan in exporting goods to the United States. In addition, the United States and Canada trade services and make investments across their borders.

Most goods enter the United States and Canada freely. However, in order to protect native agriculture and industries, tariffs are added to some goods. A **tariff** is a tax that a government charges on imports. A tariff raises the price of foreign goods, encouraging people to buy from their own country. Import quotas on goods are another way of protecting a nation's producers.

The absence of tariffs, quotas, and other trade barriers between countries is called **free trade.** People who favor such policies argue that free trade will allow a country's exports and its economy to expand. A policy that makes use of tariffs, quotas, and other trade barriers is called **protectionism.** Arguments in favor of protectionism are usually based on a nation's national security interests, the need to help developing industries, or the desire to protect jobs within the nation's industry or agriculture.

For example, most Canadian farmers want to keep import quotas on U.S. grains and farm products. U.S. produce is sometimes cheaper than Canadian produce because beginning in 1985, the U.S. government has spent billions of dollars to help U.S. farmers by subsidizing its farm exports. A **subsidy** is economic aid from the government. Another trade agreement protects the automobile industries in each country.

Four times in the past 100 years the United States and Canada have tried to establish a free-trade policy, most recently in 1987. Finally, in 1988 the U.S. Congress and the Canadian Parliament agreed to form the world's largest common market to date.

U.S. films, television, and music may be drowning Canadian culture.

Most Canadians and Americans share language, values, and wide-ranging ethnic backgrounds. Yet the people of Canada and the United States have separate and distinct identities. Despite this, most Canadian television, films, and popular music reflect American culture. For example, Canadian movie theaters show foreign films, mostly from the United States, 97 percent of the time. More than 70 percent of Canada's television programming comes from the United States, and less than 3 percent of its prime-time television features Canadian programs. More than 80 percent of all records and tapes are of foreign origin.

Three out of four books sold in Canada are imported. Foreign-owned companies, many of them American, publish almost 60 percent of Canada's school textbooks.

Not all popular culture originates in the United States, however. The National Film

U.S. Trading Partners
The chart below lists the major countries with whom the U.S. buys and sells goods.

U.S. Exports (in millions of dollars)*		U.S. Imports (in millions of dollars)*	
Country of destination:		Country of origin:	
Canada	$45,333	Japan	$81,986
Japan	26,882	Canada	68,147
Mexico	12,392	Germany	25,301
United Kingdom	11,418	Taiwan	19,771
Germany	10,561	Mexico	17,196
Netherlands	7,848	United Kingdom	15,308
France	7,216	South Korea	12,683
South Korea	6,355	Italy	10,505
Australia	5,551	France	9,962
Taiwan	5,524	Hong Kong	8,865

*1986 Figures

A movie poster shows the impact of American culture on Canada.

Board, a Canadian government agency, produces world-famous documentary films. The agency also makes animated films and full-length features of great interest to both Canadian and foreign audiences. Films made for Quebec's French-speaking audiences also tend to express Canadian subjects and concerns.

Canada says it is harmed by acid rain from the United States.

Canadians are concerned about developing their nation's wealth without injury to the land, as are people everywhere. Like the northeastern part of the United States, eastern Canada is affected by acid rain. Airborne pollutants, particularly sulfur dioxide and nitrogen oxide, come from smokestacks and car exhaust. For example, a plant for smelting nickel at Sudbury, Ontario, gives off more sulfur dioxide than any other source in North America. However, Canadians say that nearly half of their airborne pollution appears to come from factories and exhaust pipes in the Ohio River Valley in the United States.

Various factors affect a region's sensitivity to acid rain. The amount of rainfall and the thickness and mineral content of the soil are important. Soils made from limestone, such as those of the Interior Plains, tend to counterbalance the acid, lessening its effect. However, glaciers long ago scraped the limestone layer from the Canadian Shield, leaving the vulnerable bedrock granite.

Scientists in both the United States and Canada are studying ways to decrease the effects of acid rain. Canada has promised by 1994 to cut its own contribution to air pollution by 50 percent. Both countries also agreed in 1986 to take specific actions to control air pollution, including a $5 billion program of clean-coal research.

Section 3 Review

Locating Key Places
Locate the following place on the map on page 176: Sudbury, Ontario

Identifying Key Terms
Define the following terms: tariff, free trade, protectionism, subsidy

Reviewing Main Ideas
1. How are the economies of the United States and Canada tied together?
2. In what ways do U.S. films, television, and music affect Canadian culture?
3. Explain how Canada's environment is affected by the United States.

Thinking Critically: Identify Assumptions
What assumptions are being made in the following statement? "The United States needs a tariff to protect its industries from foreign competition. Without this competition, the country can decrease unemployment."

Reading Newspaper Maps

Every day newspapers provide maps to clarify and define political or other geographical situations. They are usually clear and up-to-date.

The map on this page is an example of a newspaper map that appeared in many American newspapers on August 18, 1985. The map was printed to help readers understand "the cold war over Arctic waters," a political dispute between the United States and Canada.

The map can also help you to understand the history of the conflict. For almost 500 years, sailors have been searching for a Northwest Passage that would cross North America. In nearly every attempt, the sailors were blocked by ice. Without a Northwest Passage, sailors who wanted to go from Thule, Greenland, to Point Barrow, Alaska, needed to travel thousands of miles out of their way to use the Panama Canal. Today the route through northern Canada is needed as a pathway for shipping Alaskan oil to markets in the North Atlantic Ocean.

To create a Northwest Passage, the United States Coast Guard designed a special icebreaker ship called the *Polar Sea*. The icebreaker went on its mission to clear a Northwest Passage in the ice between Greenland and Alaska in the summer of 1985.

The ship encountered ice 18 feet thick along the way, but it accomplished its mission in about two weeks. The dotted line on the map shows its route. About midway through the voyage, however, an airplane hired by some private Canadian citizens circled the icebreaker and dropped letters of protest. The protesters objected to the presence of a foreign ship in Canadian waters without official permission.

Canada had claimed control of all ocean waters up to 100 nautical miles offshore for defense and environmental purposes, and up to 200 miles in order to regulate the ocean's economic use. In effect, these claims put the entire Northwest Passage under Canadian control.

The United States has long held that the passage is an international waterway. In 1988, however, our government agreed, without recognizing claims of ownership, to seek permission before entering the Arctic waters.

Review

1. What industry would most benefit from an open passage?
2. If these were international waters, could ships of the Soviet Union also use them without permission?

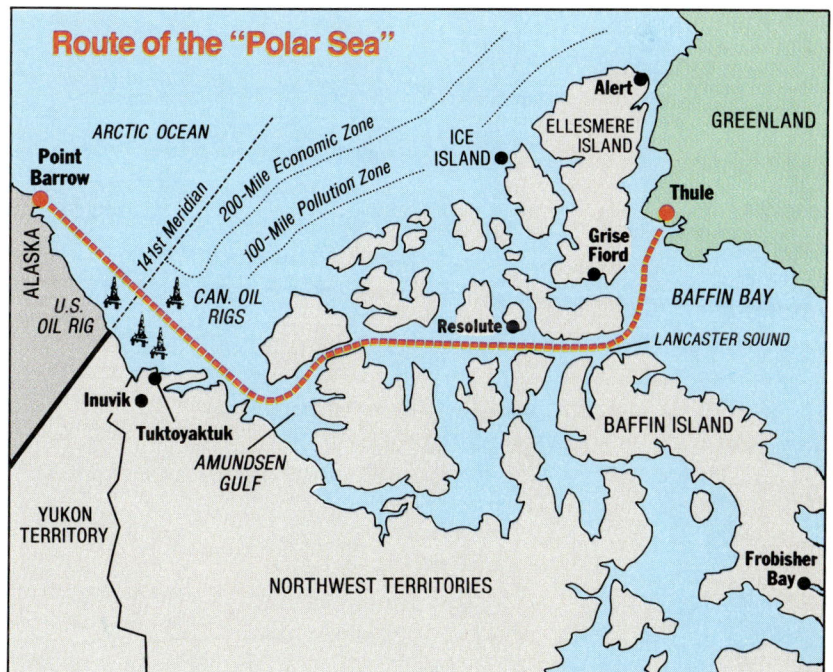

Route of the "Polar Sea"

Review

Section Summaries

1. Eastern Canada Most of the people of Newfoundland and the Maritime Provinces depend on fishing and mining for a living. Montreal, the major city of Quebec, is a center of transportation and French culture. Both Montreal and Toronto attract many Canadian and foreign tourists.

2. Western and northern Canada The Prairie Provinces—Manitoba, Saskatchewan, and Alberta—all have diverse populations and important farming and mining industries. Shipping, forestry, mining, fishing, and farming are important in British Columbia. In the Northwest and Yukon territories, minerals and petroleum are major resources.

3. Canada's relations with the United States The economies of the United States and Canada are linked in a powerful trading partnership. However, many Canadians fear that American popular culture will swamp their own film, television, and music industries. Another American import—acid rain—is even more feared and disliked.

Queen Charlotte Islands

Sea Lion

Peregrine Falcon

Blue Whale

Black Bear

Moresby Island and the many smaller islands off its coast are part of the Queen Charlotte Islands of Canada. Here can be found many unique species of plants and animals as well as other wildlife. Now this unspoiled wilderness is attracting oil and lumber companies who want to develop its rich resources.

Masset

Graham Island

Hecate

Queen Charlotte Islands

Skidegate • Sandspit

Moresby Island

Strait

Rose Harbour

N
W — E
S

0   40 Miles
0   40 Kilometers

PACIFIC OCEAN

ALASKA (U.S.)

CANADA

Queen Charlotte Islands

PACIFIC OCEAN

UNITED STATES

BRITISH COLUMBIA

© SF

Using Geography Skills

Reviewing the Map Lesson

A newspaper map like the one at left was used to clarify a debate within Canada over whether the southern part of the Queen Charlotte Islands should be opened to economic development. Use the map to answer the following questions.
1. What economic activity is suggested by the map?
2. What wildlife could possibly be endangered by economic development?
3. Off the coast of which province do the Queen Charlotte Islands lie?

Using Social Studies Skills

1. Seeing Others' Points of View. Imagine you are a member of a Québécois political party. Write and present a speech explaining why Quebec should separate from the rest of Canada. Try to anticipate the objections that Quebec's Anglophones would have to the separation and answer them in your speech.

2. Perceiving Cause-Effect Relationships. Fold a sheet of paper in half across its width. Label the top half "Before the Canadian Pacific Railroad came to Vancouver" and label the bottom half "After the Canadian Pacific Railroad came to Vancouver." Draw pictures illustrating each label.

Testing for Understanding

Locating Key Places
Match each description below with the name of the place.
1. Canadian national capital
2. site of a large nickel smelting plant
3. Manitoba's capital
4. eastern Canadian waterway
5. Nova Scotia's capital
6. Alberta's capital
7. French Acadians built dikes to reclaim land here
8. group of northern islands
a. Bay of Fundy
b. Halifax
c. St. Lawrence River
d. Ottawa
e. Winnipeg
f. Edmonton
g. Arctic Archipelago
h. Sudbury, Ontario

Recalling Key Terms
Define these terms in your own words.

Section 1
province
territory
bilingual
separatist

Section 2
métis
archipelago

Section 3
tariff
free trade
protectionism
subsidy

Reviewing Main Ideas
Section 1
1. How do natural resources shape life in Newfoundland?
2. What are the major occupations in the Maritime Provinces?
3. Why do the people of Quebec differ from other Canadians?
4. What kinds of work do the people of Ontario do?

Section 2
1. What jobs are important in the Prairie Provinces?
2. How has British Columbia's location helped its economy?
3. Why have the resources of the northern territories been developed only recently?
4. Describe how life among Canada's Inuit and Indians has changed.

Section 3
1. Tell how the economies of the United States and Canada are linked.
2. What effect does American culture have on Canada?
3. In what ways are Canada's environment affected by the United States?

Thinking Critically
1. Analyze Comparisons. Do you think a state of the United States could vote as the people of Quebec did to use a language other than English? Why or why not?

2. Make Hypotheses. Canada has 10 provinces, 2 territories, and a population of more than 27 million people. The United States has 50 states and a population of more than 240 million. What hypotheses can you make about provincial and territorial governments in Canada as compared with state governments in the United States?

Review

Summarizing the Unit

Chapter 6   The Land and People The United States and Canada possess all the major landform regions: plains, plateaus, hills, and mountains. Air masses help determine North America's climates, which in turn affect the soil and vegetation. First the American Indians and later European settlers used North America's rich resources to meet their needs. As immigrants continued to come, they brought their customs and energies, contributing to the diversity of the United States and Canada.

Chapter 7   The United States People earn a living in similar ways in each of the four census regions of the United States. Rural areas depend on primary industries—farming, fishing, forestry, and mining. People in urban areas engage in manufacturing and service industries. In the Northeast, the emphasis is on trade and finance. In the South, farming and oil-related industries are strong. Farming predominates in the Midwest, where towns like Tribune, Kansas, reflect traditional American values. In the rural West, farming and ranching are important. Electronics is one area of industrial activity.

Chapter 8   Canada Rural Canadians, like their rural American neighbors, earn a living from fishing, farming, forestry, and mining. Similarly, urban Canadians are engaged in finance, tourism, transportation, and manufacturing. The French culture exerts a strong influence, particularly in Quebec. Shipping is a major activity in British Columbia, and minerals and petroleum are the major resources of the Northwest and Yukon territories. The Inuit and Indians of northern Canada, like other Canadians, have adapted their ways of life to the modern world.

Using Writing Skills

After prewriting comes the actual writing stage of the writing process. At this stage, you will use what you've learned about prewriting to prepare a first draft manuscript.

Activity. Choose a city in either the United States or Canada. Imagine you work for the city's Chamber of Commerce and must persuade the executives of a certain company to build a plant in your city. Plan a letter that lists the city's assets and explains how these assets will benefit the company. Before you write your letter, prepare in the following ways:

1. Find out what the city has to offer as far as raw materials, a labor pool, power sources, transportation for goods and people, and other natural and human resources. Use sources like travel guides and encyclopedias to get this information. On index cards, write down the important details that you may want to use in your letter.

2. Select a company that needs what the city has to offer. You might look through a phone book to locate such a company. Then call the company's public relations office to request more information, perhaps in the form of a brochure. Read any literature you receive and take notes on index cards.

3. Outline the points you would like to put in your letter. Make the major heads main ideas and follow them with details, for example:

I. Assets of Urbia, USA
   A. Close to copper mines
   B. Surrounded by working-class suburbs
   C. Serviced by three power companies
II. Benefits to Acme Industries
   A. Accessible raw materials
   B. Large labor pool
   C. Reliable power sources

After following these steps, write your letter in convincing language. Show the company's executives that what is good for your city is good for their company.

Test

Key Terms (20 points)

Mark T if a statement is true, F if it is false. Rewrite the underlined words in all false statements to make them true.

1. The underwater part of the Atlantic Coastal Plain is the <u>fall line</u>.

2. Tornadoes are destructive winds that form over <u>tropical waters</u>.

3. The <u>conquistadors</u> were Spanish conquerors.

4. Canada's cabinet system is similar to that of the <u>U.S.</u> government.

5. Supplanting one kind of tree with another is called <u>reforestation</u>.

6. Petrochemicals are chemicals made from <u>wood or wood pulp</u>.

7. Agribusinesses produce, process, and distribute <u>food products</u>.

8. Irrigation sometimes involves tapping underground water called <u>aqueducts</u>.

9. A <u>separatist</u> is a person who wants to form a separate country.

10. <u>Protectionism</u> is a policy that makes use of tariffs and other trade barriers.

Main Ideas (40 points)

On a separate sheet of paper, complete the following sentences.

1. _____ stripped the Canadian Shield of its soil.

2. The three main types of climates in the United States are _____, mild, and dry.

3. Europeans came to the New World to find _____ and to win souls.

4. Three-fourths of all Americans and Canadians live in or near _____.

5. Major cities of the Northeast form a _____.

6. Its wide _____ areas and warm climate make the South ideal for farming.

7. Its central location made Tribune the _____ _____ of Greeley County, Kansas.

8. Western farmers and ranchers try to conserve land and _____.

9. New _____ will help the American economy compete with Japan and West Germany.

10. Its _____ at the end of the Canadian Pacific Railroad made Vancouver a major Pacific port.

Thinking Critically
(20 points)

1. Predict Effects. How would life in Canada and the United States be different if Canada had joined the rebellion against Britain in 1776? How would life be the same? List as many items as you can in separate columns. Then summarize your ideas in an essay.

2. Make Hypotheses. Look at the map on page 176 and locate the major farming regions of Canada. Explain why you think farming takes place in these areas and not in others.

Place Location (20 points)

Match the places listed below with the letters printed on the map.

1. Montreal
2. New York City
3. Houston
4. Chicago
5. Los Angeles

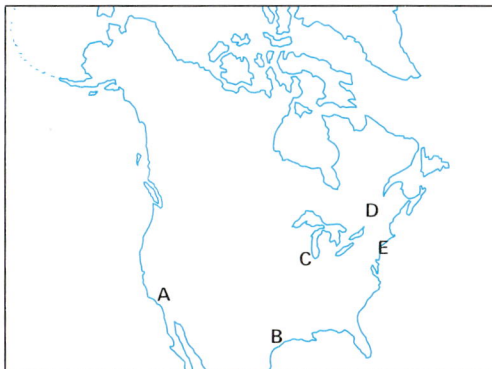

Middle and South America

In Unit 4 you will study our southern neighbors.

?>
CHAPTER 9

A Physical and Cultural Overview

In this chapter you will read about the land and people of Middle and South America.

Sections

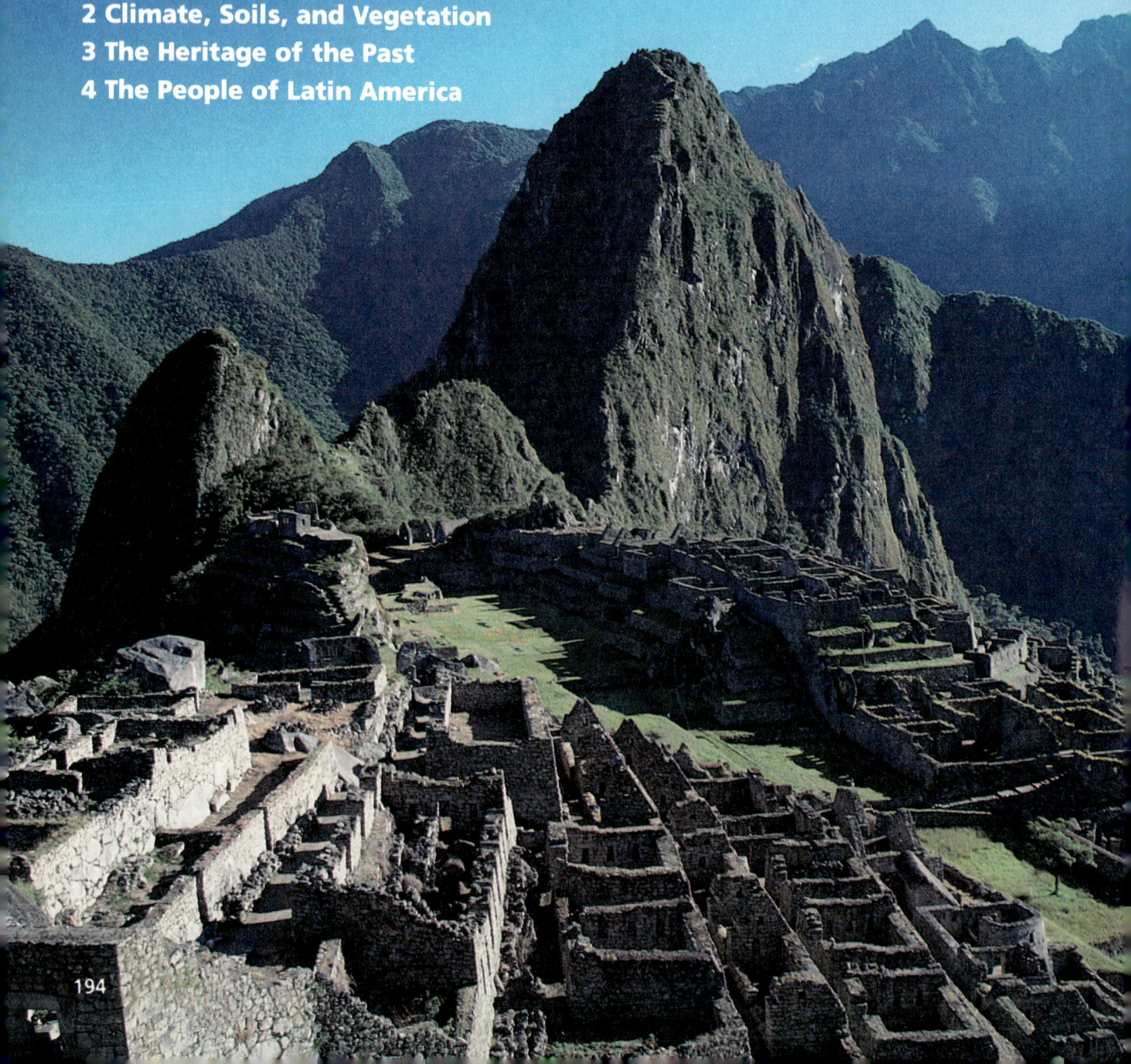

From Mountains to Plains

Preview

Key Places
Where are these places located?
1 Yucatán Peninsula
2 Amazon Basin
   See the globe below.

Key Terms
What do these terms mean?
altiplano
cordillera
isthmus

Main Ideas
As you read, look for answers to these questions.
• How was the landscape of Middle and South America formed?
• What are the main regions of Middle America?
• What are the main regions of South America?

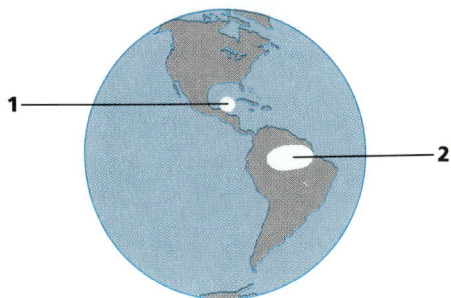

The land is a hungry woman. The forests are her hair. The grass and flowers are her skin and the lakes her eyes. Her shoulders and nose are the mountains and valleys.

This hungry woman drinks when it rains. She eats the shriveled flowers, the fallen trees, and the buried dead. Sometimes, when the wind blows at night, you can hear the woman crying for food.

Aztec legend

Internal and external forces formed the landscape.

The Aztecs, a people who ruled central Mexico from about 1300 to about 1500, explained their landscape in terms of the poetic legend you have just read. Today scientists explain the landscape of Middle and South America in a different but still dramatic way. They read its story in the region's plains, mountains, and waterways.

The region discussed in this unit is made up of Middle America—Mexico, Central America, and the West Indies—and South America. Find these places on the map on page 196. At one time Mexico and South America were united with Africa in Pangaea, but the two present-day continents split dramatically. About 200 million years ago, South America began to separate from North America. Fifty million years later, plate collisions near the western edge of South America caused the earth's crust to weaken. Eventually, volcanic activity there resulted in the formation of the rugged Andes Mountains.

Facing page: **The ruins of the ancient Inca city of Machu Picchu stand high in the Peruvian mountains.** *Page 192:* **Free-running guanacos are native to the plains and mountains of South America.**

Middle and South America
Political

- International boundaries
- ⊛ National capitals
- • Other cities

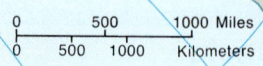

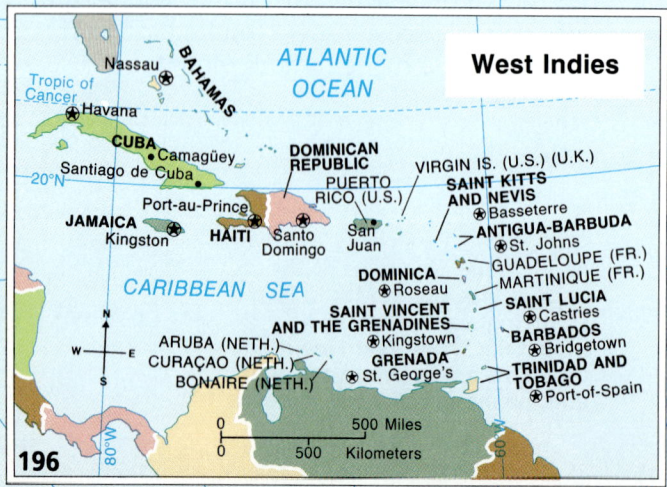

ASIA

ARCTIC OCEAN

North Pole

80°N

60°N

BERING SEA

ALASKA (U.S.)

Arctic Circle

GREENLAND (DEN.)

HUDSON BAY

LABRADOR SEA

CANADA

NORTH AMERICA

UNITED STATES

40°N

20°N

20°W

40°W

ATLANTIC OCEAN

500 1000 Miles
500 1000 Kilometers

Colorado

Rio Grande

Tijuana
Juárez
Monterrey
MEXICO
León
Guadalajara
Mexico City ⊛ Puebla
Acapulco

Gulf of Mexico

MIDDLE AMERICA

BELIZE
Belmopan ⊛
GUATEMALA
Guatemala ⊛
HONDURAS
Tegucigalpa ⊛
San Salvador ⊛
EL SALVADOR
NICARAGUA
Managua ⊛

San José ⊛
COSTA RICA
PANAMA
Panamá ⊛
Panama Canal

CENTRAL AMERICA

BAHAMAS
Havana ⊛
CUBA
HAITI
JAMAICA
DOMINICAN REPUBLIC
PUERTO RICO (U.S.)
WEST INDIES
CARIBBEAN SEA

Barranquilla
Maracaibo
Caracas ⊛
VENEZUELA
Orinoco R.
Georgetown ⊛
Paramaribo ⊛
Cayenne ⊛
FRENCH GUIANA
GUYANA
SURINAME

Tropic of Cancer
20° North Latitude

PACIFIC OCEAN

N
W E
S

0°-Equator

Medellín
Cali
Bogotá ⊛
COLOMBIA

Quito ⊛
ECUADOR
Guayaquil

GALÁPAGOS ISLANDS (ECUADOR)

Manaus
Amazon R.

SOUTH AMERICA
BRAZIL
Recife

Trujillo
PERU
Lima ⊛
Arequipa

La Paz ⊛
BOLIVIA
Sucre ⊛
Santa Cruz

Salvador
Brasília ⊛
Goiânia
Belo Horizonte
20°S

Antofagasta
PARAGUAY
Asunción ⊛
Tucumán
CHILE
Valparaíso
Santiago ⊛
Talcahuano
Córdoba
Rosario
Buenos Aires ⊛
ARGENTINA
URUGUAY
Montevideo ⊛
Mar del Plata

São Paulo
Curitiba
Rio de Janeiro
Pôrto Alegre
Paraná R.
Paraguay R.
Tropic of Capricorn

Río de la Plata
40° South Latitude

FALKLAND IS. (U.K.)
SOUTH GEORGIA I. (FALKLAND IS.)
Strait of Magellan

60°W
40°W
20° West Longitude

© SF

West Indies

ATLANTIC OCEAN

Nassau
BAHAMAS
Tropic of Cancer
Havana
CUBA
Camagüey
Santiago de Cuba
20°N
JAMAICA
Kingston
Port-au-Prince
HAITI
Santo Domingo
DOMINICAN REPUBLIC
PUERTO RICO (U.S.)
San Juan

VIRGIN IS. (U.S.) (U.K.)
SAINT KITTS AND NEVIS
⊛ Basseterre
ANTIGUA-BARBUDA
⊛ St. Johns
GUADELOUPE (FR.)
MARTINIQUE (FR.)
DOMINICA
⊛ Roseau
SAINT LUCIA
⊛ Castries
SAINT VINCENT AND THE GRENADINES
⊛ Kingstown
BARBADOS
⊛ Bridgetown
GRENADA
⊛ St. George's
TRINIDAD AND TOBAGO
⊛ Port-of-Spain

CARIBBEAN SEA

N
W E
S

ARUBA (NETH.)
CURAÇAO (NETH.)
BONAIRE (NETH.)

60°W
80°W

500 Miles
500 Kilometers

196

Two men approach a church on one of the many plateaus in the South American Andes.

At one point, the southern part of the North American plate was lifted up. Magma escaped through cracks in the earth's crust, creating volcanoes in Mexico. The uplift formed Mexico's Central Plateau. Under the ocean between North America and South America, the Cocos plate plunged beneath the Caribbean plate and elevated the land bridge known as Central America. Further plate action in the Caribbean Sea gave rise to volcanoes. Later, coral reefs formed upon their tops, thus creating the Lesser Antilles [an til'ēz].

While plate action was forming the lands of Middle America, volcanoes were erupting along the western side of South America. Some areas were covered with lava as deep as 2,000 feet.

Pressure beneath the earth's surface lifted the plain in western South America between 11,500 and 13,000 feet, forming the Altiplano of Peru and Bolivia. An **altiplano** [äl'tē plä'nō] is a high plateau or plain. On both sides of the Altiplano, folding and thrust faulting pushed up cordilleras that became parts of the Andes Mountain system. A **cordillera** [kôr'də lyer'ə] is a system of mountain ranges. Ice and water erosion from glaciers and rivers scoured sediment off the mountains and deposited it in valleys and other lowlands.

In most of the eastern part of the continent, little plate movement took place. As a result, the plateaus in eastern South America are mineral-rich shields.

Many different regions make up the Middle American landscape.

Today plates still shift beneath the surface of Middle America. This movement causes earthquakes and volcanic eruptions.

Mexico. In northern Mexico is a high central

Map Study

What are the countries in Central America? The West Indies? South America?

197

plateau cut off by bordering mountain ranges. These ranges are known as the Sierra Madre Occidental (western) and the Sierra Madre Oriental (eastern). Further south, along the Pacific Coast, is the Sierra Madre del Sur (southern).

The average elevation of Mexico's Central Plateau is about 6,500 feet above sea level. At the southern end of the Central Plateau is the Valley of Mexico, which rises to about 7,000 feet and is surrounded by volcanoes. Except for the narrow coastal plains, the only lowland in Mexico is the Yucatán Peninsula, a broad flat plain in southeastern Mexico that rises only a few feet above sea level.

Central America and the West Indies. Central America is made up of seven countries—Guatemala, Belize, Honduras, El Salvador, Nicaragua, Costa Rica, and Panama. Panama is the isthmus that joins the continents of North America and South America. An **isthmus** [is'məs] is a narrow strip of land that links two larger bodies of land.

The countries of Central America share several landform regions. Low plains lie along the Caribbean and Pacific Coast. Mountains rise farther inland and continue like a backbone down the center of Central America. Many of the mountains are active volcanoes.

Volcanoes affect the people as well as the landscape of Central America. Rich volcanic soil supports many farmers in the highlands. In addition, because so many plates converge in Central America, earthquakes are frequent and often dangerous.

The islands in the Caribbean Sea number about 7,000. These islands are sometimes called the West Indies. The islands are divided into three groups: the Bahamas, the Greater Antilles, and the Lesser Antilles.

The Bahamas are low-lying coral islands off the coast of Florida. The Greater Antilles—Cuba, Hispaniola, Puerto Rico, and Jamaica—are actually continuations of Central American mountain ranges that go under the sea and then resurface. The Lesser Antilles are a chain of volcanic islands running between the Greater Antilles and South America. Martinique, one of the Lesser Antilles, was the site of the Caribbean's worst volcanic disaster. In 1902 the island's Mt. Pelée erupted, killing nearly 40,000 people in the city of Saint-Pierre.

South America is divided into four main geographic regions.

There are four main regions. The first is northern South America and the second is western or Indian South America. The others are Brazil and southern South America.

Northern South America. The countries of northern South America are Colombia, Venezuela, and the Guianas [gē ä'nəz]—Guyana, Suriname, and French Guiana. See the map on page 196. All the countries in the northern part of South America share a narrow coastal plain along the Caribbean Sea or the Atlantic Ocean. Colombia also has a coastal plain along its Pacific Coast. A vast grassy lowland area, known as the llanos [yä'nōs] and found by the Orinoco River, extends from eastern Colombia across Venezuela. Another broad lowland occupies the basin of Lake Maracaibo in northwestern Venezuela. Lowlands are also located in southern Colombia and Venezuela.

Three branches of the Andes Mountains—the Cordillera Occidental, the Cordillera Central, and the Cordillera Oriental—stretch across western Colombia like three long fingers. A number of Colombia's mountains are volcanic. Sometimes these volcanic mountains have caused severe problems. For example, in 1985 the Nevado del

Map Study

What major river runs through Mexico? Through South America?

Middle and South America
Physical

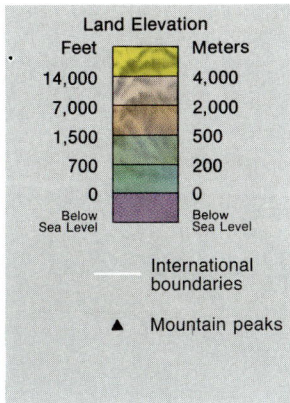

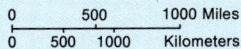

Land Elevation

Feet		Meters
14,000		4,000
7,000		2,000
1,500		500
700		200
0		0
Below Sea Level		Below Sea Level

———— International boundaries

▲ Mountain peaks

NORTH POLE

ASIA

ARCTIC OCEAN

BEAUFORT SEA

Bering Strait

Gulf of Alaska

Hudson Bay

NORTH AMERICA

PACIFIC OCEAN

ATLANTIC OCEAN

EUROPE

Arctic Circle

Tropic of Cancer

Gulf of Mexico

Bahama Is.

WEST INDIES

Cuba

Jamaica

Greater Antilles

Hispaniola

Puerto Rico

Lesser Antilles

MEXICO

Baja California

SIERRA MADRE OCCIDENTAL

SIERRA MADRE ORIENTAL

Rio Grande

Colorado R.

Gulf of California

Orizaba ▲
18,701 ft. (5,700 m)

Yucatán Peninsula

MIDDLE AMERICA

CARIBBEAN SEA

Isthmus of Tehuantepec

Volcán Tajumulco
13,845 ft. (4,220 m)

CENTRAL AMERICA

Isthmus of Panama

Panama Canal

Lake Maracaibo

LLANOS

Orinoco R.

GUIANA HIGHLANDS

Marajó Island

Galápagos Islands

Chimborazo
20,561 ft. (6,267 m) ▲

Gulf of Guayaquil

Equator

AMAZON BASIN

Amazon R.

Madeira R.

Negro R.

Xingu R.

Mt. Huascarán
22,205 ft. (6,768 m) ▲

ANDES MOUNTAINS

SOUTH AMERICA

MATO GROSSO PLATEAU

BRAZILIAN HIGHLANDS

PACIFIC OCEAN

Lake Titicaca

ATACAMA DESERT

GRAN CHACO

Paraguay R.

Paraná R.

Tropic of Capricorn

Mt. Aconcagua
22,831 ft. (6,959 m)

ANDES MOUNTAINS

PAMPAS

Río de la Plata

South Latitude

PATAGONIA

ANDES

Falkland Islands

South Georgia I.

Strait of Magellan

Tierra del Fuego

Cape Horn

N
W E
S

0	500	1000 Miles
0	500	1000 Kilometers

199

© SF

Ruiz volcano erupted. Heat from the eruption melted the volcano's ice cap, and tons of mud flowed onto the villages below.

South and east of the llanos in Venezuela are the Guiana Highlands. This ancient plateau area, which extends across Guyana, Suriname, and French Guiana, does not rise above 8,000 feet. It is rich in iron ore.

Western South America. Ecuador, Peru, Bolivia, and Paraguay make up western South America. Find these countries on the map on page 196. The dominant landscapes of western South America are the cordilleras of the Andes Mountains. The Andes run through central Ecuador and the western part of Peru, and Bolivia. Peru has more peaks that reach 20,000 feet or higher than any other Andean country. However, Cotopaxi [kō′tə pak′sē], the world's highest active volcano, is in Ecuador.

Altiplanos lie between the cordilleras in Peru and Bolivia. Lake Titicaca, the world's highest lake, is located on the altiplano along the boundary between Peru and Bolivia. In addition to the altiplano, many lower plateaus and basins are found throughout the Andes. For example, the most densely inhabited part of Ecuador is a central plateau surrounded by mountains.

Ecuador and Peru both have narrow coastal plains. Offshore lies still another part of Ecuador—the Galápagos Islands. They are named for the large turtles that live there.

The most important waterway in South America is the Amazon River. The Amazon has more tributaries, contains a greater volume of water, and drains a larger area than any other river in the world. The area drained by the Amazon and its tributaries is called the Amazon Basin. Parts of the Amazon Basin lie in Peru, Ecuador, and Bolivia, and in the northern nations of Colombia and Venezuela. About one-half of the Amazon Basin lies in Brazil.

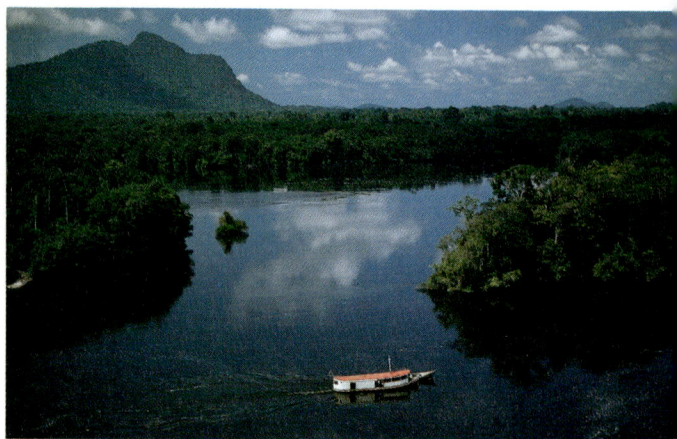

The Amazon pictured above is wider and deeper than any other river, including the Mississippi.

Great Rivers of the World

River and Continent	Approximate Length in Miles
Nile / Africa	4,200
Amazon / South America	4,000
Mississippi-Missouri / North America	3,900
Yangtze (Chang) / Asia	3,900
Congo (Zaire) / Africa	2,900
Amur / Asia	2,700
Huang / Asia	2,700
Lena / Asia	2,600
Mekong / Asia	2,600
Niger / Africa	2,600

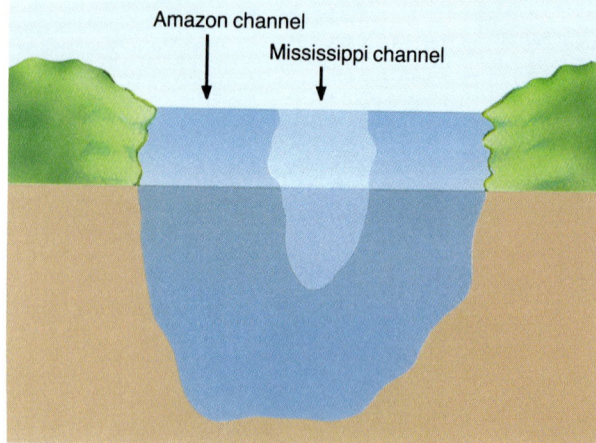

Amazon channel

Mississippi channel

Bolivia and Paraguay are landlocked countries. Bolivia's western area is made up of the altiplano and surrounding high mountains. To the southeast in Bolivia, and in western Paraguay, is the vast plain known as the Gran Chaco.

Southern South America. The countries of southern South America include Chile, Argentina, and Uruguay. Locate these countries on the map on page 196. Although Chile's width averages only about 150 miles, it is the longest country in the world. As a result, Chile has a great variety of landforms found on and near South America's coast. The rugged peaks of the Andes form Chile's eastern border. Many streams originate in these mountains and flow across a fertile valley in south central Chile to the sea. On the northern coast is the Chilean Plateau that reaches from the base of the Andes to the Pacific. Chile also includes southern coastal islands.

Argentina is the largest of the southern countries and the second largest country in South America. Argentina shares a mountainous border with Chile. Aconcagua [ä′kông kä′gwə], the highest peak in the Western Hemisphere (22,834 feet), is located in Argentina. The pampas—a vast grassy plain in central Argentina—extends northward and meets the Gran Chaco in the northern part of the country. A dry barren plateau area in southern Argentina is known as Patagonia.

Uruguay, like Paraguay, has little spectacular elevation. Uruguay's highest point is less than 2,000 feet above sea level. Low hills and plateaus are found in the northeast, and grassy, rolling plains cover the south.

Brazil. Brazil is the largest country in South America and the fifth largest in the world. Locate Brazil on the map on page 196. It spans 2,700 miles from east to west at its widest point, and its Atlantic coastline is 4,600 miles long. Brazil is so big it covers almost one-half of

South America and shares borders with every other South American country except Chile and Ecuador.

Lowlands of the Amazon Basin cover most of northern and western Brazil. The Amazon River and its tributaries have cut deep valleys across much of the basin, dissecting it into small plateaus. Also, several low mountain ranges, part of the Guiana Highlands, lie along the basin's northern border.

In the southwest are the lowlands of the Paraguay River, bordered by the vast plateau known as the Mato Grosso. The Brazilian Highlands are the upturned eastern edge of this plateau, stretching along the Atlantic Coast in the southeastern part of the country.

Section 1 Review

Locating Key Places
Locate the following places on the map on page 199: Yucatán Peninsula, Amazon Basin

Identifying Key Terms
Define the following terms: altiplano, cordillera, isthmus

Reviewing Main Ideas
1. What specific internal and external forces created the landforms of Middle and South America?
2. What are the major landform regions in Middle America?
3. Describe the four main geographic regions of South America.

Thinking Critically: Make Hypotheses
What is probably the most popular form of transportation in the Amazon Basin? Support your answer with facts from the lesson.

Climate, Soils, and Vegetation

Preview

Key Places
Where are these places located?
1 Atacama Desert
2 Patagonia
See the globe below.

Key Terms
What does this term mean?
selva

Main Ideas
As you read, look for answers to these questions.
• What climate regions cover much of Middle and South America?
• What factors create the dry areas of Middle and South America?
• Where in South America are mild climate regions located?

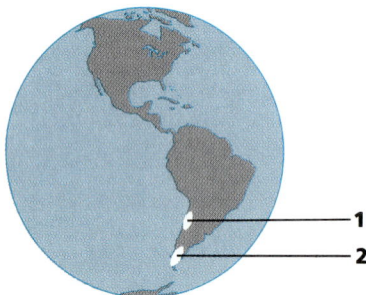

The Tambopata Wildlife Reserve, a 13,000-acre tract of unsullied rainforest in Peru has the richest animal life of any place in the world, including 566 bird species, 145 species of dragonflies, plus many other rare and endangered animals.

Ripley's Believe It or Not

Tropical climate regions cover much of this geographic realm.

Tropical rainforest and savanna climate regions prevail in the low-latitude areas of Middle and South America. Here, the sun shines directly overhead, and temperatures are high the year round. However, the rainfall and vegetation in these two climate zones are quite different.

Tropical rainforests. A tropical rainforest climate, hot and wet, is found in a band centering on the Equator, where the direct heat of the overhead sun brings daily convectional showers. It is also found along the windward side of mountains in the tropics, where trade winds loaded with moisture strike the mountain sides, rise, cool, and drop their moisture. Trade winds, you remember, blow from the northeast in the northern hemisphere and from the south-

A bulldozer clears away trees for a highway through the selva.

east in the southern hemisphere. Thus, in South America, a rainforest climate region dominates the central part of the Amazon Basin, broadening out where trade winds blow against the Andes. Point out on the map at right the east-facing trade wind coasts that also have a rainforest climate.

High heat and constant dampness in these areas produces a lush rainforest vegetation cover, called the **selva**. A characteristic tropical rainforest is described in Chapter 3, page 68. As you know, the trees are broadleaf evergreens. The tops of trees of various heights grow together to form several levels of canopies.

The selva of Middle and South America is under attack. It is being penetrated by highways and being cut down by settlers for its land and timber. Although vast areas of selva still exist, many areas of rainforest are endangered.

The loss of the rainforest would do great damage to earth's environment. The tropical rainforest is home to hundreds of species of birds and insects found nowhere else. The forests absorb carbon dioxide, rain, and sunlight. They return moisture to the atmosphere and give off oxygen, needed by all living things to sustain life. Once trees have been destroyed, there are no longer fallen leaves to replace the nutrients leached from the soil. Weeds return, but there are no deep-rooted trees to keep the soil from eroding. Sun bakes the soil, rain runs off its gullied surface, and floods result. The land is then good for neither farming nor timber.

Savannas. Savanna climate zones are found poleward of the rainforest climate. Rain comes to the savanna climate lands during the months when the sun shines from directly overhead. During the low-sun period, these lands are dry because of the influence of the thirsty trade winds. Savanna climate areas in Middle America include the entire west side of Central America (except the Isthmus of Panama), and most of

Middle and South America: Climate Regions

Tropical climates
- Tropical rainforest
- Savanna

Dry climates
- Steppe
- Desert

Mild climates
- Marine west coast
- Humid subtropical
- Mediterranean

High altitudes
- Highlands
- Uplands

Map Study

What type of climate dominates Mexico? Central America? Why do tropical climates prevail in the Amazon Basin of South America?

203

the Caribbean islands. In South America the savanna climate includes the llanos of Venezuela and the southern Guiana Highlands, most of the southern and eastern parts of the vast Amazon Basin, and the northern part of the Gran Chaco in Paraguay.

Trade winds, mountains, and cold offshore currents create dry areas.

Desert and steppe climates occur under several conditions in Latin America. Trade-wind deserts and steppes are found in northern Mexico, northeastern Argentina, and northern Chile, where drying winds blow constantly, and the sun is never directly overhead to bring a rainy season. These areas are poleward of the tropics of Cancer and Capricorn.

Rain-shadow deserts and steppes occur in areas cut off by high mountains. Winds create a desert in the lands to the west of the Andes, from almost the Equator south to about 33°, including the coasts of southern Ecuador, Peru, and northern Chile. Mountains also account for the steppe conditions of Mexico's central plateau and for the steppe and desert climates found in western and southern Argentina. There winds blow against the Andes from the west, leaving the east side of the mountains in a rain shadow.

Cold offshore currents also help to create desert conditions. The map on page 54 shows cold currents off the coasts of Baja [bä'hä] California, northern Chile, Peru, southern Ecuador, and southern Patagonia. These currents cool the winds blowing over them, making them unable to pick up moisture and ensuring that whatever onshore winds should develop will bring no rain. All of the lands where a cold current exists would be dry anyway, because either they are trade-wind deserts or are in a rain shadow or both. The cold current is the final straw, so to speak. Desert areas with a cold current offshore,

Middle and South America: Natural Vegetation Regions

- Broadleaf forest—rainforest
- Broadleaf forest—deciduous
- Broadleaf forest—other
- Needleleaf forest
- Mixed forest (broadleaf and needleleaf)
- Grassland
- Desert—little or no vegetation
- Desert—scrub with grassy patches
- High mountains (vegetation varies with elevation)

Map Study

What type of natural vegetation is most common in Mexico? What type prevails in northern South America?

like the Atacama Desert in northern Chile, are among the driest places on earth.

Deserts that receive little rain have scant thorny vegetation. Steppe lands, which get several inches of rainfall a year, grow thorny bushes and short grass but no trees except along the few and shallow streams. Irrigation provides ribbons of farming in most desert and steppe climate areas.

Mild climate zones are found in southern South America.

Mild climate zones generally lie below the Tropic of Capricorn in the southern part of South America. Summers are hot to warm and winters are never extremely cold. Since the tip of South America narrows, temperatures in the southern lands are modified by the bordering oceans.

Humid subtropical. A humid subtropical climate region extends from Paraguay eastward to the Brazilian coast, and from there southward through Uruguay to include most of northeastern and central Argentina. The northern upland margins of this area are moister, and here there are excellent stands of pine and deciduous forests. Southward the vegetation turns to grassland—lush grassland, with deep roots and fertile soils—called the pampas, where animals graze.

Mediterranean. The central valley of Chile has a Mediterranean climate much like that of southern California. In the mild, wet winters the valley comes under the influence of moist westerly winds. In the dry summers, however, it is under the influence of the drying trade winds. Short trees, shrubs, and grasses are characteristic vegetation, and the soils are highly fertile. A variety of crops can grow, especially where irrigated.

Marine west coast. A marine west coast climate region, similar to that in the northwestern United States, is located in southern Chile. Here abundant rain falls throughout the year and forests—both deciduous and evergreen—thrive . The area is too cool for agriculture, but dairying and lumbering are important industries. Limited marine west coast climate zones are also located in southern Argentina and in the uplands of southeastern Brazil.

Section 2 Review

Locating Key Places
Locate the following places on the map on page 199: Atacama Desert, Patagonia

Identifying Key Terms
Define the following term: selva

Reviewing Main Ideas
1. What climate regions are found in much of Middle and South America?
2. How are dry climate regions created in Middle and South America?
3. In what part of South America are mild climate zones found?

Thinking Critically: Make Hypotheses.
Compare the climate and vegetation regions maps in this chapter with the population distribution map on page 83. What hypotheses can you make about why people in the realm live where they do?

The Heritage of the Past

Preview

Key Places
Where were these places located?
1 Maya Empire
2 Aztec Empire
3 Inca Empire
  See the globe below.

Key Terms
What does this term mean?
creoles

Main Ideas
As you read, look for answers to these questions.
- What early civilizations existed in Mexico and South America?
- How did Europeans change Middle and South America?
- When did Middle Americans win their independence from European rule?
- Who led the struggles for independence in South America?

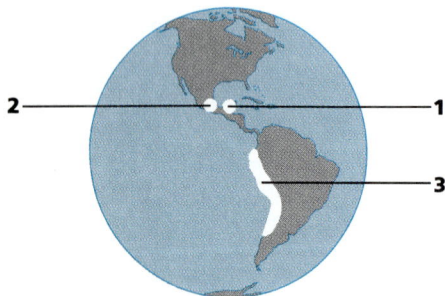

Long ago trees and flowers grew in Honduras just as they do today. Animals wandered the land and fish swam the nearby sea. But no people lived in Honduras to enjoy its beauty or to eat its fruit and game. So the Creator made a man and a woman from corn. They had teeth like ripe kernels and hair like corn silk. These were the Caribs—the earliest people of Honduras.

Carib legend

Three early civilizations flourished in Mexico and South America.
As elsewhere in the world, various peoples in Middle and South America have explained their origins in legends. Today archaeologists and other social scientists piece together the history of the early people of this region by studying their artifacts and oral traditions.

Most scientists believe that the first people to come to Middle and South America were descendants of the Asians who crossed the land bridge from Asia into North America many thousands of years ago. In San Luis Potosi, Mexico, the remains of stone tools and games from 30,000 years ago have been found—the oldest signs of people in the entire realm.

By 8000 B.C. hunters and gatherers lived in most parts of Middle and South America. Some people had already settled into farming communities and had begun growing a variety of crops including corn, beans, peanuts, squash, sweet potatoes, chili peppers, avocados, and cacao, from which chocolate is made. By about 500 B.C. groups of people in Middle and South America began to develop urban centers that were the forerunners of those of the great Maya, Aztec, and Inca civilizations.

The Mayas. At its height—A.D. 300 to 900—the empire of the Mayas extended across the Yucatán Peninsula in Mexico, and included parts of present-day Belize, Guatemala, and Honduras. The Mayas built magnificent stone temples and pyramids in cities like Chichén Itzá. They also developed a number system, a form of picture writing, and an accurate yearly calendar.

For hundreds of years, the Mayas managed to raise a variety of crops in the poor soil of the nearby forests. Archaeologists believe that about A.D. 900 the soil around the cities became exhausted and crops failed. They also believe that wars and internal rebellions weakened the empire and forced the Mayas to abandon their great cities.

The Aztecs. During the 1200s, a group of people known as the Aztecs swept into Mexico from what may now be the southwestern United States. Around 1325 the Aztecs settled near the present-day site of Mexico City. In the middle of Lake Texcoco, the Aztecs built a great city they called Tenochtitlán [tā nôch'tē tlän'].

The Aztecs conquered many other Indian groups and demanded that the conquered people give them tributes, or payments. Tributes often included cacao beans, animal hides, and gold and jade jewelry. The tributes added to the wealth of the Aztecs.

The Incas. The Incas settled near the site of Cuzco, in present-day Peru around 1200. During the early 1400s, the Incas began to dominate other Indian groups in the area. By 1500 the Incas ruled a vast South American empire that stretched for more than 2,500 miles from present-day Ecuador south through central Chile. The empire reached westward from the Andes Mountains to the Pacific Ocean.

An elaborate system of roads connected the entire empire. One road ran almost the entire length of the Pacific Coast. The Incas were clever builders. Inca engineers built suspension bridges across the deep ravines and rivers, and constructed large buildings using huge blocks of stone that were moved from the mountains with ropes and rollers. Skilled stonemasons

shaped the stones so that they fit together perfectly without the use of mortar. One of the best known Incan cities is Machu Picchu, which was built atop a high mountain in the Andes.

Europeans took control and introduced African slavery.

In 1492 Christopher Columbus landed on one of the islands in the Bahamas. He claimed the island and its gentle Arawak Indians for Spain. During Columbus's four voyages, he claimed other Bahamian islands, Cuba, Hispaniola, Domi-

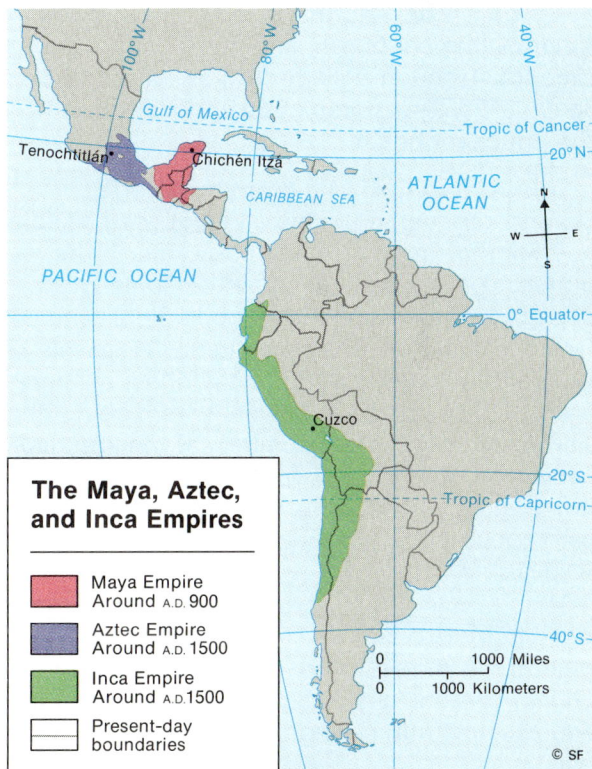

The Maya, Aztec, and Inca Empires

- Maya Empire Around A.D. 900
- Aztec Empire Around A.D. 1500
- Inca Empire Around A.D. 1500
- Present-day boundaries

© SF

Map Study

Use the map on page 196 to name the present-day countries in which these empires once reigned.

207

nica, Puerto Rico, Jamaica, Trinidad, and most of the Caribbean coast of Central America.

By the 1520s Spanish soldiers, known as conquistadors, were looking for gold in Mexico and throughout Central America. In 1521 Hernando Cortés and his army conquered the Aztec Empire and ended Aztec rule over other Indian groups. In 1534 Spanish soldiers led by Francisco Pizarro defeated the Incas, and the Inca Empire crumbled. In addition to taking control of Mexico and Peru, the Spanish founded many settlements such as Havana (Cuba), San Juan (Puerto Rico), and Granada (Nicaragua). By 1663 Spain's possessions extended through Mexico, Central America, the Caribbean, and much of South America. Through tight control on its colonies, Spain left a clear stamp of Spanish culture on the entire continent.

The Roman Catholic Church. After the Spanish conquered the Indian empires of Middle and South America, missionaries came to the region to convert the Indians to the Roman Catholic faith. The missionaries set up schools and founded hospitals. The Church also set up missions for Indians in remote areas. Some missionaries tried to protect the Indians from being enslaved. Although great numbers of Indians were converted, they did not completely give up their old religions. The Indians often blended their own rituals with Roman Catholic customs and festivals.

The Catholic Church owned much land, especially in Mexico and South America. It had huge plantations in many parts of the region. The Church became very wealthy, especially since it was exempt from paying taxes.

European colonies. The map on page 209 shows how other European nations chipped away at Spain's dominance in the New World. Portugal acquired Brazil in 1494 as a result of an agreement with Spain known as the Treaty of Tordesillas, which split South America into

Spanish and Portuguese spheres of influence. The English established a number of Caribbean colonies including Jamaica and Barbados, as well as British Honduras (present-day Belize) in Central America. The Dutch settled St. Maarten, Saba, Bonaire, Curaçao, and Aruba. France took control of almost a dozen islands, including Martinique and the western third of Hispaniola (present-day Haiti). The Guianas, on South America's northeastern coast, passed back and forth among the English, Dutch, and French.

The Indians were forced to work in mines and on plantations in the colonies. Soon European diseases, such as smallpox, and overwork killed much of the Indian population. To replace the Indian laborers, African slaves were brought to the colonies. Plantations worked by slaves were very profitable. As a result, millions of African slaves were sent to Middle and South America to do backbreaking labor.

Middle Americans became independent in the 1800s and 1900s.

During the late 1700s and the 1800s, the people of Middle and South America became familiar

Willemstad, Curaçao, reflects its Dutch origins.

with the ideas of independence that led to the American and French Revolutions. Also, the people were tired of being ruled by distant nations that restricted their trade and collected heavy taxes. The first successful revolution in the region took place in Middle America.

Caribbean independence. By 1789 slaves made up over 90 percent of the population in what is now the island nation of Haiti. These black slaves initiated the struggles for independence in Middle and South America. In 1791 the slaves staged a rebellion against their owners. In 1794 Pierre Dominique Toussaint l'Ouverture, a freed black slave, took charge of the revolt. Although he was captured and died in prison, the rebels fought on. Finally, in 1803, they gained independence from France and named their country the Republic of Haiti.

Gradually, other Caribbean colonies broke away from their European rulers. The eastern part of Hispaniola became the Dominican Republic in 1865. In 1902 Cuba gained its independence. Other colonies did not become independent until later. Jamaica was a British colony until 1962, and the Bahamas became independent of British rule in 1973. By the 1980s the French, British, and Dutch controlled only a few small island groups in the Caribbean. Puerto Rico, taken from Spain in 1898, remained a commonwealth associated with the United States.

Independence in Mexico and Central America. It took Mexico 11 years of fighting to gain its independence. In 1810 Father Miguel Hidalgo, a parish priest in the Mexican town of Dolores, rallied creoles and other groups of people in Mexico to revolt against Spain. **Creoles** were people of Spanish descent who were born in the Americas. The Spanish captured and shot Hidalgo in 1811, but his followers continued to struggle for freedom. Ten years after Hidalgo's death, Mexico was able to win its independence.

Most Central Americans also broke away from Spain in 1821. Guatemala, El Salvador, Honduras, Nicaragua, and Costa Rica united with Mexico. In 1823, however, Mexico and Central Amer-

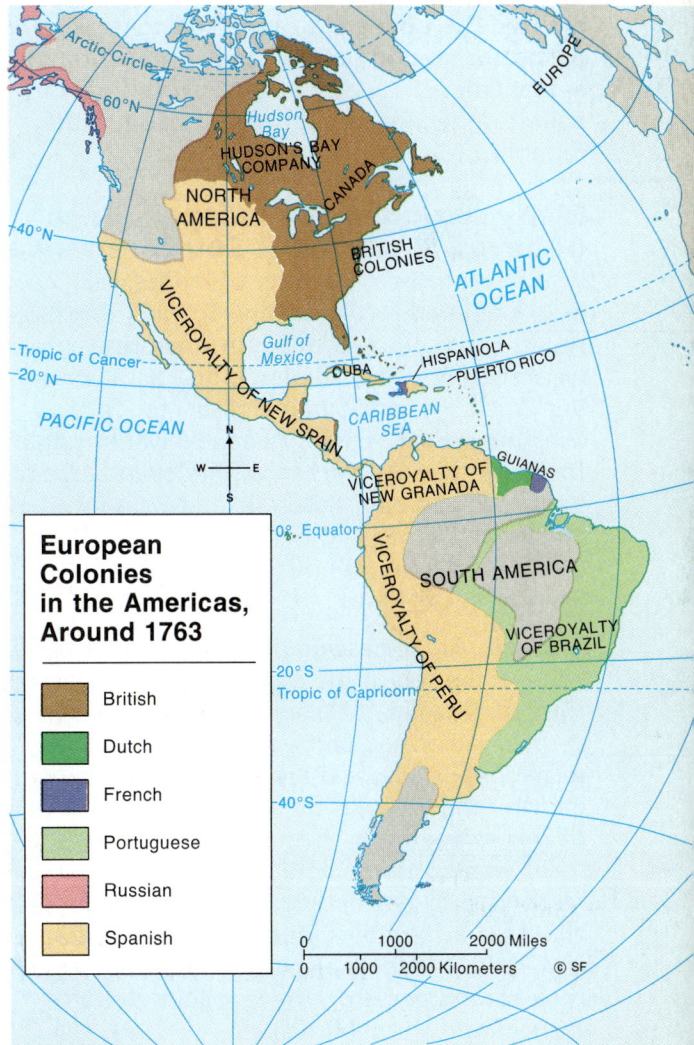

European Colonies in the Americas, Around 1763

- British
- Dutch
- French
- Portuguese
- Russian
- Spanish

0   1000   2000 Miles
0   1000   2000 Kilometers   © SF

Map Study

Which countries were the main colonizers of Middle and South America?

209

ica separated. At first the five Central American states became one republic. However, by 1839 they had formed five independent nations.

Panama became part of Colombia in 1821 and declared its independence in 1904 with help from the United States. In return Panama granted the United States use and control of part of its land to build a canal. British Honduras was the last country in Central America to gain its independence. In 1981 it became the republic of Belize.

Many struggles for independence occurred throughout South America.

In 1808 Napoleon, the ruler of France, marched into Spain and forced out the Spanish king. As a result, Spanish power in South America was weakened. Wealthy creoles, including a young Venezuelan named Símon Bolívar, fought to overthrow their Spanish rulers. Bolívar struggled for more than 20 years to win independence for Venezuela, Colombia, Bolivia, and Ecuador. Bolívar also aided another revolutionary leader—Antonio José de Sucre—in driving the Spanish out of Peru.

Brazil. Brazil became independent peacefully. Pedro I, the son of the Portuguese king, became ruler of Brazil in 1821. Fourteen years earlier, Pedro's father had opened Brazil's ports to international trade, and Brazilian merchants began to compete with the Portuguese. As a result of this competition, the new Portuguese parliament wanted to regulate Brazil's ports. Pedro I responded by demanding independence for Brazil. Brazil achieved its independence in 1823, and Pedro I became emperor. After deposing their second emperor, the Brazilians declared their nation a republic in 1889.

Paraguay, Uruguay, and the Guianas. Paraguay and Uruguay were originally parts of other South American nations. Paraguay had once been a part of Argentina but refused to

follow that country's newly independent government in 1810. The land that became Paraguay declared its own independence in 1811.

Uruguay was formed by gaining its independence from two South American nations. In the 1820s Brazil and Argentina disputed each other's claim to a large area of land between the two countries. They settled their differences by establishing the independent country of Uruguay in 1825.

Three South American countries remained European colonies into the modern era. British Guiana, now called Guyana, became independent in 1966. Dutch Guiana, now known as Suriname, gained its independence in 1975. French Guiana has self-government but still remains tied to France.

Section 3 Review

Locating Key Places
Locate these places on the globe on page 206: Maya Empire, Aztec Empire, Inca Empire

Identifying Key Terms
Define the following term: creoles

Reviewing Main Ideas
1. Who were the Mayas, Aztecs, and Incas?
2. How were the Aztec and Inca empires affected by Europeans?
3. When did most Middle American colonies become independent?
4. How did the colonies win their independence in South America?

Thinking Critically: Make Hypotheses
After the U.S. War for Independence, only two countries—the United States and Canada—were formed. In contrast, the independence movement in Middle and South America resulted in the formation of many countries. Why did these differences occur?

The People of Latin America

Preview

Key Places
Where are these places located?
1 Mexico City
2 São Paulo
3 Rio de Janeiro
4 Buenos Aires
5 Lima
See the globe below.

Key Terms
What does this term mean?
mestizos

Main Ideas
As you read, look for answers to these questions.
• What early groups in Latin America helped form its culture?
• How did later immigrants affect life in Latin America?
• What are some population trends in Latin America?
• Why are urban areas in Latin America heavily populated?

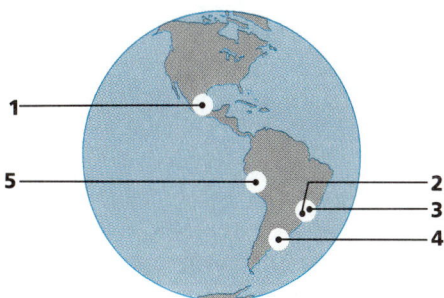

Your brother and I keep shop here and are doing well. . . . So you would give me great pleasure in leaving that misery there and coming here, because it would be greatly to your advantage. . . . Get my brother Pedro to come with you, and leave that wretched country, because it is only for people who have a lot of money, and here, no matter how poor a man may be, he never lacks a horse to ride and food to eat.

Alonso Morales

Indians, Europeans, and Africans influenced Latin American culture.

The excerpt you have just read is from a letter written in 1576 by Alonso Morales, a Spanish tailor. Morales was trying to persuade his cousin in Spain to join him in Puebla, a Spanish settlement in Mexico. Most permanent settlers in the Spanish colonies were like Morales—young male artisans. Few, however, had the opportunity to participate in governing and policymaking. Almost all decisions were made either in Spain or by government officials sent out by Spain.

Spanish and Portuguese colonists like Morales and their descendants preserved the Spanish and Portuguese languages and customs that make up a major part of the culture of Middle and South America today. The countries of Middle and South America are often known collectively as Latin America because most people there speak either Spanish or Portuguese. Both Spanish and Portuguese are derived from Latin—the language of the Roman Empire. The Roman Catholic Church in Latin America is another important legacy of the early Spanish and Portuguese colonists. Today more than 90 percent of the region's people are Roman Catholic.

Latin American Indians. The earliest cultural groups in Latin America were the Indians who lived in the cool highlands. Survival of Indian cultures in Latin America today is evident

211

in the many Indian languages that are still spoken in parts of the region. About 1,650 different Indian languages have been identified.

In some parts of Latin America, the Indians have not fared well. The Arawaks of Cuba and San Salvador, for example, were killed by overwork and European diseases before the Spanish even settled Mexico. Today only a small number of Indians still live in the West Indies.

On the other hand, the Yaqui and Tarahumara Indians of Mexico still follow their traditional ways of life. These Indian groups lived in the desert and mountain areas where the European conquerors did not want to settle. The cultures of the Maya in Guatemala and Mexico and of the Quechua and Aymará Indians who live in the Andes Mountains of Ecuador, Peru, and Bolivia continue to flourish.

Ethnic variations. Because most early Spanish colonists in Latin America were males, they often married Indian women. The children of these marriages were known as **mestizos**, people of both Indian and Spanish ancestry. Mestizos now make up the majority of people in areas where the Indian population originally flourished. In most regions mestizo families

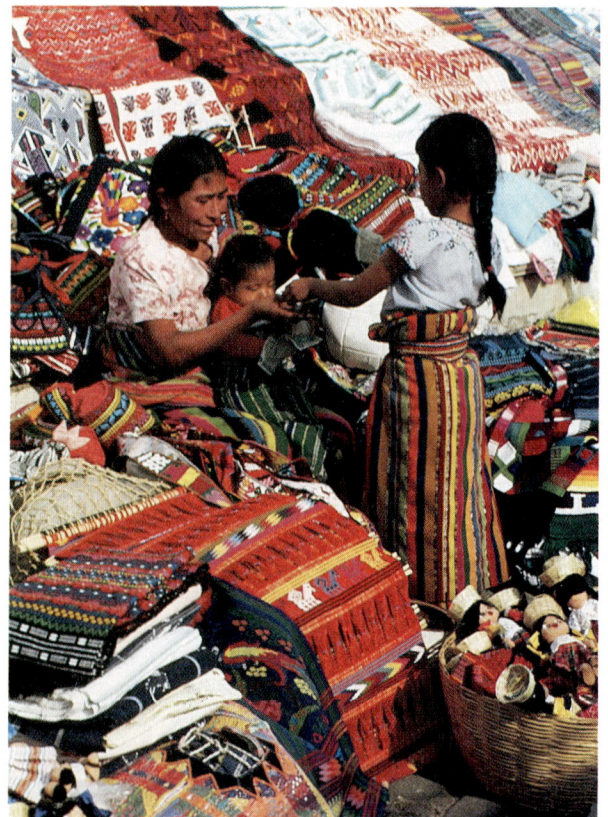

Open-air markets, like these in Colombia and Guatemala, flourish throughout Latin America. Here, people can buy various fresh fruits and vegetables, as well as intricately woven products.

speak Spanish. In Paraguay, however, the Guarani language still prevails.

Slaves who were brought to Latin America from Africa also brought ethnic variation. Today many people in Brazil and the Caribbean have mixed European and African ancestry.

Later immigrants made cultural and economic contributions.

Although most Latin Americans are of Indian, Spanish, Portuguese, or African descent, other groups settled parts of Latin America and contributed to its culture. You have already read about the Dutch, French, and British colonies in the West Indies, Central America, and the Guianas. In the 19th century, British and other European settlers came to southern South America, which seemed to them to have a climate and opportunities similar to those in the American west. Today Chile has a minority with German and English ancestry, Argentina and Uruguay have a British and Italian minority, and southern Brazil has areas of German culture.

Between 1850 and 1888, slavery was abolished in Latin America. As a result, plantation owners in the West Indies needed a new source of cheap labor. Some contracted for Chinese workers, who later settled in various parts of the region and are now owners of small businesses. Workers from India and Indonesia settled on the island of Trinidad, and in Suriname and Guyana. Their descendants now form the ethnic majority in these areas.

Twentieth-century immigration. In the early 1900s, many Turks and Syrians moved to Brazil. After the war began in 1914, Poles, Russians, and other groups from war-torn Europe also immigrated to South America. In Brazil Japanese immigrants came as pioneers to the hard-to-farm Amazon Basin and succeeded where others had failed.

During the Spanish Civil War in the 1930s, many Spanish intellectuals and professionals went to Mexico and Argentina. Later, the devastation after World War II brought many immigrants to Brazil and southern South America. Descendants of all these newcomers are now making important contributions to the arts, education, and literature of Latin America.

Growth rates and population density vary greatly.

More than 400 million people live in Latin America today. Experts predict that the population will grow to around 550 million by the year 2000.

Latin America's fastest growing areas are Mexico and Central America. Together their populations total about 108 million—more than one-quarter of all Latin Americans. Mexico's population growth rate is quite high—more than 2.5 percent. Some of the Central American countries have growth rates even higher than that of Mexico. For example, Guatemala, Honduras, and Nicaragua all have growth rates of more than 3.2 percent.

A slow-growing area in Middle America is the West Indies. Two factors contribute to the slow growth there. First, the islands that are still colonies often lose people to their ruling country. For example, people from Martinique emigrate to France. Second, the birth rate is falling because every Caribbean government—except Haiti—has an official family planning program.

Family planning programs have been instituted because, although most Caribbean countries have a low growth rate, many already have large populations. For example, the population density on Barbados is 1,522 people per square mile. Compare that number to 66—the average number of people per square mile in the United States.

The Central American countries generally have average population densities ranging from 19 in

Belize to 199 in Guatemala. Only El Salvador is very densely populated with 603 persons per square mile.

South American countries have some of the fastest, and some of the slowest, growth rates in Latin America. Countries such as Venezuela, Ecuador, Bolivia, and Paraguay all average population increases of more than 2.5 percent per year. Chile, Argentina, and Uruguay all have average population increases of less than 1.5 percent.

Generally, the countries of South America have low average population densities. Few people have settled in the rainforests around the Amazon and Orinoco rivers or in the hard-to-farm areas of the Andes and Patagonia. In addition, wide stretches of land in Brazil, Venezuela, Chile, and Argentina are used for grazing rather than for towns and cities.

Rural Latin Americans have moved to urban areas looking for jobs.

Since 1950 rural Latin Americans have been moving to urban areas in large numbers. As a result, many people in the region live in or near cities. In fact, five of the largest metropolitan areas in the world are in Latin America.

Two of these huge metropolitan areas are located in Brazil—São Paulo with 8 million residents and Rio de Janeiro with 5 million. The population in and around Buenos Aires, the capital of Argentina, is about 10 million. Lima, the capital of Peru, has about 5 million residents. The largest metropolitan area in Latin America is Mexico City with 15 million people. Experts predict that by 1990 the population of Mexico City will reach 20 million.

São Paulo, Rio de Janeiro, Buenos Aires, Lima, and Mexico City are all manufacturing centers. People who arrive in the cities from rural areas hope to find factory jobs. In many cases, however, people outnumber jobs.

The most urban South American country is Venezuela. About 85 percent of Venezuela's people live in urban areas. Shipping and off-shore oil drilling near Venezuela's seaports attract people looking for jobs.

Bolivia and Paraguay are among the least urban countries in South America. In Bolivia only 33 percent of the people are urban. Paraguay's urban population is only about 42 percent. Neither country has many resources or developed industries.

In general, about half the people who live in the West Indies live in rural areas. Because agricultural products account for much of the income in island countries, many people depend on plantation jobs rather than on jobs in the cities for their livelihood. Agriculture is also important in the Central American nations where less than half the people live in urban areas.

Section 4 Review

Locating Key Places
Locate the following places on the map on page 196: Mexico City, São Paulo, Rio de Janeiro, Buenos Aires, Lima

Identifying Key Terms
Define the following term: mestizos

Reviewing Main Ideas
1. How did the Spanish and Portuguese help form Latin America's culture?
2. Describe the contributions later immigrant groups made to Latin America.
3. What population trends vary in Latin America?
4. Why have rural Latin Americans moved to urban areas?

Thinking Critically: Identifying Assumptions
What assumptions do rural immigrants to Mexico City make? Are these assumptions valid? Explain your answer.

Understanding Altitudinal Zones

In general, maps give the observer a direct view from above the earth. To provide a different view, however, some maps—called cross sections—place the observer closer to the horizon. The cross section on this page shows a view of Mt. Orizaba, located in Mexico at 19° N.

In the world's mountainous areas, people tend to think of climate in terms of both altitude and latitude. As you read in Chapter 3, temperatures get cooler with rising elevation above sea level. As a result, South Americans are accustomed to the sight of perpetual ice and snow very near to the Equator.

In tropical regions, the mountain slope is divided into five distinct zones of altitude. As you progress up the mountain slope, these zones get colder. Note that the elevations marked as borders on the diagram below are for mountains located about 19° N or S. The zones would occur at higher altitudes as one moved toward the Equator.

In Middle and South America, the five zones are given Spanish names. The lowest zone is called *tierra caliente*, which means "hot lands." In this zone, climates and vegetation are typical of the local latitude. Crops such as bananas, sugar cane, and rice grow freely.

The second zone, called the *tierra templada* or "temperate lands," is also known as the coffee zone. This crop grows well in the warm, pleasant climate.

The third zone, called the *tierra fria* or "cold lands," usually has warm days and cool nights. This zone is best for growing potatoes, wheat, and barley.

The *puna*, or fourth zone, lies above the timberline. As a result, few trees grow in this zone. Instead, the land is used for grazing sheep and other animals.

The highest zone is called the *tierra helada* or "frozen lands." It is an area that stays covered with snow and ice.

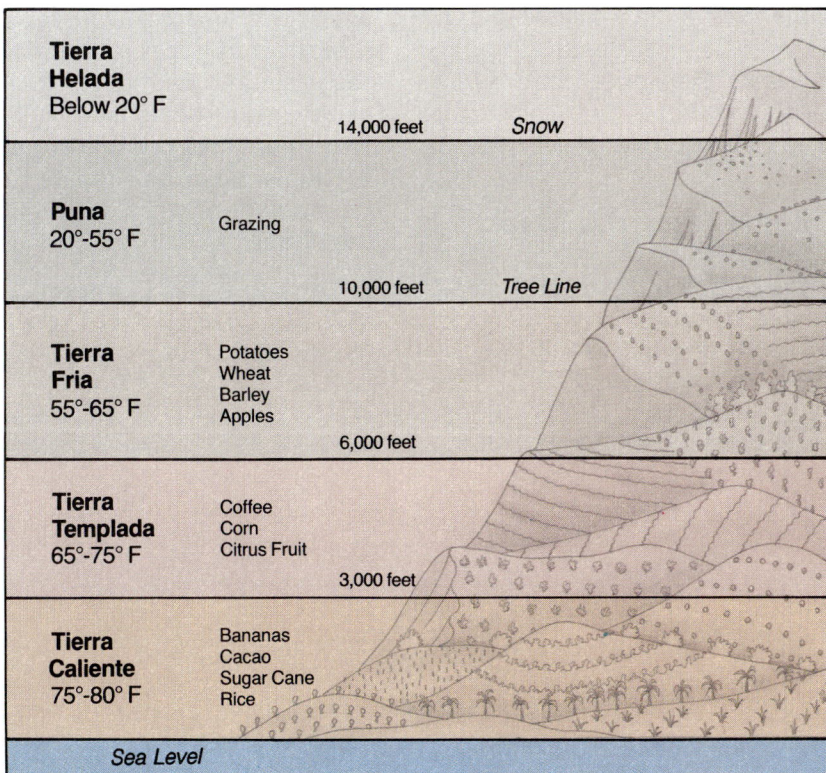

Zone	Temperature	Crops/Use	Elevation
Tierra Helada	Below 20° F		14,000 feet — Snow
Puna	20°-55° F	Grazing	10,000 feet — Tree Line
Tierra Fria	55°-65° F	Potatoes, Wheat, Barley, Apples	6,000 feet
Tierra Templada	65°-75° F	Coffee, Corn, Citrus Fruit	3,000 feet
Tierra Caliente	75°-80° F	Bananas, Cacao, Sugar Cane, Rice	Sea Level

Review

1. At 19° N, between which two elevations does the *tierra fria* occur?
2. Which zones do you think would be the best locations for large cities?
3. Which altitudinal zone occurs at 12,000 feet?
4. Which zone has the coldest average temperatures?

CHAPTER 9

Review

Section Summaries

1. From Mountains to Plains
Uplifting, volcanism, folding, faulting, and erosion created the varied landscape of Middle and South America. Plate movements in the region still build up mountains, cause earthquakes, and set off volcanic eruptions, especially in Middle America. In South America the results of plate movement are most evident in the Andes. Plains, plateaus, and a river basin are important landforms in South America.

2. Climate, Soils, and Vegetation
The climates and vegetation of Middle and South America vary widely. Many of the tropical countries have tropical rainforest or savanna climates, with canopied forests or tall grasses. Dry areas—steppes and deserts—are found in parts of Mexico and South America. Steppes have grassy patches and scrub vegetation. Cactuses and small shrubs grow in the desert. Mild climate regions, with grasses and forests, are found in southern South America.

3. The Heritage of the Past
The Mayas, Aztecs, and Incas created civilizations in Middle and South America. During the 1500s European conquerors and colonists changed the Indians' way of life and forced millions of Africans to work in Middle and South America as slaves. In the late 1700s, Middle and South Americans began their struggles against European domination. As a result, most countries in the region are independent.

4. The People of Latin America
Latin America's Indians and Spanish, Portuguese, and African immigrants all helped form Latin America's culture. Later immigrant groups made contributions in politics, business, and agriculture. Today the overall population of Latin America is growing rapidly. However, the rate of growth in some countries, especially in the West Indies, is slowing down. The density of the population also varies from country to country.

Using Geography Skills

Reviewing the Map Lesson
The slope on the tropical Grenada landscape below does not look as dramatic as the Mt. Orizaba cross section, but it does create crop variation. Using the diagram, decide if these statements are true or false. Correct any false ones.
1. Cocoa grows at the same elevation as bananas.
2. Coconuts are harvested along the coast.
3. You could expect to see coconut palms and nutmeg trees growing next to each other.

Using Social Studies Skills

1. **Sequence Historical Data.** In Section 3 of Chapter 9, find the dates and corresponding events that pertain to the wars for independence in Middle and South America. On a separate sheet of paper, arrange the dates and brief descriptions of the events along a vertical time line. Make the spaces on the time line proportionate to the number of years between the dates.

2. **Organize and Express Ideas in Written Form.** Use the information in Section 4 of

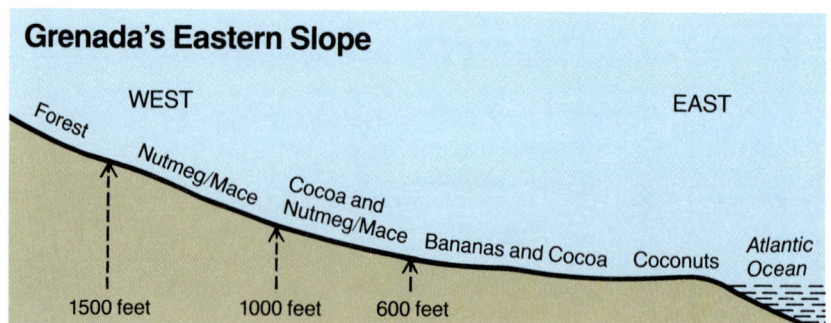

Grenada's Eastern Slope

WEST   EAST

Forest

Nutmeg/Mace

Cocoa and Nutmeg/Mace

Bananas and Cocoa   Coconuts   Atlantic Ocean

1500 feet   1000 feet   600 feet

Chapter 9 to write a paragraph describing the people of Brazil. Start by copying all sentences from the section that refer to Brazil's people. Then rewrite and rearrange the sentences to make a summary paragraph.

Testing for Understanding

Locating Key Places
Match each description below with the name of the place.
1. an Indian empire in Central Mexico
2. a desert area in Argentina
3. one of the driest places on earth
4. the largest metropolitan area in Latin America
5. a lowland area that lies chiefly in Brazil
6. an Indian empire in western South America
7. the capital and largest city of Argentina
8. Brazil's largest city
9. the capital and largest city of Peru
10. a wide plain in southeastern Mexico
a. Patagonia
b. Amazon Basin
c. Atacama Desert
d. São Paulo
e. Mexico City
f. Yucatán Peninsula
g. Aztec
h. Lima
i. Inca
j. Buenos Aires

Recalling Key Terms
Define these terms in your own words.

Section 1
altiplano
cordillera
isthmus

Section 2
selva

Section 3
creoles

Section 4
mestizos

Reviewing Main Ideas
Section 1
1. How were most of the landforms of Middle and South America created?
2. What are the major kinds of landforms found in Middle America?
3. What four geographic regions exist in South America?

Section 2
1. What climate type affects much of Middle and South America?
2. What causes dry areas to exist in parts of Middle and South America?
3. Where are mild climate regions located in South America?

Section 3
1. Why were the Mayas, Aztecs, and Incas important?

2. How did Europeans affect Middle and South America?
3. When did most of the colonies in Middle America win their independence?
4. How did the different colonies of South America gain their independence?

Section 4
1. In what ways did the Spanish and Portuguese contribute to Latin America's culture?
2. What kind of contributions did later groups of immigrants make to Latin America?
3. What are some population trends that vary greatly throughout Latin America?
4. Why have people moved from rural to urban areas?

Thinking Critically
1. **Evaluate Information.** Choose one of the statements below and support it with facts from the chapter. List the facts on a separate sheet of paper.
a. More Indians live in Mexico than in the Caribbean Islands.
b. Many immigrants to South America were from war-torn countries.

2. **Predict Effects.** Suppose a new factory is built in your neighborhood and incoming workers cause the population to double. What consequences would you predict for the area's schools, transportation system, recreational areas, and residential areas?

CHAPTER 10

Middle America

In this chapter you will learn about life in Mexico, Central America, and the West Indies.

Sections

1 **Mexico**
2 **Case Study: Mexico City**
3 **Central America**
4 **The West Indies**

SECTION 1

Mexico

Preview

Key Places
Where are these places located?
1 Mexico City
2 Yucatán
See the globe below.

Key Terms
What do these terms mean?
campesino
ejido

Main Ideas
As you read, look for the answers to these questions.
- What challenges do Mexico's history and geography present to its farmers?
- What main resources does Mexico have to improve its economy?
- How is Mexico's cultural heritage expressed?
- What issues cause friction between Mexico and the United States?

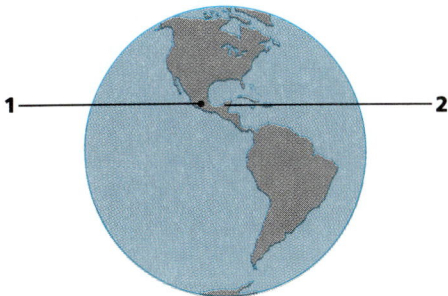

1——————————2

Here you may witness the blessings of the revolution caught in a single tear.

Mariano Azuela, *Los de Abajo*

Mexico's historical tradition and rugged terrain challenge farmers.

In 1916 Mariano Azuela, a Mexican novelist, wrote these words while in exile in Texas. He wanted to express his dissatisfaction with the achievements of the revolution that had shaken Mexico's social and political structure since 1910.

The Mexican Revolution. During colonial times, a sharp division had developed between wealthy landowners and the poor, landless peasant farmers. In 1910 the situation exploded and the peasant farmers, called **campesinos**, rebelled against the ruling class of wealthy landowners. The Mexican Revolution had officially begun. The battle cry of the campesinos was "Land and Liberty!"

Eventually, the campesinos won their liberty, and in 1917 a new constitution was written to give them their land. The 1917 constitution committed the government to redistributing Mexico's farmland. However, even though some land redistribution took place right away, it was not until 1934, when Lázaro Cárdenas became president, that it took place on a large scale.

The land was distributed into individual farms called **ejidos** [ā hē′dōs]. In one type of ejido, the people of a village work a large piece of land and share the harvest. In another type of ejido, each family in a village works its own area of land.

Facing page: Roman Catholic churches dominate townscapes all around Mexico, including this one in Taxco, near Mexico City.

Mexico, Central America, and the West Indies

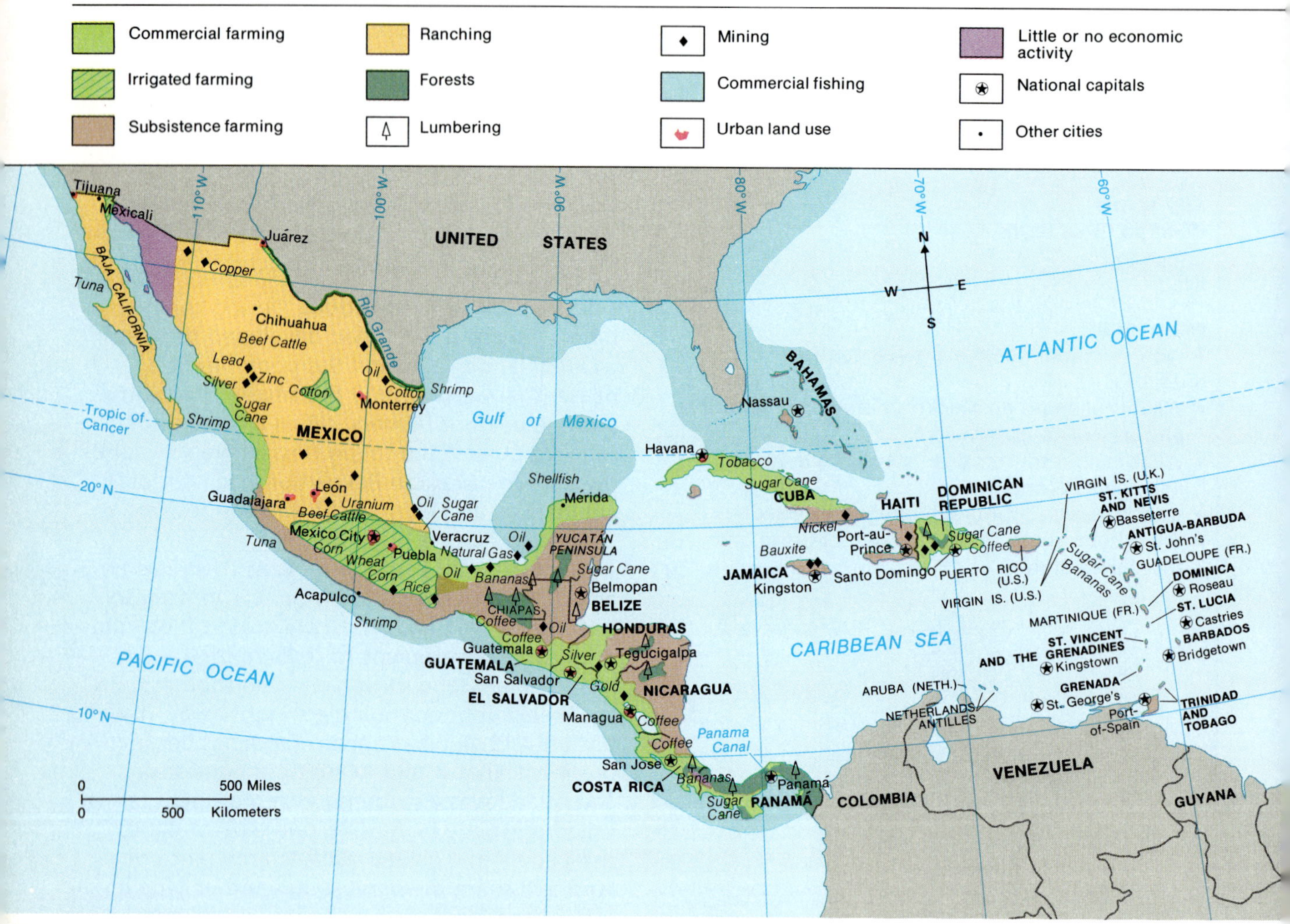

Commercial farming
Irrigated farming
Subsistence farming
Ranching
Forests
Lumbering
Mining
Commercial fishing
Urban land use
Little or no economic activity
National capitals
Other cities
110° W
100° W
90° W
80° W
70° W
60° W
N
W
E
S
UNITED STATES
Tijuana
Mexicali
Juárez
Copper
Tuna
BAJA CALIFORNIA
Chihuahua
Beef Cattle
Lead
Zinc
Silver
Cotton
Oil
Rio Grande
Monterrey
Shrimp
Sugar Cane
Tropic of Cancer
MEXICO
Gulf of Mexico
León
Uranium
Guadalajara
Beef Cattle
Mexico City
Corn
Wheat
Rice
Puebla
Veracruz
Oil
Sugar Cane
Natural Gas
Tuna
Acapulco
Shrimp
Shellfish
Mérida
YUCATÁN PENINSULA
Bananas
Sugar Cane
Belmopan
BELIZE
CHIAPAS
Coffee
HONDURAS
Guatemala
GUATEMALA
Silver
Tegucigalpa
San Salvador
Gold
EL SALVADOR
NICARAGUA
Managua
Coffee
PACIFIC OCEAN
20° N
10° N
Panama Canal
San José
Bananas
COSTA RICA
Sugar Cane
Panamá
PANAMÁ
COLOMBIA
VENEZUELA
GUYANA
0 500 Miles
0 500 Kilometers
Havana
Tobacco
Sugar Cane
CUBA
Nickel
Nassau
BAHAMAS
ATLANTIC OCEAN
HAITI
DOMINICAN REPUBLIC
Port-au-Prince
Santo Domingo
Sugar Cane
Coffee
Bauxite
JAMAICA
Kingston
PUERTO RICO (U.S.)
VIRGIN IS. (U.S.)
VIRGIN IS. (U.K.)
ST. KITTS AND NEVIS
Basseterre
ANTIGUA-BARBUDA
St. John's
GUADELOUPE (FR.)
Sugar Cane
Bananas
DOMINICA
Roseau
MARTINIQUE (FR.)
ST. LUCIA
Castries
BARBADOS
Bridgetown
ST. VINCENT AND THE GRENADINES
Kingstown
CARIBBEAN SEA
GRENADA
St. George's
ARUBA (NETH.)
NETHERLANDS ANTILLES
Port-of-Spain
TRINIDAD AND TOBAGO

Map Study

This map shows the political divisions and economic activities of Middle America. What is the capital of Mexico? What industries are located along the Mexican coastlines?

The main challenge for farmers today is that although ejidos make up about 45 percent of all of Mexico's total cropland, most of the land on the ejidos is suitable for growing only subsistence crops like corn and beans. Much of this land is dry and in need of regular irrigation.

Today commercial farms, which have most of the better quality land, grow 70 percent of Mexico's marketable food. These commercial farms are owned primarily by wealthy landowners, who can afford to buy good seeds and fertilizer and use modern irrigation and farm equipment. These farms are helping to improve Mexico's economy.

Sometimes when ejido farmers cannot grow enough food for their families, they sell their land to a commercial farmer. They then work as laborers. Other poor farmers look for work in the cities of Mexico or cross the border looking for work in the United States.

A rugged terrain. Mexico may be divided into six land regions, each presenting its own physical challenges.

The Baja California Peninsula and the mainland coastline along the Gulf of California on Mexico's west coast make up the first land region. All the land in this region is mountainous desert except along the mainland coastal strip. This coastal area contains very fertile farmland because it is irrigated by the Yacqui, Fuerte, and other rivers.

The second land region is the Central Plateau, which is in the middle of Mexico, surrounded by the mountain ranges of the Sierra Madres on all sides. The Central Plateau extends from beyond the U.S. border to Mount Orizaba. Find Mount Orizaba on the map on page 199. Some of Mexico's best farmland is found on the plateau's southern edge, where active volcanoes create fertile soil and there is good rainfall. Here corn, beans, and other crops have been grown since the earliest Indian settlements.

The Central Plateau, with its year-round mild climate, is where most of Mexico's major cities are located and where most of the people live. Mexico City, Mexico's industrial and cultural center, is located here. With about 15 million people, it is the world's first or second most populated city, depending upon the area included in the census.

Mexico's third geographical land region runs along the east coast following the Gulf of Mexico from the U.S. border to the Yucatán Peninsula. This land region is mostly dry and farming is possible only by using irrigation.

The highland areas along the southwestern section of the Sierra Madre del Sur, west of the Isthmus of Tehuantepec, make up the fourth land region. Land there is dry though farming takes place on the steep mountainsides and the flat tops of mountains.

Indians fish on Lake Pátzcuaro in Mexico's Central Plateau.

East of the Isthmus of Tehuantepec to the border of Guatemala is another group of highlands that make up Mexico's fifth land region. This region has high, flat mountaintops that are used for farming. It also has many valleys where modern farming methods and irrigation are being used to grow coffee, fruits, and other crops.

The Yucatán Peninsula is the sixth land region of Mexico. This region juts out into the Gulf of Mexico and borders Guatemala and Belize on the south.

Mexico's people, resources, and tourism help build its economy.

Even though Mexico's economy has been developing rapidly during the last 50 years, it has not kept up with its ever increasing population. Today more than 80 million people live in Mexico. By the year 2000, the population may reach 120 million.

Mexico City. Mexico's main population and industrial center is Mexico City, where 1,000 more people enter the city every day, hoping to find work. Many fail to find jobs, and housing is scarce. As a result, families build temporary shacks around the edge of the city, creating crowded, unplanned shantytowns. The Mexican government is taking steps to stimulate industrial development in other major cities such as Monterrey, Guadalajara, and Veracruz to relieve the overcrowding in Mexico City.

Natural resources. Mexico has a great variety of natural resources. Abalone, oysters, sardines, shrimp, and tuna are abundant in the coastal waters, lakes, and rivers. The seas have marlin, swordfish, and tarpon.

Mexico produces more than 40 different minerals. Since the time of the Aztecs, miners have dug gold and silver from the Mexican highlands. Today Mexico is a major producer of gold and one of the world's leading suppliers of silver.

Some of the largest industries in Mexico center around petroleum refining and the production of petroleum-based products. The discovery of major oil fields in the states of Tabasco and Chiapas and beneath the Gulf of Mexico has created jobs and the development of new industries. All oil is produced through a government-owned corporation called PEMEX. PEMEX employs more people and invests more money in industry than any other corporation in Mexico. However, because of the drop in demand for oil in the world market in the 1980s, these oil discoveries have not greatly helped the economy.

Tourism. Another major source of income and jobs in Mexico is the tourist industry. Warm, sunny climates and beautiful white beaches attract large numbers of tourists each year to resorts like Acapulco [ä′ kə pùl′kō] and Cancun [kan kün′]. These resort areas also provide jobs. Ancient Indian ruins in Mexico City, the Yucatán, and other areas of Mexico also attract scholars and tourists from all over the world. In Mexico City the Aztec ruins of the city Tenochtitlán sit alongside modern skyscrapers.

Mexico's cultural heritage is expressed through the arts.

When the Spanish missionaries arrived in Mexico in the early 1500s, they converted millions of Indians to Christianity. Today most Mexicans have a mestizo heritage, a combination of native Indian and European influences. This mestizo heritage can be seen in the cultural arts of modern Mexico.

Folk art. For more than 3,000 years the Indian artisans of Mexico have been creating beautiful art. Mexican folk artists create carved chests, lacquered trays, hand-woven and embroidered shirts, and gold and silver jewelry.

Today different areas of Mexico are known for different kinds of pottery and weaving. Mayan women on the Yucatán Peninsula make

This dramatic mural by Diego Rivera, a famous Mexican artist, depicts leaders and scenes of the Mexican Revolution.

cooking pots. Zapotec Indians of Oaxaca [wä-hä'kä] create shiny, black jars and wool rugs. Tarascan potters make figurines that look like devils and whistles shaped like owls and horses.

Fine arts and literature. Mexico has many world-famous writers and artists. Of the many writers, Octavio Paz, Carlos Fuentes, Martín Guzmán, and Mariano Azuela are just a few of the most well known.

An important influence on the arts has been the Mexican Revolution. After the revolution, efforts were made to decorate public buildings with paintings about Mexico to celebrate its his-tory. The most important artists to emerge from these efforts were Diego Rivera, José Clemente Orozco, David Alfaro Siqueiros, and Rufino Tamayo. These artists helped to bring the culture of Mexico to the rest of the world with their paintings. Their large murals, or wall paintings, have captured the interest and imagination of many.

Three issues cause friction between the United States and Mexico.

Illegal immigration, agricultural imports and

water usage challenge the relationship between the United States and Mexico. These issues are the major points of friction between the United States and our southern neighbor.

Illegal immigration. Each year thousands of jobless Mexicans cross the border into the United States looking for work. The money earned by these workers, usually from low-paying manual jobs, amounts to billions of dollars that is put back into the Mexican economy. During the 1970s jobs in the United States became scarce. Labor unions claimed that Mexican workers who had come into the United States illegally were taking jobs from U.S. citizens. In 1987 the U.S. government passed stricter laws against hiring these workers.

Agricultural imports. Mexico exports vegetables such as squash, peppers, eggplants, tomatoes and cucumbers all year long. Some farmers in the Southwest and Florida complain that low-priced Mexican vegetables create unfair competition for their own winter crops.

Water usage. Another issue yet to be resolved between Mexico and the United States is water usage. Some local governments in Mexico dispose of their sewage in rivers that flow north to the United States. As a result, California and the southwestern states are the recipients of dangerously polluted water. To help alleviate this problem, Tijuana [tē'ə wä'nə], Mexico, and San Diego, California, cooperated to build a common sewage treatment plant.

The use of the waters of the Colorado River has also caused friction between Mexico and the United States. In the United States, the Colorado River is used extensively for irrigation. Salt from the soil drains back into the river, which flows south to Mexico. (See map, page 199.)

Section 1 Review

Locating Key Places
Locate the following places on the map on page 220: Mexico City, Yucatán

Identifying Key Terms
Define the following terms: campesino, ejido

Reviewing Main Ideas
1. How are today's farmers affected by Mexico's revolutionary history and physical geography?
2. What natural resources does Mexico have to develop?
3. In what ways does Mexican art reflect the country's cultural heritage?
4. What three issues cause friction between the United States and Mexico?

Thinking Critically: Identify Assumptions
What assumptions were made when the government divided land into ejidos for the farmers? Write a paragraph to explain your answer.

This market in Oaxaca overflows with fresh farm products.

Case Study: Mexico City

Preview

Key Places
1 Tenochtitlán
2 Lake Texcoco
See the globe below.

Key Terms
What do these terms mean?
glyph
causeway

Main Ideas
As you read, look for answers to these questions.
- Why did the Aztecs establish Tenochtitlán as their capital?
- What three cultures does Mexico City reflect?
- What is life like for young people in Mexico City?

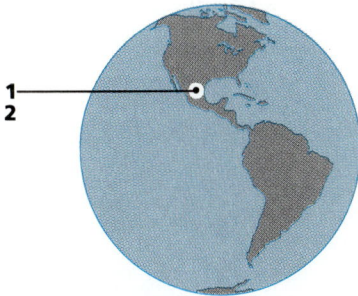

1
2

The following case study comes from three sources—"Mexico, The City That Founded a Nation," National Geographic, May, 1973; "The Aztecs," National Geographic, December, 1980; and "Two Teenagers Speak About Their Different Worlds," Scholastic Update, February 21, 1986. As you read, think about the history of Tenochtitlán, the three cultures of modern Mexico City, and some of the problems and opportunities facing teenagers who work and live in this capital city.

A legendary Aztec god told his people to establish Tenochtitlán.

The devout [religious] Aztecs were driven into the swamps of Lake Texcoco, where their hummingbird god then ordered them to look among the reeds and rushes: "Go, and go and look at the cactus, and on it . . . you shall see an eagle. It would be eating a snake and warming itself in the sun."

In the marshes of the lake they found their eagle and snake (modern Mexico's national emblem). Here they founded their capital and named it Tenochtitlán, or "place of the prickly-pear cactus." They boasted, "We shall confront all who surround us and . . . vanquish them all."

The year was A.D. 1325, according to Aztec chroniclers. During the next 194 years, the Aztecs made good their boast. Wars brought them new lands—from the Gulf to the Pacific and south to Guatemala. . . . From their new subjects the conquerors extracted tributes of food, firewood, precious metals, cloth, rare feathers, and cacao beans to be used as money. On bark paper they kept records with their **glyphs** [glifs], a cartoon way to jog the memory. Their three-city alliance—Tenochtitlán, Texcoco, and Tlacopan (now called Tacuba)—created a prosperous urban society without parallel. . . .

In 1519, Spanish conquistadors came to the Aztec capital. Bernard Díaz described the Aztec capital, Tenochtitlán, as it appeared to the Spanish. He wrote, "It was like the enchantments . . . on account of the great towers and temples . . . and buildings rising from the water . . . things never heard of, nor seen, nor even dreamed."

The leader of the conquistadors, Hernando Cortés, led his force of 400 Spaniards over a **causeway** [a road built across wet land or shallow water]. The Emperor Montezuma greeted him as a god, but Cortés took the monarch captive. Hostilities flared. Montezuma was injured and died, and the Aztecs almost annihilated the Spaniards on the *Noche Triste*—the "Night of Sadness." Cortés and his men fled, returning a year later to conquer Tenochtitlán, raze it, and build anew upon its ruins. On August 13, 1521, Cuauhtémoc, Montezuma's nephew and successor, surrendered to Cortés. Thus fell the mighty Aztec Empire.

Mexico City reflects its Aztec, Spanish, and modern heritage.

A policeman stopped the on-rushing masses of traffic while a small band of school children crossed the street to place nosegays [bouquets of flowers] before the statue of an imperious-looking Indian. They were commemorating the death of Cuauhtémoc, the last emperor of the Aztecs. . . .

It is no accident that Cuauhtémoc should be honored even as the Spaniard Hernando Cortés is virtually ignored at the scene of his greatest triumph. Though Mexicans are a product of four centuries of Europeanization . . . they do not forget their Indian past. . . . Mexico City is proud to remain, in a very real way, an Indian capital.

There are the monuments and the landmarks of the city. . . . One is the Plaza of the Three Cultures. Here, beside the partially restored

The Aztec capital of Tenochtitlán, shown in the model on the left, was destroyed in 1521. It has been replaced by the Zócalo (on the right), a public square that attracts vibrant parades such as this one commemorating the Mexican Revolution.

Aztec Pyramid and tianguis [tē an'gēs], or market, stand the Spanish Church of Santiago and the School of the Holy Cross. Along side these venerable relics rises the 20-story tower of the Ministry of Foreign Affairs. The three—tianguis, church, and tower—provide a perfect symbol of today's Mexico, a 20th-century American nation whose roots rest solidly in the rich soil of its cultural past, Indian and European.

Young people face problems and find opportunities in Mexico City.

One thousand people move to Mexico City each day. A small number will find homes on narrow Spanish-style streets, or in high-rise condominiums trimmed in glass and chrome, or among walled villas protected by armed guards. But most settle far from these symbols of wealth and progress. Instead, they will squeeze into the city's sprawling, unplanned shanty towns of cinderblock or wood-and-cardboard shacks, called Nezahualcoyotl [nə sä wäl'kō'yo tl] City.

There, Mario Vergara works in his grandparents' five table restaurant. . . . Mario, 15, works six days a week, earning about 600 pesos a day—about $1.33.

Mario's friends who work in factories can earn up to $4.44 a day. Others tend market stands, or like him, work in restaurants. Mario hopes to get a factory job in a few years. "I'd like to work with machines," he says. "There's a factory here where they make magazines." But he adds, "This work isn't boring. I like it."

. . . [Many] Mexicans prefer Nezahualcoyotl, and Mexico City, to the countryside. Since 1970, the capital's population has swelled from 9.2 million to 15 million. By 1990, experts predict the figure will hit 21.3 million, making Mexico City the world's most populous.

. . . Mario's family moved to the city 15 years ago. "There's nothing to do there," Mario says of his home village in the state of Mexico, which borders the capital.

Montserat Ceron lives just 25 miles from Nezahualcoyotl, but her life and attitudes are a world away. Montserat, 17, lives with her parents and four brothers and sisters in a house with its own garden, behind a wall in Mexico City's San Jeronimo neighborhood.

Montserat's life is active and entertaining. She studies tourism and business administration in one school and is finishing pre-college courses in another. She takes dance and French classes.

Montserat has visited the United States four times. And, the year after next, she plans to finish her education in Switzerland on a scholarship arranged by the Swiss ambassador, an acquaintance of her father's.

Montserat is comfortable with her privileges. "Sure, I have a good position," she says, "and I take advantage of it." People are poor, she insists, because they don't take advantage of opportunities.

The inability of people like Montserat to reach out to people like Mario troubles many Mexicans [and remains an important sociological problem yet to be resolved].

Section 2 Review

Locating Key Places
Locate the following places on the map on page 225: Tenochtitlán, Lake Texcoco

Identifying Key Terms
Define the following terms: glyph, causeway

Reviewing Main Ideas
1. What circumstances led the Aztecs to locate their capital at Tenochtitlán?
2. Why could Mexico City be called the "City of Three Cultures"?
3. What is life like for the poor in Mexico City? For the rich?

Thinking Critically: Recognize Values
What values are reflected in Aztec culture and in Spanish actions in the 1500s in Mexico?

Central America

Preview

Key Places
Where are these places located?
1 Nicaragua
2 Panama
See the globe below.

Key Terms
What do these terms mean?
chicle
junta
guerrilla warfare

Main Ideas
As you read, look for answers to these questions.
• Why is agriculture important to many Central Americans?
• How do nonagricultural workers in Central America make their living?
• What has caused unrest in most Central American countries?

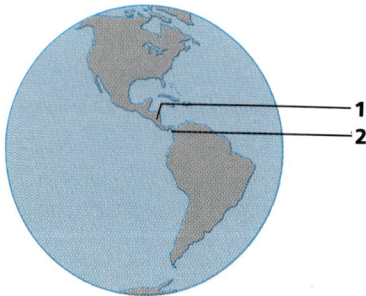

Middle America is a realm of vivid contrasts, matchless variety, turbulent history, current political turmoil, and an uncertain future.

Harm J. de Blij and Peter O. Muller,
geographers

Many Central Americans depend on agriculture to earn a living.

As de Blij and Muller conclude, the seven countries of Central America—Guatemala, Belize, Honduras, El Salvador, Nicaragua, Costa Rica, and Panama—indeed present vivid contrasts. For example, the people in each country are from many backgrounds. Guatemalans are mostly of Indian origin. Costa Ricans are mostly of European descent. Most people in Honduras, Nicaragua, and El Salvador are mestizo, and many people in Belize and Panama are of African background.

The people, natural resources, history, and governments are very different. However, despite these differences, all these countries have one thing in common—the major industry in all the Central American countries is agriculture.

Rich soils and a warm, rainy climate have helped make agriculture the economic mainstay of Central America. The rich soils are a result of the many volcanoes in the region. Abundant rainfall and warm climates in eastern Central America allow farmers to produce plentiful harvests year round. However, because of the savanna climate, with its dry season, along the Pacific Coast, farmers there depend on irrigation.

Farming and ranching. Campesinos in Central America generally raise subsistence crops such as corn, beans, and squash. Their small farms are often on the mountainsides or in high valleys. Plantation owners, on the other hand, export most of their crops, particularly to the United States. Workers on plantations in the cool highlands often raise coffee.

Plantation workers in the hot eastern lowlands along the Caribbean Sea grow bananas.

Cotton also has become increasingly important in the savanna areas along the Pacific Coast. Cotton now makes up more than 10 percent of the exports from Central America. Other major agricultural exports include sugar and rice.

Ranching is important in nearly all the Central American nations. Sheep are raised mainly for their wool, and beef is a major agricultural export. Ranches are generally located along the Pacific Coast.

Conserving soil. Forests once covered most of Central America. To make land for farming and grazing, many forests have been cleared. In addition, lumbering activities have destroyed some of the area's forests.

As a result of deforestation, much of the soil in Central America is unprotected against erosion. The heavy rains that fall in the area wash away the minerals, leaving the land infertile. Today several countries need reforestation programs to help conserve their soil.

Standards of Living in Central America

Country	Per capita income	Literacy rate	Life expectancy
Belize	$1,000	80%	60 years
Guatemala	$1,085	48%	55 years
Honduras	$ 590	55%	59 years
El Salvador	$ 854	62%	64 years
Nicaragua	$ 804	87%	58 years
Costa Rica	$2,238	90%	69 years
Panama	$1,116	87%	71 years

Central Americans also work in forestry, mining, fishing, and factories.

Besides agriculture, Central Americans work in lumbering, mining, fishing, or in factories. Forest workers harvest trees for fuel and timber. Timber and wood products are major exports from Belize, Guatemala, El Salvador, Honduras, and Panama. The chief timber trees are tropical hardwoods, such as rosewood and mahogany. However, pines, found mainly in the highlands and in northern Central America, are becoming increasingly important for the lumber industry.

Forest by-products are also valuable. For example, Indians use the gourds of calabash trees to make bowls. Other trees supply fruit. **Chicle** [chik'əl], a milky substance that comes from the sapodilla tree, is gathered in the forests of Guatemala and Belize and is used to make chewing gum.

Industries of the earth and sea. Mining is not an important industry in Central America because there are few mineral deposits in Central America. Some of the area's mineral exports are gold, silver, lead, zinc, copper, nickel, coal, and iron ore.

Most Central American countries have recently been drilling for oil. In the early 1980s, petroleum was discovered in Guatemala, but oil production has not been enough to meet domestic needs. Fuel oil is still one of the country's major imports.

Some Central Americans earn a living from the sea. Shrimp is the principal catch as well as an important export in most of the countries. Other catches on the Caribbean Coast include tuna, lobsters, snappers, and anchovies. On the Pacific Coast, fisheries harvest herring.

Industries in the cities. About 40 percent of the people in Central America live in or near cities. Many urban people work in factories, processing foods such as meat, sugar, and coffee. In addition, workers in Panama and Nicaragua are employed in the refining of imported oil. Other Central Americans work in the cement, chemical, clothing, and textile industries.

In addition, there are Indians in Guatemala who weave wool and cotton fabric on hand looms instead of on machines. Hand weaving there is a fine art. Even so, traditional Indian patterns are reproduced in factories at Quezal-tenango [ket sal'tə nāng'gō], Guatemala's textile center. Fabrics made there are sold to tourists and exported around the world.

The tourist industry thrives in Central America because people come to view the lush scenery in Costa Rica and the Mayan ruins in Guatemala and Honduras. Tourists also visit Panama to see the Panama Canal. In these areas, the tourist industry employs many workers. A number of Central Americans work for other service industries, such as government, transportation, and utilities. Trade is another important service industry, especially in Panama, where the Panama Canal attracts trading ships from around the world.

Workers in Costa Rica unload their harvest of coffee beans.

Civil war has caused unrest in most Central American countries.

Today all of the Central American countries have elected officials. For most Central Americans, however, choosing their own leaders has been a hard-won right. However, having elections has not necessarily brought democracy. There has been a long history of military rule in Central America, which some countries are now working hard to change. Costa Rica, however, has one of the most peaceful governments in Central America.

Foundations of civil war. Beginning in colonial times, Central American governments favored minorities of wealthy landowners. Government leaders denied poor Indian farmers a voice in government, and the landowners exploited the Indians for their labor. During the 1900s, an educated middle class began to demand fairer treatment for everyone.

By the mid-1900s, Central America was ripe for revolution. In most countries dictatorial juntas were in charge. A **junta** is a military group that takes over a government.

In an effort to overthrow the juntas, thousands of poor farmers and middle-class reformers resorted to fighting outside of the regular army. This type of fighting, which usually includes terrorist tactics such as harassing, ambushing, and raiding the enemy, is called **guerrilla warfare**.

Continued unrest. In several Central American countries, the guerrillas met with some success. For example, a new constitution was written for Guatemala in 1984. Two years later, Guatemalans elected a president and a congress. Salvadorans held elections, too. Despite the elections, dissatisfied guerrillas in both Guatemala and El Salvador continued to fight government supporters.

In 1984 Nicaraguans elected Daniel Ortega to the presidency. Ortega was a leader of the Sandinistas—a Marxist guerrilla group. Nicaragua's new government contributed to the general unrest in Central America during the 1980s. Sandinista leaders reputedly smuggled arms and money to guerrillas in Guatemala and El Salvador. In an effort to stop the spread of Marxist influence, the United States sponsored the contras—an anti-Sandinista group.

To try to end the hostilities in Central America, the leaders of Nicaragua, Costa Rica, El Salvador, Guatemala, and Honduras agreed to the Guatemala Plan in 1987. This plan called for a cease-fire in the civil wars, an end to aid for guerrilla fighters, and democratic reforms such as free elections. It will take time to see whether the accord will have lasting effects.

Peaceful Costa Rica. A stable government is one that is not likely to be overthrown. The most stable Central American government is that of Costa Rica. Costa Rica has been a republic since 1949, longer than any other Central American country. However, before 1949, Costa Rica had civil wars and military rule.

At that time, the government of Costa Rica eliminated its standing army in order to prevent future military takeovers. Today the country's only armed forces are civil guards who are part-time soldiers. Costa Ricans pride themselves on having more teachers than police.

Many people attribute Costa Rica's stability to its history. Its early Indians refused to be enslaved by the Spanish. Many of these Indians were killed by the Spanish or died of European diseases. Therefore, few Indians were available to work on large plantations. Instead, the economy depended on medium-sized farms worked by their Spanish owners.

As a result, Costa Rica has a long established middle class. Its per capita income is by far the highest in Central America. Costa Ricans also enjoy a fairly good standard of living. For example, they have a long life expectancy, a 90 percent literacy rate, and more doctors than any other Central American country.

Section 3 Review

Locating Key Places
Locate the following places on the map on page 220: Nicaragua, Panama

Identifying Key Terms
Define the following terms: chicle, junta, guerrilla warfare

Reviewing Main Ideas
1. Why is agriculture important throughout Central American countries?
2. In what industries are nonagricultural workers in Central America employed?
3. What factors have caused unrest in many Central American countries?

Thinking Critically: Analyze Comparisons
In this section Costa Rica was compared to other Central American countries because it has the most stable government. What factors do you think might have contributed to, and helped maintain peace in Costa Rica, and not in other countries?

SECTION 4

The West Indies

Preview

Key Places
Where are these places located?
1 Bahama Islands
2 Jamaica
See the globe below.

Key Terms
What do these terms mean?
one-crop economy   coup
light industry
heavy industry

Main Ideas
As you read, look for answers to these questions.
• Who are the people of the West Indies?
• What is the importance of agriculture to the people and the land in the Caribbean?
• What kinds of resources are developed in the West Indies?
• What is the political status of the various Caribbean governments?

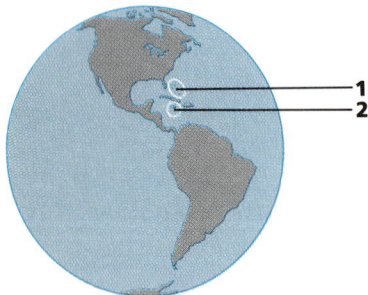

We shall speak. We shall sing.
We shall shout. Full voice, great voice,
you shall be our good and our guide.

Césaire

West Indians are descendants of European settlers and African slaves.

Césaire, a poet from the Caribbean island of Martinique, wrote these lines describing West Indian aspirations. The *we* in the poem refers to the poor of the islands who sang and shouted to raise their spirits while they slaved for colonial landowners. That same spirit helps people face the challenges of living in the West Indies today.

The West Indies are made up of the Bahamas, the Greater Antilles, and the Lesser Antilles. The Bahama Islands stretch from the southern tip of Florida to the Greater Antilles. These islands are generally considered to be part of the Caribbean even though they lie in the Atlantic Ocean.

The total population of the West Indies is about 30 million people—slightly more than the population of Central America. Cuba, with 10 million people, is the most populous Caribbean country. Only five other Caribbean places have more than 1 million residents—the Dominican Republic, Haiti, Puerto Rico, Jamaica, and Trinidad and Tobago.

The origins of the West Indians. The people of the Caribbean are often called West Indians. However, unlike Mexicans and Central Americans, few people of the Caribbean are American Indians. Many groups of Caribbean Indians were almost totally wiped out by European diseases and forced labor on plantations.

Most West Indians today are descendants of black Africans who were brought from West Africa to work as slaves on island plantations beginning in the 1700s. Other West Indians have European backgrounds. They are descendants of

British, French, Dutch, and Spanish colonists. A large number of West Indians are of mixed African and European ancestry. Some West Indians are descended from Asians, mainly East Indians, who came to work the Caribbean plantations in the later 1800s. The Asians provided cheap labor after slavery was abolished.

Cultural heritage in the Caribbean. Many islands have had more cultural contact with the European countries that colonized them than with one another. Most of the people in Cuba, the Dominican Republic, and Puerto Rico speak Spanish. However, many West Indians speak other languages. English is spoken by many people in Puerto Rico and the Virgin Islands because these islands are part of the United States. English also is the official language in Jamaica, Barbados, and the Bahamas since these islands were British colonies. In the French Antilles, the official language is French and in the Netherlands Antilles, Dutch. Many people of the Caribbean speak patois [pat'wä], a dialect that is a mixture of African languages, French, and English.

Europeans and Africans have influenced other aspects of Caribbean culture besides language. For example, cricket—a game played with a ball and a flattened bat—is popular on some Caribbean islands. Cricket was brought to the West Indies by British colonists.

African and European traditions also have affected Caribbean music. Spanish colonists brought stringed instruments to the West Indies. Later, West Indians developed their own unique instruments, such as steel drums and the three-stringed bamboo violin. African rhythms greatly influenced the calypso music that originated on Trinidad and the reggae music that began in Jamaica.

This Haitian woman carries woven baskets to market.

West Indian agricultural methods provide food but erode the land.

Many of the people of the West Indies live in rural areas. These people are often poor subsistence farmers who work as few as one or two acres. They raise yams, corn, sweet potatoes, and tropical fruits like guavas and mangoes. These small farmers use simple tools to work their land, and almost none of them have mechanized farm equipment.

Other agricultural workers are employed on large plantations. West Indian plantations produce crops such as coffee, cacao, cotton, tobacco, bananas, and sugar cane for export. Plantations in the Lesser Antilles also produce limes, nutmeg, coconuts, and pineapples.

On the island of St. Vincent, a major export crop is arrowroot. This root can be ground into a starch that is used in baby food and in producing computer paper. A number of Caribbean nations are dependent on one crop for a large part of their income. For example, Cuba is especially dependent on sugar cane. Sugar accounts for about 75 percent of Cuba's exports.

Recently, many Caribbean nations have tried to diversify their crops. A **one-crop economy**, in which only one crop provides a country's entire income, can be very risky. Diseases or other natural disasters can destroy an entire crop. Alternatively, increased competition from other countries might push down crop prices on the world market, thereby reducing the country's income. As a result, a nation's economy might be devastated.

Besides farming, ranches are found in almost all the West Indies. Hogs, sheep, and other livestock are important in Jamaica, Haiti, the Dominican Republic, and the Bahamas. Cuba is the major cattle producer.

For generations West Indian farmers have used slash-and-burn agriculture to clear land. This method involves killing a tree by slashing its bark. After the tree is dead, it is set on fire. The ashes are used to fertilize the ground. Then the farmers plant crops.

The widespread practice of slash-and-burn agriculture in the Caribbean has resulted in grasslands and farms now covering what was once forestland. In addition, burning wood for fuel has destroyed many forests. The result of all this deforestation is erosion. Heavy rains have washed much soil from the Caribbean islands because there are no tree roots to hold it in place.

Natural resources are being developed in West Indian industries.

Fishing, mining, manufacturing and tourism are the main industries in the West Indies. Fishing is an important economic activity in almost all the Caribbean islands. Shark, tuna, grouper, red snapper, and various types of shellfish are found in the coastal waters of the West Indies. The Bahamas and Cuba have especially rich fishing banks.

In the 1970s the Cuban government developed a deep-sea fishing fleet in an effort to reduce the country's dependence on sugar production. As a result, Cuba has the largest fishing industry of all the Caribbean islands.

Mining. Although mining is not an important economic activity in most of the West Indies, a few of the islands have important min-

A fisherman pulls in his catch in the Virgin Islands.

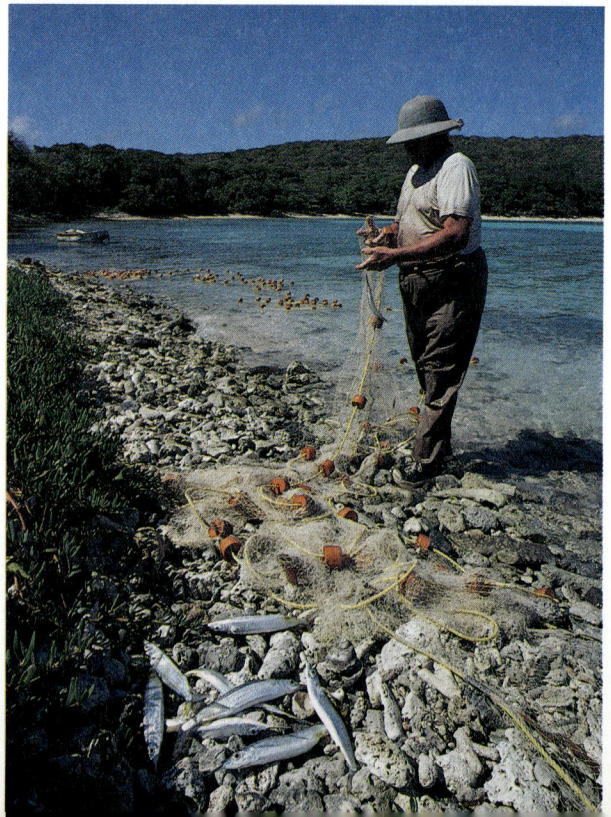

eral deposits. Miners in Jamaica extract bauxite, which is used to make aluminum. Jamaica is one of the world's leading bauxite producers, and bauxite is Jamaica's most valuable export.

Oil workers in Trinidad drill for petroleum and natural gas. The economy of Trinidad relies heavily on petroleum and petroleum products, but it is feared that the island's reserves may run dry by the middle 1990s. Another major mineral export from Trinidad is asphalt, which is mined at the island's Pitch Lake.

Cuba has some of the largest nickel reserves in the world and is one of the world's chief nickel producers. Large iron ore deposits are also found in Cuba.

Oil refining is important in the Caribbean, but most of the oil processed there has been imported. Trinidad, Puerto Rico, Jamaica, Aruba, Curaçao, and the Bahamas all have oil refineries.

Manufacturing and tourism. The chief resource used in Caribbean manufacturing is workers. Cheap and plentiful labor lures businesses from the United States mainland, and from other industrialized nations. The island governments encourage investment by foreign businesses by giving them tax breaks.

Freeport is the manufacturing center in the Bahamas. Factories in and around the city produce cement, steel piping, furniture, medicine, and processed food. Factories can operate there tax-free until 2054.

Tax breaks have encouraged producers of electronic and electrical equipment to increase their factories in Puerto Rico. Other goods manufactured by Puerto Rico include rum, clothing, medicine, metal products, and chemicals. The island is the leader in the production of consumer products like food and clothing. This type of production is called **light industry**.

The Caribbean leader in heavy industry is Cuba. **Heavy industry** is the production of heavy machinery, such as trucks and electric generators, for use in other industries. Cuban factories also produce other goods, such as processed food, textiles, and chemicals. Heavy industry has not developed in other parts of the Caribbean because there has traditionally been a small market for heavy machinery.

Perhaps the best-known resources of the West Indies are their scenic beaches, warm climates, and clear coastal waters. Large numbers of tourists visit the islands each year. As a result, shops, hotels, restaurants, and other tourist facilities are the major sources of jobs on many islands.

Caribbean governments can be divided into three groups.

Politically, there are three kinds of government in the Caribbean. The first group includes the islands that are dependencies of other countries. The second group is made up of islands that have recently become independent. The third group is made up of the countries of Cuba, Haiti, and the Dominican Republic, which established their independence long ago.

Dependencies. The Caribbean countries that are dependencies of other nations have been generally content to remain so. In most cases they manage their own local affairs but receive financial aid and military protection from their ruling power. Britain's Caribbean dependencies include the Cayman Islands, Montserrat, the British Virgin Islands, Anguilla, and the Turks and Caicos Islands. France's Caribbean dependencies are Guadeloupe and Martinique. The five Netherlands Antilles are Bonaire, Curaçao, St. Eustatius, St. Maarten, and Saba. Aruba is a separate Dutch dependency.

Puerto Rico is a U.S. commonwealth, and Puerto Ricans are U.S. citizens. They govern themselves and also send a nonvoting representative to the U.S. Congress. As a result, people and goods can travel freely between Puerto

Rico and the mainland. The United States supplies a nearby market for Puerto Rican goods, investment money for industries, and financial aid.

The Virgin Islands of St. Thomas, St. Croix, and St. John are also United States possessions. Like Puerto Rico, the people on the Virgin Islands are U.S. citizens who have a nonvoting representative in Congress.

Newly independent countries. Since the early 1960s, Britain has granted independence to a number of its Caribbean colonies. These former colonies include the Bahamas, Jamaica, Antigua and Barbuda, Dominica, St. Christopher-Nevis, St. Vincent and the Grenadines, Grenada, St. Lucia, Barbados, and Trinidad and Tobago. All these countries have parliamentary democracies like Britain's.

Some of the newly independent Caribbean countries have not had the military and financial strength to resist interference in their governments. Dominica's government experienced three attempted coups in 1980. A **coup** is a sudden takeover of an existing government. Grenada had a bloodless revolution in 1979. Four years later communists in Grenada attempted another coup. U.S. troops invaded the island to stop the apparent communist takeover.

Long-established independent countries. Cuba, Haiti, and the Dominican Republic have been independent much longer than the other West Indian nations. Cuba has been the most economically successful. Since a communist-led revolution in 1959, Cuba has received substantial military and financial aid from the Soviet Union. Cuba in turn sends aid to other communist governments in need.

Between 1957 and 1986, two dictators, President François Duvalier followed by his son Jean-Claude, ruled Haiti, which is the poorest nation in the Americas. They used their positions to become wealthy while the average Haitian struggled to survive. In 1986 the Haitians rebelled

and forced Jean-Claude Duvalier to flee the country.

Since then, Haitians have protested against their new military government. Since the rebellion, the economy has failed to improve, bringing unrest and violence.

The political history of the Dominican Republic has been one of dictatorship and revolution. Despite this turbulent history, the past 20 years have been fairly peaceful. However, during the 1980s trouble reappeared. When the price of sugar fell on the world market, the economy of the Dominican Republic became depressed. To offset the government's losses, the president raised prices for food and gasoline. These actions provoked riots and the Dominican Republic came close to another revolution.

Section 4 Review

Locating Key Places
Locate the following places on the map on page 220: Bahama Islands, Jamaica

Identifying Key Terms
Define the following terms: one-crop economy, light industry, heavy industry, coup

Reviewing Main Ideas
1. What are the origins of the Caribbean people?
2. How do the agricultural methods used in the West Indies provide food while eroding the land?
3. What resources are being developed in the West Indies?
4. What is the political status of the governments of the West Indies?

Thinking Critically: Identify Assumptions
In Section 4, you read that the Haitians are protesting their new government because the economy failed to improve after Duvalier fled the country. What assumption is being made by the people of Haiti? Justify your answer in one or two sentences.

MAP LESSON

Reading a Tourist Map

Chapultepec Park is one of Mexico City's leading attractions for residents and tourists alike. It is one of the world's greatest urban parks, housing a zoo, seven major museums, the national auditorium, and the official residence of the president of Mexico. How would you get around if you were a tourist? This map would show you the highlights to see.

This map for tourists shows only the highlights. Places of special interest are identified in the key and numbered on the map. Sometimes a sketch of the place is shown to help visitors find the place more easily.

For example, see #20, the Petroleos Monument. The key lists the places in the order one might see them on several separate visits to the park.

Your first visit, to the older section of the park, would take a whole day if you wanted to visit everything that is numbered 1 to 13. The map below could help you with the following situations.

If you start at the Diana Fountain, you would enter the park at which corner?

It would take you all day if you wanted to see all the exhibits in the world-famous collection of the Anthropology Museum. What number is it on the map?

Review

Another visit to the park might take you to attractions #14 to 17. The route is easy to get to from Hotel El Presidente Chapultepec. From there you could walk to the Restaurante del Lago for lunch and then spend the afternoon at the Museum of Natural History.
1. Which direction is the Museum from the hotel?
2. Would it be convenient for a person staying in the hotel to attend a program at the National Auditorium?
3. If a hotel guest wanted to visit the zoo, what direction would he or she walk? On which street?

Chapultepec Park

Key

1. Diana Statue and Fountain
2. Monument to the Boy Heroes
3. Statue to Simon Bolivar
4. Museum of Modern Art
5. Chapultepec Castle
6. National Museum of History
7. The Gallery of Mexican History
8. Chapultepec boating lake
9. Anthropology Museum
10. Zoo
11. Botanical gardens
12. Molino del Rey
13. Los Pinos (Presidential Residence)
14. Restaurante del Lago
15. Large boating lake in New Chapultepec Park
16. Small boating lake—landmark
17. Museum of Natural History
18. Amusement area
19. Technological Museum
20. Petroleos Monument
21. Queretaro Highway
22. Lerma water intake murals
23. National Auditorium
24. Hotel El Presidente Chapultepec

237

Review

Section Summaries

1. Mexico Mexicans face several challenges. Farmers are challenged by Mexico's historical tradition and rugged terrain. The country's people, resources, and tourism industry are helping to build an economy that has had to support a rapidly growing population. In addition, the government must deal with three issues that have been causing friction between Mexico and the United States.

2. Case Study: Mexico City The Aztec capital of Tenochtitlán was a prosperous urban society until the Spanish conquest in 1521. Today Mexico City reflects its Aztec, Spanish, and modern heritage. Young Mexicans have various problems and opportunities in Mexico City. Those from poor families live in shanty towns, and they work hard for low wages. Teenagers from wealthy families go to school and take part in many extra activities.

3. Central America Central America is an area of many contrasts. The people generally earn their living in a variety of industries, including farming, ranching, forestry, mining, fishing, manufacturing, and tourism. Many Central American countries are torn by civil war. Costa Rica, however, has had a stable and peaceful government and a successful economy.

4. The West Indies The people of the West Indies are mostly descendants of African slaves and European settlers. They speak a variety of languages. Most people live in rural areas and work on small farms or plantations. The countries of the Caribbean include dependencies of other countries, newly independent states, and independent states of long standing.

Using Geography Skills

Reviewing the Map Lesson

The Zócalo is a large plaza in Mexico City. Ever since the city was founded in 1325 this area has been the center of the city.

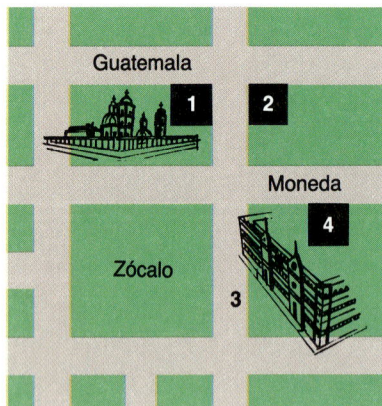

Key
1. Cathedral and Sagrario Metropolitano
2. Santa Teresa Aztec Ruins
3. National Palace
4. Cultures Museum

1. The Cathedral of Mexico is the oldest and one of the largest churches in the Americas. It is located on which side of the Zócalo?

2. The National Palace, the seat of the Mexican government, is located on which side of the plaza?

3. In 1913, when workers were digging the foundation for a new building, they uncovered a corner of the Great Pyramid from Aztec times. What number is this site on the map?

Using Social Studies Skills

1. Distinguish Fact from Opinion. Decide whether each of the following statements is a fact or an opinion:

a. The government of Mexico owns all the country's oil fields.

b. The tourist industry is a major source of jobs in Mexico.

c. The Mexican government is trying harder than any other government to create jobs for its people.

d. Mexican artists create the most beautiful pottery in the world.

e. The Aztecs had the greatest civilization in the Americas.

2. Perceive Cause-effect Relationships. In your own words, explain how the history of Costa Rica has resulted in a middle-class society.

Testing for Understanding

Locating Key Places
Match each description below with the name of the correct place.

1. swampy area where the Aztecs built their capital city
2. one of the world's leading bauxite producers
3. country where the Sandinistas are in power
4. capital city of the Aztec Empire
5. one of Mexico's major cities
6. location of the city of Freeport
7. the world's second most populated city
8. tourist area famous for its canal

a. Mexico City
b. Jamaica
c. Nicaragua
d. Lake Texcoco
e. Panama
f. Bahama Islands
g. Tenochtitlán
h. Monterrey

Recalling Key Terms
Define the following terms in your own words.

Section 1
campesino
ejidos

Section 2
glyph
causeway

Section 3
chicle
junta
guerrilla warfare

Section 4
one-crop economy
light industry
heavy industry
coup

Reviewing Main Ideas
Section 1
1. How do Mexico's land and history challenge its farmers today?
2. What are some of Mexico's natural resources?
3. How do Mexico's cultural arts express the country's heritage?
4. What are three issues that challenge the relationship between the United States and Mexico?

Section 2
1. Why did the Aztecs choose Tenochtitlán as their capital?
2. What three cultures exist side by side in Mexico City?
3. What is it like for young people who live in Mexico City?

Section 3
1. Why do Central American countries count on agriculture?
2. What nonagricultural industries are important to Central America?
3. Why is there unrest in some Central American countries?

Section 4
1. Where do most Caribbean people's ancestors come from?
2. What effect does agriculture have on the people and the land of the West Indies?
3. What human and natural resources are being developed in the West Indies?
4. What is the political status of the Caribbean countries?

Thinking Critically
1. Recognize Values. Based on the list of Mexican holidays below and on information in Section 2 of this chapter, list two values of the Mexican people. January 1 (New Year's Day), February 5 (Constitution Day), March 21 (Birthday of Benito Juárez), Easter, May 1 (Labor Day), May 5 (Anniversary of the Battle of Puebla), September 1 (President's Annual Message), October 12 (Columbus Day or Day of the Race), November 2 (Day of the Dead), November 20 (Anniversary of the Revolution), December 12 (Day of Our Lady of Guadalupe), December 25 (Christmas)

2. Make Decisions. Use an encyclopedia or other book, or call or visit a travel agent to find out about interesting tourist areas in the West Indies. Decide which country would make the best tourist spot. Write and illustrate a two-page travel brochure describing why.

South America

In this chapter you will read about the peoples and landscapes of South America.

Sections

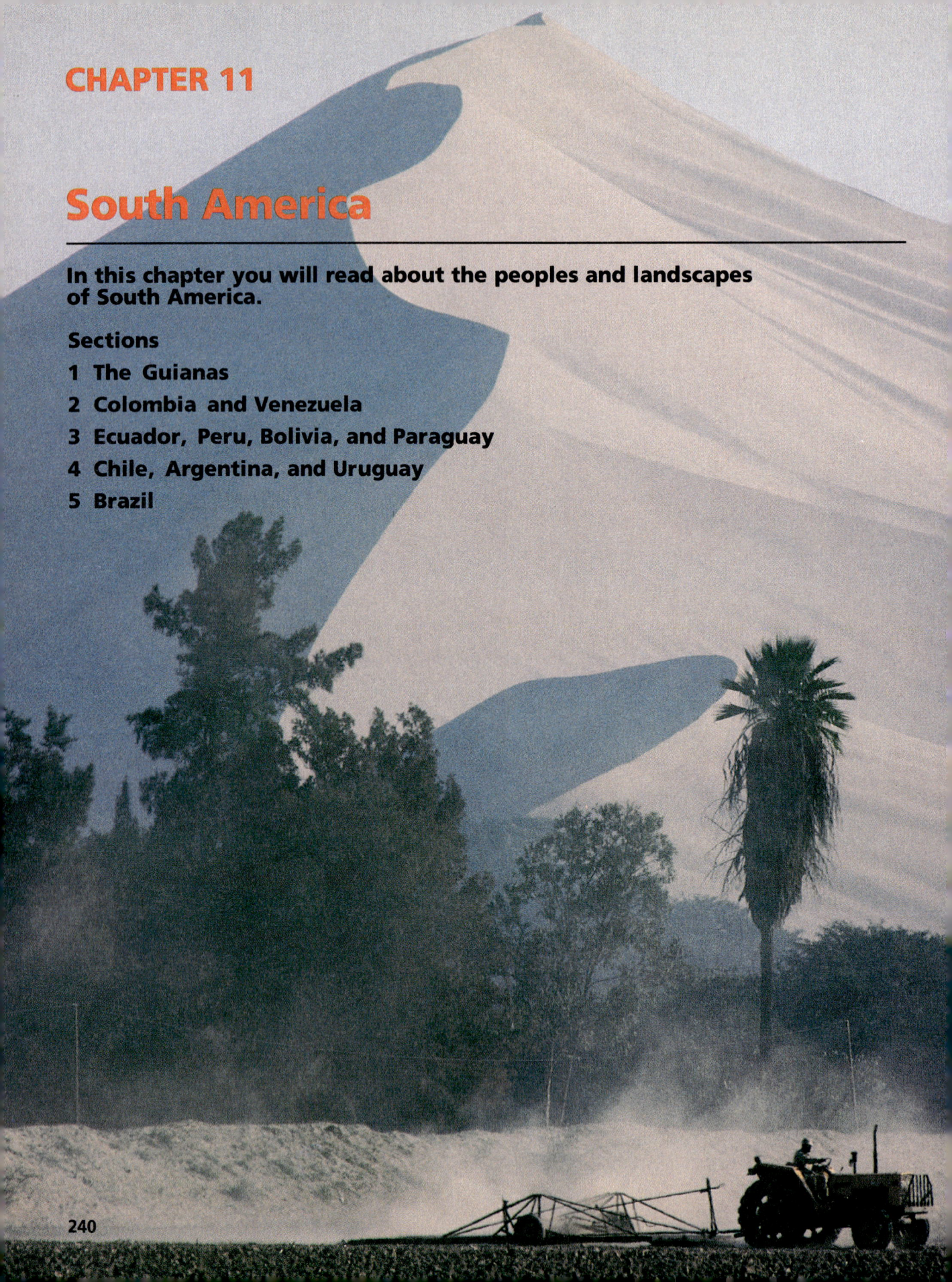

The Guianas

Preview

Key Places
Where are these places located?
1 Guyana
2 Suriname
3 French Guiana
See the globe below.

Key Terms
What do these terms mean?
plantain
bush

Main Ideas
As you read, look for answers to these questions.
- What are Guyana's main economic activities?
- In which industries do Suriname's people work?
- How is French Guiana different from the other Guianas?

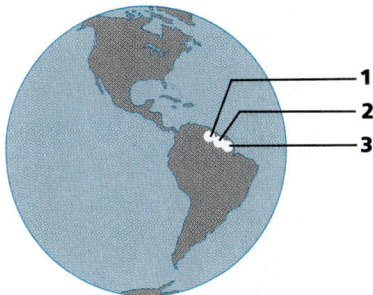

It has all the components to thrill even the most jaded explorer: a jungle that is penetrable only by motorized, native canoe; exotic birds that include parrots and macaws; stunning orchids that block your way along the river path.

Stephen Birnbaum's *South America*

Most of Guyana's people work in primary or service industries.

Travel book writer Stephen Birnbaum portrays Guyana's tropical rainforest as unspoiled and splendid. He describes the natural beauty the first settlers saw when they arrived.

Europeans first began to explore and settle the land that is now Guyana during the late 1500s. In 1581 the Dutch founded a settlement and officially claimed the area. Later in 1814 the British challenged this claim and won control of what then became the colony of British Guiana. In 1966 the colony won its independence and became the nation of Guyana.

Both the Dutch and British had established plantations on Guyana's hot, humid coasts, importing workers from their other colonies in Africa and Asia. As a result, the nearly one million people of Guyana today are descendants of not only Arawak, Carib, and Warrau Indians, but also Africans, Europeans, and Asians, particularly from India. Today about 58 percent of Guyana's people are Roman Catholic, 33 percent are Hindu, and 9 percent are Muslim.

Guyana is an Indian word meaning "land of many waters." Besides the coastal waters of the Atlantic Ocean, Guyana also has an extensive river system. The rivers transport soil and empty much of it into the Atlantic Ocean. On their

Facing page: **South American farmers face many challenges. Here a farmer plows near the sand dunes at Ica, on Peru's south coast.**

241

South America

Legend

- Commercial farming
- Irrigated farming
- Subsistence farming
- Ranching
- Forests
- Lumbering
- Hunting, fishing, and gathering
- Mining
- Commercial fishing
- Urban land use
- Little or no economic activity
- National capitals
- Other cities

Map Labels

Maracaibo · Oil · Caracas
Bananas
Coffee · Oil
Coffee · Beef Cattle · Georgetown
Gold · Orinoco · Iron Ore · GUYANA
Medellín · LLANOS · Paramaribo
Emeralds · VENEZUELA · Bauxite · Cayenne
Cali · Bogotá · SURINAME · FRENCH GUIANA (FR.)
COLOMBIA

GALÁPAGOS IS. (ECUADOR)
Quito · Coal · Rio Negro · Bauxite · Shrimp
ECUADOR · Oil · Amazon R. · Manaus · Fortaleza
Guayaquil

PACIFIC OCEAN
Trujillo · PERU · Rubber · BRAZIL · Iron Ore · Recife
Sugar Cane · Quartz Crystals · Sugar Cane
Tuna · Madeira River
Anchovies · Lima · Silver · Tocantins River · Salvador
Copper · La Paz · Nickel · Cacao
Arequipa · BOLIVIA · Goiânia · Brasília · Coffee
Lake Titicaca · Tin · Santa Cruz · Beef Cattle
Silver · Sucre · Iron Ore · Gold · Shrimp
Copper · Paraguay R. · Belo Horizonte

ATLANTIC OCEAN

Antofagasta · PARAGUAY · Sugar Cane · Fruits · Rio de Janeiro
Cotton · Coffee · São Paulo
Asunción · Itaipu Dam · Curitiba
CHILE · Cotton · Paraná R.
Córdoba · Pôrto Alegre
Valparaíso · Rosario · Sheep · URUGUAY
Santiago · Wheat · Buenos Aires · Montevideo
Copper · PAMPAS · Corn · Rio de la Plata
Talcahuano · ARGENTINA
Beef Cattle · Wheat · Mar del Plata
Oil · Natural Gas
Sheep · Tuna
Sardines · FALKLAND IS. (U.K.)

Scale
0 — 500 — 1000 Miles
0 — 500 — 1000 Kilometers

Map Study

In the Guianas, where is most commercial farming done? Which side of the continent, west or east, seems to have more productive farmland? Why do you think this would be?

242

way, the rivers leave rich deposits that make Guyana's coastal lands a fertile growing area.

Many of Guyana's people work in such primary industries as farming or mining. About one-third of the people work on plantations. Coastal farmers grow sugar cane, rice, citrus fruits, cacao, coffee, and **plantains**, a banana-like fruit. In the northeast and southwest of the country, cattle are raised on the savannas. Mining is also important. Since 1916 miners have been producing bauxite, a mineral from which aluminum is extracted. Bauxite is one of the country's major exports. Miners also extract gold, diamonds, and manganese, a mineral used in paints and chemicals.

In addition, almost 25 percent of Guyana's 850,000 people live in Georgetown, the country's national capital and chief port. Many people work in such service industries as government and commerce. The government is run by an elected president who is the majority leader of the legislature. The president appoints a prime minister who then selects a Cabinet to assist in running the government.

Suriname's diverse peoples work in primary or secondary industries.

The country just east of Guyana is now known as Suriname. It is a small country in which 80 percent of the land is covered by mountainous rainforests. As a result, most of its 400,000 people live in the flat area along the coast.

People. Suriname was a British colony until 1667 when the Dutch exchanged it for what later became the state of New York. During the early 1800s, control shifted a number of times between Britain and the Netherlands. In 1815 the Dutch gained permanent control of the area, then known as Dutch Guiana. In 1975 Dutch Guiana became independent and formally became Suriname.

The people of Suriname have varied racial and ethnic backgrounds. As in Guyana, European

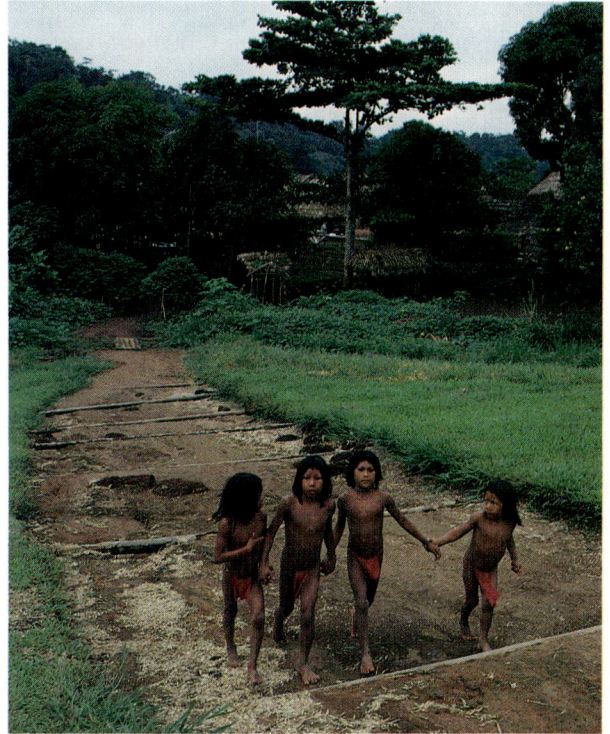

These Indian children live in Suriname's rugged interior.

settlers imported African slaves to work their plantations. During the 1600s, before the Dutch abolished slavery, a number of black African slaves escaped into the **bush**—areas of wild, unsettled forest—where some of their descendants still live today, following African tribal customs.

After a slave revolt in 1863, the Dutch brought workers from Indonesia and India to work on the plantations. The population of Suriname today reflects its history. About two-thirds of Suriname's people are of Indian descent or of mixed European and African descent. The remaining third of the population are of various ethnic backgrounds, each of which has preserved its own culture, religion, and language.

About 40 percent of Suriname's 380,000 people live in Suriname's capital and chief port, Paramaribo. In 1988 Suriname's government switched from a military to elected civilian government.

Industry. Most of Suriname's economy is based on mining and processing metals. Bauxite and aluminum provide about 90 percent of Suriname's exports.

Agriculture also plays an important role in Suriname's economy. Most farming is done in the coastal areas. One of Suriname's main exports is rice, but farmers also grow corn, coffee, bananas, cacao beans, sugar cane, and citrus fruits. In addition, the country's forests yield a variety of tropical hardwoods that are used for lumber.

About twice as many people work in manufacturing as in agriculture. They produce aluminum, processed foods, bricks, and wood products. Most of the raw materials they use come from primary industries in Suriname.

French Guiana remains a colony of France.

The French first settled what is now French Guiana in 1604 and claimed it as a colony in 1667. Except for a short time in the early 1800s, when the country was ruled by English and Portuguese armies, French Guiana has remained under French rule.

People. About 80,000 people live in French Guiana today. About 90 percent of the people live in and around the coastal capital of Cayenne. One of French Guiana's exports, cayenne pepper (a hot red pepper), is named after the capital city.

Most of French Guiana's people are descendants of African slaves brought to the colony in the 1600s and 1700s. Most of the remaining population has European, American Indian, Chinese, or African backgrounds. Although most people choose to live on the coast, the native Indians live in the dense rainforests that dominate French Guiana's interior.

Industry. French Guiana has abundant fertile soil and good rainfall in its interior. Farmers raise rice, corn, bananas, sugar cane, cacao beans, and cayenne peppers. They do not, however, raise enough to feed all the people, so much food is imported. Dense forests and rivers that are difficult to navigate have prevented further development of the fertile, well-watered soil in French Guiana's interior.

The main products of French Guiana are agricultural products, timber, and gold. Recently rice and shrimp have become important exports.

The most dramatic economic development in French Guiana is the French space center that was built at Kourou in the 1960s. The center launches and monitors satellites for businesses. The government is also developing a resort area along the coast for tourists. One well-known tourist spot is Devil's Island. It was an infamous penal colony for French prisoners from 1852 to 1946.

Section 1 Review

Locating Key Places
Locate the following places on the map on page 242: Guyana, Suriname, French Guiana

Identifying Key Terms
Define the following terms: plantain, bush

Reviewing Main Ideas
1. What are the four main occupations of the people in Guyana?
2. How do Suriname's people make a living?
3. In what ways does French Guiana differ from the other Guianas?

Thinking Critically: Assess Cause and Effect
Why do you think many people in this area are employed in primary industries?

Colombia and Venezuela

Preview

Key Places
Where are these places located?
1 Bogotá
2 Caracas

Key Terms
What do these terms mean?
llanero
barrio
hacienda

Main Ideas
As you read, look for answers to these questions.
• How do the physical and cultural features of Colombia and Venezuela compare?
• What are the chief industries of Colombia?
• Why is petroleum important to Venezuela?

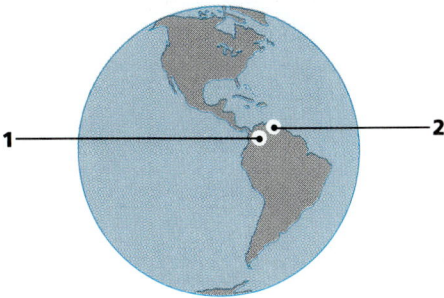

Long ago an Indian named Bochica and his wife Chia came to what is now Colombia. Bochica taught the people there to make clothing, build houses, and grow vegetables. Soon Chia grew jealous of the people.

One night as Bochica slept, Chia went to the Funza River. With a magic spell, she made the river swell between the mountains until its water covered the people's villages. Many drowned, but some people escaped up the mountains.

When Bochica saw what Chia had done, he punched holes in the mountains with his powerful fists, and the water drained away through the holes. In the place called Tequendama Falls, the water rushed wildly over the steep mountainside and is still rushing today.

Colombian legend

Colombia and Venezuela are physically and culturally alike.

This legend told by the Chibcha Indians describes Colombia's mountains, waterfalls, and peoples. It could also describe Colombia's neighbor, Venezuela.

Physical features. Both Colombia and Venezuela have Caribbean coasts, tropical rainforests, llanos (grassy, lowland areas), mountains, and impressive waterfalls. In fact, Venezuela's Angel Falls—3,200 feet high—is the world's highest waterfall.

The floods in the Colombian legend describe the floods on the llanos during the six-month-long rainy season. Flooding on these grassy plains forced the **llaneros**, or cowhands, to work without boots. They feared that if they wore boots, the leather would rot.

Colombia, however, is one-third larger than Venezuela and more mountainous. There are other physical differences as well.

In Colombia, the mountains form three major ranges with tall crests and high peaks, the highest reaching more than 19,000 feet above sea level. These ranges are referred to as the Eastern, Central, and Western cordilleras. In addition, a lower mountain chain overlooks the Pacific Ocean. As a result, highlands extend into practically every part of the country.

In Venezuela, the Andes only extend over the north and northwest and gradually disappear. The highest of these mountains is about 16,000 feet above sea level. The Guiana Highlands stretch over southern Venezuela and continue into the Guianas. The mountains in these highlands average about 8,000 feet above sea level, but generally the land is of lower elevation than in Colombia.

Cultural features. Colombia is a nation of about 30 million people; Venezuela has about 18 million. In both countries the Caribbean coast is the most densely populated region. Other densely populated areas are the Cauca and Magdalena river valleys in Colombia and the tierra templada zones of the northwestern mountains in Venezuela.

Almost 70 percent of the population in both countries is urban. The largest cities in both countries are their national capitals. Bogotá, Colombia, has 4.5 million people and is one of the great cultural centers of Latin America. Caracas, Venezuela, has a population of more than 3 million and is a commercial and industrial center.

Both Colombia and Venezuela have democratic governments. They have constitutions that guarantee freedom of religion, speech, and assembly along with other basic rights.

In both Colombia and Venezuela, three-fifths of the people are mestizos (people of both Spanish and Indian descent), about one-fifth have European (chiefly Spanish) backgrounds, and the rest of the people are of Indian or African descent. Some Indian groups, like the Ongwa of southeastern Venezuela, still follow their traditional way of life.

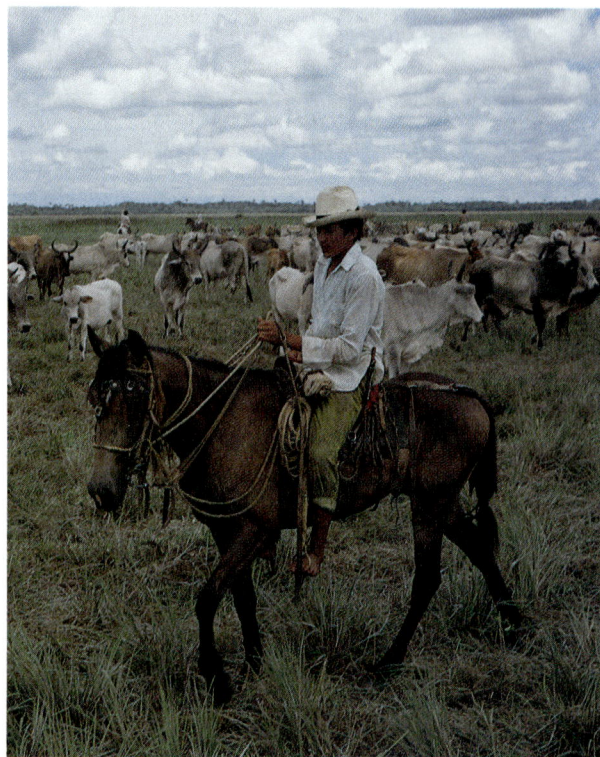

One of Colombia's llaneros watches over a herd of cattle.

Most people in the two countries speak Spanish and follow traditional Latin American cultural customs. Almost all the people of Colombia and Venezuela are Roman Catholic.

Colombia has primary, secondary, and service industries.

Colombia shares a small part of the petroleum reserves that lie in Lake Maracaibo [mar'ə kī'bō], and petroleum yields about 15 percent of Colombia's income. Some gas has been discovered in the Caribbean lowlands, and more petroleum was found between the Eastern and Central cordilleras. Pipelines transport the oil to Caribbean ports.

However, Colombia has few prospects of becoming an oil-rich nation. The country has to import petroleum to help fill its domestic energy needs. Colombia's major income comes from the mining of resources and farming.

Primary industries. Colombia produces more gold than any other country in South America. The country also has the largest deposits of platinum in the world. However, Colombia is most famous for its emeralds, the green gems that are more valuable than diamonds. Colombia supplies more than 90 percent of the world's emeralds.

In addition to a wealth of precious metals and stones, Colombia has a variety of crops. Many kinds of crops can be grown because the climate varies with the country's many elevations.

In the tierra templada zones of the mountains, coffee is grown and accounts for about 80 percent of Colombia's export income. On the Caribbean coast—the tierra caliente—farmers raise cotton, tobacco, and sugar cane for export. Flowers also are raised for export. In all regions, farmers grow corn, rice, and potatoes for domestic sale.

Secondary industries. Although not as important as mining and farming, manufacturing is increasing in Colombia. Bogotá is an industrial center as well as the national capital. Goods produced in the factories there include flour, shoes, soap, cement, and chocolate. Find Bogotá on the map on page 242. It is located on a high plateau in the Eastern Cordillera.

Medellín [med'l ēn'], the second largest city in Colombia, began as a gold mining town and has become Colombia's leading industrial center. Textile mills and steel plants are the chief factories operating there. Locate Medellín on the map on page 242. The city is located in the high valley between the Central and Western cordilleras.

Service industries. For many years, most manufactured goods traveled to markets on a combination of trains and boats. Railroads carried goods from urban factories to the Magdalena River. From there boats carried the goods to the river's mouth on the Caribbean, where they are shipped to markets worldwide. Today trains and trucks carry goods on a major railroad and highway that run along the Magdalena River valley.

Petroleum money is being used to help improve Venezuela's economy.

Ever since the discovery of petroleum in Lake Maracaibo in the 1920s, Venezuela has been paying off its debts and reinvesting in other industries. This is very important because some experts predict that Venezuela will exhaust its petroleum resources by the year 2000. Petroleum exports account for more than 70 percent of Venezuela's current income.

Raising the per capita income. Petroleum has raised the per capita income in Venezuela higher than any other Latin America country. A high per capita income can be deceiving, however, because it averages the highest and lowest incomes in a country. Actually a wide gap exists between Venezuela's rich and poor. This is true for all the South American countries. Almost all countries in the world face this problem, but in Venezuela, the oil boom has made the wealthy even richer and so has widened the gap.

Narrowing the gap between the rich and poor is Venezuela's main challenge. Class mobility is very unlikely since class is mostly determined by family ties and wealth. Today 50 percent of Venezuelans live in cities and are considered middle class or above. The rest of the people are poor. They live mostly in small rural communities.

One of the places where class differences are most obvious is in Caracas. The city has gleaming skyscrapers, palatial houses, expensive restaurants, and exclusive shops. It also has crowded **barrios,** or districts, where many people suffer from malnutrition.

Developing agriculture. For many years agriculture has been an important part of Venezuela's economy. About 20 percent of the people are farmers. Most small farms and **haciendas** (the name for large farms in Spanish-speaking South America) are clustered in the north and northwest. Now, however, the government wants farmers to cultivate the sparsely populated llanos between the mountains and the Orinoco River.

Until recently these plains have had huge cattle ranches but few people. The reason is that the area has a six-month-long dry season, making farming difficult. Recently, an irrigation system has been built on the llanos. Consequently, farmers are moving there in growing numbers.

The resources of the Guiana Highlands are also underdeveloped. If transportation were better, the tierra templada zones of these mountains would already be crowded with commercial farms. Consequently, the government is working to improve transportation into the highlands.

Some of Venezuela's aluminum is processed in this factory.

Developing mining. Presently the mineral deposits in the Guiana Highlands are more important than its farmland. Many valuable resources such as diamonds and iron ore are mined there. Some of the iron ore is used to produce steel in Venezuela. Much of it, however, is moved by rail to the Orinoco River and from there by ship to steel mills in the eastern United States.

Instead of exporting raw materials, the Venezuelan government wants to build additional factories in which to process more of its own resources. To make this possible, electricity is needed. Since 1968 the Guri Dam on the Caroni River has supplied electricity to most of Venezuela. This dam was built with private funds, but Venezuela's government has also invested in its own electrification plan to help industry in small towns and rural areas.

Section 2 Review

Locating Key Places
Locate the following places on the map on page 242: Bogotá, Caracas

Identifying Key Terms
Define the following terms: llanero, barrio, hacienda

Reviewing Main Ideas
1. Compare the physical and cultural features of Colombia and Venezuela.
2. In what industries do Colombians work?
3. How has petroleum helped Venezuela's people and industries?

Thinking Critically: Predict Effects
If petroleum prices increase dramatically, what do you think the Venezuelan government will do? Justify your prediction in a few sentences.

Ecuador, Peru, Bolivia, and Paraguay

Preview

Key Places
Where are these places located?
1 Quito
2 Lima
3 La Paz
4 Asunción
  See the globe below.

Key Terms
What does this term mean?
El Niño

Main Ideas
As you read, look for answers to these questions.
- What are Ecuador's three main geographical regions?
- What do Peru's different regions produce?
- What are the two main factors that have affected Bolivia's economic growth?
- Why are rivers Paraguay's most important physical feature?

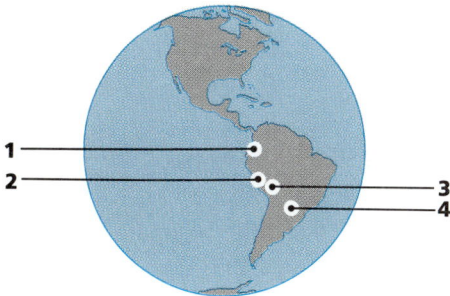

We were attempting the impossible. . . . We knew, only too well, that Sangay was inaccessible. . . . The mountain, sometimes called "the flaming terror of the Andes," had, moreover, a well-deserved reputation for being a killer.

Christopher Portway, mountain climber

Ecuador includes mountains, lowlands, and unusual islands.

Despite the mountain's killer reputation, Christopher Portway successfully climbed up Ecuador's 17,500-foot Sangay. Sangay is an active volcano in the Andes Mountains. In addition to the Andes Mountains, Ecuador also has coastal and eastern lowlands, and an unusual group of islands, the Galápagos.

The Andes Mountains. The Andes Mountains run down the center of Ecuador from north to south, covering about one-fourth of Ecuador's land area. The altiplano that lies between the mountains at between 8,000 and 10,000 feet above sea level provides flat land and a cool climate. Here farmers grow grains, vegetables, and pyrethrum [pī rē′ thrəm]—flowers used to make insecticides.

Many people who live in Ecuador's mountains are Indians who speak Quechua. This was the language of the Inca Empire, of which Ecuador was an important part. (See map, page 207.) Most of the Indians follow Roman Catholicism in combination with their Indian traditions. The people of the mountains generally work on haciendas as farmers or cattle herders.

The Andes Mountains region is an important mining and tourist region in Ecuador. The highlands contain rich deposits of gold and copper and a wealth of beautiful scenery that attracts thousands of tourists each year.

Quito [kē′tō], the capital and second largest city of this democratic country, is located in this mountain region. Quito is a major textile center with a population of about 600,000. Find it on the map on page 242.

249

The coastal lowlands. The most productive farmland in Ecuador is found in the low-lying area of the coastal plain that runs along the Pacific coast. The abundant rainfall created by cool ocean breezes and streams flowing down the Andes provide an excellent climate for growing tropical crops. Ecuador's major export crops—rice, bananas, cacao, and coffee—grow here.

Since the 1940s many people have moved to the coastal plain to farm the rich soil. Large numbers of people from the mountains and other rural areas continue to move to the area looking for jobs in Guayaquil [gwī'ə kēl'], Ecuador's largest and fastest growing city, and other coastal cities.

The eastern lowlands. The tropical rainforest region of Ecuador, called the Oriente, is located east of the Andes Highlands. It covers about half the land in Ecuador. Even though this region is mostly undeveloped because of its dense rainforests and hot climate, the discovery of petroleum has made it one of the most important regions in Ecuador.

In the 1960s petroleum was found and a pipeline was built to carry the petroleum across the Andes to the coast for export. Since then petroleum has accounted for 50 percent of Ecuador's export income. In 1987, however, Ecuador's petroleum industry suffered a major setback when an earthquake broke the pipeline.

The Galápagos Islands. These unusual islands are best known as the place where Charles Darwin first began his studies of different animal species in 1835. The Galápagos are located about 600 miles west of the mainland. Today about 6,200 people live on the islands.

The name of the islands comes from the Spanish word for turtles, *galápagos*. The islands are the home of some very unusual animals, turtles that weigh more than 500 pounds. In addition, there are penguins, mockingbirds, herons, boobies, and iguanas as long as four feet.

Peru's three distinct regions produce a variety of products.

Peru's economy depends mostly on primary industry. The coastal region produces a variety of crops and fish. The mountain region produces minerals and special wool products, and the foothills of the Andes produce petroleum.

The coastal plain. Peru's coastal plain is narrow and covers only 11 percent of Peru's land area, but it is densely populated. About 50 percent of the country's 20 million people live in this region. More than one-fourth of the people who live in the coastal plain, mostly mestizos, reside in Lima and the nearby port of Callao. Lima is Peru's national capital, the city from which the elected president and Council of Ministers run the government.

The cool Peru Current brings little rain to the coast, yet the area is striped with green oases running east to west. These oases are watered by the many streams flowing down the western

Spiny marine iguanas attract visitors to the Galápagos.

slopes of the Andes Mountains. Fields of fruit, wheat, cotton, sugar cane, and vegetables cover these oases. Much of the cotton and sugar cane are exported, but other crops are sold locally.

Peru's coastal waters are a very important part of Peru's economy. The country's fishing fleets catch huge schools of anchovies, which are ground into fish meal, one of Peru's leading exports. The fish meal is used as a high-protein livestock feed.

To protect its rich fishing waters, Peru's government has claimed the ocean within 200 miles of its coast. Fishing vessels are required to pay for fishing there and are arrested if they refuse.

A danger to Peru's fishing industry is *El Niño*. **El Niño** is an unpredictable warm current that sometimes flows into the cold Peru waters in December. This sudden temperature change causes torrential rains that often destroy nearby homes and kill the fish that the anchovies feed on. In 1972 so many of these fish were killed that the anchovies never came back in their original numbers. In spite of *El Niño*, Peru's domestic fishing industry continues to grow because of other ocean fish in the area.

The mountains. The Andes Mountains run the full length of Peru and contain a wealth of minerals. As a result, Peru is a major exporter of zinc, lead, gold, silver, copper, and iron ore. Many Peruvian towns in the Andes have developed near major mines. For example, Arequipa [ar'ə kē'pə], located in the south, has 450,000 people. Find Arequipa on the map on page 242.

Between the Western and Eastern cordilleras lies a broad altiplano. Its width averages about 200 miles and covers more than one-fourth of the country. Nearly one-half of Peru's people live here. Most are Indians who speak the Quechua and Aymará languages and live in small farm villages.

In the lower part of the altiplano, the Indians grow potatoes and some corn for their own use. In addition, citrus fruits, sugar cane, maize, wheat, rice, coffee, tea, and jute, used for making rope, are grown commercially for domestic use.

Some Andean Indians live on floating islands in Lake Titicaca.

On the grasslands of higher areas, herders graze their distinctive livestock—llamas [lä'məz] and alpacas. The llama is a South American member of the camel family. From its wool, the Indians make thick blankets. The alpaca is a domesticated animal that resembles a sheep. The Indians also use the vicuña [vi kü'nə], a wild llama-like animal with a soft, delicate wool. The wool of the vicuña is made into expensive coats. Wool from the llama, alpaca, and vicuña and the woven products made from the wool are some of Peru's main exports.

The Andes foothills. The plains area at the eastern base of the Andes Mountains is home to more than 100,000 Amazon Indians. Compared to Peru's total population of 200 million, this is a sparsely populated area. The Indians generally hunt and farm for subsistence.

The Peruvian government has tried with limited success to encourage settlers to clear the immense rainforests and jungles that impede the development of resources in this area. More recently, petroleum has been discovered and a pipeline has been built across the Andes so that it can be exported.

Bolivia's wars and limited access to resources hampered growth.

Bolivia's two main economic problems are that it has no shipping outlet and its resources are difficult to mine and harvest. In addition, though Bolivia has abundant resources, many of them are inaccessible because they are located high in the Andes Mountains.

Border and civil wars. Bolivia's war-torn history has resulted in obstacles to its economic development. In wars with Peru, Brazil, Chile, Paraguay, and Argentina, Bolivia has lost about one-half of its original territory besides losing its only seacoast to Chile in an 1883 war.

Bolivia wanted to gain access to the Atlantic through Paraguay. The two countries had been engaged in many border wars over the Gran Chaco, a fertile land area between the two countries. In the 1920s the conflicts increased when oil was discovered on the Gran Chaco. In the ensuing war, Bolivia lost much of the Gran Chaco to Paraguay.

Bolivia has been battered by domestic unrest as well. Military and civilian governments have each been toppled, and revolutionary movements have been influential. Today Bolivia has a constitution that provides for a traditional executive, legislative, and judicial branch. However, the executive branch, the president, holds most of the power in Bolivia's current government.

Natural resources. Bolivia has many resources that are difficult to mine and harvest. Many of its most valuable resources, such as silver, have been depleted. Bolivia has petroleum, timber, and fertile soils in the lowlands. How-

ever, the rugged terrain and dense rainforests prevent further development of these resources.

Mining is difficult because the minerals are high up in the Andes Mountains. Travel and transport is very difficult through the rugged terrain and dense forests. Some of Bolivia's most important mineral deposits include copper, lead, silver, tungsten, and zinc.

Since the 1900s tin has been Bolivia's major export. To ensure that all profits are used to improve the economy, the government controls the largest mines. There are tin refineries, food processing plants, and textile factories in La Paz, Bolivia's capital, and Santa Cruz, Bolivia's fastest growing city.

About 55 percent of Bolivia's 7 million people live in rural areas. The rest live in towns and cities. Bolivia has two capitals, Sucre, which is its historic capital and La Paz, which is where the government is located. La Paz has about 880,000 people, of which most are Roman Catholic. Bolivia's population is about half Indian and half mestizo.

There are three main groups of Indians. The Aymarás live in the highlands, the Quechuas live

A woman and child tend a well-stocked La Paz market stall.

in the valleys, and the Guaranis and others live in rainforests and more inaccessible lowlands.

Rivers divide Paraguay and provide transportation and irrigation.

Rivers are important to Paraguay. Paraguay's three main rivers, the Paraguay, the Paraná, and the Pilcomayo all meet at Asunción, Paraguay's capital and main port. The Paraná River flows into the Atlantic Ocean providing a shipping outlet. These rivers also divide Paraguay into two separate regions—west and east. Most people live on the east side of the Paraguay River and use it for irrigation and transportation.

Western Paraguay. West of the Paraguay River lie the low plains and desert that make up the Gran Chaco. This region covers three-fifths of Paraguay's land area. Less than 5 percent of Paraguay's 4 million people live here because of the region's harsh climate and poor transportation. Some of the people who do live on the Gran Chaco are Indians and cattle ranchers. Many are cowboys who move across the countryside from one cattle ranch to another.

Another group of people are Mennonite farmers who settled the Gran Chaco early in the 1900s. Through perseverance they have managed to make their farms productive.

A major product from this region is tannin, an acid derived from the quebracho [kā brä'chō] tree. Tannin is used as an ingredient in medicines. It is also used to strengthen and waterproof leather and to make dyes and ink.

Eastern Paraguay. East of the Paraguay River lie rolling hills and valleys. Trees cover the hilltops, and tropical forests fill the valleys. The slopes are fertile grasslands. Three-fifths of Paraguay's people live in these rural areas. Many work on haciendas raising cotton, coffee, soybeans, tobacco, and cattle for export.

Paraguay's capital, Asunción, lies in the east near the Argentine border. Most upper- and middle-class Paraguayans live there and work in service industries such as transportation, communication, and government. Most of Paraguay's people are Roman Catholic.

Paraguay's government was a military dictatorship run by General Alfredo Stroessner from 1954 to 1989. In that year he was defeated in a free election, although he retained his position as chief of the armed forces.

Wood-burning plants produced all of Paraguay's electrical power until a dam near Itaipu on the Paraná River was built under a partnership with Brazil. The dam began generating electricity in 1984, but was not yet fully operational. The building of this dam is the largest hydroelectric project in the world.

Paraguay sells electricity to Argentina and Brazil and wants to attract new industries with its inexpensive electricity. Hydroelectric power may turn out to be Paraguay's most important resource.

Section 3 Review

Locating Key Places
Locate the following places on the map on page 242: Quito, Lima, La Paz, Asunción

Identifying Key Terms
Define the following term: *El Niño*

Reviewing Main Ideas
1. What mountains run through Ecuador? Describe Ecuador's unusual group of islands.
2. What do each of Peru's regions contribute to its economy?
3. Why are Bolivia's resources underdeveloped?
4. Why are rivers Paraguay's most important resource?

Thinking Critically: Make Hypotheses
Compare the physical landscape of Bolivia with its economic output and development. What hypothesis can you make about the value of natural resources?

Chile, Argentina, and Uruguay

Preview

Key Places
Where are these places located?
1 Santiago
2 Buenos Aires
3 Montevideo
See the globe below.

Key Terms
What do these terms mean?
gaucho, *porteño*

Main Ideas
As you read, look for answers to these qustions.
- What are Chile's three main land regions?
- On what is Argentina's economy based?
- What industry is most important to Uruguay's economy?

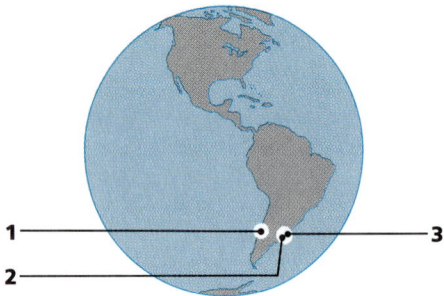

In this time of the swollen grape,
the wine begins to come to life
between the sea and the mountain ranges.

Pablo Neruda, a Chilean poet

Chile is made up of a desert, a valley, and an archipelago.

Chile has a desert in the north, a Central Valley, and thousands of islands off its southern coast. Chile's climate and land features do not provide an abundance of fertile land. However, Chile does have some world-renowned vineyards in its Central Valley. Pablo Neruda, one of Chile's most famous poets, refers to the vineyards and the Central Valley in the lines from his poem. North of the Central Valley is a desert region that is one of the driest areas in the world.

The northern desert. The northern desert region extends south from beyond the Peru border and continues to the Aconcagua [ä'kông kä'gwə] River just north of the city of Valparaíso [val'pə rī'zō]. In the north is the Atacama Desert, and just south of the Copiapo River, is the Norte Chico, an area that is less dry. In the Norte Chico, there are a few scattered farm communities where crops are grown and livestock is raised.

There are many cities and towns along the coast that contribute to Chile's growing fishing industry. Chileans catch 4 million tons of shellfish, anchovies, mackerel, and sardines every year. Fish meal is one of Chile's main exports.

Chile is the largest producer and exporter of copper in the world. It has 20 percent of the world's known supply. The city of Chuquicamata [chü'kē kə mät'ə] in the Atacama Desert has the largest open-pit copper mine in the world.

The Central Valley. The Central Valley begins at the Aconcagua River and follows the coast south to the city of Puerto Montt. It is bordered on the east by the Andes Mountains

Young musicians entertain a crowd in downtown Santiago.

and on the west by the Pacific Ocean. This region is the center of Chile's industry and agriculture and the place where three-fourths of Chile's 12 million people live.

The mild climate and flat land of the Central Valley provide a fertile area for growing crops. Wheat is the most important crop grown for domestic use. Farmers also grow corn, rice potatoes, sugar beets, grapes, peaches, and nuts. About one-third of Chile's agricultural products depend on sheep, cattle, and poultry.

To improve its economy, Chile's emphasis is on manufacturing rather than agriculture. Chile's main industrial centers are Santiago, Concepción, and Valparaíso. Santiago, Chile's capital, has a population of 4 million.

Chile's manufacturing has changed from light to heavy industry in the last 50 years. The steel industry has become increasingly important. As the importance of agriculture declines, more farmers move to the cities looking for work. Housing is scarce and most farmers do not have the skills needed for the available jobs. As a result, shantytowns surround Chile's cities.

Most of Chile's people are of mixed European and Indian heritage. Others are of European descent, mainly Spanish. Some of the Europeans are descendants of Germans, who settled mainly in the Central Valley, and Italians, British, and French, who settled in the Santiago-Valparaíso region. The remaining Chileans are descendants of the original Indians who lived in Chile when the Spanish first settled there in the 1500s.

Chile has been ruled by a military dictatorship since 1973. Recent legislatures have been run by a junta made up of army, navy, air force, and national police representatives. Plans to elect a president and to return to democracy emerge from time to time.

The archipelago. The southern portion of Chile is made up of thousands of islands. Few people live there because there is poor transportation and little cultivable land. The farmers who do live there graze sheep. This area also produces most of Chile's petroleum.

Chile also includes some islands in the South Pacific. One of these is Easter Island, which is famous for its more than 600 giant carved statues of people that stand from 11- to 40-feet high.

Argentina's land provides the basis for its economy.

Argentina can be divided into four main land regions—the Pampas, northern Argentina, the Andes Mountains, and Patagonia. Each of these areas contributes to Argentina's economy, but the most important area is the Pampas.

The Pampas. The Pampas is a grassy plain that covers about one-fifth of Argentina's land area. Find it on the map on page 242. More than 66 percent of Argentina's people live in the cities and towns of the Pampas.

Today **gauchos**, the Spanish word for cowboys, still work on some of the larger ranches, but there are no vast open areas for them to ride. Until the late 1800s, when the government divided the land into large estates, the Pampas was populated mainly by gauchos. They used to catch cattle and horses for their hides.

Buenos Aires is Argentina's capital, largest industrial and cultural center, and major port. People who work in Buenos Aires are in fact called *porteños*, which means "people of the port."

As Argentina's capital, Buenos Aires is home to the president and congress that has led the country's republican government since 1983. Before this election, Argentina had been ruled by a series of harsh military dictatorships, the most infamous of whom was Juan Perón (1946–1955). Perón's immense government spending left Argentina's economy in a slump from which it has yet to recover.

Most of Argentina's 31 million people are descendants of the Spanish and Italians who settled in the late 1800s. Some isolated Indian groups live in the Andes, Gran Chaco, and Patagonia.

The Pampas has some of the most fertile soil in the world. It provides 85 percent of Argentina's agricultural exports. The flat terrain is well suited to modern farm machinery. The main crops are wheat, corn, alfalfa, and flax, which is used to make linen cloth. Farmers also raise sheep, cattle, and hogs.

Northern Argentina. The northern region of Argentina is a lowland plain that is made up of the Gran Chaco and the Entre Ríos—the area between the Paraná and Uruguay rivers. The land of the Gran Chaco is covered with dense forests, and few people live there. In the summer heavy rains provide water for farmers to grow corn, wheat, and cotton. Farmers in the Entre Ríos graze sheep, cattle, and horses.

On the northeastern border of Argentina are the Iguacú [ē'gwä sü'] Falls. These magnificent falls are formed by 275 smaller waterfalls that descend from the Brazilian Highlands.

The Andes Mountains. The Andes Mountains form the border between Argentina and Chile. This mountainous area is mostly uninhab-

An Argentine farmer monitors his valuable corn harvest.

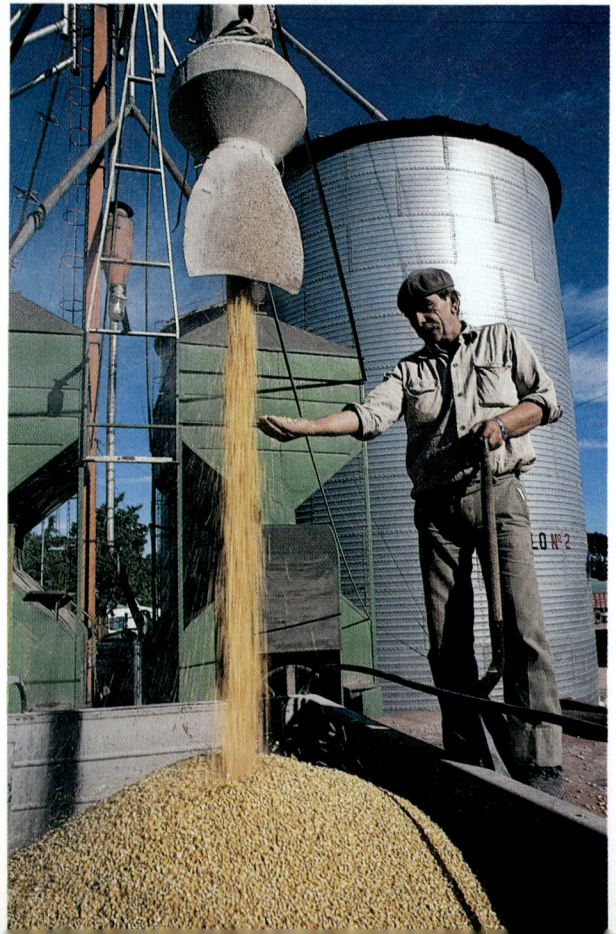

ited except for groups of Indians who graze sheep on the plateaus.

Patagonia. Patagonia is a large plateau region that covers more than one-fourth of Argentina's land area. Most of the land is too dry for farming, but there are sheep ranches in the canyons. Less than 3 percent of Argentina's people live in this region. Farmers grow apples, pears, and alfalfa, using the rivers for irrigation. There are also petroleum deposits that, when added to what is available from the Andes Mountains, provide most of Argentina's domestic needs.

Uruguay's economy is based on its cattle and sheep industry.

Uruguay's economy depends on the cattle and sheep that graze on almost all of Uruguay's land. Most of Uruguay's people work in service industries that are directly related to the sheep and cattle industry.

About 85 percent of Uruguay's people live in towns and cities, and the remaining 15 percent live in rural areas. Most Uruguayans are of Spanish and Italian descent, but there are still a very small number of Charrua Indians, the original inhabitants of Uruguay.

Agriculture. Most of Uruguay's land is a continuation of the Argentine Pampas. This land area is usually covered in grasslands, making it well suited to grazing sheep and cattle. The mild climate permits grazing all year round. Gauchos herd livestock on some of the larger ranches.

Less than one-tenth of Uruguay's land is cultivated. Most farms are in the south so that goods can be easily transported to Montevideo [mon′tə vi dā′ō], the capital and largest city, for sale in local markets. Farmers grow wheat, alfalfa, barley, citrus fruits, corn, oats, and flaxseed. Flaxseed is used to make linseed oil, a major ingredient of paint, ink, and linoleum.

Other industries. Many of Uruguay's 3 million people work in industries associated with meat or wool, such as meat-packing or textiles. Other people work in service industries such as government, trade, transportation, and tourism. Trade is very important because Uruguay imports most of the raw materials and machines needed to operate its industries. Uruguay imports all of its fuel because it has no known deposits of oil, iron, or coal.

Tourism is another very important industry in Uruguay. Resorts on the Atlantic coast bring many people from Argentina and Brazil. Uruguay has a strong middle class that enjoys a good standard of living. Its cities are modern, with beautiful parks and attractive homes. Montevideo is Uruguay's chief urban center with a population of more than one million.

Section 4 Review

Locating Key Places
Locate the following places on the map on page 242: Santiago, Buenos Aires, Montevideo

Identifying Key Terms
Define the following terms: gaucho, *porteño*

Reviewing Main Ideas
1. What main products come from Chile?
2. Why is land Argentina's most important resource?
3. Upon what is Uruguay's economy dependent?

Critical Thinking: Recognize Values
What values might be expressed in Chile's growing emphasis on manufacturing rather than agriculture?

Brazil

Preview

Key Places
Where are these places located?
1 São Paulo
2 Rio de Janeiro
See the globe below.

Key Terms
What does this term mean?
gasohol

Main Ideas
As you read, look for answers to these questions.
- Where do most of Brazil's people live?
- What are Brazil's main resources and products?

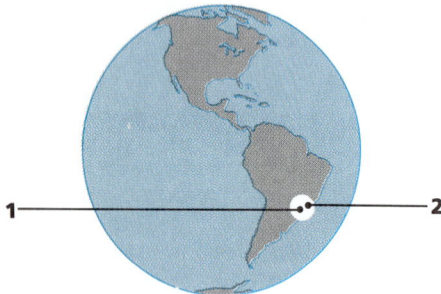

1 —————————————————— 2

No one had done it before. No one had traveled the full 4,000-mile length of the Amazon River under his own power. . . . Much of the area was unexplored and unmapped. . . . Often we could not stop to scout ahead. . . . At night we could hear the sound of the churning river beside our tents, and I would dream of kayaking into a canyon and seeing a sudden 200-foot drop ahead. I would wake up in horror.

Traveler's diary

Brazil's growing population is clustered along its coast.

This traveler's diary details a journey down Brazil's Amazon River, the deepest and widest in the world. Like the river itself, the country through which it runs is the largest in South America. In fact, Brazil is so large that it shares borders with all but two South American countries, Chile and Ecuador.

In addition, Brazil, with 140 million people, contains about half the total population of the continent. The Brazilians are primarily a European people, though many of them are of mixed European, African, and Indian descent.

Despite their diverse backgrounds, the Brazilian people have developed a common national culture. They share the Roman Catholic faith and the Portuguese language, which reflects the country's colonial history. In addition, the government holds together the separate regions of Brazil with strong central control.

Historically, Brazil has been ruled by military dictatorships or by civilian leaders backed by the military. However, a civilian government, with an elected president, has led the country since 1985.

Brazil's large population is not evenly spread over its land area. Instead, about 80 percent of Brazilians live within 200 miles of the Atlantic coast. Most live in or around such major cities as São Paulo and Rio de Janeiro. Many of the people who live away from the coasts are Indians

The lights of coastal Rio de Janeiro shine at night.

who make the Amazon Basin their home. The Amazon Basin, which extends across more than half of Brazil, is covered with tropical rainforests. Other people have taken the government's lead and moved from the crowded coast to the new capital of Brasília, located about 600 miles inland.

The Brazilian Highlands have contributed to the country's uneven population patterns. The highlands, which divide the interior plateaus from the southeastern coast, have prevented easy movement into the interior. In addition, the highlands have proven to be an important economic resource because of their vast and profitable coffee plantations. As a result, the coastal cities have grown dramatically in recent decades.

São Paulo, with 8 million people, is now the largest city, as well as manufacturing center, of Brazil. Its central location and improved communication capabilities have ensured São Paulo's position of leadership within the Brazilian economy. Rio de Janeiro, with 5 million people, is Brazil's second largest city.

Brazil, like many other South American countries, is facing increasing migration from rural to urban areas. In addition, Brazil's rate of population growth has been consistently high. As a result, São Paulo, Rio de Janeiro, and other coastal cities are fighting the problems of overcrowding and poverty that plague cities all over the South American continent.

South of São Paulo lie three Brazilian states that have traditionally made up the most European region of the country. The South, which has attracted Portuguese, German, and Italian immigrants, is a region of productive farmland that extends into the Argentine Pampas. The South also contains the Paraná River, the site of the Itaipu Dam, which is Brazil and Paraguay's joint hydroelectric power project.

In the Northeast, where Brazil juts into the Atlantic Ocean, economic situations are much different. When the Portuguese first came to Brazil, this is where they settled, later bringing African slaves to work on the area's many sugar plantations. Although the climate along the coast provides adequate rainfall for the sugar and cacao crops, the lands further inland have been hampered by severe droughts and poor soils. As a result, most of the Northeast today is overpopulated and poverty-stricken.

Brazil produces tropical crops, minerals, and precious stones.

Economically, Brazil is a developing country on the verge of becoming more developed. The country is rich in most natural resources but lacks any major supplies of oil. As a result, Brazil has had to import the oil it needs and has therefore been vulnerable to fluctuations in the world energy market. In the early 1980s, for example, Brazil had amassed a formidable national debt and was forced by its debtors to put

259

into effect a controversial austerity program designed to cut domestic spending.

Overall, however, Brazil has been building an economy based on a wide array of industries. Although agriculture and mining have long been important to the economy, manufacturing and service industries have been gaining strength.

Brazil's tropical crops, minerals, and precious stones serve as important exports. Brazil is the world's leading producer of sugar cane, and it provides about one-third of the world's coffee beans, about 3.5 billion pounds annually. Coffee is Brazil's most important export product. Rubber is another important product.

Brazil grows many crops that are exported to all parts of the world. It leads the world in the growing of bananas and oranges and is a principal grower of cacao beans, corn, cotton, lemons, pineapples, rice, and soybeans.

The center of Brazilian mining is the state of Minas Gerais [mē′nəs zhə rīs′] , one of Brazil's 23 states, located just inland of the southeastern coast. One important mineral is iron ore.

Many of the world's most beautiful gemstones, such as emeralds, aquamarines, topaz, and amethysts, come from Brazil. Diamonds are also mined in Brazil. However, most Brazilian diamonds are used for industrial purposes, such as drill bits, rather than for use in fine jewelry.

Production of oil and natural gas takes place in the state of Bahia in the northeast region of Brazil. Some recent discoveries of oil off the coast of Rio de Janeiro has also helped Brazil to meet some of its needs.

In an attempt to reduce their dependence on foreign oil, Brazil manufactures a gasoline substitute for use in their cars. More than 50 percent of Brazilian cars now run on a sugar cane based alcohol called **gasohol**. Government leaders in Brazil hope than even more cars and businesses will use gasohol in the future, further reducing the need for expensive imported oil.

Brazil is a world leader in the production of cars, chemicals, cement, and textiles. In addition, many Brazilians work in such service industries as banking, insurance, trade, and transportation.

A sloth inches slowly along a branch in the Amazon forest.

Section 5 Review

Locating Key Places
Locate the following places on the map on page 242: São Paulo, Rio de Janeiro

Identifying Key Terms
Define the following term: gasohol

Reviewing Main Ideas
1. Why do most Brazilians live along the coast?
2. Describe the products that contribute to Brazil's economy.

Thinking Critically: Make Decisions
What if Brazil's economy had to depend on only one product? Which one should it choose? Write one paragraph explaining why.

Interpreting Average Annual Precipitation Maps

Suppose you wanted to know how much rain, snow, sleet, or hail a particular place receives each year. To find out, you could use an average annual precipitation map like the one below. By studying it carefully, you might begin to see relationships between amount of precipitation and such factors as latitude, location on the continent, or elevation.

To interpret this map, begin by determining latitude. Find the Equator first. As you know, equatorial regions are usually hot and rainy. Then use the map key to find the rainfall in the Amazon River basin. Notice that the Amazon, located as it is near the Equator, has the highest amount of precipitation possible on this map (more than 80 inches).

Continental location helps give a general pattern for climate and rainfall in an area. In general, desert regions tend to appear at 30° of latitude except on the eastern side of landmasses. Locate 30° S latitude on the map, and then check to see if Brazil's land at this latitude is on the eastern

or western side of the continent.

A third factor, elevation, is also shown on this map. The Brazilian Highlands tend to be drier than the surrounding areas because the air masses drop their moisture as they are forced high above the uplands.

Review

This map shows the annual precipitation pattern for Brazil. Use the map to tell how much precipitation there is in each city.

1. Manaus
2. Recife
3. São Paulo
4. Brasília

Brazil: Annual Precipitation

Inches	Centimeters
More than 80	More than 200
60 to 80	150 to 200
40 to 59	100 to 149
20 to 39	50 to 99
Less than 20	Less than 50

CHAPTER 11

Review

Section Summaries

1. The Guianas The people of the Guianas have varied ethnic backgrounds but similar colonial histories. Only French Guiana, however remains a colony today. The coastal farmers raise crops such as rice or sugar cane. Other workers are employed in the area's manufacturing and service industries.

2. Colombia and Venezuela Colombia and Venezuela have similar natural resources, land regions, population distribution, and ethnic groups. Their economies depend on a combination of mining, agriculture, and manufacturing. The main difference between Colombia and Venezuela, however, is petroleum. Colombia has only small deposits, but Venezuela's large deposits have helped it become a wealthy country. Venezuela has successfully used petroleum money to diversify its economy.

3. Ecuador, Peru, Bolivia, and Paraguay The economies of these countries depend heavily on the primary industries of agriculture and mining. Hardy crops like coffee, sugar cane, cocoa, and wheat are grown on the slopes of the Andes Mountains. Fishing off the Pacific coast is also important. The Andes also produce a variety of minerals such as copper, gold, silver, and iron ore. All of these countries also have petroleum deposits and abundant forests.

4. Chile, Argentina, and Uruguay Land is the most important natural resource these three countries have. Crops such as cotton, fruit, sugar cane, and corn are grown. Fishing is important as well as deposits of copper, natural gas, iron ore, uranium, and petroleum. However, the most important industry in all these countries is the raising of sheep and cattle. Products from these animals are for domestic use as well as export.

5. Brazil Brazil is the largest country in South America and has half its total population. Brazil supplies the world market with many important products such as coffee, iron ore, bananas, oranges, cars, textiles, and industrial diamonds. Brazil's variety of natural resources has helped it diversify its economy.

Using Geography Skills

Reviewing the Map Lesson
Refer back to the map on page 261 to find the amount of rainfall for these two cities.
1. Pôrto Allegre
2. Rio de Janeiro

Using Social Studies Skills

1. Synthesize Information. On a separate sheet of paper, draw four boxes. At the top of each box, write Ecuador, Peru, Bolivia, or Paraguay. Beneath each heading, list the products for each country. Rank the countries' economies from least to most diversified. Explain your answer in two or three sentences.

2. Use Problem Solving Skills. You have just become the leader of Uruguay's government. You have money to improve the economy. You can either drill for oil off the Atlantic coast or irrigate the land for growing crops. Which would you do? Write one paragraph explaining what Uruguay would gain if you chose one or the other. Write a second paragraph explaining what Uruguay might lose by making your choice.

Testing for Understanding

Locating Key Places
Match the descriptions with the key places listed below.
1. the largest city in Brazil
2. the capital of Venezuela
3. Ecuador's capital and textile center
4. Brazil's second largest city
5. a former British colony on the north Atlantic coast
6. Chile's capital city
7. the capital of Peru
8. a former Dutch colony with mountainous rainforests
9. Argentina's capital
10. A French colony with dense rainforests
11. Bolivia's capital city
12. Colombia's capital and largest city
13. Paraguay's capital and main port
14. Uruguay's capital city

  a. Guyana
  b. Suriname
  c. French Guiana
  d. Bogotá
  e. Caracas
  f. Quito
  g. Lima
  h. La Paz
  i. Asunción
  j. Santiago
  k. Buenos Aires
  l. Montevideo
 m. São Paulo
  n. Rio de Janeiro

Recalling Key Terms
Define these terms in your own words.

Section 1
plaintain
bush

Section 2
llanero
barrio
hacienda

Section 3
El Niño

Section 4
gaucho
porteño

Section 5
gasohol

Reviewing Main Ideas
Section 1
1. What do Guyana's people do to make a living?
2. In what ways do Suriname's people make a living?
3. How is French Guiana unlike Guyana and Suriname?

Section 2
1. How are the physical and cultural features of Colombia and Venezuela alike? How are they different?
2. How do most Colombians make a living?
3. How has petroleum helped Venezuela's economy?

Section 3
1. What mountains and islands draw tourists to Ecuador?
2. What are the main products from each of Peru's regions?
3. What are Bolivia's major obstacles to developing its resources?
4. Why are rivers so important to Paraguay?

Section 4
1. What are some of the products that come from Chile's three land regions?
2. In what ways is land most important to Argentina's economy?
3. What are Uruguay's most important economic products?

Section 5
1. Why is most of Brazil's population clustered along the coast?
2. What products are most important to Brazil's economy?

Thinking Critically
1. **Make Decisions.** You are the head of the Venezuelan government. The price of oil has just dropped so that any oil you produce will cost more than any profits you will make. Will you stop production immediately? Explain why or why not in a paragraph.

2. **Predict Effects.** There has been a major oil discovery in the Atacama Desert. How will that affect the economy of Chile? How might it affect the people?

Review

Summarizing the Unit

Chapter 9 A Physical and Cultural Overview Scientists believe that Middle and South America's mountains, plateaus, and plains were formed by plate tectonics, volcanic action, and glaciers. The region includes tropical, dry, and mild climate zones. The Mayas, Aztecs, and Incas were the first people to establish powerful empires. European countries later ruled the region as colonial holdings. Today the countries of Middle and South America are struggling to improve their economies. The countries differ greatly in their economic development partly because of their physical features and natural resources.

Chapter 10 Middle America Mexico, Central America, and the West Indies make up Middle America. All of these countries have been influenced by various peoples, including Indians, Europeans, Africans, and Asians. The region depends mostly on agriculture, ranching, mining, forestry, fishing, tourism, manufacturing, and service industries.

Chapter 11 South America South America is a continent with a variety of vast natural resources. There is a great variance in the wealth and natural resources of the South American nations, ranging from oil-rich Venezuela, to the abundant fishing waters off the Peruvian coast, to Uruguay with its rich farm and grasslands.

Using Writing Skills

Plan a two-week itinerary for a trip to Middle and South America. An itinerary is a time and place outline of where you will be going, how long you will spend there, and what you want to see. Include travel plans for at least five different countries.

Decide which countries interest you the most. Then look at the map on page 242 to consider what arrangements you will have to make to travel from one place to another. You might be able to bicycle or take a train or you might have to travel by boat or plane.

For this assignment you have an unlimited budget. The only restriction is that you have to be back home in two weeks.

Before writing you need to do prewriting. One easy way to prepare and organize research materials is to use index cards. They will provide a basis for writing your outline.

Here are some ideas to get you started on your research:
1. Summarize the information in this unit on the countries you chose.
2. Find at least three books on each of the countries to use as references.
3. Choose at least three cities you want to visit and summarize what you will see.
4. Find out what kind of food you will be eating.
5. Call a travel agent to get brochures on your countries and find out what you might have to pay for air or water transportation.
6. If possible, use recent periodicals to find the most current information.
7. Figure out which is the best time of year to take the trip depending on climate.

Once you have gathered your information, put your notes on note cards. Then organize your note cards to formulate an outline.

When you write your first draft, remember that the most important thing is to get your ideas on paper. Don't be concerned about spelling or grammatical errors. Do remember to stick to one idea for each of your paragraphs.

The next step is to revise your draft. This is the time to correct grammar, spelling, and content errors. When you prepare your final copy include some of the following to illustrate your itinerary:
1. whole brochures or individual pictures
2. maps showing your travel plan with order and dates
3. sketches of foods or favorite sights of the countries

Test

Key Terms (15 points)
Match each term with the correct definition.
1. warm current off Peru
2. people of Spanish descent who were born in the Americas
3. a long, high valley filled with erosional materials from surrounding mountains
4. poor peasant farmers
5. a substance used to make chewing gum
a. campesinos
b. altiplano
c. chicle
d. creoles
e. *El Niño*

Main Ideas (35 points)
1. The longest and deepest waterway in South America is the _____.
a. Orinoco River
b. Gran Chaco
c. Amazon River
d. Paraná River
2. The three early civilizations of South America and Mexico were built by the:
a. Aztecs, Arawaks, Incas
b. Guaranis, Arawaks, Mayas
c. Aztecs, Mayas, Incas
d. Incas, Mayas, Arawaks
3. Which of the following groups did not help form Latin American culture?
a. Spanish
b. Portuguese
c. Inuit
d. Africans

4. The main challenge for most Mexican farmers today is:
a. a shortage of farmers
b. a shortage of cropland
c. an abundance of cropland
d. no modern irrigation or equipment
5. The Caribbean leader in heavy industry is:
a. Costa Rica
b. Cuba
c. Trinidad
d. Jamaica
6. As industrialization takes hold, more people in South American countries are moving to _____ areas.
a. urban
b. rural
c. plateau
d. mountainous
7. The place where Charles Darwin did his studies of different species is _____.
a. Easter Island
b. Galápagos Islands
c. the Bahamas
d. the Oriente

Thinking Critically (30 points)

1. Analyze Comparisons. Compare the economies of any three countries in the unit. Summarize the ways in which physical features, location, and natural resources contribute.

2. Make Hypotheses. What might Mexico be like if the Aztecs and Mayas had never settled there? Write two paragraphs explaining how the historic sites, origins of the people, economy, and culture would be different.

Place Location (20 points)
Match the places below with the letters printed on the map.
1. Mexico
2. Brazil
3. Venezuela
4. Panama
5. Bahamas

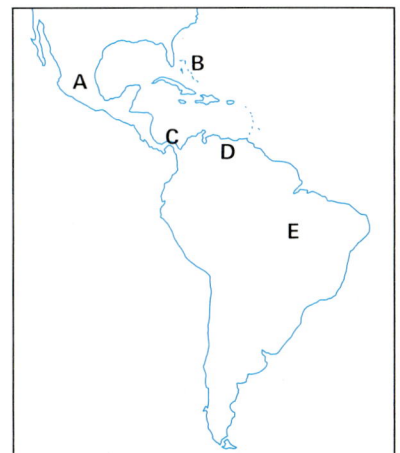

Western Europe

In this unit you will read about democratic Europe.

A Physical and Cultural Overview

In this chapter you will read about Western Europe's landscapes and cultural roots.

Sections

1 The Western European Landscape
2 Climate, Soils, and Vegetation
3 The Heritage of Western Europe

The Western European Landscape

Preview

Key Places
Where are these places located?
1 English Channel
2 North Sea
3 Iberian Peninsula
   See the globe below.

Key Terms
What do these terms mean?
peninsula
sea

Main Ideas
As you read, look for answers to these questions.
- What two geographical features give Western Europe its irregular shape?
- What advantages does Western Europe enjoy because of its nearness to the sea?
- How has Western Europe benefited from its network of rivers?
- What are the various features of Western Europe's landscape?

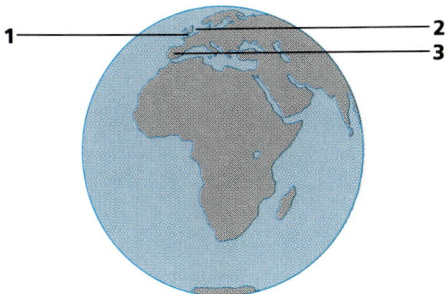

No man is an island, entire of itself; every man is a piece of the continent, a part of the main. If a clod be washed away by the sea, Europe is the less.

John Donne, "Meditations 17"

Peninsulas and islands give Western Europe its irregular shape.

As the British poet John Donne suggests, there is a certain unity to the European continent. The jutting landmasses, called **peninsulas**, are bodies of land surrounded by water on all sides but one. You are probably familiar already with several peninsulas in the United States, such as Florida, Michigan, and Alaska. In reality, the entire European continent is a great peninsula projecting westward from Asia. Refer to the world physical map on page 622 to see this huge peninsula. You'll see that Europe and Asia are not really separate continents.

Next look at the Western Europe physical map on page 272. You'll see the major peninsulas that give Europe its irregular shape—the Scandinavian and Danish peninsulas in the north, and the Iberian, Italian, and Balkan peninsulas in the south.

Every European peninsula helps define one or more seas. The word **sea** often refers to the ocean. It also refers to a large body of salt water, smaller than an ocean, that is partially or totally enclosed by land. Western Europe's northern peninsulas, for example, help define the Baltic Sea, the North Sea, and the Norwegian Sea. Its southern peninsulas help shape several small seas, such as the Adriatic, as well as the larger Mediterranean. Use the map on page 272 to locate these seas.

Facing page: **Pastoral scenes like this appear throughout Europe.**
Page 266: **In Spain the Rock of Gibraltar guards the waters between Europe and Africa.**

Western Europe
Political

International boundaries
⊛ National capitals
• Other cities

ARCTIC OCEAN

Arctic Circle

NORWEGIAN SEA

ATLANTIC OCEAN

ICELAND
⊛ Reykjavik

Faeroe Is. (Den.)

Shetland Is. (U.K.)

Hebrides Is. (U.K.)

Orkney Is. (U.K.)

NORWAY
• Bergen
• Stavanger
⊛ Oslo
• Trondheim
Narvik
Kiruna

SWEDEN
Uppsala
⊛ Stockholm
• Goteborg

FINLAND
• Oulu
• Tampere
• Turku
⊛ Helsinki

Gulf of Bothnia

BALTIC SEA

SCOTLAND
• Glasgow
• Edinburgh

NORTHERN IRELAND
• Belfast

UNITED KINGDOM
• Liverpool
• Leeds
• Manchester
⊛ Dublin
REPUBLIC OF IRELAND
• Cork
WALES
• Cardiff
ENGLAND
• Birmingham
⊛ London

NORTH SEA

DENMARK
• Ålborg
• Århus
⊛ Copenhagen
• Odense
• Malmo

• Hamburg
• Bremen

West Berlin (W. Ger.)
EAST GERMANY
POLAND

NETHERLANDS
• Amsterdam
The Hague
• Essen
• Dortmund
• Düsseldorf
• Cologne
• Bonn

BELGIUM
⊛ Brussels
LUXEMBOURG
Luxembourg

WEST GERMANY
• Stuttgart
• Munich
• Strasbourg

CZECHOSLOVAKIA

English Channel

Seine

⊛ Paris
Loire River

Bay of Biscay

• Nantes

FRANCE
• Bordeaux
• Lyon
• Toulouse
• Marseille
• Nice
Garonne River
Rhône River
⊛ Bern
• Zurich
• Geneva
SWITZERLAND
LIECHTENSTEIN
⊛ Vaduz
AUSTRIA
• Vienna
• Graz
HUNGARY

ROMANIA

• Milan
• Turin
• Venice
• Genoa
• Bologna
Po River
MONACO
⊛ Monaco
SAN MARINO
⊛ San Marino
• Florence
ITALY
⊛ Rome
VATICAN CITY
• Naples

YUGOSLAVIA

ADRIATIC SEA

BULGARIA

BLACK SEA

PORTUGAL
• Porto
⊛ Lisbon
Duero River
Tagus River
Guadalquivir River

SPAIN
• Bilbao
⊛ Madrid
• Saragossa
ANDORRA
⊛ Andorra la Vella
• Barcelona
• Valencia
• Palma
Ebro River
• Córdoba
• Seville
• Málaga
Gibraltar (U.K.)

Corsica (Fr.)

Sardinia (It.)

TYRRHENIAN SEA

Balearic Is. (Sp.)

• Palermo
Sicily (It.)

MALTA
⊛ Valletta

IONIAN SEA

ALBANIA

TURKEY
• Istanbul
• Thessaloniki

GREECE
• Patrai
⊛ Athens

AEGEAN SEA

ASIA

Crete (Gr.)

MEDITERRANEAN SEA

AFRICA

UNION OF SOVIET SOCIALIST REPUBLICS (SOVIET UNION)

Danube River
Elbe
Rhine River

0   200   400 Miles
0   200   400 Kilometers

N
W   E
S

270

© SF

Islands are also an important part of Western Europe. For historical reasons Iceland—located near Greenland—is considered part of Western Europe. Nearer to the mainland are the British Isles, whose two main islands are named Ireland and Great Britain. The English Channel separates Great Britain from the mainland.

The islands of the Mediterranean Sea have been important cultural stepping stones for thousands of years. Sicily and Sardinia, the largest two, are today part of the nation of Italy.

Western Europe enjoys both cultural and physical advantages.

No part of Western Europe is more than about 300 miles, a day's drive, from the sea. This has given Europe important cultural and physical advantages.

Historically, Europe's nearness to the ocean stimulated overseas travel and encouraged commercial and cultural exchanges. Some scholars believe that this contact with the sea encouraged Europeans to develop a venturesome psychology. Beginning in the late 1400s, the Age of Exploration led by Columbus and his colleagues opened the whole world to Europeans. They discovered that all the oceans of the earth flowed together, and thus could be reached by ships.

Western Europe's nearness to the sea also gives it the advantage of a moderate climate. Ireland even has a few palm trees growing on its southern coast. How can this be explained?

Refer to the ocean currents map on page 54. As you learned in Chapter 3, the Gulf Stream sends a huge volume of tropical water into the Atlantic. Twenty times greater than the flow of all the rivers on earth put together, this warm water spurts, like water from a hose, from the

The Rhine has long carried people and goods around Europe.

Straits of Florida all the way across the Atlantic, becoming the North Atlantic Drift. Dominant westerly winds that blow across this current bring warmth to much of Europe.

Rivers are important arteries for commerce and ideas.

Locate the Alps on the map on page 272. If you look closely, you will see that the Rhine River flows out of the Alps from Lake Constance, beginning a long journey to the North Sea. The Rhine River is famous for its wine and castles. Of even greater importance are its navigable waters, which reach into the very heart of the European continent.

As the Rhine flows along the Swiss-German border, a canal joins it from the southeast. This canal provides a link to the Rhône River, which flows all the way to the Mediterranean Sea.

The Rhine-Rhône canal is only one link in a system of canals and waterways that joins together much of the continent. By using the Main River, a major tributary of the Rhine, it is possible to go by boat from either Lake Constance or Lake Geneva to a canal that connects these waters with a third major river, the beautiful Danube.

Map Study

Which Western European countries lack a coast along a sea or ocean?

271

Western Europe
Physical

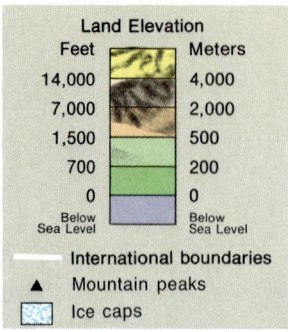

Land Elevation

Feet	Meters
14,000	4,000
7,000	2,000
1,500	500
700	200
0	0
Below Sea Level	Below Sea Level

International boundaries
▲ Mountain peaks
Ice caps

ARCTIC OCEAN

BARENTS SEA

North Cape

KOLA PENINSULA

NORWEGIAN SEA

WHITE SEA

Lofoten Islands

SCANDINAVIAN PENINSULA

Lake Onega

Gulf of Bothnia

Lake Ladoga

Åland Is.

Gulf of Finland

Arctic Circle

ATLANTIC OCEAN

Iceland
▲ Hekla
4,892 ft.
(1,491 m)

Shetland Is.

Hebrides Is.

Orkney Is.

GRAMPIAN MTS.

British Isles

Great Britain

Ireland

IRISH SEA

PENNINES

Thames River

English Channel

Channel Is.

BRITTANY PENINSULA

Loire River

Bay of Biscay

Seine River

Rhine River

JURA MTS.

Lake Geneva

CENTRAL MASSIF

Mt. Blanc
15,771 ft.
(4,807 m)

PYRENEES
▲ Pico de Aneto
11,168 ft.
(3,404 m)

Garonne R.

Duero River

IBERIAN PENINSULA

Tagus River

Guadalquivir River

Strait of Gibraltar

▲ Mulhacén
11,411 ft.
(3,478 m)

Minorca

Majorca

Ibiza

Balearic Is.

NORTH SEA

JUTLAND

Fyn

Sjaelland

BALTIC SEA

Gotland

NORTH EUROPEAN PLAIN

Elbe River

RUHR VALLEY

Danube River

Lake Constance

ALPS

Matterhorn
14,692 ft. (4,478 m)

Po River

Grossglockner
12,457 ft. (3,797 m)

Danube River

APENNINES

Corsica

Sardinia

TYRRHENIAN SEA

Vesuvius
4,190 ft.
(1,277 m)

Mt. Etna
11,122 ft. (3,390 m)

Sicily

Malta

IONIAN SEA

ADRIATIC SEA

BALKAN PENINSULA

PINDUS MTS.

AEGEAN SEA

BLACK SEA

Bosporus

Dardanelles

ASIA

Rhodes

Crete

MEDITERRANEAN SEA

AFRICA

50° North Latitude

10° West Longitude

| | 200 | 400 Miles |
| 0 | 200 | 400 | Kilometers |

272

© SF

The source of the Danube is in the Black Forest, just northwest of Lake Constance. This important river then moves eastward to the Black Sea, flowing through seven European countries. It might be called the river of capital cities—Vienna (Austria), Budapest (Hungary), and Belgrade (Yugoslavia) are all located on its banks.

These three celebrated waterways—Rhine, Rhône, and Danube—supplemented by other rivers and a network of canals, link the various parts of Europe together. As recently as 1970, about one-third of all intercity freight in Europe was carried on this system of rivers and inland waterways. Since then the use of the canals has declined somewhat because some canals are too narrow for modern barges. However, the waterways remain important arteries for commerce and the spread of ideas. The Rhine is still the most heavily traveled river in the world.

Western Europe has mountains, hills, and plains.

The landscape of Western Europe is as varied as its coastline. Mountains, hills, plateaus, and plains are distributed in a complex pattern over the continent. The ancient core of Europe is exposed in the Scandinavian Shield. Like its counterpart in Canada, the Scandinavian Shield is a stub remaining from high mountains of long ago. On its western flank are the highlands of Norway, Scotland, northern England, and Ireland. These highlands are the same age as the Appalachians, and like the Appalachians, are neither high nor rugged. Central Europe also has a core of low rounded mountains of this age.

Between these two highland areas is the North European Plain, a flat area that begins in southern England. In Western Europe the plain

Map Study

What are several mountain ranges that run through Western Europe?

also includes northwestern France, western Belgium, the Netherlands, northern Germany, Denmark, and southern Sweden. To the east the plain broadens out into Poland and the Soviet Union, clear to the Ural Mountains.

Southern Europe is dominated by a series of young mountains, still high and rugged, like those along the western edge of the American continents. The high mountains include the Pyrenees, the Alps, the Carpathians, the Apennines, the Balkan ranges, and the Pindus Mountains.

In most parts of Mediterranean Europe, the mountains come right to the sea, leaving little coastal plain. However, tucked in among the mountains and hills are three plains. The Po River Valley in Italy, the Rhône River Valley in France, and the Ebro River Valley in Spain all have broad fertile plains leading to the sea.

Section 1 Review

Locating Key Places
Locate the following places on the map on page 272: English Channel, North Sea, Iberian Peninsula

Identifying Key Terms
Define the following terms: peninsula, sea

Reviewing Main Ideas
1. What two physical features cover large portions of Western Europe? Give examples of each.
2. What cultural and physical advantages does Western Europe enjoy because of its nearness to the sea?
3. How do Western Europe's rivers enhance its culture?
4. Describe three geographical features of Western Europe's landscape.

Thinking Critically: Assess Cause and Effect
Chicago and Rome may be compared because they are located at about the same distance north of the Equator. Why do you think then that their climates vary considerably?

SECTION 2

Climate, Soils, and Vegetation

Preview

Key Places
Where are these places located?
1 Low Countries
2 Scandinavia
3 Italy
See the globe below.

Key Terms
What does this term mean?
alluvium

Main Ideas
As you read, look for answers to these questions.
• What natural feature divides Western Europe's two major climate regions?
• What climate region dominates Western Europe?
• What is the major climate region south of the Alps?
• What are the other climate regions of Western Europe?

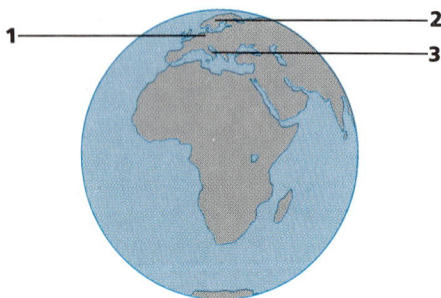

For a charming week we wandered up the valley of the Rhône, and then branching off at Leuk, we made our way over the Gemmi Pass, still deep in snow, and so, by way of Interlaken, to Meiringen. It was a lovely trip, the dainty green of the spring below, the virgin white of the winter above; but it was clear to me that never for one instant did Holmes forget the shadow that lay across him.

Sir Arthur Conan Doyle, *The Final Problem*

The Alps separate Western Europe's two major climate regions.

It was to the Swiss Alps that Sherlock Holmes and Dr. Watson made their temporary escape from Professor Moriarty. For several days they journeyed on foot through the soft, green forests, making their way from inn to inn. The jewel-like Alps towered above them, looming out of the clouds. Holmes was drawn to the forbidding Reichenbach falls, deep in the mountains, to meet his mortal enemy, Moriarty, for the last time.

Today the Alps draw tourists, artists, students, and mountaineers from the world over. A climbing party may begin from the village of Zermatt in the comfort of a warm summer's day. Several hours later, the climbers may stand on the summit of the Matterhorn, huddled and frostbitten, at the mercy of a howling snowstorm.

The Alps are more than breathtakingly beautiful and challenging. The mountains serve as a great natural wall separating Western Europe's two major climate regions—the marine west coast climate region and the Mediterranean climate region.

In the winter southern Europe is protected by the mountains from cold arctic winds, and in the summer northern Europe does not get the hot and dry weather that much of the southern latitudes experience. Locate these regions on the map on page 275. Within these regions a

274

Western Europe: Climate Regions

Dry climates

▢ Steppe

Mild climates

▢ Marine west coast

▢ Humid subtropical

▢ Mediterranean

Continental climates

▢ Humid continental, cool summer

▢ Subarctic

Polar climates

▢ Tundra

High altitudes

▢ Highlands

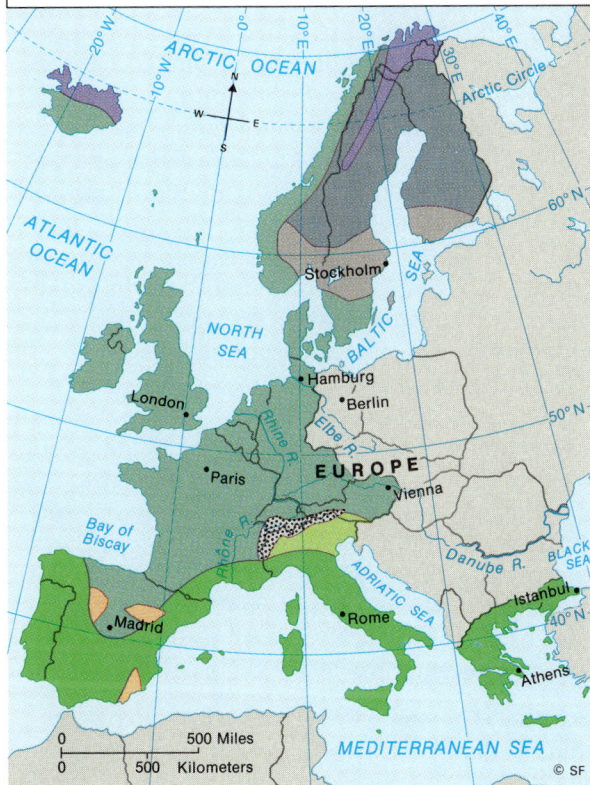

Map Study

Which two climate regions influence most of Western Europe?

variety of elevations, varying distances from the sea, and local landforms and water bodies create many minor climate variations.

Holmes and Watson, for example, experienced tremendous climatic variations as they trekked though the Swiss Alps. They had been in the highlands climate region. Locate this area on the map on page 275.

The marine west coast climate dominates Western Europe.

Moderate winters, cool summers, and abundant rainfall evenly distributed throughout the year characterize the marine west coast climate region. Westerly winds regularly blow in from the Atlantic Ocean, carrying with them the moisture picked up as they crossed the warm North Atlantic Drift. Throughout the year Western Europe remains under the influence of the westerlies and the North Atlantic Drift. As a result, temperatures are fairly mild north of the Alps, even in winter, and precipitation comes at all times of the year.

On the map you can see how the marine west coast climate extends all the way east to about 20° E longitude, aided by the broad North European Plain. If you look at the world climate map on pages 58–59, you will discover that Europe has almost as much area with a marine west coast climate as all the other continents combined. This climate region provides dependable moisture, along with moderate temperatures and a long growing season.

Vegetation. The vegetation of Western Europe is very different today than it was when people first tilled the land. In general, people have used the land in Western Europe by clearing the original forests and replacing the trees with fields and pasture lands. The clearing of the European forest began in prehistoric times and has continued up to our own century.

Europe's remaining forests may also one day be gone. Pollution from today's highly industri-

Western Europe: Natural Vegetation Regions

■ Broadleaf forest—deciduous	■ Mixed forest (broadleaf and needleleaf)
■ Broadleaf forest—other	■ Tundra
■ Needleleaf forest	▨ High mountains (vegetation varies with elevation)

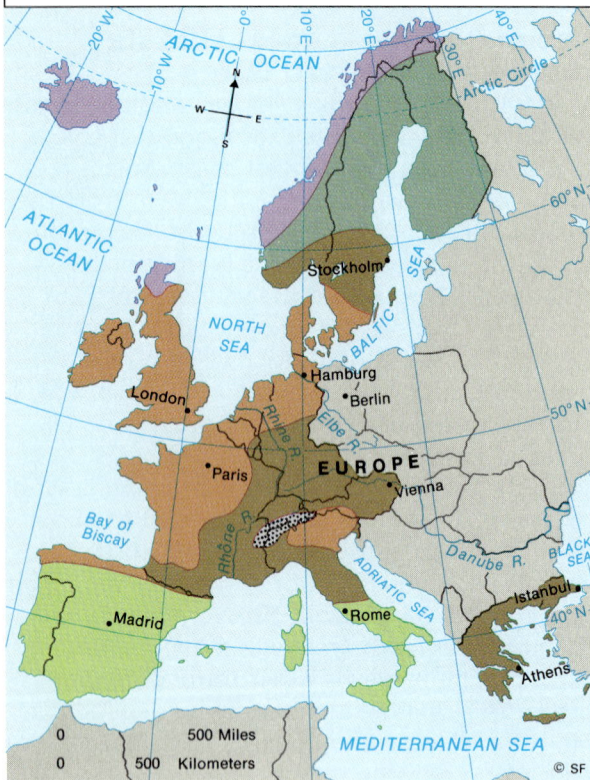

ARCTIC OCEAN

Arctic Circle

ATLANTIC OCEAN

Stockholm

NORTH SEA

BALTIC SEA

Hamburg

Berlin

London

EUROPE

Rhine R.

Elbe R.

Paris

Vienna

Bay of Biscay

Rhône R.

Danube R.

BLACK SEA

ADRIATIC SEA

Istanbul

Madrid

Rome

Athens

MEDITERRANEAN SEA

0   500 Miles
0   500 Kilometers

© SF

Map Study

What type of natural vegetation covered most of Western Europe? What types grow in northern Scandinavia?

alized Western European community poses a serious threat to the forests.

The broadleaf forest now found north of the Alps at one time covered much of France, West Germany, the Low Countries—Belgium, the Netherlands, and Luxembourg (also called Benelux, after their economic union organized in 1948)—and the British Isles. This you can see on the natural vegetation map on page 276.

The humus that formed from the leaves had made the underlying soils quite fertile. Thus, these regions were attractive to farmers, and throughout the Middle Ages (from A.D. 500 to 1500), the forest were turned into farms.

The typical landscape in this period was an isolated agricultural village, with fields and pasture on the outskirts of the community, entirely surrounded by the dark forest. Much folklore from this earlier period has survived in our own culture. Thus, to go to grandmother's house, in many stories, is to go through the sinister woods to get to the neighboring village.

Some areas of Western Europe were not forested when people first arrived. These were the broad areas of sandy meadows, or heath, along the northern fringe of the British Isles, the northern Netherlands, northern Germany, and western Denmark. Relics from the glacial period, these sandy areas are covered with low, scrubby plants such as juniper and heather. The poor soils of the heath are not well suited to farming, and few people live there even today.

Soils. The soils of the marine west coast climate region of Western Europe are adequate for strong agricultural activity, but they are not, by themselves, of great fertility. However, through the application of fertilizer and other careful farming practices, farmers in Western Europe get high crop yields from these soils.

North of the Alps, the major type of soils are gray-brown forest soils. These develop under a cover of broadleaf deciduous or mixed forests. They are acidic and somewhat leached of miner-

Purple heather grows wild in moist places of Western Europe.

als, and they benefit from the application of lime and fertilizer. Broadleaf trees, remember, provide excellent humus content for soils, but needleleaf trees, which are more common in Western Europe, result in a more acidic and less fertile soil.

One of the most fertile soils north of the mountains is alluvium. **Alluvium** is the sediment left behind where water flows slowly, as it does near the mouths of rivers. The broad delta of the Rhine River has been diked, ditched, drained, and turned into fertile polders, which are areas of reclaimed lowland. The Dutch have been applying this reclamation technique for hundreds of years, creating some of Europe's best farmland out of the alluvium-rich soil. Windmills were used to pump water out of an enclosed area to keep the drained marshes and coastal lowlands dry. There are few operating windmills any more, as they have been replaced by electric pumps.

South of the Alps is the Mediterranean climate region.

As you already learned, the Mediterranean climate zone is characterized by mild, moist winters and hot, dry summers. In the winter the westerlies prevail, and the region receives rainfall. However, the Alps and other mountains act as barriers to the Arctic blasts that often bring cold spells further to the north. Winters are warm enough, though often cloudy, to tempt northerners to spend their winter holidays along the Mediterranean.

In the summer, however, skies are clear and cloudless. The region comes under the influence of the drying trade winds, and temperatures in southern Spain, southern Italy, and southern Greece are high.

In the south, the Mediterranean open forest once had trees such as cork, oak, olive, and myrtle that could withstand the hot, dry summers. These trees had thick bark and small leaves, both of which were meant to conserve moisture. This type of woodland is called an open forest because the trees are widely spaced. Grass covers the ground between the trees.

Most of the Mediterranean open forest was removed over the centuries to make way for farmland and to use as fuel and lumber. The open forest often did not replace itself. As the large old trees were taken away, the topsoil on the steep slopes quickly washed away in the wet season. Moreover, as young trees tried to gain a foothold, they were often eaten up by sheep and goats, which have been grazing in the region for thousands of years.

The soils of the Mediterranean open forest region are not severely leached, and they are generally fairly fertile. The most fertile soils, of course, are in the alluvial valleys. In addition, some very fertile soils are the volcanic soils found especially in southern Italy and on the island of Sicily. In the hilly areas of Mediterranean Europe, however, erosion brings on the problem of thin soil covers.

Western Europe also has continental and other climates.

Refer to the climate map on page 275. Notice the sharp boundaries in the Scandinavian Peninsula, Finland, and along southern France, northern Italy, and Switzerland. These sharp climate divisions occur along mountain ranges.

Thus, the mild climates of the coastal lands of Norway contrast with the continental climates that cover most of the Scandinavian Peninsula. Humid continental, cool summer climate areas affect central Scandinavia, bringing warm moist summers and long, cold snowy winters. In these areas the forest is mixed needleleaf and deciduous, gradually becoming more dominantly needleleaf as one moves further north.

In the northern regions of Scandinavia, the subarctic climate dominates. Most of the subarctic climate area has too short a growing season to support productive agriculture. As a result, few trees have been cleared for farming. At the far northern tip of Norway and Finland is a polar climate region, with tundra vegetation. Here reindeer graze in the summer.

Several other variations in the climate pattern of Western Europe may be seen on the map on page 275. Find the steppe climate on the Iberian Peninsula. In these steppe climate regions, there is a semi-dry climate, and the vegetation cover is grass rather than trees. In the dry region of La Mancha, made famous by Cervantes and his tales of Don Quixote, windmills were used to ensure a supply of water from wells deep within the ground.

The alpine regions of France, Switzerland, Germany, Austria, and Italy all have highland climates. Valleys can be warm and pleasant in the summers, but nearby high peaks will have permanent snow. Cattle and sheep graze at high elevations in the summer but move to lower pastures in the winter.

In highland areas, like Norway, cows move down from these high summer pastures in winter.

Section 2 Review

Locating Key Places
Locate the following places on the map on page 270: Low Countries, Scandinavia, Italy

Identifying Key Terms
Define the following term: alluvium

Reviewing Main Ideas
1. Into what two climate regions do the Alps divide Western Europe?
2. What climate region covers most of Western Europe?
3. What climate region dominates the part of Europe south of the Alps?
4. Describe Western Europe's other climatic regions.

Thinking Critically: Make Decisions
You are the head of a British company whose smokestacks emit pollutants that are killing trees in Germany and Denmark. The German government has asked you to install and pay for costly antipollution devices in your factory. What options would you consider? What might your response be?

The Heritage of Western Europe

Preview

Key Places
Where are these places located?
1 Greece
2 Rome
See the globe below.

Key Terms
What do these terms mean?
classical culture
feudalism
serfs
Crusades
mercantilism
nationalism

Main Ideas
As you read, look for answers to these questions.
● What unites the diverse peoples of Western Europe?
● What is the principal religion of this geographic realm?
● How have Western European ideas affected much of the world?
● How did World Wars I and II affect Western Europe?

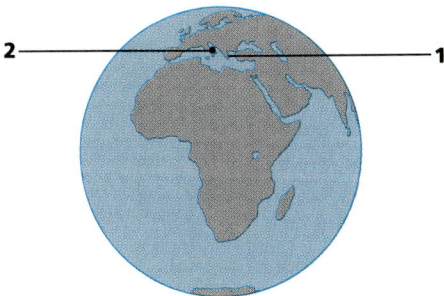

To the glory that was Greece,
And the grandeur that was Rome.

Edgar Allan Poe, "To Helen"

Most Western Europeans share a cultural heritage.

Western Europeans have many cultures and languages, but, as the poet Edgar Allan Poe suggests, they have a common heritage that is traced back to the "glory" and "grandeur" of the ancient Greek and Roman civilizations. From these two civilizations have come many of the cultural and philosophical traditions of Western Europe, including their religious and linguistic heritage.

The roots of Western European culture can be traced back to the development of the Greek civilization around 500 B.C. Over the next few centuries, Greek culture, with its many contributions in politics, philosophy, science, education, architecture, drama, and literature, spread widely from its origins in Greece to Egypt, Italy, Southwest Asia, and as far east as the Indus River.

The Roman Empire, centered on the west coast of Italy, eventually took over the Greek lands, and by 100 B.C. included almost every region that bordered the Mediterranean Sea. The Romans admired the Greek culture and adopted many of its elements. Over the years a blend of Roman and Greek culture evolved, which became known as **classical culture.** Eventually, Roman armies pushed to the Danube and Rhine rivers, and as far north as the British Isles and northern Germany. As the Romans extended their empire throughout Europe, they were responsible for spreading both classical culture and the Latin language, from which many modern Western European languages are derived.

The Roman Empire eventually collapsed in the A.D. 400s. Internal problems and invasions from Germanic tribes from northern Europe weakened and ultimately dissolved the vast empire.

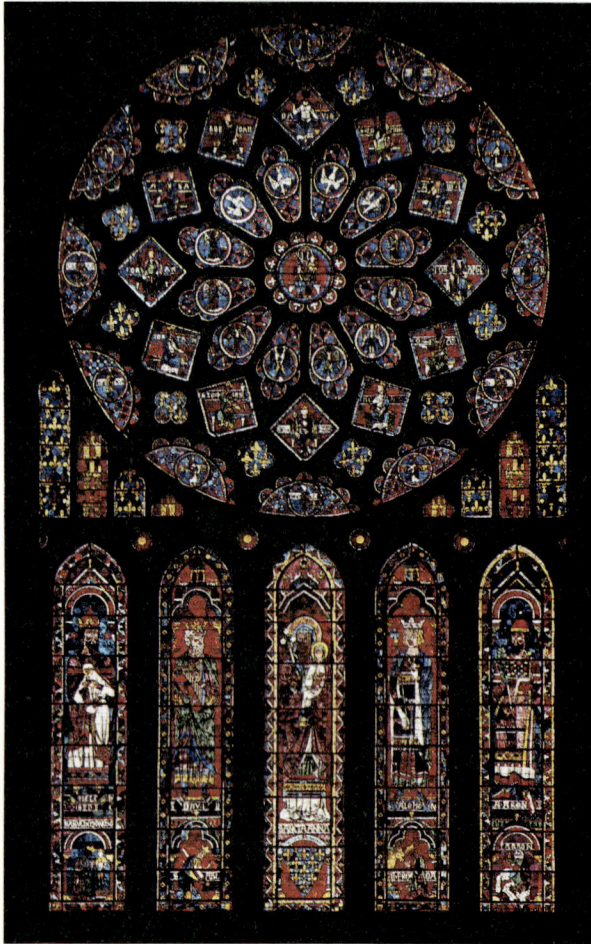

The rose window in the cathedral at Chartres and the Pietà by Michelangelo both show Christianity's influence on European art and culture.

The territory was then carved up into separate kingdoms, parts of which were eventually conquered by Muslim invaders from North Africa.

Christianity is the dominant religion of Western Europe.

The Roman Empire was also responsible for spreading Christianity throughout Western Europe. After the empire collapsed, the Christian Church remained the strongest institution uniting the realm for the next thousand years. Today most Western Europeans are Christians. Jews formed a large minority until the 1940s, when six million of them were killed in a terrible massacre known as the Holocaust. In addition, some Western Europeans are Muslim.

The origins of Christianity. This world religion is based on the life and teachings of Jesus, who was born in the Roman-controlled land of Palestine. His birth has come to signify the beginning of the Christian calendar—everything before Jesus' birth is known as B.C. (before Christ), and everything following is known as A.D. (Anno Domini, meaning "in the year of the Lord"). Christianity began as a religion among

Jews who followed the teachings of Jesus, a Jew himself.

Jesus traveled throughout Palestine, preaching the "gospel," which means "good news," to large groups of people. His teachings, like that of other Jews, condemned selfishness and violence and taught doctrines based on brotherhood. Most Jews, however, did not accept Jesus' teachings of being the Messiah ("Christ" in Greek), or "anointed one," who would usher in the Day of Judgment at the end of time.

Eventually Jesus' preaching drew criticism from both Jewish authorities and Roman rulers, who felt threatened by Jesus' following. Around A.D. 30, Jesus was crucified on the order of Pontius Pilate, a Roman governor.

The spread of Christianity. After the crucifixion, Jesus' followers continued to believe that their leader was the divine Son of God promised and sent by God to free the Jews. The New Testament of the Bible describes how Jesus rose from the dead and appeared briefly before several followers, confirming the teachings of eternal life. The Apostles, those 12 men chosen by Jesus to preach the gospel, continued the spread of Christianity.

For the first 300 years, Christians were persecuted as enemies of the Roman Empire for refusing to worship the emperor. Then, the Roman emperor Constantine converted to Christianity and granted Christians freedom of worship. This event paved the way for Christianity to become, in A.D. 395, the official religion of the Roman Empire.

By the A.D 400s, the Roman Empire had weakened, but the Church had grown in strength and numbers. It had also split into two different branches—the Western church, centered in Rome, and the Eastern church, based in Constantinople (present-day Istanbul, Turkey).

During this period, known as the Middle Ages, Western Europe was divided up among thousands of land-owning nobles. These lords, as they were called, ruled under a system of **feudalism**, in which they contracted out the use of their land to serfs. These **serfs**, who were workers belonging to the land, owed personal loyalty and manual labor to the lord, who in turned owed loyalty to the church. In this way, the Church was able to dominate many areas of life in the Middle Ages.

In addition to controlling Europe, the Church wanted to gain control over the Holy Land, the region around Jerusalem which was then under Muslim rule. To accomplish this, the Church organized several military expeditions, known as **Crusades**, which took place between 1096 and 1202.

Although the Crusaders were ultimately unsuccessful in recapturing Jerusalem, they and the rest of Europe benefited by this exposure to the Muslim world. As a result of the Crusades, many new goods and ideas were introduced into the Western European civilizations, and trade flourished across the Mediterranean.

Later, the Age of Exploration played a role in the spread of Christianity. This was a time, between 1450 and 1650, in which all the Western European countries bordering the Atlantic Ocean set off to explore and claim new lands. Christian populations grew as a result, especially in the Americas and parts of Africa and Asia.

The beliefs of Christianity. All Christians share some basic beliefs about the existence and nature of God and Jesus. However, there are many different interpretations and practices among the many different Christian groups.

Christians believe that there is one God, and that this God created and watches over the universe. They also believe in the existence and teachings of Jesus. Although some Christians view Jesus as a great but human teacher, most believe that Jesus is the divine God, appearing in human form.

In addition, most Christians meet regularly in churches to worship together, to encourage one another to follow the moral teachings of Jesus, and to act on their faith in the real world. Christian worship centers around the Bible, which includes both the Old Testament, also known as the Hebrew Bible, and the New Testament, which details the life and teachings of Jesus.

Most Christian worship also involves the participation in sacraments, which are holy acts of faith. These sacraments may include baptism, an initiation into the Christian faith, and Holy Communion, a celebration of the Lord's Supper. During Holy Communion consecrated bread and wine or grape juice is received or shared in commemoration of the last supper shared by Jesus and the Apostles on the evening before Jesus' crucifixion.

The differences within Christianity. There are three principal groups that have emerged within the Christian religion. They are the Roman Catholic, Eastern Orthodox, and Protestant churches.

The Roman Catholic and Eastern Orthodox churches had originally begun to separate in the late years of the Roman Empire. They officially split in 1054 over disagreements about the pope's authority. Roman Catholics regard the pope as the spiritual leader of their church, a position rejected by Eastern Orthodoxy.

The Protestant churches developed out of the Reformation of the early 1500s, a movement led by Martin Luther, a German priest and professor, to protest widespread corruption in the Catholic Church. Luther organized a new church in which people had a direct relationship with God. He was able to distribute his writings and gain wide support with the help of a recent invention, the printing press.

Other Christian reformers, including John Calvin, followed Luther's lead and set up separate churches as well. Today many different Protestant branches flourish, primarily in Western Europe, the United States, Canada, Africa, Australia, and New Zealand.

Western European ideas have influenced the rest of the world.

From the time of the Roman Empire, Western Europe has experienced many changes and upheavals. During the later Middle Ages (A.D. 800–1400), trade began to expand beyond the local markets, town life slowly revived, and a powerful and wealthy middle class gradually developed among merchants, artisans, and shopkeepers. From this middle class came a push for advancements in education and the arts.

A rebirth of learning. By the 1300s this desire for learning had evolved into a full-fledged movement that revitalized the culture of Western Europe. This movement, called the Renaissance [ren′ə säns′], began in northern Italy, where new wealth from trade supported the advancement of writers, philosophers, and artists. This rebirth of learning introduced secular, or nonreligious, themes and concepts.

In the wake of the Renaissance came the Age of Reason, sometimes called the Enlightenment, a time between 1700 and 1800 of great advancement in scientific and technological knowledge. This period grew out of the discoveries of some of the world's greatest thinkers—Galileo [gal′ə lē′ō], Descartes [dā kärt′], and Newton.

A time of exploration and conquest. Throughout these centuries of change within Western Europe, there was also a desire to stretch outward. Greater wealth and improved sailing technologies sent many explorers out across the Atlantic Ocean and into Africa and Asia. These explorers, mainly from Portugal, Spain, France, Britain, and the Netherlands, sailed for different purposes. These purposes revolved around the search for riches, the drive to establish colonies or to spread religion, and the desire to set up trading outposts.

These expeditions brought to Western Europe both great wealth and exposure to new lands, people, foods, goods, and ideas. They also brought about a new economic policy that controlled the way in which European countries used their newfound colonies in the 1500s and 1600s. This policy, known as **mercantilism**, was an economic system that favored a balance of exports of goods over imports and the accumulation of large stores of gold and silver.

As a result of mercantilism, colonies became very important to the Europeans. In one sense, the colonies were a source of precious metals, other raw materials, tropical crops, and slaves. In another sense, they provided ready and often closed markets for the goods manufactured by the mercantilist country.

Successive agricultural and industrial revolutions increased the advantages of Western European countries over their colonies. Improved farming technology led to increased farm production and larger and healthier populations. Innovations in industry, which first began in Britain in the late 1700s, aided the development of European monopolies on manufactured goods and the machinery to produce them.

A revolution of political thought. The Enlightenment turned the thoughts of many philosophers toward politics. In the 1600s and 1700s, such philosophers as John Locke, Baron de Montesquieu, Voltaire, and Jean Jacques Rousseau examined the rights, responsibilities, and values involved in the governing of people. As a result, the governments and societies of Western Europe and much of the Americas changed dramatically.

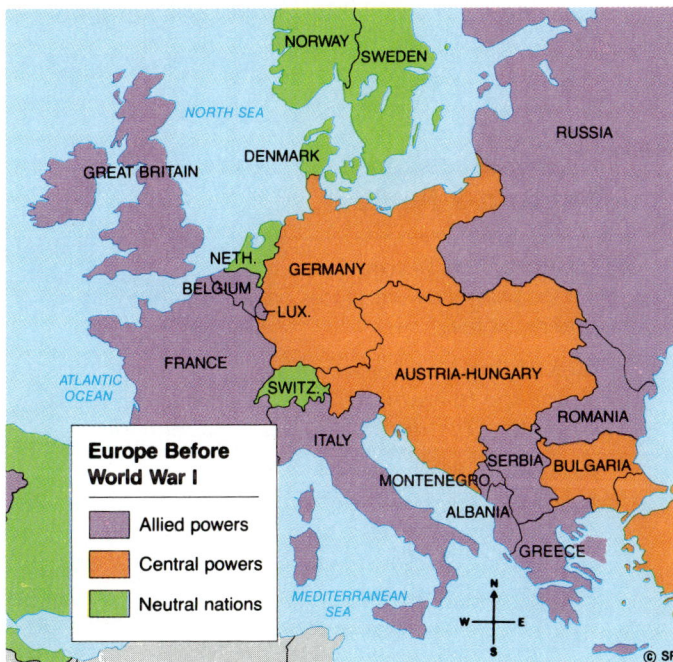

Europe Before World War I

- Allied powers
- Central powers
- Neutral nations

Europe After World War I

- New nations

Map Study

World War I, which lasted from 1914 to 1918, greatly affected European boundaries. What new political units were created after the war? From which countries was Yugoslavia formed? Poland? Czechoslovakia?

This group of philosophers endorsed democracy and the values of individual rights and freedoms that form its core. Their thoughts sparked a series of democratic revolutions against autocratic monarchies and colonial powers that spread through Western Europe. The revolutions began in Britain and led ultimately to the creation of the United States, and many other democratic governments.

Later, in the 1800s, another political movement, nationalism, swept Western Europe. **Nationalism** is a feeling of pride and loyalty that develops among a group of people who share a common language, culture, and history. This feeling usually leads them to unite under a common government to form a nation-state. Although nation-states such as Britain and France had begun to form in the Middle Ages, significant political upheavals and a greater sense of national identity characterized the 19th century. During this time, Belgium, Germany, Italy, and many other modern countries were formed.

Today many smaller groups are still seeking "national" recognition in Western Europe. This movement is closely linked to ethnic pride. For example, the Welsh and Scots in the United Kingdom and the Basques and Catalans in Spain consider themselves "nations," even though they are part of a larger country. Most Western European countries today have small or large minority groups who wish to keep their ethnic identities.

World Wars I and II affected the boundaries and identity of Europe.

As you have read, nationalism can be a force that brings people together, but it can also tear a continent apart. Both of the most terrible wars of our century, World War I (1914–1918) and World War II (1939–1945), were caused in part by nationalist passions. In turn, they played a major role in shaping the boundaries and alliances of modern Europe.

World War I changed Europe by ending the reign of four major empires (the German, Austro-Hungarian, Ottoman, and Russian) and establishing new borders. Look at the maps on page 283, before and after the war.

World War II made its mark on Europe as well. The war brought about a polarization in Europe between the democratic West, strengthened by the United States, and the communist East, dominated by the Soviet Union. One of the results of this polarization was the formation of the European Community, or European Common Market—a group of Western European nations working to unite their economic resources.

In 1989 significant political changes in the Soviet Union helped cause far-reaching changes in Eastern Europe. These nations experienced massive demonstrations that forced out hardline communist leaders.

Section 3 Review

Locating Key Places
Locate the following places on the map on page 270: Greece, Rome

Identifying Key Terms
Define the following terms: classical culture, feudalism, serfs, Crusades, mercantilism, nationalism

Reviewing Main Ideas
1. From which two ancient civilizations did the cultural heritage of Western Europe originate?
2. Describe how Christianity came to dominate Western Europe.
3. Name several influential philosophical, political, or economic ideas that originated in Western Europe.
4. What changes did World Wars I and II bring to Western Europe?

Thinking Critically: Identify Assumptions
What assumptions might people hold who are strong nationalists?

Using Block Diagrams

Suppose you were a tourist in Switzerland. You could learn how to climb the famous mountain, the Matterhorn, by looking at a block diagram. A block diagram combines the features of a map and a cross section. Although block diagrams look three-dimensional, they are really simple, shaded line drawings. These drawings give the impression that you are looking at a block cut from the earth, with both the interior and surface features shown.

The block diagram on this page shows a view of a peak like the Matterhorn, giving its main physical features. The diagram also shows how the peak's shape was affected by erosion by alpine glaciers.

At the top of the diagram is a pointed peak, or horn. It has been chiseled to a sharp point by receding glaciers, whose jagged rocks have ground away the sides of the mountain. The tops of mountains unaffected by glaciers are generally more rounded.

As the ice sheets moved down the mountain, they scooped out long, U-shaped valleys, or troughs. Some of these valleys are called "hanging valleys" because they drop off abruptly. Magnificent waterfalls tumble from the edges of the hanging valleys and spill into the troughs below.

Remains of large glaciers can be found high in the mountains. These "relic glaciers" provide meltwater that forms the streams, which spill into the troughs. Sometimes the meltwater collects, forming small lakes called "tarns." Another type of lake, found in the U-shaped lower valleys, is called a trough lake.

May Theilgaard Watts, a celebrated naturalist, called the Alps a "landscape of pockets and shelves and sheltered slits and constricted entrances." She also described the mountains as a perfect refuge for people with different ways of life and for plants and animals that could be found nowhere else.

A Matterhorn-type peak is a unique work of nature. The block diagram can only hint at its grandeur. The diagram does, however, help us understand how the peak was formed, giving us a vocabulary for the exciting sport of mountaineering.

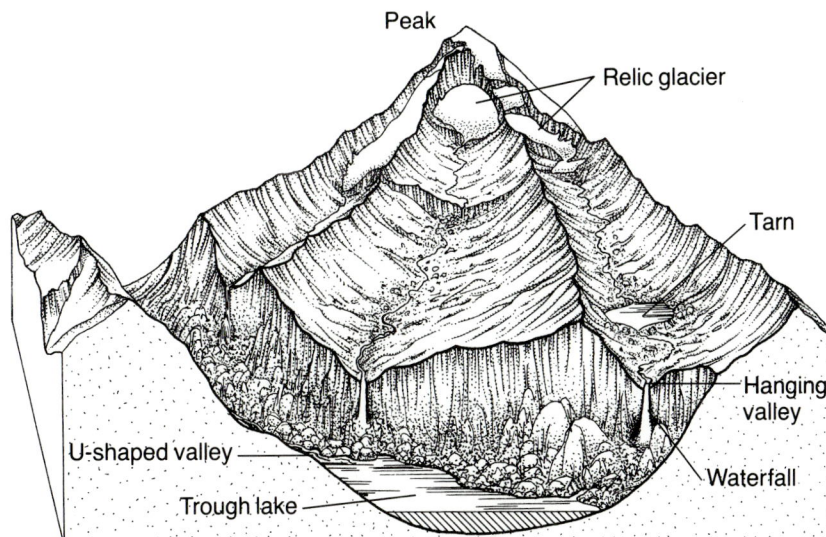

Peak
Relic glacier
Tarn
Hanging valley
Waterfall
U-shaped valley
Trough lake

Review

1. Why are there many spectacular waterfalls in mountain ranges like the Alps?

2. How can you tell whether a mountain has been glaciated?

3. Describe two kinds of lakes that you might find in the Alps.

Review

Section Summaries

1. The Western European Landscape
Western Europe can be thought of as a large peninsula with smaller peninsulas and associated islands. It is near the sea, which gives it important cultural and physical advantages. Rivers have also been important in Western Europe for commerce and the spread of ideas. In addition to interesting waterscapes, the realm has a varied landscape that includes mountains, hills, plateaus, and plains.

2. Climate, Soils, and Vegetation
The two major climates of Western Europe, marine west coast and Mediterranean, are separated by the Alps. The natural vegetation regions of the realm correspond to these climate zones, but humans have cleared much of the original forest. Western Europe also has other climate regions, including continental, polar, dry, and mild. Westerly winds and the North Atlantic Drift help keep temperatures moderate.

3. The Heritage of Western Europe
The cultural heritage of Western Europe comes from the ancient Greek and Roman civilizations. The Romans were responsible for the spread of Christianity, now the dominant religion in this geographic realm. Other Western Europeans have influenced people around the globe with their contributions to science, art, literature, philosophy, politics, and education. After World War II, Western Europe became politically separated from Eastern Europe.

Using Geography Skills

Reviewing the Map Lesson
The block diagrams below show how a landscape often reflects the different layers of rock, some harder than others, below the surface. Are these statements true or false? Correct any that are false.

1. A slope called an escarpment may form where harder rocks reach the surface.

2. According to the diagram at right, one might expect to find more hills and gently sloping valleys in a drier region.

3. The escarpment at left is steeper because there is less erosion.

Using Social Studies Skills

1. Locate and Gather Information. Think about some of the events in Western Europe's history. Pick an event which interests you and become an "expert." Use a historical atlas, an encyclopedia, or the *Readers' Guide* to help you find out all you can about your subject. Write an essay and present it to a friend. Have him or her ask questions about your topic.

2. Observe for Detail. Get together with a classmate and do the following: find some photographs of a European capital. The photos should show people going to work, buying things, and enjoying themselves. What capital city is depicted in the pictures your

Dry region

Escarpment

Resists weathering

Humid region

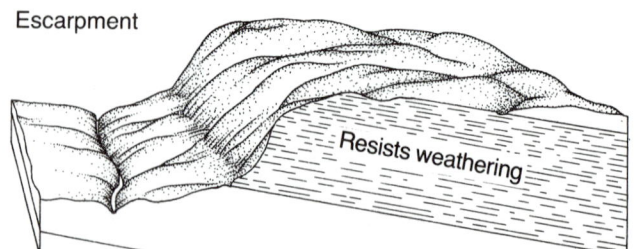

Escarpment

Resists weathering

friend gave you? Look closely for details that give you clues.

Testing for Understanding

Locating Key Places
Match each description below with the name of the place.
1. a narrow body of water that separates the British Isles from the mainland
2. the region that includes Norway and Sweden
3. boot-shaped southern country
4. a large body of water east of the British Isles
5. the center of the ancient civilization that spread Christianity
6. includes Belgium, the Netherlands, and Luxembourg
7. the center of the ancient civilization that promoted science, philosophy, and the arts
8. includes Spain and Portugal
a. English Channel
b. North Sea
c. Iberian Peninsula
d. Low Countries
e. Scandinavia
f. Italy
g. Greece
h. Rome

Recalling Key Terms
Define these terms in your own words.

Section 1
peninsula
sea

Section 2
alluvium

Section 3
classical culture
feudalism
serfs
Crusades
mercantilism
nationalism

Reviewing Main Ideas
Section 1
1. What two physical characteristics give Western Europe its irregular shape?
2. Give examples of the advantages enjoyed by Western Europe because of its nearness to the sea.
3. How have rivers benefited Western Europe?
4. What three types of landforms are evident in Western Europe?

Section 2
1. Which two climate regions are most affected by the Alps?
2. Name the primary climate region in Western Europe.
3. What climate region dominates south of the Alps?
4. What are the continent's other climate regions?

Section 3
1. Which two civilizations made significant contributions to the culture of Western Europe?
2. How did Christianity spread around Western Europe?
3. What are some philosophical, political, or economic themes that spread outward from this geographic realm?
4. How was Western Europe affected by World War I and World War II?

Thinking Critically
1. Make Hypotheses. In what ways do you think Western Europe's position near the sea and in the path of the North Atlantic Drift affected this geographical realm's economic and cultural development? Make a hypothesis that supports your opinion.

2. Recognize Values. List three or four values that are important to most people in the Western world today. Which do you think might have been influenced by the ancient civilizations of Greece and Rome?

The British Isles and Northern Europe

In this chapter you will read about the northernmost nations of Western Europe.

Sections
1 The British Isles
2 Northern Europe

The British Isles

Preview

Key Places
Where are these places located?
1 England
2 Wales
3 Scotland
4 Ireland
5 Northern Ireland
See the globe below.

Key Terms
What do these terms mean?
estuary
clan
firth

Main Ideas
As you read, look for answers to these questions.
- How are the British Isles divided geographically and politically?
- What role does England play in the United Kingdom?
- What distinguishes Wales and Scotland from the rest of the United Kingdom?
- How is Ireland divided politically?

This royal throne of kings, this scepter'd isle,
This earth of majesty, this seat of Mars,
This other Eden, demi-paradise . . .
This happy breed of men, this little world,
This precious stone set in the silver sea . . .
This blessed plot, this earth, this realm,
this England.

William Shakespeare, *King Richard II*

The British Isles have two major islands and political units.

One of Shakespeare's characters, John of Gaunt, spoke these words of endearment on his deathbed. To this day, they serve as a description of the British Isles.

The British Isles include two large islands—Great Britain and Ireland—and numerous smaller ones just west of the European mainland. The map on page 290 shows how the British Isles separate the North Sea from the Atlantic Ocean. The English Channel is the narrow strait between Britain and France.

The British Isles are divided into two major political units—the Republic of Ireland and the United Kingdom (UK). The United Kingdom, which is often referred to as Britain, includes England, Scotland, Wales, and Northern Ireland. However, Northern Ireland is part of the island of Ireland.

Britain's government today is both a constitutional monarchy and a parliamentary democracy. The country has a monarch—currently Queen Elizabeth II—as well as a constitution. Britain's constitution, unlike the Constitution of

Facing page: **An Irishman and his dog set off on a grouse hunt. The mist around them is common in the British Isles.**

289

the United States, is not a single written document. Instead, it is a collection of laws and customs that have developed over the years to limit the monarch's power. Although the monarch is officially the head of state (and of the Commonwealth), he or she has little political power. Actual power in Britain is held by Parliament.

England is the heart of Britain.

In many ways, the United Kingdom really centers on England. It is the political, economic,

The British Isles and Northern Europe

- Commercial farming
- Dairying
- Ranching
- Nomadic herding
- Forests
- ⛟ Lumbering
- ◆ Mining
- Commercial fishing
- ♥ Urban land use
- Little or no economic activity
- ✦ National capitals
- · Other cities

0   300 Miles
0   300   Kilometers

Map labels: NORWEGIAN SEA, Arctic Circle, ICELAND, ✦Reykjavik, Sheep, Cod, FAEROE IS. (DEN.), 60°N, ATLANTIC OCEAN, SHETLAND IS. (U.K.), Oil, Natural Gas, ORKNEY IS. (U.K.), Cod, Stavanger, Bergen, Trondheim, NORWAY, SWEDEN, Sheep, Reindeer, Beef Cattle, Narvik, Kiruna, Iron Ore, Luleå, Oulu, Barley, FINLAND, Copper, Beef Cattle, Barley, Tampere, Herring, Gävle, Turku, Rye, Dairying, Uppsala, ✦Helsinki, Oslo, Stockholm, Herring, Göteborg, Wheat, Dairying, BALTIC SEA, SOVIET UNION, HEBRIDES, Sheep, SCOTLAND, Coal, Cod, Glasgow, Edinburgh, NORTHERN IRELAND, Sheep, Belfast, Coal, Oil, Natural Gas, Cod, Ålborg, DENMARK, Århus, Copenhagen✦, Malmö, Odense, Potatoes, UNITED KINGDOM, Dublin✦, IRELAND, Liverpool, Leeds, Coal, Iron Ore, Natural Gas, Herring, Cork, Dairying, WALES, ENGLAND, Birmingham, Wheat, Dairying, London✦, Cardiff, Mackerel, Barley, NETH., BELG., WEST GERMANY, EAST GERMANY, POLAND, CZECHOSLOVAKIA, NORTH SEA, English Channel, CHANNEL IS. (U.K.), FRANCE, LUX., © SF

70°N, 20°W, 10°W, 0°, 10°E, 20°E, 30°E, 50°N

Map Study

This map shows the political divisions in the British Isles and Northern Europe. What two countries make up the British Isles? What resources are found off the coast of Scotland?

Tourists and pigeons alike flock to London's Trafalgar Square, which was named for Lord Nelson's famous naval battle.

and cultural heart of the United Kingdom. Geographically, England occupies the largest part of the island of Great Britain.

A varied landscape. The Pennine Hills form a kind of backbone running north and south through England. The landscape becomes most rugged in the northwest of England. To the south and east, there are lowlands that form the beginning of the North European Plain.

The Thames estuary reaches inland above the Strait of Dover to form a natural transportation route into the center of the lowlands. An **estuary** is a broad mouth of a river into which the tide flows. London's location at the end of this estuary helped make it a major port and subsequently an important commercial, governmental, and cultural center. Today it remains one of the world's great metropolitan areas, with a population of about 7 million.

North and east of London is a rural area known as East Anglia. This is the driest region in the country and a grain-producing district. The Fens is a low, marshy area south of the Wash, an indentation of the North Sea. Much of the Fens is below sea level, but it has been turned into rich farmland through artificial drainage.

An industrial economy. The beginnings of the Industrial Revolution, a period during which much of Europe made the transition from farming to industry, can be traced to the factories around Manchester, England, in the 1700s. Liverpool, a port on the Irish Sea, and Birmingham, in central England, soon became major centers of industry. Sheffield and Leeds, towns on the eastern slopes of the Pennines, also became manufacturing centers.

The Industrial Revolution helped the United Kingdom become a world power. Britain's overseas possessions became a source of raw materials and a market for manufactured goods. After World War II, however, many British colonies gained independence.

291

Today, although Britain is no longer one of the world's strongest countries, it remains one of the most powerful nations in Western Europe. With other members of the Common Market, Britain is taking strides to increase productivity. Britain's leaders hope that increased productivity, coupled with the development of new, more efficient technologies, will help the nation regain some of the economic and political power it once held.

Wales and Scotland are culturally unique regions.

Wales, bordering England on the west, and Scotland, to the north of England, are both part of the United Kingdom. Neither the Welsh nor the Scots, however, want to be called "English," preferring to retain their own unique cultural traditions.

Wales. The Severn River divides Wales from England. To the north of this large estuary is Wales, a hilly region dominated by the Cambrian Mountains and known for its rugged natural beauty. Wales is also famous for its coal deposits and fresh water, both of which supply much of Britain's needs.

The Welsh trace their origins to the Celts, who were the original occupants of the British Isles. More than half a million people speak Welsh, a Celtic language, and the Welsh have a fondness for poetry and music in their native tongue.

Coal mining, commercial fishing, and agriculture are traditional vocations in Wales. However, most people now live and work in the industrial cities such as Cardiff and Swansea.

Scotland. The Scottish Highlands are probably the best-known area of Scotland. This rugged northern region is celebrated for its clans, their tartans (plaid woolen cloth), and other aspects of the Scottish heritage. **Clans** are groups of people who are related by blood and have the same surnames. Each clan lived in the same geographic area and had a leader who was called a laird. Although some people think of

Edinburgh Castle stands upon a large rock overlooking the capital city of Scotland.

Highland culture as dating back to ancient times, scholars have shown that many aspects of this culture are less than 300 years old.

Geographically, the Scottish Highlands are composed of two separate mountain ranges divided by a narrow fault valley. Two indentations of the sea, called **firths**, occupy either end of the depression. These are called the Moray Firth and the Firth of Lorne. Between them lies Loch Ness, a narrow, deep lake that is thought by many to be the home of a large, prehistoric sea animal known as the Loch Ness monster.

The mountains on both sides of Loch Ness are rugged and swept by fierce North Atlantic winds. The thin soils of Highland Scotland support only coarse grasses, stunted trees, and heather, a low shrub, and can be used only for grazing sheep. Off the northern coast of the Highland landforms continue on the islands known as the Hebrides, the Orkneys, and the Shetlands. There fishing adds to the slender resource base.

South of the Highlands is a wide valley known as the Central Lowlands. With its rolling hills and the River Clyde, the Central Lowlands is the most fertile and most populated part of Scotland. The raising of cattle and horses is a major industry with such local breeds as Aberdeen-Angus cattle and Clydesdale horses.

Two large cities dominate these lowlands: Glasgow and Edinburgh [ed'n bėr'ō]. The port city of Glasgow grew up around its nearby coal deposits and its steelmaking and shipbuilding industry. Edinburgh, the capital of Scotland, has long been a cultural and educational center.

South of the Lowlands, the Southern Uplands continue as a series of rounded hills covered with short grass. There the economy follows traditional paths such as sheep raising. The sheep raised in this region support the famous woolen mills in the Tweed River Valley.

Large oil and gas reserves in the North Sea have made Britain self-sufficient in these power sources and have greatly boosted the country's economy. The exploitation of these resources has transformed parts of the east coast of Scotland. Fishing centers such as Aberdeen have become supply bases for offshore drilling rigs. As the world prices of petroleum declined in the late 1980s, however, development lagged.

Ireland includes the Republic of Ireland and Northern Ireland.

Ireland does not rank among the world's top 20 islands in area, yet it has exerted an influence on world culture far out of proportion to its size. Irish music, poetry, and literature have had an enormous influence.

The island of Ireland consists of two political units, each with a different religious character. The Republic of Ireland is an independent nation in which 95 percent of its people are Roman Catholic. Northern Ireland, by contrast, is a part of the United Kingdom and has a Protestant majority.

The Republic of Ireland. This nation encompasses five-sixths of the island of Ireland. It is composed of a central plateau surrounded by groups of mountains and hills. Originally, much of the land was covered with forest, but most of the trees were cut down over the centuries.

Most of the landscape remains in lush, green pasture, giving Ireland its name as the "Emerald Isle." Crops are raised in the warmer and drier eastern parts of the country. Sheep, beef cattle, and horses are the mainstays of Irish agriculture. Irish farmers are able to produce enough food for the entire country and for sizable exports as well.

The Republic of Ireland is much more than just emerald pastures. It has a number of large, modern cities. Dublin, the capital of the Republic of Ireland, is situated on the east coast. Several other manufacturing and commercial centers are located along the warmer southern coast: Wexford, Waterford, and Cork.

In the 1950s the Irish government began encouraging foreign investment in manufacturing facilities. By the 1980s the plan was a success, and the standard of living in Ireland rose dramatically. Unlike Britain, however, Ireland must import most of its fuel and other raw materials. In exchange, it exports foodstuffs and manufactured products.

Tourism is also important to the Irish economy. A picturesque landscape, a mild climate, and the Irish cultural heritage furnish the chief attractions. Because of the North Atlantic Drift and the maritime influence, the temperature rarely drops below 40° F or rises above 70° F.

Northern Ireland. For many centuries Ireland was ruled by Britain. After a long struggle for independence, three of the four parts of the island were recognized as a separate dominion in 1920 and as a completely independent republic in 1949. The northern part of the island of Ireland, called Ulster, remained a part of Britain through all these changes.

Culturally, Northern Ireland is divided between two different groups. About two-thirds of the people in the six counties of Ulster are descended from immigrants from Scotland and England. They are primarily Protestant. Today Irish Protestants loyal to the British wish to stay in the United Kingdom. There is a minority population, however, who are descended from native Irish families and who are Roman Catholic. They are often discriminated against by the Protestant majority in social, political, and economic matters. This minority group would like to be free of British influence and to join the Republic of Ireland to the south. Extremists on both sides of the dispute in Northern Ireland have used violence to voice their point of view.

The economy of Northern Ireland is dependent equally upon agriculture and manufacturing. The land itself is a continuation of Scotland's Southern Uplands, but most of the surface features are rolling hills and low mountains. Most of the land is used for fields and pastures. A variety of crops and animals are raised. Textiles are the major products of the factories. Irish linen is the most well-known product. Belfast, the largest city in Northern Ireland, is the leading manufacturing center.

Section 1 Review

Locating Key Places
Locate the following places on the map on page 290: England, Wales, Scotland, Ireland, Northern Ireland.

Identifying Key Terms
Define the following terms: estuary, clan, firth

Reviewing Main Ideas
1. What are the political and geographic parts of the British Isles?
2. In what ways does England form the center of the United Kingdom?
3. What makes Scotland and Wales culturally unique?
4. How do the two political units of Ireland differ?

Thinking Critically: Predict Effects
Demographics is the study of the size and distributions of human populations. The current majority Protestant population in Northern Ireland has voted consistently to remain part of the United Kingdom. Some demographic studies indicate that by the early 21st century, the majority population may be Catholic. What implications do you think this might have for the future of Northern Ireland?

Northern Europe

Preview

Key Places
Where are these places located?
1 Sweden
2 Norway
3 Denmark
See the globe below.

Key Terms
What do these terms mean?
social welfare
fiord
geothermal power

Main Ideas
- What do the nations of Northern Europe have in common?
- How would you describe the economies of Sweden and Norway?
- How is Finland politically oriented?
- What economic activities contribute to Denmark's prosperity?
- Why is Iceland physically unique?

It was so dark in Sarvan Viste.
Even the dogs longed for the sun.

So they sent the cowherdess, Sirka
to look for the sun.

Sirka hurried eastward. A long way she ran,
down to the sea where the forest ended.

There she saw the sun: it lay in a wooden trough
and could not shine.

Sirka wanted to punch a hole in the trough,
let out the sun. She became a bird.

That bird is now black, and lives, in the winter,
in the fast white water.

Lars Lundkvist

The nations of Northern Europe share many cultural traits.

This poem is based on a folk tale told by the Lapps, a nomadic people of the Scandinavian far north. The words of the poet, who grew up in northern Sweden, express the Lapp's deep longing for the sun during those winter months when it disappears for weeks on end.

Northern Europe is often called Scandinavia. Strictly speaking, "Scandinavia" refers to the Scandinavian Peninsula of Norway and Sweden. More loosely, Scandinavia includes Norway, Sweden, Finland, Denmark, and Iceland.

Although the nations of Scandinavia are unique in many ways, they also have much in common. Among the commonalities are the people themselves, patterns of population, language, religion, and government.

The people of Scandinavia. Present-day Norwegians, Swedes, and Danes are probably descended from tribes of reindeer hunters who lived in Scandinavia at least 12,000 years ago. The present-day peoples also have links to Germanic tribes.

The Finns moved into modern Finland in about A.D. 100. They came from south of the Gulf of Finland, an area that today is part of

295

the Soviet Union. Most of Finland's people are descended from the Finns. Unlike the Swedes, Danes, and Norwegians, who speak Germanic languages, the Finns speak a language related to Hungarian, Turkish, and Mongolian.

The land the Finns found in present-day Finland was sparsely populated by the Lapps, people probably distantly related to the Finns. The Lapps moved farther north as the Finns moved in. Some Lapps still live in the northern regions of Finland, Norway, and Sweden. Traditionally, the Lapps were nomadic hunters who followed their reindeer herds across northern Scandinavia from Norway to Russia. A few still follow this way of life. Now, however, herds are kept in a permanent pasture for about five months of the year. Most Lapps have given up the pastoral life for jobs in mining, forestry, and other industries.

Iceland is the most recently settled part of Northern Europe. Between 879 and 930, Norwegians and a few Irish and Scots settled all the land that was suitable for farming. Modern Icelanders are descended from this mixture of Nordic and Celtic people.

Patterns of population. The map on page 272 shows that lowland areas are found along the southern coasts of Norway, Sweden, and Finland. These lowland areas contain the largest concentrations of people in the area.

Denmark, the only Scandinavian country with no highland areas, is the most densely populated country in Northern Europe. Many Scandinavian people live in or near cities. Sweden's capital, Stockholm, and Denmark's capital, Copenhagen, are the two largest cities.

Government. The governments of Sweden, Norway, and Denmark are, like Britain, parliamentary democracies. They are also constitutional monarchies. The real power of government rests with an elected parliament.

Finland and Iceland are both republics. The people of these nations are governed by a president and a parliament. In Finland the president is very powerful. In contrast, the role of the president of Iceland is largely ceremonial. The real power is in the hands of the prime minister and the cabinet.

Sweden and Norway have advanced, industrial economies.

Sweden and Norway, the two countries that occupy the Scandinavian Peninsula, share a common geography. In addition, they have very similar cultural traits, economic systems, and resource bases.

Sweden. This country is sometimes called the "keystone of Northern Europe." It is the largest country in the region in both area and population. Although Sweden is somewhat larger than California, it has a much smaller population. Sweden's 8 million people represent only about one-third the number of California's citizens. Most of Sweden's population is concentrated in the cities of the southern peninsula and the towns that line the east coast.

In Sweden, the government provides many of the services that American citizens buy for themselves. The government provides for the social welfare of its people. **Social welfare** is a system under which the government provides services such as medical care and child care. The government also helps pay for the arts by funding such organizations as theaters and orchestras.

One result of the social welfare system is a society in which there are few poor people. However, in order to pay for all the services that the government provides, the tax rate is very high. In spite of heavy taxes, Sweden's economy is very strong. Its people enjoy one of the highest standards of living in the world. One reason for this is its rich and varied resource base.

Sweden has a highly productive and advanced economy. One of the country's chief resources is its highly skilled and educated population. For example, only 5 percent of the labor force now works in farming, yet they provide 90 percent of

Sweden's food needs. Most of the land on which the Swedes farm is located in the south.

The heart of the Swedish economy centers on the production of steel and the manufacture of metal products. Evergreen coniferous forests, which cover more than half of the country, are also important resources. Forest products such as lumber and wood pulp account for nearly one-fourth of Sweden's exports.

Rich ores containing iron, copper, lead, zinc, and other minerals are found in the ancient Precambrian rocks of the Scandinavian Shield. This area extends from the lake region in southern Finland to south central Sweden. It was carved by glaciers and today has little soil but is very rich in metals.

Cobblestone streets and unique shops attract visitors to Stockholm's Old Town.

Iron ores formed the basis for rapid industrialization of the Swedish economy in the late 19th century. Coal and, later, petroleum had to be imported because Sweden has almost no deposits of these important energy resources. It does have an extensive system of dams for generating electric power, but this supplies only about 15 percent of the total need. Nuclear power and the burning of wood and waste products account for an additional 15 percent. This makes it necessary to import about 70 percent of the nation's energy-producing resources.

Norway. Norway is about 30 percent smaller than Sweden. It also has only half of Sweden's population. Norway has a more rugged topography and has only a limited coastal plain in the southeast part of the country. Note how Norway reaches to the northern tip of Europe, stretching around Sweden and Finland to share a short boundary with the Soviet Union. This closeness to the Soviet Union makes Norway strategically important to the rest of Western Europe and the United States.

Norwegians enjoy a very high standard of living, partly because of their country's rich resource base. Like Sweden, Norway uses a system of high taxes to distribute its wealth through social services.

By using the map on page 290 you can trace some locations that provide other keys to Norway's economy. Within sight of the Soviet border is a major deposit of iron ore. This resource is used as a base for the nation's industry and also as a product for export. A major Norwegian steel mill is located along the coast just south of the Arctic Circle. Local limestone is used in the mill, but coal is brought by ship from several Norwegian islands in the Arctic Ocean.

Between the iron deposits and the steel mill stretches the tundra of Lapland. Like the Lapps of Sweden, the Lapps of Norway have all but

297

Fishermen in Oslo display their catch, which includes mainly fish such as capelin and cod.

fleet. It has served as one of Europe's major fish markets for a thousand years.

South and east of Bergen, the coastal valleys become wider and more productive. Forests and fields as well as industrial and shipping facilities contribute to a varied economy. Oslo, the capital and largest city of Norway, is located where several of these valleys come together to form a coastal plain.

Finland has ties to both the Soviet Union and Western Europe.

Except for a stretch of tundra in the far north, trees cover almost all of Finland's land area. Lakes, marshes, and peat bogs also cover one-fifth of the area. Over the centuries people have cleared parts of the forest for fields, pastures, and town sites. These clearings, however, account for only 12 percent of the surface.

The Baltic Sea moderates the climate of the south and southwest coasts of Finland. The winters are less severe than other areas with similar latitudes. Usually only thin ice forms on the Baltic Sea. Ships are thus able to reach the port cities of Helsinki and Turku all year long. The surrounding countryside is devoted to farms specializing in hardy crops such as rye, barley, oats, and potatoes.

Northward in Finland the farms give way to vast forests. North of 62°N the population thins and lumbering becomes the major industry. However, patches of land have been cleared for fields and pasture all the way to the Arctic Circle. Although attempts have been made to develop these frontier regions, most of the people in Finland live in the southern part of the nation. There, people rely on their skills in manufacturing, commerce, and the service industries to provide the economic base for a remarkably high standard of living.

Today Finland is a neutral nation. Its neutrality is the result of its close proximity to the Soviet Union on the east and Western Europe to the south and west. Political and economic pres-

abandoned traditional lifestyles. Few herd reindeer as their ancestors once did. Fishing is the only major occupation in Lapland.

Some farming is possible along Norway's coast above the Arctic Circle, but it becomes of major importance farther south, in the region around Trondheim Fiord. Trondheim, the nation's second largest city, is located in this area.

South of Trondheim the mountains become higher and the forests become thinner. Waterfalls, fed by glacial streams, drop over hanging cliffs into deep, crystal-clear fiords. **Fiords** are long, narrow bays bordered by steep cliffs. This region contains some of Norway's most spectacular scenery. The falling water is used for hydroelectric power to run several large aluminum and chemical plants.

Fishing, however, is the traditional livelihood of this region. Bergen, the area's chief city, is the home base for a vast North Atlantic fishing

298

sure from the Soviet Union since World War II has given Finland little choice but to remain neutral.

Finland's economy, social life, political structure, and culture all follow the Western European and Scandinavian examples. However, Finland is tied to its communist neighbor for energy supplies. One quarter of Finland's foreign trade is with the Soviet Union. Finland has a strong industrial economy based on its mineral resources and forest products. Shipbuilding today is a leading industry. Finns build ships for both the Soviet Union and Western nations.

Denmark is an urban nation with an agricultural tradition.

Denmark sits astride the straits connecting the Baltic and North seas. Its islands are like stepping stones between the Scandinavian Peninsula and the mainland of Europe.

Most of what is now Denmark was once part of the Scandinavian Peninsula. During the Ice Age, glaciers moved south from the peninsula. The deposits they left make up much of present-day Denmark.

The land in Denmark, which is primarily grassland, is almost all low and flat. People say that if the Danes stand on a box, they can see the entire country because no part of Denmark is more than 568 feet above sea level.

Denmark's grasslands have long been used for agriculture. Danish farmers in the 19th century began to specialize in products for export. Butter was the most profitable of these farm products.

Danish agriculture soon focused on dairying. Skim milk, a by-product of butter-making, was fed to the hogs. The resulting ham was of excellent quality and soon became another important export. Even today Denmark has almost as many cows as people, and the pigs outnumber

them both. Today about 75 percent of Denmark's land is used for farming. More than one-third of the nation's exports are agricultural products.

In spite of its agricultural tradition, Denmark is an urban nation. About one-fourth of all Danes live in the capital city of Copenhagen. This thriving modern city is located on the island of Sjaelland [zə' lənd]. You can see on the map on page 290 just how ideal Copenhagen's location is. A sound, or wide ocean channel, between Denmark and the Scandinavian Peninsula allows the passage of ships between the Baltic and North seas. Copenhagen's strategic location has made it a center of transportation, commerce, manufacturing, and culture.

Today Denmark is a prosperous nation that enjoys a high standard of living comparable to Norway and Sweden. Like Norway and Sweden, Denmark's prosperity is closely tied to international trade. Denmark has a large merchant marine, but most of the ships carry goods between other nations and seldom call on Danish ports. Fishing and tourism are also important segments of the economy.

Denmark has two distant, self-governing island communities—Greenland and the Faeroe Islands. Greenland is the largest island in the world. It is almost one-third the size of the continental United States. Only about 20 percent of Greenland, however, is free of the ice cap that covers the island. Significant mineral deposits are present, and some zinc and lead is mined beneath the ice.

Greenland's population of about 50,000 is composed of Eskimos, Danes, and people of mixed ancestry. Rapid cultural change has led to major problems of adjustment as Greenland attempts to become a modern community.

The Faeroe Islands, midway between Iceland and the North Sea, have an economy based on fishing and sheep raising. As a self-governing part of Denmark, the Faeroe Islands have their own flag, postage stamps, and paper money, but they use Danish coins. Denmark, however, provides the Faeroe Islands with police, courts, defense, and a foreign policy.

Iceland is an island of fire and ice.

The island nation of Iceland, home to about 250,000 people, lies between Greenland and Norway. The Norwegian Sea is to the east and the Denmark Strait is to the west. Just south of the Arctic Circle, Iceland might be considered, along with Greenland, as a stepping stone to North America.

No place on earth provides more dramatic lessons in physical geography than Iceland. This land of fire, ice, and steam sits astride two boundaries. To the north are the frigid waters of the Arctic Ocean; to the south are the warm waters of the North Atlantic Drift. Iceland sits atop the Mid-Atlantic Ridge. Thus, the eastern part of the island is part of the Eurasian plate while the western portion belongs to the North American plate.

Iceland is like a thin cap of rock and soil with fire below and ice above. Where the fire and the ice come close to each other, steam is generated and geysers and hot springs result. Sometimes the fire breaks through the crust of the earth, setting off spectacular volcanic eruptions and creating lakes of fire.

Although Iceland is located at a high latitude, the warm waters of the North Atlantic Drift make it possible for some agriculture to take place. Potatoes and turnips are common crops, but most of the available land is used to raise sheep and cows. Some specialized agriculture is also carried out in greenhouses heated with water piped from the hot springs. Flowers, vegetables, grapes, and even bananas are raised in these greenhouses.

Iceland has a narrow resource base. It has almost no forests and only one percent of its land can be used for crops. Therefore, the islanders rely heavily upon the sea for their livelihood. The processing of fish and dairy products is an important part of the economy. Fishing is the core of Iceland's economy and sheep outnumber people by four or five to one. The sheep provide wool for the famous Icelandic sweaters and are also an important food source.

Recently, the Icelandic people have harnessed geothermal and hydroelectric power sources for the production of cement, fertilizer, and aluminum products. **Geothermal power** is energy produced from heat inside the earth.

Section 2 Review

Locating Key Places
Locate the following places on the map on page 290: Sweden, Norway, Denmark

Identifying Key Terms
Define the following terms: social welfare, fiord, geothermal power

Reviewing Main Ideas
1. What are three things that the nations of Northern Europe have in common?
2. How have the economic systems of Sweden and Norway affected their people's standard of living?
3. Explain why Finland is a neutral nation.
4. What agricultural products does Denmark specialize in?
5. How is Iceland's physical geography unusual?

Thinking Critically: Recognize Values
What values are reflected in Sweden's social welfare system?

Using Subway Maps

If you were in London, Paris, or New York, and wanted a quick way to get around the city, what would you do? The first thing might be to pick up a subway map, a diagram that shows the different lines and stations that exist below the city's streets.

To read the map, note that each subway line has a different color. Note also that any station in which transfers take place is marked with an open black circle.

To use a subway map, you first need to know two things—where you are and where you want to go. Then, you can use the subway map for directions.

For example, if you were at Bond Street and wanted to go to Heathrow Airport, how would you get there? With the subway map, you could see that you could take the Jubilee line from Bond Street to Green Park. There you could transfer to the Piccadilly line, which would take you straight to the airport.

Review

Use the map and key to answer the following questions.
1. Which three subway lines cross at Oxford Circus?
2. How would you get from the Victoria station to Bond Street?
3. How would you get from Piccadilly Circus to the London Bridge station?
4. If you were on the Victoria line, to which other lines could you transfer at the Victoria station?

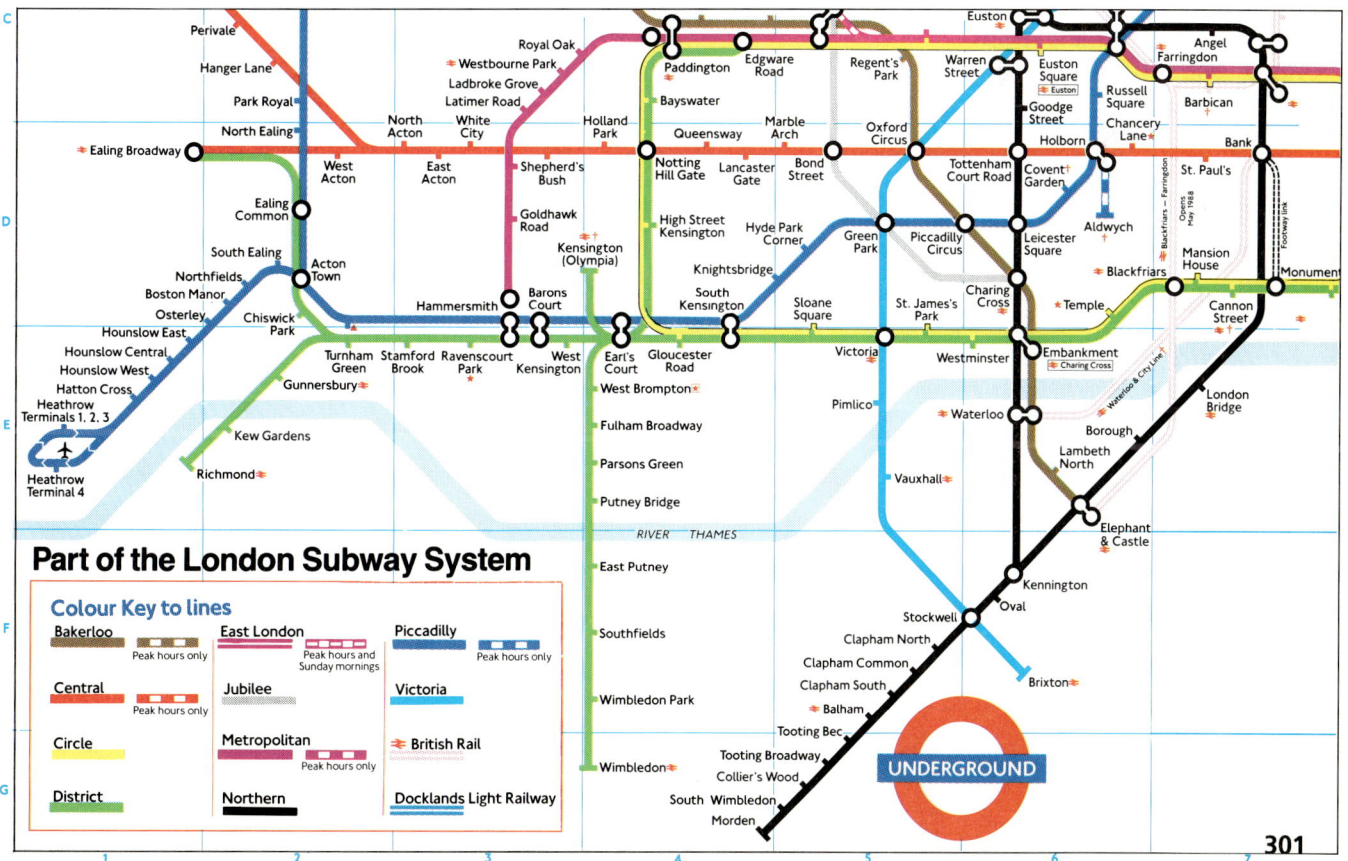

Part of the London Subway System

Colour Key to lines

Bakerloo	Peak hours only	East London	Peak hours and Sunday mornings	Piccadilly	Peak hours only
Central	Peak hours only	Jubilee		Victoria	
Circle		Metropolitan	Peak hours only	British Rail	
District		Northern		Docklands Light Railway	

UNDERGROUND

CHAPTER 13

Review

Section Summaries

1. The British Isles The British Isles consist of two large islands—Great Britain and Ireland—and many small islands. Politically, the British Isles have two major units—the Republic of Ireland and the United Kingdom (Britain). The United Kingdom includes England, Scotland, Wales, and Northern Ireland. The United Kingdom has had a tremendous influence on world culture and affairs. Ireland has made important contributions to the arts.

2. Northern Europe Northern Europe, which includes Sweden, Norway, Finland, Denmark, and Iceland, is often called Scandinavia. Sweden is an advanced industrial country with an extensive social welfare system. Norway is a strategically important, resource-rich country whose citizens enjoy a very high standard of living. Finland is a neutral country influenced by both Western Europe and the Soviet Union. Denmark is an urban country with an agricultural tradition. Denmark also has two self-governing communities—Greenland and the Faeroe Islands. Iceland, often called "the land of fire and ice," is best known for its unique physical geography.

Using Geography Skills

Reviewing the Map Lesson

Use the map on page 301 to answer these questions.
1. If you wanted to get from the Victoria station to Heathrow Airport, which two lines would you take?
2. Which four subway lines cross at the Paddington station?
3. If you are at Piccadilly Circus, which four stations are only one subway stop away?
4. If you wanted to get from Bond Street to Paddington station, at which station would you need to transfer?

Using Social Studies Skills

1. Develop Criteria for Making Judgments. You belong to a team of geographers, economists, and other social scientists who have been asked by the Norwegian government to evaluate the North Sea oil reserves. The government wants to know if it would be wise to stop drilling for oil because of the falling prices of oil on the world market. What sorts of questions would you want to ask first in order to make your report? Make a list of the kinds of questions you would want answered.

2. Perceive Cause-Effect Relationships. Give a cause for each effect.
a. Sweden has few poor people.
b. Spectacular volcanic eruptions often occur in Iceland.

Testing for Understanding

Locating Key Places
Match each description below with the name of the place.
1. Cardiff and Swansea are important commercial centers here
2. Edinburgh and Glasgow are in this country
3. a small peninsular country south of the Scandinavian Peninsula
4. a country known for its fiords
5. the part of the United Kingdom just south of Scotland
6. the smaller of the two British Isles
7. the part of Ireland that belongs to the United Kingdom
8. the largest country in Northern Europe
a. England
b. Wales
c. Scotland
d. Ireland
e. Northern Ireland
f. Sweden
g. Norway
h. Denmark

Recalling Key Terms
Define these terms in your own words.

Section 1
estuary
clan
firth

Section 2
social welfare
fiord
geothermal power

Reviewing Main Ideas
Section 1
1. What are the political units of the British Isles?
2. Why is England referred to as the "heart of the United Kingdom?"
3. How are Scotland and Wales culturally different from England?
4. In what ways are the Republic of Ireland and Northern Ireland different?

Section 2
1. What cultural traits do the countries of Northern Europe share?
2. Describe some effects of Sweden and Norway's economic systems.
3. Explain Finland's reasons for being politically neutral.

4. What agricultural products are important to Denmark's economy?
5. How is Iceland a "land of fire and ice"?

Thinking Critically
1. Make Hypotheses. Kristen's family herds reindeer in a rural area of northern Scandinavia. Her parents do not consider themselves Swedish or Finnish, and they roam in both countries. What ethnic group do you think Kristen belongs to? What changes do you think will be in store for her as she grows up?

2. Analyze Comparisons. In 1981 a Soviet submarine landed in Swedish territorial waters, near the naval base at Karlskrona. This was a major international incident and worsened relations between the two countries. Do you think this could happen between the Soviet Union and Finland? Make a list of some of your reasons.

CHAPTER 14

Continental Europe

In this chapter you will learn about the countries and cultures of Continental Europe.

SECTION 1

France

Preview

Key Places
Where are the following places located?
1 Paris
2 Marseille
   See the globe below.

Key Terms
What do these terms mean?
primate city
granary

Main Ideas
As you read, look for answers to these questions.
• Why is the city of Paris important to France?
• What are France's geographic regions?
• How do the French earn their living?

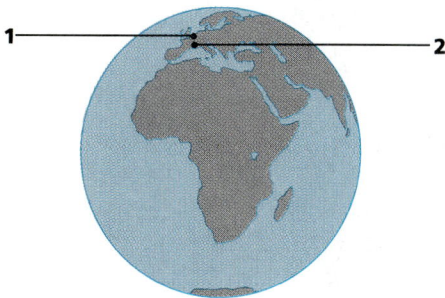

*Far, far above, piercing the infinite sky,
Mont Blanc appears,—still, snowy, and serene;
Its subject mountains their unearthly forms
Pile round it, ice and rock, broad vales between
Of frozen floods, unfathomable deeps,
Blue as the overhanging heaven, that spread
And wind among the accumulated steeps—
A desert peopled by the storms alone,
Save when the eagle brings some hunter's bone,
And the wolf tracks her there.*

Percy Bysshe Shelley, *Mont Blanc*

Paris is important because it is the cultural center of France.

Just as Mont Blanc rises above France as the country's highest peak, the city of Paris stands out as France's cultural leader. Over the years Paris has attracted thousands of writers, painters, dancers, actors, scientists, and historians from all over France and all around the world.

Paris, the nation's capital and its largest city, is the heart of France. Locate Paris on the map on page 306.

Note that Paris is on the North European Plain in the center of the Seine River valley. The area drained by the Seine and its tributaries is called the Paris Basin.

Paris captures the spirit of France in a way unmatched by most other capital cities. Nearly one in seven French citizens lives in the great city and its suburbs. In addition to serving as the cultural and governmental center of the nation, Paris is a major industrial city. Cars, books, chemicals, electronics, furniture, machinery, and a variety of other products are manufactured there.

Facing page: **This Parisian artist, across the Seine from Notre Dame, continues Europe's strong cultural tradition.**

Paris is also France's cultural center. Literature, music, and the arts have flourished there for centuries. Fashion styles set by its designers are copied in all parts of the world. The finest of French foods are served in its restaurants. Many people throughout the world look to Paris for inspiration.

Paris is what geographers call a **primate city**, one that is much larger than the second city in the nation and one that best expresses the nation's culture. Paris is the center around which the various regions of France revolve.

Why did Paris become the primate city of France? Part of the answer lies in geography.

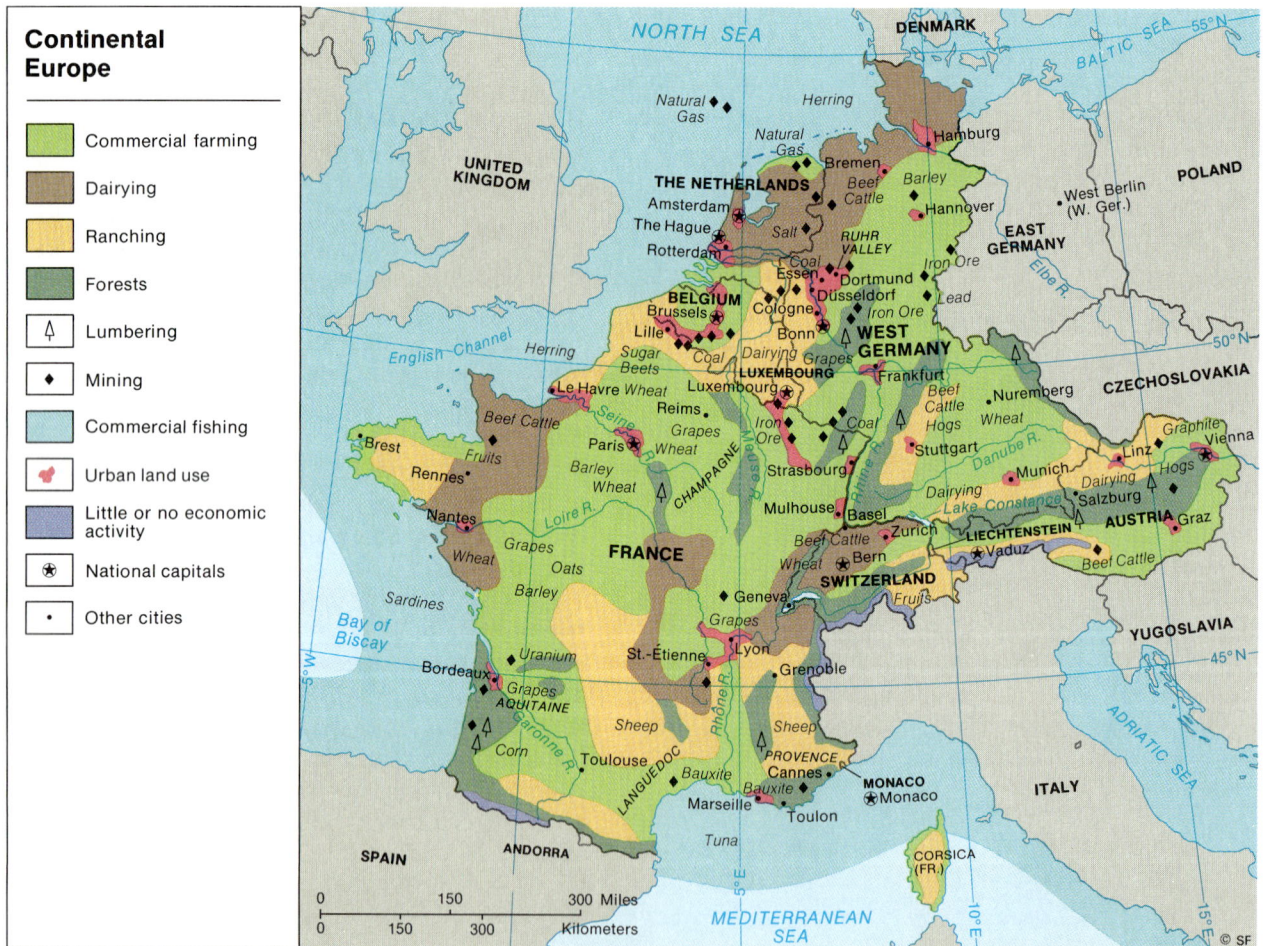

Continental Europe

- Commercial farming
- Dairying
- Ranching
- Forests
- Lumbering
- Mining
- Commercial fishing
- Urban land use
- Little or no economic activity
- ✷ National capitals
- · Other cities

NORTH SEA DENMARK BALTIC SEA 55°N

Natural Gas Herring Hamburg

Natural Gas Bremen POLAND

UNITED KINGDOM THE NETHERLANDS Beef Cattle Barley West Berlin (W. Ger.)

Amsterdam Hannover EAST GERMANY

The Hague Salt RUHR VALLEY Iron Ore

Rotterdam Coal Elbe R.

English Channel Herring Essen Dortmund Iron Ore 50°N

BELGIUM Cologne Düsseldorf Lead

Brussels Bonn WEST GERMANY

Lille Sugar Beets Coal Dairying Grapes CZECHOSLOVAKIA

Le Havre Wheat Luxembourg Frankfurt Beef Cattle Nuremberg

Beef Cattle LUXEMBOURG Reims Hogs Wheat Linz Graphite Vienna

Brest Seine Iron Ore Coal Stuttgart Munich Dairying Hogs

Rennes Paris ✷ Wheat Strasbourg Danube R. Salzburg AUSTRIA Graz

Fruits Barley CHAMPAGNE Mulhouse Basel Lake Constance LIECHTENSTEIN

Nantes Wheat Beef Cattle Zurich Vaduz Beef Cattle

Grapes Oats FRANCE Wheat Bern SWITZERLAND

Loire R. Geneva YUGOSLAVIA

Sardines Barley Grapes Fruits ADRIATIC SEA

Bay of Biscay St.-Etienne Lyon Grenoble 45°N

Bordeaux Uranium ITALY

Grapes AQUITAINE Sheep PROVENCE Cannes MONACO ✷ Monaco

Garonne R. Corn Toulouse Sheep Bauxite

LANGUEDOC Bauxite Marseille Toulon

SPAIN ANDORRA Tuna CORSICA (FR.)

MEDITERRANEAN SEA 10°E 15°E © SF

0 150 300 Miles
0 150 300 Kilometers

Map Study

What countries are included in Continental Europe? What are the major centers for urban land use in France? What other industries play a role in the French economy?

The Paris Basin is a rich agricultural region, and the Seine River provided Parisians with access to the sea. Part of the answer also lies in history. Paris was where the French kings lived.

Paris began as a fishing village on a small, boat-shaped island in the Seine River. The island, called the Île de la Cité, contains the Palace of Justice and the magnificent Cathedral of Notre Dame. Construction work on the cathedral was started in 1163. The Louvre, [lü'vrə] the palace built in the 17th century on the right bank of the river across from the Île de la Cité, is today the most celebrated art gallery in the world.

In the 19th century, Paris became the center of a worldwide empire. The city was rebuilt with grand boulevards lined with shade trees, squares filled with monuments, huge public buildings, and parks where children could play and adults could walk or sit as they pleased. The city's sewers and central marketing facilities were rebuilt as well.

France includes many different geographic regions.

France is Western Europe's largest nation. It is slightly smaller than Texas but has three and one half times as many people—about 55 million. France stretches from the North Sea to the Mediterranean Sea, giving it a variety of climates. The island of Corsica is also part of France.

France has a varied topography, the most varied of any Western European nation. French geography can best be studied by beginning with the Paris Basin and then branching out to the east, the south, the west, and the north.

The Paris Basin is often called the granary of France because its major crops are wheat, barley, and rye. A **granary** is a region that produces much grain. Farmers also grow sugar beets, and there is considerable raising of livestock as well.

To the east of the Paris Basin, the land rises in a series of foothills. This Champagne [shän-pän'yə] region leads to the Northeast Uplands. These hilly uplands end in the Vosges [Vōzh] and Jura [jür'ə] ranges, a series of low mountains that run along the border with West Germany and Switzerland.

Farmers in the Northeast Uplands grow a variety of crops, but forestry is also important. Mineral resources—including potash, iron ore, and some coal—provide the basis for such industries as chemicals and steel. As you approach the Rhine Valley, you find more and more people speaking German rather than French as their everyday language. Strasbourg, a Rhine River port, is the region's major city.

At Strasbourg, a canal connects the Rhine with a tributary of the Rhône River. The Rhône flows southward to empty into the Mediterranean. The Rhône Valley separates two upland regions: the French Alps to the east, and the Massif Central to the west.

Sidewalk cafes line many of Paris's elegant boulevards.

Mount Blanc [bläN], Europe's highest mountain, dominates the French Alps. Towering more than 15,000 feet above sea level, it is located on the border with Italy, just south of Switzerland. Because the French branch of the Alps extends southward toward the sea, the range is called the Maritime Alps, "mare" being the Latin word for sea. The mountain streams that rush down the Maritime Alps furnish electric power for the major cities of the Rhône Valley, Lyon and Marseille [mȧr sā'], as well as Paris, many miles away.

Marseille, founded by the Greeks in ancient times, is France's major Mediterranean port and the gateway to the nation's former empire in Africa. It is also an important commercial and industrial center. East of the city the mountains fall into the sea, creating the spectacular beauty of Provence [prô väNs']. Here are the popular resort cities of Cannes [kän] and Nice [nēs], as well as the tiny country of Monaco [män'ə kō]. West of the Rhône delta the slope to the coast is more gentle. Here the sandstone hills have eroded into the wide sandy beaches of Languedoc [lȧNg dôk']. West of the Rhône Valley and north of Languedoc is the Massif Central. Poor soils and rugged topography have made this a thinly populated region. However, many cattle and sheep graze its pasture lands.

West of the Massif Central are the Aquitaine lowlands. Here farmers grow a wide variety of crops—grains, vegetables, fruits, sugar beets, and tobacco. Grapes form the basis of a celebrated wine industry. The finest wines are called Bordeaux [bôr dō'], after the region's chief seaport. Cognac is a stronger Bordeaux wine named for another town in the region.

The largest city of the region is Toulouse [tü-lüz'], which specializes in manufacturing aircraft. The factories that produce the aluminum

These small stone huts in rural Aquitaine, called cabanes, house fowl or cattle.

for the planes use hydroelectric power that is generated by streams rushing down the Pyrenees. The aluminum ore is brought by canal from large deposits near Marseille. Because this mining region is called Les Baux [lā bō'], aluminum ore is commonly known as bauxite.

North of Aquitaine and the Massif Central is the Loire [lwär] Valley, a varied region of forests, pastures, fields, orchards, and vineyards. It is famous for its castles and chateaux, large palaces on country estates. Uranium deposits in the hills southeast of the city of Nantes [nänt] have enabled France to become one of the world's leading producers of nuclear power.

North of Nantes and west of the Paris Basin is a hilly region with two peninsulas that jut out into the ocean. This is the West Country of Brittany and Normandy. Thin soils and rolling terrain make dairying and livestock raising the best use of the land.

The Bretons—who are related to the Scots, Welsh, and Irish—are descended from the Celts, whose language was spoken throughout the region until Roman times. You can still hear the Breton language spoken in and around the port of Brest. The Normans are descended mostly from Viking invaders who settled in the area about a thousand years ago.

The French people make their living from farming and manufacturing.

France has a greater percent of its land suitable for agriculture than any other European country. Nearly one-third of the land is in crops. You can find farming and livestock raising in almost every region of France. You can also find several kinds of forests. Cork oaks grow along the Mediterranean. Broadleaf forests provide timber. Pines along the Aquitaine coast are a source of resins and turpentine. France's abundant mineral resources provide a good base for industry. In addition, an extensive system of railroads, highways, canals, and navigable rivers promotes trade.

France's main industrial problem is the country's lack of energy. It must import three-fourths of its energy supplies, mostly in the form of petroleum from Algeria and Persian Gulf countries. In the 1970s France announced that by the year 2000, it planned to rely on nuclear power for 30 percent of its energy requirements. At present, nuclear energy provides just 5 percent of the nation's needs.

France has a tradition of producing and distributing goods through small units. It is a nation of small farms and individual shopkeepers. The French tend to view large farms and supermarkets as a threat to the French way of life. However, this is beginning to change as the French grow increasingly interested in economic development.

Section 1 Review

Locating Key Places
Locate the following places on the map on page 306: Paris, Marseille

Identifying Key Terms
Define the following terms: primate city, granary

Reviewing Main Ideas
1. What role does Paris play in the culture of France?
2. How does the topography of France change from region to region?
3. In what industries do many of the French work?

Thinking Critically: Assess Cause and Effect
France is roughly the same size as Texas but has 3½ times as many people. Why do you think France has so many more people?

West Germany

Preview

Key Places
Where are the following places located?
1 Munich
2 West Berlin
See the globe below.

Key Terms
What do these terms mean?
fault valley
managed economy

Main Ideas
As you read, look for answers to these questions.
● Why is the Rhine River important to West Germany?
● What has made West Germany the industrial heart of Europe?
● How did Berlin become a divided city?

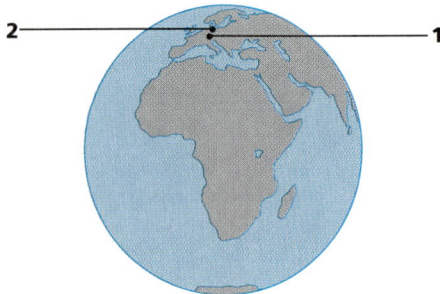

The air is cool and darkling,
And peaceful flows the Rhine;
The mountain top is sparkling,
The setting sunbeams shine.

The fairest maid is reclining
In wondrous beauty there;
Her golden jewels are shining,
She combs her golden hair.

Heinrich Heine, *The Lorelei*

The Rhine River flows through all the regions of West Germany.

The Lorelei, a famous German folk song, is but one of the many poems, operas, and novels that have the Rhine for a setting. The river has always gripped the imagination of writers and composers. Today it also serves to connect the four regions of West Germany with one another.

As you can see on the map on page 306, the Rhine is the major river of West Germany. It rises in the Swiss Alps and, after flowing through Lake Constance, forms West Germany's border with Switzerland and France. Once past a mountainous region called the Black Forest, the river enters West Germany and makes its way northward past the national capital of Bonn. After flowing through the Ruhr, it swings westward and leaves West Germany, dividing into many branches in the Netherlands.

The Rhine waters each of the four major geographic regions of West Germany. These regions are the Bavarian Uplands, the Central Uplands, the Rhine Valley, and the North German Plain.

The Bavarian Uplands. This region includes the northern slopes of the Alps east of Lake Constance. The mountains step down to the Danube River, which flows eastward along the edge of the Bavarian Uplands. Both of the region's major cities, Augsburg and Munich, are

This church stands along the Romantic Road, a scenic route through southeastern Germany.

located on tributaries of the Danube. Augsburg, founded by the Romans, was important in medieval times. Munich has dominated the region in modern times. It is the capital of Bavaria and a leading commercial and industrial city.

During the ice ages, huge Alpine glaciers covered the Bavarian Uplands. When the glaciers retreated, they left behind thin soils and rugged hills that are used mostly for pastures and hay fields. The soft wood of the pines that cover the higher slopes of the Alps encouraged the people of the region to build wooden houses with elaborately carved decorations.

The Central Uplands. The Central Uplands extend nearly 300 miles northward from the Danube through most of West Germany. Hills covered with the original broadleaf forest alternate with fertile valleys. The small farms in the valleys produce a wide variety of crops. Pastures and hay fields occupy the higher or more rugged lands. Forestry is also important.

The Central Uplands support many small cities. Some specialize in the manufacture of

certain products. Others are home to cultural institutions. Stuttgart's factories turn out electrical and photographic equipment, and the city often plays host to industrial fairs. Heidelberg's university, which dates back to 1386, was a center of the Protestant Reformation and dominated German student life during the 19th century.

The Rhine Valley. The Rhine Valley lies west of the Black Forest and extends northward to the area around Frankfurt. It is a **fault valley**. Here, an extensive section of rock dropped down as two blocks on either side were pushed upward by pressure from inside the earth. The down-faulted area then filled with sediment swept into the depression by the Rhine River.

The flat lands of the Rhine Valley are very fertile, making it West Germany's richest agricultural region. The valley also serves as a transportation corridor. Frankfurt, at the north end of the region, is a major commercial and communications center as well as the transportation hub of West Germany.

As the Rhine leaves the fault valley and enters the Central Uplands just west of Frankfurt, it cuts a deep gorge. This is the storied section of the Rhine, and the setting for Richard Wagner's famous opera, *Das Rheingold* (The Rhine Gold), about a golden treasure. For hundreds of years, tourists have traveled here by boat to view the castles perched on the rocks above the river. When the boats reach Cologne, however, most tourists leave the river. The spectacular scenery is over and an industrial belt begins.

The main part of the industrial belt is the Ruhr Valley. The Ruhr is a short tributary of the Rhine. Its valley contains the most extensive deposits of high quality coal in Europe. Eight major cities surround the coal fields, each with a concentration of steel mills, chemical plants, amd manufacturing facilities. This is the greatest urban concentration in Europe.

The North German Plain. This region extends from the Central Uplands to the North and the Baltic seas. The soils in the loess belt are very fertile. So are some of the lands near the coast. Between these two areas is a stretch of sandy and rocky glacial deposits.

Most of the people on the North German Plain live on its margins: the loess belt to the south and the coastal areas in the north. Hamburg, West Germany's largest city, is located at the end of the long Elbe River estuary. In addition to being the nation's busiest seaport, Hamburg is a major industrial center.

Four factors have made West Germany an industrial center.

West Germany today is Western Europe's leading industrial nation. In fact, it is one of the leading industrial nations in the world. Yet it was a ruined land at the end of World War II. Many of its cities and factories had been

A West German steelworker tends molten material.

bombed into rubble. It also faced the problem of feeding and housing millions of refugees from East Germany and Eastern Europe.

The emergence of West Germany out of the ruins of war has been called an economic miracle. This miracle is based on four factors.

The first is the land itself. West Germany benefits from a central location and an extensive transportation system of roads, railroads, rivers, and canals. It also has the best and most abundant supplies of coal in Europe.

The second factor is the German people and their way of life. Workers in this country of 60 million people are highly skilled, and they have a tradition of being diligent and concerned about quality. Also, the people save a large part of their earnings, which provides capital for industry.

The third factor is assistance from the United States in the period after World War II. Under the Marshall Plan, the United States gave billions of dollars to its former enemy. Within a few years, the West Germans had repaired their damaged factories and installed the most modern equipment.

The fourth factor is the government policy. When Germany was ruled by the Nazi party under Adolf Hitler, it had a **managed economy** in which prices and wages were under tight control. The government either owned or regulated most businesses. After World War II, West Germany turned more toward a free-market economy. The government still owns certain businesses, especially railroads, radio and television stations, and some firms in the aluminum and automobile industries. However, all small businesses and most large ones are run by private individuals.

West Germany's economy depends heavily on foreign trade. Although the nation has abundant coal supplies, it has almost no petroleum or natural gas. It also has to import much of its food.

During the 1960s and 1970s, West Germany was very successful at taking imported raw materials, turning them into manufactured goods, and then selling the finished products throughout the world. West German factories were so busy, in fact, that they did not have enough workers. So people from Italy, Turkey, Yugoslavia, and other nations came to West Germany to live and work. In 1985 these families made up about 8 percent of the population.

Today West Germany faces increased competition in the world market for its manufactured goods. It also faces severe problems of air and water pollution in many areas.

Berlin was divided between the West and the East after World War II.

When the German states were unified into the German Empire in 1871, Berlin was made the capital. It grew rapidly and became one of the great cities of the world.

After the victory of the Allied Powers in 1945, Berlin—like Germany itself—was split into four occupation zones. Britain, France, the United States, and the Soviet Union each controlled one zone. The Russian zone soon became the communist country of East Germany. The other three zones became West Germany, a nation strongly tied to the Atlantic countries. Berlin, although located in the middle of East Germany, remained a divided city, with the British, French, and American areas united under the name of West Berlin. West Berlin is part of West Germany, even though it is more than 100 miles away.

West Berlin was separated for 27 years from East Berlin by a fortified wall. The wall was put up in 1961 by East Germany. For several years before then, more and more East Germans had been moving into West Berlin to take advantage of its political freedom and better economic conditions. This embarrassed the communists so much that they finally decided to cut off traffic. For a time, dozens of persons attempted to break through the barrier, and many were killed by East German border guards. Beginning in

1972, however, regular visits between the two sides were permitted.

In 1989, in a sudden, dramatic reversal of policy in response to huge public demonstrations against the communist regime, East Germany opened the wall, allowing unrestricted travel between East Germany and West Germany. Thousands of East Germans quickly emigrated to West Germany, seeking work and a better life. Talks began in 1990 aimed at eventual reunification of the two Germanys.

Curiously, Berlin is not located in a rich agricultural region. Nor is it near large mineral deposits. Instead, government policies over the centuries have encouraged its growth as an administrative center, a focal point of cultural life, a manufacturing core, and a hub for railroad and highway networks. West Germany and East Germany try to make certain that Berlin keeps its standing among the major cities of Europe.

Section 2 Review

Locating Key Places
Locate the following places on the map on page 306: Munich, West Berlin

Identifying Key Terms
Define the following terms: fault valley, managed economy

Reviewing Main Ideas
1. What is the relationship between the Rhine River and the geographic regions of West Germany?
2. What four factors helped West Germany become the industrial heart of Western Europe?
3. For what reasons was Berlin divided after World War II?

Thinking Critically: Make Hypotheses
What do you think might happen to West Berlin if the wall between it and East Berlin were torn down? Give reasons for your answer.

Case Study: East Germans in West Germany

Preview

Key Places
Where are these places located?
1 West Germany
2 East Germany
  See the globe below.

Key Terms
What do these terms mean?
émigré
Eastern bloc
visa

Main Ideas
As you read, look for answers to these questions.
- How do most East Germans feel about West German society after they move West?
- What help in settling into a new life is available to new émigrés?
- What differences between East Germany and West Germany do émigrés most often cite?

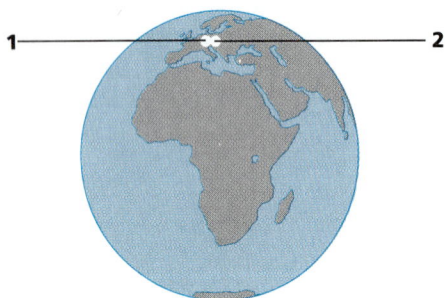

The following case study comes from the article, "Foreigners in Their Own Land," New York Times Magazine, February 16, 1986. This case study describes the hopes and problems facing East German immigrants who move to West Germany. As you read this case study, think about whether or not immigrants to the United States might have the same hopes and problems adjusting to American society.

East Germans often feel like foreigners in West Germany.

When Kai Polter and his best friend, Roland Reiss, arrived four years ago at an "emergency acceptance camp" in central West Germany, the biggest city in West Germany, Hamburg, seemed as good a destination as any, they remember thinking.

Upon arrival in West Germany, each of the émigrés receives a change of clothes, a train ticket to any West German city of his choice, "welcome money" totaling about $60, even a sightseeing tour. [An **émigré** is a person who leaves his or her own country because of political conditions and settles in another.] Because Bonn (the capital of West Germany) does not recognize the existence of East German citizenship, it also confers West German citizenship on all Germans from "over there." Jobs, however, are not conferred automatically; neither is acceptance by West Germans.

Kai Polter was a foreigner in a foreign land. Once he accepted that fact, he stopped expecting West Germans and West Germany to be like East Germans and East German society. When he went back to school to get his secondary education diploma, he found his West German classmates, too, had to learn to accept him as a foreigner.

Accepting West German classmates and neighbors as they are, Polter—who is now 22—has at last made friendships. He has also overcome his shyness and matured beyond his years. His best friend, Roland Reiss, is now a restaurant chef, but Polter no longer plans to become a draftsman. Last summer, he entered a training program to become a social worker—to help East German émigrés.

"I've been there," he says. "I know what they face and what they're going to face even after they think they're settled and established."

"Being there," for Polter as well as many East German émigrés, means a constant uphill battle. On arrival at an émigré camp, for instance, few are prepared to hear camp officials politely explain that West Germany's "economic miracle" is over. Or that unemployment is high (it is now about 9 percent). Or that they would have a hard time finding a job.

That East German émigrés are experiencing such severe social and economic problems demonstrates all too clearly just how divided the two German peoples are 25 years after the Berlin Wall went up. All told, more than half a million Germans have moved from the Communist East to the capitalist West since the Wall went up; from 1964 through 1984, an estimated 48,000 have moved in the opposite direction. Despite the efforts of the Bonn Government to promote the idea of a united Germany, probably all that East and West Germans share nowadays are a common heritage and a common language.

Private organizations and the government aid émigrés.

There are counselors for private organizations as well as Government social workers who help East German émigrés settle into their new life. But Christel Brödel is one of the few West German social workers on the public payroll who counsel only East German émigrés. Mrs. Brödel found her vocation six years ago, after noticing that East German émigrés in Hamburg, where she worked, had special problems.

A West Berliner stands before the wall that divided her city from 1961 to 1989.

Mrs. Brödel's one-room office is in the centrally situated welfare department. But her office is often empty. "They'll never come to me for their first visit of their own accord," says Mrs. Brödel. . . . "They have an ingrained distrust of anyone connected with officialdom. They assume the Government is against them, as it was against them over there."

So how does she meet her clients?

"By word of mouth," she says, "as it always is with people from the Eastern bloc. [The **Eastern bloc** refers to the communist countries of Eastern Europe.] New arrivals will meet a present or former client of mine, who will tell them I'm O.K. and that I can help them. Usually, they set up a meeting in some neutral place, like a café."

As gently as she can, she leads East German émigrés into the reality of West Germany. "One of the first things I do, after we establish a certain amount of rapport," she says, "is to take

315

them to a supermarket. Strange as it sounds, many of them don't know how to shop. At first they go crazy and start piling everything into the grocery cart. Then suddenly they realize they don't have enough money to pay for it all, and freak out and put everything back.

East Germans seem friendlier and their families seem closer.

Any conversation with an East German émigré eventually gets around to the subject of the sometimes subtle, sometimes monumental differences between the two Germanys.

"It was so different over there," says Kristine Sliwinski, who arrived in Hanover nine years ago.

"To be honest, I regret having made the move," she says. "We waited and hoped so long. Our hopes were too high and too much had changed since the war."

Asking an East German émigré what has changed since the war or how West Germany is different from "over there" generally produces the same answers.

"People are friendlier over there," says Mrs. Sliwiniski. "They stick together . . . because they need each other's support against the state. Families are closer because they usually all live together, and young people don't have as many distractions. Over here, kids grow up and move away, and old people get packed off to nursing homes. . . . I don't even know who my neighbors are here, and I had such wonderful friends over there." Like most East German émigrés who dream of moving West . . . Kai Polter's first vacation trip in 1983, was back to the Eastern bloc to be with his family for Christmas.

"I wasn't allowed back into East Germany," says Polter, "so I met my parents and brother and sister in Czechoslovakia."

Later, when his mother was dying of cancer, East German authorities denied him a visa. [A **visa** is an official document that allows a person to visit another country.] When permission

finally came through, she had already died. His visit to her grave in late 1984 made clear to him once more the extent to which Germans are divided. "The war never ended," he says matter-of-factly.

Is he an East German or a West German?

"I am both and I am neither," he replies. "It was important for me to grow up over there. And it is important for me to be here now, although one thing I've learned here is that you don't have to accept and agree with everything to belong here.

"I am a German."

Section 3 Review

Locating Key Places
Locate the following places on the map on page 306: West Germany, East Germany

Identifying Key Terms
Define the following terms: émigré, Eastern bloc, visa

Reviewing Main Ideas
1. What feeling do many East Germans have about their standing in West German society?
2. How does the government and private organizations help new émigrés?
3. How are East Germany and West Germany different, according to recent East German émigrés?

Thinking Critically: Identify Assumptions
What assumptions do East Germans make about living in West Germany? List at least two.

SECTION 4

Benelux

Preview

Key Places
Where are these places located?
1 Rotterdam
2 Brussels
See the globe below.

Key Terms
What does this term mean?
polder

Main Ideas
As you read, look for answers to these questions.
• What effect has the sea had on the Netherlands?
• How do the northern and southern parts of Belgium differ?
• What does Luxembourg have in common with its neighbors?

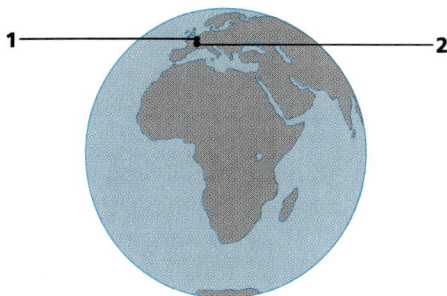

1 ——————————————— 2

In their region the ocean pours out over a vast stretch of land, at two intervals by day and by night, in a tidal wave so enormous that this eternal struggle in the course of nature makes one doubt whether the soil belongs to the land or to the sea.

Pliny, *Natural History*

The people of the Netherlands have always struggled with the sea.

More than 1,900 years ago, the Roman historian Pliny described the Dutch struggle with the sea. He told how the people chose high hills or threw up elevations higher than the highest tide on which to build their huts. Since that time, the Dutch have created more than 40 percent of their country from the sea. Both the capital of Amsterdam and the major port of Rotterdam are located on land that was formerly covered by water.

With the exception of a tiny highland province in the southeast, the land of the Netherlands may be divided into low, lower, and lowest. The low sandy plain in the eastern half of the country is generally less than 100 feet above sea level. Here and there pine forests break its gently rolling surface. Farmers fertilize and irrigate the sandy soil to support pastures and fields.

The lower land is a strip of islands and sand dunes that form the western and northern edge of the country. These sandy barriers, usually less than 25 feet above sea level, separate the North Sea from shallow inlets and lakes of brackish water. The dunelands support only a few small trees and are useless for farming.

The **polders** are the lowest land in the Netherlands. These are flat stretches of land that lie below sea level between the sandy plain and the dunelands. They were created by diking a water-covered area with dams and levees, and then draining off the excess water. Pumps operating day and night remove the excess water and send it to the North Sea. In the old days, the pumps were powered by windmills. Today they are powered by electrical and nuclear energy. Because the soil is mostly silt and the land is so flat, polder farms are among the most productive in the world.

The economy of the Netherlands was traditionally based on agriculture. Specialization developed early. Even today cheese, meat, and flowers—especially tulip bulbs—are major exports.

At present, however, the Netherlands is mostly an industrial and commercial nation. Coal deposits were found deep in the ground of the little highland province. This resource formed the basis for the development of heavy industry. About 1960 the Dutch began exploiting a huge natural gas field in the northern part of the country. It is currently the largest producing field in the world. Among the host of items manufactured in the Netherlands are steel and steel products, electronics, textiles, drugs, and chemicals. The country's location at the

Brightly colored tulips decorate this Dutch garden.

gateway to Europe has encouraged the development of commercial and transportation facilities.

The Netherlands is a land of cities. Nearly 90 percent of the people live in urban areas such as Rotterdam, The Hague [hāg], and Haarlem. Amsterdam is the largest city and the country's cultural center.

Northern and southern Belgium differ culturally and economically.

Belgium is a small country located in the coastal region between France and Germany. Although almost all Belgians are Roman Catholic, the nation is divided into two ethnic and language groups. The Flemish people, who live in the northern part of the nation, speak Flemish, which is similar to Dutch. The Walloons in the south speak French. The Flemish make up 57 percent of the population. The Walloons account for 33 percent. The remaining 10 percent are bilingual. The dividing line between the two languages runs east and west just to the south of Brussels, the nation's capital and its largest city.

The rivalry between the Flemish and the Walloons has been part of Belgian life since the kingdom was established in 1830. Political parties, trade unions, scout groups, and other organizations try to balance their membership so that both groups are represented. Laws, money, and postage stamps are printed in both Flemish and French.

In recent years the rivalry has increased because of economic changes in Belgium. Antwerp, in the Flemish-speaking area, has developed into a major port and industrial center. As a result, thousands of new jobs have been created there. At the same time, many of the country's older mines and factories, which are located in the French-speaking area, have had to close.

Belgium has three geographic regions. Flanders, the region next to the sea, is a low area of clay soils that are quite productive. Fur-

Amsterdam, in the Netherlands, is a bustling urban center.

ther inland is a central plain where the majority of the people live. The third region, south of the Meuse River, is a hilly upland with poorly drained soils. Although it supports the extensive Ardennes [är den'] Forest, the trees have little commercial value.

Luxembourg has much in common with its neighbors.

Luxembourg is a small, landlocked nation. It has much in common with its neighbors, especially Belgium. Luxembourg's northern topography is an extension of Belgium's Ardennes Uplands. In the south is a fertile, rolling plain. Like Belgium and the Netherlands, Luxembourg depends on international trade to maintain its standard of living. Also like its Benelux neighbors, Luxembourg is densely populated and highly industrialized.

At one time the iron and steel industry dominated Luxembourg's economy. However, that left the country dependent on the world price of steel. In 1962 Luxembourg passed a diversification law to give the economy more balance. New factories producing rubber and chemical products were built with government help. A new banking industry was encouraged to develop.

The 367,000 people of Luxembourg speak a dialect of German at home. Newspapers and primary schools, however, generally use the formal German language. Governmental functions and secondary schools are usually conducted in French.

Section 4 Review

Locating Key Places
Locate the following places on the map on page 306: Rotterdam, Brussels

Identifying Key Terms
Define the following term: polder

Reviewing Main Ideas
1. How have the Dutch people carried on their struggle with the sea?
2. How do the language and economy of northern Belgium differ from the language and economy of southern Belgium?
3. In what ways does Luxembourg resemble one or more of its neighbors?

Thinking Critically: Make Decisions
Suppose that the financial firm for which you work is thinking of opening up a European branch office in Antwerp. List all the arguments for this decision.

Switzerland and Austria

Preview

Key Places
Where are the following places located?
1 Geneva
2 Vienna
See the globe below.

Key Terms
What do these terms mean?
canton
neutrality

Main Ideas
As you read, look for answers to these questions.
• What effect do mountains have on Switzerland?
• How is Austria related to both the western and eastern parts of Europe?

From the pleasantly situated old town . . . a footpath leads up through shady green meadows to the foot of the mountains, which, as they gaze down on the valley, present a solemn and majestic picture. Anyone who follows it will soon catch the keen fragrance of grassy pasture lands, for the footpath goes up straight and steep to the Alps.

Johanna Spyri, *Heidi*

Switzerland's mountains influence both its languages and its economy.

Johanna Spyri's well-loved story of Heidi tells about life in the Swiss Alps. If you look at the map on page 272, you will see how the mountains stand out. The mountains, which are in the southern part of the country, make up one of Switzerland's two major regions. The northern region consists of hilly uplands. An imaginary line separating these two regions runs from the eastern tip of Lake Constance, in the northeast, to the eastern tip of Lake Geneva, in the southwest. Lake Constance borders West Germany and is part of the Rhine River system. Lake Geneva borders France and is in the Rhône River valley.

Switzerland faces in four directions, with a different language dominant on each frontier. About three-fourths of the people speak German as their first language. The other official languages are French, Italian, and Romansh, a language resembling Latin that is spoken near the Inn Valley. Switzerland's ancient Latin name, Helvetia, is used on its postage stamps and coins.

The Swiss Alps. The Swiss Alps are divided into five or six separate ranges by deep valleys. Three major passes and several minor ones make it possible to cross the Alps in several directions. The Matterhorn, Switzerland's most famous peak, and Mt. Rosa, its highest mountain, are both located in the southwest, near the border with Italy. Nearby is the resort town of Zermatt. The famous resort areas of Locarno and Lugano lie farther east, with the Alps to the north and the Po Valley to the south. Their location on the south side of the mountains gives them a much warmer climate. Still farther east is the resort town of St. Moritz. As you might imagine, tourism, throughout the seasons, is Switzerland's leading industry.

The Hilly Uplands. The nation's best farming lands lie in the hilly upland region north and west of the mountains. So do numerous long, narrow lakes. These lakes, formed by the glaciers, occupy the bottoms of valleys and are often the focus of roads and trade routes. Important cities have grown up on their shores.

Geneva and Lausanne, both popular centers for international conferences and organizations, are located on Lake Geneva. Lucerne and Zurich—the nation's largest city—are located on two separate lakes that eventually feed into the Rhine River. Bern, the capital of Switzerland, is situated near the center of the Hilly Uplands.

The Jura Mountains. An imaginary line connecting the northwestern tips of Lake Constance and Lake Geneva roughly marks the transition between the Hilly Uplands and the Jura Mountains in the northwestern corner of Switzerland. The Jura, like the Black Forest region across the Rhine in West Germany, are low, folded mountains. Most of the land is forested, with some pastures. The major city is Basel [bä'zəl], located at the southern end of the Rhine Valley. Basel is Switzerland's major river port, handling a large volume of imports and exports.

A limited resource base. Switzerland's economy is highly industrialized and highly dependent on foreign trade. Although its farmers are very productive, the nation does not raise enough food to feed its people. Nor does it have any oil, gas, or minerals to export in payment for the needed food. Although its water power and nuclear fuel generate most of its

electricity, Switzerland must import all of its petroleum and most of its raw materials. Forest products are the only significant exception.

The Swiss have approached the difficulties of a limited resource base in several ways. First, they have concentrated on manufacturing high quality, precision goods such as electronics, cameras, and watches. These take more time to make but require fewer raw materials relative to their value. Second, the Swiss labor force is highly educated and very skillful. Third, it works longer hours than in most industrial nations, averaging 45 hours a week. Fourth, the Swiss

Skiers enjoy Switzerland's idyllic mountains and villages.

have made their country a world center of such service industries as banking, insurance, and engineering. Lastly, the nation has made the most of its central location and spectacular scenery by encouraging the transportation and tourist industries.

Defending the nation. The nation of Switzerland was founded in 1291 when the inhabitants of several mountain areas decided to join together to defend their freedom from a threat by the German emperor. These original areas, plus several others, form the 22 Swiss **cantons**, each a small political division of the country.

One way the Swiss have guarded their freedom is through a strict policy of **neutrality**, by which Switzerland refuses to take part in a war between other countries. Another way to guard freedom, the Swiss believe, is a strong defense. All men between the ages of 20 and 50 belong to the Swiss army.

Austria is situated at the crossroads of Europe.

For centuries, Austria has served as a connection between the eastern and western parts of Europe. Most of the country lies in the Danube River Valley. This encouraged Austria to look eastward. At the same time, the Brenner Pass in the western part of the country links Austria to West Germany and Italy.

The landscape of Austria is similar to the high mountains and hilly uplands of Switzerland. The Austrian Alps reach their highest elevations in the center of the country. These peaks are made of hard igneous rocks. The tributaries of the Danube flow along the edge of these hard rocks, eventually reaching the fertile open Danube valley in the northern and eastern part of the country. The broad Vienna Basin, in the northeast, is Austria's leading agricultural and manufacturing region. The capital city of Vienna is located in this region. About one third of the Austrian people live in Vienna and its suburbs.

Austria's farms, especially those near Vienna and in the northern part of the country, are usually small but very productive. Farmers supply almost 90 percent of the nation's food requirements. Austria has hydroelectric power and natural gas, as well as some iron ore, coal, petroleum, and copper. Its petroleum and coal, however, need to be supplemented by imports. To pay for this, Austria's factories turn out iron and steel, chemical and forest products, and a variety of consumer goods.

In addition to foreign trade, Austria depends on tourism. Innsbruck is a world-famous resort. Salzburg has a celebrated music festival. Indeed, Austria may be called the land of music. Vienna has been a center of classical music for centuries. Among the famous composers who lived and worked in "the music capital of the world" were Mozart, Beethoven, Schubert, Haydn, Brahms, and Strauss.

Section 5 Review

Locating Key Places
Locate the following places on the map on page 306: Geneva, Vienna

Identifying Key Terms
Define the following terms: canton, neutrality

Reviewing Main Ideas
1. How do Switzerland's mountains affect its languages and its economy?
2. How has Austria's location influenced its economy?

Thinking Critically: Analyze Comparisons
Suppose you are the leader of Austria today. You notice that while Austria has been involved in numerous wars, Switzerland, which has had a policy of neutrality and military preparedness, has not. Based on what you know, how successful would you be at avoiding war if you built a strong defense and declared neutrality? Would you be as successful as Switzerland?

A Bird's-Eye View of Frankfurt

Imagine for a moment that you are looking out the window of a helicopter flying low over the city of Frankfurt, Germany. What you are seeing is a "bird's-eye view" of Frankfurt.

A bird's-eye view, like the one below, is a map-like drawing showing a small part of the earth's surface as it might look to a bird flying overhead. Bird's-eye views are used most often to show specific details in cities and towns.

The map below is called a Bollmann Plan. This map shows many of Frankfurt's historical and governmental buildings and tourist attractions that visitors might like to see.

Now take your own tour. Begin at the *Kaiserdom*, located between *Weckmarkt* and *Hollgasse*. The *Kaiserdom* is the cathedral in the city's heart.

In front of this large church is an open area with the *Rathaus*, or city hall, on one side and the Historical Museum on the other. The *Romer*, across from the Kaiserdom, is a historic meeting hall and the old city hall.

The main shopping center of the city is near the left portion of the map. Locate the large department store on a street called the *Zeil*.

Review

1. Why might a Bollmann Plan of a city be useful for a tourist to have?

2. How is a Bollmann Plan of Frankfurt different from a political map of the city?

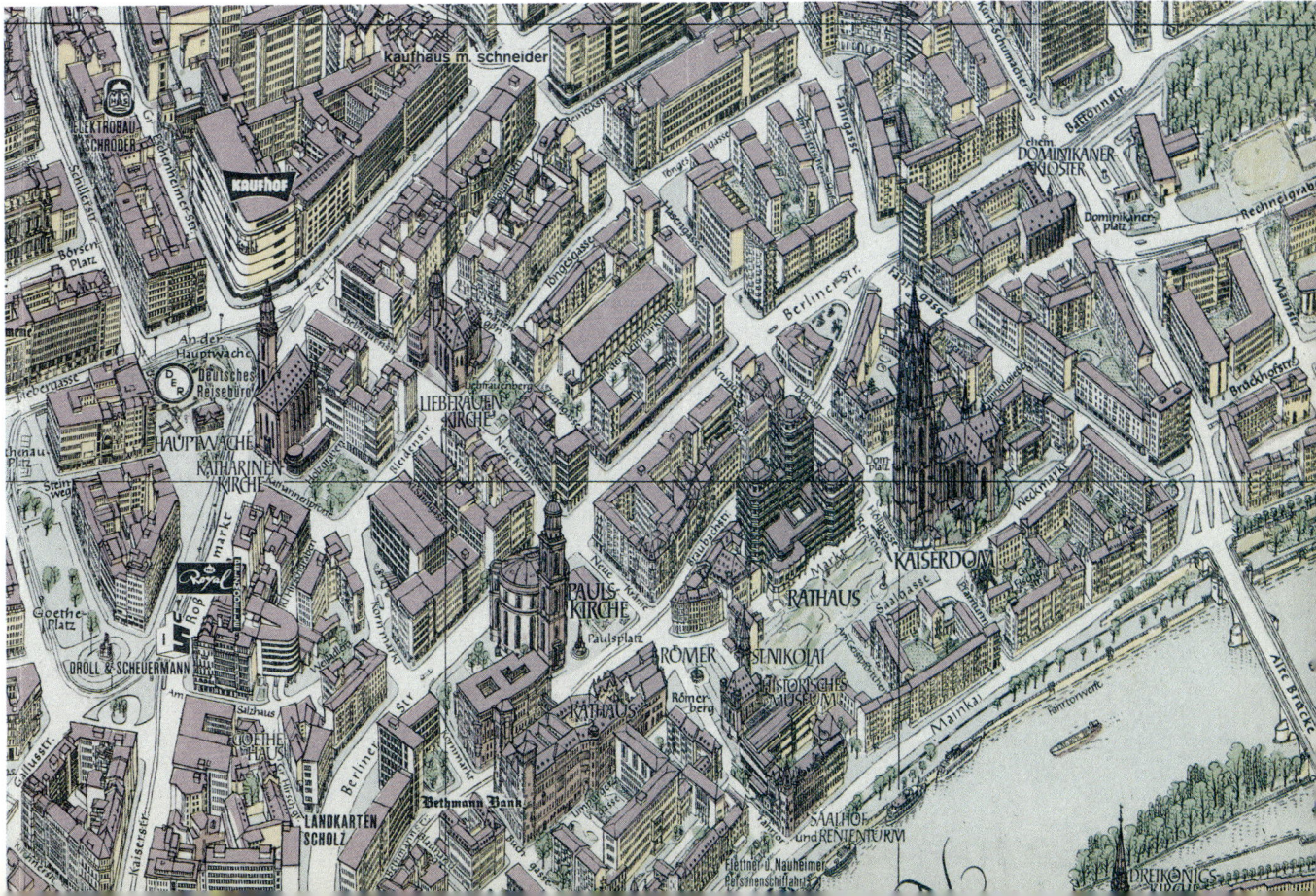

CHAPTER 14

Review

Section Summaries

1. France Paris, the capital of France and its largest city, is the cultural center of the nation. France's topography varies from plains in the north to mountains in the south and east. The people earn their living from both agriculture and industry.

2. West Germany The Rhine River connects the four major geographic regions of West Germany. The country became the leading industrial nation of Western Europe as a result of its central location, rich coal supplies, productive labor force, the Marshall Plan, and a free-market policy followed by its government. Berlin was divided between the East and the West after World War II.

3. Case Study: East Germans in West Germany Many East Germans wish to emigrate to West Germany to obtain greater freedom. However, once this move is made, some East Germans are unhappy. They are unprepared for long periods of unemployment, loneliness, and sometimes even hostility that awaits them as "foreigners."

4. Benelux The people of the Netherlands have always struggled with the North Sea and have created half their country from land that was formerly covered by water. Belgium has two regions. People in the north of Belgium speak Flemish and are more industrialized and richer than people in the French-speaking south. Luxembourg, like the other Benelux countries, depends on foreign trade and is an urban nation.

5. Switzerland and Austria Switzerland's mountains divide the country into four regions, each of which faces in a different direction and each of each speaks a different language. Austria serves as a bridge between the eastern and western parts of Europe. Both nations have a limited resource base, promote tourism, and are neutral in foreign affairs.

Using Geography Skills

Reviewing the Map Lesson

Use the map at left to answer the following questions.

1. What street passes through the middle of Schweizer Platz?

2. Name two streets that meet at Schweizer Platz.

3. Would you say that the area around Schweizer Platz is business or residential?

Using Social Studies Skills

1. Locate and Gather Information. Different reference sources can provide different kinds of information about a topic. Using a world almanac, find the most recent population count of Paris. Using an encyclopedia, find out the name of the royal family of the old Austrian Empire.

2. Perceive Cause-Effect Relationships. A lack of natural resources may sometimes have a positive effect on a nation. Choose one of the continental nations of Western Europe and write a well-organized paragraph describing what that nation's people have done to make up for a limited resource base.

Testing for Understanding

Locating Key Places
Match each description below with the name of the place.
1. primate city of France
2. a Swiss conference center
3. a communist neighbor of West Germany
4. France's major Mediterranean port
5. world's largest seaport
6. an industrial country
7. the Austrian capital city
8. the western part of a divided German city
9. the capital city of Bavaria, in southern Germany
10. Belgium's capital city

a. Paris
b. Marseille
c. Munich
d. West Berlin
e. West Germany
f. East Germany
g. Rotterdam
h. Brussels
i. Geneva
j. Vienna

Recalling Key Terms
Define these terms in your own words.

Section 1
primate city
granary

Section 2
fault valley
managed economy

Section 3
émigré
Eastern bloc
visa

Section 4
polder

Section 5
canton
neutrality

Reviewing Main Ideas
Section 1
1. Describe how Paris has affected the culture of France.
2. List the major geographic regions of France.
3. Describe the industries in the French economy.

Section 2
1. Where does the Rhine River flow in West Germany?
2. List the four factors that have made West Germany the industrial heart of Europe.
3. Why is Berlin divided into an eastern part and a western part?

Section 3
1. Describe how East Germans who have emigrated to West Germany feel about their move.
2. How does West Germany help East Germans settle into their new society?
3. How do East German émigrés view West German society?

Section 4
1. Describe the relationship between the Dutch people and the sea.
2. Compare the language and economy of northern Belgium with those of southern Belgium.
3. In what ways does Luxembourg resemble its Benelux neighbors?

Section 5
1. List two ways in which Switzerland's mountains have affected the Swiss people.
2. Why is Austria able to serve as a bridge between Eastern and Western Europe?

Thinking Critically
1. **Evaluate Sources of Information.** For a business trip to the Ruhr, which two of the following pieces of information would be most useful to you? Write a paragraph explaining your reasoning.
- a political map of Europe
- a railroad schedule for the Rhône River valley
- an article on the future of the steel industry
- a list of West Germany's major imports and exports

2. **Make Hypotheses.** Switzerland has used a strong defense to avoid wars. Based on this example, how reasonable is it to conclude that a strong defense is the key to preserving peace?

Mediterranean Europe

In this chapter you will learn about the four European countries that share characteristics called "Mediterranean."

Sections
1 Spain and Portugal
2 Greece and Italy

Spain and Portugal

Preview

Key Places
Where are these places located?
1 Bay of Biscay
2 Madrid
3 Lisbon
   See the globe below.

Key Terms
What does this term mean?
republic

Main Ideas
As you read, look for answers to these questions.
● What do the countries of Mediterranean Europe have in common?
● How has Spain changed in the past few decades?
● To which regions does Portugal belong?

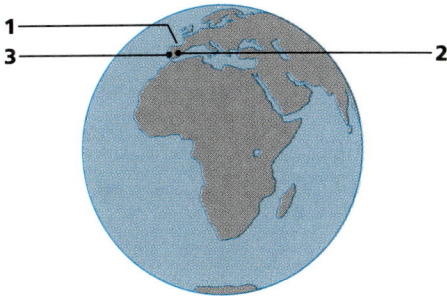

Ancha es Castilla.
The world is open to all possibilities.

Spanish proverb

Mediterranean Europe shares cultural and geographic ties.
When the Spanish sailed off to explore and colonize the New World, they left with the feeling expressed in this common saying, that their path was without obstacle. During the time of their emerging empire, the Spanish looked outward for possibilities. Now, however, Spain and the other former colonial powers of Mediterranean Europe—Portugal, Greece, and Italy—are exploring their opportunities at home.

These countries are all associated with the Mediterranean Sea, whose name means "in the middle of the land." Although the sea is located far north of the Equator, its name still makes geographical, historical, and cultural sense. Here the continents of Africa, Asia, and Europe come together, and many different cultures meet.

The western part of Mediterranean Europe, which includes Portugal, Spain, and the tiny principality of Andorra, lies on the Iberian Peninsula. This peninsula, like the rest of Mediterranean Europe, is geographically well situated. Refer to the map on page 328 to see how the peninsula's square shape suggests that the land looks out in all four directions.

Iberia's crossroads location meant that people could come from any direction to colonize the peninsula since only on the west has the land been secure. In ancient times Iberia had colonial outposts of Phoenicia, Greece, Carthage, and Rome. Between A.D. 500 and 1000, however, Germans, Berbers, and Arabs invaded the peninsula.

Facing page: In Portugal, and throughout Mediterranean Europe, fishing boats such as these move along the coast.

Spain, a former imperial power, is modernizing its economy.

An influential predecessor of modern Spain was a medieval Christian kingdom known as Castile, which was centered on the Meseta, a high semi-arid plateau that covers most of the country. Since the kingdom's capital of Toledo occupied too small a site for a large city, the nearby town of Madrid became the capital, and commercial and transportation center, of modern Spain. Today Madrid, the largest city in Spain, is a vast metropolis with more than 3 million people in this country of 39 million.

A Spanish empire. In 1469 the marriage of Princess Isabella of Castile and Prince Ferdinand of Aragon, another Christian kingdom, united the two major kingdoms of Spain. Working to create a strong, unified Spain, the two monarchs began a movement to explore and colonize the world outside of Spain. Like other imperial powers, Spain used its maritime skills, and financial and military strength, to extend its em-

Map Study

What is an important economic activity that takes place along many of the coastlines of Mediterranean Europe? How is most of the land in the Iberian Peninsula used?

Mediterranean Europe

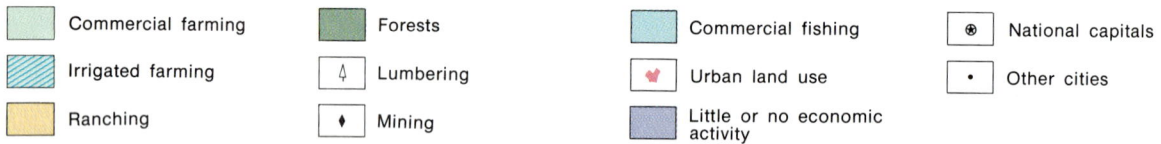

Commercial farming	Forests	Commercial fishing	⊛ National capitals
Irrigated farming	⚲ Lumbering	Urban land use	• Other cities
Ranching	◆ Mining	Little or no economic activity	

pire and Roman Catholicism around the globe. The power of the Roman Catholic Church remains with Spain to this day as 99 percent of all Spaniards are Roman Catholic.

A developing economy. Until the 1950s and 1960s, Spain relied mainly on an agricultural economy in a land poor in natural resources. The dry climate and poor soil have limited the country's production, and farming methods have only recently approached modern standards.

In the past 30 years, Spain has worked hard to industrialize and modernize its economy. The percentage of people involved in agriculture has dropped, and more people are working in manufacturing and service industries. Some important Spanish industries include tourism and automobile and ship manufacturing.

Most manufacturing firms, however, are small and technologically outdated, so Spain's industries still lag behind those of other developed countries. In 1986, however, Spain became a member of the European Community, or European Common Market.

An ethnic variety. Although the official language of Spain is Castilian Spanish, there are several large ethnic minority groups with distinct languages of their own. In Catalonia, the northeastern corner of Spain, many people speak Catalan, a language related to Spanish but more similar to French Provençal [prō′vən säl′]. Barcelona, the urban center of Catalonia, is Spain's leading seaport and industrial center.

The Basque Provinces, located in the central part of northern Spain, are home to people who speak Basque, a language that is unrelated to any other in the world. Some believe that it may be Europe's oldest spoken language. Basques are very conscious of their unique cultural and linguistic heritage and have pushed for the creation of their own independent country or autonomous state within the Spanish government.

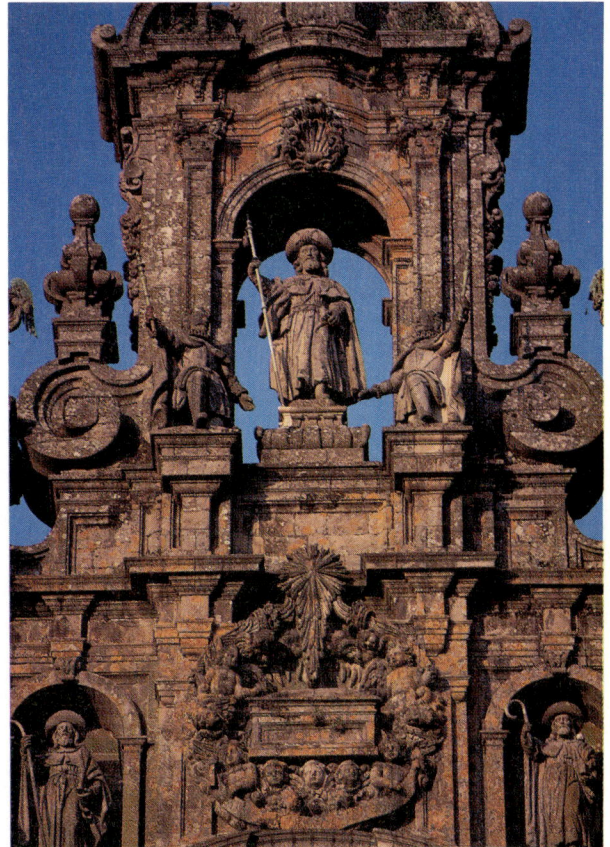

A statue of St. James adorns an ornate Spanish cathedral.

A third ethnic minority lives in Galicia, north of Portugal. Here the people speak Galician, a dialect of Portuguese.

A republican government. In 1931 a rebellion toppled the monarchy that had ruled since Ferdinand and Isabella united Spain in the late 1400s, and the Spanish Republic was born. A **republic** is a country in which the citizens elect the representatives to manage the government, which is usually headed by a president.

Five years later, however, a Spanish general named Francisco Franco revolted against the new republic and plunged the country into a civil war. His followers, called the Nationalists, eventually won the war, and Franco became dictator of Spain.

After Franco died in 1975, Spain made steady progress towards democracy. In 1979 Spain decided to recognize the geographic and cultural regions into which the country is divided. It created a federal state with strong regional governments.

This move not only quieted some of the Basque demands, but appealed to the Catalans and other regional minorities as well. Peace in Spain is an absolute necessity because of the economy's heavy dependence on tourism. In fact, Spain has more tourists each year than there are Spaniards.

Portugal has ties with both the Mediterranean and the Atlantic.

Portugal, a republic of 10 million people, occupies the southwest section of the Iberian Peninsula. Several rivers that begin in the Spanish Meseta form productive valleys as they pass through Portugal on their way to the sea. Most of the population lives in rural areas along the coast or in these agricultural valleys. The capital, Lisbon, is the country's largest city.

The two Iberian nations stand back to back rather than face to face. The rugged landscape on the border between Spain and Portugal has always made communication rather difficult between these two neighboring countries. Rather than Spain, therefore, Portugal's major trading partners are Britain, West Germany, France, and the United States.

A historic empire. You can see that Portugal faces outward, towards the Atlantic. This encouraged the development of the country's sea-based empire. Because Portugal is a small country, however, its great empire was acquired and maintained at an enormous cost.

A troubled economy. In 1984 half of Portugal's food supply had to be imported. To pay its bills, the country has developed its limited mineral resources and has nurtured some manufacturing industries.

In the last decade, Portugal has undergone major changes. The end of its empire enabled it to turn its attention to domestic political reform and modernization of its economy. As a new member of the European Community (1986), Portugal has turned its orientation around, from the wider world to the European continent.

Section 1 Review

Locating Key Places
Locate the following places on the map on page 328: Bay of Biscay, Madrid, Lisbon

Identifying Key Terms
Define the following term: republic

Reviewing Main Ideas
1. What specific ties do the countries of Mediterranean Europe share?
2. Describe how Spain's economy has moved toward industrialization.
3. How does Portugal's location foster ties with both Mediterranean and Atlantic lands?

Thinking Critically: Make Decisions
A crafts importer is planning a buying trip to Iberia. The buyer will visit Madrid first, then travel to Barcelona, Bilbao, and Porto. The person will be inspecting handicrafts locally and may visit some small isolated villages. The buyer speaks English only. Use the map on page 328 to decide how many translators may be needed during the trip.

SECTION 2

Greece and Italy

Preview

Key Places
Where are these places located?
1 Aegean Sea
2 Athens
3 Sicily
   See the globe below.

Key Terms
What does this term mean?
coalition government

Main Ideas
As you read, look for answers to these questions.
- How has Greece's position on the sea affected its development?
- What type of economy does Italy have?

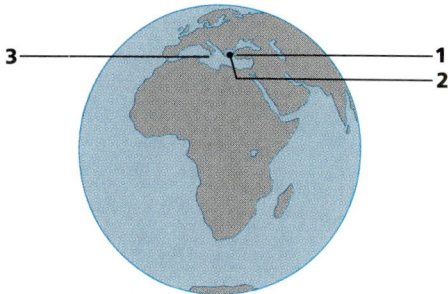

Sing in me, Muse, and through me tell the story of that man skilled in all ways of contending, the wanderer, harried for years on end, after he plundered the stronghold on the proud height of Troy.

Homer, *The Odyssey*

Greece's position has shaped its economy and culture.

These poetic lines, attributed to Homer, open one of the oldest books in the world, *The Odyssey*. According to legend, Homer was a blind Greek poet who lived around 800 B.C. *The Odyssey* is an integral part of the collection of Greek and Roman literature and philosophy that has had lasting influence on Western culture.

As you learned in Chapter 12, a central location, mild climate, and an orientation to the sea gave Greece, and its neighbor Italy, important advantages in the development of a European civilization. The Greek mainland is a series of irregular peninsulas stretching out into the Aegean and Ionian seas. The water, along with the mountains that cover 70 percent of the country's land area, divide Greece into several distinct land regions.

The focus of Greek life has traditionally been on the Aegean Sea, located between Greece and Turkey. As you can see from the map on page 328, this sea is filled with small islands, most of which belong to Greece. The islands contribute to the country's strategic location because they serve as stepping stones to Asia and as guardians to the straits that link the waters of the Mediterranean and Black seas. The Greeks also once settled much of Turkey but were pushed out in the 1920s, when modern Turkey was created.

Economy. The sea has been important to Greece's economy as well. Seafood is an important part of the Greek diet, and shipping has traditionally been a leading industry. One out of every 12 families in Greece owes its liveli-

331

hood, directly or indirectly, to the country's large merchant fleet. Interestingly enough, only one percent of the shipping involves Greek ports, since most of the ships are used to carry goods to and from foreign ports.

Agriculture in Greece is not a very productive industry because most of the land is covered by the Pindus Mountains. Much of the soil is stony, and the climate tends to be dry. In addition, Greece has poorer natural resources than most Western European countries.

Valleys provide the most fertile farmland, but many of them are small and difficult to reach by road. Northern Greece has more lowlands and more abundant rainfall than the rest of the country. As a result, the region has more potential for the expansion of agricultural production. Here, and elsewhere, Greek farmers overcome the physical limitations of the land and produce wine, wool, cheese, olives, cotton, and fruit.

Manufacturing in Greece is not a large industry, although it has grown significantly in the past 30 years. Most production is done in small shops that are often run as family businesses.

These shops, therefore, lack the economies generated by large-scale production.

Athens, the capital and largest city of Greece, contains many of these small factories, as well as some larger facilities. A growing financial district and strong tourist industry have helped push this city, and the rest of Greece, toward a more stable and industrialized economy.

People. Greece is officially a republic. It is led by a president chosen by an elected parliament. In this country where democracy was born, however, the governments have not always been democratic. Throughout its history Greece has been ruled by monarchs, the military, and by political confusion.

As you read in Chapter 12, ancient Greek civilization was one of the most advanced for its time in terms of science, philosophy, politics, and the arts. Greek thinkers such as Aristotle and Thales laid the foundation of the scientific method, and Homer's epic poems, *The Iliad* and *The Odyssey*, are viewed by many authorities as the first written tales of fiction.

This temple, just south of Athens, Greece, honors Poseidon, the Greek god of the sea. It was built in 444 B.C.

332

Today the Greek culture remains strong. Most of the population of 10 million belongs to the Greek Orthodox Church, whose beliefs and festivals are an important aspect of Greek life. Many Greeks believe in hard work and a devotion to family.

Italy, with a rich history, has a diverse economy.

The nation of Italy is composed of a boot-shaped peninsula that juts far into the Mediterranean Sea. Near the "toe" is the large island of Sicily, and just to Sicily's northwest is Sardinia. Rome, the nation's capital and one of the world's great centers of civilization, is located near the coast midway along the peninsula.

Italy has gone through many periods of unity and division. All of Italy was united under the Roman Empire, as you may remember from Chapter 12. The Roman Empire was one of the greatest and most expansive in history, and although its decline began in the A.D. 400s, the empire survived for hundreds of years. With the end of the empire, Italy was divided into a variety of small city-states, which for the next 14 centuries, fought for leadership. Only in the 1860s was the entire peninsula united into one modern state.

Italy today can be roughly divided into three geographic areas—northern, central, and southern. There are many physical, cultural, and economic differences between the regions.

Northern Italy. The northern region is Italy's industrial and agricultural center. The Po Valley, south of the Alps and north of the Apennines, is Italy's richest and most productive region. This level plain holds more than 40 percent of Italy's population of 58 million and produces nearly 60 percent of its gross national product.

The richness of the Po Valley may be explained by several factors. The level land permits intensive cultivation, and the soils, mostly alluvial in origin, are very rich. The valley enjoys

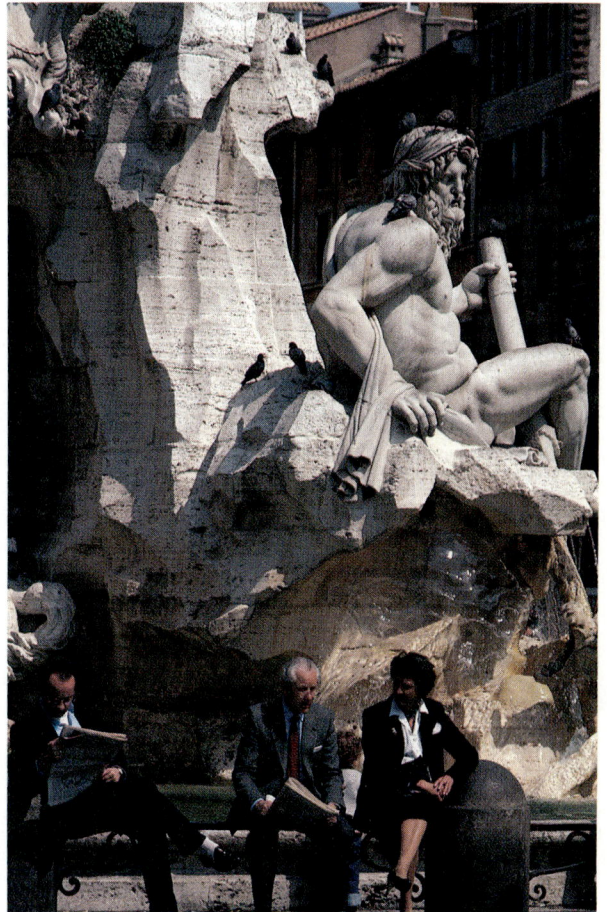

Rome's Piazza Navona reflects Italy's classical past.

a mild climate, adequate rainfall, and dependable natural irrigation.

In addition to agriculture, the Po Valley also excels in industrial development. A number of major cities—including Milan, Turin, and Genoa—and an advanced transportation network have allowed the Po Valley to develop a strong, diversified economy.

Central Italy. Central Italy is the political and cultural center of the nation. This region extends southward from the industrial Po Valley to a point just above the "spur" on Italy's boot. Mountains dominate the area, but several lowland areas and valleys have supported dense populations for thousands of years.

Florence, the major city along the Arno River, was the cradle of the Renaissance. Rome, the capital of Italy, forms the cultural and historical heart of this central region. Much of the world's great art is in Rome, as is the center of the Roman Catholic Church, the tiny self-governing state known as Vatican City. In all of Italy, 95 percent of the people are Catholic.

As the Italian capital, Rome has been at the center of the country's government. Since World War II, Italy has been a democracy. However, in this country of many different political parties, a true electoral majority is rare. As a result, following those elections in which no clear majority emerges, a cabinet is formed with a coalition government. A **coalition government** is a ruling government that is made up of many cooperating parties. Whenever these diverse political groups cannot cooperate, the government falls apart and another election must be held. Since 1945 Italy has had almost 50 such governments. However, this apparent instability has not held back Italy's economic development, at least in the northern and central regions.

Southern Italy. This region includes the lower third of the peninsula and the islands of Sardinia and Sicily. All three areas have extensive highlands, some coastal plains, and a Mediterranean climate. The summer dry season is often made longer and more severe by the rain shadow cast by the mountains.

A series of active volcanoes extends from Sicily up the west coast of the Italian Peninsula. Mt. Etna and Mt. Vesuvius have provided fertile soils, as well as dangerous living conditions.

The area around Naples combines adequate rainfall with these fertile soils and some lowland areas to produce large crops. Naples, however, like the entire southern region, is quite overpopulated and lacks adequate industry and jobs. As a result, its people do not enjoy a high standard of living. The Italian government has tried, with limited success, to encourage industrial development in the south.

The vast differences among the three regions of Italy make the economic statistics for the whole country somewhat misleading. One can point to a prosperous Italy, with a leading industrial economy, where one in four families has a second home. At the same time, one can point to massive poverty and unemployment.

Even with its problems, however, most observers are impressed with Italy's potential for the future. Although it produces only 80 percent of its needed food supply, about a fourth of its farmland is not fully utilized and some mineral resources in central Italy have yet to be developed. In addition, the country has proven to be a success at attracting tourists and exporting a variety of manufactured goods since Italian style, design, and skills are highly valued.

Section 2 Review

Locating Key Places
Locate the following places on the map on page 328: Aegean Sea, Athens, Sicily

Identifying Key Terms
Define the following term: coalition government

Reviewing Main Ideas
1. How has Greece's location affected its economic and cultural development?
2. Describe the diverse elements of Italy's economy.

Thinking Critically: Assess Cause and Effect
Use an almanac or encyclopedia to find the GNP and per capita income for Greece and Italy. Is there much difference? If so, make two headings on a sheet of paper marked "Greece" and "Italy." List some of the differences in resources and economic development that could account for the difference.

Understanding Map Bias

How might a map-maker's opinions or background influence the maps he or she draws? In reality, all maps have some bias or mental slant because of the mapmaker.

For example, note that most maps in our society are drawn with north at the top. In earlier times, however, maps were often made with east at the top because that is the direction in which the sun rises. Other mapmakers placed the direction of the prevailing winds at the top of their maps.

In fact, there is no absolutely correct way to draw a map. Thus, although the map below looks upside down to us, it is just as "correct" as the image to which we are accustomed. Such "incorrect" maps force us to look at things in new ways. Sometimes they may even help us to perceive new relationships and connections.

The Roman map below is a modern reconstruction of an ancient map thought to be drawn for Emperor Augustus about 2,000 years ago. Augustus wanted a large map of the world on display in the Forum at Rome.

In the days of Ancient Rome, people would gather around the huge map and use it to discuss contemporary affairs. Students would use it to draw their own simplified maps of the world. This map represented how the Romans viewed the world in their time.

Review

Use the Roman map to answer the following questions.
1. Which sea is placed in the middle of the world?
2. How many continents are shown on the map? Name them.
3. Which direction is at the top of the map?
4. The Mare Caspium (Caspian Sea) was once thought by the Romans to be connected to the ocean. Use the map on page 622 to determine whether or not the Romans were correct.

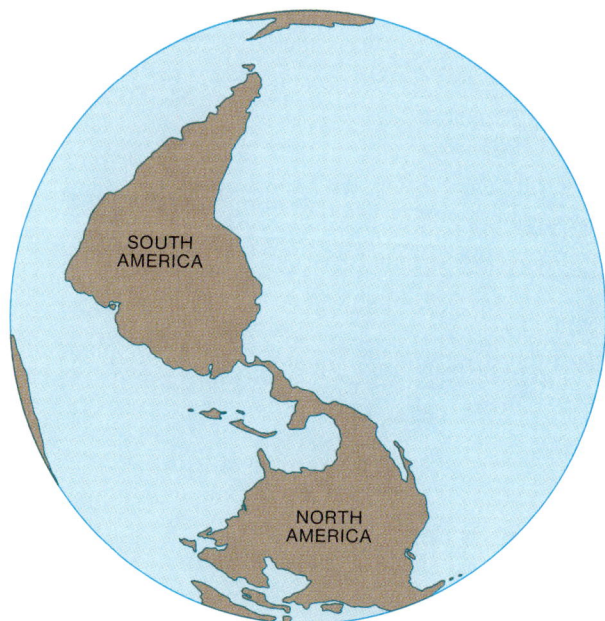

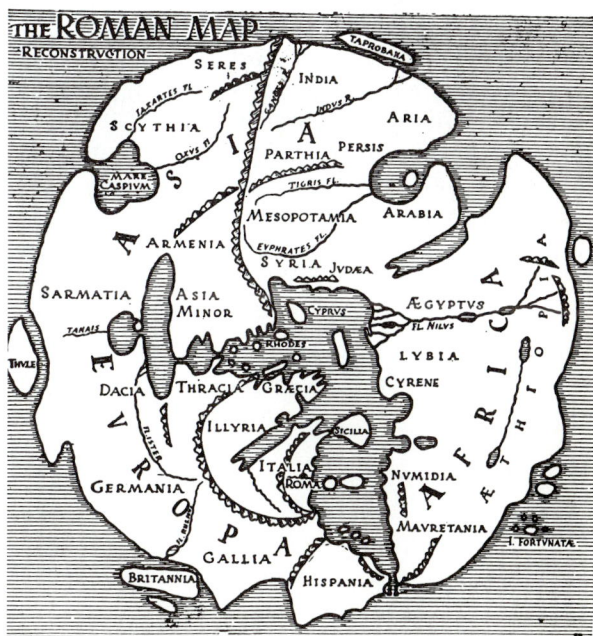

THE ROMAN MAP
RECONSTRUCTION

Review

Section Summaries

1. Spain and Portugal
The Mediterranean states share an imperial past and ties with the Mediterranean Sea. The Iberian Peninsula, with Spain, Portugal, and Andorra, makes up the western part of Mediterranean Europe. Spain is dominated by the Meseta plateau. It has been working on modernizing its economy. The rivers which flow out of Spain's Meseta form the rich valleys of Portugal, a developing republic with ties both to the Mediterranean and the Atlantic.

2. Greece and Italy
Greece and Italy are peninsular countries that jut into the Mediterranean Sea. Ancient Greek and Roman civilizations have made significant contributions to philosophy, science, politics, and the arts. Today, as in the past, the economy and culture of Greece is oriented towards its location on the sea. Its neighbor, Italy, has a diverse economy and three distinct regions.

Using Geography Skills

Reviewing the Map Lesson
The map below presents a view of the world held by Macrobius, a Roman philosopher who lived about 400 years after Emperor Augustus. He believed that another landmass, the Antipodes, balanced the known world. Use the map to answer the following questions.

1. What separated the Antipodean lands from the known world?

2. Which direction is at the top of the map?

3. What is the term used on the map to describe the cold lands near the poles?

Using Social Studies Skills

1. Organize and Express Ideas in Written Form. Choose one of the Mediterranean countries discussed in this chapter. Pick out several facts from the text that you feel are most important in describing that country. Organize those facts, and any others that you may find in other reference sources, into a clear and well-written paragraph that summarizes your country.

2. Perceive cause-effect relationships. In Athens, many of the great ancient Greek monuments are deteriorating. The buildings of the Acropolis, perhaps Greece's finest architectural treasure, are almost literally crumbling, although similar monuments in other areas are in much better condition. What do you think could be causing the damage to the Acropolis?

Testing for Understanding

Locating Key Places

1. body of water between Greece and Turkey where many islands are located

2. capital of Spain
3. Italian island just off the "toe" of the peninsula
4. capital of Greece
5. body of water along the northwestern coast of Spain
6. capital of Portugal
a. Bay of Biscay
b. Madrid
c. Lisbon
d. Aegean Sea
e. Athens
f. Sicily

Recalling Key Terms

Define these terms in your own words.

Section 1
republic

Section 2
coalition government

Reviewing Main Ideas
Section 1
1. Name some of the ties shared by the Mediterranean European countries.
2. How has the economy of Spain changed in recent years?
3. How has Portugal's location affected its ties with other parts of the world?

Section 2
1. How has the sea influenced Greece's economy and culture?
2. Why does Italy's economy vary throughout the country?

Thinking Critically

1. Evaluate Sources of Information. In this chapter's map lesson, you learned about bias on maps, which may distort the contents of maps. How might you verify, or check the facts of, the contents of a particular map?

2. Make Decisions. As you read in Section 1, the Spanish economy is heavily involved in tourism. Imagine that you live on the island of Mallorca, a quiet, lovely land of hills and beaches. Palma is the only city on the island, which is otherwise dotted with villages. A large hotel chain is seeking permission to build a resort on the Bay of Alcudia, near your village. You are on the town council. How will you vote? Explain the reasons for your choice.

UNIT 5

Review

Summarizing the Unit

Chapter 12 A Physical and Cultural Overview Western Europe may be regarded as a large peninsula with smaller peninsulas and islands. The countries have utilized rivers and seas for the spread of culture and commerce. The climates of Western Europe are generally mild, with temperatures decreasing as one moves northward or into the highlands. Many of the people of Western Europe share a common cultural heritage drawn from the ancient Greek and Roman civilizations.

Chapter 13 The British Isles and Northern Europe This northern region of islands and peninsulas has many political divisions. The United Kingdom includes Britain, Scotland, Wales, and Northern Ireland. The Republic of Ireland stands alone in the British Isles. In Northern Europe there are five countries—Sweden, Norway, Finland, Denmark, and Iceland. The countries of the British Isles and Northern Europe are generally industrialized and urban.

Chapter 14 Continental Europe The seven countries of this region occupy the central land area of Western Europe. France, West Germany, Belgium, the Netherlands, Luxembourg, Switzerland, and Austria all have related languages and cultures. They also have urban populations, industrialized economies, and diverse agricultural products.

Chapter 15 Mediterranean Europe Spain, Portugal, Greece, and Italy are the major countries of Mediterranean Europe. They lie on peninsulas along the southern edge of Western Europe and share the many benefits of their coastal location. Each country has enjoyed a rich cultural and political past. The strength of the area's economy today, however, varies from country to country, and often from region to region.

Using Writing Skills

This unit opened with an excerpt from a famous essay by John Donne that stated about Western Europe: "No man is an island, entire of itself" (See page 269.) What does this mean to Western Europe, a geographic realm that is made up of many islands and remote peninsulas?

Think about this question, and select an island of Western Europe in which you have some interest. Some possibilities include Ireland, Iceland, Mallorca, Corsica, Sicily, or one of the many Greek islands.

Activity. Research the particular island that you have chosen. Find out about its physical landscape, people, and economy. Do your research to answer this question: Is this island "entire of itself" or does it depend upon, or connect with, a larger country or government on a regular basis?

Once you've completed your research, write an essay explaining your answer to the question given. Describe how this island either maintains relationships with other peoples or survives by itself.

In writing remember first to state a clear topic sentence. Then, support that statement with interesting facts and details that relate to one another in a logical way. Finally, check your essay for spelling or grammatical errors.

Test

Key Terms (30 points)

Fill in the blank with the correct term listed below.

1. An _____ is a broad mouth of a river into which the tide flows.

2. _____ make up much of the farmland in the Netherlands.

3. Western Europe has many landmasses that jut into the sea, called _____.

4. An elected president usually heads a _____.

5. Paris, as a _____, best expresses France's culture.

6. _____ is the feeling of pride and loyalty often held by those who share a common language, culture, and history.

a. peninsula
b. nationalism
c. estuary
d. primate city
e. polder
f. republic

Main Ideas (30 points)

Select the best answer.

1. How has its nearness to the sea affected Western Europe?
a. stimulated overseas travel
b. encouraged commercial trade
c. moderated climate
d. all of the above

2. What climate type dominates Western Europe?
a. Mediterranean
b. marine west coast
c. polar
d. all of the above

3. For what policies are Scandinavian governments known?
a. capitalism
b. social welfare
c. communism
d. lack of taxation

4. What country surrounds West Berlin?
a. West Germany
b. Poland
c. East Germany
d. France

5. Which country is known for its policy of neutrality?
a. Switzerland
b. Luxembourg
c. Belgium
d. the Netherlands

6. What two seas border Greece?
a. Black and Mediterranean
b. Black and Aegean
c. Mediterranean and Aegean
d. Mediterranean and Adriatic

Thinking Critically (20 points)

1. Assess Cause and Effect. Why do you think many similarities exist between Western Europe and the United States?

2. Recognize Values. What values do you think have held Western Europe together, despite its varying landscapes, languages, and customs?

Place Location (20 points)

Match the places listed with the letters printed on the map.

1. England   **3.** Munich
2. Paris   **4.** Madrid
                   5. Athens

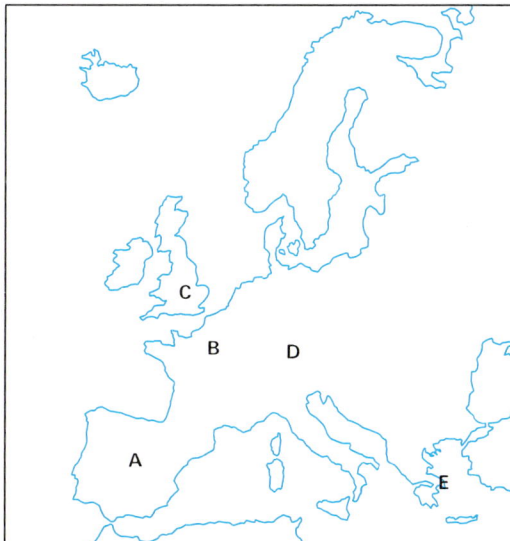

The Soviet Union and Eastern Europe

In this unit you will study nine communist countries.

341

A Physical and Cultural Overview

In this chapter you will read about the land and peoples of the Soviet Union and Eastern Europe.

Sections

1 Landscapes of Two Continents

2 Climate, Soils, and Vegetation

3 Historical Foundations

Landscapes of Two Continents

Preview

Key Places
Where are these places located?
1 Ural Mountains
2 Caucasus Mountains
3 Caspian Sea
See the globe below.

Key Terms
What does this term mean?
permafrost

Main Ideas
As you read, look for answers to these questions.
• What major mountain ranges run through the Soviet Union?
• How do the Ural Mountains divide the Great Plain?
• What major rivers flow through the Soviet Union and Eastern Europe?

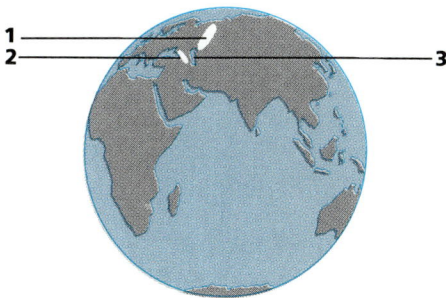

The meaning of geography in a Russian's life is most vivid in the wilderness of Siberia, so remote and deeply isolated from urban existence that its simple villages are still considered fitting punishments for common criminals and political dissidents. But their gold mines and oil fields also exert a magic pull on the frontier spirit profoundly embedded in Russian history.

David K. Shipler, *Russia*

This realm has several major mountain ranges.

If you were an ambitious peasant in Russia during the past 200 years, a tremendous frontier was open to you across the mountains. You could travel to the east, across the Ural Mountains into the part of the Soviet Union called Siberia. Siberia covers all of North Asia. Some of the frontier settlers who conquered Siberia went willingly, others were forced to go, as Shipler points out, because of criminal activity or political ideas that differed from those of the government.

Siberia is the largest region in the geographic realm of the Soviet Union and Eastern Europe. This realm includes East Germany, Poland, Czechoslovakia, Hungary, Yugoslavia, Albania, Romania, Bulgaria, and the Soviet Union. The first eight of these countries are in Eastern Europe. The last one, the Soviet Union, covers most of Eastern Europe and all of North Asia.

The realm of the Soviet Union and Eastern Europe is bordered by oceans on two sides. To the north is the Arctic Ocean. To the east is the Pacific Ocean. The other two sides of the realm are bounded by land. To the west is Western Europe. To the south is the rest of Asia.

Facing page: **Pink oleander flowers bloom on a hillside overlooking coastal Dubrovnik, Yugoslavia.** *Page 340:* **A shepherd watches over his flock on an icy stretch of Siberia.**

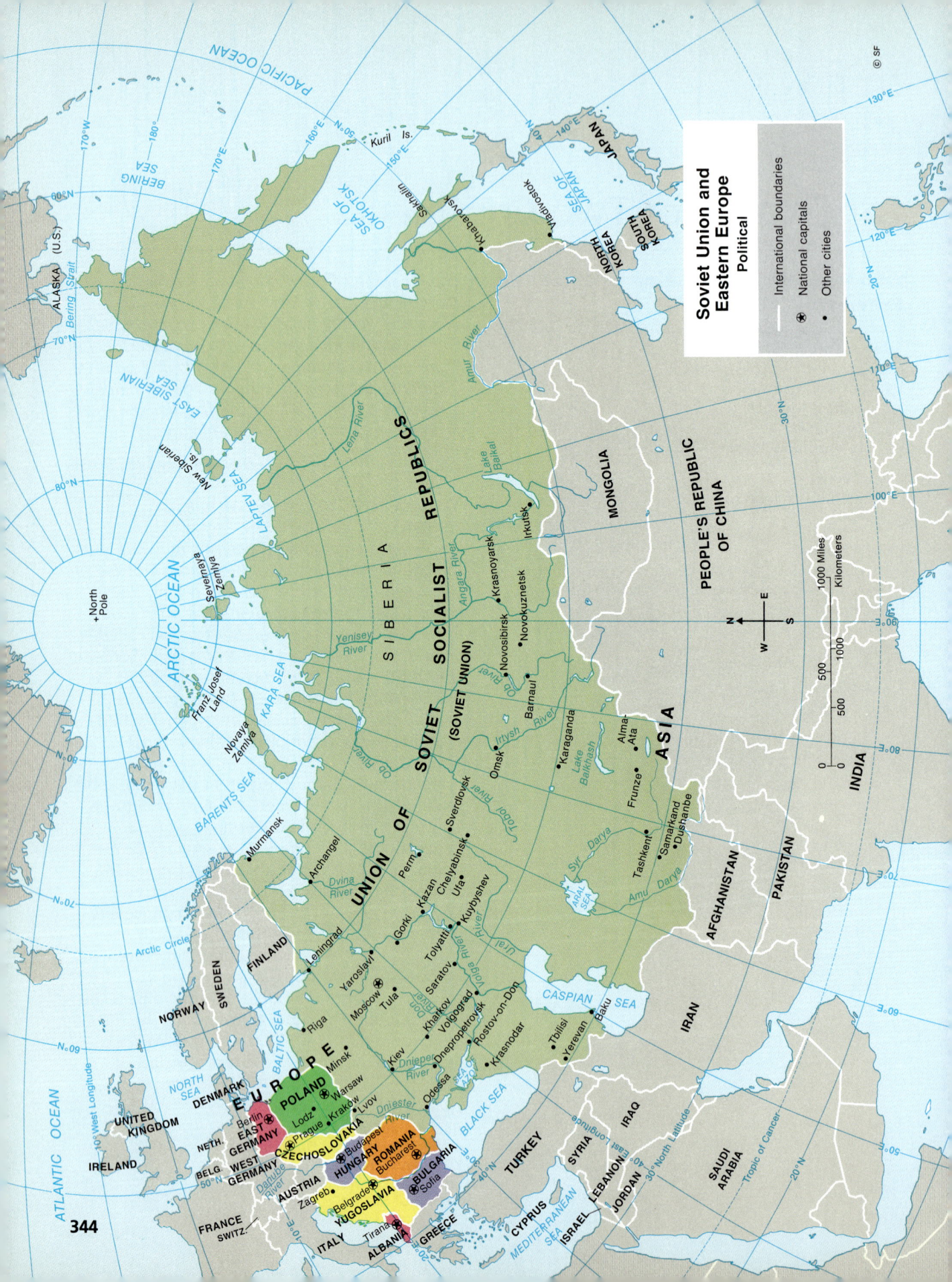

Soviet Union and Eastern Europe
Political

International boundaries
⊛ National capitals
• Other cities

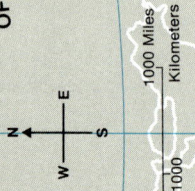

PACIFIC OCEAN

BERING SEA

SEA OF OKHOTSK

Kuril Is.

Sakhalin

JAPAN

SEA OF JAPAN

Vladivostok

Khabarovsk

NORTH KOREA

SOUTH KOREA

ALASKA (U.S.)

Bering Strait

EAST SIBERIAN SEA

New Siberian Is.

LAPTEV SEA

ARCTIC OCEAN

North Pole

Franz Josef Land

Novaya Zemlya

Severnaya Zemlya

KARA SEA

BARENTS SEA

SIBERIA

UNION OF SOVIET SOCIALIST REPUBLICS
(SOVIET UNION)

Lena River

Lake Baikal

Irkutsk

Krasnoyarsk

Angara River

Novokuznetsk

Novosibirsk

Yenisey River

Ob River

Barnaul

Irtysh River

Omsk

Karaganda

Alma-Ata

Lake Balkhash

Frunze

Tobol River

Sverdlovsk

Samarkand

Dushanbe

Tashkent

Syr Darya

ARAL SEA

Amu Darya

Ural River

Perm

Kazan

Gorki

Chelyabinsk

Ufa

Kuybyshev

Tolyatti

Saratov

Murmansk

Archangel

Dvina River

Leningrad

Yaroslavl

Moscow ⊛

Tula

Volga River

Don River

Kharkov

Volgograd

Rostov-on-Don

Krasnodar

Tbilisi

Yerevan

Baku

CASPIAN SEA

Riga

Minsk

Kiev

Dnieper River

Dnepropetrovsk

Odessa

Dniester River

BLACK SEA

Danube River

MONGOLIA

PEOPLE'S REPUBLIC OF CHINA

ASIA

AFGHANISTAN

PAKISTAN

INDIA

IRAN

IRAQ

TURKEY

SYRIA

LEBANON

ISRAEL

JORDAN

SAUDI ARABIA

Tropic of Cancer

CYPRUS

MEDITERRANEAN SEA

GREECE

FINLAND

SWEDEN

NORWAY

DENMARK

BALTIC SEA

NORTH SEA

EUROPE

POLAND

Warsaw ⊛

Lodz

Kraków

Lvov

Berlin ⊛

EAST GERMANY

WEST GERMANY

NETH.

BELG.

UNITED KINGDOM

IRELAND

ATLANTIC OCEAN

Prague ⊛

CZECHOSLOVAKIA

AUSTRIA

FRANCE

SWITZ.

ITALY

HUNGARY

Budapest ⊛

ROMANIA

Bucharest ⊛

YUGOSLAVIA

Zagreb

Belgrade ⊛

BULGARIA

Sofia ⊛

ALBANIA

Tirana ⊛

Danube

Arctic Circle

North Latitude

West Longitude

East Longitude

N E S W

1000 Miles

Kilometers

500

1000

500

0

0

344

Along the southwestern edge of the Soviet Union, near the Black Sea, are the Caucasus [kô′kə səs] Mountains. They form one of the boundaries between Europe and Asia. Farther east, the Soviet Union and China are separated by the Tien Shan [tyen′ shän′], Altai [al′tī], and Sayan mountains, and the Yablonovy Range. In the far east, the Verkhoyansk Range and other mountains rise up near the Pacific Ocean. See the map on page 346.

The Ural [yur′əl] Mountains are the major feature that divides Europe from Asia. They are located at about 60° E and run north and south for some 1,600 miles. This geographic boundary is artificial, however. Europe and Asia can also be considered one giant continent called Eurasia.

The Urals divide the Great Plain into three large regions.

North of the Urals is the Arctic Ocean. West, south, and east of the Urals are three flat regions. Together they are called the Great Plain.

West of the Urals. This region is the most densely populated of the three. Moscow—the largest city in the Soviet Union and in all of Eastern Europe—is located here. Moscow is the Soviet capital.

Most of the western region is a flat area called the North European Plain. It extends through much of the Soviet Union, Poland, and East Germany and continues westward all the way to the Atlantic coast of France.

In the Soviet Union, the North European Plain extends as far south as the Black Sea. Here it is warm and sunny. The Soviet coast of the Black Sea is covered by palm trees, fruit groves, and tourists bathing in the sun.

Map Study

🌐 **What are the eight countries of Eastern Europe?**

Sunbathers relax on the Soviet Union's warm Black Sea coast.

Bordering the North European Plain on the south are the Carpathian [kär pā′thē ən] Mountains. They run through Czechoslovakia, a small part of the Soviet Union, and Romania. South of Czechoslovakia is Hungary—a country of plains that is almost entirely surrounded by mountains. See the map on page 344. The southern part of Eastern Europe is the mountainous Balkan Peninsula.

South of the Urals. The region south of the Urals is the Central Asian Steppe. Like Wyoming or Montana in the United States, this region is "big sky country." With few trees, towns, or mountains, you can see for miles in any direction. The Central Asian Steppe, again like the western United States, was once famous for its talented horse riders.

East of the Urals. The region east of the Urals is Siberia, known for its icy winters and its tremendous size. The region is so large that it covers nine time zones. As people in eastern Siberia are going to bed, people in Moscow are just finishing lunch. The Trans-Siberian Railway,

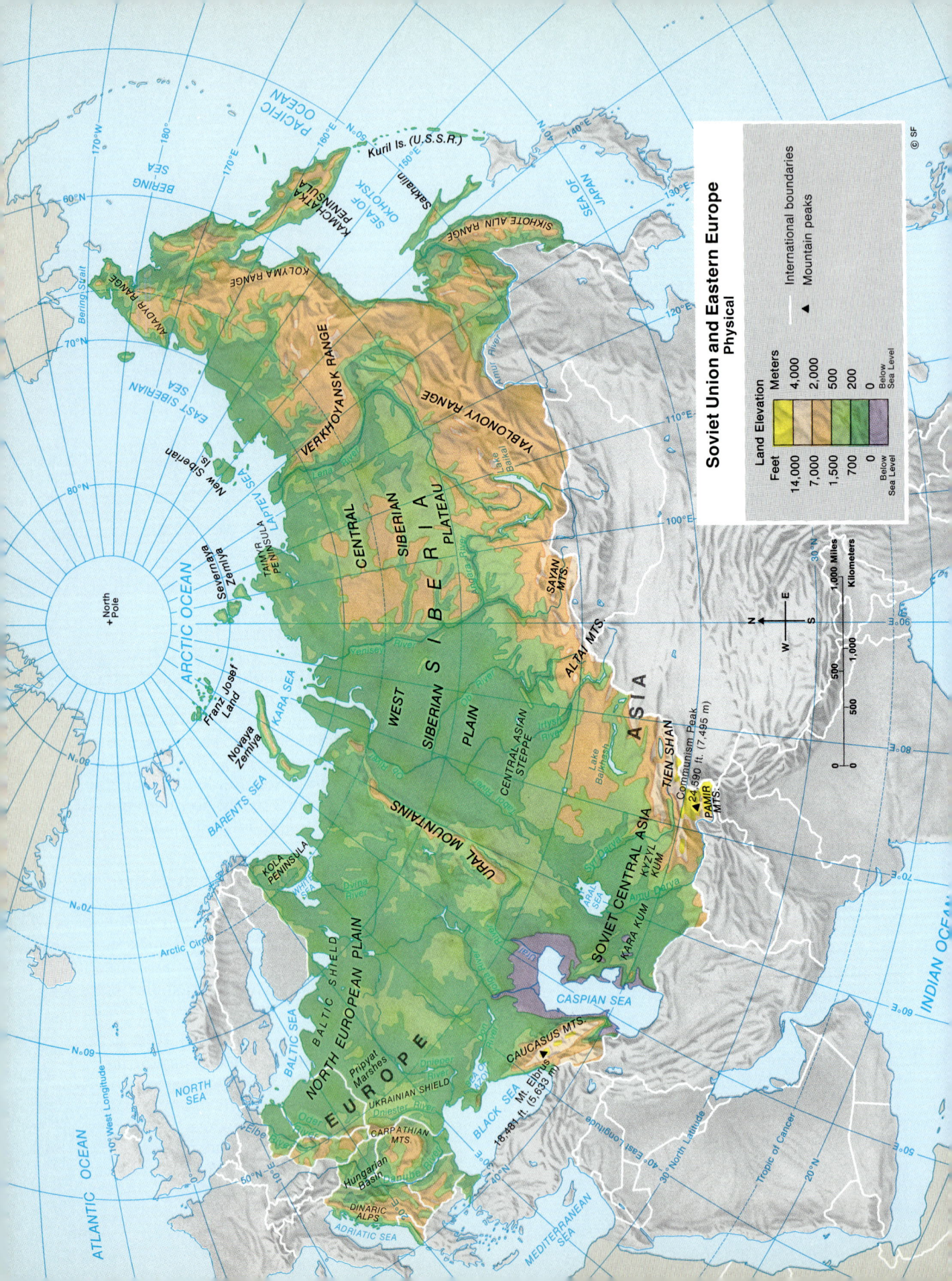

Soviet Union and Eastern Europe
Physical

© SF

Land Elevation

Feet	Meters
14,000	4,000
7,000	2,000
1,500	500
700	200
0	0
Below Sea Level	Below Sea Level

International boundaries

▲ Mountain peaks

0   500   1,000 Kilometers
0   500   1,000 Miles

N
W — E
S

PACIFIC OCEAN

Kuril Is. (U.S.S.R.)

BERING SEA

SEA OF OKHOTSK

Sakhalin

SEA OF JAPAN

KAMCHATKA PENINSULA

ANADYR RANGE

KOLYMA RANGE

SIKHOTE ALIN RANGE

Amur River

VERKHOYANSK RANGE

YABLONOVY RANGE

Bering Strait

New Siberian Is.

Lena River

Lake Baikal

CENTRAL SIBERIAN PLATEAU

S I B E R I A

TAIMYR PENINSULA

Severnaya Zemlya

LAPTEV SEA

EAST SIBERIAN SEA

ARCTIC OCEAN

North Pole

SAYAN MTS.

ALTAI MTS.

A S I A

Franz Josef Land

KARA SEA

Novaya Zemlya

WEST SIBERIAN PLAIN

Yenisey River

Ob River

Irtysh River

CENTRAL ASIAN STEPPE

Lake Balkhash

TIEN SHAN

Communism Peak 24,590 ft. (7,495 m) ▲

PAMIR MTS.

BARENTS SEA

KOLA PENINSULA

URAL MOUNTAINS

SOVIET CENTRAL ASIA

KYZYL KUM

KARA KUM

Amu Darya

Syr Darya

ARAL SEA

WHITE SEA

Dvina River

BALTIC SHIELD

BALTIC SEA

NORTH EUROPEAN PLAIN

Volga River

Don River

CASPIAN SEA

CAUCASUS MTS.

Mt. Elbrus 18,481 ft. (5,633 m) ▲

BLACK SEA

NORTH SEA

Pripyat Marshes

UKRAINIAN SHIELD

Dnieper River

Dniester River

E U R O P E

Oder River

Elbe River

Vistula River

Danube River

CARPATHIAN MTS.

Hungarian Basin

DINARIC ALPS

ADRIATIC SEA

MEDITERRANEAN SEA

INDIAN OCEAN

ATLANTIC OCEAN

Arctic Circle

Tropic of Cancer

North Latitude

West Longitude

East Longitude

which connects Moscow and the Siberian city of Vladivostok [vlad′ə vos′tok], is 5,700 miles long—about twice the distance across the United States.

Siberia is a varied region. The West Siberian Plain is flat and marshy. Farther east, the Central Siberian Plateau is a slightly elevated tableland area. Eastern Siberia is mountainous, with a jumble of ranges crisscrossing each other. On the tip of the Siberian coast is the Kamchatka [kam chat′kə] Peninsula, a part of the Pacific Ring of Fire. Thus there are many active volcanoes—a land of fire and ice.

Eight key rivers flow within the Soviet Union and Eastern Europe.

Four important rivers—the Danube [dan′yüb], the Volga [vol′gə], the Dnieper [nē′pər], and the Don—are west of the Urals. Four others—the Ob [ōb], the Amur [ä mur′], the Yenisey [yen′ə sā′], and the Lena [le′nə]—are in Siberia. Find these rivers on the map on page 346.

The Danube begins in West Germany and flows east and south into the Black Sea. Great European cities sit all along or near this river and its tributaries. Five of these cities are capitals—Budapest, Hungary; Belgrade, Yugoslavia; Sofia, Bulgaria; Bucharest, Romania; and Vienna, Austria.

The Volga, the longest river in Europe, is 2,200 miles from its headwaters to its mouth. The river flows entirely within the Soviet Union. It starts northwest of Moscow and flows east and south until it reaches the Caspian Sea.

The Ob and its tributaries drain the Western Siberian Plain. Since the area is fairly flat, the water moves slowly. Furthermore, the Ob, like most Siberian rivers, flows into the Arctic Ocean. The mouth of the Ob is clogged by ice more than 200 days each year. Like a clogged drain on a bathtub, the ice slows down the flow of the water. The slowness of the Ob causes the West Siberian Plain to be marshy. In the northern part of the plain, water remains frozen in the soil, forming **permafrost,** which is a layer of permanently frozen subsoil.

The Amur is the only major Siberian river to flow into the Pacific Ocean. The mouth of the Amur is so far north that ice blocks it much of the year. As a result, the Soviet Union has developed Vladivostok, far to the south, as its major port on the Pacific Ocean.

Section 1 Review

Locating Key Places
Locate the following places on the map on page 346: Ural Mountains, Caucasus Mountains, Caspian Sea

Identifying Key Terms
Define the following term: permafrost

Reviewing Main Ideas
1. What are the major mountain ranges of the Soviet Union and Eastern Europe?
2. Into what three large regions do the Urals separate Eastern Europe and the Soviet Union?
3. Name two major rivers in Eastern Europe and two in the Soviet Union.

Thinking Critically: Analyze Comparisons
This section compares several features of the Soviet Union and Eastern Europe with features of the United States. Use the maps on pages 125 and 346 to compare these rivers in the Soviet Union—Volga and Amur—with these in the United States—Mississippi and Columbia.

Map Study

What mountains extend along 60° E longitude dividing the Soviet Union?

Climate, Soils, and Vegetation

Preview

Key Places

Where are these places located?

1 Murmansk
2 Kara Kum
3 Pripyat Marshes
  See the globe below.

Key Terms

What do these terms mean?

taiga
peat
chernozem

Main Ideas

As you read, look for answers to these questions.

- Which region of the Soviet Union is dominated by polar climates?
- Where are the Soviet Union and Eastern Europe's continental regions located?
- Where are the Soviet Union's dry climate regions located?
- Where are the realm's mild climate regions located?

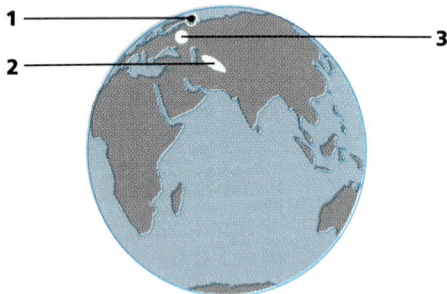

High winter came with its severe frosts. Torn, seemingly disconnected sounds and shapes rose out of the icy mist, stood still, moved, and vanished. The sun was not the sun to which the earth was used, it was a changeling. Its crimson ball hung in the forest and from it, stiffly and slowly as in a dream or in a fairy tale, amber-yellow rays of light as thick as honey spread and, catching in the trees, froze to them in midair.

Boris Pasternak, *Doctor Zhivago*

Polar climates dominate the northern edge of the Soviet Union.

An important Russian novelist, Boris Pasternak, penned these words about the frigid Soviet winter. Spring comes very late, if at all, in the tundra region. When it does, it blossoms briefly with tiny flowers of low moss and lichen [lī′kən]. The tundra runs along the Arctic Ocean across the northern Soviet Union. In this region, the average temperature may be below 0°F for five to six months each year. For only a few months does the temperature rise above freezing.

Only one port located far above the Arctic Circle is ice-free all year. The warm Gulf Stream current from the Atlantic Ocean keeps Murmansk from freezing. Because year-round ports are rare in the Soviet Union, Murmansk is an important trade and naval center.

Not far below the surface in the tundra region is permafrost. Permafrost prevents the land from supporting plants with extensive root systems.

Continental climate regions cover most of the realm.

Most of the Soviet Union and the eastern part of Eastern Europe have a continental climate. These areas have marked differences between summer and winter.

Subarctic. In the western Soviet Union, the subarctic region is very narrow. Moving eastward into Siberia, the influence of the Atlantic Ocean decreases, and the subarctic region spreads. Most of Siberia has bitterly cold winters. Summers can be hot, but they are always short.

Most of the subarctic region receives less than 20 inches of precipitation per year. However, the short summers and cold winters mean that water on the land evaporates slowly. The land is usually moist, like a sponge in a refrigerator.

Most of the subarctic region is covered by an immense forest, the **taiga** [tī′gə]. The pine, spruce, and larch trees of the taiga give shelter to fox, ermine, bear, sable, and other fur-bearing animals.

Soviet children bundle up in the cold subarctic winter.

In some subarctic areas, the organic matter in the soil decomposes so slowly that it forms peat rather than humus. **Peat** is densely packed organic matter that remains too moist to decompose. It is filled with twigs and grasses. In some areas peat is burned in electrical power-generating plants. The Soviet Union has 60 percent of the world's peat resources.

Humid continental, cool summer. South and west of the subarctic region, the warmth of the sun begins to moderate temperatures. Summers become long enough for crops to mature, and there is enough rainfall for farming. This humid continental, cool summer climate zone includes the western part of the Soviet Union and most of the North European Plain.

Humid continental, warm summer. The southwestern corner of the Soviet Union and the eastern part of the Balkan Peninsula have a humid continental, warm summer climate. This region includes most of Romania and Bulgaria. In the broad plains of this region, farmers grow wheat, corn, and some fruit crops. Northeastern Poland and part of the Soviet Union are covered by the Pripyat Marshes. Lack of good drainage makes this low land poor for farming.

The southern part of the Soviet Union is dry.

South of the continental climate region of the Soviet Union and Eastern Europe are drier climates. Forest gradually gives way to grassland, which in turn gives way to desert.

Steppe. The Central Asian Steppe stretches from the Black Sea almost to the Pacific Ocean. The climate of this region has long, hot summers. However, winters can be very cold.

The black grassland soil, called **chernozem**, is rich in humus. It is among the most fertile soils

349

in the world. About 12 percent of the Soviet Union is covered with these productive soils. In some areas the chernozem is 20 to 40 inches deep.

The warm summers and fertile lands are suitable for growing many crops. However, rainfall is undependable, and drought is a constant threat. Usually enough rain falls to support wheat and cotton crops. With irrigation, farmers can grow fruit and vegetables.

Desert. North and east of the Caspian Sea is a desert climate region. East of the sea is the Kara Kum, a desert whose name means "Black Sands." Northeast of that desert is the Kyzyl Kum, or "Red Sands."

Water is the key to farming in the desert. Most desert areas have little soil, for there is little humus from which soils can be developed. Even in oasis areas, where alluvial soils have formed, the ground tends to be salty. Evaporation of the water near the surface pulls up water from farther down in the soil. Like a wick, as moisture leaves one end, more moisture is drawn from the other end to replace it. As the water evaporates, it leaves behind the salts that were dissolved in it. With irrigation, however, some desert soils can be very productive.

Mild climates dominate Eastern Europe.

Eastern Europe has much milder climates than the Soviet Union. These countries are more like those farther west in Western Europe. Refer to the climate map on page 350.

Marine west coast. Although East Germany, Poland, Czechoslovakia, and Hungary are not on the Atlantic Ocean, they share the same marine west coast climate as Britain, France, and West Germany. Moist winds blowing in from the Atlantic give this region moderate temperatures and abundant rainfall throughout the year.

Most of the area is naturally forested land.

Map Study

What climates cover most of Eastern Europe? The Soviet Union?

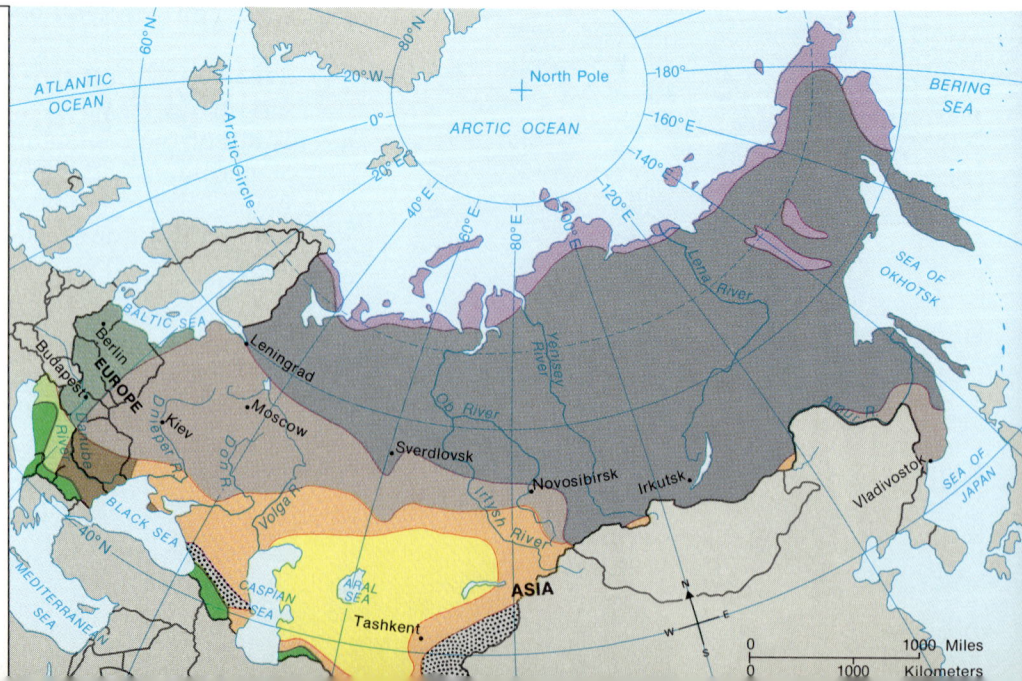

Soviet Union and Eastern Europe: Climate Regions

Dry climates
- Steppe
- Desert

Mild climates
- Marine west coast
- Humid subtropical
- Mediterranean

Continental climates
- Humid continental, warm summer
- Humid continental, cool summer
- Subarctic

Polar climates
- Tundra

High altitudes
- Highlands

However, over the centuries, people have cleared the land, and farmers grow potatoes, sugar beets, rye, and oats.

Humid subtropical. Farther south, in the Balkan Peninsula, the climate is both warm and moist. Eastern Yugoslavia and western Bulgaria have a humid subtropical climate. Corn and wheat are the chief crops, but fruit trees and grapes are grown on hillsides.

Mediterranean. Coastal areas in Yugoslavia and Albania have a Mediterranean climate. Summers are hot and dry. Winters are mild and moist. The pleasant weather makes this region popular for vacations. Two small Mediterranean climate regions on the Black Sea are especially prized in the Soviet Union. The soil and landscape of these regions are not often suitable for most grain crops, but grapes, olives, and citrus fruits do well.

Map Study

What types of natural vegetation grow in the realm's coldest areas?

Section 2 Review

Locating Key Places
Locate the following places on the map on page 344 or 346: Murmansk, Kara Kum, Pripyat Marshes

Identifying Key Terms
Define the following terms: taiga, peat, chernozem

Reviewing Main Ideas
1. Where are the polar climate regions of the Soviet Union?
2. Where are the continental climate regions of the Soviet Union and Eastern Europe?
3. Where are the dry climate regions of the realm?
4. Where are the mild climate regions of Eastern Europe?

Thinking Critically: Predict Effects
In this section and the previous section you read about the physical geography of the Soviet Union. What effects do you think these geographic features had on the people and development of the country?

Soviet Union and Eastern Europe: Natural Vegetation Regions

- Broadleaf forest—deciduous
- Needleleaf forest
- Mixed forest (broadleaf and needleleaf)
- Grassland
- Desert—little or no vegetation
- Desert—scrub with grassy patches
- Tundra
- High mountains (vegetation varies with elevation)

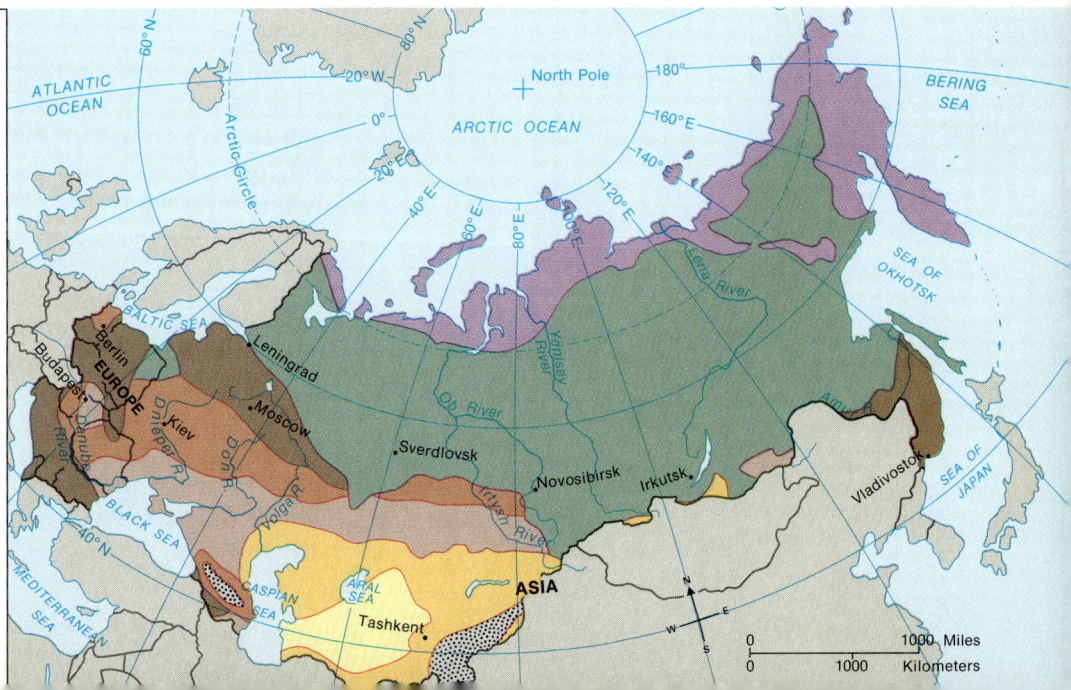

SECTION 3

Historical Foundations

Preview

Key Places
Where is this place located?

1 Moscow

Key Terms
What do these terms mean?

atheism

serf

satellite

cold war

Main Ideas
As you read, look for answers to these questions.

- When was the ethnic pattern of the Soviet Union and Eastern Europe set?
- How was the religious pattern of this geographic realm established?
- Why is the Soviet Union dominated by Russians?
- How has the political map of the Soviet Union and Eastern Europe changed since 1914?

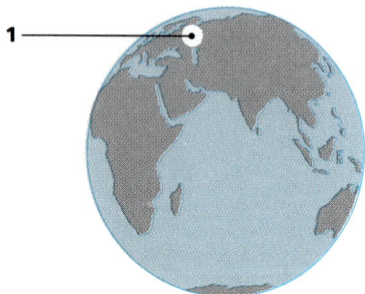

8. The Possessions of the Russian Empire extend upon the terrestrial Globe to 32 Degrees of Latitude, and to 165 of Longitude.

9. The Sovereign is absolute; for there is no other Authority but that which centers in his single Person, that can act with a Vigour proportionate to the Extent of such a vast Dominion.

Catherine the Great, *Instructions*

The ethnic pattern of this realm was set by 1600.

In 1767 the Russian ruler Catherine II wrote 655 guidelines, including these two, for a new set of laws. Her harsh command brought people of many different ethnic and political backgrounds together in one huge empire.

Long before Catherine's rule, the lands that now are part of the Soviet Union and Eastern Europe were sparsely populated. Most people lived by hunting, fishing, farming, or herding cattle.

Later, in A.D. 106 the Roman army conquered an area west of the Black Sea. The Roman soldiers who stayed in the area intermingled with the people there, forming the Romanian people.

The Slavs lived north of the Roman Empire. They farmed and hunted in the Danube River Basin and Carpathian Mountains. Between A.D. 400 and 900, the Slavs became the most widespread ethnic group in the realm. Most of the major languages spoken here are Slavic.

Groups of Slavs migrated west, south, and east from their homeland. The western Slavs were the ancestors of today's Poles, Czechs, and Slovaks. These people gave their names to two modern countries—Poland and Czechoslovakia.

The southern Slavs became the Serbs, the Croats, the Slovenes, and others who live in what is now Yugoslavia. "Yugo" is the Slavic word for southern. The eastern Slavs became the Russians, Byelorussians, and Ukrainians.

352

These three groups live in regions that are now part of the Soviet Union.

Two other important ethnic groups came from Central Asia. In the A.D. 600s, the Bulgars, a Turkic people, moved into the region west of the Black Sea. The Bulgars adopted the Slavic language of the people they conquered there. In 1908 this area became the country of Bulgaria.

In the A.D. 800s, the Magyars, another Central Asia people, invaded and terrified Europe. In the mid-900s, they settled down on the Hungarian plains. This area, now the country of Hungary, still uses the distinctive language of the Magyars.

Around 850 a Scandinavian people, called the Rus, began exploring the rivers of Eastern Europe. The Rus established a trading empire with Kiev as its capital. Their empire connected the Baltic region with the Black Sea. From those beginnings developed the Russian nation, which is the dominant part of the Soviet Union.

Religious patterns were set by the ruling powers.

Until the year A.D. 900, most of the people in what is now the Soviet Union and Eastern Europe were not Christians. The only exception was in the Balkans. Between 900 and 1100, however, the religious pattern of the realm really took shape. During these 200 years, most rulers in the realm became Christians. By custom the people who lived in an area followed the religion adopted by their ruler.

Christianity. Not all people in the realm adopted the same type of Christianity. Most in the southern and eastern part of Europe became Greek Orthodox Christians. Many people in Greece, Yugoslavia, Romania, Bulgaria, and the Soviet Union remain Orthodox even though their communist governments oppose religion.

Most in the northern and western part of the realm became Roman Catholic. Today the coun-

Orthodox Christians conduct a religious service.

tries of Poland, Czechoslovakia, and Hungary remain mostly Roman Catholic despite an official government policy of **atheism**—a disbelief in the existence of God.

Other religious groups. Three other religious influences entered the realm. One was Protestant Christianity. The Protestant Reformation began in Germany in the 1500s. Soon after, Protestant Christianity became the major religion in East Germany. In addition, many people in Czechoslovakia and Hungary also became Protestants.

A second religious influence was Judaism. Between 1300 and 1500, Jews were expelled from most of Western Europe. Many of these Jews migrated to Eastern Europe, where they formed a large part of the population. Many Jews later migrated to the United States or were killed by the Nazis during World War II. The Soviet Union still has a large Jewish population.

A third religious influence is Islam. The Ottoman Empire controlled the Balkan Peninsula for several centuries. Consequently, the country of Albania and parts of Yugoslavia and Bulgaria are predominantly Muslim today. Islam, along with Buddhism, also influenced Central Asia. Today the Soviet Union includes a large and rapidly growing Muslim population.

The Russian people gained dominance over other groups.

No single empire has ever completely dominated the land that is now the Soviet Union and Eastern Europe. As you've read, the land has always been peopled by many diverse groups.

The first people to come close to dominating the realm were the Mongols. Like the Huns before them, the Mongols were excellent horse riders and fierce warriors from the steppes of Central Asia. Under the leadership of Genghis Khan in the 1200s, the Mongols eventually united much of Eurasia into a set of allied empires.

Russian Empire. During the reign of the Mongols in the 1400s, the city of Moscow had become increasingly important. Its placement made it ideal for trade. The city is located on a tributary of the Volga River, which flows south to the Caspian Sea. It is also near the headwaters of the Don and Dnieper rivers, which flow to the Black Sea. In addition, just slightly north of Moscow are the streams flowing north to the Baltic Sea.

Moscow's location and economic power were soon matched by its political power, which continued to spread into the areas settled by Slavs. Between 1462 and 1584, two strong but brutal rulers—Ivan III (Ivan the Great) and his grandson Ivan IV (Ivan the Terrible)—greatly increased both the power and dimensions of the Russian Empire. In addition, Ivan IV proclaimed himself tsar [zär]—meaning caesar or emperor.

After the death of Ivan the Terrible in 1584, Russia's government was unstable and the nation was filled with unrest. This "Time of Troubles" continued until 1613, when a family of nobles named Romanov took control of the empire. For the next 304 years, the Romanovs ruled a growing Russian Empire. This family of rulers demanded unlimited power, claiming that an autocratic leadership would be the only way to hold the large empire together.

The Russian Empire expanded both eastward toward the Pacific Ocean and westward into Europe. The Russian tsars, including Peter the Great, realized that the nation needed a "window on the West"—a seaport from which Russia could trade with Western Europe by water. To gain such a window, each tsar tried to expand the empire, and many encouraged trade and intellectual exchange with Europe.

Throughout this period of expansion, Russia remained an agriculture-based society that was divided sharply into two classes. A few wealthy aristocrats owned most of the land. Almost everyone else was a **serf**—a person legally required to work a piece of land.

Other important empires. In the southern parts of the realm, especially in the Balkan Peninsula, the Ottoman Empire was powerful for many centuries—until the late 1800s. Although it was centered in Turkey, the Ottoman Empire at times extended to lands as far north as Hungary. (See map, page 408.) The Ottomans were Muslims, followers of the religion of Islam. Under their influence, Islam spread into southeastern Europe and made the Balkans different from the rest of Europe.

Another empire, the Austrian Empire, dominated the western edge of the realm until the 1800s. The empire, later known as the Austro-Hungarian Empire, was led by the Roman Catholic Hapsburg family.

The political map of the realm has changed dramatically since 1914.

By 1914 the Russian and the Austro-Hungarian empires controlled most of what is now the Soviet Union and Eastern Europe, except for the northwestern corner. This corner was controlled by the German Empire.

As described in Chapter 12, 1914 brought the beginning of World War I, which ended in 1918 with the establishment of several new Eastern European countries. (See the maps, page 283.)

The Russian Revolution. In 1917, as the war dragged into its third year, domestic unrest in Russia introduced a new element into Russian society. Urban workers in St. Petersburg and elsewhere had been protesting for many years because of poor working conditions and limited opportunities. In 1917, however, the protests turned into a revolution that caused the tsar, Nicholas II, to abdicate, or resign.

A temporary, or provisional government was established, but the country remained in turmoil. In October the Bolsheviks, a radical group of Marxist communists under the leadership of Vladimir Ilyich Lenin, overthrew the provisional government. Under Lenin, Russia withdrew from the war, sacrificing much of its land in the west. Lenin had to battle to control the country, and civil war continued until 1920. During this time,

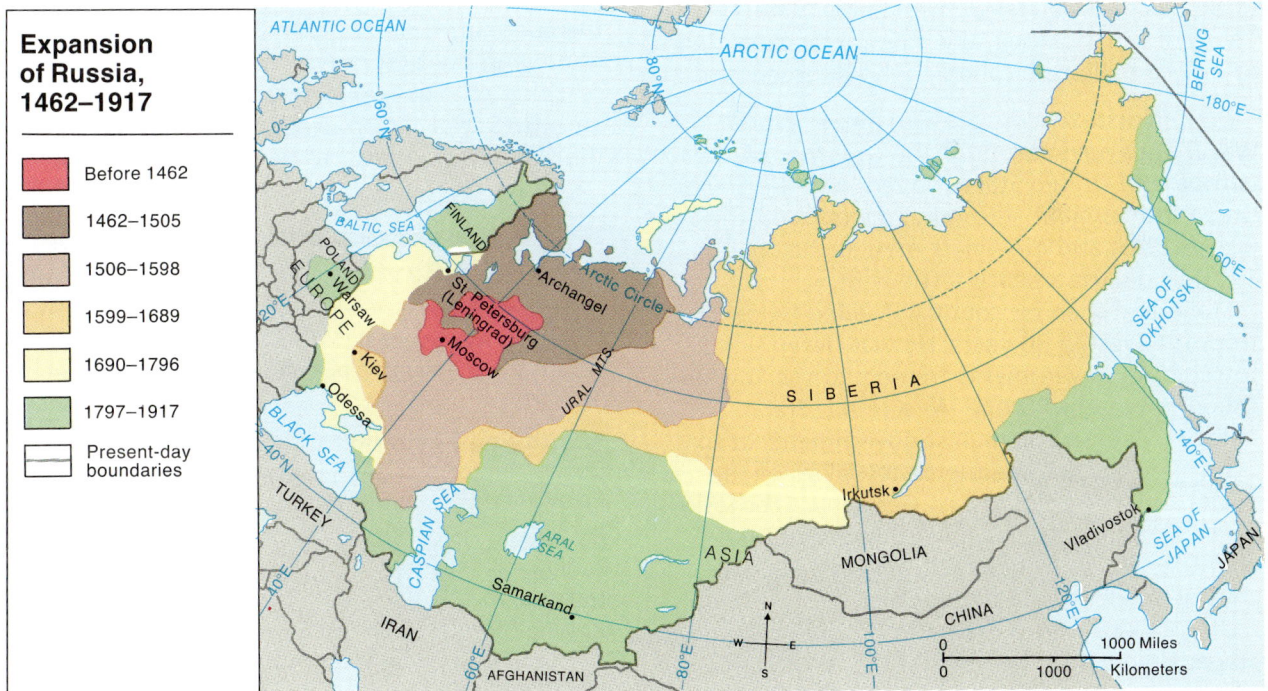

Expansion of Russia, 1462–1917

- Before 1462
- 1462–1505
- 1506–1598
- 1599–1689
- 1690–1796
- 1797–1917
- Present-day boundaries

Map Study

This map illustrates how the Russian Empire expanded its boundaries from 1462 to 1917. What color represents Russia as it was before 1462? When was most of Siberia acquired?

the United States, France, Britain, and Japan sent troops to help the anti-Lenin forces. Finally, in 1920, Lenin and his forces won, and Russia officially became a communist country.

The Soviet Union. In 1922 the country under Lenin took on a new name, the Union of Soviet Socialist Republics. The Soviet Union ruled most of the land that had been part of the Russian Empire. Russia was the largest region within the new country, and Russian the most important language. Since much of the country was not Russian, the leaders chose a name that did not mention any ethnic group. The name of the people—Soviets—reflects this same thinking.

Lenin ruled until his death in 1924. After a struggle to succeed Lenin, Joseph Stalin became the ruler of the Soviet Union. Stalin turned out to be a ruthless dictator. In the late 1930s, he "purged," or cleansed, the country by executing or exiling millions of people who opposed him.

Post-World-War-II relationships. World War II once again brought the countries of Europe, the United States, Japan, and the Soviet Union into combat. The Allied forces won the war in 1945, and diplomats met, as they had in 1919, to discuss a peace settlement.

Stalin had seen his country invaded twice from the west in 30 years. He was determined to establish governments friendly to the Soviet Union in Eastern Europe. As a result, Stalin helped establish communist governments in six countries that became the closest allies of the Soviet Union—Poland, East Germany, Czechoslovakia, Hungary, Romania, and Bulgaria. These countries were Soviet **satellites**—small countries dependent on a larger one.

These six countries in Eastern Europe and the Soviet Union were tied by treaties, economic agreements, and military arrangements. All seven countries had communist governments. Yugoslavia and Albania, however, maintained their independence.

Major changes began to take place in 1989, after Soviet leader Gorbachev moved to drastically reduce Soviet military presence in Europe. Poland elected its first noncommunist leader in 40 years. Other Eastern European nations experienced massive public demonstrations. The result was a rapid removal from power of hardline communist leaders.

Since World War II, a **Cold War**—a non-shooting war—had existed in Europe. The Soviet Union and its allies were on one side. The United States and its allies in Western Europe were on the other. To date, the two sides have fought each other economically and politically rather than militarily.

Under the dynamic new leadership of Mikhail Gorbachev, the Soviet Union in 1989 agreed to major reductions in troop strength in Eastern Europe. In a similarly dramatic domestic move, the communist party agreed to give up its monopoly on political power. In view of the far-reaching changes taking place in Eastern Europe and the Soviet Union itself, it may be said that the Cold War appears to be ending.

Section 3 Review

Locating Key Places
Locate the following place on the map on page 344: Moscow

Identifying Key Terms
Define the following terms: atheism, serf, satellite, Cold War

Reviewing Main Ideas
1. Describe three major ethnic groups in the Soviet Union and Eastern Europe.
2. What are the realm's major religions?
3. How did the Russians gain control of what is now the Soviet Union?
4. How has the political map of the realm changed since 1914?

Thinking Critically: Assess Cause and Effect
How did geography influence the expansion of Russia under the Romanovs?

Using Maps for Political Understanding: Part I

This chapter mentions the Soviet Union's need for a year-round port and how this need has affected political events. A map like the one below may be helpful in understanding this need by showing the effects of winter on major Soviet ports.

Seaports are important for the economic development of any modern nation. Ships are the most efficient way to transport bulky raw materials—such as coal, oil, and grain—and manufactured goods, especially over long distances.

The Soviet Union has a longer coastline than any other nation, yet it has only a few ports that function throughout the year. In addition, each of these ports suffers from some major handicap.

As you look at the map, note the movement of ice. Each winter the polar ice cap advances to freeze almost the entire Arctic Ocean. As a result, most of the Arctic Coast is blocked by ice for months.

Only when the warm waters of the Gulf Stream work their last bit of magic does the Arctic Ocean have an ice-free port. In these areas most of the coastline belongs to Norway.

Ice also blocks most of the Soviet coast in the north Pacific Ocean and in the eastern reaches of the Baltic Sea. Leningrad, the largest Soviet port, would be blocked by ice for three months without the help of ice breakers.

Vladivostok, on the Pacific Coast, is kept free of ice by the warm Tsushima Current that flows northward from the Sea of Japan. Unfortunately, this excellent port is thousands of miles away from most of the Soviet Union's population. On the Black Sea, the Soviet ports never freeze, but in order to reach the ocean, ships must pass through the Straits controlled by Turkey.

Review

1. Name the major Soviet port on the Arctic Ocean.
2. Why is this port ice free?
3. Is Odessa closer to the North Pole or the Equator?
4. What major Soviet ports are located on the Black Sea?

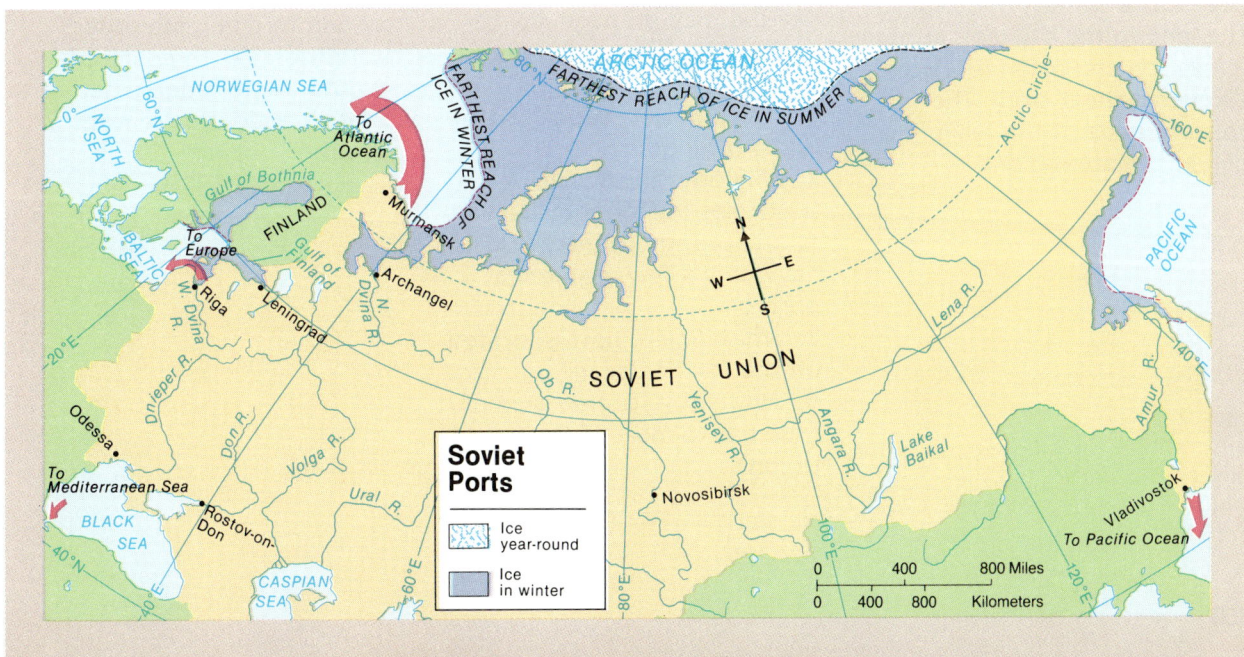

CHAPTER 16

Review

Section Summaries

1. Landscapes of Two Continents

Mountains play a large role in the Soviet Union and Eastern Europe. The Ural Mountains divide the realm into three major regions. West of the Urals are the plains and mountains of Europe, and to the south is a large steppe region. To the east is Siberia, an enormous cold region. Some major rivers of this geographic realm are the Danube, Volga, Ob, and Amur.

2. Climate, Soils, and Vegetation

This realm has four basic types of climates. The northern edge of the Soviet Union has a polar climate region, but most of the land has continental or dry climates. Generally, as you move east, away from the Atlantic Ocean, the winters get colder. The land in the dry regions has fertile soil and often produces excellent wheat crops. The western edge of the realm has milder climate regions.

3. Historical Foundations

Ethnic, religious, and political forces have shaped this realm. Ethnic groups represented are Slavic, Turkish, Albanian, Romanian, Bulgar, Hungarian, and German. Although atheism is official policy, significant numbers of people still follow traditional Christian and Jewish religions. Most people are either Catholic or Orthodox Christians. Between 1500 and 1917, the Russian Empire, led by the tsars, dominated the realm. Since 1918 the old empires have been replaced by independent countries. After World War II, the Soviet Union and six Eastern European countries became closely allied.

Using Geography Skills

Reviewing the Map Lesson

Use the map on page 357 to answer the following questions.

1. Which Soviet seaport is closest to Leningrad?

2. Why does the Soviet Union, which has the longest seacoast of any country in the world, have only a few usable seaports?

3. Which Soviet port is located on the Pacific Ocean?

4. Why is this ice-free port of little use to most of the Soviet Union?

Using Social Studies Skills

1. Draw Conclusions.

In World War II, the Soviet Union and the United States were allies. Their enemies included Germany, Bulgaria, Romania, and Hungary. In the Cold War, the Soviet Union, Bulgaria, Romania, and Hungary have been allies. Opposed to these nations have been the United States and West Germany. From this information, what can you conclude about how long alliances among countries last?

2. Develop Criteria for Making Judgments.

Historians have disagreed about Stalin's efforts to influence the governments in Eastern Europe after World War II. Some historians argued that he was justified. Others argue that he was wrong to dominate other countries. List three criteria you would use to judge whether Stalin's actions were right or wrong.

Testing for Understanding

Locating Key Places
Match each description below with the name of the place.
1. an ice-free port north of the Arctic Circle
2. major mountains east of the Black Sea
3. a slow-draining area in Poland
4. the major feature separating Asia and Europe
5. a body of water between the Soviet Union and Iran
6. the largest city in the Soviet Union
7. the dry region east of the Caspian Sea
a. Ural Mountains
b. Caucasus Mountains
c. Caspian Sea
d. Murmansk
e. Kara Kum
f. Pripyat Marshes
g. Moscow

Recalling Key Terms
Define these terms in your own words.

Section 1
permafrost

Section 2
taiga
peat
chernozem

Section 3
atheism
serf
satellite
Cold War

Reviewing Main Ideas
Section 1
1. List the major mountain ranges in the Soviet Union and Eastern Europe.
2. Describe the three regions bounded by the Ural Mountains.
3. List four major rivers of the Soviet Union and Eastern Europe.

Section 2
1. Describe where the polar climate regions are located.
2. Summarize the locations of the continental climate regions.
3. What parts of the realm are dry climate regions?
4. Where in Eastern Europe would you find mild climate regions?

Section 3
1. What are three ethnic groups found in the Soviet Union and Eastern Europe?
2. What are the major religions of the realm?
3. How did the Russians gain dominance over the land that is now the Soviet Union?
4. Describe the changes in the political map of the Soviet Union and Eastern Europe since 1914.

Thinking Critically
1. Make Decisions. In this chapter, you studied the geography, climate, and history of the Soviet Union and Eastern Europe. Write a two-paragraph statement describing where in the realm you would most like to live and at what time in history.

2. Make Hypotheses. What conclusion can you draw from the following statement? "The climates of Eastern Europe differ from those in the Soviet Union. The Mongols conquered Russia, but not all of Eastern Europe. Until Peter the Great, Russians looked east rather than west. Throughout most of the past centuries, Russians have been fighting Eastern Europeans."

CHAPTER 17

The Soviet Union

In this chapter you will learn about the Soviet Union, the world's largest country.

Sections

1 People and Life in the Soviet Union

2 The Soviet Government and Economy

3 Case Study: Soviet Youth

People and Life in the Soviet Union

Preview

Key Places
Where are these places located?
1 Ukraine
2 Byelorussia
3 Soviet Central Asia
See the globe below.

Key Terms
What do these terms mean?
anti-Semitism
dacha
link

Main Ideas
As you read, look for answers to these questions.
• What is the character of the population in the Soviet Union?
• How has the Soviet economy changed since 1917?
• What forces have influenced the Soviet way of life?

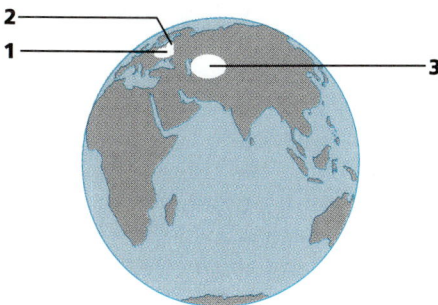

We made a revolution in 1917 to make things better, not worse. Since then we have sacrificed one generation after another. We have known nothing but hardship. Now we want to live.

Harrison E. Salisbury, *Russia*, 1944

The Soviet Union has one of the most diverse populations.

As a Soviet military officer described in Salisbury's book, the collective experience of the Soviet people has been difficult. They are a diverse people in an enormous country. The Soviet Union, with about 281 million people, is more populous than the United States. Only China and India have more people than does the Soviet Union. In addition, few countries are as ethnically diverse as the Soviet Union. More than 170 distinct ethnic groups live in the country. They speak more than 200 languages and dialects. These varied ethnic groups fall into one of three large categories.

Russians. The largest category of ethnic groups is the Russians, who make up about 50 percent of the Soviet population. Historically, most Russians lived in the region surrounding Moscow. Now, Russians live throughout the Soviet Union. Wherever they live, they hold important political and economic positions. Russian is the most widely used language in the Soviet Union. Their numbers and influences make the Russians the dominant ethnic group in the Soviet Union.

Non-Russian Slavs. A second category, about 20 percent of the population, includes all Slavs who are not Russians. Included in this cate-

Facing page: **Four hundred-year-old St. Basil's Church stands in Red Square, the cultural and physical heart of Moscow.**

gory are the Ukrainians and the Byelorussians. The Ukraine is in the southwest corner of the Soviet Union, bordering Romania. Byelorussia is in the northwest, bordering Poland.

Ukrainians and Byelorussians are closely related to the Russians ethnically. However, each group has its own distinctive history and culture. Many of them resent the dominant position of the Russians in the Soviet Union.

Non-Slavs. The third category of ethnic groups in the Soviet Union includes the 30 percent of the population who are not Slavic. Many of the people in this category, such as the Turkmen, Kirghiz, Kazakhs, and Uzbeks, are Turkic. They are ethnically related to the people of Turkey. Turkic peoples dominate Soviet Central Asia—the region east of the Caspian Sea. Most of these people are Muslim, who are the fastest growing part of the Soviet population.

Between the Black and Caspian seas are three non-Slavic groups who are not Turkic. The Georgians and Armenians are Christians, and

Included among the non-Slavic population are about 2 million Jews. Most of the Jews in the Soviet Union live in the western part of the country. **Anti-Semitism**, or prejudice against Jews, is a major problem in the Soviet Union. It is difficult for Jews to study and practice their religion and many are denied jobs because they are Jews. Thousands have asked permission to leave the country. However, the Soviet government has denied permission to most Jews who have asked to leave.

Also included among the non-Slavic groups are 5 million people who live in Estonia, Latvia, and Lithuania. These three formerly independent countries border the Baltic Sea. The Soviet Union took control of these lands at the beginning of World War II. The United States has never recognized that these areas legally belong to the Soviet Union.

Population growth. Since 1910, population growth has not been as rapid as elsewhere in the world. One reason for this is that the Slavic regions of the Soviet Union have a low birthrate. Another reason for the slow population growth this century is violence. Deaths resulting from World War I, the Russian Revolution, the Stalin purges, and World War II totaled more than 40 million. A majority of these deaths were males. After World War II, the Soviet Union had a lower percentage of males than any other large country.

Since World War II, the bulk of the Soviet population has been aging. The low birthrate in the Slavic regions has reduced the percentage of young people in the country. Improvements in medical care, food supply, and housing have improved the overall health of the population. Therefore, compared to the years before World War II, more people are surviving to old age.

The Soviet Union has changed to an industrial society.

In the 1950s public opinion surveys in the United States indicated that many people feared and disliked the people of the Soviet Union. However, people in the United States did associate one positive trait with the Soviet people: hard work. The hard work of the Soviets has helped their country advance economically.

The work force. Almost every adult in the Soviet Union has a job. Most people work 40 hours per week. Women account for more than 50 percent of the work force. As in the United States, many low-paying jobs are dominated by females. In the Soviet Union, most doctors are women, but doctors are not highly paid.

The traditional structure of the Soviet econ-

Map Study

Which part of the Soviet Union has more cities, the western or eastern part?

omy is represented by the country's symbol, the hammer and the sickle. The hammer represents factory work. Before 1917 factory workers were a small but important part of the economy. Wages were lower in Russia than in other parts of Europe. This made Russian industry competitive with industry in other countries. The poorly paid workers were among the strongest supporters of the Russian Revolution in 1917.

The sickle, a tool used to harvest grain, repre-

Soviet Union

- Commercial farming
- Irrigated farming
- Dairying
- Subsistence farming
- Ranching
- Nomadic herding
- Forests
- Lumbering
- Hunting, fishing, and gathering
- ◆ Mining
- Commercial fishing
- Urban land use
- Little or no economic activity
- ⊛ National capital
- • Other cities

Map labels: ATLANTIC OCEAN, ICELAND, GREENLAND (DENMARK), North Pole, BERING Strait, BERING SEA, Seals, Coal, UNITED KINGDOM, SVALBARD (NORWAY), ARCTIC OCEAN, NEW SIBERIAN IS., PACIFIC OCEAN, NORTH SEA, DEN., NORWAY, SWEDEN, FINLAND, Arctic Circle, FRANZ JOSEF LAND, SEVERNAYA ZEMLYA, LAPTEV SEA, Reindeer, Coal, E. GER., BALTIC SEA, BARENTS SEA, NOVAYA ZEMLYA, KARA SEA, Murmansk, Cod, Reindeer, Natural Gas, Coal, SEA OF OKHOTSK, Salmon, POLAND, Riga, Leningrad, Sugar Beets, Archangel, Reindeer, Copper, Nickel, Diamonds, Coal, SAKHALIN, Beef Cattle, Bauxite, Furs, Oil, SIBERIA, Furs, TRANS-SIBERIAN RAILWAY, KURIL IS., Coal, Minsk, BYELORUSSIA, Flax, Moscow, Iron Ore, Wheat, Dairying, Oil, Potatoes, Corn, Kiev, Barley, Gorki, Kazan, Perm, Gold, Chromite, Copper, Oil, Iron Ore, Coal, JAPAN, ROMANIA, Iron Ore, Kharkov, Titanium, Nickel, Oil, Svedlovsk, Chelyabinsk, Beef Cattle, Dairying, Krasnoyarsk, Uranium, Irkutsk, Lead, Coal, Odessa, Dnepropetrovsk, Wheat, UKRAINE, Kuybyshev, Ufa, Wheat, Omsk, Rye, Herring, Rostov-on-Don, Coal, Corn, Wheat, Volgograd, Iron Ore, Lake Baikal, Vladivostok, SEA OF JAPAN, BLACK SEA, Coal, Caviar, Gold, Sheep, Iron Ore, MONGOLIA, NORTH KOREA, TURKEY, Tungsten, CASPIAN SEA, Copper, ARAL SEA, Lead, Iron Ore, SOUTH KOREA, Tbilisi, Yerevan, Oil, SYRIA, Baku, Natural Gas, SOVIET CENTRAL ASIA, Sheep, Zinc, Rice, Alma-Ata, Coal, PEOPLE'S REPUBLIC OF CHINA, IRAQ, Oil, Cotton, Tashkent, Samarkand, IRAN, Amu Darya, AFGHANISTAN

Rivers: Dniester R., Don R., Volga R., Ural R., Ob R., Irtysh R., Tobol R., Yenisey R., Angara R., Lena R., Amur R., Syr Darya, Amu Darya, URAL MTS.

Scale: 0 500 1000 Miles; 0 500 1000 Kilometers

sents agricultural work. In 1917 about 75 percent of the people worked in agriculture. Since then, this percentage has declined. Today only about 20 percent of the people are employed in agriculture.

The economy in the Soviet Union is slowly shifting away from manual labor. Factory work, farming, and other types of manual labor are becoming more mechanized. Increasingly, new jobs in the country are in clerical work or in service work.

Vacations. Most people in the Soviet Union receive a two-week vacation each summer. Many Soviets like to spend this break from work enjoying the outdoors. Often they stay at a summer cottage—or **dacha**. For those who cannot travel to the forests, a popular series of records plays sounds you would hear hiking through the taiga and other natural settings.

Everyday life mixes traditions with new influences.

For the 300 years before 1917, the life of people in the Russian Empire changed very slowly. The traditions from this period are still important today. However, since 1917, the Soviet Union has become a communist country. This has caused people to modify many of their old customs.

Weddings. Weddings are one of the most important ceremonies in Soviet life. A modern wedding is a government function rather than a religious event. For most Soviets, their wedding is a simple ceremony conducted by a government official in a special building or room.

After the wedding the couple often visits a patriotic monument. Most couples in the Soviet Union are related to someone who died in World War II. Therefore, they often visit a memorial to the soldiers from this war and leave the flowers from their wedding.

The wedding day usually ends with a large party. A traditional party includes eating, dancing, and singing. A wedding celebration may

A wedding party conducts its visit to a political monument.

cost as much as a typical worker earns in six months. To allow the parents to prepare the wedding, the government gives them several days off from work.

Youth. In an industrial society, education is needed to perform many of the most responsible jobs. As a result, the Soviets value education highly. Teachers and parents expect young people to study hard. By the standards of schools in the United States, Soviet students have heavy homework assignments every night.

Each student in a Soviet school is part of a group of students called a **link**. All students in a link receive the same grade. This encourages students to help each other learn. However, entrance to universities is based on examinations that students take individually.

The Soviet government believes that all young people should serve society. At age 18 males enter the armed forces for two years. In addition, students who go to a government-run university are expected to pay for it by service. Many university graduates spend time helping to develop one of the new communities the government has established in Siberia.

Consumer goods. Many of the consumer goods used by people in daily life are in short supply in the Soviet Union. These goods include apartments, cars, certain foods, sporting goods, and fancy clothes.

The lack of housing is particularly severe in cities. Young adults often stay with their parents for several years before they can get their own place to live. Apartments are very small. Often several units share kitchens and bathrooms. The government owns the buildings and keeps rents very low.

The car shortage has made used cars very valuable. After ordering a new car, an individual may have to wait one year to receive it. Consequently, a used car that is immediately available sometimes sells for a higher price than a new car would.

Appliances have become increasingly common in the Soviet Union in recent years. Almost all Soviet households own a television. Most also have refrigerators and washing machines. However, only one out of five homes had a telephone in the late 1980s.

The Soviet diet is based on traditional foods, including bread, potatoes, beets, and cabbage. Improvements in the country's transportation network have made fresh fruits and vegetables from the south more available.

Lenin—the hero. Each ethnic group has its own traditional heroes. The one individual who is a hero throughout the country is Vladimir Ilyich Lenin. His body is on display at his tomb in Moscow, and each day, people wait in long lines to visit his tomb. In addition, thousands of communities have shrines dedicated to the memory of Lenin and almost every government building has his picture displayed prominently.

To the Soviets, Lenin is like a combination of three of the great heroes of the United States. Like Thomas Jefferson, Lenin developed the ideas that are the foundation of his country. Like George Washington, Lenin is perceived as the first leader of his country. Like Abraham Lincoln, Lenin held his country together when turmoil threatened to destroy it. To the diverse people of the Soviet Union, Lenin represents the unity that holds the country together.

Section 1 Review

Locating Key Places
Locate the following places on the map on page 363: Ukraine, Byelorussia, Soviet Central Asia

Identifying Key Terms
Define the following terms: anti-Semitism, dacha, link

Reviewing Main Ideas
1. What are the three main ethnic categories in the Soviet Union?
2. Summarize the shift in the Soviet economy since 1917.
3. In what ways do traditions and modern influences affect Soviet life today?

Thinking Critically: Predict Effects
What effects might there be from an aging Soviet population? List as many as you can think of.

The Soviet Government and Economy

See the globe below.

Preview

Key Places
Where are these places located?
1 Leningrad
2 Kiev
3 Novosibirsk
See the globe below.

Key Terms
What do these terms mean?
Gosplan
black market

Main Ideas
As you read, look for answers to these questions.
- What is the most powerful part of the Soviet government?
- What role does the Soviet government play in the economy?
- How has the Soviet economy changed since 1917?

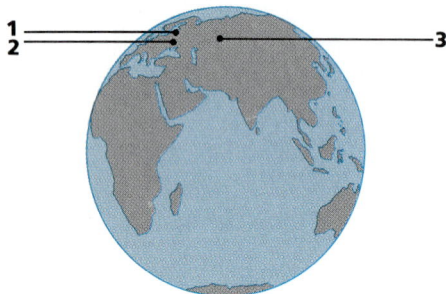

In our country the Communist Party is not only the ruling party but also the recognized leader, inspirer, and organizer of all the people's major affairs.

Leonid I. Brezhnev, *Pages from His Life*

The communist party dominates the Soviet government.

As the words of Brezhnev, the Soviet leader from 1964–1982, attest, the communist party has been a powerful institution guiding the government of the Soviet Union. Today the country is composed of 15 republics, each of which is composed of one major ethnic group. The largest of the republics is the Russian Federated Socialist Republic. Two of the republics, Byelorussia and the Ukraine, have their own seats in the United Nations. Like states in the United States, Soviet republics have some power over local issues. National issues are handled by the federal government in Moscow.

According to the constitution of the Soviet Union, the legislative power in the government lies in the Supreme Soviet. The Supreme Soviet is composed of two houses, each with 750 members. The Supreme Soviet meets for a few days twice each year.

Despite its standing in the Soviet constitution, the Supreme Soviet has little real power. The Supreme Soviet usually just ratifies decisions already made by the communist party. This party—the only party in the Soviet Union—holds the real power in the country.

Although the communist party controls the government, only about nine percent of Soviet voters are members of the party. The party carefully screens all people who apply for membership because most leadership positions are reserved for party members.

The Central Committee of the communist party appoints the Politburo, which has 18 members. In practice, the Politburo makes the major policy decisions for the Soviet government.

The Central Committee also appoints the general secretary, or chief administrator for the party. In 1985 Mikhail Gorbachev became the general secretary, later becoming the president of the Soviet Union. Gorbachev has tried to reform the government to make it more open and competitive by supporting a policy of openness in government known as *glasnost.* In 1990, for example, Gorbachev persuaded the Central Committee to agree that the communist party would surrender its historic monopoly of power in the Soviet Union. This dramatic move seemed to allow other parties to organize and seek power.

In addition to influencing the government, the communist party influences how people in the country think. The party publishes its own daily newspaper, called *Pravda,* the Russian word for "truth." The paper provides the perspective of the communist party.

The communist party influences how history and other courses are taught in school. In addition, party officials determine what types of music and painting should be acceptable and available to the people.

Soviet citizens still remember the invasions of their country during and after World War I and during World War II. In response, the Soviets have developed a large military. Only the United States has a military as powerful as that of the Soviet Union. Although the United States and the Soviet Union were allies in World War II, they have been rivals ever since. The other rival of the Soviet Union is China.

The Soviet government also believes it must defend the country internally. Through tight regulations on political protest, the Soviet government tries to reduce criticism of its policies. The government also makes widespread use of plainclothes police called the KGB, who watch citizens who are suspected of violating the law.

The Soviet government runs the economic system.

The Soviet Union's government and its economic system are based on the theories of Karl Marx, a German philosopher. Lenin adapted the ideas of Marx to local conditions.

According to Marx, in a communist economic system, individuals can own their own personal possessions, such as clothes or a car. However, all goods used to produce other goods, such as a steel mill, should be owned by the government or by groups of workers. According to Marx, all factories, farms, and stores should be operated for the good of the society.

Planning the economy. The government of the Soviet Union runs by central planning. **Gosplan** is the agency of the Soviet government that tries to control the economy. Every five years Gosplan sets out new goals and periodic quotas for the economy.

Gorbachev has supported reforms designed to increase production and decentralize economic power and planning. Recently local managers have been given more power over how their

Soviets regularly gather to read public displays of *Pravda.*

367

Soviets flock to GUM, their largest department store.

business operates. In addition, the Soviets have allowed more individually owned businesses, such as restaurants, to operate outside of central controls.

Emphasis on the future. Gosplan tries to balance the current needs of the Soviet people with the future needs of the society. The Soviets have generally decided to sacrifice current needs in favor of future rewards. That helps explain why the Soviets lead the world in production of train engines, but produce very few personal automobiles.

The shortage of consumer goods has caused development of a large **black market**—a market in illegal goods. Goods brought in from other countries, such as music or denim jeans, can be sold for high prices on the black market.

The Soviet economy has made advances since 1917.

Under the Soviet government, the lives of most Soviet citizens have improved. Before 1917 wealth was concentrated in the hands of the very rich, and most people were very poor. Since then, the Soviet Union has become a major industrial power. However, the Soviet government, with tight economic control and large defense spending, has slowed economic growth.

Agriculture. As you learned in the first section in this chapter, the Soviet Union is no longer dominated by agriculture, though farming remains a major part of the economy. Most of the farmland in the country is divided into enormous farms. State farms, or *sovkhoz*, are owned directly by the government. Collective farms, called *kolkhoz*, are owned jointly by the workers on the farm. These large farms usually produce grain crops, such as wheat.

Some of the most productive croplands are not run by the government. About 3 percent of the cropland is farmed by individuals in small plots and gardens. These plots produced 64 percent of the potato crop and about 30 percent of all other vegetables, meat, milk, and eggs produced in the Soviet Union.

Although the Soviet Union is an enormous country, less than one-quarter of the total land area can be used for agriculture. About 13 percent of the total land area is used for grazing, and about 6 percent is used for growing grain and other food crops—such as wheat, barley, and rice. About 3 percent of the land is used for raising hay and other feed crops that support the livestock industry.

Industry. Since 1917 the Soviets have emphasized the growth of the industrial sector of the economy. Today the Soviet Union leads the world in production of steel, train engines, machinery, and fertilizers. The country also produces large quantities of cement and iron. Much of the country's production is used by the military.

The industrial strength of the country results in part from the unmatched natural resources found within the Soviet Union. No other country in the world has such a large supply of so many minerals.

The largest industrial region in the country is in the center of European Russia. Since the time of the Rus, more than 1,000 years ago, the excellent water transportation in this region has made it a focal point for trade. Today cities such as Moscow, Leningrad, and Gorki use resources from around the Soviet Union to manufacture a variety of goods. Leningrad, a port city on the Baltic Sea, is the major port for this region.

A second industrial region is in the Ukraine. This region has large oil reserves and rich deposits of coal and iron ore. These deposits are used by a large steel industry. The largest city in this region is Kiev.

A third important industrial region is along the eastern side of the Ural Mountains. The Urals have large deposits of iron ore, copper, chrome, nickel, tungsten, titanium, aluminum, and gold. The Soviet Union ranks either first or second in the world in the production of each of these minerals. Many of these minerals are used in the chemical industry based here.

Other industrial cities are scattered throughout the country. For example, the city of Novosibirsk in southwestern Siberia is an important manufacturing center. The city is located where the Trans-Siberian Railway crosses the Ob River. Workers farther north ship timber, tin, and other resources down the river to Novosibirsk. Manufacturers can process these raw materials into finished products, and ship them out on the railway.

Many of the most valuable resources in the Soviet Union are in Siberia. Timber, coal, oil, and iron ore are some of the riches of this region. The Soviets may have up to 25 percent of the world's oil reserves and enough coal to last them 400 years. However, these resources are far from the population centers of the country. To make these resources useful, the Soviets have been developing transportation routes to Siberia. In addition, Siberia has long been used as the site of prison work camps. The government has sentenced many people—often for political opposition—to prison work camps in the cold north regions of this country.

Section 2 Review

Locating Key Places
Locate the following places on the map on page 363: Leningrad, Kiev, Novosibirsk

Identifying Key Terms
Define the following terms: Gosplan, black market

Reviewing Main Ideas
1. What role does the communist party have in the government of the Soviet Union?
2. Describe the role of the Soviet government in the economy of the country.
3. Summarize how the Soviet economy has changed since 1917.

Thinking Critically: Evaluate Sources of Information
The United States Constitution does not mention political parties. According to the Soviet constitution, "The Communist Party of the Soviet Union (CPSU) is the leading and guiding force of Soviet society and the nucleus of its political system, of all state and public organizations. The CPSU exists for the people and serves the people." Describe how this statement helps explain some major differences between the Soviet Union and the U.S. government.

Case Study: Soviet Youth

Preview

Key Places

Where is this place located?

1 Moscow

See the globe below.

Key Terms

What do these terms mean?

Komsomol

perestroika

icon

Main Ideas

As you read, look for answers to these questions.

- Why are the government leaders of the Soviet Union allowing Soviet youth to have more freedom?
- What factors are important in Gorbachev's plan to energize the Soviet economy and society?
- For what are Soviet youth searching?
- What forces do many blame for the restlessness of Soviet youth?
- How do Soviet youth view their leader, Gorbachev?

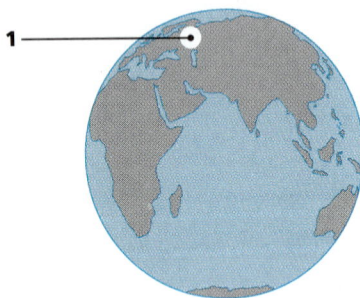

The following case study comes from the article, "Russia's Restless Youth," New York Times Magazine, July 26, 1987. This case study describes how young people in the Soviet Union feel about the changes that Gorbachev advocated. As you read this case study, think about whether Soviet teenagers are similar to U.S. teenagers.

Soviet leaders hope to regain the loyalty of Soviet youth.

On the stage of the Maxim Gorky House of Culture, beneath a red banner urging all good citizens of the Soviet Union to "fulfill the decisions of the 27th Party Congress," Anatoly Krupnov, lead singer of the Black Obelisk, is howling out the lyrics to "Disease." Bare-chested except for a guitar and chain, he struts through a cloud of artificial smoke. Below him, crowding the stage, ecstatic teenagers punch the air.

Despite the presence of wary adult chaperones and watchful young plainclothesmen, the catharsis verges briefly on the uncontrollable. The blitzkrieg [assault] of electric guitars is loud enough to drown out the sound of Bolshevik forefathers spinning in their graves.

This explosion of what used to be officially condemned as bourgeois decadence is a typical concert at Klub Vytyazi—the Warrior Club—a year-old venture in north-central Moscow. The club is sponsored by the local chapter of **Komsomol**, the Young Communist League. . . .

Even two years ago, the idea of Komsomol sponsoring a club where young people . . . listen to decadent Western music at earsplitting volume would have been inconceivable. These days it is inevitable, evidence to which Soviet officialdom is going to regain its grip on a worrisome younger generation.

Gorbachev's success depends on his ability to inspire Soviet youth.

Gorbachev's efforts to revive the Soviet Union's

A rock group entertains young people in a Moscow night club.

society from its torpor [apathy] depend to a great extent on his ability to engage the young, the only generation in which lethargy [lack of energy] and cynicism have not yet put down deep roots. It is to the young that Gorbachev most passionately addresses his pleas to work harder, speak up, take the initiative.

Gorbachev may yet rouse their interest. But so far, in the referendum on his ambitious plan for an economic renaissance—**perestroika**, or restructuring—the generation now coming of age shows every inclination to abstain.

Gorbachev's strategy for reclaiming this generation is to unswaddle them a bit, give them greater freedom and respect. But that runs against a deep grain of tradition.

Soviet youth were looking for new meaning in their lives.

Zhenia is 19 with dark curly hair and moist eyes. He puzzles his parents, a mathematics professor and an engineer, well-established party members, and it is not hard to imagine why.

"I have my own mind on various problems of the modern world," he said. "I don't agree with the peace initiatives of our country, for example. I think that nuclear weapons guarantee the peace all around the world. I think socialism isn't humane, and capitalism is the only humane system."

And Gorbachev?

"He is an idealist. He wants to make our lives better, and so he destroys the structure of our political life. Perhaps it can lead to real changes. If we can have private businesses, for example, then we will have people who will fight for their own interests. . . ."

Zhenia is exceptional in his political outlook. But in his discontent with the ideals handed down to him, he is not so unusual.

Igor M. Ilinisky, director of research for the Higher Komsomol School, recently published an unusually frank report on a poll of 1,500 teenagers. Ilinisky detected an alarming "denial of the material and spiritual achievements of socialism" and "loss of Communist convictions."

"They are looking for something. It's human nature for people to seek some belief in life. Yes, you could say that this search means something is missing."

In his search for Komsomol, Ilinisky said he discovered a fascination among young nonbelievers with the rituals of Christianity, Islam, and Judaism. "God-seeking sentiments are especially strong among young people with a higher education," Ilinisky reported. And among that group, he said, the number who wear crosses or decorate their rooms with icons has doubled in the last five years. [An **icon** is a sacred picture of Jesus Christ, an angel, or a saint, usually painted on wood or ivory.]

Some believe Russian institutions were to blame.

Casting about for the source of this malaise, Soviet analysts have discovered a general failure of the institutions designed to mold Russian

371

children into bright-eyed young Socialists. Komsomol doesn't work, school doesn't work, the army doesn't work, even work doesn't work.

Komsomol, which was Gorbachev's own springboard into the party leadership, has been widely condemned for lapsing into "formalism" and losing the interest of young people. Increasingly, they have declined to join—a few announcing their disenchantment in letters to the newspapers.

In the last two years, new leaders have been recruited, many of them bright and appealing, and in many cities Komsomol has turned its attention from civic lectures to discotheques in an attempt to ingratiate itself with disaffected youngsters.

Recently, the schools have come under assault from academic reformers, who argue that teaching is regimented and stifling, and does not encourage the creative thinking necessary if the Soviet Union is to catch up with the age of high technology. A group of innovators has been urging teachers to step down from their pulpits and develop greater intimacy with their students.

Finally, there is the question of work. That today's teenagers, unlike their parents, have not had to work to supplement the family income is a matter of national pride. But many experts fear the result has been a generation that does not know the meaning of a ruble [Soviet monetary unit], that expects to be supported well into its 20s, and then to find cushy, well-paid jobs.

Soviet youth think Gorbachev has brought change and respect.

Yuri Shchekochikhen, a commentator on youth affairs, recently invited representatives of several youth factions to meet with a group of journalists, sociologists, and psychologists at his office. The specialists were stunned when one young man arrived wearing a homemade Gorbachev button.

Indeed, young people seem to like Gorbachev personally, as a man who has brought change, energy, international respect to the Soviet Union—not to mention rock-and-roll to television. He has shaken things up, and young people like that. And occasionally you can find a flicker of idealism about Gorbachev's program as well.

"Before, a person could just sit around drinking tea all day and be paid his full salary," said Ilya, a student. . . . "Now you are paid for the work performed. I think that's good. You work for yourself and, naturally, you are more interested in what you are doing."

Section 3 Review

Locating Key Places
Locate the following place on the map on page 363: Moscow

Identifying Key Terms
Define the following terms: Komsomol, perestroika, icon

Reviewing Main Ideas
1. Why do Soviet youth have more freedoms today than in years past?
2. On whom does Gorbachev's success primarily depend?
3. In what ways are Soviet youth trying to change their lives?
4. What institutions are thought to be responsible for the restlessness among Soviet youth?
5. How do young people view Gorbachev?

Thinking Critically: Evaluate Sources of Information
Look back at the description of the poll taken by Igor Ilinsky (page 371). Based on the results of this poll, how reasonable would it be to conclude that a large number of Soviet teenagers have lost their communist convictions?

Using Maps for Political Understanding: Part II

How can maps support political understanding? As you know, maps are often used to illustrate a news or feature story about a certain part of the world. A map like the one below accompanied a feature article, written in 1986, on the relationship between the Soviet Union and Europe.

The map presents a unique perspective—that of the Soviet Union looking out. Throughout history, its size, location, and shortage of ice-free ports have all made the Soviet Union focus its energies on the land itself. As a result, the country is often described as land-based.

Lacking windows to the sea, the Soviet Union—and the Russian Empire before it—turned inward unto themselves. Instead of a society open to all visitors, the Soviet Union has been more like a fortress state.

To capture how this viewpoint might influence the Soviet view of the outside world, the mapmaker has drawn this map of Europe. Note that north is not at the top of the map. The Russians, instead of looking north toward the frozen Arctic Ocean, have traditionally sought windows to the West.

The first window, across the Baltic Sea, was developed by Peter the Great in 1703. He made St. Petersburg (now called Leningrad) the capital of the Russian Empire in an effort to introduce Western ways of life.

The second window, by land across the North European Plain, has for centuries given Russia a particular interest in Poland. It was no accident that the military alliance among the communist states in Eastern Europe was formed in Warsaw—the capital of Poland—under Russian leadership.

The third window, again by sea, is by way of the Black Sea. The Straits there are controlled by Turkey into the Aegean and Mediterranean seas.

Review

1. In recent years Turkey, Greece, Italy, France, West Germany, Britain, and several other Western European nations were joined with the United States by the NATO alliance. How does this alliance affect the Soviet windows to the West?
2. Between which two seas does Denmark control straits that are vital to Soviet ships?
3. Which country seems to occupy the center of Europe on this map?

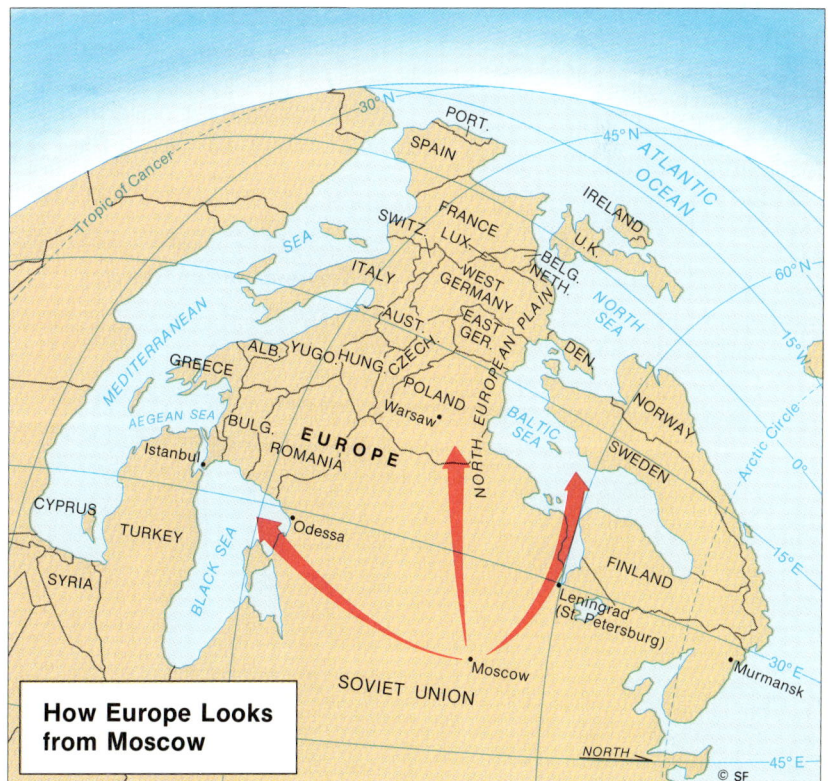

How Europe Looks from Moscow

Review

Section Summaries

1. People and Life in the Soviet Union.
The Soviet Union is a large and diverse country. The population is about 50 percent Russian, 20 percent non-Russian Slavic, and 30 percent non-Slavic. Muslims are the fastest growing part of the population. Since 1917 the Soviet Union has changed from an agricultural to an industrial economy. Everyday life in the country combines traditional customs with new influences. Lenin is the greatest hero of the country.

2. The Soviet Government and Economic System.
The most powerful force in the Soviet government is the communist party, although it has agreed to share political power with other parties. The general secretary is the leader of the party and the country. The party, through the government, also runs the country's economy. The government plans and regulates all economic activity. Although the country has made great advances since 1917, consumer goods are still in short supply. The wealth of natural resources in the country provides a strong industrial base.

3. Case Study: Soviet Youth
Mikhail Gorbachev has been reaching out to the youth of the Soviet Union by allowing them more freedoms. He is seeking their support and energy because his success in mobilizing the Soviet society and economy depends upon the young people. Recently, many Soviet youths have been questioning their government and finding interest in religion—practices some people blame on a failure of the Soviet institutions. The youths, however, seem to respect the changes that Gorbachev is bringing to their country.

Using Geography Skills
A map of the route of the Trans-Siberian Railway is helpful in understanding the political development of the Russian state. Are these statements true or false? Correct any that are false.
1. The railway closely follows the Soviet-Chinese border.
2. The railway ends in the east on the Atlantic Ocean.
3. The railway begins in Moscow.
4. The railway crosses the tundra to the Arctic Ocean.
5. The railway connects the Black and Caspian seas.

Trans-Siberian Railway

Using Social Studies Skills

1. Distinguish fact from opinion. Find an article written in a recent newspaper or magazine describing the Soviet Union. Choose ten statements from the article. Indicate whether each is primarily a fact or an opinion.

2. Synthesize information. Make a list of ten adjectives describing an individual. Include positive traits, such as hard working. Also include negative traits such as untrustworthy. Ask five people to indicate which terms generally apply to the people of the Soviet Union. Determine whether each person has a positive or a negative image of the Soviet Union. Share your results with the class.

Testing for Understanding

Locating Key Places
Match each description below with the name of the place.
1. a region east of the Caspian Sea
2. an important industrial city in Siberia
3. a major port city on the Baltic Sea
4. an important industrial city in the Ukraine
5. the location of the Klub Vytyazi

6. a region in northwestern Soviet Union
7. a non-Russian Slavic region with heavy industry
a. Ukraine
b. Byelorussia
c. Soviet Central Asia
d. Leningrad
e. Kiev
f. Novosibirsk
g. Moscow

Recalling Key Terms
Define these terms in your own words.

Section 1
anti-Semitism
dacha
link

Section 2
Gosplan
black market

Section 3
Komsomol
perestroika
icon

Reviewing Main Ideas
Section 1
1. List the three large categories of Soviet ethnic groups.
2. What important change has occurred in the Soviet economy since 1917?
3. How do traditional and modern forces influence everyday life in the Soviet Union?

Section 2
1. What organization is the most powerful force in the Soviet government?

2. Describe the role of the Soviet government in the country's economy.
3. How has the Soviet economy changed since 1917?

Section 3
1. Why have the lives of Soviet youth changes recently?
2. On what does Gorbachev's success with economic and social changes depend?
3. For what are young Soviets searching?
4. On what do many Soviets blame the changes of the young?
5. How do Soviet youth look upon Mikhail Gorbachev?

Thinking Critically
1. Analyze comparisons. Analyze the following comparison argument: "We can expect the Soviet Union to act like China in its foreign policies because the Soviets, like the Chinese, have a communist government."

2. Predict effects. Currently, much of the Soviet's industrial production goes into military spending. One reason for this is the tension between the Soviets and the United States. Predict how the Soviet economy would change if relations between the Soviets and the United States improved.

CHAPTER 18

Eastern Europe

In this chapter you will learn about the diverse communist countries of Eastern Europe.

Sections

The Countries of Northeastern Europe

Preview

Key Places
Where are these places located?
1 Warsaw
2 Prague
3 Budapest

Key Terms
What do these terms mean?
Solidarity
goulash communism

Main Ideas
As you read, look for answers to these questions.
- What makes Poland unique among the countries of Eastern Europe?
- Why is East Germany distinctive in Eastern Europe?
- How does Czechoslovakia stand out among its neighbors?
- What makes Hungary distinctive among the countries of Eastern Europe?

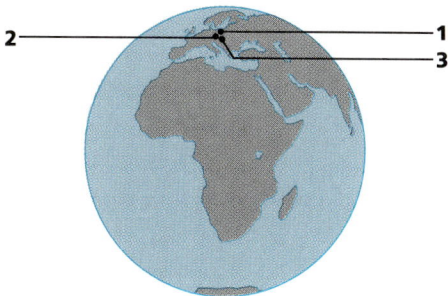

Eastern Europe today is a complex world of contrasts and contradictions—neither captive nor free, not yet affluent but no longer backward and poor.

John Dornberg, *Eastern Europe*

Poland is the most dominantly Catholic country in Eastern Europe.

The countries of Eastern Europe share many traits, but each one has its own distinctive traits. For example, Poland and five other countries have communist governments allied with the Soviet Union. However, no other country in Eastern Europe is as thoroughly Roman Catholic as Poland.

With 38 million people, Poland is the most populous country of Eastern Europe. It became Catholic at the same time it became a country. In A.D. 966, Prince Mieszko [myesh'kȯ] united the Slavic groups in the area under one government. Since Mieszko was Roman Catholic, all of the people in his country also became Catholics. Today the Roman Catholic Church remains one of the most powerful institutions in the country, affecting Poland's economic, social, and political decisions.

Economy. Most of Poland lies on the Northern European Plain. Although much of the land is flat, drainage is poor in many areas. Therefore, crops that survive in moist soil, such as potatoes, rye, and hay, are most widely grown. Poland's agricultural system is unusual for a communist country because individual farmers own more than 80 percent of the land.

In the southern part of Poland are the Carpathian Mountains, a region with large deposits of coal and iron ore. By mining and using these resources, Poland produces steel and heavy

Facing page: **Farm workers in Bulgaria tend a field on a collective near the Black Sea. Farming is important in each of the Eastern European countries.**

machinery. Poland is one of the leading shipbuilders in the world.

The main river in Poland, the Vistula, connects the coal mining region in the south with the ports on the Baltic Sea in the north. Warsaw, the capital of Poland, is located on the Vistula.

Solidarity. The port city where the Vistula flows into the Baltic is Gdansk. In 1980 meat shortages and other problems touched off a wave of strikes in Gdansk. Throughout the country factory workers and farmers joined in the protest against the economic policies of the government. The protesters formed one large union, called **Solidarity**.

The leader of Solidarity was Lech Walesa [lek vä len'sə], a worker in the shipbuilding yards of Gdansk. Solidarity succeeded in winning some economic reforms from the government, but its presence was often threatened by the Polish

People gather at an outdoor cafe in Warsaw, Poland.

government. Throughout the political turmoil that surrounded Solidarity, many Roman Catholic priests led the push for reforms.

In 1987 the Polish people voted in their first national referendum in 41 years. They defeated a government proposal of economic reforms that included large price hikes. Two years later, Solidarity took on a new role as opposition political party. In legislative elections in 1989, Solidarity won all but one of 261 contested seats. That same year, a Solidarity leader became the first noncommunist prime minister in 40 years.

East Germany is Eastern Europe's most prosperous country.

East Germany, with about 17 million people, has a population about a third the size of its neighbor, West Germany. Historically, the area that is now East Germany has been closely tied with Western Europe. The separation of East Germany from West Germany is recent—a result of World War II. At the end of the war, the Allies divided Germany into various occupied regions. The areas occupied by the United States, Britain, and France soon united and became West Germany. The area occupied by the Soviet Union became the communist nation of East Germany.

Economy. Almost all of East Germany is part of the Northern European Plain. Until 1945 this area was primarily agricultural. To this day, wheat, potatoes, and sugar beets remain important crops in East Germany.

Like Western Europe, however, the eastern part of Germany was becoming industrialized by 1945. Since the end of World War II, the communist government has emphasized industrial development. Today East Germany is a major producer of steel, chemicals, plastics, automobiles, and textiles. Industry accounts for more than 70 percent of the total production of the country. The industrial growth of the past 40 years has made East Germany the wealthiest country in Eastern Europe.

The largest industrial center in East Germany is Leipzig [līp'sig]. The East Germans face a problem with its location, however. Leipzig is located on a tributary of the Elbe River, a river that flows through West Germany before it enters the North Sea. (See the map below.) To avoid relying on a port in another country, the East Germans are developing the city of Rostock into a major port.

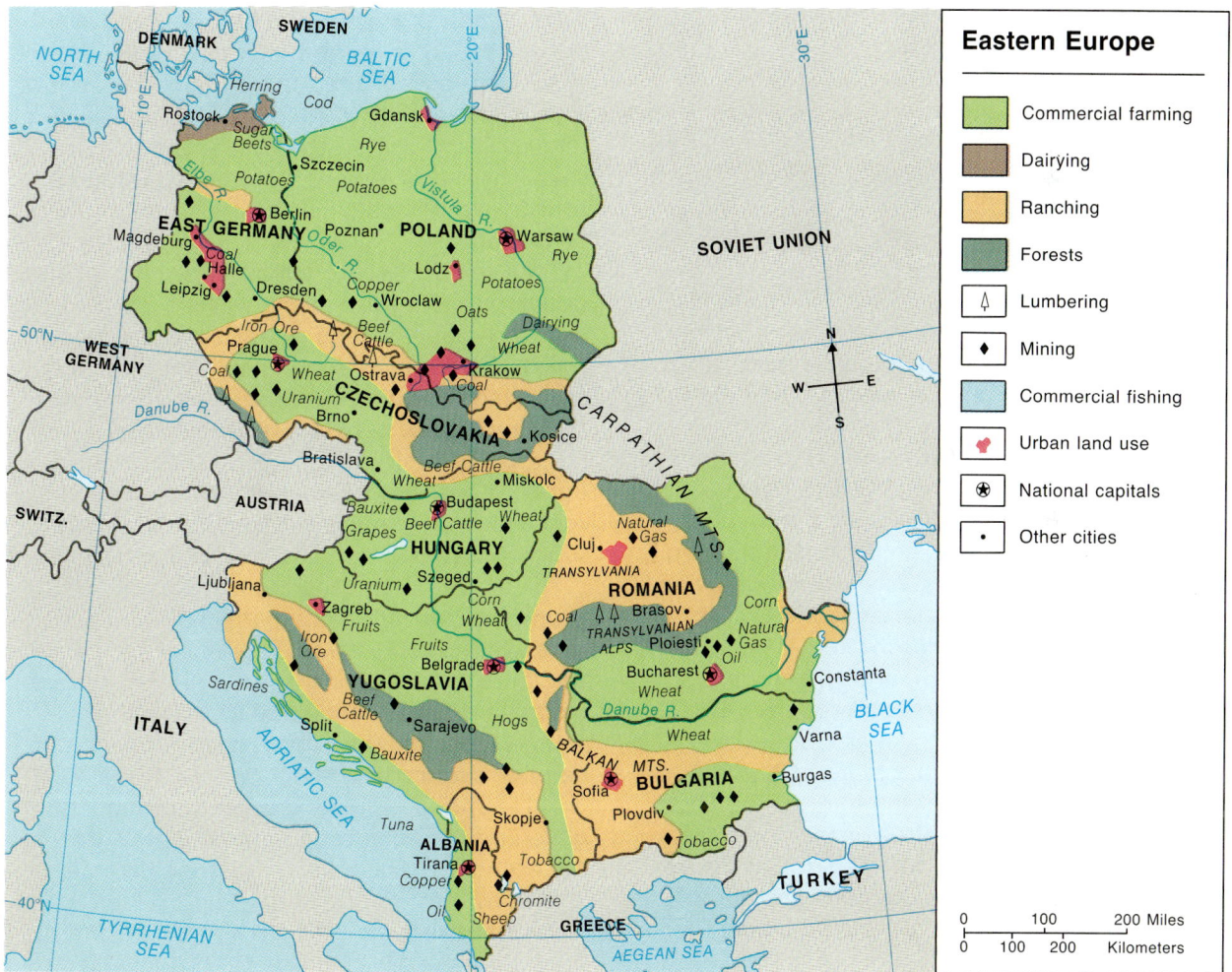

Eastern Europe

Legend:
- Commercial farming
- Dairying
- Ranching
- Forests
- Lumbering
- Mining
- Commercial fishing
- Urban land use
- National capitals
- Other cities

0 100 200 Miles
0 100 200 Kilometers

Map Study

How is most of the land in East Germany used? Where in East Germany is the city of Rostock located? What two activities take up the most land in Eastern Europe?

An East German store displays wurst, a type of sausage.

A divided country. The East German effort to develop Rostock reflects the deep division between the two Germanies. The split is even clearer in the city of Berlin. Berlin is located in the center of East Germany, but the western portion of the city is part of West Germany.

The division of Berlin is similar to the division of the rest of the country. When the four Allied armies occupied Germany after World War II, each one controlled a sector of Berlin. The three sectors occupied by French, British, and American troops became known as West Berlin. The Russian sector became known as East Berlin. In 1961 East Germany put up a fence of barbed wire between West and East Berlin to stop East Germans from leaving East Germany and moving to the West. Strongly fortified, it was known as the Berlin Wall until its gradual destruction began in 1989.

Czechoslovakia is one of the most scenic and productive countries.

The mountainous country of Czechoslovakia includes some of the most breathtaking land-scapes in Europe. In addition, the country includes beautiful old castles and buildings built more than 500 years ago. The combination of mountains and old architecture makes Czechoslovakia a country of wonderful scenery. These beautiful landscapes are found in a country that also has a developed industrial base and a strict communist government.

For almost four centuries before World War I (1914–1918), the regions now part of Czechoslovakia were part of the Austro-Hungarian Empire. Two of the regions were populated by closely related Slavic groups, the Czechs and the Slovaks. These two regions were united into one country, which today has a population of about 16 million.

The Czechs make up almost two-thirds of the population. They live in the western parts of the country—Bohemia and Moravia—where heavily forested mountains dominate. From these forests, Czechoslovakia has developed a thriving timber industry. Between the mountains is a large valley, which is used for wheat farming. Bohemia has long been an industrial area. The coal and iron deposits in the mountains have supported strong iron and steel industries.

The Slovaks live in the eastern part of the country, Slovakia. The Carpathian Mountains separate this region from the rest of the country. In general, Slovakia is more rugged and less industrial than Bohemia and Moravia. In the southern part of the region, most farmers raise dairy or beef cattle.

In the spring of 1968, the Czech communist government began to loosen its tight control of the economy. This period of change became known as the "Prague Spring."

The governments of the Soviet Union and its satellites generally opposed Czechoslovakia's reform movement. The leaders worried that the ideas of the Prague Spring could cause unrest in their own countries. To stop the reforms before they spread, the Soviet Union, and its satellites, invaded Czechoslovakia with tanks and troops. A more orthodox communist government was in place until 1989, when public pressure forced democratic reforms.

Hungary is one of the most open countries in Eastern Europe.

Hungarians are the descendants of the nomadic Magyars, a Central Asian people who invaded Europe about 1,000 years ago. Soon they settled down and began farming the rich soils of the Hungarian Basin.

Economy. Hungary is a major agricultural country. Wheat, corn, sugar beets, wine, and livestock are the leading agricultural products. Since 1950 all farms have been owned by collectives, or groups of farmers. However, these collectives allot almost 25 percent of the land to individuals for their own use.

The main water transportation route in Hungary is the Danube River, which runs right through the middle of the country. It also runs through the middle of Budapest, the only large city in Hungary. Budapest was originally two cities: Buda on the west side of the Danube River, and Pest on the east side. One of the two greatest cities of the Austro-Hungarian Empire, Budapest is still famous for its beautiful architecture and lively atmosphere.

Unlike most communist countries, the Hungarian government strongly supports private business because it wants to encourage industrial development and exports. Thus, any Hungarian with an idea for a business can apply for a loan from a government firm and use the loan to set up a new business.

The 1956 Uprising. Like Poland and Czechoslovakia, Hungary tried to make dramatic reforms. In 1956 the Hungarian communist government began to move the country away from its status as a satellite of the Soviet Union. The Soviets disapproved and sent an army of tanks and 200,000 troops into Hungary to stop the movement.

After 1956 Hungary was a steady supporter of the Soviet Union in international affairs. However, within the country, the Hungarian government was able to make some reforms. No other satellite of the Soviet Union had such a rich and varied cultural life, or allowed so much open political debate.

The result of the openness within Hungary was a modified form of communism known as **goulash communism**. Goulash is a national dish of the Hungarians, featuring many different ingredients. Like goulash, their political and economic system reflected many influences, yet remained distinctively Hungarian.

Section 1 Review

Locating Key Places
Locate the following places on the map on page 379: Warsaw, Prague, Budapest

Identifying Key Terms
Define the following terms: Solidarity, goulash communism

Reviewing Main Ideas
1. How is Poland unlike any other country in Eastern Europe?
2. What makes East Germany the most prosperous country in Eastern Europe?
3. Tell what makes Czechoslovakia a scenic and productive country.
4. Explain how Hungary is unlike the other Eastern European countries.

Thinking Critically: Make Hypotheses
The division of Germany into two parts means that no single country dominates central Europe. Suppose that Germany reunited. How might the countries of Eastern Europe react to a reunited Germany?

The Balkan Countries

Preview

Key Places
Where are these places located?
1 Transylvania
2 Adriatic Sea

Key Terms
What does this term mean?
Balkanize

Main Ideas
As you read, look for answers to these questions.
• What makes Romania unusual among the countries of Eastern Europe?
• How is Bulgaria distinct in this geographic realm?
• Why are Yugoslavia and Albania unique among their neighbors?

2————————————————1

There are few Balkan people who cannot be [happy] at festivals; but there is hardly a Balkan individual who is not at bottom a brooding skeptic. This is the mark of the past.

Edmund Stillman, *The Balkans*

Romania is one of the most diverse countries in Eastern Europe.

As writer Edmund Stillman suggests, the countries on the Balkan Peninsula have had violent and tragic histories. The region has been so divided and plagued with wars that it has given its name to a special term. Today to **Balkanize** means to divide a region into groups of people who oppose each other bitterly.

One of the Balkan countries is Romania. For such a small country, Romania has tremendous variety. The language of most Romanians is more like Italian, Spanish, and French than it is like the Slavic languages of its neighbors. Many Hungarians also live in Romania, a consequence of various border changes. Geographically, economically, and politically, this country of 23 million is quite diverse.

The diverse landscape of Romania gives it a varied economy. The country has mountains, highlands, and flat lowlands. The northwestern part of the country is a highland region—Transylvania. This region is famous for being the home of the legendary Count Dracula. The area is primarily agricultural, with corn, wheat, and sugar beets as its major crops.

The southern and eastern parts of Romania are among the flattest lands in Europe. These areas are along the Danube River and the Black Sea. Farmers raise corn and wheat along the Danube, and grapes and fruits in the warmer region near the Black Sea.

Separating Romania into two sections are the Carpathian Mountains and the Transylvanian Alps. These two mountain ranges form a horseshoe-shaped region. Along the southern side of the Transylvanian Alps, just north of the capital city of Bucharest, Romania has large oil reserves. Oil has become one of Romania's export products. However, despite its oil and mineral resources, Romania remains a poor, but industrialized country.

Since World War II, Romania had been a satellite of the Soviet Union. Even in its politics, though, Romania is diverse. Romania may have had the most rigid, repressive communist government among the satellite nations, but it was the least rigid in terms of foreign policy. The Romanians have often refused to support the Soviet Union in international affairs. In the political upset of 1989 and 1990, Romania experienced a bloody popular insurrection against armed security troops. Overcoming these forces, the Romanians ultimately executed their communist leader and sought to install a democratic government.

Members of a Romanian collective repair a road.

Language and religious heritage tie Bulgaria to the Soviet Union.

The Soviet Union has Slavic languages and an Orthodox religious heritage. The only one of its satellites that shares both of these traits is Bulgaria, a country of 9 million people. The ties in language and religion have helped make Bulgaria a strong supporter of the Soviet Union.

Bulgaria shares many other traits with the Soviet Union. Like its larger neighbor, Bulgaria was a poor, agricultural country until recently. Agriculture has never prospered in this mountainous country of few resources.

As in the Soviet Union, farms in Bulgaria are run by the government or by collectives. Similarly, Bulgarians are often allowed to have a few acres to work for themselves. Grains, fruits, and tobacco are Bulgaria's major crops.

A problem that Bulgaria shares with many Eastern European countries is ethnic conflict. During the period when Bulgaria was part of the Ottoman Empire, many Muslim Turks moved into the region. Today Bulgaria faces ongoing tensions between the non-Muslim Bulgarian majority and the Muslim Turkish minority.

Yugoslavia and Albania are both mountainous countries.

All of the Balkan Peninsula is mountainous, which makes communication and trade difficult. As a result, people who live in rugged areas often tend to be separated from their neighbors and politically independent.

Yugoslavia. A country of about 23 million people, Yugoslavia is the most ethnically diverse country in Eastern Europe. The country was formed after World War I from a variety of ethnic groups, each of which has tried to maintain its own power and identity. Consequently, Yugoslavia has a very weak central government.

The largest ethnic groups are the Serbians and the Croatians. Together, these two groups make up more than half of the population. Smaller groups include the Slovenes, Macedonians, Dalmatians, Herzegovinians, Albanians, Montenegrins, and Hungarians. The capital of Yugoslavia is the Serbian city of Belgrade.

Yugoslavia includes three major religious groups. About 50 percent of the country is

Christian Orthodox, about 30 percent Roman Catholic, and about 10 percent Muslim. The country also has three official languages, Serbo-Croatian, Slovene, and Macedonian.

Yugoslavia maintains an agricultural economy. In the east, along the Adriatic Sea, the climate is mild. Apples, plums, and grapes grow well in this region. The valley of the Danube River, in the northern part of the country, has a humid continental climate. In this region, corn, wheat, and potatoes are the major crops. Farmers in the mountains raise cattle and sheep. Although Yugoslavia is a communist country, about 85 percent of its land is owned privately.

Since World War II, Yugoslavia has become more industrial. The country produces a variety of chemicals, textiles, and machinery. In the mid-1980s, Yugoslavia began exporting cars for sale in the United States.

One area in which Yugoslavia is a world leader is in self-management. The country has tried to give workers extensive control over how factories and businesses are operated. Their experiments in self-management have been studied by many scholars and industrialists.

After World War II, Yugoslavia appeared to be developing into a satellite of the Soviet Union. However, in 1948, the country broke its ties with the Soviet Union. In foreign affairs and domestic politics, Yugoslavia is clearly separate from the Soviet Union and its allies.

Albania. Albania is a small country of about 3 million people. If Yugoslavia has emphasized independence, Albania has emphasized isolation. Culturally, Albania has long been separated from its neighbors. Albanians speak a distinctive language that is not related to those of its neighbors. In addition, Albania was part of the Ottoman Empire for about four centuries. During this time, most of its people became Muslim. Albania, then, is a Muslim country in a region dominated by Christians. Finally, Albania has also cut itself off from all major powers, including the Soviet Union.

Like Yugoslavia, Albania is a mountainous country on the Adriatic Sea. Unlike Yugoslavia, however, Albania has tried to become self-sufficient. The goal of the Albanian government is to be able to produce within the country everything its people need.

Self-sufficiency is difficult for a small country with little good cropland and few natural resources. However, Albania is now self sufficient in terms of food. By terracing mountains, Albania has improved its available croplands. Farmers grow wheat, corn, and potatoes. Many people live by grazing sheep and cattle. The largest city in Albania—the capital, Tirana—has only about 200,000 people.

Although the country is mostly agricultural, Albania has become somewhat more industrial since World War II. The government has invested much of the resources of this poor country into building railroads and highways.

Section 2 Review

Locating Key Places
Locate the following places on the map on page 379: Transylvania, Adriatic Sea

Identifying Key Terms
Define the following term: Balkanize

Reviewing Main Ideas
1. Explain how Romania is unusual among the countries of Eastern Europe.
2. Why is Bulgaria unlike its neighbors?
3. What makes Yugoslavia and Albania different from other Eastern European countries?

Thinking Critically: Assess Cause and Effect
Each of these Balkan countries has populations of diverse ethnic backgrounds because of fairly recent border changes. What have been the effects of this ethnic diversity on the countries of this realm?

Analyzing Historical Maps

How can you tell how the boundaries of a country have changed over time? Since historical maps focus on change, they are never static and can offer you some useful information.

Since historical maps feature movement, the best way to use them is to note the direction and intensity of the movements on the map. Often the mapmaker will help the reader by using a variety of arrows of different sizes, shapes, or colors.

Look carefully at the map at right, and note how Poland's territory has changed in two different ways over the last four centuries. First, it was reduced in size, and second, it shifted to the west. How might these changes be explained?

On the matter of reduced size, the cartographer has provided some hints. Note that three major cities in the Soviet Union were once included within Polish borders. Each city—Riga, Pinsk, and Kiev—serves as the center of a non-Polish ethnic group.

Since none of these cities ever had a large Polish population, you might conclude that Poland in 1569 was an empire that included extensive areas of non-Polish peoples. In fact, the reduction in area covered by the Polish state largely reflects its loss of an empire.

The shift westward of Poland's boundaries can also be partly explained by its loss of an empire. However, other factors came into play as well. To its west, Poland gained territory as a result of World War II, at the expense of what is now East Germany. At about the same time, the presence of Soviet troops in Poland played a major role in establishing the boundaries of today's Poland. Many observers felt that the traditional Russian desire for windows to the West was the major historical force behind the westward shift in the Polish territory.

When reading historical maps of this nature, you must be careful to note the dates given in the title or in the key. Because this map shows two years separated by more than four centuries, many border adjustments are not shown. Between 1772 and 1795, for example, the Polish territory was split up and taken by its three neighbors—the German (Prussian), Austrian, and Russian empires. At this time, Poland ceased to exist as a nation-state. It was not until 1918, in the aftermath of World War I, that Poland was reborn.

Review

1. Do the country's names on the map reflect present-day or historical situations?
2. Name the great river of the Polish homeland and three major Polish cities along its banks.
3. Name the present-day countries that are Poland's neighbors.

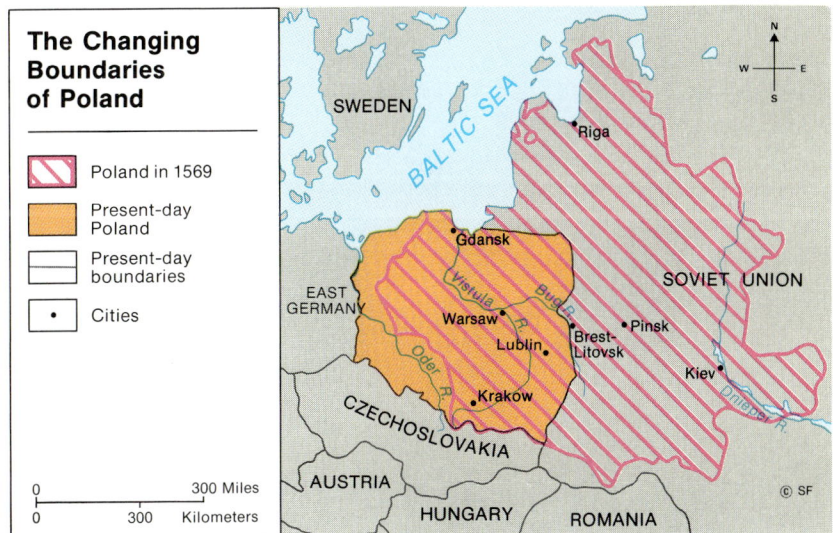

The Changing Boundaries of Poland

- Poland in 1569
- Present-day Poland
- Present-day boundaries
- Cities

SWEDEN

BALTIC SEA

Riga

EAST GERMANY

Gdansk

Warsaw

Vistula R.

Bug R.

Brest-Litovsk

Pinsk

Lublin

Oder R.

Krakow

CZECHOSLOVAKIA

AUSTRIA

HUNGARY

ROMANIA

SOVIET UNION

Kiev

Dnieper R.

© SF

0   300 Miles
0   300 Kilometers

Review

Section Summaries

1. The Countries of Northeastern Europe. All four communist countries were satellites of the Soviet Union. However, each is distinct from the others.

Poland, a firmly Roman Catholic country, has had a strong union movement, Solidarity. East Germany, split after World War II from West Germany, has become very industrial. Czechoslovakia is a relatively new country formed by joining the Czechs and the Slovaks. Hungary has long had a mixed form of government and economy that allows some private enterprise.

2. The Balkan Countries. Romania has had a sluggish but diverse economy, a rigid government, and an independent foreign policy. Like many people in the Soviet Union, Bulgarians are both Slavic and Eastern Orthodox. Yugoslavia, an independent communist country, includes many ethnic groups. Isolated from other countries, Albania, a mountainous country like Yugoslavia, has tried to become self-sufficient by refusing to rely on the aid of larger communist countries.

Using Geography Skills

Reviewing the Map Lesson

The historical map on this page shows how Eastern Europe looked at a single point in time, in 1948. Note the boundaries and other categories on the key.

1. Which country was occupied by Soviet troops in 1948?
2. Which communist countries border the Soviet Union?
3. Which country borders the Soviet Union in the northwest?

Eastern Europe in 1948

Territory added to the Soviet Union

Country occupied by Soviet troops

Other countries with communist governments

International boundaries

NORWAY

FINLAND

SWEDEN

DENMARK

BALTIC SEA

N
W E
S

U.S.S.R. (SOVIET UNION)

EAST GERMANY

POLAND

WEST GERMANY

CZECHOSLOVAKIA

AUSTRIA

HUNGARY

ROMANIA

YUGOSLAVIA

ITALY

ADRIATIC SEA

BLACK SEA

BULGARIA

ALBANIA

TURKEY

GREECE

0   200   400 Miles
0   200   400 Kilometers

© SF

Using Social Studies Skills

1. See Others' Point of View.
Six of the countries in Eastern Europe are satellites of the Soviet Union. Imagine you are a leader of one of these countries, and a group of reformers want your country to break away from the Soviets. Write a brief speech describing why you believe your country benefits from a close relationship with the Soviet Union.

2. Use Problem-Solving Skills.
Ethnic conflicts exist throughout Eastern Europe. Do library research to identify all the areas where the members of a particular ethnic group of Eastern Europe live. Draw a map showing how the borders in Eastern Europe would have to be changed so that all people in that group could be in one country.

Testing for Understanding

Locating Key Places
Match each description below with the name of the place.
1. the capital of Czechoslovakia
2. the body of water west of Yugoslavia and Albania
3. the capital of Poland
4. a city formed by uniting two older cities
5. a highland region in north-western Romania
   a. Warsaw
   b. Prague
   c. Budapest
   d. Transylvania
   e. Adriatic Sea

Recalling Key Terms
Define these terms in your own words.

Section 1
Solidarity
goulash communism

Section 2
Balkanize

Reviewing Main Ideas
Section 1
1. How does the religion of Poland make the country different from its neighbors?
2. Why is the economy of East Germany more successful than other Eastern European countries?
3. What makes Czechoslovakia a scenic and productive country?
4. Explain how Hungary is different from other countries in this geographic realm.

Section 2
1. In what way is Romania unlike other countries in Eastern Europe?
2. How is Bulgaria distinctive within Eastern Europe?
3. How are Yugoslavia and Albania different from their neighbors?

Thinking Critically
1. Make Hypotheses. Look at the map on page 344. Note the distance between the Soviet Union and each of its six satellites. Then note the distance between the Soviet Union and the three countries in Eastern Europe that are not its satellites. Use this information to propose a hypothesis to explain why some countries became satellites of the Soviet Union and others did not.

2. Make Decisions. If you were going to live in one country in Eastern Europe, which would you choose? Write a one-page essay explaining why you would choose one country over the other seven in the region.

Review

Summarizing the Unit

Chapter 16 A Physical and Cultural Overview The Soviet Union and Eastern Europe is a large, geographic realm. In fact, the Soviet Union is the largest country in the world in terms of land area. Most of the realm is affected by continental or dry climates, although much of northern Soviet Union, in Siberia, has an icy polar climate. In addition, the western edge of Eastern Europe experiences mild climates. Just as landforms and climates vary throughout the realm, ethnic groups vary as well. Most people practice either Roman Catholicism or Orthodox Christianity, although many of the communist governments officially support atheism.

Chapter 17 The Soviet Union The Soviet Union, like the rest of the realm, is a country with many diverse elements. Its population is mainly Russian and also includes other Slavic and other ethnic groups as well. The Soviet Union is officially an atheist country, but many people continue to follow the religions of Christianity, Judaism, and Islam. Although the Soviet Union has traditionally had an agricultural economy, the communist government has worked for industrial advancement. The country's wealth of natural resources has helped its industrial growth. In recent years there have been some attempts to revitalize the Soviet economy and society in general by allowing more freedoms for the people, especially the young.

Chapter 18 Eastern Europe Six Eastern European countries were communist satellites of the Soviet Union until the reforms effected by the political upheavals of 1989 and 1990. Their governments differ, however, in terms of openness and foreign policy. The other countries also have communist governments but remain more independent. Because of numerous border changes, many of the Eastern European countries contain diverse ethnic populations. Much of the region maintains an agricultural economy, though East Germany in particular has made major advancements in industry in the past 40 years.

Using Writing Skills

Throughout the last five units, you've studied and practiced prewriting and writing. In this unit you'll pull together what you've learned so far.

For the last few decades, there has been a veil of mystery surrounding the Soviet Union and Eastern Europe. The country's governments have kept much of their territory closed to journalists and photographers. As a result, people in the United States and around the world know very little about how the Soviet people really live, dress, work, or eat.

In recent years, however, the doors to the Soviet Union have begun to open wider to outsiders. Photographs are now available that show us some glimpses of Soviet life and society.

Activity. Use Chapter 17 and current library books about the Soviet Union to study photographs of Soviet life. Once your research is completed, write an essay describing your ideas of Soviet life. Think about questions like these: How do Soviet teenagers dress? What types of music do they listen to? How do they act? What do they study in school? What do they eat?

While writing, keep in mind the need for clear sentences and vivid detail. Try to create an image with your words that someone else could follow.

Test

Key Terms (20 points)
Fill in each blank with the correct term listed below.

1. A _____ country relies heavily on a larger country.

2. _____ is an influential Polish labor union.

3. A _____ provides many illegal goods for the people of the realm.

4. The _____ covers large portions of Siberia.

5. _____ tries to control the Soviet economy.

a. taiga
b. satellite
c. Gosplan
d. black market
e. Solidarity

Main Ideas (30 points)
Select the best answer for each question.

1. Which type of climate affects most of Eastern Europe?
a. polar
b. continental
c. mild
d. dry

2. How were most of the political boundaries of this realm established?
a. by ethnic group
b. by military pressure
c. by physical landforms
d. by royal decree

3. What is the ethnic majority in the Soviet Union?
a. Latvian
b. Russian
c. Turkic
d. German

4. What type of government does the Soviet Union have?
a. democratic
b. monarchy
c. republican
d. communist

5. What is the religious majority of Poland?
a. Orthodox Christian
b. Muslim
c. Roman Catholic
d. Jewish

6. Which two countries are not satellites of the Soviet Union?
a. Albania and Yugoslavia
b. Yugoslavia and Poland
c. Poland and East Germany
d. Bulgaria and Hungary

Thinking Critically
(20 points)

1. Analyze Comparisons. In this unit the communist governments of the Soviet Union and Eastern Europe were compared. Using the information in the unit, along with any other references, discuss whether the communist systems are really very similar. In what ways do they differ?

2. Evaluate Sources of Information. How does the Soviet newspaper *Pravda* differ in philosophy from most newspapers in the United States? How reliable do you think *Pravda* would be concerning information about the Soviet government or economy?

Place Location (30 points)
Match the places below with the letters printed on the map.

1. Murmansk
2. Moscow
3. Leningrad
4. Kiev
5. Warsaw
6. Transylvania

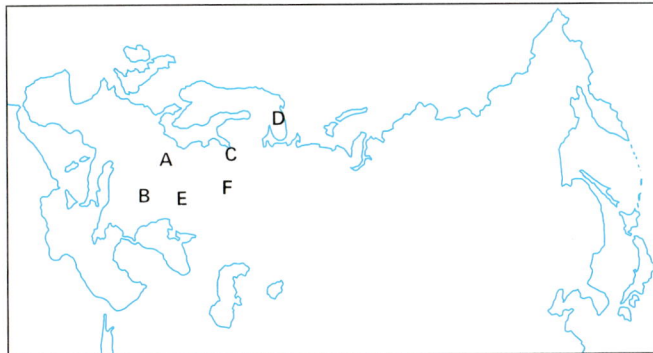

North Africa and Southwest Asia

In this unit you will read about the "Dry World."

A Physical and Cultural Overview

In this chapter you will read about the many landscapes and cultures of North Africa and Southwest Asia.

Sections

Landscapes of the Dry World

Preview

Key Places
Where are these places located?
1 Atlas Mountains
2 Anatolian Plateau
3 Afghanistan
See the globe below.

Key Terms
What do these terms mean?
wadi
erg
oasis

Main Ideas
As you read, look for answers to these questions.
- Why are North Africa and Southwest Asia sometimes called the "Dry World"?
- Where are mountains located in this region?
- What determines where people live in North Africa and Southwest Asia?

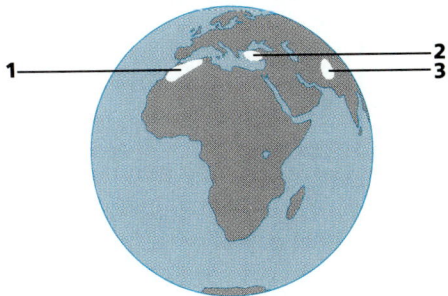

This fertile crescent . . . lies like an army facing south, with one wing stretching along the eastern shore of the Mediterranean and the other reaching out to the Persian Gulf, while the center has its back against the northern mountains.

James H. Breasted, *Ancient Times*

The deserts of this realm make up the driest inhabited land on earth.

Breasted's words are one historian's description of the fertile part of this realm. As the climate map on page 399 shows, however, most of North Africa and Southwest Asia is not fertile but rather is an immense region of desert land. That is why geographers often call this realm the "Dry World."

Throughout much of this region, there is little vegetation to hold the soil. Thus, persistent winds lift the soil and steal its moisture. When rain does fall, it comes as a torrent, sending water gushing through the **wadis**, which are dry river beds. People often drown in these violent flash floods. Soon, however, the hot sun will dry up these shallow rivers.

The Sahara. The vast Sahara is the world's largest desert. It stretches from the Atlantic Ocean to the Red Sea. This is greater than the distance between New York and San Francisco.

When people think of the Sahara, they often imagine large seas of shifting sand dunes. Actually, only about 15 percent of the Sahara is covered by such seas of sand, called **ergs**. The largest ergs are found in central Libya.

More than three-fourths of the Sahara is covered by large pebbles, gravel, and widely scattered, coarse vegetation. The rest is barren rocks. In many places, wind-blown sands have

Facing page: **Jerusalem is sacred to three religions that originated in Southwest Asia.** *Page 390:* **Green oases are scattered around Saudi Arabia.**

CHINA

UNION OF SOVIET SOCIALIST REPUBLICS
(SOVIET UNION)

A S I A

Indus River

PAKISTAN

Tropic of Cancer

20° North Latitude

ARABIAN SEA

Syr Darya

Amu Darya

Qonduz
⊛ Kabul
Mazar-e Sharif
Herat
AFGHANISTAN
Qandahar

Bandar-e Abbas

⊛ Muscat
OMAN

OMAN

SOCOTRA
(P.D.R. OF YEMEN)

INDIAN OCEAN

0° Equator

60° E

ARAL SEA

CASPIAN SEA

Meshed
⊛ Tehran
Qom
IRAN
Istahan
Kermanshah
Ahvaz
Abadan
Shiraz

UNITED ARAB EMIRATES
Abu Dhabi
Doha
QATAR
BAHRAIN
Manama
Ad Dammam

P.D.R. OF YEMEN

Sanaa

⊛ Aden
Gulf of Aden

Tabriz
Mosul
Kirkuk
⊛ Baghdad
IRAQ
Basra
Kuwait
KUWAIT
NEUTRAL ZONE
Riyadh
SAUDI ARABIA
Medina
Mecca

YEMEN
⊛ Sanaa

DJIBOUTI

SOMALIA

ETHIOPIA

KENYA

60° E

40° N

BLACK SEA

Gaziantep
Aleppo
SYRIA
Damascus
Amman
JORDAN
Jerusalem

Tigris River
Euphrates River

RED SEA

Jidda

SUDAN

40° E

Ankara
TURKEY
Konya
Adana
Bursa
Eskisehir
Izmir
Istanbul

Nicosia
CYPRUS
LEBANON
Beirut
ISRAEL
Tel Aviv-Yafo

Luxor
Aswan
EGYPT
Cairo
Giza
Al Fayyum
Al Minya
Alexandria
Suez
Nile River
Aswan High Dam
Lake Nasser

Blue Nile
White Nile

UGANDA

Lake Victoria

TANZANIA
RWANDA
BURUNDI

EUROPE

ROMANIA
BULGARIA
YUGOSLAVIA
ALBANIA
GREECE
CRETE (GREECE)

AEGEAN SEA

MEDITERRANEAN SEA

Benghazi
Ajdabiyah

LIBYA

ZAIRE

Zaire River

Congo River

CENTRAL AFRICAN REPUBLIC

P.R. OF THE CONGO

N
E
S
W

20° E

POLAND
EAST GERMANY
CZECHOSLOVAKIA
AUSTRIA HUNGARY
SWITZ.
ITALY
SARDINIA (IT.)
CORSICA (FR.)

Gulf of Sidra

Tripoli

MALTA
SICILY (IT.)
Bizerte
Tunis
TUNISIA
Sfax

CHAD

A F R I C A

Lake Chad

NIGER

CAMEROON

GABON

UNITED KINGDOM
IRELAND
NETH.
BELG.
LUX.
WEST GERMANY
FRANCE
ANDORRA
SPAIN
BALEARIC IS. (SP.)
PORTUGAL

Annaba
Constantine
Sidi Bel Abbès
Oran
Algiers
Melilla (Sp.)

Ghardaia

ALGERIA

Tamanrasset

MALI

Niger River

NIGERIA

BENIN

TOGO

BURKINA

EQUATORIAL GUINEA

SÃO TOMÉ AND PRÍNCIPE

Benue River

© SF

ATLANTIC OCEAN

40° N

20° West Longitude

Ceuta (Sp.)
Tangier
Fez
Meknés
Rabat
Casablanca
Marrakech
MOROCCO

MADEIRA IS. (PORT.)

AZORES (PORT.)

CANARY IS. (SP.)

El Aaiun
WESTERN SAHARA (MOROCCO)

MAURITANIA

SENEGAL

GAMBIA
GUINEA-BISSAU

Senegal River

GUINEA

Tropic of Cancer

20° N

20° W

North Africa and Southwest Asia
Political

—— International boundaries
⊛ National capitals
• Other cities

1000 Miles
500
0

Kilometers
1000
500
0

80° East Longitude

eroded the exposed rocks into fantastic shapes. Two mountain ranges—the Ahaggar Plateau and the Tibesti Mountains—cover part of the central Sahara. These are volcanic mountains that reach heights of 9,000 feet above sea level. This height draws a little moisture from the air, so some vegetation grows in the valleys.

Hundreds of oases are found scattered throughout the Sahara. An **oasis** is an area of sandy soil that surrounds a deep well or spring. About 90 of the larger oases are surrounded by villages, where people live and grow crops.

The deserts of Southwest Asia. In the southeastern part of the Arabian Peninsula is the Rub-al-Khali, a desert with an Arabic name meaning "empty quarter." This desert, which is almost as large as the state of Texas, has sand dunes as high as 1,000 feet. On the rocky central plateau is the Najd, which has some fertile oases.

To the north, the hot sands of the Syrian Desert cover much of Iraq, Jordan, and Syria. Across the Persian Gulf, desert landscapes continue across Iran and Afghanistan.

Many mountains surround the deserts.

The Atlas Mountains cover the northern parts of Morocco, Algeria, and Tunisia. The people of these countries call their region Djezira el-Maghrabia, meaning "Western Island." On the northern, coastal side of these mountains, moist currents cause plentiful rainfall in the winters. This area represents some of the region's best farmland.

Major mountains and highlands do not appear again until one reaches Turkey, at the east-

ern end of the Mediterranean. The high Anatolian Plateau sprawls through the heart of Turkey. Mountains cut through the southern part of this plateau, becoming extremely rugged in eastern Turkey. This highland terrain continues southeastward through the Zagros and Elburz mountains of Iran. Much of central Iran is a high plateau that is dry, rocky, and barren. This landscape continues into Afghanistan, one of the world's most mountainous countries.

The availability of water determines where people live.

In the dry lands of North Africa and Southwest Asia, the water supply determines where people make their homes. In fact, some people do not live in one place. These people are nomads who herd their grazing sheep, goats, and camels from oasis to oasis in the desert. Other people may settle around the larger oases or along the rainy coastlines. In these dry lands, the rivers are truly a lifeline to millions of people.

The 4,200-mile-long Nile River forms a long, green ribbon through the heart of Egypt. The world's longest river, the Nile River, is the center of Egypt's economy and its population.

The Nile River Valley has been a center of population since ancient times. About 5,000 years ago, the Nile River Valley was the birthplace of Ancient Egypt, one of the world's two earliest civilizations. In ancient times, yearly floods kept many people from living on the Nile Delta. Today, however, a network of dams and canals enables Egyptians to control the flooding and farm the fertile soils. More than 90 percent of Egypt's population lives in the Nile Delta or within a dozen miles of the river's lower portion.

The world's oldest civilization, that of Sumer, was born around 3500 B.C. in the valley between the Tigris and Euphrates rivers. In ancient times the land between these rivers was named Mesopotamia, or "between two rivers."

Map Study

What are the countries of North Africa and Southwest Asia? What are the capitals?

ASIA

PAMIRS
Nowshak
24,577 ft (7,485 m) ▲
HINDU KUSH
Indus River

80° East Longitude

Syr Darya

ARAL SEA

Amu Darya

REGISTAN DESERT

PLATEAU OF IRAN

DASHT-E KAVIR DESERT

ARABIAN SEA

Socotra

0° Equator

INDIAN OCEAN

60° E

20° North Latitude
Tropic of Cancer

Gulf of Oman

Strait of Hormuz

CASPIAN SEA

ELBURZ MTS.

ZAGROS MTS.

Persian Gulf

Gulf of Aden

Bab el Mandeb

40°

CAUCASUS MTS.

Ararat
17,011 ft (5,185 m) ▲

Kurdistan

Lake Urmia

Tigris River

Euphrates River

Shatt al Arab

NAJD

RUB AL KHALI

Arabian Peninsula

Asir

Farasan Is. ▲

Gulf of Aqaba

RED SEA

Hejaz

AN NAFUD

SYRIAN DESERT

Sinai Peninsula

Gulf of Suez

Suez Canal

Nile River

Blue Nile

White Nile

Lake Victoria

BLACK SEA

Bosporus

Dardanelles

ANATOLIAN PLATEAU

TAURUS MTS.

Cyprus

Rhodes

AEGEAN SEA

Crete

Nile Delta

Qattara Depression

Cyrenaica

LIBYAN DESERT

Aswan High Dam

Lake Nasser

40° N

EUROPE

40° E

20° E

MEDITERRANEAN SEA

Sicily

Malta

Gulf of Sidra

AFRICA

TIBESTI MOUNTAINS

Lake Chad

N
E
S
W

20°

Sardinia

Corsica

Balearic Is.

S A H A R A

GRAND ERG ORIENTAL

GRAND ERG OCCIDENTAL

PLATEAU OF TADEMAIT

ATLAS MTS.

Jebel Toubkal
13,665 ft (4,165 m) ▲

AHAGGAR PLATEAU

Mt. Tahat
9,573 ft (2,918 m) ▲

ERG CHECH

Niger River

Benue River

Zaïre River

Fernando Po

Príncipe

São Tomé

Congo River

Ubangi River

ATLANTIC OCEAN

20° West Longitude

Madeira Is.

Canary Is.

Azores

Cape Bojador

Tropic of Cancer

20° N

396

20° W

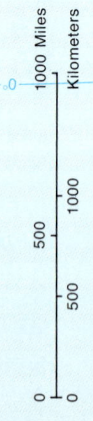

North Africa and
Southwest Asia
Physical

Land Elevation
Feet   Meters
14,000   4,000
7,000   2,000
1,500   500
700   200
0   0
Below   Below
Sea Level   Sea Level

─── International boundaries
▲ Mountain peaks

1000 Miles
1000 Kilometers
500
500
0
0

Many Christians, like these people at Yardenit, are baptized in the Jordan River.

None of the region's other rivers can compare in size to the Nile, the Tigris, or the Euphrates rivers. The Jordan River, which rises in Syria and Lebanon, flows southward for only about 220 miles before it drains into the salty waters of the Dead Sea. The Jordan is the world's lowest river. Where it flows into the Dead Sea, its elevation is nearly 1,000 feet below sea level. The river is a border between Israel and Jordan.

Other rivers, some even shorter than the Jordan River, flow off the Atlas Mountains and other highlands. In low-lying areas, many rivers dry up completely during the dry seasons or hold water only after the occasional rainstorm.

Map Study

This realm relies on its few rivers. What are some of the rivers on this map?

Section 1 Review

Locating Key Places
Locate the following places on the map on page 396: Atlas Mountains, Anatolian Plateau, Afghanistan

Identifying Key Terms
Define the following terms: wadi, erg, oasis

Reviewing Main Ideas
1. What large deserts give the region the name "Dry World"?
2. What major regions of mountains lie in North Africa and Southwest Asia?
3. What natural resource is most important to where people live in North Africa and Southwest Asia?

Thinking Critically: Assess Cause and Effect
Use what you learned in Unit 1 to decide why deserts cover so much of this realm. Is each desert caused by similar or different conditions?

Climate, Soils, and Vegetation

Preview

Key Places
Where are these places located?
1 Sahara
2 Nile Delta
   See the globe below.

Key Terms
What does this term mean?
aquifer

Main Ideas
As you read, look for answers to these questions.
• What are the predominant climates in North Africa and Southwest Asia?
• What other kinds of climate are found in this geographic realm?
• How do people adapt to the climate conditions of this realm?

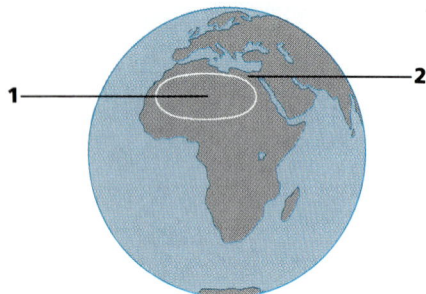

For many people the desert is an oppressive place. Their eye never steadies. The world is blank and empty. The heat by day is an unendurable agony; the cold by night an unbearable contrast. . . . The desert lover must look at these trials of the sands . . . quite differently. . . . To him the early evening, when the savagery of the sun has changed to a lambent [soft] glow filling the landscape with color, and the early morning, when the first rays of the sunrise drive away the bitter chill of the night, are like seasons of the year. Each day brings two springs to be greeted with delight.

Quentin Crewe, *In Search of the Sahara*

Dry climates are found in most of North Africa and Southwest Asia.

Crewe's description of the Sahara explores both the desert's harshness and its beauty. The words present an image of a world in which dry climates predominate. Use the climate map on page 399 to see how much of the region has desert or steppe climates.

Desert climate. In the Sahara annual rainfall averages less than eight inches. Vast areas in the eastern and western Sahara are even drier, receiving less than one inch of rain each year. Summer days in the Sahara can be very hot. The average temperature is between 90 and 110°F. In fact, the world's highest temperature, 136°F, was recorded about 40 miles south of Tripoli, Libya. On winter days, temperatures average between 50 and 60°F. At night, however, temperatures drop quickly, because there is no vegetation to help retain the sun's heat. Thus, some people call night the "winter" of the desert.

Steppe climate. A narrow line of steppe climate breaks the spell of the desert around the Atlas Mountains and along a small part of Libya's coast. Steppe climate also lines part of the Arabian Peninsula. East of the Jordan River, steppe climates line the deserts in Iran and cover most of Afghanistan.

In the steppe regions, soils are slightly better than in the deserts. The increased amount of moisture available improves the fertility of the soil. As a result, short grasses and low shrubs may grow in those areas containing soil.

There are also Mediterranean and high altitude climate regions.

Although the dry climates predominate in this part of the world, they represent just one of the many different climates found in North Africa and Southwest Asia. There are two others—Mediterranean and high altitude climates.

Mediterranean climate. Narrow zones of Mediterranean climate fringe the Mediterranean Sea in Morocco, Algeria, Tunis, Libya, Israel, Lebanon, Syria, Cyprus, and Turkey. These regions receive as much as twice the amount of rainfall as in the steppes each year. This rain comes during the winter.

The summers, in contrast, are dry. Farmers must either irrigate their crops or grow plants that are adapted to dry-summer conditions, such as olive trees or grapevines. Both of these plants have the long roots necessary to find water far below the sun-baked surface. Winter wheat, planted in the fall and harvested in late spring, also grows well in this climate.

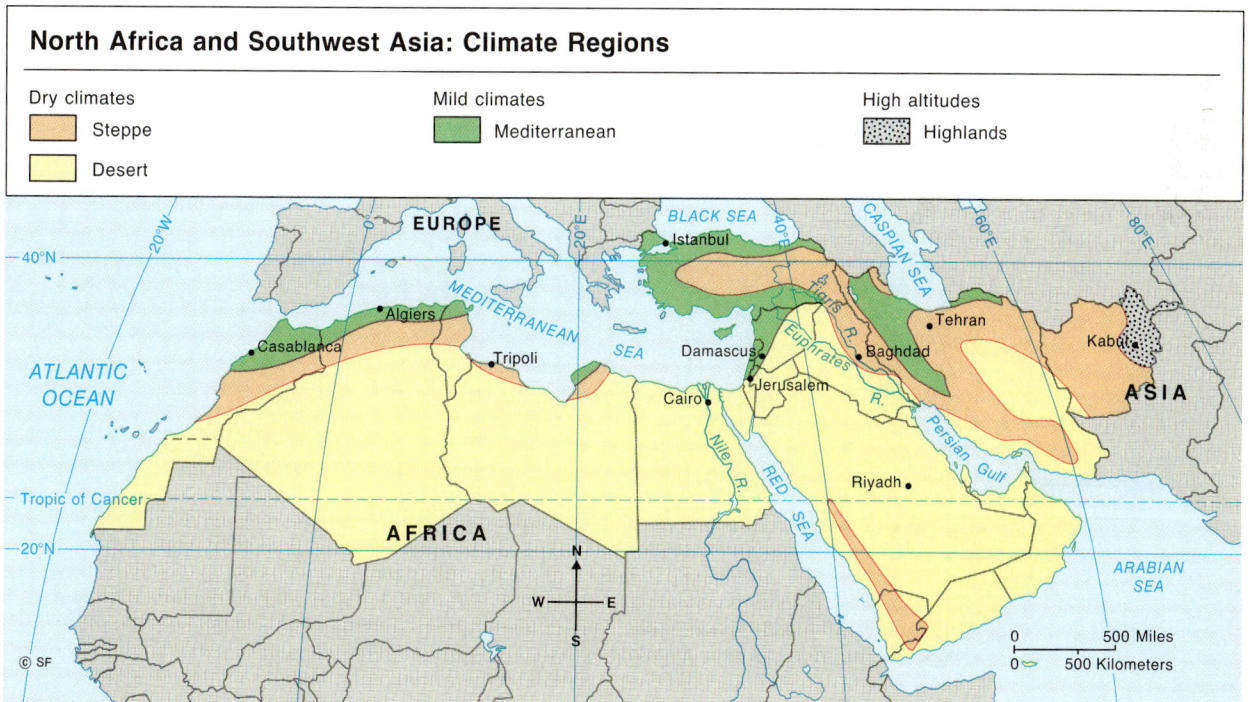

North Africa and Southwest Asia: Climate Regions

Dry climates
- Steppe
- Desert

Mild climates
- Mediterranean

High altitudes
- Highlands

EUROPE

BLACK SEA
• Istanbul

CASPIAN SEA

40°N

20°W

20°E

60°E

80°E

MEDITERRANEAN

• Algiers

SEA

Tehran •

Casablanca

Damascus •

Baghdad •

Kabul •

• Tripoli

ATLANTIC
OCEAN

Cairo •

• Jerusalem

Euphrates R.

Tigris R.

ASIA

Persian Gulf

Nile R.

RED SEA

Riyadh •

Tropic of Cancer

20°N

AFRICA

N

W   E

S

ARABIAN
SEA

0   500 Miles

0   500 Kilometers

© SF

Map Study

This map shows the various climate regions in North Africa and Southwest Asia. Which climates dominate this geographic realm?

In the wet Mediterranean regions, plentiful rainfall has created deep, fertile soils. As a result, shrubby plants often completely cover the surface of the ground. Most of these plants are able to hold water in their roots and stems, a characteristic that allows them to survive the dry summers of this region. The soils of the Mediterranean climate can be quite fertile, especially if they are irrigated.

High altitude climate. High altitude climates are found in the Atlas Mountains and in the highlands of Turkey, Iran, and Afghanistan. Here cooler temperatures in the higher elevations force clouds to condense, bringing rain to the upper slopes. The lower slopes, however, are usually quite dry. Animals are therefore taken to the higher pastures to graze.

On the northern slopes of the Atlas Mountains, rainfall is heavier than in the rest of the high altitude climate regions. Here the rainfall has helped the development of deep, fertile soils.

At the base of many of the region's mountains, an interesting situation occurs. A porous rock layer, one with many openings and passageways, absorbs rain that falls on the mountain slopes. This underground rock layer, called an **aquifer**, can lead from the base of a mountain outward to the desert beyond. There its water may come to the surface to form a natural reservoir, or it may be tapped by a line of

North Africa and Southwest Asia: Natural Vegetation Regions

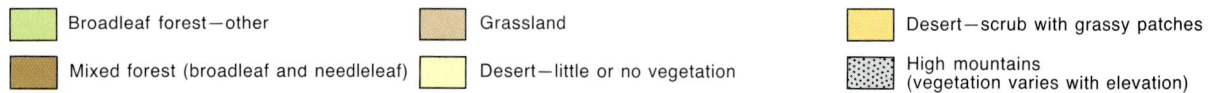

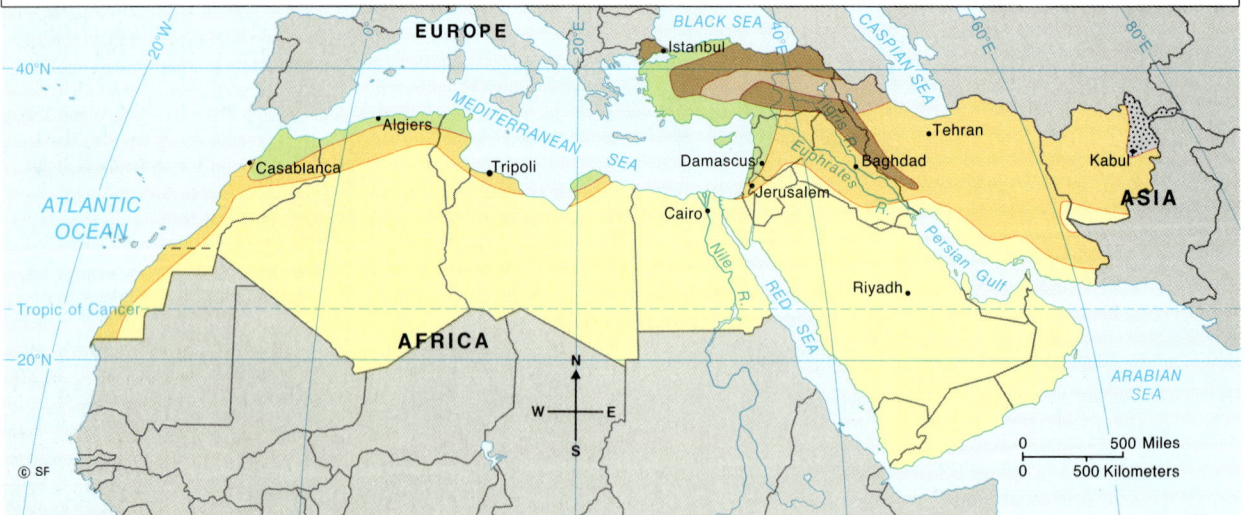

- Broadleaf forest—other
- Mixed forest (broadleaf and needleleaf)
- Grassland
- Desert—little or no vegetation
- Desert—scrub with grassy patches
- High mountains (vegetation varies with elevation)

Map Study

This map shows the different natural vegetation regions of North Africa and Southwest Asia. What type of vegetation is found in most areas of this geographic realm?

wells known as "kanats." These aquifers support oases along the bases of many mountains throughout the realm.

People have adapted in different ways to the region's climates.

Despite the dryness of this part of the world, more than half the people make their living by farming or raising livestock. Many farmers live at the subsistence level and manage to grow just enough dates, barley, wheat, and other grains to feed themselves. Goats, sheep, and chickens are their main stock animals.

In the Mediterranean climate areas, farmers can grow cash crops such as olives, citrus fruits, grapes, figs, and nuts. Israel, where agriculture has reached an advanced stage of technology, is an exporter of citrus fruits, flowers, and other crops.

To keep themselves cool and protected from the sun and dust, rural people wear traditional clothes, such as loose pants and long robes. Around their heads, they may wind long scarves.

In the cities, people depend on food from large irrigated farms that flank the river valleys, yet food imports are always needed. In many places, food production cannot keep up with rapidly growing populations. Under these circumstances, you might expect every acre of good soil to be planted in food crops, but this is not the case. In Egypt's Nile Delta, for instance, there are large cotton fields. Egypt sells the cotton to other countries to buy machinery and other products it does not produce itself.

Section 2 Review

Locating Key Places
Locate the following places on the map on page 396: Sahara, Nile Delta

Identifying Key Terms
Define the following term: aquifer

Reviewing Main Ideas
1. What are the two dry climates found in North Africa and Southwest Asia?
2. Describe the two other climate region types found in the realm.
3. How have farming techniques and lifestyles been adapted to the realm's climates?

Thinking Critically: Make Hypotheses
Egypt built the Aswan High Dam and Lake Nasser to collect the waters that used to flood the banks of the Nile each year. How do you think this dam would affect the soils north of the Aswan High Dam? Would this be an advantage or disadvantage for farmers who live along the Nile River?

Despite the dryness of most of Egypt, this village market displays fresh produce.

SECTION 3

A Common Heritage

Preview

Key Places
Where are these places located?
1 Mecca
2 Jerusalem
See the globe below.

Key Terms
What do these terms mean?
creed   sect
mosque   imam

Main Ideas
As you read, look for answers to these questions.
- What groups of people have lived in North Africa and Southwest Asia?
- What is the predominant religion in North Africa and Southwest Asia?
- What other religions are practiced in North Africa and Southwest Asia?

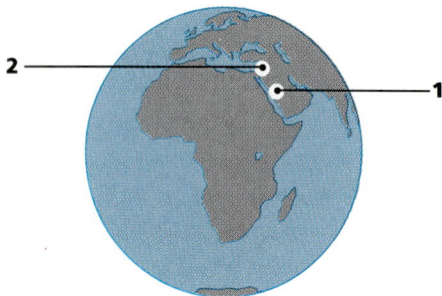

Without Enlil, the great mountain,
No cities would be built, no settlements founded,
No [trading] stalls would be built, no sheepfolds established,
No king would be raised, no high priest born
. . .
Workers [on the irrigation canals] would have neither controller nor supervisor . . .
The rivers—their floodwaters would not over-flow,
The fish of the sea would lay no eggs in the canebrake [river reed areas],
The birds of heaven would not build nests on the wide earth,
In heaven the drifting clouds would not yield their moisture,
Plants and herbs, the glory of the plain, would fail to grow.

Ancient Mesopotamian song

Many different groups of people have lived in this realm.

The words in this song are from a hymn to Enlil, the "king of heaven and earth, father to all the gods" among the people living in ancient Mesopotamia about 4,500 years ago. The song describes life in ancient Mesopotamia, the fertile valley between the Tigris and Euphrates rivers.

The city-dwellers of Mesopotamia were descended from people who once lived in the foothills of the Taurus and Zagros Mountains. The hill people were probably the world's first farmers. By about 11,000 years ago, they kept tame goats and sheep and grew plots of barley, wheat, peas, and other crops. After farmers migrated to the flatlands of Mesopotamia, they found they could grow more food than they needed. The extra food let some people become traders and live in cities.

Around 2300 B.C., nomadic invaders swept into Mesopotamia. They conquered the cities in Mesopotamia and set up the kingdom of Babylonia. Its capital was Babylon, a rich and busy trade center. The Babylonians were among several ancient groups of people known as Semites, people who speak a Semitic language.

The Semites spread throughout the lands of the eastern Mediterranean and the Arabian Peninsula. Today two Semitic languages are still spoken. One of these languages is Hebrew, the language of Israel. The other is Arabic.

People sometimes call this realm the "Arab World." Indeed, Arabs, that is, people who speak Arabic, make up almost half of the population of North Africa and Southwest Asia. However, the people of Turkey, Iran, and Afghanistan, who are not Arabs, make up more than half of the realm's total population. In addition, most of the people of Israel and Cyprus are not Arabs.

The Kaaba, in Mecca, is the most sacred shrine of Islam.

Regardless of which country they live in, all Arabs speak and write the Arabic language. This common language is a powerful unifying force. As the map on page 405 shows, this unifying force ends in the north. There the Turks speak Turkish, and most Iranians and Afghans speak Farsi or related languages. The people in Cyprus speak Greek or Turkish, and Israelis speak Hebrew.

In recent times the "Middle East" has come into use as a political name for much of the realm. The Middle East generally includes Egypt, Sudan, Israel, Jordan, Lebanon, Syria, Iraq, Iran, Turkey, Cyprus, and the Arabian Peninsula.

Islam is the religion of most of the people.

Yet another common name for North Africa and Southwest Asia is the "Muslim World." Muslims are followers of Islam, one of the world's major religions. Islam was originally the religion of the Arabs, but it has spread to other peoples both in and beyond the realm. (Pakistan, Bangladesh, and Indonesia, countries outside this realm, are also part of the Muslim world.) As the map on page 405 shows, most of the population in North Africa and Southwest Asia is Muslim.

The birth of Islam. In the 6th century, the Arabs, who lived at that time only in the Arabian Peninsula, were politically weak, divided, and leaderless. Around the year 570, Muhammad was born in the city of Mecca, a trading center near the Red Sea. As you learned in Chapter 5, Muhammad attracted many followers who believed that he was a prophet or messenger from God. The influence of the prophet Muhammad was able to pull the Arabs together, and the new faith based on his visions and teachings, called Islam, spread rapidly.

403

The spread of Islam. After the death of Muhammad in A.D. 632, Arab armies conquered a huge empire that extended across North Africa and Southwest Asia. The Arab Empire continued to expand until about 750, stretching into Spain and Portugal in 711 and on into the south of France by 719. The Arab Empire also extended into parts of Central Asia that are now in the Soviet Union and China.

Throughout the Muslim world, people took pride in their strong, unifying faith and the culture they built around it. Muslim scholars preserved the knowledge of Greece, Rome, Persia, and India. They also made their own advances in mathematics, astronomy, medicine, and literature. Cairo, Damascus, Baghdad, and Cordova all became important centers of learning with magnificent buildings and mosques.

The duties of Muslims. *Islam* is an Arabic word meaning "surrender," and its followers, the Muslims, are people who "surrender or submit completely to the will of Allah." The "will of Allah," as revealed in Muhammad's teachings, was written down in the Koran, Islam's holy book. The Koran charges Muslims with five duties, called the Five Pillars of Islam.

The first duty is to state the **creed**, or religious principle, that there is no god other than Allah and that Muhammad is Allah's messenger. The second duty is to turn toward Mecca and kneel in prayer five times daily and, on Fridays, to pray in a **mosque**, a Muslim house of worship. The other duties include giving to the poor, daytime fasting during Ramadan—the holy month—and making at least one pilgrimage, which is a religious visit, to Mecca.

Muslim differences. During his life, Muhammad did not organize a priesthood or churches. After he died, his followers quarreled about who should fill the highest office of Islam. This argument was never really settled. In time, several **sects**, or religious groups, developed, each with different interpretations of the Koran.

The majority of Muslims followed the views of the Sunni sect. The Sunni Muslims took a practical, earthly view of the world. Another sect, the Shiah, or Shiite Muslims, formed smaller, scattered minorities. The Shiites emphasized contact with Allah and sought it through **imams**, the men who lead the prayers in the mosques. The Shiites generally kept to themselves in their own mosques.

For several centuries, the differences between Sunnis and Shiites remained simply a matter of religious approach. Then, early in the 1500s, the Shah, or emperor of Persia, a Shiite, decreed that Shiah Islam was the only approved faith in his empire. His empire took in present-day Iran, Iraq, Pakistan, and part of India. As a result, Shiah Islam changed from the faith of a few scattered minorities to the faith of many.

In addition, the Persian people had their own language and ethnic background. Together, these differences in religious interpretation, language, and ethnic background created a basic conflict among Muslims. This conflict is one of the causes of the war between Shiite Iran and Sunni-dominated Iraq in the 1980s.

Christianity and Judaism are minority religions in the realm.

Along with Islam, Christianity and Judaism had their beginnings in Southwest Asia. Today each religion continues to have several million followers in this geographic realm.

Christianity. As you learned in Chapter 12, Jesus of Nazareth founded the Christian faith more than 500 years before Muhammad was born. Jesus lived and taught in present-day Israel when it was ruled by the Roman Empire. After his death around A.D. 30, Jesus' followers carried the faith throughout the northern Mediterranean and much of the world. Small groups of Christians still live in this realm, including the Maronite Christians in Lebanon and the Coptic Christians in Egypt.

Ancient Judaism. Abraham, the father of Judaism, lived around 1800 B.C. Abraham was born in Ur, one of the oldest cities in Mesopotamia. At God's bidding, he moved his family and flocks of sheep to present-day Israel, then called Canaan. His descendants became the 12 Israelite tribes later known as Hebrews or Jews.

The early Jews were nomadic herders. Faced with food shortages, many of them moved to Egypt, where they lived for several hundred years. Later they were reduced to slavery. Around 1250 B.C. the great Jewish leader Moses led his people out of Egypt, across the Sinai Desert, and back to Canaan. This land became the land of Israel.

Around 900 B.C. Israel split into two nations: Israel and Judah. Israel was destroyed in 722 B.C., but Judah survived until 586 B.C. At that time, the Babylonians attacked, destroying the Jews' capital city of Jerusalem, leveling the temple, and carrying many Jews to Babylonia as captives. After Persia conquered Babylonia around 550 B.C., many Jews returned to Judah. This land became a Roman province in 64 B.C.

The Jews rebelled against Roman rule because

North Africa and Southwest Asia: Religions and Languages

Islam

▢ Sunnis ▢ Judaism ✡ ▢ Christianity ✝

▢ Shiites

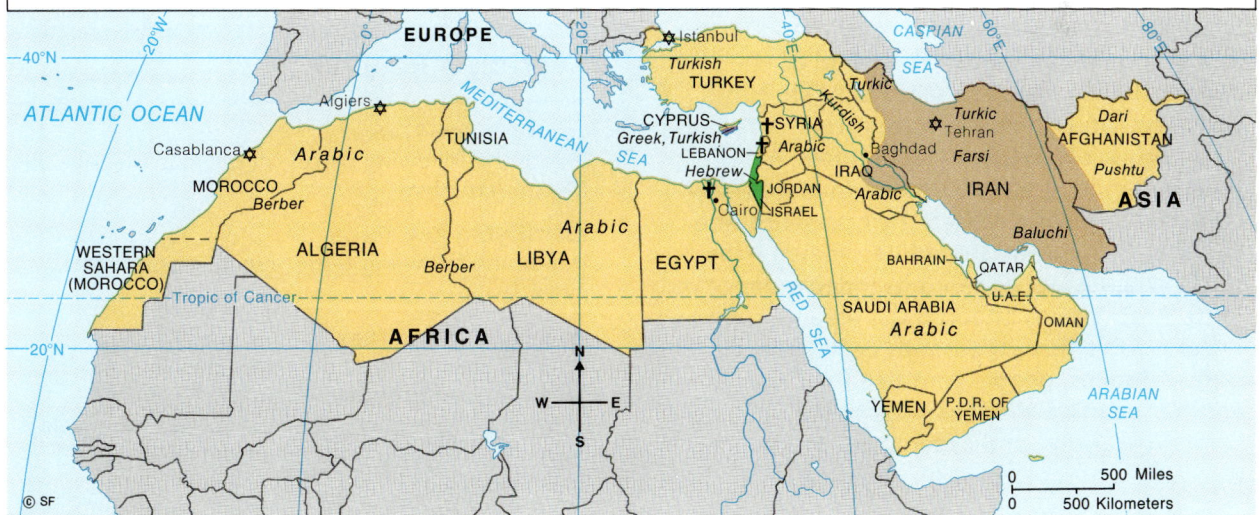

Map Study

This map illustrates the religious diversity of North Africa and Southwest Asia. What is the dominant religion? Where are the centers of Judaism and Christianity located?

the Romans tried to force the Jews, who believed in one God, to worship the many Roman gods. In A.D. 70. Roman armies destroyed Jerusalem and its temple. After another unsuccessful revolt in A.D. 135, most Jews were driven from their homeland, which was renamed Palestine.

Modern Israel. Over the centuries, Jews settled in different countries all over the world. They held on to their religious beliefs, however, and dreamed of regaining their homeland. Beginning in the late 1800s and especially after World War II, many thousands of Jews returned to Palestine.

However, many Arabs lived in Palestine, and they, too, viewed it as their homeland. In 1948, shortly after World War II, the United Nations tried to solve the problem. Palestine was divided into Jewish areas and Arab areas. The Jews called their new nation Israel. Since its founding, hundreds of thousands of Jews from all over the world have moved to Israel.

Jews and Arabs had generally lived amiably together for centuries in North Africa and Southwest Asia. Muhammad taught and Muslims acknowledge that the one God of the Jews and the Christians is the same as Allah. However, Jews and Christians were often treated as second-class citizens by Muslim rulers. After Jews began moving to Palestine in large numbers, many Arabs resented their presence and felt that the country should become an Arab state. When Israel declared its independence in 1948, Arab armies attacked the area.

During this time, thousands of Palestinians became refugees, people who flee their homes for another country. War has since broken out on several occasions, and Israel is still officially at war with a number of Arab countries.

Beliefs of Judaism. Moses was an important Jewish leader. During the Exodus, or journey out of Egypt, Moses told the Jews that they had made a covenant—a formal agreement—with God. According to Moses, God had promised to give them a new land in Israel and to watch over them—if they worshipped God and obeyed the Ten Commandments and other laws. Jews believe that God wants all people to work for a just society that treats everyone with respect.

The Ten Commandments are a set of rules for ethical conduct that are important to both Jews and Christians today. They formed the basis for a code of Jewish law and custom, which was subsequently developed and recorded in the Hebrew Bible. The Hebrew Bible is what Christians call the Old Testament.

The Hebrew Bible has three parts: the Torah, the Prophets, and the Writings. The first five books make up the Torah—the Hebrew word for teaching—and describe both the early history and basic laws of Judaism. The middle books of history and moral teachings are called the Prophets, and the last are the Writings.

Another important collection of writings is the Talmud, which is a series of interpretations and applications of Jewish law and custom.

Section 3 Review

Locating Key Places
Locate the following places on the map on page 394: Mecca, Jerusalem

Identifying Key Terms
Define the following terms: creed, mosque, sect, imam

Reviewing Main Ideas
1. What are the major groups of people living in North Africa and Southwest Asia?
2. What is the main religion practiced in the realm?
3. What other religions exist in North Africa and Southwest Asia?

Thinking Critically: Make Decisions
Which is the best name for North Africa and Southwest Asia—the Arab World, the Muslim World, or the Dry World? Give reasons for your answer.

Conflicts and Alliances

Preview

Key Places
Where is this place located?
1 Persian Gulf
See the globe below.

Key Terms
What does this term mean?
caliph

Main Ideas
As you read, look for answers to these questions.
- How were national boundaries created in North Africa and Southwest Asia?
- How do political concerns affect the realm?
- What is the primary natural resource of North Africa and Southwest Asia?

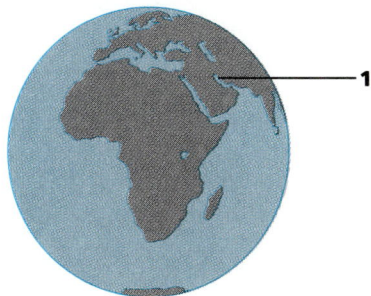

Why does Southwest Asia deserve attention? This is not a rich land either in agriculture or commerce. Except for fabulous reserves of oil, the area is poor in mineral wealth. . . . Something else must characterize Southwest Asia, for it has been the goal of world conquerers since the days of Alexander the Great. Part of the answer lies in its strategic location; here is one of the world's great crossroads.

George B. Cressey, *Crossroads*

Tradition and conquest shaped today's national boundaries.

If you look at the map on page 394, you can see what the geographer George Cressey means when he calls Southwest Asia a "crossroads." This whole area forms a land bridge that connects three continents—Africa, Europe, and Asia. Many civilizations have used this land bridge as a foundation for huge empires.

One such empire was the Arab, or Muslim Empire built by Muhammad and his followers. Much of the empire's unity died with Muhammad's successors, however, since they could not decide on who should be the empire's rightful **caliph** [kā'lif], or supreme religious and political leader. After A.D. 750 the Arab Empire gradually became divided into smaller parts. Much of it was later conquered by Turks and Mongols.

The Ottoman Empire. By the end of the 1500s, the Ottoman Turks, originally invaders from Central Asia, built an empire that united much of the realm. Find the limits of this empire on the map on page 408. The Ottomans were Sunni Muslims, and they fought, but never completely subdued, Shiite Persia, along their eastern frontier.

The Ottoman Turks also colonized much of Eastern Europe. The Ottoman Empire lasted, at least in name, until the early 1900s. By then, many local rulers held actual power. After World War I (1914–1918), the empire was disbanded, and modern Turkey was established.

The Arabian Peninsula and Iran. Local rulers controlled coastal portions of the Arabian Peninsula long before Muhammad. After converting to Islam, they ruled under Muslim titles, such as sheik, emir, or sultan. To this day, there remain the Sultanate of Oman, the Emirate of Qatar, and the Sheikdom of Kuwait. The large country of Saudi Arabia did not come into being until the 1920s, when the region was conquered by Abd al-Aziz ibn Saud.

Iran, too, can trace its modern boundaries to ancient times. Persia, as Iran was known until 1925, had a civilization that rivaled ancient Greece. Persians built and lost many empires but managed to fight off the Arab and Ottoman empires.

European colonization. In the 1800s and early 1900s, European nations took over North Africa and drew the straight-line boundaries shown on the map on page 394. It was easy for them to draw such boundaries through the empty desert because they doubted anyone would ever fight over the land.

During World War I, the remnants of the Ottoman Empire joined Germany, and as a result, were on the losing side when the war ended. Western European nations then took over the Ottoman Empire's lands at the eastern end of the Mediterranean Sea.

Persia, too, lost some of its territory because of European influence. Throughout the 1800s the Russians wanted to expand their empire

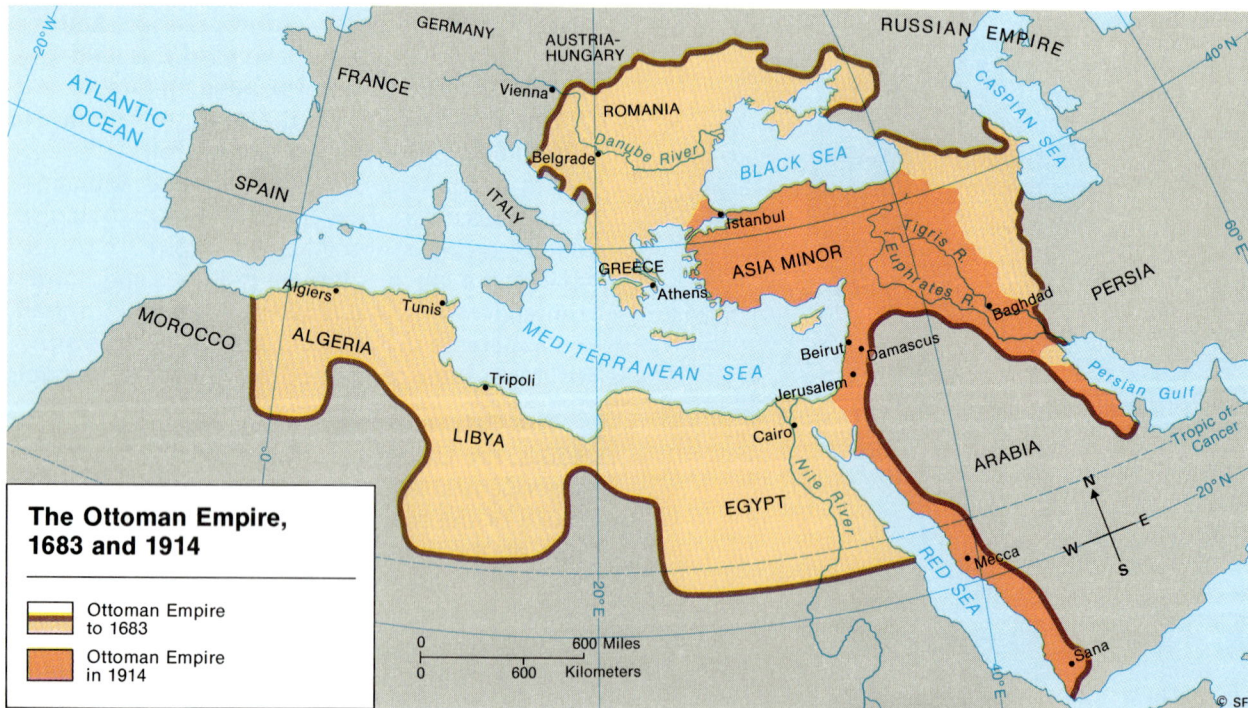

The Ottoman Empire, 1683 and 1914

- Ottoman Empire to 1683
- Ottoman Empire in 1914

0   600 Miles
0   600 Kilometers

Map Study

This map shows the Ottoman Empire at its peak in 1683 and in its decline in 1914. What present-day regions were influenced by the Ottoman Empire at its peak?

Oil refineries illustrate an industry that has both united and divided this area.

through Persia to the open sea-lane of the Persian Gulf. Britain wanted to stop them. The present borders of Iran resulted largely from a treaty between the Russians and the British.

Unsettled boundary questions. After World War II (1939–1945), the North African and Southwest Asian nations became independent. However, ongoing boundary disputes still exist between Iran and Iraq, between Morocco and Algeria, between Libya and Tunisia, and between Israel, Syria, and Jordan.

Political concerns both unite and divide the people.

Rulers of the emirates and sultanates of this area rule their countries like absolute kings. A radical military figure, Colonel Muammar el-Qaddafi, has led Libya since 1969. Kings also rule in Saudi Arabia, Morocco, and Jordan. In

Saudi Arabia, for example, the king is both a political and religious leader.

Israel is a democracy with many political parties. Egypt and Algeria are limited democracies, in that they have elected parliaments and presidents but have only one political party from which to choose. Yet another political system exists in Iran, where a Shiite religious leader has led the government since a revolution in 1979.

One of the most pressing concerns among Arab states is their relationship with Israel. Arab attitudes toward Israel partly reflect concern for the Palestinian refugees who left the area when Israel was created in 1948. Some refugee leaders formed the Palestinian Liberation Organization, or PLO, to work toward the creation of their own country. The PLO is a member of the Arab League, but league members disagree on the PLO's demands for a Palestinian state to replace Israel.

409

The World's Known Reserves of Oil and Natural Gas

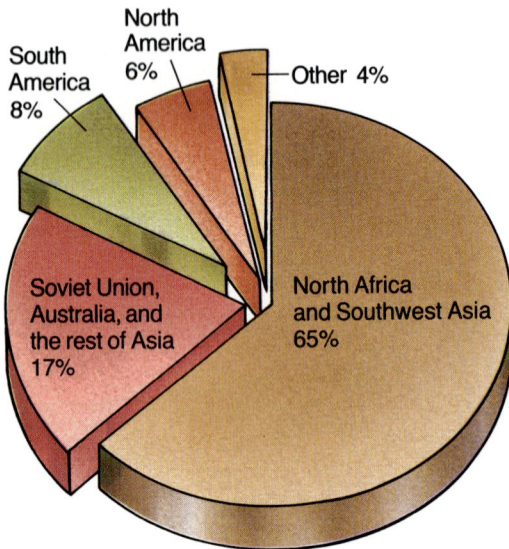

Oil is the realm's most important natural resource.

It is estimated that about two-thirds of the world's total oil reserves are held by nations in the Muslim World. As a whole, this region is not rich in mineral resources. Oil, however, is different. The countries surrounding the Persian Gulf have enormous oil reserves. Saudi Arabia has the largest reserves, but Kuwait, Iraq, Iran, and the United Arab Emirates all have vast oil deposits. In addition, Libya and Algeria are major oil producers. Since 1960 these countries have joined with such other oil-producing nations as Venezuela and Nigeria to form the Organization of Petroleum Exporting Countries (OPEC) in an effort to increase their political influence.

Over the years the billions of dollars raised by oil exports have brought great changes and many outward signs of modernization, particularly in the cities. In urban areas, freeways, traffic lights, schools, and hospitals are common. In the rural areas, change is coming more slowly.

In the 1970s high world oil prices brought sudden, enormous wealth to the Arab oil states and Iran. The situation also brought more contact with foreign influences. For example, the Arabs needed skilled technicians and workers to run the oil fields of the Arabian Peninsula. Lacking enough trained workers locally, the Arabs recruited workers from the West and from such Asian countries as Pakistan, India, the Philippines, and South Korea. With these foreigners came non-Islamic lifestyles, which the Arab states try to keep from influencing their societies.

In the 1980s ongoing conflicts threatened the continued supply of oil from Southwest Asia. For example, Iran and Iraq have been at war for many years. As a result, oil ships and rigs have been attacked, and many outside countries have become involved.

Section 4 Review

Locating Key Places
Locate the following place on the map on page 396: Persian Gulf

Identifying Key Terms
Define the following term: caliph

Reviewing Main Ideas
1. What forces created the boundaries of modern nations in North Africa and Southwest Asia?
2. How have political concerns divided the Arab people? How have they united them?
3. What are some of the changes that have resulted from the high price of oil in the 1970s?

Thinking Critically: Make Hypotheses
Many of the world's developing nations are beginning to use chemical fertilizers, some made from oil, and modern farm machinery in an effort to grow more food for their growing populations. How do you think these countries would be affected by rising oil prices?

Using Time Zones Maps

Suppose that you wanted to make a phone call to a friend who was an exchange student in Cairo. How would you know the best time to make the call?

A time zones map could tell you what the difference in time is between your home and Egypt. We know that the earth rotates on its axis once every 24 hours. To divide the world up into time zones, you might expect that you would just need to divide the 360 degrees of latitude on the earth by the 24 hours of the day. Each zone would then cover 15 degrees.

A glance at the map below tells you that things aren't that simple. People living in different areas have decided that they would like to be in different time zones. As a result, the time zones map has many irregularities.

In addition, many people around the earth have decided to observe traditional ways of keeping time. In Saudi Arabia, for example, some cities set their own time, marking noon as the time when the sun is directly overhead.

Now, back to your phone call. On the map, note that Cairo is marked 2 P.M. Let's say that you are calling from New York City, which is marked 7 A.M. Therefore, it is seven hours later in Cairo.

Review

If it is 12:00 noon in Cairo, what time is it in . . .
1. Moscow?
2. Ottawa, Canada?
3. Los Angeles?
4. Canberra, Australia?
5. Mexico City?

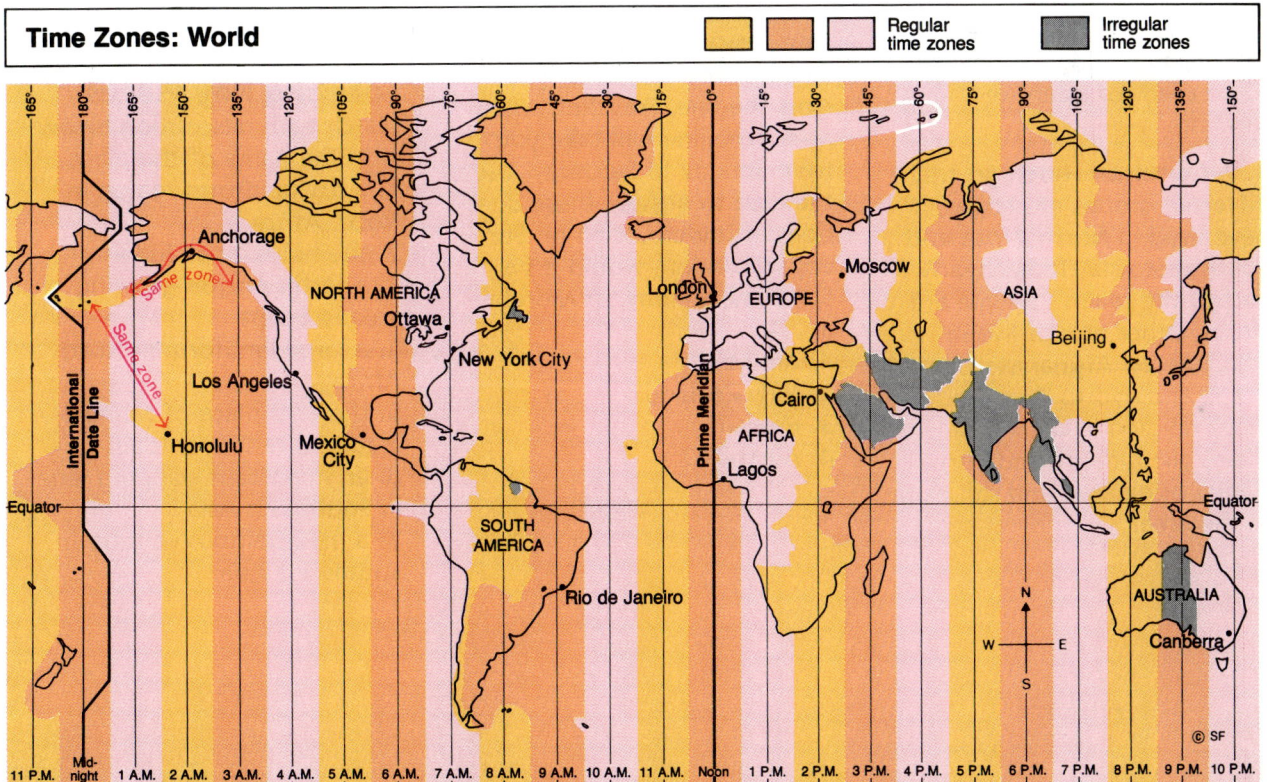

Time Zones: World Regular time zones Irregular time zones

CHAPTER 19

Review

Section Summaries

1. Landscapes of the Dry World North Africa and Southwest Asia are sometimes called the "Dry World" because their vast deserts make the realm the world's driest inhabited land. Many mountain ranges surround the deserts. In this realm, water supply determines where people live.

2. Climate, Soils, and Vegetation Dry climates, desert and steppe, predominate in the realm. There are also areas with Mediterranean and high altitude climates. People have adapted to the different climate types with their clothing and farming techniques. Irrigation allows the rich alluvial soils, found along river banks, to be used for intensive farming.

3. A Common Heritage Many different groups of people have lived in North Africa and Southwest Asia. Today nearly half of the realm's people are Arabs. Other groups live in Iran, Turkey, Afghanistan, Israel, and Cyprus. The predominant religion in the realm is Islam, but Judaism and Christianity originated and still exist in the area.

4. Conflicts and Alliances Modern boundaries were shaped by both tradition and by conquest. Political concerns that either unite or divide include boundary disputes, different forms of government, and relations with global powers. High oil prices brought wealth, and contact with non-Islamic ways of life.

Using Geography Skills

Reviewing the Map Lesson

Find the International Date Line on the map on page 411. It is the ending line for measuring time zones. When you cross the line, the day of the week changes. If you travel west toward the line on Sunday, it is Monday after you cross the line. Traveling east across the line will take you from Sunday to Saturday. Use the map to answer these questions. If it were noon on Sunday in London, would it be Saturday, Sunday, or Monday in . . .
1. Alaska?
2. New Zealand?
3. Hawaii?
4. Australia?

Using Social Studies Skills

1. Synthesizing Information. You've now read about the land, climate, and vegetation in this realm. Choose one country and write a paragraph about the way that nation is affected by its land, climate, and vegetation.

2. Sequencing Historical Data and Information. This chapter describes a number of events that helped shape the heritage of the people living in this realm. Use your text and, if necessary, an encyclopedia, to order the key events, from earliest to most recent.

Testing for Understanding

Locating Key Places
Match each description below with the name of the place.
1. a dry landform region in North Africa
2. the holy city of Judaism
3. a fertile cotton-growing area in Egypt
4. a large landform in North Africa
5. the birthplace of Muhammad and center of Islam
6. an important shipping lane in Southwest Asia
7. a mountainous country in Southwest Asia

8. a high, flat landform in Turkey
a. Atlas Mountains
b. Anatolian Plateau
c. Afghanistan
d. Sahara
e. Nile Delta
f. Mecca
g. Jerusalem
h. Persian Gulf

Recalling Key Terms
Define these terms in your own words.

Section 1
wadi
erg
oasis

Section 2
aquifer

Section 3
creed
mosque
sect
imam

Section 4
caliph

Reviewing Main Ideas
Section 1
1. What are the major deserts in the realm?
2. Where are the major groups of mountains located?
3. What is a major determinant of where people live in the realm?

Section 2
1. What is the most common type of climate in this realm?
2. What are two other climate regions found in the area?
3. Describe some ways that people adapt to climate in this realm.

Section 3
1. Who are the main groups of people in North Africa and Southwest Asia?
2. What is the predominant religion in the realm?
3. What other world religions were born in Southwest Asia?

Section 4
1. How were modern boundaries created in this realm?
2. How have political concerns affected the Arab people?
3. What changes have occurred recently in the realm because of oil wealth?

Thinking Critically
1. Identify Assumptions. Imagine that you found the following passage in a newspaper article: "Oil wealth has brought many benefits to the Arab people. One of the most important is the chance to learn more about modern ways. Trucks and automobiles have replaced the balky camel in many rural areas. Inspired by the example of foreign workers, many women have given up their traditional robes and veils for stylish suits and dresses." What assumption or assumptions was this writer making?

2. Predict Effects. Many scientists predict that, if demand for oil continues at the present rate, the world's oil reserves will be exhausted early in the next century. What effects might this have on industrialized nations? On Arab oil-producing nations?

North Africa

In this chapter you will read about the five Arab nations of North Africa.

Sections

SECTION 1

Egypt and Libya

Preview

Key Places
Where are these places located?
1 Suez Canal
2 Egypt
3 Cairo
4 Libya
See the globe below.

Key Terms
What do these terms mean?
fellahin   minaret
muezzin   bazaar

Main Ideas
As you read, look for answers to these questions.
- Why does Egypt depend on the Nile?
- Where do most Egyptians live?
- What is the greatest challenge today for Egypt?
- How is Libya governed?
- How does Libya use its oil income?

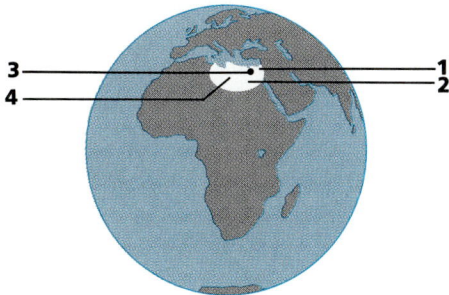

And thus, O Ruler of the Faithful, Egypt presents in turn the picture of a dry, sandy waste, of a stretch of silver water, of a swamp covered with thick mud, of a lush green meadow, of a garden rich with many flowers, and again of spreading fields covered with resplendent [splendid] crops.

Amr ibn el As, around A.D. 639

Egypt depends on the Nile for its existence.

From the words of Amr ibn el As—the Muslim general who conquered Egypt—you can see why 2,500 years ago Herodotus gave Egypt the name "Gift of the Nile." Without the Nile, Egypt would be almost entirely desert, except for scattered oases. One of the river's gifts was the rich alluvial soils deposited by the annual floods. These soils allow the country to be a leading producer of cotton, rice, and oranges. Another gift was the long stretch of waters that flow smoothly between the cataracts and the Mediterranean Sea. Ships have sailed these waters for more than 6,000 years.

Modern Egypt also owns another important waterway—the Suez Canal. If you look at the map on page 416, you can see the 118-mile canal located between the Gulf of Suez and the Mediterranean Sea. Built in the mid-1800s, this canal is one of the world's busiest waterways. It connects the Mediterranean Sea with the Indian Ocean and East Asia. Tolls from the Suez Canal are an important part of Egypt's income.

Most of the people in Egypt live near the Nile.

The Nile influences Egyptians in yet another way—nearly all the people of Egypt live on just 3.5 percent of the country's land, either along

Facing page: **Women in Morocco carry firewood gathered from scrub trees. Desert vegetation covers much of North Africa.**

the Nile or the Suez Canal. Only a small percentage of Egypt's population lives in the deserts or mountains away from the Nile.

About half of all Egyptians live in rural areas, with most of them living in crowded villages along the Nile. The rural villagers are peasant farmers called **fellahin**. The fellahin usually live in homes made of sun-dried brick and farm in fields rented from landowners. The rest of those in rural areas are Bedouin nomads—desert herders who consider themselves to be the true Arabs. The Bedouins travel around in search of land on which to feed their camels, goats, and sheep.

Nearly half of all Egyptians live in large cities. The two largest are Cairo and Alexandria. The cities are filled with a variety of people—wealthy landowners, middle-class people in service or technical fields, and poor, unskilled, and illiterate workers.

Cairo. The national capital, Cairo, is also Africa's largest city. With nearly 13 million people, Cairo is the home of more than a fourth of all Egyptians. In the newer, western half, skyscrapers cast gleaming reflections in the Nile.

Modern buildings house the president and the lawmakers of the national parliament, key people in a government that is officially called "democratic socialist." In this system, only one person can run for president, and the person must be nominated by at least two-thirds of the

North Africa

Commercial farming	Nomadic herding	⚲ Lumbering	Commercial fishing	Little or no economic activity	⊛ National capitals
Irrigated farming	Forests	♦ Mining	Urban land use		• Other cities

AZORES (PORT.)

ATLANTIC OCEAN

MADEIRA IS. (PORT.)

CANARY IS. (SP.)

PORTUGAL SPAIN ITALY GREECE TURKEY

Grapes Citrus Fruits

Ceuta (Sp.) Melilla Algiers Annaba Bizerte
Tangier (Sp.) Oran Constantine Tunis MALTA CYPRUS SYRIA
Tuna Barley Iron Ore Sfax MEDITERRANEAN SEA LEBANON IRAQ
Rabat Wheat Oujda Sidi Bel Abbès Dates TUNISIA ISRAEL JORDAN
Casablanca Sheep Tripoli Cotton, Port Said
Safi Meknès Oranges Alexandria Suez Canal
Marrakech MOROCCO Ghardaia Benghazi Giza Suez
Agadir Phosphates Ajdabiyah Al Fayyum Cairo SAUDI ARABIA
Sardines Goats Natural Gas Al Minya Rice
Camels ALGERIA Natural Gas Tanda Corn
El Aaiun Oil Dates Oil EGYPT
WESTERN SAHARA (MOROCCO) LIBYA Dates Luxor
Tropic of Cancer Camels Aswan
Tamanrasset Lake Nasser Aswan High Dam
MAURITANIA Iron Ore
MALI CHAD SUDAN RED SEA
NIGER Nile River

0 500 Miles
0 500 Kilometers

Map Study

Find the capital of each North African country. How are the locations of the capitals alike? What agricultural activity takes place in much of North Africa?

Egyptian legislature and approved by a majority of voters. The president may serve an unlimited number of terms and appoint a vice-president and cabinet of choice. The president also has the power to dismiss the legislature—most of which is elected by the voters—at will and run the government by legal decree.

Cairo's museums display many treasures from Egypt's glorious past. The dry desert air around the Nile has helped to preserve many artifacts and records of life in ancient Egypt. The Great Pyramid at nearby Giza and the Great Sphinx have attracted many tourists over the years. In and around Cairo, factories process cotton and other textiles, sugar, chemicals, paper, iron, and steel.

In the eastern Old Quarter of Cairo, narrow, winding streets connect buildings that were built centuries ago. Five times a day, **muezzins**, or criers, climb into the **minarets**—the slender towers of Cairo's many mosques—to call Muslims to prayer. Many streets in the Old Quarter are filled with outdoor shopping areas called **bazaars**.

Alexandria. Cairo's neighbor to the north is Alexandria, Egypt's second largest city and home to 2.3 million people. Founded in 332 B.C. by the Greek conquerer Alexander the Great, Alexandria was a great center of Greek learning in ancient times. Today it is Egypt's major port and second largest industrial center. Besides two oil refineries, Alexandria contains textile plants, an automobile factory, and a cottonseed oil processing plant.

Egypt's growing population is a challenge to its four regions.

Egypt is one of the most populous countries in North Africa. Currently, Egypt's population has been growing at the rate of about 1.5 million people each year. Every year the growing popu-

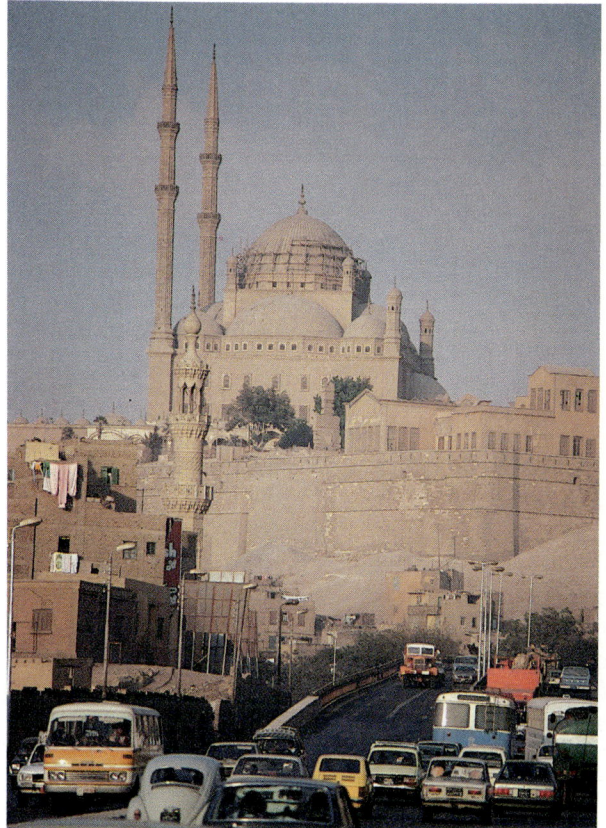

A high fortress called the Citadel surrounds the Muhammad Ali mosque in Cairo.

lation forces more of the fellahin to leave their villages for the cities, where they hope to find jobs.

Egypt's cities cannot supply enough jobs for all of these people, however. Often, the new arrivals join the many jobless and homeless people already living in slums or makeshift shacks. This rapid population growth is Egypt's greatest challenge. To supply more food and jobs, Egypt will need to develop the resources of each of its regions.

Lower Egypt and Middle Egypt. Lower Egypt is the area of the Nile Delta. Middle Egypt

417

Egypt's Predicted Population Growth

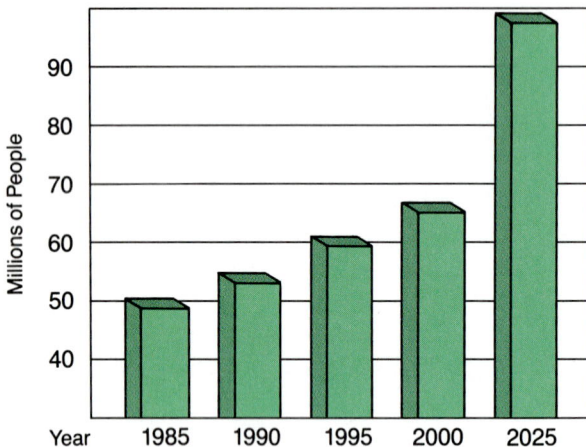

Chart: "Egypt's Predicted Population Growth" — bar graph. Y-axis: Millions of People (40, 50, 60, 70, 80, 90). X-axis: Year (1985, 1990, 1995, 2000, 2025).

lies along the Nile between Cairo in the north and Luxor in the south. Lower Egypt produces most of the cotton that Egypt sells to other countries for cash. Because cotton prices often fluctuate on the world market, cotton is an unreliable source of income.

Egypt, however, needs the money brought in by the cotton, so its farmers are still draining and irrigating more delta lands for cotton production. As a result, people are migrating to the Nile Delta in great numbers. Some geographers predict that half of Egypt's population will be living there by the middle of the 1990s. Together, Lower Egypt and the intensively farmed lands of Middle Egypt will probably be Egypt's core area for some time.

Upper Egypt. This region is the area of the Aswan High Dam and Lake Nasser. For many centuries the Nile River flooded each year, fertilizing Egypt's farmland. Now the yearly floods are controlled by the Aswan High Dam and have been used to irrigate 2 million acres of formerly dry land, doubling food production. Rice, wheat, and oranges are the major food crops of this region. Modern irrigation methods and the

warm climate let farmers harvest as many as three crops in one year.

Hydroelectric generators on the dam have also created electric power for rural farms and for industry. Even so, Egypt's food production has not kept up with the needs of its growing population. The country has had to spend much of its cash income on food imports, leaving little money for building industries that would strengthen the economy.

The dam has also brought some negative changes. Some of these are discussed in the case study that follows this section. In the past the Nile flooded every year, renewing the fields and replacing soil lost to erosion. Today the flooding is controlled by dams. As a result, the fellahin have to buy expensive fertilizers to enrich their fields.

Lake Nasser is in danger of "silting up," or becoming clogged by trapped river mud. The dam has also stilled the rushing floodwater that cleansed the river. By forcing the Nile to flow more slowly, the dam has harbored diseases and parasites found in still or slow-moving waters. People now stand a greater risk of becoming sick from using the water.

The Sinai Peninsula. Egypt's few oil reserves are found mostly in the Sinai Peninsula. Income from exported oil is a valuable addition to Egypt's economy. The Sinai Peninsula also has some small coastal fishing villages and some farming villages where water is available. About a fourth of the people living in the peninsula are Bedouin nomads.

The Western Desert. The desert lands west of the Nile make up about two-thirds of Egypt's total land area. At present only about 2 million people live in this huge area. The most populous place is the Al Fayyum Oasis near Middle Egypt. Egyptians have built canals that carry water from the Nile into a depression in the land that lies about 150 feet below sea level. The flooded depression had created an artificial lake and oases, where about a million people farm for a living.

The Western Desert has other land below sea level areas, including a large region called the Qattara Depression. There remains the possibility of channeling some of Lake Nasser's water into these spots for further desert irrigation.

Libya, rich in oil, has been run by a radical leadership.

Nearly 95 percent of Libya is desert. People can farm only in the Mediterranean and steppe climate regions along the northern coast and around the few oases deep in the Sahara. Although Libya is much larger than Egypt, Egypt has ten times more people. The reason is, of course, that Egypt has a huge source of fresh water, the Nile, that Libya lacks. Libya, however, has something that Egypt lacks—huge oil reserves.

Libya was ruled by the Turks from the 1500s until 1911. In 1912 it became an Italian colony. After 39 years under Italian rule, Libya became independent. In 1951 it set up a traditional Islamic monarchy to govern the country. It was

Ancient and modern worlds meet in Egypt. North of the Aswan Dam (left), used mainly to make electricity, are temple ruins at Luxor.

419

during this rule, in 1959, that rich oil fields were discovered in north central Libya. Soon oil money was flowing rapidly into the country.

In 1969 the military, led by Colonel Muammar el-Qaddafi, overthrew the monarch, King Idris I. They replaced him with a Revolutionary Command Council headed by Qaddafi, who has run the country ever since. Qaddafi has favored radical—or extreme—means to promote various causes, including support of terrorist groups in many countries, and opposition to Israel, Western nations, and Western influences. As a result, Libya's relations with the United States have been hostile. In the early 1980s Libya sent military troops into Chad, its southern neighbor, but suffered a major defeat in 1987.

Libya's radical policies have helped to divide the Arab world. Although some Arab countries have at times sympathized with Libyan causes, many have rejected Qaddafi's violence.

Libya has used its oil income to build its economy and buy arms.

Libya's main natural resource is oil. Today income from oil makes up about 80 percent of the country's revenue. Since most Libyans are farmers in a country in which only 8 percent of the land is arable, oil money has brought new wealth to the country. However, only about 50,000 of the country's 4 million people work in the oil fields. Most people still work on the land, usually raising cattle, sheep, or goats on land that is too dry for crops.

Overall, about 75 percent of the population lives along the Mediterranean coast. About one million of these people live in the nation's capital and largest city—Tripoli. Most of the remaining people live near the northeast coast. These two regions make up the most fertile land areas of the country. The rest of the people either live in two desert oasis regions in the southeast and in the southwest, or travel the desert lands as nomads.

Since the discovery of oil, lifestyles in Libya have begun to change. People who have traditionally led lives grazing animals or growing crops have begun to leave their farms and move to the cities. European clothing and customs have become more common than in the past. Qaddafi, however, has tried to keep most Western influences away from this primarily Arab and Muslim population.

Oil income has been used by the government to drill hundreds of new water wells, build new irrigation canals, and construct dams and roads. For example, irrigation canals now tap the huge underground lake beneath the Al Kufrah Oasis in the southwest. In addition, much of the money brought in by oil sales has been used to buy warplanes and advanced weapons and military technology from industrialized nations.

Section 1 Review

Locating Key Places
Locate the following places on the map on page 416: Suez Canal, Egypt, Cairo, Libya

Identifying Key Terms
Define the following terms: fellahin, muezzin, minaret, bazaar

Reviewing Main Ideas
1. In what ways has Egypt been dependent upon the Nile?
2. Where in Egypt do most people live?
3. What is an important challenge facing Egypt today?
4. Describe the leadership of Libya.
5. How has oil money been spent by Libya?

Thinking Critically: Recognize Values
What values are reflected in the government policies of Egypt and Libya?

Case Study: Tanda, Egypt

Preview

Key Places
Where are these places located?
1 Nile Valley
2 Tanda, Egypt
   See the globe below.

Key Terms
What do these terms mean?
chevron
millennia
water table

Main Ideas
As you read, look for answers to these questions.
• What are the homes of the well-to-do like in Tanda?
• How has El Arous changed irrigation methods for the farmers of the Nile Valley?
• What new problem faces the farmers of Tanda?

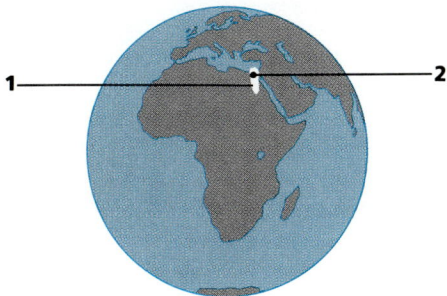

The following case study comes from the article, "The Nile Valley," by Bret Wallach. The source of the article is Focus, *Spring, 1986. This case study describes life in Tanda, Egypt, a village located in the Nile Valley. As you read, think about how important the Nile River is to the people who live in Egypt's desert regions.*

The well-to-do live in comfortable homes with simple furnishings.

Even in the Nile Valley, the Sahara feels very close. It is not so evident from the express trains whose tracks hug the river as they run up and down the valley, or from the narrow strip of cultivated land, 5 or 10 miles wide, that runs along the left bank of the Nile for hundreds of miles. The countryside here is laced with canals and irrigation fields. Yet come into a village and you know that you are in a desert settlement. Mudbrick buildings line the sun-baked, dusty dirt roads. There is no greenery; the only color comes from people—mostly children. . . .

A village elder in one such village, Tanda, invited us into his two-story mudbrick home. The front door led straight into a room for barnyard animals—in this case a female donkey. . . . Her coat had just been elaborately shaved into a pattern of decorative **chevrons** [a design shaped like an upside down "V"]. Off to the left was a small receiving room, a good twelve feet high in the search for coolness. Chairs and sofas solidly lined the walls. There was a worn carpet on the floor, and surprisingly, a telephone on a small table covered with an oilcloth. As in so many other homes of the well-to-do in poor countries, the room was lit by fluorescent tubes; its window shutters were tightly closed, and pictures of a Coptic saint . . . decorated the walls. [The Coptic Church is the national Christian Church of Egypt.]

421

Traditional wells are still used to obtain water in the Nile Valley. Cattle-driven wells like this one have been used for many thousands of years.

We were permitted to go upstairs. Part of the upstairs was open to the sky; a door led to the four rooms in which the family lived. Here were some modern conveniences: an electric refrigerator, a television, modern plumbing. I opened a shuttered window and looked down a vacant street. From a back landing the view was equally quiet, with just enough space between the neighboring houses for chicken coops.

El Arous provides the water for irrigation of farm fields.

Following the visit we joined officers from Egypt's irrigation ministry and headed for the "bride" canal—"El Arous" in Arabic. El Arous is a branch of the great Ibrihimiya Canal, which was built in the mid-nineteenth century and transformed the agricultural calendar of a great slice of middle Egypt. Lands that for **millennia** [thousands of years] had been irrigated once a year by floods were hereafter irrigated eleven months of the year with water drawn from the river far upstream. El Arous enabled two irrigated crops to be grown annually: cotton in summer and corn in winter.

Since its completion, the El Arous canal has experienced little change. . . . For a century, water has been released into the canal for ten days out of every twenty, year-round save for January. Along its course, farmers use diesel pumps to lift the water into ditches. Most of the ditches are long enough to serve twenty or more farmers who long ago worked out an arrangement for sharing the water. . . .

The rising water table is a new problem facing the farmers.

In the past the farmers often fought over water, but the Aswan High Dam put an end to most of the fights. Now the problem, in fact, is quite the opposite: there is so much water, and the farmers irrigate so frequently, that the water table is rising. [The **water table** is the depth below which the ground is thoroughly saturated with water.]

Along the El Arous the fields are white with salt. How high is the water table? A farmer pointed to a hole he had dug, and it was nearly full of water—full to within a foot of the surface. It was not rainwater or canal spillage; it was simply groundwater. Crop yields are suffering, but it would do no good for him alone to reduce the amount of water he applies to his fields; the rising water table is a community problem.

One of the proposed solutions for the drainage is being tried at El Arous. The head of the canal that serves the area will be permanently plugged. Henceforth, the farmers will depend entirely on about 50 wells being drilled on the orders of the Ministry of Irrigation. Use of the groundwater will cause the water table to gradually fall. . . . What is in the scheme for the Tanda farmers? From now on they will no longer have to lift water: El Arous will be rebuilt and the pumps will discharge at the new built up level. Gravity will do the rest.

There are still many unknowns with the project; the working out of a new irrigation schedule, the regulation and maintenance of pumps. But most problematic is coordination of the irrigation ministry's plans with the local farmers. The farmers depend on irrigation water in a more direct and inescapable way than almost any other group of people on earth. . . .

As it is, it seems probable that the project will be abandoned before it begins to operate or, if pushed to completion, that it will eventually fail, and the farmers will . . . restore the system of their fathers.

Section 2 Review

Locating Key Places
Locate the following places on the map on page 416: Nile Valley; Tanda, Egypt

Identifying Key Terms
Define the following terms: chevron, millennia, water table

Reviewing Main Ideas
1. What features characterize the homes of the well-to-do people in Tanda?
2. Why is El Arous important to the farmers of the Nile Valley?
3. Why is the rising water table a problem for farmers of the Nile Valley?

Thinking Critically: Assess Cause and Effect
Explain the cause-and-effect relationship between irrigation and the rising water table described in the case study. What do you predict will happen if a plan to lower the water table isn't put into operation soon?

Morocco, Algeria, and Tunisia

Preview

Key Places
Where are these places located?
1 Morocco
2 Algeria
3 Tunisia
   See the globe below.

Key Terms
What do these terms mean?
constitutional monarchy
maquis

Main Ideas
As you read, look for answers to these questions.
• Who were the early settlers of the Maghreb?
• What are the landscapes and resources like in Morocco?
• How is Algeria divided into regions?
• What goals has Tunisia adopted?

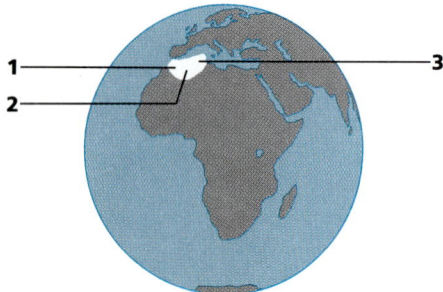

The successive civilizations coming from the out-side have been for the Berbers like outer garments under which body and soul remain unchanged.

André Julien

The Berbers were the earliest settlers of northwestern Africa.

The words of this French historian, André Julien, describe the Berbers—a group of people who first settled the northwestern coast of Africa. This region is known as the Maghreb [mä'greb], an area that includes Morocco, Algeria, and Tunisia. The Maghreb, which means "the West" in Arabic, got its name from early Arab travelers who thought that the scattered settlements in this area represented the westernmost point of civilization.

The Berbers probably migrated to the Maghreb from Southwest Asia about 4,000 years ago. No one is sure, however, because the Berbers do not have a written language. Their history is passed down by storytellers. Berbers have traditionally been herders or farmers who lived in small fortlike villages. Many have re-tained this lifestyle to this day, still possessing the fine skills of horse handling of their ances-tors. An independent people, the Berbers for many centuries resisted waves of invaders, including the powerful Roman Empire.

When Arab invaders reached the Maghreb in the late 600s, the Berbers became their allies. Together, Arabs and Berbers formed the Moor-ish Empire of North Africa. In 711 a Moorish army crossed the Strait of Gibraltar and gained control of Spain and Portugal. From the 8th to 11th centuries, most of this part of southern Europe was under Muslim rule. During this era, Spain became a great center of learning and ar-tistic achievement. The distinctive work of Moorish architects can still be seen in Spain and Portugal. Their buildings are characterized by complex lacy carvings, elaborate tilework, and refreshing courtyards.

Centuries later, the tables were turned, and in the period between 1830 and 1912, the Maghreb became part of the French Empire. Hundreds of thousands of French colonists moved to North Africa. Although France gave up these colonies in the 1950s and 1960s, Morocco, Algeria, and Tunisia still show the mark of French culture.

Morocco is a nation of diverse landscapes and resources.

Although Morocco gained its independence from France in 1956, some French people still live in this country. Since the early 1960s, Morocco has had a **constitutional monarchy**, in which the king appoints and controls a Council of Ministers, and the people elect the lawmakers. This government has traditionally held a moderate position in the Arab-Israeli conflicts of this geographic realm.

Each of Morocco's diverse regions has its own unique landscapes and resources. If you look at Morocco on the map on page 416, you will see that it has a very long Atlantic coast and short Mediterranean coast. In the middle of the country, the rugged Atlas Mountains take over. Near Tangier, the nine-mile-wide Strait of Gibraltar separates Africa from Europe.

The Atlas Mountains. The Atlas Mountains cover the center of Morocco proper. About a third of Morocco's 25 million people are Berbers who live in the mountains, where they herd sheep for a living. They generally speak various Berber dialects. Most other Moroccans speak Arabic, the official language of the country.

Mountain winters are bitterly cold, and snow may drift up to seven feet deep in January and February. Sometimes helicopters are needed to

Skilled horseback riding has long been a tradition among Moroccan Berbers.

drop supplies to snowbound herding families. During the rest of the year, paved roads and highways through the mountains are open and used often by skiers, fishers, and other vacationers.

The northwestern Atlas Mountains have large deposits of phosphates—Morocco's major mineral resource, and an important export that is used primarily in fertilizers. This country produces and exports more phosphates than any other country in the world.

South and east of the mountains. The Saharan side of Morocco's Atlas Mountains is dry, and the sparse population lives around several oases. On the Atlantic side, the southern lowlands are also fairly dry. Herders graze sheep, goats, and cattle here and in pastures that extend up the mountain slopes.

Morocco's Atlantic coast. Most Moroccans live north and west of the mountains. Northern Morocco's Mediterranean climate has warm beaches and commercial farms. Inland from the Mediterranean, higher lands are covered with forests of cork oaks. Northern Morocco centers on Tangier, located on the coast. Tangier is an international trade center, and many foreigners live there.

Morocco's core area spreads southward from Tangier. On the coast, Rabat, the capital, and Casablanca, the nation's largest city, experience cool breezes and fog from the Atlantic Ocean. Casablanca, with 2 million people, is the commercial center of Morocco. Casablanca and Rabat both contain manufacturing plants that produce cork, phosphate fertilizers, flour, refined sugar, and canned foods.

The cool waters of the Atlantic have enabled Moroccans to build a sizable fishing industry. The country's other leading industries include tourism and the production of such handicrafts as wool rugs, leather goods, silver jewelry, and brasswork. A portion of these goods are bought by tourists, most of whom are from Europe.

In the spring melting snow from the mountains helps water the Atlantic coast—the country's most important farming region. During the French colonial days, Moroccans developed modern, commercial farms. Today farmers work fields of wheat, barley, and potatoes, groves of citrus fruit, and vineyards in the large core area. Other crops include olives, figs, dates, rice, and a wide variety of vegetables. Morocco's farmers export fruits, vegetables, and flowers.

Algeria is divided into northern and southern regions.

Despite its long and bitter war for independence in the late 1950s and early 1960s, Algeria developed a special relationship with France after the war. The French bought most of Algeria's new-found oil reserves and supplied more imports to Algeria than any other country. Many Algerians moved to France to work, and French advisers helped Algerians improve their farming efficiency.

When the Algerians won their independence, they established a republican government. The government is led by a powerful president and legislature who are elected from one political party. The party supports socialism in which the government owns the nation's means of production.

Algeria has the largest territory of all the countries of North Africa and Southwest Asia. About 90 percent of this territory is covered by desert—the Sahara. As a result, most of Algeria's population of 23 million live in the north near the Mediterranean coast in a region called the Tell. The population, which is now about half that of Egypt, is growing at one of the world's highest rates.

The Tell Atlas region. The Atlas Mountains form several parallel ranges across Algeria's north. The most northern range, called the Tell Atlas, slopes down toward the Mediterranean Sea and has a Mediterranean climate. The farming region of the Tell Atlas makes up Algeria's

Algeria's vineyards flourish in the Tell Atlas region.

government ordered many of the vineyards to be uprooted. Some of the vineyards were later replanted, on the understanding that Muslims would not drink the wine. Algeria again became an important producer of wines. The Soviet Union has been a major customer for Algerian wines.

The Tell, as the whole coastal region is known, produces many other kinds of crops, including wheat, barley, potatoes, tomatoes, citrus fruits, dates, and figs. However, this comparatively small area cannot feed all the people. In an average year, Algeria must spend about 20 percent of its money on food imports.

Most of Algeria's people live in the Tell, which holds most of the country's towns and cities. Nearly 70 percent of all Algerians live in urban places. The coastal capital, Algiers, has a population of about 3 million, and the leading port, Oran, has a population of about 1 million.

The southern side of the Tell Atlas slopes down to a region of high-elevation grasslands. The land then rises again in the parallel range of the Saharan Atlas. Here the good soils, adequate water, and productive farmlands fade out. The farming areas that do exist here stand out against a background of forest, grassland, and **maquis**—the dense growth of small trees and shrubs often found in Mediterranean climates. Herds of sheep and goats graze on the mountain slopes.

Iron ore deposits also lie in the western and eastern zones of the Atlas region. Algeria fosters its economy by mining these ores.

Saharan Algeria. The Sahara begins south of the Saharan Atlas range. Along the foot of the mountains stands a string of oases. Some of them are quite large, with several million date palms growing on irrigated lands. Paved roads, railways, and air transport connect these northern desert regions and help attract tourists who

"breadbasket." Moist air blown off the Mediterranean produces rain, and rain-fed streams flow through the farmlands.

These favorable conditions attracted many French farmers during the colonial period. They laid out many grape vineyards and made wine one of colonial Algeria's major exports. This industry changed soon after independence. Since Islam prohibits the use of alcohol, the Muslim

427

stay in the oasis hotels. Deeper in the desert, nomadic herders and camel caravans crisscross the desert lands.

Algeria has two major oil fields—both located in the Sahara. One is deep in the desert near the midpoint of Algeria's boundary with Libya. A pipeline carries this oil through Tunisia to the coast for overseas shipment. The second major oil field is farther west and north in the Sahara. Pipelines transport this oil to the port of Skikda, on the Algerian coast. The northern Sahara also has large supplies of natural gas that is piped to the coast. Together, oil, natural gas, and refined oil products account for about 95 percent of Algeria's exports.

Tunisia has adopted goals of modernization.

The Atlas Mountains come to an end in the northwestern part of the small country of Tunisia. The northern quarter of Tunisia has moist, Mediterranean climate conditions. As a result, it is densely populated and intensively cultivated. The capital, Tunis, lies along the coast near the site of ancient Carthage. For hundreds of years, Carthage controlled trade in the Mediterranean until it was destroyed by its rival, the Romans, in 146 B.C. Rainfall decreases in the middle quarter of Tunisia, where steppe conditions prevail. The southern half of Tunisia is in the Sahara.

Stable leadership. After Tunisia became independent in 1956, it elected Habib Bourguiba president. He remained in office until 1987, when he was deposed in a coup. During his rule, Tunisia experienced great change. French and Arab cultures were both encouraged to develop.

Women received the right to vote, and public education was expanded throughout the country for both boys and girls. Tunisian universities graduate more scholars and technicians than the country can use. Many of them move to other African countries to find jobs.

Although industry did not greatly increase, the government strengthened agriculture to the point that nearly a third of the country—a very high percentage for the "Dry World"—is productive farmland. About half the fields grow new, more productive varieties of wheat and barley. There is still room, however, for more efficiency.

Industry and tourism. Oil exports, producing about 40 percent of its foreign income, have bolstered Tunisia's economy. Phosphates, iron ore, lead, and zinc also bring in money.

Tourism is another major source of income. Many fine resort hotels have been built along the Mediterranean coast, and a network of paved roads and railroads make it easy for tourists to explore the country.

Section 3 Review

Locating Key Places
Locate the following places on the map on page 416: Morocco, Algeria, Tunisia

Identifying Key Terms
Define the following terms: constitutional monarchy, maquis

Reviewing Main Ideas
1. Describe the lifestyle of the first people of the Maghreb.
2. What are some of the different landscapes of Morocco?
3. Describe the two regions into which Algeria is divided.
4. What has Tunisia tried to do in the last 30 years?

Thinking Critically: Recognize Values
How are Muslim values evident in Algeria's management of its productive farmland? Think of an example of values affecting agriculture or another industry in your own community or state.

Comparing Maps

Suppose that you wanted to know why people live where they do. How might you find out? One solution would be to compare two maps. In this way you could see how one aspect of geography relates to another.

The two maps on this page will help you answer your question. First, look carefully at the top map. Next, take the same care in analyzing the bottom map. Then, compare the two maps to find relationships.

The top map shows the generalized land use pattern in northern Africa. Most of the land is used for nomadic herd-

ing. Large areas are also listed as having little or no economic activity.

The bottom map shows the population distribution in North Africa. As with other such maps, dots illustrate where clusters of people live. People can be found throughout the region, but the population in the Sahara is so sparse that it does not show up on the map. In the densely populated areas along Egypt's Nile River, however, the dots are so close together that you can trace the course of the river.

When comparing the two maps, it becomes clear that most people in North Africa

live in areas of urban land use or commercial farming. Many of the mining areas have fewer than 10,000 residents, so no red dot appears.

Review

Tell whether the following statements are true or false. Then rewrite the false statements to make them true.
1. Algeria's herding areas support large populations.
2. In Tunisia most people live in the zone of commercial agriculture.
3. Well-populated urban areas tend to be located on a coast or near a river.
4. Most of the people in Egypt live near mining areas.

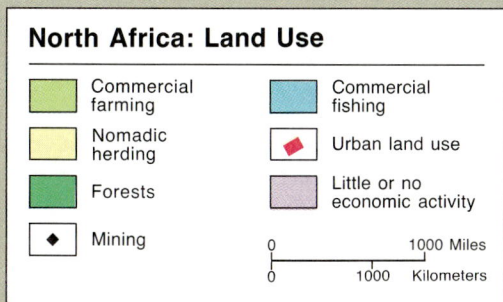

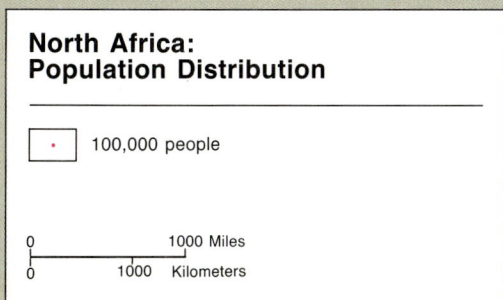

North Africa: Land Use

North Africa: Population Distribution

CHAPTER 20

Review

Section Summaries

1. Egypt and Libya Egypt has depended upon the Nile River for many centuries for fresh water and transportation. Most of the nation's rapidly growing population lives near the river, farming the fields made fertile by the river's annual floods. Egypt's western neighbor, Libya, is a desert country rich in oil. Its radical leadership has used its oil money to strengthen the economy and to buy weapons.

2. Case Study: Tanda, Egypt Tanda, Egypt, is a village in the Nile River Valley, where irrigation makes the dry soil productive for farming. In Tanda there are people who live comfortably with modern conveniences. El Arous is an irrigation canal that has allowed two different crops to be grown in a year. Along El Arous, the rising water table presents a problem to farmers who find that their fields are too wet.

3. Morocco, Algeria, and Tunisia These three nations form the Maghreb region of North Africa—the home of the Berbers. Morocco has been slow to develop its resources of productive farm areas and phosphates. Algeria has two main regions, a productive farming region in the north and a dry region in the south with oil deposits. Tunisia's main asset has been its stable government over the past 30 years. Tunisia has improved farming and education, and encouraged the oil and tourism industries.

Using Geography Skills

Reviewing the Map Lesson

Compare the climate regions map on page 399 with the population distribution map on page 429 to answer the following questions.
1. In which climate region do most of the people in North Africa live?
2. Which climate region covers most of the land with little or no population?
3. Why is there a population cluster in Egypt's desert climate region?

Using Social Studies Skills

1. Locate and Gather Information. In this chapter you've read about Egypt's population growth. Use a world almanac or encyclopedia to find the most recent population counts for each of the countries in this realm. Use this information to make a chart comparing the different countries and their populations.

2. Perceive Cause-Effect Relationships. North Africa contains some of the world's most extreme climates and physical landscapes. Using the maps in this chapter, and in Chapter 19, figure out how an area's physical environment affects how and where people live. Write a short paragraph explaining your findings.

Testing for Understanding

Locating Key Places

Match each description below with the name of the place.
1. an oil-rich desert country with a radical leadership
2. the largest nation in North Africa

3. a farming village along the Nile River
4. the country with the Nile River
5. the westernmost nation of the Maghreb
6. the capital of Egypt
7. a small modernizing nation
8. an important Egyptian waterway
9. a fertile area around an Egyptian river
a. Suez Canal
b. Egypt
c. Cairo
d. Libya
e. Nile Valley
f. Tanda, Egypt
g. Morocco
h. Algeria
i. Tunisia

Recalling Key Terms
Define these terms in your own words.

Section 1
fellahin
muezzin
minaret
bazaar

Section 2
chevron
millennia
water table

Section 3
constitutional monarchy
maquis

Reviewing Main Ideas
Section 1
1. How has the Nile been important for Egypt?
2. Near what natural resource do most Egyptians live?
3. What major challenge are Egypt's regions facing today?
4. How is Libya governed today?
5. What are the main ways that Libya has used its oil income?

Section 2
1. Describe the homes of wealthy citizens of Tanda.
2. What does El Arous provide for farmers in the Nile Valley?
3. What effects has the rising water table had on farming in the Nile Valley?

Section 3
1. Who are the Berbers?
2. What are Morocco's major land areas?
3. How do the two regions of Algeria differ?
4. How has Tunisia changed in the past three decades?

Thinking Critically
1. Make Hypotheses. Use the map on page 416 to measure the width of the Strait of Gibraltar. Why do you think many earlier empires wanted to control the land that is now Morocco? What would happen if any country managed to block this channel?

2. Make Decisions. This chapter described the influence of the Muslim religion on the economies of the nations in North Africa. Suppose, based on this information, someone concluded that in all nations religion is an important influence on economics. How reasonable is that generalization?

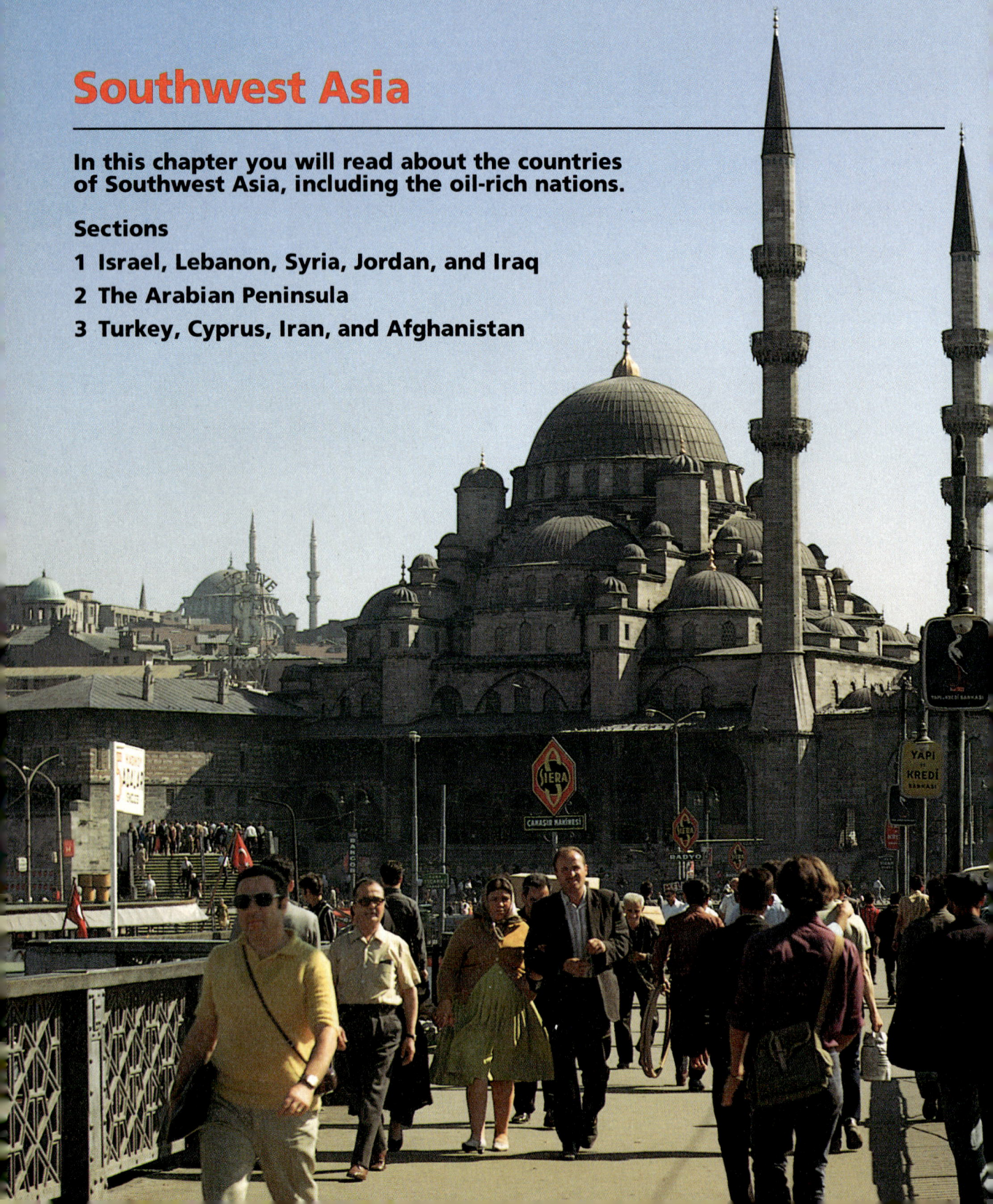

Southwest Asia

In this chapter you will read about the countries of Southwest Asia, including the oil-rich nations.

Sections

1 **Israel, Lebanon, Syria, Jordan, and Iraq**

2 **The Arabian Peninsula**

3 **Turkey, Cyprus, Iran, and Afghanistan**

SECTION 1

Israel, Lebanon, Syria, Jordan, and Iraq

Preview

Key Places
Where are these places located?
1 Israel
2 Lebanon
3 Syria
4 Jordan
5 Iraq
  See the globe below.

Key Terms
What do these terms mean?
kibbutz
anarchy

Main Ideas
As you read, look for answers to these questions.
• How has Israel developed its economy?
• How has Lebanon fared since it became independent in 1943?
• How is Syria governed?
• What has Jordan's king worked to achieve?
• How have Iraq's oil revenues been used?

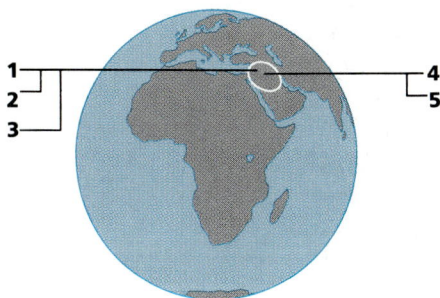

In the early days the Hebrews . . . spoke of their new home as a 'land flowing with milk and honey'. . . . But Palestine, though not without its rugged beauty . . . is far from being a garden spot. It has always required persistence and patience to wring a living from these stubborn hills, and the land has therefore nurtured deep faith and profound gratitude.

The Dartmouth Bible

Israel has developed its economy despite constant political conflicts.
More than 3,000 years ago, the Hebrews, or Jews, celebrated their exodus from Egypt to their new home in Palestine. Jews celebrated a second homecoming in 1947 when the United Nations voted to divide British-controlled Palestine into separate Arab and Jewish states. In 1948 Israel declared its independence and dedicated itself to building a new nation.

Physical and human geography. The tiny country of Israel is about the size of the U.S. state of New Jersey. It can be divided into four main regions. A narrow, fertile coastal plain extends north and south from the city of Haifa and contains most of Israel's farms and industries.

Through the center of the country runs the Galilean–Judean Highlands, which include Jerusalem, the capital. In the northeast, lowlands make up the Jordan River Valley. In the south, a desert called the Negev covers about half of Israel's land area.

Jews, many of them immigrants from other countries, make up more than 80 percent of Israel's population. Arabs and other non-Jewish groups make up the rest of the population.

Facing page: **Mosques are characteristic of Southwest Asia. This mosque is one of about 500 in Istanbul, Turkey.**

433

Although Hebrew and Arabic are the official languages, many different languages are spoken, and newspapers in ten different languages are published.

About 90 percent of Israel's people live in towns and cities. The large coastal cities of Tel Aviv-Yafo and Haifa are major manufacturing as well as population centers.

Economic development. What Israel lacks in natural resources has been made up by the determination and skill of its labor force. It has been said that Israel made the desert bloom,

Southwest Asia

▨ Commercial farming	▨ Nomadic herding	♦ Mining	▨ Little or no economic activity
▨ Irrigated farming	▨ Forests	▨ Commercial fishing	✴ National capitals
▨ Ranching	⌂ Lumbering	🐾 Urban land use	• Other cities

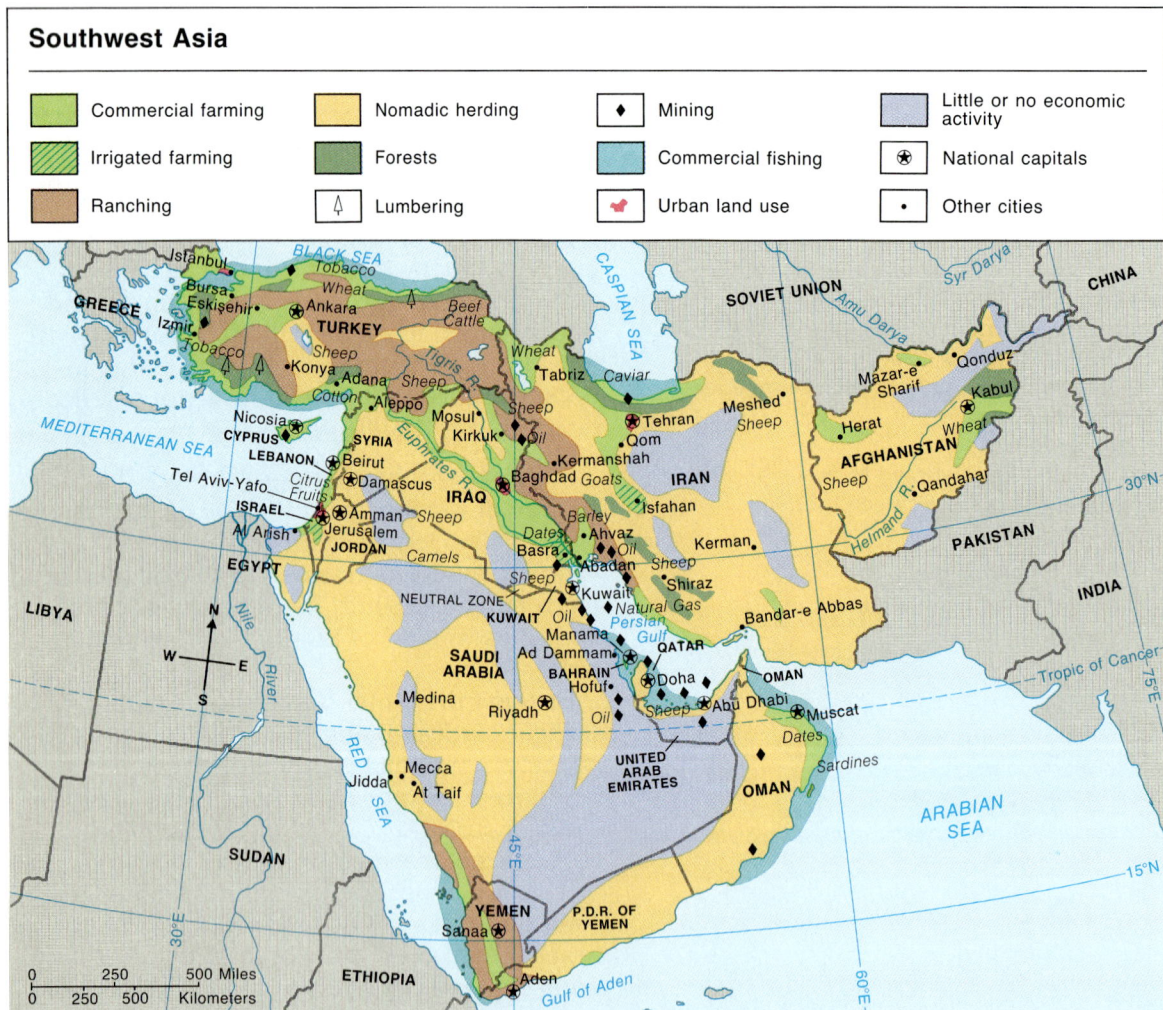

Map Study

Which countries in Southwest Asia border the Mediterranean Sea? Which countries border the Persian Gulf? What mineral is found in many places throughout Southwest Asia, especially along the Persian Gulf?

434

and in many places this is true. The National Water Carrier—a network of canals, pipelines, and tunnels that carries water from the Sea of Galilee in the north to the southern Negev—has enabled Israel to cultivate much of its desert lands. Products made by skilled workers also contribute to Israel's economy. The country exports such products as electronic equipment, textiles, chemicals, and military equipment.

About 5 percent of Israelis live on cooperative farms called kibbutzim. On a **kibbutz**, men and women work together for the cooperative. In return, they receive housing, food, education, health care, and child care.

Israel's farmers use modern equipment and techniques to produce grain, tobacco, olives, wine, vegetables, and citrus fruits. The country grows more than three-fourths of the food it needs, and relies on income from food exports for the cost of importing other food products.

Political conflicts. The day after Israel declared its statehood in 1948, the country was invaded by Egypt, Jordan, Lebanon, Syria, Iraq, and Saudi Arabia. This first of several Arab-Israeli wars ended after six months. During this war, Jordan occupied the region now known as the West Bank. The Arab countries continued to try to destroy Israel, and war broke out again in the 1950s, in 1967, and in 1973. In each war Israel captured territory from its neighbors.

In 1979 President Jimmy Carter of the United States helped forge the Camp David Accords peace agreement, which ended the state of war between Israel and Egypt. Israel then withdrew its forces from Egypt's Sinai Peninsula, with the exception of the Gaza Strip.

Israel still controlled a part of Syria called the Golan Heights. From Jordan, Israel had taken the West Bank. The people living in these areas, occupied by Israeli defense forces, increasingly fought for self-rule. Today relations between Israel and some Arab states remain tense.

Oranges rank as one of Israel's major crops. These will be processed for their juice.

Lebanon's economy has suffered greatly because of internal warfare.

When Lebanon became independent from French rule in 1943, the small country seemed headed for prosperity. Compared with other countries of the "Dry World," Lebanon receives substantial moisture. The soils of the Bekaa Valley—lying between two mountain ranges—are fertile and productive. More than a third of this mountainous country is suited to farming.

In 1943 Beirut, the capital city, was a beautiful, modern city and regional financial center with fine schools, hospitals, homes, and hotels. Today civil war has destroyed much of its beauty, and neighborhoods are divided by rival military groups.

Despite the years of civil war, however, the Lebanese population is one of the best educated and most highly skilled in the Arab world. Almost all the Lebanese are Arabs, but almost half of them are Christians rather than Muslims. The Muslims are divided into Sunnis [sù'nēs], Shiites [shē'īts], Druze [drüz], and other Islamic sects. In addition, small groups of people follow other faiths.

For a time the Christians and Muslims lived together peacefully. However, the 1943 constitution gave the most important political positions to the Christians. As the Muslim population became the clear majority, the Muslims called for more political power. Meanwhile, after various Arab-Israeli wars and other turmoil, about 400,000 Palestinians moved into Lebanon. As the Palestine Liberation Organization (PLO) gained power in southern Lebanon, tensions began to build among various Lebanese groups.

In 1975 a civil war broke out between Christians and Muslims. Syria sent troops to help the government try to restore order. Meanwhile, the PLO in Lebanon tried to attack Israel. In retaliation, Israel invaded Lebanon in 1982 to try to defeat the PLO. Soon after, the United Nations and many individual nations sent peacekeeping forces. These troops were withdrawn when Muslims took over the government in 1984.

By the late 1980s, Lebanon was a fragmented, crippled country. Israel had withdrawn, but fighting among Lebanese groups continued. Syrian armies continued to try to keep peace. Beirut, home of 40 percent of all Lebanese, was wrecked and filled with refugees. **Anarchy**— the absence of a system of government and law—reigned. The economy, which once had strong banking, food-processing, textile, chemical, and oil refining industries, lay in ruins.

Syria is an Arab country reliant upon agriculture.

As in Israel and Lebanon, Syria's narrow strip of coastal lowlands soon gives way to a mountain zone. Many towns and cities, from the important city of Aleppo in the north to the capital of Damascus in the south, lie on the eastern side of the mountains. These urban centers are built around oases that have supplied trading caravans for centuries. The oases get their water

from rain that soaks into the side of the mountains and then comes back to the surface along the base of the mountains.

Little rain falls on the east side of Syria's mountains. As one moves eastward, the land grows drier until the desert takes over again in central and eastern Syria. The Euphrates River crosses Syria's desert region. Although the country's arid and semiarid regions are sparsely populated, many farms and settlements lie along the Euphrates and its tributary, the Khabur River. There are also numerous oasis villages.

Near the town of Thawrah, Syrians have built a dam across the Euphrates and are constructing

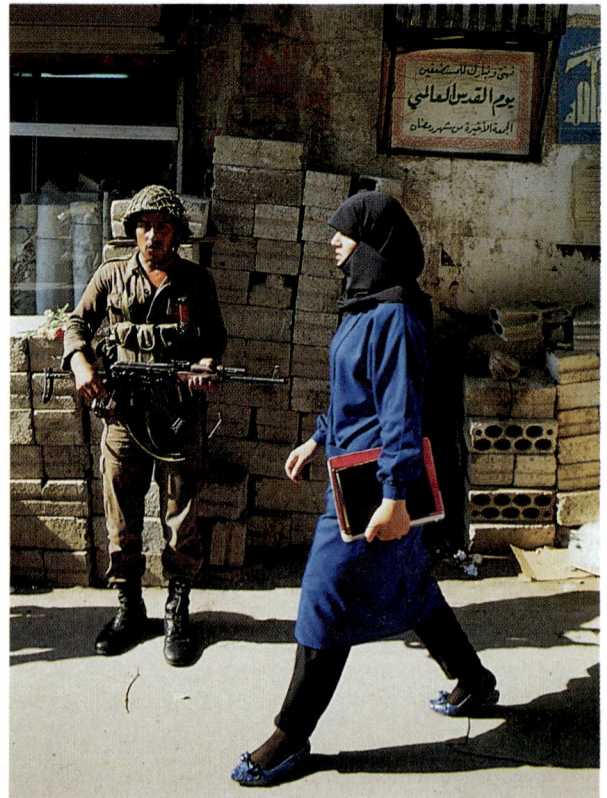

A Lebanese student walks along a street patrolled by a Syrian soldier in Beirut.

a large irrigation system. This development program will greatly expand Syria's farmlands.

An agricultural economy. Syria depends largely on farming and livestock for its income. Its leading farm crops are wheat, barley, cotton, olives, and fruits and vegetables. In addition, herders raise large numbers of sheep and cattle.

The Syrian government has been working to increase industrial production. For a long time, the country has manufactured textiles based on its wool and cotton production. It exports some oil from reserves in the north, but a general lack of major mineral deposits hampers industrial growth.

An Arab country. In this country of 11 million people, more than 90 percent of Syrians speak Arabic and consider themselves to be Arabs. About half of the population lives in rural areas—most living in small villages. Some Bedouin nomads travel the desert regions. The rest of the Syrians live in cities or towns.

As in most of Southwest Asia, Islam is the primary religion of Syria. Eighty-seven percent of Syrians are Muslim, and most of them belong to the Sunni sect. Other religions that are represented in the country are Judaism and Christianity—Greek, Armenian, and Syrian Orthodox faiths primarily.

Syria has a socialist government headed by a president. Syria's president runs the country as head of the Baath party, the only political party allowed to exist in Syria. Party members dominate the government, which controls the country's political and military power. The party also controls much of Syria's economy.

Jordan's King Hussein has tried to achieve modernization.

When Jordan became independent from Britain in 1946, it was an isolated Arab country with a small population of Bedouin nomads, a few small towns, and few paved roads. In 1948 during the first Arab-Israeli war, Jordan annexed the region west of the Jordan River, thus gaining a large population of farmers and urban Arabs. It also gained many Arab refugees from the area that became Israel. Together these groups are known as Palestinians. Today Jordan's population is about 4 million.

Although nearly 90 percent of Jordan is desert, a relatively moist area stretches along the eastern side of the Jordan River and the Dead Sea. Amman, the capital, is in this region, along with most of the country's farmland.

Jordan has enjoyed stable leadership under King Hussein, who assumed rule in 1953. With the help of grants, loans, and food from the United States and other countries, Hussein has modernized many aspects of Jordan. His government developed the port of Aqaba on the Gulf of Aqaba, Jordan's only outlet to the sea. It improved railroads, paved roads, and developed phosphate mines near the Dead Sea. Jordan exports phosphate along with some of its farm products, including wheat, olives, fruits, and vegetables.

In 1967 Jordan attacked Israel and lost the region west of the Jordan River now known as the West Bank. This area contained about a third of its population, many of its farms, and some mineral deposits.

In 1979 fighting between the PLO and the Jordanian army broke out. Within a year, the king's forces had gained control, and many Palestinians left Jordan for Lebanon and other Arab countries. During the 1980s King Hussein made great efforts to find a permanent solution to ongoing boundary disputes with Israel. Meanwhile, peaceful temporary solutions have continued to hold.

Iraq's oil revenues have been spent on weapons.

The ruins of ancient Mesopotamian civilization—in the Tigris-Euphrates river valley—lie within the heart of modern Iraq. Each year, river flooding renews the fertile alluvial soils of the valley with a fresh layer of silt.

About three-fourths of Iraq's population clusters on farms and in village settlements along the riverbanks and irrigation canals between Basra, near the Persian Gulf, and Baghdad, the capital located on the Tigris River near the center of the country. Most of the remaining people live in the northern mountains. The large western and southern desert regions are thinly settled.

Iraq has large oil deposits near Baghdad, and during the 1970s earned much foreign income from high oil prices. At the time, it used the money to improve its irrigation systems and agriculture. The Iraqis also made plans to build roads and bring electricity to remote villages.

An important minority group. Arabs make up about 70 percent of Iraq's population. About 5 percent of them are Christians but most are Muslims. About 55 percent of the Muslims are Shiites, and the rest are Sunni.

The most important non-Arab ethnic group— the Kurds—lives in the northern mountains near Turkey and makes up about 18 percent of Iraq's population. The Kurds are Sunni Muslims who speak the Kurdish language, which is related to Farsi. Until World War I, the Kurds were mainly nomadic herders who lived in an area called Kurdistan. This area has since been divided among Turkey, Iran, Iraq, and Syria. There are now about 5 million Kurds living in these four countries. The Kurds have struggled to get their own territory and government.

War with Iran. During the 1970s Iraq fought to put down a Kurdish revolt. When Iran supported the Kurds, Iraq bombed Kurdish villages inside Iran. Iraq and Iran then quarreled over rights to the Shatt-al-Arab waterway. This waterway—Iraq's outlet to the Persian Gulf—

forms part of the common boundary between Iraq and Iran. In 1980 open warfare broke out, and as the 1980s progressed, the fighting spread into the Persian Gulf, involving such foreign countries as Kuwait and the United States.

Shiite-Sunni religious differences also played a powerful role in the Iraq-Iran war. Both countries claim to have God on their side. About a million people on both sides have been killed or wounded, and many villages have been ruined. Iraq's economy has also suffered. Oil revenues intended for modernization projects have gone instead to weapons.

Section 1 Review

Locating Key Places
Locate the following places on the map on page 434: Israel, Lebanon, Syria, Jordan, Iraq

Identifying Key Terms
Define the following terms: kibbutz, anarchy

Reviewing Main Ideas
1. In what ways has Israel worked to develop its economy?
2. How has Lebanon changed since 1943?
3. Describe Syria's system of government.
4. What goals has Jordan tried to work toward?
5. How has Iraq's oil income been used?

Thinking Critically: Make Hypotheses
Based on what you have read in this section about the economic effects of warfare, how reasonable is it to conclude that wars generally hurt economies?

SECTION 2

The Arabian Peninsula

Preview

Key Places
Where are these places located?
1 Arabian Peninsula
2 Strait of Hormuz
   See the globe below.

Key Terms
What does this term mean?
welfare state

Main Ideas
As you read, look for answers to these questions.
• How have oil riches affected Saudi Arabia?
• How has Kuwait benefited from its oil revenues?
• What are the other Persian Gulf states?
• How have oil revenues affected Oman?
• What do the two Yemens have in common?

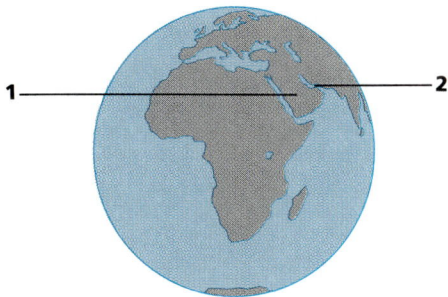

[When Saudi Arabia's King Ibn Saud was] Paid $250,000 in gold for the concession [right] to look for black gold, [he] hoped in his heart for water, it is said. But oil it was, popping the first cracks in old Arabia and opening the way to the new.

National Geographic, October 1987

Oil riches have brought a blend of old and new to Saudi Arabia.

Saudi Arabia's oil is found in its Eastern Province, along the Persian Gulf. This is where U.S. geologists began their oil explorations in the 1930s and where Saudi Arabia's oil-boom cities and industries are centered today.

Historically, the Arabian Peninsula was a land of a few settled oases and many different nomadic tribes. Each Bedouin tribe had its own defined wells and territories—where they herded sheep and goats. Camels, the "desert ships," carried Bedouin belongings from camp to camp. In their desert life, Bedouins developed a code of behavior that stressed hospitality, self-reliance, and loyalty.

In the 1700s a powerful and wealthy Bedouin family, the Saud family, gained control of most of the peninsula. A century later, the Egyptians defeated the Sauds and drove them out. The Sauds returned in the early 1900s and conquered most of the peninsula. In 1932 their leader, King Ibn Saud, founded the present kingdom of Saudi Arabia, named for the Saud family.

The Saud family still rules Saudi Arabia as a traditional monarchy. There is no constitution; there are no political parties, no elections, and no lawmaking representatives. Instead, the laws are based on Islamic commands and Bedouin traditions.

Oil and its impact. Oil was discovered in Saudi Arabia in 1936, and commercial production began during World War II. After the war,

439

the Arabian American Oil Company—Aramco—sent many technicians into the country. Aramco also trained many young Saudis. Saudi Arabia soon became one of the world's richest countries and the world's largest exporter of oil. Saudi Arabia now holds the controlling interest in Aramco.

The Saudis have spent their oil money on modernization projects. They have provided for basic economic needs such as roads, water supplies, and electrical and telephone service. They also provide education for all children. Because they know that the oil reserves will run out one day, the Saudis are also working to develop manufacturing and industry, especially chemicals and fertilizers.

Oil has also changed Saudi culture by bringing the Saudis into contact with foreign men and women. Oil has drawn people from the United States, Pakistan, Korea, France, Greece, Italy, and many other countries for work. Since most of Saudi Arabia follows the guidelines of Islam, there are certain restrictions that must be observed by all—Muslim or not. For example, people are not allowed to drink alcohol and women cannot drive cars. On the other hand, foreigners and Saudis alike shop in modern, air-conditioned supermarkets featuring imported foods and other products.

Throughout the years, the motto of Saudi rulers has been "modernization without Westernization." They have tried to preserve traditional family customs and conservative religious values despite such foreign influences as non-Arab workers, television, and technology.

Religious and political power. Almost all of Saudi Arabia's 11 million people are Muslims, primarily Sunni. As the protector of Islam's holiest places—Mecca and Medina—the king of Saudi Arabia has a powerful voice in Arab affairs.

Because of its wealth and religious role, Saudi Arabia is also a major political power in the Arab world. It was one of the founding members of the Arab League, and it has played an important role in OPEC. Despite maintaining good relations with the United States, Saudi Arabia opposed the Camp David Accords and still opposes Israel.

If you look at the map on page 434, you can see how Saudi Arabia faces Iran across the Persian Gulf. Saudi tankers must pass through the narrow Strait of Hormuz [hȯr′məz′] before they can reach the open sea. For this reason, Saudi Arabia has developed strong armed forces that can defend its tankers and oil installations.

Kuwait has thrived on its oil riches.

Wedged between Saudi Arabia and Iraq, the tiny country of Kuwait has been independent from British protection since 1961. Kuwait has only 1.8 million people, but its oil reserves—discovered in the 1930s—are about one-fifth of the world's known oil reserves.

Kuwait's emir, or ruler, receives half the country's oil income. This money has been used to modernize the country and build what is sometimes described as a "welfare state." In a **welfare state**, the government provides many basic necessities. Kuwait pays for all medical services and offers free education through the university level. In addition, telephone service is free.

Kuwait, however, faces several challenges. One is the large number of foreigners working in its oil fields. The Kuwaitis are outnumbered by foreigners whose customs often clash with Islamic ways. Kuwait's location on the Persian Gulf has also presented a challenge. In the Iraq-Iran war, Kuwaiti oil tankers have been endangered by rockets and mines used by the two nations in their struggle for control of the gulf.

Traditional and Western dress blend in Kuwait, as is common in the Arabian Peninsula.

Bahrain, Qatar, and the United Arab Emirates are Persian Gulf states.

Bahrain, like Kuwait, is an Arab emirate. This nation of 400,000 people is made up of 11 small islands off the coast of Saudi Arabia. Bahrain has a strong modern economy because of large natural gas and oil reserves. In addition, the country's refineries process Saudi Arabian oil before it is sent to overseas markets.

Qatar is a tiny emirate on a peninsula of the Arabian Persian Gulf. Its population numbers fewer than 300,000, with 80 percent of the people being foreign oil workers. The emir and his council have invested much of the country's oil money in development projects and services for the people of Qatar.

The United Arab Emirates is a union formed in 1971 of seven small Arab states. The individual states vary in size and oil production, and maintain their own local governments. The union allows joint policies in foreign relations, defense, and development.

Oman's oil revenues have not significantly changed the country.

Oman is a small oil-rich desert country located in the southeast corner of the Arabian Peninsula. Its location made it an important player in the sea trade until the 1800s when its sailing ships couldn't compete with faster steam-powered ships.

Oman's location has other consequences as well. A small, detached part of the country is situated on the Strait of Hormuz—the pathway of oil between the Persian Gulf and the Arabian Sea. In addition, Oman is one of the hottest countries on the earth, with temperatures often reaching 130° F.

Oman is governed by a monarch called a sultan. Although oil exports yield about 95 percent of all export income, Oman is still an isolated, undeveloped country. Most people—about 90 percent—live in rural areas, farming, fishing, or living as nomads. As with the rest of the peninsula, most of Oman's population is Arab and Muslim.

South Yemen and North Yemen are both poor Arab nations.

The two countries at the southern corner of the Arabian Peninsula are the People's Democratic Republic of Yemen—often called South Yemen—and the Yemen Arab Republic—called North Yemen. Muslim Arabs dominate both of these small nations, but they are divided into many diverse tribes and sects.

South Yemen. Since gaining independence from Britain in 1967, South Yemen has experienced little but strife and revolution. Struggles for power have placed many internal groups in conflict with one another. In addition, border conflicts have brought fighting between the two Yemens.

The fighting has destroyed much of the economic structure built during the period of British rule. South Yemen has no oil, very little industry, and few human or natural resources. Since 1975 the country has been governed by the United Political Organization National

Men and women browse through an outdoor market in North Yemen.

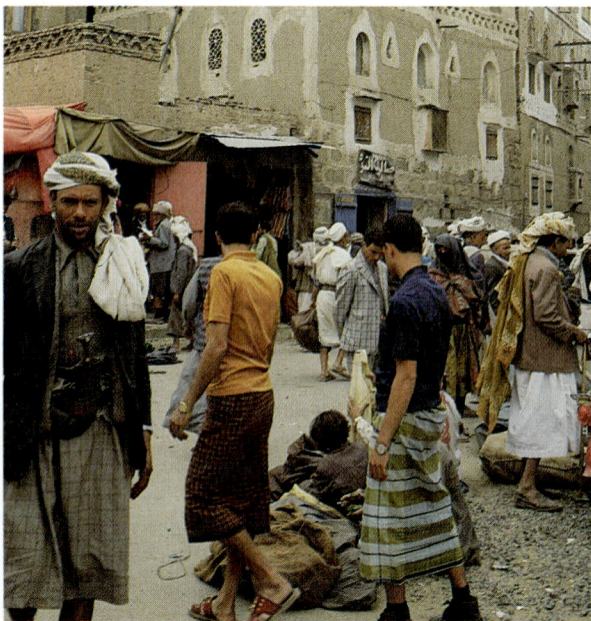

Front—the only political party. This leadership supports communist ideas and maintains ties to the Soviet Union.

North Yemen. At first glance, this country might seem to have the same economic problems as South Yemen. It has virtually no industry, and its only known mineral exports are oil and salt. Yet North Yemen has something its neighbor lacks—a fertile, mountainous region that receives enough rainfall to support both a profitable coffee crop for export and a large population.

North Yemen, like its neighbor, has experienced civil war among opposing political groups—in particular, during the 1960s and early 1970s. Politically, however, North Yemen has taken the opposite course from South Yemen. The government has friendly relations with the United States and with Saudi Arabia. As a result, it receives large amounts of food and other financial assistance.

Section 2 Review

Locating Key Places
Locate the following places on the map on page 434: Arabian Peninsula, Strait of Hormuz

Identifying Key Terms
Define the following term: welfare state

Reviewing Main Ideas
1. In what ways has the discovery of oil affected Saudi Arabia?
2. What benefits has Kuwait received from oil?
3. What are three other Persian Gulf States in Southwest Asia?
4. Describe Oman's economy and how oil plays a part in it.
5. How are the two Yemens alike? How are they different?

Thinking Critically: Make Hypotheses
Reread the quotation on page 439. Then use what you have learned about the geography of this realm to decide why the Saudi Arabian king hoped the geologists would find water.

Turkey, Cyprus, Iran, and Afghanistan

Preview

Key Places
Where are these places located?
1 Turkey
2 Black Sea
3 Iran
   See the globe below.

Key Terms
What do these terms mean?
secular
mullah

Main Ideas
As you read, look for answers to these questions.
• How did Kemal Atatürk affect Turkey?
• Why has Cyprus had a troubled history?
• How has Iran been governed?
• How have cultural differences affected Afghanistan?

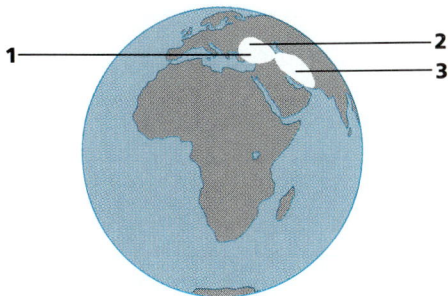

He was the "father sun" who could burn the enemies of one's childhood, but he was also the "mother sun" who could warm and soothe the child that remains within everyone. It was said that one could no more look directly into his blue eyes than one could gaze into the sun without blinking.

The Immortal Atatürk

Atatürk set Turkey on a path toward modernization.

The words of Vamik D. Volkan and Norman Itzkowitz in their biography, *The Immortal Atatürk*, describe the personal magnetism of Mustafa Kemal. In 1935 the Turkish Assembly gave him a new name, Kemal *Atatürk*, or "the father of Turkey." As a young army officer, Atatürk had seen the disintegrating Ottoman Empire fight on the losing side of World War I. Atatürk rallied the Turkish people and drove the European armies out. In 1923 Turkey declared itself an independent republic, and Atatürk became its president.

Atatürk wanted the Turkish people to forget the past—shaped mainly by Islam—and build a new, modern state. One of his first acts was to choose a new capital—Ankara. Ankara's central location, he reasoned, made it closer to all the people. The old capital, Istanbul (known in Europe as Constantinople), had been the capital of the Ottoman Empire since the mid-1400s.

Atatürk also made Turkey a **secular** nation— one in which government and religion are separate. Islam was no longer the official religion, and the state took over the religious schools. To make Turkey more westernized, the government recognized women's rights and encouraged both men and women to dress in European styles instead of the clothing required by Islamic custom. The government also changed the written Turkish language from Arabic script to the Roman alphabet.

The economy. Kemal Atatürk set two goals for Turkey's economy. The first was to grow enough food for the people. The second was to become industrialized. Today Turkey is still working to achieve these goals.

Although about 55 percent of Turkey's people live in cities or towns, the rest live in small villages or on farms. Two ethnic minorities—the Kurds and the Armenians—live in the high eastern mountains.

Turkey's best farmland is located on the low fertile plains and valleys in the west. In this region, a Mediterranean climate supports such crops as fruits, vegetables, cotton, and tobacco—many of which are important farm exports. On the inland plateaus of Anatolia, a steppe climate supports wheat, barley, and livestock herding. In most years Turkey's farmers can grow enough food to feed its population of 52 million. Farmers on the plateaus, however, lack irrigation systems that could protect their crops from long, frequent droughts.

Turkey's mineral resources include copper, chromium, iron ore, mercury, and manganese.

Istanbul, Turkey
(Mediterranean)

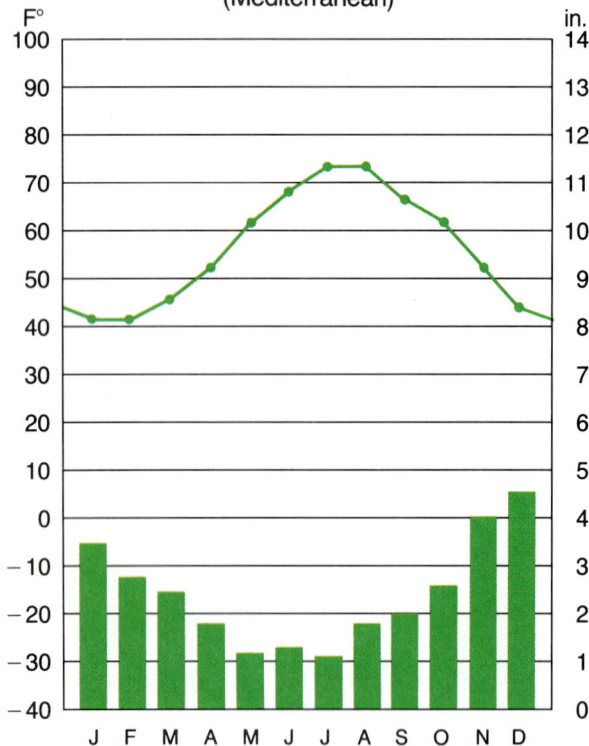

Ankara, Turkey
(Steppe)

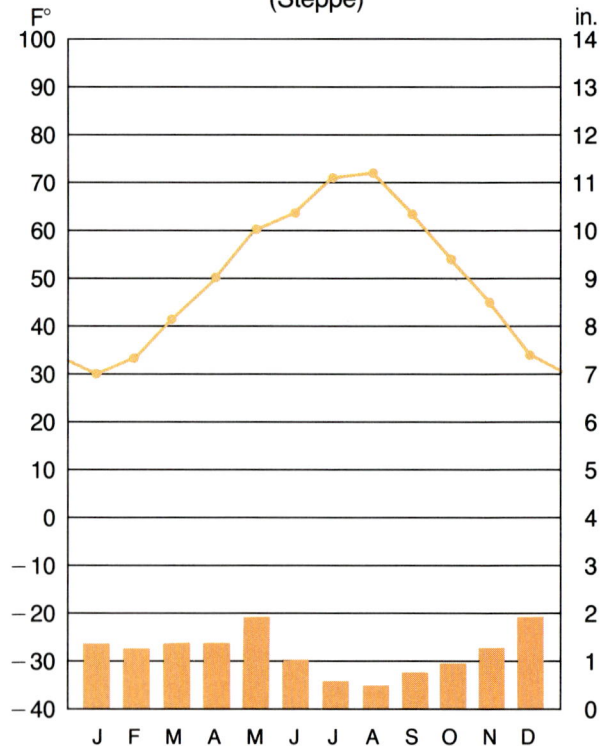

Climate graphs like the ones above are useful in describing the climate of a specific place. Each graph uses a line to show average monthly temperature and bars to show average monthly precipitation. Letters along the bottom of the graphs stand for each month of the year beginning with *J* for January. Each graph also tells in which climate region the city lies. Study each graph. How does Istanbul's climate differ from Ankara's climate?

The mountainous east contains a little oil and natural gas. Turkey exports some of its resources and keeps some for its own industries, such as steel mills and textile mills. Ankara is an important industrial center. Istanbul, Turkey's largest city, is a center for both trade and industry in the highly developed and densely populated west.

Since the 1940s the number of people living in urban areas has increased dramatically. The industries in the cities, however, cannot provide enough jobs for the population. As a result, many Turks have gone to other countries—such as West Germany, France, Australia, and Canada—to work.

International relations. Turkey lies in one of the world's most strategic locations. It has coasts along three seas and shares borders with the Soviet Union, Greece, Bulgaria, Iran, Iraq, and Syria. Turkey also spans the narrow entrance to the Black Sea. This waterway is the Soviet Union's only year-round outlet to the sea. By international agreement, this waterway is open to all ships. Turkey's alliance with Western nations, however, has strained relations with the Soviet Union.

Much of Turkey was originally settled by Greeks, and Turkey has a long history of conflict with Greece. As recently as 1987, there was a dispute over their common boundary in the Aegean Sea. Conflicts on the island nation of Cyprus have also involved the Turks.

Cyprus has been troubled by ethnic conflicts.

Geographically, Cyprus is a part of Asia. As you can see on the map on page 434, this small island nation lies close to Turkey and Syria. However, about 80 percent of the country's 700,000 people are descended from Greeks. Most Greek Cypriots are Christians. On the other hand, most Turkish Cypriots are Muslims.

Tensions between Greek and Turkish Cypriots did not end when independence from Britain came in 1960. Greek Cypriots still wanted Cyprus to become a part of Greece. When Greek Cypriots overthrew the government in 1974, Turkey invaded. In 1975 Turkish Cypriots declared their independence, but only Turkey recognized the new state.

Before its civil strife, Cyprus had a strong economy based on farming, tourism, and the export of copper, iron ore, and fruits and vegetables. Since the mid-1970s, many Cypriots have left to find jobs in other parts of the world.

Iran has had dictatorial governments.

Iran is a nation of 45 million people. Most of Iran's best farmlands—and most of its people—lie in a narrow strip of lowlands along the Caspian Sea. (See map, page 434.) Here enough rain falls to raise rice, tobacco, and mulberry leaves, on which silkworms feed. Iran's silkworm industry has been famous for centuries. The rest of Iran is mostly desert or steppe. In these dry areas Iranians are either nomadic herders or farmers who depend on irrigation and oases for water. Oil, Iran's most important resource, was discovered in 1908.

The Shah and the Shiite revolution. In the 1920s Iran, like Turkey, had a ruler who hoped to modernize a traditional Muslim state. Iran's ruler, a former army officer, was Reza Pahlavi. In imitation of the ancient Persian emperors, he used the title "Shah." His son, Muhammad Reza Pahlavi, took the throne in 1941.

Like his father before him, the new Shah devoted some of Iran's oil riches to economic and social reforms. He tried to improve the status of women, education, and public health. He also took land from wealthy landowners and redistributed it among poor farmers.

Many Iranians believed that some of these changes violated fundamental Islamic teachings.

Among the Shah's opponents were **mullahs**—religious scholars and leaders. The Shah offended the mullahs further by taking property away from the mosques. He established a police state, and his secret police imprisoned, tortured, and killed thousands of opponents. Many Iranians fled, including a mullah named Ayatollah Ruhollah Khomeini.

In 1979 Shiite revolutionaries overthrew the Shah. Khomeini returned to Tehran—the capital—and took control. Thousands of the Shah's supporters were killed or imprisoned. Modernization programs were ended, and Iranians were forced to follow the Ayatollah's strict interpretation of Islamic law.

War with Iraq. The Shah had tried to make Iran a military giant. Huge sums of oil money had been spent to buy weapons and to build a large army and air force. When Khomeini came to power, this military power became his.

In 1980 Iraqi troops invaded the Iranian-held portion of the Shatt-al-Arab, and in retaliation, Iran invaded Iraq. Since then, hundreds of thousands of young Iranian soldiers have willingly died in battle, believing that they would go straight to Heaven. Iraq and Iran have destroyed each other's major oil ports, and the fighting continues in the Persian Gulf.

Cultural differences have weakened Afghanistan.

A nation of 19 million people, Afghanistan is a landlocked country that shares boundaries with Iran, Pakistan, China, and the Soviet Union. It is a land of high mountains and deep valleys.

For centuries the people of Afghanistan lived in isolation. Many nomadic caravans moved across the country in search of water and pasture. Except for Kabul [kä'bül], the capital, most towns in Afghanistan remained small.

The Afghans are Muslims, mostly Sunnis. About half are from the Pathan—or Pushtu—ethnic group, but there are many other ethnic

divisions. Cultural differences have sparked tribal conflicts and civil wars throughout Afghanistan's history, and renewed power struggles erupted in Kabul in the 1970s.

In 1979 the Soviet Union entered the conflict on the side of one of the Afghan factions. As a close neighbor, the Soviet Union has always played an important role in Afghan affairs. The allied Soviet and Afghan forces planned to create a modern, secular communist state.

Soviet-controlled forces moved to take control. Anti-Soviet Afghans across the open countryside rebelled, and a war began. Afghan Mujahedeen—"holy warriors"—attacked Soviet supply carriers, and the Soviets bombed and devastated hundreds of villages. The war in Afghanistan dragged on through the 1980s, claiming thousands of lives and destroying the fragile Afghan economy. Today several million Afghan refugees live in Pakistan, hoping to return to their country.

Section 3 Review

Locating Key Places
Locate the following places on the map on page 434: Turkey, Black Sea, Iran

Identifying Key Terms
Define the following terms: secular, mullah

Reviewing Main Ideas
1. What did Kemal Atatürk contribute to Turkey?
2. What have been sources of conflict in Cyprus?
3. Describe the history of rule in Iran.
4. What has been the result of cultural differences in Afghanistan?

Thinking Critically: Recognize Values
Compare the modernization attempts of Saudi Arabia (modernization without westernization) and Turkey. What different values are evident in each country's actions?

MAP LESSON

Using Maps to Understand Economic Development

Suppose you wanted to find out how much a country had developed in a certain period of time. How could you learn? Maps might be able to get you started.

Economic development means the change from a traditional economy to a modern one. The facilities and institutions needed to support a modern economy—telephone and power lines, and transport systems—are called an infrastructure. Roads are an important part of that infrastructure.

Maps of roads provide a good way to gauge a country's economic development.

In a modern economy, individual villages and cities become less self-sufficient and more connected with one another. Roads provide a means of communication and travel.

On the map, note that in 1963 Saudi Arabia's roads went from seaports to selected cities in the nation's interior. It was not possible to cross the nation on a paved road.

By 1985, however, Saudi Arabia had changed dramatically. Most parts of the country were connected to each other by a network of roads. In the

process, cars replaced camels as the major means of travel. Saudi Arabians went from having fewer than 50,000 automobiles in 1963 to having more than 4 million in 1985.

Review

1. In 1963 could pilgrims from Riyadh use a paved road to get to the holy places of Mecca?
2. Which part of Saudi Arabia remains without a road network? Why might this be?
3. Why do you think Saudi Arabia developed so much in these 22 years?

Saudi Arabia's Roads, 1963

Saudi Arabia's Roads, 1985

Review

Section Summaries

1. Israel, Lebanon, Syria, Jordan, and Iraq These five Middle Eastern nations have been involved in many territorial conflicts. Israel has been able to develop its economy despite wars and tension with Arab neighbors. In contrast, Lebanon has been devastated by internal warfare. Syria and Jordan, despite involvement in Arab-Israeli disputes, have tried to modernize their agricultural economies. Iraq, on the other hand, has spent much of its revenues from rich oil deposits on weapons.

2. The Arabian Peninsula Oil is the major resource of this desert peninsula. The Arab countries of this region—Saudi Arabia, Kuwait, the Persian Gulf states, Oman, and North and South Yemen—all receive revenue from oil. The oil industry has brought large numbers of foreigners to the area. Some countries, like Saudi Arabia, have tried to modernize their economies and establish social welfare programs without changing their traditional societies.

3. Turkey, Cyprus, Iran, and Afghanistan These non-Arab countries of northern Southwest Asia have been involved in many territorial and ethnic disputes. Turkey has been on a path toward modernization, and away from strict Islamic rule, since Kemal Atatürk became president in 1923. Ethnic and cultural differences have divided Cyprus and Afghanistan. In Iran, a powerful dictatorial government has pursued war policies against Iraq throughout the 1980s.

Using Geography Skills

Reviewing the Map Lesson

The map below shows a causeway that was built to connect the island nation of Bahrain with the Arabian mainland.

The Bahrain Causeway

The causeway—a sign of economic development—was built to improve communication, travel, and defense.

1. In which directions does the causeway run?
2. Which two nations does the causeway connect?
3. What body of water does the causeway cross?

Using Social Studies Skills

1. Draw Conclusions. After Israel was founded in 1948, hundreds of thousands of Jews moved there from Europe, the United States, North Africa, Iraq, and other countries. How do you think these immigrants helped Israel's economy? Why were there relatively few cultural conflicts—even though people came from very different countries? Summarize your answer in a paragraph.

2. Synthesize Information. In this chapter, you have read how efforts to modernize Islamic economies have sometimes caused cultural conflicts. What advice would you give to an Islamic ruler who wanted to modernize the economy without challenging traditional values? Summarize your answer in a written paragraph.

Testing for Understanding

Locating Key Places
Match the description with the key places listed below.

1. a narrow waterway used by ships leaving the Persian Gulf for the open seas

2. a desert kingdom rich in phosphates

3. landform with some of the world's richest oil reserves

4. a Middle Eastern country formed for religious reasons

5. the site of ancient Mesopotamia

6. the Soviet Union's only year-round outlet to the sea

7. an oil-rich country with a dictatorial leadership

8. an Arab country beseiged by civil war

9. a mountainous northern country

10. an agriculturally based Arab socialist country

a. Israel
b. Lebanon
c. Syria
d. Jordan
e. Iraq
f. Arabian Peninsula
g. Strait of Hormuz
h. Turkey
i. Black Sea
j. Iran

Recalling Key Terms
Define these terms in your own words.

Section 1
kibbutz
anarchy

Section 2
welfare state

Section 3
secular
mullah

Reviewing Main Ideas
Section 1
1. What measures has Israel used to develop its economy?
2. What has happened in Lebanon since its independence?
3. How is Syria governed?
4. What has Jordan's King Hussein attempted to achieve?
5. How has Iraq spent its oil revenues?

Section 2
1. How has the discovery of oil affected Saudi Arabia?
2. What has Kuwait gained from its oil supplies?
3. Name three other Persian Gulf states in Southwest Asia.
4. What kind of economy does Oman have? How is it affected by oil?
5. What characteristics are shared by North and South Yemen?

Section 3
1. What effects did Kemal Atatürk have on Turkey?
2. What issues have caused conflict in Cyprus?
3. How has Iran been governed?
4. What have cultural differences led to in Afghanistan?

Thinking Critically
1. Predict Effects. Shortly after World War II, the Soviet Union demanded the right to control eastern Turkey and build military bases along the entrance to the Black Sea. Turkey reacted by asking the West for help and joining NATO, the Western military alliance. What might have happened if the Soviet Union had got its way?

2. Identify Assumptions. What assumptions does the writer make in the following passage?
"Iran lost much when it overthrew the Shah of Iran. The Shah's only goal was to bring his nation into the world's community of strong, modern, Westernized states. However, his people clung to their outmoded, traditional ways. In the Shah's place, they chose a religious fanatic, a man who believed that Western ways are the work of Satan. Under his emotional and unthinking rule, Iran lost the little progress the Shah had made."

Review

Summarizing the Unit

Chapter 19   A Physical and Cultural Overview This realm is often called the "Dry World" because much of it is desert. As a result, populations cluster around water supplies. Although desert climates are the most common, steppe, Mediterranean, and high-altitude climates are also found. The Arabic language and the Islamic faith make up this geographic realm's common heritage, but Jews, Christians, and other minorities also live in the region. The people in this region have often been divided over boundaries, foreign relations, religion, and politics.

Chapter 20   North Africa Like the rest of this realm, North Africa is very dry. Water and oil are two natural resources that have allowed countries to develop their farmland and their economies. In Egypt the Nile River is the center of both population and industry. In Libya oil provides revenues that are used both to bolster the economy and finance military activities. The western part of the region— the Maghreb—includes Morocco, Algeria, and Tunisia. These three countries share a rich history and a desire to modernize.

Chapter 21   Southwest Asia Most of the oil-rich Southwest Asian countries maintain agricultural economies in which people work as farmers and herders. Israel, an exception, has built its economy using advanced techniques in agriculture and industry. Except for Israel, Islam is the primary religion, though pockets of Christianity and Judaism exist throughout the area. Oil remains an important resource. It has brought great wealth and change to much of the region. Change from foreign influence, however, is not always welcome. In Saudi Arabia and Iran, for example, leaders discourage the customs of the western world in favor of strict adherence to Muslim values and practices.

Writing for Understanding

After prewriting and writing— which you've worked on in the last six unit reviews—the third step in the writing process is revising. This step involves many activities—reading and conferring, making changes, proofreading, and producing a final, improved version of the original draft.

(1) Read and confer. In this activity you first reread over your rough draft and correct any obvious errors. Then you have a conference with one or more other students who read your writing and suggest ways to improve it.

(2) Make changes. In this step you consider your classmates' suggestions and decide whether they are useful. Then you make the necessary changes.

(3) Proofreading. This activity gives you the chance to check for spelling, grammar, and content errors. Some common methods are reading aloud, following a checklist of questions, and checking a dictionary.

(4) Make a final copy. In the final copy, you would make sure that all of your changes are made, and that your writing is as clear and interesting as possible.

Activity. Choose a country in North Africa or Southwest Asia. Write a paragraph detailing its cultural or physical geography, using the chapter or other resources for information. Then meet with a partner to swap paragraphs and make suggestions. Finally follow the steps listed to develop the best possible paragraph.

Test

Key Terms (20 points)

Match each term with the correct definition.

1. poor farmers in Egypt
2. a fertile area that surrounds a desert well or spring
3. a cooperative farm in Israel
4. a division or group within a larger religion
5. a slender, high tower of a Muslim mosque

a. oasis
b. sect
c. fellahin
d. minaret
e. kibbutz

Main Ideas (30 points)

1. The world's largest desert is the _____.
a. Syrian Desert
b. Rub-al-Khali
c. Sahara
d. Gobi
2. A major North African population center is the delta of the

_____.
a. Tigris River
b. Nile River
c. Euphrates River
d. Jordan River

3. The most common climate in this realm is _____.
a. steppe
b. Mediterranean
c. high altitude
d. desert
4. Members of the most prominent religion in this geographic realm are _____.
a. Muslims
b. Hindus
c. Christians
d. Jews
5. The Moorish empire was built by Arabs and _____.
a. Turks
b. Kurds
c. Persians
d. Berbers
6. One of Atatürks's major reforms was _____.
a. making Islam the state religion of Iran
b. outlawing the Ottoman Empire
c. making Turkey a secular state
d. building new religious schools

Thinking Critically
(20 points)

1. **Evaluate Sources of Information.** Which map would be most useful if you were trying to explain how people live in this geographic realm—a physical map, a population density map, a political map, or a climate map? Explain your answer.

2. **Make Hypotheses.** Why do you think Islam has played such an important role in North Africa and Southwest Asia? How have the religion's values and customs shaped much of this region's history and culture?

Place Location (30 points)

Match the places listed below with the letters on the map.

1. Nile Delta
2. Persian Gulf
3. Libya
4. Morocco
5. Israel
6. Arabian Peninsula

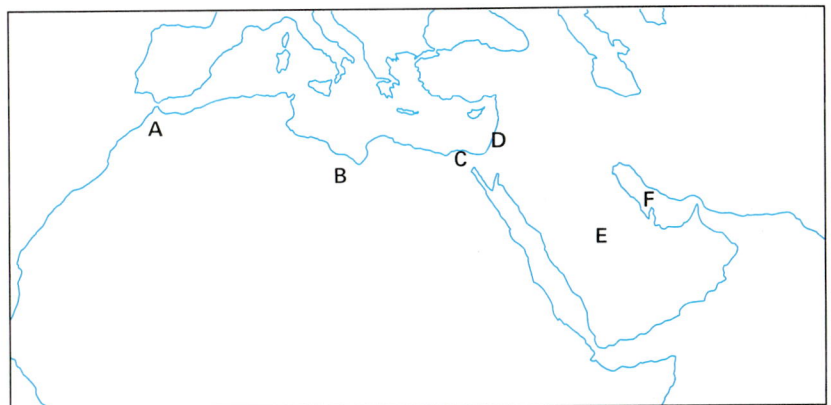

Sub-Saharan Africa

In this unit you will study the area south of the Sahara.

A Physical and Cultural Overview

In this chapter you will learn about Africa south of the Sahara.

Sections
1 Landforms
2 Climate, Soils, and Vegetation
3 Civilizations and Colonizations
4 Africa for Africans

Landforms

Key Places
Where are these places located?
1 Madagascar
2 Niger River
3 Congo (Zaire) River
4 Zambezi River

Key Terms
What do these terms mean?
escarpment
rift valley

Main Ideas
As you read, look for answers to these questions.
- How do Africa's coastline and mountains differ from those of other continents?
- What is Africa's main landform region?
- What is unusual about Africa's rivers, lakes, and valleys?

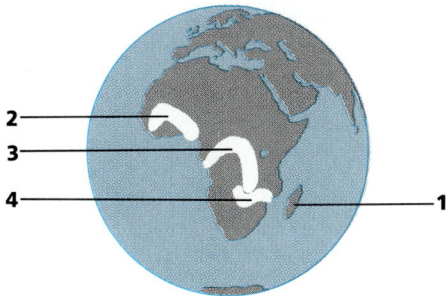

Nkosi Sikelel' Afrika. . . .

God bless Africa.

God bless the sun-scorched Karoo [plateau] and the green of the Valley of a Thousand Hills. God bless the mountain streams that chatter impudently when they are high in the hills and are young, but roll lazily from side to side like old women in the Great Plains. . . . God bless this Africa of heat and cold, and laughter and tears, and deep joy and bitter sorrow.

Richard Rive, *African Song*

Africa has a smooth coastline and no long mountain chains.

Imagine yourself riding in a spacecraft, approaching the earth. A few swirls of clouds hang over the blue oceans, but you can see the continents quite clearly. As you orbit the earth in preparation for landing, you are reminded that our planet has a land hemisphere and a sea hemisphere. The Pacific Ocean is almost half the orbit. Then there is mostly land.

Coming closer to earth, you begin to see more detail. You may see the high, arid plateaus of southern Africa and the meandering rivers described by Richard Rive. Africa, you begin to realize, is different from the other continents. Africa lies at the middle of the land hemisphere, surrounded by all the other landmasses. Africa is the only landmass without a Pacific Ocean coastline. Africa also impresses you with its bulk. It is large. Only Asia is larger.

The coastline of Africa also differs from those of the other continents. Africa has few deep bays, peninsulas, or islands. Only one really

Facing page: Shepherds look toward a lonely landscape in a scene common to much of Africa.
Page 452: Tailings, or residue, from a gold mine create a steep slope in South Africa.

Sub-Saharan Africa
Political

— International boundaries
✪ National capitals
• Other cities

0   400   800 Miles
0   400   800 Kilometers

EUROPE

ASIA

ATLANTIC OCEAN

MEDITERRANEAN SEA

RED SEA

Gulf of Aden

INDIAN OCEAN

ATLANTIC OCEAN

SAHARA

Tropic of Cancer

40°N

40°N North Latitude

20°N

Equator

20°S

Tropic of Capricorn

40°S

MOROCCO
WESTERN SAHARA (Morocco)
ALGERIA
TUNISIA
LIBYA
EGYPT
Lake Nasser

MAURITANIA
Nouakchott
CAPE VERDE
MALI
Tombouctou
NIGER
Agadez
Zinder
CHAD
AFRICA
SUDAN
Port Sudan
Omdurman
Khartoum
Asmara
El Obeid
Atbara River
Lake Tana
Socotra (P.D.R. of Yemen)

Dakar
SENEGAL
GAMBIA
Banjul
Bissau
GUINEA-BISSAU
Bamako
Ségou
Niamey
Ouagadougou
BURKINA FASO
Zaria
Kano
N'Djamena
Sarh
Addis Ababa
Dire Dawa
DJIBOUTI
Djibouti
Hargeisa
SOMALIA
ETHIOPIA

Conakry
GUINEA
Kankan
Freetown
SIERRA LEONE
Bouaké
Yamoussoukro
Monrovia
LIBERIA
Abidjan
CÔTE D'IVOIRE (IVORY COAST)
GHANA
BENIN
TOGO
Lomé
Accra
Porto Novo
Ogbomosho
Ibadan
Lagos
Cotonou
Sekondi-Takoradi
Lake Volta
NIGERIA
Abuja
Benue River
CENTRAL AFRICAN REPUBLIC
Bambari
Bangui
Lake Chad

CAMEROON
Douala
Yaoundé
Malabo
EQUATORIAL GUINEA
São Tomé
SÃO TOMÉ AND PRINCIPE
Libreville
GABON
P.R. OF THE CONGO
Brazzaville
Kinshasa
CABINDA (Angola)
Kananga
Mbuji-Mayi
ZAIRE
Kisangani
Zaire River
Congo River
Kasai River
Ubangi River

Luanda
Lobito
ANGOLA
Huambo
Likasi
Lubumbashi
Kitwe
Ndola
ZAMBIA
Lusaka

UGANDA
Kampala
Lake Albert
Lake Victoria
RWANDA
Kigali
BURUNDI
Bujumbura
Mwanza
TANZANIA
Arusha
Dodoma
Zanzibar
Dar es Salaam
Lake Turkana
KENYA
Nakuru
Nairobi
Mombasa
Kismaayo
Mogadishu
Lake Tanganyika

MALAWI
Lilongwe
Blantyre
Lake Nyasa
MOZAMBIQUE
Beira
Harare
ZIMBABWE
Bulawayo
Victoria Falls
Lake Kariba
Zambezi River
Limpopo River

NAMIBIA (South Africa)
Walvis Bay (South Africa)
Windhoek
BOTSWANA
Serowe
Gaborone
Johannesburg
Soweto
Pretoria
Maputo
Mbabane
SWAZILAND
Maseru
LESOTHO
Bloemfontein
SOUTH AFRICA
Durban
Umlazi
Mdantsane
Cape Town
Port Elizabeth
Orange River
Vaal River

COMOROS
Moroni
SEYCHELLES
Antsiranana
Mahajanga
MADAGASCAR
Antananarivo
Toamasina
Toliary
Réunion (Fr.)

Senegal River
Niger River
Nile River
White Nile
Blue Nile

N W E S

456

© SF

large island, Madagascar, lies off the southeastern coast. When you compare Africa with our own North American continent, you see that Africa has nothing like Hudson Bay, the Caribbean Islands, or Baja California.

You may notice that something else is missing in Africa. In North America you saw the Rocky Mountains stand out like a backbone from north to south across the continent. Long, narrow-ridged mountain chains also lie like great folds across South America, Europe, Asia, and Australia. Africa has no long mountainous backbone. The Atlas Mountains in the north seem to be an extension of Europe's Alpine system. The Cape Mountains in the south are relatively low. If you look closely, you can see tall mountains clustered in eastern Africa, but these are mainly volcanic cones.

Africa is a plateau continent.

If Africa has no long mountain chains to dramatize its surface features, then what landforms do stand out? Africa, particularly Sub-Saharan Africa—that part south of the Sahara—is almost entirely plateau. You can see on the map on page 635, however, that the plateau in southern and eastern Africa is higher than the plateau in the north. This upland, with an average elevation of 3,000 feet, earns Africa its name as the "plateau continent."

If you look for plains on the map, you find them mostly along the coastline. Often these coastal plains form a narrow band that ends abruptly not far inland. There the land slopes sharply upward in a long **escarpment**, or steep cliff. South of the Equator, Africa's many miles of escarpment are especially pronounced. In South Africa, the country at Africa's southern

Map Study

Name the countries that are bisected by the Equator. Which is the largest?

Victoria Falls lies between Zambia and Zimbabwe.

tip, the land rises sharply in a series of cliffs and low mountains called the Great Escarpment.

The African plateau is not flat and featureless. In addition to being higher in the east than in the west, the plateau sinks into basins or other large areas with lower altitudes. Three of these depressions lie in the north, centered on Mali, Chad, and Sudan. The largest, the Congo Basin, lies in central Africa. Another basin centers on the Kalahari Desert in the south. Use the map on page 458 to locate these areas of depression.

Sub-Saharan Africa
Physical

Land Elevation

Feet		Meters
14,000		4,000
7,000		2,000
1,500		500
700		200
0		0
Below Sea Level		Below Sea Level

—— International boundaries

▲ Mountain peaks

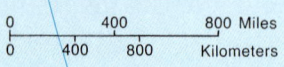

EUROPE

ASIA

ATLANTIC OCEAN

Azores

Madeira Is.

Canary Is.

Cape Verde

Strait of Gibraltar

ATLAS MOUNTAINS

MEDITERRANEAN SEA

Gulf of Sidra

Suez Canal

Nile River

Lake Nasser

RED SEA

Tropic of Cancer

40°N

40° North Latitude

20°N

S A H A R A

AHAGGAR PLATEAU

TIBESTI MOUNTAINS

LIBYAN DESERT

ENNEDI PLATEAU

NUBIAN DESERT

GÉZIRA

S A H E L

AÏR MASSIF

Lake Chad

Senegal River

Niger River

JOS PLATEAU

ADAMAWA MTS.

Benue River

Lake Tana

Ras Dashen 15,158 ft. (4,620 m) ▲

Bab el Mandeb

Gulf of Aden

Socot

ETHIOPIAN HIGHLANDS

HORN OF AFRICA

SOMALI PENINSULA

Blue Nile

White Nile

Atbara River

Cape Lopez

Mt. Cameroon 13,353 ft. (4,070 m) ▲

Bioko

Príncipe

São Tomé

Gulf of Guinea

Black Volta

White Volta

CONGO BASIN

Ubangi River

Zaire River

GREAT RIFT VALLEY

Lake Albert

Lake Victoria

Lake Turkana

Margherita Peak 16,762 ft. (5,109 m) ▲

Mt. Kenya 17,058 ft. (5,199 m) ▲

Mt. Kilimanjaro 19,340 ft. (5,895 m) ▲

Pemba

Zanzibar

MITUMBA MTS.

Lake Tanganyika

Seychelles

Equator

0°

ATLANTIC OCEAN

Congo River

Kasai River

KATANGA PLATEAU

BIÉ PLATEAU

Cape Delgado

Comoro Is.

Lake Nyasa (Lake Malawi)

Lake Kariba

Zambezi River

OKAVANGO SWAMP

Victoria Falls

Mozambique Channel

Madagascar

Mauritiu

Reunion

20°S

Tropic of Capricorn

KALAHARI DESERT

NAMIB DESERT

Limpopo River

Orange River

Vaal River

GREAT ESCARPMENT

DRAKENSBERG RANGE

GREAT KARROO

Cape of Good Hope

INDIAN OCEAN

N
W   E
S

0 400 800 Miles
0 400 800 Kilometers

© SF

40°S

Rivers, lakes, and valleys cut through the African plateau.

Your list of Africa's unique physical features is far from complete. Its large rivers, long lakes, and high-walled valleys are also noteworthy.

Twisting and turning rivers. Find the Niger River on the map on page 458. The Niger rises in highlands only 200 miles from the Atlantic Ocean and flows northeast toward the Sahara. On the edge of the desert it creates an inland delta, as if it were flowing into some inland lake. The Niger is flowing into one of the basins you just read about, the one centered on Mali. Then the Niger makes a drastic change in direction. The river descends over waterfalls and rapids and heads southeast and then south until it empties into the Gulf of Guinea. There it creates a second delta.

On the map on page 458, find Africa's other great rivers—the Nile in the northeast, the Congo near the Equator, and the Zambezi in the southeast. Follow the path of each river. Notice that the Congo is called the Zaire [zä ir'] as it flows through the nation of Zaire. Note that the Nile, the Congo, and the Zambezi twist and turn like the Niger.

Long, narrow lakes and valleys. Look again at the map on page 458 and locate the lakes that begin in Ethiopia and curve southward in chainlike fashion to the Zambezi River. Except for Lake Victoria in the middle, these lakes are all long and narrow, like fingers. The lakes often lie in steep, high-walled trenches.

Many more such trenches extend over the same area. In fact, series of parallel trenches cut across eastern Africa and extend northward

4,000 miles through the Red Sea and into parts of Israel and Jordan in Southwest Asia. Together they make up the Great Rift Valley system. A **rift valley** is formed when a long, narrow section of the earth's crust sinks below the surrounding area. Eastern Africa's long lakes and the Red Sea are the bottoms of rift valleys filled with water. Some of Africa's dry rift valleys have grassy floors 20 to 60 miles across. Their walls may rise almost straight up to the surface of the high plateau. In other valleys, the walls ascend in a more gradual, stairstep fashion.

Section 1 Review

Locating Key Places
Locate the following places on the map on page 458: Madagascar, Niger River, Congo (Zaire) River, Zambezi River

Identifying Key Terms
Define the following terms: escarpment, rift valley

Reviewing Main Ideas
1. In what ways do Africa's coastline and mountains compare to those of other continents?
2. What major landform dominates the African landscape?
3. What special features distinguish Africa's major rivers and its eastern lakes and valleys?

Thinking Critically: Evaluate Sources of Information
Suppose you planned to visit Tanzania, Kenya, and Zambia and want to do some research about the physical features you will see in each country. Which of the following sources would best suit your needs? Explain your answer.
- a political map of Africa like the one on page 456
- a physical map of Africa like the one on page 458
- an atlas with physical and political maps of each country in Africa
- a physical map of the Great Rift Valley in Tanzania

Map Study

Find the Great Rift Valley in Africa. What lakes are located within it?

Climate, Soils, and Vegetation

Preview

Key Places
Where are these places located?
1 Kalahari Desert
2 Namib Desert

Key Terms
What does this term mean?
veld

Main Ideas
As you read, look for answers to these questions.
- Why are latitude and altitude important in learning about Africa?
- What are Africa's main forms of natural vegetation?
- What vegetation other than rainforest and grassland does Africa have?

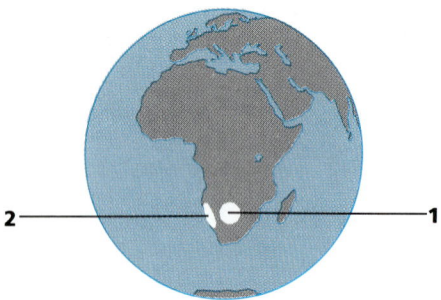

If you want to speak to God, speak to the winds.

The rain forms dark clouds in the sky for the sake of those who are deaf; it rumbles for the sake of the blind.

African proverbs

Both latitude and altitude affect Africa's climates.

In the movies, Africa is a wild land of thickly overgrown jungle with treacherous swamps and tangled vines. Moisture drips from every bush and tree. This fantasy world bears no relation to the real Africa. Part of the continent does have a tropical rainforest climate. However, as you can see from the map on page 461, tropical rainforest occupies only about one-seventh of Africa's total area. Most of the continent south of the Sahara has tropical savanna or dry steppe climates. Because so much of Africa has dry climates, winds bearing moisture are much sought after, as the African proverbs suggest.

Africa lies squarely across the Equator. A large part of Africa lies to the south of the Equator, and an even larger part lies to its north. Sub-Saharan Africa begins near the point where the Tropic of Cancer crosses the continent in the north. The Tropic of Capricorn crosses southern Africa. Because most of Africa lies within the tropics, you can assume that this continent has hot or warm climates.

The map on page 461 shows that, except for small areas along the northern and southern coasts, Africa's climates are either dry or tropical. The map key tells you that the tropical climates are of two types: tropical rainforest and savanna. In the tropical rainforest regions, rain falls year-round. Savanna climates have a season of heavy rainfall followed by a dry season.

As you can see from the map, the dry climate regions are generally away from the Equator. The closer one comes to the Equator, the more tropical and more humid the climate is apt to

Sub-Saharan Africa: Climate Regions

Tropical climates
- Tropical rainforest
- Savanna

Dry climates
- Steppe
- Desert

Mild climates
- Marine west coast
- Humid subtropical
- Mediterranean

High altitudes
- Highlands
- Uplands

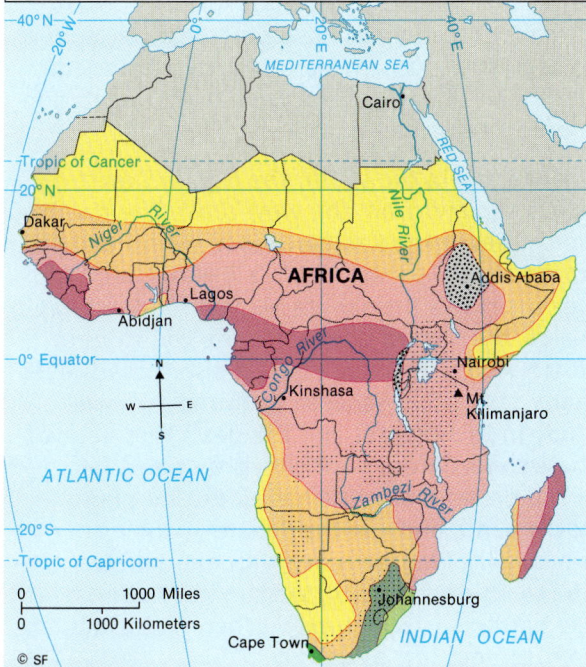

Map Study

Where is Sub-Saharan Africa's largest rainforest climate region?

be. Rainfall is uneven, and many areas have either too much rain or too little. Rainfall also varies from year to year.

Even at the Equator, Africa has some relatively cool areas. That is because part of the African plateau lies at high elevations, and moun-

tainous areas reach higher. As you have read, places with high elevations are cooler than lower areas nearby. In eastern Africa, Mount Kilimanjaro [kil'ə mən jär'ō] and Mount Kenya, in sight of the Equator, are permanently capped with snow.

Most of the continent is rainforest or grassland.

Compare the map on page 461 with the map showing Africa's natural vegetation on page 462. You can see from this comparison that Africa's climate regions and natural vegetation regions follow similar patterns. On the map showing natural vegetation, find the region around the Equator west of the rift valleys. Africa's largest rainforest is located here. Notice that this vegetation region takes in much of the Congo (Zaire) Basin and extends north along the coast in western Africa. Smaller areas of rainforest are found along river valleys in eastern Africa and in Madagascar.

Grasslands make up by far the greatest part of Africa south of the Sahara, as you can see from the map on page 462. Directly north and south of the Equator, the grasslands have a tropical savanna climate. The term *savanna* is often applied to the land and vegetation as well as the climate region. In South Africa, the savanna is called the **veld** [velt], from a Dutch word meaning "field."

Savanna. The savanna country is open with wide spaces between low trees or bushes. This is the Africa of the grass-eating zebras and antelope and of the lions and leopards that hunt them.

If you were to travel from the rainforest to the savanna, you would smell the difference in the air and feel it on your skin. During the short rainy season, the vegetation is green and full. When the rains give way to the dry season, which happens once or twice a year, the parched air is often tinged with the smoke of

461

Sub-Saharan Africa: Natural Vegetation Regions

Key:
- Broadleaf forest—rainforest
- Broadleaf forest—deciduous
- Broadleaf forest—other
- Grassland
- Desert—little or no vegetation
- Desert—scrub with grassy patches
- High mountains (vegetation varies with elevation)

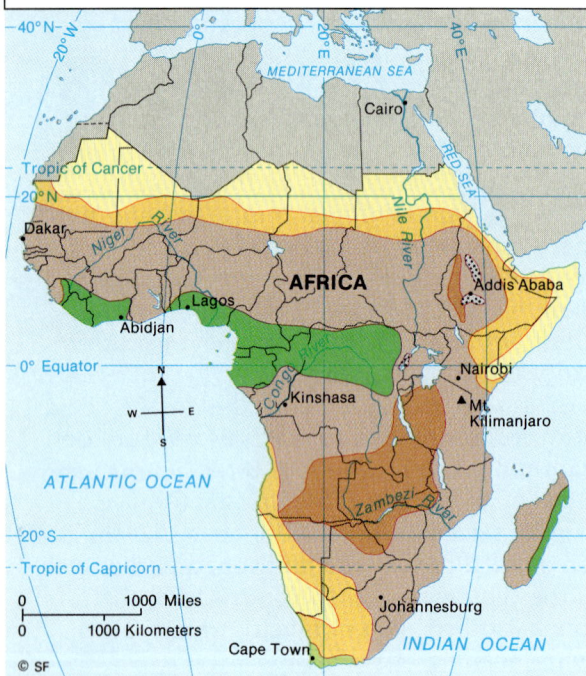

Map labels: 40°N, 20°W, 20°E, 40°E, MEDITERRANEAN SEA, Cairo, Tropic of Cancer, 20°N, RED SEA, Dakar, Niger River, Nile River, AFRICA, Addis Ababa, Lagos, Abidjan, Congo River, 0° Equator, Nairobi, Kinshasa, Mt. Kilimanjaro, ATLANTIC OCEAN, Zambezi River, 20°S, Tropic of Capricorn, 0 1000 Miles, 0 1000 Kilometers, Johannesburg, INDIAN OCEAN, Cape Town, © SF

Map Study

Use the key to describe desert vegetation in Sub-Saharan Africa.

grass fires. Days are warm all year. Nights are relatively cool.

Steppe climates. Farther north and south, away from the Equator, the grass of the savanna thins to scrub. These areas have dry

steppe climates. The trees have all but disappeared. Shade is hard to find. Sparse patches of grass are separated by bare, sandy soil. Days are hot, and nights are cool, even cold. It rains very little in the steppe. Most people herd livestock—goats especially but also some sheep and cattle.

Africa also has deserts and broadleaf vegetation.

Africa has many regions that are neither rainforest nor grassland. Much of Africa is desert. Large highland areas have broadleaf deciduous forests. The southern tip of Africa has a Mediterranean climate where the natural vegetation is broadleaf evergreen shrubs.

Deserts. In the south, the Namib Desert reaches inland from the west coast. The Kalahari Desert lies in the Kalahari Basin, inland and east of the Namib. In the north, a narrow band of steppes meets the Sahara. As you read in Chapter 19, the Sahara dominates the countries of North Africa. This huge desert also spreads over many of the Sub-Saharan countries you will study in this chapter and the next. Find each of these desert areas on the map on page 458.

The desert landscape has almost no plants. Rocks, sand, and—in the Sahara—stony cliffs prevail. The climate is dry with extreme temperatures. During the day, the sun's radiation heats the barren surface quickly. When night falls, the heat escapes just as quickly.

Broadleaf deciduous forests. In the highlands of eastern and central Africa are large regions where deciduous forests are the natural vegetation. Many of the forests have been leveled, though, so farmers can plant crops. Some highland soils are fertile and productive. In other cases, the soil is thin and poor. When the trees are gone, the soil often washes away.

A region of low broadleaf vegetation. In Chapter 19 you read about the narrow band of Mediterranean climates along the northern coast of Africa. Along the southern coast, South Africa also has an area of Mediterranean climate. Here broadleaf evergreen shrubs are the natural vegetation. Cool, moist air from Antarctic seas drifts into regions of the Cape Ranges. Skiers find snow on the higher slopes almost year-round.

Section 2 Review

Locating Key Places
Locate the following places on the map on page 458: Kalahari Desert, Namib Desert

Identifying Key Terms
Define the following term: veld

Reviewing Main Ideas
1. How do latitude and altitude affect Africa's climate patterns?
2. How is the vegetation of Africa's savanna climate region different from that of its steppe climate region?
3. Name and describe the location of three desert areas in Sub-Saharan Africa.

Thinking Critically: Analyze Comparisons
Imagine that an agricultural representative has been sent by an African nation's government to several rainforest villages with modern fertilizers, tools, and planting information. What points could the representative make to convince farmers who have practiced shifting agriculture for generations to adopt new methods? What points might the farmers make to support their traditional way of life?

Savanna with low trees creates a habitat for giraffes in Kenya's Meru National Park.

Civilizations and Colonizations

Preview

Key Places
Where are these places located?
1 Pate
2 Mogadishu
3 Tombouctou
4 Cape of Good Hope

Key Terms
What do these terms mean?
city-state
imperialism
ethnic group

Main Ideas
As you read, look for answers to these questions.
- What effect did trade have among the early Africans?
- How did the coming of Europeans in the 1400s affect Africa's trading empires?
- How did Europeans change Sub-Saharan Africa after 1850?

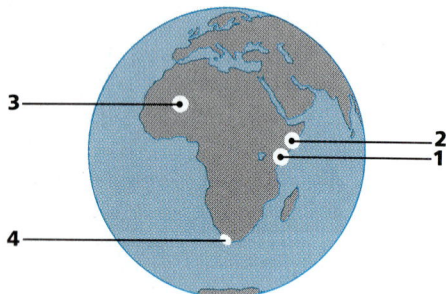

All the world paid them homage
  And their world was straight ahead of them.
  They walked with heads held disdainfully
  And eyes closed in scorn.
Swinging their arms and arching their necks
  While behind and in front crowds
    accompanied them.
  And everywhere they had seats of honor
  And troops of soldiers to attend them.
Their lighted houses were aglow
  With lamps of crystal and brass.
  The nights were as the day.
  Beauty and honor surrounded them.

Sayid Abdallah, *Utendi wa Inkishafi*

Trade helped early Africans achieve a high level of civilization.

Sayid Abdallah, an African poet in the early 1800s, lived in an early African trading community. Abdallah came from Pate, an island city along Africa's eastern coast. Pate reached its peak as a trading center between 1200 and 1500 when the city was governed by the rich rulers honored in the poem. By Abdallah's time, his city was falling into ruin, as other African city-states and empires had flourished and fallen for centuries. A **city-state** is an independent state consisting of a city and the territories depending on it.

The city-states of eastern Africa. During the time of the Roman Empire, about 2,000 years ago, iron from mines in Central Africa was reaching Arabia, India, and perhaps China. African traders brought the metal from inland regions to cities along the eastern coast. Pate, Mogadishu [mog′ə dē′shü], Mombasa, and Kilwa still stand at the sites of some of these ancient cities. At the ancient ports, Indian and Arabian ships picked up African iron, copper, gold, and ivory and carried it across the Indian Ocean to foreign lands.

The empires of western Africa. Trade was equally important in western Africa. Trade routes there centered inland in the towns and cities on the southern fringes of the Sahara. There, wrote one Arab historian, "the camel caravans of the desert met the boatmen of the Niger and their canoes."

In time, the market centers became rich and powerful cities. Tombouctou [tông bŭk tü'], near the Niger River, was one of these trading cities. Find Tombouctou on the map on page 465 and follow the path by river and camel caravan from the Gulf of Guinea to the Mediterranean port of Ceuta. Control of the north-south

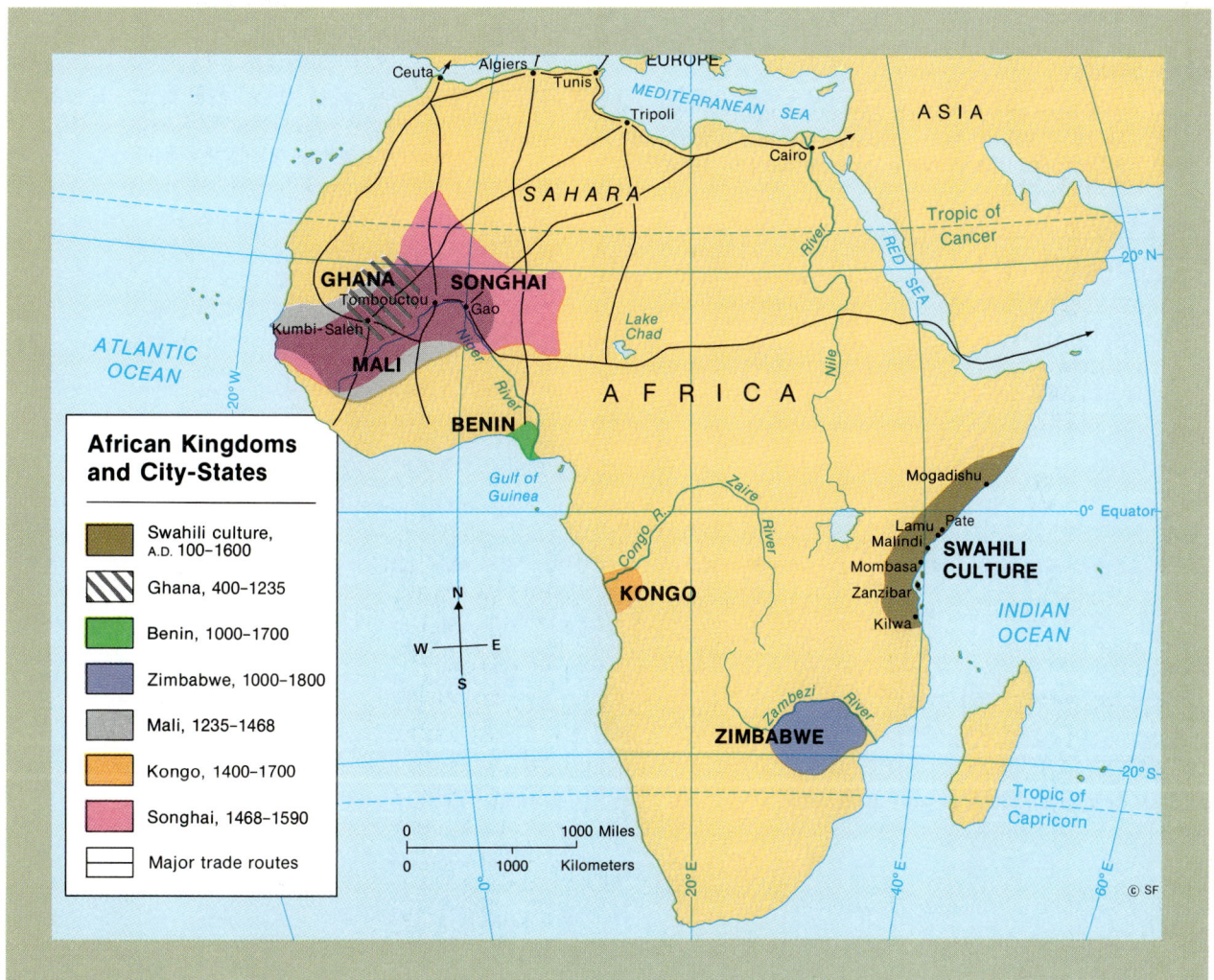

African Kingdoms and City-States

- Swahili culture, A.D. 100–1600
- Ghana, 400–1235
- Benin, 1000–1700
- Zimbabwe, 1000–1800
- Mali, 1235–1468
- Kongo, 1400–1700
- Songhai, 1468–1590
- Major trade routes

Map Study

The map shows Africa's major kingdoms and city-states and their major trade routes. Which kingdoms were located in West Africa? Which of these was established first?

trade enabled African rulers to establish large empires in the savanna grasslands. The first such empire, Ghana, was founded about A.D. 400. Find Ghana on the map on page 465. Where is Ghana located in relation to Tombouctou?

Ghana fell to Muslim armies from the north in 1235, and a larger empire, Mali [mä'lē], took its place. Mali controlled the north-south trade from the 1200s to the 1400s. Mali collapsed in 1468 to be replaced by yet another trading empire, Songhai [song'hī].

The coming of Europeans weakened African trading centers.

Portuguese sea captains began exploring Africa's coast in the mid-1400s, and by 1498 one

Map Study

The map shows which European nations ruled colonies in Africa in 1914. Which two nations held the most land? How many African countries were independent in 1914?

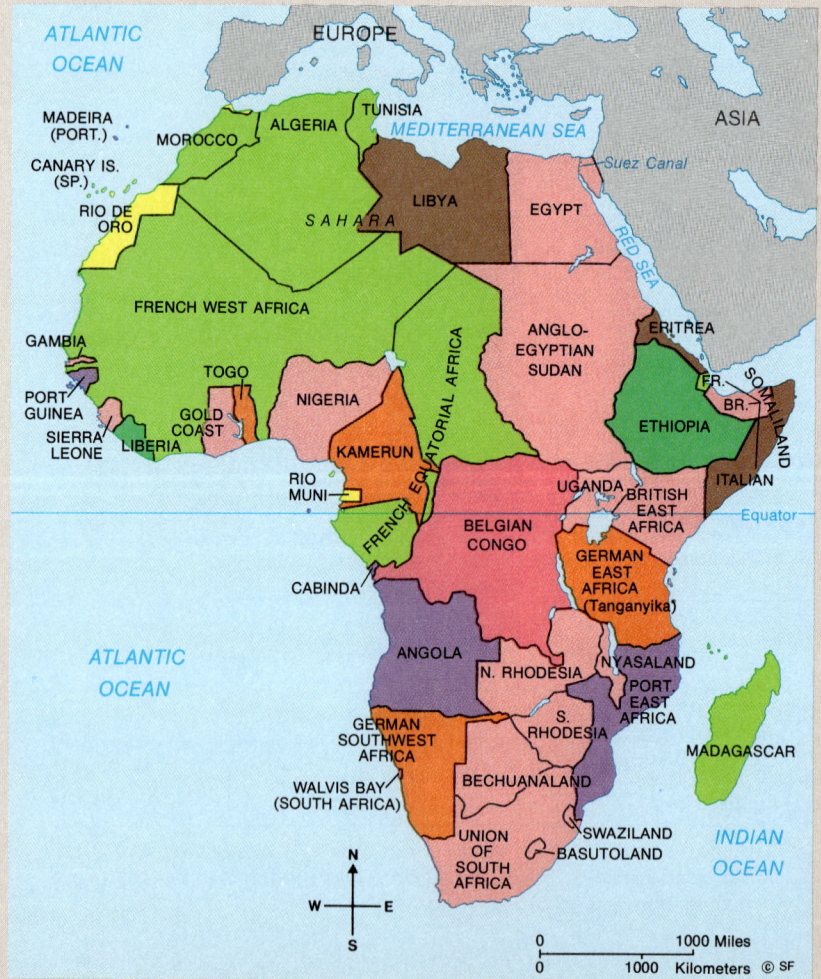

Africa in 1914

- Belgian
- British
- French
- German
- Italian
- Portuguese
- Spanish
- Independent

ATLANTIC OCEAN
EUROPE
ASIA
MADEIRA (PORT.)
MOROCCO
ALGERIA
TUNISIA
MEDITERRANEAN SEA
CANARY IS. (SP.)
RIO DE ORO
LIBYA
EGYPT
Suez Canal
SAHARA
RED SEA
FRENCH WEST AFRICA
ANGLO-EGYPTIAN SUDAN
ERITREA
GAMBIA
PORT. GUINEA
TOGO
GOLD COAST
NIGERIA
FRENCH EQUATORIAL AFRICA
FR. SOMALILAND
BR.
SIERRA LEONE
LIBERIA
KAMERUN
ETHIOPIA
RIO MUNI
UGANDA
BRITISH EAST AFRICA
ITALIAN
Equator
BELGIAN CONGO
GERMAN EAST AFRICA (Tanganyika)
CABINDA
ATLANTIC OCEAN
ANGOLA
N. RHODESIA
NYASALAND
PORT. EAST AFRICA
GERMAN SOUTHWEST AFRICA
S. RHODESIA
MADAGASCAR
WALVIS BAY (SOUTH AFRICA)
BECHUANALAND
SWAZILAND
INDIAN OCEAN
UNION OF SOUTH AFRICA
BASUTOLAND
N
W   E
S
0   1000 Miles
0   1000   Kilometers   © SF

of them—Vasco da Gama—made the first European voyage around the Cape of Good Hope, near Africa's southern tip, to India. The Portuguese attacked and took a number of African ports including, in 1506, the city-state of Pate. Soon, Portuguese, Dutch, and British trading vessels were seen regularly off the coast.

The developing trade affected Africa more than it did Europe. The northern trade routes across the Sahara became less important, and the large and powerful empires died out. African traders along the coasts south of the Sahara now handled the exchange of trade items from the interior.

The Portuguese and other Europeans also began enslaving black Africans in the 1500s. Portuguese, Dutch, British, and Spanish sea captains carried off Africans captured along the coasts or bought from African slave traders farther inland. These captives, at first by the thousands and then by the millions, were crowded into miserable slave ships and carried to European colonies in the Americas.

Europeans established colonial rule in Africa after 1850.

A handful of Europeans had led exploring parties inland from Africa's east and west coasts by 1800. Further explorations in the 19th century helped set the stage for European control of Africa. The Europeans' policy of extending their rule over other countries and colonies is known as **imperialism**.

Britain assumed control of the southern tip of Africa in 1814. The Portuguese, French, Belgians, Germans, and the British had greatly enlarged other coastal outposts by the late 1800s and were turning them into colonies. Before pushing farther inland, the European powers met at Berlin in 1884, to plan their strategy. The nations at the Berlin Conference drew lines across a map of Africa planning how best to divide it among themselves. By 1914 the map of Africa looked like the one on page 466.

Europeans drew their boundaries with little knowledge of or regard for African history, culture, or ethnic groups. An **ethnic group** is a group of people who share similar cultural or racial backgrounds.

As European armies, mining companies, government officials, farmers, teachers, and missionaries brought colonial people into their fold, the boundaries Europeans imposed often broke up ancient ethnic groupings. At the same time, members of two or more traditionally rival groups often had to work together under the same colonial rulers. For example, the Hausa [hau'sə] people were split among several countries when the British colony of Nigeria was being established in the late 1800s and early 1900s. At the same time, Nigeria brought together in one nation more than 250 different ethnic groups.

Section 3 Review

Locating Key Places
Locate Pate, Mogadishu, and Tombouctou on the map on page 465. Locate the Cape of Good Hope on the map on page 458.

Identifying Key Terms
Define the following terms: city-state, imperialism, ethnic group

Reviewing Main Ideas
1. How did trade influence the development of early Africa?
2. In what ways did the coming of Europeans in the 1400s affect Africa's trading empires?
3. How did Europeans change Sub-Saharan Africa politically after 1850?

Thinking Critically: Identify Assumptions
European penetration into Sub-Saharan Africa began early. The Europeans named parts of western Africa the Gold Coast, the Pepper Coast, the Ivory Coast, and the Slave Coast. Write a paragraph explaining why the Europeans chose those names. Which of the names still exist?

Africa for Africans

Key Places
Where are these places located?
1 Zimbabwe
2 Zaire

Key Terms
What do these terms mean?
secede   official language
mixed economy   animism

Main Ideas
As you read, look for answers to these questions.
- How did Africa change politically in the 1950s and 1960s?
- How did the new African nations work to change their economies?
- How can Africa's cultural diversity be described?

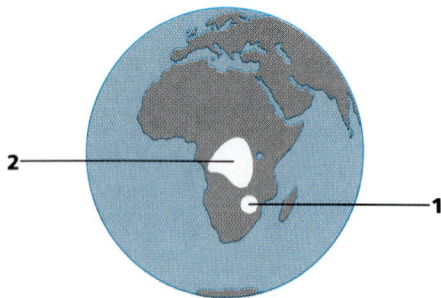

Ohoho akyi mpa asem.

After a stranger has gone, there is always something to be said about him, good or bad.

Ashanti proverb

Africans moved toward political independence.

The "stranger"—the Europeans who first came to Sub-Saharan Africa in the 1500s—had stayed too long, in the opinion of most African leaders. Africans struggled successfully to throw off colonial rule in the 1950s and 1960s. When this rule finally ended, few Africans could find anything good to say about colonialism.

During the colonial period, European powers forced Africans into labor, deprived them of their freedoms, and settled on the best land. The Europeans, however, did improve health conditions, education, and the distribution of food. Ironically, these very actions contributed to a rising awareness of the injustices of colonial rule and a determination to end it.

Moves toward independence. Even before World War II, African freedom movements had arisen all over the continent. The leader of one of the first successful African independence movements came from the land of the Ashanti [ə shän′tē]. Kwame Nkrumah [kwä′mä en krü′mə] was the prime minister of the Gold Coast, a British colony in western Africa. In their colonies, the British often chose African leaders like Nkrumah to rule on behalf of the British Crown. Nkrumah led the Gold Coast to full independence from Britain in 1957. The citizens of the Gold Coast promptly renamed their new nation Ghana, after the ancient empire that once ruled that part of western Africa.

Encouraged by Ghana's example, other African leaders strengthened their demands for independence. Over the next five years alone, more than two dozen African colonies became independent nations. More new countries were created in the 1960s and 1970s.

In most instances the transfer of political power to the new African nations was peaceful. The British, for example, helped their African colonies plan for new governments before leaving. The Portuguese and the French were less willing to surrender their colonies. Africans in Cameroon fought a four-year battle to expel the French. Angola and Mozambique struggled against Portuguese forces until 1975 before they gained independence. Today Namibia is the only African territory that is not independent. Namibia is dominated by neighboring South Africa.

As the map on page 456 shows, many new names appeared for Africa's nations and national capitals. Compare this map with the map of Africa in 1914 on page 466. How have the boundaries of African countries changed since independence?

Conflicts after independence. The transition to independent status was most difficult where large numbers of Europeans had settled and developed strong commercial interests. British settlers in the southern African country that is now Zimbabwe [zim bä'bwe], for example, declared their independence from Britain in 1965. However, they tried to keep the government in the hands of the white minority. Only after years of civil war did black citizens of Zimbabwe, who formed the majority of the population, gain their full civil rights. Independence was achieved in 1980.

Zaire's experiences reflect the difficulties African nations experienced on achieving independence. These difficulties resulted in part because the political boundaries drawn earlier by European nations enclosed diverse groups who could not agree on how to share power. For example, the Belgian Congo—now Zaire—became an independent nation in 1960. Immediately the

Kwame Nkrumah, center, led the movement for Ghana's independence.

province of Katanga (now called Shaba) tried to secede. To **secede** means to withdraw formally from an organization. Within weeks, the new nation was fighting a civil war. Leaders asked the United Nations (UN) to restore order. Three years and many battles later, UN armies ended Katanga's secession.

African nations worked to improve their economies.

Africa's new governments faced major economic problems after independence. When European managers and technicians left, many industries and large farms suffered. Living standards in at least 20 of the countries declined steadily. In addition, poorly planned programs for economic development left some African nations burdened with billions of dollars in debt.

Economic potential. The continent, of course, has many of the mineral resources needed to build industries. It has some large oil reserves and great potential for hydroelectric power because of the many waterfalls along its rivers.

However, the colonial era left behind an economic system unsuited to the needs of Africans. Exporting raw materials and cash crops was the European system, and it proved difficult to change. Providing raw materials and cash crops for industry works well if such commodities sell for a good price. Exports provide cash to build new industries and buy spare parts. If the prices for exports fall, a country may go into debt.

Economic development plans sometimes went wrong. Money for new construction and other projects seldom helped the majority of the population. Africa's 20 poorest countries owed $40 billion in foreign debt by the late 1980s.

On the other hand, some African nations worked to strengthen agricultural development and improve the land. For example, farmers were encouraged to plant trees, dig simple irrigation systems, and build terraces. In Burkina Faso, farmers built stone dikes across their fields to keep rain from carrying away topsoil. In fields with the dikes, harvests more than doubled. Zimbabwe suffered from drought in 1985 but was able to sell surplus corn to other African nations in 1986 after its government supplied farmers with cheap fertilizer.

Improved economic performance. Some new African nations, such as Angola, Benin, Congo, Mozambique, and Tanzania, adopted

A street in Accra, Ghana's capital, bustles with life. African cities are growing faster than any others in the world.

Soviet-style socialist economies—a form of command economy in which the government owns the factories and transport system and controls the distribution of goods and services. Major businesses such as commercial plantations, mines, lumbering operations, and textile mills were owned and operated by the government. By the late 1980s, many state-owned businesses were losing money and dragging down the overall economy. Several socialist African nations decided to move toward a **mixed economy**—that is, an economy that combines some government planning with free enterprise. For example, the governments of Ghana, Ivory Coast, Tanzania, and Togo began selling some state-owned industries to private owners. Under private ownership, industries began to show a profit, creating jobs for Africans and increasing exports.

Population pressures. Economic decisions must take into account population growth. The population of Africa, especially in its cities, is growing faster than anywhere in the world. Population pressures are severe not only in the cities but also in the rural areas where eight out of ten Africans live.

Remember that Africa's climates and soils can not generally support large, dense farming populations. Rainfall is too uncertain, and soils are often too poor. What seems like a sparsely populated region may, in fact, be overcrowded. Africa has experienced devastating droughts over the last 20 years. When crops fail, people often migrate to the cities where they hope to make a better living. The cities, however, can provide few jobs, and most of the migrants live in slums.

Many languages and religions reflect Africa's cultural diversity.

If you travel in the United States, you expect to be able to communicate in English wherever you go. Imagine what it would be like if the people in the next town spoke a language different from yours. This is frequently the case in Africa.

Traditional and official languages. More than 800 different languages are spoken in Africa today. Small ethnic groups of only a few thousand people may speak a separate language. Many African languages belong to the Bantu language family. Even so, these languages may sound no more alike than English and Greek, for example. English and Greek also came from a common language family. The chart on page 483 lists some common English words of Bantu origin.

A modern country in which people speak many different languages needs an **official language** for use in government, business, and higher education. A number of African countries have chosen the language of their former colonial rulers for this purpose. Thus you would speak English if you went to Nigeria, French in Zaire, Portuguese in Angola, and Spanish in Equatorial Guinea. Sometimes two official languages are used—the colonial language plus a local one. In Kenya, both English and Swahili are official languages. Swahili is a Bantu language with many Arabic words mixed in and can be traced back to early trading contacts with the Arabs. All in all, Africa is a place with a large number of languages.

Traditional, Islamic, and Christian religions. Religion is a vital part of everyday life in African cultures. Beliefs differ from group to group, but many features are held in common. In many traditional religions, the souls of the dead and spirits of nature play an important role. A religion of this kind is called **animism**.

The traditional African religions usually begin with human beings at the center of a universe created by a Supreme Being, or God. Between humans and God are the spirits of ancestors, who act as go-betweens when necessary. The ancestors also act as intermediaries between an

The antelope represents the spirit of farming in dance headdresses of the Bambara, an ethnic group in Mali.

third of the Africans practice traditional animist beliefs. Yet even where the people have converted to Islam or Christianity, their beliefs blend with ancient traditions.

Even highly westernized Africans honor traditional religious practices as a sign of respect. For instance, when a whale died some years ago on a beach near Accra, Kwame Nkrumah, who was then Ghana's president, attended the funeral of the whale together with members of his cabinet. Many coastal people believe the whale is the king of the sea and that the spirit of the whale will help their fishing villages.

Section 4 Review

Locating Key Places
Locate the following places on the map on page 456: Zimbabwe, Zaire

Identifying Key Terms
Define the following terms: secede, official language, animism

Reviewing Main Ideas
1. In what ways did Africa change politically in the 1950s and 1960s?
2. How did the new African nations work to improve their economies?
3. What aspects of African life show the diversity of its cultures?

Thinking Critically: Make Hypotheses
Business people from industrialized nations have the large capital assets that Africans generally do not have to invest in privately owned industries. At least for a while, this will mean that foreigners will have a large stake in Africa's free-enterprise ventures. Some Africans worry that this situation could open the door to new, commercial colonialism. Suppose that you are a cabinet member of an African state that is turning toward free enterprise. Prepare a written proposal outlining how you think your government can regulate foreign business owners so that they strengthen the economy without endangering your government's own supremacy.

individual and less powerful spirits that are thought to inhabit mountains, rivers, trees, and animals.

About one-third of all Africans are Muslims. Islam is strongest in the countries of the northern steppe and savanna regions and in eastern Africa. Another one-third of the population follows one of the various Christian faiths introduced during the colonial period. The remaining

472

Comparing Ethnic and Political Boundaries on Maps

Have you ever wondered how the boundaries of countries are drawn? To what are they tied or related? Political boundaries tend to be sharp lines on maps, neatly separating one country from another. Sometimes these boundaries are even apparent on the landscape itself. They may follow a river or a coastline.

In Kenya, however, as you can see on the map below, the boundaries are not tied to any physical landforms. Some wind through mountains and others seem to be a series of straight lines made with a ruler. The outline of Kenya, as with many countries, ends up looking like a piece from a jigsaw puzzle.

Although many of the political boundaries in Kenya seem clear, they do not always mesh with the boundaries and territories established by the country's many ethnic groups. In some regions, particularly in urban and coastal areas, people from many different groups live together in multiethnic neighborhoods.

In other areas, however, each ethnic group lives within a particular territory. The boundaries between these ethnic areas are seldom sharply defined. They shade into one another, change from time to time, and often overlap in disputed areas.

Why is there such a gap between political and ethnic boundaries in Kenya? Kenya was made a British colony in 1895 and became an independent country in 1963. The political boundaries drawn at those times often paid little attention to the existing patterns of settlement. Boundaries sometimes ran through the middle of an established territory.

The situation was made even more difficult in areas where the people practiced nomadic herding. These pastoral people traditionally moved their herds from place to place, sometimes crossing the new international boundaries established by the Europeans. In this way, some Somali people became citizens of Kenya instead of Somalia.

The Turkana and the Masai are important pastoral groups. They have at times come into conflict with one another over herding territory.

In addition to these two groups, there are the Kikuyu. The Kikuyu are a farming people who form Kenya's largest ethnic group. They dominate the Kenyan government and live throughout the country. Traditional enemies of the Kikuyu are the Luo, a group of farmers who live in a well-defined area.

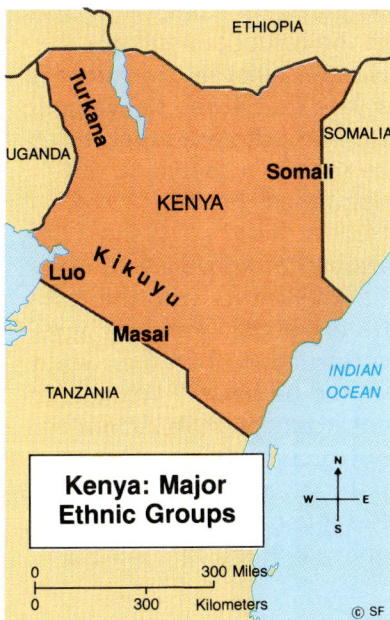

Kenya: Major Ethnic Groups

ETHIOPIA

Turkana

UGANDA

SOMALIA

Somali

KENYA

Luo

Kikuyu

Masai

TANZANIA

INDIAN OCEAN

Kenya: Major Ethnic Groups

N
W   E
S

0   300 Miles
0   300 Kilometers

© SF

Review

1. Between which two countries are the Masai divided?
2. If Lake Turkana had been used as a boundary, in which country would the people for which it is named live?
3. Besides the Masai, which other ethnic group is shown as being split by politics?
4. In which two countries do these people primarily live?

473

Review

Section Summaries

1. Landforms Africa is a plateau continent, with a smooth, steeply sloping coastline and no long mountainous backbone. Major rivers include the Niger, the Congo (or Zaire), and the Zambezi. The Great Rift Valley is a series of parallel trenches that cut through eastern Africa and extend through the Red Sea and into parts of Southwest Asia.

2. Climate, Soils, and Vegetation Africa's latitude dictates warm or hot climates, moderated in some areas by high elevations. Tropical rainforests grow near the Equator, but grasslands are Sub-Saharan Africa's main form of natural vegetation. Deciduous forests, grasses, shrubs, or scrub grow in other regions with steppe, desert, marine west coast, and Mediterranean climates. Most soils are not very fertile.

3. Civilizations and Colonizations Farming and trading communities led to the development of large city-states in Sub-Saharan Africa beginning about A.D. 400. European ships began visiting African coasts during the 1400s, disrupting local trading patterns. European nations colonized almost the entire continent during the 1800s and early 1900s, further disrupting African life and cultures.

4. Africa for Africans Beginning in 1957, Sub-Saharan colonies became independent in steady succession. Unstable governments, rapid population growth, drought, and war have all slowed economic growth, but some important gains have occurred. Africa's many languages and its traditional, Islamic, and Christian religions complicate and enrich the lives of its people.

Using Geography Skills
Reviewing the Map Lesson
Use the map on page 473 and the map on page 456 to answer these questions.
1. What are the five major ethnic groups in Kenya?
2. Which Kenyan boundary was formed by a line of latitude?
3. Which Kenyan border was formed by a line of longitude?

Using Social Studies Skills
1. Translate Information from One Medium to Another. Use an encyclopedia, almanac, or other reference book to find the dates of independence in the countries listed. Record the information on a time line.

Botswana   Malawi
Congo   Nigeria
Ghana   Senegal
Kenya

2. Draw Inferences. Not long after the new nation of Kenya held its first elections for members of the legislature (National Assembly), a Kenyan newspaperwoman printed an article containing these sentences: "Even if it were a matter of kindness, there ought to have been a woman in the National Assembly. I wonder whether the public is aware that at the Kenya polls, women, who are supposed to be socially subservient, outnumbered the men . . . by three to two? . . . If the women of Kenya are to identify themselves with the task of Nation building and social reconstruction, then their voice should be heard." What inference can you make about the outcome of Kenya's first election? What can you infer about the role of women in Kenya's political life?

Testing for Understanding

Locating Key Places
Match each description below with the name of the place.

1. formerly the Belgian Congo
2. a major African river that flows toward the Sahara
3. a desert region east of the Namib
4. an urban cultural and trading center of western Africa
5. Africa's southern tip
6. the largest island of continental Africa
7. a trading city on the eastern African mainland made important by central African iron
8. an island-city and trading center in eastern Africa
9. flows through the nation of Zaire
10. a southern African country where the black majority fought for civil rights
11. a major river in southeastern Africa
12. a desert region reaching in from Africa's southwest coast

a. Madagascar
b. Niger River
c. Congo (Zaire) River
d. Zambezi River
e. Kalahari
f. Namib
g. Pate
h. Mogadishu
i. Tombouctou
j. Cape of Good Hope
k. Zimbabwe
l. Zaire

Recalling Key Terms
Define these terms in your own words.

Section 1
escarpment
rift valley

Section 2
veld

Section 3
city-state
imperialism
ethnic group

Section 4
secede
mixed economy
official language
animism

Reviewing Main Ideas
Section 1
1. Tell how Africa's coastline and mountains are different from those of other continents.
2. Describe Africa's major landform.
3. What is unusual about Africa's major rivers and its eastern lakes and valleys?

Section 2
1. In what ways do latitude and altitude affect Africa's climate patterns?
2. Tell how the vegetation in Africa's savanna climate region is different from that of its steppe climate regions.
3. Name and tell the location of Africa's three desert areas.

Section 3
1. In what ways did trade influence the development of early Africa?
2. Describe how the coming of the Europeans in the 1400s affected Africa's trading empires.
3. What did the Europeans do to politically change Sub-Saharan Africa after 1850?

Section 4
1. How did Africa change politically in the 1950s and 1960s?
2. How have the new African nations been working to change their economies?
3. What aspects of African life reflect the diversity of its cultures?

Thinking Critically
1. Analyze Comparisons.
Why does population density tend to be low where shifting agriculture is practiced as compared with other forms of subsistence agriculture?

2. Assess Cause and Effect.
How might Africa's physical and cultural geography both promote and discourage unity on the continent?

West and Central Africa

In this chapter you will read about life today in West and Central Africa.

Sections

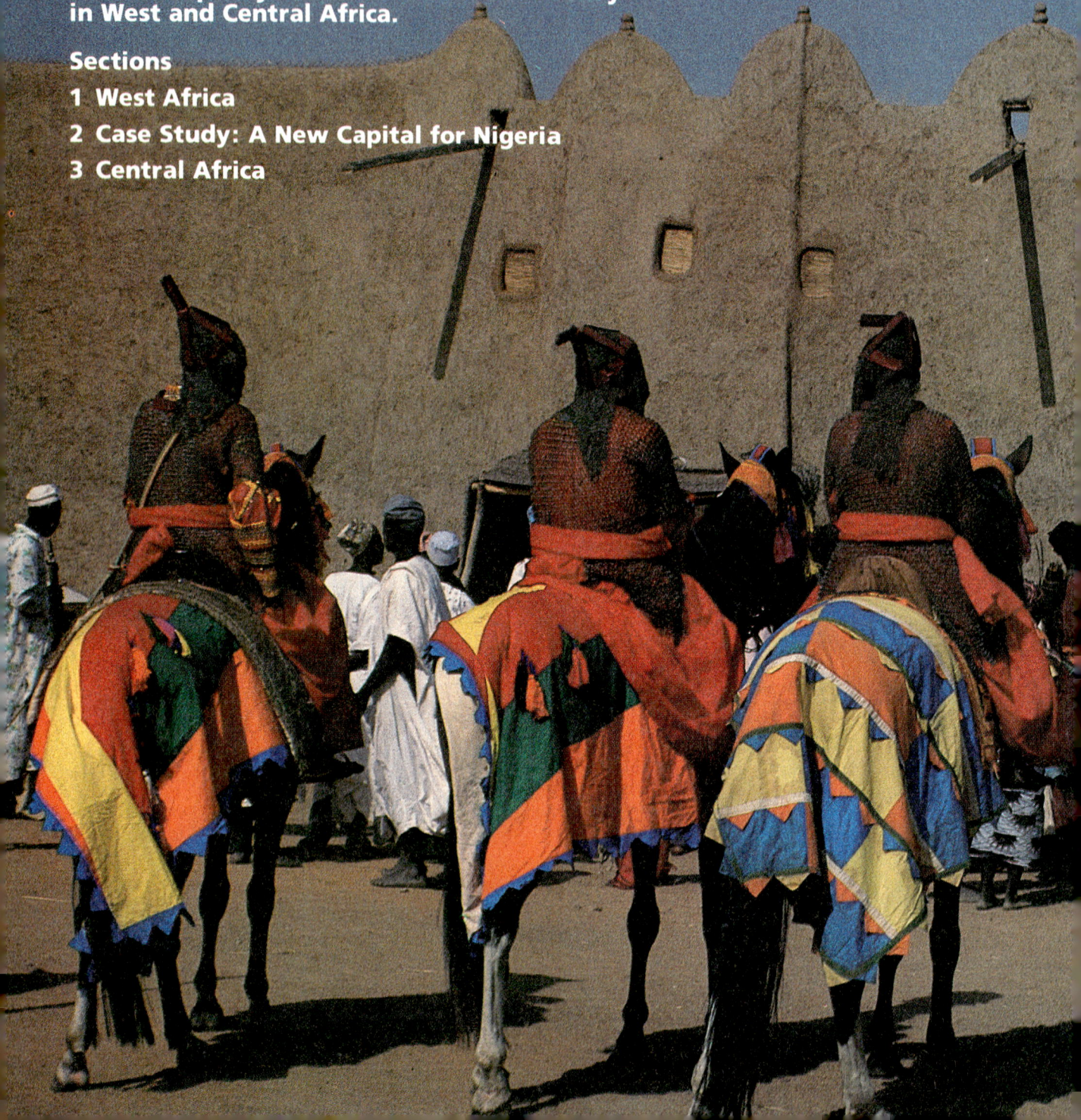

West Africa

Preview

Key Places
Where are these places located?
1 Sahel
2 Dakar
3 Abidjan
4 Lagos
  See the globe below.

Key Terms
What do these terms mean?
periodic market   harmattan
desertification   plural society

Main Ideas
As you read, look for answers to these questions.
- What activity connects the nations of western Africa?
- What natural feature dominates Mauritania, Senegal, Mali, Niger, and Chad?
- How do the people of the Sahel make a living?
- How do the coastal countries of western Africa differ from the countries of the Sahel?
- Why is Nigeria important economically?

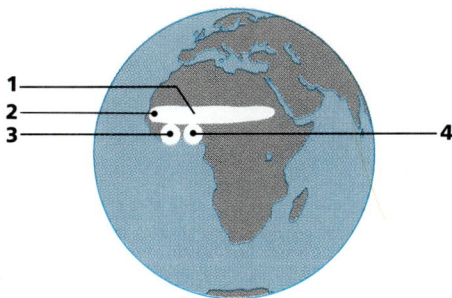

It was [my father's and uncles'] custom every market-day to go and trade. . . . [They] sold cotton and sugar-cane and they bought food and kolanuts and tobacco-flowers to take home to the women. . . . When it was market-day in Kudan, they went there to trade; at Dan Sambo market too they would trade and wear their fine clothes and ride their horses.

Baba of Karo, a Hausa woman
from Nigeria

Trade connects the 16 diverse nations of West Africa.

You read in Chapter 22 that the inhabitants of the Sahara more than a thousand years ago traded salt from the desert for the gold and ivory of the forested coastlands. To this day, trade links West Africa's coastal rainforests with its midland savannas and its arid north. Traders who cannot understand each other's languages use English, French, or the language of the Hausa people. The Hausa language is spoken and understood from northern Nigeria to Senegal.

Look at the map on page 478 and find the 16 countries that make up West Africa. These countries can be divided into two groups: seven dry countries in which the Sahara dominates, and nine more humid countries. The seven dry countries are Mauritania, Senegal, Gambia, Mali, Niger, Burkina Faso, and Chad. The nine wetter countries are Guinea-Bissau, Guinea, Sierra Leone, Liberia, Ivory Coast, Ghana, Togo, Benin, and Nigeria.

The map of West Africa shows its countries, capitals, and land use, but it cannot tell the complete story of how the people live. Most people in this part of Africa are rural farmers. Like the Hausa farming family to which Baba of

Facing page: **Fulani riders wear ceremonial dress in Cameroon. The Fulani people live in Central and West Africa.**

West and Central Africa

Legend:
- Commercial farming
- Irrigated farming
- Subsistence farming
- Nomadic herding
- Forests
- Lumbering
- Hunting, fishing, and gathering
- Mining ◆
- Commercial fishing
- Urban land use
- Little or no economic activity
- National capitals ✹
- Other cities •

Map labels:

MEDITERRANEAN SEA
MOROCCO
TUNISIA
ALGERIA
LIBYA
EGYPT
WESTERN SAHARA (MOROCCO)
Tropic of Cancer
Iron Ore
MAURITANIA
Copper
SAHARA
Nile R.
20°N
Nouakchott
Camels
MALI
Tombouctou
Uranium
NIGER
Camels
Sheep
CHAD
SUDAN
Blue Nile
White Nile
CAPE VERDE
Praia
Tuna
SENEGAL
Dakar
Peanuts
Banjul
GAMBIA
Bissau
GUINEA-BISSAU
Senegal R.
Bamako
Millet
Rice
Niger R.
Niamey
Lake Chad
Kano
N'Djamena
Bauxite
Rice
Ougadougou
BURKINA
Millet
NIGERIA
Cotton
GUINEA
Conakry
Freetown
IVORY COAST
Cacao
Coffee
SIERRA LEONE
Monrovia
LIBERIA
TOGO
BENIN
Cacao
Lome
GHANA
Accra
Abidjan
Tuna
Porto Novo
Cacao
Ibadan
Lagos
Tin
Abuja
Oil Palm
Benue R.
CAMEROON
CENTRAL AFRICAN REPUBLIC
Bangui
Oil
Malabo
Natural Gas
Yaoundé
EQUATORIAL GUINEA
São Tomé
SÃO TOMÉ AND PRÍNCIPE
Cacao
Ubangi R.
Gold
L. Albert
UGANDA
0° Equator
Libreville
P.R. OF THE CONGO
Rubber
Zaire R.
Oil Palm
Tin
RWANDA
GABON
Oil
Uranium
Congo R.
Brazzaville
ZAIRE
BURUNDI
TANZANIA
CABINDA (ANGOLA)
Cassava
Kinshasa
Matadi
Kananga
Diamonds
Lake Tanganyika
SHABA
Tin
KATANGA PLATEAU
ATLANTIC OCEAN
Manganese
Cobalt
Lubumbashi
Copper
ANGOLA
ZAMBIA
Zambezi R.
NAMIBIA (SOUTH AFRICA)
BOTSWANA
ZIMBABWE
© SF

N W E S

| 0 | 500 | 1000 Miles |
| 0 | 500 | 1000 Kilometers |

40°N
20°W
20°E
20°N
0° Equator
20°S

Map Study

The eastern boundary of Nigeria and the southern boundary of Chad separate West Africa from Central Africa. Mineral riches make mining an important economic activity in West and Central Africa. What minerals are mined in Nigeria? What minerals are mined in Zaire?

Karo belonged, the peasant farmers make weekly markets a focal point of their lives.

Suppose you were to visit a local market in Nigeria, for example. The village would be filled with bustling crowds. Wole Soyinka [wō′lā shō-yin′kə], winner of the Nobel Prize for Literature in 1986, described the market in his childhood village, Aké [ä kä′]:

> The earthy smell of yam powder assailed my nostrils long before I came on it, piled high in calabash trays. And SALT! Nobody surely, not even the whole of Aké could eat so much salt in a hundred years, yet I came on the piles stall after stall. It gave way to a variety of tubers, vegetables, dried fish and crayfish, then the stalls of meat with men flashing long, two-edged knives among slabs of meat.

Not every village has a market every day. Instead, a village may have one every three or four days. Neighboring villages will have their markets on other days. This pattern of trade results in rotating, or **periodic markets**.

Women frequently control the sales in the periodic markets. In many African cities, market women have become successful and wealthy. Even the socialist governments in some African countries have been unable to control the prices charged by the market women.

Buyers and sellers meet at a West African city market.

The Sahara dominates five nations in West Africa.

The Sahara is a dominant feature of Mauritania, Senegal, Mali, Niger, and Chad. Gambia and Burkina Faso [bėr kē′nä fä′sō], lie in the savanna region but are also arid and hot. All these countries include areas of sandy plain and grassland as well as desert.

In West Africa, people call the margins of the Sahara "the Sahel". This is an Arabic word that means "border"—a good name for the zone where the land changes from habitable to desert-dry. Life in the Sahel is not easy. Water is the essence of life, and everywhere water is scarce. The countries of the Sahel take in an area about half the size of the United States, but their total population—about 28 million—is about one-tenth the size of the U.S. population. Most people live in clusters where water can be found for cattle and goats and for raising a few crops.

Rivers and streams and scattered oases make survival possible in the Sahel. Yet the people live constantly under the threat of drought. Rainfall is unpredictable. Where the average annual rainfall is 8 inches, for example, only 3 or 4 inches may fall in some years. Another year perhaps 20 inches may fall.

The 1970s and 1980s brought catastrophe to the Sahel. By 1974 many places had gone for six years with almost no rain. In Niger alone, 2 million people were starving, along with countless cattle and goats. Then between 1981 and 1984 the worst droughts of the 20th century struck again. By the mid-1980s, at least 1 million people had died of starvation. Famine threatened 30 million more.

Although Africa's drought broke in the late 1980s, famine and malnutrition persisted. Drought and desertification still hold the people of the Sahel in their grip. **Desertification** means the drying up of comparatively moist areas along the margins of a desert. Close grazing by goats, which eat even the roots of plants, only hastens the drying process. The Sahara is gradually growing larger through desertification in the Sahel.

The people of the Sahel are primarily farmers.

The desert regions of the Sahel contain vast stores of iron ore, copper, and other minerals, but this wealth has yet to be tapped. As you can see from the map on page 478, the people at the edge of the Sahara are mainly subsistence farmers, practicing oasis agriculture.

Mauritania, Senegal, and Gambia. Among the countries on the Sahara's margin, Mauritania, Senegal, and Gambia have the advantage of an Atlantic coastline. Mauritania is three-fourths desert. Most of its population clusters along the Senegal River in the south.

Dakar, the capital of Senegal, is a bustling port city with more than a million inhabitants. Three-fourths of the people of Senegal farm for a living. They grow millet, peanuts, rice, and cassava—a root eaten like potatoes.

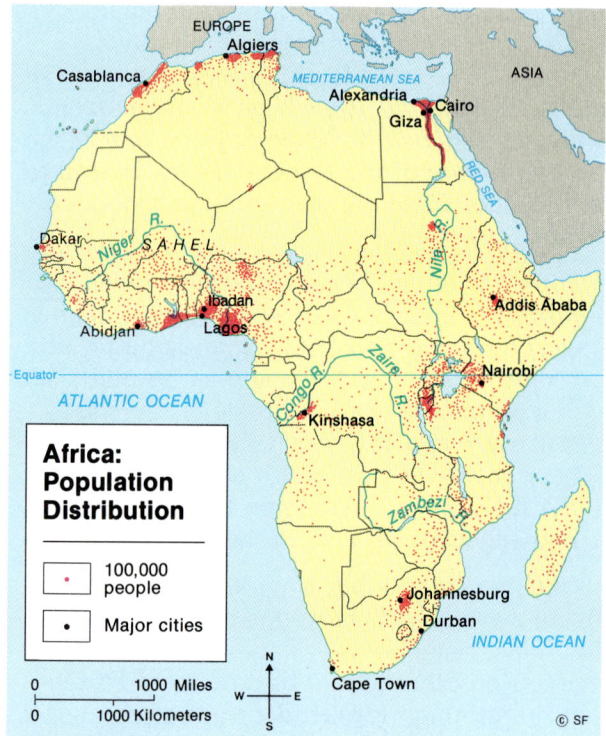

Africa: Population Distribution

·	100,000 people
•	Major cities

0   1000 Miles
0   1000 Kilometers

Map Study

Where do most of the people in West Africa live?

A look at the map on page 478 shows that Senegal almost completely surrounds Gambia. Senegal and Gambia agreed in 1982 to form a confederation uniting their communications, transportation, and defense systems. Economic union will come next. Then the two nations will be united under one flag as Senegambia. Neither country is rich, but family ties ease the burdens of poverty here as they do elsewhere in Africa. For example, a wealthy Senegalese importer recently had a dozen families of relatives living temporarily in the courtyard of her home. She explained to a journalist, "Our dream is always to have enough wealth to redistribute. Here we are judged by how we treat our kinfolk."

Mali, Niger, and Chad. The northern part of Mali, Niger, and Chad is the heart of the Sahara. South is savanna country. In Mali and Niger, the Niger River cuts through the land like a stream of life. If you look at the map on page 478, you will see that the capital cities of both Niger and Mali are built on the Niger River.

Burkina Faso. The landlocked country of Burkina Faso is more southerly and therefore more moist than other countries of the Sahel. Parts of Burkina Faso are densely populated. However, about a third of the country cannot be inhabited because of the severe diseases that affect the area. In tropical areas impure water and disease-bearing insects cause diseases like malaria, sleeping sickness, and river blindness, which blinds many adults. A program for treating river blindness was tried out in the 1970s. The program involved spraying rivers and treating patients to kill the wormlike, early form of the insect that transmits the disease.

The coastal countries are greener and more densely populated.

Along the coast the land is green with palm trees and grass and crops. The coastal countries are much more heavily populated than the countries of the Sahel as you can see from the map on page 480.

The coast has a rainy season that brings 100 inches of rain to Sierra Leone and as much as 50 inches to many other places. The rainy season extends from June to September. Then, during the fall, the clouds are driven off by a drying wind, the harmattan. The **harmattan** blows from the Sahara and along the northwest coast of Africa, signaling the onset of winter.

When you look at the map on page 478, you see that the coastal countries are often narrow with short coastlines. Their boundaries begin at the coast and go almost straight inland. Today, if you were to travel along the coast from west to east, you might hear Portuguese, French, and English spoken along with African languages. Just as European languages are spoken in Africa, African languages have influenced European languages. The chart on page 483 lists some words that have come into the English language from West Africa.

Ivory Coast. Ivory Coast (Cote d'Ivoire) is about as large as the U.S. state of New Mexico and has 10 million people. Ivory Coast is not rich. However, political stability, strong ties with the West, and wise economic management have raised its standard of living. Today Ivory Coast is the world's largest producer of cacao, from which chocolate and cocoa are made.

The capital and modern port of Abidjan [ab i-jän'] lies in the south, on the coast. Abidjan has become an important industrial center where aluminum is made, automobiles are assembled, and many products are exported.

Ghana. Ghana, the Ivory Coast's eastern neighbor, is smaller but more densely populated with 14 million people. Kwame Nkrumah had bright dreams for Ghana when he became its first president in 1960. His government built extensive harbor facilities at Tema [tä'mə], a seaport in the southeast. The city, he hoped, would handle trade for most of the rest of West Africa as well as for Ghana itself. Nkrumah's government also began building automobile assembly plants and steel and chemical industries so that the country would not have to depend so heavily on cacao, its major export. To meet the need for electric power, a huge dam was built across the Volta River. Its electricity is used to make aluminum from Ghana's large bauxite deposits.

Because of corruption and the buildup of large debt, Ghana's economy did not grow as quickly as hoped. A military council ousted Nkrumah in 1966, beginning the first of several periods of military rule.

With 14 million inhabitants, Ghana has the second largest population in West Africa. More than two-thirds are farmers.

Smaller coastal nations. Like Nigeria, Ghana, and Ivory Coast, the six smaller coastal nations have distinct histories and cultures and different political and economic systems today. As with the other coastal countries, their national capitals and densest populations lie to the

A cacao harvest in the Ivory Coast rainforest yields the ingredient from which chocolate is made.

south, along the Gulf of Guinea. Their people are mostly farmers, and their governments have had unrest and many changes.

The country of Liberia, for example, is the oldest black republic in Africa. Liberia was settled by freed slaves from the United States beginning in 1821. Descendants of the black settlers from the United States make up about 5 percent of Liberia's population, but they controlled the government until 1980. Then the army established a military government.

Another coastal nation, Togo, was once a German colony. After Germany's defeat in World War I, Togo fell under British and French control. The British part later joined Ghana. The French part became a republic in 1960. Like several other new African republics, Togo owned and operated the nation's industries under a socialist system. Many industries operated at a loss. In the late 1980s, Togo moved to sell many companies to private industry. In fact, Togo has been at the forefront of the African trend toward free enterprise.

Oil-rich Nigeria is Africa's most populous nation.

Nigeria is Africa's most populous country and the world's tenth most populous. Nigeria is also one of Africa's most outstanding economic powers. The map on page 478 shows that Nigeria extends deep into the interior. Thus the natural environments of the forested, green south are quite different from those of the dry north.

The Ibo [ē'bō] of southeastern Nigeria are one of the country's four great national cultures. In the southwest the Yoruba [yor'ə bə] have their historic home. In the north live the Hausa and the Fulani [fü'lä nē]. Together these four groups number more than two-thirds of the entire Nigerian population of 91 million. The remaining population is divided into nearly 250 other ethnic groups, making Nigeria one of the world's important **plural societies**—ones including numerous cultural groups.

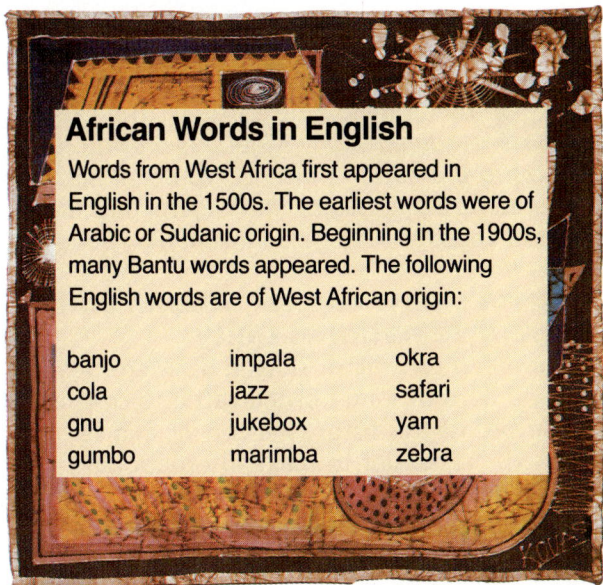

African Words in English

Words from West Africa first appeared in English in the 1500s. The earliest words were of Arabic or Sudanic origin. Beginning in the 1900s, many Bantu words appeared. The following English words are of West African origin:

banjo	impala	okra
cola	jazz	safari
gnu	jukebox	yam
gumbo	marimba	zebra

The Niger coming in from the northwest and its tributary, the Benue [bān'wā], coming from the east form a Y-shaped river system across the heart of Nigeria. North of the point where they flow together is a zone of severe tsetse-fly [tset'sē flī] infestation. The tsetse fly causes sleeping sickness and a similar disease that attacks livestock.

In the south, the oil palm is the basis of life for many people. The tree provides building materials and fibers for mats, and its pulpy fruit and kernels produce oils used for margarine, soap, and a whole range of other purposes. Along with its agricultural products, Nigeria has long exported tin, coal, and other minerals.

Lagos, on the southwest coast, is Nigeria's capital. Ibadan, a traditional city of the Yoruba about 90 miles north of Lagos, has become one of Africa's largest cities. Kano, one of the ancient caravan stops in the north, also is an important manufacturing center. Textile factories, metal works, car and truck assembly plants, and food-processing industries are located in and around these cities.

The discovery of large oil and natural gas reserves in the 1950s changed Nigeria's economy. Rich deposits of these fuels lie in the area of the Niger River's delta. Nigeria received a huge income from these exports in the 1970s. Oil income helped finance other industries, new roads and railroads, and improved health, housing, and education. When the price of oil dropped in the 1980s, Nigeria's economy suffered. Soon political problems resulted in a military takeover of the government. In an effort to strengthen Nigeria's economy, its government made plans to sell many state industries to private investors.

Section 1 Review

Locating Key Places
Locate the following places on the map on page 478: Sahel, Dakar, Abidjan, Lagos

Identifying Key Terms
Define the following terms: periodic market, desertification, harmattan, plural society

Reviewing Main Ideas
1. How does trade link nations in West Africa?
2. What natural feature dominates Mauritania, Senegal, Mali, Niger, and Chad and how does it affect life in these countries?
3. What kind of farming is practiced by the people of the Sahel?
4. Explain how the coastal countries of West Africa differ from the countries of the Sahel.
5. Give two reasons why Nigeria is important economically.

Thinking Critically: Assess Cause and Effect.
Refer to the maps on pages 478 and 480 to list the factors that cause people to live where they do in West Africa.

Case Study: A New Capital for Nigeria

Preview

Key Places
Where is this place located?
1 Abuja, Nigeria
See the globe below.

Key Term
What does this term mean?
bureaucratic

Main Ideas
As you read, look for answers to these questions.
- What is the symbolic value of moving Nigeria's capital to Abuja?
- What entertainment and recreation opportunities does Abuja have to offer?

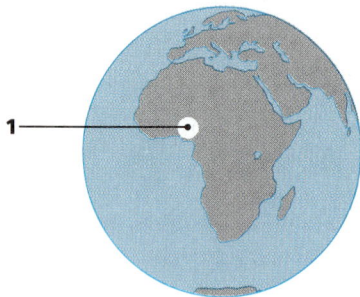

The following case study is from the article, "A 'Big Bore,' á la Brasília, in the Middle of Nigeria," in the New York Times, *June 25, 1987. The case study tells why Nigeria is moving its capital to the nation's interior, as Brazil has done. Before you begin, find Nigeria and the cities of Lagos and Abuja on the map on page 478.*

Nigeria's new capital, Abuja, will symbolize national unity.

A European contractor slowed his Mercedes to allow a herd of long-horned cattle to cross a boulevard of this future metropolis and re-marked, "It's easier to make international calls than at home."

With telephone and water systems in place for 1.5 million people, Abuja [ə bü'jə], population 15,000, is growing in fits and starts toward its future as the capital of Nigeria, black Africa's most populous and most powerful nation.

In the sparsely populated, wooded savanna of central Nigeria, gray concrete building skeletons are rising floor by floor, and giant bulldozers are scraping out four-lane expressways, following a blueprint drawn up a decade ago by an American company.

The construction of Abuja near the geographic center of this fractious [unruly] West African nation has symbolic value, as did the construction in the 1960s of Brasília, in Brazil's undeveloped interior.

"Abuja is meant to be a symbol of our unity—Lagos is on the periphery [edge] of our country," said Commodore Hamza Abdullahi, Minister for the Federal Capital Territory, referring to Nigeria's capital on the Atlantic coast 300 miles southwest of here [Abuja].

By building the new capital on a site where no ethnic groups had laid claims, Nigeria's leaders hope to inspire people to rise above ethnic and religious divisions that have tormented the nation since independence from Britain in 1960.

A sign marks the site for a government building in Abuja.

. . . "Abuja is Unity," proclaims a large billboard painted in the green and white national colors at the start of a 23-mile expressway leading from the Abuja International Airport to the new capital.

When the American company drew up the master plan for Abuja, Nigeria was at the height of its oil boom. The city was designed to be home to 250,000 people this year [1987] and 1.5 million by the year 2000. . . . Nigeria's oil revenues dropped to $5.6 billion last year, from $26 billion in 1980. From 1983 to 1985, most construction here was frozen. Commodore Abdullahi scaled down some of the designs, with a priority of completing old projects before beginning new ones. . . .

Four thousand housing units have been completed. And this year, the first seed of bureaucratic life was planted in the future capital. [**Bureaucratic** has to do with the officials running government bureaus.] The first two ministries, Trade and Internal Affairs, moved here. Two more of Nigeria's 20 ministries, Finance and Industry, are to move here by the end of the year.

This week, Commodore Abdullahi vowed to

have 75 percent of the ministries here by 1990, the target date for the official transfer of the capital from Lagos. A city of five million people, Lagos is often criticized for its inconveniences—traffic jams, open sewers, and erratic telephone service. But some civil servants are not eager to be pioneers in this infant city, even to escape Lagos's urban headaches. . . .

Recreation and entertainment in Abuja are not yet developed.

[Abuja's] two hotels . . . hold the city's only restaurants. Four banks are scheduled to open branches later this year. Meanwhile, the shopping district on Festival Road remains quiet.

Every Friday afternoon, the Nigerian Airways flight to Lagos is filled. . . . There are no movie theatres here yet. Foreign construction engineers who live in compounds, called life camps, take pride in their large and varied video-cassette collections. When a visitor asked a hotel desk clerk last week where to go for entertainment, the reply was, "Home."

Section 2 Review

Locating Key Places
Locate the following place on the map on page 478: Abuja, Nigeria

Identifying Key Terms
Define the following term: bureaucratic

Reviewing Main Ideas
1. Explain the symbolic value of Abuja.
2. Why might people not like living in a city with few opportunities for entertainment and recreation?

Thinking Critically: Analyze Comparisons
Find the states of New York, Ohio, Illinois, Michigan, Minnesota, Iowa, Alabama, Louisiana, and Texas on the map on pages 624–625. Locate the capital city for each state. None of these capitals is the largest city in its state. Based on what you have read in this case study, what may have been some of the reasons why each city became the state capital?

485

SECTION 3

Central Africa

Preview

Key Places
Where are these places located?
1 Zaire
2 Cameroon
3 Gabon
See the globe below.

Key Terms
What do these terms mean?
nationalize
tontine

Main Ideas
As you read, look for answers to these questions.
• What is Central Africa's main landform feature?
• Which is the largest Central African country?
• What countries lie north and west of Zaire?

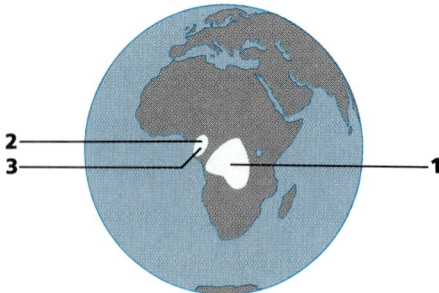

When I die, don't bury me under forest trees,
I fear their thorns.
When I die, don't bury me under forest trees,
I fear their dripping water.
Bury me under the great shade trees in the
market.
I want to hear the drums beating,
I want to feel the dancers' feet.

Traditional Kuba poem, Zaire

Central Africa's main landform feature is the Congo Basin.

Central Africa spreads across the continent's equatorial heartland. The huge Congo Basin is the main landform feature of Central Africa, also sometimes referred to as Equatorial Africa. The Congo Basin is the area drained by the Congo (Zaire) River and its tributaries. As the Kuba poem suggests, rainforests are the main form of natural vegetation.

Conditions of low latitude combined with low altitude hold special challenges for the countries of Central Africa: Cameroon, the Central African Republic, Equatorial Guinea, Gabon, Congo, and Zaire. Off the coast lies the tiny island country of São Tomé and Príncipe. Find these countries on the map on page 478. The dense vegetation makes it difficult to build and maintain modern systems of transportation and communication. Many communities are relatively isolated. Infertile soils often add to the problem of modern development. Like other wet, tropical areas, Africa is also a breeding place for many disease-carrying insects.

Zaire is central Africa's largest country in population and in area.

Zaire's 33 million people give it the largest population of any central African country. Zaire also covers the largest land area.

Zaire's modern history. During the earliest colonial days, the king of Belgium personally owned the land that is now Zaire. Ruthlessly, the king controlled the lives of the people, ordering them to gather wild rubber from the forests and kill elephants for their ivory. Many Africans died under the king's policies, and the Belgian government assumed control in 1908. The discovery of copper on the Katanga Plateau brought powerful Belgian mining companies into the southeastern area today known as Shaba [shä′bə].

As you read in Chapter 22, civil war broke out in Zaire immediately after independence. At the end of the war, Joseph Mobutu [mō bü′tü] seized control and has been president ever since. Mobutu has held tight military control

A family in southern Zaire crosses an open-pit mine.

and allowed no political parties to oppose him. He has also nationalized most of Zaire's industries. To **nationalize** means to convert from private to governmental ownership and control land, industries, railroads, or other concerns.

Zaire's economic advancement. Although the majority of Zaire's people are subsistence farmers, Zaire has vast potential for development. A massive dam on the Zaire River generates hydroelectric power. The Zaire River and its branches form the basis for transportation.

With cool highlands around its rim ranging to hot lowlands, Zaire can grow many kinds of crops. Zaire's mineral resources include gold and diamonds. Shaba Region contains cobalt, zinc, manganese, tin, and iron as well as copper.

Four countries lie north and west of Zaire.

In colonial days, much of the land north of the Congo River belonged to France. Today the French lands are divided among four countries: Congo, Gabon, Cameroon, and the Central African Republic.

Congo. Brazzaville, the capital city of Congo, lies across the Congo River from Zaire's capital, Kinshasa. More than a third of the population lives in Brazzaville, and more people arrive each year hoping to find work. At Brazzaville goods carried by boat down the Congo are loaded onto the railroad that runs to the ocean port of Pointe-Noire [pwänt nwär′], a major import-export center for much of Central Africa.

About half of Congo is forest-covered, and wood exports bring a major source of foreign income. Congo has some limited oil and gas resources that the United States is helping to develop. During the 1970s, the relatively stable military government had an economic agreement with the Soviet Union that helped build hospitals and a few factories for refining sugar, processing palm oil, and making cloth.

Timber is one of Gabon's many resources. Along the coast, logs are loaded onto ships.

Gabon. Gabon presents a picture very different from its neighbors for one major reason: rich mineral resources. Like Congo, Gabon is heavily forested, and until the 1960s its main export was timber. The country has had a stable civilian government since independence in 1960, when it began almost immediately to develop the country's mineral riches. These resources include oil reserves along the coast and huge iron ore deposits. Gabon's government has also developed its large deposits of uranium and manganese along with smaller supplies of gold.

Cameroon. French colonists left Cameroon with some small beginnings of manufacturing and agricultural development, which civilian leaders have built on since independence in 1960. Cameroon's economic growth rate in the 1980s was higher than any other African nation. The growth came in part, many economists said, because of Cameroon's tontines. A **tontine** [tän tēn'] is a kind of informal savings and loan association in West and Central Africa. Members can borrow money to buy a taxi, start a business, or for some other project.

The Central African Republic. In the Central African Republic, the equatorial rainforest yields to the savanna. The variety of climates and natural vegetation gives the country more economic possibilities. A few plantations raise cotton, coffee, and rubber for export. However, most of the people are subsistence farmers living in small farming villages. Traditionally, the women have been the farmers, raising sorghum, peanuts, and bananas. The men hunt and fish. The mineral resources of the Central African Republic include diamonds, uranium, iron ore, and coal.

Section 3 Review

Locating Key Places
Locate the following places on the map on page 478: Cameroon, Gabon, Zaire

Identifying Key Terms
Define the following terms: nationalize, tontine

Reviewing Main Ideas
1. Describe Central Africa's main landform feature.
2. What are some economic advantages of Zaire?
3. Name four countries that lie north and west of Zaire and tell one advantage of each country.

Thinking Critically: Analyze Comparisons
Recall what you learned about the attitude of Nigeria's leaders toward government-owned industries in that country. Compare the governments of Nigeria and Zaire in this regard. Then compare Zaire's major economic activities and physical geography with Nigeria's. Summarize your findings in a paragraph. Conclude by saying whether or not you think Zaire will follow Nigeria's example.

Using Remote Sensing Images

Suppose you wanted to find out how certain land and water areas are being used in Africa. One way you could find out is by studying a "remote sensing image." This term refers to a satellite picture that measures heat, light, and other forms of radiation.

The image on this page shows the paths of the Niger (left center) and Bani (bottom center) rivers as they flow through the West African country of Mali. The dark reds indicate marsh vegetation growing like islands in the wetlands. The lighter reds show cultivated fields and grasslands, and the lightest colors indicate sparse steppe vegetation.

From the image, you can pick up information about this area of Mali. Both rivers flow into this large depression to form a vast inland delta 600 miles from the sea. Three different ethnic groups use the inland delta. At different times of the year, the land is used alternately for fishing, grazing, and cultivation.

Review

Describe the vegetation type at these locations:
1. the northwest corner
2. along the Niger as it moves up from the southwest corner
3. in the middle of the wetlands in the northwest

Review

Section Summaries

1. West Africa Trade connects the countries of West Africa. This area includes seven countries of the dry north (mainly the Sahel) and nine moister countries. The Sahara dominates the Sahel, a fragile environment along the southern edge of the desert where drought and desertification often threaten life. The nine moister countries have relatively large, diverse populations. Nigeria, with Africa's largest population, has great potential based on urban industries, oil, and other minerals.

2. Case Study: A New Capital for Nigeria Nigeria plans to move its capital from the bustling port city of Lagos, on its southwestern coast, to a centrally located, planned capital, Abuja. Nigeria's leaders want the new capital as a symbol of national unity. When the first government ministries

moved to the new capital in 1987, Abuja had few restaurants and no theaters. Most people wanted to return to Lagos for their weekends.

3. Central Africa The Congo Basin—the huge, bowl-shaped region drained by the Congo (Zaire) River—is the main landform region of Central Africa. Zaire, Central Africa's largest country, exports many minerals from the Shaba region. North and west of Zaire are Cameroon, the Central African Republic, Equatorial Guinea, Gabon, and Congo. Off the coast lies São Tomé and Príncipe. Cameroon's economy is based on manufacturing and agriculture. Most people in the Central African Republic are subsistence farmers. Gabon has rich mineral resources, and Congo exports wood.

Using Geography Skills

Reviewing the Map Lesson

Use the remote sensing image on page 489 to answer the following questions.
1. Which color represents land on which crops are grown?
2. Which color indicates the wettest areas on the image?
3. Which color shows areas where there is little vegetation?

Using Social Studies Skills

1. See Others' Point of View. In the United States, many farmers live on and work separate, family-owned farms. Most African farmers live in villages in which the land is communally held and the whole group shares common rights to its resources. Suppose you are a farmer in Zaire. Write a letter to a farmer in the United States explaining why you think your system of land ownership is better for you than the U.S. system.

2. Analyze Information. Read a recent newspaper or weekly news magazine to find out which West and Central African countries are in the news. Select information from one or more articles and then write an editorial explaining the "geographic story" behind the events of the day. You may want to consider such things as (a) location, (b) population patterns, (c) resources, (d) colonial heritage.

Testing for Understanding

Locating Key Places
Match the description with the places listed below.
1. the future capital of Nigeria
2. a West African country in which tontines have helped strengthen the economy
3. the Senegalese capital and major port
4. the capital and major port in Ivory Coast
5. the capital of Nigeria until 1990
6. a West African country that began developing its mineral riches after it gained independence
7. the southern margins of the Sahara
8. Central Africa's largest country in both land area and population
a. Sahel
b. Dakar
c. Abidjan
d. Lagos
e. Abuja
f. Cameroon
g. Gabon
h. Zaire

Recalling Key Terms
Define these terms in your own words.

Section 1
periodic market
desertification
harmattan
plural society

Section 2
bureaucratic

Section 3
nationalize
tontine

Reviewing Main Ideas
Section 1
1. Tell how trade links the nations of West Africa.
2. What natural feature dominates Mauritania, Senegal, Mali, Niger, and Chad and how does it affect life in these countries?
3. In what ways are the coastal countries of West Africa different from the countries of the Sahel?
4. Why is Nigeria important economically?

Section 2
1. According to Nigeria's leaders, what is the symbolic value of the new capital at Abuja?
2. Tell why people might not enjoy living in a city like Abuja, where they have as yet little opportunity for recreation and entertainment.

Section 3
1. What is Central Africa's main landform feature?
2. What are some of Zaire's economic advantages?
3. Identify four countries that lie north and west of Zaire. What is one advantage of each country?

Thinking Critically
1. **Make Hypotheses.** Most African railroads were built during colonial days to carry raw materials from the interior to the coast. How would the location of the railroads affect trade between African nations today? African countries still trade vital resources with former colonial rulers. How do their railroads help explain this pattern?

2. **Predict Effects.** Explain why you would agree or disagree with this statement: If the vast majority of the people in Africa had a high-school education, the most serious national problems would soon be corrected.

East and Southern Africa

In this chapter you will read about life today in East and Southern Africa.

Sections
1 East Africa
2 Southern Africa

East Africa

Preview

Key Places
Where are these places located?
1 Khartoum
2 Lake Victoria
See the globe below.

Key Terms
What do these terms mean?
villagization
ujamaa village

Main Ideas
As you read, look for answers to these questions.
• What role does Sudan's location play?
• What countries make up the Horn of Africa?
• What economic ties bind the countries of East Africa nearest the Equator?

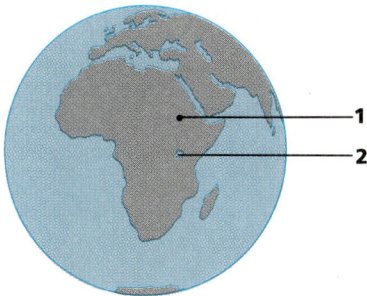

Kharita [a map] *is not necessary. We use the sun by day and the stars by night to go.*

Truck driver in western Sudan

Sudan is divided into a dry north and a wet south.

Centuries ago Muslim pilgrims from the western savanna traveled along the southern edge of the Sahara toward the Nile River and eventually across the Red Sea to Mecca on the Arabian Peninsula. The pilgrims took their bearings from the sun by day and the stars by night like the Sudanese driver of a market truck following the same lonely track today. As the pilgrims moved eastward, they saw much that was as familiar to them as their western homelands. At last they would find the place known today as Khartoum [kär tüm′], the capital of the modern country of Sudan. Here the White Nile and the Blue Nile join as they flow north to the Mediterranean Sea.

If the pilgrims had turned southward at Khartoum, instead of continuing their journey to Mecca, what a different world they would have seen. After crossing a moist, grassy area, they would have come to steep escarpments opening onto high plateaus. The heart of East Africa would have spread before them, with its snow-capped volcanoes, lake-filled valleys, and broad savannas.

Modern Sudan. Today Sudan is a large country, the largest in area in all of Africa. Its north is vastly different from its south. The north is dry and parched, but the south often suffers from too much water. There the White Nile divides into innumerable channels and creates a vast swampland called the Sudd.

Sudan's cultures also are divided north and south. The Nubians, who have lived in the

Facing page: **Nairobi's skyline forms a backdrop of contrast for Nairobi National Park in Kenya.**

East and Southern Africa

Legend:

- Commercial farming
- Irrigated farming
- Subsistence farming
- Ranching
- Nomadic herding
- Forests
- Lumbering
- Mining
- Commercial fishing
- Urban land use
- Little or no economic activity
- National capitals
- Other cities

Scale:
0 — 500 — 1000 Miles
0 — 500 — 1000 Kilometers

Map labels:

ALGERIA, LIBYA, EGYPT, Tropic of Cancer, 20°N

NIGER, CHAD, Lake Chad

Gold, Port Sudan, RED SEA, Dates, Cotton, Omdurman, Khartoum, SOCOTRA (P.D.R. OF YEMEN), DJIBOUTI

NIGERIA, Benue R., Niger, CAMEROON, CENTRAL AFRICAN REPUBLIC, Ubangi R.

Sheep, SUDAN, Millet, Chromite, White Nile, Blue Nile, Lake Tana, Beef Cattle, Djibouti, SOMALIA, Addis Ababa, ETHIOPIA, Coffee, Sheep

P.R. OF THE CONGO, GABON, Zaire R., Congo R.

Copper, UGANDA, KENYA, Mogadishu, 0° Equator, Kampala, Coffee, Tea, Lake Victoria, Nairobi, Fruits, INDIAN OCEAN

ZAIRE, RWANDA, Kigali, Coffee, Bujumbura, BURUNDI, Coffee, Diamonds, Mombasa, Sisal, SEYCHELLES, Victoria

Kasai R., Lake Tanganyika, Dodoma, TANZANIA, Cloves, ZANZIBAR, Dar es Salaam, Tea, Sugar Cane

Mackerel, ATLANTIC OCEAN, Luanda, Coffee, Diamonds, Cotton, ANGOLA, Sugar Cane, Corn, Copper, Lake Nyasa, MALAWI, Lilongwe, Cashews, Moroni, COMOROS

Oil, ZAMBIA, Iron Ore, Lusaka, Zambezi, Tobacco, MOZAMBIQUE, Sugar Cane, Coffee

Copper, NAMIBIA (SOUTH AFRICA), Diamonds, Gold, Harare, ZIMBABWE, Antananarivo, Rice, 20°S, MAURITIUS, MADAGASCAR, REUNION (FR.), Port Louis

Uranium, WALVIS BAY (SOUTH AFRICA), Windhoek, BOTSWANA, Limpopo R., Platinum, Tropic of Capricorn

Beef Cattle, Gaborone, Pretoria, Maputo, Mbabane, SWAZILAND, Johannesburg, Sheep, Gold, Uranium, Coal, Diamonds, Orange R., Diamonds, Iron Ore, Maseru, LESOTHO, Durban, Bloemfontein, SOUTH AFRICA, Sheep, Fruits, Grapes, Cape Town, Port Elizabeth

20°E, 40°E, 60°E

N, W, E, S (compass)

Map Study

East Africa includes Sudan, Ethiopia, Djibouti, Somalia, Kenya, Uganda, Tanzania, Rwanda, and Burundi. Find these countries on the map. Which East African country is farthest south? The other countries on the map make up Southern Africa. Which Southern African countries are landlocked?

northern part for millenia, have evolved a culture that is both Arab and African. Different ethnic groups live in the south, including the Dinka and the Nuer who retain their traditional animist beliefs. Nubian rulers from time to time have tried to impose Muslim ways on their southern subjects. Civil wars, even today, mark southern resistance to the north's domination.

Sudan's economy. Throughout Sudan, most people live by farming and herding. Cotton grows on the irrigated farmland of the Gezira [jə zir'ə] Plain between the White Nile and the Blue Nile. The region also produces millet, sorghum, and gum arabic, a sap from acacia [ə kā'shə] trees used in candy and medicine.

The droughts of the early 1970s and 1980s brought famine to about 4 million Sudanese. Surprisingly enough, while people were starving, Sudan had a record cotton harvest.

How could this happen? Like many African countries, Sudan has a cash-crop economy. Sudan's government encouraged farmers to grow cotton for export in order to get foreign currency. Sudan was able to increase its food production enough by 1986 to put a year's supply of grain in reserve. However, by the late 1980s, Sudan still carried a heavy burden of foreign debt.

The dependence on cash crops causes severe problems for many African countries. Economists say that world supplies and the availability of substitutes usually determine prices for such raw materials as cotton. However, from the Africans' point of view, wealthy nations dominate the world markets, controlling the demand, price, and other market factors. From this perspective, low prices for raw materials are seen by many African leaders as just another way to keep their nations in poverty.

Ethiopia, Djibouti, and Somalia make up the Horn of Africa.

East of Sudan lie Ethiopia, Djibouti [ji bü'tē], and Somalia. This area is referred to as the Horn

A Somali family receives aid during a drought.

of Africa because of the shape of its eastern tip, which you can see on the map on page 494.

Somali herders use the Ethiopian borderlands, and Ethiopia and Somalia fought for possession of this region during the 1970s. Both countries have also laid claims to Djibouti in the past. Djibouti's capital city, also named Djibouti, is a port on the Gulf of Aden and the nation's main source of income.

Ethiopia, with 36 million people, is the third most populous country in Africa, following Nigeria and Egypt. Ethiopians became Christians during their 4th-century contacts with Rome. Later, Muslim invaders took over the coastal areas. Ethiopia's Christian leadership was able to control the Muslims and resist European colonization in the 1800s.

Like Sudan, Ethiopia has been plagued with severe droughts since the early 1970s. Ethiopia's high plateaus usually have ample moisture, however. Soils are fertile. Coffee, figs, grapes, and citrus fruits grow there as well as wheat and barley. Why then is Ethiopia not a bread-basket for all of East Africa? There are several reasons. For one thing, large parts of Ethiopia are covered by rugged mountains and arid plains suitable at best for herding cattle and sheep. Even in the fertile highland areas, population growth has led to deforestation and soil erosion. The country also has not built roads in the rugged highlands, so food distribution remains difficult even when crops are good. In addition, poor political leadership has contributed to economic stagnation.

The drought of 1984 brought famine and starvation to Ethiopia. Ethiopia's leaders began to resettle farmers from drought-stricken areas. Under this program, called **villagization**, some farmers who had been working small, scattered family plots were moved to farming villages, where they would have to spend their time working in communal fields. The farmers resisted villagization.

The countries nearest the Equator have close economic ties.

Five countries lie close to the Equator in East Africa: Kenya, Uganda, Tanzania, Rwanda, and Burundi. Use the map on page 494 to locate these countries and find the different ways that people use the land there. As you read in Chapter 22, Arab traders and the people of eastern Africa formed distinctive Swahili cultures in part of this region. British and German colonization brought still more cultures and economic ties.

Kenya's people and economy. About 40 main ethnic groups and many subgroups live in Kenya. The Kikuyu [ki kü'yü] are the dominant group. The farming Luo live near Lake Victoria, and the cattle-herding Masai [mä sī'] live to the south. (See map, page 473.)

Jomo Kenyatta, a Kikuyu, led the war against Kenya's European settlers shortly before independence. When independence came in 1963, Kenyatta led the new nation until his death in 1978. Then his vice-president, Daniel arap Moi [moi], assumed the office.

Kenya's economic policies since independence have encouraged private ownership of business and allowed farmers to work their own farmlands. Agriculture and tourism are the main sources of income. In the cool highlands, farmers cultivate tea and coffee for export as well as sisal [sis'əl], a fiber used to make twine.

Volcanic peaks in Kenya rise against vast expanses of savanna, where many species of wildlife roam free in reserves set aside for them. These national parks attract thousands of visitors from around the world, and tourists provide Kenya's major source of income.

Because of population growth, Kenya's government has considered opening some of the restricted parks to create more farmland.

The Masai people of Kenya farm as well as raise livestock.

Destroying the habitat of the herds would cut off Kenya's valuable tourist income and bring death to the animals. Thus the problems of Kenya's farmers concern not only its own government but also environmentalists throughout the world.

Uganda's people and economy. When British colonizers reached Uganda in the 1890s, they found the BaGanda had built a rich trading kingdom along Lake Victoria. Under colonial rule, the British favored the BaGanda. When Uganda became independent, the BaGanda were a powerful people in a thriving economy based on cotton, coffee, tea, tobacco, and sugar production.

Ethnic groups in northern Uganda controlled the army after independence, and they resented the BaGanda influence. Idi Amin [e'dē ä mēn'], a military officer from the north overthrew the government and began a terrible reign of destruction in which 300,000 of his opponents were killed. With Tanzania's help, Ugandans finally ousted Amin in 1979. In the late 1980s, a new government worked to rebuild Uganda's economy.

Tanzania's people and economy. Julius Nyerere [nī râr'ē] led the new nation of Tanzania until 1985. He wanted to make Tanzania self-sufficient by turning it into a strong agricultural nation, and he began a program that provided a model for Ethiopia's program of villagization. Under Nyerere's plan, 90 percent of Tanzania's farmers were eventually moved to new villages called **ujamaa** [ü jä mä'] **villages**. Ujamaa is a Swahili word meaning "neighborliness, or mutual aid." In the ujamaa villages, the farmers live and work as a community to grow food for themselves and another crop to sell. The government invested much money in wells, electricity, and sewage systems in 8,300 ujamaa villages. However, most farmers had to be forced to leave their ancestral lands. Some people lost their lives when their homes were burned or bulldozed. Productivity dropped, and farm output has markedly declined.

Tanzania fought a costly war in the late 1970s to keep Uganda from taking part of its land in the north. Tanzania is still trying to rebuild its economy, and like some other African nations has begun to favor free enterprise over government-run industries. By the late 1980s, Tanzania had sold many government business interests and was looking for foreign managers to revive its game reserves and tourist lodges.

Section 1 Review

Locating Key Places
Locate the following places on the map on page 494: Khartoum, Lake Victoria

Identifying Key Terms
Define the following terms: villagization, ujamaa village

Reviewing Main Ideas
1. Tell how the northern part of Sudan differs from the southern part.
2. Describe the countries that make up the Horn of Africa.
3. What are three ways in which the countries of East Africa nearest the Equator are tied together?

Thinking Critically: Make Hypotheses
A grassland region called the Serengeti Plain stretches across portions of Kenya and Tanzania between Lake Victoria and Mount Kilimanjaro. The Serengeti has long abounded with great game herds. One reason wildlife has survived in the Serengeti is that these animals, unlike cattle, are not vulnerable to diseases carried by the tsetse fly. Now Africans cannot safely herd cattle there. If the tsetse fly is eventually eliminated, what do you think will happen to the animals of the Serengeti Plain?

Southern Africa

Preview

Key Places
Where are these places located?
1 South Africa
2 Angola
3 Mozambique
See the globe below.

Key Terms
What do these terms mean?
Afrikaner
apartheid
sanction
copra

Main Ideas
As you read, look for answers to these questions.
- From what parts of the world did South Africa accumulate its diverse population?
- Who brought apartheid to South Africa?
- What do Namibia, Zimbabwe, and Zambia have in common?
- How have their wars for independence affected Angola and Mozambique?

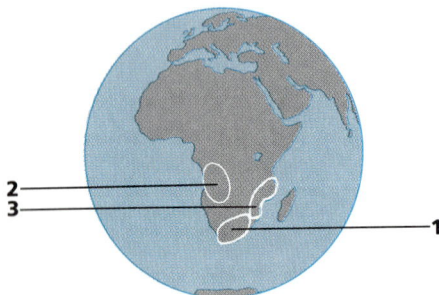

When my father taught me history, I began to understand. I remember distinctly, for instance, how he taught us about the nine Xhosa [kō'sä] wars. Of course we had textbooks, naturally written by white men, and they had their interpretation, why there were nine "Kaffir" wars. ["Kaffir" has been used as a derogatory term for blacks in South Africa.] Then he would put the textbook aside and say: "Now, this is what the book says, but the truth is: these white people invaded our country and stole the land from our grandfathers.". . . That's how he taught us our history.

Winnie Mandela, *Part of My Soul Went with Him*

People from Africa, Europe, and Asia have settled in South Africa.

Southern Africa is a region torn by a deep and continuing struggle between the black majority and a white minority in South Africa and Namibia. Each group has its own interpretation of history and its own vision of the future, as black liberation leader Winnie Mandela implied. The struggle between the black majority and the white minority has an important effect not only on South Africa but on its relations with its neighbors. The country of South Africa is the chief political and economic power in southern Africa. None of the other countries— Zimbabwe, Zambia, Botswana, Lesotho, Swaziland, Angola, Malawi, Mozambique, and Madagascar—are completely free from its influence.

South Africa's land and climate. As you read in Chapter 22, South Africa's climate is generally cooler and more varied than in other African countries. The city of Cape Town on the Atlantic coast has a Mediterranean climate. The interior and economic heartland of the country are its high, grassy velds. The veld is a plateau region where wheat, corn, fruit, and other crops are grown and sheep and cattle are raised. South Africa's vast mineral resources are also concentrated in the velds, especially in the regions around the city of Johannesburg. Find Cape Town and Johannesburg on the map on page 494.

South Africa is the world's largest supplier of gold and diamonds. It also has rich reserves of copper, iron ore, manganese, chromium, platinum, asbestos, nickel, and other minerals needed by many nations for their national defense.

South Africa has built a powerful industrial economy on this strong agricultural and mineral base. The most highly urbanized country in Africa, it produces iron and steel, cars, textiles, chemicals, and all the other products of a modern industrialized country. So far, however, modern South Africa's successes have been overshadowed by interracial conflicts that limit human and economic growth for its people.

South Africa's people. Small groups of Africans, the San, were living around the Cape of Good Hope when the Dutch began to settle there in 1642. The San were forced to retreat into the Kalahari Desert. As the Dutch expanded their settlement, they came into conflict with powerful Bantu-speaking groups like the Xhosa, Sotho, and Zulu. Then the British arrived in 1806, claimed the Cape, and opened sugar plantations on the eastern coast. The British brought in Hindu laborers from their colony in India. Thus South Africa of the 1800s held many cultures—African, European, and Asian. Africans were by far the largest group.

South Africa's fabulous diamond resources were discovered in 1870, and 16 years later its rich gold deposits were found. Fortune seekers from all over the world rushed to the veld. The diamond rush created the town of Kimberley. Witwatersrand, or the Rand—the ridge on which Johannesburg is located—was soon recognized as the world's greatest gold-bearing district.

South Africa became a British colony in 1902 after the Boer War—a fierce war between the British and the Afrikaners over South Africa's mineral wealth. The **Afrikaners** are the descendants of the Dutch settlers. South Africa was given its independence in 1910, with people of British descent in control of the government. The balance of power shifted after the 1948 election when the Afrikaners outnumbered the English representatives in the South African national government.

Afrikaners began a policy of apartheid.

After 1948 the Afrikaners adopted the policy that South Africa should keep the racial groups in groups in its society separated. They named their policy **apartheid** [ə pärt′hāt], an Afrikaner word meaning "separateness." The overall plan of apartheid was to maintain four separate social and political communities within South Africa. The four communities were the 24 million black South Africans, the 5 million white South Africans, the 3 million "Coloureds" (people of

Workers pour molten gold at a Johannesburg smelting plant.

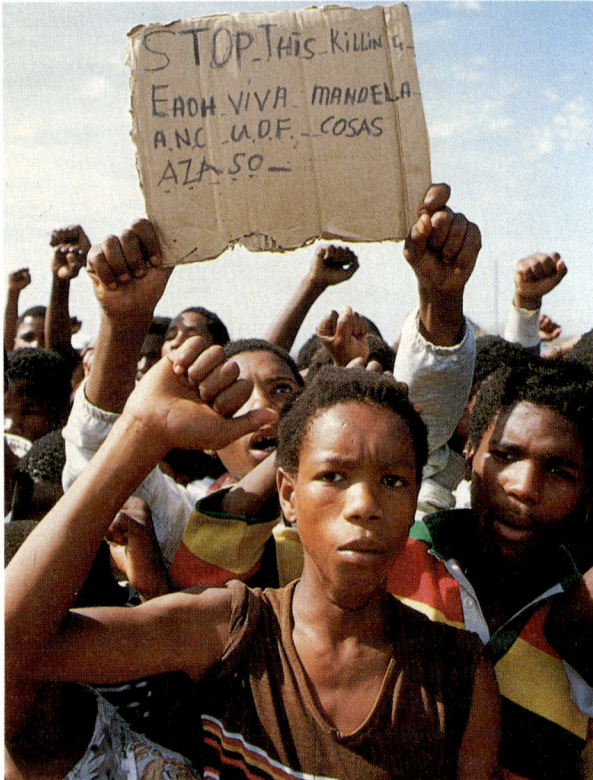

Black South Africans demonstrate against apartheid.

mixed racial backgrounds), and the 1 million Asians, mostly Indians.

South African blacks were to be assigned their own territories, or "homelands," within South Africa. Each black person would be considered a citizen of his or her particular homeland, not of South Africa, and would not have political rights in South Africa's national government.

According to this plan, South Africa's black population was assigned ten homelands. Together the homelands make up about 15 percent of South Africa's land.

In addition to creating inequalities in land distribution, apartheid policies resulted in some 200 other laws aimed at further segregation.

Black South Africans, Asians, and people of mixed racial background were needed and allowed to work in the mines, factories, farms, and to act as household servants. However, blacks had to carry passbooks describing where they were going when they were outside their homelands. Apartheid laws kept blacks, "Coloureds," and Asians from sharing restaurants, schools, or other public facilities with white South Africans.

People living in the homelands were crowded together on lands poor in farming and mineral resources and far from industry and transportation networks. Thus they had little chance for becoming self-sufficient. The men often had to work in the mines and cities, separated from their families in the homelands.

Many people within South Africa and around the world protested and condemned apartheid. As a result of these protests, the government agreed to drop the passbook laws. Now, all South Africans must carry a Uniform Identity Document, regardless of race. Schools and neighborhoods, however, are still mostly segregated, and black South Africans cannot vote in national elections. Black political leaders and students have resisted the government's policies with strikes and other demonstrations. This has often led to violence and police repression. Many black South Africans, including young children, have been imprisoned, killed, or injured. Black leaders, including Anglican Archbishop Desmond Tutu and political activist Nelson Mandela, recently released from a 27-year imprisonment, continued to work for change.

Western governments, including that of the United States adopted sanctions to hasten the end of apartheid. **Sanctions** are actions—usually economic restrictions—taken by nations in hopes of forcing another nation to obey international law. As a result of the sanctions, many U.S. companies have discontinued business operations in South Africa and cut their investments in its economy.

500

South Africa's policies strongly affect nearby countries.

The territory of Namibia and the independent countries of Botswana, Lesotho, and Swaziland are almost completely overshadowed by South Africa. The countries of Zambia, Zimbabwe, and Malawi form a buffer zone between South Africa and the rest of the continent.

Many people in these countries depend on jobs in South Africa to support their families, and these countries provide markets for South Africa's manufactured goods. South Africa has resisted any changes in these countries that would affect its economic interests. Except for Namibia, all of South Africa's neighbors have black-majority governments that are opposed to

Scattered trees provide wood for a settlement in Namibia.

apartheid. South Africa wants to discourage them from aiding black guerrillas fighting to overthrow its white-minority rule.

Namibia. Although large in area, Namibia is mostly desert and sparsely populated, but it has valuable mineral deposits.The UN is trying to get South Africa to grant independence to Namibia, and Namibians are fighting a guerrilla war against South African soldiers. South Africa agreed to grant Namibia its freedom in 1990.

Zimbabwe. As you read in Chapter 22, the black citizens of Zimbabwe fought a strong minority of white inhabitants before gaining independence. Rich in minerals and farmlands, Zimbabwe attracted many European settlers during its days as a British colony. Mines were developed, and large farms raised tobacco, cotton, sugar, tea, coffee, and wheat. The Europeans also started many manufacturing plants. The black people had low-paying, menial jobs and lived in poverty compared to the white minority.

The civil war shattered Zimbabwe's economy. In recent years, however, the farm economy has improved, and Zimbabwe resumed the export of minerals. The new nation has been able to feed its own people and is beginning to realize the potential of becoming a leading African nation.

Zambia. Zambia became independent in 1964, shortly before the civil war began in Zimbabwe. Zambia chose to join the Commonwealth of Nations, a group of independent countries with ties to Britain. Zimbabwe, Botswana, Lesotho, Swaziland, and eight other African nations, all former colonies of Britain, also belong to the Commonwealth. Zambia, like many Commonwealth countries, trades heavily with its former ruler.

Zambia shares the mineral-rich belt that begins in the Shaba Region of Zaire and runs southward through Zambia and into Zimbabwe.

The region produces copper, zinc, lead, manganese, vanadium, and cobalt. Although Zambia has a good income from its mineral exports, most of its population live on subsistence farms remote from the major roads, railroads, and the capital city, Lusaka.

Madagascar. In early geologic times, Madagascar was attached to the African mainland, near Mozambique. Its high savannas and eastern escarpment make its physical geography similar to the continent's. The country's 10 million people, however, are mainly of Southeast Asian ancestry rather than African. Agriculture employs most of Madagascar's workers today, and coffee, cloves, vanilla, and cotton are major exports.

Wars have hurt the economies of Angola and Mozambique.

Angola and Mozambique, on opposite coasts of the continent, were both Portuguese colonies. Use the map on page 494 to find Angola, south of the Congo River on the Atlantic coast, and Mozambique, bordering the Indian Ocean.

Angola. Angola is a large country well endowed with natural resources. The land is fertile savanna, where coffee, cotton, tobacco, and sugar cane can grow. Angola also has deposits of iron ore, manganese, diamonds, and oil. The oil fields lie in its small territory of Cabinda, north of Zaire's corridor to the sea.

War and unrest continued after Angola's independence from Portugal in 1975. Rebel groups in the south and east opposed the new president, a communist, who took office without an election. The rebels began a civil war that has not yet been settled. The president asked for and received help from Cuba and the Soviet Union. The rebels received help from South Africa and the United States. Years of fighting have weakened Angola's economy.

Mozambique. When Mozambique's war for independence ended in 1975, its new leaders also planned to install a communist system. Rebels immediately challenged the new president. South Africa has supported the rebels for years, keeping the country in turmoil. In addition to the fighting, Mozambique suffered years of devastating drought.

Despite its problems, Mozambique still has a substantial rail system for transporting goods to the port cities of Beira and Maputo. The country also has coal and other minerals. Large farms near the Zambezi and Limpopo rivers can produce cash crops of cashew nuts, sugar, cotton, tea, and **copra**—dried coconut meat used for its oil.

Section 2 Review

Locating Key Places
Locate the following places on the map on page 494: South Africa, Angola, Mozambique

Identifying Key Terms
Define the following terms: Afrikaner, apartheid, sanction, copra

Reviewing Main Ideas
1. From what parts of the world and when did South Africa accumulate each of its main population groups?
2. What group established South Africa's policy of apartheid? How has this policy worked in practice?
3. Explain what effect South Africa's policies have had on Namibia, Zimbabwe, Zambia, and other nearby nations.
4. Why have the economies of Angola and Mozambique suffered since independence?

Thinking Critically: Make Hypotheses
South Africa's government has often scorned other world nations' criticisms of its racist policies, even going so far as to say that South Africa can "go it alone" in the world. List as many reasons as you can why you think the South African government would take this attitude.

Understanding Political Maps

Suppose you wanted to collect an accurate political map of every country in the world. For a country like the United States, you would have little problem finding a map that is commonly accepted.

For other countries, however, political conflicts could make your search difficult. Border and territorial disputes, as well as one's definition of a country, all affect mapmaking.

By common definition, a country has four characteristics. They are a territory with defined boundaries, an independent government with a recognized leadership, a population, and an independent foreign policy. If any of these basic elements are missing, then a country's existence may be questioned.

The "homelands" of the Republic of South Africa are a case in point. More than 70 percent of the people living in this country are black. In the 1970s, however, the white-minority government took steps to strengthen its control.

These steps included setting up ten "homelands" for the different ethnic groups that make up South Africa's black population. Use the map on this page to identify each homeland.

Fifty-one percent of South Africa's black population has been assigned to an "official"

residence in the homelands. However, most of the land of the homelands is unproductive.

As a result, most male residents leave to find work in South Africa's larger cities, where their families are not allowed to live. Thus, families are separated, and the homelands are filled primarily with women and children.

The South African government has given independence to four homelands so far—Transkei, Bophuthatswana [bō pü'tä tswä'nä], Venda, and Ciskei. The independence of these homelands, however, has not been recognized by the United States, the United Nations, and almost all other countries of the world. The only official maps to show the "homelands" as separate nations are those published in South Africa.

Review

1. Which homelands have land along the Indian Ocean coast?
2. Which homeland is closest to Pretoria?
3. What are two formally independent countries that lie within South Africa's borders?

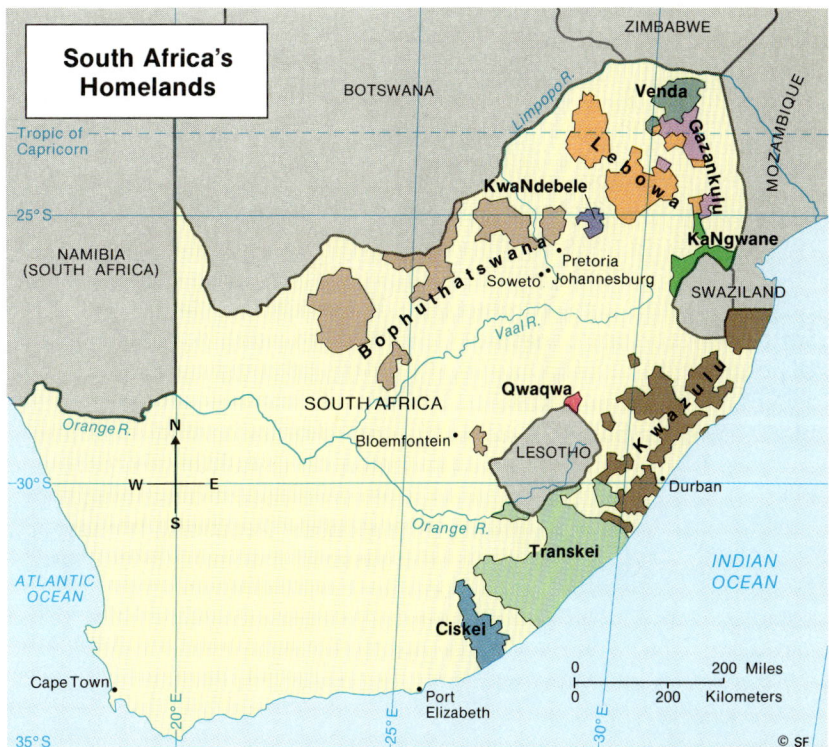

South Africa's Homelands

Review

Section Summaries

1. East Africa Sudan, with both Muslim Nubians and Africans holding animist beliefs, is a transition zone to other parts of Africa. Civil strife, population growth, and poor political leadership have kept Ethiopia from developing its rich agricultural potential. Kenya depends strongly on savanna tourism and agriculture. Uganda's people and economy fell into disarray under an unstable government. Tanzania's planned villages, meant to increase agricultural output, have disrupted that nation's economy.

2. Southern Africa The white minority controls South Africa's government and mineral and agricultural riches through the system of apartheid. Black South Africans, however, are fighting for their rights. All of southern Africa feels the influence of South Africa. The territory of Namibia remains under South African control despite UN opposition. After a civil war against white domination, black-ruled Zimbabwe is now

trying to rebuild its potentially strong economy. Zambia's copper and other minerals give it important advantages. The island nation of Madagascar has an agricultural economy with many people of Asian descent. Civil wars have continued in Angola and Mozambique. Both countries have mineral resources and fertile farmland.

Using Geography Skills

Reviewing the Map Lesson

Use the map on page 503 to answer the following questions.
1. How do the shapes of the homelands compare to the shapes of most countries?
2. What three homelands lie in the far northeast corner of South Africa?
3. Which two homelands border Lesotho?

Using Social Studies Skills

1. Locate and Gather Information. The list below names some ethnic groups of East Africa. Select one group and use your library to find information on its culture. Prepare a written report describing the people's traditions, homes, art, ways of making a living, and

how they are adjusting to the new Africa. Include a map locating their traditional homelands in your report.

Amhara	Luo
Dinka	Masai
Kikuyu	Somali

2. Translate Information from One Medium to Another. The list below gives some important metals and the estimated percentages of the world's total reserves that lie in African countries. Make bar graphs showing African reserves compared to world totals. Underline the names of southern African countries on your graphs.

Chromium: South Africa, 91%; Zimbabwe, 2%
Cobalt: Zaire, 50%; Zambia 13%
Gold: South Africa, 53%
Manganese: South Africa, 41%; Gabon, 11%
Platinum: South Africa, 79%

Testing for Understanding

Locating Key Places
Match the descriptions with the key places listed below.
1. a former Portuguese colony bordering the Indian Ocean
2. Africa's southernmost country
3. where the White Nile joins the Blue Nile
4. the site of the BaGandas' trading kingdom
5. a former Portuguese colony on the Atlantic Ocean
a. Khartoum
b. Lake Victoria
c. South Africa
d. Angola
e. Mozambique

Recalling Key Terms
Define these terms in your own words.

Section 1
villagization
ujamaa village

Section 2
Afrikaner
apartheid
sanction
copra

Reviewing Main Ideas
Section 1
1. In what way is northern Sudan different from southern Sudan?
2. Which countries make up the Horn of Africa?
3. Name three ways in which the countries of East Africa nearest the Equator are tied together.

Section 2
1. When did South Africa accumulate each of its main population groups? From what parts of the world did they come?
2. What group began South Africa's policy of apartheid? Tell how this policy has worked in practice.
3. How have South Africa's policies affected Namibia, Zambia, Zimbabwe, and other nearby countries?
4. Explain why the economies of Angola and Mozambique have suffered since independence.

Thinking Critically
1. **Identify Assumptions.** How does Tanzania's ujamaa village experiment reflect the traditional African values holding that land should be owned in common and worked for the benefit of all? What other values would have led so many of Tanzania's farmers to want to remain on their ancestral lands rather than move to the ujamaa villages?

2. **Predict Effects.** How do you think South Africa's economy and its various social groups would be affected if other world nations did not buy its exports?

505

Review

Summarizing the Unit

Chapter 22 A Physical and Cultural Overview High plateaus cut by the Great Rift Valley give Africa a unique landscape. Although located in or near the tropics, the continent has savanna, steppe, and desert climates as well as tropical rainforests. Farming and trading communities led to the growth of city-states and empires beginning A.D. 400. In the 19th century, Europeans drew new boundaries in Africa to section off their colonies. New African nations gained independence beginning in the 1950s. Since then they have striven to build their economies while retaining their African identities.

Chapter 23 West and Central Africa West Africa stretches from Chad westward to the Atlantic. Its northern countries take in the fragile, sparsely settled Sahel. The more densely populated and moister countries have great social and economic variety. Nigeria has the largest population in Africa and the advantage of rich oil deposits. Its leaders are building a new capital, Abuja, with national unity as a principal object. The Congo Basin is the main landform feature of Central Africa. Mineral-rich Zaire is central Africa's largest country.

Chapter 24 East and Southern Africa Sudan's northern desert and more moist south contrast with Ethiopia's potentially productive highland farms and with the savannas and volcanic mountains of East Africa. South Africa has productive farmlands, rich mines, and modern cities and industries, all controlled by the ruling white minority left from early Dutch and British settlement. Black South Africans make up most of the country's labor force and are battling for their political, social, and economic rights. Overshadowed by South Africa's policies, many countries of Southern Africa have suffered wars and unrest. Zambia, Angola, Mozambique, and Zimbabwe all have fertile lands and good mineral resources to strengthen their economies.

Writing for Understanding

Revising and polishing your work can turn a poor report into an excellent one. Proofreading—reading the report carefully and marking errors to be corrected—is an important step in the revision process. As you proofread, use a dictionary to check the spelling of any words about which you are uncertain. Make sure that you use the correct punctuation, and eliminate any run-on sentences or sentence fragments.

Activity. Read the following story about market women in West Africa. Then copy the story on a separate paper, using the proofreaders' marks that you can find in most dictionaries or English textbooks to correct any errors that you find.

Ghana's Market Women
The socialist governments in many African countries have tried to control the market women. They have not succeded. Ghana's president in 1979, for instance, bulldozed the women's stalls in Ghana's capital, Accra [ə krä']. And whipped those women who disregarded governmint price controls. The next morning. The women set up their businesses again amid the rubble the president gave in. He not only lifted price controls. But also built the women a new markit center with concrete floors and a steel roof.

Test

Key Terms (20 points)
Match each definition with its correct term.

1. grassland with some trees, brush, and wet and dry seasons
2. traditional beliefs in spirits and ancestors
3. South Africa's policy of racial separation
4. results when a long section of the earth's crust falls below the surrounding area
5. to convert private land or industries to government control

a. rift valley
b. savanna
c. animism
d. nationalize
e. apartheid

Main Ideas (40 points)
On your paper, record the letter of the response that best completes the sentence.

1. A great _____ dominates Sub-Saharan Africa.
a. plateau
b. escarpment
c. mountain chain
d. valley

2. The most important factor in determining African climates is the _____.
a. Tropic of Capricorn
b. altitude
c. Sahara
d. Tropic of Cancer

3. Control of _____ gave ancient savanna empires much power and wealth in western Africa.
a. migrations
b. ironworking
c. trade
d. colonies

4. The new nations of Africa began to gain independence from European powers during the _____.
a. 1890s
b. 1920s
c. 1950s
d. 1970s

5. Nigeria faced severe economic setbacks when the price of _____ went down.
a. copra
b. oil
c. copper
d. cloth

6. Fertile highlands in _____ offer opportunities for a rich agricultural economy.
a. Somalia
b. Sudan
c. Ghana
d. Ethiopia

7. Zaire's location on the Congo (Zaire) River and its immense _____ provide the backbone for its economy.
a. rail system
b. ujamaa villages
c. mineral wealth
d. irrigated farmlands

8. South Africa retained its political control of _____ into the 1980s.
a. Zambia
b. Zimbabwe
c. Angola
d. Namibia

Thinking Critically
(20 points)
1. Analyze Comparisons. Compare the physical geography and resources of Kenya with those of Zaire.
2. Make Hypotheses. Why is it difficult to describe the people of Sub-Saharan Africa on a country-by-country basis?

Place Location (20 points)
Match the places listed below with the letters printed on the map.
1. Madagascar
2. Congo (Zaire) River
3. Lagos
4. Khartoum
5. Lake Victoria
6. South Africa

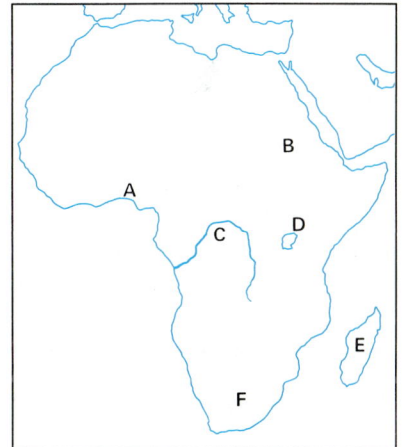

South, East, and Southeast Asia

In this unit you will read about the world's most crowded region.

A Physical and Cultural Overview

In this chapter you will learn about the physical and cultural geography of South, East, and Southeast Asia.

Sections
1 The Land and Water
2 Climate, Soils, and Vegetation
3 Cultural Beginnings and Religions
4 From Past to Present

The Land and Water

Key Places
Where are these places located?
1 Plateau of Tibet
2 Himalayas
3 Deccan Plateau
See the globe below.

Key Terms
What do these terms mean?
subcontinent
loess
dike

Main Ideas
As you read, look for answers to these questions.
• How do plate tectonics affect the Asian rimland?
• What major plateaus mark the Asian landscape?
• Where are important plains regions found in the Asian rimland?

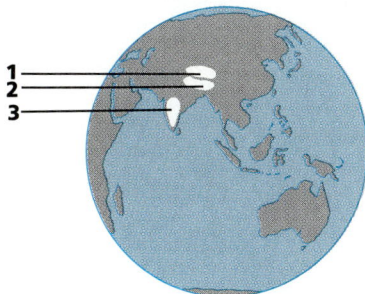

As you climb, they climb.

French description of the Himalayas

Plate movements in the Asian rimland created huge mountain ranges.

People have long tried to find words to describe the awe they feel as they approach and ascend the Himalayas. Some French travelers may have captured the feeling best in the simple description you have just read. One may first glimpse the Himalayas a hundred miles from their southern slopes. That first sighting often appears as gleaming, sparkling patches of snow that seem to loom almost overhead and sit among the clouds. As one moves upwards, the glistening snowy patches seem to rise higher and higher rather than closer to the climber.

As you can see on the map on page 514, the Himalayas lie between China and India. These mountains, the highest in the world, mark the dividing point between South Asia and East Asia, two of the three subregions that make up the great Asian rimland. The Asian rimland includes South Asia, East Asia, and Southeast Asia. These subregions contain all the countries lying on the Asian continent southeast of the Soviet Union's portion of Asia. South Asia includes India, Pakistan, Nepal, Bhutan, Bangladesh, and Sri Lanka. East Asia includes China, Mongolia, Japan, Taiwan, North Korea, and South Korea. Southeast Asia includes the countries of Burma, Thailand, Laos, Vietnam, Cambodia, the Philippines, Malaysia, Singapore, Brunei, and Indonesia. Locate each of the countries on the map on page 512.

Plate tectonics and mountain building.

India and portions of other South Asian countries were once part of the ancient super-

Facing page: **The bronze Great Buddha in Japan attracts many Asian followers.** *Page 508:* **This volcano in Java dwarfs visitors to this fiery area.**

511

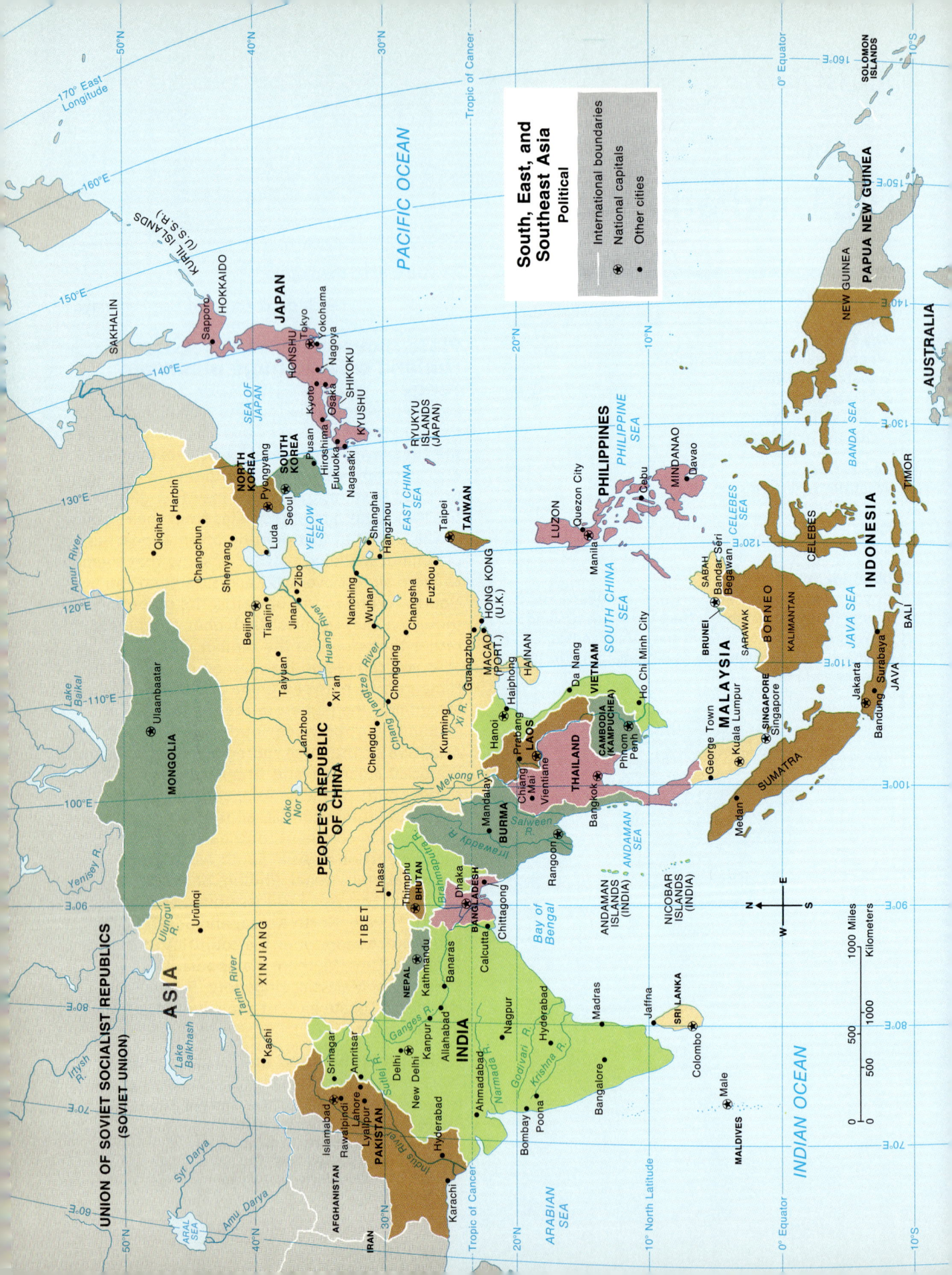

South, East, and
Southeast Asia
Political

International boundaries
National capitals
Other cities

PACIFIC OCEAN

SOLOMON ISLANDS

PAPUA NEW GUINEA
NEW GUINEA
AUSTRALIA

170° East Longitude
160°E
150°E
140°E
130°E
120°E
110°E
100°E
0°
160°E
150°E
140°E
130°E
120°E
110°E
100°E
90°E
80°E
70°E
Equator

50°N
40°N
30°N
20°N
10°N
Tropic of Cancer
Equator
10° South Latitude

SAKHALIN
KURIL ISLANDS (U.S.S.R.)
HOKKAIDO
Sapporo
JAPAN
HONSHU
Tokyo
Yokohama
Nagoya
Kyoto
Osaka
SHIKOKU
Hiroshima
Fukuoka
Nagasaki
KYUSHU
SEA OF JAPAN
RYUKYU ISLANDS (JAPAN)

NORTH KOREA
Pyongyang
SOUTH KOREA
Seoul
Pusan
YELLOW SEA
EAST CHINA SEA

Qiqihar
Harbin
Changchun
Shenyang
Luda
Beijing
Tianjin
Jinan
Zibo
Shanghai
Hangzhou
Taiyuan
Nanching
Nanjing
Wuhan
Changsha
Fuzhou
Taipei
TAIWAN
Xi'an
Chongqing
Guangzhou
HONG KONG (U.K.)
MACAO (PORT.)
HAINAN

Huang River
Chang (Yangtze) River
Xi R.

Lanzhou
Chengdu
Kunming

PEOPLE'S REPUBLIC OF CHINA

MONGOLIA
Ulaanbaatar

UNION OF SOVIET SOCIALIST REPUBLICS (SOVIET UNION)
ASIA

Lake Baikal
Amur River
Yenisey R.
Irtysh R.
Lake Balkhash
ARAL SEA
Syr Darya
Amu Darya

Ulungur R.
Tarim River
Urümqi
Kashi
XINJIANG
Koko Nor

TIBET
Lhasa

Thimphu
BHUTAN
Kathmandu
NEPAL
Banaras
Allahabad
Kanpur
Delhi
New Delhi
Srinagar
Amritsar
Islamabad
Rawalpindi
Lahore
Lyalpur
Hyderabad
Karachi
PAKISTAN
AFGHANISTAN
IRAN

Brahmaputra R.
Ganges R.
Sutlej R.
Indus River
Narmada R.
Godavari R.
Krishna R.

INDIA
Ahmadabad
Bombay
Poona
Bangalore
Nagpur
Hyderabad
Madras

Dhaka
BANGLADESH
Chittagong
Calcutta
Bay of Bengal

Mandalay
BURMA
Rangoon
Irrawaddy R.
Salween R.
Mekong R.

Chiang Mai
Vientiane
LAOS
Luang Prebang
THAILAND
Bangkok
CAMBODIA (KAMPUCHEA)
Phnom Penh
VIETNAM
Hanoi
Haiphong
Da Nang
Ho Chi Minh City

ANDAMAN SEA
ANDAMAN ISLANDS (INDIA)
NICOBAR ISLANDS (INDIA)

SOUTH CHINA SEA

PHILIPPINES
LUZON
Quezon City
Manila
Cebu
MINDANAO
Davao
PHILIPPINE SEA

MALAYSIA
George Town
Kuala Lumpur
SINGAPORE
Singapore
SARAWAK
BRUNEI
Bandar Seri Begawan
SABAH
BORNEO
KALIMANTAN

INDONESIA
SUMATRA
Medan
JAVA SEA
CELEBES SEA
CELEBES
Jakarta
Bandung
Surabaya
JAVA
BALI
BANDA SEA
TIMOR

SRI LANKA
Jaffna
Colombo
MALDIVES
Male

INDIAN OCEAN
ARABIAN SEA

N E S W

1000 Miles
Kilometers
500
500
1000
0
0

30°N
20°N
10° North Latitude
Tropic of Cancer

continent of Gondwanaland. As you learned in Chapter 2, certain landmasses broke off and drifted away from Gondwanaland. A plate of the earth's crust carrying both India and Australia moved north and east. The Indian part of that plate rammed into Asia. The South Asian lands that thus attached to the Asian continent are often called the Indian subcontinent. A **subcontinent** is a landmass that is very large, but smaller than a continent.

The plate collision between Asia and the Indian subcontinent formed great chains of high, rugged mountains. "The Roof of the World" is a phrase often used to describe a range of high mountains, called the Pamirs, which mark the boundary between Pakistan, Afghanistan, China, and the Soviet Union. Find this range on the map on page 514. From the Pamirs, a vast web of mountain ranges extends in all directions. The Hindu Kush project to the west, the Karakoram to the east, the Tien Shan to the northeast, and the Himalayas to the southeast.

Crustal plates are moving toward each other in East Asia too, under the Pacific Ocean. The underwater collisions are pushing up large mountains. As they rise from the ocean floor, their peaks break through the surface waters as islands. Japan, Taiwan, and the Philippines are the crests of mountains rising from the ocean depths.

Perils in the Ring of Fire. Plate movements make earthquakes and volcanic eruptions a threat to peoples everywhere in the Asian rimland. No place on earth, however, faces greater peril from these disasters than East Asia. China and the rest of East Asia are part of the "Ring of Fire," the earthquake and volcano zone that encircles the Pacific Ocean. Not surprisingly the Chinese have pioneered in earthquake research. The first earthquake measuring device was built in China nearly 2,000 years ago. The elaborate work of art below is an ancient Chinese earthquake detector from A.D. 132. The Chinese government today operates many scientific stations, where people work to predict earthquakes.

Three major plateau regions mark the Asian landscape.

Three large plateaus border on the highlands of the Asian rimland. In East Asia, mountain ranges surround two large plateau regions, each with

At the slightest tremor, one of these dragons drops a ball to sound a unique earthquake alarm.

Map Study

Which countries are located in South Asia? East Asia? Southeast Asia?

South, East, and Southeast Asia
Physical

Land Elevation

Feet	Meters
14,000	4,000
7,000	2,000
1,500	500
700	200
0	0
Below Sea Level	Below Sea Level

— International boundaries
▲ Mountain peaks

PACIFIC OCEAN

170°East Longitude
160°E
150°E
140°E
130°E
120°E
110°E
100°E
90°E
80°E
70°E
60°E

170°East Longitude

Kuril Islands
Sakhalin
Hokkaido
Honshu
Mt. Fuji 12,388 ft. (3,776 m)
Shikoku
Kyushu
SEA OF JAPAN
Korean Peninsula
Ryukyu Is.
Taiwan
Formosa Strait
EAST CHINA SEA
YELLOW SEA
Manchuria
DA HINGGAN MTS.
WUYI MTS.
QIN MTS.
SICHUAN BASIN
Huang River
Chang (Yangtze) River
Han R.
YUNNAN PLATEAU
Hainan I.
Gulf of Tonkin
SOUTH CHINA SEA
Luzon Strait
Luzon
Mindoro
Panay
Negros
Cebu
Samar
Leyte
Philippine Islands
Mindanao
Mt. Apo 9,692 ft. (2,954 m)
PHILIPPINE SEA
Halmahera
Molucca Islands
BANDA SEA
Puncak Jaya 16,503 ft. (5,030 m)
New Guinea
New Ireland
New Britain
ARAFURA SEA
AUSTRALIA

SAYAN MTS.
ALTAI MTS.
Ulungur R.
JUNGGAR BASIN
TIAN SHAN
Tarim River
TAKLA MAKAN (DESERT)
KUNLUN MTS.
PAMIR MTS.
HINDU KUSH
Mt. Godwin Austen (K2) 28,250 ft. (8,611 m)
KARAKORAM RANGE
Nanda Devi 25,645 ft. (7,817 m)
HIMALAYAS
Mt. Everest 29,028 ft. (8,848 m)
PLATEAU OF TIBET
Hkakabo Razi 19,296 ft. (5,881 m)
QILIAN MTS.
Koko Nor
GOBI
MONGOLIAN PLATEAU
Lake Baikal
Lake Balkhash
Irtysh R.
Yenisey R.
Amur River
Syr Darya
Amu Darya
ARAL SEA

ASIA

Indus River
THAR DESERT
BALUCHISTAN PLATEAU
Ganges River
Brahmaputra R.
Irrawaddy R.
Salween R.
Mekong R.
Mouths of the Ganges
Narmada R.
Godavari R.
Krishna R.
DECCAN PLATEAU
WESTERN GHATS
EASTERN GHATS
Coromandel Coast
Malabar Coast
Sri Lanka
Bay of Bengal
Andaman Is.
Nicobar Is.
ANDAMAN SEA
Isthmus of Kra
Gulf of Thailand
Malay Peninsula
Strait of Malacca
Sumatra
Krakatoa I.
Java
JAVA SEA
Bali
Sumbawa
Sumba
Flores
Sumba
Timor
Celebes
CELEBES SEA
SULU SEA
Palawan
Borneo
Mt. Kinabalu 13,431 ft. (4,094 m)
Sunda Islands
East Indies

Laccadive Is.
Maldive Is.
ARABIAN SEA
INDIAN OCEAN

N E S W

0 500 1000 Miles
0 500 1000 Kilometers

50°N
40°N
30°N Tropic of Cancer
20°N
10°N
0° Equator
10°S

ASIA
AUSTRALIA

60°N
50°N
40°N
30°N
20°N North Latitude
10°N
Tropic of Cancer

impressively high elevations. In South Asia, a third major plateau region is surrounded by hills.

East Asia's plateaus. To the north of the Himalayas lies the great Plateau of Tibet, a giant tableland that extends for about 1,000 miles from east to west. As you can see from the map on the opposite page, this plateau sits 14,000 feet above sea level. Strong, biting winds howl across the rugged surface of the plateau and completely close off mountain passes during intensely cold winters. The few people who inhabit the Plateau of Tibet live in one of the world's harshest environments.

Northeast from the Plateau of Tibet lies the Mongolian Plateau. The Mongolian Plateau covers a large portion of northern East Asia. This region is not as high or rough as the Plateau of Tibet, but it, too, is cold, windswept, and dry. The Gobi, a desert with stretches of flat rock and gravel surfaces, occupies part of the Mongolian Plateau. Winter winds from Soviet Siberia blow across the Gobi and carry tons of fine, yellow silt called **loess** [lō′is] into northeastern China. Plains and smaller plateau regions in this part of China have a loose covering of yellow loess ranging from 100 to 1,000 feet thick. Not surprisingly, winter dust storms are frequent and severe in many parts of northeastern China.

The Deccan Plateau. The Deccan Plateau takes up the center of India's large, triangle-shaped peninsula. Elevations on the Deccan Plateau are fairly low and the surface is often gentle and rolling. Hills called the Western Ghats line the Deccan's western boundaries. From there the plateau slopes off gradually toward the east. While the subcontinent was drifting toward Asia millions of years ago, great lava flows poured across the northwestern corner of the plateau and left a deep, rich covering of dark soil. The southern parts of the Deccan were not so fortunate. Soils there are much less fertile.

The Asian rimland's major plains regions are found along rivers.

Tracing the major rivers on the map of the Asian rimland on page 514 will lead you to the largest and most important plains and lowlands. Note that these major rivers begin either in the Himalayas or in the Plateau of Tibet.

Rivers of South Asia. Three rivers flow through the northern part of the Indian subcontinent. They are the Indus, the Ganges, and the Brahmaputra rivers. All three rivers begin in the Himalayas and swell with water from melting mountain snows each spring. Find these rivers on the map. Notice how the plains surrounding the Indus and Ganges rivers form an open corridor of lowlands reaching from the mouth of the Indus to the mouth of the Ganges. The Ganges joins the Brahmaputra to form the Ganges-Brahmaputra delta at the head of the Bay of Bengal. The level terrain and rich soil of this long corridor supports a multitude of farmers.

Rivers of East Asia. East Asia's major river valleys and plains center in eastern China. Several lowland river systems wind through northeastern China, north of the Korean Peninsula, but the most important ones are farther south. The main rivers to remember are the Huang River and the Chang (Yangtze) River. Follow their paths from the highlands of western China eastward to the sea on the map on page 514.

The Huang River flows sluggishly through many miles of loess soils before it enters China's

Map Study

In which mountain range is Mt. Everest located? What major rivers run in East Asia?

A Chinese ship, called a junk, sails on the Huang River.

broad eastern plain. It picks up a yellow-brown silt that colors the waters of the river and the Yellow Sea into which it empties. Silt that filters to the bottom of the Huang River has over the centuries built up the height of the riverbed and caused it to flood disastrously again and again. Since very early times, the Chinese have fought the floods by building walls of earth, or **dikes**, along the river to keep it inside its banks. In some places, the dike-enclosed Huang River now rises 12 feet above the land areas it crosses.

The Chang River, one of the world's longest, crosses China's eastern plain at its southern end.

Unlike the Huang River, the Chang moves swiftly and has a number of high waterfalls and treacherous rapids. These lie far inland, however, so boats and ships can travel on the Chang in the eastern lowland reaches.

Rivers of Southeast Asia. Several rivers create level lands for people in Southeast Asia also. The Mekong River and its tributaries create a large plain that covers most of the broad peninsula at the southeast corner of the mainland. Find the Mekong River on the map on page 514. You can see that it begins in the Plateau of Tibet. West of the Mekong, the Irrawaddy River flows through a long narrow plain in Burma used for farming.

Section 1 Review

Locating Key Places
Locate the following places on the map on page 514: Plateau of Tibet, Himalayas, Deccan Plateau

Identifying Key Terms
Define the following terms: subcontinent, loess, dike

Reviewing Main Ideas
1. Which mountains in the Asian rimland are the highest in the world? What are the dangers created by plate movements in the Asian rimland?
2. Name three large plateaus in South, East, and Southeast Asia.
3. What major rivers flow through the plains regions of South, East, and Southeast Asia?

Thinking Critically: Evaluate Sources of Information
Suppose you were assigned to prepare a report on farming in South Asia. As part of your research, you locate an article written by an agriculture professor that describes a year-long study of farming along India's west coast. You also locate a book that tells about farming in each of the countries on the Indian subcontinent. Which source of information would be more useful for your report? Explain your reasons.

SECTION 2

Climate, Soils, and Vegetation

Preview

Key Places
Where are these places located?
1 Ganges-Brahmaputra delta
2 Borneo
See the globe below.

Key Terms
What do these terms mean?
monsoon
paddy

Main Ideas
As you read, look for answers to these questions.
● What part of the Asian rimland has a warm, tropical climate?
● What parts of the Asian rimland have mild climates?
● Where are the Asian rimland's deserts and steppes?
● What is the climate in the Asian rimland's highland region?

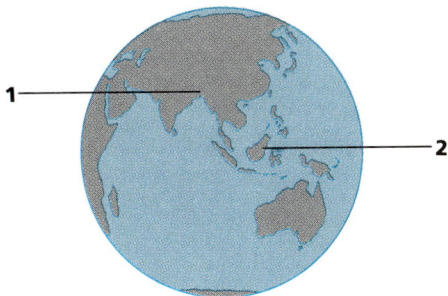

The Chinese would say: "Have you eaten rice?"
Americans would say: "Hello, how are you?"

The Chinese would say: "I can't eat my rice."
Americans would say: "I'm not feeling well."

The Chinese would say: "I've broken my rice bowl."
Americans would say: "I've lost my job."

Adapted from *Things Chinese* by Rita Aero

South and Southeast Asia have mostly warm, tropical climates.

Rice is important to people everywhere in the Asian rimland. This grain, along with wheat, has been a staple food in Asia for thousands of years. In China, where more rice is grown than in any other nation, the importance of rice is shown in the everyday language of the Chinese.

Much of the Asian rimland has the right kind of climate for growing rice. However, the Asian rimland is not a one-climate culture region any more than it is a one-crop region. Wheat, millet, soybeans, corn, and other grains are also grown. Climate regions in the Asian rimland range from tropical to dry.

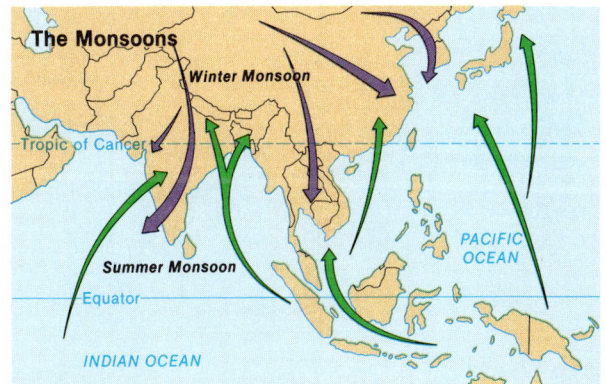

The Monsoons

Winter Monsoon

Tropic of Cancer

Summer Monsoon

Equator

PACIFIC OCEAN

INDIAN OCEAN

Map Study

The arrows show the summer and winter monsoons. Which bring wetter weather?

517

Tropical rainforest. If you trace the Tropic of Cancer and the Equator on the map on page 514, you will see that Southeast Asia and most of South Asia are in the tropics. The climate map on page 518 shows that the islands and coastal areas of Southeast Asia, the west coast of India, and the Ganges-Brahmaputra delta are tropical rainforest regions. Although the forests in western India and on the Ganges-Brahmaputra delta lands were cleared centuries ago for rice fields, many heavily forested areas still stand in Southeast Asia. Southeast Asians often live in wooden houses raised above the ground on wooden stilts to catch cooling breezes in the hot, muggy climate.

Tropical savanna. Throughout the Asian rimland, **monsoons**, or seasonal winds of the Indian Ocean, regulate climate patterns and peoples' lives. In the rimland's tropical regions, the monsoons create definite wet and dry seasons in the savanna areas you see on the map on page 518. These wet and dry seasons govern the success of much of Asian agriculture.

The monsoon is a seasonal wind that changes direction twice a year. From April to October, the wind blows from the southwest, off the Indian Ocean and toward the land. These winds, called the summer monsoon, carry warm, moist air inland and brings heavy rains to most of South Asia, South China, and much of Southeast

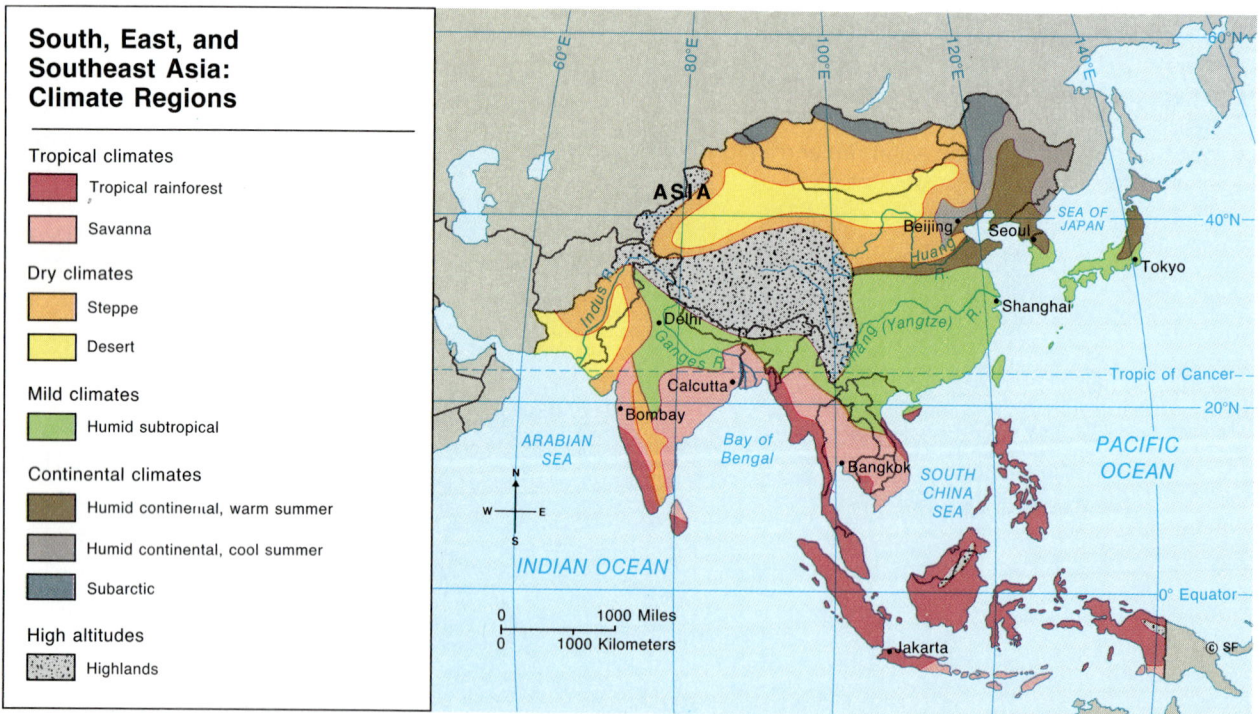

South, East, and Southeast Asia: Climate Regions

Tropical climates
- Tropical rainforest
- Savanna

Dry climates
- Steppe
- Desert

Mild climates
- Humid subtropical

Continental climates
- Humid continental, warm summer
- Humid continental, cool summer
- Subarctic

High altitudes
- Highlands

Map Study

The geographic realm of South, East, and Southeast Asia has a wide range of climates. What climate dominates Southeast Asia? What climate appears in southern Japan and Korea?

Asia. You can see the effect the summer monsoon has on Bombay, India, by studying the climate graph on page 539. By November the winds reverse and begin to blow from the northeast. This northeast wind, called the winter monsoon, pushes cool, dry air over most of South Asia and much of Southeast Asia and carries rain to Indonesia and northern Australia.

Farmers living in monsoon lands depend on the rains to water their crops. Everyone living in monsoon lands, in fact, needs the water to replenish a dwindling winter supply. Not even expert meteorologists, however, can accurately predict the coming of the rains. Some years the summer monsoon is late—late enough to cause severe droughts and crop failure. Once the rains arrive, they nourish and refresh people as well as crops.

Forests of low-growing thorn and scrub trees covered India's savannas long ago, but most of this vegetation was all destroyed to make room for crop growing. The lava-rich soils in the northwest hold moisture well and support many valuable cotton fields. In the other parts of India's savanna climate region, the people grow rice. Here as in Southeast Asia's savanna areas, the farmers quickly plant their seedlings during the rainy season and store runoff waters to use during the dry season.

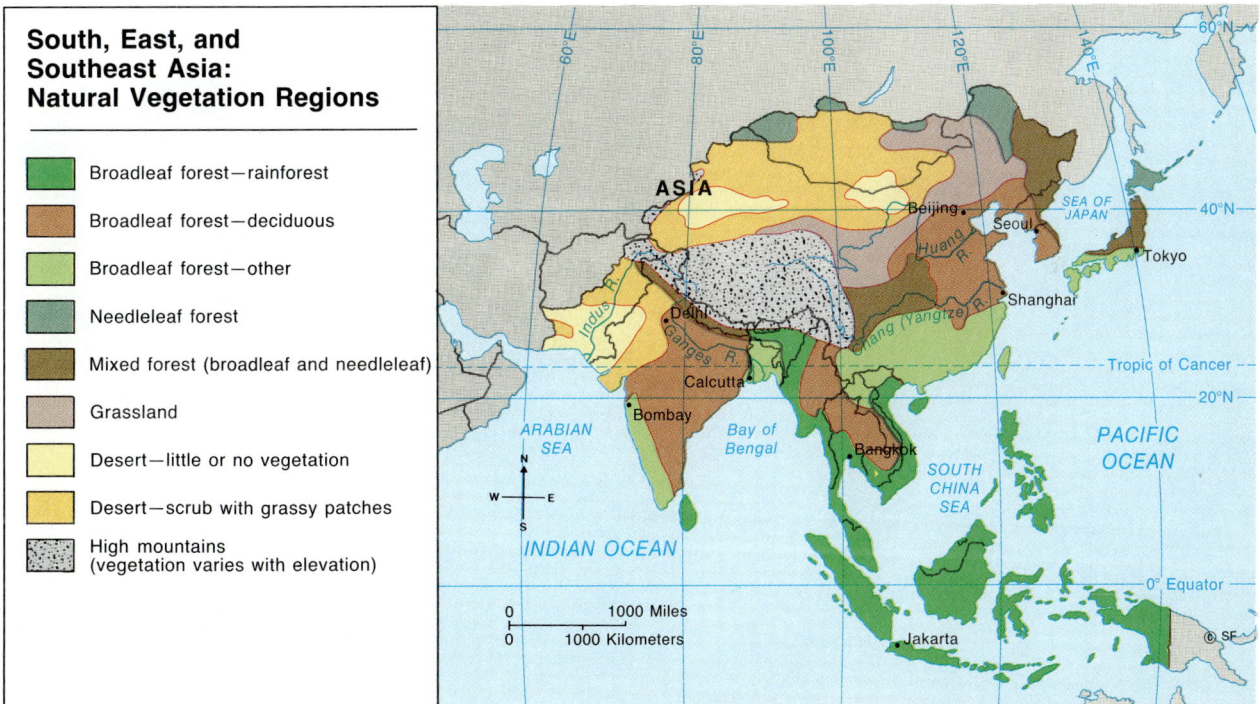

South, East, and Southeast Asia: Natural Vegetation Regions

- Broadleaf forest—rainforest
- Broadleaf forest—deciduous
- Broadleaf forest—other
- Needleleaf forest
- Mixed forest (broadleaf and needleleaf)
- Grassland
- Desert—little or no vegetation
- Desert—scrub with grassy patches
- High mountains (vegetation varies with elevation)

0   1000 Miles
0   1000 Kilometers

Map Study

This geographic realm also has many types of natural vegetation. What types of vegetation are found in India? Describe the natural vegetation in Southeast Asia.

Northern India and southeastern China have mild climates.

A mild climate region begins north of the Tropic of Cancer and spreads from west to east across northern India. Small portions of Southeast Asia, all of southeast China, and southern Japan and South Korea also have mild climates the year round. Winters seldom bring freezing temperatures. Warm to hot temperatures prevail for 10 months of the year. Rain falls the year round, but the monsoon influence means that winters are drier than summers.

The drier conditions in northwestern India and northern Pakistan favor wheat rather than rice. Elsewhere in the mild climate areas, however, farmers grow rice. All of the subtropical regions would be forest covered if they had not been cleared for farming.

The subtropical lowland plains and southern uplands in southeastern China are China's "rice bowl." In April, China's rice farmers repair the small, earthen ridges that enclose their paddies. A **paddy** is a field that can be flooded with three to six inches of water in which rice plants

Workers bend to plant rice in the shadows of the unique limestone hills near Guilin in southern China.

grow. When the ridges are secure, the farmers send water from streams and canals into the paddies. Then they begin the process of planting rice.

In May men, women, and children work quickly to place tender young rice seedlings into the paddies. They bend to do the transplanting by hand and often wear peaked hats with broad rims to shield them from warm, gentle rains. The rice grows over the summer, when there is scarcely a breeze. Thermometers may read higher than 100° F, with the humidity as high as 90 percent. When the heads of the rice plants grow heavy, the farmers drain the paddies. They let the rice become golden and mature, and then they harvest it.

Agriculture is year-round work in subtropical China. After the rice harvest, farmers begin immediately to prepare their fields for their winter crops. Many farmers plant beans, but in the southernmost regions farmers practice double cropping of rice. This means that they get two and in some places even three crops of rice in one year.

Deserts and steppes lie in the Indus Valley and in East Asia's interior.

Moisture-bearing monsoons die out or fail to reach some areas of the Asian rimland. Dry steppe and desert conditions claim the Indus River valley, the Mongolian Plateau, and wide bands of northern and western China. In India the Western Ghats deprive a long strip of the Deccan Plateau of monsoon moisture and make crop growing even more fragile than in surrounding savanna areas. Pakistan would be a largely barren desert were it not for the life-giving waters and fertile alluvial soil deposits of the Indus River and its tributaries.

In the northern interior of East Asia, the vast steppe of Central Asia widens into the steppes of Mongolia. In some places the lack of moisture discourages almost all plant life. In other areas desert scrub and low grass cover the

ground. These northern steppes are cold as well as dry. In winter blasts of wind from Siberia make numbing temperatures seem even more severe. As in Central Asia, East Asia's steppes are the traditional homelands of nomadic herders.

Steppe and desert conditions extend into northern China and across the northern loop of the Huang River and its loess soil areas. Winters in northern China are very cold, and the ground is frozen for a full three months. In the northeast, where continental climates occur (see the climate map on page 518), snowfalls are heavy.

Winds off the Pacific Ocean bring moisture during the warmer months also, and sometimes during a few summer weeks even the dry steppes of northern China catch these winds. When this happens the rains can be violent and destructive. Fields of wheat, millet, and other cool-climate crops may be flooded out. The Huang River's waters can swell and spill over or break through the dikes to bring utter calamity. Farmers in northern China must work as hard at tending the containing walls of the Huang as they do at tilling their crops. Northern China's climate can also swing the opposite way. Some summers have hardly any rain, and crops wilt in drought. The loess soils of northern China are very fertile, but even they cannot produce when the weather does not cooperate.

Most highlands are cold and often snow-covered.

The map on page 518 shows two places in the Asian rimland that fall into a high-altitude climate region. The central part of the island of Borneo in Southeast Asia is high enough to experience a climate change with altitude. On the mainland, a huge highland climate region covers the Plateau of Tibet and its adjacent mountain ranges. If you traveled to these two high-altitude climate regions, you would be struck by the sharp contrast between climate conditions.

Prayer flags reach to Potala Palace in Lhasa, one of the few cities in Tibet's highlands.

The strip of highland climate on Borneo is a mountain range with dense rainforest vegetation. There, you would need light clothing and rain gear.

In the highlands of the mainland, however, cool clothing would be the last thing you would want. Climate conditions there are subarctic. Snow cover is permanent over much of the windswept countryside, and winter temperatures can drop as low as −40° F. In some places, however, sunny slopes and sheltered valleys have more moderate conditions. Summer days in southern Tibet, for instance, have been known to warm up to 68° F. The few people who live in this sparsely settled environment cluster in such isolated spots. Tibet is nearly twice as large as Texas, but the 3 million people of Tibet scarcely add up to the number of people living in the Texas cities of Dallas and Fort Worth alone.

The high-altitude climate regions of mainland Asia take in a huge expanse. In the north they border on vast and forbidding steppes and deserts. The inhospitable environments of the high altitude and dry regions often acted as barriers between East Asians and peoples living to the west, in Western Asia and Europe. For many centuries civilizations flourished in both East and West with little knowledge of one another's cities, beliefs, or technology.

Section 2 Review

Locating Key Places
Locate the following places on the map on page 514: Ganges-Brahmaputra delta, Borneo

Identifying Key Terms
Define the following terms: monsoon, paddy

Reviewing Main Ideas
1. Where are the Asian rimland's tropical rainforest regions?
2. Where does Asia have mild climates?
3. Where are the Asian rimland's desert and steppe climate regions?
4. What kind of climate is found in the Plateau of Tibet and its adjacent mountain ranges?

Thinking Critically: Predict Effects
In a sentence or two, tell how the timing of the summer monsoon affects the lives of people in South and Southeast Asia.

SECTION 3

Cultural Beginnings and Religions

Preview

Key Places
Where are these places located?
1 Indus River
2 Great wall of China
See the globe below.

Key Terms
What do these terms mean?
caste system
guru

Main Ideas
As you read, look for answers to these questions.
• How did early peoples of the Asian rimland contribute to the beginnings of civilization?
• What major religions originated in South Asia?
• What religions developed in East Asia?

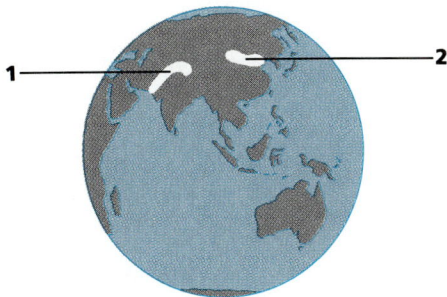

What I do not wish to have done unto me, I likewise wish not to do unto others.

Confucius, 5th century B.C.

Two ancient civilizations were located in the Asian rimland.

You probably recognize the ancient saying you've just read as a version of what Christians call the "golden rule." It dates back to the Chinese teacher Confucius, one among several of the world-famous philosophers and religious leaders who lived long ago in the Asian rimland. You may remember from Unit 2 that several of the world's major religions began in the Asian rimland. In addition, two important civilizations began in this part of the world.

The Indus Valley civilization. The valley of the Indus River and portions of northwestern India were the site of a great urban civilization that developed around 3000 B.C. In time its two largest cities, Mohenjo-Daro [mō hen'jō dä'rō] and Harappa, dominated an area larger than either ancient Egypt or Mesopotamia. Archaeological diggings showed that the cities were carefully planned with brick drainage systems and streets laid out in a grid pattern. In the surrounding countryside, villagers grew wheat, barley, fruits, and were probably the first farmers ever to cultivate cotton. Indus ships left magnificent ports and sailed to the Persian Gulf carrying ivory, precious gems, and fine cotton cloth to exchange for goods from Mesopotamian cities.

The Indus Valley civilization flourished until around 1750 B.C. Scholars are still unsure about the causes that brought about its decline and fall. One explanation holds that changes in the course of the Indus River may have resulted in a loss of water supply, thus cutting off a vital key to survival. It is known, however, that around 1500 B.C. tribes of invaders from Central Asia called Aryans invaded the Indus and Ganges plains regions.

The Aryans had a culture much different from the Indus Valley people. The Aryans were cattle herders. Cattle and bulls gave them food and clothing and measured an individual's wealth and prestige. The invasion of the Aryans marks the final decline of the early Indus urban development.

The Huang River civilization. Far to the east of the Indus Valley, another civilization began to develop around 7,000 years ago when people settled in villages along the Huang River in China. The villagers began taming the river floods and grew millet and other grains in the fertile, easily worked loess soils. From these early beginnings Chinese culture took root and eventually spread east and south to develop into the oldest continuous civilization in the world.

The written history of China began around 1500 B.C. Carvings on bones from this period are the first samples of Chinese writing. China's written language over the centuries helped to tie its people together. Even though people in different parts of China could not understand each other's spoken dialects, they all used the same written language and so could communicate through reading and writing.

The Grand Canal, begun around A.D. 500, also helped tie different parts of China together. Eventually this human-made waterway connected the Huang River with the Chang (Yangtze) River. The canal was a major carrier of goods and people until railroads were built around 1900.

Since the earliest farmers settled in northern China, nomads from the Asian steppes raided these settlements. The Chinese built walls around their fields and villages to defend themselves. By about 200 B.C., the Huns, a warlike Central Asian people, increased the threat against China's northern cities and villages. The Chinese began to connect their fortifications into the Great Wall of China.

The Great Wall still stands, its total length extending from west to east nearly 1,500 miles. Built of granite blocks, wood, and trampled earth, the wall stands from 15 to 50 feet high and is about 15 feet wide across its top. In ancient times, Chinese farmers in fields behind the wall had to be prepared to drop their labors at a moment's notice. From their battle stations atop the wall they tried to fend off fierce attackers.

Hinduism and Buddhism originated in South Asia.

The Aryans left a lasting imprint on the Indian subcontinent. Some scholars say that Indian culture and history began with the Aryan invasion. Although the Aryans left no cities, statues, or other such artifacts, they did leave a rich legacy of sacred writings. From these writings came the teachings of Hinduism, one of the world's oldest faiths.

A Hindu priest, in traditional attire, conducts a wedding ceremony in northern India.

Hinduism. Hinduism gave India both religious beliefs and a way of life. Hinduism teaches that people and animals have eternal souls that move in endless cycles of reincarnation. After death, the soul of someone who has led a good life may move upward and enter another body at a higher level of society. A life of bad behavior may have the opposite effect. Hindus believe that when a person's soul reaches a state of spiritual perfection, it ascends to the same level of existence as Brahma, the Hindu god.

Another important part of Hinduism is the caste [kast] system. The Hindu **caste system** divides society into four main ranks. From highest to lowest, caste groupings include (1) priests and **gurus**, the religious teachers of Hinduism, (2) rulers and warriors, (3) merchants and land-owners, and (4) farmers, workers, and servants. Below the caste members are the untouchables, or people of no caste. To them, in the past, fell such responsibilities as cleaning, garbage removal, and working with animal hides.

Hindus believe that people enter a caste at birth. Caste membership then determines every person's occupation, choice of marriage partners, and other aspects of everyday life. In recent decades India's caste practices have broken down considerably, especially in cities. The government outlawed untouchability in 1950. In Indian villages, however, many of the age-old caste traditions are still observed.

Buddhism. Hinduism was already firmly established in India by the time the Buddha, meaning the "Enlightened One," began preaching in 528 B.C. Buddhism teaches that people should strive to end all attachment to worldly things. Only then will they reach a state of peace and happiness. For a while Buddhism won over many Hindus in India. In time, however, Hinduism enfolded many Buddhist beliefs, and the religion disappeared almost completely in

India. Meanwhile, Buddhism spread across Central, East, and Southeast Asia and is practiced today by about 250 million people in these regions.

Confucianism, Taoism, and Shintoism developed in East Asia.

About the same time that the Buddha began his ministry in South Asia, philosophers in China were also pondering and teaching lessons on the meaning of life. The two greatest Chinese teachers were Confucius, the founder of Confucianism, and Laozi [lou'dzu'], the founder of Taoism.

Confucianism. Kong Fuzi, known to the West as Confucius, lived from 551 to 479 B.C. His philosophy, known as Confucianism, emphasizes rules of conduct rather than religious beliefs. Confucianism teaches that all people must strive to be kind, righteous, wise, and trustworthy. In relating to others, friends are equals. Husbands, however, have complete authority over wives, fathers over children, older brothers over sisters and younger brothers, and rulers over subjects. According to Confucius, if those in authority behaved with goodness and subjects behaved with loyalty, there would always be peace and harmony in the world.

Confucius' guidelines reinforced ideas about the family that were already strong in China before his lifetime. The Chinese family was very close-knit, and every member shared its possessions and wealth. A father ruled a family as an emperor, and every individual tried to bring honor upon his or her relatives.

Taoism. Confucianism teaches people how to live peaceably with each other. Taoism, however, teaches people how to find inner peace and personal contentment. Laozi, said to have lived about the same time as Confucius, presumably fostered Taoism. The *Tao*, or "the way," focuses on an attempt to live simply and at one

A torii, or gate, leads to a Shinto shrine in Kyoto, Japan.

Shinto shrines today stand in lovely natural settings across Japan. They are traditional symbols of Shinto beliefs.

Over the centuries, Shintoism absorbed many ideas from Confucianism, Buddhism, and Taoism. Thus, there are many Japanese who practice both Buddhist and Shinto rituals and who emphasize Confucian ideals about behavior and the family.

Asia's Hindu, Buddhist, Taoist, and Shinto shrines often contrast with the bustle of the 20th-century civilization that surrounds them. They still, however, carry deep meaning. For hundreds of millions of Asians, religion, family, and tradition continues to be the center of life as they have been for centuries.

Section 3 Review

Locating Key Places
Locate the following places on the map on page 512: Indus River, Great Wall of China

Identifying Key Terms
Define the following terms: caste system, guru

Reviewing Main Ideas
1. What two ancient civilizations developed in South and East Asia?
2. What are the major beliefs of Hinduism and Buddhism?
3. How are Confucianism, Taoism, and Shintoism different from one another?

Thinking Critically: Recognize Values
The teachings of Confucius commonly take the form of sayings. One of the sayings in a collection called the *Analect* is as follows: "A man who has committed a mistake and doesn't correct it is committing another mistake." What values are being stressed in this saying?

with nature. Unlike Confucianism, which emphasizes the importance of social duties, Taoism encourages a person to withdraw from society and live close to nature.

Most Chinese followed both Confucianism and Taoism. When Buddhist missionaries brought their religion to China after the A.D. 1st century, many Chinese added yet a third belief to their codes of conduct and spiritual lives.

Shintoism. Shintoism, or the "Way of the Gods," was an early Japanese belief system. The spirits of gods were said to rest in mountains, rivers, the sky, and even grass and trees. Many

From Past to Present

Preview

Key Places
Where are these places located?
1 China
2 India
3 Japan
   See the globe below.

Key Terms
What does this term mean?
emissary

Main Ideas
As you read, look for answers to these questions.
- What paved the way to contacts between Europe and South, East, and Southeast Asia?
- Who set up colonies in South, East, and Southeast Asia?
- What kinds of governments and economies do these Asian countries have?
- How does the population of South, East, and Southeast Asia compare with other regions of the world?

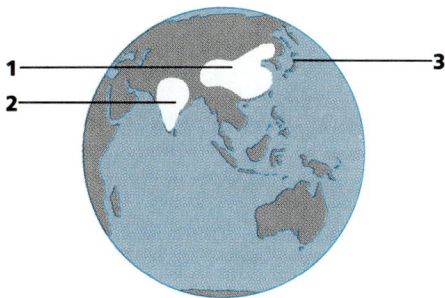

The travelers never tire of describing Pegu [a city in Burma]—the long moat full of crocodiles, the walls, the watchtowers, the gorgeous palace, the great processions with elephants . . . and [nobles] in shining robes, the shrines filled with . . . gold and gems, the unending hosts of armed men, and the [grand spectacle] of the king himself.

European visitors' impressions of Burma, around 1500

European explorers found their way to South, East, and Southeast Asia.

Europeans of the 1500s and 1600s regarded sailing trips to South, East, and Southeast Asia as romantic adventures. For the first time in history, Westerners were getting on-the-scene looks at cultures and civilizations edging the Indian and Pacific oceans. However, this was by no means the first contact between East and West.

Ancient East-West contacts. As early as the 3rd or 4th centuries B.C. Chinese traders were sending silk overland to the West, where wealthy Romans eagerly bought it. In return, metal items and gems from the West traveled eastward. In addition, China, India, and other ancient civilizations often sent **emissaries**, or official representatives, to explore foreign territories. They hoped their emissaries would return with knowledge of new philosophies, religions, or magical practices. In these ways European and Asian civilizations learned of each other's existence, but little else.

Various factors such as nomadic invasions, political turmoil, and Arab control of land and sea trade in Asia's southwest led to centuries of separation between Europeans, Indians, Chinese, and other Asians. Trade items passing overland by way of caravans still reached Mediterranean markets but direct contacts were nonexistent.

527

Later contacts. Europe's knowledge of South, East, and Southeast Asia began to grow during the 1300s. Much of this interest developed after Marco Polo, a member of an Italian merchant family, spent several years in China. People all over Europe marveled at the descriptions of China's wealth in his book of 1298. By the 1400s Europeans were caught up in voyages of discovery that eventually brought thousands to the shores of almost all Asian lands. In 1497–1498 the Portugese explorer Vasco da Gama sailed around Africa and across the Indian Ocean to India. In the centuries following his voyage, many European vessels made regular trips to India, Southeast Asia, and finally on to China and Japan.

Map Study

This map shows how foreign countries controlled much of South, East, and Southeast Asia in 1914. Which countries influenced the Philippines? India? Korea?

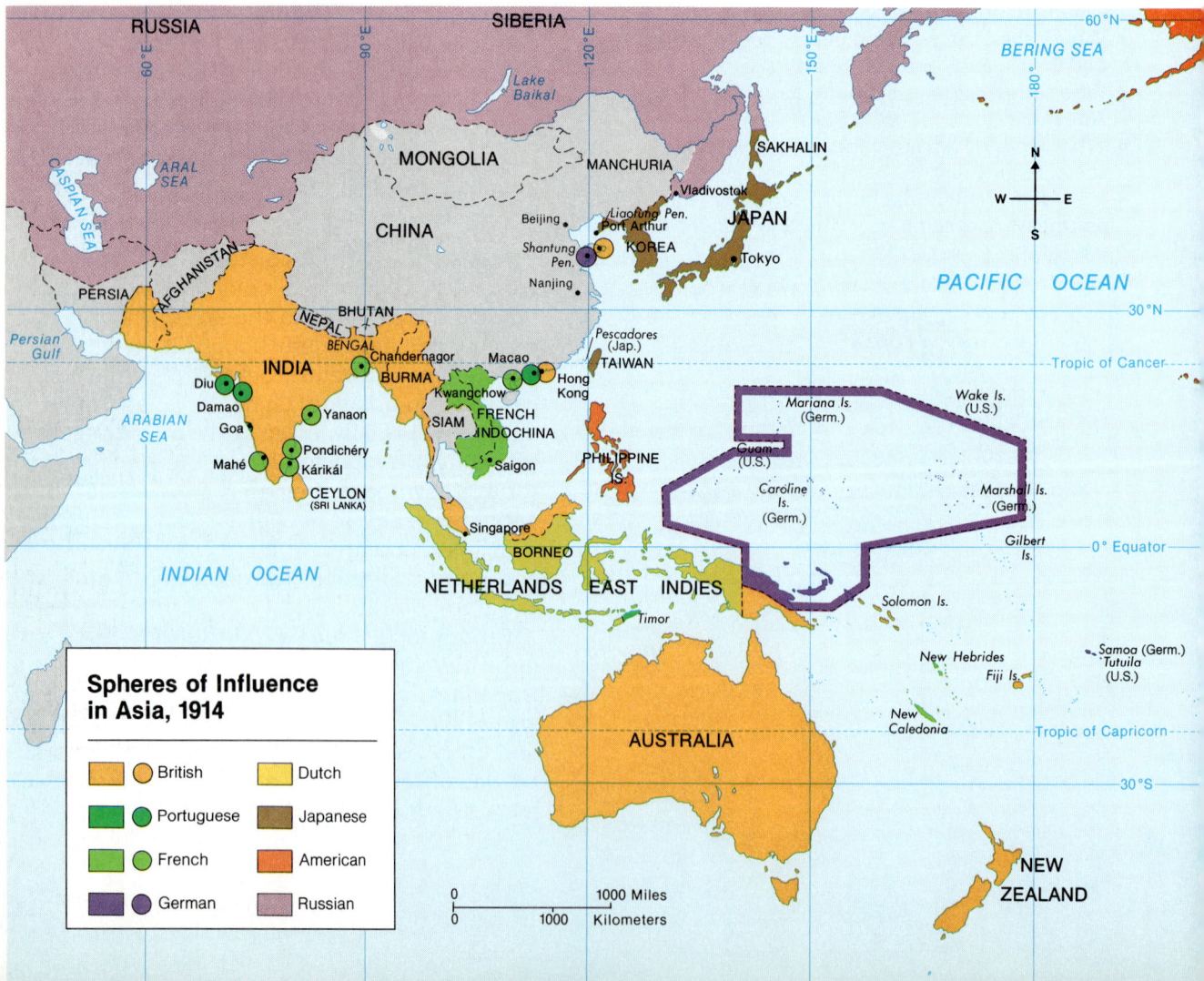

Spheres of Influence in Asia, 1914

European powers set up colonies in Asia.

Portuguese settlers and missionaries arrived along the coasts of India, Southeast Asia, and southern China. Political struggles in Europe, however, reduced Portugal's power, so it soon lost its early lead to other European nations in claiming Asian colonies.

Between about 1600 and 1900, Britain, France, Spain, and the Netherlands built huge colonial empires in Asia. The British acquired present-day Pakistan, India, Bangladesh, Sri Lanka, Burma, Malaysia, Singapore, Brunei, and Hong Kong. The Dutch claimed most of the islands in present-day Indonesia. The Spanish took over the Philippines, and the French conquered what is now Vietnam, Laos, and Cambodia.

European powers did not colonize China, but by 1900, their military and industrial might had brought the Chinese largely under their control. Thailand and Japan managed to avoid European colonization and maintain their independence, and Japan took over Korea and Taiwan as colonies.

Asian countries have a variety of governments and economies.

As in Africa, independence came to Asian nations after the end of World War II. The boundaries of the new nations closely followed colonial boundaries drawn by the Europeans, but some of those boundaries later changed.

Current political patterns. Forms of government vary considerably among the countries in South, East, and Southeast Asia. Japan and India are both strongly democratic. A number of other countries have democratic constitutions but in fact are ruled by military leaders with broad powers. Pakistan, for example, is ruled by a general who seized power in 1977. China, North Korea, Mongolia, and the Southeast Asian countries of Vietnam, Laos, and Cambodia all have communist governments.

China is by far the most populous communist nation in the world. Its relations with neighboring communist countries are not always friendly. Beginning in the 1960s, Chinese and Soviets were often at odds, with troops stationed along both sides of their borders. By the late 1980s, however, there were signs that the Chinese and Soviets were interested in improving relations.

Growing industrial strength. The countries of the Asian rimland are at various levels of economic development. Japan has been an industrial nation for at least a century. Today Japanese industrial wealth ranks alongside that of the United States and Western Europe.

Since the 1960s and 1970s China and India have both built strong heavy industries. In recent years South Korea, Taiwan, Hong Kong, and Singapore have become major manufacturing and trading centers. Their consumer-goods industries, such as electronics, clothing, and footwear, combined with Japan's manufactured exports have greatly increased the number of Asian items for sale around the world. By the 1980s the value of trade goods exchanged across the Pacific Ocean for the first time exceeded the value of exchange centered on Atlantic Ocean ports. The United States is the leading importer of Asian goods. You probably own several items of clothing and audio equipment that were made in Asian countries.

More than half of all people live in South, East, and Southeast Asia.

The countries of South, East, and Southeast Asia take up about 14 percent of the earth's total land area. However, about 54 percent of all the world's people make their homes here. China, with a population of 1 billion, and India, with a population of 767 million, rank as the world's two most populous nations. Together they account for more than a third of the world's 5 billion people. Both countries have supported large populations for at least 2,000 years, but modern medical technology has lowered their death rates and swelled their numbers during the last half of the 20th century.

Uneven distribution. As the population map on page 83 shows, people do not spread evenly over Asia's land areas. The Plateau of Tibet and the dry areas of western China cover a huge land area, yet they are almost empty of human settlement. This means that most of China's huge population lives in the eastern half of the country. In other countries, people tend to cluster in the river valleys and on level plains. One such population cluster covers the Ganges-Brahmaputra delta, which India shares with Bangladesh. In Southeast Asia, the island of Java, which is rich in fertile, volcanic soils, is much more densely populated than many larger islands.

High densities. As you might expect, population densities in some places in South, East, and Southeast Asia are the highest in the world. Along the Ganges basin in India, the delta area in Bangladesh, and portions of China's Huang and Chang rivers, as many as 2,000 or more peo-

ple crowd into a single square mile. Such densities take on special meaning when you consider that these are nearly subsistence farming areas. By comparison, a square mile of cropland in the United States or Canada may be worked by only three or four families.

Population growth rates are still rising in many parts of Asia. As in other areas, many Asians have migrated from rural areas to cities. South, East, and Southeast Asian countries contain many of the world's largest cities, yet outside of Japan, Singapore, and Hong Kong, all the Asian countries are predominantly rural and agricultural. In most areas peasants practice subsistence or commercial farming using traditional methods and tools. Some farmers, however, work on modern commercial farms or on plantations, such as the rubber plantations of Malaysia.

Chinese child care workers wheel around members of the world's largest population.

Section 4 Review

Locating Key Places
Locate the following places on the map on page 512: China, India, Japan

Identifying Key Terms
Define the following term: emissary

Reviewing Main Ideas
1. In what two ways did European and Asian civilizations first learn of each other's existence?
2. Which European nations set up colonies in the Asian rimland?
3. Which two Asian rimland countries are the strongest democracies? Which countries have communist governments?
4. How large a percentage of the world's people live in the Asian rimland? Which two countries are the most populous?

Thinking Critically: Predict Effects
Write a short paragraph explaining how China's huge population might offer both advantages and disadvantages for developing new factories and industries.

Analyzing Cartograms

A cartogram is a graph which is made to look like a distorted map. Cartograms can be used to display many different kinds of data. The cartogram on this page, for example, compares the population of the world's nations.

To analyze a cartogram, begin by studying its key. The key at the bottom of the cartogram on this page shows a square that represents 50 million persons. Each nation's population is then indicated by a rectangle. These rectangles are assembled in a way to make the chart look like a map of the world.

Cartograms such as this one help us perceive the world's nations in terms of population rather than land area. Greenland on a conventional land-area map is a large island. On this cartogram Greenland is a speck, just to the right of Canada and too small even to be labeled. Europe is the smallest continent in area, but in population it outranks, by far, every continent except Asia. Asia, however, assumes the dominant role on this cartogram. It has more people than the rest of the world combined.

Cartograms can yield information both at a glance and after careful study. For example, you can easily see in a glance that China is the world's most populous country. Now look more carefully and you will see that almost all of North and South America and Africa could be fitted into China's box.

Review

Study the cartogram to compare the populations of the following pairs of nations. For each pair, tell which nation has more people.
1. Japan or Mexico
2. France or Bangladesh
3. Indonesia or Poland
4. Canada or the Philippines
5. Vietnam or Norway, Sweden, Denmark, and Finland combined
6. South Korea or South Africa
7. Taiwan or Cuba
In these comparisons, are the largest nations always in Asia?

Countries According to Size of Population

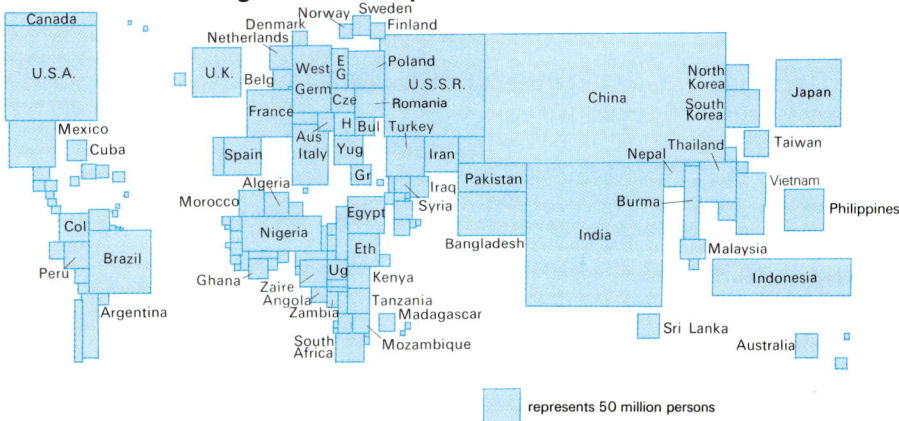

represents 50 million persons

CHAPTER 25

Review

Section Summaries

1. The Land and Water The Himalayas are at the center of a huge mountain cluster separating South, East, and Southeast Asia from western lands and marking the division between South Asia and East Asia. In South Asia, the Deccan Plateau covers much of the Indian subcontinent. East Asia's huge plateau region takes in the Plateau of Tibet, the Mongolian Plateau, and the southern highlands in China. The Huang, Chang, Indus, Ganges, Brahmaputra, Mekong, and Irrawaddy rivers all run through fertile plains regions.

2. Climate, Soils, and Vegetation Tropical rainforest and savanna climates cover much of South Asia and Southeast Asia. Much of the rainforests have been cleared for agriculture. Mild climates persist in southeastern China and across the Ganges-Brahmaputra delta. Steppes and deserts lie in northern and northwestern parts of East Asia as well as in the Indus Valley. The highlands of Tibet are bitterly cold, snow-covered, and windblown.

3. Cultural Beginnings and Religions Two of the world's earliest civilizations developed in the Indus Valley and along the Huang River. From Aryan writings came Hinduism, which remains a major religion in South Asia. Buddhism made longer lasting impressions in East and Southeast Asia. East Asians also developed other religious and ethical systems such as Confucianism, Taoism, and Shintoism.

4. From Past to Present By the early 1900s, European powers had colonized South Asia and most of Southeast Asia. Now independent, the countries of South, East, and Southeast Asia have a variety of governments and economies. More than half the world's people live in this culture region.

Using Geography Skills

Reviewing the Map Lesson

Use the cartogram on page 531 to find the most populous country in the following continents.
1. North America
2. South America
3. Africa
4. Asia

Using Social Studies Skills

1. Organizing and Expressing Ideas in Written Form. Imagine you have recently returned from a trip to China during which you traveled from north to south. You have a friend who is about to make a similar journey in the summer. Write a letter to your friend telling about the kind of clothing to take along.

2. Translating Information from One Medium to Another. Make a climate graph like the ones on page 444 using the data below about Jakarta, Indonesia. You may use graph paper to make the grid for your graph. Make a bar graph to show Jakarta's precipitation. Using the same grid, make a line graph to show temperature.

Jakarta

	average monthly temperature	average monthly precipitation
Jan.	77.9	13.0
Feb.	77.9	12.8
Mar.	78.0	7.8
Apr.	79.5	5.1
May	79.7	4.0
June	79.2	3.7
July	78.6	2.6
Aug.	79.0	1.7
Sept.	79.7	2.9
Oct.	79.9	4.5
Nov.	79.3	5.5
Dec.	78.4	8.5

Testing for Understanding

Locating Key Places
Match each description below with the name of the place.
1. a river in China that carries yellow silt
2. a barren, windswept steppe and desert in the northern part of East Asia
3. the site of an early civilization in South Asia
4. a plateau bordering the northern Himalayas
5. a river that joins the Brahmaputra

a. Ganges River
b. Plateau of Tibet
c. Mongolian Plateau
d. Indus Valley
e. Huang River

Recalling Key Terms
Define these terms in your own words.

Section 1
subcontinent
loess
dike

Section 2
monsoon
paddy

Section 3
caste system
guru

Section 4
emissary

Reviewing Main Ideas
Section 1
1. What great mountain range and natural perils result from tectonic activity in South, East and Southeast Asia?
2. What are the three large plateaus in South, East, and Southeast Asia?
3. Name the major rivers of South, East, and Southeast Asia.

Section 2
1. Describe the location of tropical rainforest climate regions in South, East, and Southeast Asia.
2. Where are climates mild in South, East, and Southeast Asia?
3. What places in South, East, and Southeast Asia have desert and steppe climate regions?
4. What climate conditions are most common on the Plateau of Tibet and its adjacent mountain ranges?

Section 3
1. Identify two ancient civilizations that developed in South and East Asia.
2. What are the major beliefs and social guidelines contained in Hinduism?
3. How does Confucianism contrast with Taoism?

Section 4
1. In what two important ways did Europeans and Asians first begin to learn about each other?
2. Name four European nations that set up colonies in South, East, and Southeast Asia.
3. Which two major Asian countries have highly democratic governments? Which countries have communist governments?
4. What portion of the world's 5 billion people live in South, East, and Southeast Asia? Which two countries have the largest populations?

Thinking Critically
1. **Make Hypotheses.** Why was the development of a written language important in China's history?

2. **Recognize Values.** Why could a Chinese person follow Confucianism, Taoism, and Buddhism without experiencing conflicts in his or her religious life?

CHAPTER 26

South Asia

In this chapter you will learn about India and India's neighbors in South Asia.

Sections

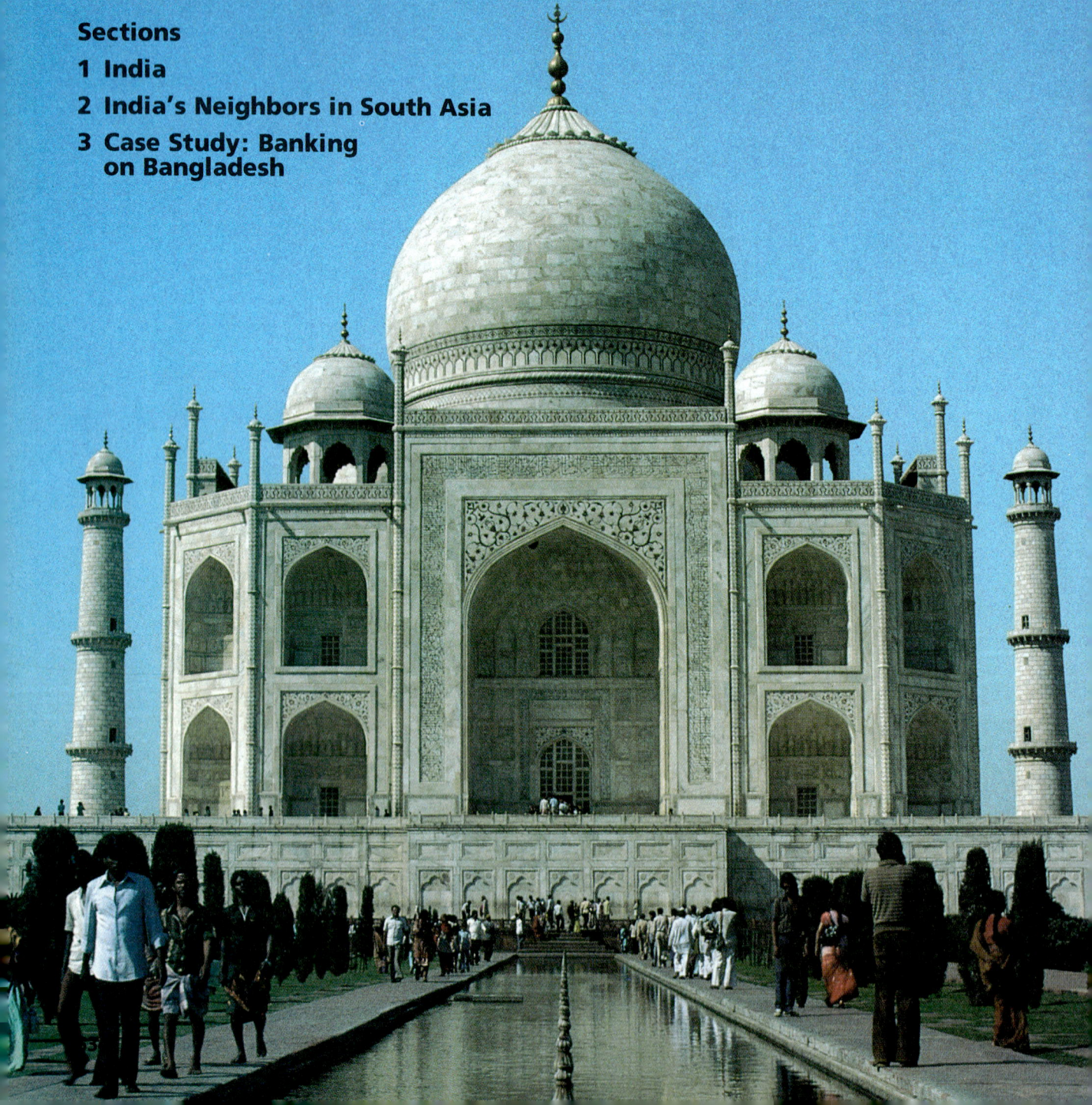

India

Preview

Key Places
Where are these places located?
1 Bombay
2 Calcutta
3 New Delhi
See the globe below.

Key Terms
What do these terms mean?
sari
millet
jute

Main Ideas
As you read, look for answers to these questions.
- What major empires rose in India before it became a British colony?
- What changes did the British bring to India?
- When did India gain its independence?
- Where do most of the people of India live?
- What challenges has India faced since independence?

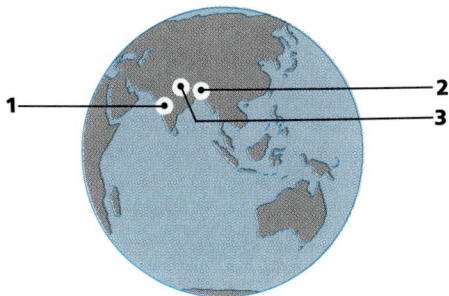

All sects [religious groups] deserve reverence for one reason or another. By thus acting a man exalts his own sect and at the same time does service to the sects of other people.

Asoka, an ancient Indian emperor

The memory of Asoka lives over the continent of Asia, and his edicts still speak to us in a language we can understand and appreciate. And we can still learn much from them.

Jawaharlal Nehru, India's first prime minister

Three major empires rose in India before the coming of the British.

Asoka and Nehru are two of the many people famous in India's history. Asoka [ə sō′kə] was an emperor who ruled India in ancient times. In his words and actions, Asoka urged acceptance of all people and faiths. During his rule he brought unity and peace to India. Jawaharlal Nehru [nā′rü] was a modern-day Indian leader. After India became an independent nation in 1947, Nehru served as India's first prime minister. Nehru's words remind us that India's history dates back thousands of years.

Indian empires. Beginning in the 1st century B.C., three major empires rose and fell in India. The first was the Mauryan [mä′ur̄ yən] Empire, which lasted from about 320 to 184 B.C. One of the Mauryan emperors was Asoka. Asoka used military force to expand the Mauryan Empire until it included all but the southern part of India. About ten years into his reign, Asoka gave up warfare and became a devout Buddhist. For the rest of his life, he concentrated on spreading his faith rather than on military conquests.

Facing page: **The beauty of the Taj Mahal is known worldwide. It was built in the 1600s as a tomb for an Indian ruler's wife.**

After Asoka's death in 232 B.C., the Mauryan Empire began to lose power. The last Mauryan emperor was assassinated in 184 B.C. India then underwent a long period of invasions and foreign rule. This period lasted until about A.D. 200, when northern India divided into many small kingdoms. In the 4th century a new line of kings, the Guptas, came to power and launched the beginning of the Gupta Empire.

The Gupta Empire flourished from A.D. 320 to 500. Gupta emperors ruled India during a period called the golden age of Hindu culture. Art, literature, music, and learning flourished under Gupta rulers. Hinduism became the religion of most of the people, as Buddhism became important mostly in Asian lands to the east.

During the period between 1000 and 1500, Muslim invaders from Afghanistan and Central Asia established many small kingdoms in India. The third major empire in India began around 1500 when a Central Asian Muslim ruler named Babur invaded India and began the Mughul

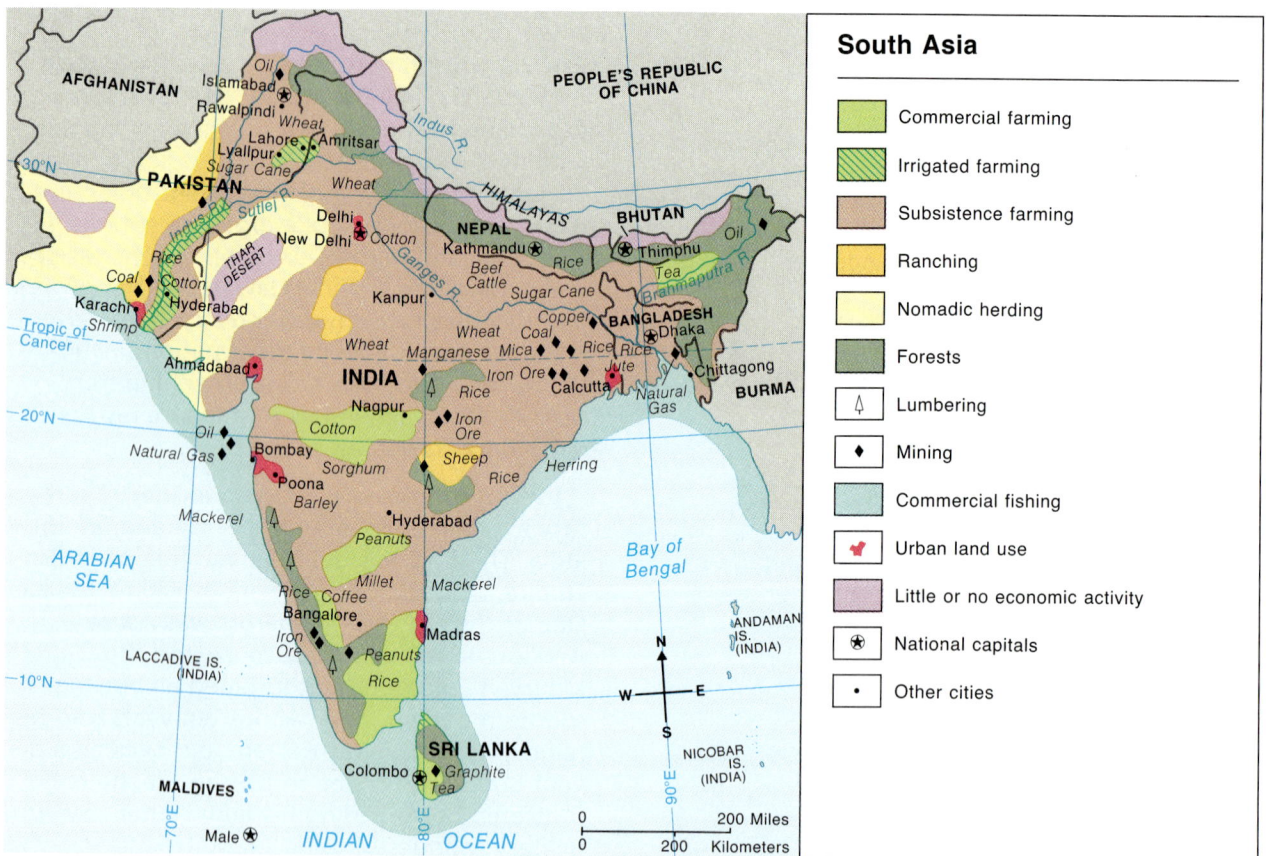

South Asia

- Commercial farming
- Irrigated farming
- Subsistence farming
- Ranching
- Nomadic herding
- Forests
- Lumbering
- Mining
- Commercial fishing
- Urban land use
- Little or no economic activity
- National capitals
- Other cities

Map Study

You can see from the map that much of South Asia's land is used for farming. In what countries does commercial farming take place? How is land used in Bangladesh?

[mü'gul] Empire. India remained under Mughul control until the empire broke apart about 1750.

The coming of the British. During the same centuries that the Mughuls were building their Indian empire, European trading ships were arriving along India's coasts. The British soon overcame their Portuguese, Dutch, and French rivals to Indian trade. The break-up of the Mughul Empire allowed the British to gain power in India.

British involvement in India first began with a rich, powerful business group called the British East India Company. The East India Company set up trading stations along India's coasts, from which it obtained fine woven cottons and other village handicrafts carried from inland. When company representatives began moving inland, they came into conflict with Indian cultural traditions and local rulers. To end the strife, the British government in 1857 ended the East India Company's control over India. Britain then made India a colony ruled directly by the British Crown.

British rule brought both good and bad changes to India.

India underwent many changes under British colonial rule. On the positive side, the British helped to unify India by bringing almost all of the subcontinent under one authority. The introduction of English also helped to unify India. Before the arrival of the British, there had been no single language all Indians could speak. The British also built roads, railways, and irrigation systems throughout India. Colonial doctors improved medical facilities.

British rule had some bad results as well. Before the British arrived, Indian merchants along the coasts had long been trading Indian village products for goods from Southeast Asia. British colonists took over this trade. The British also ended the village handicraft industries that had

flourished for centuries. The British then turned India into a supplier of raw materials for the growing textile industry in England. India also became a market for English manufactured goods.

India became an independent nation in 1947.

British rule did much to tie the Indian subcontinent together. The people of India, though, looked forward to the time when they would govern themselves. Many saw the British as outsiders who discriminated against Indians. Beginning in the 1870s, a nationalist movement began that ended when Britain agreed in 1945 to give India full independence.

Mohandas K. Gandhi [gän'dē] became known to the world as the leader of the Indian independence movement. Starting around 1920 he led a campaign of nonviolent resistance against the British. Millions of Indians followed Gandhi's methods, based on principles of nonviolence and truth. Gandhi also worked for a united country where all Indians would live in peace.

When preparations for self-government began, however, it became increasingly clear that political unity on the subcontinent would not come about. The people in the western part of British India were almost all Muslims, who insisted they would never be part of a Hindu-dominated state. Another cluster of Muslims occupied the area around the Ganges-Brahmaputra delta. The people in the rest of British India were predominantly Hindus.

In 1947 British and Indian leaders made the difficult decision of drawing a boundary that separated the subcontinent's people into two nations. One was the large, predominantly Hindu nation of India. The other was Pakistan, ruled by Muslims. The newly created nation of Pakistan included the huge cluster of Muslims living in the east. Thus the new Muslim country actually had two widely separated geographic sectors—West Pakistan and East Pakistan.

The creation of India and Pakistan did not take place peacefully. Even before the partition, riots between Hindus and Muslims had broken out throughout India. After the partition, horrible killings and widespread violence occurred as Hindus and Muslims migrated into their newly formed countries. About 15 million people were uprooted, and at least 500,000 people died.

During the late 1960s, East Pakistan rebelled against West Pakistan over language and cultural differences. With the help of India, East Pakistan in 1971 became the independent country of Bangladesh. West Pakistan then became known simply as Pakistan.

Most Indians live in traditional villages.

For hundreds of millions of Indians, life in villages continued despite the political events that swirled around them for centuries. Although India now has many large cities, about 70 percent of the population lives in its half million villages. Most villages have less than a thousand people. Many are centuries old.

Village life. An individual village household usually includes three generations—children, parents, and grandparents. Farming is a major way of earning a living. Modern facilities are few. Villagers may carry water in pottery jugs from a village well or pump.

People of the villages dress simply, but also according to local traditions. Women typically wear a long piece of cloth draped around the body in a **sari**. The way they arrange their saris depends on where they live. Village men wrap a piece of cloth loosely between their legs and around the waist. With this they wear a simple shirt. Workingmen in cities sometimes wear the same type of garment.

Urban life. About 30 percent of India's population lives in urban areas. Most of India's big cities stand along the coastline or on the Ganges plain. Some Indian cities are among the most populated in the world. Calcutta, on the Ganges-Brahmaputra delta, and Bombay, on the west coast, each have more than 10 million people. The city of Delhi and its neighbor, the capital city of New Delhi, have a combined population of more than 7 million.

Traditional and modern India meet—and often collide—in its great cities. Pushcarts and wagons compete with automobiles, buses, and bicycles for space on the streets. Shirt-and-tie

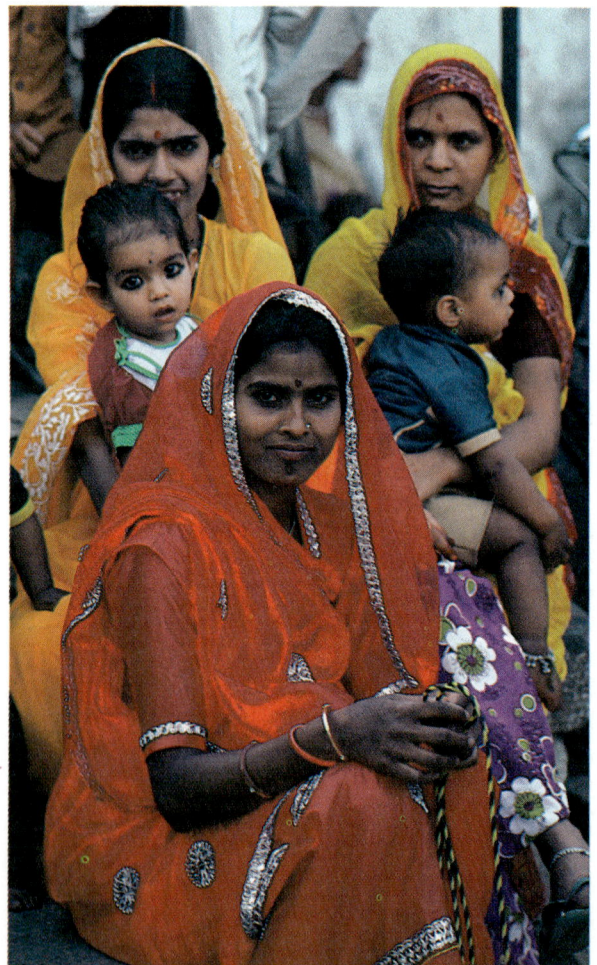

These northern Indians are dressed in saris.

office workers buy vegetables at open-air stalls where villagers bring their produce in the mornings. New high-rise buildings shade lovely homes styled after early Indian architecture. Former British colonial office buildings contrast with modern buildings.

Problems of poverty and overcrowding also beset Indian cities. Thousands of homeless people fill many Indian cities. Some of the homeless live on city sidewalks. Others live in makeshift shelters or in crowded apartment buildings.

India has faced major challenges since independence.

When India became independent in 1947, many challenges faced the new nation. Since independence India has worked to develop its economy and build its industries. As a developing nation, India continues to face challenges. India's population growth rate, for example, greatly concerns its leaders. The national government has taken various steps to try to reduce its present growth rate. Another challenge for India is the problem of poverty and crowded living conditions in cities.

Challenges of democracy. India has become the world's largest democracy. Like the United States, India is a federal republic. This means that the country is divided into a number of different states, generally based on regional similarities. Each state has a separate government that makes many independent decisions. Maintaining a democracy of 767 million people has been an important accomplishment for India. Its challenges include a diverse population that speaks many different languages. In addition, illiteracy has been a concern.

Challenges in agriculture. The task of increasing agricultural output is one of India's biggest challenges. Acre for acre, India's farms produce less than farms in almost any other part of the Asian rimland. Farmers generally use age-old methods that are unproductive by modern standards. Even where machines are available and fields are sizable, the equipment may be out-of-date. Poor subsistence farmers cannot afford to buy the fertilizers and implements needed to increase the yield of their crops.

Bombay, India
(Tropical savanna)

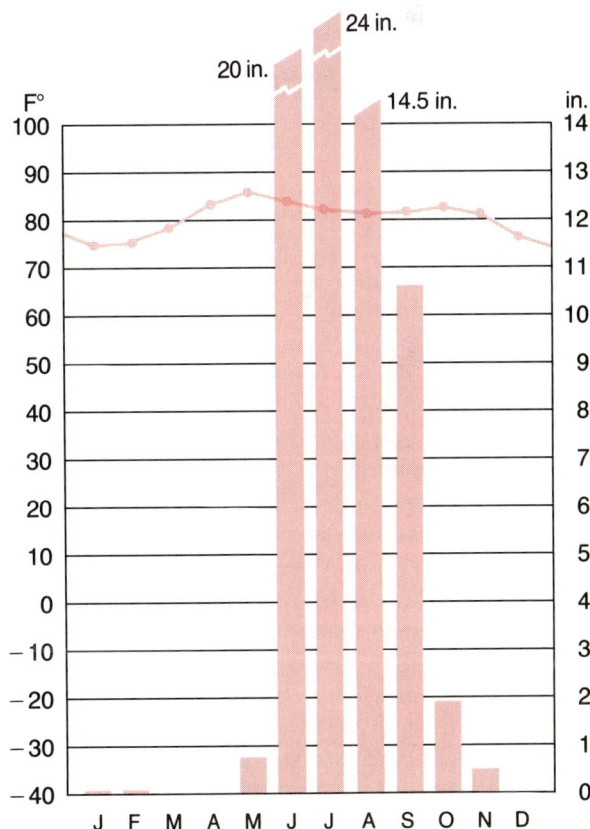

The success of much of India's agriculture depends on the arrival of the monsoon. The bars on this graph show when rain is due in Bombay, which lies in a rice-growing region.

Most of the people of India
farm for a living.

put is among the world's largest. India mines and exports iron ore, coal, manganese, copper, mica (used in electronics parts), and other raw materials. Japan is a major buyer of these exports. A strong mineral base also helped India build its own new factories. Large iron and steel complexes as well as chemical, engineering, and food-processing industries have all been built since 1947.

Already the total amount of goods India produces exceeds that of some the world's most industrialized nations. India's population, however, is so large that the GNP per person is still very low. Thus India falls into the modern world's category of developing nations. The government is trying to expand industry in the cities. In the villages it is also encouraging the handicraft industries that were so successful before the colonial period.

India's major crops include rice, millet, and wheat. (**Millet** is a type of cereal grass that produces very small, edible seeds.) These grains make up the main diet of subsistence farmers who grow them. There are also some commercial farms that supply food for urban areas. In favorable years, India grows enough food to export surpluses and save some for reserve. Thus even in years of drought, India generally can feed itself. Funds that formerly paid for food imports can now go toward buying other essentials needed to build a modern economy.

India's commercial farms produce a number of crops that bring in much-needed cash. India is among the world's top exporters of tea, cotton, and **jute**, a strong fiber used for making rope and coarse fabrics such as burlap. Its coffee, spices, and peanuts also sell in world markets. Still India's potential—and need—for increasing production on both subsistence and commercial acreage is vast. Although India usually can feed itself, many of its people are too poor to eat well. Malnutrition is common.

Advances in industry. India's industrial out-

Section 1 Review

Locating Key Places
Locate the following places on the map on page 536: Bombay, Calcutta, New Delhi

Identifying Key Terms
Define the following terms: sari, millet, jute

Reviewing Main Ideas
1. Describe briefly the three major empires that rose in India before the arrival of the British.
2. What were some positive and negative results of British rule in India?
3. What three countries were formed after Britain agreed to India's independence?
4. Where do 70 percent of all Indians live?
5. What are some of the challenges that India has faced since 1947?

Thinking Critically: Predict Effects
You have read that India's leaders want to rebuild village handicrafts industries. If they succeed, how might the nation's economy, its cities, and its villagers be affected?

India's Neighbors in South Asia

Preview

Key Places
Where are these places located?
1 Pakistan
2 Sri Lanka
See the globe below.

Key Terms
What do these terms mean?
martial law
graphite

Main Ideas
As you read, look for answers to these questions.
● What kind of goverment and economy does Pakistan have?
● What is Bangladesh like?
● How have ethnic disputes affected Sri Lanka?
● What similarities and differences exist between Nepal and Bhutan?

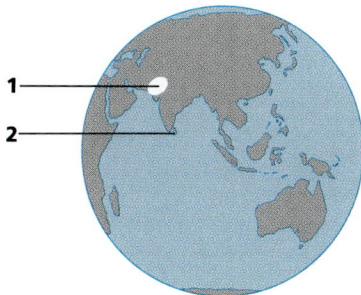

One walks here in the footsteps of Alexander the Great, and in the paths of caravans that carried silk and gold, ivory and jewels to and from China.

National Geographic, May 1981

Pakistan is an Islamic republic dependent upon agriculture.

The description you have just read conveys the sense of the past in Pakistan, India's neighbor to the northwest. Pakistan as a modern nation has existed only since 1947, but the history of its land dates back thousands of years. Inside Pakistan's boundaries lies the site of the Indus Valley civilization, one of the earliest civilizations in the world. In 326 B.C. Alexander the Great conquered what is now Pakistan. The Mauryan Empire, the Gupta Empire, and the Mughul Empire, which you read about earlier in this chapter, all included land that now lies within Pakistan.

Pakistan's government. Pakistan became an independent country in 1947. The events that led to the republic's founding date back to the early 1900s. The nations of India, Pakistan, and Bangladesh did not exist then. These present-day nations made up a single colony ruled by Britain. As you read earlier, India and Pakistan were created in 1947 when Britain agreed to grant its colony independence. Indians adopted a democratic government under which church and state are separate. Unlike India, Pakistan became an Islamic republic in which Muslim religious law plays an important part in how the country is to be governed.

Pakistan today remains an Islamic republic. In 1977, however, control of the government passed from civilian to military hands. General Mohammad Zia [zē'a] declared himself president and set up **martial law**, that is, rule by the military with military courts instead of the usual civil authorities.

Pakistan's economy. Pakistan's economy is based on agriculture, and most of the people work in farming. Pakistani farmers grow a great deal of cotton along with large food crops of rice, wheat, and sugar cane. They export both raw cotton and rice. Production in the north is much greater than in the south, where the irrigation works are outdated. Although there are successful commercial farmers, most rural Pakistanis live on small farms, grow their own food, and sell part of their crop for cash.

Pakistan also has built new industries. The first were textile mills for making cotton cloth and clothing. Pakistan now exports both finished cotton goods as well as raw cotton. Its most developed industrial center is Karachi. Located west of the Indus River delta, Karachi is also Pakistan's major port. The city's industries assemble cars, make steel, and process food.

Bangladesh is a poor, crowded nation of farmers.

Imagine a country the size of Iowa with 104 million people—or about 40 percent of the entire U.S. population. That is Bangladesh, one of the most densely populated and poorest countries

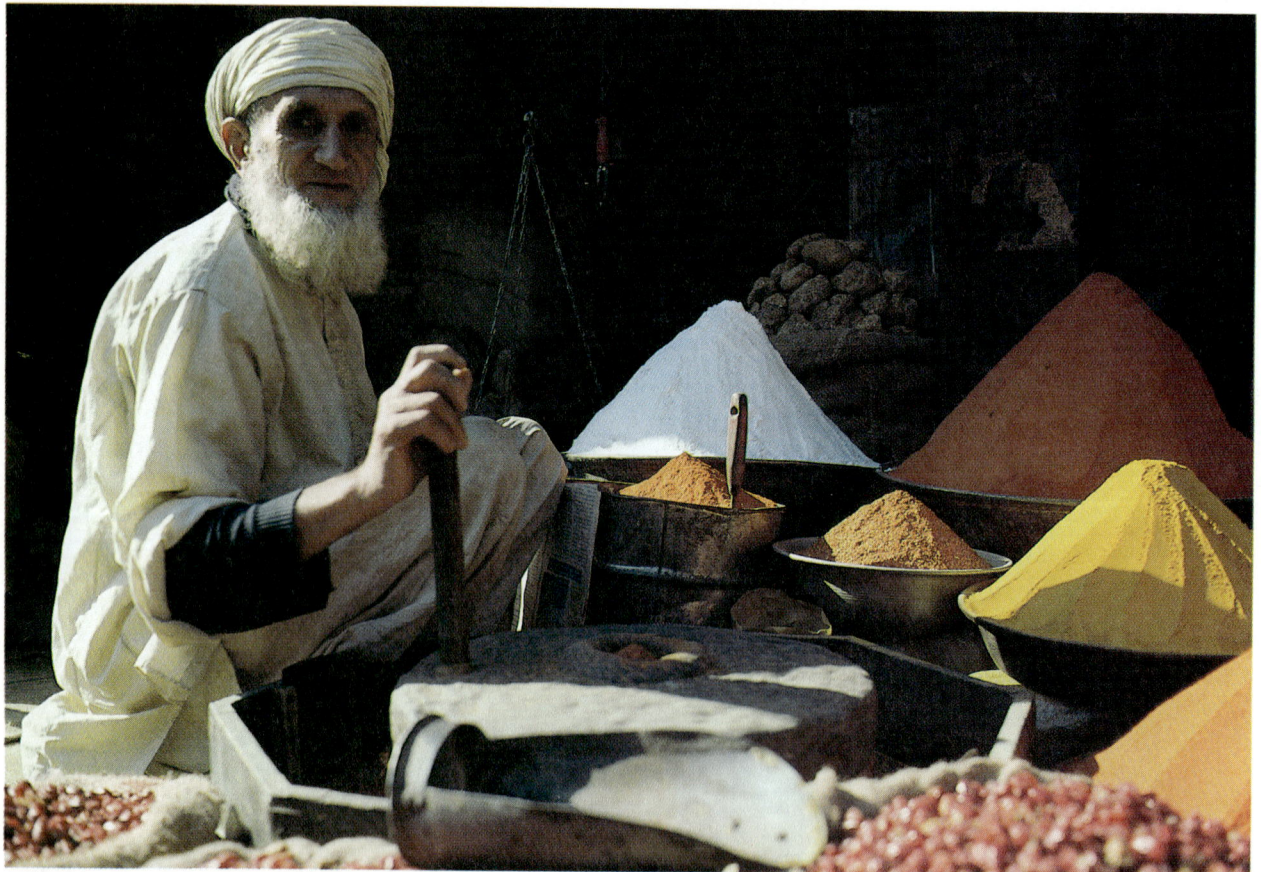

Pyramids of colorful fabric dyes surround a merchant at a market in Lahore, Pakistan. Lahore is a center of the textile industry.

in the world. About 13 percent of its people live in cities. The capital and largest city, Dhaka, holds most of the urban dwellers.

Farming in Bangladesh. The alluvial soils of Bangladesh are very fertile, and most of the land is flat. Thus practically every available square foot of land is under cultivation. In Chapter 25 you read that double-cropping of rice takes place in parts of Asia. In Bangladesh the warm, humid climate and the fertile alluvial soils allow millions of farmers to practice triple cropping. They harvest three crops of rice from the same piece of land in the same year.

Still Bangladesh usually needs to import food from other countries. With its large population and small land area, the country cannot always grow enough food for its people. Natural disasters, too, have played their role. Most of the southern part of the country lies less than 13 feet above sea level. In 1970 more than 200,000 people were killed when a cyclone struck the coast and flooded the level farmlands.

Politics and government. Political problems have beset Bangladesh since it declared its independence from Pakistan in 1971. Military leaders took office in 1975, and years of violence and bloodshed followed as different generals fought for power. A civilian president was ousted in 1982 in a coup led by Lieutenant General Hossain Mohammad Ershad. Ershad appointed himself president in 1983 and has ruled the country since then under martial law.

Ethnic disputes have troubled the island nation of Sri Lanka.

Ancient Hindu legend tells that "glorious Lanka was like the garden of the sky." Poised like a teardrop pendant in the Indian Ocean, the island was known in ancient times as a land of pearls and peacocks, gems and spices, lovely lagoons, and forested mountains.

Economic activities. Sri Lanka has built an agricultural economy based on tea, rubber, and coconut plantations. Exports of these plantation products, especially tea, still earn most of Sri Lanka's foreign income. The country also exports **graphite**, from which pencil "lead" and lubricating oils are made. The island has few known mineral deposits, and industrial development is scant.

The people grow rice as their staple food, but not enough to feed all of the population. The government has invested in new irrigation projects in dry northern lands and given aid to poor farmers. Population growth, however, has outstripped the gains made.

Ethnic conflicts. About 17 million people live in Sri Lanka. Two major ethnic groups make up the population. The largest group, about 75 percent of the population, are the Sinhalese, who practice Buddhism. About 20 percent of the population are Tamils, most of whom are Hindus and live in the north. Earlier conflicts between the Tamils and the Sinhalese grew worse during the 1980s when some Tamils began demanding their own separate, northern country. Tamil extremists led terrorist attacks, which the Sinhalese met with rioting and revenge attacks. India intervened to help stabilize the country in preparation for peace talks. The overall situation threatened the stability and economic well-being of Sri Lanka.

Nepal and Bhutan have similar economies and different religions.

The mountain lands of Nepal and Bhutan both received British protection during the colonial period. The British recognized Nepal's complete independence in 1923 and Bhutan's in 1949. Today both countries are governed by kings who are assisted by national legislatures.

Nepal. Nepal is about the size of the state of Wisconsin, but its 16 million people give it an

ern border. Tourism brings in important foreign cash.

Bhutan. Bhutan is much smaller than Nepal. Its land area is only a third as large, and its population density is only a fourth as great. About 70 percent of the people are Buddhists, and almost all the rest are Hindus.

As in Nepal, about 90 percent of the people farm for a living, mainly in fertile valleys. Large, fortresslike Buddhist monasteries overlook farm-and-village landscapes. Bhutan's remoteness and quiet beauty attract a steady flow of tourists, who also buy the products of the country's handicraft industries.

Section 2 Review

Locating Key Places
Locate the following places on the map on page 536: Pakistan, Sri Lanka

Identifying Key Terms
Define the following terms: martial law, graphite

Reviewing Main Ideas
1. How is Pakistan governed? What is the basis of its economy?
2. How has land area and population affected the economy of Bangladesh?
3. What led to ethnic conflicts in Sri Lanka?
4. How are the countries of Nepal and Bhutan alike? How are they different?

Thinking Critically: Make Hypotheses
When Pakistan was created in 1947, about 750 miles separated East Pakistan from West Pakistan. Control of the government, the economy, and the armed forces were based in West Pakistan. Although the people of West Pakistan and East Pakistan shared the same religion, they spoke different languages. Using these facts, make a hypothesis on why East Pakistan broke away from West Pakistan to form the separate nation of Bangladesh.

Climbers in Nepal follow a snowy trail to Mount Everest.

average population density four times greater than Wisconsin's. Nearly 90 percent of the people are Hindus. Most are farmers working in valleys cradled by the Himalayas.

Rice is the staple crop for the Nepalese. Most of the rice crop grows on or at the base of the south-facing Himalayan slopes in southern Nepal. Unlike many Asian countries, Nepal has been able to feed itself in most years. Widespread clearing of forests on southern Himalayan hillsides has added to the available farmland and boosted food supplies.

Subtropical southern slopes and snowcapped mountaintops make Nepal a land of great contrast and scenic wonder. Mount Everest, the world's highest mountain, rises along its north-

Case Study: Banking on Bangladesh

Preview

Key Places
Where is this place located?
1 Bangladesh

Key Terms
What do these terms mean?
philanthropist
independent contractor
collateral

Main Ideas
As you read, look for answers to these questions.
- What is helping change the lives of poor people in Bangladesh?
- How did one man begin the system of loaning money to the poor?
- How have the bank loans been used?
- How have the borrowers' lives changed?

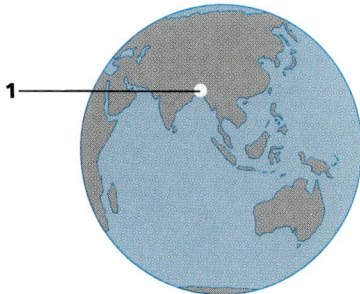

The following case study comes from the article, "Banking on the Poor," Chicago Tribune, October 27, 1987. This case study describes how one person, Mohammad Yunus, helped the people in the district of Tangail, Bangladesh, gain self-confidence and obtain a standard of living few could ever hope to reach. As you read this case study, think about how what Mohammed Yunus did in Bangladesh might work in other poor areas.

Bank loans are helping the poor of Bangladesh.

Imagine living on $140 a year.

Not a month. A year.

That's the average income of the average Bangladeshi. And half of the nearly 110 million people squeezed into this country the size of Wisconsin don't do that well. For many, the possibility of of getting ahead is beyond imagining. In a country known mainly for floods and famines, survival is hard enough.

In a small but impressive way, though, the plight of some of this nation's poorest is changing, not through charity, welfare or foreign aid but through a renegade [not typical] bank created out of social conscience by an academician from a well-to-do family.

"Being poor is like being at the bottom of a well," Mohammad Yunus, the bank's founder, likes to say. "We can throw down a rope—that's credit. Whether the poor grabs the rope is up to them. If you transfer this resource to a poor person and this person is intelligent and has skill, then you can trust that this person will take advantage of the trust you've placed in them. Credit for self-employment is a fundamental human right."

This man and his bank have succeeded in helping the supposedly helpless poor of

545

Bangladesh improve their lives where dozens of other well-intentioned but inappropriate efforts have failed.

The unorthodox blend of traditional banking and social service has been successful enough to attract the attention of governments, community organizations and philanthropists around the world. [A **philanthropist** is a person who gives large sums of money to worthy causes.]

A professor loaned poor people money to run their own businesses.

It began like this: One day in 1975 some poor women in the village of Jobra, in southeastern Bangladesh, were going about the business of surviving. They were making bamboo stools when Yunus, then an economics professor from nearby Chittagong University, approached them.

How much did they earn? he asked, in their dialect.

Half a taka a day, they replied—a penny.

A trader supplied their materials and took a substantial cut of the price they were paid.

"What if you could buy your own materials? How much could you earn then?" he asked them.

They looked at him disbelievingly; they could never afford the materials, they said.

Yunus persisted. "How much would the materials cost?"

One or two dollars, they said. They could earn more as independent contractors, 5 cents a day, maybe more. [An **independent contractor** is a person who supplies his or her own materials and then produces a product for sale.]

Yunus found 42 illiterate but skilled women in similiar straits in the village. They had no means of obtaining the small sum needed to become self-employed.

Reaching into his own pockets, the professor became a banker and lent the Jobra women a total of $60 interest-free. Some borrowers bought rice, husked it and sold the cleaned grains. Others made puffed rice and sweets, earthenware or woven mats. Some bought baby goats or chickens. They repaid their loans, pennies at a time, on schedule. Heartened, Yunus approached bankers.

Eventually, he found a bank willing to risk a few hundred dollars on loans to Jobra villagers, provided he guarantee the loans. Yunus signed the papers, but how could he ensure repayment?

Credit, Yunus decided, would be extended only to those villagers considered landless, those with less than a half-acre of cultivable land.

Facing page: **Borrowers from the Grameen Bank, mostly women, gather for a meeting. The center picture shows a typical farm in Bangladesh.**

Their reputations would be their collateral. [**Collateral** is something of value pledged to secure a loan.] To qualify, they would have to form groups of five men or women. Each group would decide which two members would receive loans first. If the first two repaid on schedule, the next two would receive loans, then the final member. If either of the first two didn't repay on schedule, no one else would receive a loan.

Yunus christened [named] his experiment the Grameen (Rural) Bank Project and tested it in other villages from 1976 to 1978. In 1979 the Central Bank of Bangladesh agreed to back the program in Tangail, a district (like a state) northwest of Dhaka, the capital.

Eleven years after the bankers first scoffed at Yunus' proposition, the proof is in the passbooks. Grameen Bank has more than $6 million in savings and monthly disburses $1.3 million in loans to landless Bangladeshi.

Loans have been used to launch hundreds of projects.

The loans have been used to launch hundreds of projects: making furniture, fans, mats, quilts, rickshaws, garments, baskets, cradles, snacks, rope, candles, toys, fish nets, farm implements, jewelry, and more. Borrowers raise animals, fodder, fruits, cotton, sugar cane, and vegetables with discount seeds provided by the bank. They distribute newspapers and trade spices, betel nuts, leather, yarn, and dried fish. They drive rickshaws and bullock carts.

More than 70 percent of the borrowers are women; in one district women account for 82 percent of the loans. This is in a country where only 7 percent of the women are employed, where females are more poorly nourished than males, and where cultural and religious traditions oppress women in a dozen ways.

Thanks to Grameen Bank, "Women are gaining more autonomy [independence]. Social scientists had predicted we'd break up the family structure, but just the opposite has happened. The ties between husband and wife have become stronger."

The borrowers have pride in their accomplishments.

In spite of the strides she has made economically and personally, Rezia Begum and most of the other Grameen Bank loanees remain impoverished. "Another bank still wouldn't consider us loanworthy," she acknowledges.

But that doesn't diminish her pride and wonder at how far she has come. When she was a maid, living on table scraps and under a shelter of banana leaves, she never imagined a bank might take a chance on her.

"I never dreamed of it. It was beyond our comprehension."

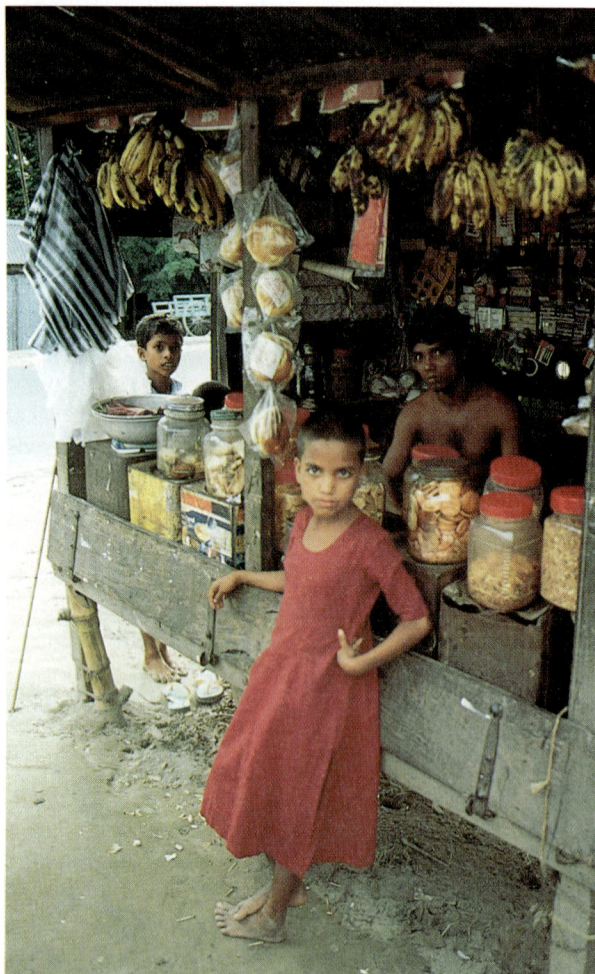

A Grameen Bank loan helped this family open a food shop.

Section 3 Review

Locating Key Places
Locate the following place on the map on page 536: Bangladesh

Identifying Key Terms
Define the following terms: philanthropist, independent contractor, collateral

Reviewing Main Ideas
1. Why are the lives of some people in Bangladesh changing?
2. How were the poor helped by Mohammad Yunus?
3. In what ways have the villagers used the loans?
4. How have the loans changed the lives of the borrowers?

Thinking Critically: Evaluate Sources of Information
Based on the information in this section, how reasonable is it to conclude that on the whole the people of Bangladesh are improving their standard of living?

Using Special-Purpose Maps

The chapter you have just read presents a great deal of information about the religions of South Asia. What kind of map would help you visualize where these religions are located? The answer is a special-purpose map like the one on this page. A special-purpose map illustrates one particular aspect of a region, often omitting almost every other feature. The map on this page, for example, shows the location of South Asia's major religions. Notice that the only other feature shown on the map is the political boundary of each South Asian country. All other features are omitted in order to simplify the map.

An essential step in using a special-purpose map is to check the key to make sure you understand how the map presents information. The map on this page uses colors to show the major religions of South Asia. Capital letters mark places where a religion dominates a small area.

Special-purpose maps have many different uses. For instance, you can use the map on this page to note the major religion of each nation. You can also find out which religion dominates South Asia as a whole.

Another way to use a special-purpose map is to make comparisons. For example, compare India and Pakistan. India's major religion is Hindu, but with every other religion having at least one area of dominance. In contrast, Pakistan's major religion is Islam with a small area of Hinduism close to India's western border.

Review

Use the map on this page to answer the questions.
1. What is the major religion in Nepal?
2. What is the major religion in Bangladesh?
3. Where is Christianity practiced in India?

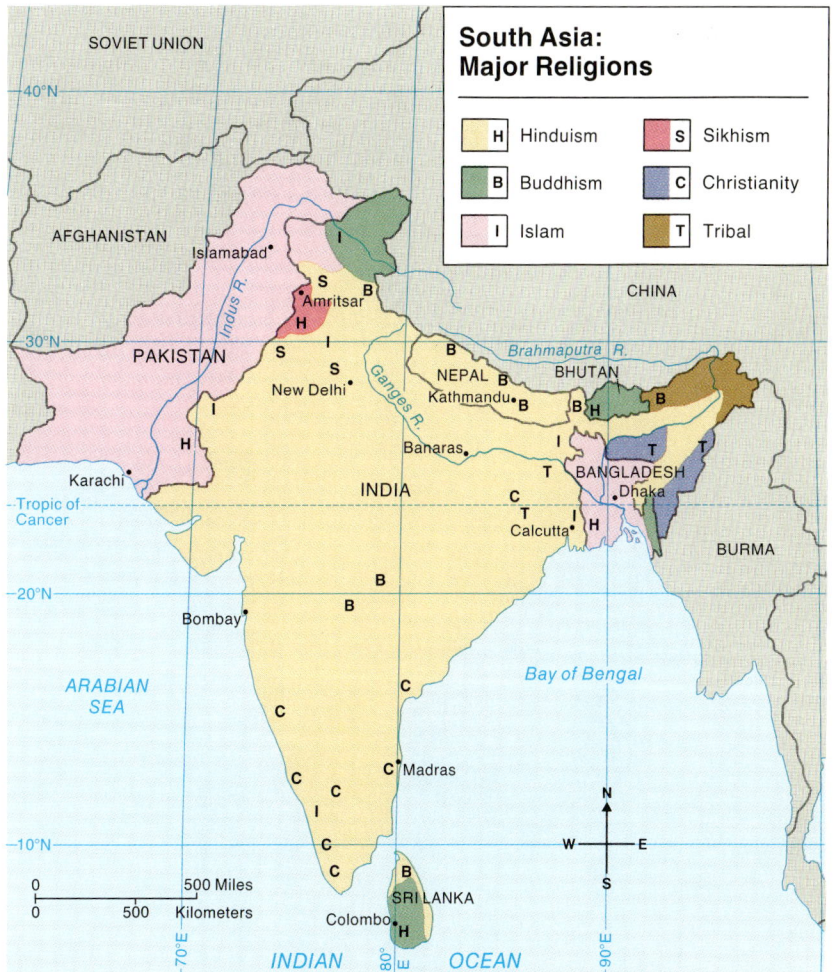

South Asia: Major Religions

H	Hinduism	S	Sikhism
B	Buddhism	C	Christianity
I	Islam	T	Tribal

SOVIET UNION

AFGHANISTAN

Islamabad

PAKISTAN

New Delhi

Amritsar

Karachi

CHINA

NEPAL

Kathmandu

BHUTAN

Banaras

BANGLADESH

Dhaka

INDIA

Calcutta

BURMA

Bombay

ARABIAN SEA

Bay of Bengal

Madras

SRI LANKA

Colombo

INDIAN OCEAN

Indus R.

Ganges R.

Brahmaputra R.

Tropic of Cancer

40°N

30°N

20°N

10°N

70°E

80°E

90°E

500 Miles

500 Kilometers

N

S

E

W

549

Review

Section Summaries

1. India The Mauryans, the Guptas, and the Mughuls each built strong empires in India before the coming of the British in the mid-1700s. India became a British colony in 1867. Since winning independence in 1947, India has maintained the world's largest democracy. It has also worked to build its economy. Most Indians live in villages, where farming is a main economic activity. About 25 percent of the population lives in urban areas, where many industries have developed.

2. India's Neighbors in South Asia India's neighbors in South Asia are Pakistan, Bangladesh, Sri Lanka, Nepal, and Bhutan. Agriculture is a major economic activity in these countries. Pakistan and Bangladesh both have military governments. The island country of Sri Lanka has been troubled by ethnic conflicts.

3. Case Study: Banking on Bangladesh Loans from a bank are helping to change the lives of people in Tangail, a district in Bangladesh. Mohammad Yunus, the bank's founder, began in 1975 to lend poor people money to start their own businesses. Borrowers have started hundreds of projects and have taken much pride in their accomplishments.

Using Geography Skills

Reviewing the Map Lesson

Use the special-purpose map below to tell whether the following statements are true or false. Then rewrite the false statements to make them true.

1. The Indian Tamils are mainly Hindus.
2. The low country Sinhalese dominate the northern coastal region.
3. Sri Lanka's interior has small, isolated areas where Ceylon Tamils live.
4. Both types of Sinhalese live mostly in central and southern Sri Lanka.

Using Social Studies Skills

1. Organize and Express Ideas in Written Form. Suppose that you are a travel agent arranging tours in South Asia. Write an article that tells what tourists might see in each country. Include at least two facts about each country. Use your textbook to help you.

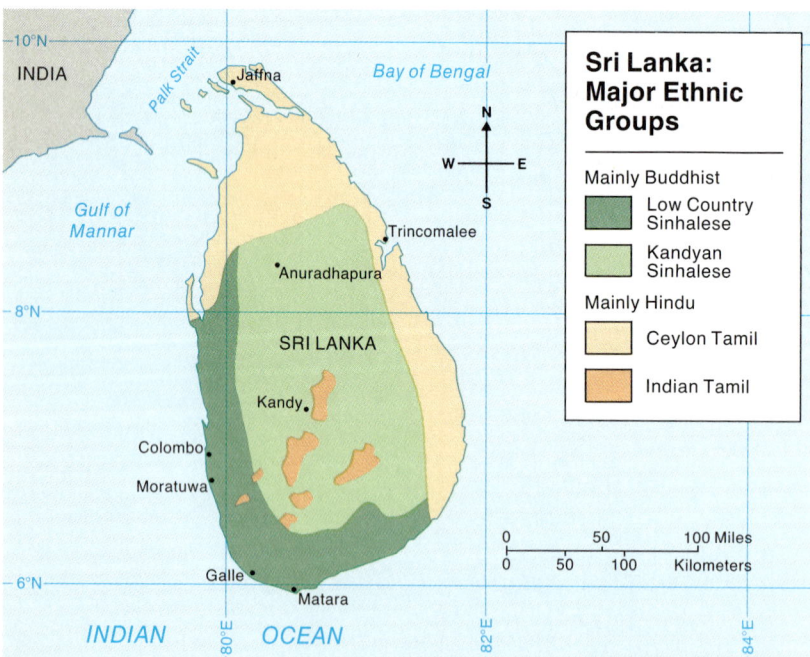

Sri Lanka: Major Ethnic Groups

Mainly Buddhist
Low Country Sinhalese
Kandyan Sinhalese
Mainly Hindu
Ceylon Tamil
Indian Tamil

2. Synthesize Information. Make a chart that shows facts about South Asian countries. For each country, include the population, capital, major economic activities, major physical features, and a brief statement about the country's history. Use maps, your textbook, and reference books to locate the facts you need. Then use your chart to write a paragraph that compares similarities and differences among the South Asian nations.

Testing for Understanding

Locating Key Places
Match the description with the key places listed below.
1. an Indian city located on the Ganges-Brahmaputra delta
2. an Islamic republic northwest of India
3. an agricultural country independent since 1971
4. the capital of India
5. a city located on India's west coast
6. an island country that exports tea and rubber
a. Bombay
b. Calcutta
c. New Delhi
d. Pakistan
e. Sri Lanka
f. Bangladesh

Recalling Key Terms
Define these terms in your own words.

Section 1
sari
millet
jute

Section 2
martial law
graphite

Section 3
philanthropist
independent contractor
collateral

Reviewing Main Ideas
Section 1
1. Identify and briefly describe the three major empires that rose in India before India became a British colony.
2. List some positive and negative effects of British rule on India.
3. What three present-day nations grew out of British India?
4. Where do most of India's people live?
5. What challenges has India faced since independence?

Section 2
1. Describe the government and economy of Pakistan.
2. How does Bangladesh's small size and large population affect that country's economy?
3. Why has Sri Lanka experienced ethnic conflicts?
4. How are Nepal and Bhutan alike and different?

Section 3
1. What has happened to change the lives of some people in Bangladesh?
2. How did Mohammad Yunus help the poor of Bangladesh?
3. How have bank loans been used in Bangladesh?
4. How have the loans affected the lives of the borrowers?

Thinking Critically
1. Recognize Values. Small families, a single language, and complete land redistribution might improve conditions in India. Why do India's leaders not pass laws that would force the people to rapidly adopt such reforms?

2. Make Hypotheses. Suppose the British had left India without drawing the lines of partition. What do you think might have happened on the subcontinent? Give reasons for your answer.

CHAPTER 27

East Asia

In this chapter you will read about China, Japan, North Korea, South Korea, Mongolia, and Taiwan.

Sections

1 **China**

2 **North Korea, South Korea, Mongolia, and Taiwan**

3 **Japan**

China

Preview

Key Places
Where are these places located?
1 Beijing
2 Shanghai
3 Hong Kong
   See the globe below.

Key Terms
What do these terms mean?
dynasty   revolution
dynastic cycle   collective

Main Ideas
As you read, look for answers to these questions.
• What part did emperors play in shaping Chinese history?
• How did China become a communist nation?
• What are China's main economic activities?
• How does communism affect family life in China?
• How does Hong Kong relate to China?

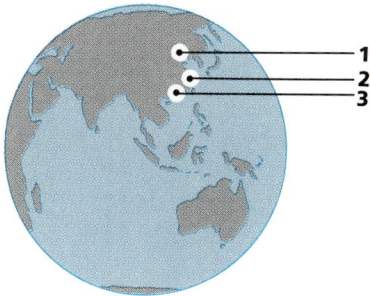

[A local ruler] asked whether there were any form of encouragement by which he could induce the common people to be respectful and loyal. The Master said, Approach them with dignity, and they will respect you. Show piety towards your parents and kindness towards your children, and they will be loyal to you. Promote those who are worthy, train those who are incompetent; that is the best form of government.

The Analects of Confucius, 5th century B.C.

Emperors ruled China until 1911.
For centuries, the teachings of Confucius lay at the heart of Chinese political and social ideas. Today China's rulers follow the ideas of a very different philosopher, Karl Marx. The writings of Marx were studied by revolutionaries bent on creating a China totally unlike the China of the past. The nation they formed is the most populous communist country in the world. The political systems they established began a new era in China's long history.

China has a written history that dates back about 3,500 years. The people who lived in China developed a rich civilization unlike any other. They built magnificent cities, wrote poetry, wove intricate silk fabrics, and developed styles of painting, porcelain making, and architecture that were widely imitated around the world. The early Chinese also made many important contributions in science and technology, including the "four inventions" of paper, printing, gunpowder, and the magnetic sailing compass.

China's history until 1911 can be seen as a series of dynasties. A **dynasty** is a succession of rulers who belong to the same family. Dynastic rule in China followed a pattern called the

Facing page: Traditional Chinese opera features elaborate make-up and beautifully decorated costumes.

dynastic cycle. Each dynasty was strong and powerful when it first began its rule. Then, over a period that sometimes lasted for centuries, the dynasty grew weak from rebellions and invasions and, sometimes, poor rulers. Finally, the dynasty fell. A new dynasty took its place, beginning the cycle again. Absolute power within the dynasty belonged to the emperor, whose orders were carried out by a vast system of government officials.

Between 1500 B.C. and A.D. 1911, the Chinese made great advances in art, science, and many

East Asia

Commercial farming

Irrigated farming

Subsistence farming

Nomadic herding

Forests

Lumbering

Hunting, fishing, and gathering

Mining

Commercial fishing

Urban land use

Little or no economic activity

National capitals

Other cities

Map Study

China is the largest country in East Asia. Other East Asian countries are Japan, Mongolia, Taiwan, and North and South Korea. What is China's capital?

other fields. The impact of some of their contributions is still felt today.

The people of the Shang dynasty, for example, created fine bronze vases and jade carvings that are admired in museums around the world. The Shang dynasty, the first in China, ruled from about 1500 to 1027 B.C. During the Zhou [jō] dynasty, great teachers such as Confucius developed standards of behavior that influence Chinese people today. The Zhou dynasty ruled China between 1027 and 256 B.C.—longer than any other Chinese dynasty.

Many advances were made during the Qin [chin] dynasty and the Han dynasty. The Qin dynasty (221–206 B.C.) gave China a uniform system of weights and measures. During Qin rule

The Great Wall of China is a lasting reminder of how people can change physical landscapes.

the Great Wall of China was built as barrier against invasions from China's north and west. During the more than 400 years of Han rule between 202 B.C. and A.D. 220, the Chinese invented paper and wrote the world's first dictionary.

The Tang dynasty ruled China from A.D. 618 to 907 during what historians call a golden age for China. Education and literature—especially poetry—flourished during this period. The Chinese also invented printing and paper money during the Tang dynasty.

In 960 the Song dynasty came to power. Its emperors ruled until 1279. The Song dynasty ranks as one of the greatest artistic periods in world history. Song artists and craft workers excelled at painting and porcelain making.

In 1279 the Song dynasty fell to the Mongols, a group of nomad conquerors from Central Asia. The Mongol dynasty in China began in 1279 when Kublai Khan [kü′ blī kän′], a powerful Mongol emperor, brought all of China under his control. Over time, the Mongols adopted Chinese ways of life and so were absorbed into Chinese culture. The Chinese, however, saw the Mongols as intruders. In 1368 a Chinese army expelled Mongol rulers, and a new Chinese dynasty called the Ming took over.

In 1644 the Manchus, a nomadic tribe from Manchuria, overthrew the Ming and began the Manchu dynasty. The Manchu dynasty was the last dynasty to rule China. The Manchus were overthrown in 1911 by a group of nationalists who believed that China should become a nation in which the people, not emperors, ruled. Nationalist leaders then established a republic—the first in China's history.

A revolution transformed China into a communist nation.

The nationalists who made China a republic never succeeded in gaining full control of the government. In 1921 the Chinese Communist party formed and began planning a revolution to bring communism to China. A **revolution** is a complete overthrow of an established government or political system. Nationalists and Communists fought each other in a power struggle that lasted until 1949. By then the Communists had taken over most of China. Their leader, Mao Zedong [mou'tse'tùng'], proclaimed the birth of the People's Republic of China.

Many changes took place in China under communist rule. Farmland became collectively owned by the peasants, who were organized onto huge agricultural **collectives.** This was land that used to belong to individual families. Under the communist system, major industries became the property of the government. The government also took control of banking, communication, and foreign trade.

In some ways Chinese life improved under the communists. Millions of Chinese had died of famine in earlier years, for example, and the communists' agricultural programs helped increase food production. Health care improved, and efforts were made to raise the literacy rate.

China's transformation into a communist nation involved great human suffering, however. When the communists redistributed farmland to the peasants, several million landlords were killed. Between 1966 and 1969, thousands lost their lives when Mao carried out a "Cultural Revolution" to rid the party of those perceived as straying from the communist way.

Mao remained head of China's communist party until his death in 1976. A new group of top leaders soon came to power. In 1978 they announced a plan to forge China into a leading world power by the year 2000. Known as the "Four Modernizations," the plan focused on modernizing agriculture and industry, strengthening military forces, and making advances in science, technology, and medicine. To reach this goal, China invited American, Japanese, and European companies to help build its economy. The government also raised factory outputs and farm production by introducing labor incentives.

A high school student in China leads his class in exercises.

China's main economic activities are agriculture and manufacturing.

Under the communists, China made agriculture and manufacturing its primary economic activities. Steps to increase agricultural output began under Mao when peasants were organized onto huge collectives known as communes. Each commune contained as many as 20,000 people. Work was carried out by teams, with assignments that ranged from gathering wood to building small-scale rural factories. Peasants were also expected to work in the fields. For their efforts they received free food and clothing, housing, and a small state salary.

Agriculture in China. Farmland in China is still collectively owned. National leaders since Mao, however, changed the system of labor. Communes were abolished in favor of township governments, under which farm families are assigned their own plots of land. They can pass this land to their children, but they cannot sell it. Farm families are responsible for turning over

lies are responsible for turning over a fixed amount of their crop to the government. Anything they produce beyond that amount may be kept for themselves or sold for profit. This system has resulted in much higher agricultural yields for the nation.

At the same time, many rural villagers have raised their incomes and standard of living. Some own television sets and modern appliances. Others add to their personal incomes by running such small businesses as repair shops.

Most of the farming in China takes place in the country's eastern third. This part of the country has land best suited for growing crops.

The southern part of China's farming region, with its humid subtropical climate and fertile soils, produces major rice crops. China raises more rice than any other country in the world, largely because in the south two crops of rice can be harvested each year. Wheat ranks as the main crop in the northern part of China's farming region. The Chinese also raise large quantities of corn, soybeans, cotton, and tea. In addition to raising most of the world's rice, China also leads the world in the production of cotton.

Manufacturing in China. After some 40 years of enormous effort, China has built a full

Billboards in Guangzhou, advertising watches, cameras, and sport shoes, reflect China's plans to provide more consumer goods.

range of heavy industries. Industrial centers produce iron and steel, chemicals, tractors, trucks, and irrigation equipment. Textile mills are also a very important industry.

China's efforts in industrialization have drawn large numbers of workers to Shanghai, Beijing, and other cities. Although three out of every four Chinese live in rural areas, China has many very large cities, including more than 33 cities with populations of more than a million. China's largest city is Shanghai, with a population of 12 million. More than 9 million people live in Beijing, China's capital.

Communist rule strongly influences family life in China.

China's communist system affects many aspects of Chinese family life. Before 1949 three-generation households were common in China, with parents, grandparents, and children living under one roof. Now most Chinese live as nuclear families of parents and children. To decrease China's population growth rate, the government encourages people to marry later and have just one child. Single-child families receive income bonuses, better health care, and a free education for the child. Parents with more than two children pay heavy income taxes. Under China's government, people must work where they are needed.

However, in 1989 protests occurred in several Chinese cities. As the world kept watch, thousands of students peacefully occupied Beijing's Tiananmen Square and demanded democratic reforms. After some hesitation, China's leaders sent in army troops to crush the demonstrations. Thousands of protestors were killed or arrested.

China will regain the British colony of Hong Kong in 1997.

A small reminder of European colonialism in Asia lies along China's southern coast. It is the British colony of Hong Kong. Hong Kong's 400 square miles take in a small peninsula and several islands at the mouth of the Xi [shē] River. The British leased most of Hong Kong from China in 1898. The rest of the colony had been acquired by Britain in 1841 and 1860. China has announced that it will reclaim Hong Kong when Britain's 99-year lease expires in 1997.

Today 6 million people live in Hong Kong's almost completely urbanized landscape. Nearly 99 percent of them are Chinese.

Hong Kong has developed an enormously rich economy. The British gave free enterprise every opportunity to thrive. With its huge labor force, Hong Kong drew many Western manufacturing companies. "Made in Hong Kong" appears on hundreds of goods sold all over the world.

Section 1 Review

Locating Key Places
Locate the following places on the map on page 554: Beijing, Shanghai, Hong Kong

Identifying Key Terms
Define the following terms: dynasty, dynastic cycle, revolution, collective

Reviewing Main Ideas
1. How was China ruled before 1911?
2. What changes took place in China under its communist government?
3. What crops and industrial products help make agriculture and manufacturing important to China's economy?
4. Name two ways that the Chinese government has affected family life in China.
5. In what way is Hong Kong linked to China?

Thinking Critically: Evaluate Sources of Information
In 1948 Mao said, "We have always maintained that the revolution must rely on the masses of the people, on everybody's taking a hand, and have opposed relying merely on a few persons issuing orders." Based on what you have read in this section, do you think this statement applies to China?

North Korea, South Korea, Mongolia, and Taiwan

Preview

Key Places
1 North Korea
2 South Korea
3 Mongolia
4 Taiwan
See the globe below.

Key Terms
What do these terms mean?
demilitarized zone
urbanization

Main Ideas
As you read, look for answers to these questions.
• How does North Korea differ from South Korea?
• How has Mongolia developed its economy?
• What kind of government and economy is found in Taiwan?

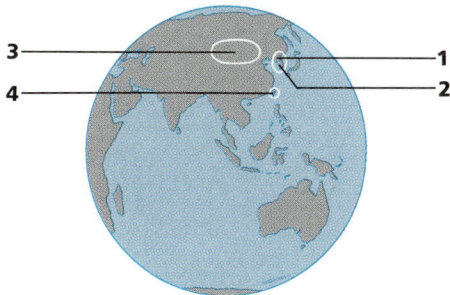

When whales fight, the shrimp gets hurt.

Korean proverb

North Korea and South Korea differ in government and economy.

Korea was a single country from about A.D. 735 to 1910. Like a shrimp among whales, Korea has often felt the influence of larger, more powerful nations, especially China and Japan. After Japan was defeated in World War II, Korea was released from a period of Japanese control that had begun in 1910. Korea then became caught between the United States and the Soviet Union. In 1945 Korea was divided in half with Soviet troops occupying the north and American forces in the south. Each side set up a government aligned with its own. By 1948 Korea was officially divided into two separate countries, communist North Korea and noncommunist South Korea.

In 1950 North Korean troops invaded South Korea. This invasion led to a three-year war in which United Nations countries, mainly the United States, helped South Korea fight against North Korea. China fought on the side of the North Koreans. The Korean War ended in 1953 with a stalemate. The line where the fighting stopped forms the present-day boundary between North Korea and South Korea. A small strip of land called a **demilitarized zone**, where no troops are allowed, lies on either side of the boundary. Although populated by people of the same ethnic and language groups, the two countries have remained enemies.

North Korea. North Korea has the larger territory, but its population of 21 million is half that of South Korea. About half of the people live along North Korea's western coast. The nation's capital, Pyongyang, and the most important industrial centers are found in this part of North Korea. Also located on the western coast is most of North Korea's farmland. Some farmland and industrial centers are found on North

559

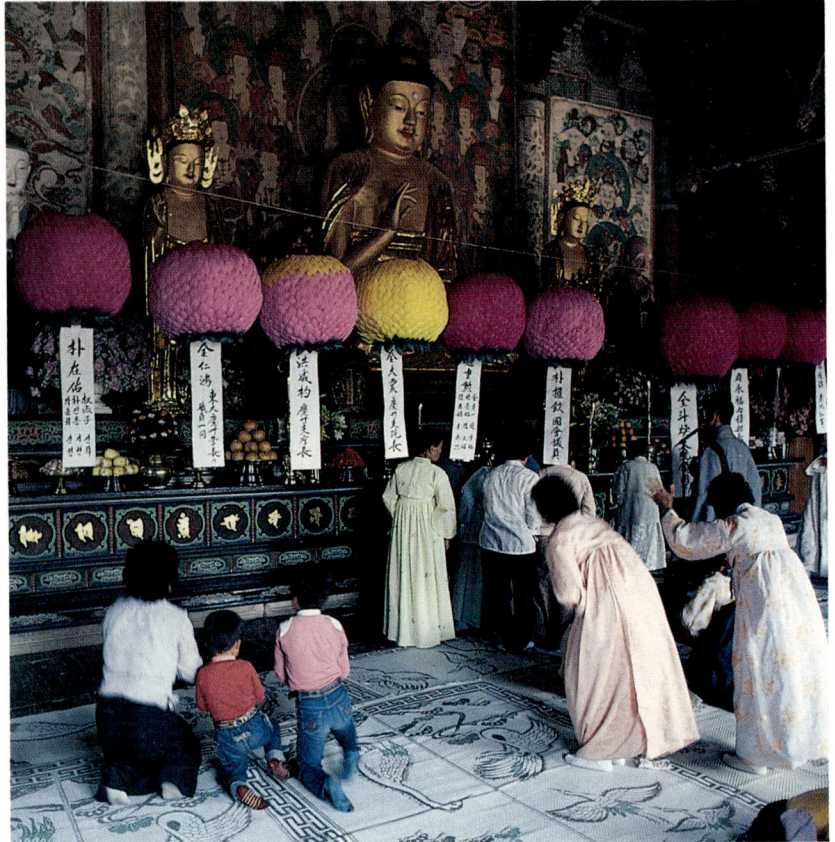

South Korean Buddhists worship at a temple. Buddhism is one of South Korea's main religions.

Korea's eastern coast, too. Forest-covered mountains make up the rest of the country. About 40 percent of North Korea's population lives in urban areas.

North Korea's economy relies more on industry than agriculture. Industry accounts for about 70 percent of the country's gross national product. The government has placed more emphasis on heavy industries than on consumer goods. Industrial production centers on iron and steel making, machinery for factories and farms, and textiles. Other industries make chemicals, cement, cars, and trucks.

Two resources have helped North Korea build a strong industrial base. First, the country has a rich supply of minerals. Iron and coal as well as lead, zinc, gold, and graphite provide valuable raw materials for industry. Second, North Korea's rivers are used to create a large supply of electric power.

Agriculture accounts for about 20 percent of North Korea's GNP and employs about half of North Korea's workers. As in many other Asian countries, rice is the leading crop. Where rice cannot be grown, farmers raise wheat, corn, cotton, and tobacco. Farmland is owned by the government and divided into collectives. Each collective includes about 300 families who farm about 3,500 acres. Like farmers in China, North Korean farmers must deliver a certain amount of their production to the government. The farmers are paid in cash or in crops.

South Korea. Like North Korea, South Korea also has worked hard to build industries. South Korean industries produce chemicals, machinery, and metal. South Korea's economy, however, differs from that of North Korea. North Korea's per capita GNP is almost $450. South Korea's, however, is nearly $2,110. In addition, South Korea has developed service industries, which account for nearly 50 percent of South Korea's overall GNP. South Korea also places more emphasis on producing consumer goods than does North Korea. South Korea's economy has grown dramatically in recent years, and the country is now considered one of the world's developed nations.

A major difference between North Korea's and South Korea's economy stems from the two countries' political systems. Under North Korea's communist system, the government owns and operates the industries. Under South Korea's capitalist system, most industries are privately owned. Although its government has remained staunchly anticommunist, South Korea has been troubled by leaders who proclaimed military rule and bypassed the election process. Widespread protests in 1987 forced the government to hold the first election in 16 years in which the people chose their own president.

As in North Korea, agriculture in South Korea centers on rice. Farmers also raise barley, corn, millet, and soybeans. Farms in South Korea are privately owned and so are much smaller than North Korean collectives. Each farm covers a few acres. Most of South Korea's farmland stretches along the country's eastern and western coasts. About 30 percent of the South Korean labor force works in agriculture.

Mongolia has worked to build cities, industries, and agriculture.

Mongolia is a semiarid, landlocked country about four times the size of California. Mongolia fell under Chinese rule during the Manchu dynasty. In the 1920s, when Nationalists and

Communists were fighting each other for control of China, the Soviet Union helped the Mongolians form their own communist nation. Despite its ethnic and cultural ties with China, Mongolia has worked to develop its economy with much assistance from the Soviet Union.

The people of Mongolia have traditionally lived as nomadic herders on the country's vast grasslands. Livestock raising, in fact, is still Mongolia's chief economic activity. Fewer people than in the past live as nomads, however. About half of Mongolia's 2 million people live on livestock farms set up by the government. Each farm is owned cooperatively by the people who live there. Livestock herders raise camels, horses, cattle, sheep, and goats. Most of the animals are owned by the government, and a small number are privately owned. Communist party officials issue orders on the management of livestock. Mongolia has about 20 million animals, including more than 14 million sheep.

With the help of Soviet experts, Mongolians have begun to develop agriculture. An area in

Nomadic homes in Mongolia are tentlike dwellings called *yurts.*

north central Mongolia near the Soviet border is now a center for growing grain.

Mongolia's government is also working to build cities and industries. About half of all Mongolians live in urban areas. Towns and cities are scattered over the country's steppes and semideserts. The largest city is Ulaanbaatar [ü'län bä'tôr], which also is Mongolia's capital. Many of its high-rise buildings have been built in the last 20 years. Factories in Mongolia produce textiles, such as carpets, building materials, and processed foods. **Urbanization**, or the process of becoming urbanized, has changed the lives of the once nomadic Mongolians.

Industrialized Taiwan is home to the Chinese Nationalist government.

Lying in the South China Sea about 90 miles off China's coast is the island of Taiwan. Find Taiwan on the map on page 554. In 1949, when Chinese Communists succeeded in their effort to set up a communist government in China, about 2 million members of the Chinese Nationalist party fled to Taiwan. As you read earlier, the Communists and Nationalists in China fought each other for control of China. Once in Taiwan, the Nationalists set up the noncommunist Republic of China and claimed to be the legal government of mainland China as well as Taiwan. Meanwhile, the People's Republic of China made the same claim.

Most nations supported the Nationalists and recognized their government in Taiwan. In 1971, however, the United Nations admitted Communist China as a member and expelled Nationalist China. During the 1970s dozens of countries recognized the People's Republic of China as the sole legal government of the Chinese people. The United States ended diplomatic relations with Taiwan in 1978 and granted full recognition to the People's Republic in 1979.

More than 80 percent of the people in Taiwan live in the urban areas of their island's warm, fertile coastal plain. With much aid from the United States, the Taiwanese have built a strong, industrialized economy based on trade. Apart from some coal and hydroelectric power, few natural resources are found on the island. Thus Taiwan imports the raw materials it needs to produce manufactured goods. Taiwan's industries make textiles, electronic equipment, chemicals, plastics, and processed foods.

Eighty-five percent of the population of Taiwan are native Taiwanese. Taiwan, however, is officially considered by both Nationalists and Communists as a part of China. In the late 1980s, a native Taiwanese became president for the first time since the Nationalists took over the island. Taiwan's first native national leader succeeded the island's Nationalist president, who died in 1988.

Section 2 Review

Locating Key Places
Locate the following places on the map on page 554: North Korea, South Korea, Mongolia, Taiwan

Identifying Key Terms
Define the following terms: demilitarized zone, urbanization

Reviewing Main Ideas
1. How are the governments and economies of North Korea and South Korea different from one another?
2. What steps has Mongolia taken to build its economy?
3. How did Taiwan acquire its present form of government? What kind of economy does Taiwan have?

Thinking Critically: Analyze Comparisons
Compare North and South Korea using information in this section. Write a short paragraph that explains why the countries are different.

Japan

Key Places
Where are these places located?
1 Honshu
2 Tokyo
See the globe below.

Key Terms
What does this term mean?
shogun

Main Ideas
As you read, look for answers to these questions.
- How many main islands make up Japan?
- How did Japan change between the 17th and 20th centuries?
- What is the basis of Japan's economy?
- What are living standards like in Japan?

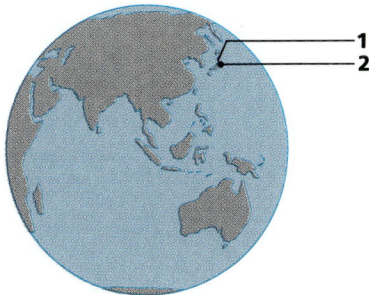

I passed by the beach
At Tago and saw
The snow falling, pure white
High on the peak of Fuji.

Yamabe No Akahito, 8th century

Japan has four main islands.

The poem you have just read tells about Mount Fuji, whose beautiful volcanic peak is a famous symbol of Japan. The poem's brevity also reflects the concerns with space that the Japanese have held throughout their history because of their island location.

Japan consists of four large islands and nearly 4,000 small islands that stretch in an arc reaching from the eastern tip of the Soviet Union almost as far south as Taiwan. Part of the Pacific Ring of Fire, the islands are mountainous, volcanic, and subject to earthquakes. Northernmost Japan has short summers and long, cold winters. The southernmost islands have subtropical conditions warm and moist enough for double cropping of rice.

The largest of Japan's four main islands is Honshu. More than 75 percent of Japan's 121 million people live on Honshu. Tokyo, Japan's capital and largest city, lies on Honshu's east coast. Also located on Honshu are most of Japan's major cities. The cities of Yokahama, Kobe, Osaka, and Nagoya are major metropolitan areas.

The much less densely populated island of Hokkaido [hō kī′dō] lies north of Honshu. Its farms produce dairy products, barley, corn, potatoes, and some rice. Hokkaido also has important coal reserves and extensive forests, a major source of timber for Japanese homes.

At its southern end, Honshu is bordered by a broad bay called the Inland Sea. To the south of the Inland Sea lies the island of Shikoku. Because Shikoku has no really good ports, small boats carry tea, tobacco, rice, camphor, fruits, and other products of Shikoku across the Inland Sea to Japan's large export harbors.

Japan's southernmost large island is Kyushu [kyü'shü]. Mountainous and forested, Kyushu also has several large cities and good ports. Kyushu's curved west coast is an important farming region. About 10 percent of all the people in Japan live on Kyushu, which ranks as Japan's most populated main island after Honshu.

Japan grew from an isolated nation to a leading world economy.

Geography has played a major role in Japanese history. Japan's island location allowed the Japanese to isolate themselves from the rest of the world in past times. Japan's nearness to China, however, resulted in many contacts between the Chinese and Japanese. During the 600s, for example, Japan sent a delegation to China to learn about Buddhism. In addition to Buddhism, the Japanese borrowed other things from China, including styles of architecture and methods of government.

More than 250 years of isolation began in the early 1600s when Japan entered a period known as the Tokugawa Shogunate [tō kū gä'wä shō'gun it]. **Shoguns** had ruled Japan since A.D. 1192 when the emperor named the first shogun, or supreme general, as absolute ruler of the entire country. The emperor then became a figure-

Mount Fuji, a famous landmark in Japan, is the country's highest mountain. It is located on the island of Honshu.

head. During the Tokugawa Shogunate a strong central government kept Japan shut off from contact with the outside world. Foreign trade was greatly reduced, and foreign missionaries were either expelled from the country or killed. The shoguns also executed Japanese who had become Christian converts. In this way, the Tokugawa shoguns erased the influence of Europeans who had come to Japan to spread Christianity and, with it, Western ideas.

Japanese isolation ended rather suddenly in the mid-1800s, however. During the 1850s warships from the United States sailed into a number of Japan's harbors. American representatives on board requested trading rights with Japan. Japan's leaders, recognizing that resistance to Western military power and technology would fail, agreed to trade with the United States and other Western powers.

The Meiji Era. By the early 1860s, Japan seemed on the verge of becoming just another European or American colony. New Japanese leadership, however, set Japan on a new course aimed at keeping the country independent. In 1868 a group of young revolutionaries overthrew the old rulers, who had kept Japan closed off from foreigners. The young reformers wanted to remake Japan along Western models. They said that if Europeans could make ships and trains and modern weapons, so could the Japanese. The modern reform movement begun in the late 1860s is known as Japan's Meiji [mā'jē] Era.

Reformers began to take steps to build Japan's economy. Japanese leaders sent people to Europe to study industry and technology and to learn how to build modern factories. Japan already had a huge labor force of workers. By the late 1800s, Japan was making light industrial products, such as textiles, that could compete on world markets.

Imperial Japan. At the beginning of the 20th century, Japan's industrial and military

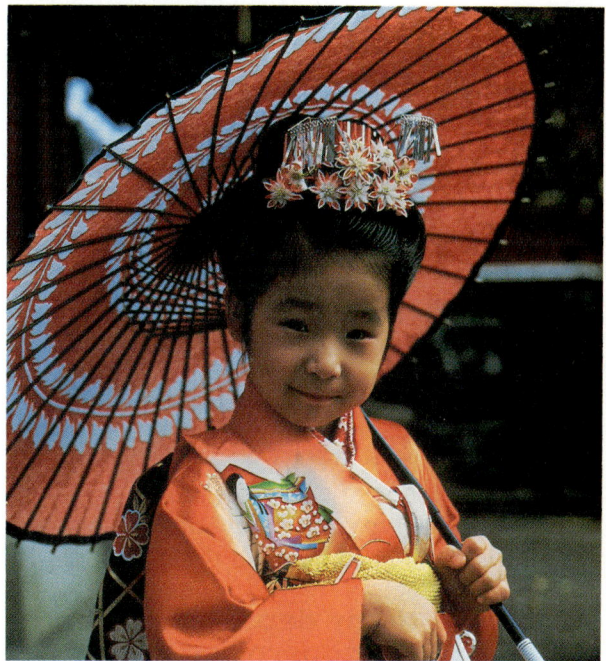

Traditional dress, worn mainly on ceremonial occasions, is an important aspect of Japanese culture.

might surpassed that of all its Asian neighbors. By 1910 the Japanese had seized and colonized the Ryukyu Islands to the south as well as Taiwan and Korea. In 1931 Japan invaded and occupied Manchuria, a northeastern province of China. Japan also invaded eastern coastal areas of China in 1937. When World War II began, Japan continued to expand its Asian empire by conquering territory in Southeast Asia.

In 1941 Japan attacked a U.S. naval base at Pearl Harbor, Hawaii, in an attempt to cripple American naval capability. This attack brought the United States into World War II. For four years Japan and the United States fought in the western Pacific. The Japanese finally surrendered in 1945 after the United States dropped two atomic bombs on Japan, one on Hiroshima and one on Nagasaki.

Postwar Japan. Japan's economy and most of its major cities were ruined after World War II. The United States kept troops and advisers in Japan long enough for the people to form a new, democratic government, with an emperor as a figurehead, and to begin to be able to feed and house their population. In 1951 Japan again became a fully self-governing nation.

The Japanese since World War II have opposed renewal of their military power. Instead the people have poured their energies into a massive economic effort. The United States emerged from World War II as the world's modern industrial leader. This time instead of going to Europe, Japanese went to the United States to gain knowledge of the latest technology. They also looked to the United States as the world's richest market open to them.

Japan's economy depends on trade, industry, and modernized farming.

Japan's economy now touches virtually all corners of the earth. State-of-the-art electronics, automobiles, cameras, watches, and countless other high-quality products made in Japan are in demand all over the world. Japan is the main exporter of foreign goods to the United States. In fact, people in the United States buy nearly half of Japan's exports. Japan's economic success has boosted the country's gross national product to third place. Only the United States and the Soviet Union have a higher GNP.

Trade with foreign nations is central to Japan's economy. Japan buys the iron ore, copper, coal, aluminum, and other minerals its industries need from other countries of the world. Australia, for example, sells many of its mineral exports to Japan. Since there are few known oil deposits in or near Japan, the Japanese must also import huge amounts of petroleum for fuel. Japan has built a fleet of huge tankers that carry oil from the Persian Gulf states to Japanese ports.

Manufacturing is one of Japan's most important economic activities. With its imported resources, Japan makes such export products as iron and steel, automobiles, ships, electronic equipment and computer parts. Japanese manufacturers sell some of these goods in Japan itself, of course, but most of these products are sold in the United States and other foreign countries. The money the foreign countries pay for Japanese goods in turn pays for more imported raw materials. Thus, Japan could not survive without large foreign markets.

Japan must also import food to feed its people as well as raw materials for its factories. Nearly 75 percent of Japan's land is too mountainous for farming, and when other areas also unsuited for crops are subtracted, there is not enough farmland left to feed all the people.

Even though Japan must import food, its own farms supply two-thirds of its food needs. Agricultural efficiency is another one of Japan's remarkable success stories. Japan uses 90 percent of its scarce farmlands for growing food crops. Farmers use modern machines adapted to the soils and sizes of their fields, apply fertilizers,

Computers are among Japan's
many high-technology products.

People view cherry blossoms near Tokyo. Cherry blossoms, which bloom only briefly, are a Japanese symbol of the brevity of life.

and practice double-cropping wherever possible. More than half of Japan's farmlands are irrigated, and careful terracing of slopes adds still more needed acreage. Japanese farmers' up-to-date methods make high crop yields possible. An acre of rice land in Japan produces three times more grain than an acre in India, for instance.

Rice is grown on more than half of Japan's farmland, but wheat, barley, and potatoes are also important crops. Meat is scarce and high priced, but fish is plentiful and reasonably affordable. Coastal and inland fishing, along with deep-sea fishing in the world's oceans, helps supply protein for Japanese diets.

Most Japanese enjoy a high standard of living.

About 75 percent of Japan's 121 million people live in urban areas. Most Japanese, whether urban or rural, enjoy a high standard of living that combines traditional and modern ways.

Life in Japan's urban areas. Use the map on page 554 to find Tokyo, Japan's capital. Tokyo is part of the world's largest megalopolis, which includes the cities of Yokohama and Osaka.

Urban life in Japan can be characterized by life in Tokyo. As in many of the world's large cities, high-rise buildings and skyscrapers dominate Tokyo's central business district. Most of the people who work in Tokyo commute to their jobs using trains, subways, cars, buses, and bicycles. City restaurants serve everything from Japanese cuisine to French pastry to American fast food. The people in Tokyo and in many other Japanese cities wear Western-style clothes. On ceremonial occasions, however, the Japanese typically wear traditional clothing.

Housing in Japan's urban areas includes modern apartments and small houses. A typical house is made of wood and has a tiled roof. Television sets, audio systems, and electric appliances can be found in most urban homes. Although traditionally the Japanese sit on the floor on cushions and sleep on the floor using quilts, the use of Western-style furniture has also become common.

Life in rural Japan. Farmers and workers in small factories make up most of Japan's rural population. Some rural Japanese also work along the coast as fishers. Rural homes are usually traditional. Television sets and cars are also common in rural Japan. Many families have two cars, just like American families.

Living with Japan's problems. Japan's high standard of living is not without problems. Rapid industrial growth has led to major air and water pollution that government regulations have reduced but not erased. Industrialization has also resulted in severe housing shortages, especially in large urban centers such as Tokyo. In recent years, an increased demand for homes in Tokyo has driven the prices of houses so high that most people cannot afford to own them. In the late 1980s houses in a suburb about 90 minutes from downtown Tokyo started at $1 million. Many people are forced to live far from central Tokyo in order to find an affordable home.

People, buildings, traffic, and signs fill a Tokyo landscape.

Section 3 Review

Locating Key Places
Locate the following places on the map on page 554: Honshu, Tokyo

Identifying Key Terms
Define the following term: shogun

Reviewing Main Ideas
1. Describe Japan's four main islands.
2. In what ways did Japan change in the mid-1800s? How did Japan change after World War II?
3. What activities are important to Japan's economy?
4. What are Japan's living standards like? What are some recent problems brought on by Japan's rapid industrialization?

Thinking Critically: Predict Effects
Suppose the United States decided to raise the taxes its citizens pay on such imported "luxury" goods as automobiles, cameras, and consumer electronic goods. How would this action affect Japan? How would it affect American consumers? What would the long-term effects probably be?

MAP LESSON

Using a Metropolitan Map

A metropolitan map shows a major city and its surroundings. Such a map is essential for navigating the urban landscape. If you live or work anywhere near or in a major city, you're certain from time to time to need a metropolitan map. If you ever visit a major city, either in this country or abroad, one of your first concerns will likely be where to find such a map.

Metropolitan maps vary in size and detail. Highly detailed maps often unfold to poster size. Other maps, like the one on this page, are smaller and show less detail. This map, for instance, focuses primarily on Tokyo. Surrounding cities appear as dots, although many like Yokohama are part of a huge metropolitan area. Most metropolitan maps, however, commonly show a city boundary, transportation routes, and such cultural features as parks and airports.

Uses for metropolitan maps are as varied as the maps themselves. Such maps are often used to find a highway route to a particular destination. Tourists in major cities usually use metropolitan maps to orient themselves. These maps often are available in different languages.

Review

1. Does Haneda Airport lie within Tokyo's city boundary?
2. What transportation routes link the Imperial Palace and Chiba?

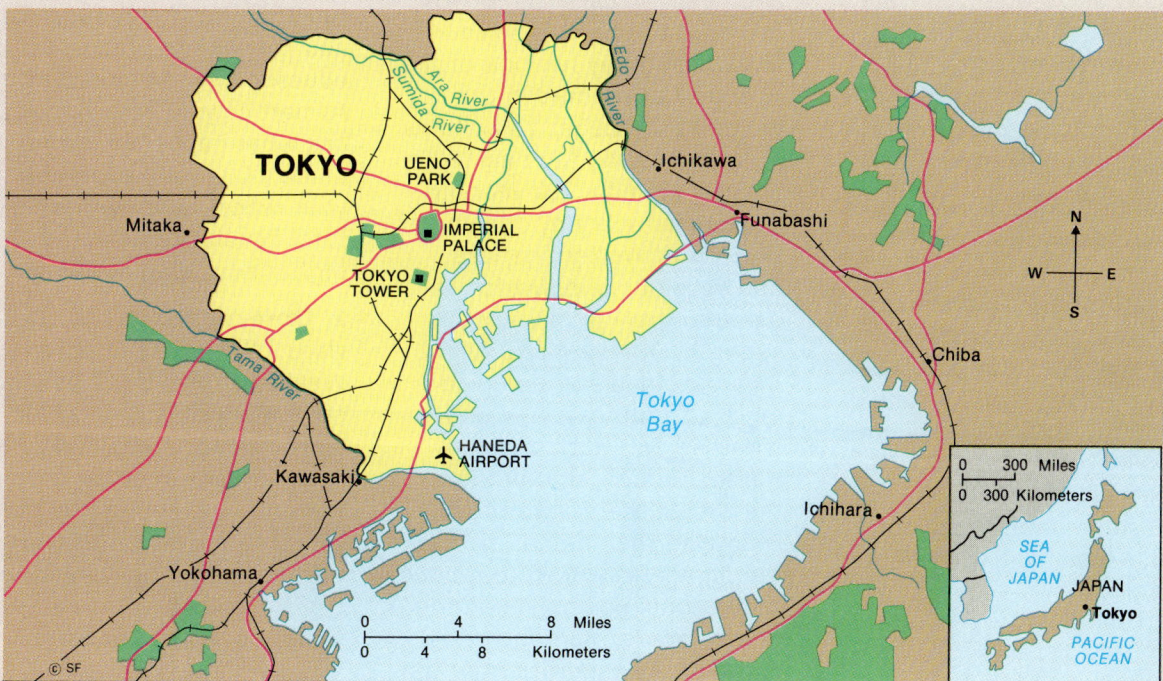

Tokyo, Japan

- Tokyo city boundary
- Highways and major streets
- Railroads
- Airport
- Points of interest
- Woods, parks, and gardens
- Other cities over 100,000

Review

Section Summaries

1. China Beginning in 1500 B.C., China was ruled by a series of dynasties in which emperors had the highest power. Dynastic rule ended in 1911 when the Chinese Nationalists overthrew the government. China became a communist nation in 1949 after the Nationalists were defeated by the Chinese Communist party. Communist rule changed China in many ways, some positive and some negative. Now agriculture, manufacturing, and other economic activities are directed by the government. In addition, virtually all aspects of private life are strongly affected by the government. Hong Kong, once Chinese territory and now a British colony, will be reclaimed by China in 1997.

2. North Korea, South Korea, Mongolia, and Taiwan Location and political systems distinguish these East Asian countries. North and South Korea occupy a peninsula extending from China's northeast. North Korea is governed by communists. South Korea's government, however, is anticommunist. North and South Korea have both worked hard to build their economies, although South Korea's economy has grown more rapidly than North Korea's. Mongolia is a landlocked country between the Soviet Union and China with a Soviet-aligned communist government. Taiwan is an island off China's southeastern coast. Taiwan's government was set up in 1949 by Chinese Nationalists who fled mainland China. Although Taiwan, like South Korea, is a highly industrialized country, Mongolia is just beginning to build industries and cities.

3. Japan Four large islands and nearly 4,000 small islands make up this East Asian country, which today has one of the strongest economies in the world. Japan began to build its economy during the mid-1800s when it ended a 250-year-old isolationist policy by opening trade with Western nations and developing industries. Japan also grew in military strength. During World War II, Japan invaded and occupied much of Southeast Asia and launched an attack on Pearl Harbor, Hawaii, that brought the United States into the war. Following their defeat in 1945, the Japanese worked to rebuild their economy, now reliant on foreign trade, manufacturing, and agricultural efficiency. As a result, most Japanese enjoy a high standard of living.

Using Geography Skills

Reviewing the Map Lesson

Refer to the map lesson on page 569 to answer the following questions.
1. What does a metropolitan map show?
2. What features are commonly shown on metropolitan maps?
3. How does the map show cities near Tokyo?
4. How many cities does the map show outside Tokyo?

Using Social Studies Skills

1. Locate and Gather Information. Do library research and prepare an oral report on education in communist China. As part of your research, find out what happened during China's Cultural Revolution. In your report tell how the Cultural Revolution affected higher education in China.

2. Observe for detail. Declare a "Japanese Import Weekend." For one weekend carry a pencil and notepad with you. Jot down every Japanese product that you use or see someone else using. Then compare your list with your classmates', noting similarities and differences. Write a brief summary of your findings.

Testing for Understanding

Locating Key Places
Match each description below with the name of the place.
1. a British colony
2. the largest of Japan's four main islands
3. a landlocked communist country north of China
4. Japan's capital
5. China's capital
6. an island governed by the Chinese Nationalists
7. a communist country that makes up the northern half of the Korean Peninsula
8. China's largest city
9. a noncommunist country whose capital is Seoul

a. Beijing
b. Shanghai
c. Hong Kong
d. North Korea
e. South Korea
f. Mongolia
g. Taiwan
h. Honshu
i. Tokyo

Recalling Key Terms
Define these key terms in your own words.

Section 1
dynasty
dynastic cycle
revolution
collective

Section 2
demilitarized zone
urbanization

Section 3
shogun

Reviewing Main Ideas
Section 1
1. Tell how China was ruled before 1911.
2. What changes did the communists bring to China?
3. What are China's major crops and industrial products?
4. In what ways has the Chinese government affected family life in China?

Section 2
1. How do the governments and economies of North and South Korea differ?
2. What has Mongolia done to build its economy?
3. Why is Taiwan's government run by Chinese Nationalists?

Section 3
1. Name and give the location of Japan's four main islands.
2. What steps did the Japanese take to rebuild their economy after World War II?
3. What are Japan's main economic activities?
4. What percentage of Japan's population lives in urban areas? How has rapid industrialization affected Japan's urban areas?

Thinking Critically
1. Predict Effects. For many centuries, the Japanese have eaten mainly rice, vegetables, and fish. Part of the reason is that Buddhist beliefs, strong in Japan, forbid the eating of meat. Since the 1950s, however, the Japanese people have been eating more meat and dairy products. What reasons can you give for this change in diet?

2. Make Hypotheses. Mongolia was ruled by China from the 1180s to 1911. When Chinese Nationalists overthrew the Manchu Dynasty in China, Mongolia began a struggle for independence with much encouragement from the Soviet Union. In 1942 Mongolian and Soviet communists established Mongolia as a communist nation. Today the Soviet Union keeps 60,000 troops along the Mongolian-Chinese border. Why do you think this is so?

CHAPTER 28

Southeast Asia

In this chapter you will read about the ten resource-rich countries of Southeast Asia.

Sections

The Mainland Countries of Southeast Asia

Preview

Key Places
Where are these places located?
1 Vietnam
2 Laos
3 Cambodia
See the globe below.

Key Terms
What does this term mean?
insurgent

Main Ideas
As you read, look for answers to these questions.
- What was the outcome of the war between North Vietnam and South Vietnam?
- What tragic events occurred in Cambodia during the 1970s and 1980s?
- What kind of government and economy does Laos have?
- What are Burma's religious and economic characteristics?
- What are Thailand's religious and economic characteristics?

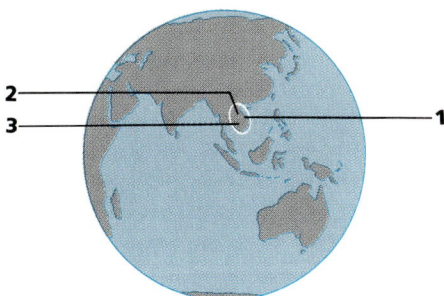

After all this agony of fighting—mostly for reasons they do not understand and for [political ideas] that make no village sense—the resilient, desperate, durable little peasants of South Vietnam dream only of peace. Peace for them means no longer losing sons, food, and savings to rival armies, a chance to grow and eat crops.

C. L. Sulzberger, American newspaper columnist writing from South Vietnam in 1965

Vietnam united under a communist government after years of warfare.
At the time Sulzberger wrote the words you have just read, North and South Vietnam were fighting a bitter war. Communist leaders of North Vietnam and South Vietnamese communists were trying to overthrow South Vietnam's noncommunist government. The United States took up the cause of the noncommunist South Vietnamese government in the 1960s. After some ten painful years of warfare, however, little if any progress had been made, and U.S. armed forces withdrew from Vietnam in 1973. In 1975, the South Vietnamese government fell, and all of Vietnam came under communist rule.

Like most Southeast Asian countries, Vietnam has a largely peasant agricultural economy with rice as the major crop. Vietnam's rice production centers on the flatlands of the Red River Valley in the north and on the broad Mekong River delta in the south. During the war, many peasants in the south left their fields and fled to Saigon, now called Ho Chi Minh City. Afterwards the communists tried to get the peasants to return to farming in order to relieve severe food shortages.

By the end of the 1980s, new communist leaders began to gain power in Vietnam. On a mod-

Facing page: Buddhist temples, this one in Thailand, are found throughout much of Southeast Asia. Buddhism is an important religion in Southeast Asia.

Southeast Asia

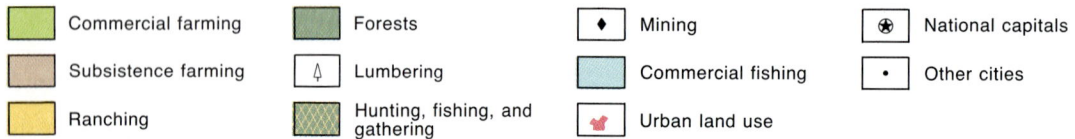

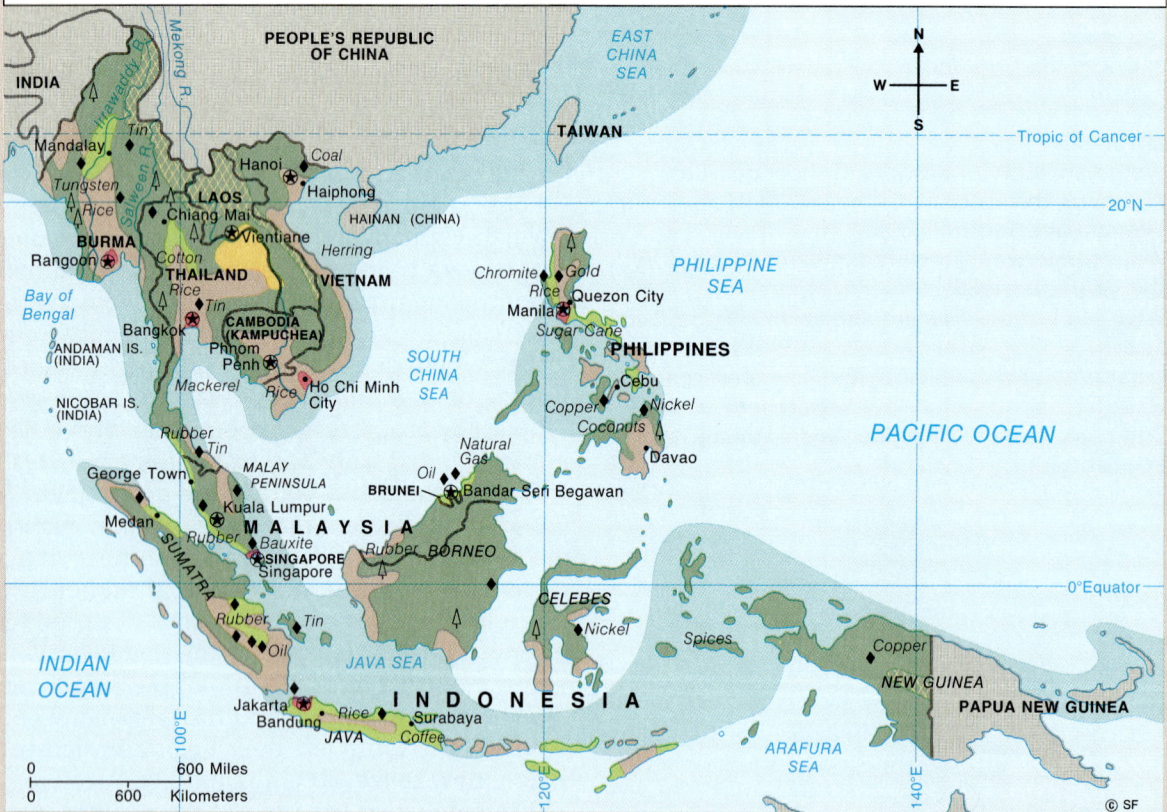

▢	Commercial farming	▢	Forests	◆	Mining	⊛	National capitals
▢	Subsistence farming	△	Lumbering	▢	Commercial fishing	•	Other cities
▢	Ranching	▢	Hunting, fishing, and gathering	🐦	Urban land use		

PEOPLE'S REPUBLIC OF CHINA

EAST CHINA SEA

INDIA

TAIWAN

Tropic of Cancer

Mandalay ◆

Tin

Hanoi •

Coal

HAINAN (CHINA)

20°N

Tungsten △

Rice

Haiphong

LAOS

Chiang Mai •

BURMA

Vientiane ⊛

Herring

PHILIPPINE SEA

Rangoon ⊛

Cotton

THAILAND

Rice

VIETNAM

Chromite ◆ Gold

Rice

Quezon City

Bay of Bengal

Bangkok ⊛

Tin

Manila ⊛

ANDAMAN IS. (INDIA)

CAMBODIA (KAMPUCHEA)

Phnom Penh ⊛

Sugar Cane

PHILIPPINES

Mackerel

Rice

Ho Chi Minh City

SOUTH CHINA SEA

Cebu •

NICOBAR IS. (INDIA)

Copper ◆

Coconuts

◆ Nickel

Rubber

Tin

Davao •

PACIFIC OCEAN

George Town •

MALAY PENINSULA

Natural Gas

Oil ◆

BRUNEI

Kuala Lumpur ⊛

Bandar Seri Begawan ⊛

Medan •

Rubber

Bauxite

MALAYSIA

Rubber

BORNEO

SINGAPORE ⊛

Singapore

SUMATRA

△

0°Equator

CELEBES

Rubber

Tin

◆ Nickel

Spices

Copper ◆

INDIAN OCEAN

Oil ◆

JAVA SEA

NEW GUINEA

Jakarta ⊛

I N D O N E S I A

PAPUA NEW GUINEA

Bandung •

Rice

Surabaya •

JAVA

Coffee

ARAFURA SEA

0 ——— 600 Miles
0 ——— 600 Kilometers

100°E *120°E* *140°E*

© SF

Map Study

Ten countries make up Southeast Asia. Five countries—Burma, Thailand, Laos, Cambodia, and Vietnam—lie between India and China. The rest of Southeast Asia is located mainly between the Indian and Pacific oceans. Which countries are located on archipelagos?

est level the new leaders introduced incentives to increase economic production. The new leaders also began permitting foreigners and Vietnamese people who had left to enter the country and invest in or manage factories.

Revolution destroyed Cambodia's social and economic order.

For many years after gaining independence from France in 1954, Cambodia was a peaceful, even tranquil agricultural country on part of the large fertile plain created by the Mekong River. Disaster befell Cambodia, however, during the Vietnam War. First, in 1970, the Cambodian army took over the government. Then in 1975 communist revolutionaries called the Khmer Rouge, meaning "Red Cambodians," assumed control. Bent on creating a new, peasant-based society, the Khmer Rouge drove the urban, westernized population into the countryside, even emptying hospitals into the streets. During the period of Khmer Rouge rule, between one and two million Cambodians died through starvation, disease, and murder.

In the late 1970s, Vietnam drove out the Khmer Rouge and stationed troops in Cambodia to make sure that Cambodian insurgents would not overthrow a new, Vietnamese-supported government. An **insurgent** is a person who rises in revolt. In the late 1980s, Cambodia was still reeling from more than a decade of terror. Vietnamese forces continued their occupation. Many Cambodian refugees had fled north into Thailand, where they lived in camps near the border. The economy was disrupted, and once self-sufficient Cambodia had to import food.

Communist Laos lags in development.

Laos is the only landlocked country in Southeast Asia. It is also the poorest. The country has a population of 4 million, 85 percent of whom live in the rural forested highlands. The country has no railroads, few paved roads, and very little industry. It does have mineral resources, however, in the form of tin, iron ore, copper, manganese, and gold deposits. The economy of Laos relies on agriculture. Rice is the major product, and farmers also grow corn, cotton, citrus fruits, and coffee.

France governed Laos as a colony between 1893 and 1949. In 1954 Laos became an independent country. Four years later civil war broke out as government forces and communist

Cyclists and pedestrians cross a central market in Ho Chi Minh City, Vietnam.

Thais in Bangkok leave the main train station.

troops fought for control of the country. The communists won, and in 1975 Laos became a communist country.

Burma is a Buddhist nation with an agricultural economy.

Anyone entering Burma's capital, Rangoon, is reminded that more than 85 percent of the nation's people are devout Buddhists. The huge Shwe Dagon [shwā′ də gän′], a Buddhist shrine built centuries ago, dominates the city.

Since 1962 Burma has been a socialist republic, most of the time under military rule. The government adopted a closed-door policy that restricted visits by foreigners. The government also took over industries and tried to make the country as self-sufficient as possible.

Burma can easily produce enough to feed itself on the fertile soils of the Irrawaddy and Salween river valleys. Burma's main crop is rice, much of which is exported. Other crops include sugar cane, cotton, and peanuts. Burma has valuable mineral resources such as copper and lead in its forested mountains.

Thailand is a Buddhist nation with a healthy economy.

The people of Thailand, a name that means "land of the free," are proud that their country managed to hold off European colonists, borrowed modern ways, and still preserved many family and other social traditions. Buddhism is Thailand's major religion. Ethnically about 75 percent of the people are Thais, living and farming mostly in the fertile plains along the Chao Phraya [chaú prī′ə] River. The remaining 25 percent include people from China, other Southeast Asian countries, India, and Europe. Officially Thailand is ruled by monarchs, but in practice a military government is in control.

Thailand enjoys a comparatively healthy economy. It exports huge amounts of rice, especially to Japan. Teak from northern forests, rubber from southern plantations, oil and natural gas from the Gulf of Thailand also bring in export income.

Section 1 Review

Locating Key Places
Locate the following places on the map on page 574: Vietnam, Laos, Cambodia

Identifying Key Terms
Define the following term: insurgent

Reviewing Main Ideas
1. How did Vietnam change after the Vietnam War?
2. What happened to the people and government of Cambodia during the 1970s?
3. Who governs Laos? Describe its economy.
4. Describe religious and economic life in Burma.
5. What is Thailand's major religion? What products does it sell?

Thinking Critically: Evaluate Sources of Information
Reread the quotation about Vietnam on page 573. How do you think the author felt about the effects of the Vietnam War?

Malaysia, Singapore, Brunei, the Philippines, and Indonesia

Preview

Key Places
Where are these places located?
1 Malay Peninsula
2 Borneo
3 Java
See the globe below.

Key Terms
What does this term mean?
bauxite

Main Ideas
As you read, look for answers to these questions.
- Where is Malaysia located?
- What kind of economy has Singapore developed since independence?
- Why is Brunei rich?
- What goals has the Philippines strived to reach?
- What are two important economic assets for Indonesia?

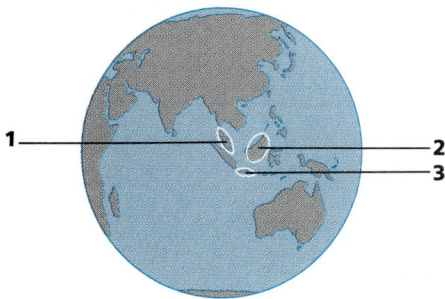

Singapore will give you an opportunity to see a state in transformation. For while in many tropical countries you can almost watch the grass grow, here you can watch the buildings grow. Hotels, apartments, offices, and shopping blocks spring up at an incredible rate. Even the island itself is growing—outward—as land is reclaimed from the sea on which to build multi-laned highways, parks, and new building developments.

Fodor's Southeast Asia

Malaysia is a prosperous nation on the Malay Peninsula and Borneo.

The words you have just read describe changes in Singapore, the smallest country in Southeast Asia. As in Singapore, many changes have taken place in Malaysia, Brunei [brü nī'], the Philippines, and Indonesia since these countries became independent.

Malaysia became an independent country in 1963. Before independence the country had been a colony under British rule. As you can see from the map on page 574, Malaysia's boundaries are somewhat unusual. Part of Malaysia lies on the southern end of the Malay Peninsula. Another part lies 500 miles to the east, on the island of Borneo in the South China Sea.

Malaysia has developed a healthy economy since becoming independent. Its farms do not produce quite enough to feed all the people, but exports earn the money to buy what is still needed. These exports include rubber, palm oil from coconuts, timber, and tin. Malaysia leads the world in producing natural rubber. In recent years Malaysians have also developed petroleum and iron ore deposits.

Malaysia has a richly mixed population of 16 million people. About 45 percent of all the people are Malays, making up the nation's largest ethnic group. The second largest ethnic group are the Chinese, who make up about 36 percent of the population. South Asians, mainly Indians, account for another 9 percent of the population. Chinese Malaysians work mostly in commerce, trade, and banking in Malaysia's cities. The Malays are traditionally farming villagers.

Religious preferences add further diversity. The Malays practice Islam, the country's majority religion, but the Chinese follow mainly Buddhist, Confucian, and Taoist beliefs. Most of the Indians are Hindus, and many people in Malaysia's portion of Borneo are animists.

The people of Malaysia are governed under a constitutional monarchy. A king serves as head of state and a prime minister serves as head of government. The prime minister carries out the laws made by Malaysia's parliament in the capital city of Kuala Lumpur [kwä′lə lüm′pur′].

Singapore has built an industrial economy since its independence.

Like Malaysia, Singapore also had been ruled by the British. Located at the tip of the Malay Peninsula, Singapore was a part of Malaysia between 1963 and 1965. In 1965, however, Singapore became a separate country. Governed as a parliamentary republic, Singapore has grown in economic strength since independence.

Thriving trade and industries have helped Singapore build its economy. When Singapore was under British rule, it was one of the world's busiest ports. Goods passing back and forth between East Asia and the West were transferred from ships stopping at Singapore. Singapore is still an important port, but since 1965 it has become a modern industrial area as well. Its people built oil refineries, chemical plants, shipbuilding operations, and many factories.

The people of Singapore enjoy the highest standard of living in Southeast Asia. Singapore has a population of 3 million people, most of whom live in the capital and only city, also called Singapore. Chinese make up about 80 percent of all the population. Most of the rest of the people are Malay, Indian, or European. The people of Singapore are governed under a parliamentary republic.

Oil makes the small Muslim nation of Brunei a rich country.

Brunei, a tiny country located along the northern coast of Borneo, is Southeast Asia's boom country. Until oil was discovered in Brunei in 1929, life moved according to old traditions. Today modern high-rise buildings tower over once sleepy villages. Brunei's rich oil reserves have been well developed and bring large export incomes.

Large buildings border a waterfront in Singapore's financial district.

578

Brunei has a very small population, only 220,000 people, half of whom have Chinese ethnic backgrounds. The majority of the people practice Islam, and a sultan heads the Muslim-styled government. Brunei became free of British control in 1984.

The Philippines has strived for democratic government and economic growth.

The Philippines consists of more than 7,000 islands stretching between the Philippines Sea and the South China Sea. Most of the islands are too small and mountainous to support many people. Thus nearly 95 percent of the Filipinos, as the inhabitants of the Philippines are called, live on about a dozen of the country's islands.

A wide, intensively farmed plain on the main island of Luzon is the heartland of the Philippines. Nearly 10 percent of the people live in or near Manila, the Philippines' capital and industrial center, located in southern Luzon.

Colonial heritage. Spain ruled the Philippines for 300 years before the United States took over in 1898. The Spaniards left a strong colonial imprint, including many converts to the Roman Catholic religion. The Spaniards also set up a system that gave large holdings of land to rich landlords and left poor peasants to tend the fields and commercial plantations. The Americans found it difficult to change this unbalanced situation. Even after the Philippines became an independent democracy in 1946 the gap between the few very rich people and the many poor remained wide.

Economic potential and political unrest. Today about half of all the Filipino workers farm on level plains and terraced hillsides. Farmers raise enough rice to feed everyone, but many people do not have balanced diets. Commercial plantations grow export crops of sugar cane, pineapples, coconut, and abaca, a plant that provides fiber used in making rope.

The Philippines has considerable potential for developing industries, which it must do to keep pace with its rapidly growing population. The islands contain deposits of iron ore, coal, copper, gold, and other minerals. For a long time, the gap between rich and poor, however, has held back development. Corrupt government leaders also discouraged social and economic progress.

In 1986 President Corazón Aquino [kō'rä sôn' ä kē'nō] took office. Her election came after several years of antigovernment protests and violence. She promised greater social democracy and economic reforms. Before moving ahead in these areas, however, she and her administration had to deal with much political unrest. Armed supporters of former government leaders, minority Muslim rebels, and a growing segment of communist insurgents all challenged the Aquino government.

Indonesia's size and natural resources are economic assets.

Indonesia scatters across some 13,000 islands, forming part of the largest archipelago on the earth. At 788,421 square miles, Indonesia covers more land than Mexico. Indonesia also has a dense population. Its island of Java is one of the world's most densely populated places. Close to two-thirds of Indonesia's 164 million people live on Java.

Economic riches. Mineral deposits on Indonesia's islands are some of the best in the world. Indonesia is a leading producer of tin and also sells large amounts of bauxite to other countries. **Bauxite** is a claylike mineral from which aluminum is obtained. Indonesia gets much revenue from its extensive oil and natural gas deposits in many places but especially off the eastern and southern coasts of Sumatra.

Two-thirds of Indonesia's workers are agricultural laborers, but some food imports are still needed. Java's rice paddies and terraced hillsides

Indonesian Hindus gather at a festival.

are intensively cultivated. Commercial plantations produce sugar cane, tea, coffee, coconut palm products, and rubber.

Less than 10 percent of Indonesia's workers as yet can find jobs in industry. Indonesia processes some of its own agricultural products and refines some mineral ores for export.

People and political contests. Most of Indonesia's people are Malays. There are also some sizable minorities of Chinese and Indians. For the past 500 years, most of the people have practiced the Muslim religion, but there are many strong reminders of earlier Buddhist and Hindu influence. The small island of Bali, just east of Java, for instance, has a solidly Hindu society with many colorful ceremonies and Hindu dances.

Indonesia went through some turbulent times after gaining independence from the Netherlands. In the early 1960s, communist insurgents almost gained control of the government. By 1967 an anticommunist government assumed power, but only after its soldiers had hunted down and killed more than 300,000 communists or people suspected of being communists.

"Unity in Diversity" is Indonesia's national motto. It seems to say that the country is determined to hold together. With its large territory and rich resources, Indonesia has the potential for being a leading country in the world.

Section 2 Review

Locating Key Places
Locate the following places on the map on page 574: Malay Peninsula, Borneo, Java

Identifying Key Terms
Define the following term: bauxite

Reviewing Main Ideas
1. Describe Malaysia's location in Southeast Asia.
2. What industries have helped strengthen Singapore's economy since 1965?
3. What drives Brunei's economy?
4. What social, political, and economic problems have the Philippines tried to correct?
5. Why might Indonesia play a leading role among Southeast Asian nations?

Thinking Critically: Analyze Comparisons
In a few sentences answer these two questions: How are the territories occupied by Malaysia and Indonesia alike? How are they different? What part does geography play in your comparison?

Using Maps to Understand Military History

In the early 1960s, the United States began to send American troops into South Vietnam. Our goal was to prevent the downfall of South Vietnam's government, which was under attack from communist-trained South Vietnamese rebels. These rebels, known as the Viet Cong, were supported by North Vietnam's communist government. The Viet Cong and North Vietnam sought to unite all of Vietnam under communist rule.

By 1968 more than half a million American soldiers were fighting in Vietnam, against both Viet Cong and North Vietnamese troops. Despite our involvement, the South Vietnamese government grew weaker. In 1969 the United States slowly began to withdraw troops, and in 1973 the last American ground troops left Vietnam after a cease-fire had been arranged. Two years later, in 1975, the South Vietnamese government in Saigon fell, and Vietnam became one country under communist rule.

Knowledge of the Vietnam War is important in understanding contemporary American history as well as recent Asian history. One way to reinforce knowledge of the Vietnam War is to use a map like the one on this page.

This map was drawn to accompany a written account of the Vietnam War. Like any map showing military action, it stresses location and movement. First, the map shows the location of North and South Vietnam. Second, it uses symbols to locate major battles and U.S. air bases. Third, the map uses red arrows to show movement—in this case, the movement of supplies from North Vietnam to South Vietnam along the Ho Chi Minh Trail. Location of battles and movement of troops and supplies are common features on all military maps.

CHINA

U.S. air raids
1966–1968, 1972

Hanoi

Haiphong

Gulf of Tonkin

Gulf of Tonkin incident
1964

LAOS

Vientiane

NORTH
VIETNAM

Mekong River

DEMILITARIZED ZONE (DMZ)

17th Parallel

Hue
Tet offensive 1968

THAILAND

Invasion
of Laos
1971

Ho Chi Minh Trail

Bangkok

CAMBODIA

Invasion
of Cambodia
1970

SOUTH
VIETNAM

Cam Ranh Bay

*Gulf of
Thailand*

Phnom Penh

Saigon
Tet offensive 1968
Fall of Saigon 1975

Mekong Delta

SOUTH CHINA
SEA

N
W   E
S

**The Vietnam
War, 1964–1975**

✳ Major battles

▲ U.S. air bases

0   75   150 MILES
0   75   150 KILOMETERS

Review

1. Through what two countries were supplies moved from North Vietnam into South Vietnam?
2. Describe the location of Saigon, where the South Vietnamese government fell in 1975.

Review

Section Summaries

1. The Mainland Countries of Southeast Asia
Vietnam, Cambodia, Laos, Burma, and Thailand all lie on Southeast Asia's mainland. Vietnam, Cambodia, and Laos came under communist governments after breaking free of French colonial rule and fighting internal conflicts. Burma, a former British colony, and Thailand, never colonized, are both Buddhist strongholds. Both countries are major rice producers and have valuable mineral resources.

2. Malaysia, Singapore, Brunei, the Philippines, and Indonesia
Island locations define many of these Southeast Asian countries. Malaysia, located on the Malay Peninsula and the island of Borneo, has a strong economy based on rubber, tin, and a variety of other exports. Singapore, at the tip of the Malay Peninsula, has built an economy based on industries. Brunei is located on the island of Borneo and has oil deposits that have made the country rich. The Philippines has progressed economically but has faced social and political unrest. Indonesia is a huge archipelago with valuable mineral resources.

Using Geography Skills

Reviewing the Map Lesson
Use the map on page 581 to answer the questions.

1. What symbol is used to show the movement of supplies from North Vietnam to South Vietnam?

2. What two countries share South Vietnam's western border?

3. In 1968 North Vietnam and the Viet Cong launched major attacks against South Vietnamese cities. The campaign began at the start of Tet, Vietnam's new year celebration. Especially hard hit were the cities of Saigon and Hue [hwā]. Describe Hue's location in South Vietnam.

Using Social Studies Skills

1. Sequence Historical Data and Information
The following statements about the Philippines appear in an incorrect order. Read each statement first. Then, on your paper, write the letter of each statement in the order in which it occurred.

a. Japan occupied the Philippines during World War II.

b. Following the Spanish-American War, Spain ceded the Philippines to the United States.

c. Spanish explorers established a Philippine settlement in 1565.

d. The United States granted full independence to the Philippines after World War II.

2. Perceive Cause-and-Effect Relationships.
A *cause* is a person, idea, or event that produces an effect. An *effect* is the result of an event, idea, or action. Listed below are two effects that have taken place in Vietnam since 1975 and two causes. For each effect, write the letter of its cause.

Effects

a. About one million South Vietnamese, mostly small business owners and their families, fled from Vietnam beginning in 1978.

b. Vietnam has relied heavily on financial aid from the Soviet Union.

Causes

c. Efforts by the communists to rebuild Vietnam's economy have met with little success.

d. Vietnam's communist government began nationalizing, or taking over, all businesses in Vietnam in 1978.

Testing for Understanding

Locating Key Places

Match the descriptions with the key places listed below.

1. a country taken over by the Khmer Rouge during the 1970s
2. the most densely populated island of Indonesia
3. the only landlocked country in Southeast Asia
4. a large island on which Brunei and portions of Indonesia and Malaysia lie
5. where part of Malaysia's territory is located
6. a country that shares its western border with Laos and Cambodia

a. Vietnam
b. Cambodia
c. Laos
d. Malay Peninsula
e. Borneo
f. Java

Recalling Key Terms

Define these terms in your own words.

Section 1
insurgent

Section 2
bauxite

Reviewing Main Ideas
Section 1

1. How did the Vietnam War change Vietnam?
2. What disorders did Cambodia suffer during the 1970s and 1980s?
3. What form of government does Laos have? Describe its economy.
4. What religion dominates Burma? How does Burma support itself?
5. Name Thailand's major religion and chief exports.

Section 2

1. On what lands does Malaysia lie?
2. What are some major industries developed by Singapore since 1965?
3. What is the basis of Brunei's economy?
4. What social, political, and economic problems have the Philippines worked to solve?
5. What are some of Indonesia's geographic and economic strengths?

Thinking Critically

1. **Analyze Comparisons.** In a brief paragraph, tell how Indonesia's experience with communist forces differed from that in the countries of Laos, Cambodia, and Vietnam.

2. **Make Hypotheses.** Write a statement or two that tells where Southeast Asians of Chinese ethnic background have settled and what kinds of economic activities they have practiced. Cite evidence from at least one Southeast Asian country to support your statement.

Review

Summarizing the Unit

Chapter 25   A Physical and Cultural Overview Major physical features of South, East, and Southeast Asia include such mountains as the Himalayas, which are the highest in the world. Plateaus and plains are also major landforms in South, East, and Southeast Asia. From north to south, climate regions include steppe, desert, highlands, humid subtropical, savanna, and tropical rainforest. Two of the world's earliest civilizations developed in South Asia and East Asia. Hinduism, Buddhism, and other important religions also developed there. Today the countries of this culture region have a variety of governments and economies.

Chapter 26   South Asia South Asia includes the countries of India, Pakistan, Bangladesh, Nepal, Bhutan, and Sri Lanka. India was governed under a series of empires until the mid-1700s. It became a British colony in 1857. The present-day countries of India, Pakistan, and Bangladesh were formed from British India. Today agriculture is a major economic activity in all three nations. Agriculture also is important in Nepal, Bhutan, and Sri Lanka. India has made rapid gains in industrial output. This huge nation is the world's largest democracy.

Chapter 27   East Asia East Asia includes China, North Korea, South Korea, Mongolia, Taiwan, and Japan. China is a communist nation whose economy is directed by the government. North Korea and Mongolia also have communist governments. North Korea's economy centers on industry. Mongolia has long depended on livestock raising, although the country is working to build industries. Both South Korea and Taiwan have anticommunist governments and industrialized economies. Japan, which has one of the strongest economies in the world, built economic strength through foreign trade, manufacturing, and agricultural efficiency.

Chapter 28   Southeast Asia The countries of Southeast Asia spead across the peninsulas and islands wedged between India and China. Vietnam, Laos, and Cambodia endured years of warfare before their present communist governments were in place. Burma, Thailand, and Malaysia have maintained stable governments and have prosperous economies built on rice and other agricultural products. Indonesia is a large island country that has developed its valuable mineral resources. The island nation of the Philippines has recently faced political unrest.

Using Writing Skills

So far you have practiced three steps in the writing process—prewriting, writing, and revising. The last and final step is presenting. In this step, you share or present your writing to an audience of one or more.

Activity. To master the presenting step, first divide into groups and choose a country you have studied in this unit. Then choose a topic about that country—such as its landforms or cultural traditions—on which to write a report. Be sure to follow the strategies you have learned for prewriting, writing, and revising. You might then divide your report into parts for each group member to write.

Finally, choose a way to present your work. Suppose your report is about foods people eat in China. Here are some ways to present such a report:
- Display your report on a bulletin board, using pictures and maps to show what people eat in different parts of China.
- Publish a magazine with a special issue on Chinese food.
- Send your report to a Chinese restaurant. Ask for recipes of dishes described in the report.
- Present your report as a television news broadcast.

Test

Key Terms (20 points)

Fill in each blank with the correct terms listed below.

1. The _____ is a seasonal wind that changes direction twice a year.

2. _____ is the complete overthrow of an established government or political system.

3. Plate tectonics formed the Indian _____.

4. A _____ is a large farm owned and operated by a large group of people.

5. Under _____, people are ruled by the military.

a. subcontinent
b. monsoon
c. martial law
d. collective
e. revolution

Main Ideas (30 points)

Choose the answer that best completes each sentence.

1. The Plateau of Tibet lies in
a. southern India.
b. Southeast Asia.
c. East Asia.
d. Indonesia.

2. Hinduism and Buddhism originated in
a. South Asia.
b. East Asia.
c. Southeast Asia.
d. Japan.

3. After gaining independence, India adopted
a. a socialist government.
b. a communist government.
c. an Islamic government.
d. a democratic government.

4. Mao Zedong was a leader in
a. India.
b. Japan.
c. China.
d. Taiwan.

5. Ships, automobiles, rice, and electronics equipment are products of
a. Mongolia.
b. Burma.
c. Laos.
d. Japan.

6. Sumatra, Java, and Borneo are names of Southeast Asian
a. religions.
b. islands.
c. ethnic groups.
d. cities.

Thinking Critically
(20 points)

1. Analyze Comparisons.
In what ways are the histories of Vietnam and Korea alike? In what ways do they differ? How does government and politics figure in your comparison?

2. Distinguish Fact from Opinion. Tell whether the following statements are facts or opinions. Then briefly explain how each fact might be proved.

a. Mongolia and Laos are landlocked countries.

b. China is the largest country in South, East, and Southeast Asia.

c. Hindu and Muslim leaders should have agreed to make British India one country instead of two.

d. The natural vegetation of most of Southeast Asia is rainforest.

Place Location (30 points)

Match the places below with the letters printed on the map.

1. Japan
2. Ganges River
3. Chang (Yangtze) River
4. Vietnam
5. Taiwan
6. Beijing

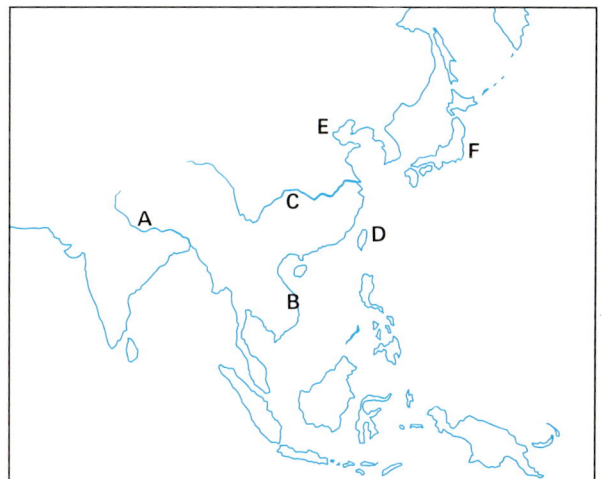

Australia and the Southern Realm

In this unit you will learn about the lands "Down Under".

Australia and New Zealand

In this chapter you will read about the physical and cultural landscape of Australia and New Zealand.

Sections

Landscapes, Climate, Soils, and Vegetation

Preview

Key Places
Where are these places located?
1 Great Dividing Range
2 Great Barrier Reef
3 Tasmania
   See the globe below.

Key Terms
What do these terms mean?
artesian well
barrier reef
marsupial

Main Ideas
As you read, look for answers to these questions.
● How have Australia and New Zealand's landscapes been shaped?
● What are Australia's main physical-geographic regions?
● What climate regions dominate Australia?
● What other climate regions cover parts of this geographic realm?
● What is responsible for Australia and New Zealand's unique wildlife?

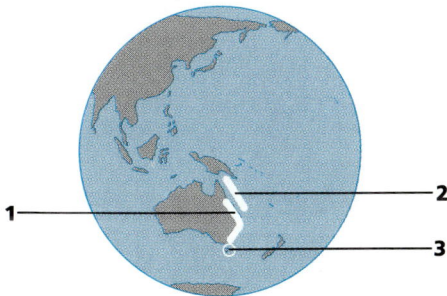

To my mind the exterior aspects and character of Australia are fascinating things to look at and think about, they are so strange, so weird, so new, so uncommonplace, such a startling and interesting contrast to the other sections of the planet.

Mark Twain, *Following the Equator*

Australia and New Zealand have been shaped differently.

As Mark Twain pointed out, Australia is a remarkable contrast to the rest of the planet, including its neighbor, New Zealand. For one thing, Australia is the only inhabited continent that lies entirely in the Southern Hemisphere. Both Australia and New Zealand lie southeast of Asia, between the Indian Ocean and the Pacific Ocean. Australia's northern coasts are washed by warm equatorial waters and draped by tropical forests. its southern shores face the cold Antarctic Ocean. Not far from Melbourne—the second largest city in Australia—thousands of penguins make their nests. Australia is truly a land of contrasts.

   The shaping of Australia. The continent of Australia is quite different from the surrounding regions. Although its neighbors in Southeast Asia are volatile parts of the Pacific Ring of Fire, Australia is quite stable. It was shaped primarily by weathering and erosion. It is a very old continent. The mountains along its eastern rim are as old as the Appalachians and are rounded and worn down. Australia was already an old landmass when it broke away from Gondwanaland.

Facing page: Skyscrapers rise behind the sail-like roofs of the Sydney Opera House in Sydney, Australia. *Page 586:* Trees and a cloud-streaked sky enliven an Australian desert.

589

Australia and Oceania
Physical—Political

Land Elevation

Feet	Meters
14,000	4,000
7,000	2,000
1,500	500
700	200
0	0
Below Sea Level	Below Sea Level

International boundaries

⊛ National capitals

• Other cities

▲ Mountain peaks

EASTER I. (CHILE)

PITCAIRN (U.K.)

Marquesas Is.

Tuamotu Archipelago

FRENCH POLYNESIA (FR.)

Society Is. Tahiti

Line Islands

COOK ISLANDS (N.Z.)

NIUE (N.Z.)

TOKELAU (N.Z.)

AMERICAN SAMOA (U.S.)

WESTERN SAMOA Apia ⊛

TONGA Nuku'alofa ⊛

K I R I B A T I

PACIFIC OCEAN

Hawaiian Is.

HAWAII (U.S.)

MIDWAY IS. (U.S.)

WAKE I. (U.S.)

MARSHALL ISLANDS

Majuro ⊛

Tarawa ⊛

NAURU Yaren ⊛

TUVALU Funafuti ⊛

WALLIS AND FUTUNA (U.K.)

FIJI Suva ⊛

Port- Vila

VANUATU

Loyalty Is. NEW CALEDONIA (FR.)

SOLOMON ISLANDS Honiara ⊛

Kolonia ⊛

FEDERATED STATES OF MICRONESIA

NORTHERN MARIANA ISLANDS (U.S.)

GUAM (U.S.)

Caroline Is.

Palau

TRUST TERRITORY OF THE PACIFIC ISLANDS (U.S.)

PHILIPPINE SEA

A S I A

Bismarck Archipelago

PAPUA NEW GUINEA

New Guinea Mt. Wilhelm ▲ 14,875 ft. (4,508 m)

Lae

Port Moresby

CORAL SEA

Great Barrier Reef

TIMOR SEA

Darwin

GREAT SANDY DESERT

GIBSON DESERT

GREAT VICTORIA DESERT

Great Australian Bight

AUSTRALIA

Alice Springs

Lake Eyre

GREAT ARTESIAN BASIN

GREAT DIVIDING RANGE

Murray

Brisbane

Newcastle

Sydney Canberra ⊛ Mt. Kosciusko ▲ 7,360 ft. (2,230 m)

Melbourne

Adelaide

Perth

TASMAN SEA

Tasmania Hobart

INDIAN OCEAN

NEW ZEALAND

Auckland

North Island

Wellington ⊛

South Island Christchurch

Mt. Cook 12,420 ft. ▲ (3,764 m)

CHATHAM IS. (N.Z.)

N E
W S

Equator

Tropic of Cancer

Tropic of Capricorn

30°N
15° North Latitude
15° South Latitude
30°S
45°S

120°W
135°W
150°W
165° West Longitude
180°
165° East Longitude
150°E
135°E
120°E

15°N
0°

0   500   1000 Miles
0   500   1000   Kilometers

© SF

The shaping of New Zealand. New Zealand lies east of Australia, more than a thousand miles across the Tasman Sea. New Zealand is an archipelago made up of two large islands and many small ones.

Plate tectonics have greatly affected New Zealand's landscape. New Zealand is part of the Pacific Ring of Fire. In fact, its two main islands, the North Island and the South Island, lie along a crustal plate boundary—on two separate plates that are moving in two different directions. In sharp contrast to Australia, New Zealand exhibits crustal instability. Earthquakes and volcanic activity rock the country from time to time.

Great active glaciers still carve the land in New Zealand. In the southwest, the island's coastline is fiorded. Glaciers cut deep valleys here, which were later flooded by the sea. This area is appropriately called "Fiordland," and it is one of the world's most spectacular landscapes.

Australia has four main physical-geographic regions.

Australia is divided into four major regions—the Great Dividing Range, Tasmania, the Central Lowlands, and the Western Plateau. The highest relief occurs in the east where the Great Dividing Range rises. Off the northeastern coast extends the Great Barrier Reef.

Great Dividing Range. From the Cape York Peninsula in the north to the state of Victoria in the south lies the Great Dividing Range. It is a series of weathered plateaus and mountain ranges whose highest point, Mount Kosciusko [kos′ē us′kō] in the south, is only 7,310 feet. The spectacular Australian Alps are the highest part of the Great Dividing Range.

Map Study

The map shows Oceania as well as Australia and New Zealand. Where are most Australian and New Zealand cities located?

Tasmania. Off the south coast of the mainland, across the Bass Strait, lies Australia's island state, Tasmania. This island is a piece of the Great Dividing Range, separated from the mainland by the strait but high enough to rise above the sea.

Central Lowlands. This region includes great grassland pastures and fertile river plains just west of the Great Dividing Range. In the southern lowlands lies the great Murray River and its tributary, the Darling. The 1,600-mile-long Murray River is sometimes called the Mississippi of Australia. The name comes from its early importance for trade and communication and because of the many paddle steamers that once moved up and down the river. The Murray River Basin receives its water from the western slopes of the Great Dividing Range.

Northward lies the Great Artesian Basin. Here surface water is less common. To supply water for their millions of cattle and sheep, ranchers depend on artesian wells. **Artesian wells** are deep-bored wells that bring underground water to the surface.

Western Plateau. This vast region occupies the entire western two-thirds of the continent. Here, millions of years of erosion have created a stark, beautiful landscape and have exposed Australia's most ancient rocks. In the interior of the Western Plateau lies famous Ayers Rock, the world's biggest rock, rising like an island above the surrounding flatlands. Much of this region is barren, with little soil. The rocks contain many minerals, so that the region has economic importance despite its emptiness.

Great Barrier Reef. Off Australia's northeastern coast is the Great Barrier Reef. When a rocky surface lies just below sea level along a tropical coast, small marine animals attach themselves to it. Their skeletons accumulate over many thousands of years, creating a coral reef. The water is so shallow that ships cannot cross the reefs, so the name **barrier reef** is used for many offshore coral reefs. The longest and largest of all the world's reefs is Australia's Great Barrier Reef. It extends for 1,250 miles along the coast. Crystal-clear waters, vivid colors, and abundant, varied marine life have made the Great Barrier Reef one of the world's greatest tourist attractions. People come from all over the world to explore its underwater treasures.

Australia's dry climate regions dominate the continent.

More than any other continent, even Africa, Australia is dominated by desert. More than one-third of the continent receives less than 10 inches of rain each year. At this latitude, the sun's rays are intense, so what little rain there is evaporates quickly. In the desert regions, the soil is generally poor. The interior of Australia is fairly productive, however, because the rocks of the desert contain valuable minerals.

The grasses of the steppe can support large herds of livestock, provided the animals do not stay in the same area too long. Tens of millions of sheep and cattle move across the "Outback," as this interior region of Australia is called. The use of the grazing lands is carefully controlled on vast ranches, called "stations."

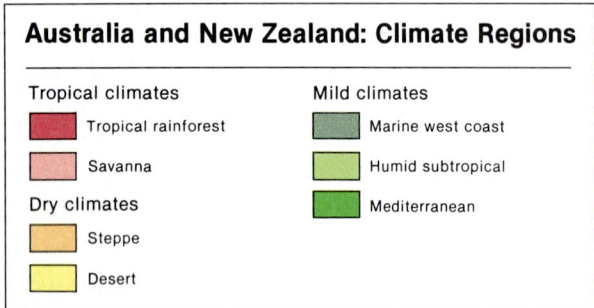

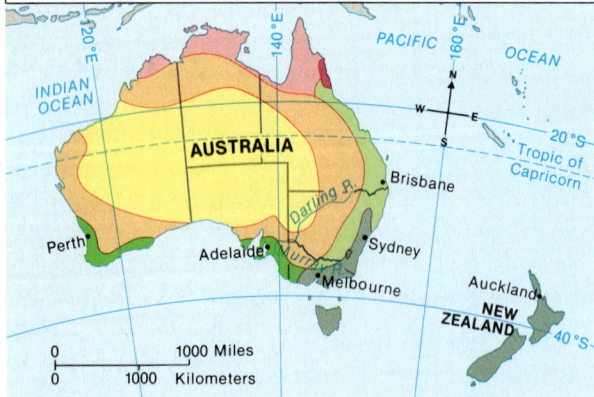

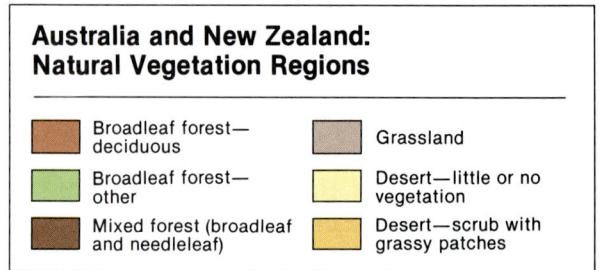

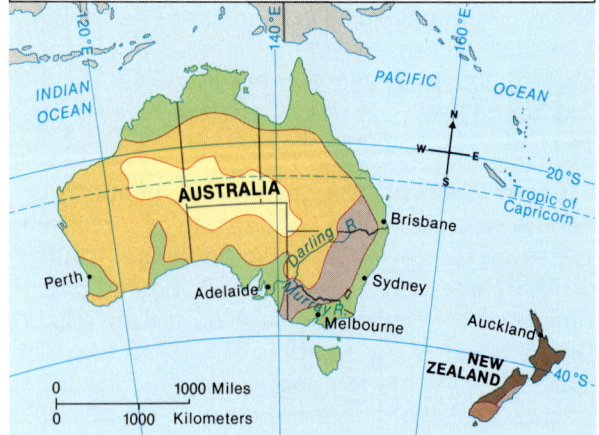

Australia and New Zealand: Climate Regions

Tropical climates
- Tropical rainforest
- Savanna

Dry climates
- Steppe
- Desert

Mild climates
- Marine west coast
- Humid subtropical
- Mediterranean

Australia and New Zealand: Natural Vegetation Regions

- Broadleaf forest— deciduous
- Broadleaf forest— other
- Mixed forest (broadleaf and needleleaf)
- Grassland
- Desert—little or no vegetation
- Desert—scrub with grassy patches

Map Study

Describe the climate and vegetation of central Australia. How does the climate and vegetation of northern Australia differ from that of southern Australia?

Tropical and mild climate regions cover parts of the realm.

Just as dry climates dominate Australia, mild climates prevail in New Zealand. In addition, mild climates cover the southern and southeastern coasts of Australia—where most people live.

Australia. As the map on page 592 shows, in northern Australia a tropical savanna region reigns. The climate here is affected both by southeast trade winds and monsoons. Northern Australia has two seasons, the "Dry" (winter) and the "Wet" (summer). The north coastal areas are not only moist but also very warm. The soils here are not very fertile. They are leached of nutrients like soils in other savanna climate areas in the world.

In eastern Australia, between the Great Dividing Range and the coast, cooler conditions prevail. Soils here are better, rainfall moderate, and farming more dependable than in the savanna.

Along part of Australia's south coast, the climate is comparable to that of the northwest coast of the United States. A marine west coast climate dominates Tasmania, as well as a strip of land along the southeast coast.

Continuing west along the coast, a Mediterranean climate region—with its hot, dry summers and mild, wet winters—appears. This climate occurs principally in two areas where specialized farming has developed.

Australia's vegetation reflects its climatic patterns. The "empty heart" of the country is encircled by the grasses and shrubs of the steppe. Along the coastal rim, where rainfall is higher, the vegetation is more dense and varied. Rainforest cloaks many peaks of the Great Dividing Range, especially in Queensland, but also in parts of Tasmania.

Elsewhere, the eucalyptus forest dominates. The eucalyptus is the "signature" tree of the Australian landscape. Three out of four trees in Australia are eucalyptus. The more than 700

Eucalyptus leaves are the main food of koalas.

species of eucalyptus range from the 300-foot karris and blue gums of the southern coast to the dwarf scrub of the interior.

New Zealand. On the two main islands of New Zealand, climates are generally moist and are classified as marine west coast. Because they are fairly small, the islands lie exposed to the westerly winds that prevail in these latitudes. In addition, New Zealand has high mountains. As a result, moist air coming off the ocean is pushed upward, causing much precipitation—especially

593

on the west-facing slopes. Areas east of the islands, to the mountains' leeward side (the side away from the wind), tend to be somewhat drier. In general, the North Island, being lower and flatter, is drier than the South Island.

The native vegetation of New Zealand consists of mixed evergreen forest covering about two-thirds of the country. Because of New Zealand's isolated location, plant species developed here that are unknown to the rest of the world. Today dense "bush" remains only in areas unsuitable for settlement and in parks and reserves.

Isolation is responsible for the realm's unique wildlife.

The wildlife of Australia and New Zealand is of special interest. In Australia there are about 240 species of mammals native to the continent, more than half of which are marsupials. **Marsupials** are animals that carry their young in pouches. The most common of these is the kangaroo, an animal capable of hopping at speeds of up to 40 miles per hour. Koalas, wom-

bats, and Tasmanian devils are other Australian marsupials.

Australia is also the home of the world's only primitive, egg-laying mammals—the duck-billed platypus and the echidna, which is also known as the spiny anteater. New Zealand has unique wildlife as well. The islands are home to the kiwi, an unusual flightless bird, and many other rare species of plants and animals. One New Zealand native, now extinct, was the moa, a huge ostrichlike bird.

Scientists believe that Australia and New Zealand's unique animal life resulted from the continent's lengthy period of isolation after the breakup of the supercontinent of Gondwana-land. Although marsupials all but disappeared on other landmasses, Australia's marsupials were free to develop unrestricted by competition from other groups of mammals.

Section 1 Review

Locating Key Places
Locate the following places on the map on page 590: Great Dividing Range, Great Barrier Reef, Tasmania

Identifying Key Terms
Define the following terms:
artesian well, barrier reef, marsupial

Reviewing Main Ideas
1. How has the land of Australia and New Zealand been shaped?
2. Describe Australia's four main physical-geographic regions.
3. What climate regions cover most of Australia?
4. Describe Australia and New Zealand's mild climate regions.
5. Why is Australia and New Zealand's wildlife unique?

Thinking Critically: Predict Effects
If the factors that formed the landscapes of Australia and New Zealand continue to operate, what long-term effects could we expect for the two countries?

A baby kangaroo, called a *joey*, naps in its mother's pouch.

The People of Australia and New Zealand

Preview

Key Places
Where are these places located?
1 Sydney
2 Melbourne
3 Auckland
   See the globe below.

Key Terms
What does this term mean?
Aborigine

Main Ideas
As you read, look for answers to these questions.
- Who were the first people in Australia and New Zealand?
- How were Australia and New Zealand later populated?
- Where do most Australians and New Zealanders live?
- How do most Australians and New Zealanders make a living?

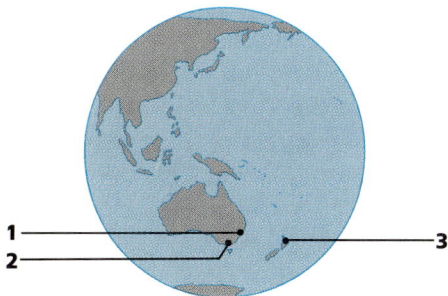

Australian history is almost always picturesque; indeed, it is so curious and strange, that it is itself the chiefest novelty the country has to offer. It is full of surprises, and adventures, and incongruities, and contradictions, and incredibilities; but they are all true, they all happened.

Mark Twain, *Following the Equator*

The first inhabitants were Aborigines and Maori.
Today both Australia and New Zealand have primarily European populations. In the past, however, their populations were quite different.

Australia. The first people to live in Australia—called **Aborigines**—arrived about 40,000 years ago. A second wave of Aborigine settlers arrived 25,000 to 30,000 years ago. Scientists think these people may have come to the continent by way of a temporary land bridge from New Guinea during glacial times. This second wave were the ancestors of today's Aborigines.

When European settlers first arrived during the late 1700s, there were probably 300,000 Aborigines in all of Australia. Most lived in small groups because water was scarce and food was limited. They built no permanent villages and subsisted on hunting and gathering.

In some parts of Australia, however, aboriginal groups were freer to expand. The most complex aboriginal culture was found in the far north. Here the Aborigines had had centuries of contact with Chinese, Malay, Indonesian, and Macassan sailors, traders, and fishers.

New Zealand. In New Zealand, the Maori, a Polynesian people, were the first settlers. They are believed to have arrived on the islands around A.D. 900, preceding Europeans by about 900 years. When European seafarers first saw New Zealand during the 1600s and 1700s, there may have been more than 200,000 Maori, most of them living on the North Island. They built fortified villages with large, wooden houses and

Traditional wood carvings decorate this Maori meeting house.

public places. They farmed the land, hunted the wildlife, and were skilled canoeists.

The lands were later populated by convicts and immigrants.

Although Dutch explorers were the first to visit Australia in 1606, the British were the first to found permanent settlements on the continent that had once been known as Terra Australis Incognita, or Unknown South Land. The British were the first Europeans to settle in New Zealand as well. Today both countries remain primarily European.

Australia's convict heritage. In 1788 several boatloads of exiled British prisoners, along with a small company of marines and their families, arrived where Sydney now stands. Some of the prisoners were put into penal camps, but most were assigned to work on farms or public works projects where living conditions were wretched.

Word of Australia's possibilities—especially concerning the discovery of gold in 1851—sailed back to Britain, and the flow of free settlers increased. By 1859, as in the United States, the British had established six colonies in Australia, covering the entire continent. Gradually the British granted these colonies the rights of self-government. In 1901 they united to form the Commonwealth of Australia—now a federation of six states and two territories. The Australians retained the British monarch as the official head of state but elect a prime minister and parliament to actually run the country. In addition, English was made the official language.

Later immigration. Australia's penal origins are now a distant memory. For a long period, the country, fearing an Asian invasion, limited immigration to "Europeans with the needed skills." This "White Australia" policy received much criticism and was changed in 1966. Today non-Europeans can and do apply for immigrant status. In particular, many Asian immigrants have settled in Australia in recent years. The country has also been a haven for political refugees.

As a result of these long-term policies, the population of Australia is remarkably homogeneous. About 80 percent of the population of 16 million originally came from the British Isles. Most of the remaining Australians are Europeans—coming from Italy, Greece, Germany, Yugoslavia, and other nations—or Asians. Aborigines now make up about 1 percent of the population.

New Zealand. In New Zealand, too, the mainly English settlers struggled to overcome native opposition. When they arrived about 1840, the Europeans met with skilled Maori warriors. The Maori fought hard, but they lost ground steadily in the face of European numbers, firepower, and diseases.

Recently, the position of the Maori has begun to improve. Although some are poor and separated from the mainstream culture, many have become partners in the new society. Dame Kiri Te Kanawa, a Maori, is now one of the most famous opera singers in the world. Today there are about 300,000 Maori in New Zealand, which has a population of 3 million.

Most Australians and New Zealanders live in cities and towns.

In both of these countries, most people live in urban areas—89 percent in Australia and 85 percent in New Zealand. In Australia most of the cities and towns are located on the southeastern coast. (See the map below.) In New Zealand the population is more spread out.

Australia. Like the United States, Australia has a fairly short history of urban development.

It is, however, one of the most urbanized countries in the world—with almost 90 percent of the population living in cities.

Two cities, Sydney and Melbourne, are the largest. Sydney, with about 3.6 million people, is the capital of the state of New South Wales and the oldest and largest Australian city. Melbourne, the capital of Victoria, has a population of about 3.4 million. In many ways Melbourne has the appearance of a British city. Because of past rivalries between these two leading cities, a third city, Canberra, replaced Melbourne as the federal capital in 1927.

New Zealand. Like Australia, most of New Zealand's population lives in cities near a coast. Most people live on the North Island, which has a milder climate, more suitable land for farming, and more industrial development than the South Island. The country's largest city is Auck-

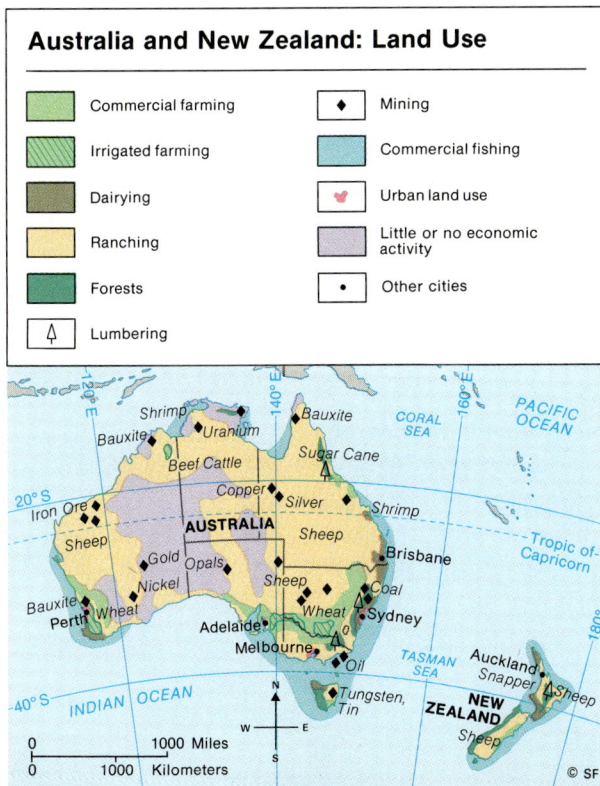

Australia and New Zealand: Land Use

Commercial farming	Mining
Irrigated farming	Commercial fishing
Dairying	Urban land use
Ranching	Little or no economic activity
Forests	Other cities
Lumbering	

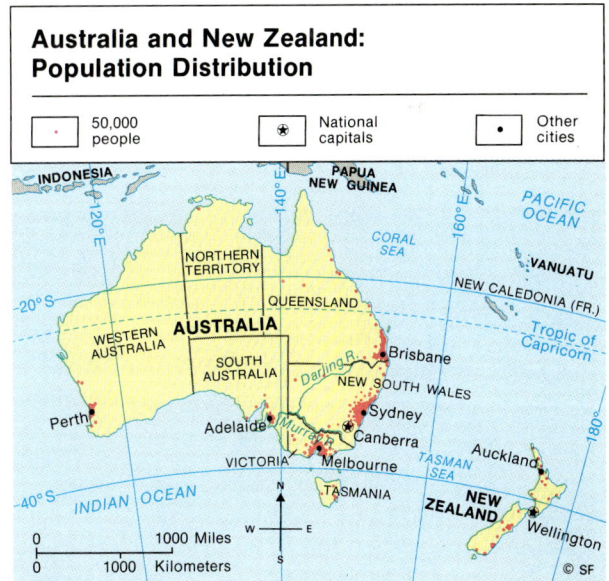

Australia and New Zealand: Population Distribution

50,000 people	National capitals	Other cities

Map Study

Compare New Zealand's population distribution with Australia's. What similar land uses do you find?

597

land, a northern port city and industrial hub with about 860,000 people. Another North Island city, Wellington, is the nation's capital with a population of about 340,000.

New Zealand, like Australia, is a former British colony that has retained ties to Britain. It is a constitutional monarchy in which the British monarch reigns with little real power. The government is run by an elected prime minister and parliament, and an appointed Cabinet.

Over the years New Zealand has formed a society in which equal rights and benefits are valued. It became the first nation—in 1893—to give women the vote, and has strong social security and public health programs.

Most people work in farming, mining, or manufacturing.

Both Australia and New Zealand have strong economies that are heavily based on products taken from or raised on the land. The raising of sheep, for example, is an important industry in both countries, with sheep outnumbering Australians by ten to one. Wool from the sheep is a profitable export for both countries.

Australia. Although sheep raising was the first large-scale venture in Australia, the country's largest source of export income is now from minerals. Australia is rich in mineral resources—including coal, iron ore, bauxite, and uranium. Farming and ranching are important industries as well, with much of the product being shipped out as export. As a result, Australia has quickly become one of the richest, most developed countries in the world.

New Zealand. The rich New Zealand land serves as the basis of the country's economy. Farming, forestry, fishing, and foreign trade make up the major industries. The country's mild climate and fertile soil allow for strong farm production. As a result, New Zealand exports wool, meat, timber, and dairy products to places around the globe.

Section 2 Review

Locating Key Places
Locate the following places on the map on page 590: Sydney, Melbourne, Auckland

Identifying Key Terms
Define the following term: Aborigine

Reviewing Main Ideas
1. How were Australia and New Zealand first settled?
2. Who were the later groups of people to arrive? From what countries did they come?
3. In Australia and New Zealand, where do most people live?
4. In what industries do most Australians and New Zealanders work? What products do they export?

Thinking Critically: Recognize Values
Based on what you have read in this section, what are some of the things that many Australians value?

Ranchers in Australia shear a sheep to remove its wool, or fleece.

Reading Ocean Floor Maps

More than 70 percent of the earth's surface is covered by water. How could you picture this vast area on a map? In the last few decades, explorations have been going on to map the ocean floor.

Although the mapping is not yet complete, it is now possible to get a general impression of what the bottom of the ocean looks like. The map below presents a view of one part of the ocean floor.

The earth's seabed is just as varied and interesting as the surface above the water. Note the vast plains, shallow basins, deep trenches (subduction zones), and islands that peek up above the ocean surface. In fact, the deepest point on earth—36,198 feet below sea level—lies south of Guam (a U.S. territory) in the Mariana Trench.

Note as well the region between Australia and New Guinea. Scientists believe that in the past this area was used as a land bridge by ancient peoples, including the Aborigines.

Review

1. Which trench on the map is farthest east?
2. Name three basins.

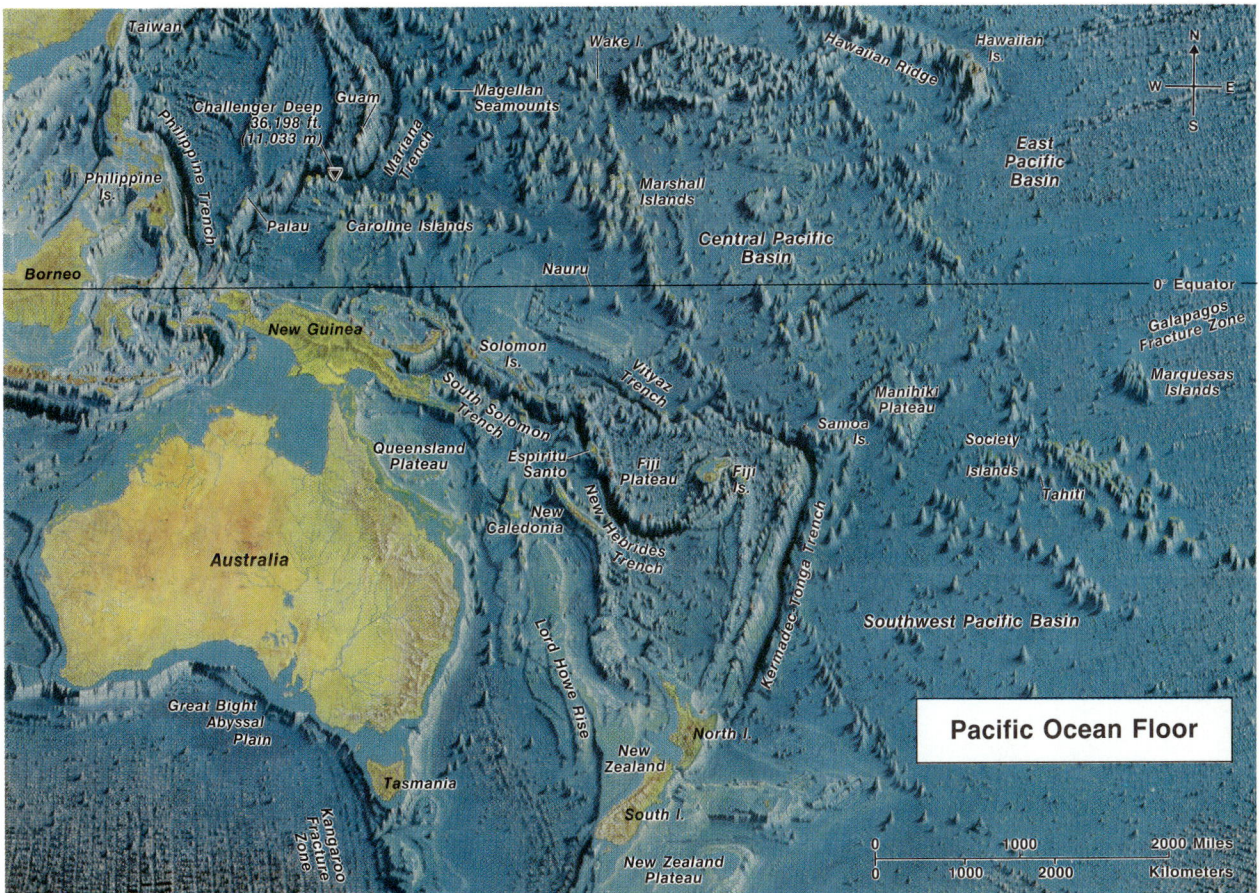

Pacific Ocean Floor

Review

Section Summaries

1. Landscapes, Climate, Soils, and Vegetation.
The landforms of Australia and New Zealand were shaped differently—those in Australia by weathering and erosion, and those in New Zealand by plate and glacier movement. Australia is dominated by dry climates since much of the continent is a desert. All of New Zealand and the southeastern coast of Australia are different since they enjoy mild climates. The isolation of Australia and New Zealand has allowed the development of unique species of wildlife, including marsupials, egg-laying mammals, and flightless birds.

2. The People of Australia and New Zealand.
Both Australia and New Zealand were primarily populated by immigrants. The very first migrants to the area were Aborigines and Maori. Later, Europeans—mainly British—came in large numbers. Today most Australians and New Zealanders live in cities and towns. This urban population is concentrated in Australia on the southeastern coast, and in New Zealand on North Island. Both countries though independent have maintained close ties with Britain. The economies of Australia and New Zealand rely mainly on primary industries—farming, ranching, and mining—and manufacturing.

Using Geography Skills

Reviewing the Map Lesson
Use the ocean floor map on page 599 to answer the following questions.
1. What are some of the landforms found on the bottom of the ocean?
2. What ocean floor features lie between the Solomon Islands and Australia?
3. What ocean floor feature is east of the Philippine Islands?

Using Social Studies Skills

1. Draw Conclusions. Compare the climate map and the vegetation map on page 592, and the population distribution map on page 597. Why do you think most Australians live where they do?

2. See Others' Points of View. The Australian Aborigines and New Zealand Maoris have had experiences similar to those of our Native Americans. Research the past and present conditions of either the Aborigines or the Maori. Find out how they have fared when faced with modern development and how they feel about their current situation.

Testing for Understanding

Locating Key Places
Match each description below with the name of the place.
1. an island state of Australia
2. a landform made of coral
3. the largest city in Australia
4. a large landform that splits Australia
5. the second largest city in Australia
6. the largest city in New Zealand
a. Great Dividing Range
b. Great Barrier Reef
c. Tasmania
d. Sydney
e. Melbourne
f. Auckland

Recalling Key Terms
Define these terms in your own words.

Section 1
artesian well
barrier reef
marsupial

Section 2
Aborigine

Reviewing Main Ideas
Section 1
1. What has shaped the landforms of Australia and New Zealand?
2. What are Australia's five main geographic regions?
3. Which climate region dominates Australia?
4. Where are the mild and tropical climate regions?
5. What has caused the realm's wildlife to be unique?

Section 2
1. Who were the first settlers of these two countries?
2. Who were the next groups to settle the land? From where did these later settlers come?
3. In which regions do most Australians and New Zealanders live?
4. How do most Australians and New Zealanders make a living, and what products do they export?

Thinking Critically
1. Analyze Comparisons. Australia has often been compared to the United States. Both have had a frontier image and both enjoy many open spaces. In what ways is the western and northern "frontier" of Australia like, and different from, the western "frontier" of the United States of the 1800s?

2. Evaluate Sources of Information. This chapter's map lesson introduced the mapping that is currently being done on the ocean floor. In what ways might an accurate map of the ocean floor be useful to you or to scientists?

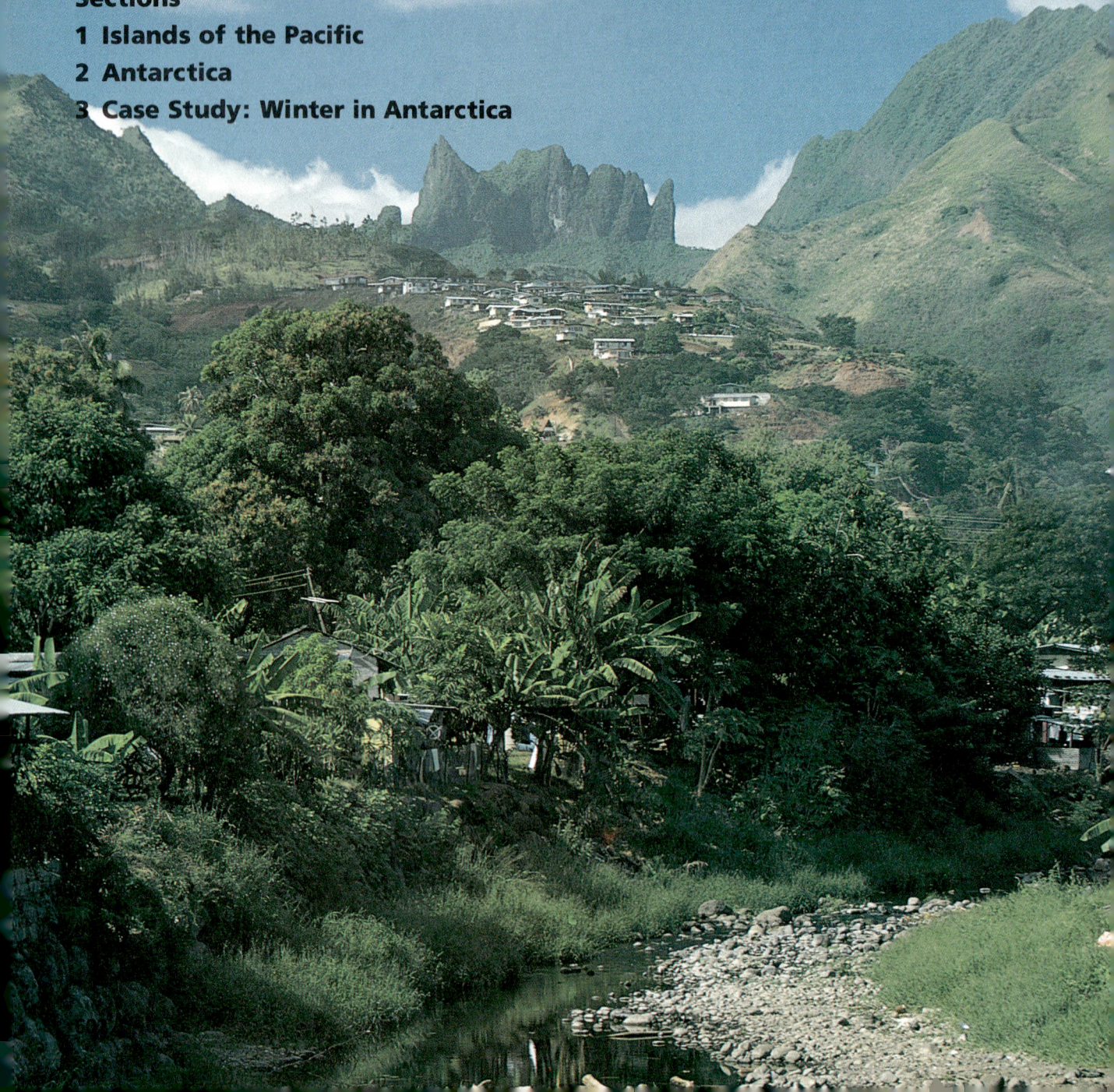

CHAPTER 30

The Southern Realm

In this chapter you will read about the Pacific Islands and the "Frozen Continent."

Sections

1 Islands of the Pacific

2 Antarctica

3 Case Study: Winter in Antarctica

Islands of the Pacific

Preview

Key Places
Where are these places located?
1 Melanesia
2 Polynesia
3 Micronesia
See the globe below.

Key Terms
What does this term mean?
atoll

Main Ideas
As you read, look for answers to these questions.
- How many types of islands are there in the Pacific?
- How do the cultures and economies of the three Pacific regions differ?

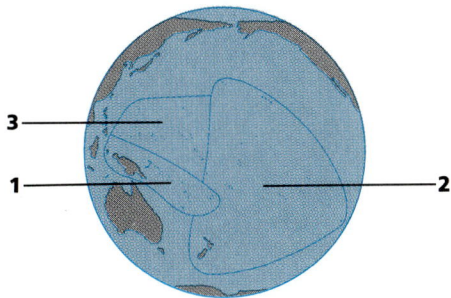

I wish I could tell you about the South Pacific. The way it actually was. The endless ocean. The infinite specks of coral we called islands. Coconut palms nodding gracefully toward the ocean. Reefs upon which waves broke into spray, and inner lagoons, lovely beyond description. I wish I could tell you about the sweating jungle, the full moon rising behind volcanoes, and the waiting.

James Michener, *Tales of the South Pacific*

Two types of islands, volcanic and coral, lie in the Pacific.

Michener's "endless ocean," the Pacific, is larger than all the landmasses combined. It covers one third of the entire planet, and extends from the Arctic to Antarctica. Its waters range from frigid polar to warm equatorial. Great currents move these waters constantly, driven by winds upon which seafarers have always depended.

Most of the islands in the Pacific are small, but as a group, called Oceania [ō'shē an'ē ə], they are quite significant. Many geographers number the islands of Oceania at around 10,000, though the number depends upon one's definition of an island. Some geographers include in the count any rocks that stand above the waves, which doubles this number to more than 20,000. If you were to fly over the ocean, you would soon recognize that these islands are of two distinct types—volcanic and coral.

Volcanic islands. These islands are tall and mountainous, rising high above the water. The volcanoes from which they are formed actually stand on the ocean floor, with their tips sometimes rising thousands of feet above the ocean's surface. On Hawaii, one of the larger Pacific

Facing page: Like many volcanic islands in the Pacific, Tahiti is characterized by lush vegetation and steep terrain.

603

islands, two volcanoes stand more than 13,600 feet high and are frequently blanketed by snow.

When the trade winds, coming off the warm ocean, rise against these volcanic slopes, much rain falls. This moisture, and the fertile volcanic soils, support dense vegetation. As you fly over the islands, you can distinguish the direction of the prevailing wind by the types of vegetation. The windward sides of the islands are densely forested and green, and the leeward sides, away from the wind, are much drier.

Coral islands. Many Pacific islands are **atolls**, which are flat islands, usually ring-shaped, that just barely rise above the surface of the ocean. They are often ringed by a pale, submerged shelf. These islands are made of living coral that forms in the ring of submerged volcanoes. Coral islands tend to be drier than

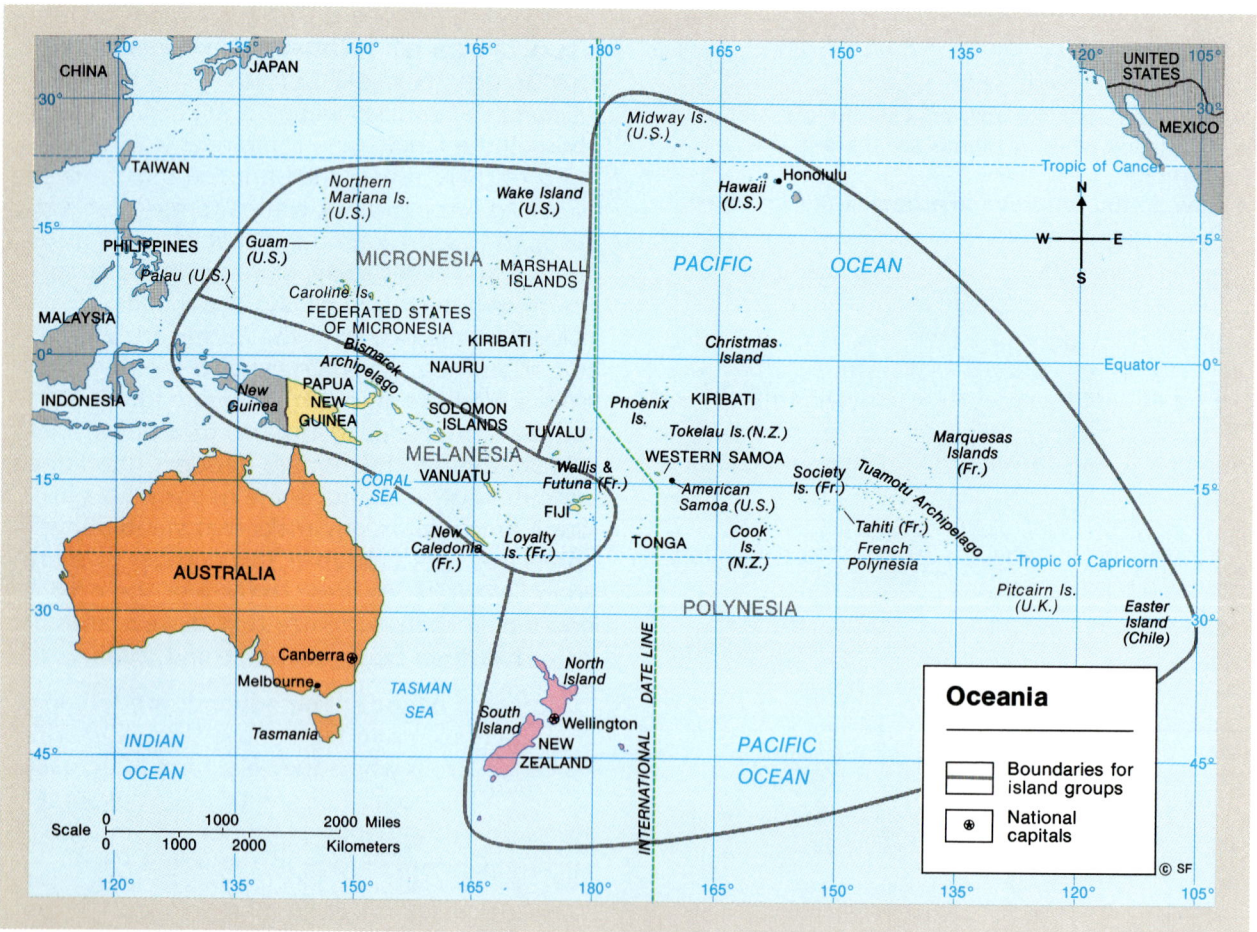

Map Study

The Pacific Islands are divided into three geographic regions: Melanesia, Micronesia, and Polynesia. How are these regional boundaries shown? Which region is largest?

volcanic ones. Their soils are generally poor, unable to support much vegetation.

The three Pacific regions differ tremendously.

Although the Pacific realm consists of thousands of scattered islands, three geographic regions are recognized. These regions—Melanesia, Polynesia, and Micronesia—are based on the distribution of the peoples and cultures of the Pacific. Within each region are varied cultures and governments, all of which have been influenced by colonial rule.

Melanesia. The islands of the Pacific were first populated by people from Asia. The earliest of these people, the Melanesians, may have reached the islands as long as 50,000 years ago. The Melanesian islands include New Guinea, just north of Australia, and the islands extending southeastward from there. The Melanesian peoples are distinguished by their dark complexions. "Mela" is Greek for "black," and "nesia" comes from the Greek word for "islands."

New Guinea, the largest island in the Pacific, has rugged, forested mountains, deep valleys, and swampy coastal lowlands. Most of its 6 million inhabitants live in small, isolated villages, between which communication is poor. There are few roads on which to travel. More importantly, because there are more than 700 different languages spoken on New Guinea, people have difficulty speaking to one another.

After a period of colonial rule by the Netherlands, the western half of the island now belongs to Indonesia and is called Irian Jaya, or West Irian. The eastern half, now called Papua New Guinea, became an independent country in 1975.

Many other groups of Melanesian islands have recently gained their independence from colonial powers, including the Solomon Islands, Vanuatu [vä'nü ä'tü] (formerly called the New Hebrides Islands), and Fiji. Fiji and the Solomons had been held by the British, and Vanuatu by joint British and French rule.

The economic strength of these island groups varies. Fiji, which has a mixed Melanesian, Polynesian, and Indian population of 700,000, has a decent economy based on tourism, sugar cane, and light industry. Vanuatu and New Caledonia both have important mineral deposits.

Polynesia. After the Melanesians, the next people to migrate from Asia settled on many different islands, thus their name "poly" for "many." Polynesia is the largest region of the Pacific realm, extending all the way from the Hawaiian Islands to New Zealand and Easter Island. (See the map on page 604.)

There is more cultural unity among the islands of Polynesia than in Melanesia. Early Polynesians sailed the Pacific waters in huge double canoes, guided by maps made of bamboo sticks and shells. They traded with faraway islands and settled newly discovered lands. In this way Polynesian culture traveled from island to island.

Today Polynesia includes many different political units. One group of islands, Hawaii, is one of our 50 states. Other islands are dependencies of various foreign countries. For example, American Samoa is a dependency of the United States, Easter Island of Chile, and French Polynesia of France. New Zealand, Western Samoa, Tuvalu [tü vä'lü], and Tonga are independent. Tonga, an archipelago of 170 islands and 107,000 people, has the Pacific's only surviving monarchy.

Most Polynesians live in Hawaii or New Zealand. The other countries combined have less than 170,000 people.

Many of the Polynesian islands, including Tahiti in French Polynesia, are known for their appeal to tourists in search of scenic beauty and sunny beaches. Other spots, such as Pago Pago [päng'ō päng'ō] in American Samoa, are known for their excellent ports. Industry in the islands consists of fishing, tourism, and the cultivation of bananas, pineapples, and coconuts.

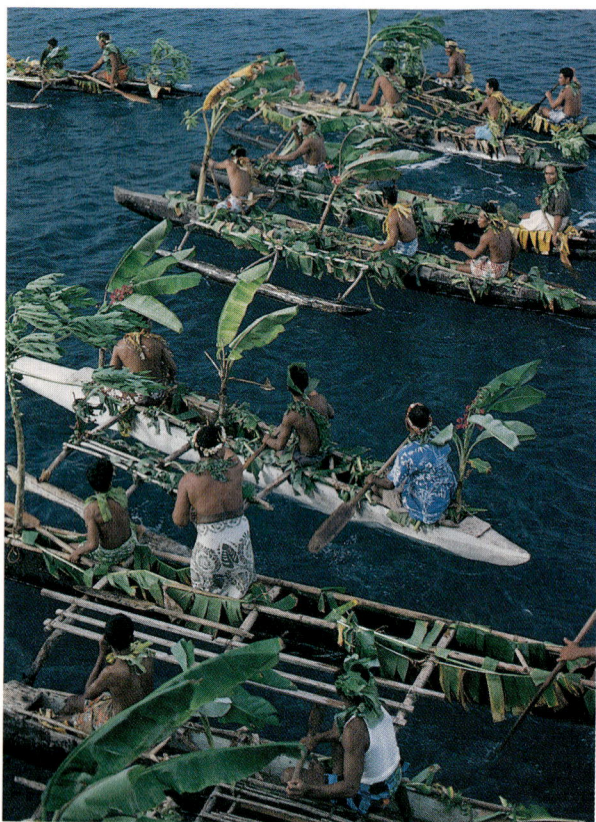

A floating welcome committee in Tuvalu awaits an incoming ship.

Micronesia. After the Melanesians and Polynesians, the last Asian people to settle on Pacific islands were the Micronesians. The Micronesian region lies north of Melanesia and west of Polynesia. The regional name of Micronesia refers to the small size of each of the islands.

Much of Micronesia is closely associated with the United States. Almost half of all Micronesians live on Guam in the Mariana Islands. Guam is a U.S. territory, with 115,000 people, that houses a large American military base. Guam became a U.S. territory in 1898, after the Spanish-American War. Much of Micronesia became part of the U.S. Trust Territory of the Pacific after World War II. During that war, the Pacific islands were badly damaged in the fighting between Japan and the United States.

In taking responsibility for this region, the United States asked the people of the islands to decide their political futures. The Northern Mariana Islands elected to become a commonwealth of the United States. The Marshall Islands, the Federated States of Micronesia, and Palau [pä lou'] chose to become independent republics. These countries continue to receive assistance from the United States.

Two former British dependencies, Kiribati [kir'ə bäs] and Nauru [nä ü'rü], have also recently become independent. Kiribati, with 68,000 people, is mainly a cluster of 16 small coral islands, formerly known as the Gilberts, in southeastern Micronesia. However, the country extends eastward along the Equator almost 2,000 miles to include 17 other tiny islands. Nauru, a country of 8,000, has rich phosphate deposits, that make it the wealthiest Pacific island.

Section 1 Review

Locating Key Places
Locate the following places on the map on page 604: Polynesia, Micronesia, Melanesia

Identifying Key Terms
Define the following term: atoll

Reviewing Main Ideas
1. Describe the two types of islands found in the Pacific.
2. How do the regions of Melanesia, Polynesia, and Micronesia differ?

Thinking Critically: Make Hypotheses
Why do you think that the United States, France, and other countries are interested in maintaining close ties with these tiny Pacific islands?

Antarctica

See the globe below.

Preview

Key Places
Where are these places located?
1 Ross Ice Shelf
2 Transantarctic Mountains
See the globe below.

Key Terms
What do these terms mean?
ice shelf
pack ice

Main Ideas
As you read, look for answers to these questions.
- How does Antarctica compare with the Arctic?
- What is Antarctica called?
- How are Antarctica's landforms divided?

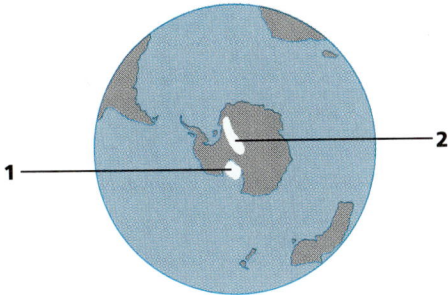

The Clowds near the horizon were of a perfect Snow whiteness and were difficult to be distinguished from the Ice hills whose lofty summits reached the Clowds. The outer or Northern edge of this im nence Ice field was composed of loose or broken ice so close packed together that nothing could enter it; about a Mile in began the firm ice, in one compact solid boddy and seemed to increase in heights as you traced it to the South; In this field we counted Ninety Seven Ice Hills or Mountains, many of them vastly large.

Captain James Cook, *Journals II,* January 1774 (original spelling and capitalization retained)

Antarctica is far different from the Arctic.

As described in his journal, the English explorer Captain Cook and his crew were the first recorded humans to cross the Antarctic Circle, entering a world of "cold so intense as hardly to be endured." Since then, many explorers and scientists have traveled to this frigid continent. In fact, Antarctica is a region where the political geography is just beginning to be established. It is the earth's last frontier.

Although Antarctica means "opposite to the Arctic," the two polar regions do have some characteristics in common. They are both intensely cold, with howling winds that drive blinding snow. During the winter months, the sun fails to rise above the horizon, and all is dark. In contrast, during the summer months, Antarctica experiences days of 24-hour light.

The differences, however, between the northern and southern polar regions are significant. The Arctic is a frozen ocean surrounded by sparsely populated land, but Antarctica is a continent—the fifth largest—almost completely covered with ice, surrounded by water, and with no permanent population. In addition, Antarctica is far colder than the Arctic, with temperatures ranging as low as 126 degrees below zero, the world's lowest recorded temperature.

Antarctica is often called the "Frozen Continent."

More than 95 percent of Antarctica is covered by a huge ice sheet. This great continental ice sheet contains about 7 million cubic miles of ice, representing 90 percent of the world's ice. The ice is shaped like a giant dome, thickest in the middle of the continent, where it is as much as

two miles thick, and thinner near the edges. Antarctica has been called the "Frozen Continent" because of its icy landscapes and climate.

Ice floats in water. As a result, when the Antarctic ice sheet reaches the edge of the continent, it settles on the water and creates a unique "landform" called an **ice shelf**. There are two huge ice shelves and several smaller ones in Antarctica. The largest, the Ross Ice Shelf, is named after an early British explorer named James Clark Ross. The ice on this ice shelf measures about 4,000 feet thick near the south-

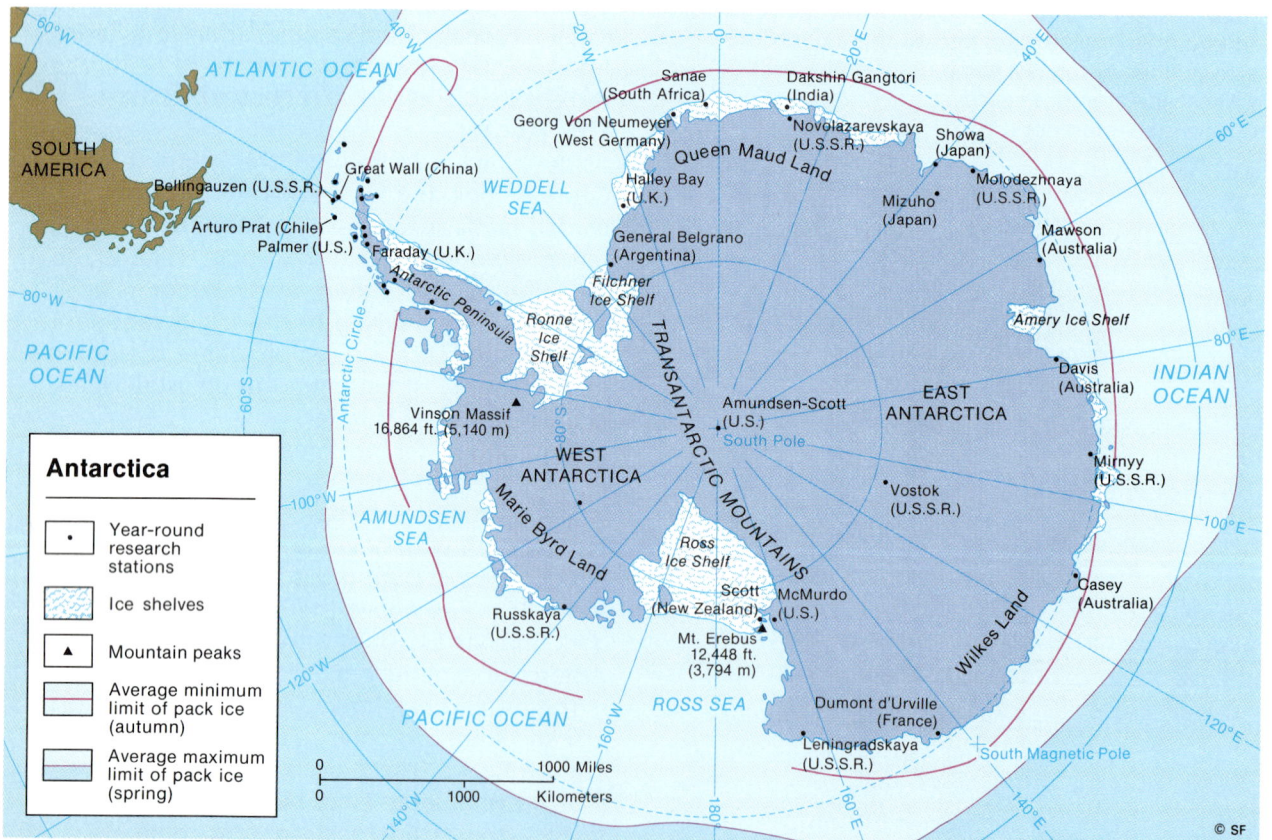

Map Study

Which is larger, West Antarctica or East Antarctica? Which countries have research stations on the Ross Ice Shelf? Which station is located at the South Pole?

A party of penguins and a seal greet an Antarctic diver.

which extends northward toward South America. Some geographers believe that the Antarctic Pensinsula is a continuation of the Andes Mountains.

Antarctica, with an average height of 7,000 to 8,000 feet, is the world's highest continent. Asia, the next highest, averages only about 3,000 feet. Only a tiny portion of Antarctica is exposed rock. Tall mountains, including some active volcanoes, stand out above the ice.

Antarctica affects life and landforms all over the planet. Annual variations in the amount of precipitation in Antarctica are reflected in global weather variations. The frozen continent serves as an important test site for climate researchers. Many scientists are also using Antarctica as a research laboratory to find out how the ozone layer of the earth may be affected by such chemical substances as fluorocarbons.

of the continent. Toward the sea, it thins to about 600 feet.

Ice shelves move slightly as they are "fed" from the land side and lose pieces to the seaward side. The pieces that break off and float away are icebergs. The ice shelves are stable enough, however, to maintain research stations and associated facilities.

Because snow is continually falling in the interior, the great dome of ice and its ice shelves keep slowly spreading outward. At the edge of the ice sheet and its shelves, large pieces of ice break off, then crowd together. The resulting mass of ice chunks is called **pack ice**, a ring of which surrounds Antarctica and makes shipping both dangerous and difficult.

Antarctica has two main regions.

Physical geographers have concluded that, under the ice, Antarctica is divided into two main regions, West Antarctica and East Antarctica. These regions are separated by the 1,900 mile-long chain of the Transantarctic Mountains. East Antarctica is believed to have been attached to Africa and Australia as part of Gondwanaland. West Antarctica includes the Antarctic Peninsula,

Section 2 Review

Locating Key Places
Locate the following places on the map on page 608: Ross Ice Shelf, Transantarctic Mountains

Identifying Key Terms
Define the following terms: ice shelf, pack ice

Reviewing Main Ideas
1. In what ways does Antarctica compare with the Arctic?
2. Why is Antarctica sometimes called the "Frozen Continent"?
3. Describe the different regions and landforms of Antarctica.

Thinking Critically: Assess Cause and Effect
In this section Antarctica was compared to its opposite polar region, the Arctic. Refer to the world population distribution map on page 83 to verify that many more people live nearer to the Arctic than to Antarctica. Name several major population centers that lie north of 40°N. Name any that lie south of 40°S. What can you conclude?

609

Case Study: Winter in Antarctica

Preview

Key Places
Where is this place located?
1 Antarctic Peninsula
   See the globe below.

Key Terms
What do these terms mean?
ctenophore
krill
diatom

Main Ideas
As you read, look for answers to these questions:
- What was the mission of the scientists who went to Antarctica?
- Why are krill important?
- Why was fishing exciting to the scientists?
- What did the voyage of the *Polar Duke* achieve?

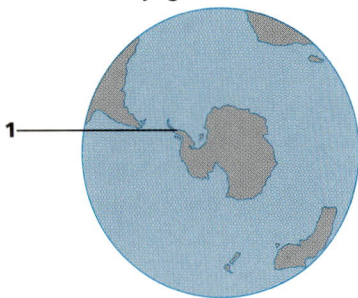

1

The following case study comes from the article, "A new ship tests the rigor of winter in the Antarctic," from the Smithsonian *magazine, November, 1986. This case study describes the voyage of the* Polar Duke *in Antarctic waters, as experienced by one of the participants of the voyage. After you read this case study, compare your previous perceptions of Antarctica with your new knowledge.*

The mission was to explore Antarctic marine life in winter.

The big red ship turned into the full force of the Antarctic winter. It was like walking into a fist. Books and charts flew and crashed. The ship heaved up and down, and buried its prow in a vast gray wave. The wind took the shards of water and threw them, at 65 knots, straight at the bridge [knots are nautical miles per hour]. The flying water caught the shine of the searchlights and flung it against the windows, flooding the pilothouse with noise and light.

The water drained away in foam. But on masts, superstructure, winches, bits, rails and all unheated windows some remained, turned to crystal by the cold, adding another layer to the ship's burden of ice.

Time and dates were never important on this journey, a winter voyage across the Antarctic Circle. The degrees and minutes written on the gray screen of the satellite navigation system, not the clock, would record the success or failure of everyone's mission: to take the detailed and intricate observation of marine science into the virtually unknown winter of Antarctica.

Scientists have spent winters in Antarctica since 1898, when the ship *Belgica* was stuck in the ice for a year, but most have been restricted to icebound bases. This was one of the first times ever that a research vessel had intentionally steamed into the sea ice in this daunting season.

Icebergs are a common sight and an ever-present danger for polar voyages.

"The scientific merit of this trip is primarily the season," said Donald Siniff, a noted mammalogist from the University of Minnesota who had sent three scientists on the trip to study seals. "It is also the opportunity to work with other teams, which allows us to get an ecosystem-peek at things." For the National Science Foundation's Division of Polar Programs, it was a chance to see just how capable its new ship [the *Polar Duke*] really was.

The least scientific pursuit on the ship was weather prediction. The captain and the barometer were seldom right about what was coming. The day he thought it would blow, the air and sea remained utterly placid. Nor did the temperatures ever plummet to the depths we had expected. Usually it was about 20 degrees F and on the most bitter night it only got down to zero.

Krill are food for every creature in the Antarctic.

Away from the ship's rumble, Antarctica was quiet. The ice cakes had been bashed together by storms; deep slush filled the space between them. A swell ran sluggishly through this mass and whispered in the slush.

The bottoms of what looked like flat ice cakes on the surface were humped and jagged beneath. They were made of ice chunks jammed together by wind and waves. "It's like a low overcast with improbable clouds," Richard Moe said. "The ctenophores were all out, combing their tresses."

Ctenophores are small jellyfishlike animals with long tentacles, with which they catch things to eat. Their presence here was significant. They were eating young krill and the krill were eating diatoms. [**Krill** are shrimplike animals that are eaten by whales and other sea animals. **Diatoms** are microscopic, one-celled water algae with hard shells.] Even in this time of winter, at the very beginning of the season of light, the food chain was evident.

Krill could be called the rice or wheat of the Antarctic ecosystem: they are a staple of almost every other creature's diet. They are also the most important Antarctic resource to the rest of the world.

Krill have been kept alive for months in tanks without food; they molted [shed their shells] and diminished in size, consuming themselves. The transparent bellies of most of the animals we caught were clear and empty as glass, and the water in which they swam was almost barren. A major objective of the trip had been to see whether krill spend the winter in the sea as they do in a tank—fasting—and now it seemed that perhaps the krill were indeed shrinking through the winter, eating nothing.

That didn't mean that nothing was eating them.

Fishing was exciting because each catch was new and unique.

Fishing, which usually happened at night, was also attended by scientists from other projects, because bringing up the net from that mysterious Antarctic bottom never ceased to be exciting. "Nobody knows what's there at this time of year," said Gerardo Chin-Leo before the ship's first trawl. [A ship trawls when it drags a net along the bottom of the sea.] "Could be tennis shoes for all we know."

The net never brought up a shoe, but one night it caught a nightmare: at 12:30 A.M. the net came up from the depths bearing an enormous jellyfish. Its body was ten gallons of glop, its tentacles were 50 feet long and it looked like the genesis of a terrible dream, a creature of grasping slime.

Little stones, algae, sea urchins, worms and young fish were the normal catch. During the whole voyage the four fishermen dissected and froze all or parts of more than 2,500 fish. . . .

One objective was to find out if the fish were eating krill in the winter; some northern rockfish eat very little during the cold season. But from the larval fish up to the adults, stomachs were often stuffed with krill cocktail. "Clearly," said John Konecki of the University of Washington, "the krill must be around here, because these guys are chowing down."

The *Polar Duke* surpassed its goal of crossing the Antarctic Circle.

Leaving Palmer, the *Polar Duke* sought to establish its own winter range, the habitat in which it might hope to work regularly in the future. This trip had revealed as many questions as answers, so if the data gathered in this month of work was to become part of a comprehensive knowledge of the Antarctic winter, it would have to be supplemented. This could not be an isolated event; it must be a beginning.

At 66 degrees 10 minutes south, we saw open water for the last time. Pushing through ice, the ship slowed, from eight knots to four, from four to two. All movement of the sea's swell vanished in the ice, but still the ship pushed south. Seals appeared on floes less and less often and we only occasionally saw a penguin. At last the ice seemed barren but for the rich brown soup of the diatoms in the wake. Then, on a quiet evening, the captain wrote in the log: "0345 GMT. V/L crossed Antarctic Circle." The ship had penetrated the boundary of the winter night and surpassed its goal.

"That's it," the captain said. The *Polar Duke* slowly turned around, to go back to two weeks' more research and to the long journey home. At 67 degrees 45.75 minutes south, winter had won.

Section 3 Review

Locating Key Places
Locate the following place on the map on page 608: Antarctic Peninsula

Identifying Key Terms
Define the following terms: ctenophore, krill, diatom

Reviewing Main Ideas
1. Why did the scientists on the *Polar Duke* go to Antarctica?
2. Describe the relationship between krill and other marine life.
3. What activity did the scientists find exciting?
4. What did the voyage of the *Polar Duke* accomplish?

Thinking Critically: Predict Effects
What effect do you think the extinction of krill in Antarctica would have on the food chain there? Give examples from the case study that support your hypothesis.

Using Polar Maps

Who owns Antarctica, and all its mineral riches? This question has been at the heart of a conflict that has gone on since the 1940s. To understand the situation, you need to consult a polar map.

Polar maps have one of the earth's poles at their center. These maps have some special characteristics. Take direction, for example. If the South Pole is at the center of the map, then any move you'd make from the center, or pole, would be toward the north.

Polar maps often distort shapes and distances as they reach the lower latitudes. The parallels, however, always appear as concentric circles, just as they appear on a globe. The meridians likewise appear correctly as straight lines that cross the parallels at right angles.

The map at right is a political polar map of Antarctica. It shows the claims that countries have made on this frozen continent. Seven countries, shown on the map, have made official claims on the land and its contents. In addition, five other countries—the United States, the Soviet Union, Belgium, France, Japan, and South Africa—have been involved in Antarctic research and exploration projects.

In 1959 these 12 countries made an agreement to delay the settlement of the individual claims for 30 years. At that time, they would meet to discuss their claims. In addition, they agreed to maintain the continent as a place of peace and research. They were never to use the continent for nuclear testing or other military purposes.

Today there are no permanent settlements on Antarctica, but there are many research stations and observation sites. The countries involved in research have agreed to share their scientific findings. They have studied the wildlife, vegetation, landforms, climate, and ozone status of Antarctica. Already they have found gold, silver, copper, and iron.

Review

1. Within which circle does almost all of Antarctica lie?
2. Which three countries hold claims on the Antarctic Peninsula?
3. Which U.S. research facility is shown on the map?
4. Which country claims the largest portion of Antarctica?
5. Does the United States hold an official claim on any land in Antarctica?

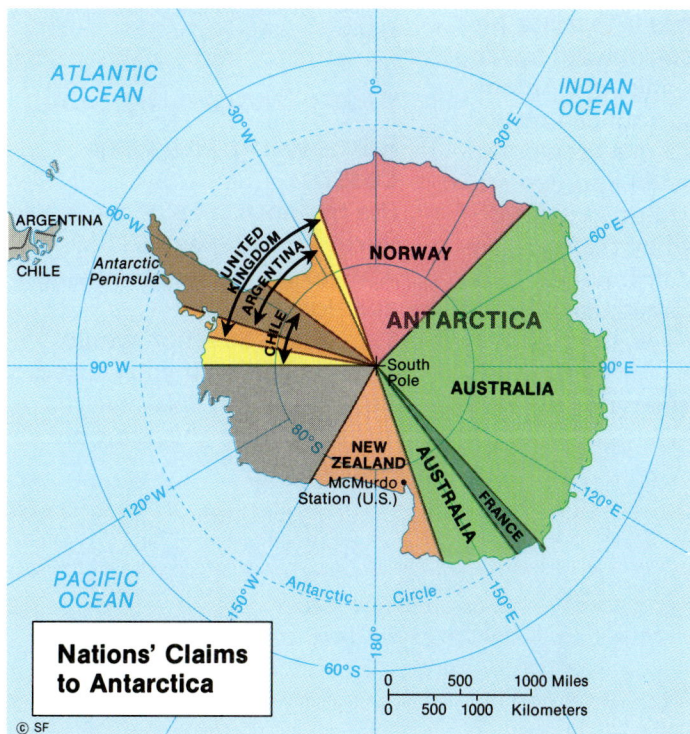

Nations' Claims to Antarctica

613

Review

Section Summaries

1. Islands of the Pacific. The Pacific Ocean, the largest ocean in the world, contains more islands than any other ocean. There are two types of islands in the Pacific: volcanic and coral. The three main regions into which the Pacific is divided are Melanesia, Polynesia, and Micronesia. In these three regions today, there are different cultures and forms of government, as a result of their history and colonial status.

2. Antarctica. This frozen continent and its surrounding seas form an icy realm far different from the Arctic. The biggest difference is that the Arctic is water surrounded by land and some people, but Antarctica is land surrounded by water and almost no people. Antarctica is divided into two main regions, West and East, which are separated by the Transantarctic Mountains. Huge amounts of accumulated ice on top of the tall mountains make Antarctica the highest continent. Antarctica is rich in minerals, including gold, silver, iron, and copper.

3. Case Study: Winter in Antarctica. The *Polar Duke*, a ship designed for Antarctic research, set off on a journey in the 1980s to explore marine life in the winter of this frozen continent. The scientists aboard took samples of fish and other sea animals, whose bodies offered evidence of a marine ecosystem based upon the consumption of a tiny animal called krill. The scientists aboard the *Polar Duke* had surpassed their goal by crossing the Antarctic Circle.

Using Geography Skills

Reviewing the Map Lesson

Use the polar map of the North Pole on page 637 of the Atlas to answer the following questions.
1. In which direction would you be heading if you started from the North Pole and moved toward any point on the map?

2. Are the parallels on this polar map concentric circles?
3. Does the North Pole lie on land or in water?
4. Name the landmass or body of water on which it lies.

Using Social Studies Skills

1. Locate and Gather Information. The Ross Ice Shelf is the largest flat-surfaced body of floating ice in the world. About how big is it? On the west side of the ice shelf there is a sound where the United States had a research station. What is the name of the sound? What other countries had research stations there? The Ross Ice Shelf was also traditionally the gateway for exploration of Antarctica. Amundsen and Scott began their fateful race on the ice shelf. Where were they racing? Who won the race? What other interesting information can you find about the Ross Ice Shelf? Use an almanac, encyclopedia, book, or other reference source to answer these questions.

2. Detect Stereotypes. The islanders of the South Pacific are often stereotyped as easy-going, gentle natives with flowers in their hair, sitting under the coconut palms or dancing around the fire. Is this stereotype accurate? Why or why not? Use reference sources to find the necessary evidence to support your conclusion.

Locating Key Places
Match each description below with the name of the place that appears in the next column.
1. named for the dark complexions of its inhabitants
2. large, famous sheet of floating ice
3. a region of small islands
4. range that separates the regions of our fifth largest continent
5. part of Antarctica that reaches toward South America
6. the largest Pacific island region

a. Melanesia
b. Polynesia
c. Micronesia
d. Ross Ice Shelf
e. Transantarctic Mountains
f. Antarctic Peninsula

Recalling Key Terms
Define these terms in your own words.

Section 1
atoll

Section 2
ice shelf
pack ice

Section 3
ctenophore
krill
diatom

Reviewing Main Ideas
Section 1
1. What are the two types of islands found in the Pacific?
2. Describe the different cultures of the three distinct regions of the Pacific islands.

Section 2
1. How are Antarctica and the Arctic alike? How are they different?

2. Why does Antarctica have the name "Frozen Continent"?
3. What are the two main regions of Antarctica?

Section 3
1. What was the purpose of the *Polar Duke* voyage?
2. What is the importance of krill to marine life?
3. Why did the scientists find fishing in Antarctica interesting?
4. What were the achievements of the *Polar Duke* voyage?

Thinking Critically
1. Predict Effects. What do you think would happen if the immense stores of ice on Antarctica began to melt?

2. Make Hypotheses. You have read about Antarctica and why it is of great interest to people around the world. For what reasons does Antarctica affect the world around it?

UNIT 10

Review

Summarizing the Unit

Chapter 29   Australia and New Zealand Lying southeast of Asia between the Indian and Pacific oceans, Australia and New Zealand share some physical and cultural characterstics and differ in others. Australia was shaped by weathering and erosion; in contrast, New Zealand's landforms were formed by plate and glacier movements. A mild climate characterizes New Zealand. Australia, however, has dry, tropical, and mild climates. Both countries have unique wildlife. Aborigines were the first people to settle in Australia, and the first settlers in New Zealand were the Maori. The two countries were later populated mainly by the British. Most Australians and New Zealanders live in cities and towns and work in manufacturing, farming, or mining. Both countries are independent but have maintained close ties with Britain.

Chapter 30   The Southern Realm This geographic realm consists of the Pacific Islands and the continent of Antarctica. The Pacific Islands are of two types, volcanic and coral, and are grouped into three main regions—Melanesia, Polynesia, and Micronesia. These regions have varied governments, all of which have been influenced by colonial rule, and different cultures, reflecting their different ethnic origins. Unlike the Arctic, Antarctica is land surrounded by water, with no permanent inhabitants. Antarctica's mineral-rich land has two main regions, West Antarctica and East Antarctica, over which lies a huge, thick ice sheet. In the 1980s scientists aboard the *Polar Duke* explored Antarctica's marine life.

Writing for Understanding

Presenting, the final step in the process of writing about geography, is an opportunity to come up with some creative ways to share your writing with your chosen audience.

Written work can be presented in many ways: in a play, newspaper, or magazine that you create, or as a radio show or television broadcast.

Sometimes your topic can inspire a way to present. For example, a report comparing the Australian cities of Sydney and Perth might be presented as a series of letters exchanged between two imaginary people, one from each city. The letters might be read aloud or displayed on a bulletin board, complete with "snapshots" clipped from travel brochures.

Activity. Suppose all of the members of your class have worked together to write a report on Polynesian food. On a separate sheet of paper, describe at least four ways the report could be presented. Try to think of presentations that your class actually has the means to carry out. When you are finished, share your ideas with other students. Use your imagination!

Test

Key Terms (40 points)

Match each definition with its correct term.

1. an off-shore coral reef that cannot be crossed by ships
2. a flat island, usually ring-shaped, that just barely rises above the ocean surface
3. provides a source of water for ranchers in Australia's Great Artesian Basin
4. an animal that carries its young in a pouch
5. a mass of ice chunks ringing Antarctica
6. an original inhabitant of Australia
7. shrimplike animals that are eaten by whales and other sea animals
8. the part of the Antarctic ice sheet that settles on the water along the edge of the continent

a. atoll
b. ice shelf
c. pack ice
d. krill
e. artesian well
f. barrier reef
g. marsupial
h. Aborigine

Main Ideas (40 points)

On your paper, record the letter of the response that best completes the sentence.

1. The Australian Alps are part of the _____.
a. Central Lowlands
b. Great Dividing Range
c. Western Plateau
d. Great Barrier Reef

2. Most of Australia has a _____ climate.
a. Mediterranean
b. marine west coast
c. mild
d. dry

3. Most people in Australia live _____.
a. on the southeastern coast
b. on the western coast
c. in the interior
d. on the northern coast

4. The main purpose of the Polar Duke voyage was _____.
a. making weather predictions
b. exploring marine life in summer
c. building a research station
d. exploring marine life in winter

Thinking Critically (10 points)

1. **Evaluate Sources of Information.** On your paper, write the letter of the source that would provide the most complete information on the physical geography of Australia.
a. a travel book about Australia
b. a tourist just returned from a two-month trip along Australia's southeastern coast
c. a 200-page book on the land and climate of Australia written by a geographer
d. a scientific report documenting the satellite imaging of Australia

2. **Make Hypotheses.** You learned in Chapter 29 that most people in Australia live along its southeastern coast from north of Brisbane to northwest of Adelaide. Using what you know about Australia's history, climate, and landforms, write a brief paragraph that tells why Australians live where they do.

Place Location (10 points)

Match the places listed below with the letters printed on the map.
1. Great Barrier Reef
2. Tasmania
3. Sydney
4. Melbourne
5. Auckland

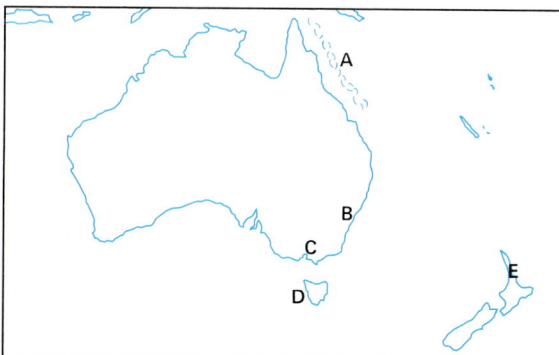

617

ATLAS AND REFERENCE SECTION

Contents

The Atlas and Reference Section includes a variety of materials to help you learn geography. Here you will find political and physical maps, tables of facts about countries, pronunciation guides, and more.

Facts About Countries 638
This section includes the flag, capital, area, population, major or official languages, and important products of each country or dependency.

Gazetteer 646
The Gazetteer is a geographical dictionary. Here you will find the latitude/longitude locations and brief descriptions of the key places in *Scott, Foresman World Geography.* Page references indicate a map on which the key place is located.

Glossary 651
The Glossary gives the pronunciations, parts of speech, and definitions of the key words in the text. Page references are also included.

Index 657
The Index lists page references for places, topics, and people to help you locate information in the book. Pronunciations are also included.

The World: Political

PACIFIC OCEAN

ATLANTIC OCEAN

NORTH AMERICA

SOUTH AMERICA

ANTARCTICA

Arctic Circle

80°N

60°N

140° West Longitude

40° North Latitude

Tropic of Cancer

20°N

0° Equator

20°S

Tropic of Capricorn

40°S

60°S

Antarctic Circle

80°S

180° 160°W 140°W 120°W 100°W 80°W 60°W

Alaska (U.S.)

Aleutian Islands

CANADA

UNITED STATES

MEXICO

Midway Islands (U.S.)

Hawaii (U.S.)

KIRIBATI

POLYNESIA

WESTERN SAMOA

American Samoa (U.S.)

TONGA

French Polynesia (FRANCE)

Easter Island (CHILE)

Galapagos Islands (ECUADOR)

Bermuda (U.K.)

BAHAMAS

CUBA

HAITI

DOMINICAN REPUBLIC

Puerto Rico (U.S.)

ST. KITTS AND NEVIS

ANTIGUA-BARBUDA

DOMINICA

ST. VINCENT AND THE GRENADINES

BARBADOS

GRENADA

TRINIDAD AND TOBAGO

JAMAICA

BELIZE

Virgin Is. (U.S.-U.K.)

GUATEMALA

HONDURAS

ST. LUCIA

EL SALVADOR

NICARAGUA

COSTA RICA

PANAMA

VENEZUELA

GUYANA

SURINAME

FR. GUIANA (FRANCE)

COLOMBIA

ECUADOR

PERU

BRAZIL

BOLIVIA

PARAGUAY

CHILE

URUGUAY

ARGENTINA

Falkland Islands (U.K.)

South Georgia (Falkland Is.)

Greenland (DEN)

Azores (POR)

CAPE

Central America and the West Indies

UNITED STATES

Gulf of California

Gulf of Mexico

NORTH AMERICA

MEXICO

Tropic of Cancer

30°N

20°N

10°N

110°W 100°W 90°W 80°W 70°W 60°W 50°W

BAHAMAS

CUBA

HAITI

DOMINICAN REPUBLIC

Puerto Rico (U.S.)

Virgin Is. (U.S.)

ANTIGUA-BARBUDA

Guadeloupe (Fr.)

DOMINICA

Martinique (Fr.)

ST. LUCIA

BARBADOS

ST. KITTS AND NEVIS

ST. VINCENT AND THE GRENADINES

GRENADA

TRINIDAD AND TOBAGO

JAMAICA

ATLANTIC OCEAN

CARIBBEAN SEA

West Indies

BELIZE

GUATEMALA

HONDURAS

EL SALVADOR

NICARAGUA

COSTA RICA

PANAMA

Panama Canal

Central America

PACIFIC OCEAN

VENEZUELA

COLOMBIA

SOUTH AMERICA

GUYANA

SURINAME

0   500 Miles
0   500 Kilometers

N
W   E
S

ICELAND
NORWAY
SWEDEN
FINLAND
Arctic Circle
80°N
60°N
UNITED KINGDOM
DENMARK
IRELAND
NETHERLANDS
EAST GERMANY
POLAND
UNION OF SOVIET SOCIALIST REPUBLICS (SOVIET UNION)
BELGIUM
LUX.
WEST GERMANY
EUROPE
CZECHOSLOVAKIA
HUNGARY
MONGOLIA
FRANCE
SWITZERLAND
AUS.
YUGOSLAVIA
ROMANIA
BULGARIA
ASIA
40°N
SPAIN
ITALY
ALBANIA
GREECE
TURKEY
PORTUGAL
NORTH KOREA
JAPAN
MOROCCO
MALTA
CYPRUS
SYRIA
IRAQ
IRAN
AFGHANISTAN
PEOPLE'S REPUBLIC OF CHINA
SOUTH KOREA
LEBANON
ISRAEL
JORDAN
KUWAIT
PACIFIC OCEAN
ALGERIA
LIBYA
EGYPT
BAHRAIN
QATAR
PAKISTAN
NEPAL
BHUTAN
Tropic of Cancer
20°N
TUNISIA
UNITED ARAB EMIRATES
Northern Mariana Islands (U.S.)
Wake Island (U.S.)
MARSHALL ISLANDS
WESTERN SAHARA (MOROCCO)
SAUDI ARABIA
INDIA
BANGLADESH
BURMA
TAIWAN
Guam (U.S.)
MICRONESIA
MAURITANIA
OMAN
LAOS
SENEGAL
YEMEN
P.D.R. OF YEMEN
THAILAND
VIETNAM
PHILIPPINES
Palau (U.S.)
FEDERATED STATES OF MICRONESIA
GAMBIA
MALI
NIGER
AFRICA
DJIBOUTI
CAMBODIA (KAMPUCHEA)
GUINEA-BISSAU
BURKINA FASO
SRI LANKA
BRUNEI
KIRIBATI
GUINEA
NIGERIA
CHAD
SUDAN
ETHIOPIA
MALAYSIA
SIERRA LEONE
CÔTE D'IVOIRE (IVORY COAST)
BENIN
CENTRAL AFRICAN REPUBLIC
SINGAPORE
Equator
0°
GHANA
LIBERIA
TOGO
CAMEROON
ZAIRE
UGANDA
SOMALIA
MALDIVES
NAURU
EQUATORIAL GUINEA
P.R. OF THE CONGO
RWANDA
KENYA
MELANESIA
SÃO TOMÉ AND PRÍNCIPE
GABON
BURUNDI
PAPUA NEW GUINEA
SOLOMON ISLANDS
TUVALU
Cabinda (ANGOLA)
TANZANIA
SEYCHELLES
INDONESIA
ANGOLA
MALAWI
ZAMBIA
MOZAMBIQUE
COMOROS
INDIAN OCEAN
VANUATU
FIJI
20°S
ATLANTIC OCEAN
NAMIBIA (SOUTH AFRICA)
ZIMBABWE
BOTSWANA
MADAGASCAR
MAURITIUS
New Caledonia (FRANCE)
Tropic of Capricorn
SWAZILAND
AUSTRALIA
SOUTH AFRICA
LESOTHO
N
W E
S
Tasmania
NEW ZEALAND
40°S

0 1000 2000 Miles
0 1000 2000 Kilometers
Scale accurate for the Equator

60° South Latitude
Antarctic Circle
20°W
0°
20°E
40°E
60°E
80°E
100°E
120°E
140° East Longitude
160°E
180°
© SF
ANTARCTICA
80°S

Prime Meridian

Europe

SWEDEN
FINLAND
Arctic Circle
60°N
NORWAY
NORTH SEA
BALTIC SEA
IRELAND
UNITED KINGDOM
DENMARK
U.S.S.R.
NETHERLANDS
ATLANTIC OCEAN
BELGIUM
EAST GERMANY
POLAND
50°N
LUX.
WEST GERMANY
CZECHOSLOVAKIA
FRANCE
AUSTRIA
HUNGARY
SWITZERLAND
ROMANIA
PORTUGAL
ITALY
YUGOSLAVIA
BLACK SEA
SPAIN
BULGARIA
ALBANIA
40°N
MEDITERRANEAN SEA
GREECE
TURKEY
N
W E
S
0 500 Miles
0 500 Kilometers

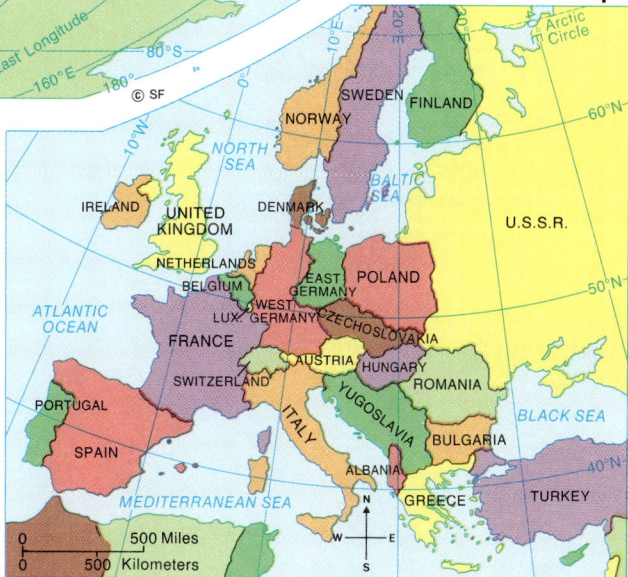

Southwest Asia

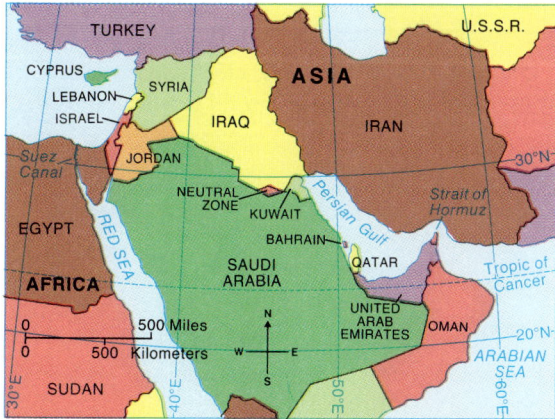

TURKEY
U.S.S.R.
CYPRUS
SYRIA
ASIA
LEBANON
ISRAEL
IRAQ
IRAN
Suez Canal
JORDAN
30°N
NEUTRAL ZONE
Persian Gulf
Strait of Hormuz
KUWAIT
EGYPT
BAHRAIN
RED SEA
SAUDI ARABIA
QATAR
Tropic of Cancer
AFRICA
UNITED ARAB EMIRATES
OMAN
20°N
ARABIAN SEA
SUDAN
N
W E
S
0 500 Miles
0 500 Kilometers
30°E
40°E
50°E
60°E

The World: Physical

ARCTIC OCEAN

180°
160°W
140° West Longitude
80°N
GREENLAND
Arctic Circle Yukon R.
BERING
60°N
SEA
Gulf of
Alaska
Hudson
Bay
ALEUTIAN IS.
NORTH
Great Lakes St. Lawrence R.
AMERICA
ROCKY MOUNTAINS
APPALACHIAN MTS.
40° North Latitude
PACIFIC
OCEAN
ATLANTIC
OCEAN
Mississippi R.
Rio Grande
Gulf of
Mexico
WEST
Tropic of Cancer
20°N
HAWAIIAN
ISLANDS
INDIES
CARIBBEAN SEA
GUIANA
HIGHLANDS
Amazon River
0°
Equator
SOUTH
ANDES
AMERICA
BRAZILIAN
HIGHLANDS
20°S
ATACAMA
DESERT
MOUNTAINS
Tropic of Capricorn
Paraná R.
PACIFIC
OCEAN
40°S

60°S
Antarctic Circle
80°S
ANTARCTICA
160°
140°W
80°W

Land Elevation

Feet		Meters
10,000		3,000
5,000		1,500
2,000		600
500		150
0		0
Below Sea Level		Below Sea Level

Ice-covered land

International boundaries

0   500   1000   1500 Miles
0 500 1000 1500   Kilometers

Scale accurate for the Equator

ARCTIC OCEAN

BARENTS SEA

ICELAND

NORTH SEA

BALTIC SEA

NORTH EUROPEAN PLAIN

EUROPE

ALPS

CAUCASUS MTS.

BLACK SEA

MEDITERRANEAN SEA

ATLAS MTS.

SAHARA (DESERT)

ARABIAN DESERT

AFRICA

Niger R.

Nile R.

RED SEA

Congo R.

Lake Victoria

ATLANTIC OCEAN

KALAHARI DESERT

MADAGASCAR

URAL MTS.

Ob R.

Volga R.

Lena R.

Arctic Circle

Lake Baikal

ASIA

GOBI (DESERT)

PLATEAU OF TIBET

HIMALAYAS

THAR DESERT

Huang R.

Chang (Yangtze) River

Ganges R.

Tigris R.

Euphrates R.

CASPIAN SEA

SEA OF JAPAN

EAST CHINA SEA

ARABIAN SEA

Bay of Bengal

SOUTH CHINA SEA

PHILIPPINE ISLANDS

PACIFIC OCEAN

INDIAN OCEAN

AUSTRALIA

GREAT VICTORIA DESERT

Darling R.

80°N

60°N

40°N

Tropic of Cancer

20°N

Equator

20°S

Tropic of Capricorn

40°S

0°

0° 20°E 40°E 60°E 80°E 100°E 160°E 180° 80°N

Prime Meridian

60°South Latitude

Antarctic Circle

80°S

ANTARCTICA

20°W 20°E 40°E 60°E 80°E 100°E 120°E 140° East Longitude 160°E 180°

N
W   E
S

© SF

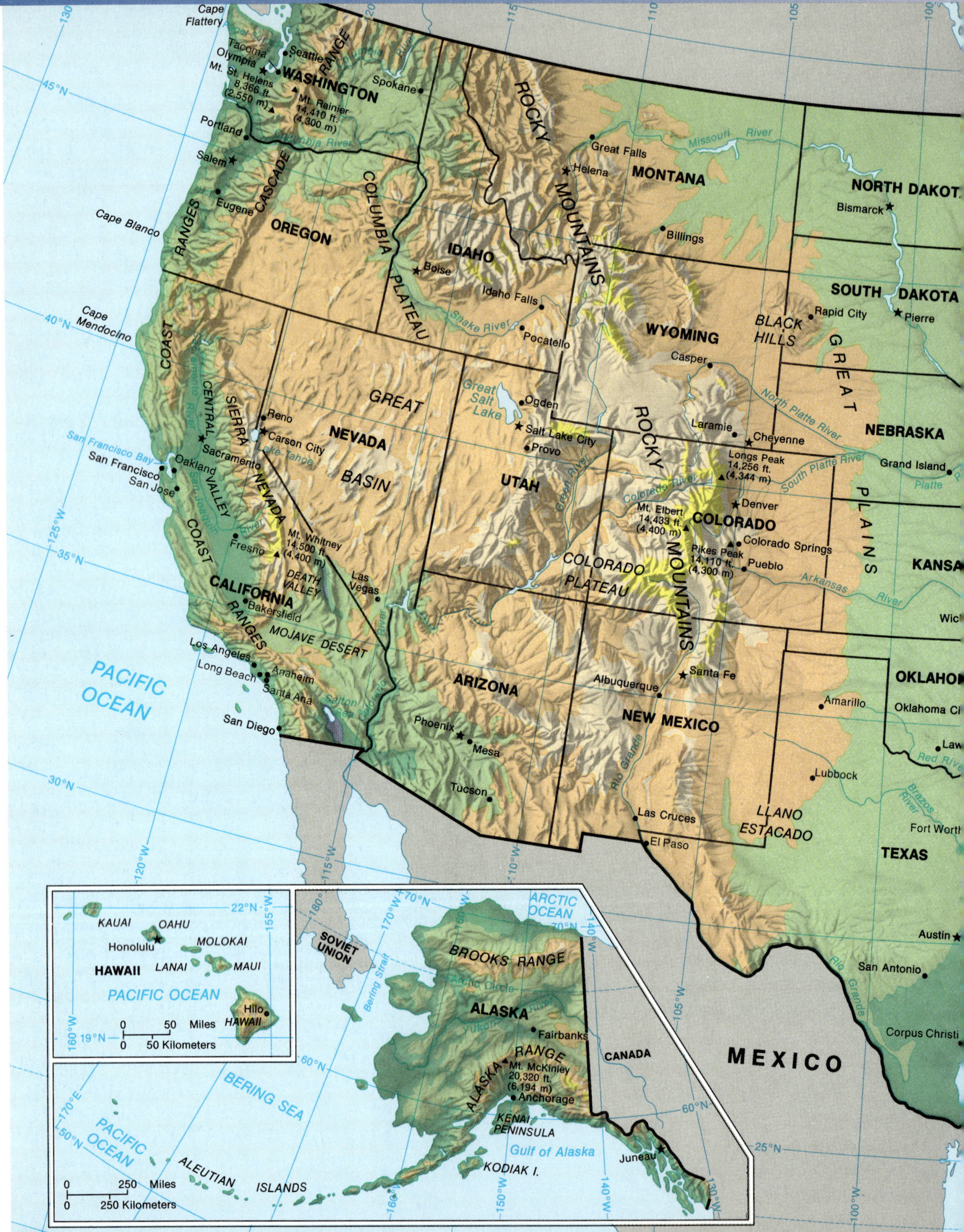

PACIFIC OCEAN

Cape Flattery
Olympia
Tacoma
Seattle
Spokane
WASHINGTON
Mt. St. Helens 8,366 ft. (2,550 m)
Mt. Rainier 14,410 ft. (4,300 m)
Portland
Salem
Eugene
Cape Blanco
OREGON
CASCADE RANGES
COLUMBIA PLATEAU
Columbia River
ROCKY MOUNTAINS
Great Falls
Helena
MONTANA
Billings
Missouri River
NORTH DAKOTA
Bismarck

Cape Mendocino
COAST RANGES
IDAHO
Boise
Idaho Falls
Snake River
Pocatello
WYOMING
Casper
Laramie
Cheyenne
BLACK HILLS
Rapid City
Pierre
SOUTH DAKOTA
GREAT
North Platte River
NEBRASKA
Grand Island
Platte

Reno
Carson City
Lake Tahoe
Sacramento
CENTRAL VALLEY
SIERRA NEVADA
NEVADA
GREAT BASIN
Great Salt Lake
Ogden
Salt Lake City
Provo
UTAH
Green River
ROCKY
Longs Peak 14,256 ft. (4,344 m)
Mt. Elbert 14,433 ft. (4,400 m)
Denver
COLORADO
Colorado Springs
Pikes Peak 14,110 ft. (4,300 m)
Pueblo
South Platte River
Arkansas River
PLAINS
KANSAS
Wic

San Francisco Bay
San Francisco
Oakland
San Jose
Fresno
Mt. Whitney 14,500 ft. (4,400 m)
DEATH VALLEY
Bakersfield
CALIFORNIA
COAST RANGES
Los Angeles
Long Beach
Anaheim
Santa Ana
San Diego
MOJAVE DESERT
Las Vegas
Salton Sea
Colorado River
COLORADO PLATEAU
MOUNTAINS
Albuquerque
Santa Fe
Amarillo
OKLAHOMA
Oklahoma Ci
Law
Red Riv

ARIZONA
Phoenix
Mesa
Tucson
NEW MEXICO
Rio Grande
Las Cruces
El Paso
LLANO ESTACADO
Lubbock
Brazos River
Fort Worth
TEXAS
Austin
San Antonio
Rio Grande
MEXICO
Corpus Christi

PACIFIC OCEAN

KAUAI
OAHU
Honolulu
MOLOKAI
HAWAII
LANAI
MAUI
Hilo
HAWAII
PACIFIC OCEAN
0 50 Miles
0 50 Kilometers
22°N
19°N
155°W
160°W

SOVIET UNION
Bering Strait
ARCTIC OCEAN
BROOKS RANGE
Arctic Circle
ALASKA
Yukon River
Fairbanks
ALASKA RANGE
Mt. McKinley 20,320 ft. (6,194 m)
Anchorage
KENAI PENINSULA
CANADA
Gulf of Alaska
Juneau
KODIAK I.
BERING SEA
ALEUTIAN ISLANDS
PACIFIC OCEAN
0 250 Miles
0 250 Kilometers
50°N
60°N
70°N
25°N

CANADA

MINNESOTA
WISCONSIN
MICHIGAN
MAINE

nd Forks
Duluth
Lake Superior
Augusta
Lewiston
Portland

argo
St. Paul
Minneapolis
Green Bay
Lake Michigan
Lake Huron
Burlington
Montpelier
VT NH
Concord
Manchester
Boston
Cape Cod

oux Falls
IOWA
Madison
Milwaukee
Grand Rapids
Lansing
ADIRONDACK MTS
Albany
Worcester
MA
Providence
RI

Cedar Rapids
Rockford
Chicago
Gary
Fort Wayne
Detroit
Rochester
Syracuse
Buffalo
NEW YORK
Hartford
Bridgeport
LONG ISLAND

Des Moines
Davenport
Peoria
Lake Erie
Lake Ontario
New York City
Jersey City
Newark
Trenton
NEW JERSEY

Omaha
ncoln
CENTRAL
ILLINOIS
INDIANA
OHIO
Toledo
Cleveland
Akron
PENNSYLVANIA
Pittsburgh
Harrisburg
Philadelphia
Wilmington
DELAWARE
Dover

Springfield
Indianapolis
Cincinnati
Columbus
Wheeling
WEST VIRGINIA
ALLEGHENY MTS
WASHINGTON D.C.
Baltimore
Annapolis
MARYLAND

Kansas City
Missouri River
St. Louis
PLAINS
Louisville
Frankfort
Lexington
Huntington
Charleston
VIRGINIA
Richmond
DELMARVA PENINSULA
Chesapeake Bay

Topeka
Kansas City
Jefferson City
MISSOURI
KENTUCKY
APPALACHIAN MTS
PIEDMONT
Newport News
Norfolk

Springfield
OZARK PLATEAU
Ohio River
Nashville
Knoxville
BLUE RIDGE MTS
Mt. Mitchell 6,684 ft. (2,030 m)
Winston-Salem
Greensboro
Raleigh
Cape Hatteras

Tulsa
ARKANSAS
TENNESSEE
NORTH CAROLINA
Charlotte

Fort Smith
Little Rock
Memphis
Huntsville
Greenville
PIEDMONT
SOUTH CAROLINA
COASTAL PLAIN
Cape Fear

Pine Bluff
MISSISSIPPI
ALABAMA
Birmingham
Atlanta
Columbia
Charleston

as
Shreveport
Jackson
Meridian
Montgomery
GEORGIA
Macon
Savannah

LOUISIANA
PLAIN
Biloxi
Mobile
Columbus
COASTAL

Baton Rouge
New Orleans
COASTAL
Tallahassee
Jacksonville
Cape Canaveral

Houston
Gulf of Mexico
Mississippi Delta
FLORIDA
Tampa
St. Petersburg
FLORIDA PENINSULA
Fort Lauderdale
Miami
Florida Keys
Straits of Florida

ATLANTIC OCEAN

St. Lawrence River
Bay of Fundy
Atlas

40°N
35° North Latitude
70° West Longitude
Tropic of Cancer

The United States: Physical–Political

Land Elevation

Feet	Meters
10,000	3,000
7,000	2,000
3,000	1,000
700	200
(Sea Level) 0	0 (Sea Level)
Below Sea Level	Below Sea Level

International boundaries
State boundaries
National capital
State capitals

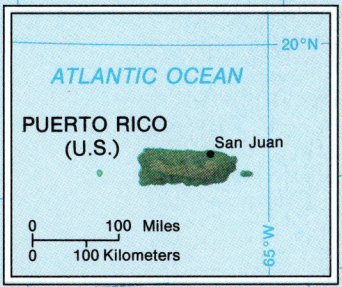

0 100 200 Miles
0 100 200 Kilometers

ATLANTIC OCEAN
20°N
PUERTO RICO (U.S.)
San Juan
0 100 Miles
0 100 Kilometers
N S E W

CUBA

625

ASIA

ARCTIC OCEAN

BERING SEA

BEAUFORT SEA

• Barrow

ALASKA (U.S.A.)

• Fairbanks

• Anchorage

• Dawson

Gulf of Alaska

• Juneau

Arctic Circle

Greenland (Denmark)

Iceland

• Thule

Baffin Bay

• Godthåb

CANADA

• Churchill

Hudson Bay

LABRADOR SEA

• Goose Bay

• Edmonton

• Calgary

• Regina

• Winnipeg

• Victoria

• Vancouver

Puget Sound

• Seattle

• Portland

Columbia River

GREAT LAKES

• St. John's

St. Pierre and Miquelon (Fr.)

PACIFIC OCEAN

• Quebec

• Montreal

• Ottawa ✸ Laval

• Minneapolis • St. Paul

• Halifax

North York

Mississauga Hamilton Toronto

• Milwaukee London

• Chicago Detroit Cleveland Buffalo

• Boston

Toledo Pittsburgh New York City

Columbus Newark Philadelphia

Cincinnati Baltimore

• Salt Lake City

San Francisco • Oakland

• San Jose

• Denver

• Omaha

Kansas City St. Louis

Indianapolis

Washington, D.C. ✸

UNITED STATES

Missouri R.

Colorado R.

Ohio R.

• Norfolk

ATLANTIC OCEAN

• Los Angeles

• Long Beach

• San Diego

• Tijuana

• Albuquerque

• Phoenix

• Tucson

• Mexicali

• Tulsa

• Nashville

• Memphis

• Greensboro

Raleigh

• Charlotte

30° North Latitude

120° West Longitude

• El Paso

• Juárez

Fort Worth • • Dallas

• Atlanta

• Jacksonville

Bermuda (U.K.)

• Chihuahua

• Austin

Rio Grande

• Houston

• San Antonio

• New Orleans

Gulf of California

• Torreón

• Monterrey

Gulf of Mexico

• Miami

• Nassau

Tropic of Cancer

MEXICO

• San Luis Potosí

• Tampico

• Guadalajara

Mexico City ✸ • Veracruz

• Puebla

• Mérida

• Havana

CUBA

BAHAMAS

ANTIGUA-BARBUDA

✸ St. Johns

DOMINICAN REPUBLIC

ST. CHRISTOPHER AND NEVIS

• Basseterre

Port-au-Prince

HAITI

San Juan

Santo Domingo

Puerto Rico (U.S.A.)

DOMINICA

✸ Roseau

• Acapulco

Kingston ✸

JAMAICA

WEST INDIES

CARIBBEAN SEA

SAINT LUCIA

✸ Castries

SAINT VINCENT AND THE GRENADINES

✸ Kingstown

N W E S

• Belmopan

BELIZE

• Guatemala City

GUATEMALA ✸

• Tegucigalpa

HONDURAS

San Salvador

EL SALVADOR ✸

NICARAGUA

Managua ✸

Curaçao (Neth.)

Aruba (Neth.)

BARBADOS

• Bridgetown

GRENADA

✸ St. George's

TRINIDAD AND TOBAGO

• Port-of-Spain

San José ✸

COSTA RICA

• Panamá City

PANAMA

SOUTH AMERICA

North America
Political

— International boundaries
✸ National capitals
• Other cities

| 0 | 250 | 500 Miles |
| 0 | 250 | 500 Kilometers |

626

ASIA

ARCTIC OCEAN

Bering Strait

BERING SEA

BEAUFORT SEA

BROOKS RANGE

Pt. Barrow

ALASKA PENINSULA

ALASKA RANGE

Mt. McKinley

Kodiak

Gulf of Alaska

COAST MOUNTAINS

Alexander Arch.

Queen Charlotte Is.

Vancouver I.

Puget Sound

Yukon

Mackenzie

Great Bear Lake

Great Slave Lake

Peace

Lake Athabasca

Reindeer Lake

Saskatchewan

Lake Winnipeg

CANADIAN SHIELD

Hudson Bay

Queen Elizabeth Is.

Victoria I.

Baffin I.

Baffin Bay

Greenland

Iceland

Arctic Circle

LABRADOR SEA

UNGAVA PENINSULA

LABRADOR

LAURENTIAN SHIELD

Newfoundland

Gulf of St. Lawrence

Davis Strait

CASCADE RANGE

Mt. Rainier

ROCKY MOUNTAINS

GREAT BASIN

Great Salt Lake

SIERRA NEVADA

Mt. Whitney

WRANGES

DEATH VALLEY

MOHAVE DESERT

GRAND CANYON

COLORADO PLATEAU

Colorado

Snake R.

GREAT PLAINS

BLACK HILLS

Missouri

Platte

INTERIOR

CENTRAL PLAINS

PLAINS

OZARK PLATEAU

Arkansas

Red R.

Lake Superior

Lake Michigan

Lake Huron

Lake Erie

Lake Ontario

Lake of the Woods

APPALACHIAN MTS.

PIEDMONT

COASTAL PLAIN

Cape Cod

Long I.

Chesapeake Bay

Cape Hatteras

Bermuda Is.

ATLANTIC OCEAN

PACIFIC OCEAN

Pt. Conception

Eugenia Pt.

BAJA CALIFORNIA

Gulf of California

SIERRA MADRE WEST

Cape San Lucas

CENTRAL PLATEAU

SIERRA MADRE EAST

Rio Grande

COASTAL PLAIN

Gulf of Mexico

FLORIDA PENINSULA

Cape Canaveral

YUCATÁN PENINSULA

Bahama Is.

Tropic of Cancer

Cuba

West Indies

Jamaica

Greater Antilles

Hispaniola

Puerto Rico

Leeward Is.

CARIBBEAN SEA

Lesser Antilles

Windward Is.

Mt. Orizaba

ISTHMUS OF TEHUANTEPEC

CENTRAL AMERICA

Nicaragua

ISTHMUS OF PANAMA

Panama Canal

SOUTH AMERICA

Equator

North America
Physical

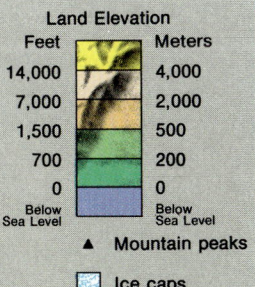

Land Elevation

Feet	Meters
14,000	4,000
7,000	2,000
1,500	500
700	200
0	0
Below Sea Level	Below Sea Level

▲ Mountain peaks

Ice caps

0 250 500 Miles
0 250 500 Kilometers

White lines represent international boundaries

627

© SF

NORTH AMERICA

CENTRAL
AMERICA

CARIBBEAN SEA

Barranquilla
Cartagena
Maracaibo
Valencia
Caracas

Medellín

VENEZUELA

Ciudad Guayana

GUYANA
Georgetown

Coco Is.
(Costa Rica)

Cali
Bogotá

COLOMBIA

Paramaribo
Cayenne
SURINAME
FRENCH
GUIANA
(Fr.)

ATLANTIC

OCEAN

Equator
Galápagos Is.
(Ecuador)

Quito

ECUADOR

Guayaquil

Iquitos

Manaus

Amazon R.

Belém

Trujillo

PERU

BRAZIL

Recife

PACIFIC

OCEAN

Callao
Lima

Cuzco

Arequipa
La Paz

BOLIVIA
Sucre

Salvador

Brasília

Belo Horizonte

Antofagasta

PARAGUAY

São Paulo
Santos

Rio de Janeiro

Asunción

Tropic of Capricorn

CHILE

Tucumán

Paraná R.

N

W   E

S

Córdoba

Pôrto Alegre

Valparaíso
Santiago

Rosario

URUGUAY
Buenos Aires
La Plata
Montevideo

Concepción

ARGENTINA

Bahía Blanca

Punta Arenas

Falkland Is.
(U.K.)

South America
Political

—— International boundaries
⊛ National capitals
• Other cities

0   200   400   600 Miles
0 200 400 600
Kilometers

NORTH AMERICA

CENTRAL
AMERICA

CARIBBEAN SEA

GUAJIRA PENINSULA

10° North Latitude

10°N

Coco Is.

ATLANTIC
OCEAN

LLANOS

Lake Maracaibo

GUIANA HIGHLANDS

Angel Falls

Equator 0°

Galápagos Is.

Mt. Chimborazo

A M A Z O N

Marajó I.

0°

Gulf of Guayaquil

B A S I N

Cape São
Roque

Aguja Point

ANDES

Mt. Huascarán

10° South Latitude

MATO GROSSO PLATEAU

São Francisco

10°S

PACIFIC

OCEAN

MOUNTAINS

Mt. Ancohuma

Lake Titicaca

BRAZILIAN

ATACAMA DESERT

HIGHLANDS

20°S

MOUNTAINS

GRAN CHACO

20°S

Tropic of Capricorn

Iguaçu Falls

Cape Frio

N

ANDES

W E

MOUNTAINS

30°S

S

Mt. Aconcagua

PAMPAS

30°S

Río de la Plata

40°S

Blanca Bay

40°S

San Matias Gulf

Chiloé I.

Colorado

PATAGONIA

Gulf of San Jorge

| 0 | 200 | 400 | 600 Miles |
| 0 | 200 | 400 | 600 Kilometers |

Strait of Magellan

Falkland Is.

50°S

Strait of Magellan

Tierra del Fuego

Cape Horn

60°S

90°W   80°W   70°W   60°W   50°W West Longitude   40°W   30°W

South America
Physical

Land Elevation

Feet		Meters
14,000		4,000
7,000		2,000
1,500		500
700		200
0		0
Below Sea Level		Below Sea Level

▲ Mountain peaks

White lines represent
international boundaries

Europe
Political

- — International boundaries
- ⊛ National capitals
- • Other cities

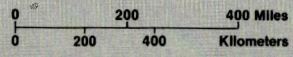

ARCTIC OCEAN

70°N

30°W

20°W

10°W

0°

10°E

20°E

30°E

40°E

50°

60°N

50°N

40°N

30°N

Arctic Circle

ICELAND
⊛ Reykjavik

NORWEGIAN SEA

Faeroe Is. (Den.)

Shetland Is. (U.K.)

ATLANTIC OCEAN

Hebrides Is. (U.K.)

Orkney Is. (U.K.)

NORWAY
• Bergen
⊛ Oslo

SWEDEN
• Stockholm ⊛

FINLAND
Helsinki ⊛
• Leningrad

Orust I. (Sweden)

• Moscow ⊛

BALTIC SEA

UNION OF SOVIET SOCIALIST REPUBLICS (SOVIET UNION)

Volga River

SCOTLAND
• Glasgow

NORTHERN IRELAND
• Belfast

UNITED KINGDOM

• Dublin ⊛
REPUBLIC OF IRELAND

WALES

ENGLAND
• Manchester

• London ⊛

NORTH SEA

DENMARK
Copenhagen ⊛

• Hamburg
Elbe

NETHERLANDS
The Hague ⊛ • Amsterdam ⊛

EAST GERMANY
East Berlin ⊛

POLAND
Warsaw ⊛

Vistula River

Oder River

Dnieper River

• Essen • Dortmund
• Dusseldorf
Brussels ⊛ • Bonn
BELGIUM
LUXEMBOURG
Luxembourg ⊛

• Prague ⊛
CZECHOSLOVAKIA

Dniester River

WEST GERMANY

Seine River

• Paris ⊛

Loire River

Rhine River

Danube River

• Munich

Vienna ⊛

AUSTRIA

HUNGARY
Budapest ⊛

ROMANIA
Bucharest ⊛

BLACK SEA

Bay of Biscay

FRANCE

• Bordeaux

Garonne River

Rhône River

Zurich •
LIECHTENSTEIN
Vaduz ⊛
Bern ⊛ **SWITZERLAND**

• Milan
Po River
• Turin
• Genoa

SAN MARINO
San Marino ⊛

YUGOSLAVIA
Belgrade ⊛

Danube River

BULGARIA
Sofia •

• Marseille
• Monaco
MONACO

PORTUGAL
Madrid ⊛

Ebro River

⊛ Andorra la Vella
ANDORRA
• Barcelona

ITALY

Corsica (Fr.)

VATICAN CITY ⊛⊛ • Rome

ALBANIA
Tirana •

GREECE

Istanbul •
TURKEY

ASIA

Tagus River

• Lisbon ⊛

SPAIN

Guadalquivir River

• Córdoba

Balearic Is. (Sp.)

Sardinia (It.)

• Naples

Athens ⊛

Nicosia •

CYPRUS

Gibraltar (U.K.)

• Palermo

Sicily (It.)

N
W E
S

Crete (Gr.)

MALTA • Valletta

MEDITERRANEAN SEA

AFRICA

| 0 | 200 | 400 Miles |
| 0 | 200 | 400 Kilometers |

Europe
Physical

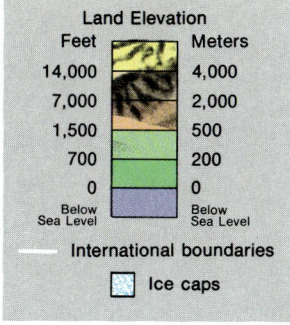

Land Elevation

Feet		Meters
14,000		4,000
7,000		2,000
1,500		500
700		200
0		0
Below Sea Level		Below Sea Level

—— International boundaries

Ice caps

ARCTIC OCEAN

North Cape

BARENTS SEA

KOLA PENINSULA

NORWEGIAN SEA

WHITE SEA

SCANDINAVIAN PENINSULA

Gulf of Bothnia

Lake Onega

Lake Ladoga

Gulf of Finland

Volga River

Arctic Circle

Iceland

ATLANTIC OCEAN

Shetland Is.

Hebrides Is.

Orkney Is.

NORTH SEA

BALTIC SEA

NORTH EUROPEAN PLAIN

Great Britain

British Isles

Ireland

IRISH SEA

Thames River

English Channel

Seine River

Loire River

RUHR VALLEY

Elbe River

Oder River

Vistula River

Dnieper River

Dniester River

CARPATHIAN MTS.

BRITTANY PENINSULA

Garonne River

Danube River

Central Massif

ALPS

HUNGARIAN BASIN

TRANSYLVANIAN ALPS

Danube River

Po River

PYRENEES

DINARIC ALPS

ADRIATIC SEA

BALKAN MTS.

BLACK SEA

IBERIAN PENINSULA

Corsica

APENNINES

APENNINE PENINSULA

BALKAN PENINSULA

ASIA

Sardinia

Balearic Is.

PINDUS MTS.

AEGEAN SEA

Guadalquivir River

TYRRHENIAN SEA

IONIAN SEA

Sicily

Crete

Cyprus

Malta

MEDITERRANEAN SEA

AFRICA

Bay of Biscay

| 0 | 200 | 400 Miles |
| 0 | 200 | 400 | Kilometers |

631

Asia
Political

- International boundaries
- ⊛ National capitals
- • Other cities

| | 1,000 Miles |
| 500 | 1,000 |
| Kilometers |
| 0 | 500 | 1,000 |

ARCTIC OCEAN

PACIFIC OCEAN

North Pole

International Date Line

Aleutian Is. (U.S.A.)

BERING SEA

Kuril Is. (U.S.S.R.)

SEA OF OKHOTSK

Magadan

Verkhoyansk

Khabarovsk

Vladivostok

Amur River

Lena River

Yenisey River

Ob' River

Arctic Circle

SIBERIA

Irkutsk

Lake Baikal

Novosibirsk

Omsk

UNION OF SOVIET SOCIALIST REPUBLICS (SOVIET UNION)

URAL MOUNTAINS

Sverdlovsk

Tashkent

TURKESTAN

ARAL SEA

CASPIAN SEA

BLACK SEA

BALTIC SEA

EUROPE

North Latitude

MEDITERRANEAN SEA

AFRICA

Ankara
TURKEY
Nicosia
CYPRUS
LEBANON
Beirut
Damascus
SYRIA
Amman
JORDAN
Jerusalem
ISRAEL
EGYPT
Baghdad
IRAQ
Abadan
Kuwait
KUWAIT
Neutral Zone
Manama
BAHRAIN
Riyadh
QATAR
Doha
SAUDI ARABIA
Mecca
YEMEN
Sana'a
P.D.R. OF YEMEN
Aden
RED SEA
Abu Dhabi
UNITED ARAB EMIRATES
Muscat
OMAN
Socotra (P.D.R. of Yemen)
ARABIAN SEA

IRAN
Tehran

AFGHANISTAN
Kabul

PAKISTAN
Islamabad
Lahore
Karachi

JAMMU AND KASHMIR

New Delhi

INDIA

NEPAL
Kathmandu

BHUTAN
Thimphu

BANGLADESH
Dhaka

Calcutta

Bombay

Madras

Laccadive Is. (India)

MALDIVES
Male

SRI LANKA
Colombo

Ganges River

Brahmaputra R.

Indus R.

Bay of Bengal

Andaman Is. (India)

Nicobar Is. (India)

INDIAN OCEAN

Equator

MONGOLIA
Ulaanbaatar

PEOPLE'S REPUBLIC OF CHINA

TIBET
Lhasa

MANCHURIA
Harbin

Great Wall

Beijing
Tianjin
Huang River
Nanjing
Wuhan
Shanghai
Chang (Yangtze) R.
Changsha
Chongqing
Guangzhou
HONG KONG (U.K.)
MACAO (Port.)

NORTH KOREA
Pyongyang
SOUTH KOREA
Seoul

JAPAN
Tokyo
Yokohama
Osaka

Ryukyu Is. (Japan)

EAST CHINA SEA

TAIWAN
Taipei

SOUTH CHINA SEA

BURMA
Rangoon

LAOS
Vientiane

THAILAND
Bangkok

VIETNAM
Hanoi

CAMBODIA (KAMPUCHEA)
Phnom Penh

Ho Chi Minh City

Mekong R.

REPUBLIC OF THE PHILIPPINES
Manila

BRUNEI

MALAYSIA
Kuala Lumpur

SINGAPORE
Singapore

Sumatra

Java

Jakarta

Kalimantan

Celebes

INDONESIA

Timor

AUSTRALIA

PACIFIC OCEAN

Tropic of Cancer

632

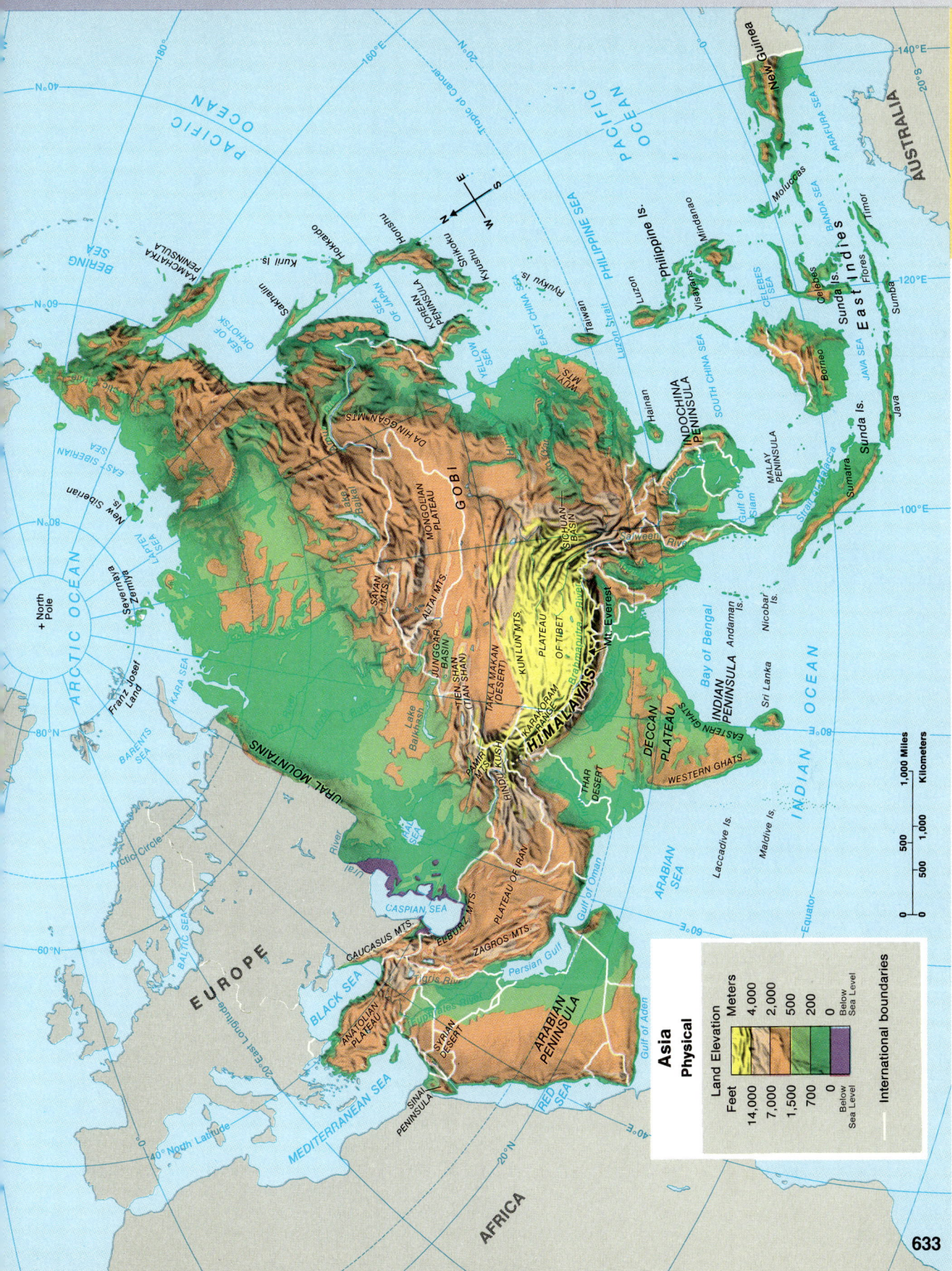

Asia
Physical

Land Elevation

Feet	Meters
14,000	4,000
7,000	2,000
1,500	500
700	200
0	0
Below Sea Level	Below Sea Level

International boundaries

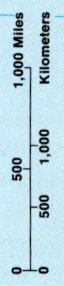

1,000 Miles

1,000 Kilometers

500

1,000

500

0

0

Africa
Political

EUROPE

ATLANTIC OCEAN

ASIA

MEDITERRANEAN SEA

Azores (Port.)

Madeira Is. (Port.)

Algiers · Tunis
Oran
Casablanca · Rabat
Marrakech

TUNISIA
Tripoli
Benghazi

MOROCCO

Canary Is. (Sp.)

El Aaiun

WESTERN SAHARA (Morocco)

ALGERIA

LIBYA

Alexandria
Cairo
Giza

Suez Canal

EGYPT

ASWAN HIGH DAM
Lake Nasser

Nile River

Tropic of Cancer

MAURITANIA

Nouakchott

MALI
Tombouctou

NIGER

CHAD

Port Sudan

RED SEA

CAPE VERDE
Praia

Dakar
SENEGAL
GAMBIA
Banjul
Bissau
GUINEA-BISSAU
Bamako
Senegal River
Niger River

Niamey

Omdurman · Khartoum

Atbara River

GUINEA
Conakry
Freetown
SIERRA LEONE

Ouagadougou
BURKINA FASO

Zaria · Kano

AFRICA
N'Djamena

SUDAN

Blue Nile

White Nile

Lake Tana

DJIBOUTI Djibouti

So (P.D Ye

GHANA
TOGO
BENIN
Yamoussoukro
Monrovia
LIBERIA
Abidjan
CÔTE D'IVOIRE (IVORY COAST)
Lomé
Porto Novo
Accra
Ibadan
Lagos
Cotonou
NIGERIA
Abuja
Benue River
Lake Volta

Addis Ababa

ETHIOPIA

SOMALIA

Mogadishu

CAMEROON
Bangui
CENTRAL AFRICAN REPUBLIC
Malabo
EQUATORIAL GUINEA
Yaoundé

Ubangi River

São Tomé
SÃO TOMÉ AND PRINCIPE
Libreville
P.R. OF THE CONGO
Equator

GABON

Zaire River

Congo River

UGANDA
Kampala
Lake Albert
Lake Victoria
KENYA
Nairobi

Lake Turkana

Brazzaville · Kinshasa

ZAIRE
RWANDA Kigali
Bujumbura **BURUNDI**

Mombasa

CABINDA (Angola)

Luanda

Kasai River

TANZANIA
Dodoma
Zanzibar
Dar es Salaam

Lake Tanganyika

ATLANTIC OCEAN

ANGOLA

MALAWI
Lilongwe
Lake Nyasa

Moroni
COMOROS

ZAMBIA
Lusaka
Zambezi River

Victoria Falls
Lake Kariba

Harare

ZIMBABWE
MOZAMBIQUE

Antananariv
MADAGASCAR

Réu (Fr

NAMIBIA (South Africa)

BOTSWANA

Limpopo River

Tropic of Capr

Walvis Bay (South Africa)
Windhoek

Gaborone
Pretoria
Johannesburg
Maputo
Mbabane **SWAZILAND**

Vaal River
Orange River

Bloemfontein
Maseru
LESOTHO
Durban

SOUTH AFRICA

Cape Town
Port Elizabeth

INDIAN OCEAN

SEYCH

Gulf of Aden

Legend

——	International boundaries
⊛	National capitals
•	Other cities

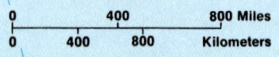

0   400   800 Miles
0   400   800   Kilometers

N
W — E
S

© SF

ATLANTIC OCEAN

EUROPE

ASIA

MEDITERRANEAN SEA

Azores

40°N

Madeira Is.

Strait of Gibraltar

ATLAS MOUNTAINS

Canary Is.

Gulf of Sidra

LIBYAN DESERT

Suez Canal

Tropic of Cancer

S A H A R A

AHAGGAR PLATEAU

TIBESTI MOUNTAINS

NUBIAN DESERT

Lake Nasser

RED SEA

20°N

Cape Verde

Senegal River

S A H E L

Niger River

Lake Chad

GEZIRA

Gulf of Aden

Lake Tana

ETHIOPIAN HIGHLANDS

HORN OF AFRICA

SOMALI PENINSULA

Lake Volta

Volta River

Benue River

Mt. Cameroon

Ubangi River

GREAT RIFT VALLEY

Lake Turkana

São Tomé

Cape Lopez

CONGO BASIN

Lake Albert

Mt. Kenya

Equator 0°

Lake Victoria

Mt. Kilimanjaro

Zanzibar

Kasai River

ATLANTIC OCEAN

Lake Tanganyika

Cape Delgado

KATANGA PLATEAU

Comoro Is.

Lake Nyasa / Lake Malawi

Mozambique Channel

Madagascar

Lake Kariba

Zambezi River

OKAVANGO SWAMP

Victoria Falls

20°S

NAMIB DESERT

KALAHARI DESERT

Limpopo River

Tropic of Capricorn

Orange River

Vaal River

DRAKENSBERG RANGE

GREAT KARROO

N
W   E
S

INDIAN OCEAN

Cape of Good Hope

Africa
Physical

Land Elevation

Feet	Meters
14,000	4,000
7,000	2,000
1,500	500
700	200
0	0
Below Sea Level	Below Sea Level

—— International boundaries

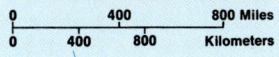

Miles: 0 — 400 — 800
Kilometers: 0 — 400 — 800

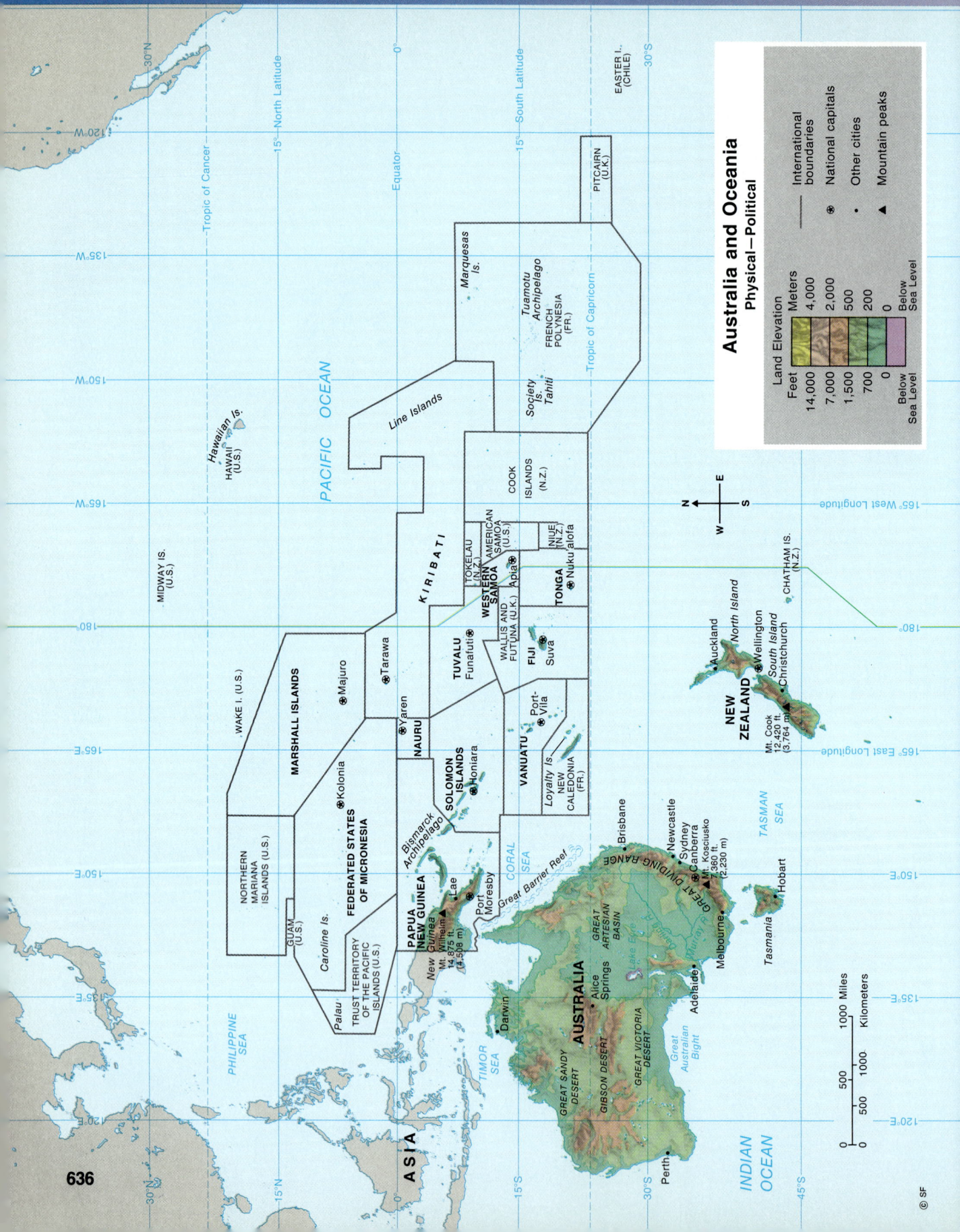

Australia and Oceania
Physical–Political

Land Elevation

Feet	Meters
14,000	4,000
7,000	2,000
1,500	500
700	200
0	0
Below Sea Level	Below Sea Level

International boundaries

⊕ National capitals

· Other cities

▲ Mountain peaks

PACIFIC OCEAN

EASTER I. (CHILE)

PITCAIRN (U.K.)

Marquesas Is.

Tuamotu Archipelago

FRENCH POLYNESIA (FR.)

Society Is. Tahiti

Tropic of Capricorn

Line Islands

COOK ISLANDS (N.Z.)

Hawaiian Is.
Hawaii (U.S.)

MIDWAY IS. (U.S.)

K I R I B A T I

TOKELAU (N.Z.)

AMERICAN SAMOA (U.S.)

WESTERN SAMOA
⊕ Apia

NIUE (N.Z.)

TONGA
⊙ Nuku'alofa

WAKE I. (U.S.)

MARSHALL ISLANDS

⊕ Majuro

· Tarawa

· Yaren
NAURU

TUVALU
Funafuti ⊕

WALLIS AND FUTUNA (U.K.)

FIJI
⊙ Suva

NORTHERN MARIANA ISLANDS (U.S.)

FEDERATED STATES OF MICRONESIA

⊕ Kolonia

Caroline Is.

GUAM (U.S.)

TRUST TERRITORY OF THE PACIFIC ISLANDS (U.S.)

Palau

SOLOMON ISLANDS
· Honiara

Bismarck Archipelago

VANUATU
⊙ Port-Vila

Loyalty Is.
NEW CALEDONIA (FR.)

CORAL SEA

CHATHAM IS. (N.Z.)

NEW ZEALAND

Auckland
North Island
· Wellington
South Island
Christchurch ▲
Mt. Cook 12,420 ft. (3,764 m)

PAPUA NEW GUINEA
· Lae
Port Moresby
New Guinea ▲ Mt. Wilhelm 14,875 ft. (4,508 m)

PHILIPPINE SEA

TIMOR SEA

A S I A

AUSTRALIA

Darwin ·

Alice Springs ·

GREAT SANDY DESERT

GIBSON DESERT

GREAT VICTORIA DESERT

Great Australian Bight

Perth ·

INDIAN OCEAN

GREAT ARTESIAN BASIN

GREAT DIVIDING RANGE

Lake Eyre

Murray R.

▲ Mt. Kosciusko 7,360 ft. (2,230 m)

Brisbane ·

Newcastle ·
Sydney ·
Canberra ⊕

Melbourne ·

Adelaide ·

Hobart ·
Tasmania

TASMAN SEA

Great Barrier Reef

1000 Miles

500 1000 Kilometers

0 500 1000

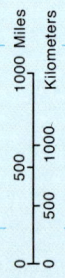

© SF

SEA OF OKHOTSK

ASIA

UNION OF SOVIET SOCIALIST REPUBLICS
(SOVIET UNION)

Moscow

EUROPE

Archangel

Leningrad

Novaya
Zemlya

KARA
SEA

BARENTS
SEA

FINLAND

LAPTEV
SEA

Severnaya
Zemlya

Franz Josef
Land

Murmansk

BALTIC SEA

New
Siberian
Is.

Hammerfest

SWEDEN

NORWAY

Narvik

Bergen

NORTH
SEA

80°N

Svalbard
(Norway)

NORWEGIAN
SEA

EAST
SIBERIAN
SEA

Arctic Circle

Paris

North Pole

London

CHUKCHI SEA

ARCTIC OCEAN

UNITED
KINGDOM

BERING SEA

Bering Strait

Nome

Barrow

BEAUFORT
SEA

Ellesmere I.

ICELAND

Reykjavik

Denmark Strait

ATLANTIC
OCEAN

ALASKA
(U.S.)

Mt. McKinley
20,320 ft.
(6,194 m)

Greenland
(Denmark)

Thule

20°W

Mt. Logan
15,520 ft.
(5,950 m)

Arctic Archipelago

Baffin
Bay

PACIFIC
OCEAN

Victoria I.

Baffin I.

Davis Strait

Godthåb

Mackenzie R.

CANADA

NORTH AMERICA

LABRADOR
SEA

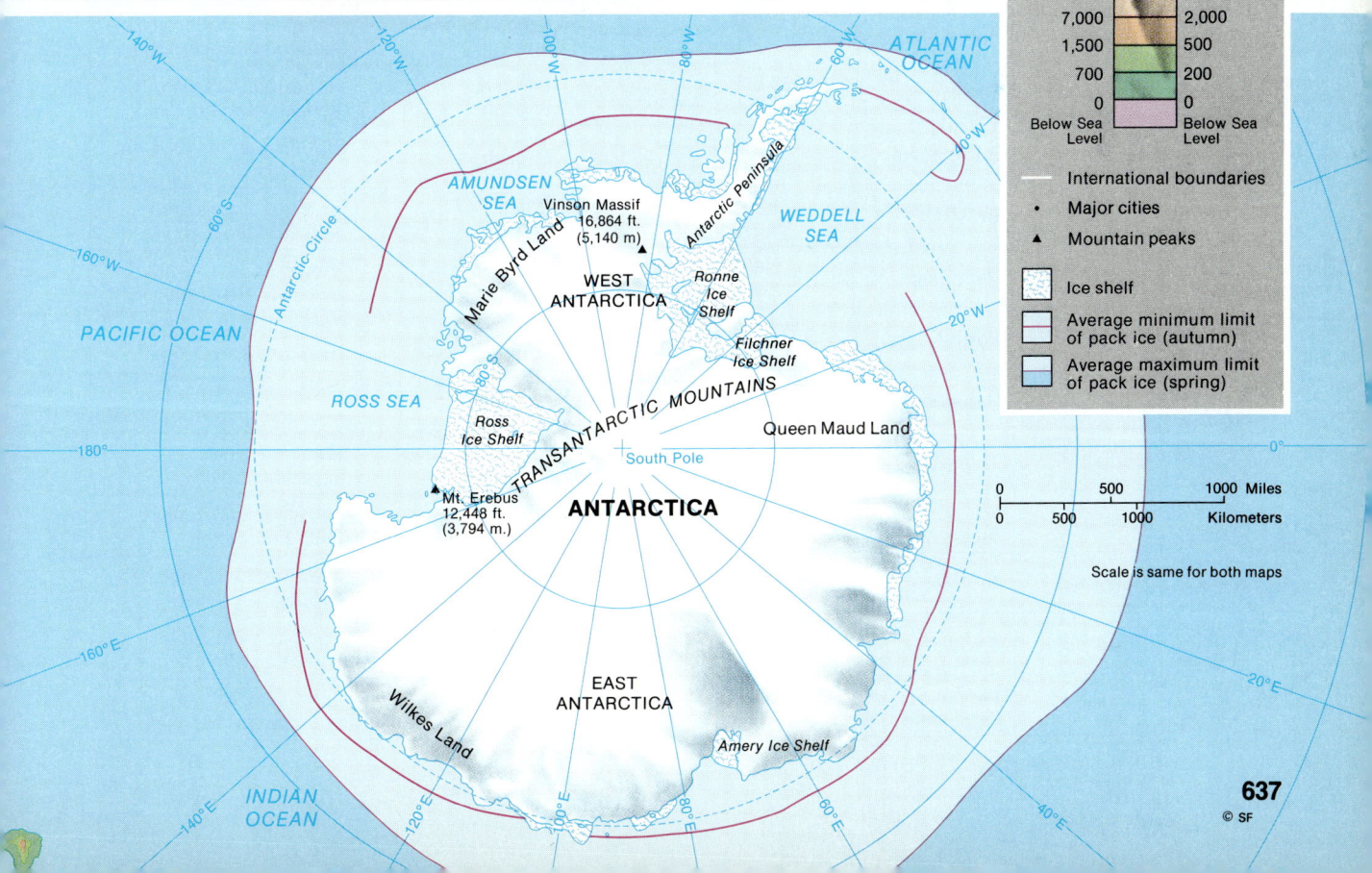

ATLANTIC
OCEAN

140°W

120°W

AMUNDSEN
SEA

WEDDELL
SEA

Antarctic Circle

160°W

Vinson Massif
16,864 ft.
(5,140 m)

Antarctic Peninsula

Marie Byrd Land

WEST
ANTARCTICA

Ronne
Ice
Shelf

20°W

PACIFIC OCEAN

Filchner
Ice Shelf

ROSS SEA

TRANSANTARCTIC MOUNTAINS

Queen Maud Land

180°

Ross
Ice
Shelf

South Pole

0°

Mt. Erebus
12,448 ft.
(3,794 m.)

ANTARCTICA

160°E

EAST
ANTARCTICA

20°E

Wilkes Land

INDIAN
OCEAN

Amery Ice Shelf

140°E

120°E

60°E

40°E

Polar Regions
Physical–Political

Land Elevation

Feet		Meters
14,000		4,000
7,000		2,000
1,500		500
700		200
0		0
Below Sea Level		Below Sea Level

—— International boundaries

• Major cities

▲ Mountain peaks

Ice shelf

Average minimum limit
of pack ice (autumn)

Average maximum limit
of pack ice (spring)

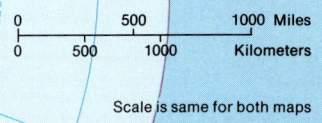

0	500	1000 Miles
0	500	1000 Kilometers

Scale is same for both maps

637

© SF

Facts About Countries

Flag	Country or Dependency	Capital	Area	Population	Major or Official Languages	Important Products
	Afghanistan	Kabul	250,000 (mi²) 647,497 (km²)	19,000,000	Pushtu, Dari Persian	carpets, natural gas, fruit, salt, coal, wheat
	Albania	Tirana	11,099 28,748	3,000,000	Albanian	minerals, metals, olives, cereals, tobacco, lumber
	Algeria	Algiers	919,591 2,381,741	23,000,000	Arabic, French	wheat, barley, petroleum, wine, fruit, iron ore
	Andorra	Andorra la Vella	175 453	47,000	French, Spanish	livestock, tobacco, cereals, potatoes, iron ore
	Angola	Luanda	481,351 1,246,700	8,000,000	Bantu languages, Portuguese	coffee, diamonds, cotton, oil, fish, iron ore
	Anguilla (UK)	The Valley	35 91	8,000	English	fruit, vegetables, lobsters, fish, salt
	Antigua and Barbuda	St. Johns	171 442	83,000	English	cotton, clothing, rum, molasses, sugar, bananas
	Argentina	Buenos Aires	1,068,297 2,766,889	31,000,000	Spanish	meat, wool, hides, wheat, corn, fruit, vegetables
	Australia	Canberra	2,967,895 7,686,848	16,000,000	English	wheat, wool, livestock, metal ores, coal, bauxite
	Austria	Vienna	32,374 83,849	8,000,000	German	lumber, metal products, paper, textiles, food
	Azores (PO)	Ponta Delgada	902 2,335	280,000	Portuguese	farm products, fish, fruit, grains
	Bahamas	Nassau	5,380 13,935	232,000	English	pharmaceuticals, salt, fish, lobsters, rum
	Bahrain	Manama	254 659	400,000	Arabic, English, French	petroleum products, fish, aluminum processing
	Bangladesh	Dhaka	55,598 143,998	104,000,000	Bengali, English	jute goods, tea, fish, leather, seafood, hides
	Barbados	Bridgetown	166 431	280,000	English	clothing, molasses, rum, sugar, fish, lime
	Belgium	Brussels	11,781 30,513	10,000,000	Dutch, French	precious stones, iron and steel products
	Belize	Belmopan	8,867 22,965	161,000	English, Spanish	molasses, rice, lumber, livestock, fish, fruit
	Benin	Porto-Novo	43,483 112,622	4,000,000	French, others	palm oil, cotton, cocoa beans, fish, iron ore
	Bermuda (UK)	Hamilton	20 53	60,000	English	perfumes, petroleum products, pharmaceuticals
	Bhutan	Thimphu	18,147 47,000	1,000,000	Dzongkha, Nepali	lumber, fruit, coal, vegetables, cement
	Bolivia	La Paz, Sucre	424,163 1,098,581	7,000,000	Spanish, Quechua, Aymara	petroleum, tin, gold, lead, zinc, coffee
	Botswana	Gaborone	231,804 600,372	1,000,000	English, Setswana	livestock, diamonds, copper, nickel, salt
	Brazil	Brasília	3,286,473 8,511,965	140,000,000	Portuguese	iron ore, steel, motor vehicles, coffee, sugar
	Brunei	Bandar Seri Begawan	2,226 5,765	221,000	Malay, English, Chinese	petroleum, rubber, lumber, rice, pepper, bananas

(UK) United Kingdom   (PO) Portugal

Flag	Country or Dependency	Capital	Area	Population	Major or Official Languages	Important Products
	Bulgaria	Sofia	42,823 (mi²) 110,912 (km²)	9,000,000	Bulgarian	farm products, minerals, machinery, equipment
	Burkina Faso	Ouaga-dougou	105,869 274,200	8,000,000	French, others	livestock, cotton, peanuts, sesame, grains
	Burma	Rangoon	261,216 676,552	37,000,000	Burmese	teak, rice, sugar, precious stones, rubber
	Burundi	Bujumbura	10,747 27,834	5,000,000	Kirundi, French	cotton, hides, tea, coffee, bananas, grain
	Cambodia (Kampuchea)	Phnom Penh	69,898 181,035	6,000,000	Khmer	fish, rubber, paper, timber, rice, sugar
	Cameroon	Yaoundé	183,568 475,442	10,000,000	English, French, others	cotton, coffee, cocoa beans, tea, rubber
	Canada	Ottawa	3,851,791 9,976,139	27,000,000	English, French	motor vehicles, machinery, lumber, metal ores
	Canary Islands (SP)	Las Palmas	2,808 7,273	1,000,000	Spanish	fish, fruit, grains, wine, vegetables, sugar
	Cape Verde	Praia	1,557 4,033	356,000	Portuguese	fish, shellfish, salt, bananas, coffee, sugar
	Cayman Islands (UK)	Georgetown	100 259	20,000	English	turtle products, fish, lobsters
	Central African Republic	Bangui	240,534 622,984	3,000,000	French, Sango	coffee, diamonds, cocoa beans, lumber, cotton
	Chad	N'Djamena	495,752 1,284,000	5,000,000	French, Arabic, others	livestock, cotton, rice, animal products, fish
	Chile	Santiago	292,256 756,945	12,000,000	Spanish	paper, lumber, copper, iron, nitrates, fish
	China	Beijing	3,705,390 9,596,961	1,000,000,000	Mandarin Chinese, others	farm products, petroleum, minerals, metals
	Colombia	Bogotá	439,735 1,138,914	30,000,000	Spanish	petroleum, coffee, sugar, cotton, textiles
	Comoros	Moroni	719 1,862	469,000	Arabic, French	vanilla, copra, cloves, perfume essences, sugar
	Congo	Brazzaville	132,046 342,000	2,000,000	French, Lingala, Kokongo	lumber, petroleum, cocoa beans, palm oil, sugar
	Cook Islands (NZ)	Avarua	93 241	21,000	English	citrus, clothing, canned fruit, vegetables
	Costa Rica	San José	19,575 50,700	3,000,000	Spanish	livestock, sugar, cocoa beans, coffee, palm oil
	Cuba	Havana	44,218 114,524	10,000,000	Spanish	sugar, rice, citrus, tobacco, nickel, fish
	Cyprus	Nicosia	3,572 9,251	700,000	Greek, Turkish	cereals, citrus, grapes, potatoes, copper, cement
	Czechoslo-vakia	Prague	49,370 127,869	16,000,000	Czech, Slovak, Hungarian	iron and steel, machinery, beer, wheat, potatoes
	Denmark	Copenhagen	16,629 43,069	5,000,000	Danish	machinery, textiles, dairy products, clothing
	Djibouti	Djibouti	8,494 22,000	481,000	Arabic, French, Afar, Somali	salt, livestock, hides
	Dominica	Roseau	290 751	88,000	English, French patois	cocoa beans, lime juice, bananas, pumice, fruit

(SP) Spain   (NZ) New Zealand

Flag	Country or Dependency	Capital	Area	Population	Major or Official Languages	Important Products
	Dominican Republic	Santo Domingo	18,816 (mi²) 48,734 (km²)	7,000,000	Spanish	coffee, tobacco, bauxite, nickel, sugar, cocoa
	Ecuador	Quito	109,483 283,561	10,000,000	Spanish, Quechua	bananas, coffee, cocoa beans, fish, petroleum
	Egypt	Cairo	386,659 1,001,449	48,000,000	Arabic	cotton, textiles, chemicals, rice, petrochemicals
	El Salvador	San Salvador	8,124 21,041	6,000,000	Spanish	cotton, coffee, sugar, livestock, lumber, rice
	Equatorial Guinea	Malabo	10,830 28,051	282,000	Spanish, Fang, Bubi	lumber, coffee, cocoa beans, bananas, fish
	Ethiopia	Addis Ababa	471,776 1,221,900	36,000,000	Amharic, others	hides, coffee, oilseeds, fruits, vegetables, metals
	Falkland Islands (UK)	Stanley	4,700 12,173	3,000	English	wool, hides, whales
	Fiji	Suva	7,056 18,274	700,000	Fijian, Hindi, English	copra, sugar, gold, lumber, bananas, ginger
	Finland	Helsinki	130,128 337,032	5,000,000	Finnish, Swedish	lumber, paper, manufactured goods, glassware
	France	Paris	211,207 547,026	55,000,000	French	machinery, clothing, farm products, textiles
	French Guiana (FR)	Cayenne	35,135 91,000	82,000	French, Creole	shrimp, rice, lumber, gold, bauxite, sugar
	French Polynesia (FR)	Papeete	1,544 4,014	166,000	French, Polynesian languages	coconuts, citrus, bananas, sugar, vanilla, pearls
	Gabon	Libreville	103,346 267,667	1,000,000	French, Bantu languages	coffee, petroleum, lumber, manganese, iron ore, gold
	Gambia	Banjul	4,361 11,295	751,000	English, others	fish, peanuts, cotton, grains, livestock
	Germany, East	East Berlin	41,767 108,178	17,000,000	German	machinery, precision instruments, textiles
	Germany, West	Bonn	95,976 248,577	60,000,000	German	manufactured goods, chemicals, motor vehicles
	Ghana	Accra	92,099 238,537	14,000,000	English, others	lumber, petroleum, gold, manganese, cocoa beans
	Greece	Athens	50,944 131,944	10,000,000	Greek	textiles, minerals, fish, fruit, cotton, tobacco
	Greenland (DE)	Godthab	840,000 2,175,600	54,000	Danish, Greenlande	metallic ore, fish, fish products, seals
	Grenada	St. George's	133 344	116,000	English	cocoa beans, citrus, fish, nutmeg, bananas, sugar
	Guadeloupe (FR)	Basse-Terre	687 1,779	335,000	French, Creole	fruits, vegetables, sugar, vanilla, cocoa beans, fish
	Guam (US)	Agana	212 549	115,000	Chamorro, English	palm oil, fish, copra, citrus, bananas, sugar
	Guatemala	Guatemala	42,042 108,889	9,000,000	Spanish, Indian languages	cotton, sugar, livestock, bananas, coffee, lumber
	Guinea	Conakry	94,925 245,857	6,000,000	French, Fulani, others	bauxite, fruit, coffee, iron ore, rice, bananas
	Guinea-Bissau	Bissau	13,948 36,125	640,000	Portuguese	peanuts, palm oil, fish, shrimp, lumber, coconuts
	Guyana	Georgetown	83,000 214,969	1,000,000	English, Hindi, Urdu	bauxite, aluminum, sugar, rice, shrimp, coffee

Flag	Country or Dependency	Capital	Area	Population	Major or Official Languages	Important Products
	Haiti	Port-au-Prince	10,714 (mi²) 27,750 (km²)	7,000,000	French, Creole	coffee, sugar, rice, textiles, bauxite
	Honduras	Tegucigalpa	43,277 112,088	5,000,000	Spanish, Indian languages	bananas, coffee, sugar, lumber, livestock
	Hong Kong (UK)	Victoria	403 1,045	6,000,000	Chinese, English	textiles, clothing, electronic goods, cameras, shoes
	Hungary	Budapest	35,919 93,030	11,000,000	Hungarian	consumer goods, tools, machinery, wheat, fruit
	Iceland	Reykjavik	39,768 103,000	245,000	Icelandic	fish, livestock, dairy products, chemicals
	India	New Delhi	1,269,339 3,287,590	767,000,000	Hindi, others	clothing, textiles, jute, machinery, cars, steel
	Indonesia	Jakarta	788,421 2,042,012	164,000,000	Bahasa Indonesia, others	petroleum, tin, lumber, rubber, tea, rice
	Iran	Tehran	636,293 1,648,000	45,000,000	Farsi, Kurdish, Azerbaijani	wheat, petroleum, livestock, textiles, cement
	Iraq	Baghdad	167,925 434,924	16,000,000	Arabic, Kurdish	petroleum, cement, livestock, cotton, textiles
	Ireland	Dublin	27,136 70,283	4,000,000	Irish, English	chemicals, dairy products, textiles, machinery
	Israel	Jerusalem	8,019 20,770	4,000,000	Hebrew, Arabic	citrus, chemicals, clothing, machinery, food products
	Italy	Rome	116,303 301,225	58,000,000	Italian	clothing, shoes, textiles, machinery, foods, cars
	Ivory Coast (Cote d'Ivoire)	Abidjan	124,503 322,463	10,000,000	French, others	lumber, coffee, cocoa beans, sugar, cotton
	Jamaica	Kingston	4,244 10,991	2,000,000	English	bauxite, bananas, sugar, citrus, rum, cocoa beans
	Japan	Tokyo	143,750 372,313	121,000,000	Japanese	cars, metal products, textiles, electronics
	Jordan	Amman	37,737 97,740	4,000,000	Arabic	phosphates, fruits, olives, copper, sulfur
	Kenya	Nairobi	244,960 582,646	20,000,000	Swahili, Bantu languages, English	livestock, coffee, tea, hides, cement, sugar
	Kiribati	Bairiki	281 728	68,000	English, Gilbertese	copra, fish, mother-of-pearl, phosphates
	Korea, North	Pyongyang	46,540 120,538	21,000,000	Korean	chemicals, minerals, rice, wheat, cement
	Korea, South	Seoul	38,025 98,484	42,000,000	Korean	machinery, steel, clothing, footwear
	Kuwait	Kuwait	6,880 17,818	2,000,000	Arabic, English	petroleum, shrimp, fertilizer
	Laos	Vientiane	91,429 236,800	4,000,000	Lao	lumber, tin, coffee, textiles, fruits, rice
	Lebanon	Beirut	4,015 10,400	3,000,000	Arabic, French	textiles, fruits, lumber, jewelry, cotton, tobacco
	Lesotho	Maseru	11,720 30,355	2,000,000	English, Sesotho	livestock, diamonds, hides, wool, wheat
	Liberia	Monrovia	43,000 111,800	2,000,000	English, others	lumber, iron ore, gold, cocoa beans, coffee, fish
	Libya	Tripoli	679,359 1,759,540	4,000,000	Arabic	petroleum, olives, dates, barley, citrus fruit

Flag	Country or Dependency	Capital	Area	Population	Major or Official Languages	Important Products
	Liechtenstein	Vaduz	61 (mi²) 157 (km²)	27,000	German	chemicals, metal products machinery, optical lenses
	Luxembourg	Luxembourg	998 2,586	367,000	Luxembourgish, German, French	chemicals, steel, oats, barley, potatoes, wheat
	Macao (PO)	Macao	6 16	320,000	Chinese, Portuguese	manufactured goods, fish, electronic goods, clothing
	Madagascar	Antananarivo	226,657 587,041	10,000,000	Malagasy, French	chromium, graphite, cloves, cotton, coffee
	Malawi	Lilongwe	45,747 118,484	8,000,000	English, Chichewa	fish, tobacco, peanuts, fertilizer, textiles
	Malaysia	Kuala Lumpur	127,316 329,749	16,000,000	Malay, Chinese, Tamil, English	petroleum, lumber, tin, rubber, palm oil, textiles
	Maldives	Male	115 298	177,000	Divehi	coconuts, fish, millet, breadfruit, vegetables
	Mali	Bamako	478,764 1,240,000	8,000,000	French, others	fish, livestock, cotton, peanuts, textiles, rice
	Malta	Valletta	122 316	360,000	Maltese, English	manufactured goods, ships, textiles, fruits
	Marshall Islands	Majuro	70 183	31,000	English, others	copra, tortoise shell, mother-of-pearl, fish
	Martinique (FR)	Fort-de-France	425 1,102	329,000	French, Creole	bananas, rum, sugar, pineapples, vegetables
	Mauritania	Nouakchott	397,953 1,030,700	2,000,000	Arabic, French	copper, iron ore, dates, cereals, vegetables
	Mauritius	Port Louis	790 2,045	1,000,000	English, others	molasses, sugar, tea, iron ore, rice, fish
	Mexico	Mexico City	761,601 1,972,547	80,000,000	Spanish, Indian languages	cotton, petroleum, corn, livestock, coffee, minerals
	Micronesia	Kolonia	280 726	80,000	English, others	copra, fish, handicrafts
	Monaco	Monaco-Ville	.73 1.90	26,000	French, Monégasque	industrial products, chemicals, perfume
	Mongolia	Ulaanbaatar	604,247 1,565,000	2,000,000	Mongolian	livestock, wheat, oats, footwear, minerals
	Montserrat (UK)	Plymouth	40 104	14,000	English	cotton, mangoes, citrus, livestock, potatoes
	Morocco	Rabat	172,413 446,550	25,000,000	Arabic, Berber, French, Spanish	phosphates, citrus, carpets, chemicals
	Mozambique	Maputo	309,494 801,590	14,000,000	Portuguese, Bantu languages	cotton, cashew nuts, sugar, copra, tea
	Namibia (SA)	Windhoek	318,259 824,292	1,000,000	Afrikaans, English, others	sheepskins, diamonds, uranium, copper, lead
	Nauru	Yaren	8 21	8,000	Nauruan, English	phosphates
	Nepal	Katmandu	54,362 140,797	17,000,000	Nepali, Newari	rice, lumber, grain, sugar, jute, cotton
	Netherlands	Amsterdam, The Hague	16,041 41,548	14,000,000	Dutch	manufactured goods, foods, flower bulbs
	Netherlands Antilles (NE)	Willemstad	308 800	223,000	Dutch	phosphates, sugar, fruits, vegetables, fish

(SA) South Africa   (NE) Netherlands

Flag	Country or Dependency	Capital	Area	Population	Major or Official Languages	Important Products
	New Caledonia (FR)	Nouméa	7,358 (mi²) 19,058 (km²)	148,000	French, Melanesian languages	nickel, coffee, copra, chrome, iron, cobalt
	New Zealand	Wellington	103,736 268,676	3,000,000	English, Maori	lumber, dairy products, wool, manufactured goods
	Nicaragua	Managua	50,193 130,000	3,000,000	Spanish, Indian languages	coffee, cotton, sugar, chemicals, livestock
	Niger	Niamey	489,189 1,267,000	6,000,000	French, Hausa, others	coal, iron, uranium, peanuts, livestock
	Nigeria	Lagos	356,667 923,768	91,000,000	English, others	petroleum, lumber, tin, cotton, palm oil
	Northern Marianas (US)	Saipan	185 480	18,000	Chamorro, English	copra, livestock, fish, fruits, vegetables
	Norway	Oslo	125,182 324,219	4,000,000	Norwegian, Lapp	petroleum, lumber, fish, ships, chemicals
	Oman	Muscat	105,000 271,950	1,000,000	Arabic	petroleum, fish, asbestos, dates
	Pakistan	Islamabad	310,402 809,943	103,000,000	Urdu, English, others	cotton, rice, fish, sugar, leather
	Palau (US)	Koror	191 494	16,000	English, others	bauxite, yams, copra, fruits, fish, handicrafts
	Panama	Panama City	29,761 77,082	2,000,000	Spanish, English	bananas, sugar, rice, coffee, lumber, corn
	Papua New Guinea	Port Moresby	178,259 461,691	4,000,000	Melanesian languages, English	cocoa beans, copra, lumber, copper, rubber
	Paraguay	Asunción	157,047 406,752	4,000,000	Spanish, Guarani	livestock, tobacco, cotton, oilseeds, lumber
	Peru	Lima	496,222 1,285,216	21,000,000	Spanish, Quechua, Aymara	coffee, cotton, sugar, fish, copper, silver
	Philippines	Manila	115,830 300,000	57,000,000	Pilipino, English, others	lumber, sugar, textiles, coconuts, tobacco
	Poland	Warsaw	120,725 312,677	38,000,000	Polish	machinery, textiles, coal, iron, steel
	Portugal	Lisbon	35,552 92,082	10,000,000	Portuguese	cork, fish, wine, olives, textiles
	Puerto Rico (US)	San Juan	3,435 8,897	3,000,000	Spanish, English	chemicals, clothing, fish, electronic goods, sugar
	Qatar	Doha	4,247 11,000	300,000	Arabic	petroleum, fish, steel
	Réunion (FR)	Saint-Denis	969 2,510	571,000	French, Creole	sugar, beans, vanilla, molasses, rum, bananas
	Romania	Bucharest	91,699 237,500	23,000,000	Romanian, Hungarian, others	lumber, petroleum, coal, machinery, minerals
	Rwanda	Kigali	10,169 26,338	6,000,000	Kinyarwandu, French	coffee, tea, beans, potatoes, livestock
	St. Christopher and Nevis	Basseterre	100 258	50,000	English	molasses, sugar, cotton, salt, fish, spices
	St. Helena (UK)	Jamestown	47 122	5,000	English	fruits, vegetables, handicrafts
	St. Lucia	Castries	238 619	130,000	English, French patois	bananas, coconuts, fish, cocoa beans, spices
	St. Vincent and the Grenadines	Kingstown	150 390	138,000	English	bananas, arrowroot, copra, nutmeg, sugar

Flag	Country or Dependency	Capital	Area	Population	Major or Official Languages	Important Products
	Samoa, American (US)	Pago Pago	76 (mi²) 198 (km²)	34,000	Samoan, English	tuna, pet food, fish meal, handicrafts
	Samoa, Western	Apia	1,093 2,831	163,000	Samoan, English	copra, cocoa beans, lumber, bananas
	San Marino	San Marino	23 61	21,000	Italian	lime, building stone, wheat, textiles, wine
	São Tomé and Príncipe	São Tomé	372 964	106,000	Portuguese	copra, palm oil, cocoa beans, lumber, bananas
	Saudi Arabia	Riyadh	829,996 2,149,690	11,000,000	Arabic	petroleum, cement, dates, chemicals, livestock
	Senegal	Dakar	75,750 196,192	7,000,000	French, Wolof, others	phosphates, fertilizer, peanut oil, cotton, fish
	Seychelles	Victoria	108 280	69,000	English, French	copra, vanilla, fish, livestock, cinnamon
	Sierra Leone	Freetown	27,699 71,740	4,000,000	English, Mende, others	coffee, cocoa beans, fish, ginger, peanuts, sugar
	Singapore	Singapore	224 581	3,000,000	English, Chinese, Malay, Tamil	manufactured goods, fish, electronic goods, textiles
	Solomon Islands	Honiara	10,983 28,446	273,000	Melanesian languages, English	lumber, fish, copra, rice, palm oil, spices
	Somalia	Mogadishu	246,199 637,657	6,000,000	Somali	spices, iron ore, livestock, bananas, peanuts
	South Africa	Capetown, Pretoria	471,443 1,221,037	33,000,000	Afrikaans, English, Bantu languages	gold, diamonds, uranium, wool, fruits, chrome
	Spain	Madrid	194,896 504,782	39,000,000	Spanish, Catalan, Galician, Basque	footwear, fruit, vegetables, cars, clothing
	Sri Lanka	Colombo	25,332 65,610	17,000,000	Sinhala, Tamil, English	rubber, tea, graphite, petroleum, spices, fish
	Sudan	Khartoum	967,495 2,505,813	22,000,000	Arabic, others	livestock, peanuts, copper, cotton, sesame seeds
	Suriname	Paramaribo	63,251 163,820	460,000	Dutch, Surinamese, English	aluminum, bauxite, citrus, lumber, shrimp, sugar
	Swaziland	Mbabane	6,704 17,363	671,000	English, Siswati	coal, iron ore, citrus, cotton, livestock, sugar
	Sweden	Stockholm	173,731 449,964	8,000,000	Swedish	lumber, motor vehicles, machinery, iron and steel
	Switzerland	Bern	15,941 41,288	6,000,000	German, French, Italian	precision instruments, dairy products, chemicals
	Syria	Damascus	71,498 185,180	11,000,000	Arabic	clothing, fruits, vegetables, cotton, petroleum
	Taiwan	Taipei	13,885 35,961	20,000,000	Mandarin Chinese	electrical machinery, footwear, textiles, citrus
	Tanzania	Dar es Salaam	364,898 945,087	22,000,000	Swahili, Bantu languages, English	diamonds, cashews, sisal, cloves, coffee, tea
	Thailand	Bangkok	198,456 514,000	54,000,000	Thai, Chinese	rubber, tapioca, tin, rice, textiles, lumber
	Togo	Lomé	21,925 56,785	3,000,000	Ewe, Mina, others	coffee, cocoa beans, rice, phosphates, cotton, iron
	Tonga	Nuku'alofa	290 751	107,000	Tongan, English	coconuts, bananas, vanilla, pineapples, papayas, fish

Flag	Country or Dependency	Capital	Area	Population	Major or Official Languages	Important Products
	Trinidad and Tobago	Port-of-Spain	1,981 (mi²) 5,130 (km²)	1,000,000	English, Hindi	ammonia, fertilizer, petroleum, sugar, rice
	Tunisia	Tunis	63,379 164,152	7,000,000	Arabic, French	textiles, phosphates, olive oil, fertilizers
	Turkey	Ankara	301,381 780,576	52,000,000	Turkish	fruits, textiles, foods, livestock, cotton, nuts
	Turks and Caicos (UK)	Grand Turk	166 430	8,000	English	salt, crayfish, conch shells, fish
	Tuvalu	Funafuti	10 26	8,000	Tuvaluan, English	bananas, handicrafts, copra, postage stamps
	Uganda	Kampala	91,343 236,880	15,000,000	English, Swahili, others	cotton, coffee, tea, tobacco, sugar, textiles
	Union of Soviet Socialist Republics	Moscow	8,649,490 22,402,200	281,000,000	Russian, Ukrainian, others	petroleum, machinery, lumber, grains, cotton
	United Arab Emirates	Abu Dhabi	32,278 83,600	1,000,000	Arabic, others	petroleum, fish, pearls, dates, tobacco, fruits
	United Kingdom	London	92,247 244,100	56,000,000	English, Welsh, Gaelic	chemicals, foods, iron and steel, motor vehicles
	United States of America	Washington, D.C.	3,615,105 9,363,123	240,000,000	English	aircraft, chemicals, machinery, grain, fruits
	Uruguay	Montevideo	68,037 176,215	3,000,000	Spanish	livestock, wool, leather, textiles, wheat, rice
	Vanuatu	Port-Vila	5,700 14,763	138,000	Bislama, English, French	fish, copra, cocoa beans, livestock
	Vatican City	Vatican City	.17 .44	1,000	Italian, Latin	coins, postage stamps
	Venezuela	Caracas	352,143 912,050	18,000,000	Spanish	petroleum, iron ore, coffee, cocoa beans
	Vietnam	Hanoi	127,242 329,556	60,000,000	Vietnamese	coal, minerals, fruits, vegetables, rice, rubber
	Virgin Islands (UK)	Road Town	59 153	12,000	English	fruits, vegetables, livestock, coconuts
	Virgin Islands (US)	Charlotte Amalie	133 344	107,000	English	manufacturing, petroleum refining, fruits, sugar
	Yemen, North	Sanaa	75,289 195,000	6,000,000	Arabic	coffee, cotton, wheat, hides, fruits, vegetables
	Yemen, South	Aden	128,559 332,968	2,000,000	Arabic	fish, salt, petroleum products, dates, cotton
	Yugoslavia	Belgrade	98,766 255,804	23,000,000	Serbo-Croatian, Slovene, others	processed foods, lumber, chemicals, shoes, fruits
	Zaire	Kinshasa	905,563 2,345,409	33,000,000	French, Bantu languages	copper, diamonds, cobalt, petroleum, coffee
	Zambia	Lusaka	290,584 752,614	7,000,000	English, Bantu languages	cobalt, lead, zinc, cotton, chemicals
	Zimbabwe	Harare	150,803 390,580	9,000,000	English, Shona, Sindebele	cotton, fruits, sugar, copper, chrome, nickel

Countries

Gazetteer

Pronunciation Key

a hat	i it	oi oil
ā age	ī ice	ou out
ä far	o hot	u cup
e let	ō open	ù put
ē equal	ô order	ü rule
èr term		

ch child	a in about
ng long	e in taken
sh she	ə = i in pencil
th thin	o in lemon
ŦH then	u in circus
zh measure	

The key to the pronunciation of foreign sounds is on page 657 of the Index.

Abidjan [ab'i jän'], a seaport and capital of the Ivory Coast, on the west coast of Africa. (5°N/4°W), pp. 478, 634

Abuja, Nigeria [a bü'jə], the future capital of Nigeria located in the center of the nation, in West Africa. (8°N/8°E), p. 478

Adriatic Sea [ā'drē at'ik], an arm of the Mediterranean Sea, between Italy and Yugoslavia. (43°N/16°E), pp. 328, 631

Aegean Sea [i jē'ən], a sea between Greece and Turkey. (37°N/25°E), pp. 328, 631

Afghanistan [af gan'ə stan], a mountainous country in Southwest Asia, between Pakistan and Iran. (33°N/65°E), pp. 394, 632

Algeria [al jir ē ə], a country in north Africa, on the Mediterranean Sea. (35°N/3°E), pp. 394, 634

Alps, the highest mountains in Europe. They extend from eastern France through Switzerland, southern West Germany, Austria, and northern Italy. (47°N/8°E), pp. 26–27, 631

Amazon Basin [am'a zon, am'ə zen], the area in South America drained by the Amazon River and its tributaries in Brazil, Peru, Ecuador, Bolivia, Colombia, and Venezuela. (8°S/70°W), pp. 199, 629

Anatolian Plateau [an'ə tō'lē ən pla-tō'], a high plateau in central Turkey. (32°N/34°E), pp. 396, 633

Andes [an'dēz], a mountain range in South America that runs north and south near the Pacific coast. It is the world's longest mountain range and second tallest after the Himalayas. (20°S/68°W), pp. 26–27, 629

Angola [ang gō'lə], a country in southwestern Africa, on the Atlantic coast. (12°S/18°E), pp. 494, 634

Antarctica [ant'ärk'tə kə], an ice-covered continent that makes up 9 percent of the world's land, near the South Pole. (90°S), p. 26–27, 608

Antarctic Circle [ant'ärk'tik sėr'kəl], the imaginary boundary of the south polar region, running parallel to the Equator. (66½°S), pp. 26–27, 622

Antarctic Peninsula [ant'ärk'tik pə-nin'sə lə], a peninsula extending from the Antarctic continent northward toward South America. (67°S/60°W), pp. 608, 637

Appalachian Mountains [ap'ə-lā'chən], a mountain range in eastern North America, extending from Canada to the southern United States. (38°N/80°W), pp. 125, 627

Arabian Peninsula [ə rā'bēən pə-nin'sə lə], a large peninsula in Southwest Asia between the Mediterranean Sea, the Red Sea, and the Indian Ocean. (30°N/45°E), pp. 396, 633

Arctic Archipelago [ärk'tik är'kə-pel'əgō], a large group of islands in the Arctic Ocean. (70°N/75°W), pp. 176, 637

Arctic Circle [ärk'tik sėr'kəl], the imaginary boundary of the north polar region, running parallel to the Equator. (66½°N), pp. 26–27, 637

Asunción [ä sün' syön'], the capital of Paraguay, located in the east of the country. (25°S/57°W), pp. 242, 628

Atacama Desert [ät'ə käm'ə], a long, narrow desert in northern Chile. (24°S/69°W), pp. 199, 629

Athens [ath'ənz], the capital of Greece, located in the southeast part of the country. (38°N/24°E), pp. 328, 630

Atlantic Ocean, one of the four oceans of the world, east of North and South America and west of Europe and Africa. (20°W), pp. 54, 622

Atlas Mountains, a mountain range in northwest Africa. (33°N/3°W), pp. 396, 635

Auckland [ôk'lənd], an important seaport in northern New Zealand. (37°S/175°E), pp. 590, 636

Aztec Empire [az'tek em'pīr], the empire of the Aztec civilization near the present-day site of Mexico City. (19°N/99°W), p. 207

Bahama Islands [bə hä'mə], a chain of 700 islands in the West Indies that makes up the independent country of the Bahamas. (24°N/75°W), pp. 220, 626

Bangladesh [bäng'glə desh'], a country in south Asia on the Bay of Bengal; formerly part of India. (24°N/90°E), pp. 536, 632

Beijing [bā'jing'], the capital of China; located near the northeastern coast. (40°N/116°E), pp. 554, 632

Bering Strait [bir'ing strāt], a narrow strait between the Bering Sea and the Arctic Ocean. (66°N/170°W), pp. 125, 624

Biscay, Bay of [bis'kā, bis'kē], an inlet of the Atlantic Ocean, north of Spain and west of France. (45°N/5°W), p. 328

Black Sea, an inland sea between southeastern Europe and western Asia. (43°N/35°E), pp. 346, 631

Bogotá [bō'gə tä'], the capital of Colombia, located in the central part of the country. (5°N/74°W), pp. 242, 628

Bombay [bom bā'], a port city in western India on the Arabian Sea. (19°N/73°E), pp. 536, 632

Borneo [bôr'nē ō], an island in Southeast Asia; includes the country of Brunei and parts of Malaysia and Indonesia. (1°N/115°E), pp. 514, 574

Boston [bô'stən, bos'tən], a seaport city and capital of Massachusetts in the northeastern United States. (42°N/71°W), pp. 147, 624

Brussels [brus'əlz], the capital of Belgium, in the central part of the country. (51°N/4°E), 306, 630

Budapest [bü'də pest], the capital of Hungary, located on the Danube River. (47°N/19°E), pp. 379, 630

Buenos Aires [bwā'nəs er'ēz; bwā' nəs ar'ēz], the capital of Argentina, in the eastern part of the country. (34°S/58°W), pp. 242, 628

Byelorussia [byel'ə rush'ə], an area of the Soviet Union in the northwestern part of the country. (54°N/35°E), p. 363

Cairo [kī'rō], the capital of Egypt, on the Nile River; Africa's largest city. (30°N/31°E), pp. 416, 634

Calcutta [kal kut'ə], a seaport on the eastern coast of India, near the Bay of Bengal. (23°N/88°E), pp. 536, 632

Cambodia [kam bō'dē ə], a country in Southeast Asia. (12°N/105°E), pp. 574, 632

Cameroon [kam'ə rün'], a country in Central Africa. (6°N/12°E), pp. 478, 634

Cape of Good Hope [gùd hōp], a cape near the southwestern tip of Africa. (34°S/16°E), pp. 458, 635

Caracas [kə rä′kəs], the capital of Venezuela, in the northern part of the country. (10°N/67°W), pp. 242, 628

Caspian Sea [kas′pē ən], an inland sea between Europe and Asia in the Soviet Union and Iran. (43°N/50°E), pp. 346, 632

Caucasus Mountains [kô′kə səs], a mountain range in the Soviet Union and Turkey that provides part of the division between Europe and Asia. (43°N/45°E), pp. 346, 633

Central Valley [sen′trəl val′ə], a valley in California, (38°N/121W), p. 624

Chiapas [chē äp′əs], the southernmost state of Mexico. (17°N/93°W), p. 220

Chicago [shə kô′gō], city in northeastern Illinois in the United States. (42°N/88°W), pp. 155, 624–625

China [chī′nə], the world's most populous country, located in East Asia. (30°N/110°E), pp. 554, 632

Colorado Plateau [kol′ə rad′ō pla-tō′], a plateau west of the Rocky Mountains in the western United States. (37°N/110°W), pp. 125, 624–625

Colorado River [kol′ə rad′ō], a large North American river flowing from northern Colorado into the Gulf of California. (39°N/105°W), pp. 125, 624–625

Columbia Plateau [kə lum′bē ə pla-tō′], a dry region between the Rocky Mountains and the Cascade Range in the western United States. (40°N/114°W), pp. 125, 624

Congo (Zaire) River [kong′gō (zä ir′)], a large river in central Africa, flowing from southeastern Zaire to the Atlantic Ocean. (3°S/17°E), pp. 458, 634

Dakar [dä kär′], a seaport and capital of Senegal in West Africa. (15°N/17°W), pp. 478, 634

Deccan Plateau [dek′ən, de kan′], a plateau in south central India. (18°N/78°E), pp. 514, 633

Denmark [den′märk], a Scandinavian country in northern Europe, between the Baltic and the North seas. (55°N/9°E), pp. 290, 630

Detroit [di troit′], a city in southeastern Michigan, in the United States. (42°N/83°W), pp. 155, 624

Earth [ėrth], the planet on which we live; the fifth largest planet in the solar system. p. 4

East Asia [ēst ā′zhə], the eastern region of Asia consisting of China, Japan, North and South Korea, and Taiwan. (35°N/110°E), pp. 554, 632

East Coast [ēst kōst], the eastern section of the United States bordering the Atlantic Ocean. p. 37

East Germany [ēst jėr′ mə nē], a country in central Europe south of the Baltic Sea. (52°N/12°E), pp. 379, 630

Edmonton [ed′mən tən], the provincial capital of Alberta, Canada. (53°N/113°W), pp. 176, 626

Egypt [ē′jipt], a country in eastern North Africa. (28°N/31°E), pp. 416, 634

England [ing′glənd], the largest, more southern, division of Great Britain. (53°N/2°W), pp. 290, 630

English Channel [ing′glish chan′l], a strait between England and France. (50°N/2°W) pp. 272, 631

Equator [i kwā′tər], an imaginary line dividing the earth into the Northern and Southern hemispheres. (0° latitude), pp. 9, 622

Euphrates River [yü frā′tēz], a river in Southwest Asia that flows from Turkey through Syria and Iraq into the Persian Gulf. (31°N/47°E), pp. 396, 633

Europe [yür′əp], the continent west of Asia. (50°N/20°E), pp. 270, 630

France [frans], an industrialized nation in Western Europe. (47°N/3°E), pp. 306, 630

French Guiana [french gē ä′nə], a French territory in northern South America. (4°N/53°W), pp. 242, 628

Fundy, Bay of [fun′dē], an inlet of the Atlantic Ocean in southeast Canada between New Brunswick and Nova Scotia. (45°N/64W), p. 176

Gabon [gà bôN′], a country in Central Africa on the Atlantic Ocean. (0°S/10°E), pp. 478, 634

Ganges-Brahmaputra Delta [gan′jēz′brä′mə pü′trə del′tə], the delta formed by the Ganges and Brahmaputra rivers in Bangladesh and India. (24°N/89°E), p. 514

Geneva [jə nē′və], a city in southwestern Switzerland. (46°N/6°E), p. 306

Gobi [gō′bē], a high desert that covers most of Mongolia in East Asia. (45°N/110°E), pp. 26–27, 633

Great Barrier Reef [grāt bar′ē ər rēf], the longest coral reef in the world, near the northeast coast of Australia. (18°S/147°E), pp. 590, 636

Great Basin [grāt bā′sn], a bowl-shaped region in the western United States, part of the Intermontane Region.

Great Dividing Range [grāt dəvīd′ing rānj], a mountain system in eastern Australia. (26°S/149°E), pp. 590, 636

Great Lakes, a group of five lakes south of Hudson Bay in North America; includes Lakes Ontario, Erie, Huron, Michigan, and Superior. (45°N/83°W), pp. 125, 626

Great Wall of China, a wall about 1,500 miles long in north and northwest China built in the 200s B.C. p. 632

Greece [grēs], a country in southeastern Europe on the Mediterranean Sea. (40°N/23°E), pp. 328, 630

Greenland [grēn′lənd], an arctic island in northeastern North America; the largest island in the world. (66°N/45°W), pp. 26–27, 626

Guatemala [gwä′tə mä′lə], a country in northwestern Central America. (16°N/90°W), pp. 220, 626

Gulf Coast [gulf kōst], the southeastern region of the United States bordering the Gulf of Mexico. (30°N/88°W), p. 37

Gulf Stream [gulf strēm], a warm current in the Atlantic Ocean that flows north from the Gulf of Mexico along the eastern United States toward the British Isles. p. 54

Guyana [gī an′ə], a country in northern South America. (5°N/59°W), pp. 242, 628

Halifax [hal′ə faks], a seaport in southeastern Canada, the capital of Nova Scotia. (45°N/64°W), pp. 176, 626

Hawaii [hə wī′e], one of the United States, made up of a group of islands in the north Pacific Ocean. (20°N/157°W). pp. 162, 624

Himalayas [him ə lā′əz], a mountain range in Central Asia that includes the 200 highest peaks in the world. (29°N/84°E), pp. 26–27, 514, 633

Hong Kong [hong′kong′, hông′kông′], a British dependency on the southeastern coast of China encompassing a small peninsula and several islands. (22°N/114°E), pp. 554, 632

Honshu [hon′shü], the largest of Japan's four main islands. (36°N/138°E), pp. 554, 633

Houston [hyü′stən], the largest metropolitan area in the southern United States, in southeastern Texas. (30°N/95°W), pp. 150, 624

Huang River [hwäng′], a river in China that begins in the Plateau of Tibet and empties into the Yellow Sea. (32°N/110°W), pp. 514, 633

Iberian Peninsula [ī bir′ē ən pə nin′sə-lə], a peninsula in southwestern Europe bordered by the Mediterranean Sea and the Atlantic Ocean and containing the countries of Spain, Portugal, and Andorra. (40°N/5°W), pp. 272, 631

Inca Empire [ing′kə em′pīr], the empire of the ancient South American civilization of the Incas, who settled around Cuzco in present-day Peru. p. 207

India [in′dē ə], a large country in South Asia. (20°N/78°E), pp. 536, 632

Indianapolis [in′dē ə nap′ə lis], the capital of Indiana, in the United States. (40°N/86°W), pp. 155, 624

Indus River [in′dəs], a river flowing from western Tibet through Kashmir and Pakistan into the Arabian Sea. (24°N/68°E), pp. 514, 633

Iran [i ran′, i rän′], a country in Southwest Asia, south of the Caspian Sea. (33°N/53°E), pp. 434, 632

Iraq [i rak′, i räk′], a country in Southwest Asia, west of Iran. (33°N/44°E), pp. 434, 632

Ireland [īr′lənd], one of the British Isles, divided into the Republic of Ireland and Northern Ireland. (53°N/8°W), pp. 290, 630

Israel [iz′rē əl], a country in Southwest Asia on the Mediterranean Sea. It was the ancient kingdom of the Jews. (32°N/35°E), pp. 434, 632

Italy [it′l ē], a country in southern Europe on the Mediterranean Sea. (42°N/13°E), pp. 328, 630

Jamaica [jə mā′kə], an island in the West Indies south of Cuba. (18°N/77°W), pp. 220, 626

Jamestown, Virginia [jāmz′toun′, vər jin′yə], the first permanent English colony established in North America in 1607. (37°N/76°W), p. 132

Japan [jə pan′], a country made up of four large islands and many smaller ones in the western Pacific Ocean off the east coast of Asia. (36°N/136°E), pp. 544, 632

Java [jä′və, jav′ə], the main island of Indonesia, southeast of Sumatra. (7°S/110°E), pp. 574, 632

Jerusalem [jə rü′sə ləm], the capital of Israel, in the eastern part of the country; a holy city for Jews, Christians, and Muslims. (32°N/35°E), pp. 433, 632

Jordan, a country in Southwest Asia east of Israel. (31°N/36°E), p. 434, 632

Kalahari Desert [kä′la här′ē], a large desert in southern Africa covering much of Botswana. (23°S/22°E), pp. 458, 623, 635

Kansas City [kan′zəs sit′ē], a city in western Missouri, in the United States. (39°N/98°W), pp. 155, 624

Kara Kum [kär′ə küm′], a desert in the Soviet Union east of the Caspian Sea. (39°N/60°E), p. 346

Khartoum [kär tüm′], the capital and largest city of Sudan in East Africa; (16°N/33°E), pp. 494, 634

Kiev [kē′ef, kē ev′], a city in the southwestern Soviet Union. (50°N/30°E), p. 363

Lagos [lä′gōs, lā′gos], the capital of Nigeria; on the southwest coast, in West Africa. (6°N/3°E), pp. 478, 634

Lake Texcoco [tā skō′kō], a lake in central Mexico where the Aztecs built their capital city of Tenochtitlan. (25°N/103°W), p. 225

Lake Victoria [vik tôr′ē ə], a lake in East Africa in Uganda and Tanzania. (1°S/40°E), pp. 494, 635

Laos [lä′ōs, lā′os], a country in Southeast Asia west of Vietnam. (18°N/105°E), pp. 574, 632

La Paz [lä päs′], one of two capitals of Bolivia (Sucre is the other), in the western part of the country. (16°S/68°W), pp. 242, 628

Lebanon [leb′ə nən], a country in Southwest Asia on the Mediterranean Sea north of Israel. (34°N/36°E), pp. 434, 632

Leningrad [len′ən grad, len′ən gräd], a port city on the Baltic Sea in the northwestern Soviet Union. (60°N/30°E), pp. 363, 630

Libya [lib′ē ə], a country in North Africa west of Egypt. (27°N/17°E), pp. 434, 634

Lima [lē′mə], the capital of Peru, in the western part of the country. (12°S/77°W), pp. 242, 628

Lisbon [liz′bən], the capital of Portugal, in the southwestern part of the country. (39°N/9°W), pp. 328, 630

Los Angeles [lôs an′jə ləs, lôs an′jə lēz′], a large city in southwestern California, the second largest city in the United States. (34°N/118°W), pp. 162, 624

Low Countries, the countries of Belgium, the Netherlands, and Luxembourg in western Europe. (51°N/5°E), p. 270

Madagascar [mad′ə gas′kər], a large island country in the Indian Ocean, off southeastern Africa. (20°S/47°E), pp. 456, 634

Madrid [mə drid′], the capital of Spain, in the central part of the country. (40°N/40°W), pp. 328, 630

Malay Peninsula [mā′lā, mə lā′], a peninsula in Southeast Asia, north of Sumatra. (5°N/103°E), pp. 514, 633

Marseille [mär sā′], a seaport in southeastern France on the Mediterranean Sea. (43°N/5°E), pp. 306, 630

Maya Empire [mī′ə, mä′yə], the empire of the Mayan civilization, which extended across the Yucatán Peninsula in Mexico and part of Central America. p. 207

Mecca [mek′ə], the religious capital of Saudi Arabia, in the western part of the country. (21°N/40°E), pp. 434, 632

Melanesia [mel′ə nē′zhə], a group of islands in the Pacific Ocean, north of Australia including New Guinea. (4°S/155°E), p. 604

Melbourne [mel′bərn], a seaport in southeastern Australia. (38°S/145°E), pp. 590, 636

Mexico City [mek′sə kō], the capital of Mexico, in the central part of the country. (19°N/99°W), pp. 220, 626

Miami [mī am′ē, mī am′ə], a city in southeastern Florida, in the United States. (26°N/80°W), pp. 150, 624

Micronesia [mī′krō nē′zhə], a group of islands in the Pacific Ocean north of Melanesia. (11°N/160°E), p. 604

Mogadishu [mog′ə dē′shü], the capital and principal port of Somalia, on the Indian Ocean. (2°N/45°E), pp. 494, 634

Mongolia [mon gō′lē ə], a country in Central Asia north of China and south of the Soviet Union. (47°N/103°E), pp. 554, 632

Montevideo [mon′tə vi dā′ō], the capital, seaport, and largest city in Uruguay. (35°S/56°W), pp. 242, 628

Montreal [mon′trē ôl′], a city in Canada on the St. Lawrence River. (46°N/74°W), pp. 176, 626

moon [mün], a heavenly body that revolves around the earth. p.5

Morocco [mə rok′ ō], a country in western North Africa. (32°N/6°W), pp. 416, 634

Moscow [mos′kou, mos′kō], the capital of the Soviet Union, in the western part of the country. (56°N/38°E), pp. 363, 630

Mount Kilimanjaro [kil′ə mən jär′ō], a mountain in Tanzania near the Kenyan border. (4°S/37°E), pp. 458, 635

Mozambique [mō′zam bēk′], a country in southern Africa, bordering the Indian Ocean. (19°S/35°E), pp. 494, 634

Munich [myü′nik], a city in southern West Germany's Bavarian Uplands. (48°N/12°E), pp. 306, 630

Murmansk [mèr′mansk′], a seaport and railroad terminus in the northwestern Soviet Union. (69°N/33°E), p. 363

Namib Desert [nä mib′], a desert in southern Africa reaching inland from the west coast. (22°S/15°E), pp. 458, 635

New Delhi [del′ē], the capital of India, in the northern part of the country. (28°N/77°E), pp. 536, 632

New Orleans [ôr'lē ənz, ôr lēnz, ôr'lənz], a seaport city in southeastern Louisiana, in the United States. (30°N/90° W), pp. 150, 624

New York City, a seaport city in southeastern New York State; the largest city in the United States. (41°N/74°W), pp. 147, 624

Nicaragua [nik'ə rä'gwə], a country in Central America north of Costa Rica. (12°N/85°W), pp. 220, 626

Niger River [nī'jər], a river flowing from West Africa into the Gulf of Guinea. (6°N/7°E), pp. 458, 635

Nile Delta [nīl], the fertile region at the mouth of the Nile River in Africa. (31°N/31°E), pp. 396, 635

Nile Valley [nīl], the fertile banks of the Nile River in Africa. (25°N/32°E), p. 396

Northern Ireland [nôr'THərn īr'lənd], a self-governing district in northeastern Ireland that is part of the United Kingdom of Great Britain and Northern Ireland. (55°N/7°W), pp. 290, 630

North Korea [nôrth kô rē'ə], a country on the Korean Peninsula north of the 38th parallel. (40°N/127°E), pp. 554, 632

North Sea, a part of the Atlantic Ocean east of Great Britain, west of Denmark, and south of Norway. (56°N/4°E), pp. 272, 631

Norway [nôr'wā], a mountainous country in northern Europe on the Scandinavian Peninsula. (63°N/11°E), pp. 290, 630

Novosibirsk [nō'vō si birsk'], a city in southwestern Siberia in the Soviet Union. (55°N/83°E), pp. 363, 632

Ottawa [ot'ə wə, ot'ə wä], the capital city of Canada, located in southeastern Ontario. (45°N/76°W), pp. 176, 626

Pacific Ocean [pə sif'ik], one of the four oceans of the world; bordered on the east by North and South America and on the west by Asia and Australia. (10°N/140°W), pp. 21, 620

Pakistan [pak'ə stan, pä'kə stän], country in South Asia west of India. (30°N/70°E), pp. 536, 632

Panama [pan'ə mä, pan ə mä'], a Central American country on the Isthmus of Panama. (9°N/80°W), pp. 220, 626

Paris [par'is], the capital and largest city of France, in the northern part of that country. (49°N/2°E), pp. 306, 630

Patagonia [pat'ə gō'nē ə], a barren region in southern Chile and Argentina. (45°S/69°W), pp. 199, 629

Pate [pät], an island city-state off Africa's eastern coast that reached its peak between A.D. 1200 and A.D. 1500. p. 465

Persian Gulf [pėr'zhən], a part of the Arabian Sea between Iran and the Arabian Peninsula. (27°N/50°E), pp. 396, 633

Philadelphia [fil'ə del'fē ə, fil'ə-del'fyə], a city in southeastern Pennsylvania, in the United States. (40°N/75°W), pp. 147, 624

Piedmont [pēd'mont], an area of foothills between the Appalachian Mountains and the Atlantic Coastal Plain of the United States. (36°N/80°W), pp. 125, 627

Pittsburgh [pits'bėrg'], a city in southwestern Pennsylvania, in the United States. (37°N/95°W), pp. 147, 624

Plateau of Tibet [ti bet'], the world's highest plateau, located in western China north of the Himalayas. (35°N/90°E), pp. 514, 633

Polynesia [pol'ə nē'zhə], a vast group of islands in the central Pacific Ocean; includes New Zealand and Hawaii. (10°S/162°W), p. 604

Prague [präg], the capital of Czechoslovakia, in the western part of the country. (50°N/14°E), pp. 379, 630

Prime Meridian [prīm mə rid'ē ən], an imaginary line that acts as the starting point for measuring longitude on the globe; also known as the Greenwich Meridian. (0° longitude). pp. 10, 620

Pripyat Marshes [prip'yət], a marsh region in northeastern Poland and the western Soviet Union. (52°N/28°E), p. 346

Quito [kē'tō], the capital of Ecuador, in the northern part of the country. (0°S/78°W), pp. 242, 628

Rio de Janeiro [rē'ō dā zhə ner'ō], a port city in southeastern Brazil. 23°S/43°W), pp. 242, 628

Rocky Mountains [rok'ē], the longest mountain system in North America, extending from Alaska to New Mexico. (55°N/121°W) pp. 125, 627

Rome [rōm], the capital of Italy; the city from which the Roman Empire expanded. (42°N/12°E), pp. 328, 630

Ross Ice Shelf [rôs], the largest ice shelf in Antarctica. (80°S/180°E), pp. 608, 637

Rotterdam [rot'ər dam], the world's largest seaport, in the southwestern Netherlands. (52°N/4°E), p. 306

Sahara [sə her'ə, sə har'ə], the world's largest desert, in northern Africa. (25°N/5°E), pp. 58–59, 635

Sahel [sä hel'], a semiarid region of Africa consisting of the southern margins of the Sahara. pp. 478, 635

St. Lawrence River, a river in southeastern Canada flowing from Lake Ontario into the Gulf of St. Lawrence. (49°N/66°W, pp. 176, 627

Santa Clara County, [san'tə klar'ə], a region in northern California, in the United States. (37°N/122°W), p. 161

Santiago [san'tē ä'gō], the capital of Chile in the central part of the country. (33°S/71°W), pp. 242, 628

São Paulo [soun pou'lù], a city in southeastern Brazil; the largest city in South America. (24°S/47°W), pp. 196, 242, 628

Saudi Arabia [sä ü'dē ə rä'bē ə], a country on the Arabian Peninsula in Southwest Asia. (26°N/44°E), pp. 434, 632

Scandinavia [skan'də nā'vē ə], a region in northern Europe made up of Norway and Sweden, but sometimes including Denmark, Finland, and Iceland. (64°N/12°E), pp. 290, 630

Scotland [skot'land], a division of Great Britain north of England. (57°N/4°W), pp. 290, 630

Shanghai [shang'hī'], a seaport in eastern China. (31°N/121°E), pp. 554, 632

Sicily [sis'ə lē], an island in the Mediterranean Sea near Italy. (37°N/14°E), pp. 328, 630

South Africa [south af'rə kə], a country in southern Africa. (32°S/17°E), pp. 494, 634

South Asia [south ā'zhə], the Asian continent south of the Himalaya Mountains, including India, Pakistan, Bangladesh, Nepal, and Sri Lanka. pp. 536, 632

South Korea [south kô rē'ə], a country on the southern Korean Peninsula south of the 38th parallel. (36°N/128°E), pp. 554, 632

Soviet Central Asia, the region of the Soviet Union north and east of the Caspian Sea. (50°N/60°E), p. 363

Soviet Union [sō'vē et yü'nyen], the Union of Soviet Socialist Republics, a nation of Eastern Europe and North Asia, the largest country in the world in size. (60°N/100°E), pp. 363, 630, 632

Sri Lanka [srē'läng'kə], an island country in the Indian Ocean near southern India. (7°N/81°E), pp. 536, 632

Strait of Hormuz [hôr′müz′], a narrow channel connecting the Persian Gulf and the Arabian Sea. (26°N/56°E), p. 396

Sudbury, Ontario, a city in southeastern Canada. (46°N/81°W), p. 176

Suez Canal [sü ez′ kə nal′], a canal in Egypt connecting the Mediterranean and the Red seas. (30°N/33°E), p. 416

sun, the brightest heavenly body in the sky, the star around which the earth and other planets revolve and which supplies them with light and heat. p. 4

Sunbelt, the southern and southwestern United States. p. 136

Suriname [sùr′ə nam], a country in northern South America. (4°N/56°W), pp. 242, 628.

Sweden [swēd′n], a country on the Scandinavian Peninsula in northern Europe. (57°N/15°E), pp. 290, 630

Sydney [sid′nē], a seaport in southeastern Australia. (34°S/151°E), pp. 590, 636

Syria [sir′ē ə], a country in Southwest Asia south of Turkey. (35°N/38°E), pp. 434, 632

Taiwan [tī′wän′], an island country near southeastern China. (23°N/121°E), pp. 554, 632

Tanda, Egypt [Tän′də], a village in Egypt's Nile Valley. (26°N/31°E), p. 416

Tasmania [taz mā′nē ə], an Australian island off the southern coast. (40°S/146°E), pp. 590, 636

Tenochtitlán [tā nōch′tē′tlän], the capital of the Aztec Empire, now the site of Mexico City. (19°N/99°W), p. 207

Tigris River [tī′gris], a river in Southwest Asia that flows from southeastern Turkey through Iraq into the Persian Gulf. (37°N/42°E), pp. 396, 633

Tokyo [tō′kē ō, tō′kyō], the capital of Japan. (36°N/140°E), pp. 554, 632

Tombouctou [tông bük tü′], a city in central Mali near the Niger River; an ancient trading center. (17°N/3°W), pp. 478, 634

Toronto [tə ron′tō], a port city in Canada on Lake Ontario. (44°N/79°W), p. 176

Transantarctic Mountains, a mountain range that divides Antarctica into two main regions. pp. 608, 637

Transylvania [tran′səl vā′nyə], a highland region in Romania. (45°N/25°E), p. 379

Tribune, Kansas [trib′yün], a rural town in west central Kansas, in the United States. (39°N/100°W), p. 158

Tropic of Cancer [kan′sər], the parallel at 23½° north latitude. (23½°N), pp. 47, 620

Tropic of Capricorn [kap′rə kôrn], the parallel at 23½° south latitude. (23½°S), pp. 47, 620

Tunisia [tü nē′zhə], a country in North Africa, on the Mediterranean Sea. (33°N/9°E), pp. 416, 634

Turkey [tėr′kē], a country in southeastern Europe and Southwest Asia. (39°N/36°E), pp. 434, 632

Ukraine [yü krān′], southwestern part of the Soviet Union bordering Romania. (49°N/32°E), p. 363

United States, a country in North America composed of 50 states, including Alaska lying west and northwest of Canada, and Hawaii, an island group in the Pacific Ocean, the District of Columbia, Puerto Rico, and other possessions. (37°N/96°W), pp. 122, 624–625

Ural Mountains [yür′əl], a mountain range in the western Soviet Union that forms the northern boundary between Europe and Asia. (60°N/59°E), pp. 346, 633

Vancouver [van kü′vər], a seaport in southwestern British Columbia, Canada. (49°N/123°W), pp. 176, 626

Vienna [vē en′ə], the capital of Austria, in the northeastern part of the country. (48°N/16°E), pp. 306, 630

Vietnam [vē et′näm′], a country in Southeast Asia that was divided into a communist north and an anticommunist South from 1954 to 1976. (19°N/106°E), pp. 574, 632

Wales [wālz], a division of Great Britain west of England. (52°N/3°W), pp. 290, 630

Warsaw [wôr′sô], the capital of Poland, in the eastern part of the country. (52°N/21°E), pp. 379, 630

Washington, D.C. [wosh′ing tən], the capital of the United States, covering the federal District of Columbia. (39°N/77°W), pp. 150, 624

West Berlin [bər lin′], the western sector of the city of Berlin, belonging to West Germany but located 100 miles inside East Germany. (52°N/13°E), p. 306

West Coast, the western edge of the continental United States, bordering the Pacific Ocean. p. 37

West Germany [jėr′mə nē], a country in west central Europe, the part of Germany that came under American, British, and French control after World War II. (52°N/9°E), pp. 306, 630

Winnipeg [win′ə peg], a city in southeastern Manitoba, Canada. (50°N/97°W), pp. 176, 626

Yucatán Peninsula [yü′kə tan′], a peninsula of southeastern Mexico and northern Central America. (18°N/90°W), pp. 220, 627

Zaire [zä ir′, zar], the largest country in Central Africa, formerly the Belgian Congo. (3°S/23°E), pp. 478, 634

Zambezi River [zam bē′zē], a river flowing from northwestern Zambia in southern Africa into the Indian Ocean. (19°S/36°E), pp. 458, 635

Zimbabwe [zim bä′bwe], a country in southern Africa. (20°S/30°E), pp. 474, 634

Glossary

Pronunciation Key

a hat	i it	oi oil
ã age	ī ice	ou out
ä far	o hot	u cup
e let	ō open	ù put
ē equal	ô order	ü rule
ėr term		

ch child	a in about
ng long	e in taken
sh she	ə = i in pencil
th thin	o in lemon
ŦH then	u in circus
zh measure	

The key to the pronunciation of foreign sounds is on page 657 of the Index.

A

aborigine [ab′ə rij′ə nē], *noun*, an original inhabitant of a country or area, especially as distinguished from European or other colonists. p. 595

Afrikaner [af′rə kä′nər], *noun*, a person born in South Africa of Dutch descent; Boer. p. 499

agribusiness [ag′rə biz′nis], *noun*, the business of producing, processing, and distributing agricultural products. p. 156

alliance [ə lī′əns], *noun*, a joining of independent nations by a treaty. p. 167

alluvium [ə lü′vē əm], *noun*, the sediment, in the form of sand, silt, mud, etc., left behind where water flows slowly, as near the mouths of rivers. p. 277

alpine glacier [al′pīn glā′shər], a block of ice that forms at high elevations when more snow falls than melts in a year's time. p. 35

altiplano [äl′ti plä′nō], *noun*, a high plateau or plain. p. 197

anarchy [an′ər kē], *noun*, the absence of a system of government and law. p. 436

animism [an′ə miz′əm], *noun*, a traditional religion in which the souls of the dead and the spirits of nature play important roles. p. 471

anti-Semitism [an′ti sem′ə tiz′əm], *noun*, prejudice against Jews. p. 362

apartheid [ə pärt′hāt], *noun*, the policy of racial separation in South Africa; an Afrikaner word meaning "separateness." p. 499

aquifer [ak′wə fər], *noun*, an underground layer of porous rock that contains water; a desert aquifer can support an oasis, well, or natural reservoir. p. 400

archipelago [är′kə pel′ə gō, är′chə-pel′ə gō], *noun*, a group of many islands. p. 182

artesian well [är tē′zhən], a deep-bored well that brings underground water to the surface. p. 591

atheism [ā′thē iz′əm], *noun*, a disbelief in the existence of God. p. 353

atoll [at′ol, at′ôl; ə tol′, ə tôl′], *noun*, a flat, ring-shaped coral island enclosing or partly enclosing a lagoon. p. 604

authoritarian system [ə thôr′ə ter′ē-ən], government in which one or a few individuals have complete, or nearly complete, power. p. 103

B

Balkanize [bôl′kə nīz], *verb transitive*, to divide a region into groups of people who oppose each other bitterly. p. 382

barrier reef [bar′ē ər rēf], a coral reef, created by the accumulation of the skeletons of small marine animals on a rocky surface just below sea level along a tropical coast. p. 592

barrio [bär′ē ō], *noun*, a district of a city or town; a slum section. p. 248

bauxite [bôk′sīt, bō′ zīt], *noun*, the claylike mineral from which aluminum is obtained; aluminum ore. p. 579

bayou [bī′ü], *noun*, a sluggish, marshy inlet or outlet of a lake, river, or gulf in the south central United States. p. 151

bazaar [bə zär′], *noun*, an outdoor shopping area consisting of a street or streets filled with small shops and booths. p. 417

bilingual [bī ling′gwəl], *adjective*, able to speak another language as well as or almost as well as one's own. p. 177

biome [bī′ōm], *noun*, a large plant community that shares common plant and animal life and a distinctive climate. A desert and a rainforest are two kinds of biomes. p. 65

black market, a market in illegal goods; also, the selling of goods at illegal prices or in illegal quantities. p. 368

bureaucratic [byùr′ə krat′ik], *adjective*, having to do with a system of government by groups of officials or with the officials themselves. p. 485

bush, *noun*, an area of wild, unsettled forest. p. 244

C

cabinet system [kab′ə nit], a form of government in which the officials who hold the executive powers of the government are directly responsible to the legislature, or lawmaking body. p. 138

caliph [kā′lif], *noun*, the former title of the supreme religious and political leader of a Muslim state. p. 407

campesino [käm pä sē′nō], *noun*, the Spanish word for farmer or peasant. p. 219

canton [kan′tən, kan′ton], *noun*, a small part or political division of a country. p. 322

caste system [kast], the system of social groupings into which Hindus are divided. By tradition, a Hindu is born into a caste and cannot rise above it. p. 525

causeway [kôz′wā′], *noun*, a raised road or path, usually built across wet ground or shallow water. p. 226

census [sen′səs], *noun*, an official count of the population of a country or a district. p. 86

chernozem [cher′nə zem′], *noun*, the fertile black soil of certain steppe regions. p. 350

chevron [shev′rən], *noun*, a design shaped like an upside-down "V." p. 421

chicle [chik′əl], *noun*, a milky substance that comes from the sapodilla tree and is used in making chewing gum. p. 229

chip [chip], *noun*, in electronics, a small piece of semiconductor material, usually silicon, that processes or stores information in a computer. p. 164

city-state [sit′ē stāt], *noun*, an independent state consisting of a city and the territories that depend on it. p. 464

clan [klan], *noun*, a group of people who are related by blood and have the same surname. p. 292

classical culture [klas′ə kəl kul′chər], the blend of ancient Roman and Greek literature, art, and customs. p. 279

coalition government [kō′ə lish′ən], a ruling government made up of many cooperating parties. p. 334

Cold War, the contest for power between the communist nations headed by the Soviet Union and the nations of the West headed by the United States that began after World War II; a nonshooting war fought economically and politically rather than militarily. p. 356

collateral [kə lat′ər əl], *noun*, something of value pledged to secure a loan. p. 547

collective [kə lek′tiv], *noun*, a farm, factory, or other organization owned, worked, or managed cooperatively. p. 556

command economy, an economic system in which most of the factors of production are owned by the government. p. 108

communism [kom′yə niz′əm], *noun*, a governmental system that combines authoritarian political and socialist economic philosophies. Land, factories, and other means of production are owned by the community as a whole or by the state. p. 103

compression [kəm presh′ən], *noun*, a force that makes an object smaller through applied pressure or squeezing. p. 29

conquistadors [kon kwis′tə dôrz, kon kē′ stə dôrz], *noun*, *plural*, the Spanish conquerors in North or South America during the 1500s. p. 133

constitutional monarchy [kon′stə-tü′shə nəl mon′ər kē], monarchy in which the ruler has only those powers given by the constitution and laws of the nation. p. 425

continental ice sheet [kon′tə nen′tl], one of the many huge blankets of ice, some measuring more than two miles thick in places, that covered the earth thousands of years ago. p. 34

continental shelf [kon′tə nen′tl], the margin of the continent that extends underwater beyond the shoreline, sloping gradually out and ending in an abrupt descent to deeper water. p. 121

convection [kən vek′shən], *noun*, the transfer of heat from one place to another by the circulation of heated particles of a gas or liquid. p. 20

convection rainfall [kən vek′shən], the rainfall that occurs as the result of convection forces in the air. Air heated by the sun rises. As the air rises, it cools and its saturation point is lowered. This results in both condensation and precipitation. p. 60

copra [kō′prə], *noun*, the dried meat of coconuts from which coconut oil is obtained. p. 502

cordillera [kôr′də lyer′ə], *noun*, system of mountain ranges. p. 197

core [kôr], *noun*, the innermost portion of the earth. p. 18

Coriolis effect [kôr′ē ō′lis], the tendency of winds to bend because of the earth's rotation. The Coriolis effect causes wind and water to veer to the right in the Northern Hemisphere and to the left in the Southern Hemisphere. p. 52

county seat [koun′tē], the town or city where the county government is located. p. 159

coup [kü], *noun*, a sudden takeover of an existing government. p. 236

creed [krēd], *noun*, a statement of the main point or points of religious belief of a church; a religious principle. p. 404

creole [krē′ōl], *noun*, in Mexico, a person of Spanish descent who was born in the Americas. Descendants of the early French or Spanish settlers in Louisiana and French or Spanish people born in Latin America or the West Indies are also known as creoles. p. 209

Crusades [krü sādz′], *noun*, *plural*, the Christian military expeditions organized between the years 1096 and 1270 to recover the Holy Land from the Muslims. p. 281

crust [krust], *noun*, the very thin layer of solid rock that makes up the surface of the earth. p. 18

ctenophore [ten′ə fôr, ten′ə fōr], *noun*, a small marine animal resembling a jellyfish, with long tentacles that are used to catch food. p. 611

cultural diffusion [kul′chər əl di-fyü′zhən], the process by which a culture trait or innovation moves from one culture to another. p. 94

cultural feature [kul′chər əl fē′chər], a physical or social structure, such as a city, religion, or form of architecture, that humans use to organize and change the natural world. p. 5

culture [kul′chər], *noun*, everything that a society has learned and passed along to its members; the way of life of a given people at a given time. p. 93

culture hearth [kul′chər härth], the center and major source of a particular culture; a place from which new ideas, values, and practices have spread. p. 94

D

dacha [dä′chə], *noun*, a summer cottage in the country or suburbs, in the Soviet Union. p. 364

deciduous [di sij′ü əs], *adjective*, dropping leaves annually. Maples, elms, and most oaks are deciduous trees. p. 68

demilitarized zone [dē mil′ə tə rīzd′], an area where no troops are allowed. p. 559

democracy [di mok′rə sē], *noun*, a government that is run by the people who live under it, in which the people rule either directly through meetings that all may attend or indirectly through the election of representatives. p. 103

demographic transition [dē′mə-graf′ik, dem′ə graf′ik], the four basic stages of population change found in countries as they move from low-technology agricultural to high-technology industrial and service societies. p. 87

deposition [dep′ə zish′ən, dē′pə-zish′ən], *noun*, the laying down of rock fragments in a new location. p. 32

desertification [di zėrt′ə fə kā′shən], *noun*, the drying up of comparatively moist areas along the margins of a desert, generally caused by overuse by people and animals. p. 480

diatom [dī′ə tom], *noun*, any one of a class of microscopic, one-celled water algae with hard shells. p. 611

dike [dīk], *noun*, a bank of earth or a dam constructed to prevent flooding of low-lying lands by a river or the sea. p. 516

dry farming, the practice of farming without irrigation, depending entirely on melting snow and rainfall to provide moisture for crops. One method of dry farming involves leaving part of a field fallow so that the soil absorbs moisture to nourish the crop planted the next year. p. 163

duty [dü′tē, dyü′tē], *noun*, a tax, especially a tax on articles imported, or brought into, a country. p. 157

dynastic cycle [dī nas′tik], the pattern followed by dynastic rule in China, whereby a dynasty started out strong and powerful, but eventually grew weak and fell. A new dynasty took its place, repeating the cycle. p. 554

dynasty [dī′nə stē], *noun*, a succession of rulers who belong to the same family. p. 553

E

Eastern Bloc [ē′stərn blok], the communist countries of Eastern Europe. p. 315

ecosystem [ē′kō sis′təm, ek′ō sis′təm], *noun*, a physical environment with the community of various organisms that inhabit it. An ecosystem could be a lake, a vacant lot, a desert, etc. p. 38

ejido [ā hē′dō], *noun*, Spanish, an individual farm. p. 219

electronics [i lek′tron′iks, ē′lek-tron′iks], *noun*, the branch of physics that deals with the production, activity, and effects of electrons in motion through vacuums, gases, or semiconductors, and which makes such machines as transistors, lasers, computers, and television possible. p. 147

elevation [el′ə vā′shən], *noun*, the distance above or below sea level. p. 25

El Niño [el nē′nyō], *noun*, a warm current that flows into the cold Peru waters each December, causing a sudden temperature change that results in torrential rains. p. 251

embargo [em bär′gō], *noun*, an order of a government forbidding merchant ships to enter or leave its ports; any restriction put on commerce by law; trade restrictions. p. 167

émigré [em′ə grā], *noun*, a person who leaves his or her own country because of political conditions and settles in another country. p. 314

emissary [em′ə ser′ē], *noun*, an official representative sent on a mission or errand. p. 527

equinox [ē′kwə noks], *noun*, either of the two times in the year when the sun is directly over the Equator and day and night are of equal length; equinoxes occur about March 21 and about September 21. p. 48

erg [èrg], *noun*, a large sea of shifting sand dunes in a desert. p. 393

erosion [i rō′zhən], *noun*, a gradual wearing away by glaciers, running water, waves, ice, or wind. p. 32

escarpment [e skärp′mənt], *noun*, a steep slope or cliff. p. 457

estuary [es′chü er′ē], *noun*, a broad mouth of a river into which the tide flows. pp. 151, 291

ethnic group [eth′nik], a group of people who share similar cultural or racial backgrounds. p. 467

F

fall line, the place that marks the end of layers of hard rock of a plateau and the beginning of a softer rock layer of a plain. Generally many waterfalls and rapids form along this line. p. 122

fallow [fal′ō], *adjective*, plowed and left unseeded for a season or more. p. 159

faults, *noun*, *plural*, fractures, or breaks, in the earth's crust. p. 30

fault valley, a valley created when a section of rock drops down as sections on either side are pushed upward by pressure from inside the earth. p. 311

fellahin [fel′ə hēn′], *noun*, *plural*, the peasant farmers or laborers in Egypt and other Arabic-speaking countries. p. 416

feudalism [fyü′dl iz′əm], *noun*, the social, economic, and political system of western Europe in the Middle Ages in which the lords ruled by contracting out the use of their land in return for personal loyalty and manual labor. p. 281

fiord [fyôrd, fyōrd], *noun*, a long, narrow bay of the sea bordered by steep cliffs. p. 298

firth [fèrth], *noun*, a narrow arm or indentation of the sea. p. 293

folds, *noun*, *plural*, a series of giant wrinkles that occurs when pressure forces the surface rock of a plate to compress. The earth's great mountain ranges are folds. p. 29

foreign trade zone, an area in the United States where importers pay no customs duties, or taxes on imported goods. p. 157

forest conversion [kən vèr′zhən], the process of supplanting one kind of tree with another. p. 151

fossil [fos′əl], *noun*, hardened remains or traces of an ancient plant or animal found in the layers of the earth. p. 19

free trade, the absence of tariffs, quotas, and other trade barriers between countries. p. 184

freeway [frē′wā′], *noun*, a high-speed highway with no tolls, stoplights, or stop signs. p. 165

front, *noun*, the area created when masses of dissimilar air meet, and the boundary between them becomes unstable. p. 55

G

gasohol [gas′ə hôl, gas′ə hol], *noun*, a fuel for cars, composed of gasoline and ethyl alcohol. p. 260

gaucho [gou′chō], *noun*, a cowboy on the southern plains of South America. p. 256

geothermal power [jē′ō thèr′məl], energy produced from heat inside the earth. p. 300

glyph [glif], *noun*, any symbol used to represent a name, word, or message. p. 225

Gosplan [gos′plan, gôs′plän], *noun*, the agency of the Soviet government that controls the economy through five-year plans that have goals and periodic production quotas. p. 367

goulash communism [gü′läsh], in Hungary, the modified form of communism resulting from reforms within the country. p. 381

granary [gran′ər ē, grā′nər ē], *noun*, a region that produces much grain; also a storehouse for grain. p. 307

graphite [graf′īt], *noun*, a soft, black form of carbon with a metallic luster, used for lead in pencils and for lubricating oils. p. 543

greenhouse effect, the effect of carbon dioxide and water vapor in the atmosphere as they trap solar radiation much as the glass of a greenhouse does; the result can produce a change in world climate. p. 39

gross national product (GNP), the total worth of all goods and services produced in a country in a year. p. 111

ground water, water that flows or seeps downward and saturates the soil. p. 163

guerrilla [gə ril′ə], *noun*, a member of a band of fighters who annoy the enemy by sudden raids and ambushes. Guerrillas are not part of a regular army. p. 167

guerrilla warfare [gə ril′ə], a type of fighting outside of the regular army, which usually includes such terrorist tactics as harassing, ambushing, and raiding the enemy. p. 231

guru [gü′rü, gù rü′], *noun*, a religious teacher or guide in Hinduism. p. 525

H

hacienda [hä′sē en′də], *noun*, the name for a large ranch or farm in Latin America. p. 248

harmattan [här′mə tan′], *noun*, a drying wind that blows from the Sahara along the northwest coast of Africa and signals the onset of winter. p. 481

heavy industry, industry that manufactures such products as machines or steel for use by other industries. p. 235

hemisphere [hem′ə sfir], *noun*, one half of a globe formed by a line passing through the center. The Equator is an imaginary line that divides the earth into the Northern and the Southern hemispheres; the Prime Meridian divides the earth into the Western and Eastern hemispheres. p. 9

hills, *noun*, *plural*, raised parts of the earth's surface, lower than mountains and often rounded at the tops. p. 25

huipil [wē pēl′], *noun*, ceremonial clothing, rich in symbolism, woven by the Maya people of ancient Mexico and worn also by their modern Mexican descendants. p. 104

human geography [hyü′mən jē og′rə-fē], branch of geography that deals with the ways humans organize or change the natural world. Human geographers study such features as cities, religions, agriculture, or architecture, and political, economic, historical, and social structures. p. 5

humus [hyü′məs], *noun*, the dark brown or black part of soil formed from decayed plants and animals, containing valuable plant foods. p. 64

hurricane [hèr′ə kān], *noun*, a wind having a speed of more than 70 miles per hour; a tropical cyclone, or windstorm, originating in the West Indies, usually accompanied by violent thunderstorms. p. 127

hydrologic cycle [hī′drə loj′ik], the process through which water changes its form as it continuously circulates between the earth and the atmosphere; the water cycle. p. 51

I

ice shelf, a unique "landform" that results when the Antarctic ice sheet reaches the edge of the continent and settles on the water. p. 608

icon [ī′kon], *noun*, a picture or image of Christ, an angel, or a saint, usually painted on wood or ivory, and regarded as sacred in the Eastern Orthodox Church. p. 371

imam [i mäm′], *noun*, in the Muslim religion, the person who leads the prayers in a mosque. p. 404

Glossary

653

imperialism [im pir'ē ə liz'əm], *noun,* the policy of extending the rule or authority of one country over other countries. p. 467

independent contractor [in'di pen'-dənt kon'trak tər], a person who supplies his or her own materials and produces a product or service for sale. p. 547

insurgent [in sėr'jənt], *noun,* a person who rises in revolt; a rebel. p. 575

isthmus [is'məs], *noun,* a narrow strip of land with water on both sides, connecting two larger bodies of land. p. 198

J

junta [jun'tə, hùn'tə], *noun,* a political or military group that takes over a government and holds power after a revolution, p. 230

jute [jüt], *noun,* a strong fiber, obtained from two tropical plants, used for making rope and such coarse fabrics as burlap. p. 540

K

kibbutz [ki büts'], *noun,* an Israeli communal settlement, especially a farm cooperative. p. 435

Komsomol [kom'sə mol], *noun,* the Young Communist League, a Soviet organization for youth between 15 and 28. p. 370

krill [kril], *noun, plural,* shrimplike animals that are eaten by whales and other sea animals. p. 611

L

language family, the grouping to which languages with similar vocabularies and structures belong. p. 97

latitude [lat'ə tüd, lat'ə tyüd], *noun,* distance north or south of the Equator, measured in degrees. The Equator represents zero degrees latitude; either pole is located 90 degrees latitude from the Equator. p. 8

light industry, industry that manufactures products, such as shoes or food, for use by consumers. p. 235

lingua franca [ling'gwə frang'kə], any language that is widely used as a means of communication among speakers of different languages. p. 99

link [lēngk], *noun,* a student group to which individual students belong in a Soviet school. All students in a link receive the same grade, thus encouraging them to help one another. p. 365

llanero [yä nãr'ō], *noun,* in Spanish America, a cowhand who works in the llanos (grassy, lowland areas). p. 245

loess [lō'is, les], *noun,* a fine, yellow silt, usually deposited by the wind. p. 515

longitude [lon'jə tüd, lon'jə tyüd], *noun,* distance east or west on the earth's surface, measured in degrees from the Prime Meridian, which passes through Greenwich, England. p. 8

M

managed economy, an economy in which the government controls prices and wages, and either owns or regulates most businesses. p. 312

mantle [man'tl], *noun,* the thick layer of very hot and heavy liquid rock lying between the earth's crust and its core. p. 18

maquis [mä kē'], *noun,* the dense growth of small trees and shrubs often found in Mediterranean climates. p. 427

market economy, an economic system in which the four factors of production—land, labor, capital, and entrepreneurship—are owned by individuals. p. 108

marsupial [mär sü'pē əl], *noun,* any of an order of mammals having a pouch in which the incompletely developed young are carried. Kangaroos and opossums belong to this order. p. 594

martial law [mär'shəl], rule by the military with military courts instead of the usual civil authorities. p. 541

megalopolis [meg'ə lop'ə lis], *noun,* a large metropolitan area encompassing several cities. p. 84

mercantilism [mėr'kən ti liz'əm, mėr'kən tī liz'əm], *noun,* the economic system of Europe during the period of exploration that favored exports over imports and the accumulation of large amounts of gold and silver. p. 283

meridian [mə rid'ē ən], *noun,* an imaginary line that runs north and south on the globe, meets at the two poles, and is used to measure longitude. The Prime Meridian is the starting point for measuring longitude. p. 8

mestizos [me stē'zōz], *noun, plural,* persons of mixed descent, especially of Spanish and American Indian ancestry. pp. 180, 212

métis [mā tēs'], *noun,* (in Canada) a person of European (especially French) and American Indian descent. p. 180

metropolitan area [met'rə pol'ə tən], area or region that includes a large city and its suburbs. p. 84

middle latitudes, the zone lying between 30° and 60°N and 30° and 60°S of the Equator. p. 47

migration [mī grā'shən], *noun,* the movement and settlement of people from one place to another. p. 87

millennia [mə len'ē ə], *noun, plural,* thousands of years. p. 422

millet [mil'it], *noun,* a type of cereal grass that produces very small, edible seeds. p. 539

minaret [min'ə ret'], *noun,* a slender tower of a mosque with one or more projecting balconies, from which a muezzin, or crier, calls the people to prayer. p. 417

mixed economy, an economy that combines some government planning with free enterprise. p. 471

monsoon [mon sün'], *noun,* a seasonal wind of the Indian Ocean and southern Asia that blows from the southwest from April to October and from the northeast during the rest of the year. p. 518

mosque [mosk], *noun,* a Muslim house of worship. p. 404

motif [mō tēf'], *noun,* a distinctive figure in a design or painting. p. 104

mountains, *noun, plural,* the natural landforms that reach heights of thousands of feet above sea level. p. 25

muezzin [myü ez'n], *noun,* the crier who calls Muslims to prayer five times a day. p. 417

mullah [mul'ə, mùl ə], *noun,* (in Muslim countries), a title of respect for one who is learned in or teaches the sacred law; a religious scholar or leader. p. 446

N

nationalism [nash'ə nə liz'əm], *noun,* a feeling of pride and loyalty that develops among a group of people who share a common language, culture, and history; patriotic feelings. p. 284

nationalize [nash'ə nə līz], *verb transitive,* to bring land, industries, railroads, etc., under the control or ownership of a nation's government. p. 487

natural feature [nach'ər əl fē'chər], a landform, water body, climate, geologic event, or vegetation pattern occurring in nature. p. 5

natural growth rate, the measure of population growth or decline taken by determining the difference between the crude birth rate and the crude death rate. p. 87

neutrality [nü tral'ə tē], *noun,* a national policy to not take part directly or indirectly in a war between other nations. p. 322

O

oasis [ō ā'sis], *noun,* an area of sandy soil that surrounds a deep well or spring and provides a fertile place where people can live and grow crops. p. 395

official language [ə fish'əl lang'gwij], the language used in government, business, and higher education in a country where people speak many different languages. p. 471

one-crop economy, an economic system through which a country or region depends on only one crop for its entire income. p. 234

P

pack ice, the mass of ice chunks at the edge of the ice sheet and its shelves formed as large pieces of ice break off and crowd together. p. 609

paddy [pad'ē], *noun*, a field, enclosed by small, earthen ridges, that can be flooded for growing rice. p. 520

parallel [par'ə lel], *noun*, an imaginary line running east and west around the earth, parallel to the Equator, used to measure degrees of latitude. p. 8

peat [pēt], *noun*, densely packed organic matter that remains too moist to decompose; may be used as a fertilizer or as fuel. p. 349

peninsula [pə nin'sə lə, pə nin'syə lə], *noun*, land surrounded by water on all sides but one. p. 269

per capita income (PCI), the value of goods and services available for each person in a country. p. 111

perestroika [pe're stroi'kə], *noun*, the restructuring of the Soviet economy. p. 371

periodic market [pir ē od'ik], a rotating market that occurs where a village has its market every three or four days and neighboring villages have their markets on the other days. p. 478

permafrost [pèr'mə frôst'], *noun*, a layer of permanently frozen subsoil, found throughout most of the arctic regions. pp. 63, 347

petrochemical [pet'rō kem'ə kəl], *noun*, chemical made from petroleum or natural gas, including plastic, paint, and fertilizer. p. 153

philanthropist [fə lan'thrə pist], *noun*, a person who gives large sums of money to worthy causes. p. 546

physical geography [fiz'i kəl jē og'rə-fē], branch of geography that deals with landforms, water bodies, climates, geologic events, and vegetation patterns that occur in nature. p. 5

plains, *noun, plural*, flat or gently rolling lands that are generally low in elevation. p. 25

plantain [plan'tən], *noun*, a bananalike fruit from a tropical plant of the same family as the banana. p. 243

plateaus [pla tōz'], *noun, plural*, flat areas that rise higher in elevation than the surrounding area; tableland. p. 25

plate tectonics [plāt tek ton'iks], the theory that the earth's crust is composed of plates, whose movements have created mountains, ocean trenches, and major faults. p. 20

plural society [plùr'əl], a society that includes many cultural groups. p. 482

polar regions [pō lər], the zone located from 60°–90°N and 60°–90°S, called the "high latitudes." These regions are the coldest on earth. p. 47

polder [pōl'dər], *noun*, flat stretches of low land located between a sandy plain and dunelands, reclaimed from the sea or other body of water and protected by dikes. p. 317

population density [pop'yə lā'shən den'sə tē], the average number of people living within a certain measured area. p. 81

population distribution [pop'yə-lā'shən dis'trə byü'shən], the way in which people are spread out over the earth. p. 81

porteño [pôr tān'yō], *noun*, the Spanish word meaning "a person of the port." p. 256

precipitation [pri sip'ə tā'shən], *noun*, the depositing of moisture in the form of rain, snow, sleet, hail, or dew. p. 52

prevailing winds [pri vāl'ing], the most dominant winds in any area. p. 52

primate city [prī'māt], a city that is much larger than the second city in the nation and best expresses the nation's culture. p. 306

protectionism [prə tek'shə niz'əm], *noun*, an economic policy of taxing foreign goods through the use of tariffs, quotas, and other trade barriers so that people are more likely to buy goods made in their own country. p. 185

province [prov'əns], *noun*, one of the main political divisions of a country, similar to states in the United States. p. 175

R

rain shadow, an area that has relatively light rainfall because it is sheltered from rain-bearing winds by a mountain slope. The air has lost its moisture in moving up and over the mountain. p. 56

reforestation [rē fôr ist ā'shən], *noun*, the replanting of forests. p. 146

region [rē'jən], *noun*, a part of the earth that is marked by features, either physical or cultural, that make it different from neighboring areas. p. 6

relative humidity [rel'ə tiv hyü mid'ə-tē], the amount of moisture actually in the air compared to the amount the air can hold at a given temperature. p. 51

republic [ri pub'lik], *noun*, a nation or state in which the citizens elect representatives to manage the government, which is usually headed by a president. p. 329

resource [ri sôrs', rē'sôrs], *noun*, any supply, skill, or aid that will meet a need. Resources can be natural, human, or capital, such as finances or machinery. p. 107

revolution [rev'ə lü'shən], *noun*, a complete overthrow of an established government or political system. p. 556

rift valley, a valley formed when a long, narrow section of the earth's crust sinks below the surrounding area. p. 459

S

sanction [sangk'shən], *noun*, an action, usually economic restrictions, taken by nations in hopes of forcing another nation to obey international law. p. 500

sari [sär'ē], *noun*, a long piece of cloth draped around the body, typically worn by women in India. p. 538

satellite [sat'l ĭt], *noun*, a small country dependent on a larger, more powerful country, especially a country under the control of the Soviet Union. p. 356

sea, *noun*, the great body of salt water that covers almost three-fourths of the earth's surface; the ocean. Also, a large body of salt water, smaller than an ocean, partly or wholly enclosed by land. p. 269

secede [si sēd'], *verb intransitive*, to withdraw formally from an organization. p. 469

sect [sekt], *noun*, a division or group within a larger religion with its own interpretations of religious doctrine. p. 404

secular [sek'yə lər], *adjective*, not religious or sacred. A secular nation is one in which government and religion are separate. p. 443

selva [sel'və], *noun*, the lush rainforest vegetation cover produced by the high heat and humidity in certain areas of Latin America. p. 203

separatist [sep'ər ə tist], *noun*, a member of a group that wishes to withdraw or separate from a larger group. p. 178

serf [sèrf], *noun*, in the Middle Ages, a person legally required to work a piece of land. A serf could not leave the land. pp. 281, 354

shifting cultivation [kul'tə vā'shən], *noun*, type of farming in which fields are cleared by cutting down large trees and burning the area. The field is used for crops for a few years and then another area is cultivated. p. 131

shogun [shō′gun, shō′gün], *noun*, the supreme general of the Japanese army. The shoguns were the real rulers of Japan for hundreds of years. p. 564

site [sīt], *noun*, a specific place; location. p. 84

situation [sich′ü ā′shən], *noun*, the position of a specific place in relation to the surrounding region. p. 84

social welfare, a system under which the government provides services such as medical care and child care. p. 296

Solidarity [sol′ə dar′ə tē], *noun*, in Poland, the large union formed by farmers and factory workers to protest the economic policies of the government. p. 378

solstice [sol′stis], *noun*, one of the two days a year when either the North or South Pole is as close to the sun's rays as it will be all year. In the Northern Hemisphere, June 21 or 22, the summer solstice, is the longest day of the year and December 21 or 22, the winter solstice, is the shortest. The reverse is true in the Southern Hemisphere. p. 48

speculator [spek′yə lā′tər], *noun*, an individual who buys and sells land with the hope of making a profit from future price changes. p. 159

subcontinent [sub kon′tə nənt], *noun*, a landmass or region that is very large but smaller than a continent. p. 513

subduction [sub′duk shən], *noun*, the process whereby one of the earth's plates is forced beneath the edge of another plate. p. 22

subsidy [sub′sə dē], *noun*, a grant or contribution of money, especially one made by a government; economic aid. p. 185

superconductor [sü′pər kən duk′tər], *noun*, a material that conducts electricity without resistance. p. 170

T

taiga [tī′gə], *noun*, the swampy, coniferous, evergreen forest land of the subarctic regions, especially in the Soviet Union. p. 349

tariff [tar′if], *noun*, a tax that a government charges on imports. p. 185

territory [ter′ə tôr′ē], *noun*, land or region. In Canada, an area with a limited governmental structure in which relatively few people live. p. 175

timberline [tim′bər līn′], *noun*, the boundary on mountains and in polar regions beyond which trees will not grow because of the cold. p. 131

tontine [ton tēn′], *noun*, a kind of informal savings and loan association in West and Central Africa; members can borrow money for various projects. p. 488

tornado [tôr nā′dō], *noun*, an extremely violent and destructive wind extending down from a mass of dark clouds as a twisting funnel and moving over the land in a narrow path. p. 126

trade deficit [def′ə sit], the condition that arises when the value of a country's imports exceeds the value of its exports. p. 169

tropics [trop′iks], *noun*, *plural*, the zone closest to the Equator, extending from 30°N to 30°S; usually hot all year. p. 47

U

ujamaa village [ü′jo mo′o], in Tanzania, a communal farming village created by the government where the farmers live and work to grow food for themselves and to sell. *Ujamaa* is a Swahili word meaning "neighborliness," or "mutal aid." p. 497

urbanization [ėr′bə nī zā′shən], *noun*, the process whereby a place takes on the characteristics of a city, or a person learns to live in a city. p. 562

V

veld [velt], *noun*, the open, grass-covered plains, or savanna, of southern Africa often having bushes but few trees. p. 461

vestment [vest′mənt], *noun*, a robe or a gown worn on a ceremonial occasion. p. 106

villagization [vil′ij ə zā′shən], *noun*, the resettlement program in Ethiopia under which farmers from drought-stricken areas were moved from small family plots to farming villages with communal fields. p. 496

visa [vē′zə], *noun*, an official document that allows a person to visit another country. p. 316

W

wadi [wä′dē], *noun*, in North Africa and Southwest Asia, a dry river bed through which water flows during periods of heavy rainfall. p. 393

water table, the depth below which the ground is thoroughly saturated with water. p. 423

weathering [weᴛн′ər ing], *noun*, the destructive or discoloring action of air, water, frost, etc., especially on rocks; the breakup of rocks into fragments. p. 32

welfare state, a nation whose government provides for the welfare of its citizens through such free services as education, social security, unemployment insurance, and medical treatment. p. 440

Index

Pronunciation Key
The index tells you where to find maps (*map*), photographs (*photo*), charts (*chart*), diagrams (*diagram*), and definitions (*def.*). Pronunciations are respelled in the familiar Thorndike Barnhart pronunciation key in the *Scott, Foresman Advanced Dictionary,* shown to the right. For some foreign words in *Scott, Foresman World Geography,* the pronunciation given is not the local pronunciation but an Anglicized version, one acceptable to educated Americans.

Some words and names, taken from foreign languages, are spoken with sounds that do not otherwise occur in English. Symbols for these sounds are given in the keys as "foreign sounds."

a hat	i it	oi oil
ā age	ī ice	ou out
ä far	o hot	u cup
e let	ō open	ů put
ē equal	ô order	ü rule
ėr term		

ch child	a in about
ng long	e in taken
sh she	ə = i in pencil
th thin	o in lemon
ŧH then	u in circus
zh measure	

Foreign Sounds
Y as in French *du.*
Pronounce (ē) with the lips rounded as for (ü).

à as in French *ami.*
Pronounce (ä) with the lips spread and held tense.

N as in French *bon.*
The N is not pronounced, but shows that the vowel before it is nasal.

For names in mainland China, pronounce 'q' like the 'ch' in 'chin', 'x' like the 'sh' in 'she', 'zh' like the 'j' in 'jam', and 'z' as if it were spelled 'dz'. In general, pronounce 'a' as in 'father', 'e' as in 'but', 'i' as in 'keep', 'o' as in 'or', and 'u' as in 'rule'.

Index

Acknowledgments

QUOTED MATERIAL

3 Michael Collins, CARRYING THE FIRE: AN ASTRONAUT'S JOURNEY. New York: Farrar, Strauss & Giroux, Inc., 1976. **17** Jules Verne, JOURNEY TO THE CENTER OF THE EARTH, 1864. **25** James Michener, HAWAII. New York: Random House, Inc., 1959. **32** James Michener, HAWAII. New York: Random House, Inc., 1959. **37–40** Excerpts from "Shrinking Shores," TIME, August 10, 1987. Copyright © 1987 Time Inc. All rights reserved. Reprinted by permission from TIME. **50** Excerpt from SCIENCE DIGEST. May 1984. **57** From EGYPT'S DESERT OF PROMISE by Farouk El-Baz, NATIONAL GEOGRAPHIC, February 1982. Copyright © 1982 National Geographic Society. Reprinted by permission. **81** Zagreb, Yugoslavia, Associated Press news article, CHICAGO TRIBUNE, July 12, 1987. **93** Quotation by E. T. Hall cited in "A Plea for True Global History," Theodore R. Von Lane, WORLD HISTORY BULLETIN. Spring 1987, vol. IV, no. 2. **104–106** From "Garments Offer Fresh Look at Ancient Maya" by John Noble Milford, The *New York Times*, September 29, 1987. Copyright © 1987 by the New York Times Company. Reprinted by permission. **121** From "Prairie" in CORNHUSKERS by Carl Sandburg, copyright 1918 by Holt, Rinehart and Winston, Inc.; renewed 1946 by Carl Sandburg. Reprinted by permission of Harcourt Brace Jovanovich, Inc. **127** Aline Amon Goodrich, "Rain Song" from THE EARTH IS SORE. Copyright © 1981 Aline Amon Goodrich. Reprinted with the permission of Atheneum Publishers, an imprint of Macmillan Publishing Company. **132** Excerpt from AMERICA AT 1750 (introduction) by Richard Hofstadter. **145** Rachel Carson, "Our Ever-Changing Shore," HOLIDAY, July 1958. **149** Margaret Mitchell, GONE WITH THE WIND. New York: Macmillan Publishing Company, 1936. **158–160** From "The Simplest of Counties" by Bret Wallach, FOCUS, Summer 1987. Copyright © 1987 by The American Geographical Society. Reprinted by permission. **180** Mary Hiemstra, GULLY FARM. Toronto: McClelland and Stewart Ltd. 1955. **184** Hugh MacLennan, THE COLOUR OF CANADA. Boston: Little, Brown and Company, 1967. **202** RIPLEY'S BELIEVE IT OR NOT. New York: Pocket Books, Inc., 1978. **211** Alonso Morales letter written in 1576 cited in THE CAMBRIDGE ENCYCLOPEDIA OF LATIN AMERICA AND THE CARIBBEAN. New York: Cambridge University Press, 1985. **219** Mariano Azuela, Los de Abajo, 1916. **225–227** From p. 723, 726. From AZTECS by Bart McDowell, *National Geographic Magazine*, December 1980. Copyright © 1980 by National Geographic Society. Reprinted by permission. **228** Harm J. de Blij and Peter O. Muller, GEOGRAPHY: REGIONS AND CONCEPTS. New York: John Wiley & Sons, 1985. **232** Aime Cesaire cited in THE CAMBRIDGE ENCYCLOPEDIA OF LATIN AMERICA AND THE CARIBBEAN. Cambridge University Press, 1985. **241** Stephen Birnbaum, BIRNBAUM'S SOUTH AMERICA: 1988 TRAVEL GUIDE SERIES. Boston: Houghton Mifflin Company, 1987. **314–316** From "Foreigners in Their Own Land" by Ernest Gill, *The New York Times Magazine*, February 16, 1986. Copyright © 1986 by The New York Times Company. Reprinted by permission. **331** Homer, THE ODYSSEY translated by Robert Fitzgerald. New York: Doubleday and Company, Inc., 1961. **343** David K. Shipler, RUSSIA: BROKEN IDOLS, SOLEMN DREAMS. New York: TIMES BOOKS, 1983. **343** Boris Pasternak, DOCTOR ZHIVAGO. New York: Pantheon Books, 1958. **352** "Catherine's 'Instructions'" from DOCUMENTS OF CATHERINE THE GREAT. ed. by W.R. Reddaway. New York: Macmillan Publishing Company, 1931. **361** Harrison E. Salisbury, RUSSIA. New York: Atheneum Publishers, 1965. **370–372** From "Russia's Restless Youth" by Bill Keller, *The New York Times Magazine*, July 26, 1987. Copyright © 1987 by The New York Times Company. Reprinted by permission. **377** John Dornberg. EASTERN EUROPE: A COMMUNIST KALEIDOSCOPE. New York: The Dial Press, 1980. **382** Edmund Stillman. LIFE WORLD LIBRARY: THE BALKANS. New York: Time, Inc., 1964. **393** James Henry Brestead, ANCIENT TIMES: A HISTORY OF THE EARLY WORLD. Boston: Ginn and Company. **398** Quentin Crewe, IN SEARCH OF THE SAHARA. New York: Macmillan Publishing Company, 1983. **402** Sumerian hymn from THE SUMERIANS: INVENTORS AND BUILDERS by Elizabeth Lansing. McGraw-Hill. **407** George B. Cressey, CROSSROADS: LAND AND LIFE IN SOUTHWEST ASIA. New York: Harper & Row, Publishers, Inc. 1960. **415** Amr ibn el As quoted in Emil Ludwig's: THE NILE. New York: Viking Press, 1937. **421–423** From "The Nile Valley" by Bret Wallach, FOCUS, Spring, 1986. Copyright © 1986 by The American Geographical Society. Reprinted by permission. **424** Quotation by Andre Julien cited in NORTH AFRICA by Mario Rossi. New York: Doubleday & Company, Inc., 1974. **433** THE DARTMOUTH BIBLE. Boston: Houghton Mifflin Company, 1950. **443** Vamik D. Volkan and Norman Itzkowitz, THE IMMORTAL ATATURK, Chicago: University of Chicago Press, 1984. **455** Richard Rive, AFRICAN SONGS. Seven Seas Publishers, 1963. **460** Kofi Asare Opoku, SPEAK TO THE WINDS. New York: William Morrow & Company, 1975. **464** Saiyid Abdallah, "Utendi wa Inkishafi," translated by L. Harrier, SWALHILI POETRY. New York: Oxford University Press, 1962. **468** R. Sutherland Rattray, ASHANTI PROVERBS. New York: Oxford University Press. **477** Mary F. Smith, BABA OF KARO: A WOMAN OF THE MUSLIM HAUSA. London: Faber & Faber Ltd., 1954. **479** Wole Soyinka, AKE: THE YEARS OF CHILDHOOD. London: Rex Collings, Ltd., 1981. **484–485** From "A Big Bore," a la Brasilia, in the Middle of Nigeria," by James Brooke, *The New York Times*, June 25, 1987. Copyright © 1987 by The New York Times Company. Reprinted by permission. **486** "Death" from JEUNE AFRIQUE. **498** Winnie Mandela, A PART OF MY SOUL WENT WITH HIM. New York: W.W. Norton, 1985. **517** Rita Aero, THINGS CHINESE. New York: Doubleday & Company, Inc., 1980. **527** F.S.V. Donnison, BURMA. New York: Praeger Publishers, 1970. **541** S. Ellis and James L. Stanfield, "Pakistan Under Pressure" NATIONAL GEOGRAPHIC, May 1981. **545–548** From "Banking on the Poor" by Magda Krance. Reprinted by permission of the author. **553** Arthur Waley, trans., THE ANALECTS OF CONFUCIUS. New York: Macmillan Publishing Company, 1939. **559** Korean proverb cited in KOREA, Hans Johannes Hoefer. Hong Kong, Apa Productions Ltd., 1981. **563** "I passed by the Beach" by Yamabe No Akahito from Kenneth Rexroth, ONE HUNDRED POEMS FROM THE JAPANESE. Reprinted by permission of New Directions Publishing Corporation. All rights reserved. **573** C.L. Sulzberger cited in SOUTHEAST ASIA by Tillman Durdin. New York: Atheneum, 1966. **577** FODOR'S SOUTHEAST ASIA 1985. New York: Fodor's Travel Guides, 1984. **589** Mark Twain, FOLLOWING THE EQUATOR **595** Mark Twain, FOLLOWING THE EQUATOR **603** James Michener, TALES OF THE SOUTH PACIFIC. New York: MacMillan Publishing Company, 1947. **610–612** From "A new ship tests the rigor of winter in the Antarctic" by Michael Parfit. Appeared in SMITHSONIAN, November 1986. Reprinted by permission of the author.

ILLUSTRATIONS

COVER Joe Devenny/The Image Bank **ii** E. Nagele/FPG **v(t)** George Holton/Photo Researchers **v(b)** Robert Frerck/Odyssey Productions, Chicago **vi** David Muench/The Image Bank **vii** Stuart Cohen **viii(t)** F. Roiter/The Image Bank **viii(b)** John Eastcott/Yva Momatiuk/Woodfin Camp & Associates **ix** Eric Preau Sygma **x(t)** W. Campbell/Sygma **x(b)** Joseph F. Viesti **xi** G.R. Roberts **1** NASA **2** Richard Howard **16** Pete Turner/The Image Bank **23** Tony Stone Worldwide/Masterfile **26(t)** J.C. Criton/Sygma **26(c)** Cary Wolinsky/Stock Boston **26(b)** Jim Pickerell 1985/Click/Chicago Ltd. **28** G.R. Roberts **33** Harald Sund **35** Joseph F. Viesti **38** Bill Ross/Woodfin Camp & Associates **39** Connie Geocaris/Click/Chicago Ltd. **44** E.R. Degginger **49** R. Rowan/Alpha/FPG **61** Claude Beziau/Gamma-Liaison **62** FPG **65** Kenneth W. Fink/Berg & Associates **68** Rudi Von Briel **71** F. Gohier 1984/Photo Researchers **77-78** Mike Yamashita **80** Joseph F. Viesti **86** McNeil/Miller/H. Armstrong Roberts **92** Owen Franken **95** W. Campbell/Sygma **101** Alain Nogues/Sygma **102** Dickman/Gamma-Liaison **105(l,r)** Used by permission of the publisher Harry N. Abrams, Inc., NY, from the book *Living Maya*. Text © 1987 Walter F. Morris, Jr. Photographs © 1987 Jeffrey Jay Foxx, All rights reserved. **109** Smetzer/Click/Chicago Ltd. **116** Robert Maas **118-119** E. Otto/Miller Comstock, Inc. **120** J.P. Laffont/Sygma **124** Lynn M. Stone **129** Choice Photos/Berg & Associates **135** Nebraska State Historical Society, Solomon D. Butcher Collection **137** Norma Morrison/Hillstrom Stock Photos **139** Lee Balterman/Marilyn Gartman Agency **140(l)** Courtesy U.S. Capitol Historical Society, National Geographic Photographer George F. Mobley **140(r)** © 85 Tibor Bognar/Miller Comstock Inc. **144** Baron Wolman **148** Bill Nation/Sygma **151** A. Weems/Woodfin Camp & Associates **152** Randy Taylor/Sygma **157** Milt & Joan Mann/Cameramann International, Ltd. **159** Courtesy *Greeley County Republican*, Tribune, Kansas **163** Milt & Joan Mann/Camermann International, Ltd. **165** Baron Wolman **167** J. Langeuin/Sygma **169** Al Satterwhite/The Image Bank **171** U.S. Dept. of the Interior, Geological Survey **174** Henry Georgi/Miller Comstock, Inc. **178** Derek Caron/Masterfile **179** Mike Dobel/Masterfile **181** Alec Pytlowany/Masterfile **182** Sherman Hines/Masterfile **186** REFX Reflexion/Miller Comstock **192-193** Victor Englebert **194** Robert Frerck/Odyssey Productions, Chicago **197** Loren McIntyre/Woodfin Camp & Associates **200** Loren McIntyre/Woodfin Camp & Associates **202** Loren McIntyre **208** Gale Zucker 1987/Stock Boston **212(l)** Telegraph Colour Library/Masterfile **212(r)** Photri/Spillane/Marilyn Gartman Agency **218** Hans Blohm/Masterfile **221** Victor Englebert **223** Robert Frerck/Odyssey Productions, Chicago **224** Robert Frerck/Odyssey Productions, Chicago **226(l)** Instituto Nacional de Antropologia e History, Mexico **226(r)** Robert Frerck/Odyssey Productions, Chicago **230** Nicholas Devore III/Bruce Coleman Inc. **233** Masterfile **234** Cary Wolinsky/Stock Boston **237** From *The Easy Guide to Mexico City* by Richard Bloomgarden. Used with permission. **238** From *The Easy Guide to Mexico City* by Richard Bloomgarden. Used with permission. **240** Robert Frerck/Odyssey Productions, Chicago **243** John Blaustein 1980/Woodfin Camp & Associates **246** Victor Englebert **248** Milt & Joan Mann/Cameramann International, Ltd. **250** ANIMALS ANIMALS/M.A. Chappel **251** Robert Frerck/Odyssey Productions, Chicago **252** Robert Frerck/Odyssey Productions, Chicago **255** D. Goldberg/Sygma **256** Robert Frerck/Odyssey Productions, Chicago **259** W. Fischer/FPG **260** Wolfgang Kaehler **266-267** Robert Frerck/Odyssey Productions, Chicago **268** Mike Mazzaschi/Stock Boston **271** D & J. Heaton/Click/Chicago Ltd. **277** Photri/Marilyn Gartman Agency **278** G.R. Roberts **280(l)** Chartres Cathedral. Scala/Art Resource, NY **280(r)** Vatican. Scala/Art Resource, NY **286** McGraw-Hill Book Co. Used with permission. From *Physical Elements of Geography* by Finch, Trewartha, Robinson and Hammond. 4th edition. **288** Brian Seed/Click/Chicago Ltd. **291** Milt & Joan Mann/Cameramann International, Ltd. **292** Milt & Joan Mann/Cameramann International, Ltd. **297** Bruno Widen/Click/Chicago Ltd. **298** Kim Hart/Black Star **301** George Philip & Son Ltd. **304** Eric L. Ergenbright **307** George Hunter/Click/Chicago Ltd. **308** Bruno Barbey/Magnum Photos **311** Owen Franken **312** Milt & Joan Mann/Cameramann International, Ltd. **315** 1983 Christopher Morris/Black Star **318** Dennis Stock/Magnum Photos **319** Milt & Joan Mann/Cameramann International, Ltd. **321** 1985 John Anderson/Click/Chicago Ltd. **323-324** Copyright Bollmann-Bildkarten-Verlag, 3300 Braunschweig, Germany **326** Joseph F. Viesti **329** Robert Frerck/Odyssey Productions, Chicago **332** Robert Frerck/Odyssey Productions, Chicago **333** Joseph F. Viesti **335** Erwin Raisz, General Cartographer. From *Maps* by Michael & Susan Southworth. Permission McGraw-Hill **340-341** Howard Sochurek/Woodfin Camp & Associates **342** Dallas & John Heaton/Click/Chicago Ltd. **345** P. Vauthey/Sygma **349** Sovfoto **353** Novosti/Sovfoto **360** Peter W. Gonzalez **364** Alain Nogues/Sygma **367** Peter W. Gonzalez **368** Fabian/Sygma **371** Frederique Hibon/Sygma **376** Owen Franken/Sygma **378** Bernard G. Silberstein/Shostal Associates **380** 1986 Chris Niedenthal/Black Star **383** Owen Franken/Sygma **390-391** Minosa-Scorpio/Sygma **392** Travelpix/FPG **397** Milt & Joan Mann/Cameramann International, Ltd. **401** Milt & Joan Mann/Cameramann International, Ltd. **403** 1984 Robert Azzi/Woodfin Camp & Associates **409** Cynthia Johnson Gamma-Liaison **414** Craig Aurness/Woodfin Camp & Associates **417** Tom Zimberoff/Sygma **419(l)** J. Alex Langley/Click/Chicago Ltd. **419(r)** Robert Frerck/Click/Chicago Ltd. **422** Owen Franken/Sygma **425** L. Isy-Swart/Image Bank **427** Marc Riboud/Magnum Photos **432** Ron Snipe **435** Milt & Joan Mann/Cameramann International Ltd. **436** M. Attar/Sygma **441** H.D. Bollinger/The Image Bank **442** Claude Salhani/Sygma **452-453** Milt & Joan Mann/Cameramann International, Ltd. **454** James R. Holland/Stock Boston **457** Milt & Joan Mann/Cameramann International, Ltd. **463** Robert Frerck/Odyssey Productions, Chicago **469** UPI/Bettmann Newsphotos **470** William Campbell/Sygma **472** Collection Sylvia & Michael Horowitz, Photo by David Tuttle **476** Michael Fogden Bruce Coleman Inc. **479** Robert Frerck/Odyssey Productions, Chicago **482** Marc & Evelyne Bernheim 1981/Woodfin Camp & Associates **485** W. Campbell/Sygma **487** Alex Webb/Magnum Photos **488** Bruno Barbey/Magnum Photos **489** NASA, From Mission to Earth: Landsat Views the World **492** M. Amin/Camerapix **495** Ilka Ranta/Woodfin Camp & Associates **496** Robert Frerck/Odyssey Productions, Chicago **499** A. Tannenbaum/Sygma **500** A. Tannenbaum/Sygma **501** Peter Marlow/Sygma **508-509** Joseph F. Viesti **510** J. Kugler/FPG **513** © Paulus Leeser **516** Lowell Georgia/Photo Researchers **520** Hiroji Kubota/Magnum Photos **522** Marc Riboud/Magnum Photos **524** Robert Frerck/Odyssey Productions, Chicago **526** J. Kugler/FPG **530** J.P. Laffont/Sygma **531** George Philip & Son Ltd. **534** Galen Rowell/Alpha/FPG **538** Robert Frerck/Odyssey Productions, Chicago **540** Marilyn Silverstone/Magnum Photos **542** Robert Frerck/Odyssey Productions, Chicago **544** © Chris Noble 1987 **546(all)** Beryl Goldberg Photographer © 1987 **548** Beryl Goldberg Photographer © 1987 **552** A. Giampiccolo/FPG **555** John Henebry **556** Bruno Barbey/Magnum Photos **557** Ira Kirschenbaum/Stock Boston **560** Milt & Joan Mann/Cameramann International, Ltd. **561** Howard Sochurek/Woodfin Camp & Associates **564** Steve Young/Taurus Photos, Inc. **565** Travelpix/FPG **566** Milt & Joan Mann/Cameramann International, Ltd. **567** Milt & Joan Mann/Cameramann International, Ltd. **568** Philip J. Griffiths/Magnum Photos **572** Joan Dunlop/Hillstrom Stock Photos **575** Kevin McKiernan/Time Inc. **576** William D. Middleton/Hillstrom Stock Photos **580** Ron Snipe **586-587** Cynthia Clampitt **588** Shostal Associates **593** ANIMALS ANIMALS/Alan G. Nelson **594** ANIMALS ANIMALS/Mickey Gibson **596** Shostal Associates **598** G.R. Roberts **599** © Marie Tharp **602** Milt & Joan Mann/Cameramann International, Ltd. **606** Milt & Joan Mann/Cameramann International, Ltd. **609** W. Curtsinger/Photo Researchers **611** W. Curtsinger/Photo Researchers **618** Joe Devenny/The Image Bank